THE CAMBRIDGE HISTORY OF
SCIENCE FICTION

The first science fiction course in the American academy was held in the early 1950s. Since then, science fiction has become a recognized and established literary genre with a significant and growing body of scholarship. *The Cambridge History of Science Fiction* is a landmark volume as the first authoritative history of the genre. Over forty contributors with diverse and complementary specialities present a history of science fiction across national and genre boundaries, and trace its intellectual and creative roots in the philosophical and fantastic narratives of the ancient past. Science fiction as a literary genre is the central focus of the volume, but fundamental to its story are its non-literary cultural manifestations and influence. Coverage thus includes transmedia manifestations as an integral part of the genre's history, including not only short stories and novels but also film, art, architecture, music, comics, and interactive media.

GERRY CANAVAN is an associate professor of twentieth- and twenty-first-century literature in the Department of English at Marquette University. He is the co-editor, with Kim Stanley Robinson, of *Green Planets: Ecology and Science Fiction* (2014) and, with Eric Carl Link, of *The Cambridge Companion to American Science Fiction* (2015). His first monograph is *Octavia E. Butler* (2016).

ERIC CARL LINK is Professor of American Literature and Dean of the College of Arts and Sciences at Purdue University Fort Wayne. His many publications include *The Vast and Terrible Drama: American Literary Naturalism in the Late Nineteenth Century* (2004), *Understanding Philip K. Dick* (2010), and *Crosscurrents: Readings in the Disciplines* (2012). He is the editor or co-editor of numerous volumes, including *The Cambridge Companion to American Science Fiction* (co-edited with Gerry Canavan, 2015).

THE CAMBRIDGE
HISTORY OF
SCIENCE FICTION

★

Edited by

GERRY CANAVAN

Marquette University
and

ERIC CARL LINK

Purdue University Fort Wayne

CAMBRIDGE
UNIVERSITY PRESS

University Printing House, Cambridge CB2 8BS, United Kingdom

One Liberty Plaza, 20th Floor, New York, NY 10006, USA

477 Williamstown Road, Port Melbourne, VIC 3207, Australia

314–321, 3rd Floor, Plot 3, Splendor Forum, Jasola District Centre,
New Delhi – 110025, India

79 Anson Road, #06–04/06, Singapore 079906

Cambridge University Press is part of the University of Cambridge.

It furthers the University's mission by disseminating knowledge in the pursuit of
education, learning, and research at the highest international levels of excellence.

www.cambridge.org
Information on this title: www.cambridge.org/9781107166097
DOI: 10.1017/9781316694374

First published 2019

Printed in the United States of America by Sheridan Books, Inc.

A catalogue record for this publication is available from the British Library.

Library of Congress Cataloging-in-Publication Data
NAMES: Canavan, Gerry, editor. | Link, Eric Carl, editor.
TITLE: The Cambridge history of science fiction / edited by Gerry Canavan, Eric Carl Link.
DESCRIPTION: Cambridge ; New York, NY : Cambridge University Press, 2019. |
Includes bibliographical references and index.
IDENTIFIERS: LCCN 2018012832 | ISBN 9781107166097
SUBJECTS: LCSH: Science fiction – History and criticism.
CLASSIFICATION: LCC PN3433.5 .C36 2018 | DDC 809.3/8762–dc23
LC record available at https://lccn.loc.gov/2018012832

ISBN 978-1-107-16609-7 Hardback

For Sarah Link, Nathaniel Link, Natalie Link, and Nolan Link, who make life worth living and who are the best of companions on this generation starship called Earth.

For my parents, who got me every book I ever asked for. And for Jaimee Hills, Zoey Canavan, and Connor Canavan, and another trillion years.

Contents

Contents

Contents

Contents

Illustrations

Notes on Contributors

BRENT RYAN BELLAMY is Assistant Professor of Speculative Literature at Trent University. His work can be read in the forthcoming *Loanwords to Live With: An Ecotopian Lexicon* (co-edited with Matthew Schneider-Mayerson) and a special issue of *Science Fiction Studies* on climate crisis (with Veronica Hollinger, November 2018). His book *Remainders of the American Century: Post-Apocalyptic Novels in the Age of US Decline* is under advanced contract.

PAUL BOOTH is an associate professor of media and cinema studies in the College of Communication at DePaul University, specializing in fandom, new media, games, technology, popular culture, and cultural studies. He is the author of *Digital Fandom: New Media Studies*, which examines fans of cult television programs, and of *Time on TV: Temporal Displacement and Mashup Television*, which compares time travel on television with social media. His latest book, *Companion to Media Fandom and Fan Studies*, was published in 2018.

MARK BOULD is Reader in Film and Literature at the University of the West of England, Bristol. One of the founding editors of the journal *Science Fiction Film and Television*, he co-edits the *Studies in Global Science Fiction* monograph series. His most recent books are *Solaris* (2014), *SF Now* (2014), and *Africa SF* (2013).

ANDREW M. BUTLER is a senior lecturer at Canterbury Christ Church University and one of the editors of *Extrapolation*. He has written extensively on science fiction and related genres; his most recent books are *Eternal Sunshine of the Spotless Mind* (2014) and *Solar Flares: Science Fiction in the 1970s* (2012).

RITCH CALVIN teaches at Stony Brook University. His work has appeared in *Science Fiction Studies, Extrapolation, Femspec, Utopian Studies, The Journal of the Fantastic in the Arts, Science Fiction Film and Television, The New York Review of Science Fiction*, and *The SFRA Review*. He co-edited a collection of essays for studying and teaching science fiction in 2014. His monograph, *Feminist Science Fiction and Feminist Epistemology: Four Modes* was published by Palgrave Macmillan in 2016.

GERRY CANAVAN is an associate professor in the English Department at Marquette University, specializing in twentieth- and twenty-first-century literature. An editor at

Extrapolation and *Science Fiction Film and Television*, he has also co-edited *Green Planets: Ecology and Science Fiction* (2014) and *The Cambridge Companion to American Science Fiction* (2015). His first monograph, *Octavia E. Butler*, appeared in 2016 in the Modern Masters of Science Fiction series at University of Illinois Press.

GREG CONLEY is an instructor at Bluegrass Community and Technical Colleges and Eastern Kentucky University. Specializing in transatlantic speculative fiction from the late nineteenth and early twentieth centuries, he has explored the figure of the extra-terrestrial from the Gothic period to the present.

NICOLE DE FEE is an associate professor in the English Department at Louisiana Tech University. Her research focuses on nineteenth-century American Literature, Herman Melville, and American literary naturalism, alongside science fiction and horror.

JANE DONAWERTH, Professor Emerita of English and Affiliate in Women's Studies, University of Maryland, is the author of *Frankenstein's Daughters: Women Writing Science Fiction*, co-editor of *Utopian and Science Fiction by Women: Worlds of Difference*, and co-author with Kate Scally of "'You've found no records': Slavery in Maryland and the Writing of Octavia Butler's *Kindred*" in *Extrapolation* (2017). She has been awarded the International Association for the Fantastic in the Arts Scholarship Award for career work in gender and SF.

REBECCA EVANS is an assistant professor in the English department at Winston-Salem State University. She researches and teaches twentieth- and twenty-first-century American literature as it intersects with social and environmental justice; she is currently working on a book manuscript that shows how contemporary American writers experiment with speculative genres in order to make structural and environmental violence legible to readers.

PAWEL FRELIK is Associate Professor of American Media and the Director of the Video Game Research Center at Maria Curie-Skłodowska University in Lublin. His research interests include science fiction, video games, fantastic visualities, digital media, and transmedia storytelling, and he has published widely in these fields. He serves on the advisory boards of *Science Fiction Studies, Extrapolation*, and *Journal of Gaming and Virtual Worlds*, and is the co-editor of the New Dimensions in Science Fiction book series at the University of Wales Press. In 2013–14, he was President of the Science Fiction Research Association (SFRA). In June 2017, he received SFRA's Thomas D. Clareson Award for service to the field.

MICHAEL FUCHS is a fixed-term assistant professor in American Studies at the University of Graz. He has co-edited six volumes, most recently *Intermedia Games – Games Inter Media: Video Games and Intermediality* (2019), *Space Oddities: Difference and Identity in the American City* (2018), and a special issue of the *European Journal of American Studies* on animals in American television (2018). He is currently working on a monograph on urban spaces in horror films and a project on animal monsters in American culture.

TERRY HARPOLD teaches science fiction, image-text studies, and climate studies at the University of Florida. The author of *Ex-foliations: Reading Machines and the Upgrade Path* (2008) and co-editor of *Collectionner l'Extraordinaire, sonder l'Ailleurs: Essais sur Jules Verne en hommage à Jean-Michel Margot* (2015), his published science fiction scholarship includes studies of European and Anglo-American SF (especially of the long nineteenth and early twentieth centuries), the illustrated Jules Verne, and historical and contemporary environmental humanities.

DAN HASSLER-FOREST works as an assistant professor in the Department of Media and Cultural Studies at Utrecht University. He has published books and articles on comics, transmedia storytelling, superhero movies, critical theory, and fantastic world-building, and is one of the editors of *Science Fiction Film and Television*.

RACHEL HAYWOOD FERREIRA is Associate Professor of Spanish and Portuguese at Iowa State University. She is co-editor of the book series Studies in Global Science Fiction and of the journal *Extrapolation*, serves on the editorial boards of *Science Fiction Studies, Journal of the Fantastic in the Arts, Zanzalá – Revista Brasileira de Estudos de Ficção Científica,* and *Alambique: Revista Académica de Ciencia-Ficción y Fantasía / Jornal Académico de Ficção Científica e Fantasia,* and is subeditor for Latin American and Iberian science fiction for *The Encyclopedia of Science Fiction.* She is the author of *The Emergence of Latin American Science Fiction* (2011). Her current book project is provisionally titled *Latin American Science Fiction in the Space Age.*

KAREN HELLEKSON has published widely in the fields of science fiction and fan studies, and is the founding co-editor of the journal *Transformative Works and Cultures.* She is also the co-editor, with Kristina Busse, of *The Fan Fiction Studies Reader* (2014).

JEFFREY HICKS is an assistant professor of English at Los Angeles City College. His work has appeared in *The Cambridge Companion to the City in Literature* (2014) and *Marxism and Urban Culture* (2014). His research interests include dystopian literature and film, urban literature and film, and New Wave science fiction.

DAVID M. HIGGINS is the Speculative Fiction Editor for the *Los Angeles Review of Books*. He teaches English at Inver Hills College in Minnesota, and his research examines imperial fantasies in postwar American culture. Higgins's article "Toward a Cosmopolitan Science Fiction" won the 2012 SFRA Pioneer Award for excellence in scholarship. He has published in journals such as *American Literature, Science Fiction Studies, Paradoxa,* and *Extrapolation,* and his work has appeared in edited volumes such as *The Cambridge Companion to American Science Fiction.*

VERONICA HOLLINGER is Emerita Professor of cultural studies at Trent University in Ontario. She is a long-time co-editor of *Science Fiction Studies,* co-editor of *The Wesleyan Anthology of Science Fiction,* and co-editor of five scholarly collections. Her publications include essays on contemporary SF theory and criticism, queer and feminist SF, Chinese SF, posthumanism, the anthropocene, cyberpunk, and postmodernism.

AARON KASHTAN is a visiting assistant professor in composition and rhetoric at Miami University of Ohio. His research focuses on the material, digital, and multimodal rhetoric of comics. His first book, *Between Panel and Screen: Comics, the Future of the Book, and the Book of the Future*, currently under review, examines what comics can tell us about the effect of digital media on the material experience of reading. His second book project will examine comics as a site of nostalgia for handwriting in contemporary American culture.

LEE KONSTANTINOU is Associate Professor of English at the University of Maryland, College Park, and Senior Humanities Editor at the *Los Angeles Review of Books*. He wrote the literary history *Cool Characters: Irony and American Fiction*, and the novel *Pop Apocalypse*. With Samuel Cohen, he co-edited the collection *The Legacy of David Foster Wallace*. He is currently working on a book project entitled "The Cartoon Art: Comics in the Age of Mass High Culture."

MALISA KURTZ received her PhD from Brock University in Interdisciplinary Humanities. Her work focuses on the intersection of science fiction, globalization, and postcolonialism. She has published in *Paradoxa, Science Fiction Studies* and *Journal of the Fantastic in the Arts*, and co-edited *Notions of Genre: Writings on Popular Film Before Genre Theory* (2016) with Barry K. Grant.

LAUREN J. LACEY is Associate Professor of English and co-director of Women's and Gender Studies at Edgewood College in Madison, Wisconsin, where she regularly teaches courses in contemporary literatures, feminist theory, and speculative fiction. She is author of *The Past That Might Have Been, the Future That May Come: Women Writing Fantastic Fiction, 1960s to the Present* (2014). Her current project examines how posthuman relationships negotiate power dynamics in contemporary fiction.

BROOKS LANDON teaches in the University of Iowa English Department. He has written widely on aspects of science fiction literature and film.

ROB LATHAM is the author of *Consuming Youth: Vampires, Cyborgs, and the Culture of Consumption* (2002), co-editor of *The Wesleyan Anthology of Science Fiction* (2010), and editor of *The Oxford Handbook of Science Fiction* (2014) and *Science Fiction Criticism: An Anthology of Essential Writings* (2017). He was a senior editor of the journal *Science Fiction Studies* for two decades. Currently, he is planning a volume on the work of Robert Silverberg and is completing a second book manuscript on New Wave science fiction.

ISIAH LAVENDER III is Associate Professor of English at Louisiana State University, where he researches and teaches courses in African-American literature and science fiction. In addition to his book *Race in American Science Fiction* (2011) and edited collections *Black and Brown Planets: The Politics of Race in Science Fiction* (2014) and *Dis-Orienting Planets: Racial Representations of Asia in Science Fiction* (2017), his publications on science fiction include essays and reviews in journals such as *Extrapolation, Journal of the Fantastic in the Arts*, and *Science Fiction Studies*. He's currently working on his second monograph, *Classics of Afrofuturism*.

MICHAEL LEVY was a prolific writer and editor of science fiction criticism, as well as the longtime managing editor of *Extrapolation*. He passed away in 2017.

HUA LI is Associate Professor of Chinese at Montana State University. She published her monograph *Contemporary Chinese Fiction by Su Tong and Yu Hua: Coming of Age in Troubled Times* in 2011, and has authored journal articles and book chapters on various topics in contemporary Chinese fiction and cinema. She has carried out research on Chinese science fiction since 2014, and has published journal articles and book chapters on such Chinese science fiction writers as Liu Cixin and Xu Nianci. She is currently working on a book manuscript on Chinese science fiction in the 1980s.

ERIC CARL LINK is Professor of American Literature and Dean of the College of Arts and Sciences at Purdue University Fort Wayne. He is the author of several books, including *Understanding Philip K. Dick* (2010), *The Vast and Terrible Drama: American Literary Naturalism in the Late Nineteenth Century* (2004), *Neutral Ground: New Traditionalism and the American Romance Controversy* (co-authored with G. R. Thompson, 1999), and *Crosscurrents: Readings in the Disciplines* (co-authored with Steven Frye, 2012). He is the editor or co-editor of numerous volumes, including *The Cambridge Companion to American Science Fiction* (co-edited with Gerry Canavan, 2015), *Critical Insights: Herman Melville* (2012), *Critical Insights: The Red Badge of Courage* (2010), *Taming the Bicycle: Essays, Stories, and Sketches* by Mark Twain (2009), and the fourth edition of the *Norton Critical Edition of The Red Badge of Courage* (2008).

ROGER LUCKHURST is Professor of Modern and Contemporary Literature at Birkbeck College, University of London, and the editor of *The Cambridge Companion to Dracula* and *Science Fiction: A Literary History* (both 2017). He has written books on telepathy, mummy curses, and zombies, and has edited Lovecraft, Stoker, and H. G. Wells in Oxford World's Classics. His latest book is *Corridors: Passages in Modernity* (2019).

SHANNON DAVIES MANCUS is a PhD candidate in the Department of American Studies at the George Washington University. Her dissertation, "Appealing to Better Natures: Genre and the Politics of Performance in the American Environmental Movement, 1990–Present," examines the political implications of how different genres act as structuring mechanisms for narratives that compete to define the moral and philosophical parameters of the modern environmental movement. She is particularly interested in how those genres influence performances and media framing.

PAUL MARCH-RUSSELL is the editor of *Foundation: The International Review of Science Fiction* and the general editor of *SF Storyworlds*. His most recent book publications are *Modernism and Science Fiction* (2015), *The Postcolonial Short Story*, co-edited with Maggie Awadalla (2013), and *Legacies of Romanticism*, co-edited with Carmen Casaliggi (2012).

LARISA MIKHAYLOVA is a Russian philologist, literary critic, and translator. She teaches world literature of the twentieth century and science fiction in the Department of Journalism at Moscow State University. She edits the Russian SF magazine *Supernova*.

GRAHAM J. MURPHY is a professor with the School of English and Liberal Studies (Faculty of Business) at Seneca College in Toronto. He co-edited *Cyberpunk and Visual Culture* (2018) and *Beyond Cyberpunk: New Critical Perspectives* (2010), co-authored *Ursula K. Le Guin: A Critical Companion* (2006), and has written numerous articles that have appeared in diverse anthologies and peer-review journals. He is an assistant editor for *Journal of the Fantastic in the Arts* and sits on the editorial advisory boards of *Science Fiction Studies* and *Extrapolation*.

HUGH CHARLES O'CONNELL is an assistant professor of English at the University of Massachusetts Boston. His current research project focuses on the relationship between speculative fiction and speculative finance. His essays on utopianism, British SF, and postcolonial SF appear in *Postcolonial Literary Inquiry, Paradoxa: The Futures Industry, CR: The New Centennial Review, Modern Fiction Studies*, and *The Journal of Postcolonial Writing*. His essay, "Mutating Towards the Future," received Honorable Mention for the 2013 Science Fiction Research Association Pioneer Award.

ERIC C. OTTO is an associate professor of environmental humanities in the Department of Integrated Studies at Florida Gulf Coast University, where he also directs the General Education Program. He is the author of *Green Speculations: Science Fiction and Transformative Environmentalism* (2012).

MICHAEL R. PAGE is the author of three monographs: *The Literary Imagination from Erasmus Darwin to H. G. Wells* (2012), *Frederik Pohl* (2015), and *Saving the World Through Science Fiction: James Gunn, Writer, Teacher and Scholar* (2017). He has edited *The Man with the Strange Head and Other Early Science Fiction Stories* by Miles J. Breuer (2008) and has edited and annotated an edition of James Gunn's 1951 master's thesis, *Modern Science Fiction: A Critical Analysis, The Seminal 1951 Thesis* (2018). Page teaches science fiction and holds an administrative position in the English Department at the University of Nebraska.

ANDREW PILSCH is an associate professor of English at Texas A&M University. He is the author of *Transhumanism* (2017).

SALVATORE PROIETTI teaches American literature at the University of Calabria. His main areas of research include SF, early-republican US culture, Thoreau, and Twain. He is the author of *Storie di fondazione: Letteratura e nazione negli Stati Uniti post-rivoluzionari* (Foundation Stories: Literature and Nationhood in Post-Revolution America, 2002) and *Hippies: Le culture della controcultura* (Hippies: The Cultures of the Counterculture, 2003, 2008), as well as of numerous articles on SF in Italian and English.

STEFAN "STEVE" RABITSCH is a fixed-term assistant professor in American Studies at the University of Graz and teaches courses in American cultural history at the University of Klagenfurt. His first monograph, *Star Trek's Secret British History*, was published in 2019. He has also co-edited *Set Phasers to Teach! The Use of Star Trek in Research and Teaching* (2018) and *Fantastic Cities: American Urban Spaces in Science Fiction, Fantasy, and Horror* (forthcoming). His research and his classes are dominated by American cultural studies, with a focus on science fiction studies across media.

SEAN REDMOND is Professor of Screen and Design at Deakin University, Australia. He is the editor of *Liquid Metal: The Science Fiction Film Reader* (2005), co-editor (with Leon Marvell) of the *AFI Film Reader: Endangering Science Fiction Film* (2015), and author of *Liquid Space: Science Fiction Film and Television in the Digital Age* (2017). He edits the online open-access science fiction studies journal *Deletion* and has published in such landmark journals as the *Cinema Journal*, the *New Review of Film and Television*, *Thesis 11*, and *Social Semiotics*. He is currently working on a monograph on loneliness in science fiction film.

JOHN RIEDER is a professor of English at the University of Hawaii at Mānoa, author of *Science Fiction and the Mass Cultural Genre System* (2017) and *Colonialism and the Emergence of Science Fiction* (2008), recipient of the Science Fiction Research Association's Pilgrim Award in 2011, and a member of the editorial board of *Extrapolation*.

REBEKAH SHELDON is an assistant professor of English at Indiana University. Her first book, *The Child to Come: Life After the Human Catastrophe* (2016), received an honorary mention for the Science Fiction and Technoscience Studies Program Award from the University of California at Riverside. She has published essays on science fiction in *Science Fiction Studies*, *The Cambridge Companion to Contemporary American Science Fiction*, and *ADA: Journal of Gender, New Media, and Technology*.

W. ANDREW SHEPHARD is a PhD candidate in the Department of English at Stanford University. His research interests are broadly concerned with modes of genre fiction such as science fiction, fantasy, and horror in their various media forms, including prose, film, television, and graphic narrative. He is particularly interested in these genres' engagements with race, gender, and sexuality.

SHERRYL VINT is Professor of Media and Cultural Studies at the University of Calfornia, Riverside, where she directs the Speculative Fiction and Cultures of Science Program. She is an editor of *Science Fiction Studies*, and was an editor of *Science Fiction Film and Television*, which she co-founded, for a decade. Her publications include *Bodies of Tomorrow* (2007), *Animal Alterity* (2010), and *Science Fiction and Cultural Theory: A Reader* (2015).

RYAN VU received his PhD from the Program in Literature at Duke University. His work focuses on the historical rise of fantastic literature during the Enlightenment in Britain and France.

PHILLIP E. WEGNER is the Marston-Milbauer Eminent Scholar and Professor of English at the University of Florida, as well as the founder and director of the Working Group for the Study of Critical Theory. He is the author of four books: *Imaginary Communities: Utopia, the Nation, and the Spatial Histories of Modernity* (2002), *Life Between Two Deaths: US Culture, 1989–2001* (2009), *Periodizing Jameson: Dialectics, the University, and the Desire for Narrative* (2014), and *Shockwaves of Possibility: Essays on Science Fiction, Globalization, and Utopia* (2014), and the editor of a new edition of Robert C. Elliott's *The Shape of Utopia* (2013), *Darko Suvin: A Life in Letters* in *Paradoxa* (2011), a special issue of *ImageText*, "Anime and Utopia" (2010), and the forthcoming *The Next Generation: Emerging Voices in Utopian Studies*.

NATHANIEL WILLIAMS completed his PhD at the University of Kansas and is a fulltime lecturer for the University Writing Program at the University of California, Davis. He is the author of *Gears and God: Technocratic Fiction, Faith, and Empire in Mark Twain's America* (2008) and essays in *American Literature, Utopian Studies, Nineteenth-Century Contexts*, and elsewhere. He has been awarded a Horatio Alger Fellowship for the study of popular American culture and an honorable mention for *American Literature*'s Norman Foerster Prize. He serves on the advisory board of the Gunn Center for the Study of Science Fiction.

RHYS WILLIAMS is Lord Kelvin Adam Smith Research Fellow at Glasgow University. He completed his PhD in English Literature at the University of Warwick on the subject of contemporary science fiction and radical politics in 2014. His work is broadly concerned with the relationship between fantasy and social change, radical politics, pedagogy, and the politics of the imagination; he also writes about science fiction and utopianism. His current project is on how we imagine our alternative energy futures.

Acknowledgments

The editors are tremendously grateful to everyone who made this volume possible, a list of contributors and benefactors far too large to properly or adequately name. In particular we would like to thank the editorial staff at Cambridge University Press for supporting this project from inception to execution, especially Ray Ryan and Edgar Mendez; the anonymous readers from the Press, who provided us with very useful feedback on our initial proposal; the research assistants at Marquette University who helped us gather, process, and organize the immense bibliographic footprint of this volume, Elliott Neal, Sarah Holland, Sarah Bublitz, Kenny Guay, and Justice Hagan; Sarah Lambert, Caroline Drake, Neil Wells, and Jaimee Hills; and our families, for putting up with this mammoth project in our lives and allowing us the space to get the project done. Last and best of all we would like to thank the incredible contributors to this volume, who have produced both brilliant scholarship and brilliant *revisions* for us (sometimes on very tight deadlines), who have taught us so much about the genre we love, and who have together produced a wonderful history of SF that, we hope, will be read and enjoyed by scholars, students, and fans for many years to come. Thanks so much, to all of you.

Eric Carl Link
Purdue University Fort Wayne
Gerry Canavan
Marquette University

Chronology

1929   David H. Keller, "The Conquerors"
        Leslie F. Stone, "Letter of the Twenty-Fourth Century"
1930   Lilith Lorraine, "Into the 28th Century"
        Olaf Stapledon, *Last and First Men*
        John Taine, *The Iron Star*
        Philip Wylie, *Gladiator*
        Astounding Science-Fiction launches
        The Comet appears, the first science fiction fanzine
1931   Edmond Hamilton, "The Man Who Evolved"
        H. P. Lovecraft, "The Whisperer in Darkness"
        George S. Schuyler, *Black No More*
        Frankenstein (dir. James Whale)
1932   Aldous Huxley, *Brave New World*
        Amelia Long Reynolds, "Omega"
1933   John W. Campbell, "Twilight"
        Laurence Manning, *The Man Who Awoke*
        Philip Wylie and Edwin Balmer, *When Worlds Collide* (sequel *After Worlds Collide*
        [1934])
1934   Murray Leinster, "Sidewise in Time"
        E. E. Smith, "Lensman" series (multiple sequels)
        Donald Wandrei, "Colossus"
        Stanley G. Weinbaum, "A Martian Odyssey"
        Flash Gordon debuts
        DC Comics founded (as National Allied Publications)
1935   John W. Campbell, "Night"
        Sinclair Lewis, *It Can't Happen Here*
        Nat Schachner (as Chan Corbett), "When the Sun Dies"
        Olaf Stapledon, *Odd John*
1936   H. P. Lovecraft, "At the Mountains of Madness"
        George S. Schuyler, *Black Empire*
        Things to Come (dir. William Cameron Menzies)
1938   John W. Campbell, Jr. (as Don Stuart), "Who Goes There?"
        Lester del Rey, "Helen O'Loy"
        John Campbell becomes editor of *Astounding Science-Fiction*
        Superman debuts in *Action Comics* #1
        Orson Welles, *War of the Worlds* radio hoax
1939   L. Sprague De Camp, "Lest Darkness Fall" (novel 1941)
        Dalton Trumbo, *Johnny Got His Gun*
        Stanley G. Weinbaum, *The New Adam*
        Marvel Comics founded (as Timely Comics)
        New York World's Fair
        The first Worldcon is held in New York City
1940   Robert A. Heinlein, "The Roads Must Roll"
        Robert A Heinlein, "'If This Goes On – '"
        A. E. van Vogt, *Slan* (book 1946)
        Superman radio series premieres

1941	Isaac Asimov, "Nightfall"
	Robert A. Heinlein, "Universe"
	Robert A. Heinlein, "By His Bootstraps"
	L. Sprague De Camp, *Lest Darkness Fall*
	Theodore Sturgeon, "Microcosmic God"
1942	Isaac Asimov, "Foundation" (book 1951)
	Robert A. Heinlein, *Beyond This Horizon* (book 1948)
1943	Ayn Rand, *The Fountainhead*
1944	C. L. Moore, "No Woman Born"
1945	Murray Leinster, "First Contact"
1946	Groff Conklin, ed., *The Best Science Fiction* (anthology)
	Raymond J. Healy and J. Francis McComas, eds. *Adventures in Time and Space* (anthology)
1947	Robert A. Heinlein, *Rocket Ship Galileo*
1948	Shirley Jackson, "The Lottery"
	Judith Merril, "That Only a Mother"
	B. F. Skinner, *Walden Two*
1949	Everett Bleiler and T. E. Dikty, eds. *The Best Science Fiction Stories*
	George Orwell, *Nineteen Eighty-Four*
	H. Beam Piper, "He Walked Around the Horses"
	George R. Stewart, *Earth Abides*
	Jack Vance, "The Kind of Thieves"
	Magazine of Fantasy and Science Fiction launched
1950	Isaac Asimov, *I, Robot* (linked collection)
	Ray Bradbury, *The Martian Chronicles* (linked collection)
	Judith Merril, *Shadows on the Hearth*
	Jack Vance, *The Dying Earth*
	Galaxy Science Fiction launched (dir. Irving Pichel)
	Destination Moon (dir. Irving Pichel)
1951	Ray Bradbury, *The Illustrated Man* (loosely linked collection)
	John Wyndham, *The Day of the Triffids*
	The Day the Earth Stood Still (dir. Robert Wise)
1952	Ray Bradbury, "A Sound of Thunder"
	Philip José Farmer, "The Lovers"
	Vladimir Nabokov, "Lance"
	Clifford D. Simak, *City* (linked collection)
	Theodore Sturgeon, "The World Well Lost"
	Osamu Tezuka, *Astro Boy v.1* (anime premiered 1963, remakes in 1980 and 2003, movie in 2009)
1953	Alfred Bester, *The Demolished Man*, winner of the first Hugo Award for Best Novel
	Ray Bradbury, *Fahrenheit 451*
	Arthur C. Clarke, *Childhood's End*
	Hal Clement, *Mission of Gravity*
	Ward Moore, *Bring the Jubilee* and "Lot" (sequel, "Lot's Daughter," 1954)

Philip José Farmer, *Strange Relations* (linked collection)
Walter M. Miller, Jr., *A Canticle for Leibowitz*
Theodore Sturgeon, *Venus Plus X*
The Time Machine (dir. George Pal)

1961   Gordon R. Dickson, *Naked to the Stars*
Harry Harrison, *The Stainless Steel Rat*
Robert A. Heinlein, *Strangers in a Strange Land*
Zenna Henderson, *Pilgrimage: The Book of the People* (linked collection)
Stanslaw Lem, *Solaris* (transl. US 1970)
Cordwainer Smith, "Alpha Ralpha Boulevard"
Leó Szilárd, "The Voice of the Dolphins"
Fantastic Four debut in *Fantastic Four #1*

1962   J. G. Ballard, *The Drowned World*
Philip K. Dick, *The Man in the High Castle*
Naomi Mitchison, *Memoirs of a Spacewoman*
Madeline L'Engle, *A Wrinkle in Time*
Eric Frank Russell, *The Great Explosion*
The Manchurian Candidate (dir. John Frankenheimer)
The Jetsons premieres
Spacewar! (first computer game)

1963   Kurt Vonnegut, *Cat's Cradle*
The Outer Limits premieres
First broadcast of *Doctor Who*

1964   Philip K. Dick, *Martian Time-Slip*
Robert A. Heinlein, *Farmham's Freehold*
Dr. Strangelove (dir. Stanley Kubrick)
New York World's Fair

1965   Philip K. Dick, *Dr. Bloodmoney*
Harlan Ellison, "'Repent, Harlequin!' Said the Ticktockman"
Harry Harrison, "The Streets of Ashkelon"
Frank Herbert, *Dune*, winner of the first Nebula Award for best novel
Jack Vance, *Space Opera*
Donald A. Wollheim and Terry Carr, eds., *The World's Best Science Fiction: 1965* (anthology)
Lost in Space premieres

1966   Samuel R. Delany, *Babel-17*
Philip K. Dick, "We Can Remember It For You Wholesale"
Harry Harrison, *Make Room! Make Room!*
Robert A. Heinlein, *The Moon Is a Harsh Mistress*
Damon Knight, ed., *Orbit I* (annual original anthology)
Frederik Pohl, "Day Million"
Thomas Pynchon, *The Crying of Lot 49*
Keith Roberts, "The Signaller"
Star Trek first broadcast in the USA

1967   Samuel R. Delany, *The Einstein Intersection*
Philip Jose Farmer, *Riders of the Purple Wage*

Ursula K. Le Guin, "The Ones Who Walk Away from Omelas"

Thomas Pynchon, *Gravity's Rainbow*

Mack Reynolds, *Looking Backward, from the Year 2000*

Alice Sheldon (as James Tiptree, Jr.), *Ten Thousand Light Years from Home* (collection) and "The Women Men Don't See"

Ian Watson, *The Embedding*

Sleeper (dir. Woody Allen)

Soylent Green (dir. Richard Fleischer)

Science-Fiction Studies begins publication

1974   Suzy McKee Charnas, *Walk to the End of the World*

Joe Haldeman, *The Forever War*

Ursula J. Le Guin, *The Dispossessed*

Larry Niven and Jerry Pournelle, *The Mote in God's Eye* (sequel *The Gripping Hand* [1993])

Land of the Lost premieres

1975   Ernest Callenbach, *Ecotopia*

Samuel R. Delany, *Dhalgren*

Salman Rushdie, *Grimus*

Joanna Russ, *The Female Man*

Pamela Sargent, ed., *Women of Wonder: SF Stories by Women About Women* (anthology)

Robert Shea and Robert Anton Wilson, *Illuminatus!*

Space Is the Place (dir. John Coney, featuring jazz musician Sun Ra)

The Rocky Horror Picture Show (dir. Jim Sharman)

1976   Octavia E. Butler, *Patternmaster*

Samuel R. Delany, *Triton*

Marge Piercy, *Woman on the Edge of Time*

Alice Sheldon (as James Tiptree Jr.), "Houston, Houston, Do you Read?"

Logan's Run (dir. Michael Anderson)

1977   Mack Reynolds, *After Utopia*

Joanna Russ, *We Who Are About To . . .*

Alice Sheldon (as James Tiptree, Jr.), "The Screwfly Solution"

Leslie Marmon Silko, *Ceremony*

Close Encounters of the Third Kind (dir. Steven Spielberg)

Star Wars (dir. George Lucas, sequels *The Empire Strikes Back* [1979] and *The Return of the Jedi* [1983])

1978   Stephen King, *The Stand*

Vonda MacIntyre, *Dreamsnake*

Dawn of the Dead (dir. George Romero)

Invasion of the Body Snatchers (dir. Philip Kaufman)

Battlestar Galactica (original series) premieres

Space Invaders (Taito Corporation)

1979   Douglas Adams, *The Hitch-Hiker's Guide to the Galaxy* (film 2005)

Octavia E. Butler, *Kindred*

John Crowley, *Engine Summer*

Sally Miller Gearhart, *The Wanderground*

Frederik Pohl, *Gateway*
Mack Reynolds, *Lagrange 5*
Kurt Vonnegut Jr., *Slaughterhouse-Five*
Alien (dir. Ridley Scott, sequel *Aliens* [1986])
Mad Max (dir. George Miller, sequels *Mad Max 2 – The Road Warrior* [1981], *Beyond Thunderdome* [1985], *Fury Road* [2015])
Star Trek: The Motion Picture (dir. Robert Wise)
Superman (dir. Richard Donner)

1980   Gregory Benford, *Timescape*
Suzy McKee Charnas, *The Vampire Tapestry*
Gene Wolfe, *The Shadow of the Torturer* (first volume of *The Book of the New Sun*)
Missile Command (Atari)

1981   C. J. Cherryh, *Downbelow Station*
Philip K. Dicks, *VALIS*
William Gibson, "The Gernsback Continuum"
Salman Rushdie, *Midnight's Children*
Vernor Vinge, "True Names"

1982   Brian W. Aldiss, *Helliconia Spring* (Helliconia 1)
Hayao Miyazaki, *Nausicaä of the Valley of the Wind* (film 1984)
Katsuhiro Ôtomo, *Akira v.1* (film 1988)
Blade Runner (dir. Ridley Scott)
E.T. the Extra-Terrestrial (dir. Steven Spielberg)
The Thing (dir. John Carpenter)
TRON (dir. Joseph Kosinski)
EPCOT Center opens
International Association for the Fantastic in the Arts founded

1983   David Brin, *Startide Rising*
Born in Flames (dir. Lizzie Borden)
WarGames (dir. John Badham)
V and *The Day After* premiere

1984   Octavia E. Butler, "Blood Child"
Samuel R. Delany, *Stars in My Pocket Like Grains of Sand*
Gardner Dozois, ed., *The Year's Best Science Fiction: First Annual Collection* (anthology)
Suzette Haden Elgin, *Native Tongue*
William Gibson, *Neuromancer*
Gwyneth Jones, *Divine Endurance*
Frederik Pohl and Elizabeth Anne Hull, eds., *Tales from the Planet Earth* (anthology)
Kim Stanley Robinson, "The Lucky Strike" and *The Wild Shore*
The Brother from Another Planet (dir. John Sayles)
The Terminator (dir. James Cameron, multiple sequels)

1985   Margaret Atwood, *The Handmaid's Tale*
Greg Bear, *Blood Music* and *Eon*
Orson Scott Card, *Ender's Game* (multiple sequels) (film 2013)
Don DeLillo, *White Noise*

Ursula K. Le Guin, *Always Coming Home*
Alan Moore and Dave Gibbons, *Watchmen*
James Morrow, *This Is the Way the World Ends*
Carl Sagan, *Contact*
Lewis Shiner and Bruce Sterling, "Mozart in Mirrorshades"
Bruce Sterline, *Schismatrix*
Kurt Vonnegut, *Galápagos*
Back to the Future (dir. Robert Zemeckis, sequels 1989 and 1990)
Brazil (dir. Terry Gilliam)

1986   Lois McMaster Bujold, *Ethan of Athos*
Orson Scott Card, *Speaker for the Dead*
Ken Grimwood, *Replay*
Pamela Sargent, *The Shore of Women*
Joan Slonczewski, *A Door into Ocean*
Bruce Sterling (ed.), *Mirrorshades* (anthology)
Metroid (Nintendo)

1987   Iain M. Banks, *Consider Phlebas*
Octavia E. Butler, *Dawn* (sequels *Adulthood Rites* [1988] and *Imago* [1989])
Pat Cardigan, *Mindplayers*
Judith Moffett, *Pennterra*
Lucius Shepard, *Life During Wartime*
Michael Swanwick, *Vacuum Flowers*
Robocop (dir. Paul Verhoeven)
Star Trek: The Next Generation and *Max Headroom* premiere
Mega-Man (Capcom)

1988   John Barnes, *Sin of Origin*
Terry Bisson, *Fire on the Mountain*
David Markson, *Wittgenstein's Mistress*
Masamune Shirow, *Ghost in the Shell* (film 1995; sequels *Ghost in the Shell: Stand Alone Complex* [2002], *Ghost in the Shell: Arise* [2013])
Sheri S. Tepper, *The Gate to Woman's Country*
They Live! (dir. John Carpenter)
Mystery Science Theater 3000 premieres

1989   Orson Scott Card, *The Folk of the Fringe*
Geoff Ryman, *The Child Garden*
Dan Simmons, *Hyperion*
Bruce Sterling, "Dori Bangs"
Sheri S. Tepper, *Grass*
Dingbo Wu, ed., *Science Fiction from China* (anthology)
Batman (dir. Tim Burton)
Alien Nation and *Quantum Leap* premiere

1990   David Brin, *Earth*
Colin Greenland, *Take Back Plenty*
Kim Stanley Robinson, *Pacific Edge*
Sheri. S. Tepper, *Raising the Stones*

1991   Stephen Baxter, *Raft*
       Emma Bull, *Bone Dance*
       Pat Cadigan, "Dispatches from the Revolution"
       Ted Chiang, "Understand"
       Michael Crichton, *Jurassic Park* (film 1993)
       Karen Joy Fowler, *Sarah Canary*
       Gwyneth Jones, *White Queen* (Aleutian Trilogy 1)
       Nancy Kress, "Beggars in Spain"
       Marge Piercy, *He, She and It*
       Brian Stableford, *Sexual Chemistry: Sardonic Tales of the Genetic Revolution* (collection)

1992   Derrick Bell, "The Space Traders"
       Greg Egan, *Quarantine*
       Maureen McHugh, *China Mountain Zhang*
       Horacio Moreno, ed., *Más Allá* (*Far Beyond* in English) (anthology)
       Kim Stanley Robinson, *Red Mars* (sequels *Green Mars* [1994] and *Blue Mars* [1996])
       Starhawk, *The Fifth Sacred Thing*
       Neal Stephenson, *Snow Crash*
       Vernor Vinge, *A Fire Upon the Deep*
       Connie Willis, *Doomsday Book*
       The X-Files premieres

1993   Eleanor Arnason, *Ring of Swords*
       Octavia E. Butler, *Parable of the Sower* (sequels *Parable of the Talents* [1998] and *Parable of the Trickster* [unfinished])
       Nicola Griffith, *Ammonite*
       Peter F. Hamilton, *Mindstar Rising*
       Lois Lowry, *The Giver* (film 2014)
       Horacio Moreno, ed., *Lo Fantastico* (*The Fantastic* in English) (anthology)
       Paul Park, *Coelestis*
       Star Trek: Deep Space Nine premieres
       Doom (id Software, multiple sequels) and *X-Wings* (LucasArts, multiple sequels)

1994   Kathleen Ann Goonan, *Queen City Jazz*
       Greg Egan, *Permutation City*
       Elizabeth Hand, *Waking the Moon*
       Jonathan Lethem, *Gun, with Occasional Music*
       Mike Resnick, *A Miracle of Rare Design*
       Melissa Scott, *Trouble and Her Friends*
       Babylon Five premieres

1995   Greg Egan, *Permutation City*
       Tim LaHaye and Jerry Jenkins, *Left Behind*
       Ken MacLeod, *The Star Fraction* (Fall Revolution 1)
       Daniel Quinn, *Ishmael*
       Melissa Scott, *Shadow Man*
       Neal Stephenson, *The Diamond Age*
       Neon Genesis Evangelion premieres in Japan (dir. Hideaki Anno)

Cixin Lui, *The Three-Body Problem* published in China (sequels *The Dark Forest* [2008], *Death's End* [2010]) (trans. Ken Liu)

2007 Michael Chabon, *The Yiddish Policeman's Union*
Junot Díaz, *The Brief Wondrous Life of Oscar Wao*
Portal (Valve, sequel *Portal 2* [2011]), *Bioshock* (2 K Boston, multiple sequels), and *Mass Effect* (Bioware, multiple sequels)

2008 Paul Auster, *Man in the Dark*
Paolo Bacigalupi, *Pump Six*
Ted Chiang, "Exhalation"
Suzanne Collins, *The Hunger Games* (multiple sequels, film 2012)
John Rieder, *Colonialism and the Emergence of Science Fiction*
Nisi Shawl, *Filter House*
Sleep Dealer (dir. Alex Rivera)
WALL-E (dir. Andres Stanton)
Fringe and *Star Wars: The Clone Wars* premiere
Braid (Number None, Inc.) and *Spore* (Maxis Corporation)

2009 Paolo Bacigalupi, *The Wind-Up Girl*
Stephen King, *Under the Dome*
Avatar (dir. James Cameron)
Star Trek (dir. J. J. Abrams, sequels 2013 and 2016)
Dollhouse premieres
Andrew Hussie, *Homestuck*
Minecraft (Mojang)
District 9 (dir. Neill Blomkamp)

2010 Andrea Hairston, *Redwood and Wildfire*
Nnedi Okorafor, *Who Fears Death*
Charles Yu, *How to Live Safely in a Science Fictional Universe*
Eliezer Yudkowsky, *Harry Potter and the Methods of Rationality*
Inception (dir. Christopher Nolan)
Pumzi (dir. Wanuri Kahiu)

2011 Lauren Buekes, *Zoo City*
Ernest Cline, *Ready Player One*
Rachel Haywood Ferreira, *The Emergence of Latin American Science Fiction*
Stephen King, *11/22/63*
Nnedi Okorafor, "Hello Moto"
Colson Whitehead, *Zone One*
Rise of the Planet of the Apes (dir. Rupert Wyatt, sequel 2014)
Black Mirror premieres

2012 Samuel R. Delany, *Through the Valley of the Nest of Spiders*
Grace Dillon, ed., *Walking the Clouds: An Anthology of Indigenous Science Fiction*
Junot Díaz, "Monstro"
Ken Liu, "The Paper Menagerie"
Nnedi Okorafor, ed., *AfroSF: Science Fiction by African Writers* (anthology)
Kim Stanley Robinson, *2312*
John Scalzi, *Redshirts*
Brian K. Vaughan and Fiona Staples, *Saga*

Andy Weir, *The Martian* (film 2015)
The Avengers (dir. Joss Whedon)
Looper (dir. Rian Johnson)
Star Wars Episodes VII–IX announced

2013   Bill Campbell and Edward Austin Hall, eds., *[Mothership]: Tales From Afrofuturism and Beyond*
Karen Joy Fowler, *We Are All Completely Beside Ourselves*
Anne Leckie, *Ancillary Justice* (sequels *Ancillary Sword* [2014] and *Ancillary Mercy* [2015]
Ken Liu, "Mono no aware"
Balogun Ojetdae, ed., *Steamfunk!*
Elysium (dir. Neill Blomkamp)
Her (dir. Spike Jonze)
Pacific Rim (dir. Guillermo del Toro)
Rick and Morty premieres (created by Dan Harmon and Justin Roiland)
Injustice: Gods Among Us (DC Entertainment)
Steven Universe premieres (created by Rebecca Sugar)
Gravity (dir. Alfonso Cuarón)

2014   Octavia E. Butler, *Unexpected Stories*
Nnedi Okorafor, *Lagoon*
Jeff VanderMeer, *Annihilation* (film 2018)
Captain America: The Winter Soldier (dir. Anthony Russo and Joe Russo)
The Guardians of the Galaxy (dir. James Gunn)
Interstellar (dir. Christopher Nolan)

2015   Paolo Bacigalupi, *The Water Knife*
Ted Chiang, "The Great Silence"
N. K. Jemisin, *The Fifth Season* (sequels *The Obelisk Gate* [2016] and *The Stone Sky* [2017]), the first trilogy to win three consecutive Hugo Awards
Hao Jingfang, "Folding Beijing" (trans. Ken Liu)
Nnedi Okorafor, *Binti*
Kim Stanley Robinson, *Aurora*
Neal Stephenson, *Seveneves*
Jurassic World (dir. Colin Trevorrow)
Ex Machina (dir. Alex Garland)
Star Wars: The Force Awakens (dir. J. J. Abrams)

2016   Ken Liu, ed. and trans., *Invisible Planets: Contemporary Chinese Science Fiction in Translation* (anthology)
Ada Palmer, *Too Like the Lightning*
Nisi Shawl, *Everfair*
Colson Whitehead, *The Underground Railroad*
Stranger Things premieres (dirs. Matt and Ross Duffer)
Independence Day: Resurgence (Roland Emmerich)
No Man's Sky (Hello Games)
Overwatch (Blizzard Entertainment)
Arrival (dir. Denis Villeneuve)
Rogue One: A Star Wars Story (dir. Gareth Edwards)

On Not Defining Science Fiction:
An Introduction

ERIC CARL LINK AND GERRY CANAVAN

The very idea of assembling a history of science fiction suggests a fundamental question: of what, exactly, is this a history? In one sense, the history of science fiction is the history of something that still feels relatively new. Not as new as some things – postmodernism, for instance, or the Internet – but certainly newer than many other topics that warrant enshrining between the boards of a Cambridge History. In another sense, however, one might suggest that humans have engaged with science fiction for centuries. Science fiction, in one form or another, is something artists have seemingly always participated in, but which was named less than a century ago, and thus it is an aesthetic with a chrome sheen of newness, and long and complicated trails of glory that extend back into the annals of artistic expression to Mary Shelley, or Thomas More, or even as far back as the ancient epic, depending on one's critical vantage point. This tension between science fiction's relative newness and the complicated network of definitions of the science fiction aesthetic that have managed to push debates over the origin of the category back to Gilgamesh and the Book of Genesis will receive no particular special pleading here: histories of artistic categories almost all share the difficulty of setting definitional borders. Yes, science fiction, like anything else, has its own set of nuances and particularities, but the debates engendered by such nuances are not so different from the debates that have ensued over the definition of romanticism or postmodernism or "the medieval" or "Europe" or any of several dozen other aesthetic categories of varying size, shape, and global impact.

In keeping with romanticism, postmodernism, and other complicated genres, movements, and aesthetic categories, the origin story of science fiction has been told and retold more times than DC Comics has reinvented the origin of Wonder Woman. It sometimes seems that science fiction has as many proposed origin points as it has critics. Do we begin with Hugo Gernsback, whose editorial and curatorial work in the American pulp magazines of the 1920s and 1930s helped crystallize science fiction as a recognizable and distinct literary genre? Do we begin with H. G. Wells – who introduced some of the best-loved tropes of the genre, like alien invasion and time travel – or go still further back, to Jules Verne, or to Edgar Allan Poe, or to Mary Shelley? Can we ignore the flying cities and horse civilizations of Jonathan Swift as proto-science fictions, which (like our own contemporary versions) satirically presented our own foibles and illusions to us as if for the first time? In his 1979 *Metamorphoses of Science Fiction*, Darko Suvin, one of the key figures in the initial establishment of science fiction studies as an academic discipline,[1] posits More's *Utopia* as the starting point for science fiction and utopian writing both – though Suvin elsewhere suggests that perhaps the Epic of Gilgamesh, the Tower of Babel, the Book of Revelation, and the Garden of Eden could all themselves be thought of as proto-science-fictions too, at least from a certain point of view. Perhaps "science fiction" is only the latest iteration of some larger tendency of the human imagination that in some sense truly is innate and transhistorical.

Wherever one begins, it is clear that the story of science fiction is transnational and transmedia, cutting across the easy and well-policed boundary lines that typically structure academic departments. It is a history that has roots in the philosophical and fantastic narratives of the ancient past, and which continues not only to flourish in the twenty-first century but to serve as a cross-cultural language spoken throughout every corner of the globe. When the study of science fiction literature entered the academy in the 1950s and 1960s – slowly and hesitatingly at first, but gaining in status and momentum throughout the last quarter of the twentieth century – it became increasingly evident to students of science fiction that it was not merely the literature of imaginary objects, but a literature that evolved out of, and celebrated, the human compulsion to push beyond the horizon of the real in order to gain new perspective on human nature and experience. This compulsion has manifested itself in every major twentieth- and twenty-first-century cultural enterprise, from literary production to the visual arts, to music, architecture, and interactive media. From the vantage point of the first quarter of the twenty-first century, the contributions of science fiction to human intellectual and cultural endeavor are clearly not something one can capture through mere description of the forms, tropes, and conventions of science fiction literature. It is no longer adequate to approach the study of

---

[1] See Gerry Canavan, "The Suvin Event," in Darko Suvin, *Metamorphoses of Science Fiction* (New York: Ralahine Utopian Studies, 2016 [1979]).

science fiction simply as the description of some particular and peculiar enterprise, at the fringes of culture; instead, one must tell the story of the evolution of the transnational and multimedia manifestations of science fiction as it has intersected with the larger cultural movements and socio-political fluctuations of its age. It is this intellectual history – the history of the century-old, many-headed *project* of science fiction, writ large – that *The Cambridge History of Science Fiction* seeks to narrate.

Since the formal study of science fiction first established itself in the academy, science fiction has shifted from a position on the margins of scholarly discourse to the position it holds at present as a recognized and established literary genre that has generated a significant and growing body of scholarship. As a field of study, it has proven both popular and provocative: courses in science fiction are now taught at colleges and universities through-out the United States, Europe, and beyond, and narratives in a variety of media – print, film, music, art, architecture – that engage the conventions and ideas of science fiction are pervasive in contemporary culture. Meanwhile, scholarship on science fiction has gone well past its infancy, and is now entrenched in the academy, with numerous high-quality books published by academic presses on the subject every year, several major academic journals devoted to the topic – including *Science Fiction Studies, Extrapolation, Foundation, FEMSPEC, The New York Review of Science Fiction, Science Fiction Film and Television, Journal of the Fantastic in the Arts,* as well as the trade journal *Locus* – and courses at both the undergraduate and graduate levels on the subject being offered at universities across the United States and abroad. The Science Fiction Research Association (SFRA) and International Association for the Fantastic in the Arts (IAFA) both boast strong member-ship, holding annual conferences which attract scholars from around the world. Scholarly books on science fiction run the gamut from monographs that pursue a particular idea or thesis, through edited collections of essays, to a growing body of reference works, encyclopedias, guidebooks, and so forth. Thus, with the maturation of the study of science fiction – and its ongoing and profound popularity in American and world pop culture – the time for serious consideration of the history of science fiction has hit a kind of critical mass.

***

In this *Cambridge History of Science Fiction*, as will become evident, the editors have taken an inclusive approach to science fiction, but not so inclusive as to make science fiction out of literally anything. The boundary line between inclusion and exclusion from the category is one of the key debates that emerge from among the array of definitions offered by critics of science fiction over the past century. The sweep of these many definitions have been discussed numerous times by other critics and will not be repeated here. Nevertheless, there will be value to examining a few definitions of science fiction in order to draw from them some of the broad definitional principles that frame *The Cambridge History of Science Fiction*.

As others have pointed out over the past several decades, there is a certain wit and charm to the notion that, as Damon Knight somewhat famously suggested in 1952, science fiction is "what we point to when we say it."[2] But this formulation has little value as a critical tool, whatever its value might be in highlighting the complicated marketing and cultural factors that feed into the discussion between *genre* and *non-genre* science fiction. Likewise, the division among authors and critics over the decades between the relative merits of the labels *science fiction, speculative fiction*, and even *structural fabulation*, not to mention the entertaining tensions between "sci-fi" and "SF" (vs. "sf") and the wretched "SyFy" and beyond, all point to the range of nuances that characterized, in part, the various attempts by different groups – authors, academics, fandoms, detractors – to situate science fiction and determine its boundaries (much less determine its relationship to adjacent genre categories like *fantasy, horror, noir, romance, realism*, and so on).[3]

There is a certain logic to Knight's quip, however. Not only does SF remain deeply imbricated in its relationship to a marketing category – SF is, as much as anything else, a *brand* – SF in the main is something that, in this twenty-first century, is readily recognizable to both academic and non-academic communities. Much of this is due to the fact of the pervasive nature of the SF aesthetic in modern culture, coupled with the array of tropes and conventions that have characterized the aesthetic for a century or more – from bug-eyed monsters to spaceships to physics-defying wormholes and warp drives. If there is a spaceship, a ray gun, an alien – it's SF. Arguments tend to occur around the fringes, and often occur at the point of overlap with

---

[2] Damon Knight, *In Search of Wonder: Essays on Modern Science Fiction* (Chicago: Advent Publishers, 1967), p. 1. For a brief survey and discussion of the many different attempts to define science fiction in the twentieth century, see the entry on "Definitions of SF" in the *Encyclopedia of Science Fiction* (see www.sf-encyclopedia.com/entry/definitions_of_sf). See also the "Science Fiction" entry in Gary K. Wolfe's *Critical Terms for Science Fiction and Fantasy* (New York: Greenwood, 1986). Another good entry point into the critical literature on the definition of science fiction is James Gunn and Matthew Candelaria, eds., *Speculations on Speculation: Theories of Science Fiction* (Lanham, MD: Scarecrow Press, 2005).

[3] As will soon become evident, in these pages we will favor SF as the catch-all term.

related genres. Many utopian novels are in some fashion or another SF novels, for sure, but not all of them. What must a utopian novel have in order for it to make sense to call it SF? Even more pointed are debates related to the role of *science* in SF. It is well documented that some of the earliest claims on behalf of the category – from Gernsback and others – stressed that the science of SF must have a certain underlying credibility to it. Not in the way that the recent "mundane" science fiction movement would define it, of course – but there was a kind of claim of extrapolative veracity to the science in science fiction that almost aligned the movement, in a way, with the generous claims made by Émile Zola on behalf of *Le roman expérimental* in the late nineteenth century (an unlikely pairing on the surface, perhaps, but there is an odd kinship to be found here, too).

Yet, as any reader of SF knows, claims for the veracity or extrapolative "reasonableness" of the *science* in science fiction are instantaneously problematic. SF has little to do with real scientific investigation, and many texts routinely considered among the greatest instances of the category are scientifically quite silly. Moreover, whole subgenres of SF – the time travel fantasy, for instance – have little or nothing to do with "science." Indeed, if science is in any way the key to understanding science fiction, one might have to lop off whole subcategories, like the alternative history novel, which may seem perfectly fine when the novel is Philip Roth's *The Plot Against America* (2004) but which seems decidedly problematic when one is considering Philip K. Dick's *The Man in the High Castle* (1962) – and which seems inevitably to lead us to the absurdity of declaring that a foundational science fictional text like *Star Wars* isn't *actually* SF because, because, because . . .

The issues that have arisen from the "science" of SF lead numerous critics and authors over the twenty-first century to shift toward substitute labels and reconceptualizations, with *speculative fiction* now the dominant alternative. SF, too, has come to be a convenient shorthand symbol for the entire aesthetic category, precisely *because* it sidesteps the entire *science v. speculative* debate while still recognizing some inherent coherence to the concept itself.[4] Even if we can successfully sidestep the science debate, attempts to define SF still have plenty of other academic questions to answer: for instance, what distinguishes SF from fantasy, and is SF a subset of fantasy, or vice versa, or are they actually separate categories that perform different cultural and intellectual work? For many genre questions, these oppositions

---

[4] As Gary K. Wolfe has noted, it's likely that SF is "almost universally favored in the science-fiction community" precisely because the two letters don't really stand for anything. See "Coming to Terms," in Gunn and Candelaria, eds., *Speculations on Speculation*.

are not simply academic questions but fiercely debated moral allegiances; genre work both inside and outside the academy has typically proceeded from the assumption that certain genres are "good" for us (politically, ethically, cognitively, you name it) and that others are "bad" – a critical impasse that is only now being moved beyond.

Several attempts to provide a working definition of SF have produced compelling results. Perhaps the best known attempt within academic circles is the definition provided by Darko Suvin: "SF is, then, a literary genre whose necessary and sufficient conditions are the presence and interaction of estrangement and cognition, and whose main formal device is an imaginative framework alternative to the author's empirical environment."[5] Suvin uses this idea of a dialectical interplay between cognition and estrangement, between similarity and difference, between science and fiction, as the focal point for extended discussion in *Metamorphoses of Science Fiction* on the utopian nature of SF and how it differs both from realist writing and from other varieties of the fantastic. Central to Suvin's definition is the concept he introduces of the *novum* – the new thing – the element or elements introduced into a work of science fiction that sets it apart from the zero world – that is, the consensus, empirical world we inhabit.

This definition has been the subject of considerable analysis and debate, and is commonly used as a starting point for analysis of the genre even by those who ultimately reject Suvin's terms – but, as influential as Suvin's work on this topic has been, his is only one of dozens of attempts to precisely define what SF is, and what it isn't, over the past century. In his Pioneer-Award-winning essay "On Defining SF, or Not: Genre Theory, SF, and History" – now the spine of his paradigm-shifting monograph *Science Fiction and the Mass Cultural Genre System* (2017) – John Rieder offers a schema for understanding how to understand SF as a "historical process":

(1) sf is history and mutable;
(2) sf has no essence, no single unifying characteristic, and no point of origin;
(3) sf is not a set of texts, but rather a way of using texts and drawing relationships among them;
(4) sf's identity is a differentially articulated position in an historical and mutable field of genres;

---

[5] Darko Suvin, *Metamorphoses of Science Fiction: On the Poetics and History of a Literary Genre* (New Haven: Yale University Press, 1979), pp. 7–8.

(5) attribution of the identity of sf to a text constitutes an active intervention in its distribution and reception.[6]

In the spirit of Rieder's analysis, therefore, we might sidestep this now-routinized definitional pitfall by noting that all compelling attempts to define SF as "the literature of x" seem to truly capture a core element of many of the texts – broadly conceived to include art, literature, film, music, architecture, video games, and more – that comprise the category, but nonetheless they all fall short of being descriptive of everything we could conceivably associate with the category or they are so broad as to encapsulate far more than we would typically associate with the category (and even, sometimes, both at the same time).

Taking our cues from Knight, Rieder, Suvin, and Carl Freedman, among others, the editors of this *Cambridge History of Science Fiction* understand the term "SF" to in general denote a very broad category of aesthetic enterprise that posits some discontinuity with the empirical world – as opposed to continuity with the empirical world – and further understand that the nature of that discontinuity is in alignment with a principally post-Enlightenment value system that is oriented toward naturalized as opposed to supernaturalized extrapolation. SF and fantasy are not diametrically opposed, we would suggest, but exist along a spectrum of discontinuity, where the discontinuities described in the narrative – in the spirit of Suvin's cognitive estrangement and especially Freedman's "cognition effect"[7] – are either more or less domesticated within a more or less rational metanarrative framework. Thus the ghosts of *A Christmas Carol* might well be a barred term for SF, while the ghosts of *Ghostbusters* slip through – and the dreamlike time travel of *A Connecticut Yankee in King Arthur's Court* indeed feels less like SF to us than the technologically fueled time travel of *The Time Machine* and *Back to the Future*. But even these sorts of bare, gestural demarcations feel highly provisional, subject to change at any moment – and certainly at the mercy of some persuasive argument to the contrary. The true, absolute essence of SF, that odd, unnamable thing we feel we recognize immediately when we see it, is

---

[6] John Rieder, "On Defining SF, or Not: Genre Theory, SF, and History," *Science Fiction Studies* 37, 2 (July 2010), pp. 192–3.

[7] See Carl Freedman, *Critical Theory and Science Fiction* (Middletown, CT: Wesleyan University Press, 2000), p. 18: "All these examples suggest that cognition proper is not, in the strictest terms, exactly the quality that defines science fiction. What is rather at stake is what we might term ... the *cognition effect*. The crucial issue for generic discrimination is not any epistemological judgment external to the text itself or the rationality or irrationality of the latter's imaginings, but rather ... the attitude of the text itself to the kind of estrangements being performed."

always moving away from us at warp speed; its shields are up and its cloaking device is fully engaged.

Thus the editors of the present volume have no intention of answering all of the questions above, nor of settling the debate, *per se*, regarding the definition of SF. Instead, we take SF as a historical process in which many sorts of people have intervened – or can be seen, retroactively, to have been intervening – in different ways, to different extents, as far back as human memory goes. And as our writers in the coming chapters capably demonstrate, these sorts of debates among writers, critics, and fans are themselves a key part of the history of this or any genre. Thus in one telling SF can be seen to trace its DNA back to the speculative narrative writing of the ancient epic – but in another it is a specifically post-Enlightenment or specifically *modernist* narrative product, emerging slowly out of the transformative political and economic conditions of the nineteenth century before achieving a kind of cultural saturation in the twentieth and twenty-first. One telling might emphasize its European, or even Anglo-American, roots – while another might center the science fictional imaginations of France, Germany, Russia, Latin America, America, China, or Japan, while still another might see SF as emerging precisely out of the transnational and indeed transhistorical crosscurrents of global fandom.

Our study traces these myriad and overlapping interventions in SF history – in casting SF as a historical process – through three general periods: "Before the New Wave," "The New Wave," and "After the New Wave." We have chosen this organizational structure to reflect the central importance of the New Wave as a turning point in the genre's development and history, not simply in terms of the changing creative output of (some of) its writers but also in the shift in SF's reception in culture, particularly in the academy. Science fiction studies, as an academic discipline, itself begins during the New Wave, and remains strongly informed by New Wave concerns about utopia and empire, while continuing to focus a tremendous amount of attention on 1970s New Wave writers like Philip K. Dick, Ursula K. Le Guin, Samuel R. Delany, and Octavia E. Butler to this day. For the person interested in science fiction in an academic context, we feel that special attention to the New Wave is required to make sense of the traditions and practices of SF scholarship that originated in that time. The preferred themes, tropes, and literary-cultural forms of SF completely transformed during the revolutionary decade of the New Wave, with contemporary work tending to follow in that mold. The sorts of demographic changes in authorship and readership (especially around increased diversity and inclusivity) that now structure the field also begin in earnest during that time, producing an SF imagination that can finally be said to be, for the first time, truly global.

Across each of three divisions, we focus on the major texts and trends of each historical moment. We also trace a number of recognizable "arcs" on crucial subtopics across our chapters: the history of non-literary media forms, especially film and television; the large impact of fandom and fan practices on the history of the field; the contributions of nonwhite and nonmale authors; and the critical history of science fiction studies. Alongside the chronological trajectory, we have also made space for breakout chapters on particularly crucial themes, such as war, consumerism, postmodernism, and environmentalism. We hope these embedded mini-arcs provide useful historical subnarratives that tell part of the immense larger story that is SF – a symphony in which even a critical volume as large and as daunting as a Cambridge History can strike only the most hesitant opening note.

PART I

★

BEFORE THE NEW WAVE

Science Fiction before Science Fiction: Ancient, Medieval, and Early Modern SF

RYAN VU

What do we have to gain by projecting the term "science fiction" onto literary eras that predate the nineteenth century, before not only the earliest texts it was intended to describe, but even before "science" and "fiction" acquired their current definitions? The further into the past we look, the further we get from the supposed epistemological rupture that gives SF coherence as a distinct narrative genre. Whatever historical event "modernity" might be thought to refer to – the Renaissance, the Enlightenment, the rise of capitalism – the notion of a radical break with a premodern past is essential to Hugo Gernsback's 1926 definition of "scientifiction."[1]

No "prehistory" of SF can liberate us from our guiding assumptions, but in forcing us to redefine our terms it becomes a constructive, even necessary project. This chapter's premise is that "science fiction before science fiction" is a worthwhile object of scholarly inquiry precisely for the ways it challenges SF theory's most fundamental concepts. For example, Brett Rogers and Benjamin Stevens's recent use of Theodore Sturgeon's term "knowledge fictions" aims at extending SF studies into the classical period, encompassing narratives of epistemological questioning in general over any particular modality.[2] Such a wide net could encompass the earliest recorded myths and fables; SF would then name a tendency inherent to narrative itself rather than a distinct genre or even literary mode.

The polar opposite approach is critical historicism, which restricts SF to the period of its emergence as a self-conscious genre in the twentieth century or by tracking its rise through the nineteenth, moving in parallel with the

---

[1] Hugo Gernsback, "A New Sort of Magazine," *Amazing Stories* 1 (April, 1926), p. 3, quoted in Gary Westfahl, *Hugo Gernsback and the Century of Science Fiction* (Jefferson, NC: McFarland and Company, 2007), p. 20.

[2] Brett Rogers and Benjamin Stevens, *Classical Traditions in Science Fiction* (Oxford: Oxford University Press, 2015).

development of the realist novel.[3] Adam Roberts has attempted to split the difference between the two camps by locating the beginnings of SF in the seventeenth-century imaginary voyage, born out of the spread of Copernicanism in Britain and France and the literary revival of Lucianic satire.[4] His work has the advantage of drawing meaningful historical connections between the conventional period of SF's rise and the whole tradition of Western rationalism, from the Greeks and Romans to the Renaissance and Enlightenment. Refusing to treat SF as a purely secular phenomenon, it also provocatively roots the genre's later concerns in the metaphysical consequences of the Protestant reformation. While this conception unfortunately limits the history of SF to Europe and the West, it remains the most productive theorization of "early SF."

My guiding ambition, however, is to take as ecumenical a view as possible, providing an overview of ancient, classical, and early modern texts that have been or could be counted as twentieth-century SF's antecedents without endorsing any one definitional paradigm. Neither teleological nor strictly linear, this account will traverse multiple genres and lines of scholarship, from philosophical dialogue to travel satire to utopian fiction and beyond.

Classical / Antique: Myth, Travelers' Tales, Imaginary Voyages

The traveler's tale and its close cousin the imaginary voyage are the oldest literary genres consistently associated with SF. Existing in some form as long as storytelling itself, both center on travel to far-off places and exciting adventures, separated not by any explicit formal difference but by the inherently ambiguous criteria of tone and plausibility. For the contemporary reader, empirical veracity is of secondary consequence to formal and thematic interpretation. Through narrating an encounter with the unknown other, they enabled reflection on the familiar, allowing not only for wonder and the utopian imagination but also parody and satire. Like SF, the voyage was inherently epistemological, confronting the reader/listener with layers

---

[3] John Rieder offers the most convincing recent historicist account of SF's relationship to other narrative genres, by separating the commercial genres of mass culture (SF, detective fiction, etc.) and the classical genres (tragedy, comedy, satire) inherited by the literary academy into historically distinct but interrelated genre systems. See John Rieder, *Science Fiction and the Mass Cultural Genre System* (Middletown, CT: Wesleyan University Press, 2017).

[4] Adam Roberts, *The History of Science Fiction* (Basingstoke: Palgrave Macmillan, 2006), p. 42.

of interpretive ambiguity: between experience and invention, earnestness and irony, knowledge, speculation, and pure fantasy.

While it may not include the first voyage fiction, Greco-Roman literature does constitute the best-preserved archive extending before the first millennium CE. The episodes of the *Odyssey* (around 700–675 BCE) suggest the existence of a lively oral tradition of voyage tales by the eighth century BCE while serving as a root for countless later works. Ancient Greek philosophy is distinguished by a commitment to materialism as early as Thales's positing of water as the universal substance of nature (620–546 BCE) and his criticisms of mythology. Perhaps the most convincing basis for locating the earliest examples of "proto-SF" within Greco-Roman voyage literature is its close dialogue with the earliest philosophy of nature.

Our story is complicated by the fact that the oldest imaginary voyage preserved in its entirety is a parody of travel narratives written by historians and poets alike. The Assyrian rhetorician and satirist Lucian's *True Histories* (*Verae Historiae*, second century CE) begins with the disclaimer that everything that follows is a lie. "So," he concludes, "I am writing about things I neither saw nor experienced nor heard about from others, which moreover don't exist, and in any case could not exist. My readers must therefore entirely disbelieve them."[5] The narrative accordingly spins uninhibited fantasy for comic effect: a voyage in search of a continent beyond the western sea is delayed by a war between the people of the Moon and Sun, a sojourn in the belly of a whale, and a stopover on the Isle of the Blessed (the paradisiacal afterlife in Greek mythology). Employing fiction to interrogate the ambiguous distinction between *historia* (history) and *mûthoi* (myth), the *True History* was the chief surviving example of Menippean satire to inform the early modern lunar voyage, *Gulliver's Travels*, and the multitude of satirical imaginary voyages published in the early modern period. Its skeptical mockery of philosophers echoes Aristophanes's (fifth century BCE) attacks on Socrates in the comedy *Clouds*, while the narrative format parodies contemporary travelers' tales. Neither *True History* nor Lucian's later *Icaromenippus*, the two earliest texts commonly identified as SF or proto-SF, are straightforward advocates for rationalism or materialism; their thoroughgoing skepticism takes aim at the speculative flights of philosophers and utopians as well as the poetic license assumed by writers of history.

The Moon served as the ideal destination for Lucian's satirical purposes. It occupied a liminal position in the geocentric cosmology of Aristotle, marking

---

[5] Lucian, *Selected Dialogues* (Oxford: Oxford University Press, 2006), p. 204.

the border between terrestrial and celestial regions. The sublunar domain, consisting of the four primary elements (earth, fire, water, air), was subject to constant change – birth and decay – while the planets, sun, and stars, composed of a fifth element called quintessence, moved along perfect, eternal orbits. The mere notion of planetary inhabitants was as unthinkable as travel beyond the lunar border. The Moon itself was a more ambiguous prospect. The earliest canonical source for the notion that the Moon is a world like the Earth is Plutarch's *On the Face in the Moon* (second century CE), a fantastic philosophical dialogue that includes a detailed description of its surface and the argument that life on the Moon is no less plausible than life in the ocean (populating it, as per tradition, with "daemons," or human souls).[6] But even if the Moon could theoretically be reached from Earth, actual travel would require extraordinary means. This made it an open invitation to the speculative imagination, and the perfect target for a critique of the same.[7]

As a potential alternative world, the Moon also has long existed in a reflexive relationship with Earth, providing a critical vantage point on terrestrial customs and foibles. En route to the Moon, the narrator of *Icaromenippus* initially indulges in this imaginary perspective, looking down on earthly affairs with ironic detachment as a "colony of ants."[8] Yet despite riding on the stolen wings of an eagle and a vulture (a parody of Icarus), the merely human narrator can never reach the heights of the gods. The lunar goddess Selene, tired of being the object of idle speculation, begs the narrator to ask Zeus to silence the arrogant philosophers. *Icaromenippus* closes with an impassioned speech by Zeus denouncing their hypocrisy. The fable's defense of the gods and critique of philosophy at once undermines SF's speculative aims and serves as a distant precursor to countless later SF stories about humanity's overreach.

Closely related to the imaginary voyage, the utopia is the other major classical genre most often associated with SF. Though the utopian imagination has often been identified as SF's central feature, the history of utopian literature is better understood as a parallel genre history with occasional overlap than a direct antecedent (or, as in Darko Suvin's provocation, a subgenre of SF[9]). Some, like the ideal cities outlined in Plato's *Republic*

---

[6] Plutarch, *Moralia, Vol. xii* (London: William Heinemann, 1960–2004), p. 179.
[7] Plutarch's dialogue includes a mythical traveler's tale that claims among other things that the Moon is the abode of spirits due to its intermediate status; this tale is likely one of Lucian's sources and his targets.
[8] Lucian, *Selected Dialogues*, p. 54.
[9] Suvin, *Metamorphoses of Science Fiction: On the Poetics and History of a Literary Genre* (New Haven: Yale University Press, 1979), p. 13.

(*c.* 380 BCE) and *Laws*, are only lightly fictionalized and lean toward the programmatic. More ambiguous in intent are the utopian episodes within longer voyage fiction by Euhemerus, Iambulus, and Antonius Diogenes, which only survive in fragments or secondhand summaries by Diodorus Siculus (first century BCE)[10] and Photius (810–893 CE).[11] All are framed as ethnographic accounts of exotic travel to isolated societies, from Iambulus's tale of sun-worshipping natives on the islands of Ethiopia[12] to Euhemerus's rational multiethnic paradise[13] to the close encounter with the Moon described by Diogenes.[14] These writers took their cues from historian and ethnographer Hectaeus of Abdera (fourth century BCE), who, in treatises on Egypt and the mythical far northern island of Hyperborea,[15] freely mixed fact, speculation, and invention.[16] For the Greeks, natural phenomena were more subject to variation in the climates of India, Persia, and Africa than in the temperate Mediterranean.[17] The "edges of the earth" beyond the *oikoumene* (known or inhabited world) thus gave writers license to imagine strange alternate worlds, in the process reflecting on current philosophical, anthropological, and other theories in a manner that would be repeated in medieval and early modern voyage fiction and is comparable to twentieth-century SF visions of alien cultures.

Though Lucian mocks these earlier writers for employing the rhetoric of history to spin implausible tales about inaccessible places,[18] it is unclear how straightforwardly they were ever intended. For instance, according to Photius, Diogenes himself ironically cites Antiphanes of Berge (fourth century BCE) as an influence,[19] a writer so famous for unbelievable travel tales

---

[10] *Bibliotheca historica* (60–30 BCE).

[11] *Bibliotheca / Myriobiblion* (820–827).

[12] *Islands in the Sun* (165–50 BCE).

[13] The island of Panchaea in *Hiera Anagraphe* ("The Sacred Inscription," *c.* 300 BCE). The islanders believe that Greek gods were originally great kings and heroes who had been deified over time.

[14] In the 24-volume *The Wonders Beyond Thule* (possibly second century CE).

[15] An island supposed to lie beyond the north of Britain.

[16] As of course did Diodorus, in whose *Bibliotheca* Hectaeus's work survives in fragments and summaries.

[17] See James Romm, *The Edges of the Earth in Ancient Thought: Geography, Exploration, and Fiction* (Princeton: Princeton University Press, 1992) pp. 82–108 for an overview of ancient thought regarding the wonders of India.

[18] See the Greek rhetorical distinction between *historia*, including historical narrative and recorded knowledge, and *mûthoi*, which can refer to myth, fable, and fiction. Romm, *Edges of the Earth*, p.10.

[19] Antonius Diogenes, *The Wonders Beyond Thule*, trans. Gerald N. Sandy in B. P. Reardon, ed., *Collected Ancient Greek Novels* (Berkeley, CA: University of California Press, 1989), p. 782.

that "bergaizein," an Attic verb for outlandish lying, was coined after the town of his birth.[20] *True Histories* distinguishes itself from its targets by commenting on its own invented status, its primary subject being the ambiguous relationship between written narrative and the experiential world. For Lucian, to distinguish clearly between history and poetry is narrative interpretation's most urgent task.[21] Lucian's criticisms marked out an as-yet-undefined territory by highlighting fiction's unstable position half-way between truth and lies.[22]

Medieval Europe

The medieval period is traditionally left out of SF histories. If we understand the genre to be rooted in the rationalist, empiricist project of the Enlightenment, the long interregnum between the decline of Rome and the Italian Renaissance would not seem a promising place to look. But more recent scholarship has complicated this assumption. The conventions of medieval romance continue to structure SF narratives, intentionally and otherwise, and the rational imagination of alternate worlds figured strongly in medieval natural philosophy.[23] If we wish to understand how the histories of science and fiction intersect, we can little afford to ignore this pivotal epoch.

Among the most influential medieval texts of interest to SF scholars is Cicero's "Dream of Scipio," a brief concluding fragment from his six-volume political-philosophical dialogue *De re publica* (54–51 BCE). Preserved with extensive commentary by Macrobius (*c.* 400 CE), this text became a primary vessel for the survival of Neoplatonist and Stoic philosophy within medieval Christian thought. While the Neoplatonic privileging of consciousness over observable material phenomena may seem anathema to natural science, in this pre-Enlightenment context it enabled the speculative, imaginative thought about nature that would later be associated with SF.

Likewise, dream visions are framed around mystical experience rather than rational extrapolation. Yet this conceit is precisely what enabled them to

---

[20] Stephanus Byzantius, *Strabo.*

[21] His position is further elaborated upon in his essay "How to Write History" in Lucian, *Selected Dialogues*, pp.181–202.

[22] Georgiadou and Larmour trace this interest to Dio Chrysotom's introduction to his *Oration* 5 ("Libyan Myth"), in which he argues that the earliest myths were created as allegories, using lies to convey a truth. See Aristoula Georgiadou and David H. J. Larmour, *Lucian's Science Fiction Novel. True Histories: Interpretation and Commentary* (Leiden: Brill, 1998), p. 4. Lucian's truth is a negative, critical one.

[23] Edward Grant, *A History of Natural Philosophy* (Cambridge: Cambridge University Press, 2007), p. 225.

explore analogous metaphysical and cosmological ideas. The "Dream of Scipio" imagines that Scipio, the Roman conqueror of Carthage, is visited in his dreams on the eve of victory by his adoptive grandfather. Together they look down on the Earth from the heavens. "The starry spheres," Scipio notes, "were much larger than the earth; indeed the earth itself seemed to me so small that I was scornful of our empire, which covers only a single point, as it were, upon its surface."[24] Just as the gods did for Lucian, the parable's Neoplatonist metaphysics, urging the reader to take inspiration from the unchanging perfection of the stars over mutable earthly matter, invoke cosmic scales to deflate human ambition. Along with updating the fragment's cosmology in terms of Ptolemy's complex system of epicycles, Macrobius's commentary includes theories of dream analysis and allegory that bear striking similarities to later discussions of fantastic fiction, arguing that outlandish narratives, through proper interpretation, revealed moral and spiritual truths.

Accounts of distant travel, firsthand and otherwise, continued to be important vehicles for reflection on the changing status of knowledge about the world and humankind's place within it. Highly popular, illustrated bestiaries included detailed descriptions of flora and fauna within Europe along with accounts of natural wonders beyond the borders of Christendom. They were organized like encyclopedias, with each entry merging natural history with Christian symbolism and morality. For medieval Christians, nature was not governed by observable, universal laws but by the will of God to instruct mankind. While there was a gradual embrace of nature's predictability as more Greek and Arabic texts on natural history and philosophy were translated into Latin in the twelfth century,[25] deviations were still thought possible, and (as with the ancient Greeks) were believed to be increasingly common the further one traveled. The center of epistemic authority for both bestiaries and travel tales wavered between references to canonical texts[26] and personal observation[27] with no clear demarcation between fact and fiction. Boundary-mixing in all ways, creatures such as

[24] Cicero, *The Republic*, in Loeb Classical Library, 213, trans. C. W. Keyes (Harvard: Harvard University Press), p. 269.

[25] Lorraine Daston and Katherine Park, *Wonders and the Order of Nature* (New York: Zone Books, 1998), pp. 109–20.

[26] Aristotle's *History of Animals* (fourth century BCE) and Pliny the Elder's *Natural History* (77–79 CE) were major sources; formal predecessors include *Physiologus* (anonymous, second – fourth century CE), Isidore of Seville's *Etymologiae* (seventh century CE), and Bartholemus Anglicus's *De proprietatibus rerum* (1240 CE).

[27] See discussion of Albertus Magnus in Karen Meier Reeds and Tomomi Kinukawa, "Medieval Natural History," in *The Cambridge History of Science* (Cambridge: Cambridge University Press, 2013), pp. 575–8.

basilisks, centaurs, and the leucrota (a composite of hyena, lion, horse, and stag with the ability to mimic human speech)[28] were typically conceived as animal–human hybrids. The experience of wonder at these monstrous races was considered morally valuable insofar as it provoked the recognition of mortal ignorance.[29] Accounts of the marvelous and strange in nature, whether encyclopedic or narrative in structure, thrived well into the seventeenth century. The best-known fictional travelogue to draw on bestiaries, romances, folklore, encyclopedias, and (perhaps) firsthand experience alike is the fourteenth-century *Travels of Sir John Mandeville* (1357–71). Also borrowing heavily from recent travel writing by Odoric of Pordenone and Marco Polo, the *Travels* claims to tell of an English knight's journeys across North Africa and Asia and his encounters with the great Khan of China, a Brahminic utopia, cannibals, automata, and headless humanoids with their faces on their chests, among other outlandish adventures. Its precise relationship to actual experience continues to be the subject of debate; Christopher Columbus believed he was following Mandeville's directions to the "Isle of Cathay" when he sailed west in 1492.

Medieval accounts of the marvelous could defer authority to canonical texts from antiquity, but a few such narratives strove to be convincing on their own terms. The tale of the "Green Men of Woolpit," first mentioned by English historians William of Newburgh[30] and Ralph of Coggeshall,[31] is distinguished by the chroniclers' insistence on eyewitnesses. Though they differ in key details, both versions are set in the middle of the twelfth century and tell of a green-skinned boy and girl found in a ditch in the East Anglian village of Woolpit. Though they initially spoke an unknown language, they were made accustomed to English ways, eventually losing their green color.[32] The girl describes their home as a world where the Sun never rises. This tale would later be referenced by Francis Godwin and others (see below) and is considered one of the earliest non-mythical accounts of an extraterrestrial encounter.

---

[28] Royal MS 12 C XIX, ff 6r–94v. 1200–1210. British Library Manuscripts, www.bl.uk/manuscripts/FullDisplay.aspx?ref=Royal_MS_12_C_XIX (last accessed June 20, 2018).

[29] Following St. Augustine. See Daston and Park, *Wonders and the Order of Nature*, pp. 39–48.

[30] Chapter 27 of *Historia rerum Anglicarum*.

[31] In his contributions to the *Chronicon Anglicanum* between 1187 and 1224.

[32] For a detailed analysis of both versions and the history of their reception (from which my summary is derived), see Mary Baine Campbell, "'Those two green children which Nubrigensis speaks of in his time, that fell from heaven', or the Origins of Science Fiction," in Carl Kears and James Paz, eds., *Medieval Science Fiction* (London: King's College London, Centre for Late Antique and Medieval Studies, 2016), pp. 117–32.

Though exotic travel writing often borrowed from romance, this capacious form (along with the *chanson de geste*) is overall perhaps too distant from philosophical reflection on the natural world to warrant direct consideration in a history of SF. Yet many SF subgenres owe it an immense formal debt.[33] Ranging in subject from the legendary exploits of Alexander the Great to Arthurian legend to courtly love, its emphasis on heroic adventure and worlds beyond experience make romance an important ur-mode for science fictional narratives.

The twelfth century also marked the appearance of automata in romances. The production of automata, or machines that at least appeared to be self-operating, had flourished in ancient Greece and Rome, and continued in the Byzantine, Islamic, and Mongol empires. For high medieval writers artifacts such as singing mechanical birds and water clocks were the objects of uncomfortable fascination with Eastern knowledge of the natural world, suggestive of decadence if not diabolic influence.[34] If projected back into antiquity, however, they could be understood in more positive terms as a cultural inheritance. Examples range from the spectacular Byzantine court in *Le Voyage de Charlemagne à Jérusalem et à Constantinople* (The Journey of Charlemagne to Jerusalem and Constantinople, mid-twelfth century) to the life-size (and superhumanly skilled) human automata in the *Roman de Troie* (The Romance of Troy, c. 1165). In *Lancelot do lac* (Lancelot of the Lake, c. 1220) Lancelot battles copper knights who are later revealed to be animated by demons.[35] Medieval notions of causality were not restricted to natural laws or physical processes, but the ambiguous, liminal position automata occupied between life and death, natural creation and artificial mimic, or between natural and demonic agency bears a structural resemblance to modern fantasies of androids.

Early Science Fiction Beyond Europe

While the origins of SF as a modern literary institution are firmly rooted in the United States and Europe, the genre's worldwide spread has prompted the search for antecedents in early literatures outside this narrow region.

---

[33] See Kathryn Hume, "Medieval Romance and Science Fiction: The Anatomy of a Resemblance," *Journal of Popular Culture* 16, 1 (1982), pp. 15–26 for a comparison of narrative tropes common to SF and romance.

[34] See the discussion in E. R. Truitt, *Medieval Robots* (Philadelphia: University of Pennsylvania Press, 2015), pp. 37–9 and 58–60, as well as Park and Daston's reading of the automata in the Khan's palace as featured in Mandeville's *Travels*, pp. 92–3.

[35] Truitt, *Medieval Robots*, pp. 58–60.

Most commonly cited are stories that strongly resemble SF in their particulars but function according to the logic of myth and folklore, without sustained development of what we might recognize as proto-scientific concepts. A striking example can be found in the oldest surviving written fiction of Japan (*monogatari*). In "Tale of the Bamboo Cutter" (tenth century CE), an old bamboo cutter discovers a thumb-sized infant inside a glowing bamboo plant. In a mere three months, she grows into a woman whose beauty is renowned throughout the land, despite the bamboo cutter's efforts to keep her hidden. The middle section consists of a series of episodes in which noble suitors try and fail to win her heart. By the tale's conclusion she has grown dissatisfied with earthly life, and discovers she is actually from the Moon. The tale ends with the Moon men carrying her off on a beam of light.

The *Ramayana* and other Sanskrit epics mention flying machines (*vimana*), which, though they are attributed to the magic of the gods, are described convincingly enough to have inspired a cottage industry of New Age speculations on "ancient astronauts."[36] In a subsection of the *Lokapannatti*[37] devoted to the exploits of the great Indian king Ashoka, there is a story involving a treasure of Buddhist relics guarded by robots (*bhuta vahana yanta* or "spirit movement machines") with a lengthy digression on the robots' origin as stolen Roman technology.[38] The tale is notable for the way its speculative technology is the product of human craftsmanship rather than divine intervention, and as an interesting example of exoticization of the West from the East. The Daoist text *Lie Zi*[39] includes a brief story about an artificer in the Zhou court who builds an automaton so convincingly human-like that the king has to be shown its internal workings to accept its artificial nature. In this case the automaton serves as a metaphor for human behavior as having exclusively natural causes.[40]

---

[36] This notion was spread by the *Vaimānika Shāstra*, a detailed aeronautics manual composed in Sanskrit by an early twentieth-century mystic who claimed to have learned the secrets of ancient air travel from channeling Hindu sages.

[37] A Theravadan Buddhist text composed in the Pali language in Burma in the eleventh or twelfth century but using much older Sanskrit sources and Indian traditions.

[38] John Strong, *Relics of the Buddha* (Princeton, NJ: Princeton University Press, 2004), pp. 133–6.

[39] Probably written in the third century BCE, *Lie Zi* was compiled in the fourth century CE and attributed to Lie Yukou, fifth century BCE. The story is "Yanshi." Joseph Needham, *The Shorter Science and Civilization in China* (Cambridge: Cambridge University Press, 1978), p. 92. See also Regina Kanyu Wang, "A Brief Introduction to Chinese Science Fiction," *Mithila Review* 9 (2017), http://mithilareview.com/wang_11_16/.

[40] Along the same lines, elsewhere in the *Lie Zi* is the story of a physician who exchanges two mens' hearts, effectively exchanging their minds (Needham, *Science and Civilization*, p. 93).

If medieval Islamic culture contains the most familiar examples of pre-modern or proto-SF, this is no doubt due to the formative influence of the Islamic Golden Age on the development of modern science in Europe. We can extend this influence to imaginative literature through the pivotal role played by the *1,001 Nights*, a collection of folk tales first translated into Arabic in the early eighth century.[41] Though of more obvious relevance to fantasy than SF, cosmic travel ("The Adventures of Bukulayia"), a flying horse statue that functions like a jet plane ("The Ebony Horse"), and a lost city full of ingenious devices made out of brass ("The City of Brass") are only a few wonders that bear more than a passing resemblance to SF, even if their mechanisms aren't explained in great detail. Certainly the trope of rapid travel between worlds or physical metamorphosis enabled by a device, whether it be mechanical or magical, is central to the tales of marvelous adventure that form the generic root of much SF.[42] Antoine Galland's translation into French in the early eighteenth century first introduced the *Nights* to Europe, its first step in becoming one of the first classics of world literature.

Other Arabic texts of immense importance to SF are Ibn Tufayl's *Hayy Ibn Yaqzan* and especially Ibn al-Nafis's *Theologus Autodidactus* (The Self-Taught Theologian, 1268–77).[43] Both are desert island stories, philosophical thought experiments that use the conceit of a solitary autodidact to evaluate the role of experience in the development of thinking consciousness. Considered the first novel in Arabic, *Hayy Ibn Yaqzan* is named after its central character, an abandoned boy raised by a gazelle.[44] After her death, he is driven to comprehend the mutable physical world through careful observation, beginning with the dissection of his "mother." His capacity for reflection then leads him to a concept of God and eternal truth. Intended as a critical response to Ibn Tufayl's text that privileges revelation (mediated through development as a social being, not merely a reasoning observer), the *Theologus Autodidactus*

---

[41] The oldest extant Syrian manuscripts of the *Nights* claim to have been translated from a Persian text, and the stories themselves have been traced to Arabic, Persian, Indian, Jewish, and many other sources.

[42] Discovered in 1933 and recently translated into English for the first time, the collection *Tales of the Marvellous and News of the Strange* is another medieval Arabic story collection of interest to SF and fantasy scholars from roughly the same period as the *Nights*. See *Tales of the Marvellous and News of the Strange*, ed. and trans. Malcolm C. Lyons (London: Penguin Classics, 2016).

[43] The Latin title is how it was known in Europe.

[44] Upon translation into Latin in 1671 and English in 1708, it also inspired Daniel Defoe in his writing of *Robinson Crusoe* (1719), another desert island tale typically cited as the first English novel.

includes more overtly science fictional elements such as the spontaneous generation of the protagonist in a cave. Of special interest is al-Nafis's vision of apocalypse, informed by both scripture and natural philosophy and including such pulpy details as the rise of a race of mutants and the coming to power of sex-crazed lesbians. Both texts use the narrative development of a wholly fictional character to work through philosophical, scientific, and theological ideas. In this way they take a step further than dream visions, travelers' tales, or inherited folk tales toward the marriage of fictional narrative and learned yet imaginative speculation that characterizes modern SF.

Early Modern Science Fiction

What we might identify as "early SF" in the early modern period was indebted to classical and antique literary forms. This was certainly true during the initial period of classical knowledge's revival and its challenge to scholasticism. The eighteenth century saw the rise of empiricism and the emergence of the novel as the dominant fictional genre for depicting social and historical reality, but the preferred narrative templates for the philosophical and speculative imagination remained those of the ancients, not the moderns. SF has always been formally anachronistic; from nineteenth-century "scientific romance" to the early twentieth-century pulps, SF only truly began to embrace literary modernism during modernism's postwar decline. Likewise, the lunar societies, journeys underground, and hermaphroditic Australian utopias of early modern imaginative literature were not straightforwardly progressive; readers of these texts must be sensitive to the contradictory ways in which they respond to the uncertain status of new knowledge.

At times this ambivalence was a result of the threat of censorship and reprisal. Many works that embraced potentially controversial ideas were circulated anonymously in manuscript form before posthumous publication, even in relatively tolerant Protestant countries like England and the Netherlands. The contradictory effects of religious, political, and epistemological upheaval determined the subtle layers of signification in Johannes Kepler's *Somnium* (The Dream, 1634). The product of decades of work, *Somnium* was initially composed in 1608 from his suppressed 1593 Tübingen university thesis and published only in 1634, a few years before Kepler's death. Modeled on Cicero, Plutarch, and Galileo,[45] it is an exhaustively footnoted,

---

[45] Galileo published the results of his telescopic investigations of the Moon in the *Sidereal Messenger* (1610), which Kepler publicly defended. They also maintained a correspondence and regularly commented on each other's work.

speculative survey of the Moon's topography nested within three allegorical frames: a dream (1) about a book by a young Icelandic student named Duracotus (2) whose pagan mother summons a lunar daemon to describe the nature of the Moon to him in a vision (3). The story's selenocentric cosmological perspective avoids explicitly confirming or denying the heliocentric implications of Copernicus's *De revolutionibus* (On the Revolution of the Holy Spheres, 1543). Still, taking the Moon seriously as an astronomical object – a physical place with its own geography and its own elevated perspective on the Earth – already ceded ground to Copernican theory's most radical interpretation by suggesting an entirely material universe in which the Earth was not the privileged epistemological center. The multiple narrative frames, the mixture of precise descriptive detail, exobiological speculation about lizard-like creatures, and the Plutarchian notion that daemons populate the dark side of the Moon meant that the text could not be reduced to either astronomical treatise or allegory.

Though *Somnium* was perhaps too singular and elaborate to be a model for later works, hermeneutic complexity was typical of early SF. This extends to the more popular imaginary voyage fiction, which saw a major resurgence throughout the period following two distinct but interrelated events: the (so-called) discovery of the New World in 1492 and the publication of Copernicus's heliocentric theory of the cosmos (*De revolutionibus*) in 1543. Though earthly island settings were always more common, the Moon's liminality continued to make it an important imaginary destination, especially for metaphysically and/or politically sensitive reflections; the Moon could increasingly be used not only in support of a revolution in theology and cosmology but in challenging Europe's place in the world.[46]

As much as any single genre could, the lunar voyage inaugurated early modern SF. Adam Roberts notes[47] that the majority of early modern SF was produced in England and France, and of the two foundational lunar voyages one is English and the other French: Francis Godwin's *The Man in the Moone* (1638) and Cyrano de Bergerac's *L'Autre monde ou les états et empires de la Lune* (*The Other World*, or, *The States and Empires of the Moon*, 1657). Both are picaresque satires indebted to Lucian, whose Menippean model provided early modern writers with an omnivorously flexible genre that appealed to

---

[46] Some historians have suggested the notion of the Moon as a world like the Earth was more important than the encounter with the New World, which had comparatively little effect. See Michael Ryan, "Assimilating New Worlds in the Seventeenth Century," *Comparative Studies in Society and History* 23, 4 (October 1981), pp. 519–38; 519.

[47] Roberts, *The History of Science Fiction*, pp. 81–2.

a learned readership in order to undermine intellectual pretentions. But they reverse the targets of Lucian's critique; just as thoroughly skeptical, their exploration of the lunar world turns a critical eye on the hubris of European cultural orthodoxies that were being challenged by new intellectual currents. The worlds they depict are aimed more at destabilizing any unitary perspective than straightforward advocacy of a coherent worldview or utopian arrangement.

The anonymously published diversion of an Anglican bishop, Godwin's playful tale is in the "Spanish style" of picaresque, sending its narrator Domingo Gonsales from St. Helena in the East Indies to the Moon to imperial China and then back to Europe. Gonsales is carried to the Moon from a mountaintop by a flock of migrating geese, upon which he encounters a lunar society that immediately tries him for the heresy of believing their world to be a Moon to his Earth rather than vice versa. The confrontation between geocentrism and selenocentrism revealing their mutual absurdity would become the most commonly recurring trope of the subgenre. The rest of Godwin's short work is filled with observations on natural philosophy, theology (the lunarians are Christian, reconciling plurality with Christ's redemption of mortal sin), linguistics (they speak a universal musical language that the narrator compares to Chinese), and politics, all of which are couched in self-reflexive doubt.

This skeptical decentering is carried to a further extreme by the infamous French libertine Cyrano, whose lunar adventure follows some of the same plot points – his narrator makes his way to the Moon via an improbable contraption (fireworks in this case) and is put on trial for believing the lunar world to be Earth's Moon (and, in an intertextual joke, is imprisoned with Gonsales) – but draws on a wider and more eclectic set of literary and philosophical references. The second volume departs from the observable almost entirely by setting the adventure on the Sun, with such mystically tinged adventures as an allegorical battle between a salamander and a remora and a conversation with the spirit of Descartes. Though it may seem unserious to the reader of modern SF, the lack of distinction between theological, proto-scientific, literary, and merely fanciful elements in these texts may have been their most subversive feature in the context of intense seventeenth-century social and intellectual upheaval.

Godwin's and Cyrano's scattered utopian speculations are subordinated to a picaresque sequence in which nearly every narrative event or observation is immediately undercut, creating an atmosphere of perpetual doubt. Other potential examples of early SF were more didactic and stressed the coherence of a utopian totality. Utopian literature began as a subset of the imaginary voyage narrative with Thomas More's *Utopia* (1516). Inspired by Socrates's meditations on an ideal state in Plato's *Republic*, More uses a New World voyage as a framing device for the detailed discussion of an alternative society. Exploring the consequences of one or two key ideas in the context of a totally integrated social world makes the utopia an important cousin of SF. The Dominican friar and philosopher Tommaso Campanella's *La Citta Del Sole* (The City of the Sun, 1602) inscribes the totality of human knowledge on the walls of its ideal city, conceived as a series of painted concentric circles, each reflecting a different category.[48] The utopian vision of a city organized around learning and the study of nature was tremendously influential. A successor text more immediately relevant to the history of SF is Francis Bacon's unfinished *New Atlantis* (1627). The fictional counterpart to his earlier manifesto for experimental science, an important early work in the history of scientific method, *New Atlantis* describes a secret college on the mythic New World island of Bensalem called Solomon's House.[49] Presented as the ideal institutional model for the natural sciences, its disciplined structure, dividing the study of nature into distinct fields, prefigured the Royal Society of London. The Duchess of Newcastle Margaret Cavendish's eccentric *The Description of a New World, Called the Blazing World* (1666), also originally affixed to a natural philosophic treatise, stands out in this context as an attack on the all-male Royal Society for excluding her. She imagines two contiguous planets joined by their respective North and South Poles. The "blazing world" is populated by several species of animal–human hybrids and a (handsome) human ruler who chooses Cavendish's narrator as his wife and queen shortly after a shipwreck on her world lands her in his court. In a departure from the standard utopian protagonist, hers is no passive observer but actively judges and revises the natural philosophic ideas of the ape-men, bird-men, and other denizens of the imperial court. Through spirit communication she makes contact with Cavendish herself, and together they construct "immaterial" worlds according to their own desires. The novella ends with the protagonist leading an army from the Blazing World into battle with her home world's enemies. Cavendish's text at once endorses monarchy

---

[48] Though he was branded as a heretic, Campanella's ideas about the centrality of the senses to true knowledge were highly influential on early theorists of the new science; he even makes an appearance in the second volume of Cyrano's lunar voyage as the narrator's primary guide and interlocutor on the Sun.

[49] Frances Yates links *New Atlantis* to the intellectual Protestant cults of Rosicrucianism and Freemasonry in *The Rosicrucian Enlightenment* (London and New York: Routledge, 2002), pp. 164–9.

(she and her husband supported the Stuarts against Cromwell) and celebrates the world-creating power of the liberated imagination, through which anyone "may create a world of what fashion and government he will."[50]

The imaginary voyage continued to be the parent genre for imaginative fiction in the eighteenth century. Most voyages still took place to distant islands and unexplored continents. The single most significant, for SF and mainstream literary scholars alike, is *Gulliver's Travels* (1726/1735). Jonathan Swift arranges Lemuel Gulliver's accidental odyssey into four parts, each centered on a different imaginary country. Swift distinguishes himself from the mass of neo-Menippean imaginary voyage satirists of the period by how fully realized his invented worlds are despite their obviously fantastical contents. Prose satirists and fantasists alike learned from Swift that the thicker the descriptive detail and more compelling the narrative action, the stronger the resulting satire, capable of taking aim at targets both specific and broad. The second two parts are most immediately germane to the history of SF. Both, like Lucian's satires, attack blinkered or excessive forms of intellectualism. On the floating island of Laputa, subject of the first section of the third part, an immoderate obsession with theoretical sciences such as mathematics and astronomy is joined with practical ineptitude and tyrannical dependency on the cities below. The encounter in part four with the Houyhnhnms, a race of intelligent horses, ends in tragedy, as their utopian society is based on an innately superior faculty of moral reason. Despite Gulliver's desire to assimilate, they conclude he and his entire civilization are barbaric, banishing him among their enemies the primitive Yahoos, humanlike animals who are entirely subject to their passions. While there is little in the *Travels* that would remind a twentieth-century reader of SF, Swift's improvements to the imaginary voyage satire lie at the foundation of the genre. Utopian and dystopian civilizations were no longer simple mirrors of European society, but were logically extrapolated from specific cultural and moral traits, a far more sophisticated basis for the construction of imaginary worlds.

Lunar voyages in the eighteenth century were concentrated in Britain and were variations on the examples set by Godwin and Swift. As with Godwin, the Moon was often one destination alongside exotic islands or nations on Earth. Their engagement with early natural science or philosophy was typically minor, instead emphasizing allegorical satire of contemporary politics. The anonymous *Voyage to Cacklogallinia* (1727), for instance, references

---

[50] Margaret Cavendish, *The Blazing World and Other Writings* (London: Penguin Classics, 1994), p. 185.

the South Sea Bubble with an island race of giant chickens who send the narrator to the Moon in search of gold. *The Consolidator* (1705), one of Daniel Defoe's genre experiments, is an elaborate (and today barely decipherable) work of anti-Tory propaganda in the form of an extended description of an antediluvian Chinese spacecraft constructed with lunar science.

Other lunar voyages are simply more didactic versions of Godwin's original with cosmetic differences.[51] The popularity of this primarily satirical mode of lunar voyage spread across the channel, and includes Cornelie Wouters, Baron de Wasse's *Le Char Volant; ou, Voyage dans la lune* (The Flying Chariot; or Voyage to the Moon, 1783) and the first Polish example of early SF, Michal Dymitr Krajewski's *The Life and Adventures of Wojciech Zdarzynski* (1785). Two German entries stand out for expanding the scope of the genre from the Moon to Mars, both via hot air balloon. Eberhard Kindermann's *Die geschwinde Reise auf dem Lufft-schiff nach der obern Welt* (The Swift Journey by Air-Ship to the World Above, 1744) predates the maiden voyage of the Montgolfière brothers' balloon in 1783[52] and is the first imaginary voyage to worlds beyond the Moon. *Reise eines Erdbewohners in den Mars* (Journey of an Earth-Dweller to Mars, 1790) by Carl Ignaz Geiger moves through three dystopian and one utopian Martian nation in a Swiftian satirical allegory of fractious German politics.

Still more capacious were the new planetary romances and dream visions centered in France. Concentrated more toward the second half of the eighteenth century following the wider adoption of Newtonianism, they (like Isaac Newton himself[53]) combined natural philosophy with theology and metaphysical speculation, at times finding inspiration in alchemy and Cabala. Athanasius Kircher's cosmological dialogue *Itinerarium exstaticum*

---

[51] Anonymity remained a feature of the genre, though by this time it was in order to protect its authors from their satirical targets. When available, their authors' names are likely to be pseudonyms. A full account of such lunar voyages can be found in Marjorie Nicolson, *Voyages to the Moon* (New York: Macmillan, 1948).

[52] A pivotal event for the European imagination, the hot air balloon quickly became a common device in imaginary voyages. The two most significant in English from the period are *A Journey Lately Performed Through the Air in an Aerostatic Globe* (1784), in which the narrator travels to Uranus (albeit a moon-like Uranus that orbits the Earth and doesn't rotate on its own axis) and *A Voyage to the Moon, Strongly Recommended to All Lovers of Real Freedom* (1793).

[53] For a brief overview of Newton's interest in alchemy as part of a chapter surveying early modern science's vexed relationship with the occult, see Paul Kléber Monod, *Solomon's Secret Arts: The Occult in the Age of Enlightenment* (New Haven: Yale University Press, 2013), pp. 103–5. Betty Jo Teeter Dobbs argues that Newton sought a total system of truth that would synthesize physics, astronomy, philosophy, and alchemy in *The Janus Faces of Genius: The Role of Alchemy in Newton's Thought* (Cambridge: Cambridge University Press, 1991).

(The Ecstatic Journey, 1656), between an interstellar traveler and an angelic guide, is an important root text, along with the writings of Emmanuel Swedenborg, the Swedish polymath and Neoplatonist mystic whose psychedelic visions of the cosmos, Heaven, and Hell inspired (and enraged) figures as diverse as William Blake and Immanuel Kant.[54] Charles Tiphaigne de la Roche's *Amilec, ou, La Graine d'hommes* (Amilec, or the Seeds of Mankind, 1753) is a dream vision based on an extended analogy between the nature of the universe and biological growth ("generation"); Amilec, the story's guide, is a spirit being or *génie* ("genius"), who plays a similar tutelary role to the spiritual guides in Kepler's, Kircher's, and Cyrano's works. The grand tour of *Voyages de milord Céton dans les sept planètes* (The Voyages of Lord Ceton to the Seven Planets, 1765–6) by Marie-Anne de Roumier-Robert is likewise led by a *génie* ("Zachiel"), but, following the examples of Cyrano and the Chevalier de Béthune's action-packed planetary romance *Rélation du monde de mercure* (The World of Mercury, 1750), has more narrative momentum. Lord Céton and his sister Monime, refugees from Cromwell's Puritan revolution, are taken by Zachiel on a journey through a populated solar system. Each planet is the site of new adventures and moral and political lessons, all directed at Monime, who by novel's end is revealed to be heir to the throne of Georgia. Roumier-Robert's references tend more toward classical mythology and seventeenth-century French historical romance than natural philosophy. But, like *Blazing World*, her *Voyages* is significant as an early attempt to order knowledge in terms of female power.

Roumier-Robert's romance is in conversation with Bernard Le Bouvier de Fontenelle's influential *Entretiens sur la pluralité des mondes* (Conversations on the Plurality of Worlds, 1686), a playfully seductive dialogue in which the author introduces the latest cosmological theories of the Académie des Sciences to an inquisitive Marquise. The text popularized the notion of a cosmopolitan universe filled with intelligent life as the logical consequence of a plurality of worlds. The alternative – a barren, lifeless cosmos – would be sheer waste, irreconcilable with the God of Enlightenment reason. Similarly essayistic, lightly fictionalized cosmic voyages include Jesuit theologian Gabriel Daniel's *Voyage au monde de Descartes* (Voyage to the World of Cartesius, 1692), a critique of Descartes via a fictional cosmos constructed according to Cartesian principles, and the Dutch astronomer Christiaan

---

[54] His *De Telluribus in Mundo Nostro Solari* (1758) is a visionary exploration of the notion of a plurality of inhabited worlds within an infinite universe. The central text of Swedenborgian cosmology is *Arcana Coelestia* (1749–56).

Huygens's *Cosmotheoros* (1698), which chastises Fontenelle for failing to cleanly separate rational deduction from imaginative license.

Alien visitors to Earth in the early modern period are comparatively rare. Most appear in French literature, part of a strong tradition of Orientalist novels about Eastern travelers to Europe and their satirical observations of local mores. Voltaire's *Micromégas* (1752) is the best-known example. A novella about an exile from a planet orbiting Sirius and his travels through our solar system, it employs the vast scales of the new astronomy to highlight European provincialism. The Sirian's 20,000-foot height makes him beyond gigantic on Earth, where he is shocked to learn the miniscule Earthlings (so small he can hear them only by fashioning a funnel out of his thumbnail) are actually sentient. Louis-Guillame de La Folie's *Le Philosophe sans prétention ou L'homme rare* (The Unpretentious Philosopher, or The Rare Man, 1775) describes a denizen of Mercury's experience of European society after crash landing on Earth. Perhaps the most interesting aspect of the story for SF scholars is La Folie's unusually forward-thinking means of space flight – a wingless, electrically powered ship – and his informed representation of Newtonian physics.

There remained regions on Earth's surface that were *terra incognita*, objects for the imagination of radical alterity just as they were in ancient and medieval times. The most important of these were known as the "antipodes," a theoretical landmass thought to cover the opposite end of the globe, and a subject of debate as early as the ancient Greeks.[55] Like the Moon, the antipodes were often thought unreachable, uninhabitable, or both. And as with the Moon, the question of the antipodes did not become a pressing one until the sixteenth century, when new empirical discoveries came into conflict with scholastic doctrine. In the nearly two hundred years between Amerigo Vespucci's journey to the southern tip of South America in 1502 and James Cook's voyage up the east coast of Australia in 1770, a number of fictional works appeared that used the antipodes as a basis for social and philosophical speculation. Distinct from lunar and planetary voyages, these tended to be more concerned with anthropology than epistemology, exploring the pre-Rousseauian notion that "primitive" cultures encountered by European explorers might possess both physical and moral superiority in spite of – or perhaps because of – their isolation from European modernity and religious institutions.[56]

---

[55] The first surviving direct reference is in Plato's *Timaeus*, though the notion was also attributed to Pythagoras. Matthew Boyd Goldie, *The Idea of the Antipodes: Places, People, and Voices* (London: Routledge, 2014), p. 25.

[56] David Faussett, *Images of the Antipodes in the Eighteenth Century: A Study in Stereotyping* (Amsterdam, Atlanta, GA: Rodopi, 1995), pp. 1–38.

Most simply used the antipodes as a convenient basis for an "inverted world" of utopian satire, Joseph Hall's anonymously published *Mundus alter et idem* (The Discovery of a New World, 1605) being the prime example. Anticipating Swift, Hall describes an Australian continent divided into a number of kingdoms, each organized by a dominant satirical trait: Crapulia is full of gluttons, Moronia full of fools, etc. More fully fleshed out worlds are offered by Denis Vairasse's *Histoire des Sevarambes* (*History of the Sevarambians*, first volume in English 1675, both volumes in French 1679) and Gabriel de Foigny's *La Terre australe connue* (*The Southern Land, Known*, 1693). Both feature journeys to the Austral continent and encounters with prelapsarian utopian races – in effect, Earthbound aliens.

The best of the eighteenth-century antipodean romances are Robert Paltock's *Life and Adventures of Peter Wilkins* (1751) and Nicolas-Edme Restif de la Bretonne's *La Découverte australe par un homme-volant* (The Discovery of the Austral Continent by a Flying-Man, 1781). Both maintain the centrality of sexuality to their anthropological imaginaries, but for them sexuality is a means of exchange between European explorers and antipodean races. The first several chapters of *Wilkins* follow the model set by *Robinson Crusoe* (1719): Peter Wilkins is led by a series of accidents from England to Africa to the South Pole, where its magnetic pull draws him into an underground grotto. The narrative shifts into colonial adventure fantasy when he meets and soon mates with a female member of a winged race of humanoids. Raising an interspecies family with her and devising artificial wings for himself leads him to her country; there heroic adventures ensue in which Wilkins spreads Enlightenment values, frees a slave population, and reconciles two warring underground nations. Bretonne, mainly known for anti-Sadean erotica, was a late inheritor of the libertine tradition. His protagonist is more intentional than Wilkins, inventing a flying suit (inspired by entomological research) to abscond with his illicit love. Their travels are similarly wide-ranging, and while Bretonne's climactic utopia is a little imaginatively thin, the animal–human hybrid creatures his travelers encounter throughout their adventures combined with a sexualized cosmogony (God is likened to seminal fluid) suggest a quasi-evolutionary process interweaving the biological with the social.

The move underground in Paltock's Australian romance was far from an isolated episode. The first main source of inspiration for the literary tradition of subterranean romance was Kircher's *Mundus Subterraneus* (The Underground World, 1665), an account of a vast underground network of canals based on his observations of craters caused by eruptions at Mount

Vesuvius and Mount Etna. Its eclectic contents range from quasi-alchemical explanations for earthquakes and volcanoes to fantastical descriptions of dragons and other mythical creatures partly derived from giant fossils. Another important source was Royal Society member Edmond Halley's explanation for changes in Earth's magnetic field, in which the interior of the Earth was hollow, consisting of rotating concentric spheres (which he thought were probably inhabited). Kircher's countryman Hans Jacob von Grimmelshausen's picaresque novel *Simplicius Simplicissimus* (Simplicissimus the Vagabond, 1668/1671) has a brief episode in a fantastic underground world inhabited by water-spirits, and Charles de Fieux, Chevalier de Mouhy's swashbuckling Orientalist fantasy *Lamékis, ou les voyages extraordinaires d'un Egyptien dans la terre interieure* (Lamékis, or the Extraordinary Voyages of an Egyptian to the Interior World, 1735–8) likewise makes a few excursions underground. Perhaps the first true Hollow-Earth fiction, however, and certainly the first to take a proto-scientific approach, was Simon Tyssot de Patot's *La Vie, les aventures et le voyage de Groenland du Révérend Père Cordelier Pierre de Mésange* (The Life, Adventures, and Trip to Greenland of The Reverend Father Cordelier Pierre de Mésange, 1720). An earlier work, *Voyages et aventures de Jacques Massé* (The Voyages and Adventures of Jacques Massé, 1714–17), is primarily set in the antipodes but concludes with the discovery of a prehistoric Lost World underground.

The best-known of these stories is strongly indebted to Swift: Danish writer Ludwig Holberg's *Nikolai Klimi iter subterraneum* (The Journey of Niels Klim to the World Underground, 1741/1745). Protagonist Niels Klim falls through a hole in the North Pole into a solar system orbiting an internal sun. He lands on the planet Nazar in the kingdom of Potu, a quasi-utopian society of intelligent trees, going on to encounter the denizens of the other underground planets as he rises and falls from power. *A Voyage to the World in the Centre of the Earth* (1755), the first Hollow-Earth fiction in English, is a fairly typical utopian tale of an underground society without private property. The great libertine and memoirist Giacomo Casanova experimented with the premise in *Icosaméron* (1787). A hermaphroditic miniature race called "Megamicres" ("big-littles," contrasting their eighteen-inch height with their moral greatness) lives underground on an island floating on the concave interior of our Earth. Casanova grounds his vision in the Bible rather than natural philosophy. Yet he is far from consistent, his descriptions of Megamicre civilization and physiology vacillating between utopian and dystopian, scriptural and naturalistic. The Megamicres are peaceful, predating original sin, yet they are also capitalistic and hierarchical; when his

English surface world protagonists take power they bring technological improvements along with tyrannical subjugation.

Toward the end of the eighteenth century, romance literature set in the distant future became increasingly popular, sparked by the onset of the French Revolution.[57] Louis Sébastien Mercier's *L'An 2440* (*The Year 2440*, 1771, expanded 1786), the most successful of these works, is a pro-Revolutionary utopia (or uchronia) set in a far future Paris after a religion of reason has supplanted Catholic superstition, transforming French society. Initially banned in both France and Spain, Mercier's work eventually became one of the bestselling novels of its time, taking on tremendous cultural importance as a concrete, sensory representation of the abstract moral principles advocated by Rousseauians such as Mercier. Like the imaginary voyage, *L'An 2440* aims at exploring imaginary possibilities. Unlike them, it explicitly links the utopian imaginary to the present, moving from the allegorical to the extrapolative. Ironically, to do so Mercier invokes the age-old framing device of the dream vision – dissatisfied with eighteenth-century life, a narrator imagines a better world – while constructing that world in terms of the modern urban tableau that would be the subject of the great nineteenth-century realists. This great shift in the architecture of the possible was not the reduction of radical alterity to the merely probable, but the subjection of imagination to historical cognition. Perhaps more than anything else, this is the precondition for SF as we know it today.

---

[57] Roberts, *The History of Science Fiction*, pp. 83–4.

2

Interrelations: Science Fiction and the Gothic

ROGER LUCKHURST

How best to articulate the relationship between the non-Realist popular genres of the Gothic and SF? This has been a fraught question. For Brian Aldiss, SF is the rather disappointing offspring of the older, more eminent Gothic. He defines SF as "the search for a definition of man and his status in the universe which will stand in our advanced but confused state of knowledge (science), and is characteristically cast in Gothic or post-Gothic modes."[1] For Darko Suvin, pioneer genre critic, SF was absolutely *divorced* from the Gothic, and he relentlessly pitched its science against superstition, natural law against supernatural transgression, reason against magic, expansive radicalism against contractive conservatism. Suvin's neat binaries insist that SF projects a future through rational, "cognitive" extrapolation from the present, while the Gothic regards the present as haunted by the nightmare of history, and cowers as it awaits its fearful returns. The Gothic was thus one of Suvin's politically and conceptually "invalidated" genres, declared "delusional" along with fantasy and fairy tales and expelled from the Party of properly rigorous SF.[2]

Even in times less anxious to legitimate the study of popular fiction, and where boundaries are not so determinedly constructed, mined, barb-wired, and patrolled, finding terms can still be difficult. Should the long history of fictions generative of the eventual emergence of SF be called "proto-SF," or is this, as Arthur Evans complains, "intrinsically biased and dismissive; it implies that *true* science fiction came into being only at some later date"?[3] But is "early SF" – Evans's suggestion – distinct from the Gothic, or entirely blended with it?

---

[1] Brian W. Aldiss, *Billion Year Spree* (London: Weidenfeld & Nicholson, 1973), p. 8.
[2] Darko Suvin, *Positions and Presuppositions in Science Fiction* (Basingstoke: Macmillan, 1988), p. 72.
[3] Arthur B. Evans, "Preface" to *Vintage Visions: Essays on Early Science Fiction* (Middletown, CT: Wesleyan University Press, 2014), p. viii.

All origin stories rightly deserve suspicion. Scholars of the Gothic get just as annoyed about the critical shorthand that suggests the genre bursts complete from Horace Walpole's anxious state of persecution in 1764 – which produced, mysteriously complete, the nightmare vision of *The Castle of Otranto* – just as much as those historians of SF who wish to complicate the primogeniture of H. G. Wells's *The Time Machine* in the 1890s or Hugo Gernsback's *Amazing Stories* in the 1920s. And if it is inevitable that any discussion of the imbrication of the Gothic and SF must address the impact of Mary Shelley's *Frankenstein* (1818), given the multiple lines of influence that stream out of that extraordinary text, Shelley is hardly the virgin mother of SF either.

This chapter will propose that we read Gothic fiction and SF as always interrelated responses to a self-reflexive, scientific modernity that begins in the eighteenth century. John Clute has suggested that "the genres of the Fantastic began to be invented in tune with the changing world after 1750, and the story devices of the Fantastic constitute a series of exorbitant utterances of that change."[4] Both the Gothic and SF are *proleptic* genres that use, as Walpole put in his Preface to *Otranto*, "the great resources of fancy" to respond to that change, since "a strict adherence to common life" (or what will come to be called Realism, the dominant form of the literary novel of the bourgeois public sphere) cannot always necessarily register the accelerations of modernity arising from scientific and technological change.[5] Although using different cognitive and affective tenors, both genres lever open imaginative possibilities at the boundaries of advancing knowledge, exploiting ungrounded phases of "extraordinary" science where norms are unravelling and have not quite yet established a new norm.[6]

Gothic and SF always share this context of transformation – modernity's ceaseless creative destruction – but engender different imaginative inflections of it. A useful analogy might be that they are different refractions of the same light, co-existing and often overlapping on the same spectrum, with some frequencies easy to differentiate and others much less so. It is only latterly that our critical spectrographs have insisted on absolute demarcations: Gothic and scientific romances, "terror novels" or phantasmagoric tales,

---

[4] John Clute, *The Darkening Garden: A Short Lexicon of Horror* (Cauheegan: Payseur and Schmidt, 2006), p. 53.

[5] Horace Walpole, "Preface to the Second Edition," in W. S. Lewis, ed., *The Castle of Otranto* (Oxford: Oxford World's Classics, 2008), p. 9.

[6] Terminology of "normal" science and "phases of extraordinary science" are taken from Thomas Kuhn, *The Structure of Scientific Revolutions* (Chicago: Chicago University Press, 1970).

and poetry and prose inspired by the discoveries of natural philosophy and the new sciences were all often jumbled together before the emergence of distinct genre categories in the late nineteenth century.

I am therefore interested in this chapter in the period between the definitive arrival of the Gothic craze in the 1790s and the emergence of a distinctive "scientific romance" in the new magazine markets of the 1880s. This is the epoch where fantastical genres were a "tangled bank," to use Charles Darwin's famous phrase.[7] After a generation of academic criticism devoted to severe taxonomic demarcations, the efflorescence of "recombinant genre fiction" at the turn of the millennium ("stories which effectively decompose and reconstitute genre materials") suggests that we are gleefully returning to this entangled state, delighted or terrified once more by the generative hybridity of our current accelerationist times.[8]

Let's start with this intoxicating passage from 1774:

> The rapid progress of knowledge, which, like the progress of a wave of the sea, of sound, or of light from the sun, extends itself not this way or that only, but *in all directions*, will, I doubt not, be the means, under God, of extirpating *all* error and prejudice, and of putting an end to all undue and usurped authority in the business of *religion*, as well as of *science*; and all the efforts of the interested friends of corrupt establishments of all kinds will be ineffectual for their support in this enlightened age ... The English hierarchy ... has equal reason to tremble even at an air-pump, or an electrical machine.[9]

This prefacing statement from Joseph Priestley's book of chemical and other experiments hedges its bets a little, yet spells out fairly overtly the revolutionary potential of the new knowledge, tying the advance of science and mechanism to political transformation. Priestley was a dissenting theologian, natural philosopher, one of the chemists who isolated oxygen, a theorist of electricity, a liberal political theorist, and defender of free inquiry in all areas of knowledge. He was part of the radical dissenting culture in England that drove the Industrial Revolution among the mercantile middle class. He welcomed the French Revolution, a stance condemned by the prominent conservative writer and politician Edmund Burke in his *Reflections on the*

---

[7] For a reflection on the "tangled bank" image, see Gillian Beer, *Darwin's Plots: Evolutionary Narrative in Darwin, George Eliot, and Nineteenth-Century Fiction* (Cambridge: Cambridge University Press, 1983).

[8] Gary Wolfe, "Maleboge, or the Ordnance of Genre," *Conjunctions* 39 (2002), p. 415. See also Robin Mackay and Armen Avanessian, eds., *#Accelerate: The Accelerationist Reader* (Falmouth: Urbanomic, 2014).

[9] Joseph Priestley, *Experiments and Observations on Different Kinds of Air* (1774), extracted in Tim Fulford, ed., *Romanticism and Science 1773–1833*, Vol. 1 (London: Routledge, 2002), p. 60.

Revolution in France (1790), a book that explicitly named and denounced Priestley. On the anniversary of the storming of the Bastille in 1791, a carefully orchestrated mob in Birmingham targeted dissenters and radicals, and Priestley's church and family home – including his laboratory – were razed to the ground. This event was recalled by Samuel Taylor Coleridge in "Religious Musings," in which he praised Priestley as a "patriot, and saint, and sage" of "heavenly Science" who had been attacked by a "blind multitude" in "vain hate."[10] In this juncture science, politics, theology, aesthetics, and poetry flow seamlessly together.

The story of scientific modernity in the eighteenth century is often channeled through Michel Foucault's investigation of the rise of taxonomy, ordering, separation, and distinction in *The Order of Things*, where it is through the imposition of disciplinary "grids that order manifests itself in depth as though already there," and Man is famously dethroned as "probably no more than a kind of rift in the order of things."[11] For the modern Gothic, it might be that systems of modern taxonomy in botany or biology or ethnology actively generate new kinds of monsters, horrific chimera that are produced by category error or boundary transgression of the grids themselves (hence Foucault's productive reflections on "Monsters and Fossils" in *The Order of Things*).

But another way of grasping the interplay of Gothic, romanticism and science is to see it as a much more fluid, unbounded series of interactions before the full institutional and disciplinary formation of what Bruno Latour calls the "modern constitution" tried to enforce demarcations between nature and culture, science, and poetry. Latour envisages a world less of bounded, essential objects and distinct categories of knowledge than of "risky attachments" and "tangled objects" that have "no clear boundaries, no well-defined essences, no sharp separation between their own hard kernel and their environment. It is because of this feature that they take on the aspect of tangled beings, forming rhizomes, and networks."[12] It is with this view of entanglement that science, the Gothic, romantic science, and the scientific romance could be regarded as occupying the same set of networks, sharing

---

[10] Samuel Taylor Coleridge, "Religious Musings" (1796), in Lewis Patton and Peter Mann, eds., *The Collected Works of Samuel Taylor Coleridge*, Vol. 1 (London: Routledge & Kegan Paul, 1971), lines 395, 225, 400–1.

[11] Michel Foucault, *The Order of Things: An Archaeology of the Human Sciences* (London: Tavistock, 1970), pp. xx, xxiii.

[12] Bruno Latour, *The Politics of Nature: How to Bring the Sciences into Democracy* (Cambridge, MA: Harvard University Press, 2004), pp. 22, 24.

many of the same nodes yet put together in different but overlapping distributions or patterns.

Let's not think of the Gothic as simply or solely the *underside* of the Enlightenment (a common reading of Goya's famous etching called "The sleep of reason produces monsters"), or of romanticism *and* science, but instead of something like a "Neural Romanticism," a literary mode fully imbricated in the ferment of ongoing scientific revolutions in botany, biology, geology, anthropology, and psychology at the end of the eighteenth century.[13] Another good example would be Erasmus Darwin, the medic, inventor, engineer, and pioneering botanist, who explored the theological scandal of the hybridization of plants to express an early version of the evolutionary transformism more commonly associated with his grandson Charles, but did so principally through the medium of poetry. Darwin, a friend of Priestley (and fellow member of Birmingham's Lunar Society), was also denounced in the political paranoia of the 1790s as a dangerous Jacobin revolutionary from the very top of the reactionary government. In *The Temple of Nature* (1791), Darwin's major poetic paean to evolution, he spoke of

> Organic life beneath the shoreless waves
> Was born and nurs'd in Ocean's pearly caves;
> First forms minute, unseen by spheric glass,
> Move on the mud, or pierce the watery mass . . .
> Thus . . .
> Imperious man, who rules the bestial crowd,
> Of language, reason and reflection proud . . .
> Arose from rudiments of form and sense,
> An embryon point, or microscopic ens![14]

Key elements of the craze for Gothic "terror novels" of the 1790s, which erupted after the sensational success of Ann Radcliffe's *Mysteries of Udolpho* (1794), can be correctly portrayed as a counterrevolutionary response to the dangerous enthusiasms of modern thought in politics and science, a retrenchment of cautious Protestant reformism. Yet the clear connections between the new sciences and political radicalism also fomented another kind of Gothic text, and it is from this milieu that Mary Shelley's *Frankenstein* emerged.

---

[13] See Alan Richardson, introduction to *British Romanticism and the Science of Mind* (Cambridge: Cambridge University Press, 2001).
[14] Erasmus Darwin, The Temple of Nature in *The Poetical Works of Erasmus Darwin*, Vol. III (London: Johnson, 1806), lines 295–8, 309–10 and 313–14. For commentary, see Michael Page, *The Literary Imagination from Erasmus Darwin to H. G. Wells: Science, Evolution, and Ecology* (Aldershot: Ashgate, 2012).

Frankenstein

The origin myth of *Frankenstein* is that it was produced from Mary's disordered nightmare and pushed into narrative form in the ghost-story writing contest started amongst the party at the Villa Diodati in 1816 that included Lord Byron, Percy Shelley, William Polidori, and Claire Clairmont. The group had spooked themselves over a French collection of Teutonic terror tales, *Fantasmagoriana*, first published in 1812. The Frankenstein story drives a certain narrative of the Gothic as symptomatic of conflicted unconscious desires and anxieties, the young Mary surrounded by dead babies and suicides, seemingly perpetually pregnant and in exile from England in the company of Europe's most notorious pair of libertines. This Diodati origin story was encouraged by Mary Shelley herself to some extent in the 1831 Preface, but it has since been established with the recovery of the 1818 text that she was contriving to downplay the revolutionary scientific currents that thrill through that first anonymous publication of the novel.

Frankenstein's scandal is that it is an entirely secular horror, the experiments of Victor Frankenstein stripped of any theological frame. His story conforms to the structure of human hubris punished, the "over-reacher" myth, but it is more Greek than Christian and there is no Mephistopheles in this Faustian pact, no supernatural plane of divine intervention or demonic punishment – only the brute biological dyad of creature and creator, locked in a deathly pursuit that leads them beyond any possible social existence and into the sublime, icy wastes.

"Whence, I often asked myself, did the principle of life proceed?"[15] Victor Frankenstein's question is not posed in vague, metaphysical or theological terms, but (after a false start dabbling in alchemy) becomes a question to be addressed through the upstart new sciences of anatomy and physiology. The first leads to "days and nights in vaults and charnel houses" (34) observing "the natural decay and corruption of the human body" (33). The latter is more dangerous, since it probes for the very "causes and generation of life" (34). Frankenstein's confession skips over the investigation and unlocking of the spark of life itself and speaks only of the eventual epochal discovery that he "possesses the capacity of bestowing animation" upon dead matter (35).

This is the proleptic leap of an imagination bathed in fraught contemporary scientific debates in London. Controversies swirled around medical anatomical training and the dissection of the human body; within ten

---

[15] Mary Shelley, *Frankenstein 1818 Text*, ed. Marilyn Butler (Oxford: Oxford World's Classics, 2008), p. 33. All further page references are to this edition and given in the text.

years, the constraint on using the bodies of executed prisoners only would produce the enduring Gothic horror of the Edinburgh "body-snatchers," Burke and Hare, who short-circuited the laborious business of digging up fresh bodies in graveyards and began suffocating victims to supply to anatomical schools. Biology – a new and curious word entering the language in the 1810s – was mapping the complex nervous system of the human body, and finding powerful analogies between electricity and nervous stimulus of bodies even after death. And this was the decade when mechanical engineers were transforming the industrial landscape (resulting also in the mysterious working-class resistance movement of machine wreckers who called themselves Luddites), while the engineers and artisans studying electricity were figures frequently suspected of harbouring dangerously materialistic and godless ideas that linked them to continental radicalism.

How this intense and unstable period fed into Shelley's *Frankenstein* has long been studied.[16] Among the scientific spectacles of London around that time was Giovanni Aldini's notorious demonstration of the nervous re-animation of a just executed man by the application of "Galvanic fluid" through the newly invented battery, muscular movements that were so extensive, Aldini claimed, "as almost to give an appearance of re-animation."[17] Aldini himself spoke in obscurely proleptic terms, promising perhaps the full restoration of "vitality" in the near future. Scientific and imaginative projections traversed the same space. But it is worth emphasizing again the very concrete proximity of the Shelleys to these overlapping circumstances in London.

For instance, after his expulsion from Oxford in 1811, Percy Shelley arrived in London and toyed with training in surgery, attending the lectures of John Abernethy at St Bartholomew's hospital. The "demonstrator" at these lectures was William Lawrence, who treated both Percy and Mary Shelley medically over the next few years. In the 1810s, Lawrence, who had already translated some suspiciously atheistical German works of comparative anatomy, was to become a leading representative of modern, materialist science, openly opposed to theological claims, and politically radical. He conducted a very public dispute with his former master, John Abernethy, over vitalism.[18]

---

[16] See, for example, Iwan Rhys Morus, *Frankenstein's Children: Electricity, Exhibition, and Experiment in Early-Nineteenth-Century London* (Princeton: Princeton University Press, 2014).

[17] "An Account of Experiments Performed by J. Aldini" (1803), extracted in Fulford, ed., *Romanticism and Science*, p. 288.

[18] See Sharon Ruston, *Shelley and Vitality* (Basingstoke: Palgrave, 2005).

In 1816, two years before *Frankenstein*, Lawrence delivered two lectures at the Royal College of Surgeons, the latter called "On Life." In it, Lawrence rejected the vitalist notion of life as a "particular principle" that operated in "apparent exception to general laws," and instead merely argued that "Life is the assemblage of all the functions, and the general result of their exercise."[19] The "vital impulse" was not a divine spark, but purely a biological fact, transmitted from parents to offspring: "life proceeds only from life."[20]

As to the nature of life itself, Lawrence said: "We do not profess to explain how the living forces ... exert their agency." He continues proleptically, in a way that sketches out the space of imaginative possibility for *Frankenstein*:

> But some are not content to stop at this point; they wish to draw aside the veil from nature, to display the very essence of the vital properties, and penetrate to their first causes; to shew, independently of the phenomena what is life, and how irritability and sensibility execute those purposes.[21]

He rather dismissed the hypothesis linking vitality to electricity, but did not suggest there was any transgression in pursuing these researches. The reckless Victor Frankenstein, meanwhile, pursues just these questions in shuttered secrecy.

Lawrence's following *Lectures*, published in 1819, were so overtly anti-theological, materialist, and radical in their conception that Lawrence was subject to a vicious conservative press campaign, in which he was denounced for his "infidel" tendencies, French Jacobinism and his "infamous attempt of demoralizing mankind."[22] He was forced to withdraw the book (although it circulated in cheap pirate editions and was read among radical groups and scientific artisans) and began the task of burying his radical roots to become a respectable reformist baronet of the establishment over the next forty years. There was a lesson for his patient Mary Shelley in covering over the tracks of dangerous texts written in youthful political fervour.

In the novel, it is not only Victor Frankenstein who is the inadvertent scientific radical. His creature is even more thoroughly a materialist, perhaps inevitably so. The creature's narrative of his unsentimental education in human cruelty, in the political monstering of the Other, comes in part

---

[19] William Lawrence, *An Introduction to Comparative Anatomy and Physiology, Being the Two Introductory Lectures delivered at the Royal College of Surgeons on the 21st and 25th March, 1816* (London: J. Callow, 1816), pp. 122, 120

[20] Ibid., pp. 141, 142.

[21] Ibid., p. 165.

[22] These citations come from Hugh J. Luke, "Sir William Lawrence, Physician to Shelley and Mary," *Papers on English Language and Literature* 1, 2 (1965), p. 147.

through reading Count Volney's *Ruins of Empire* (1791), a Jacobinical denunciation of the rise and fall of imperial power published two years into the French Revolution and produced by contemplating the "ruins and sepulchres" of fallen civilizations, written among the collapsed stones of Luxor and Palmyra.[23] In *Frankenstein*, the creature listens to long expositions on Volney, while hiding in the forest. "Man is governed . . . by natural laws, regular in their operation," Volney declares. "Let man study these laws, let him understand his own nature, and the nature of the beings that surround him, and he will know the springs of his destiny."[24] This is not the lumbering imbecile of James Whale's 1932 adaptation, cursed with a criminal's brain, but a principled radical only constructed as "evil" by man's arbitrary laws.

Frankenstein's creature is a monster in that it is a "mosaic being," a composite formed of hybrid parts, a walking crisis of category.[25] Yet this has made the creature a perfect emblem for thinking through what monsters knot together when we read the sciences and scientific fictions as parts of the same network rather than in discrete categories. "Such a monster," Latour suggests, "cannot be stabilized in any of the great metaphors we usually employ. It is at the same time machine, market, code, body and war."[26] SF and the Gothic often abject liminal, transitional, hybrid beings: this is one influential trajectory out of the modern mythos of *Frankenstein*. But read in the context of Neural Romanticism, the text also centres on what Donna Haraway suggests is a "hopeful monster," pointing the way towards a different understanding of hybrid being: "We are *all* in chiasmatic borderlands, liminal areas where new shapes, new kinds of action and responsibility, are gestating."[27]

It is difficult but perhaps also pointless to try to parse separate lines of Gothic or science-fictional progeny from Mary Shelley's text. Victor Frankenstein spawns a line of chillingly indifferent vivisectionists that passes down through Dr. Benjulia in Wilkie Collins's *Heart and Science* (1883),

---

[23] C. F. Volney, *The Ruins; or, A Survey of the Revolutions of Empires* (London: Davison, 1819), p. 8.

[24] Ibid., p. 10.

[25] See Stephen T. Asma, *On Monsters: An Unnatural History of Our Worst Fears* (Oxford: Oxford University Press, 2009).

[26] Michel Callon and Bruno Latour, "Unscrewing the Big Leviathan: How Actors Macro-Structure Reality and How Sociologists Help Them to Do So," in K. Knorr-Cetina and A. Cicourel, eds., *Advances in Social Theory and Methodology: Toward an Integration of Micro- and Macro-Sociologies* (London: Routledge & Kegan Paul, 1981), p. 294. This paper is often taken to be the founding essay of Latour's "Actor-Network Theory."

[27] Donna Haraway, "The Promises of Monsters: A Regenerative Politics for Inappropriate/d Others" in Lawrence Grossberg et al., eds., *Cultural Studies* (London: Routledge, 1992), p. 314.

Dr. Wycherley in Charles Reade's *Hard Cash* (1863) to Robert Louis Stevenson's Dr. Jekyll (1886) and Arthur Machen's nasty experimentalists in *The Great God Pan* and *The Inmost Light* (1894), via H. G. Wells's Dr. Moreau (1896), to H. P. Lovecraft's "Herbert West – Reanimator" (1931), an old school body-snatcher. But amongst the mad doctors, there are also fictions about doctors who are heroic visionaries, who use a wider conception of the scientific spectrum to expand the boundaries of Nature and embrace what ossified convention has deemed "supernatural," from Sheridan Le Fanu's Dr. Hesselius to Bram Stoker's Professor Van Helsing to Algernon Blackwood's psychical detective John Silence and William Hope Hodgson's Carnacki, "the ghost finder" who neatly fuses the scientific and occult with his handily electrified pentacle for defense against malign obtrusions from other dimensions. This list bounces unpredictably between Gothic and SF, transgressing any definitions that are too pedantically drawn.[28]

In context, *Frankenstein* provides a precise lesson in understanding how these branches of the literary Fantastic can multiply, like symbionts in a shared ecology, in the gaps or intervals of rapidly transforming sciences, levering open spaces of proleptic fantasy where possibilities that hover on the edge of realization can be imagined.

Gothic Science

The natural philosopher William Whewell coined the word "scientist" in 1833. Although it was rarely used in the nineteenth century, this was part of a critical moment of institutionalization of science, with the formation of the British Association for the Advancement of Science in 1831, which began to meet annually in ever-larger conferences, with increasingly differentiated panels, to consolidate scientific authority in the public sphere. The British Medical Association was formed in 1832, transforming the social and professional standing of medicine. The introduction of educational structures for science teaching and new kinds of research funding from central government followed in the 1860s. Similar institutional formations occurred across Europe and America, contributing to the "rise of the professional society."[29]

One might be forgiven for thinking that this marks the beginnings of the formal demarcations that stopped the chaotic (if creative) inter-mixings of

---

[28] For a more exhaustive account see Christopher Frayling, *Mad, Bad and Dangerous? The Scientist and the Cinema* (London: Reaktion Press, 2006).

[29] Harold Perkins, *The Rise of Professional Society: England since 1880* (London: Routledge, 1989).

Neural Romanticism. With science finally secured as a possible vocation, Max Weber argued in 1918, comes the "disenchantment of the world," the sorting of knowledge from belief.[30] But demarcations take a long time to establish, and are rarely left uncontested; they cannot maintain stability for long since living sciences are always in a process of self-transformation. Indeed, creating thresholds for professional participation and boundaries to mark out legitimacy effectively generates challenges from those now deemed "outside" the new orthodoxy. The shadowlands between amateur and professional, orthodox and heterodox knowledge, the natural and the supernatural, authenticated and disavowed or "marginal" sciences – all of these continued to be deeply contested throughout the Victorian period.

Let's take mesmerism as an example of where natural and supernatural claims constantly blurred, despite innumerable attempts to fix and police the boundaries of orthodoxy in biology, medicine, and scientific psychology. Because of the strangely suspensive, inter-subjective state of trance, rival sciences of mind, fictions of the Gothic and emergent SF remained maddeningly indistinguishable in this area long into the early twentieth century.

In the 1780s, the unorthodox Viennese medic, Franz Anton Mesmer, travelled to Paris to demonstrate his practice of treating illnesses through the manipulation of what he called "animal magnetism."[31] Mesmer's theory was that he was manipulating an invisible, super-subtle fluid, passing its energy from his own body to those of his patients with whom he developed a *rapport*. They were cured of their various debilities by a restorative jolt to their depleted energy. Since this theory emerged in parallel with rival theories about electricity, magnetism, Galvanism, and other speculations about subtle vital energies, it entered a lively arena of debate. However, a Royal Commission investigating Mesmer's claims in 1784 absolutely rejected both theory and practice. Mesmer was already selling his "secret" methods of manipulation at a high price to initiates in the manner of a "quack" remedy or initiation into an occult group and in defiance of emergent protocols of transparency in scientific practice. But, rather more urgently, an unpublished annex to the 1784 report privately expressed alarm that Mesmer was treating women patients in states of defenceless trance, inducing in them "crises" or hysterical reactions that seemed worryingly

---

[30] Max Weber, "Science as a Vocation," in *From Max Weber: Essays in Sociology*, trans. H. Gerth and C. Wright Mills (London: Routledge, 1948), pp. 129–56.
[31] See Robert Darnton, *Mesmerism and the Era of Enlightenment in France* (Cambridge, MA: Harvard University Press, 1968) and Adam Crabtree, *From Mesmer to Freud: Magnetic Sleep and the Roots of Psychological Healing* (New Haven: Yale University Press, 1994).

close to states of orgasmic ecstasy ("When this kind of crisis is approaching, the countenance becomes gradually inflamed, the eye brightens, and this is the sign of natural desire," the Commissioners warned).[32] Just as the Gothic wave crested, Mesmer provided a model for the alluring foreigner who manipulated mysterious, occult forces that could induce a trance state that dissolved the will and in doing so particularly menaced female virtue. That is the model of the evil hypnotist, via Svengali and Count Dracula, down to the present day.[33]

Mesmer was soon hounded out of town, and yet his French followers repeatedly claimed to present evidence of the objective phenomenon of trance states and its potential curative power. In 1811, the Marquis de Puységur dismissed Mesmer's theory that a physical fluid was being transferred and laid the groundwork for the idea that the curative power of *rapport* in trance came from psychological *suggestion*. Even so, Puységur continued to observe remarkable phenomena associated with trances, including "clairvoyance" and an odd sharing of mental states between the mesmerist and the mesmerized. This penumbra of the sensational and occult meant that repeated commissions in France rejected the existence of the phenomena again in 1826 and 1837.

In England, mesmerism had been demonstrated in the 1810s (and seen by Percy Shelley, amongst many others), but with the rise of professional medicine and the rejection of dangerous and metaphysical continental ideas it was resolutely banished from orthodox medicine. This set the scene for a major controversy in the early 1840s about where to draw the line of legitimacy. Professor John Elliotson of University College not only accepted the curative power of trance, but proceeded to demonstrate mesmeric cures in the wards of the hospital attached to University College, the rationalist, "godless" college. His forced resignation pushed mesmerism firmly into the marginal sciences, and it became a discredited popular treatment.[34] However, Elliotson had powerful allies. Charles Dickens not only accepted the theory of mesmerism but practiced it himself, energetically mesmerizing the alluring Madame de la Rue over several years from 1842 and reporting in detail on the *rapport* that connected them even as far apart as London and Italy. In 1845, Dickens

---

[32] Annex to the report, quoted in Alfred Binet and Charles Féré, *Animal Magnetism*, 3rd edn. (London: Kegan Paul International Scientific Series, 1891), p. 20.

[33] See Daniel Pick, *Svengali's Web: The Alien Enchanter in Modern Culture* (New Haven: Yale University Press, 2000).

[34] For this history, see particularly Alison Winter, *Mesmerized: Powers of Mind in Victorian Britain* (Chicago: University of Chicago Press, 1998).

reported that such was his mesmeric power that he had accidentally entranced his wife instead of Madame de la Rue, much to his harried wife's consternation and annoyance.[35] Rationalist and political economist Harriet Martineau also published her famous "Letters on Mesmerism" in 1844, claiming various debilities were substantially improved by treatment. In 1845, Edgar Allan Poe published "The Facts in the Case of M. Valdemar," in which a mesmerist suspends a dying man in a mesmeric trance, allowing him to speak, impossibly, from beyond the grave. Edward Bulwer-Lytton, a writer interested in both scientific and occult matters, and in the vanishing point between them, published a host of Gothic tales where mesmerism played a central role, including "The Haunted and the Haunters" and *A Strange Story*.[36] At the same time, a new generation of professional medics and psychologists were suggesting a rational, physiological basis for "magnetic sleep," which they named "neurypnology" or, more catchily, "hypnosis." For a science hopelessly entangled in the occult, these new coinages that proposed a workable physiological thesis were ignored for over thirty years.

The eminent physiologist and ardent anti-clerical materialist Jean-Martin Charcot lent his authority to the objective phenomenon of trance in 1882, finally discarding mesmerism but embracing hypnotism. Trance finally became a fact of neurological science. Charcot considered susceptibility to trance a likely sign of degenerative biological weakness and incipient hysteria, although rival schools proposed that the power of *suggestion* was universal. Yet even at this late stage, the natural and the supernatural blurred. Experiments under Charcot's stern control included claims to have observed clairvoyance, mind-reading, and the transfer of hysterical symptoms *between patients*. Some of the leading English experimentalists in hypnosis were some of the founding members of the Society for Psychical Research in 1882. F. W. H. Myers and his brother, the doctor A. T. Myers, experimented with "hypnotism at a distance," trying to hypnotize patients across the distance of the English Channel. In the same year, F. W. H. Myers coined the term "telepathy" to describe "communications outside the recognized channels of sense," which he considered to have been objectively proved by experiments with the science of hypnotism.[37] Psychical research was

[35] See Fred Kaplan, *Dickens and Mesmerism: The Hidden Springs of Fiction* (Princeton: Princeton University Press, 1975).

[36] See Bruce Wyse, "Mesmeric Machinery: Textual Production and Simulacra in Bulwer-Lytton's 'The Haunted and the Haunters: or, The House and the Brain,'" *Victorian Review* 30, 2 (2004), pp. 32–57.

[37] See Roger Luckhurst, *The Invention of Telepathy 1870–1902* (Oxford: Oxford University Press, 2002).

established by pioneering dynamic psychologists and energy physicists who hoped to scientize and naturalize the supernatural. Although it initially offended Spiritualists by suggesting that their claims of contacting the dead were probably merely evidence of unusual but "natural" psychological sensitivities, many researchers, like Myers, came to believe that they had scientific proof of life after death.

The transition from mesmerism to hypnotism in the late nineteenth century opened a place for competing theories to which contemporaneous Gothic fictions and scientific romances extensively contributed. The Gothic tenor of the fevered, delirious enchantments in, say, Grant Allen's "The Pallinghurst Barrow" (1892) or Arthur Conan Doyle's "The Parasite" (1894), or Bram Stoker's *Dracula* or Richard Marsh's *The Beetle* (both 1897) were mixed into the public discourse with imperious denunciations of hypnotism as "the new witchcraft" by none other than the editor of the *British Medical Journal*, official organ of the British Medical Association.[38] At the same time, revelations of the potentially transformative power of what Myers called "the subliminal mind" inspired some to consider this hyper-sensitivity or perhaps even telepathic powers of the mind to be fugitive signs of an evolutionary advance to the next stage of humanity.

This curious mix of biology, psychology, scientific romance, SF, utopianism, and, sometimes, a scientized theology became a central motif of later SF writings. You can find this from A. E. van Vogt's *Slan* (1946), to Arthur C. Clarke's *Childhood's End* (1951), to John Wyndham's *The Chrysalids* (1955) and beyond. Typically, this later phase of SF on expanded mental capacities spills over the edges of pulp fiction and into a strange "real" existence in the interstices of psychological and para-psychological research. Van Vogt set up the Nexial Institute to teach the "general semantics" that lay behind the self-transformation fantasies often found in the pages of *Astounding Science Fiction*. It was a forerunner of the more notorious science-fictional psychological science of Dianetics, a form of training enthusiastically endorsed by John W. Campbell, the editor of *Astounding SF*, in 1950, and a method that soon transformed into the religion of Scientology. This weird moment has its roots in the phase of "extraordinary" psychological science in the late nineteenth century.

All of this is to suggest that the arrival of the "scientific romance" in the 1880s was not some kind of decisive new generic formation, breaking from

---

[38] Ernest Hart, *Hypnotism, Mesmerism and the New Witchcraft*, enlarged edn. from 1896 (New York: Da Capo Press reprint series, 1982).

the Gothic. Charles Howard Hinton, the first to use the phrase "scientific romance" in a book title in 1886, was writing odd sketches that mixed fiction, philosophical Socratic dialogues, speculations in the higher mathematics on the possibility of a fourth dimension, and the occult theories of professional astronomer and Spiritualist Johann Zöllner, who proposed that multiple dimensional mathematics could explain apparently supernatural phenomena. These kinds of theories and fictional experiments fed directly into the framework Wells constructed a few years later for *The Time Machine*, the "scientific romance" he sent in homage to both fiction writer Grant Allen and eminent man of science T. H. Huxley.[39]

As in the case of the Neural Romantics, this is a period of frenetic scientific discovery, multiple theories, and proleptic visions of a scientific future just on the brink of emergence, and fictions in many registers exploited these exploded intervals in contemporary knowledge, snatching a re-enchantment of the world from the very jaws of what was meant to be rationalist disenchantment. I contend that it is from these bleeding edges that we can best grasp the border zones from which Gothic and SF emerge together, inextricably entwined. Separating them out like some peculiar Maxwell's demon not only seems fruitless theoretically but counters the actual history of genre.

---

[39] See Mark Blacklock, *The Emergence of the Fourth Dimension: Higher Spatial Thinking in the Fin de Siècle* (Oxford: Oxford University Press, 2016).

3

European Science Fiction in the Nineteenth Century

TERRY HARPOLD

Defining the canon of nineteenth-century European SF seems to lead, inevitably, to also embracing doubtful analogies and inventive anachronisms. Hugo Gernsback's endorsement of "the Jules Verne, H. G. Wells, and Edgar Allan Poe type of story" as the model for what Gernsback christened "scientifiction" – later "science fiction" – is telling in this regard.[1] Verne, Wells, and Poe *are* among the precursors of modern SF, but in most respects they are dissimilar from each other. Many other, equally dissimilar, figures also contributed to the incunable period of SF, the complexity of which confounds such comparisons.[2]

Labels such as "proto-SF," "early SF," or "Victorian SF" – the last of which is too closely associated with one national tradition to be generally useful – may help to mark the field's development. But they also beg the question of what SF was, really, during this early phase when it had no widely accepted name, a concern at least since Félix Bodin's description of the problem in *Le Roman de l'avenir* (*The Novel of the Future*, 1834). (Bodin offers the label *roman futuriste* ["futurist novel"].) Recurring thematic and stylistic elements, and several of the field's foundational texts, date to the beginning of the century or a little before. Brian Aldiss (in *Trillion Year Spree*) credits Mary Shelley's *Frankenstein, or The Modern Prometheus* (1818) as the first work of true SF. Brian

---

[1] Gary Westfahl, *Hugo Gernsback and the Century of Science Fiction* (Jefferson, NC: McFarland & Co., 2007).

[2] Brian Aldiss and David Wingrove, *Trillion Year Spree: The History of Science Fiction* (London: Gollancz, 1986); Paul K. Alkon, *Science Fiction Before 1900: Imagination Discovers Technology* (New York: Routledge, 2002); Istvan Csicsery-Ronay, Jr., *The Seven Beauties of Science Fiction* (Middletown, CT: Wesleyan University Press, 2008); Brian Stableford, *New Atlantis: A Narrative History of Scientific Romance* (Rockville, MD: Wildside Press, 2016); Brian Stableford, *The Plurality of Imaginary Worlds: The Evolution of French Roman Scientifique* (Tarzana, CA: Black Coat Press, 2016); Jacques Van Herp, *Panorama de la science-fiction: Les thèmes, les genres, les écoles, les problèmes* (Verviers: Marabout Université, 1975); Pierre Versins, *Encyclopédie de l'utopie, des voyages extraordinaires et de la science fiction* (Lausanne: Éditions l'Age d'Homme, 1984).

Stableford (in *The Plurality of Imaginary Worlds*) pushes the origins back earlier, for example, to Nicolas-Edme Restif de la Bretonne's *La Découverte australe par un homme-volant* (*The Discovery of the Austral Continent by a Flying-Man*, 1781). Jean Baptiste Cousin de Grainville's *Le Dernier Homme* (*The Last Man*, 1805) and Julius von Voss's *Ini, Roman aus dem 21sten Jahrhundert* (*Ini, A Novel of the Twenty-First Century*, 1810) are other candidates for early priority. But, as shown below, other elements now considered characteristically science fictional are rare before the second half of the century, and novelty has its privileges. The label "scientific romance," used from mid-century onward for mostly British authors, was rejected by many to whom it was applied, such as Wells, who found "romance" too backward-looking. The French *roman scientifique* ("scientific novel" *and* "scientific romance") dodges retrospection a little – the etymologies of *roman* and *romance* are tangled – but "scientific" is the problem term here; the label also was applied to naturalist authors such as Émile Zola because their depictions of the influences of heredity and environment were considered *scientifically* accurate. The French *merveilleux scientifique* ("scientific marvel fiction"), associated with authors J.-H. Rosny aîné and Maurice Renard, is too self-consciously anti-Vernian to be of much use outside that context. Disagreements about the pertinent traits of the emerging European literature left an opening for twentieth-century Americans like Gernsback and Golden Age editor John W. Campbell to name and circumscribe the field's content and method.

In the context of the nineteenth century, then, "SF" becomes a placeholder for a radically diverse, inconsistent field of literary production that emerged, haltingly, out of traditions of utopian fiction, satirical *contes*, and imaginary voyages, and in relation to other literary movements such as romanticism, realism, naturalism, and early modernism. (The porousness of boundaries here is discernible in the number of "literary" authors who tried their hand at SF: Honoré de Balzac [*Le Centenaire, The Centenarian*, 1822], Guy de Maupassant ["Le Horla," "The Horla," 1887], George Sand [*Laura, Voyage dans le cristal, Laura, Journey in the Crystal*, 1864], and Émile Zola [the unfinished *Quatre Évangiles, The Four Gospels*, 1899–1903], among others.) More directly, SF emerged in connection with the century's passion for the popularization of science and technology.[3] Popularization had begun in the eighteenth century with the publication of Denis Diderot's *Encyclopédie, ou dictionnaire raisonné des sciences, des arts et des métiers* (*The Encyclopedia, or the*

---

[3] Daniel Fondanèche, *La Littérature d'imagination scientifique* (Amsterdam: Editions Rodopi, 2012).

Rational Dictionary of the Sciences, Arts and Crafts, 1751–72), and it expanded during the nineteenth century as popular-scientific media multiplied and were consumed avidly by middle and working classes that imagined their economic futures to be tied to technological innovation.[4]

A new image of the scientist emerges from the century's fiction and nonfiction: the professional, secular agent of scientific naturalism and progress. He – almost always the scientist is male – works in the new idioms of astronomy, chemistry, and physics, and with the new technologies of steam-power and electricity. New methods or inventions in the fictional life of the scientist – a novel form of transportation, a source of power, a mysterious ray – may be necessary to his adventures but they are not sufficient. They are more the stage props of the fiction, as Poe (no stranger to genre invention) might have observed: "the wheels and pinions – the tackle for scene-shifting – the step-ladders and demon-traps" of emergent SF,[5] they signify the *science* of the fiction less than does an implicit or explicit technoscientific worldview, which need not involve any hardware, or any scientists. For example, Hollow Earth and prehistoric fiction featured little scientific apparatus, but the nine-teenth-century variant of the former and all of the latter genre are unthink-able without the century's geological and paleontological revolutions. Similarly, nascent SF's extraordinary voyages (under the seas, over land, in the air, into space) are applications of actual innovations in transportation (steam-driven locomotives and ships, balloons), or those, such as heavier-than-air flight, that were believed by century's end to be practicable.

Commercial and National Contexts

Late nineteenth-century European SF was read in contexts of mass literacy and mass production that had not existed at the end of the eighteenth century. Improved literacy rates, especially among working classes and women and children, a change accelerated by the introduction of compulsory primary education in most of Europe, and the rise of a culture of private recreational reading, resulted in an expanded reading public.[6] Improvements in paper manufacture and printing technologies dramatically reduced the

---

[4] Aileen Fyfe and Bernard Lightman, eds., *Science in the Marketplace: Nineteenth-Century Sites and Experiences* (Chicago: University of Chicago Press, 2007).

[5] Edgar Allan Poe, "The Philosophy of Composition," in J. Gerald Kennedy, ed., *The Portable Edgar Allan Poe* (New York: Penguin, 2006), pp. 543–54.

[6] Martyn Lyons, *Readers and Society in Nineteenth-Century France: Workers, Women, Peasants* (New York: Palgrave, 2001); David Vincent, *The Rise of Mass Literacy: Reading and Writing in Modern Europe* (Cambridge: Polity, 2000).

costs of publishing. The relaxing of press censorship laws, particularly in France, released a flood of new newspapers and magazines. The rise of major publishing houses such as Hetzel et Cie (France), Routledge (Britain), and Tauchnitz (Germany), the emergence of independent booksellers, and changes in the retail trade that had begun in the late eighteenth century, increased competition for readership and the range and variety of available texts.[7] Publishers often multiplied editions of successful titles in different formats targeted at different audiences. (Verne's publisher Hetzel was the master of this technique.) Contracts for translation rights – and outright piracy, even after the Berne Convention of 1885 – ensured that many popular authors were read internationally. SF found an important footing in new serial formats, in French *feuilletons* and in magazines such as the *Magasin d'éducation et de récréation* (1864–1916), in which most of Verne's fiction first appeared, and in British periodicals such as *The Strand* (1891–1950) and *Pearson's Magazine* (1896–1939), in which works by George Griffith, Wells, and others were serialized. Similarly, SF became a fixture of "railway literature," reprint series that included hundreds of titles, published by Routledge (1848–98), Hachette (1853–69), and Reclam (1867–), and sold at train stations and from street kiosks. Over the course of the century, innovations in lithography, wood engraving, electrotyping, and photo-mechanical reproduction fostered an explosive growth in illustrated books and periodicals, to which SF storyworlds appeared particularly well suited. (Verne's *Voyages extraordinaires* [*Extraordinary Voyages*, 1863–1905] include nearly 5,000 illustrations, as many as one for every six to eight pages of text.) A few SF authors, such as illustrator–satirist Albert Robida, were acknowledged masters of polymedial storytelling.

The success and reach of the individual national traditions during the nineteenth century had less to do with the appeal of authors than with the character of the nations' respective publishing sectors, prevailing (and often changeable) state censorship laws, and the openness of literary institutions to new genres.[8] France and England dominate; there are few German contributions of note before late in the century, and fewer from Italy and Spain.

---

[7] Michael F. Suarez, S. J. and H. R. Woudhuysen, eds., *The Book: A Global History* (Oxford: Oxford University Press, 2013), especially the chapters on regional and national histories.

[8] Anindita Banerjee, *We Modern People: Science Fiction and the Making of Russian Modernity* (Middletown, CT: Wesleyan University Press, 2013); Andrea Bell and Yolanda Molina-Gavilán, eds., *Cosmos Latinos: An Anthology of Science Fiction from Latin America and Spain* (Middletown, CT: Wesleyan University Press, 2003); Franz Rottensteiner, ed., *The Black Mirror and Other Stories: An Anthology of Science Fiction from Germany and Austria* (Middletown, CT: Wesleyan University Press, 2009); Versins, *Encyclopédie, passim.*

Russia, the source of a rich SF tradition in the Soviet era, produced a handful of significant works before the twentieth century. Notwithstanding, Wells and Verne towered over other authors and their outsized roles contributed to the greater influence of British and French SF, respectively. Wells's stature explains his reputation as a founding figure of SF, though less than a half of his published work fits even a generous definition of the field. Verne's more than fifty novels and collections of short stories so dominated the Francophone sphere that most French SF into the first decades of the twentieth century was written in imitation of, or conscious opposition to, his example.

World-building

The imagined terrains of nineteenth-century SF describe a world made significantly smaller by new technologies of movement and communication, and the first evidences of the coming globalization of politics and economies.[9] These were accompanied by changes in the understanding of time, particularly after the adoption of a worldwide system of time zones and the setting of Greenwich as the prime meridian (1884). The modern extraordinary voyage is in these regards an exercise in spatial exhaustion and temporal compression, and the conveyances that make this possible – locomotives, steamships, submarines, balloons, and heavier-than-air craft – are there to support the exercise with improved efficiency and speed. (*Outer* space travel plays a minor role in the literature before mid-century.) Verne's Phileas Fogg (*Le Tour du monde en quatre-vingt jours* [*Around the World in Eighty Days*, 1873]) is the first railway-timetable automaton, active on a global – literally a globetrotting – scale, and the movements and actions of science-fictional subjects after him are similarly calibrated to standardized relations of space and time.

This exhaustion of space and compression of time tends also toward the establishment of technoscience as the basis of verismilitude. Verne's novels, for example, are robustly intertextual, interpolating details from actual scientific journals, maps, and gazeteers.[10] His most successful imitators, such as Georges Le Faure (*Voyages scientifiques extraordinaires* [*Extraordinary Scientific Voyages*, 1892–4]) and Paul d'Ivoi (*Voyages excentriques* [*Eccentric Voyages*, 1894–1914]), followed this formula. Their roles in the origins of hard SF are

[9] Armand Mattelart, *Networking the World, 1794–2000*, trans. Liz Carey-Libbrecht and James A. Cohen (Minneapolis, MN: University of Minnesota Press, 2000).

[10] Darko Suvin, *Metamorphoses of Science Fiction* (New Haven: Yale University Press, 1979), p. 150.

marked not in the fictive hardware – mere wheels and pinions – but in the intimate join of an author's text with his or her scientific sources. This method of interpolation can also reach across a shared storyworld. Verne's later novels cite events of earlier novels in narrative asides or footnotes, with no distinction made between them and the real scientific documents and historical events that are also cited.

Other Histories

Advances in geology and paleontology laid the foundation for another relation of time and space that became a feature of prehistoric and future history SF. Superposed strata represent deep time in overlapping layers rather than serial vignettes (à la Bayeaux Tapestry, or comics, or film), and early SF often used geologic imagery to flag the passage of time. Pierre Boitard's *Paris avant les hommes* (*Paris Before Man*, 1861) relies on both stratigraphic and serial forms (the Talmudic demon Asmodeus gives a geology lesson to the narrator in a dream); so does Verne's *Voyage au centre de la terre* (*Voyage to the Center of the Earth*, 1864), in which the hero imagines history running in reverse to the origin of the solar system while floating on the surface of a vast ocean in an underground grotto. Only after Wells's description in *The Time Machine* (1895) of "night [following] day like the flapping of a black wing" do representations of time travel turn from stratigraphic to proto-cinematic sequences, doorways, corridors, and the like.

Writers sourced their early visions of deep time from popularizers like Camille Flammarion, Louis Figuier (*La Terre avant le déluge* [*Earth Before the Deluge*, 1863]), George Lyell (*Geological Evidences of the Antiquity of Man*, 1863), and Franz Unger (*Die Urwelt in ihren verschiedenen Bildungsperioden* [*The Primitive World in Its Different Periods of Development*, 1851]). At mid-century those scholars were still trying to reconcile Biblical creation myths with the new scientific evidence. As agreement coalesced around a much older geologic history than indicated by the Bible, the influences of the creation narrative on SF diminished. At the same time, influences of modern paleontology and the theory of natural selection were increasingly felt. (Charles Darwin's *The Origin of Species* [1859] and *The Descent of Man* [1871], and Thomas Henry Huxley's *Man's Place in Nature* [1863] are key texts here.)

Prehistoric SF, strictly speaking, emerges with Boitard's *Paris before Man*, Adrien Arcelin's *Solutré, ou les chasseurs de rennes de la France centrale. Histoire préhistorique* (*Solutré, or, the Reindeer Hunters of Central France, a Prehistoric*

Story, 1872), and Élie Berthet's *Paris avant l'histoire* (*Paris Before History*, 1885).[11] J.-H. Rosny aîné's *Vamireh* (1892) and *Eyrimah* (1895) are the most important works of the genre before his landmark *La Guerre du feu* (*The Quest for Fire*, 1909). The scientific accuracy of these stories is thin; they are for the most part romances with prehistory as the exotic locale. Often, the genre draws on contact episodes (see p. 63 below) for narrative tension, when protagonists meet other hominids more or less advanced than they on the evolutionary scale, or are banished from their tribes because they represent improbable leaps of evolution. (Henry Curwin's whimsical *Zit and Xoe. Their Early Experiences* [1886–7] is one of the first examples of this now-familiar outcast motif.) Contact stories drift into variations on lost race fiction or musings on the supposed primitivism of non-whites – Verne's *Le Village aérien* (*The City in the Treetops*, 1901) combines both – as well as transparent miscegenation fantasies. Wells's *The Island of Doctor Moreau* (1896), though it foregrounds critiques of scientific hubris and vivisection, owes much to this crossing of motifs, as do the melodramatic *Hémo* (1886), by Émile Dodillon, and "L'Homme-singe" ("The Ape-Man," 1894), by Han Ryner, similar stories of scientists' meddling with the human–animal divide. Robert Louis Stevenson's *Strange Case of Dr. Jekyll and Mr. Hyde* (1886) mixes anxieties about this divide with class conflict. Elsewhere in Britain, worries over distinctions between the higher primates manifested as satire: the anonymous *The Gorilla Origins of Man* (1871), in which a simian race determines that humans are the product of a rape of a gorilla, and Arthur Montagu Brookfield's *Simiocracy* (1884), in which orangutans are given voting rights in Britain and proceed to take over the government.

An important distinction between pre- and post-Darwinian SF is that future humans may be physically or socially transformed by evolution, or contemporary humans may be replaced by others better suited to a changed world. Wells's *The Time Machine* (1895) is the best-known example. Ernest George Harmer's "Professor Bommsenn's Germs" (1887), in which an agricultural lab experiment produces a new species superior to humans, is another. W. H. Hudson's *A Crystal Age* (1887), an early work of ecological SF, envisages a pastoral utopia in which humans are physically unchanged but live like social insects. Similarly, artificial life may appear equal to human life or evolve to potentially surpass it. E. T. A. Hoffmann's Olimpia in "Der Sandman" ("The Sandman," 1816) and Auguste Villiers de l'Isle-Adam's

---

[11] Nicholas Ruddick, *The Fire in the Stone: Prehistoric Fiction from Charles Darwin to Jean M. Auel* (Middletown, CT: Wesleyan University Press, 2009).

Hadaly in *L'Ève future* (*The Future Eve*, 1886) are early examples of the "uncanny valley" of almost-human robots. Samuel Butler's *Erewhon* (1872) includes "The Book of the Machines," which predicts their eventual rise to become the planet's pinnacle species. W. Grove's *The Mexican Mystery* (1881) and *The Wreck of the World* (1889) describe industrial machinery developing sentience and vying with humans for dominance. In Didier de Chousy's *Ignis* (1883), mechanical "Atmophytes," automata essential to the novel's technological utopia, demand autonomy from human control. Wells's "The Lord of the Dynamos" (1895) is a counter-example that treats machinic agency as a conceit of the preindustrial imagination.

For most of the century, imagined leaps between epochs rarely involved the use of hardware. *The Time Machine* is an exception, but it was not the first: Enrique Gaspar y Rimbau's *El anacronópete* (*The Anachronopete*, 1887), published one year before Wells's *The Chronic Argonauts*, is the earliest example of time travel with a machine. More common are stories of time travel through suspended animation. In Faddei Bulgarin's *Plausible Fantasies, or a Journey in the Twenty-Ninth Century* (1924), the nineteenth-century narrator drowns in the frozen Gulf of Finland. Accidentally enveloped in a miraculous herb that keeps him alive, he awakens in an Edenic Siberia transformed by geoengineering. In Jane C. Loudon's *The Mummy!* (1827), the body of Cheops (Khufu, pharaoh of the Fourth Dynasty) is reanimated in the year 2137 to observe technologies and social mores dramatically changed from Loudon's day. In Louis Henri Boussenard's *Dix Mille Ans dans un bloc de glace* (*Ten Thousand Years in a Block of Ice*, 1890) and A. Vilgensofer's *La Terre dans cent mille ans* (*The Earth in a Hundred Thousand Years*, 1893) the traveler is resurrected from similar forms of interrupted consciousness. Wells uses drug-induced sleep to achieve the temporal crossing in *The Sleeper Awakes* (original version 1898–9, rewritten 1910). Hudson relies on a centuries-long coma in *A Crystal Age*, as does William Morris in *News from Nowhere* (1890). Telepathic connections are another path to the future. In Antonio Flores's speculative history of the nineteenth century *Ayer, hoy y mañana, ó La fé, el vapor y la electricidad* (*Yesterday, Today, and Tomorrow, or Faith, Steam, and Electricity*, 1863–4), the spirit of Merlin dictates the narrator's account of a future Madrid whose citizens travel on elastic sidewalks and whose skies are full of hot-air balloons.

The political and military ferment of post-Napoleonic Europe offered ample raw material for visions of the future. France careened from Empire to Republic, back, and back again. The Risorgimento unified Italy. The German Confederation, initially a bulwark against Austrian and

Prussian dominance, gave way to the North German Confederation and then to the German Empire. German unification was hastened by the Franco-Prussian War, which shamed the French with the loss of Alsace-Lorraine and set a fuse for the First World War. Spain lost most of its North and South American colonies early in the century, was divided by failed liberal revolutions against its monarchs, became a short-lived Republic, restored the Bourbons to power, and lost the last of its colonies in the Spanish–American War (1898). Portugal's empire collapsed with Brazil's declaration of independence in 1822 and later losses of territories in Africa to the British. The global military and economic dominance of the British Empire increased to an unprecedented degree under Victoria, especially in South Asia and Africa. After the Berlin Conference of 1884–5, the Congo Free State became the personal property of Leopold II of Belgium, initiating the cruelest colonial experiment of the modern age. Soon thereafter, the rest of Africa was seized and divided among the other European powers. Nicholas II became Tsar of Russia (1894), rejecting last-chance reforms to improve the lot of peasants and workers.

Alternate histories and uchronian fantasies flourished. ("Uchronia," meaning "fictional times," was coined by Charles Renouvier in his 1876 novel *Uchronie*.) The first significant entry in this genre was Louis Geoffroy's 1836 *Histoire de la monarchie universelle: Napoléon et la conquête du monde, 1812–1832* (*Napoleon and the Conquest of the World, 1812–1832*), in which Napoleon's invasion of Russia is a success. The Emperor then invades England and becomes the benevolent dictator of a united world. Geoffroy's novel was the first of many future histories turning on alternative outcomes of the Napoleonic Wars.

Future wars fought with new, more terrible weapons were common after mid-century.[12] These stories were to a large degree stimulated by actual advances in long-range artillery (decisive in the Crimean and Franco-Prussian Wars), military transport, telegraphy and balloon reconnaissance, and early developments in chemical and air weaponry. Hermann Lang's *The Air Battle* (1859), about aerial warfare in the sixty-eighth century, was an important anticipation. More influential was George Chesney's *The Battle of Dorking* (1871), an international bestseller about a Prussian invasion of Britain that established the genre's perennial theme of German military superiority. Louis Tracy and M. P. Shiel's *An American Emperor* (1897) and *The Lost*

---

[12] I. F. Clarke, *Voices Prophesying War: Future Wars, 1763–3749* (Oxford: Oxford University Press, 1993).

Provinces (1898) imagine turning the tables: on behalf of France the American hero Vansittart uses armored vehicles to retake Alsace-Lorraine from the Germans.

Verne's *Les Cinq Cents Millions de la Bégum* (*The Begum's Millions*, 1879) and Barillet-Lagargousse's *La Guerre finale* (*The Final War*, 1885) shifted the emphasis from prospective national conflicts to the profitability of war, with stories of mad inventors willing to sell their weapons (giant cannons, earthquake machines) to the highest bidder. Camille Debans's *Les Malheurs de John Bull* (*The Misfortunes of John Bull*, 1884) and Verne's *Face au drapeau* (*Face the Flag*, 1896) featured, unusually, French military geniuses and inventors of super-weapons. In addition to building spacecraft and airplanes, Mikhail Ossipov, the hero of Henry de Graffigny and George Le Faure's *Aventures extraordinaires d'un savant russe* [*The Extraordinary Adventures of a Russian Scientist*, 1889–96] creates "selenite," an apocalyptic explosive that threatens the entire Earth. In contrast, Verne's Baltimore Gun Club novels (*De la Terre à la lune, Autour de la lune, Sans dessus dessous* [*From the Earth to the Moon*, 1865; *Around the Moon*, 1870; *Topsy-Turvy*, 1889) are puckish satires of the American military-industrial complex, which must find new uses for its munitions after the Civil War. Robida's *La Guerre au vingtième siècle* (*War in the Twentieth Century*, 1887) is in a darker vein, combining outright farce, Robida's whimsical illustrations, and appalling accounts of massacres by mechanical, chemical, and biological weapons during wars for control of Africa and Europe.

Robur, the half-crazed inventor of Verne's *Robur-le-conquérant* (*Robur the Conqueror*, 1886), pointedly does not use his aeronef, the *Albatross*, for war. (In the 1904 sequel, *Maître du monde* [*Master of the World*], there is no ambiguity about Robur's madness or the menace of his airplane-automobile-speedboat-submarine, the *Terror*.) In other novels aerial bombardment is common and devastating, as, for example, in Lang's *The Air Battle* and the jingoistic *La Guerre en ballon* (*War by Balloon*, 1889) by Émile-Auguste-Cyprien-Driant ("Captain Danrit"). George Griffith's *The Angel of the Revolution* (1893) depicts the world-ending power of aerial weaponry *and* a scenario in which it may be used to keep the peace, themes that Wells would explore more deftly in *The War in the Air* (1908) and, much later, in *The Shape of Things to Come* (1933). Nemo, inventor of literature's most famous submarine, uses the *Nautilus* chiefly as a defensive weapon (Verne's *Vingt Mille Lieues sous les mers* [*Twenty Thousand Leagues Under the Sea*, 1870]). But in Georges Le Faure's *La Guerre sous l'eau* (*War Beneath the Water*, 1890) an international federation builds a super-submarine, the *Vindex*, to attack the German Navy. Captain Danrit's *La Guerre fatale: France–Angleterre*

(*The Inevitable War: France–England*, 1901–2) features French submarines defeating the British Navy.

In nationalist and colonial imaginaries, technological progress often joined with genocidal fantasies of conflict and dispossession. Danrit, who wrote more future war fiction than any other author of the period, was also a contributor to that verminous subgenre, the race war narrative, penning such titles as *L'Invasion noire* (*The Black Invasion*, 1895–6) and *L'Invasion jaune* (*The Yellow Invasion*, 1905). Jules Lermina's *La Bataille de Strasbourg* (*The Battle of Strasbourg*, 1892) probably invented modern race war narrative with his account of Asia rebelling against European imperial might. In Kenneth Mackay's *The Yellow Wave* (1895) Britain, battling Russia in India, turns its attention from Australia, leaving the colony open to Chinese invasion. Race war stories were generally cautionary tales, in which the nonwhite other is discovered to be more cunning and/or more technologically advanced than white Europeans and the latter, weakened by decadence, manage to prevail by undeserved good fortune or timing. In M. P. Shiel's *The Yellow Danger: The Story of the World's Greatest War* (1899), European civilization is saved by the intervention of a plague to which whites are immune. Camille Mauclair's *L'Orient vierge* (*The Virgin Orient*, 1897) describes a united Europe in the year 2000 making a pre-emptive strike against insubordinate Asia.

Promises of technological progress also fed peaceable, sometimes ambiguous, visions of the future.[13] Von Voss's *Ini, a Novel of the Twenty-First Century*, perhaps the first German SF novel, describes a technological utopia ruled by a benevolent aristocracy whose members are raised anonymously among free and happy citizens. Bulgarin's *Plausible Fantasies, Incredible Implausibles* (1828), and *A Scene from the Private Life* (1828), and Vladimir Odevsky's *The Year 4338: Petersburg Letters* (*c.* 1835), depict global societies modeled on nineteenth-century Russia, except that the workers and serfs are content because new technologies have improved their welfare. Nikolai Chernyshevski's unfinished *What Can Be Done?* (1863) imagines a distant future, also Russophile, in which citizens live in a stateless, classless, agrarian society. In Émile Souvestre's *Le Monde tel qu'il sera* (*The World as It Shall Be*, 1846), one of the first European dystopias, a young couple sleep in a mesmeric trance until the year 3000. They awaken to discover that corporations have wrested effective power from national governments by influencing tax policies, chipping away at the social safety net, controlling the mass media, and

---

[13] John Rieder, *Colonialism and the Emergence of Science Fiction* (Middletown, CT: Wesleyan University Press, 2008).

encouraging frenzied consumerism. Robida's *War in the Twentieth Century* and *La Vie électrique* (*Electric Life*, 1892) satirize in a lighter vein the unfreedoms of future consumer societies driven by acquisitive impulses. In contrast, Morris's *News from Nowhere* envisages a classless utopia, in which there is no private property and individual reward is found in creative and pleasurable labor.

Sometimes the future includes more equal relations between the sexes. Robida's novels feature female protagonists who are free to pursue careers and financial independence. In Florence Dixie's *Gloriana, or the Revolution of 1900* (1890), a successful women's suffrage movement lead by a charismatic prime minister, a woman disguised as a man, results in a prosperous twenty-first-century Britain governed by women. Hudson's *A Crystal Age* resolves conflicts between the sexes more radically, by way of a sexless matriarchy in which only the Queen and her consort are allowed to reproduce. Other pseudo-feminist scenarios include (un)healthy measures of masculine priority and *ressentiment*. The socialist utopia of Morris's *News from Nowhere* frees women from legal bondage to men but confines them to the roles of child-bearers and helpmates. Elizabeth Burgoyne Corbett's *New Amazonia: A Foretaste of the Future* (1889) takes place in an "Amazonian" utopia, the former Ireland, in the year 2472. Men may be citizens but they have no political power, women practice "nerve regeneration" to keep their youth, and euthanasia to weed out imperfect citizens. A male visitor from the nineteenth century is outraged by his subordinate status and is sent back to the past. Similarly, a male visitor to the 1999 world of Henri Desmarest's *La Femme future* (*Woman of the Future*, 1890) encounters a dictatorship of women in which they control all business ventures and dress as men, and the powerless men are forced into arranged marriages. In the "Great Transition" of Walter Besant's *The Revolt of Man* (1882) all political and cultural authority is transferred to women – even God has been replaced by an ideal "Perfect Woman" – and men are allowed only to be physical laborers. Scientific and artistic advancement has stopped because "women, who can receive, cannot create," and thus the men rebel to reinstate patriarchy and reboot progress.

Towering hyperdense, hygienic urbanism is a mainstay of cityscapes of the pulp SF era. This is not the case for SF during most of the nineteenth century, when European cities, subject to unregulated growth, unprecedented crowding, poverty, disease, and crime, and massive displacements of the working classes during periodic bursts of urban renewal, provided mostly negative anticipations of future urban life. In William Delisle Hay's *The Doom of the*

Great City, Being the Narrative of a Survivor, Written A.D. 1942 (1880), the sudden suffocation of all of London by clouds of fog and soot is the outward sign of an inner miasma of economic and moral conflict and decay. (Hays's readers would have been reminded of events of the summer of 1858, when unusually hot weather and the Thames, choked with industrial effluent and untreated human waste, had combined to produce The Great Stink.) The degraded conditions of most of Victorian London, and the capital and social costs of Baron Haussmann's renovation of Paris during the Second Empire projected futures that would be more, not less, stratified by class and opportunity. Some future fictions imagine sparsely inhabited agrarian utopias, though it is not always clear how the needed reduction in population to allow this to happen has been achieved. (The above- and below-ground realms of the year 802,701 in Wells's *The Time Machine* represent both suspect visions of the future city.) The prospect of Paris's renovation elicited some positive predictions: Théophile Gautier's "Paris futur" ("Future Paris," 1851) imagines an open, clean, climate-controlled city lit by towering lighthouses, in which citizens live prosperous and contented lives. The story is one of the earliest to predict that Paris would become an open port connected to the Atlantic. But Haussmannization generally inspired negative visions. Fernand Giraudeau's "La Nouvelle Cité" ("The New City," 1868) describes a Paris that is overcrowded, hectic, and in economic and social crisis owing, simultaneously, to unregulated capitalism and despotic trade unionism. Science, art, and the life of the mind are in decline because the populace is distracted by prurient media spectacles. Verne's *Paris au XXe Siècle* (*Paris in the Twentieth Century*, 1863, posthumously published in 1995) mourns the city's overtaking by unchecked capitalism, technology, and the "demon of electricity." More hopeful, Albert Bleunard's *La Babylone électrique* (*Babylon Electrified*, 1888) displaces the story of extreme urban renewal to the site of ancient Babylon, renamed "Liberty" and constructed with electricity and a version of thermonuclear power. Nilo María Fabro's *En el planeta Marte* (*On the Planet Mars*, 1890) shifts the utopian city to Mars, where the post-literate inhabitants receive their news by gramophone and telephone, and travel the canals by electric ship and the cityscapes of slender aluminum palaces via moving sidewalks. Rudimentary contact has been made with Earth, whose primitive technologies and brutal social orders the Martians view with dismay. Paolo Mantegazza's *L'Anno 3000* (*The Year 3,000*, 1897) describes Andropolis, the government seat of Earth's United Planetary States. The city's thoroughly modern citizens have access to unlimited clean energy, eat healthful synthetic foods, live in plastic and steel houses, and share abundant leisure time to enjoy virtual reality entertainments.

Contact

SF's visions of the other during the century were shaped by transformed conditions of imperial, urban, industrial, and economic life. Obdurate race and class barriers remained, however, and are frequent subtexts of contact SF. Chattel slavery, abolished in most European colonies before the middle of the nineteenth century, persisted longer in the Americas and Africa. Other and new forms of bondage were also durable: serfdom in Russia, effective peonage of criminal debtors and industrial workers throughout Europe. Well-trodden stories of meetings with fantastic beings were given new meaning by the expansion of colonial territories and the emergence of new anthropological thinking, often laced with dubious assumptions about race and racial differences. An important influence was the "plurality of worlds" debate, on the question of whether life is unique to Earth or might also occur elsewhere.[14]

An early example of otherworldly contact SF is Willem Bilderdijk's *Kort verhaal van eene aanmerklijke luchtreis, en nieuwe planeetontdekking* (*A Short Account of a Remarkable Aerial Voyage*, 1813), about a balloon trip to a previously unknown satellite of Earth found to harbor life. Until late in the century, such stories of balloon voyages between worlds were not unusual, as the absence of rocket technology proved a conceptual block for authors. (Edmé Rousseau's *Voyage à Venus* [*Voyage to Venus*, 1865] is an exception, perhaps the first serious description of rocket-propelled space travel.) In Charles Guyon's *Voyage dans la planète Venus* (*Voyage to the Planet Venus*, 1888) a dirigible crosses interplanetary space to reach an Earthlike civilization more advanced than ours. During the transit the passengers remain in a comatose state to avoid breathing in the vacuum of space. Verne's *Hector Servadac* (1877), discussed below, pokes fun at these scenarios.

Telepathic communication and astral projection provided alternative methods of travel. In Humphrey Davy's *Consolations in Travel; Or, the Last Days of a Philosopher* (1838), the narrator's psychic connection with an intelligence called "The Genius" reveals humanity's prehistory and the civilizations of Saturn, Jupiter, Mars, and Venus, each of which is inhabited by human

[14] Michael J. Crowe, *The Extraterrestrial Life Debate, 1750–1900* (New York: Dover Publications, 1999).

creatures at different stages of moral and intellectual evolution. (A common conceit of early contact narratives is that life develops in parallel everywhere; inhabitants of other worlds are very nearly like us, only more or less advanced.) Flammarion's *Lumen* (1872) features a series of psychically transferred dialogues on the plurality of worlds debate, with descriptions of alien inhabitants, the then-novel idea that their bodies would be specifically adapted to their physical environments, and one of the earliest discussions in fiction of faster-than-light travel. In Flammarion's *Urania* (1889), the muse of astronomy visits a younger version of the author and takes him on a tour of several solar systems. The novel's publication coincided with the 1889 opposition of Mars that had brought to popular attention Giovanni Schiaparelli's discovery of Martian *canali* ("channels" or "gullies," widely mistranslated as "canals"); the novel describes speculative Martian life and civilization in detail. Jean Chambon's *Cybèle: Voyage extraordinaire dans l'avenir* (*Cybèle: An Extraordinary Voyage into the Future*, 1891) combines space and time travel with the conceit of parallel development, as the narrator travels psychically to a distant double of Earth in its future state.

Kurd Lasswitz's *Auf zwei Planeten* (*Two Planets*, 1897) introduces some hard SF elements: a balloon expedition to the Earth's north pole is captured in the antigravity field of a Martian space station. From there, the adventurers travel by rocket to Mars, which is described as formerly wet and warm but now increasingly cold and dry. The Martians use their superior military technology to help the Germans defeat the British Royal Navy. Wells's *The First Men in the Moon* (1901) used the gravity-negating alloy Cavorite to journey to the Moon and back. (Robert Cromie's *A Plunge into Space*, 1890, had used a similar antigravity gimmick for his Mars voyage.) Wells's novel is also noteworthy as one of the first contact narratives to depict aliens as large insects.

Henri de Parville's *Un Habitant de la planète Mars* (*An Inhabitant of the Planet Mars*, 1865) flipped the direction of the journey with an account of a mummified Martian found inside a meteorite fallen to Earth. Wells's *The War of the Worlds* (1897) also brings the Martians to us, combining the contact scenario with future and race war elements. The Martians are monstrous, nearly invulnerable to human weapons, and in the end defeated thanks to terrestrial microbes. In C. I. Defontenay's alien-civilization-in-a-bottle *Star, ou Psi Cassiopeia* (1854), contact is made indirectly, through a cache of "Starian books" found in a meteorite. Charles Cros's *Études sur les moyens de communication avec les planètes* (*A Study of the Means of Communication with the Planets*, 1869) was the earliest proposal to establish communication between worlds via optical telegraphy and mathematically coded messages. His idea was widely reported and Cros incorporated it into several short stories. A version of his proposed apparatus appears in Pierre de Sélènes's *Un Monde inconnu* (*An Unknown World*, 1896), which also uses a clever intertextual stratagem: the heroes renovate the abandoned giant cannon from Verne's lunar novels in order to reach the Moon.

Contact scenarios, mostly of the entranced-visitor-to-a-utopian-world sort, had been an element of inner- and Hollow-Earth fiction since Ludvig Holberg's *Nicolaii Klimii iter subterraneum* (*The Journey of Niels Klims to the Underground World*, 1741) and Giacomo Casanova's *Icosameron* (1788).[15] Inhabitants of De Sélène's lunar utopia are found to have retreated to the Moon's interior when its once lush surface cooled. Verne's *Journey to the Center of the Earth* includes an encounter with a primeval giant herding mammoths on the shores of the inner sea. Edward Bulwer-Lytton's *The Coming Race* (1871) introduced Vril, the energy source of the Vril-ya, a secret utopian society of the inner Earth, thereby spawning whole literatures of esoteric Hollow Earth and lost race fantasy.

A few narratives depict contact with creatures strangely or terrifyingly different from humans. E. A. Abbott's *Flatland* (1884) and Charles Howard Hinton's *A Plane World* (1884) describe friendly communications with worlds of fewer or more dimensions than our own. On the side of terror, Maupassant's "The Horla" and Wells's *The War of the Worlds* are key works. The most extreme SF visions of this kind are Rosny aîné's "The Xipéhuz" (1887), "Another World" (1895), and "The Cataclysm" (1896), in which the other resides in our reality but is unintelligible, or in a parallel reality that we can barely perceive, or its arrival changes the physics of our reality. "The Xipéhuz" is noteworthy for the titular creatures' total lack of anthropomorphic qualities.

Apocalypse

World-ending scenarios during the century warn of humanity's inability to control its worst instincts, or even survive in a scientific universe in which its priority appears increasingly uncertain. Grainville's prose-poem *The Last Man* is one of the earliest SF apocalypses: a meditation on the catastrophe of the French Revolution, an affirmation of Christian redemption, and a future history stocked with flying machines, life extension, and a prediction of our

[15] Guy Costes and Joseph Altaïrac, *Les Terres creuses: Bibliographie commentée des mondes souterrains imaginaires* (Amiens: Encrage, 2007); Peter Fitting, ed., *Subterranean Worlds: A Critical Anthology* (Middletown, CT: Wesleyan University Press, 2004).

demise from our successes. For the latter downbeat note Grainville draws on Thomas Malthus's forecast of a human population time bomb and resulting overcrowding and famine (*An Essay on the Principle of Population*, 1798, 1803). In Richard Jefferies's *After London* (1885), nature reclaims England after an unspecified ecological crisis; unchecked vegetation overruns abandoned towns and cities and humans lapse into barbarism. Robert Cromie's *The Crack of Doom* (1895) links future apocalypse to abyssal past in the story of a scientist who decides to use his discovery of atomic energy to restore Earth to its etheric origins, before the emergence of life or the formation of matter. Leopoldo Alas's "Cuento futuro" ("Future Story," 1886) features a comparable backward-looking end, in which a scientist cures the stultifying boredom of a future utopia by electrocuting everyone but his spouse and himself. The story shifts to a second Garden of Eden created for the couple by God. The woman again eats a forbidden apple but this time God kicks out only the new Eve, and the man and woman are separated forever. Mary Shelley's *The Last Man* (1826) describes a worldwide plague at the end of the twenty-first century. Plagues are frequent in future war fiction, where diseases spread quickly in devastated cities, but here the infection is terminal for everyone but the lone immune survivor.

The century's earliest planetary collision story is probably Antoine Rey-Dussueil's *La Fin du monde, histoire du temps présent et des choses à venir* (*The End of the World, Story of the Present and The Things to Come*, 1831), in which Biela's Comet lays waste to the planet, leaving one man and three women as survivors. (The comet famously did intersect with the Earth's orbit in 1832, though a month ahead of the Earth.) Verne incorporated glancing blows and lesser collisions in two novels, *Hector Servadac* (1877) and *La Chasse au météore* (*The Meteor Chase*, 1901, published in 1908). In the former, French, English, and Russian military personnel stationed near Gibraltar are carried off on the comet Gallia for a two-year tour of the solar system before the comet again passes near the Earth and they manage to make the hop between worlds by balloon. *The Meteor Chase* is a comic satire of financial greed: the meteor is made of gold and the protagonists race to its landing site to secure the fallen riches for themselves. In Félicien Champsaur's "Le Dernier Homme" ("The Last Man," 1886), the oxygen-rich tail of a passing comet overstimulates Earth's inhabitants: every human except one man dies in paroxysms of passion; Paris becomes a primeval rainforest; the survivor reverts to an ape-like mental and physical state. The episode is revealed to be a dream. In M. P. Shiel's *The Purple Cloud* (1901), a polar explorer is the apparent lone survivor of Earth's passage through a cloud that kills all animal life.

Anticipating staple scenes of later "cozy catastrophes"[16] he wanders in a state of madness, availing himself of now-abundant consumer goods and senselessly destroying entire cities for the pleasures of oblivion. He later meets a woman who also survived the cloud because she was kept prisoner in a cellar; they determine to restart human civilization.

Other novels take a longer view of cometary collision. In George Griffith's *Olga Romanoff* (1894), Martian astronomers warn the Earth of an impending collision in the twenty-first century. The humans interrupt their prolonged warring to build a shelter deep in the Earth in which to wait out the calamity. Flammarion's *Omega* (1894) treats a pending collision in the twenty-fifth century as the opportunity to refocus human activity on its physical and spiritual improvement. Wells's "The Star" (1897) describes the global destruction produced by an errant star's near-miss of Earth. As the few survivors settle at the now temperate poles, Martian astronomers conclude from a distance that the only significant effects of the crisis are a slight melting of the Earth's icecaps.

Some ends are more whimper than bang. In the 1860s and 1870s, physicist Sir William Thomson, Lord Kelvin, published a series of articles estimating the age of the Sun at between 100 and 500 million years, and predicting that it will be extinguished within a few million years. His conclusions were based on faulty assumptions but the specter of a failing Sun provided the basis for a number of end-time scenarios. The most important of these is the penultimate chapter of Wells's *The Time Machine*, in which the Traveller journeys thirty million years into the future, to the silent shore of a frigid sea below a dim red sun. The only sign of life is a repulsive, football-shaped creature hopping fitfully in the surf. Solar decline comes earlier in Gabriel de Tarde's *Fragment d'Histoire Future* (*Fragment of a Future History*, 1896.) In the year 2489, a global utopia is threatened by a sudden drop of temperature. European survivors flee the advancing ice to North Africa, where they construct a giant concrete bunker and later tunnel into the Earth to make use of its inner heat. The "Martians" of Vladislav Uminsky's *In the World of the Future: From the Lives of the Martians* (1896) are the future descendants of the first terrestrial explorers of Mars. They huddle in their colony's ruins, awaiting effects of the heat death that has already extinguished life on Earth. Uminsky's novel anticipates, in a fatalist mood, the turnabout that Ray Bradbury signals in "The Million Year Picnic" (*The Martian Chronicles*, 1950): humans who have left their homeworld behind will in time become the other.

---

[16] Aldiss and Wingrove, *Trillion Year Spree: The History of Science Fiction*, pp. 293–4.

Closer at hand, other scenarios of world's end, products of the national hubris, reckless ambition, and technologies of slaughter that had made future war fiction seem plausible, would soon be acted out on the Western and Eastern Fronts. Wilfred Owen's comparison of No Man's Land to the lunar surface – "gray, cratered like the moon with hollow woe, / and pitted with great pocks and scabs of plagues" – is more aware of the cruel analogy and disproportion of the imaginary and the real than any description of that surface in Verne or Wells.[17] During the First World War the brutal fantasies of a Chesney, a Shiel, a Danrit, or a Lermina, and the less toxic but still xenophobic projections of a Lasswitz or a Wells, were realized without recourse to invaders from the Far East or another world. There was more than enough depravity and racial animus in "civilized" Europe to transport millions to landscapes more truly desolate than any predicted by the previous century's fictions.

[17] "The Show" (1917), *The Collected Poems of Wilfred Owen* (New York: New Directions, 1965), pp. 50–1.

4

Inventing New Worlds: The Age of Manifestos and Utopias

RHYS WILLIAMS

It is not what man has been, but what he will be, that should interest us.
H. G. Wells

Introduction

From *Frankenstein* (1818) to *The Time Machine* (1895), candidates for the ur-text of SF top and tail the nineteenth century, and mark the era within which SF emerged as a discernible genre. Central to the development of the genre, especially during the Victorian period, is the concept of utopia. It is nearly impossible to distinguish the utopian impulse from the science fictional during its early years, and almost as hard to prise apart literature from manifesto. As one commentator noted in 1891: "The prophetic romance is indeed becoming a feature of the literature of to-day, but we must note that as a rule it is also propagandist romance."[1] The aim was not only speculation, but also intervention. So what was it about the nineteenth century that necessitated the emergence of the science-fictional imagination, and why was it entwined with utopianism?

Roger Luckhurst has outlined four preconditions essential to the emergence of SF.[2] Along with the extension of literacy and primary education to the majority of the population (Britain and the United States), and the arrival of cheap new magazines that, as a publication format, demanded formal innovation, Luckhurst notes two further shifts. First, the "arrival of scientific and technological institutions" that train a generation of scientific workers, engineers and teachers from the lower-middle class. These new educational institutions present a challenge to the traditional sources of cultural

---

[1] Matthew Beaumont, *Utopia Ltd: Ideologies of Social Dreaming in England, 1870–1900* (Boston: Brill, 2005), p. 5.
[2] Roger Luckhurst, *Science Fiction* (Malden, MA: Polity, 2005), p. 16.

authority – a tradition with elitist roots in classical education, of which Matthew Arnold may be taken as the contemporary image and defender. Second, Luckhurst cites the visible transformation of the lived world by technological and scientific innovation, which "begin to saturate the everyday life experience of nearly all with Mechanism." Marshall Berman paints a picture of that vigorous tumult:

> the highly developed, differentiated and dynamic new landscape ... a landscape of steam engines, automatic factories, vast new industrial zones; of teeming cities that have grown overnight, often with dreadful human consequences ... an ever-expanding world market embracing all, capable of the most spectacular growth, capable of appalling waste and devastation, capable of everything except solidity and stability.[3]

The fact that this description would work as the prologue to an SF story speaks volumes about the deep conceptual relationship between the Industrial Revolution and SF as a genre. But not only was the mega-novum of the Industrial Revolution driving a fundamental rearrangement of lived experience and social life, but another, prior revolution had already shattered the sanctity of traditional political order:

> With the French Revolution and its reverberations, a great modern public abruptly and dramatically comes to life. This public shares the feeling of living in a revolutionary age, an age that generates explosive Upheavals in every dimension of personal, social and political life.[4]

These twin revolutions, products of the bourgeoisie and the creative destruction of capitalism, engendered the experience of fundamental instability that Marx and Engels captured with their famous phrase "all that is solid melts into air."[5]

Finally, intersecting with the technological and the political vectors of change came a third just as formidable: the biological, that of the human being itself. This is to be understood in two overlapping senses. Firstly, the idea that humankind was possessed of a basic and fixed character was to become a site of contention. The key question was whether human nature could be molded (and thus improved) through changes to the social order, or whether it was fixed, with the less palatable elements requiring repression via the strictures of civilized society. Secondly, the publication of Charles

---

[3] Marshall Berman, *All That Is Solid Melts Into Air: The Experience of Modernity* (London: Verso, 2010), p. 19.
[4] Ibid., p. 17.
[5] Karl Marx and Friedrich Engels, *Communist Manifesto*, 1848, www.marxists.org/archive/marx/works/1848/communist-manifesto/cho1.htm (last accessed April 2018).

Darwin's *On the Origin of Species* (1859) throws the fixity of the physical human body into flux, transforming the very substrate of humanity as it stood into a mere milestone on a long and inscrutable evolutionary trajectory.

The technological, the political, and the biological: each of these in their own way had been sources of stability – for both society and the individual – and each, in the course of the nineteenth century, is irrevocably historicized. As the present became visibly different from the remembered past, the future opened up as a space of difference and possibility: from new gadgets to new governance, from the promise of a better humanity to the threat of a species unrecognizable. It is to this new space of speculation, structured by the myriad intersections of these three primary vectors, that literature and culture turns in the nineteenth century – not only to guess at the future, but also to try to make sense of a present unmoored and in crisis, and to exert influence on the direction of change where it could.

Naming the Novel of the Future

Mostly ignored upon its release, but now firmly established as a vital part of the canon of SF pre-history, *The Novel of the Future* (*Le Roman de l'avenir*) by Félix Bodin made its appearance in France in 1834. It owes its importance less to the half-hearted novel indicated by the title and more to the preface, which is both a description and a prescription for a new kind of literature: for Bodin, novels about the future are the future of the novel.

The preface identifies two popular attitudes towards the future at work in the literature of the time: "ameliorist" (optimist) and "pejorativist" (pessimist).[6] For Bodin these attitudes had led to a preponderance of literature in either the utopian or the apocalyptic mode. Uninterested in these extremes, Bodin wanted to "get to grips with the living creation of an ordinary world to come"; he advocated for the *novel* of the future, speculative but steeped in the realism of the novel form.[7] Bodin wanted literature that contained within itself both the promise and the threat of modernity, in which the political, technological, and biological foundations of the age were thrown wide open to the possibility of change.

Bodin expected the novel of the future to capture the poetry and marvel of the modern age, and move beyond the drag of classical standards and forms. Rather than be concerned with prediction or speculation as such, the future

---

[6] Félix Bodin, *The Novel of the Future*, trans. Brian Stableford (Encino, CA: Black Coat Press, 2008), n.p.
[7] Ibid., n.p.

novel should "recapture, in appropriate images acceptable to the modern world, imaginative equivalents of older sources of poetic emotion that can no longer serve as material for the novelist's art."[8] This anticipates Baudelaire's famous demand to move beyond the stagnant ideals of classical art and capture the poetry of modernity in the transient markers of the contemporary. As Bodin states: "If ever anyone succeeds in creating the novel, the epic of the future, he will have tapped a vast source of the marvellous, and of a marvellous entirely in accord with verisimilitude."[9] Here, realism and the modern marvelous are seen as inextricable, a precursor to Darko Suvin's efforts to distinguish SF from other fantastical genres by its realism.[10]

Yet the relationship between SF and realism has never been straightforward. Literary realism distinguishes itself by adherence to the details of the present – by creating a verisimilitude that appears to reflect the present. The realism of SF is of another order, and has to do with acknowledging deeper truths of historical movement and instability over replicating a tableau of the present. The same questions would animate H. G. Wells at the turn of the century, framed by this time as a debate between realism and romanticism. Disdaining romanticism as having little or no connection with reality, Wells also railed against a realism that presented its reality as immutable. For Wells, "strict realism is too much restriction, just as romance is excess of freedom," and when he wrote realism, "he never accepted the material conditions of reality depicted therein as permanent."[11] As he stated:

> The Novel in English was produced in an atmosphere of security for the entertainment of secure people who liked to feel established and safe for good. Its standards were established within that apparently permanent frame and the criticism of it began to be irritated and perplexed when, through a new instability, the splintering frame began to get into the picture. I suppose for a time I was the outstanding instance among writers of fiction in English of the frame getting into the picture.[12]

The three revolutions – the political, technological, and biological – provide the "new instability" that Wells mentions, and open up the possibility of SF

[8] Paul K. Alkon, *Origins of Futuristic Fiction* (Athens, GA: University of Georgia Press, 1987), p. 253.

[9] Ibid., p. 245.

[10] See Christine Brooke-Rose, *A Rhetoric of the Unreal* (Cambridge: Cambridge University Press, 1981).

[11] Simon J. James, *Maps of Utopia: H. G. Wells, Modernity and the End of Culture* (Oxford: Oxford University Press, 2012), p. 12.

[12] H. G. Wells, *Experiment in Autobiography* (1934), https://gutenberg.ca/ebooks/wellshg-autobiography/wellshg-autobiography-00-h-dir/wellshg-autobiography-00-h.html (last accessed May 30, 2018).

which, from its inception, aims at a more profound realism by placing the present within a timeframe that acknowledges its own transience. This "realism" cannot be achieved directly – one must go some distance in order to turn around and see things properly – and in Bodin's preface we find the tension that haunts and structures SF to the present day. In Darko Suvin's infamous "cognitive estrangement" are the later echoes of Bodin's framing of the future novel as a "hoax," but a serious one.[13] Bodin sees these tales as tall, but also as having purpose: "a means of gripping and stirring imaginations and hastening the progress of humanity ... more powerful than the finest displays of theoretical systems," establishing the didactic purpose that continues to re-emerge in critical claims for the importance of SF.

The times call forth SF as a necessary mode. This new present brings with it a newly widespread type; SF emerges through the demand for a mode of expression suited to the new rise of the scientific mind-set on the one hand, and the new importance of the future on the other. In his lecture *The Discovery of the Future* (1902), Wells posited a fundamental distinction between two types of mind – one that reads the present through the past, and one that reads the present through the future.[14] For Wells, the latter was the more powerful and appropriate mind, that of a leader rather than a follower, since "modernity" for Wells was when the future outweighed the past in determining action and morals in the present. This split between dispositions cuts along the same dividing line as a broader social split between Culture and Mechanism, the latter a growing and not always welcome influence on the former. The privileged place of SF, then and now, is to be the meeting ground for these often-antagonistic points of view.

Enter Mechanism

As the Industrial Revolution brought increasingly dramatic and widespread changes to the lived environment and the way of life of most in the United Kingdom and the United States, the question over the future direction of technological progress became central. Humanity's power, both destructive and productive, was massively increased by the new inventions, but these also fed back into the organization of social life. In "Signs of the Times" (1829) Thomas Carlyle wrote about the onset of "The Mechanical Age," starting an

[13] See Darko Suvin, *Metamorphoses of Science Fiction* (New Haven: Yale University Press, 1979).

[14] See H. G. Wells, *The Discovery of the Future*, https://archive.org/stream/discoveryoffu turoowelliala/discoveryoffuturoowelliala_djvu.txt (last accessed May 30, 2018).

influential discourse about how Mechanism suffused not only "the external and physical" but the internal and spiritual also.[15] According to Carlyle, Mechanism changed the whole manner of existence: everything from the forms of industrial production to the interior self. The specialization of labor became more pronounced, and the submission of the individual to the machine – memorably captured by Charlie Chaplin in his classic *Modern Times* (1936) – led to both celebration and denunciation of the new "rational" organization of labor and life.

Most utopian visions of the period fell on one or the other side of the fence. Marx noted how "Machinery, gifted with the wonderful power of shortening and fructifying human labour, we behold starving and overworking it . . . All our invention and progress seem to result in endowing material forces with intellectual life, and stultifying human life into a material force."[16] Yet many, including Marx, felt that technology would provide liberation from toil, even if it had not yet lived up to that promise. That most famous of nineteenth-century utopias, Edward Bellamy's *Looking Backward* (1888), is paradigmatic in this regard. Bellamy's future city of Boston is highly rational, organized, and stuffed with machines. For Bellamy, labor would never become a thing of pleasure, but instead must be reduced and made as bearable as possible through labor-saving machinery and early retirement. While everyone has to work in Bellamy's Industrial Army, the necessity is kept to a minimum, which must have seemed heavenly from the contemporary perspective.

Horrified by what he saw as a future "organized with a vengeance," William Morris sketched the opposite vision in his reply to Bellamy – *News From Nowhere*.[17] For Morris, work was unbearable only because of the alienation from the products of labor that capitalism enforced, and the needless production of goods for false or induced desires. The machinery and the rational, specialized organization of the workforce that came with the modern era were a disaster. They led to the making of partial, fragmented people, who worked to make things they didn't need, and in whom no love of their work was possible. Following John Ruskin, Morris admired the Gothic style, and understood it to be representative of, and to have emerged from, a more holistic and organic social whole than the fragmented and

---

[15] See Thomas Carlyle, "Signs of the Times" (1829), www.victorianweb.org/authors/carlyle/signs1.html (last accessed May 30, 2018).

[16] Karl Marx, "Speech at Anniversary of *The People's Paper*," www.marxists.org/archive/marx/works/1856/04/14.htm (last accessed May 30, 2018).

[17] William Morris, "Review of Bellamy's *Looking Backward*," www.marxists.org/archive/morris/works/1889/backward.htm (last accessed May 30, 2018).

divided present. Under changed conditions, art would become simply "the expression of man's pleasure in labour," and people would take great pleasure in their work-as-art.[18] The utopia pictured by Morris is thus a pastoral one, where urban centers have dissolved, life has returned to a more rustic organization, and there is no machinery beyond what is considered genuinely useful. These latter are labor-saving devices for the meanest jobs, workshop machines for large-scale work, and transportation such as barges for the river. In a bit of a cheat, these are all run on a mysterious new form of energy, about which we get no details. Even these devices are not so common, however, and we follow the narrator journeying to the countryside to help bring in a harvest by hand, rather than use a harvester. Most work, in moderation, is pleasurable for Morris, in a way reminiscent of Marx's Communist Man who hunts in the morning, fishes in the afternoon and critiques in the evening.

Together these two visions covered the "technical premises and sensual horizons" of socialist utopian possibility; "each lacks what the other has."[19] While Morris's view of a sustainable small-scale future may well be gaining the upper hand in a twenty-first-century imaginary plagued by climate change, Bellamy's urban techno-utopia was certainly the more commonly adopted initially. If we look ahead to Wells, we find a faith in "a steady increase in this proportion of mechanical energy, in this emancipation of men from the necessity of physical labour. There appears no limit to the invasion of life by the machine."[20] Wells had no time for Morris's argument, claiming it required the "Olympian unworldliness of an irresponsible rich man ... playing at life" to imagine "that all toil may be made a joy."[21] Wells certainly dabbled in dystopian visions of Mechanism – in *The Time Machine*, for example, or *The Sleeper Awakes* (1899), in which a serious case of technological gigantism has captured the masses – but his later utopian visions embrace it. He understood himself to be the latest in a line of techno-utopians, stating that "Cabet, who first in a Utopian work insisted upon the escape of man from irksome labors through the use of machinery ... is the great primitive of modern Utopias, and Bellamy is his American equivalent."[22] Wells was, if not the first, then one of the best to practice the art of speculation based upon technological advance. His work *Anticipations* (1905) is a masterclass. It begins

---

[18] William Morris, "Preface to *The Nature of Gothic* by John Ruskin," www.marxists.org /archive/morris/works/1892/ruskin.htm (last accessed May 30, 2018).
[19] Suvin, *Metamorphoses of Science Fiction*, p. 185.
[20] H. G. Wells, *A Modern Utopia* (London: Penguin, 2006), p. 71.
[21] Ibid., p. 72.
[22] Ibid., p. 72.

with modes of transport as the most fundamental drivers of change, and moving from there it builds layer by layer, from urban organization to work styles to ideologies, a picture of the future a century hence. *Anticipations* provides a glimpse of just how Wells composed his "sociological novels" and is, in the earlier chapters at least, uncannily accurate, predicting motorways and urban sprawl to a tee.

The most radical thought on technological change that is a precursor to later SF hides in a lone chapter of Samuel Butler's satirical utopian masterpiece *Erewhon* (1872). Before writing his utopia, Butler contributed a series of essays to *The Press*, a New Zealand journal, to which country Butler had moved in order to try to make money by raising sheep. In these essays and the novel, Butler takes the idea of the evolution of machines far beyond his contemporaries. The first, "Darwin Among the Machines" (1863) announces his theme of the machine as an advanced evolutionary species, with human selection (as opposed to natural selection) guiding their development. Butler predicts, accurately enough, that the development of machines will follow certain trends; the large will become smaller, and they will develop self-regulating and self-acting powers akin to intellect. In time the machines will hold power over humanity and "we shall find ourselves the inferior race." The article ends with a clarion call to arms: against machines "war to the death must be instantly proclaimed."[23]

He softens his tone in the second article, "Lucubratio Ebria" (1865), now seeing machines as extensions and additions to the human. His argument here is remarkable for prefiguring the idea of cyberculture in its insistence that changes to the body, such as mechanical prostheses, entail changes to the mind and character, and humanity itself will come to adapt and change through such feedback to suit the mechanical environment it constructs for itself. Humans become a "vertebrate machinate mammal," changing in a dialectic with the technology it produces.[24] Here Butler grasps the true consequences of the theory of evolution in combination with technological innovation in a way that outstrips the imagination of his contemporaries, and even much SF produced to this day.

In the third article, "The Mechanical Creation" (1865), he produces a combination of his previous positions, suggesting "an eventual development of mechanical life, far superior to, and widely differing from, any yet known" and foreseeing the development of the "steam engine of today into

---

[23] Samuel Butler, "Darwin among the Machines" (1863), http://nzetc.victoria.ac.nz/tm/scholarly/tei-ButFir-t1-g1-t1-g1-t4-body.html (last accessed May 30, 2018).

[24] Samuel Butler, "Lucubratio Ebria" (1865), http://nzetc.victoria.ac.nz/tm/scholarly/tei-ButFir-t1-g1-t1-g1-t5.html (last accessed May 30, 2018).

the mechanical prodigies which are to come as the spade to the steam engine, as the ovum to the human being."[25] Humans cannot help but hasten their own supersession by technology for Butler as "man is committed hopelessly to the machines."[26] Finally, all this is brought together in *Erewhon*, where a counter-argument is provided that machines, however developed, are only servants. Butler answers this chillingly:

> But the servant glides by imperceptible approaches into the master; and we have come to such a pass that, even now, man must suffer terribly on ceasing to benefit the machines. If all machines were to be annihilated at one moment, so that not a knife nor lever nor rag of clothing nor anything whatsoever were left to man but his bare body alone that he was born with, and if all knowledge of mechanical laws were taken from him so that he could make no more machines, and all machine-made food destroyed so that the race of man should be left as it were naked upon a desert island, we should become extinct in six weeks. A few miserable individuals might linger, but even these in a year or two would become worse than monkeys. Man's very soul is due to the machines; it is a machine-made thing: he thinks as he thinks, and feels as he feels, through the work that machines have wrought upon him, and their existence is quite as much a *sine qua non* for his, as his for theirs.[27]

The entwining of humanity and their machines – not a one-way relationship of domination, but a tangled web in which the changers are in turn changed – is here captured with lucid and prescient clarity. From this position spring all the utopian and dystopian possibilities of contemporary SF that face the challenge of conceiving this dialectic; from the diminished individual chained to the conveyor belt, to the almost-magic of one who wields advanced technology, Butler captures an early sense of what Heidegger would come to call "enframing." The way in which Mechanism changed humanity was a flash point for debate over the direction of culture and society, and over just what kind of human it was desirable to produce.

Mechanism, Culture, and the New Man

So Mechanism clashed with the gate-keepers of Culture, and accrued

a whole range of metaphorical associations that constructed it as one of the opposites of civility and culture: Mechanism was industrial, harsh, inflexible,

---

[25] See Bruce Mazlish, "Butler's Brainstorm," in Darren Tofts, ed., *Prefiguring Cyberculture: An Intellectual History* (Cambridge, MA: MIT Press, 2002), pp. 228–39; pp. 231–3.
[26] Ibid., p. 236.
[27] Samuel Butler, *Erewhon* (1872), www.marxists.org/reference/archive/butler-samuel/1 872/erewhon/ch24.htm (last accessed May 30, 2018).

undifferentiated, exterior, superficial, vulgar, lowly, wrecking of spirit. In Britain, the "mechanical arts" carried the resonance of the artisan, low on the social scale and even lower in the symbolic capital by which cultural value was discriminated.[28]

The rising star of Science and the established star of Culture (the bastion of the upper-classes, educated in the Classics and the Arts) tussled for authority. In his Belfast Address in 1874, physicist John Tyndall famously argued for the superior authority of science over religious explanation. T. H. Huxley wrestled with Mathew Arnold, the former claiming science as necessary to the proper cultivation and perfection of spirit, the latter that art and poetry must always supersede the close technical knowledge of science. A newly expanded literate public occasioned a debate as to what the "masses" should be reading, with the rising novel form seen in the main as "lowly" and unworthy in comparison with the classics and the works of sages such as Arnold and Ruskin. For Arnold, fiction simply wasn't literature. H. G. Wells straddled the cultures in terms of class, in terms of what was popular and what was refined, and in terms of the science and art debate. He was firmly on the side of science as the modern mode of knowledge, but in his work he aimed for a balance of scientific insight and beauty – a balance that remains the zenith for the best of SF.

Wells wrote particularly for a new category of individuals who were direct products of the age of Mechanism. In his *Anticipations* he gave voice to the expectation that the rapid proliferation and increased innovation in technology would give rise to a new class of rational, scientifically minded men, trained in rational and empirical thought, and indeed much of the new literacy came from the founding of numerous workers' universities and technical colleges, which trained the mechanics and engineers that were to populate Wells's utopian future. He saw himself in them: "my own culture and turn of mind . . . is probably akin to that of a respectable mechanic of the year 2000."[29] This self-projection was not limited to Wells. The late Victorian utopia generally "invests in its reader the hope that, collectively, they will form the nucleus of the ideal society that it has outlined."[30] Morris is perhaps the significant exception here; Suvin notes that he rejects Victorian mores and "explores the meaning and price of brotherhood in terms of an intimate neighborliness," not to mention that his utopia requires a violent

---

[28] Luckhurst, *Science Fiction*, p. 4.
[29] H. G. Wells, *Anticipations* (1902), www.gutenberg.org/files/19229/19229-h/19229-h.htm (last accessed May 30, 2018).
[30] Beaumont, *Utopia Ltd*, p. 9.

revolution, the likelihood of which was neutered by other, more ameliorating visions such as Bellamy's.[31]

In his New Men Wells placed great faith – too much faith. He saw their rational approach to life as eradicating out of necessity the irrational problems that beset humanity. The impression we get of them as people, and their romantic pairings especially, is as grey as can be, though he imputes great poetry to their being and doing, of the *Übermensch* type.[32] Wells claims that from their empirical observations, these new men will possess a moral certainty of the matter and the purpose of the world, and from here a partial understanding of the purpose of God. These men will then be free to do as they wish, secure in the knowledge that they are bound to act in accordance with the world and God's own desired directions, their actions both affirming and creating reality as the foundation and arbiter of right. In one of his earliest utopias, *In the Days of the Comet* (1906), Wells depicts the effects of this newfound rationality as an atmospheric one, caused by an alien gas introduced by the titular comet. Everything is new, fresh, clean, and crisp – from grass and birdsong to morals and human organization: clarity is the keyword. This vision of a rational future society freed from the murk of past errors had a lot of currency during the nineteenth century, reaching apotheosis in the grandeur of the Crystal Palace and its legacy.

A Rational Future

While the future was a space of speculation throughout the nineteenth century, the early to mid-Victorian narrative of history was overwhelmingly one of ceaseless progress and development. If we can take the attitude of one of the century's great rationalizers, John Stuart Mill, as paradigmatic, the early Victorians looked forward to a future "so firmly grounded in reason and the true exigencies of life, that they shall not, like all former and present creeds, religious, ethical, and political, require to be periodically thrown off and replaced by others."[33] The future was to be one where Enlightenment values reigned supreme, where social life was organized on a truly rational basis which accorded the greatest happiness to the greatest number, and where Britain in particular could look forward to ever-growing prosperity. This promise reached its material apotheosis in the mid-century Great

---

[31] Suvin, *Metamorphoses of Science Fiction*, p. 191.

[32] www.gutenberg.org/files/19229/19229-h/19229-h.htm (last accessed May 30, 2018).

[33] John Stuart Mill, *Autobiography* (1873), www.utilitarianism.com/millauto/five.html (last accessed May 30, 2018).

Exhibition (1851), housed in that superlatively modern building, the Crystal Palace. Following on from the so-called "Hungry Forties," and marking the beginning of an era of liberal triumph that emerged from the defeated revolutions of 1848, the Great Exhibition promised that "after a decade of deprivation, now there would be plenitude, and not merely plenitude but organized plenitude, structured abundance."[34] The Exhibition represented that most science-fictional of Enlightenment hopes, the "triumph of techne over matter" – not only in the abundant commodified fruits extracted from nature through new production techniques, but also in the better adminis-tration and civilizing of people.[35]

While the New York World's Fair of 1939 is well known to be a moment of great science fictional importance, in fact, it was "one of the end-points of an eighty-year-old tradition in world's fairs that figured globalized capital and transnational encounters in consistently sfnal modes."[36] The Great Exhibition presented a utopian vision of a world united by free-trade, and pointed to a glorious future via its spatial organization into timelines of civilizing progress, from primitive East to advanced technological West. This arrow of humanity pointed to the undiscovered future, ripe for science-fictional imagining, and pre-loaded with a sense of proper direction. The dream of Prince Albert, whose initial agitation brought the Great Exhibition into being, demonstrates the vision behind it:

> We are living at a period of most wonderful transition which tends rapidly to the accomplishment of that great end to which, indeed, all history points – the realisation of the unity of mankind. Not a unity which breaks down the limits, and levels the peculiar characteristics of the different nations of the earth, but rather a unity the result and product of those very national varieties and antagonistic qualities ... The great principle of division of labour, which may be called the moving power of civilisation, is being extended to all branches of science, industry and art. Whilst formerly the greatest mental energies strove at universal knowledge, and that knowledge was confined to the few, now they are directed to specialities, and in these again even to the minutest points; but the knowledge acquired becomes at once the property of the community at large.[37]

---

[34] Karen Chase and Michael Levenson, "Mathew, the Prince, and the Poor: The Great Exhibition of Power and Dispossession," in James Buzard, Joseph W. Childers, and Eileen Gillooly, eds., *Victorian Prism: Refractions of the Crystal Palace* (Charlottesville: University of Virginia Press, 2007), pp. 123–37; p. 124.

[35] Ibid., p.125.

[36] Roger Luckhurst, "Laboratories for Global Space-Time: Science-Fictionality and the World's Fairs, 1851–1939," *Science Fiction Studies* 39 (2012), pp. 385–400; p. 387.

[37] Chase and Levenson, "Mathew, the Prince," p. 127.

Greater unity and productivity through greater rationalized division, specialization, and organization: a vision of the future as a "perfectly articulated apparatus, differentiated into gracefully moving parts."[38] The dream appeared inclusive – not only were the backward countries of the globe to be brought into the embrace of the future, but also those unfortunates – whom Jack London and H. G. Wells later called "The People of the Abyss" – nestled in the very heart of Britain's cities, and so vividly described in a number of publications during the century, perhaps most famously Henry Mayhew's *London Labour and the London Poor* (1851).

The Great Exhibition also marked the beginning of an era of liberal triumph that emerged from the defeated revolutions of 1848. This lasted some twenty years, and in the early 1870s began to wane. The malaise that set in was social as well as economic, as the newly emergent powers of American and German industry threatened the position of Britain as world-leader, and caused a crisis of confidence in British capital. There followed a sustained economic crisis, with a sequence of recessions from the 1870s onwards. Socialist movements proliferated across Europe, fomenting unrest among the working classes and multiplying utopian visions of post-capitalism. After the Parisian Communards' experiment with proletarian democracy in 1871, there were riots and protests in Britain and the United States, including the New Unionism of the 1880s in the former and the flashpoint of the infamous 1886 Haymarket affair in the latter. Yet the revolution never came, making this period a good fit with Fredric Jameson's description of social conditions ripe for utopianism:

> [A period of] great social ferment but seemingly rudderless, without any agency or direction: reality seems malleable, but not the system; and it is that very distance of the unchangeable system from the turbulent restlessness of the real world that seems to open up a moment of ideational and utopian-creative free play in the mind itself or in the political imagination.[39]

The vastly popular utopianism of these latter decades – the great socialist visions of Bellamy and Morris not least among them – were a mark of the achievements of socialism, but also a mark of its failure to take advantage of the real-life political opportunities held out by the recession and general unrest. Rather than exacerbate the unrest, the utopias of the *fin de siècle* can be understood as mitigating it. As Matthew Beaumont puts it:

> Socialism appealed to intellectuals of the middle class to the extent that it opened up the possibility of ameliorating the capitalist system; but it tended

---

[38] Ibid., p. 128.
[39] Fredric Jameson, "The Politics of Utopia," *New Left Review* 2, 25, pp. 35–54, p. 45.

to appall them to the extent that it threatened to overthrow it altogether . . . In the dehiscent climate of the time, the future itself functioned as a new semantic figure in which their tension was articulated.[40]

Bellamy's vision of a bloodless revolution, where "the Marxist threat of the slaughter of the bourgeoisie was dispelled, the class war would not materialise, and the dictatorship of the proletariat would never be installed" was clearly appealing to the comfortable strata of society, particularly in such volatile times.[41] Morris forms a rare and honorable exception, with his insistence on the need for revolution.

The impact of the Crystal Palace as a symbol of a rationally organized future cannot be overestimated; organizing humanity's crooked timber into straight lines was a dream that echoed through the age. In his influential utopian SF text *What Is to Be Done?* (1863), the radical critic and editor Nikolai Chernyshevsky conceived of a future world littered with Crystal Palaces, each building a self-contained city, with all mod-cons, from workshops to ballrooms, and each surrounded by lush countryside, gardens, woods, and lakes. Thousands of people live in each megastructure, and they are imagined to be completely satisfied; benefiting from the latest innovations in agriculture and industry (such innovations as the Great Exhibition took pride in), they lead full lives under the guidance of a benign and rational governing body. Later, Bellamy's *Looking Backward* would present a technologically suffused world of "overriding rationalism," in which social relations were reduced "to a well-ordered mechanism": a utopia, according to Raymond Williams, without desire.[42] Beginning with his *A Modern Utopia* (1905), H. G. Wells would produce vision after vision of, in the acerbic words of the Manuels, "a dynamic technological society of joy and endless movement run by an ascetic elite of Samurai . . . a banality subsequently repeated for decades in scores of his novels and essays."[43] These crystal utopias of Taylorism turned ugly in the twentieth century, from Yevgeny Zamyatin's *We* (1924) to Aldous Huxley's *Brave New World* (1932), but opposition to them long predates these dystopias. Contemporaries of the Great Exhibition took aim, perhaps most famously Dostoyevsky in *Notes from the Underground* (1864), who despised Chernyshevsky's vision of a perfect techno-pastoral order, and feared it as "the Crystal Palace, eternally indestructible . . .

[40] Beaumont, *Utopia Ltd*, p. 4.
[41] Frank E. Manuel and Fritzie P. Manuel, *Utopian Thought in the Western World* (Cambridge, MA: Harvard University Press, 1979), p. 761.
[42] Raymond Williams, *Tenses of Imagination* (London: Peter Lang, 2010), p. 101.
[43] Manuel and Manuel, *Utopian Thought*, p. 776.

something at which you cannot secretly stick out your tongue, or make gestures of defiance."[44] The rationally organized future, where desire and satisfaction were to be nothing more than 2+2=4, was not to everyone's taste.

Radical Futures

The nineteenth century was a time of burgeoning rational futures, rationally organized, and full, it must be said, of men. Women in the literature are love interests at best, a peccadillo for a utopian traveler, a reason to maintain interest, a cause for husbandly duty, or a nod to the "romance" of scientific romances. But gender roles and the traditional family were feeling the centrifugal tug of revolution as much as anything else, and women were writing SF that was in many ways too radical for the men to contemplate. Mary Wollstonecraft's manifesto of the movement for women's liberation, *A Vindication of the Rights of Women* (1792) heralded the publication of future visions that incorporated the new possibilities of the political, technological, and biological revolutions to raise questions about domesticity, domestic labor, motherhood, and the social position of women in general.

The best-known example is also the latest: Charlotte Perkins Gilman's *Herland* (1915). Considered the "prototype for later feminist utopias," *Herland* presents an all-female society that has existed for 2000 years in isolation, reproducing through parthenogenesis.[45] The story follows a fairly typical structure, where three men stumble upon the utopia and are introduced to it. The women are excited at the prospect of male company again, and make relationships with them. Each man holds different attitudes towards the women, with one – a chauvinist type – expelled from the land at the end for attempting to rape his wife. The all-female social order is an ideal one, free of supposedly masculine traits such as conflict and domination. While the influence of *Herland* is tremendous on later science-fictional utopias, from Joanna Russ's *Female Man* to Marge Piercy's *Woman on the Edge of Time*, it grew and took ideas from a tradition of feminist utopias that preceded it.

Parthenogenesis is also how the women of Mary Bradley Lane's *Mizora: A Prophecy* (serialized 1880–1) reproduce. A Hollow-Earth tale, *Mizora* holds up science and technology as a great liberator; all housework is automated,

---

[44] Fyodor Dostoevsky, *Notes from the Underground*, trans. Jane Kantish (Oxford: Oxford World's Classics, 1991), p. 35.

[45] Frances Bartkowski, *Feminist Utopias* (Lincoln, NE: University of Nebraska Press, 1989), p. 16.

and there are televisions, airships, and picture-phones. The female race is constantly being improved through education and genetic manipulation, demonstrating an embrace of the Darwinian principles, yet at the same time Lane presents human history as an argument for the elimination of men, taking a rather troublingly essentialist view of male and female characteristics in the process.

A less essentialist view of character is taken in the earlier *Man's Rights; Or, How Would You Like It?* (1870) by Annie Denton Cridge. This consists of five dream voyages to Mars, in which traditional gender roles are reversed and again, machinery and industrial organization have freed the men (née women) from their housework. Earlier still, in 1836, is Mary Griffith's *Three Hundred Years Hence*, in which technological progress has led to a utopia where a new power source is discovered, and runs new automatons that have liberated women from their roles but not enfranchised them just yet. But perhaps the most radical of the lot is a short story by Lydia Maria Francis Child, an abolitionist, women's rights activist, and Native American rights activist. "Hilda Silfverling: A Fantasy" (1845) sees the titular character fall pregnant to a man who then dies at sea before they can marry. When her "disgrace" is discovered, she is sentenced to death, but the sentence is commuted in favor of cryogenically freezing her body after she has given birth, as an experiment. Two hundred years later she awakes in a much more liberated society, and ends up living a happy and, we assume, sexually fulfilled life with a charming rogue who is also her great-grandson.

This alternative stream of utopian thought was lost for a long time, buried under other political priorities by a patriarchally inclined canon, but was rediscovered after the strong re-emergence of women's movements in the 1960s. What these works show clearly is the profound radicalism that utopian thought is capable of when not in the hands of those in charge. From Mary Griffith on, SF by women was "a far more socially activist genre than that written by men."[46]

Beyond a Conclusion

After the potential of technology and politics to alter the human world, we come at last to the final frontier that all SF tends towards: the world beyond the human. Utopias concern themselves with the perfectibility of human

---

[46] Bruce H. Franklin, *Future Perfect: American Science Fiction of the Nineteenth Century* (New Brunswick, NJ: Rutgers University Press, 2010), p. 313.

character, but if these hopes and dreams were made possible by the historical perspective granted by the nineteenth century, they were also thoroughly undermined by it. The notion of human progress depends upon a recognizable humanity that is progressing, and the still-undigested truth of evolution is that humanity is a mere moment in a long and unfinished process. Edward Bulwer-Lytton's *The Coming Race* (1871) presents the reader with the discovery of a powerful utopian race underground, but rather than providing a learning experience it instead threatens human extinction. J.-H. Rosny aîné's "La Morte de la Terre" (1910) is set in a far future when humanity is about to die from lack of water, while a new ferrous species rises. And yet, despite foreseeing its extinction, these visions are still tied to humanity as such. Is the post-human where SF and utopianism part ways definitively? In a short article, "Man of the Year Million" (1893), H. G. Wells describes a vision of evolved humanity in the distant future. Living by their brains rather than their brawn, they end up resembling calm, smooth, and disturbing babies with overgrown heads and few defining features. Wells's Eloi are somewhere towards this, and his Martians too. This is the real horizon opened up by Darwin's discovery, and one that SF will explore from Wells onwards.

But utopia, it seems, is for people. In *Anticipations* and "Discovery of the Future," Wells sees the essential posthuman nature of SF. He admits clearly that his New Republic is by no means the end, only the furthest he can imagine, needing some stable "man" to build upon. What comes beyond there is unknown:

> We perceive that man, and all the world of men, is no more than the present phase of a development so great and splendid that beside this vision epics jingle like nursery rhymes and all the exploits of humanity shrivel to the proportion of castles in the sand.[47]

Where SF and utopianism were tightly woven in the infancy of the genre, the making-unstable of humanity reveals that the horizons of SF extend far beyond that of the utopian, into a realm unimaginable. And yet even this might be reclaimed if we consider utopia – in its origins, in the nineteenth century, now and in the future – to be a joyous relation to the present that calls for its own expansion, no matter what shape it takes.

---

[47] https://archive.org/stream/discoveryoffuturoowelliala/discoveryoffuturoowellia
la_djvu.txt (last accessed May 30, 2018).

5

War Machines and Child Geniuses: American Edisonades

NATHANIEL WILLIAMS

John Clute coined the term "Edisonade" in 1993's *Encyclopedia of Science Fiction* out of a need to recognize a neglected subfield of nineteenth-century American literature. The label signifies "Any story which features a young US male inventor hero who uses his ingenuity to extricate himself from tight spots" by building a weapon, transportation device, or some combination of both, typically set during their audience's present featuring then-cutting-edge steam or electric power.[1] Clute's neologism uses Thomas Alva Edison's persona to define these works, which is appropriate given their celebration of the inventor as independent professional, as financial success story, and as (generally) a force for good in the world. And yet the term doesn't quite convey the true heart of Edisonades or the likely source of their continued allure for some readers, which could perhaps be better articulated in a punchier, synechdochial phrase like "Giant Mechanical Spiders!" or "Flying Battleships with 100 Propellers!" Edisonades overflow with such miraculous inventions. They are both the United States' answer to Jules Verne and the nineteenth-century American antecedent of modern steampunk. They carry their era's cultural baggage, often in matter-of-fact ways that can unnerve modern readers.

As such, Edisonades occupy the space where "deservedly obscure" meets "culturally relevant" meets "kind of nifty." In their time, public figures maligned them for their portrayals of bloodthirsty violence and greed.[2] Others have dismissed them for being Victorian kitsch, for their unrigorous science, inelegant writing, and formulaic plots; even sympathetic historians

---

[1] John Clute, "Edisonade," in John Clute and Peter Nicholls, eds., *The Encyclopedia of Science Fiction*, 3rd edn. (New York: St. Martin's Press, 1993), p. 368.
[2] The era's most famous anti-dime-novel book was moralist and postmaster Anthony Comstock's *Traps for the Young* (1883). Another dismissive article appeared in an 1879 issue of *The Atlantic Monthly*. See Bill Brown, *Reading the West: An Anthology of Dime Novel Westerns* (Boston: Bedford/St. Martin's, 1997), pp. 2–3.

must acknowledge their frequent imperialistic tone and racist portrayals of non-white characters.[3] They may face some disdain simply because of their packaging; most Edisonades appeared in cheap, ephemeral, mass-produced formats aimed at a juvenile market, without high literary aspirations. Precisely because of these origins, however, they also showcase America's relationship with technology, expansion, and identity in telling ways.

Origins

The ur-Edisonade contains all these features. That book, *The Steam Man of the Prairies* (1868) by Edward Sylvester Ellis, tells the tale of a disabled boy, Johnny Brainerd, who invents and builds a steam-driven automaton, uses it to travel out West, finds gold, fights native peoples, and returns a hero. As such, it encompasses the post-Civil War United States' anxieties regarding expansion, disability, technology, civil rights, and capital acquisition. The book is less significant for its themes than its role in inspiring a succession of subsequent boy inventor novels that pervaded the market-place, more famous as a bellwether than as a conceptual masterpiece or "good read." Unlike other contenders for the title of first American SF novel, such as Charles Brockden Brown's *Weiland* (1798) and Edgar Allan Poe's *Narrative of Arthur Gordon Pym* (1838), Ellis relies heavily on technology for his plot and portrays inventive tinkering with unambiguous praise. From this perspective, it marks the ideal place to begin a study of US postbellum SF.

When it was published in 1868, *The Steam Man of the Prairies* had a ripped-from-the-headlines relevance, at least for readers in the greater New Jersey area. That January, local newspapers reported that inventor Zadoc P. Dederick had created an automaton, over seven feet tall, powered by steam but designed to mimic human motion. The steam man came complete with a larger boiler that served as his stomach and a top hat that operated as smokestack.[4] While some controversy surrounds whether the steam man actually worked or not, the idea of a steam-powered humanoid able to navigate any terrain while hauling a carriage or cart pervaded the area, inspiring Edward Ellis to write about it for the Beadle and Adams dime-

---

[3] See Everett F. Bleiler, *Science-Fiction: The Early Years* (Kent, OH: Kent State University Press, 1990), pp. 549–50; J. B. Dobkin, "Treatment of Blacks in Dime Novels," *Dime Novel Round-Up* 55 (August 1986), pp. 50–6; and Jess Nevins, *Encyclopedia of Fantastic Victoriana* (Austin, TX: Monkeybrain Books, 2005), pp. 280–1.

[4] Everett F. Bleiler, "From the Newark Steam Man to Tom Swift," *Extrapolation* 30, 2 (1989), pp. 101–2.

novel publishing company. As dime-novel historians have shown, many authors borrowed from recent news items to generate plots in time to meet stressful publishing deadlines, and Ellis's transformation of Dederick's invention into fiction typified the process.[5] The book's appearance, however, coincided with major cultural transformations that probably gave it resonance. Bill Brown, for example, has noted that the novel presents technology capable of overcoming both the "loss of slave labor" and "the notorious loss of limbs" caused by the Civil War.[6] Moreover, it came at a time when many Americans looked to the still-open West as a place of opportunity, providing a predominantly urban and juvenile audience with escapist views of the frontier.[7]

Like many Edisonades that follow, *The Steam Man of the Prairies* is highly episodic. Hero Johnny Brainerd hitches his cart to the steam man and meets a miner, Baldy Bicknell, who immediately requests – in the kind of dialect prose common to the era's fiction – to buy the invention because "Thar's three of us goin' out to hunt fur gold, and that's jist the thing to keep the Injins back an' scart."[8] When first encountered, the steam man seems valued as much for its ability to terrorize the native population as its ability to traverse wide swaths of land. During one of his expeditions, Brainerd meets a "huge hunter" who, like Baldy, immediately wants to use the steam man to "chase redskins."[9] Brainerd outwits the hunter's attempt to steal the invention. Other episodes feature Brainerd hunting buffalo, confronting and killing a grizzly bear, and other typical Western dime-novel adventures. Ultimately, the heroes find their canyon encampment blocked by native would-be assailants; with regret, Brainerd fires up the steam man's boiler to full power and sends him rushing into the barricade where he explodes, resulting in his opponents' mass murder.[10] He saves the day for his white comrades, and uses the gold to pay for an expensive formal education, concluding the text in standard rags-to-riches style.[11]

---

[5] See, for example, Michael Denning, *Mechanic Accents: Dime Novels and Working-Class Culture in America* (London: Verso, 1987), pp. 17–24, and J. Randolph Cox, "Nick Carter, Fact or Fiction: The Historical Context of the American Dime Novel," *Dime Novel Round-Up* 54, 3 (1985), p. 51.

[6] Bill Brown, "Science Fiction, the World's Fair, and the Prosthetics of Empire, 1910–1915," in Amy Kaplan and Donald E. Pease, eds., *Cultures of United States Imperialism* (Durham, NC: Duke University Press, 1993), p. 132.

[7] Brown, *Reading the West*, p. 5.

[8] Edward S. Ellis, *The Huge Hunter; or, The Steam Man of the Prairies* (New York: Beadle and Adams Publishers, 1870), p. 25.

[9] Ibid., p. 71.

[10] Ibid., p. 99.

[11] Ibid., p. 100.

Perhaps the first significant, long-term influence of Ellis's novel comes in its hero, Johnny Brainerd. "This dwarf," the novel states, "small and mis-shapen as he was, was gifted with a most wonderful mind. His mechanical ingenuity bordered on the marvelous."[12] He is beloved by his friends and his doting mother. At only fifteen years old, Brainerd's intellect and engineering ability far surpass his peers. The steam man is initially proposed by his mother simply to find something to occupy her brilliant son, who has already proved his mechanical prowess many times over.[13] Thus, *The Steam Man of the Prairies* shapes the archetypal American "boy-genius" persona. Inventor stories that follow it repeatedly borrow this concept: each hero is distinguished by youth and engineering intelligence.

In a publishing move designed to give old material a fresh appearance, dime-novel stories were frequently retitled when re-released. *The Steam Man of the Prairies* subsequently appeared seven times with three different titles between 1868 and 1904.[14] When reprinted in 1876, it was retitled *The Huge Hunter; or, The Steam Man of the Prairies*, an odd renaming given that the huge hunter character appears in only a single chapter. Nevertheless, this repri-nting had the most lasting influence because, within weeks of its appearance, one of Beadle and Adams's competitors printed an imitation entitled *The Steam Man of the Plains; or, the Terror of the West*. Tousey Press serialized it between February 28 and April 24, 1876, then republished it as a standalone novel in their flagship *Five Cent Wide Awake Library*.[15] While Beadle and Adams's *Steam Man* was a one-off story, Frank Tousey and writer Harry Cohen (under the pseudonym Harry Enton) turned the concept into a series, unleashing a succession of invention stories starring boy hero Frank Reade. *The Steam Man of the Plains* introduces sixteen-year-old Reade, a New Yorker who builds his steam man and takes him to Missouri, where he and his cousin fight natives, chase buffalo, and find treasure. Reade differs little from Johnny Brainerd, with one exception: he inhabits a normalized "able" body, which robs Enton's novel of the cyborgian potential found in Brainerd's self-transformation from disabled "dwarf" to frontier hero through his utilization of his steam man.[16] In fact, Reade's physical heroics could be transplanted

[12] Ibid., p. 18.
[13] Ibid., p. 20.
[14] See Bleiler, "From the Newark Steam Man to Tom Swift," pp. 105, 113.
[15] Bleiler, *Science-Fiction*, p. 548.
[16] For more on prosthesis in Ellis, see Brown, "Science Fiction," pp. 130–3. Nearly a century later, TV series *The Wild, Wild West* (1965–9) used the concept of a disabled "dwarf" inventor using technology in the post-Civil War frontier in recurring villain Miguelito Loveless.

into any cowboy dime novel, such as when "the plucky inventor" confronts one outlaw: "Frank leaped backwards, ripped forth a revolver, and sent a heavy ball tearing through the robber's shoulder .... [He] leaped lightly over the prostrate form and dashed out."[17] Enton's steam man story emphasizes frontier heroics, its inventor a mundanely rugged, masculine protagonist.

Tousey slowly developed a series of Frank Reade novels. The third, *Frank Reade and his Steam Tally-Ho* (1881), was the first story ascribed to Tousey's house pseudonym "Noname," rather than Enton, and its authorship is still uncertain. The new attribution, however, signals that the publisher was interested in "branding" Frank Reade, attaching it to a single author's name regardless of which author wrote the actual story. Luis Philip Senarens, an experienced dime novelist but only sixteen years old at the time, eventually took over the series and wrote most or all of the 180+ Reade tales. As Bleiler and others have noted, the Senarens era brought two major changes that affected Edisonades forever. First, he made the hero Frank Reade, Jr., son of the now rich-and-famous inventor from previous stories. Doing this erased the rags-to-riches element so central to Ellis's and Enton's boy inventor stories. In the first of these, *Frank Reade, Jr. and his Steam Wonder* (1882), the son wins his father's approval by building a fast, bulletproof all-terrain vehicle and venturing West himself. Undeniably, the series' emphasis on youth became stronger as "Jr." became part of nearly every subsequent story's title. The second major change occurred in the next storyline, *Frank Reade, Jr., and his Electric Boat* (1882). As the title indicates, the invention has a new power source – electricity – and travels on water rather than land. From this moment on, Senarens's stories rely primarily on electrical power and feature all sorts of vehicles: airships, submarines, bicycles, "electric buckboards," and other oddities. Each adventure highlights a different single device, with Reade, Jr.'s adventures serialized regularly in the dime-novel weekly *The Boys of New York* throughout the remainder of the 1880s. No longer reliant on steam and possessing crafts that traverse sea and air, Frank Reade, Jr.'s adventures gradually expand beyond the Wild West and into every corner of the world. This era yields iconic titles such as *From Pole to Pole; or, Frank Reade, Jr.'s Strange Submarine Voyage* (1890) and *Frank Reade, Jr. and his Electric Air Yacht; or, The Great Inventor Among the Aztecs* (1891). On September 24, 1892, the Reade series blazed another trail by becoming

---

[17] Harry Enton, "The Steam Man of the Plains; or, The Terror of the West," *Wide Awake Library* 541 (January 24, 1883), p. 5. Northern Illinois University Libraries. http://dimeno vels.lib.niu.edu.

the first regularly published science fiction series when Tousey released the *Frank Reade Library*, a weekly dime-novel series devoted exclusively to the boy inventor's exploits, each issue offering one, approximately 40,000-word story in its entirety.[18]

If there is an actual "boy genius" in the Edisonades' history, it is Senarens himself. The Brooklyn-born writer began his career writing for dime novels at age fourteen, helping to support a family that had lost its father, a former tobacco merchant from Cuba, when Senarens was a child.[19] During the first year of the *Frank Reade Library*'s publication, young Senarens wrote at minimum a long novella-length story from start to finish every two weeks. If this weren't enough work, the Reade stories' success inspired the publisher to create a second "boy-inventor" hero, Jack Wright, whose exploits were serialized in *The Boys' Star Library* beginning in 1891 and ultimately produced 121 separate stories.[20] While each story was attributed to "Noname" and some writers have dismissed Senarens's claims that he wrote all of them, the handful of profiles published about Senarens during his lifetime never failed to note his creative abundance.[21] His obituary noted he'd written 1,500 books under twenty-seven pseudonyms.[22] In 1920, future *Amazing Stories* editor Hugo Gernsback christened him the "American Jules Verne" in *Science and Invention* for his "prophetic" and "prolific" career in technology fiction.[23]

Proliferation

As Reade's and Wright's stories became a cottage industry, Edisonades' conventions congealed quickly. No longer rags-to-riches tales or overt considerations of prosthetic normalization, their controlling themes become youth and autonomous power, particularly technology's ability to facilitate the latter. Nearly all scholars agree that they operated as imperialist fantasies during the two decades leading up to the United States becoming an actual global empire

[18] See Sam Moskowitz, *Explorers of the Infinite* (Cleveland: World Publishing Company, 1963), p. 120.

[19] "Biography of Lu Senarens," *Dime Novel Round-Up* 114 (March 1942), p. 10. See also E. F. Bleiler, "Introduction," in *The Frank Reade Library*, 10 vols. (New York: Garland, 1979), Vol. 1, p. viii.

[20] Bleiler, *Science-Fiction*, pp. 558–9.

[21] See, for example, Elizabeth Alden, "A Writer of a Thousand Thrillers," *The American Magazine* 91, 4 (April 1921), p. 57.

[22] "L. P. Senarens Dies; Dime Novel Author," *New York Times* (December 28, 1939), p. 21.

[23] "An American Jules Verne" (unsigned editorial), *Science and Invention* 8, 6 (October 1920), p. 622.

after 1898's Spanish–American War.[24] Their narrative relies on the same appeal to technocracy that factors into nearly all imperial endeavors, as "civilized" technology colonizes the other. Reade's and Wright's electric and aerial/nautical technology provides them with access to all corners of the globe, giving them power to violently assert control once there.

The storylines rely heavily on readers' ability to empathize with a protagonist who can use technology not simply to "even the odds" but actually to overwhelm his attackers – technocracy at its most extreme. In each dime-novel Edisonade, the invention operates as staging ground for weaponry. For example, Frank Reade, Jr.'s first escapade in his "Steam Wonder" features several attacks by Native Americans portrayed as one-dimensional, barbaric villains who try to break into the vehicle. "I'll give 'em a scare," Reade announces, before turning on their antagonists a hose that pumps "a stream of boiling water upon them."[25] The brutality of Reade's counter-attacks on assailants is exacerbated by each vehicle's near-invulnerability; their crews never quite seem in *real* danger. In *Frank Reade and His Adventures with His Latest Invention* (1883), for example, Reade travels in an enormous electric tricycle encased by a bulletproof mesh cage to protect the passengers.[26] When attacked by another indigenous group, Reade runs an electric current through the wire cage around the tricycle: "The six savages who had laid hands on the tricycle were instantly killed. They dropped to the ground in their tracks, and remained as motionless as only the dead can."[27] It is possibly the earliest incident of mass electrocution in American letters, predating Twain's use of the concept in *A Connecticut Yankee in King Arthur's Court* (1889) by six years. Similarly, in 1893's *Frank Reade, Jr., in the Sea of Sand*, the inventor pilots an airship and discovers a race of desert giants called Barokites. When they attack, Reade simply takes to the sky: "Knowing that the bows and arrows of the Barokites could do no harm, Frank Reade Jr. held the ship suspended. Then he worked the electric gun, and before such a fearful instrument of death the Barokites could not stand."[28] In 1896, Senarens sent his boy inventors to his father's homeland,

---

[24] For examples, see Bleiler, *Science-Fiction*, pp. 549–50; Brown, *Reading the West*, p. 360, and Clute, "Edisonade," p. 370.

[25] Noname, *Frank Reade, Jr. and his Steam Wonder*, in E. F. Bleiler, ed., *The Frank Reade Library*, 10 vols. (New York: Garland, 1979), Vol. II, 20, p. 5.

[26] Noname, *Frank Reade, Jr. and his Adventures with his Latest Invention*, in Bleiler, ed., *The Frank Reade Library*, Vol. II, 24, p. 3.

[27] Ibid., p. 6.

[28] Noname, *Frank Reade, Jr., in the Sea of Sand; and his Discovery of a Lost People*, in Bleiler, ed., *The Frank Reade Library*, Vol. IV, 49, p. 23.

having both of them aid the Cuban revolution against Spain and interact with some of the actual generals in that conflict. While the author's incorporation of the very real conflict into his dime-novel plot is fascinating, the outcomes are essentially the same. Jack Wright, for example, discovers Spanish troops preparing to shoot a group of Cuban patriots, including elderly women. He promptly pilots the airship above them and mows the Spanish troops down with a "rapid-fire electric gun" that discharges 3,000 shots at a rate of 560 per minute.[29] Each incident plays out a fantasy of technocratic power.

Obviously, there is an ethno-nationalist appeal underscoring the technocracy; perhaps audiences could justify unequal violence against Native Americans, Mexicans, prehistoric giants, and Spanish soldiers in a country whose definition of "American" was overwhelmingly Anglo-Protestant.[30] The stories, however, often try to temper their overt racism with appeals to ethnic dignity. In the first Senarens-penned story, Reade chastises his cousin, who wants to shoot the first Native American he sees: "Father warned me against firing on Indians just because they were Indians. They are human beings as well as ourselves."[31] Such language continues even as he scalds, shears the heads of, and kills native peoples in subsequent adventures. Similarly, the most infamous Jack Wright storyline features him aerially bombing a large settlement of African-American criminals – a horrifying racist fantasy. The story, however, begins with Wright confronting and striking a white man he finds beating an unarmed black man, suggesting that Wright's violence is only aimed at criminals and bullies, regardless of ethnicity.[32] This widely divergent portrayal of race is most apparent in Senarens's three Edisonades set during the Cuban Revolution, where he demeans Spanish troops, but portrays real-life Cuban officers, including mulatto general Antonio Maceo, as romanticized heroes of the George Washington mold. Like the America of their era, the books' racism is tangible and often internally conflicted.

More than anything, these narratives value independence. A motif recurs in the novels when someone – a government official, a millionaire stockbroker, *et al.* – offers to buy the inventor's creation. The answer is always

---

[29] Noname, *The Flying Avenger; or, Jack Wright Fighting for Cuba* in *The Boys' Star Library* 376 (April 10, 1896), p. 11.

[30] See, for example, Susan K. Harris, *God's Arbiters: Americans and the Philippines, 1898–1902* (New York: Oxford University Press, 2011) pp. 71, 143–4, and Walter Benn Michaels, *Our America* (Durham, NC: Duke University Press, 1995), pp. 23–4.

[31] Noname, *Frank Reade, Jr. and his Steam Wonder*, p. 8.

[32] Noname, *Jack Wright and His Flying Torpedo; or, The Black Demons of Dismal Swamp* in *Pluck and Luck* 278 (September 30, 1903), p. 4. Originally printed in *Boys' Star Library* on November 3, 1893, Bleiler calls it "an extreme example of bigotry" in *Science-Fiction*, pp. 560–1.

"No." Autonomy is worth its weight in gold in Edisonades, though it is enabled only by the fact that the boy inventor's family is already rich. Similarly, the regularly appearing sidekicks – bickering ethnic "types" used primarily for comedic purposes – are all adults.[33] For example, Jack Wright's companions are an "old salt" sailor named Tim Topstay and a Dutch electrician named Fritz. Each man speaks in heavy dialect, has his own area of expertise, but is not in control of the journey's goals or destination. That's Jack's business. Each older man is subordinate to the "boy inventor," suggesting to readers that technical know-how can grant a young man power to boss around grown-ups.

The success of the Reade and Wright series inspired imitators that further reveal the era's publishing techniques and cultural obsessions. Street and Smith publishers developed a series in their *Nugget Library* featuring young inventor "Tom Edison, Jr." Eleven stories appeared between 1891 and 1892, during the boy-inventor craze's zenith.[34] The titular hero's father is an inventor, although the story elucidates that he is *not* Thomas Alva Edison. (*Nugget Library* used a similar marketing tactic with boxing stories featuring "John L., Jr.," whose name suggested filial kinship with then-heavyweight champ John L. Sullivan.) If the character's name weren't enough of a draw, stories were attributed to pseudonym "Philip Reade," implying a connection with Tousey's boy inventor.[35] Despite these attempts at coat-tailing, the still-unknown author(s) used interesting narrative techniques to distinguish them from other Edisonades. *Tom Edison Jr's Electric Sea Spider; or, The Wizard of the Submarine World*, for example, is written in the present tense with long paragraphs, eschewing the dialogue-heavy, single-sentence paragraphs found in Senarens. Tom invents an aluminum craft that propels itself along the sea's surface with its legs, similar to a water bug.[36] He also fights another super-scientist, a US-educated Chinese pirate named Kiang Ho, who has invented a "Sea Serpent" submarine and duels with Tom using electric guns on the ocean floor.[37] Ho is one of the first Yellow Peril antagonists in

---

[33] Letter columns from *Boys of New York* indicate that at least some readers genuinely admired the sidekicks. See Sara Lindey, "Boys Write Back: Self-Education and Periodical Authorship in Late-Nineteenth-Century Story Papers," *American Periodicals* 21, 2, pp. 72–88.

[34] J. Randolph Cox, *The Dime Novel Companion* (Westport, CT: Greenwood Press, 2000), pp. 94–5.

[35] See Bleiler, *Science-Fiction*, p. 615.

[36] Philip Reade, *Tom Edison Jr's Electric Sea Spider; or, The Wizard of the Submarine World* in *Nugget Library* 134, (February 11, 1892), p. 3. http://jessnevins.com/edisonade/electric seaspider.html.

[37] Ibid., pp. 13–14.

Western fiction, predating Sax Rohmer's Fu Manchu by a decade.[38] Not long after Tom Edison, Jr.'s final story appeared in *New York Five Cent Library*, Street and Smith debuted a new boy inventor, "Electric Bob," whose adventures are so idiosyncratic that many scholars read them as Edisonade parodies.[39] Most of Bob's vehicle/weapons are giant, motorized animals. For example, his thirty-foot-tall electric ostrich's gizzard contains an "enlarged revolver cylinder, holding twenty-five Winchester rifle cartridges"; the ostrich also serves as a camera, with a telescopic neck and a lens in its mouth.[40] Street and Smith's willingness to call attention to the outright absurdity of Edisonades is, of course, a backhanded compliment of the subgenre's success.

Beyond dime-novel publishing, technocratic fiction developed a readership over the same time frame. Most notable were, inevitably, Jules Verne's translated novels. Scholars debate how much Verne's work influenced American Edisonades and vice versa, with some writers noting mutual inspiration, culminating in Sam Moskowitz's unsubstantiated claim that Verne wrote a complimentary letter to "Noname."[41] It is certainly true that *Frank Reade, Jr. and his Air-Ship* appeared in 1883, and, thus, predates by three years Verne's *Robur the Conqueror*, still often misidentified as the "first" flying-machine tale. Regardless, nineteenth-century Americans who would never touch a dime novel devoured Verne's technophilia and were introduced to lunar voyages, submarines, and airships through his writing. Verne's American success came with problems. His popularity resulted in the hasty release of twelve translated novels between 1872 and 1874.[42] Verne's French publisher wanted his work to have educational appeal, suitable for young readers, and English translators took this sanitizing further.[43] Regularly, 20 to 40 percent of Verne's original novel was deleted in English translations – often passages with linguistic subtlety or with musings regarding science's impact on empire or religion – with entirely new paragraphs composed and added by

---

[38] See Bleiler, *Science-Fiction*, p. 617.

[39] Bleiler calls them "obviously largely tongue-in-cheek." See Bleiler, *Science-Fiction*, p. 742. See also Nevins, *Encyclopedia*, p. 282.

[40] *Electric Bob's Big Black Ostrich; or, Lost on the Desert* in *New York Five Cent Library* 55 (August 26, 1893), p. 3. jessnevins.com/edisonade/edisonade.html.

[41] Moskowitz, *Explorers of the Infinite*, p. 109.

[42] Jean-Marc Lofficier and Randy Lofficier, *French Science Fiction, Fantasy, Horror and Pulp Fiction* (Jefferson, NC: McFarland and Company, 2000), p. 736.

[43] See Brian Stableford, "Science Fiction Before the Genre," in Edward James and Farah Mendelsohn, eds., *The Cambridge Companion to Science Fiction* (Cambridge: Cambridge University Press, 2003), p. 21; and Arthur B. Evans, "Jules Verne's English Translations," *Science Fiction Studies* 32 (2005), pp. 80–104.

translators.[44] Verne's influence was enormous but, at least in America, some undeserved taint of juvenile, pulpy writing clung to him.

A case in point was the major US writer of non-dime-novel Edisonades who dismissed Verne as "the rampaging French lunatic" in private letters.[45] That man was Samuel Clemens, better known as Mark Twain, who penned Victorian America's greatest technocratic novel, A Connecticut Yankee in King Arthur's Court (1889). Twain's protagonist, Hank Morgan, becomes the American über-technocrat, and his campaign to use technology to secularize and democratize sixth-century England brings Edisonade complexities to their fatalistic head. True, Morgan does not build a machine to reach his remote destination; he's hit on the head by an angry subordinate's crowbar at Hartford's Colt Arms Factory and travels through time/space to Arthurian times. From a practical perspective, however, Morgan behaves identically to other inventors upon reaching his destination. He immediately states that he will "boss the whole country inside of three months; for I judged I would have the start of the best educated man in the kingdom by a matter of thirteen hundred years."[46] In fact, he perceives King Arthur's world as analogous to the Wild West, full of "savages" who need to be tamed and believing that his technological edge will enable this.[47] Prone to pyrotechnics, he blows up court magician Merlin's castle to discredit him.[48] He fixes a monastery's well using simple plumbing, but then sets off fireworks above it while uttering mock incantations to awe the locals.[49] As Morgan passes off technology as supernatural power, he justifies it as necessary to rid England of its traditions of inherited royalty and the Church's absolute authority. This is, of course, the voice of a colonizer, and also of the secular technologist, assured that his testable, materialist worldview is superior to ideas built on "weak" foundations like faith, tradition, or fear.[50] Despite his

---

[44] Evans, "Jules Verne's English Translations," pp. 80, 89.
[45] Samuel Langhorne Clemens to Jane Lampton Clemens, February, 23, 1878. Mark Twain Papers, University of California at Berkeley.
[46] Mark Twain [Samuel Langhorne Clemens], A Connecticut Yankee in King Arthur's Court, ed. Bernard L. Stein (Berkeley: University of California Press, 1979), p. 17.
[47] See Kerry Driscoll, "'Man Factories' and the 'White Indians' of Camelot: Re-reading the Native Subtext of A Connecticut Yankee in King Arthur's Court," The Mark Twain Annual 2 (2004), pp. 7–23; and Gregory M. Pfitzer, "'Iron Dudes and White Savages in Camelot': The Influence of Dime-Novel Sensationalism on Twain's A Connecticut Yankee in King Arthur's Court," American Literary Realism 27, 1 (Fall 1994), pp. 42–58.
[48] Twain, A Connecticut Yankee, pp. 57–9.
[49] Ibid., pp. 219–24.
[50] Studies of A Connecticut Yankee's complex treatment of imperialism include Harris, God's Arbiters, pp. 85–9; Hsuan Hsu, Sitting in Darkness: Mark Twain's Asia and Comparative Racialization (New York: New York University Press, 2015), pp. 112–19; and John

ability to bring a handgun to a jousting match and build an electrified trench around his assembled forces, Morgan fails because his hubristic technocracy isn't enough to create lasting change; indeed, contrary to the progressivist spirit of most Edisonades, Twain's version ends in a horrific massacre after Morgan's introduction of electric wire, minefields, and the Gatling gun to Camelot.[51]

There is no proof that Samuel Clemens ever read dime-novel Edisonades which, given the scrutiny to which his reading habits have been subjected, suggests he at most generally knew *of* them.[52] Indisputably, however, Twain's own Vernian balloon voyage, *Tom Sawyer Abroad* (1894), is conversant with Edisonades and appeared in *The St. Nicholas Magazine*, a periodical designed to supplant violent dime novels by giving children more genteel reading material.[53] In it, Twain makes his most famous character the mouthpiece of American exceptionalism and technocracy. Finding himself in control of a fantastic aerial vehicle, Tom Sawyer pilots the craft to the Middle East, where he schemes ways to make money by selling Saharan sand as a souvenir and drops ex-slave Jim atop the Sphinx.[54] When angry Egyptians shoot at Jim, Tom explains that the United States will no doubt demand an "indemnity" payment. Technology allows Tom to see the world, but his jingoistic worldview goes along with him. The critical Edisonade had arrived.

Influence

Between the weekly *Frank Reade Library*'s 1892 appearance and *Tom Sawyer Abroad*'s 1894 publication, Frederick Jackson Turner delivered his famous 1893 oration announcing the closing of the North American frontier. By then, Edisonades had been portraying American technocrats in international escapades for two decades, in some ways preparing the US audience for global super-powerdom beyond the now-closed US West. The legacy of Edisonades shows in several strands of early twentieth-century SF.

Carlos Rowe, *Literary Culture and US Imperialism: From the Revolution to World War II* (Oxford: Oxford University Press, 2000), pp. 123–7.

[51] Twain, *A Connecticut Yankee*, pp. 391, pp. 418–40.

[52] See, for example, Alan Gribben, *Mark Twain's Library: A Reconstruction*, 2 vols. (Boston: G. K. Hall and Company, 1980) and Albert Bigelow Paine, *Mark Twain's Notebook* (New York: Harper and Brothers, 1935). For a contrasting view, see Pfitzer, "Iron Dudes," pp. 44–6.

[53] Albert E. Stone, Jr., *The Innocent Eye: Childhood in Mark Twain's Imagination* (Hamden, CT: Archon, 1970), p. 104.

[54] Mark Twain, *Tom Sawyer Abroad and Tom Sawyer, Detective* (Berkeley: University of California Press, 1990), pp. 90–3.

Dime novels had proved that a "boy inventor" series could have appeal, and publishers adapted it for a new generation. In 1910, as dime-novel publishing waned, the Stratemeyer Syndicate brought out the Tom Swift series of juvenile books, introducing probably the best-known "boy inventor" of the twentieth century. Swift is an all-American boy with a penchant for engineering. Like Frank Reade, he's the son of a rich, successful inventor, often accompanied by older male sidekicks who are awed by his talent. Like the Reade series, every story was attributed to a pseudonym ("Victor Appleton") to ensure brand consistency. As Bleiler has shown, American SF writers like Isaac Asimov and Robert Heinlein didn't know Reade or Wright, but they adored Tom Swift and the character's faith in technology informed their juveniles and Golden Age SF.[55] While not all strictly Edisonades, multiple juvenile series featuring technophilic youths – The Boy Inventors, The Aeroplane Boys, The Radio Boys – appeared in the same era, some predating Swift.[56] Stratemeyer brought out The Motor Boys, then The Motor Girls series, ensuring that young, female readers wouldn't be left out of the technocratic fiction rage. Many series showcasing young women as aviators and auto enthusiasts followed.[57] Juvenile technology literature – starring juvenile protagonists – was built on the Edisonades' template.

Later popular fiction that drew from the invention tales' tradition was typically more willing to overtly name real inventors and to consider the genre's imperial implications. When tapped by the *New York Evening Journal* to write an Americanized sequel to H. G. Wells's just-released opus *The War of the Worlds*, astronomy journalist Garrett P. Serviss conceived of an American counterattack against Mars led by Thomas Alva Edison. Unlike Street and Smith's dime novels, Serviss fictionally portrayed the *real* Edison, along with President William McKinley, Lord Kelvin, and Wilhelm Roentgen. After surviving the Martian invasion of Wells's novel, Edison creates a rocketship and develops spacesuits and "disintegrator guns." This announcement ignites imperial zeal among Earthlings: "Let us go to Mars. We have the means. Let us beard the lion in his den. Let us ourselves turn conquerors."[58] What follows plays as a revenge fantasy, with its longing for conquest of remote locales played out on interplanetary levels. (The era's

[55] Bleiler, "From the Newark Steam Man to Tom Swift," p. 112.
[56] See Francis J. Molson, "The Boy Inventor in American Series Fiction: 1900–1930," *Journal of Popular Culture* 28, 1 (Summer 1994), pp. 31–48.
[57] See Sherrie A. Inness, "On the Road and in the Air: Gender and Technology in Girls' Automobile and Airplane Serials, 1909–1932," *Journal of Popular Culture* 30, 2 (Fall 1996), pp. 47–60.
[58] Garrett P. Serviss, *Edison's Conquest of Mars* (Burlington, Ontario: Apogee, 2005), p. 18.

other major narrative using a real-life scientist, *To Mars with Tesla* from the dime-novel series *New Golden Hours* in 1901, focused more on exploration than conquest.)

Instead of sending their imaginary war machines off to distant locales, early SF works began to consider the possibility of attack from the outside. The ensuing preparedness SF – with its paranoia and incorporation of "Yellow Peril" motifs – drew from the Edisonades' well. J. H. Palmer's *The Invasion of New York; or, How Hawaii was Annexed* (1897), for example, imagines a one-year-away future of 1898, with America attacked by Japan in Hawaii and by Spain on the East Coast, actions that force the United States to become an imperial force around the globe.[59] Palmer's introduction tells readers to consider his book carefully, because such events are "quite possible"; lest this be lost on readers, Palmer ends with the maxim, "In time of peace, prepare for war."[60] Jack London's 1910 short story "The Unparalleled Invasion" charts a similar course with more ironic subtlety. Like Palmer and other future-war authors, London takes the voice of a historian from that future, looking back on the events. London, for example, calmly explains how war against imperial China in 1976 leads the United States to conduct the first germ-warfare experiment by aerially bombing Peking with glass containers of smallpox, cholera, and others.[61] Reade, Jr.'s massacre of Barokites seems humane in contrast. Former successful dime-novelist H. Irving Hancock's four-volume, hard-bound *Conquest of the United States* novel series told a preparedness narrative with juvenile heroes. A class of Gridley High School cadets are led by West Point grads during a German invasion of the US East Coast. In the first book, America loses most of New England in the battle, leading one cadet to note ominously "If the people everywhere had been as busy as the Gridley folks, we'd have had a big and trained volunteer army ... that Germany wouldn't have dared to attack."[62] These works applied Edisonade imagery to voice anxieties about the buildup of imperial powers around the globe in the early twentieth century. By the First World

---

[59] See John Rieder, *Colonialism and the Emergence of Science Fiction* (Middletown, CT: Wesleyan University Press, 2008), pp. 138–9. American colonialism in Hawaii also figured into Twain's composition of *A Connecticut Yankee*. See Gerry Canavan, "Science Fiction in the United States," in Priscilla Wald and Michael A. Elliott, eds., *The American Novel, 1870–1940* (Oxford: Oxford University Press), p. 379.

[60] J. H. Palmer, *The Invasion of New York; or, How Hawaii Was Annexed* (London: F. Tennyson Neely, 1897), pp. iii, 248.

[61] Jack London, "The Unparalleled Invasion," 1910, in James Banks, ed., *The Science Fiction Stories of Jack London* (New York: Citadel Publishing, 1993), pp. 112–13.

[62] H. Irving Hancock, *The Invasion of the United States; or, Uncle Sam's Boys at the Capture of Boston* (Philadelphia: Henry Altemus Company, 1916), p. 88.

War, these strands of the Edisonades' influence comingled, with boy inventor Tom Swift deciding to "do his bit" in the Great War by building a tank that travels twice as fast as British tanks, with "a number of machine guns" and "crushing power" to allow the infantry to follow it through enemy lines.[63] The global conflict anticipated by Edisonades had ultimately come.

Today, the flaws of the nineteenth-century Edisonades seem to outweigh their pleasures, and it would be easy to incorrectly dismiss them the way tastemakers of their own era did. Simply providing a list of the subgenre's landmark achievements, such as the codification of the "boy genius" or the first SF series, only validates them slightly, as does choosing to celebrate only their proto-steampunk imagery. In truth, the elements that most perturb modern readers – unreflective technocracy, nationalist entitlement, racial insensitivity – still pervade the United States and (depressingly) suggest the present has not grown as far from the past as it *should* have. For better or worse, this desiderium may be Brainerd, Reade, Jr., and their ilk's greatest legacy.

---

[63] Victor Appleton, *Tom Swift and his War Tank; or, Doing his Bit for Uncle Sam* (New York: Grosset & Dunlap Publishers, 1918), p. 104.

6

Afrofuturism in the Nineteenth and Twentieth Centuries

W. ANDREW SHEPHARD

In his initial coinage of the term, Mark Dery defined Afrofuturism as "speculative fiction that treats African-American themes and addresses African-American concerns in the context of twentieth-century technoculture."[1] It has thus conventionally been discussed as a post-Second World War phenomenon, due in no small part to the influx of luminaries such as Samuel R. Delany and Octavia E. Butler from the 1960s onward. Recounting a point once made by Harlan Ellison, Delany notes:

> We know of dozens upon dozens upon dozens of early pulp writers only as names: they conducted their careers entirely by mail – in a field and during an era when pen names were the rule rather than the exception. Among the "Remington C. Scotts" and the "Frank P. Joneses" who litter the contents pages of the early pulps, we simply have no way of knowing if one, three, or seven of them – or even many more – were blacks, Hispanics, women, Native Americans, Asians, or whatever. Writing is like that.[2]

As such, it is impossible to construct a full history of the African diaspora's participation in the speculative tradition; however, considerable strides have been made in recent years to reprint and recuperate speculative works by black authors from the beginning of the genre. Likewise, several significant works of Afrofuturist fiction by non-black authors have been recently recovered.

Race and Revolution in the Nineteenth Century

Any discussion of the US Afrofuturist tradition should probably begin with Martin Delany. A prominent abolitionist, journalist, physician, explorer, Civil

---

[1] Mark Dery, "Black to the Future: Interviews with Samuel Delany, Greg Tate, and Tricia Rose," in Mark Dery, ed., *Flame Wars: The Discourse of Cyberculture* (Durham, NC: Duke University Press, 1997), p. 180.
[2] Samuel R. Delany, "Racism and Science Fiction," in Sheree R. Thomas, ed., *Dark Matter: A Century of Speculative Fiction from the African Diaspora* (New York: Warner Books, 2000), p. 380

War veteran, and writer of political tracts, in many ways, Delany's resume calls to mind the polymath heroes of the American pulp tradition. In addition to these accomplishments, his advocacy for repatriation of African Americans to Africa has led him to be regarded as the father of black nationalism.[3] His sole work of fiction, *Blake, or The Huts of America*, was one of the first novels published by an African-American author and is arguably the first work of speculative fiction published by an African American. The novel was serialized in part in *The Anglo African Magazine* from January to July 1859, before being published in its entirety in *The Weekly Anglo-African* from November 1861 to May 1862. It remained out of print for over a century until it was rediscovered and published in book form for the first time in 1970.

The plot concerns Carolus Henrico Blacus, a black man born and educated in Cuba, later anglicized to Henry Blake when he is enslaved in the United States. When his wife is separated from him and sold to a new master in Cuba, Blake escapes captivity and travels both to Africa and throughout the American South, fomenting a rebellion amongst his fellow slaves, which eventually develops into an international movement as they eventually join forces with Cuban slaves rebelling against Spanish rule. The narrative draws considerable inspiration from the slave rebellions of the early nineteenth century. Blake's fellow revolutionaries express "sacred reverence" for famous slave revolt leaders "Nat Turner, Denmark Veezie (Vesey), and General Gabriel (Prosser)" and the "noble, self-emancipated nation" of Haiti is shown equally high regard.[4] Likewise, the mention of Liberia's "praiseworthy efforts to develop their own nationality" and economy based on "the staple products of their native Africa" gesture towards a utopian possibility in pan-Africanism that is congruent with Delany's political tracts.[5] Sadly, contemporary readers may never know if this utopian future comes to pass; as of this writing, the final six chapters of the novel are still unrecovered, leaving Blake's revolutionaries on the eve of a tremendous battle.

---

[3] Delany's noteworthy nonfictional writings include *The Condition, Elevation, Emigration and Destiny of the Colored People of the United States Politically Considered* (1852), a book-length pan-Africanist manifesto, his *Official Report of the Niger Valley Exploring Party* (1861), detailing his exploits as the leader of the first scientific expeditionary party to Africa from the Western hemisphere, and *Principia of Ethnology: The Origin of Races and Color* (1879), a scientific treatise exploring the biological origins of racial difference. For a more thorough discussion of Delany within the context of black nationalism, see Paul Gilroy, *The Black Atlantic: Modernity and Double Consciousness* (Cambridge, MA: Harvard University Press 1993.), pp. 19–29.

[4] Martin R. Delany, *Blake, or The Huts of America* (Boston: Beacon Press, 1970 [1859; 1861–2]), pp. 113, 289.

[5] Delany, *Blake*, p. 289.

The end of Reconstruction in the American South ushered in a particularly tumultuous era for black Americans, one commonly known as "the nadir of American race relations."[6] During this period, the country experienced record numbers of lynchings and race riots, as well as modes of legalized discrimination in the form of segregationist Jim Crow laws designed to circumvent the Fourteenth and Fifteenth Amendments to the US Constitution on the state level. White supremacy also commonly found expression in the popular culture of the era: in the racial caricature of the minstrel tradition, as well as novels like King Wallace's *The Next War* (1892), about a failed murder plot against white southerners enacted by freed blacks, and Thomas Dixon's *The Clansman* (1905), which portrayed a south besieged by exploitative northern industrialists and lawless, predatory blacks prone to abducting and raping white women. D. W. Griffin's *Birth of a Nation* (1911), the filmic adaptation of Dixon's novel, was so popular that it led to a resurgence for the Ku Klux Klan in the south.

Perhaps it is unsurprising, then, that black speculative visions proliferate during this time period – particularly of utopias. As noted by critic M. Giulia Fabi, black utopians of the era generally seem "less convinced of the liberatory potential of technological progress than their white counterparts," instead embracing "a radical this-worldiness" that focuses more on effecting societal change through shifts in ideology.[7] A prime example would be *Iola Leroy* (1892), a novel by prominent activist, poet, and fiction writer Frances E. W. Harper that is arguably the first Afrofuturist work written by a black woman. The novel's plot concerns a young woman of mixed race who belatedly discovers her heritage after the death of her plantation-owning father, a revelation which considerably complicates both her life and legal status as a free woman. The novel primarily follows the conventions of the "tragic mulatto/a" narratives so popular in this period, with Iola virtuously resisting both the temptation to pass as white and the sexual predations of men looking to exploit her precarious status. However, the novel eschews the obligatory tragic ending typical to the genre, by allowing its heroine to establish a community for freed slaves to live productively and without molestation. Moreover, this community is remarkably gender egalitarian,

---

[6] The term "nadir of American race relations" was coined by American historian Rayford Logan, referring to the period which began with the end of Reconstruction in the South and lasted into the early twentieth century, during which racism in the United States was at its worst. See Rayford W. Logan, *The Negro in American Life and Thought: The Nadir 1877–1901* (New York: The Dial Press, Inc., 1954).

[7] M. Giulia Fabi, *Passing and the Rise of the African American Novel* (Urbana and Chicago: University of Illinois Press, 2001), p. 46.

with women serving in prominent positions as activists, educators, and physicians. While not science fictional, Harper's novel is certainly a radical vision for her time.

Borrowing from a different set of literary traditions, Edward A. Johnson's *Light Ahead for the Negro* (1904) and Roger Sherman Tracy's *The White Man's Burden: A Satirical Forecast* (1915) both appropriate the genre of "future history" popularized by Edward Bellamy's seminal utopia *Looking Backward: 2000–1887* (1888). But while many future histories, at best, ignored the race question and, at worst, actively proposed eugenicist solutions to it, both of these works propose very different societies from their contemporaries. Johnson's vision proves the more straightforward of the pair, largely following the conventions of the subgenre while redirecting its focus to racial matters. It concerns Gilbert Twitchell, an idealistic young white man teaching at a Negro school in Georgia to carry on his father's abolitionist legacy. A freak occurrence on a dirigible flight leads to him falling into a state of suspended animation and waking up one hundred years in the future. As in Bellamy's novel, Johnson's protagonist is informed of the changes in this new world largely through long passages of expository description. Such changes include considerable advances for African Americans including educational initiatives and remarkable successes in the agricultural industry, as well as the medical and legal professions. Yet, as Mark Bould notes, *Light Ahead* is oddly conciliatory in tone, seemingly "a sentimental and affective utopia for white sympathies and sympathizers"[8] in its insistence that blacks are fundamentally docile people who are "[not] able to make any concerted movement on their own behalf."[9]

Though probably authored by a white man, Roger Sherman Tracy's *The White Man's Burden* (originally published under the pseudonym T. Shirby Hodge) presents a radical take on the future history that is much more overtly critical of white supremacy.[10] Tracy's unnamed narrator, a white man living in 1910 New Hampshire, awakens to find himself in fifty-first century Africa, since transformed into an anarchist utopia. A black scientist

---

[8] Mark Bould, "Revolutionary African-American Sf Before Black Power Sf," *Extrapolation* 51, 1 (2010), p. 65.

[9] Edward A. Johnson, *Light Ahead for the Negro* (New York: The Grafton Press, 1904), p. 45.

[10] Though biographical information on Roger Sherman Tracy is somewhat scarce, his father Rev. Ebenezer Carter Tracy is confirmed to be white. This, coupled with Roger Tracy's status as a Yale-educated doctor in the nineteenth century, suggests that he was probably a white man. See "Rev Ebenezer Carter Tracy," www.findagrave.com/cgi-bin/fg.cgi?page=gr&GRid=115963122 (last accessed September 25, 2017). See also "Tracy Family Papers (MS 816)," Yale University Library, Manuscripts and Archives, http://hdl.handle.net/10079/fa/mssa.ms.0816 (last accessed September 25, 2017).

by the somewhat improbable name of George Washington Bonaparte Andrews has discovered and cornered the market on a source of unlimited renewable energy, which has given African Americans a significant technological advantage. The result is a massive political upheaval, which leads to the founding of a black separatist state in the United States, a costly and attritional race war in which blacks win the right to repatriate to Africa, and the forcible expulsion of whites from Europe and Asia by a coalition of Pan-Asian militants. On the surface, the premise of Tracy's novel bears a strong resemblance to the types of paranoid racial fantasies that proliferated in Western SF during this period, such as the "Yellow Peril" stories which demonized East Asian peoples. However, a more subversive motive on the author's part is quickly revealed. That the founder of this new society possesses a name which combines one of the founders of American democracy with a famously imperialistic tyrant serves as a sly commentary that the differences between the two may not be as dramatic as Americans would like to believe. Moreover, it implies that this new society may not represent as dramatic a shift away from the old regime as it initially seems.

Rather than a straightforwardly dystopian scenario in which whites are blameless victims, the novel presents us with some rather uncomfortable parallels to the history of the African diaspora. The blacks of Tracy's future have used their technological advantage to render Europeans and those of European descent into abjection and statelessness. When the narrator arrives in this radically different future, he is almost immediately discriminated against – told that he is a member of an "inferior race" whose "mental powers are probably not sufficient" to understand the information being imparted to him.[11] Thus, any white reader of the text is placed in the uneasy position of experiencing the condescending rhetoric and systemic oppression endured by blacks for centuries. This and the inversion of other familiar tropes of nineteenth-century racism, such as the Social Darwinist argument of blacks' inherent criminality, hint at an effort to defamiliarize and deconstruct contemporary racial attitudes.

Of the "nadir-era" writers, Sutton E. Griggs particularly merits special attention. Over the course of five novels, as well as numerous essays, sermons, and political tracts, Griggs consistently and tenaciously grappled with the race question. His later novels, *The Hindered Hand* (1905) and *Pointing the Way* (1908), focus on repatriation to Africa and jurisprudent measures to

---

[11] Roger Sherman Tracy, *The White Man's Burden: A Satirical Forecast* (Boston: The Gorham Press, 1915), pp. 45, 46.

improve the conditions of African Americans – the latter text is often remarked upon for its extraordinary prescience with regard to the strategies it imagines. However, Griggs's first novel, *Imperium in Imperio* (1899), is his most significant. It concerns two black men – Belton Piedmont, an educator, dark-skinned and born to poverty, and Bernard Belgrave, a wealthy mulatto turned politician – who join a secret society of African Americans that has existed within the United States from its inception. Both characters represent the type of inspirational, high-achieving "New Negro" expected to uplift the race at the turn of the century. Indeed, as Lisa Yaszek notes, the mythical founder of the Imperium, "a negro scientist who won an international reputation by his skill and erudition ... [and by] the publication of a book of science which outranked any other book of the day," is likely to be a reference to Benjamin Banneker – the famous black astronomer and planner of Washington DC.[12] The reference serves as a reaffirmation of black tech-noscientific genius not often acknowledged in this era. However, Griggs also seems to fall back on familiar stereotypes. Belgrave's plot, in which his wife elects to kill herself instead of "destroying the Negro race" through miscegenation,[13] calls to mind the familiar "tragic mulatto" plot with the added wrinkle of scientific racism. Likewise, Belgrave's descent into madness and mobilization of the Imperium against the US government ultimately transforms the narrative from the celebratory to the cautionary. The novel ends somewhat ambiguously, with the Imperium on the eve of war with the United States, the conspiracy having been exposed by a dissenter within its own ranks.

Conjure Tales at the End of the Nineteenth Century

The post-Civil-War period also generated a great deal of interest in black folklore and folk tradition – particularly with regard to conjure, a syncretic folk magic tradition blending elements of West African, Native American, and European beliefs. As conjure scholar Jeffrey Anderson notes, local regional distinctions in the South were under threat of being homogenized away by the industrialization process.[14] The 1890s, in particular, saw a surge

---

[12] Lisa Yaszek, "The Bannekerade: Genius, Madness, and Magic in Black Science Fiction," in Isiah Lavender III, ed., *Black and Brown Planets* (Jackson: University Press of Mississippi, 2014) p. 19.

[13] Sutton E. Griggs, *Imperium in Imperio* (New York: The Modern Library, 2003 [1899]), p. 119.

[14] Jeffrey E. Anderson, *Conjure in African American Society* (Baton Rouge: Louisiana State Press, 2005), p. 4.

of anthropological fieldwork by blacks investigating their own culture, in the interest of preserving these traditions. In addition to the articles on conjure lore published by black periodicals like *The Southern Workman*, white authors begin to extensively utilize black folk traditions for the purposes of "local color" in their own regional literatures. This takes the form of ethnographic studies such as those by W. D. Weatherford and Niles Nelson Page, as well as collections of black folklore – with the most popular of the era being Joel Chandler Harris's Uncle Remus tales. Seeing a marketplace demand for conjure-related fiction, black authors begin to produce similar works.

The most successful of such authors was Charles W. Chesnutt, whose collection *The Conjure Woman* (1898), deliberately patterns itself after the plantation fiction of the era. The story cycle concerns a white northern couple who move to the fictional southern town of Patesville, NC after purchasing a plantation there. Their groundskeeper Julius McAdoo, formerly enslaved upon the plantation, ingratiates himself to his new employers by regaling them with tales of its antebellum years, often involving conjure and miraculous transformations, as well as other familiar elements from black folklore such as "ha'nts" (ghosts). While Chesnutt's Julius stories bear some structural similarities to the Uncle Remus tales of Joel Chandler Harris, Chesnutt's tales quite slyly subvert the conventions of the plantation genre as typically practiced by white authors. Julius's tales are inevitably told with an ulterior motive in mind and he frequently comes out ahead of his white patrons. Moreover, the tales themselves use fantastical conceits to communicate ugly truths about the realities of slavery in a form more palatable for white readers. In his private journal, Chesnutt states: "The object of my writings would be not so much the elevation of the colored people as the elevation of the whites ... "[15] In a sense, Julius's narrative trickery can be said to reflect that of his creator.

Paul Laurence Dunbar, one of the most prolific and commercially successful black authors at the turn of the twentieth century, published several stories about conjure in his collection *In Old Plantation Days* (1903). Like Chesnutt, Dunbar makes extensive use of eye dialect, mostly in the spoken dialogue of his black characters. However, Dunbar's tales make little effort to subvert the established conventions of the plantation genre – stories like "Dandy Jim's Conjure Scare" and "The Brief Cure of Aunt Fanny" invoke the familiar tropes of kindly, paternalistic masters and child-like, contentedly

[15] Charles W. Chesnutt, "From His Journal, Spring 1880," in Robert B. Stepto and Jennifer R. Greeson, eds., *The Conjure Tales* (New York and London: W. W. Norton & Company, 2012), p. 168.

loyal slaves with little irony. Conjure is typically revealed to be unambiguously rooted in superstition, its efficacy within the slave community primarily owing to the placebo effect.[16]

Other authors move the conjure tale to settings beyond the plantation. Alice Dunbar-Nelson, wife of Paul and an accomplished writer in her own right, also tried her hand at the genre with "The Goodness of St. Rocque" (1899), in the collection of the same name. Nelson eschews both the plantation setting and the peculiar institution that was its trademark in favor of a different genre – a love story. The tale concerns a young Creole woman in nineteenth-century New Orleans who procures the services of a conjure woman to help win back a suitor who has quite literally been bewitched by another woman. Later authors would transport the conjure tale northward, in the wake of the Great Migration, which brought hundreds of thousands of rural blacks from the south to major northern cities. Rudolph Fisher's Harlem-based detective novel, *The Conjure Man Dies* (1933), follows John Archer and Perry Dart, a medical doctor and a homicide detective as they investigate the apparent murder of N'Gana Frimbo, a neighborhood root doctor. Their investigation becomes complicated when Frimbo seemingly rises from the dead and proceeds to assist in solving his own murder, all the while having lively debates with Archer on metaphysics. This novel was followed by "John Archer's Nose," a second Archer and Dart mystery, also concerning conjure; a third tale in the series, titled "Thus Spake the Prophet," was planned, but remained uncompleted at the time of Fisher's death.[17]

Afrofuturism and the Niche Genre Market

Fisher's Archer and Dart stories could be considered part of a larger trend happening contemporaneously, one of black authors putting their own subversive spins on established genre fiction conventions. The early twentieth century would see the emergence of a popular fiction market aimed at black readers, bolstered by such magazines as *The Crisis* and *Colored American Magazine*. The editor of the latter, Pauline Elizabeth Hopkins, is arguably one of the most accomplished black writers and editors of this era. Her fifth and final novel, *Of One Blood; or The Hidden Truth*, was serialized in *Colored*

---

[16] Paul L. Dunbar, "In Old Plantation Days," in Gene A. Jarrett and Thomas L. Morgan, eds., *The Complete Stories of Paul Laurence Dunbar* (Athens, OH: Ohio University Press, 2005 [orig. 1903]), pp. 202–314.
[17] John McCluskey, "Introduction," in *City of Refuge: The Collected Stories of Rudolph Fisher* (Columbia and London: University of Missouri Press, 2008), p. 28.

American from 1902 to 1903. It is generally acknowledged as the first "lost race" novel written by a black author, a significant distinction indeed; it is estimated that roughly a tenth of SF published before 1930 fell into this genre.[18]

The plot concerns Reuel Briggs, a brilliant young physician with an interest in spiritualism and psychic phenomena, passing for white in Boston. Desiring to make money for his impending marriage to his former patient turned fiancée, Dianthe, Reuel finds himself on an expedition to Africa. Reuel eventually stumbles upon the long-lost city of Telassar, a technologically advanced African society, which recognizes him as the reincarnation of the Meriotic king Ergamenes, prophesized to restore them and Africans the world over to greatness. The novel is a bricolage of several popular genres. The adventures of Reuel and his compatriots in Africa call to mind the adventure fiction of H. Rider Haggard, with its reincarnation plot being an almost certain reference to Haggard's popular novel *She* (1888); Dianthe's ordeal as a prisoner in the home of Reuel's treacherous friend Aubrey Livingston retrofits the Gothic tradition. Likewise, the novel's interest in spiritualism and psychic phenomena shows the influence of William James's writings on these subjects.

As Deborah McDowell notes in her introduction, the novel's messianic overtones reflect the influence of Ethiopianism, a popular notion amongst Afrocentrists of the era inspired by the Biblical passage, "Princes shall come out of Egypt; Ethiopia shall soon stretch out her hands unto God" (Psalms 68:31).[19] The discourse of Ethiopianism tended to evoke the country as a synecdoche for the continent of Africa more broadly, a habit probably derived from the discussion of Ethiopia in the Bible and in the writings of ancient Greek historians such as Diodorus and Pliny. Hopkins follows suit in this regard, conflating the Ethiopia of her contemporary moment with the ancient Nubian trading empires that were based in what is now modern-day Sudan. The result is a novel which succeeds at evoking a mythic African past to inspire its African-American readership, but at the expense of historical and geographic accuracy. The novel also serves as a companion piece to Hopkins's nonfiction writing being published at the time, much of which was devoted to recuperating the historical legacy of the African diaspora. In

---

[18] John Rieder, *Colonialism and the Emergence of Science Fiction* (Middletown, CT: Wesleyan University Press, 2008), p. 34. See also, again, Bould's "Revolutionary African-American SF."

[19] Deborah McDowell, "Introduction" in *Of One Blood* (New York, London, Toronto, and Sydney: Washington Square Press, 2004), p. xix.

particular, her pamphlet "A Primer of Facts ... " (1905) makes extensive reference to Ergamenes and the history of the Ethiopian people.[20]

Though he is better known for his activist work and sociological writing, W. E. B. Du Bois was quite a prolific author of fiction – much of it falling within the speculative genres. His best-known speculative work, "The Comet" (1920), concerns Jim, a black man, and Julia, a white woman, who find themselves the sole survivors in New York City after poison gas from a low-flying comet wipes out the city's population. Ironically, the citywide annihilation becomes something of a eucatastrophe for Jim, carrying the fringe benefit of wiping out the racist social structures that so narrowly circumscribed his life. Dining in a previously segregated but now abandoned restaurant, Jim muses that "yesterday, they would not have served me."[21] The disaster also opens other possibilities. As Jim and Julia spend more time together, both are forced to reconsider racial prejudices that have been deeply instilled in them by society and to consider the possibility of repopulating the Earth together. This development is thwarted by the revelation that the world outside the city has been unaffected by the comet; the return of white supremacy is seen at the end of the story when Jim is threatened with lynching for simply being in the presence of a white woman.

Du Bois' other major published work of speculative fiction is his second novel, *Dark Princess* (1928), a book which the author himself professed to be his "favorite" but was poorly received by many critics of the time. The novel concerns a young black medical student named Matthew Townes, expelled from medical school owing to segregationist policies which prevented him from taking an obstetrics class necessary to complete his degree. He decamps for Berlin, where a chance encounter with the Princess Kautilya of India leads him to join an international consortium of colonized nations aiming to strike back against Western imperialism. The two are separated by a number of contrivances, including Townes's incarceration after a failed bombing attempt on the Ku Klux Klan and a run for congress. They are reunited on a farm owned by Townes's mother in Virginia, where Kautilya gives birth to a son, the maharajah of her kingdom in India, amidst a "score of men clothed in white with shining swords" in a scene seemingly inspired by the Christian

---

[20] Pauline E. Hopkins, "A Primer of Facts Relating to the Early Greatness of the African Race and the Possibility of Restoration by its Descendants" in Ira Dworkin, ed., *The Major Nonfiction Works of Pauline E. Hopkins* (New Brunswick, NJ and London: Rutgers University Press, 2007 [orig. 1905]).

[21] W. E. B. Du Bois, "The Comet," in Sheree R. Thomas, ed., *Dark Matter: A Century of Speculative Fiction from the African Diaspora* (New York: Warner Books, 2000), p. 8.

nativity.[22] There is the implication here of a redemptive possibility in African Americans joining the larger world community, which is congruous with Du Bois' activist work on the Pan-African congress. However, the novel also represents a reproach to other black leaders with whom Du Bois disagreed. In particular, Lovie Gibson singles out the charismatic, but demagogically inclined activist Perigua as "a contrivance of the worst in both [Marcus] Garvey and [Walter] White."[23]

Perhaps the most prolific black speculative fiction writer of the early twentieth century was George Schuyler. In addition to his prodigious output of journalistic and political writing, Schuyler also published a substantial amount of popular fiction – much of which was serialized under various pseudonyms in the *Pittsburgh Courier*, a prominent black-run newspaper, as opposed to the traditional publication vehicles for SF. His most famous science fictional work, *Black No More* (1932), imagines a near future in which a white scientist named Junius Crookman invents a process which swiftly and affordably turns black people white, radically disrupting the racial dynamics of the United States virtually overnight. The novel mainly follows the picaresque adventures of Max Disher, a black con man, who undergoes the treatment and takes advantage of the ensuing racial chaos to rise to the top ranks of the Knights of Nordica – a fictionalized version of the Ku Klux Klan – ultimately undermining the organization from within. Schuyler also uses his fantastical conceit to satirize what he perceived as the civil rights movement's exploitation of everyday blacks.

Prominent figures such as W. E. B. Du Bois and Marcus Garvey are caricatured in the form of Dr. Shakespeare Agamemnon Beard and Santop Licorice, respectively; and of the National Social Equality League, a thinly disguised take on the National Association for the Advancement of Colored People (NAACP) and the National Urban League (NUL), Schuyler writes: "While the large staff of officials was eager to end all oppression and persecution of the Negro, they were never so happy and excited as when a Negro was barred from a theater or fried to a crisp."[24] Indeed, many of the passages of the novel seem an extension of Schuyler's journalistic muckraking; in discussing the famous scene in which two white men presumed to be

---

[22] W. E. B. Du Bois, *Dark Princess: A Romance* (Jackson: Banner Books, 1995), p. 310.
[23] Lovie N. Gibson, "W. E. B. Du Bois as a Propaganda Novelist," *Negro American Literature Forum* 10, 3 (1976), p. 77.
[24] George S. Schuyler, *Black No More: Being an Account of the Strange and Wonderful Workings of Science in the Land of the Free, AD 1933–1940* (Boston: Northeastern University Press, 1989), p. 80.

blacks who have undergone the Crookman process are lynched by an angry mob, Samuel Delany notes that "Schuyler simply used accounts of actual lynchings of black men at the time, with a few changes in wording."[25]

Schuyler's focus on racial matters became increasingly international throughout the 1930s, in the wake of his brief and dissatisfying association with Marcus Garvey's Back to Africa movement, as well as the Second Italo-Ethiopian War (1935–6) – a galvanizing event for the African diaspora that was initiated by fascist Italy's swift and brutal conquest of Hailee Selassie's Ethiopia. Schuyler said of the invasion: "It would be a major catastrophe for the darker peoples of the world … if Ethiopia should be defeated and subjugated by the Italians. This is the opinion of every intelligent colored person in the world today, and for once that view of the majority is correct."[26] This fascination with Africa is reflected in a series of tales about the continent serialized in the *Pittsburgh Courier* through the 1930s. Notable examples include "Golden Gods: A Story of Love" (December 1934 to February 1935), a "lost race" tale about an African-American woman who stumbles upon a map to a mysterious city, and "The Beast of Bradhurst Avenue" (March to May 1934), concerning the murder of an African princess in Harlem which leads to the discovery of a bizarre series of experiments by a German mad scientist attempting to transplant the brains of black women into dogs.

But his most significant work on the subject of Africa is the two Henry Belsidus stories, serialized in the *Courier* from 1936 to 1938 and reprinted as the single volume *Black Empire* in 1991. In the first story, "The Black Internationale" (November 1936 to July 1937), a young black journalist stumbles upon and is forcibly conscripted into a worldwide conspiracy led by the sinister but ingenious Dr. Henry Belsidus. The plan is to destabilize Western Europe and the United States in order to facilitate the liberation of Africa for all black people. Belsidus is aided in this conspiracy by his network of brilliant black engineers, chemists, pilots, and soldiers – essentially, Du Bois' Talented Tenth as radicalized insurgents. The serial ends with Belsidus having violently reclaimed Africa from European colonists and established a pan-African empire. He then declares himself an interim dictator, with the justification that "the Negro is not used to freedom" and that it is only until the new society "consolidates its power."[27]

[25] Delany, "Racism," p. 384.
[26] Quoted in "Introduction," *Ethiopian Stories*, ed. Robert A. Hill and R. Kent Rasmussen (Boston: Northeastern University Press, 1994), p. 1.
[27] George S. Schuyler, *Black Empire* (1936–38), ed. Robert A. Hill and R. Kent Rasmussen (Boston: Northeastern University Press, 1991), p. 141.

The sequel, "Black Empire" (October 1937 to April 1938), skips ahead a few months to show the thriving new society, rife with such technologies as hydroponic vegetable gardens and solar powered machinery, as well as radio and television stations far in advance of the communications technology available contemporaneously to the novel's writing. The society is threatened by the cessation of in-fighting between the European powers, who have joined forces to invade Africa and retake their colonies. This threat is vanquished by Belsidus' deployment of nefarious new weapons, including plague-carrying rats dropped on major European cities and solar-powered death rays. The tone of these stories is difficult to gauge. On one hand, there is a kind of gleeful *Schadenfreude* to the affair, which is unmistakable. However, there are troubling overtones of fascism, which contradict Schuyler's own disparagement of such movements in his unpublished essay "The Negro Flirts with Fascism." It is difficult to tell whether Schuyler's tale is one of caution or simply revenge.

Afrofuturism and Mainstream Literature

While many black authors subverted the conventions of genre fiction to serve their agendas, others incorporated Afrofuturist themes and elements into more mainstream literary works. In his introduction to the thirtieth anniversary edition of *Invisible Man*, Ralph Ellison remarked "a piece of science fiction was the last thing I set out to write."[28] Nonetheless, many critics, including Lisa Yaszek and Greg Tate, have identified it as one of the seminal works of Afrofuturism. Episodes commonly cited in support of this claim typically include the harrowing, surreal "Battle Royale" chapter, in which black men are pitted against each other in animalistic underground boxing matches, or Chapters 10 and 11, in which "the protagonist's identity is scraped away in the basement of the paint factory."[29] One might also include the protagonist's marijuana-fueled vision of a female ancestor, as well. Though Ellison's unnamed protagonist states upfront that he is neither "a spook like those who haunted Edgar Allan Poe; nor ... [a] Hollywood-movie ectoplasm,"[30] the novel relies heavily on the metaphor of "invisibility" to highlight the estranging effect of being black in early twentieth-century America.

[28] Ralph Ellison, "Introduction," in *Invisible Man* (New York: Vintage International, 1995 [1982]), p. xv.
[29] Quoted in Dery, "Black to the Future," p. 208.
[30] Ellison, *Invisible Man*, p. 3.

In her analysis of the text, Yaszek argues that "what Ellison's protagonist is looking for is the possibility of a black future that, in the 1930s of the novel, he cannot find. In each case his dreams of self-realization are thwarted because he is treated as little more than a blank slate upon which institutional authority projects its own vision of the future."[31] Indeed, much of the novel can be read as critiquing the various political activist movements available to blacks during the 1930s. This is most clearly reflected in the novel's portrayal of the Brotherhood, the leftist political organization with which the protagonist becomes affiliated in the second half of the novel. Despite the Brotherhood's seemingly anti-racist stance, the protagonist becomes dissatisfied with the organization's increasingly exploitative attitude towards himself and black people in general. In light of Ellison's own less than satisfactory experience with the Communist party in the 1930s and 40s, many scholars have interpreted the Brotherhood as the author's critique of that movement and its efforts to recruit African Americans in the early twentieth century.[32] Likewise, the figure of Ras the Exhorter serves as an unflattering analogue to Marcus Garvey and his militant black nationalism, here portrayed as leading to little more than madness and death in the apocalyptic race riot of the novel's climax. The protagonist eventually rejects both of these futurisms as unusable, opting instead for a period of "hibernation" in a New York tenement basement, surreptitiously siphoning power from the city grid and planning his next move.

Taking us into the era of the Civil Rights movement is William Melvin Kelley's remarkable first novel, *A Different Drummer* (1962). Like Ellison's *Invisible Man*, Kelley's novel skirts the line of the preternatural without crossing over into the overtly science fictional. Set in a fictional Gulf coast state in an alternative 1957, the novel concerns Tucker Caliban, a young black farmer and the great-grandson of a legendarily defiant African chief, who one day without warning decides to salt his fields, kill his livestock, and burn down his home before leaving the state for parts unknown. His actions precipitate the mass flight of the state's entire black population, who depart under similarly mysterious circumstances. Despite its fantastical premise, Kelley's tale owes a considerable debt to modernist authors such as William Faulkner. The story is told elliptically and non-linearly; the actions of the black characters are rendered only from the perspective of their baffled

---

[31] Lisa Yaszek, "An Afrofuturist Reading of Ralph Ellison's *Invisible Man*" (2005), *Rethinking History* 9,2–3, p. 304.
[32] See Barbara Foley, "Ralph Ellison as Proletarian Journalist," *Science & Society* 62, 4 (Winter 1998–9).

white neighbors and the events leading up to the exodus are gradually illuminated through flashbacks. A flashback to Tucker's ancestor, "the African," and his legendary flight through the south, stirring up insurrection in his wake, would seem to imply a metaphysical connection between those events and Tucker's contemporary act of rebellion. While drawing inspiration from earlier historical phenomena such as the Great Migration and the then-nascent Civil Rights movement, Kelley imagines something slightly more utopian in its possibilities. Like Schuyler's fiction, Kelley's novel expresses skepticism about the hierarchy of the Civil Rights movement, with one character remarking that "[the] leadership has followed in the footsteps of the negro overseers of plantation times. Each is out for himself and money is the thing."[33] Yet, as David Bradley points out in his foreword to the novel, "Tucker [does not] guide anyone. People follow him, but without his knowledge, certainly without his instigation."[34] Tucker's exodus is a model of anarchy without chaos, disobedience without disorder, and a civil rights movement without the somewhat elitist notion of the Talented Tenth to guide it.

Afrofuturism and the Science Fiction Community

The early days of genre SF were often not kind to black people in terms of representation. Indeed, Lisa Yaszek has noted that Stanley Weinbaum's "A Martian Odyssey" (1934), famous for being the first sympathetic portrayal of an extraterrestrial in science fiction, also establishes that being's intelligence by using Africans as a negative point of comparison.[35] However, moving into the 1940s and 50s, one begins to see a nascent awareness in the SF community with regard to racial matters. The famous "Carl Brandon" hoax perpetuated by Terry Carr and Pete Graham is a strong example. The incident involved two white members of fandom fabricating a fictional African-American reader and amateur SF writer who became an active participant of fan culture in the mid-1950s. His witty, incisive satires of works like Poul Anderson's *Brain Wave* helped to challenge many underlying assumptions about race that often went unnoticed in the genre. Prominent fan Walt Willis would say of "Brandon": "This handsome young soft-spoken Negro with his lazily brilliant wit and thoughtful mind was an asset to fandom ... Carl Brandon doesn't

---

[33] William M. Kelly, *A Different Drummer* (New York: Anchor Books, 1989 [1962]), p. 157.
[34] Ibid., p. xxv.
[35] Lisa Yaszek, "Afrofuturism, Science Fiction, and the History of the Future," *Socialism and Democracy* 20, 3 (2006), p. 45.

exist; very well, it is necessary to create him."[36] Brandon's legacy lives on the SF community today. In 1999, the Carl Brandon Society was formed at the feminist SF convention Wiscon, its self-proclaimed goal to "help build awareness of race and ethnicity in speculative literature and related fields."[37] In 2005, the society developed two awards, the Carl Brandon Parallax Award for "works of speculative fiction by a self-identified person of color" and the Kindred Award for "any work of speculation fiction dealing with themes of race and ethnicity; nominees may be of any racial group."[38]

Allen DeGraeff's anthology *Humans and Other Beings* (1961) collects several SF works that significantly grapple with issues of race, either directly or through the use of science fictional conceits such as aliens, published over the previous two decades. Particularly noteworthy stories in this collection include: George P. Eliot's "NRACP" (1949), a bleak tale in which a relocation program for African Americans secretly transports them to a facility where they are slaughtered for meat; and Ray Bradbury's pair of tales "Way up in the Air" (1952) and "The Other Foot" (1955). The former offers a vision of the future in which, fed up with the persistence of racial discrimination, African Americans pool their money together to build rockets to flee Earth in favor of Mars. In the second, the prosperous Martian colony established by African Americans is disrupted when white refugees from an Earth that has been ravaged by nuclear war show up requesting sanctuary.

Arthur C. Clarke's classic novel *Childhood's End* (1953) deploys an unusual narrative structure for science fictional works of the era, eschewing a singular protagonist in favor of a penumbra of perspectives from around the world. Yet, the novel's climax is focalized from the perspective of Jan Rodricks, an African-American scientist who manages to become the last surviving member of the human race after the event which transforms Earth's children. That a black man is authorized to give the last word on human civilization as we know it is significant progress. Theodore Sturgeon's *More Than Human* (1953), a novel which involves the merging of six superhuman individuals into the next stage of human evolution, includes a pair of teleporting African-American twins as part of the newly emerging gestalt organism. Sturgeon seems to imply that in order to truly evolve as a species, humanity will have to move past race-based discrimination. And Alfred Bester's magnum opus, *The Stars My Destination* (1956), tackles the legacy of racial discrimination

---

[36] Quoted in Andre M. Carrington, *Speculative Blackness: The Future of Race in Science Fiction* (Minneapolis and London: University of Minnesota Press, 2016), p. 61.

[37] http://carlbrandon.org/about/ (accessed September 17, 2017).

[38] http://carlbrandon.org/awards/ (accessed September 17, 2017).

subtly through the contentious relationship between its protagonist, Gully Foyle, and Robin Wednesbury, a black psychic whom he brutally rapes and later coerces into serving as his etiquette coach/accomplice. Robin's role as both Foyle's slave and his educator functions as an acknowledgment of the notions of the "White Man's Burden" used to justify slavery and colonialism, as well as a satirical refutation of them. Moreover, in light of Foyle's description as the "stereotype common man,"[39] it is telling that his redemption and the salvation of the human race both hinge upon Robin's forgiveness.

Filmic representations of Afrofuturist themes were relatively scarce in the early days of SF cinema, as the lack of people of color behind the camera often significantly impacted the types of stories that were told about them onscreen. Ranald MacDougall's *The World, the Flesh and the Devil* (1959) is a notable exception. A loose adaptation of M. P. Shiel's "last man" novel *The Purple Cloud* (1901), the film updates the story's setting to contemporary America as a means of exploring race relations. It concerns Ralph Burton (Harry Belafonte), an African-American mining engineer who finds himself one of the last people on Earth when nuclear war wipes out the majority of the human population while he is trapped in a mine. Burton travels to New York City looking for other survivors, where he encounters Sarah Crandall, a young white woman whom he befriends and with whom he shares a mutual attraction.[40]

Like Du Bois' "The Comet," MacDougall's film uses the conceit of a post-apocalyptic New York as a means of exploring the role of social reinforcement in the perpetuation of racism as well as the taboo of race mixing. However, here the chief obstacle to the pairing is Burton's own reluctance, one rooted in his awareness of how it might be received by other survivors should they encounter them. Burton's suspicions are sadly confirmed with the appearance of Ben, a third survivor who happens to be white; the ensuing rivalry for Sarah's affections ultimately escalates to an attempt on Burton's life. Tragedy is narrowly averted by Burton's refusal to participate in the

---

[39] Alfred Bester, *The Stars My Destination* (New York: Vintage Books, 1996 [1956]), p. 22.

[40] Though the element of a black protagonist is a later addition by the filmmakers, it is worth noting that the novel's author, born Matthew Phipps Shiell [*sic*] (1865–1947) in the West Indies is believed to be of Creole ancestry. His mother, Patricia Blake, was identified as "free" on her birth records, indicating that she was probably descended from slaves. Shiel himself seemed to self-identify as white and would later attribute his darker features as "a dash of Spanish blood." For further information about Shiel's racial background and how it might have impacted his fiction, see Amy J. Ransom, "Yellow Perils: M. P. Shiel, Race, and the Far East Menace," in Isiah Lavender III, ed., *Dis-Orienting Planets: Racial Representations of Asia in Science Fiction* (Jackson: University Press of Mississippi, 2017), p. 74.

violent conflict and Ben shamefully agreeing to cease hostilities in response; the film ends on a note of reconciliation, with the two of them joining hands with Sarah and walking off together, a caption stating "The Beginning" emerging in the final frames before the credits.

The film received mixed reviews upon its release, with many critics expressing disappointment at the ending's decidedly compromised statement on race relations, particularly the lack of consummation of the love story between Burton and Sarah. Belafonte, who also served as an uncredited producer on the film, expressed similar sentiments: "Not only do I agree, but I said as much to [producer] Sol Siegel, while we were making the film. And the protests of [co-stars] Inger Stevens and Mel Ferrer were even stronger than mine. They had a wonderful basis of a film there, but it didn't happen."[41] In spite of this compromise, the film was still poorly received by audiences in many parts of the American South because of the suggestion of racial mixing. Nonetheless, the film succeeds in providing a black SF protagonist who is shown not only to be the most technologically competent character in the story (Burton manages to restore power to the buildings where he and Sarah reside, as well as the radio equipment which allows them to contact other survivors), but the sole party responsible for preserving the knowledge of the previous civilization through his project of salvaging books from the New York public libraries. For a film produced before 1960, this is no small accomplishment.

Conclusion

Until fairly recently, the early Afrofuturist tradition has been marginalized for a variety of reasons. For much of literary history, black authors or those who sought to address black concerns were deliberately swept to the periphery of the literary world, especially in SF, where the myth that black people never read the genre inscrutably persisted. The speculative works produced by blacks often went unacknowledged as such because they appeared in publications that were not part of the mainstream SF community. Add to this mixture SF's own status as an often ghettoized genre, ignored for its contributions to literature, and one practically has a recipe for literary neglect. The texts listed here are not only compelling in their own right, but form an

---

[41] Quoted in Stéphanie Larrieux, "The World, the Flesh, and the Devil: The Politics of Race, Gender, and Power," *Quarterly Review of Film and Video* 27:2 (2010), p. 142. See also Arnold Shaw, *Belafonte: An Unauthorized Biography* (Philadelphia: Chilton Company, 1960).

interesting "shadow-canon" to the existing archive of race literature: one in which tragic mulattos can rescue themselves and racial passing can be affected en masse. The speculative in many of these cases helps to unpack the familiar conventions of mainstream literature in ways which reveal the tacit assumptions lying behind them or provide a welcome respite from the real.

7

Science Fiction, Modernism, and the Avant-Garde

PAUL MARCH-RUSSELL

As the art historian Rory O'Dea has argued, SF is "intimately connected to modernism" since they "both share a conceptual logic that is shaped by the scientific worldview of the Enlightenment and its instrumentalism in the ensuing Industrial Revolution."[1] Citing both Clement Greenberg and Joanna Russ, O'Dea continues by arguing that SF provided the postwar land artist Robert Smithson with "a main line to modernism's unconscious desires and secret logics,"[2] namely, the twin poles of immanence and transcendence. This chapter begins with contemporary responses to the Paris World Fair of 1900 and, in particular, to the Eiffel Tower, opened eleven years earlier. As Robert Hughes has argued, the Tower "seemed to gather all the meanings of modernity together,"[3] and became an object of fascination for writers such as Guillaume Apollinaire and Blaise Cendrars, as well as artists such as Robert Delaunay. Speculating later upon what these meanings might be, Roland Barthes argued that the Tower embodied a "mythic combat . . . between the base and summit,"[4] which is to say, between an immanent history experienced amongst the crowds at ground level and a transcendent mythology the further that the individual leaves behind the crowd and scales the heights of the Tower. In this chapter, I argue that this dialectic between immanence and transcendence is not only integral to modernism's relationship to modernity but also to its relationship to SF. To make that case, I shall examine the interaction between SF and the avant-garde – from literature to painting, architecture, and cinema – as an example of the science-fictionalization of modernist culture during the first decades of the twentieth century.

---

[1] Rory O'Dea, "The Other Side of Robert Smithson's Mirror-Travel," in Sarah J. Montross, ed., *Past Futures: Science Fiction, Space Travel, and Postwar Art of the Americas* (Cambridge, MA: MIT Press, 2015), p. 109.

[2] Ibid.

[3] Robert Hughes, *The Shock of the New*, 2nd edn. (London: Thames and Hudson, 1991), p. 9.

[4] Roland Barthes, *The Eiffel Tower and Other Mythologies*, trans. Richard Howard (Berkeley: University of California Press, 1997), p. 150.

Technoculture and the Paris World Fair

The *Exposition Universelle* held in Paris in 1900 confirmed that city's emerging status as the preeminent cultural capital of the modernist period.[5] In perhaps the most famous response to the *Exposition*, the American intellectual Henry Adams distinguished between what he termed "the Dynamo and the Virgin." Upon encountering "the great hall of dynamos," Adams experienced a spiritual awakening akin to "the force of the Virgin ... still felt at Lourdes."[6] However, although the machine's immense power inspired a sense of infinite wonder, it lacked the reproductive capabilities of the Virgin: "the greatest and most mysterious of all energies."[7] While Adams idolized the figure of the Virgin, he condemned the sterility of the machine, a sexlessness that he found elsewhere in American art, language, and education.[8] In place of sexual desire, there existed instead the gratification of mathematical precision as embodied by the dynamo.

Although Adams's technophobia is one of the more sophisticated accounts of the anti-machinist tendency that Adam Roberts associates with high modernism,[9] and its influence has been profound on such later writers as Thomas Pynchon, it nevertheless projects North American anxieties regarding what Leo Marx once termed "the technological sublime" on to what was otherwise a European and global event.[10] By contrast, the Mexican poet Amado Nervo, reporting on the *Exposition* for the newspaper *El Imparcial*, explicitly compared the Eiffel Tower to one of H. G. Wells's tripods from the recently published *The War of the Worlds* (1898): "Could this gigantic steel organism perhaps be the famous tripod where a Martian observes from his watchtower?"[11] Nervo, coming from a country economically and technologically deprived in part because of its more powerful Northern neighbor, described technology as "the poetry of human effort" and, in his 1917 poem "El gran viaje" ("The great journey"), dreamt: "Who will become, in a not too distant future, / the Christopher Columbus of some planet?"[12] Against

---

[5] See, for example, Roger Shattuck, *The Banquet Years: The Origins of the Avant-Garde in France, 1885 to World War I* (London: Jonathan Cape, 1969).

[6] Henry Adams, *The Education of Henry Adams* (New York: The Modern Library, 1931), pp. 380 and 383.

[7] Ibid., p. 384.

[8] Ibid., p. 385.

[9] Adam Roberts, *The History of Science Fiction* (Basingstoke: Palgrave Macmillan, 2006), pp. 158–63.

[10] Leo Marx, *The Machine in the Garden: Technology and the Pastoral Ideal in America*, 2nd edn. (New York: Oxford University Press, 2000), p. 195.

[11] Quoted in Miguel Ángel Fernández Delgado, "*Saudado* for Space, Utopia, and the Machine in Latin American Art," in Montross, ed., *Past Futures*, p. 55.

[12] Quoted in ibid., p. 51.

the backdrop of the Mexican Revolution, the technological utopianism of Nervo's writing would feed into later Latin American art movements, such as the Madí group based in Buenos Aires, and focused around the visionary artist Gyula Kosice who, in 1944, proclaimed: "Man will not end on Earth."[13]

A third point of view on the *Exposition* came from the Belgian poet, Emile Verhaeren, writing for the *Mercure de France* which, between 1898 and 1899, had published Wells's *The Time Machine* as well as Alfred Jarry's semi-serious response, "How to Build a Time Machine":

> When, on the eve of the fifteenth of April, Paris quivered from a frightening fury of work, when all construction sites on the Champ-de-Mars and the Invalides howled and the night seemed to be ablaze with fire, who could call himself a poet and not be swept away by these maelstroms of laboring, sweating, shouting and panting masses towards a new and profound art?[14]

Now largely forgotten, Verhaeren's poetry – in which he celebrated the late but rapid industrialization of Brussels – was widely translated, although only selectively in English, and in 1911 he was nominated for the Nobel Prize. In his most celebrated collections, *The Hallucinated Countryside* (1893) and *Tentacular Cities* (1895),[15] Verhaeren imported a Whitmanesque sense of onward and upward expansion in place of the voguish symbolism of French city-poets such as Charles Baudelaire, Jules Laforgue, and Stephane Mallarmé:

> And it's you, you cities, . . .
> Who have concentrated in yourselves enough humanity,
> Enough red force and new clarity,
> To ignite with fertile fever and rage
> The patient or violent brains of those
> Who discover the rule and hold
> the world within themselves.[16]

Although critics such as Vera Castiglione regard Verhaeren as a catalytic figure upon the development of Futurism (he was read and admired by F. T. Marinetti), his avant-garde moment was soon overtaken by modernists

---

[13] Quoted in ibid., p. 53. Kosice subsequently designed what he called "hydrospatial cities," effectively orbiting space colonies, an example of which he sent to Ray Bradbury in 1980.

[14] Quoted in Vera Castiglione, "A Futurist before Futurism: Emile Verhaeren and the Technological Epic," in Günter Berghaus, ed., *Futurism and the Technological Imagination* (Amsterdam: Rodopi, 2009), p. 110.

[15] In retrospect, it is tempting to read Verhaeren's use of the tentacular in light of China Miéville's claim that it represents the emblematic trope of the crisis of modernity at the turn of the twentieth century. See, in particular, Miéville, "M. R. James and the Quantum Vampire," in Robin Mackay, ed., *Collapse IV* (Falmouth: Urbanomic, 2008), p. 105.

[16] Quoted in Castiglione, "A Futurist before Futurism," p. 107.

who sought to describe the exhilaration of speed and travel at the level of form as well as content. Nonetheless, as a kind of anti-symbolist, Verhaeren remains significant: his many-tentacled cities are not to be read as a symbol for something else (a mood, atmosphere, or attitude) but at face value; the clunky literalism of Verhaeren's verse becomes paradoxically – like the language of pulp SF – a style in itself. This might also explain, in retrospect, Verhaeren's surprising popularity in Continental Europe. His poetry had a similar effect to novels such as Jules Verne's *Journey to the Center of the Earth* (1863) and *Twenty Thousand Leagues Under the Sea* (1870), which, with their exploration of vast time-scales, spatial distances, and futuristic modes of transport, not only inspired and communicated real-world science but also acclimatized their readers to new perceptions of space and time – a spatio-temporal experience also consolidated in such events as the *Exposition Universelle* and the beginnings of cinema.[17]

To that end, Verhaeren (like Marinetti after him) could be said to have taken literally the following claim from J.-K. Huysmans's *Against Nature* (1885): "Does there exist, anywhere on this earth, a being conceived in the joys of fornication and born in the throes of motherhood who is more dazzlingly, more outstandingly beautiful than the two locomotives recently put into service on the Northern Railway?" Although the erotic descriptions of the two engines as respectively "an adorable blonde with a shrill voice," "muscles of steel" and "steaming flanks," and "a strapping saturnine brunette given to uttering raucous, guttural cries,"[18] relay the sadomasochistic desires of Huysmans's anti-hero, the decadent aesthete Des Esseintes, they nevertheless prefigure Marinetti's fetishization of the motorcar as a "snorting beast" with "swollen breasts," "more beautiful than the *Victory of Samothrace*."[19] If Huysmans intended his novel to be a satire of aestheticism, that purpose was lost on Marinetti and Verhaeren, for whom, like so many readers, the novel was perceived as a decadent Bible. As with Verhaeren's use of the tentacular, Huysmans's ironic salute to techno-

---

[17] On the science-fictional qualities of world fairs, see Roger Luckhurst, "Laboratories for Global Space-Time: Science-Fictionality and the World's Fairs, 1851–1939," *Science Fiction Studies* 39.3 (2012), pp. 385–400. On the relationship between cinema and early SF, see Ian Christie, *The Last Machine: Cinema and the Birth of the Modern World* (London: BBC Books, 1994), pp. 27–33.

[18] J.-K. Huysmans, *Against Nature*, trans. Robert Baldick (London: Penguin, 2003), p. 23.

[19] F. T. Marinetti, "The Founding and Manifesto of Futurism" (1909), in Lawrence Rainey et al., eds. *Futurism* (New Haven: Yale University Press, 2009), pp. 49 and 51. See also "To My Pegasus" (1908), in Marinetti, *Selected Poems and Related Prose*, ed. Luce Marinetti, trans. Elizabeth R. Napier and Barbara R. Studholme (New Haven: Yale University Press, 2002), pp. 38–9, an earlier version of which Marinetti read to Jarry in 1903.

fetishism was taken literally and turned into a founding principle by avant-gardists such as Marinetti.

The Science Fictionality of the Avant-Garde

No better place for this literalism can be found than in Marinetti's novel, *Mafarka the Futurist* (1909), which, like all of his early works, was first published in French. Written in the same year as the Italian Futurist movement was officially launched, Marinetti's novel dramatizes his theoretical and polemical claims. Set like Raymond Roussel's *Impressions of Africa* (1910) in an imaginary African state,[20] *Mafarka the Futurist* is a violent and deeply misogynistic text that seeks to hybridize technological modernity with the spirit of primitivism, then at its height as an artistic movement following such works as Pablo Picasso's *Les Demoiselles d' Avignon* (1907). Such hybridization, as Robert Young suggests, is implicated in the illicit colonial anxieties and desires surrounding miscegenation;[21] it is no coincidence that, as a child, Marinetti was drawn erotically to his Sudanese nurse. Unlike Roussel, who culled whatever knowledge of Africa he had from travel books, Marinetti was born in Egypt and liked to consider himself as North African. To that end, the African warlord Mafarka, resplendent in his violent and sexual exploits, can be read as an idealized version of Marinetti himself.

Mafarka's dream, though, is for his "sun-warmed soul" to "give birth to a son, who flies on tuneful wings!"[22] By an act of pure will, he imagines into being Gazourmah, "twenty cubits tall" with "mighty arms" that "can power wings more vast than all the tents of the Bedouin and all the roofs of your huts" (145). His purpose is to demonstrate to his people that they too can "give birth without resorting to the woman's vulva," "shape everything around us and endlessly renew the face of the earth," and extinguish romantic love for "the sublime voluptuousness of Heroism" (146). The misogyny of Mafarka's act, echoed in the Futurist Manifesto and ridiculed by Marinetti's former lover, the poet Mina Loy, as "notifying women's wombs / of Man's immediate agamogenesis,"[23] speaks to a latent dream of male reproduction to

[20] On Roussel's novel as a work of science fiction, see Paul March-Russell, *Modernism and Science Fiction* (Basingstoke: Palgrave Macmillan, 2015), pp. 42–3.

[21] Robert J. C. Young, *Colonial Desire: Hybridity in Theory, Culture and Race* (London: Routledge, 1995), esp. pp. 6–19.

[22] Marinetti, *Mafarka the Futurist*, trans. Carol Diethe and Steve Cox (London: Middlesex University Press, 1998), p. 123. Subsequent citations are given in the text.

[23] Mina Loy, "Lions' Jaws," in Roger L. Conover, ed., *The Lost Lunar Baedeker* (Manchester: Carcanet, 1997), p. 47.

be found elsewhere in early SF, from Mary Shelley's *Frankenstein* (1818) to Villiers de l'Isle-Adam's *Tomorrow's Eve* (1886), Wells's *The Island of Doctor Moreau* (1896), and Maurice Renard's *Doctor Lerne* (1909), the prevalence of which indicates not only the patriarchal structures that informed the rise of both modernism and SF but also the extent to which the hopes and aspirations of technoculture were informed by such fantasies. These desires are given hyperbolic manifestation in Marinetti's novel when, after Mafarka has listed all the advantages of how he has designed the architecture of his son's body, "Gazourmah's leathery, copper-coloured penis stiffen[s] like a sword" (189), Mafarka hungrily kisses him to "Drain myself into you" (196) only to be killed in suitably Oedipal fashion, and Gazourmah launches himself destructively into the air:

> The firmament? I am its master! My great wings can beat a hundred times for each of my breaths. My breathing makes forests lean over, because my lungs are huge and adapted to the unbreathable atmospheres that I shall have to pass through when I dive into the sidelong red glance of Mars! But first I must conquer the scarlet Emperor's capital! (205)

The imperialistic and phallocentric desires, more ambiguously handled in modernist SF novels such as Blaise Cendrars's *Moravagine* (1926) and Alfred Jarry's *The Supermale* (1902),[24] nevertheless make manifest the tendencies toward male supremacy and the objectification of the female or colonial Other to be found elsewhere in the modernist avant-garde and in early pulp SF (as exemplified by the John Carter novels of Edgar Rice Burroughs). The all-too obviously phallic symbol of the rocket, the INTEGRAL from Yevgeny Zamyatin's *We* (1921), built with the purpose of "integrat[ing] the indefinite equation of the universe,"[25] ironically embodies this principle.

During his time in Paris in the early 1900s, Marinetti published in magazines such as *La Plume* and *Mercure de France*, both of which also printed the criticism and fiction of Jarry, in particular, excerpts from his time-traveling, multi-dimensional novel, *Exploits & Opinions of Dr. Faustroll, Pataphysician* (1911). Jarry formed part of a network of Dadaists and proto-surrealists that also included Guillaume Apollinaire, Marcel Duchamp, Francis Picabia, and Raymond Roussel. The last, deeply indebted to Verne, influenced the others through his bizarre descriptions of impossible machines that hinted at secret

---

[24] On the former, see March-Russell, *Modernism and Science Fiction*, pp. 139–41; on the latter, see March-Russell, "Atrocious Objects: The Colonial Imaginary in Verne, Roussel, Jarry and Ballard," in Rick McGrath, ed., *Deep Ends 3* (Toronto: Terminal Press, 2016), pp. 196–203.
[25] Yevgeny Zamyatin, *We*, trans. Clarence Brown (London: Penguin, 1988), p. 3.

desires, a libidinal economy reflected also in the punning self-referentiality and self-sufficiency of his texts.[26] As Duchamp later claimed, "It was fundamentally Roussel who was responsible" for his masterpiece, *The Large Glass (The Bride Stripped by Her Bachelors, Even)* (1915–23), since "he produced something that I had never seen … The madness of the unexpected."[27] As Linda Dalrymple Henderson has described, the scientific and quasi-scientific literature that both Jarry and Roussel were steeped in resurfaces in the conceptual art of Duchamp,[28] but their effect upon him was more galvanic than originary. His earlier paintings such as *Nude Descending a Staircase (No. 2)* and *Bride* (both 1912) – with their evocations of biomechanical forms, chronophotography, X-Rays, and what the British physicist Sir William Crookes termed "radiant matter" – locate Duchamp's art within the intersection between the avant-garde and contemporary science. Duchamp's subsequent claim that *Bride* enabled him to see "the fourth dimension in his work" for the first time links his art to a whole gamut of hyperspatial fictions and theories in literature, philosophy, mathematics, and the visual arts at the turn of the century.[29] These texts included not only the work of Jarry and Wells but also SF stories by such modernist writers as Wells's close friends Joseph Conrad and Ford Madox Ford (*The Inheritors* [1901]), as well as May Sinclair ("The Finding of the Absolute" [1923]) and Allen Upward (*The Discovery of the Dead* [1910]).[30] Duchamp's migration to New York City in 1915, alongside fellow writers and artists such as Loy and Picabia, helped to disseminate these ideas within the American avant-garde scene.[31]

While the biomechanical artworks of Duchamp and Picabia tend to focus on the representation of sexual drives from a male point of view, Loy's cyborg poetry signifies a more emancipatory potential. Although the eponymous "human cylinders" of her 1917 poem indulge in sexual gratification as "the lucid rush-together of automatons," their objectification as machines

---

[26] For further details, see Mark Ford, *Raymond Roussel and the Republic of Dreams* (Cornell: Cornell University Press, 2000).

[27] Quoted in Linda Dalrymple Henderson, *Duchamp in Context: Science and Technology in the Large Glass and Related Works* (Princeton: Princeton University Press, 1998), pp. 51–2.

[28] Ibid., pp. 40–57.

[29] Quoted in ibid., p. 13. See also Mark Blacklock, *The Emergence of the Fourth Dimension: Higher Spatial Thinking in the Fin de Siècle* (Oxford: Oxford University Press, 2018) and Henderson, *The Fourth Dimension and Non-Euclidean Geometry in Modern Art* (Princeton: Princeton University Press, 1983).

[30] See March-Russell, *Modernism and Science Fiction*, pp. 31–40.

[31] For further details, see Dickran Tashjian, *Skyscraper Primitives: Dada and the American Avant-Garde, 1910–1925* (Middletown, CT: Wesleyan University Press, 1975).

allows Loy to strip away the sentimental veil of romantic love and to view their behavior starkly and coldly. In so doing, she nonetheless hints at the intimacy of "one opulent wellbeing" hidden by such automatism. The participants lean "brow to brow ... Over the abyss of the potential,"[32] evoking a problem in the theory and understanding of another's consciousness that underlines not only Adolfo Bioy Casares's modernist dystopia, *The Invention of Morel* (1940), but also the later SF of Philip K. Dick, most obviously *Do Androids Dream of Electric Sheep?* (1968).

Loy's use of the cyborg both prefigures the science-fictional theories of feminist thinkers such as Shulamith Firestone and Donna Haraway and sets her apart from her male contemporaries. For them, the merger of human and machine resulted in either the techno-fetishism of Marinetti or the alienated, abstracted figures that occur in the early work of Wyndham Lewis, for example, in his play *Enemy of the Stars* (1914) or the city painting, *The Crowd* (1915). Karel Čapek's popularization of the word "robot," meaning a serf or slave, following the international success of his Expressionist play, *R.U.R.* (1920), encapsulated the sense of alienation experienced by Anglo-American audiences living under the conditions of technological modernity. The word's fast acceptance into the critical vocabulary of modernists as politically diverse as Lewis and John Dos Passos indicates its usage as a kind of shorthand for the dehumanizing effects of urbanization and bureaucratization from which movements such as modernism had emerged. Its adoption signifies the extent to which modernist discourse also transected the science-fictional to represent the rapid transformations within urban society.

For Lewis, in particular, the unthinking automatism represented by the robot encapsulated the process that he termed "the piecemealing of the personality": the delusional and farcical belief that humans retain individual agency when, on the contrary, under the technological and bureaucratic forces of modernity, they are merely automata performing the part of being "human." Lewis's blurring of man and machine clearly invokes an uncanny, proto-science fictional lineage of mechanical dolls in literature that include Olympia in E. T. A. Hoffmann's "The Sandman" (1817), the gynoid Hadaly in Villiers's *Tomorrow's Eve*, and the murderous chess-player in Ambrose Bierce's "Moxon's Master" (1899). However, what distinguishes Lewis's critique from these fantastical doppelgangers is his conception of a fully networked society: "By his education he has been made into an ingeniously

---

[32] Loy, "Lions' Jaws," p. 40.

free-looking, easy-moving, "civilized," gentlemanly Robot. At a word . . . at the pressing of a button, all these hallucinated automata, with their technician-trained minds and bodies, can be released against each other."[33] Such a vision not only contrasts with Marinetti's fetishized description of the power station worker ("These men have finally won the joy of living behind walls of iron and glass"),[34] it also evokes E. M. Forster's networked dystopia in "The Machine Stops" (1909) as well as prefiguring the genetically and socially conditioned citizens of Aldous Huxley's *Brave New World* (1932), and even the two-minute hate in George Orwell's *Nineteen Eighty-Four* (1949) or the Nova Police in William Burroughs's *The Ticket That Exploded* (1962). Indeed, it is only the grotesquerie of Burroughs's fiction that can match Lewis's unrepentant vision: the final reconciliation between Vashti and Kuno in Forster's fable, the instinctual vitality of Huxley's Savage, and the doomed love affair between Orwell's Winston and Julia would, for Lewis, be unpardonable concessions to an illusory romanticism.

Yet, despite the hellish premonition of Lewis's automated society, a more optimistic version of a technological social network was being proposed in pre-Soviet Russia. As McKenzie Wark has recently noted, Alexander Bogdanov, one of the key members of the Bolshevik Party while its leadership was in exile after the failed revolution of 1905, fell out with Lenin because dialectical materialism failed to "criticize the dialectic in the light of labor and scientific experience . . . labor's experience in and against nature."[35] Instead, influenced on the one hand by Darwinist ideas of evolution and adaptation (popularized further by the early Russian translations of Wells's novels), and on the other hand, by Ernst Mach's relativistic approach to the scientific study of reality, Bogdanov proposed new ways of "organizing knowledge" (*tektology*) and practicing culture (*proletkult*) seen from the point of view of labor.[36] These ideas Bogdanov initially sketched out in his utopian novel, *Red Mars* (1908).

Upon arriving on the planet, Bogdanov's narrator is taken on a guided tour by the Martian engineer, Menni. In particular, he is shown the factories where the men work harmoniously with the machines: "To an outsider the threads connecting the delicate brains of the men with the indestructible organs of the machines were subtle and invisible."[37] This

[33] Wyndham Lewis, *The Art of Being Ruled* (London: Chatto and Windus, 1926), pp. 111–12.
[34] Marinetti, "Selections from *Le Futurisme*" (1911), in Rainey *et al.*, eds., *Futurism*, p. 101.
[35] McKenzie Wark, *Molecular Red: Theory for the Anthropocene* (London: Verso, 2015), p. 24.
[36] Ibid., p. 13.
[37] Alexander Bogdanov, *Red Star*, trans. Charles Rougle (Bloomington: Indiana University Press, 1984), p. 65. Subsequent citations are given in the text.

harmony arises from the replacement of paid labor with voluntary service: "work is a natural need for the mature member of our society, and all overt or disguised compulsion is quite superfluous" (66). Martian industry has been organized around the distribution, rather than the division, of labor so that each worker is free to change occupation as and when he chooses: "The central statistical apparatus takes constant note of this, transmitting the data hourly to all branches of industry" (66). Extrapolating from the real-world technology of the telephone exchange, Bogdanov imagines a global communication network forty years before the publication of Norbert Weiner's *Cybernetics* (1948): "One of these apparatuses connected Menni's house with the Communications Center, which was in turn joined to all the cities of the planet ... Several finely gridded screens showed a reduced image of illuminated rooms full of large metal machines and glass equipment attended by hundreds of workers" (62). Consequently, the Martians are able to monitor the changing work patterns and to evenly distribute the labor according to need via a constant updating of statistical information. Whereas Zamyatin's *We* will see the dystopian potential in this system via the imposition of the Table of Hours, a regulated and centralized clock-time and a Taylorist code of efficiency, Bogdanov's utopia has not been imposed from above but has emerged from below, according to the needs of labor and its relationship to the external environment. For Wark then, "the Bogdanovian future" is one where "workers cease to be workers, organizers of their particular labor alone, but become co-creators of the whole of social organization."[38] One effect of this social change is to dissolve the division of labor between writers and engineers, a distinction already being toyed with by American modernists such as Dos Passos, Ernest Hemingway, Ezra Pound, and William Carlos Williams.[39] However, in contradistinction to their vision of the writer-as-technician, let alone Bogdanov's dream of a workforce liberated through scientific management, the engineering paradigm that would catch on within the SF pulps was wholly indebted to the instrumentalism of the modernist architectural landscape.[40]

[38] Wark, *Molecular Red*, p. 28.
[39] See, for example, Cecelia Tichi, *Shifting Gears: Technology, Literature, Culture in Modernist America* (Chapel Hill: University of North Carolina Press, 1987), esp. chapters 4 and 5.
[40] For a discussion of how the language of the pulps, albeit in this case crime fiction, complemented the streamlining of modern urban design, see William Marling, *The American Roman Noir: Hammett, Cain, and Chandler* (Athens, OH: University of Georgia Press, 1995), pp. 39–52 and 72–88.

The Modernist/SF City

In his poem, "Brooklyn Bridge" (1925), Bogdanov's fellow Russian Vladimir Mayakovsky imagines the attempt of a future geologist to decode the remains of American civilization from its ruined infrastructure:

> By the leads
>   of electrical strands –
> I know –
>   it's the era
>   following steam –
> it's when
>   people
>   already
>   yelled over radio,
> it's when
>   people
>   already
>   flew by plane.[41]

Much as Wells does with his Time Traveler, Mayakovsky projects his poetic alter ego forwards in time to a post-capitalist moment (perhaps also when Communism is triumphant), in order to pick through the ruins of Western modernity. As in American modernist texts, such as Dos Passos's *Manhattan Transfer* (1925) and Hart Crane's *The Bridge* (1930), Mayakovsky imbues the architectural icon of the Brooklyn Bridge with a mythic quality, one though that is then lapped and ruined by the ephemeral passage of history. Although the works of Crane and Dos Passos often teeter on the fantastical, most notably in Crane's poem, when Poe's ghost appears in the New York subway, Mayakovsky moves into the science-fictional to explore the relationship between myth, history and capital in a narrative pattern characteristic of SF.[42]

This tension underwrites the often science-fictional dreams of modernist architecture and urban design. The German architect and SF writer, Paul Scheerbart, sought to do away with "the present 'brick' culture of the city,"[43] the consequence of the railways and the Industrial Revolution, and to introduce "a glass culture": "the new glass environment will completely transform mankind" (74). Owing to the special properties of glass and the additional

---

[41] Vladimir Mayakovsky, *My Discovery of America*, trans. Neil Cornwell (London: Hesperus, 2005), pp. 126–7.

[42] See, especially, Tom Shippey, "The Fall of America in Science Fiction," in Tom Shippey, ed., *Fictional Space* (Oxford: Basil Blackwell, 1991), pp. 104–32.

[43] Paul Scheerbart, *Glass Architecture*, ed. Dennis Sharp (New York: Praeger, 1972), p. 71. Subsequent citations are given in the text.

effects of lighting and colors, Scheerbart imagines a bejeweled Earth: "We should then have a paradise on earth, and no need to watch in longing expectation for the paradise in heaven" (46). Instead, the inhabitants of Venus and Mars "will stare in wonder and no longer recognize the surface of the earth" (66). Scheerbart applies the effects of glass, light, and color to other kinds of fortification – domes and towers – and to industrial machinery: boats, cars, planes, trains, and factories. He even speculates, thanks to the imperviousness of reinforced concrete, "floating architecture": "The buildings can obviously be juxtaposed or moved apart in ever changing patterns, so that every floating town could look different each day" (59). Glass confers not only a sense of timelessness but also lightness: an ethereal quality that, as Scheerbart suggests, could with the application of color create "ghostly" illuminations (57), a somber and spectralized modernity.

Scheerbart's ideas inspired Bruno Taut's "Glass House" displayed at the Cologne Werkbund Exhibition in 1914 (around which were inscribed the words of Scheerbart: "Colored glass destroys all hatred at last"). Reyner Banham speculates that Scheerbart and Taut may have inspired the earlier incarnations of the Bauhaus School, since Walter Gropius was in close contact with Taut and the journal, *Der Sturm*, which had originally published Scheerbart's theories; two designs by Mies van der Rohe for glass skyscrapers in 1919 and 1921 suggest some affinity with Scheerbart.[44] On the other hand, the therapeutic uses of colored glass as a building material is prominently used in Bogdanov's *Red Mars*, while the notion of a domed city occurs in two of Wells's lesser-known but, at the time, widely read dystopias, "A Story of the Days to Come" (1897) and *When the Sleeper Wakes* (1899). The latter's architectural look, modeled upon the New York skyline, with single-seater aircraft flitting between the buildings, is clearly replicated in Fritz Lang's *Metropolis* (1927).

Furthermore, "reinforced concrete, iron, glass, textual fibers" reoccur as the building materials in Antonio Sant'Elia's manifesto of Futurist architecture. However, whereas Scheerbart seeks harmony, Sant'Elia reproduces the Futurist mantra of constant dynamism: "oblique and elliptical lines are dynamic"; "only from the use and disposition of raw, naked, or violently colored materials can the decorative value of Futurist architecture be derived"; "our houses will last less time than we do. Every generation will have to make its own city anew."[45] This perpetual revolution, by which the energies of Futurism will be renewed, not only complements the sense that

---

[44] Reyner Banham, *Theory and Design in the First Machine Age*, 2nd edn. (Oxford: Architectural Press, 1962), p. 267.

[45] Antonio Sant'Elia, "Futurist Architecture" (1914), in Rainey *et al.*, eds. *Futurism*, p. 201.

the modern city is in a constant state of flux (pictorially represented by such works as Umberto Boccioni's *The City Rises* [1910] and *The Street Enters the House* [1911]) but is underlined with the death-drive that Tim Armstrong regards as a constituent element of Futurist aesthetics: "a sense of the end of the human, and of a present moment that is freed from the drag of the past."[46] Such sentiments would later resurface within New Wave SF, most notably J. G. Ballard's *Crash* (1973), but for now Futurism's architectural influence would be chiefly felt on the Russian Suprematist movement led by Kasimir Malevich.

Like Futurism, Suprematism sought to negate the past and to celebrate man's multiple technological extensions. In that respect, Malevich's "suprematist manifesto" (1924) is little different from the Cubo-Futurist broadside, "A Slap in the Face of Public Taste" (1917), but like Velimir Khlebnikov's manifesto, "Trumpet of the Martians" (1916), it rapidly becomes more science fictional:

> The new dwellings of man lie in space. The Earth is becoming for him an intermediate stage ... The new man's provisional dwellings both in space and on Earth must be adapted to the aeroplane. A house built in this way will still be habitable tomorrow. Hence we Suprematists propose the objectless planets as a basis for the common creation of our existence.[47]

Inspired as much by Russian cosmism as the revolutionary promise of new technology, Suprematist art and architectural design constantly seek to depart the gravitational pull of both the Earth and the *ancien regime*. Malevich, for instance, divided his designs between what he called "architectons," plaster models of towers and tall buildings with cuboid and circular shapes, and "planits," sketches of futuristic houses that seem barely tied to the Earth. Christine Lodder suggests that they could be compared to satellites and quotes Malevich accordingly:

> The Earth and the Moon – perhaps a new Suprematist satellite can be built between them, equipped with all the elements, which will move in orbit, creating its own new path ... Suprematist forms, as an abstraction, have achieved utilitarian perfection. They are no longer in contact with the Earth and may be examined and studied like any planet or entire system.[48]

---

[46] Tim Armstrong, "Technology: 'Multiplied Man,'" in David Bradshaw, ed., *A Concise Companion to Modernism* (Oxford: Blackwell, 2003), p. 161.

[47] Kasimir Malevich, "Suprematist Manifesto Unovis (excerpt)," in Ulrich Conrads, ed., *Programs and Manifestos on 20th Century Architecture* (Cambridge, MA: MIT Press, 1971), pp. 87–8.

[48] Quoted in Christine Lodder, "Living in Space: Kazimir Malevich's Suprematist Architecture and the Philosophy of Nikolai Fedorov," in Charlotte Douglas and Christine Lodder, eds., *Rethinking Malevich* (London: Pindar Press, 2007), p. 197.

To that end, Suprematism as both theory and practice can be read as the systematization of earlier proposals along these lines: Anton Lavinsky's 1923 plan for a city on springs or Georgy Krutikov's 1928 thesis for a "Flying City," both of which had more in common with the SF of pioneering rocket scientist Konstantin Tsiolkovsky than they did with the goals of the First Five-Year Plan. The most significant example, though, of Suprematist intervention into popular Russian culture was Alexandra Exter's costume designs for the Martian populace in Yakov Protazanov's film version of *Aelita* (1924), as well as the set designs of Exter's former pupil, Isaak Rabinovich. Not only does the model of the Martian city suggest some affinity with one of Malevich's architectons, the dehumanized appearance of the soldiers and workers juxtaposed with the elegant yet angular costumes of the aristocracy and their servants strikingly enforces their characterization and rigid social position.[49]

Le Corbusier, who visited the architectural school where Krutikov wrote his thesis, can be seen as encapsulating many of these science-fictional tendencies; the development of the so-called "international style" is its nadir. His manifesto, *Toward a New Architecture* (1923), begins with a celebration of American engineers; the adoration bestowed upon the design of factories and grain silos echoes (but also caricatures) the work of American artists such as Charles Demeuth and Charles Sheeler, who were attempting to articulate a distinctive cultural idiom from the industrial landscape. The engineering paradigm permits Le Corbusier to propose the importance of geometry, grids, and straight lines in urban design, as well as the need for a concerted plan imposed from above by the technocratic elite, an obsession with mathematical logic and hierarchical thinking already critiqued in Zamyatin's *We*. Having regulated city planning, Le Corbusier supplants the inchoate bustle of the crowd with the streamlined energy of the automobile and the aeroplane, the two recurring emblems of technological modernity from the Futurists onwards, denoting speed, transcendence, and personal freedom. (In his subsequent writings, Le Corbusier will include private landing strips at the top of tall buildings, again evoking the iconography of Lang's *Metropolis*.) At the same time, Le Corbusier sees the mass production of housing as solving the alleged problems of communal life, including that of the proletariat. While on the one hand Le Corbusier regards the egalitarianism of rationally organized, collective households as removing the social

---

[49] For further discussion, see Christie, "Down to Earth: *Aelita* Relocated," in Richard Taylor and Ian Christie, eds., *Inside the Film Factory* (London: Routledge, 1991), pp. 80–102.

distinctions between the proletariat and the bourgeoisie (not unlike the numbered citizens of Zamyatin's One State), on the other hand, he believes in a planned, graduated hierarchy between the social and economic classes, again, not unlike the predetermined hierarchy of Huxley's *Brave New World*. In *The Radiant City* (1933), Le Corbusier appropriates some aspects of Ebenezer Howard's turn-of-the-century plans for "Garden Cities," such as the incorporation of tree-lined avenues, so as to ameliorate the harshness of strict geometry. Similarly, this use of rationally organized nature as part of a technocratic urban design resurfaces in the look of W. C. Menzies's film *Things to Come* (1936).[50]

Le Corbusier's elevation of the architect-as-engineer not only complements the writer-as-technician but also resembles both the Wellsian notion of the technocratic "samurai" and the libertarian heroes of Ayn Rand's right-wing fantasies. The premature utopianism – that is to say, the implicit dystopianism – of his ideas was indicated by Wells when he complained that the design of *Things to Come* "could never get beyond contemporary modernism" into a radically alternative vision of the future.[51] Just as Le Corbusier embodies so much of the science-fictional tendencies of the avant-garde, so too can his theories be inverted to reveal their latent dystopianism. New Wave texts, such as Thomas M. Disch's *334* (1972) and tech-noir films, most notably *Blade Runner* (1982), have gained considerable mileage from such an inversion.[52] Curiously then, despite the sometimes explicitly science-fictional content of the popular modernism of the 1939 New York World's Fair (thereby squaring a circle inaugurated by the 1900 *Exposition Universelle*),[53] this inversion – rather than its often ecstatic progressivism – is the avant-garde's most conspicuous legacy within contemporary SF.

---

[50] On the modernist influences in *Things to Come*, see Christopher Frayling, *Things to Come* (London: BFI Publishing, 1995).

[51] Quoted in Keith Williams, *H. G. Wells, Modernity and the Movies* (Liverpool: Liverpool University Press, 2007), p. 120.

[52] See also Janet Staiger, "Future Noir: Contemporary Representations of Visionary Cities," in Annette Kuhn, ed., *Alien Zone II* (London: Verso, 1999), pp. 97–122.

[53] On the 1939 World's Fair, see Andrew Ross, *Strange Weather: Culture, Science and Technology in the Age of Limits* (London: Verso, 1991), pp. 101–36.

8

The Gernsback Years: Science Fiction and the Pulps in the 1920s and 1930s

BROOKS LANDON

The feature novellette in the October 1938 *Astounding Stories* – the leading pulp SF magazine of the day, edited by the soon-to-be preeminent editor of SF's "Golden Age," John W. Campbell – was "Hunger Death," written by a promising writer who would himself go on to SF prominence, Clifford D. Simak. *Astounding* was one of several American pulp magazines in the 1930s dedicated exclusively to publishing SF. Those specialized SF magazines were part of a much larger pulp industry, featuring dozens of different magazines, direct descendants of nineteenth-century dime novels, publishing fiction on a wide range of popular topics such as westerns, detective stories, and true romance. Distinguished by their cheap price (made possible by cheap, coarse wood pulp paper with usually untrimmed edges to the pages), and usually a seven-by-ten-inch size, the pulps generally featured simple action narratives. They varied in length, but usually ranged between 144 and 200 pages, containing serialized novels, single issue novelettes, and short stories, with issues usually costing between fifteen and twenty-five cents. Most – though not all – pulp narratives featured rudimentary characterization and simplistic plots that valued action over ideas. Frank Munsey is generally credited with initiating the pulp-fiction era when he made *Argosy* an all-fiction magazine in 1896, and the pulps remained a staple of popular literature well into the late 1940s.

"Hunger Death" opens with a familiar figure, Old Doc Trowbridge, an elderly drunk small town doctor – only this small town, New Chicago, is on Venus, and its inhabitants are Iowa farmers, lured to the planet by lying land agents who falsely promised them that the soil and climate on Venus would allow them to raise lucrative crops no longer possible in the worn-out soil of Earth. Instead, their traditional crops of corn have been wiped out by too much rain and displaced by an invasive plant called "polka-dot weed." These weeds apparently originated from 5,000-year-old seeds brought to Venus from Mars by a somewhat crackpot botanist, disgraced for his wild theories and now dead, who believed the seeds were from plants developed by a now long disappeared race of tyranical Martian scientists, the Genziks, ostensibly overthrown and killed by other Martians. The Genziks, one lost race, were possibly originally inhabitants of Earth's Atlantis, another lost race, and had used their knowledge of science to enslave other Martian races.

Shift to the offices of the Earth newspaper, *The Evening Rocket*, where a familiar crusty-editor-type is bribing an equally familiar cynical-ace-reporter-type to go to New Chicago to try to discover why its inhabitants were apparently immune to a mysterious deadly pandemic sweeping Earth and other planets – the "Hunger Disease," which so speeded up human metabolism to make victims insatiably hungry for the week or so in which they dramatically age and then die. Once on Venus, the reporter points the old doctor to the unlikely fact that the hated polka-dot weeds, eaten by locals as a cheap green, prevent and cure the Hunger Disease. Then the greedy land agents of the unscrupulous Venus Land Company, who had lured the Iowa farmers to Venus, try to reclaim the land on which the polka-dot weeds grow, figuring on unimaginable profit for holding a monopoly on a miracle cure. Back on Earth, the crusty editor, using his investigative knowledge of political misdeeds, quasi-blackmails the Chief Justice of the Interplanetary Court into issuing an injunction which would prevent the Venus Land Company from seizing the Iowa farmers' land. Those Midwestern-nice farmers then declare they only want a fair price for the now invaluable polka-dot weeds. Meanwhile, it turns out that there *are* survivors of the ancient Genzik Dynasty, who have hidden in the Martian desert for thousands of years and who have now engineered and spread the Hunger Disease as part of their plan to reassume power on Mars and subjugate Earth and Venus. These survivors send an armed rocket to New Chicago, determined to kill the inhabitants of the town and eradicate all polka-dot weeds to insure the deadly efficacy of the Hunger Disease. *Another* familiar stock character, a former skilled rocket pilot now turned formidable town marshal, Angus MacDonald, first helps run off the land agents, then gives his life to save the farmers, avenging the death of his son at the hands of the Genziks by crashing a rocket into their spaceship.

The point of this extended, all-too-detailed synopsis of a smorgasbord narrative that mashes up stereotyped characters is to suggest the difficulty of citing any particular pulp magazine narrative of the 1920s or 1930s to support any prescriptive norms about or criticism of SF. By the time "Hunger Death" appeared, nearly 400 issues of specialized SF pulp magazines had already been published, containing over 2,000 stand-alone or serialized narratives, written by some 500 different authors.[1] Many more SF narratives had appeared in general purpose or other specialized pulps, such as *Weird Tales*, where more than 200 SF stories were published between 1923 and 1930. It is easy to imagine "Hunger Death" appearing in almost any adventure magazine of the time, and possibly even a Western pulp; indeed, since, as Jess Nevins has revealed, some 60 percent of pulp SF narratives were published in general pulp magazines outside those devoted solely to SF, it would not have been surprising to find this story in any pulp that carried adventure or mystery stories.[2] Nor do summaries of the stories in the pulps tell the full story of the phenomenological impact of these magazines, whose covers, interior illustrations, science factoids, editorial content, readers' columns, and even advertisements created a comprehensive experience for readers. Brian Attebery underscores this point when he notes "the artwork, the scientific articles, the almost interchangeable stories and even the advertising in the pulp magazines represented a single continuous flow of information about the technological future."[3] Most readers in the original audience for these magazines read every page and followed many pulps of the time, receiving a composite experience rarely captured by brief histories of the impact and influence of the pulps.

Neither a celebration of technology nor a showcasing of gadgets, "Hunger Death" features a plot that is essentially a paean to investigative journalism, celebrating the hard-nosed decency of both a newspaper editor and an ace reporter who save humanity on Earth, Venus, and Mars. Two different kinds of stock antagonists, one a Depression-era cliché of corporate greed, the other a staple of several SF lost-race mythologies, provide the evil these journalists combat. The plot of this story turns on a scientifically implausible disease and an even less plausible cure, the polka-dot weed, neither described nor explained in even remotely plausible terms. Moreover, apart from being very difficult to fit into any of the narrative formulas generally used to

---

[1] Throughout this essay I draw repeatedly from Everett F. Bleiler's indispensable overviews and annotated bibliographies of early SF narratives: Everett F. Bleiler, *Science-Fiction: The Early Years* (Kent, OH: Kent State University Press, 1990); Everett F. Bleiler with the assistance of Richard J. Bleiler, *Science-Fiction: The Gernsback Years: A Complete Coverage of the Genre Magazines Amazing, Astounding, Wonder, and Others from 1926 through 1936* (Kent, OH: Kent University Press, 1998). Bleiler counts 345 issues of specialized science fiction pulps by 1936, and I have added 1937 and 1938 issues of *Amazing, Astounding,* and *Wonder* to his count.

[2] Jess Nevins, "Pulp Science Fiction," in Rob Latham, ed., *The Oxford Handbook of Science Fiction* (Oxford: Oxford University Press, 2014), pp. 93–103.

[3] Brian Attebery, "The Magazine Era: 1926–1960," in Edward James and Farah Mendlesohn, eds., *The Cambridge Companion to Science Fiction* (Cambridge: Cambridge University Press, 2003), p. 36.

describe pulp SF, "Hunger Death" would seem to fly in the face of most of the science fictional norms and ethos associated with the efforts of Hugo Gernsback, founding publisher and editor in 1926 of *Amazing Stories*, generally agreed to be the first pulp magazine solely devoted to SF, and the man widely regarded, for better or for worse, as the "father" of American magazine SF.[4]

After an early career as an electrical inventor (batteries) and a home radio enthusiast and entrepreneur, Gernsback – who had come to America from Luxembourg in 1904 when he was twenty – turned to publishing a series of technical magazines focused on radios. His first magazine was *Modern Electrics* (1908), and it was succeeded by *The Electrical Experimenter* (1913), and then *Science and Invention* (1920). Also enthusiastic about stories that contained information and speculation about science, Gernsback tried his hand at writing a novel of technological prophecy, *Ralph 124C 4+*, which he published serially in his *Modern Electrics*, and he frequently ran SF stories to promote interest in science in his magazines, including a long series of science-fictional stories about "Dr. Hackensaw's Secrets" by Clement Fezandié. Then, in August 1923, he dedicated an entire issue of *Modern Electrics* to "scientific fiction." In April 1926 he published a new magazine devoted to SF, *Amazing Stories*, effectively establishing a clear market outlet for pulp SF, a market he continued to expand with seven subsequent SF pulps of varying success: *Amazing Stories Annual* (1927), *Amazing Stories Quarterly* (1928), *Science Wonder Stories* (1929), *Air Wonder Stories* (1929), *Scientific Detective Monthly* (1930), *Science Wonder Quarterly* (1929), and *Wonder Stories* (1930).

Gernsback did more to shape the future of SF than did any other single writer or editor during the 1920s and well into the 1930s, yet he remains one of the most controversial figures in SF history, serving as a convenient lightning rod for criticism of the pulp era. He was reviled as "Hugo the Rat" by H. P. Lovecraft and some of the other writers he published, who claimed he withheld payment for their stories until threatened with legal action. Gernsback has been blamed by other critics, including the dean of British SF, Brian Aldiss, for the "hijacking" of American SF from its more proper European antecedents and the subsequent "ghettoization" of American SF as superficial and puerile. Aldiss has famously declared Gernsback "was one of the worst disasters ever to hit the science fiction field," charging that the "technological romanticism" of the "low" pulp SF "conveniently labeled

---

[4] Gernsback's *Amazing* was in fact not characteristic of the pulps, insofar as it was printed on better paper than the cheap wood pulp paper for which the pulps were named, its edges were trimmed, and its "bedsheet" dimensions were larger than the dimensions of most pulps.

Gernsbackian" was responsible for stealing SF's "European heritage" and "transforming it, vulgarizing it and changing it beyond recognition,"[5] a view largely shared by other British SF critics such as Brian Stableford and Edward James. Against the fulminations of Aldiss et al. (including a number of American critics), the indefatigable and largely compelling American scholar Gary Westfahl has made a rigorous and persuasive case for Gernsback's key role in the positive codification of SF both as a genre and as an attitude toward the world.[6]

Accordingly, any serious look at the development of SF in the 1920s and 1930s must navigate Gernsback's complicated legacy. What we now recognize as "early" SF or "proto-SF" existed long before Gernsback in numerous forms at various lengths in numerous countries, as earlier chapters in this volume make clear. But the American SF of the 1920s and 1930s was particularly shaped by writers, publications, and social movements in the nineteenth century.[7] H. Bruce Franklin has claimed that "science fiction was somewhere near the center of nineteenth-century American literature," specifying that there "were few prominent nineteenth-century American writers of fiction who did not write some science fiction or at least one utopian romance."[8] Starting in the mid-nineteenth century, dime novels, each presenting a single action-oriented story, were direct ancestors of the pulps; dime-novel stories following the travel adventures of young inventors such as Frank Reade and Jack Wright popularized the Edisonade formula that would reappear in the pulps. Those stories of young inventors and their marvelous creations – usually some form of mechanized transportation – led directly to the Stratemeyer Syndicate's long-running Tom Swift series. Though lacking interior illustrations, dime novels sported always exciting and eventually brightly colored covers that frequently depicted fantastic air ships, submarines, and fabulously imaginary mechanized land vehicles. The sale of

[5] Brian Aldiss with David Wingrove, *Trillion Year Spree: The History of Science Fiction* (New York: Atheneum, 1986), pp. 202–3.

[6] Gary Westfahl, *Hugo Gernsback and the Century of Science Fiction* (Jefferson, NC: McFarland, 2007); Gary Westfahl, *The Mechanics of Wonder: The Creation of the Idea of Science Fiction* (Liverpool: Liverpool University Press, 1998); Gary Westfahl, "The Mightiest Machine: The Development of American Science Fiction from the 1920s to the 1960s," in Eric Carl Link and Gerry Canavan, eds., *The Cambridge Companion to American Science Fiction* (Cambridge: Cambridge University Press, 2015), pp. 17–30.

[7] For brief overview histories of the science fiction Gernsback "inherited," see Aldiss and Wingrove as well as Edward James, *Science Fiction in the Twentieth Century* (Oxford: Oxford University Press, 1994).

[8] H. Bruce Franklin, *Future Perfect: American Science Fiction of the Nineteenth Century – An Anthology* (New Brunswick, New Jersey: Rutgers University Press, 1966), p. 3.

hundreds of millions of copies of dime novels helped shape the mass popular audience that subsequently turned to the pulps. Cultural historian Andrew Ross argues that early twentieth century American SF was part of "widely shared social fantasy."[9] Ross challenges the linear received history of early American SF as developing from pulp naïveté through Campbell's "Golden Era." To Ross's larger view of Gernsbackian SF, we should add the precedent and continuing influence of the Technological Utopians, best remembered in the nineteenth century for Edward Bellamy's *Looking Backward* (1888) and represented in the mid-1930s Technocracy movement.[10] Salient characteristics of the pulp SF of the period also reflect the paradigm shift detailed by Cecilia Tichi in her *Shifting Gears: Technology, Literature, Culture in Modernist America*, where she traces the widespread rise of metaphors tied to gear and girder technology and explains how the engineer supplanted the frontiersman as the new American twentieth-century mythic hero.[11]

When Gernsback launched *Amazing Stories* he also intensified a lifelong effort to create and codify norms for SF as a type of literature. Famously specifying that his commitment to "scientifiction" centered on "the Jules Verne, H. G. Wells, and Edgar Allan Poe type of story – a charming romance intermingled with scientific fact and prophetic vision," Gernsback fervently believed that "science fiction is an idea of tremendous import" and "an important factor in making the world a better place to live in, through educating the public to the possibilities of science and the influence of science on life."[12] Gernsback wanted SF to predict new scientific and technological discoveries (as he had done in *Ralph 124C 4+*) and hoped to inspire young readers to try their hands at science by offering them stories that could actually instruct them about ways to do so. He did also want SF stories to be entertaining literature, but seemed considerably less interested in literary quality than in science boosterism. However, before he could educate the reading public to this importance, he needed to educate pulp writers to his conviction and that proved difficult. So he initially countered the absence of writers who could provide the kind of

---

[9] Ross's essay first appeared in *Critical Inquiry*, 17, 2 (Winter 1991), pp. 411–33 and was republished in Andrew Ross, "Getting Out of the Gernsback Continuum," *Strange Weather: Culture, Science and Technology in the Age of Limits* (London: Verso, 1991), pp. 101–36.

[10] See Howard P. Segal, *Technological Utopianism in American Culture* (Syracuse, NY: Syracuse University Press, 2005).

[11] Cecilia Tichi, *Shifting Gears: Technology, Literature, Culture in Modernist America* (Chapel Hill: University of North Carolina Press, 1987).

[12] Hugo Gernsback, "A New Sort of Magazine," *Amazing Stories*, 1, 1 (April 1926), p. 5.

stories he desired by publishing reprints of the exemplars he had identified. Bleiler identifies reprints of twenty-three works by Wells, seven works by Verne, and six works by Poe. Gernsback also reprinted A. Merritt's popular "The People of the Pit" and "The Moon Pit" that had previously appeared in *All-Story*, Murray Leinster's "The Runaway Skyscraper," and Ray Cummings's "The Girl in the Golden Atom," both previously published in *Argosy*. He also reprinted Garrett P. Serviss' "A Columbus of Space" and "The Second Deluge" and "The Land That Time Forgot," and a combination of three previous stories by Edgar Rice Burroughs. While Gernsback's efforts may not have led directly to any new inventions or turned many to science, they did help create an enthusiastic cadre of SF readers and fans who kept alive his utopian zeal and promoted his belief in a populist ethos which felt science was too important to be left only to professionally trained and educated scientists.

The pulp market for writers at the time consisted of general fiction magazines such as *Argosy*, *All-Story*, and *Adventure*, plus specialized magazines featuring westerns, detective stories, love stories and even more specialized topics such as trains and air combat. *Thrill-Story*, for a brief run starting in 1919, even specialized in fantastic stories that included some SF. Professional writers who regularly published in those magazines might occasionally try their hand at a story based in some way on science or technology, but only a very few writers consistently produced stories in that loosely understood category, referred to variously as "different stories," "off-trail stories," and few, if any, of those stories shared Gernsback's desire for rigorous science. The problem with finding new material was compounded by the fact that Gernsback was a penurious editor and professional pulp writers could not afford to shape their stories to his science-oriented norms, so even established writers such as Cummings, Merritt, and Leinster who leaned toward stories that contained science fictional elements were slow to write for him. Edgar Rice Burroughs, the American master of the scientific romance, appeared in Gernsback's magazines only in reprint. Gernsback's formal desiderata was for an "ideal proportion" in SF stories of 75 percent literature interwoven with 25 percent science, although the stories he published rarely, if ever, met that ideal proportion, and the narrative "interweaving" of science and literature remained distinctly crude. For all his prescriptions and pronouncements, Gernsback exerted only limited immediate influence on the development of the genre. As Gary Westfahl has detailed, even the writers who tried to write for Gernsback actually adopted strategies of "avoidance" and "distraction" to slip their stories past his prescriptive requirements.[13] Indeed, if Mike Ashley is right in arguing that Gernsback's goals for all of his publishing, whether technical or fiction magazines, were to educate and stimulate, few of the original fictional narratives he published came close to that mark.[14] Still, Gernsback articulated his vision for SF to an extent unmatched by any other writer or editor of his time.

Gernsback's SF magazines met different fates, as he lost control of his Experimenter Publishing Company and the relatively successful *Amazing* series in 1929; *Air Wonder Stories* and *Scientific Detective Monthly* failed quickly, and he sold *Wonder Stories* to Beacon publishing in 1936, which continued publishing the magazine as *Thrilling Wonder Stories*. The ups and downs of Gernsback's publishing career reveal much about his determination and business acumen, but what is important is that his persistence in publishing specialized SF magazines revealed a publishing niche that soon attracted more specialized SF pulps, such as *Astounding Stories of Super Science* (1931), *Astonishing Stories* (1931), and *Startling Stories* (1939), which established a stable enough market for newer writers themselves to specialize in SF. Moreover, Gernsback helped readers who were fans of SF to organize into clubs, ultimately establishing SF fandom as a distinguishing component of and influence on the genre. His invitations to readers to comment on the stories in *Amazing* in a "Discussion" section (where the addresses of letter writers allowed fans to get in touch with each other) and his creation in 1934 of the Science Fiction League, designed to be an umbrella organization for SF clubs, contributed to the sense among SF fans that they were joined in an elite enterprise. However, heated disagreement about the exact nature of this enterprise quickly led to disputes among fan clubs or factions, with perhaps the best-known between the left-leaning progressive Futurians and the more traditional New Fandom exploding at the first Worldcon in 1939. Early members of the Science Fiction League, such as Raymond A. Palmer, whose self-published *The Comet* (1930) is frequently cited as the first SF fanzine, played important roles in the creation of SF fandom, with many (such as Palmer, Robert W. Lowndes, Bob Tucker, and Donald A. Wollheim) eventually becoming notable SF writers and editors.

Not all American SF in the 1920s and 1930s appeared in the pulps, and numerous masterpieces of the emerging genre appeared in novels and other media, but accounts of this formative era tend to focus on Gernsback,

---

[13] Westfahl, *The Mechanics of Wonder*, pp. 145–50.
[14] Mike Ashley and Robert A. W. Lowndes, *The Gernsback Days: A Study of the Evolution of Modern Science Fiction from 1911 to 1936* (Holicong, PA: Wildside Press, 2004).

frequently at odds with each other.[15] SF literary history has failed to arrive at any broad consensus of Gernsback's role in the development of SF beyond agreeing on his central role in establishing a marketing space for SF as a publishing category and initiating discussions that continue until today about the norms of SF as a literary genre. Sidestepping arguments about the value of Gernsback's prescriptions for SF, Everett F. Bleiler locates his accomplishment in non-literary terms: "Essentially, his contribution first to American cultural history, then to world cultural history, was establishing a commercial entity that was capable of growth. He brought together under a single canopy many varied sorts of fantastic fiction and presented it in such a way that it could survive."[16] Crediting Gernsback with creating "the language and ideological rhetoric of SF," Farah Mendlesohn specifies that he "established the parameters within which the field's critical debates took place and hosted the community of highly vocal readers and writers that we now call 'fandom.'"[17] It seems safe to say that Gernsback's more abstract eventual impact on SF was huge, as his somewhat inchoate dedication to science spread over the years of the 1920s and 1930s to fans who began demanding "better" science in SF stories, to writers who began providing the "better" science readers wanted, and to editors who gradually accepted the scientific ethos Gernsback called for, while blending it with the higher literary standards to which he had paid lip service, but had failed to deliver.

The garish covers of SF pulps, particularly the reds and yellows of Frank R. Paul's iconic covers, have been memorialized in so many coffee table books and on so many Internet sites that we run the risk of thinking that SF pulp magazines were more prominent in the overall pulp industry than they actually were. For all of the discussion of Gernsback and the busy history of the rise and fall of publishers, editors, and individual pulp SF magazines, it is important to remember that SF was never a large part of pulp magazine history, at least as determined by sales and readership. "During the 1926–1936 period," Jess Nevins details, "SF pulps never had more than seven percent of the overall market and were never higher than the sixth most popular genre, trailing far behind the detective/mystery, romance, spicy and western genres."[18] Nevins explains that throughout the "Gernsback Era," "science

---

[15] For a balanced general overview of this period, see: Roger Luckhurst, *Science Fiction* (Malden, MA: Polity Press, 2005). See also Paul Carter, *The Creation of Tomorrow: Fifty Years of Magazine Science Fiction* (New York: Columbia University Press, 1977).
[16] Bleiler, *Science-Fiction: The Gernsback Years*, p. xxiii.
[17] Farah Mendlesohn, "Fiction, 1926–1949," in Rob Latham, ed., *The Oxford Handbook of Science Fiction* (Oxford: Oxford University Press, 2014), p. 54.
[18] Nevins, "Pulp Science Fiction," p. 97.

fiction remained less important to the industry than all other genres; at the high point there were fewer SF pulps than those of any other major genre."[19] His striking conclusion: "As far as most pulp writers and editors were concerned, Gernsback might as well not have existed."[20]

Once relieved of the focus on Gernsback, attention on American SF in the 1920s and 1930s can be concentrated on a relatively small group of writers, three or four major pulp magazines, four or five editors, and a handful of narratives of lasting significance. Basically, there were three "brands" of SF pulps, *Amazing, Astounding,* and *Wonder,* although changes in publishers and editors led to distinct stages in each brand. Gernsback controlled *Amazing Stories* and its quarterly and annual supplements for only three years, before Teck Publishing seized control, establishing one of Gernsback's former assistants, the already ancient Dr. T. O'Conor Sloane as editor. Under his plodding guidance, *Amazing* stagnated and slowly deteriorated until 1938, when the creative and increasingly controversial Raymond A. Palmer assumed its editorship. When he lost control of *Amazing* in 1929, Gernsback quickly (within a couple of months) launched two new SF ventures, *Science Wonder Stories* and *Air Wonder Stories,* which soon collapsed into *Wonder Stories,* edited by Charles D. Hornig, until 1936, when Gernsback sold the magazine to Beacon Publications, which retitled it *Thrilling Wonder Stories,* turning editorship over to Mort Weisinger.

Astounding, added almost by accident in 1930 to a stable of eleven other specialty pulps published by Clayton, was clearly oriented more to action and adventure stories than science under the editorship of Harry Bates, until it was taken over by Street and Smith in 1933, when new editor Frederick Orlin Tremaine initiated his "thought variant policy," which injected considerable new life into SF publishing. Tremaine promised that each issue of *Astounding* would contain at least one example of a "thought variant" story, a new kind of SF that would free authors from the usual blend of science and fiction to give increased focus to an unexplored idea or a new twist on an older idea, usually with sociological implications, as opposed to the "tired" stock stories about interplanetary conflict, deadly insects, time machines, space pirates, and evil aliens that had already become the norm in SF. This policy effectively freed writers from an obligation to scientific plausibility if they could deliver a story that had what SF critics, in later years, would identify as a "sense of wonder." For example, in 1934, Jack Williamson's "Born of the Sun" recast the

---

[19] Nevins, "Pulp Science Fiction," p.98.
[20] Nevins, "Pulp Science Fiction," p. 97.

planets as eggs of the Sun that could hatch giant winged dragons, Howard W. Graham's "The Wall" explored the idea of a totally impenetrable paint that cut off parts of New York from the rest of the city, and John Russell Fearn's "The Man Who Stopped the Dust" imagined eradicating dust by destroying the electrons within the dust molecules. As ambiguous as the concept of the thought variant was, it immediately excited readers and inspired writers to expand their vision of what SF could address. Perhaps the most celebrated change in editorship, not just for *Astounding*, but for all SF pulps, came in 1937, when Tremaine turned the editorship of *Astounding* over to a young John W. Campbell, who led magazine SF into its "Golden Age" in the 1940s with his promotion of future SF greats such as Robert Heinlein, Isaac Asimov, A. E. van Vogt, and Theodore Sturgeon – as the next chapter will discuss.

Tracking the major SF pulp writers of the period is complicated by the fact that most employed pseudonyms, allowing editors sometimes to publish as many as three different stories by the same writer in a single issue. This was also a time of frequent collaborations under a single pseudonym. The number of significant pulp writers of SF can be loosely grouped into three periods, the first composed of writers who were already publishing pulp fiction and transitioned into SF in the years between 1927 and 1930, the second composed of writers who more and more identified themselves as SF writers in the years between 1931 and 1936, and the third composed of writers who came to prominence or remained significant after 1936. Bleiler identifies Miles J. Breuer, David H. Keller, Captain S. P. Meek, Ed Earl Repp, A. Hyatt Verrill, and Harl Vincent in that first group, while John W. Campbell, Nat Schachner, Jack Williamson, Edmond Hamilton, Raymond Z. Gallun, and Stanton Coblentz were the most prominent in the second generation. After 1936, Gallun and Williamson remained prolific, and were joined by Murray Leinster, C. L. Moore, Ross Rocklynne, Frank Belknap Long, John Beynon Harris, and Clifford Simak. Of course, the writer whose work famously spanned all three periods, E. E. "Doc" Smith, the "father of space opera," whose incredibly popular "Skylark" stories first appeared in *Amazing* in 1928, remained a major force in pulp SF until after the Second World War. And the writer who may have had the greatest impact on future directions of SF was Stanley G. Weinbaum, whose "Martian Odyssey" in the July 1934 *Wonder Stories* attracted immediate acclaim and continues to be considered an SF classic for its innovative depiction of odd alien life forms, including a sympathetic and richly textured depiction of a brave and intelligent alien at a time when "bug-eyed monsters" were more the norm.[21] Writers whose work starting appearing in 1938 and 1939, but who became the celebrated nucleus of *Astounding's* Campbell-orchestrated "Golden Age" in the 1940s and 1950s included Robert Heinlein, Isaac Asimov, L. Sprague de Camp, L. Ron Hubbard, Henry Kuttner, Fritz Leiber, Theodore Sturgeon, and A. E. van Vogt.

While most of the pulp SF written in the 1920s and 1930s deserves the Bleiler dismissal as "routine," there were a few stories that have deservedly achieved "classic" status and remain of interest today. Gernsback's *Ralph 124C 4+*, while crudely written, offered strikingly accurate predictions of some two dozen future technologies. E. E. (Doc) Smith's Skylark stories established space opera protocols that continue to be invoked in film and TV today. Edmond Hamilton and Jack Williamson joined Smith in establishing the popularity of space opera, and Hamilton's "The Man Who Evolved" (1931) is remembered for its imagination of a scientist's acceleration of human evolution in fifty million year increments, each increment exploring the implications of massively developed brainpower, until at 300 million years a cycle of evolution is completed. Stanley G. Weinbaum's "Martian Odyssey" (1934) and Lester Del Rey's "Helen O'Loy" (1938) are the two period stories chosen by the Science Fiction Writers of America for enshrinement in *The Science Fiction Hall of Fame, Volume I* (1970), while John W. Campbell, writing as Don A. Stuart, made "Twilight" (1934) a memorable and frequently reprinted vision of a far future in which machines have almost supplanted humans. Stuart also gave us "Who Goes There?" (1938), now better known through film adaptations *The Thing from Another World* (dir. Christian Nyby and Howard Hawk, 1951) and *The Thing* (dir. John Carpenter, 1982). C. L. Moore is remembered for her pioneering exploration of sexuality and addiction in an update to the Medusa myth, "Shambleau," published in *Weird Tales* in 1934, and her "The Bright Illusion," published in *Astounding* in 1934, although both these supernatural narratives are only borderline SF.

Jane L. Donawerth has provided an important correction to the widely shared assumption that women SF writers were largely silent during the pulp era, and it is worth noting that Gernsback was quite comfortable publishing SF by women writers. While their numbers were probably limited to fewer than a dozen, women writers in the pulp produced noteworthy stories that directly continued the technological utopian fictions of the late nineteenth century and paralleled the campaigns documented by Cecilia Tichi in which

---

[21] Sadly, Weinbaum died in 1935, robbing science fiction of a voice that could have significantly hastened its maturity, both as a genre and as a literary form.

women's magazines constructed women as "domestic engineers," aligning science and technology with domestic issues. Donawerth cites stories by women writers of the period, particularly Leslie F. Stone and Claire Winger Harris, that romanticized science and technology in the manner of their male counterparts, but that also romanticized alien life forms and offered views of technologized domestic spaces, duties, and topics such as future food and childbirth in ways quite different from the concerns of male pulp writers.[22] Stone's "The Conquest of Gola," published in *Wonder Stories* in 1931, and Harris's "The Ape Cycle," published in *Science Wonder Stories* in 1930, are of particular interest.

While the story of the pulps is largely the story of the development of American SF in the 1920s and 1930s, there were a number of significant publications and events during the period outside the pulp tradition. Outside the United States, works by Karel Čapek (*R.U.R.*, 1921), Yevgeny Zamyatin (*We*, 1924), Olaf Stapledon (*Last and First Men*, 1930; *Star Maker*, 1937), and Aldous Huxley (*Brave New World*, 1932) tremendously impacted the reach and reputation of SF. In the United States, works that preceded and obviously influenced the pulps included Garrett P. Serviss's *Edison's Conquest of Mars* (1898) and *The Second Deluge* (1912). Philip Wylie's *Gladiator* (1930) developed the superman theme and Wylie and Edwin Balmer's *When Worlds Collide* (1933) and *After Worlds Collide* (1934) popularized astronomical apocalypse. Largely forgotten, but intriguing for the influence it might have had on the development of SF, was Stanley Weinbaum's fascinatingly bleak, but intriguingly mature *The New Adam* (1939), lavishly advertised to little avail in the pages of *Amazing* by editor Ray Palmer as "a masterpiece of scientific fantasy" and "a literary event of the first magnitude." For all his genius, Weinbaum's mutant intellectual superman in *The New Adam*, Edmond Hall, finds no satisfaction in riches and power, and cannot overcome sexual desire and needs of the body, leading him to calm despair and suicide.

Readership of pulp SF magazines paled in comparison to the movie audiences who experienced SF icons, ideas, and themes in films such as *Metropolis* (dir. Fritz Lang, 1927), *Just Imagine* (dir. David Butler, 1930), *Frankenstein* (dir. James Whale, 1931), *King Kong* (dir. Merian C. Cooper and

---

[22] See Donawerth's "Science Fiction by Women in the Early Pulps, 1926–1930," in Jane L. Donawerth and Carol A. Kolmerten, eds., *Utopian and Science Fiction by Women* (Syracuse, NY: Syracuse University Press, 1994), pp. 137–52; and Jane L. Donawerth, *Frankenstein's Daughters: Women Writing Science Fiction* (Syracuse, NY: Syracuse University Press, 1997), as well as her chapter in this volume. Bleiler lists some forty pulp SF stories by women writers, including Lilith Lorraine, Sophie Wenzel Ellis, and Amelia Reynolds Long.

Ernest B. Schoedsack, 1933), *Things to Come* (dir. William Cameron Menzies, 1936), and the serials *Flash Gordon* (dir. Frederick Stephani and Ray Taylor, 1936) and *Buck Rogers* (dir. Ford Beebe, 1939). So inspirational was its construction of the future that celebrated SF writer and editor Frederik Pohl claims that he saw *Things to Come* some thirty-three times *before he stopped counting*. And, of course, it is hard to overstate the eventual impact of the Orson Welles *Mercury Theatre on the Air* radio production of *War of the Worlds* (1938), the most famous but only one of many radio productions of SF stories in the 1930s.

Even more telling for its indication of the cultural footprint of SF at the end of the period is H. Bruce Franklin's provocative claim that the "principal form of SF in 1939" was in fact the New York World's Fair, "The World of Tomorrow."[23] And included in the contents of the Westinghouse Time Capsule buried at the 1939 fair – not to be opened until 6939, five thousand years in the future – was the October 1938 issue of *Amazing Stories*.

---

[23] H. Bruce Franklin, "America as Science Fiction: 1939," in George Slusser, Eric S. Rabkin, and Robert Scholes, eds., *Coordinates: Placing Science Fiction and Fantasy* (Carbondale: Southern Illinois Press, 1992), p. 108.

9

Astounding Stories: John W. Campbell and the Golden Age, 1938–1950

MICHAEL R. PAGE

In the late 1930s American magazine SF experienced a monumental shift in its development when John W. Campbell joined the editorial staff of *Astounding Stories* in September 1937, replacing F. Orlin Tremaine as editor in 1938 when Tremaine became editorial director at Street and Smith. Campbell remained *Astounding*'s editor until his death in 1971. Over the course of the first five years of Campbell's editorship, *Astounding* became the fulcrum of SF's Golden Age, as a host of new writers – including Isaac Asimov, Robert A. Heinlein, Theodore Sturgeon, and A. E. van Vogt – exploded upon the scene and dominated the field for the next fifty years. Three factors were of particular importance to the emergence of the Golden Age at this moment. First, the SF magazine phenomenon was itself entering its teens, the first magazine, *Amazing Stories*, having been launched in 1926. Second, Campbell had been one of the leading SF writers throughout the 1930s in his two personas: through the super-science stories under his own name and the more introspective and philosophical idea-driven stories under the pseudonym Don A. Stuart. Before Campbell, the top editors of SF – Hugo Gernsback, T. O'Conor Sloane, Harry Bates, F. Orlin Tremaine – were all middle-aged men, and had all been in the magazine business for other reasons; with the exception of Gernsback, editing SF was for them merely a job. For Campbell it was different: SF was a way of life. This directly correlates with the third significant factor that shaped the Golden Age: an emerging generation of writers, some of whom, like the SF magazines, were still teenagers, who grew up reading the early SF magazines and whose intellectual and emotional lives were largely shaped by the dreams and insights of the earlier magazine writers.

When Campbell was hired, *Astounding* began serializing *Galactic Patrol* (August 1937 – February 1938), the first of E. E. "Doc" Smith's *Lensman* novels featuring the intrepid superman Kimball Kinnison. Although the pulpy *Lensman* series is ostensibly representative of SF's earlier era, in many ways it registers an important preoccupation of Campbell's Golden Age in its depiction of a transcendent human mental evolution and a galactic-spanning human exceptionalism. Campbell would go on to publish three more novels in the series over the course of the 1940s: *Gray Lensman* (October 1939 – January 1940), *Second Stage Lensman* (November 1941 – February 1942), and *Children of the Lens* (November 1947 – February 1948). In the *Lensman* saga Smith created a wide-screen vision of a galaxy-spanning human future in which humans would be actively engaged with a panoply of other sentient beings, politically, economically, and technologically, and develop themselves further along a progressive evolutionary trajectory. This dream of human progressive development was among the central myths of Campbell's Golden Age, as Alexei and Cory Panshin have argued,[1] and it appealed to Campbell's human exceptionalism: in spite of humanity's relatively recent emergence on the galactic scene, Kimball Kinnison is the highest-rated intelligence in the galaxy (though he still, more or less, behaves like a depression-era white American). What Smith lacked in literary style and characterization, he made up for in his sweeping plotting and in the introduction of SF ideas, which Darko Suvin has famously defined as novums.[2]

Campbell spent six months apprenticing under Tremaine before taking over the editorial reins for the March 1938 issue. To mark this change, Campbell immediately changed the magazine's title from *Astounding Stories* to *Astounding Science-Fiction* to demarcate the changes ahead in the magazine, which included plans to usher in a new, mature phase of SF. In his first official editorial (he's credited with having unofficially written those in the issues during his Tremaine apprenticeship), titled "Science-Fiction," Campbell emphasized the importance of replacing *Stories* with *Science-Fiction*, to more clearly state the content of the magazine to the uninitiated reader: "Science is the gateway to the future; its predictions alone can give us some glimpse of times to come. Therefore, we are adding the word 'science' to our title, for the man who is interested in science must be interested in the future, and appreciates that the old order not only does change, but must change."[3] Among Campbell's other changes to the magazine, the most significant, perhaps, was moving "The Editor's Page" to the front of the magazine to lead off every issue. Before the November 1938 issue the editorial was often

[1] Alexei and Cory Panshin, *The World Beyond the Hill: Science Fiction and the Quest for Transcendence* (Los Angeles: J. P. Tarcher, 1989).
[2] Darko Suvin, *Metamorphoses of Science Fiction* (New Haven: Yale University Press, 1979), pp. 63–84.
[3] John W. Campbell, "Science-Fiction," *Astounding* (March 1938), p. 37.

buried in the interior of the magazine, presumably wherever there was open space. Whereas previously the Editor's Page had not been much more than filler, in Campbell's *Astounding* it became the standard bearer. By putting it at the front of the magazine, Campbell more clearly established the voice and direction of *Astounding* – and his own centrality to the project. As time went on, Campbell's editorials got longer and became the center point for ideas and debates within the magazine. Some of Campbell's key editorials from these early years include "Fantastic Fiction" (June 1938), "Future Tense" (June 1939), "Robots" (November 1939, which inspired Asimov), "Atomic Power to Space" (July 1940, where he's already discussing U-235), and "History to Come" (May 1941, where he introduces Heinlein's Future History chart and describes SF as "'period pieces,' historical novels laid against a background that hasn't happened yet").[4]

Tremaine had left Campbell with a good magazine, the best in the field, although Tremaine's own editorial attention had waned. And since 1934, Tremaine had been publishing stories that were already pointing toward the new, mature SF of Campbell's vision, exemplified by the work of Don A. Stuart (Campbell himself), including the classics "Twilight" (November 1934), "The Machine" (February 1935), and "Forgetfulness" (June 1937). In Campbell's sixth issue, he published his paradigmatic Don A. Stuart story "Who Goes There?" (August 1938), which would set the tone for what Campbell expected *Astounding* to become. "Who Goes There?" takes place in an isolated research station in the interior of Antarctica – the story appears to be Campbell's response to H. P. Lovecraft's *At the Mountains of Madness*, which Tremaine published in *Astounding* in 1936 – where the researchers have discovered a wrecked alien spacecraft that has been buried in the ice for twenty million years, and an alien corpse frozen a few yards away from the craft. Upon being taken back to base camp, the alien thaws out and comes to life. The alien is intelligent, cunning, malevolent, and telepathic, and is able to absorb and mimic the physical and mental structures of other lifeforms, making it a threat to the entire human species. Utilizing reason and prompt and unwavering action, the men of the station must combat this *thing* and keep it from escaping from the isolation of the camp into the temperate zones of the planet, or all life on Earth will face extinction. The story is a brilliant meditation on scientific inquiry, human perseverance, the competent man, evolution, and cosmic chance. Campbell constructs an unforgettable environment of claustrophobia and paranoia that forges an ideal combination of tension, suspense,

[4] John W. Campbell, "History to Come," *Astounding* (May 1941), pp. 5–6.

and curiosity. "Who Goes There?" stands as the model-type story for Campbell's new *Astounding* aesthetic. Uncomfortably present also is Campbell's celebration of the "blonde beast" superman in the depiction of McReady, "a figure from some forgotten myth, a looming, bronze statue that held life, and walked," illustrating that Campbell's human exceptionalism was exceptionally white.[5] Campbell published one last Stuart story in *Astounding* in the March 1939 issue, the seldom anthologized "Cloak of Aesir," a follow-up to the October 1937 story "Out of Night." Like "Who Goes There?," "Cloak of Aesir" is also paradigmatically Campbellian in many ways, including the championing of human perseverance and the evolution of transcendent powers of the mind. The story is set 4,000 years after the conquest of Earth by a matriarchal alien species, the Sarn. The Sarn live for thousands of years and have enslaved humanity and bred them into passivity, but because humans are on a faster life-cycle, over the thousands of years of oppression, humanity has evolved and developed psi powers – a theme that would become one of Campbell's hobby-horses in later years. In this, humanity achieves rebirth and breaks the hold of the decadent Sarn. Here Campbell introduces the theme of an underground rebellion overcoming oppression, a central theme in much later SF, and particularly evident in Golden Age *Astounding*.

New Writers

Four months after the appearance of "Cloak of Aesir," Campbell introduced two new writers, A. E. van Vogt and Isaac Asimov, in the July 1939 issue. Asimov's "Trends" is a powerful depiction of science and rationality under threat from the forces of religious fundamentalism and conservatism at the moment of the first spaceflight. Van Vogt's inaugural story "Black Destroyer" is one of the great classics of the genre. Like "Who Goes There?," which is an obvious influence, it pits a crew of competent human beings against an alien menace. In this case, the alien is the cat-like Couerl, one of the last of its kind, a species that has ravished its civilization and planet in an unceasing hunger for "id" (which turns out to be phosphorus). As in "Who Goes There?," the competent crew of the *Space Beagle* thwart the superior Couerl by applying a philosophical-methodological synthesis called Nexialism, which allows the resident Nexialist, Grosvenor, to outthink the alien and trick it into a lifeboat, where after a moment of spatial disorientation, it commits suicide

[5] John W. Campbell, "Who Goes There?," in *The Best of John W. Campbell* (New York: Ballantine, 1976), p. 291.

before the *Space Beagle* can blast it into oblivion. Like Campbell, van Vogt effectively creates suspense and tension, although van Vogt's narrative tension comes from a rapid-fire sequence of ideas and narrative twists, whereas Campbell's is more introspective and precise. The influence of "Black Destroyer" (and its lesser-anthologized follow-up "Discord in Scarlet" (December 1939)) can be seen in such later alien contact dramas as Mario Bava's *Planet of the Vampires* (1965), the first-aired *Star Trek* episode, "The Man Trap" (1966), and Ridley Scott's *Alien* (1979). Van Vogt was *Astounding*'s great dreamer and became the Campbell writer known for creating strange alien vistas and fast-paced, nearly incomprehensible tales of human supermen.

On the heels of the introductions of Asimov and van Vogt, the August issue introduced the writer who, next to H. G. Wells, is arguably the single most significant writer in the SF genre: Robert A. Heinlein. Heinlein's first story "Life-Line" does not fully convey the narrative and ideational power of his achievement, but it is nonetheless a story where the competent Heinleinian voice establishes itself. "Life-Line" is also the beginning point of Heinlein's "Future History," his near-future stories set in a shared background. The story centers on the social consequences of a transformative invention, another theme central to the *Astounding* aesthetic. In the September issue, Campbell published Theodore Sturgeon's first story, "Ether Breather." These three consecutive issues introduced four of the most important innovators in the field: van Vogt, the dreamer, Asimov, the scientific rationalist, Heinlein, the politically informed competent man, and Sturgeon, the empathetic stylist. These four and several others, including L. Sprague De Camp, Lester Del Rey, Ross Rocklynne, Clifford D. Simak, Malcolm Jameson, L. Ron Hubbard, Nelson Bond, and Cleve Cartmill, made up the core of Campbell's contributors before the war.

Heinlein soon emerged as the most significant. One additional minor Heinlein story appeared in 1939, but Heinlein's centrality to *Astounding* was secured in the first issue of the new decade with the appearance of "Requiem" (January 1940), the story of aged financier D. D. Harriman making his first and final journey to the Moon. In "Requiem," Heinlein created a future *realism* that gives an extra layer of authenticity and believability to his stories; his is a lived-in future. Heinlein's first serial, *If This Goes On . . .* (February – March 1940) began in the next issue. In it, Heinlein depicts a near-future in which America has been taken over by a theocratic dictatorship led by evangelist Nehemiah Scudder, and the rationalist rebellion that overcomes it. Heinlein's political fable continues to resonate. As 1940 progressed, Heinlein contributed "The Roads Must Roll" (June 1940), "Coventry" (July 1940), and "Blowups

Happen" (September 1940) to *Astounding*. "The Roads Must Roll" is one of the paradigmatic engineering stories in the genre, centered on the economic and political disruptions that emerge when a society becomes dependent on complex, intertwined advanced transportation technologies and the men who keep them running. "Blowups Happen" is one of the earliest stories to engage with the social and political consequences of the use of atomic energy. After "Blowups Happen," atomics becomes a central concern in *Astounding*. At the beginning of 1941, Heinlein's novel *Sixth Column* (January – March 1941) was published under the pseudonym Anson MacDonald. *Sixth Column* was developed from Campbell's unpublished – and even more egregiously racist – novella "All," involving an invasion and occupation of North America by a Pan-Asian dictatorship. A small group of American military and scientific men and women gather at a hidden enclave in the Rockies, where they hatch a plan to cast out the invaders by forming a new religion and utilizing an advanced energy weapon developed at the enclave. Later in the year, Heinlein's novel *Methuselah's Children* (July – September 1941) introduced Lazarus Long (whose history is fully rendered in the later novel *Time Enough for Love* [1973]) and the other long-lived and super-intelligent members of the Howard families. *Methuselah's Children* plays with then popular ideas about eugenics (also prevalent in van Vogt's stories) and evokes the frontier theme when the persecuted Howards flee Earth in a generation starship. Other stories appeared under the Heinlein and MacDonald bylines in 1941, including "Solution Unsatisfactory" (May 1941), another paradigmatic early atomics story that anticipates the politics of the Cold War, and "By His Bootstraps" (October 1941), one of the greatest time-paradox stories ever written. Both these stories appeared under the MacDonald pseudonym because they shared their respective issues with what is, for many, Heinlein's greatest early achievement: the generation starship story "Universe" (May 1941) and its sequel "Common Sense" (October 1941). "Universe" is the quintessential "conceptual breakthrough" story, involving Hugh Hoyland and his quest to understand the enclosed world he lives in. Hoyland's coming-of-age journey leads him to befriend the mutants of the upper decks, led by the memorable two-headed Joe-Jim, and eventually to find that their world is, in fact, a starship. "Common Sense" depicts Hugh's struggle to convince others of the reality of the ship; failing that, he and a small band of others escape in a shuttle and land on another world. Like no other story, perhaps, "Universe" and its sequel are the quintessential representations of Golden Age *Astounding*. By the end of 1941, Japan had attacked Pearl Harbor and Heinlein abruptly got involved in war work and ceased writing, although a few remaining stories appeared in 1942, including the utopian novel *Beyond This Horizon* (April – May 1942) and the novella "Waldo" (August 1942). When Heinlein returned to writing after the war, he had mostly left Campbell and *Astounding* behind, having found his way into the greener markets of the mainstream and book publication.

While Heinlein dominated *Astounding* for the first two years of the 1940s, van Vogt further established himself as the heir of the gosh-wow "sense of wonder" school. Van Vogt's serial *Slan* (September – December 1940) appeared at the end of 1940 and quickly became a favorite among SF fandom, inspiring the mantra "fans are slans," as many SF readers identified with the persecuted outsider hero Jommy Cross. Slans are mutated humans possessing super intelligence, but those with golden tendrils (not unlike Couerl's tentacles) also have telepathic capabilities, and they are brutally hunted to near extinction by "normal" humans. Fast-paced, suspenseful, and endearing, *Slan*, like most of van Vogt's work, has the mesmerizing quality of dreams. A similar vibe of outsiderism and super intelligence appears in the novella "Asylum" (May 1942), in which a pair of human-like "energy vampires" descend upon Earth and pull the life force out of human victims. Their presence awakens the super intelligence of newsman Bill Leigh, thus aggregating into another van Vogtian fantasy of human-accelerated mental evolution. Van Vogt's next major achievement was "The Weapon Shop" (December 1942), a libertarian narrative of an underground movement overcoming authoritarianism. Van Vogt's superman theme is developed further in a number of stories and novels throughout the decade, most notably in *The World of Null-A* (August – October 1945) and its sequel *The Players of Null-A* (October 1948 – January 1949), featuring the paradigmatic superman Gilbert Gosseyn, the Clane series, consisting of *Empire of the Atom* (1946–7) and *The Wizard of Linn* (April – June 1950), and perhaps his bizarrest expression of the theme in *The Book of Ptath* (October 1943), which appeared in the final issue of *Astounding*'s fantasy companion magazine *Unknown*.

But of all those writing for Campbell before the war, the writer who was most shaped by Campbell's editorial guidance was Isaac Asimov. Under Campbell's tutelage, Asimov created the quintessential symbol of a technological future in his Robot series (even if Campbell actually rejected the first robot story, "Robbie," which appeared in *Super Science Stories* in September 1940 instead). The first two contributions to the series published in *Astounding*, "Reason" and "Liar!," appeared in back-to-back issues in the spring of 1941. "Reason" (April 1941) introduces the put-upon robot-engineer team Donovan and Powell, who must match wits with robot QT-1, "Cutie," who has reasoned that imperfect humans can't possibly have created a superior creation such as itself. Set on a solar energy relay station whose proper function is critical for Earth's well-being, the story involves Donovan and Powell's efforts to prove that Cutie was designed, manufactured, and constructed by humans. In the end they fail, but the zealous robot fulfills its task anyway, having reasoned that it should "keep the dials at equilibrium in accordance with the will of the Master."[6] "Liar!" (May 1941) examines the personal anguish of Asimov's robot psychologist Susan Calvin. The story involves RD-34, "Herbie," a robot that is able to read minds. But in order to follow the First Law of Robotics – "A robot may not injure a human being, or, through inaction allow a human being to come to harm" – Herbie tells the staff of US Robots & Mechanical Men, Inc. what they want to hear. In Dr. Calvin's case, this involves encouraging her secret romantic feelings for her younger colleague Milton Ashe. When the robot's deceptions are unmasked, a deeply embarrassed Dr. Calvin destroys the robot's positronic brain. All the robot stories that Asimov wrote for Campbell hinge in some way or another on a complication with the Three Laws of Robotics; six more robot stories appeared in *Astounding* during the decade, and, along with "Robbie," were published in 1950 as *I, Robot*, still one of the genre's essential texts.

In September 1941, Asimov's "Nightfall" appeared as the cover story. Widely recognized as one of the greatest SF stories of all time, "Nightfall" is set on the planet Lagash, which has six visible suns in the sky, leaving the planet constantly illuminated. Therefore, Lagashian culture has developed a deep-seated psychological phobia for darkness and a divergent technological development, among other things. The story is set just before the moment when the Lagashian suns align with an otherwise unseen moon, causing an eclipse, which has historically led to the collapse of Lagashian civilization on a cycle of 2049 years and a near-complete obliteration of the historical record. What is perhaps the most potent image in the story, if not in all of SF, comes at the conclusion when the panicked Lagashian scientists experience not the anticipated full darkness, but rather the revelation of the panorama of stars set against the night sky, overwhelming them with the knowledge that the universe is a much vaster place. The scene is an awe-inspiring example of Campbellian "sense of wonder," rivaling the moment in "Universe" when Hugh opens the viewport on the Captain's veranda and sees space for the first time. But in Asimov's oddly paranoid vision, the Lagashians fall into madness, failing to achieve epiphany from the sublime

---

[6] Isaac Asimov, "Reason," in *I, Robot* (New York: Fawcett, 1970), p. 62.

vision of the stars. Aside from the startling ending, the story is also notable for establishing Asimov's style; most of the story's action occurs as rational dialogue and declarative exposition. Asimov further honed this style in later years, as he became a great communicator of science, publishing much nonfiction alongside his later SF.

Perhaps surpassing both the robot stories and "Nightfall" is Asimov's *Foundation* series (1942–50), which first appeared with the titular story in the May 1942 issue. Seven more *Foundation* stories appeared throughout the Golden Age decade and were soon gathered together in book form in three volumes, *Foundation* (1951), *Foundation and Empire* (1952), and *Second Foundation* (1953). Asimov later added several novels to the series in the 1980s and 1990s, beginning with *Foundation's Edge* (1982), which tied it together with the Robot series and the Empire series, forging a belated continuity among the series. What sets Asimov's space epic apart from, say, Smith's *Lensman* saga, is Asimov's focus on the larger social, scientific, and historical forces that impact civilization, in contrast to Smith's focus on the exploits of a superhero. Thus, like the innovations introduced in Heinlein's "Future History," *Foundation* is an exercise in world-building, creating a plausible future history and a plausible social science (psychohistory) that offers an analytical approach to historical crisis set against the backdrop of the galaxy. The influence of *Foundation* can be seen in subsequent Galactic Empire/space epics, most especially Frank Herbert's *Dune* (1965). Central to the argument in *Foundation* is the idea of the underground movement of scientists working to maintain civilization during a dark age or to overthrow repressive forces, an idea, as seen above, taken through varying permutations in the works of Heinlein and van Vogt.

A few months before the momentous appearances of Asimov, van Vogt, Heinlein, and Sturgeon in *Astounding*, Campbell launched a companion fantasy magazine, *Unknown*. In many ways, *Unknown* was of equal importance in the development of the SF and fantasy fields. In its pages, Campbell, among other achievements, nurtured the development of what is now called urban fantasy, and insisted that writers applied the same analytical logic and rigor to their fantasy stories that they would apply to SF. Most of Campbell's writers wrote stories for both magazines. Sturgeon's early work was, largely, better suited for the fantasy magazine, where his classic monster story "It" appeared in the August 1940 issue. The slightly later "Killdozer!" (November 1944) might have appeared in *Unknown* had it not ceased publication owing to wartime paper shortages. In all, Sturgeon appeared in *Unknown* sixteen times. That's not to say that Sturgeon could not produce the kind of hard SF stories suited to *Astounding* in these early years. "Microcosmic God" (April 1941) – a rationalistic twist on the "mad scientist" cliché that dominated 1930s SF cinema: it is not the scientist who is mad, but the exploitative banker who monetizes his discoveries for greed and power – remains one of the classic engineering stories from the period. The story involves an isolated scientist who bioengineers creatures he calls neoterics that, through an accelerated evolutionary cycle, create an unlimited energy source and, ultimately, the means for advanced space travel. After the war, Sturgeon became one of *Astounding*'s most important contributors with such stories as "The Chromium Helmet" (June 1946), "Maturity" (February 1947), "Mewhu's Jet" (November 1946), "Tiny and the Monster" (May 1947), and the significant nuclear war stories "Memorial" (April 1946) and "Thunder and Roses" (November 1947).

Other Key Campbell-Era Writers

Two other writers were important to the development of *Unknown* and the subsequent development of fantasy fiction: Fritz Leiber and L. Sprague De Camp. Like many writers in Campbell's stable, Leiber and De Camp wrote for both magazines. In *Unknown*, Leiber's Fafhrd and the Grey Mouser stories (1940–3) took sword and sorcery in a new direction: the short story "Smoke Ghost" (October 1941) is a foundational work of urban fantasy, and the novel *Conjure Wife* (April 1943) is a classic example of applying Campbellian logic to a traditional fantasy trope, in this case witchcraft. Leiber also made major contributions to *Astounding* during the war years. His novel *Gather, Darkness!* (May–July 1943) is one of the first to depict a future society forged in the aftermath of atomic war, while *Destiny Times Three* (March–April 1945) expands and develops the concept of parallel universes. De Camp's major work before the war appeared mostly in *Unknown*, including the Harold Shea stories "The Roaring Trumpet" (May 1940), "The Mathematics of Magic" (August 1940), and *The Castle of Iron* (April 1941), and the novel *Land of Unreason* (October 1941), all in collaboration with Fletcher Pratt. But De Camp's most important contribution is the alternate history novel *Lest Darkness Fall* (December 1939) involving a contemporary archaeologist thrust back to the era of the Roman Empire, where he introduces several techno-logical and social innovations that prevent the collapse into the Dark Ages. At the end of the decade, De Camp returned to *Astounding*, publishing the first of his Viagens Interplanetarias series, "The Animal-Cracker Plot" (July 1949) and *The Queen of Zamba* (August – September 1949), a model for the world-building planetary adventures that came to dominate *Astounding/ Analog* in later decades.

Veteran writer Jack Williamson was another who flourished in both *Astounding* and *Unknown*. Williamson had been a prolific pulpster throughout the thirties in both the SF and the fantasy fields and had been a major contributor to *Astounding* during the Tremaine years, publishing the *Legion of Space* series (1934–9) and *The Legion of Time* (May – July 1938). In *Unknown*, Williamson's modern werewolf novel *Darker Than You Think* (December 1940) was, along with Leiber's *Conjure Wife*, an important milestone in the development of modern horror and urban fantasy. In *Astounding*, Williamson's story "Breakdown" (January 1942) – which provides some of the background for Williamson's later collaboration with James Gunn, *Star Bridge* (1955) – is another remarkable prewar story that, like Asimov's *Foundation*, has its basis in theories of cyclical history. After experiencing a case of writer's block, which would trouble him periodically for the next few decades, Williamson, on Campbell's suggestion, began the *Seetee* series in 1943, which, in turn, provided the source material for Williamson's syndicated comic strip *Beyond Mars* (1952–5). The *Seetee* stories (1942–9) introduced the concept of contraterrene matter (antimatter) and became a discussion point for possible ways to mine alternative energy sources from space. Williamson's most famous contribution to *Astounding* came after the war. "With Folded Hands" (July 1947) is one of the great technological dystopias to come out of Campbell's *Astounding* and it is a direct response to Asimov's optimistic robot stories. Williamson wondered if the prime directive for robots to protect humans from harm might not lead to complete annihilation of human autonomy. In the story, the robots follow their benign imperative to its ultimate conclusion, rendering humans helplessly trapped by robot control. When Campbell wanted a sequel, he talked Williamson into creating a way out in the serial ... *And Searching Mind* (March – May 1948): that humans would develop powers of the mind and thus be able to destroy their robot caretakers. Thus, the reluctant Williamson contributed one of the first major statements of Campbell's growing obsession with psi powers, although as shown earlier, the seeds of this obsession were in Campbell's own stories at the beginning of the Golden Age.

Another writer who flourished in *Unknown* and then made additional major contributions to *Astounding* after the war was the enigmatic L. Ron Hubbard. Like Williamson, Hubbard was a veteran pulpster, having begun his career in the adventure pulps in 1934. When Campbell took over at *Astounding*, Hubbard began submitting; his first story, "The Dangerous Dimension," appeared in July 1938, the fifth issue under Campbell's control, and was soon followed by a serial entitled *The Tramp* (September – November 1938). Hubbard's 1940 novel *Final Blackout* (April – June 1941), starkly portraying the rise of a dictator in England after a world war, appeared on the heels of Heinlein's *If This Goes On*. Hubbard also had a number of short novels in *Unknown*, including *Slaves of Sleep* (July 1939), *Death's Deputy* (February 1940), *Fear* (July 1940), and *Typewriter in the Sky* (November – December 1941). After the war, Hubbard returned to the pages of *Astounding* with the serial *The End is Not Yet* (August – October 1947) – a surprisingly excellent Cold War anticipation suggesting a political-military-industrial conspiracy against right-thinking scientists – the *Ole Doc Methuselah* stories (1947–50), and the interstellar romp *To the Stars* (February – March 1950), before the controversial, landmark publication of his article "Dianetics: The Evolution of a Science" in the May 1950 *Astounding* quickly moved Hubbard out of the SF magazines and into the world of pop psychology.

Other significant writers were publishing some of their greatest work in the pages of *Astounding* during the 1940s. Clifford D. Simak, a newspaperman from Minnesota, came into his own as a Campbell writer after an inauspicious beginning in the early thirties. Simak began contributing to *Astounding* regularly in 1938 and his somewhat clunky novel *Cosmic Engineers* (February – April 1939) is an early example of the new approach cultivated by Campbell. However, Simak's *City* stories (1944–7) are of a different magnitude and are among the great early SF works that develop an environmental consciousness. *City* is also a deeply compassionate series and counters some of the cold scientism often conveyed by Campbell's editorials and the more rationalistic stories in the magazine. The *City* series posits a future in which humans depart Earth for other planets or retreat into dream chambers, leaving Earth to their faithful servants, the dogs and the robots. Simak was deeply troubled by the destruction brought on by the war, and the pastoral *City* stories are his elegiac response. Like Asimov's *Foundation*, Simak provided interstitial chapters for book publication that further link the stories into a future history narrative. Lester Del Rey's first story "The Faithful," was also a poignant story about dogs and the legacy of humanity, and it appeared in the second issue under Campbell's direction in April 1938. At the end of the year, Del Rey's classic (and sexist) robot-wife story "Helen O'Loy" (December 1938) capped off Campbell's first year as *Astounding*'s editor. Del Rey's most significant contribution to Campbell's magazines was the long novella "Nerves" (September 1942), which accurately portrays a crisis at an atomic power plant when the atomic pile collapses. Starkly realistic, "Nerves" is the quintessential story of competent technicians and medical staff working efficiently to avert disaster. The story was published three years before the dropping of the atomic bomb. The most controversial atomic story during the war years was, however, penned by one of Campbell's writers who never rose to the level of fame and production that the other luminaries so far discussed did. Cleve Cartmill's "Deadline" (March 1944) is the sole work on which his reputation lies, even though he contributed a number of other stories to Campbell's magazines during the Golden Age. "Deadline" involves an alien war and the development of a super weapon utilizing the isotope U-235. The story got the attention of the FBI, who showed up at Campbell's office and at Cartmill's front door in Los Angeles.[7]

With many of his writers involved in the war, Campbell increasingly relied on the husband and wife team Henry Kuttner and Catherine L. Moore to fill the magazine during the war years. Moore began publishing in the early 1930s with her unforgettable Northwest Smith stories in Weird Tales (1933–6). Kuttner got his start in 1936 with the Weird Tales classic "The Graveyard Rats," but most of his early work was unimpressive. Kuttner and Moore married in 1940 and became major contributors to Astounding in 1942, mainly under the pseudonyms Lewis Padgett and Laurence O'Donnell, although an occasional story appeared under one or the other's own name. The most significant of these is certainly Moore's "No Woman Born" (December 1944), about a famous dancer who after a theatre fire has had her brain transferred into a cybernetic body. It brings new and deeper layers to the psychological interface between humans and advanced robotic technologies introduced in Asimov's robot stories. Among the Padgett stories are "The Twonky" (September 1942), "Mimsy Were the Borogoves" (February 1943), and the comic Professor Gallagher series (1943–8). All are notable as dramas of technological befuddlement, in which humans are faced with technologies beyond their cognitive apprehension. These stories anticipate the works of such contemporary writers as Bruce Sterling, Cory Doctorow, and Charles Stross. Perhaps the most harrowing of the Padgett stories in this register is the later story "Private Eye" (January 1949), which offers an important insight into the problems of a society that develops ubiquitous electronic surveillance technologies. After the war, Kuttner and Moore engaged with the crisis of atomic war that became a central part of Astounding's discourse. "Vintage Season" (September 1946), the "Baldy" stories (1945–53) collected in Mutant,

---

[7] Albert I. Berger, The Magic That Works: John W. Campbell and the American Response to Technology (San Bernadino: Borgo, 1993), pp. 60–9.

The Fairy Chessmen (January – February 1946), and *Tomorrow and Tomorrow* (January – February 1947), all explore apocalyptic and post-apocalyptic scenarios. Atomic holocaust also lurks in the background of their novel *Fury* (May – July 1947), set on a terraformed Venus centuries after humanity has destroyed the Earth through atomic war.

Two classic stories from the war years by veteran writers, Fredric Brown's "Arena" (June 1944), later adapted into a famous *Star Trek* episode, and Murray Leinster's "First Contact" (May 1945), are also central to the Golden Age canon. "Arena" depicts a confrontation between humanity and malevolent alien invaders. The story is a problem-solving exercise as the human Carson must figure out a way to defeat the alien and save humanity within the confines of an enclosed arena established by superior intelligences that have the power to eradicate the losing species from the galaxy. "First Contact," published nearly a year after "Arena," takes a different tack. In it, Leinster suggests that space-faring humans and aliens may have more in common than not, and that the real question will be how to establish communication. The problem-solving in this story leads to mutual understanding and accord. Leinster's March 1946 story "A Logic Named Joe" has achieved classic status in recent years for its depiction of a future responding to the consequences of ubiquitous personal computer technology linked by a vast network.

After the war, a number of important stories engaged with the crisis of atomic war. Theodore Sturgeon's lyrical "Thunder and Roses" (November 1947) is a poignant warning about the possibility of mutually assured destruction and illustrates the no-win nature of this scenario in a climactic moment where an individual must act on behalf of the species instead of the nation to avert extinction by *not* allowing the launch of a retaliatory strike, murdering a fellow soldier in the process. Judith Merril's domestic drama "That Only a Mother" (June 1948) shows the impact the bomb and perpetual war might have on the family psyche; it is a succinct and biting critique of patriarchal attitudes and their threat to species survival. Poul Anderson's first story, "Tomorrow's Children" (March 1947), written with F. N. Waldrop, raises the ethical dilemma that must be faced when most children are mutated following atomic war. H. Beam Piper's first story, "Time and Time Again" (April 1947), also contributes to the atomic dialogue in a wish-fulfillment plot involving a soldier in a future atomic war being thrust back in time and into his adolescent self, where he makes plans to change the world before the atomic holocaust happens. Wilmar H. Shiras's "In Hiding" (November 1948) also suggests that atomics could lead to mutation, but unlike Merril's limbless baby, Shiras's "children of the atom" could hide in plain sight. Shiras's vision of a positive evolutionary outcome to the dangerous direction atomic research and contemporary political tensions were leading gave hope for the future during a time when species extinction seemed inevitable.

The Close of the Golden Age Decade

Although *Astounding*, and, for a time, its companion, *Unknown*, dominated the decade of the 1940s, other SF magazines and their editors made important contributions as well. Frederik Pohl, Robert Lowndes, and Donald A. Wollheim, central figures in the New York City fan group the Futurians, each edited magazines in the early forties, before the United States joined the war. Pohl's *Astonishing Stories* and *Super Science Stories* published early work by Asimov, James Blish, Leigh Brackett, Ray Bradbury, and C. M. Kornbluth, among others, as well as work by *Astounding* writers which Campbell may have passed on. Lowndes edited *Future Fiction* and *Science Fiction Quarterly* from 1941 to 1943, then revived both again in the early 1950s. Wollheim's early magazines *Cosmic Stories* and *Stirring Science Stories* each ran for only a handful of issues in 1941 but are notable for publishing a number of Kornbluth's early stories. The field's oldest magazine, *Amazing Stories*, under the editorship of Ray Palmer, was mostly considered down-market during the decade, although it sold well by exploiting the bizarre "Shaver Mystery" conspiracy theory. *Planet Stories*, launched at the end of 1939, focused primarily on planetary adventure, but the magazine became especially important in the late 1940s for publishing a number of Ray Bradbury stories, several of which made their way into *The Martian Chronicles* (1950). *Thrilling Wonder Stories*, which began life as a pair of Hugo Gernsback magazines in 1929, and its companion *Startling Stories*, founded in 1939, were solid magazines through-out the 1940s, but were especially good – at times nearly rivaling *Astounding* – after Sam Merwin, Jr. became editor in 1944. Some of the most significant works from these magazines include Kuttner and Moore's "Call Him Demon" (*Thrilling Wonder*, Fall 1946), Sturgeon's "The Sky was Full of Ships" (*Thrilling Wonder*, June 1947), Heinlein's "Jerry was a Man" (*Thrilling Wonder*, October 1947), Bradbury's " . . . And the Moon Be Still as Bright" (*Thrilling Wonder*, June 1948) and several more later published in *The Martian Chronicles* and *The Illustrated Man* (1951), Fredric Brown's *What Mad Universe* (*Startling*, September 1948), Arthur C. Clarke's *Against the Fall of Night*

(*Startling*, November 1948) and "History Lesson" (*Startling*, May 1949), and the first stories of James Gunn.

As the decade concluded, Asimov completed the *Foundation* series and Heinlein returned to *Astounding* with the two-part serial "Gulf." It seems fitting that the December 1949 issue of *Astounding* contains the concluding segment of "Gulf" and the second part of the final *Foundation* serial " . . . And Now You Don't," as the Golden Age's two greatest writers put capstones on the decade of SF's greatest achievement. These were signals that *Astounding*'s Golden Age was coming to an end. Two new magazines were about to challenge *Astounding*'s dominance in the field, *The Magazine of Fantasy and Science Fiction* and *Galaxy*. That December issue also contained James Schmitz's novella "The Witches of Karres," a story that signaled one of the new directions that Campbell's editorial preferences would take. Schmitz's amusing galactic adventure involving three waifs with psychic powers encapsulates Campbell's increasing obsession with psi and a penchant for world-building galactic stories removed from the immediate problems facing humanity on Earth. The publication of Hubbard's Dianetics article in the May 1950 issue further marked an end to the Golden Age. Campbell's influence would continue, and his increasingly cantankerous voice would be heard, but the SF community would no longer listen quite as devotedly as it once did.

Indeed, as Campbell continued to edit *Astounding*, later changing its name to *Analog* in 1960, his views on race, social justice, civil society, the military, American exceptionalism, economics, and science and technology became increasingly (and overtly) right-wing and authoritarian; alienating, in turn, many of his former writers, and much of the new generation of SF readers, who favored the implicit left-libertarianism found in the Golden Age era of the magazine and/or the social justice movements emerging in the 1950s. *Astounding* remained a top magazine throughout the 1950s, in spite of the calcification of Campbell's views, in part because of the continued presence, from time to time, of the Golden Age writers, now in their maturity, and the emergence of new writers of significance who still found a mentor in Campbell – James Blish, Algis Budrys, Harry Harrison, Chad Oliver, and Robert Silverberg, for example. In general, the fiction in *Astounding/Analog* by the 1960s echoed Campbell's shift to the right and his various hobby-horses, although, certainly, gems would appear periodically (*Dune*, Anne McCaffrey's early *Pern* stories, and early stories by James Tiptree, Jr., for example), as would stories that challenged Campbell's political and social proclivities (notably, the economic stories of card-carrying socialist Mack

Reynolds). And, whereas Campbell's editorials of the Golden Age 1940s were often inviting and inspiring, the editorials of the 1950s all too often bordered on the lunatic fringe of pseudoscience, and many of those of the 1960s were ugly screeds on right-wing intolerance and military aggression. Although this evolution should not wholly dampen Campbell's editorial achievements, especially those during the Golden Age, it certainly should give us pause for reassessment.

The number of significant writers who shaped the field and the volume of classics that appeared in Campbell's *Astounding* and *Unknown* during the 1940s is truly an astounding achievement, much of it brought together by the editorial gifts of John W. Campbell. The Golden Age of *Astounding* is the ground zero of the SF genre, where many of the genre's central ideas came to full fruition. Campbell's Golden Age remains a central locus point in the history of SF and its importance cannot be overestimated.

Science Fiction in Continental Europe before the Second World War

SALVATORE PROIETTI

For the literary historian, the very notion of "SF in Europe" can be a challenge. Can so many different languages generate a field that can be grasped as a single unit? The proposition seems dubious. Moreover, even insofar as the vague concept of "Europe" can be used as an organizing principle, additional risks present themselves. Prewar European SF *could* be presented as a sparse list of Great Authors addressing Lofty Themes, against a background of self-evidently inferior and deservedly forgotten potboilers, often associated with reactionary politics – or else it *could* be a magma of isolated entities, single writers, and national traditions (some quite crowded) that can only be analyzed in isolation. Either model *could* further assume, as many apparently have, that the postwar emergence of specialized markets and the dominance of Anglophone SF in the later half of the twentieth century has doomed these traditions to marginality.

Nonetheless, refusing to take literary history as a zero-sum game, I would contend that the field of "science fiction in continental Europe" can indeed be postulated, and that SF history can only benefit from a widened megatext, countering tendencies towards erasure of non-Anglophone SF. Coming to terms with such a transnational fuzzy set requires something similar to what Franco Moretti has called "distant reading": the willingness "to focus beyond units that are smaller or larger than the text: devices, themes, tropes – or genres and systems."[1] Facing two world wars; the crisis of *fin-de-siècle*

In a virtually boundless corpus, secondary readings are endless. Among so many explorers of European SF, I would like to acknowledge the inspirational work of a number of scholars: Mike Ashley, Mark Bould, John Clute, Arthur B. Evans, Jean-Marc Gouanvic, Edward James, Andrew Milner, Franz Rottensteiner, Brian Stableford, and Darko Suvin, as well as (in memoriam) Everett F. Bleiler, I. F. Clarke, Jacques Sadoul, George Slusser, and Riccardo Valla. I also wish to warmly thank Andy Sawyer and the SF Collection at the University of Liverpool.

[1] Franco Moretti, "The Slaughterhouse of Literature," *Modern Language Quarterly* 61 (2000), p. 216.

empires; the rise of finance capitalism; epoch-defining scientific-technological breakthroughs; the Soviet revolution; major working-class and socialist movements; wildly heterogeneous – often *within* individual countries – patterns of class structure, social mobility, and literacy; as well as internal divides stemming from the rise of Fascism, Nazism, Stalinism, and the horrors of the Holocaust, European SF before the Second World War found multitudinous trajectories both inside and outside the terms of the high-modernist literary canon.

Constellations

Fuzzy as it was, European SF had its centers: beyond the obvious predecessors Edgar Allan Poe, Jules Verne, and H. G. Wells, the shared background also included Jonathan Swift and the utopian-dystopian tradition, and Mary Shelley and the Gothic, as well as late nineteenth-century figures ranging from H. Rider Haggard and Arthur Conan Doyle to Camille Flammarion, Albert Robida, and J.-H. Rosny aîné. At the turn of the century, the future-war subgenre was a cross-continental endeavor to which virtually all countries and languages contributed, with Germany a likely second after the United Kingdom in terms of participation.

With at least French, German, and Russian writers reaching beyond national boundaries, frequent translations across European languages could ensure some degree of common awareness. As tokens of this awareness, in 1903 Alfred Jarry traced a genealogy of *romans scientifiques* from Cyrano de Bergerac through Villiers de l'Isle-Adam to Wells, and from 1909 on Maurice Renard theorized the *roman merveilleux-scientifique*, followed in the 1920s to 1930s by Régis Messac's pioneering critical work and Antonio Gramsci's nods towards proto-SF in his *Prison Notebooks*.

Popular periodicals in Europe at the time were usually generalist in nature, mixing exotic adventures with nonmimetic genres – but, gradually, increasing degrees of specialization among periodicals appeared. In Germany, Karl Hans Strobl's magazine *Der Orchideengarten* (1919–21) was a bridge between pulp and expressionism (also in illustration), with SF included as a variant of the weird-Gothic. In other magazines, SF was featured alongside popular science. This was the case in Russia, with *Mir Prikliuchenii* (*World of Adventures*) from 1910, whose mastermind, Iakov Perelman, had connections with Alexander Bogdanov and Konstantin Tsiolkovsky; in the late 1920s, *Vsemirnyi sledopyt* (*The World Pathfinder*) was a bestseller, and throughout the decade the SF community was strong enough to support a full-fledged magazine, *Selena*. A similar didactic attempt to join popular science and SF emerged in Sweden, with Otto Witt's *Hugin* (1916–20) – and, much later, between 1940 and 1947, Sweden produced what can be called the first "modern" SF magazine with the first series of the *Jules-Verne Magasinet*.

Among countries in which equivalents of English-language pulp heroes were being published, Germany was the most prolific. Around 1910 the adventures of Kapitän Mors featured a variant of Verne's Captain Nemo, a heroic redresser of wrongs, whose airship often led to space adventures, and whose stories were strongly disliked by authorities. In the 1930s, the Nazis remained lukewarm even towards some of Mors's frankly racist successors, from Sun Koh, "the heir of Atlantis," to the even worse Jan Mayen, "lord of atomic power." This mode of German SF output probably peaked with the career of Hans Dominik, who from 1922 on produced a prodigious number of SF adventures (in which the Atlantis motif was often deployed as a strategy to ground racial mystique), often including fights in which German nationalism and outright white racism stood on the "good" side. (Working in a similar register were the SF juveniles of Denmark's Niels Meyn, a Nazi activist during the Second World War.)

Overall, though, I would not take the shades of nationalism and racism in the German-language SF translated in Hugo Gernsback's US magazines (e.g., by Ludwig Anton, Bruno H. Bürgel, Otto Willi Gail, Otfried von Hanstein, and ranging from space adventure to utopia) as conclusive evidence of their authors' pro-Nazi sympathies (though it is the case for Friedrich Freksa). This is a major difficulty the contemporary reader has in approaching this period: the overawing presence of ethnic/national stereotyping, not just in overtly fascist writers (from Marinetti to "Volt," Daudet, and Pierre Benoît) but also in an author like Bernhard Kellermann who was despised by the Nazis (and who eventually chose to live in East Germany). The difficulty becomes even greater when it comes to exoticism and Orientalism: lost-race primitivist dreams receive a new colonialist boost from Benoît, but later find a new anarchist-pacifist use in Han Ryner, while alien princesses feature in both Bogdanov and Alexei Tolstoy.

At the turn of the century, both Tsiolkovsky and Kurd Lasswitz choose faraway uninhabited places in Himalaya and the Arctic as starting points for their space visions, a political unconscious in action in the hope of – or illusion of – an empire without colonialism. For many writers of the period, the political orientation of SF is above all cosmopolitan, and their outlook is transnational, even when their plots aren't; Wells's dream of a socialist

Europe or world-state haunts myriad utopias and adventures, reaching beyond specific national subtexts. Individual national responses are of course endless: among "minor" traditions, the rise of Portugal's *estado novo* dictatorship is accompanied by a flurry of utopias-dystopias, while Flemish and Dutch SF produces some relevant global catastrophes. The local seems privileged in short-story humor, as illustrated by Spain's Wenceslao Fernández Flórez, Bulgaria's Svetoslav Minkov, and Holland's "Samuel Falkland" and "Belcampo."

In this period, though, the dominant form of SF production in Europe is the novel, and generic mixtures are very frequent. This included Voltairian/Swiftian allegorical satire (Hungarian Frigyes Karinthy and Spain's Luis Araquistáin), religious fantasy (Anatole France), adventure (Thea von Harbou's *Frau im Mond* is actually an adventure thriller for its first two-thirds), or animal stories (whose most famous example may be Josef and Karel Čapek's satirical *Ze života hmyzu* (1921; translated into English as *The Insect Play*). A particular favorite was mystery-detective fiction. In Soviet Russia, a "red detective" motif was crucial to many social and technological apocalypses. In Austria, Leo Perutz's 1923 *Der Meister der Jüngsten Tages* (*The Master of the Day of Judgment*) is a detective novel whose villain produces a drug that induces apocalyptic visions and madness – the only SF foray for a crucial Viennese Jewish author of important magical realism – and many popular mysteries of the 1910s and 1920s by Otto Soyka involved hypnosis or mind control.

On the other hand, different shades of the fantastic incorporated SF motifs. In horror, Germany's Hanns Heinz Ewers's 1911 *Alraune* opened the period with a supernatural plot generated by a hubristic scientist, and French Belgium's Jean Ray's 1945 *Malpertuis* closed it with Greek gods trapped in modern times, inside the bodies of artificial humans; in the 1910s to 1920s the short fiction of Poland's Stefan Grabiński found railways and trains a constant source of the uncanny. There was something dystopian in the dreamlike topology of Austrian artist Alfred Kubin's 1909 *Die antere Seite* (*The Other Side*), a novel admired by Franz Kafka, whose own 1919 "In der Strafkolonie" ("In the Penal Colony") and the posthumous, unfinished *Das Schloss* (*The Castle*, written in the early 1920s) similarly showcase oppressive polities in elusive, ungraspable lands.

In many such novels, the norm appears very removed from the Wellsian model of a single idea that dominates the plot, replaced by apparently rambling, chaotic narratives. To pick a famous Czech example, Karel Čapek's 1922 *Krakatit* is a cautionary tale focused on the possession of a destructive "atomic" explosive, but one that builds into the narrative a complicated array of love affairs that are totally unrelated to the SF novum. I would hypothesize this type of cross-generic proliferation as part of a general trend in classic European realism, marked by the overwhelming role of "fillers" over "turning points,"[2] especially in stories that strive to portray social dioramas. Here, the SF novum sometimes appears as one center among others, or at least not the generative engine for the whole narration, while in other cases novums are manifold, experimentalism turning Bakhtinian in works such as Čapek's *War with the Newts* (1936) or Renard's *The Blue Peril* (1911).

One final general point is that analyzing this corpus requires revising many assumptions about the high–low divide; popular does necessarily imply lowbrow, and the latter was often a way out of "reactionary modernism." The case of SF theatre is the most obvious. Other challenges are presented by French SF, in which a figure like Gustave Le Rouge develops from the same bohemian circle as avant-garde author Blaise Cendrars; a criminal mastermind like Fantômas draws the attention of Cendrars, Guillaume Apollinaire, René Magritte and numerous French literati; and in 1936 we find Jacques Spitz among contributors, along with prominent figures in surrealist circles, to the magazine *Inquisitions* of the Groupe d'Études pour la Phénoménologie Humaine with a piece on "Quantum Theory and the Problem of Knowledge." In Russia, SF was a field that in different roles often involved heretic figures of the revolution, starting with Bogdanov. Among other things European SF contributed to a democratic, dissenting radicalism that contemporary cultural and political systems were increasingly marginalizing.

Visions

Speed, light, empire, and the working classes – the rhetorical and conceptual icons of modernity are at stake in SF, whose own icon of space travel was also undergoing a sea-change. The subgenre was revamped in the almost non-narrative novel by astronautics pioneer Tsiolkovsky's *Vne Zemli* (*Beyond the Planet Earth*), begun in 1896 and completed in 1920), in which a group of scientists build a rocket in a Himalayan castle, first effecting an orbital flight then reaching the Moon and initiating a space program; in a continuing traffic between science and SF, after participating in early films, he inspired the research of Hermann Oberth, science consultant to Lang's *Frau im Mond*.

[2] Franco Moretti, "Serious Century," in Franco Moretti, ed., *The Novel, Vol. I: History, Geography, and Culture* (Princeton: Princeton University Press, 2006), pp. 364–400.

Tsiolkovsky's enthusiasm was contagious throughout Europe (e.g., in this vein work by Victor Anestin and Henri Stahl, pioneers of Romanian SF, and by Ukrainian Volodymyr Vladko).

Responding to the rise of photography and cinema, and adding aerospace technology and astronomy to the mix, the sublime ecstasy of the visual is at the heart of early SF: this is of course notoriously foregrounded in SF film. Against the idealizations of literary humanism, early SF is a powerfully transmedia endeavor (whose precursor is Albert Robida's 1879 *Saturnin Farandoul*, in which illustrations are inseparable from the narration). Paul Scheerbart is a novelist who belongs to the history of illustration (his 1907 *Jenseits-Galerie* is a portfolio of alien creatures) and architecture as well; a cult hero like Fantômas generated immediate transmedia franchises (from film to comics) in multiple languages; Vicente Blasco Ibáñez's 1922 *El paraíso de las mujeres* (*The Paradise of Women*) is initially conceived as a screenplay (by the Spanish author of many worldwide bestsellers filmed in Hollywood); many novels (beside the Lang/von Harbou collaborations, by Benoît, Renard, Rosny, Ewers, Kurt Siodmak, Tolstoy, and Italian novelist "Yambo," a pioneering filmmaker as Enrico Novelli) were immediately filmed, and so belong to the histories of both film and print.

Among literary authors problematizing the visual itself, Maurice Renard stands out. Many chapters of his 1911 *Le Péril bleu* (*The Blue Peril*) comprise long aerial views; his 1928 *Un Homme chez les microbes* (*A Man among the Microbes*), opens with a section entitled "Cinematographic (Why Not?) Prologue"; and in his 1933 *Le Maître de la lumiére* (*The Master of Light*) a scientist creates "luminite," a sort of light-slowing glass that allows observers to look at the past (and solve a 100-year-old murder, resulting in the protagonist's marriage). Less daringly, J.-H. Rosny aîné's 1913 glum *La Force mystérieuse* (*The Mysterious Force*) describes a threatening disruption of the spectrum of light, perhaps caused by aliens from another dimension; Earth freezes because of the disappearance of infrared wavelengths, and civilization degenerates through a defeated social upheaval to pastoral stagnation, though a group of scientists and heroes reestablish control when the effect vanishes.

In 1921, Renard himself wrote the novella "L'Homme truqué" ("The Doctored Man"), in which the emphasis on sight brings about one of the very first cyborg tales. This is a tragic story of a wounded First World War soldier found with artificial eyeballs – a German scientist has implanted "electroscopic eyes" into the soldier, which even allow him to see synesthetically and to glimpse energy forms, but the soldier can't filter or control his visions, and may be seeing invisible beings. Meanwhile, one of France's most popular heroes was a cyborg: from 1908, Jean De La Hire (a Nazi supporter during the Second World War) wrote his novels on *Nyctalope*, a superhero with an artificial heart and other enhanced organs, who possesses night vision, and spends his time fighting villains (dictators, mad scientists) and aliens.

Love and the Alien

The interplay of mutual gazes in *The War of the Worlds* is part of Wells's legacy to the larger field of continental SF.[3] As early as 1897, Lasswitz's *Aus zwei Planeten* (*Two Planets*) had staged a meeting with "good" humanoid Martians, fighting scarcity and lack of water through advanced technology, traveling in space via an antigravity substance named Stellit and building a station around Earth. The novel explores themes of self-determination and freedom through its portrayal of a Martian society of multiple little states that, in the name of scientific research, have moved beyond Darwinian struggle; the Martians choose Germans as possible pupils, ambiguously thinking of establishing a protectorate over humans. They find Earth people, though, carry the seeds of corruption and tyranny – though peace is eventually achieved, and symbolically underlined by an interspecies couple.

Renard's *Le Péril bleu* explicitly challenges colonialist rhetoric (his title a play on "Yellow Peril"), first by presenting Earth (embodied in rural France) as the prey of impalpable beings from an ethereal dimension, who attack humans like fishermen in the ocean. From the perspective of the "alien" Sarvants, an insect/arachnid interconnected group-mind very similar to Wells's Martians, the human conquest of the air is like an invasion of crabs. When, however, the Sarvants come to understand that humans are intelligent and can suffer, they stop their experiments, and the novel closes with the option of a shared planet. This optimistic motif resurfaces in 1943 with Spitz's *Les Signaux du soleil* (Signals from the Sun) as well, in which prospectors from Mars and Venus start extracting oxygen and nitrogen from Earth's atmosphere; when scientists successfully convey to the aliens that humans are intelligent, they stop.

Visual communication is the trope in Maurice Leblanc's 1919 *Les Trois Yeux* (*The Three Eyes*), in which contact with three-eyed Venusians is established thanks to images reflected on a surface covered with a substance discovered

---

[3] For a survey of the amazing scope of his influence, see Patrick Parrinder and John S. Partington, eds., *The Reception of H. G. Wells in Europe* (London: Thoemmes Continuum, 2005).

by the scientist protagonist. Confidence in science is key to this cluster. Danish poet Sophus Michaëlis's 1921 *Himmelskibet* (The sky ship), a novelization of his script for the film with the same title (dir. Holger-Madsen, 1918, titled *A Trip to Mars* in English), is a space opera, in which a sort of airship called *Excelsior* brings a group of disaffected scientists to Mars, where they meet highly advanced humanoids racialized in an Egyptian motif (pyramid-like temples with astronomical observatories on top). These humanoids are pacifist, vegetarian, and even-tempered: they represent a possible evolutionary future for humanity. Friendship with beautiful, luminous Martians is also the theme of J.-H. Rosny aîné's 1925 *Les Navigateurs de l'infini* (*The Navigators of Space*). Rather than the specifics of the *voyage* (though the novel is credited with the first use of the word "astronautics"), it is the *aliens* who are central for Rosny. The Martian "tripods" are dying out, but a new species called "Zoomorphs" is emerging. If the latter remain unknown, the former return in the posthumously published sequel, *Les Astronautes* (*The Astronauts*), in which a Martian father brings his daughter to Earth to get ready to repopulate Mars; parthenogenesis via thought applies on Mars: the male's desire is enough, even with an Earthman – a misogynous twist to a daring dream of interspecies mix.

Even more directly, the alien gaze is at the core of Paul Scheerbart's 1913 *Lesabéndio*; the inhabitants of Scheerbart's "asteroid" Pallas live a utopian life in the name of transparency, and their attempt to reach their star by building an immense tower is a sign of their intrinsic innocence that bears comparison with both Winsor McCay's Little Nemo and Italo Calvino's later *Cosmicomics*. Their quest for beauty in an upward technological thrust, grounded in Scheerbart's contemporary writings on "glass architecture" – an influence on Walter Benjamin – might well be the conceptual opposite to all that was leading to Theodor Adorno's later "negative" views of modernity.

Evolution

Before the Zoomorphs, the French-Belgian Rosny had been the bard of evolutionary anthropology, and many of his works reveal a sort of innocent Darwinism, which he extended from the remote past to the remote future. His 1909 *La Guerre du feu* (*The Quest for Fire*) staged a conflict over the disappearance of fire, leading to the prehistoric humans' intuition of their place in evolution. On the other hand, his 1910 *La Mort de la terre* (*The Death of the Earth*) was the portrait of the dying humanity in a desert earth, a veritable tour de force of neologisms describing a humanity endowed with a communication network called Grand Planétaire – and who practice routine euthanasia for the unfit – who face the emergence of virtually incomprehensible beings called *les ferromagnétaux*. The novel concludes with final acceptance of the end of history, though the mutant protagonist's fusion with the energy of the new beings will allow a changed "humanity" to be part of the future. French SF produced at least another strong proto-posthuman tale in Han Rymer's *Les Surhommes* (*The Superhumans*), a sort of Stapledonian scientific romance, describing the evolution of future species.

Evolution seems to wrap up and subsume all the themes of Karel Čapek's 1921 play *Rossumovi univerzální roboti* (*RUR*), which famously coined the term "robot" (Čapek credited the suggestion to his brother Josef). Set in a faraway island, it focuses on the exploitation of the synthetic workers, grown in vats, whose alienation is reflected in a programming that does not include sexual activity though they are physically sexed. The robots eventually rebel and wipe out humanity after developing emotions; the embedded love story between two robots is the harbinger of their evolutionary leap.

Experiments in evolution are at the heart of Mikhail Bulgakov's two 1925 plays, *Rokovye jajca* (*The Fatal Eggs*) and *Sobach'e serdse* (*The Heart of a Dog*), both Faustian tales with comedic touches, based on Wells's *Moreau* and *Food of the Gods* (alluded to in the former), with eugenic attempts at developing new creatures and skeptic retorts to the Soviet self-confidence in the creation of a "new humanity." In the latter, the ironic self-awareness of the dog is a forceful estranging viewpoint judging humanity, even though there is no classic rebellion.

In the development of images of evolution, the 1930s seem to do away with a linear progressive model, emphasizing ambiguity instead. In Karel Čapek's 1936 masterpiece *Válka s mloky* (*The War with the Newts*), the story of discovery and exploitation of the sentient animals leads first to the advancement of their culture and then to war, the polyphonic formal complexity a counterpart of the metaphor's ambivalence. The satire (ranging from nationalism and racism to consumerism) and the shades of predatory Nazism are embodied both by us and by the newts. A similar emphasis can be detected in Austrian Egon Friedell's *Die Reise mit der Zeitmaschine* (*The Return of the Time Machine*) (post-humously published in 1946, after Friedell committed suicide to avoid arrest by the Nazis, but written in the 1930s), one of the very few time-travel stories in this period in which the machine itself is at the center. The back-and-forth travels reveal a notion of resistance of time which is both pessimistic and optimistic; these adventures lead to repeated hypotheses that the nightmare of the Eloi and Morlocks might be only an alternative future, or that there might be a utopian alternative after them. Notable other examples of the very few time-travel stories from this period include Antoni Słonimski's 1924 *Torpeda czasu* (Time torpedo) and René Barjavel's 1944 *Le voyageur imprudent* (*Future Times Three*), the former a Wellsian attempt to eliminate war, the second a humorous romp; both feature a character who eventually erases himself from history. In 1945, Hungarian SF histories mention László Gáspár's *Mi I. Adolf* (We, Adolf I), among the very earliest alternate histories depicting a Nazi-dominated postwar Europe.

Spaces

Spatial travel (on Earth and in outer space) is possibly the most contested terrain in SF, as it brings both promise and unease. Narratives that focus on Earth travel manifest either conservative or pessimistic attempts to engage in transatlantic communication. These narratives range from Luigi Motta's 1912 *Il tunnel sottomarino* (The undersea tunnel), with the villain discovering and destroying Atlantis, to Kellermann's 1913 *Der Tunnel* (*The Tunnel*), in which the builder is an idealist who wishes to reach the center of the New World (incarnated in New York and the show-business), but the workers revolt, and by the time the tunnel actually opens it has been superseded by air travel. Here the tunnel seems a token of a growing feeling of inferiority on Europe's side. A similar moment of failure occurs in Luigi Motta and Calogero Ciancimino's *Il prosciugamento del Mediterraneo* (The draining of the Mediterranean), which deals with the creation of cultivable lands after a war has destroyed all great European cities, resulting in the economic domination of the United States thanks to electric planes and ships – but the collapse of the Gibraltar dam thwarts the effort. Less glum is Maurice Leblanc, French creator of the hugely popular, ironically anarchistic, gentleman-thief Arsène Lupin, in his 1920 *Le Formidable Evénement* (*The Tremendous Event*), in which an earthquake creates a land link between Britain and France, resulting in the emergence of new lands to cultivate, a lawless site of discovery and possible freedom. The only significant techno-optimistic view is the German future emigré to the United States Kurt Siodmak's 1931 *F.P.1 antwortet nicht* (*F.P.1 Does Not Reply*), which depicts an air station facilitating transatlantic connections (and air-carrier ships). *Il paese senza cielo* (*The Country Without a Sky*), written in 1939 by the Italian Giorgio Scerbanenco, another antifascist whose later career would peak in the hard-boiled crime fiction genre, is a global gallery of extraordinary inventions, with a war between the United States and the Natives (who eventually win).

The triumph of colonialist ideology is Benoît's 1919 *L'Atlantide* (*Queen of Atlantis*), a lost-race tale in which a French soldier is kidnapped by the evil princess Antinea (whose name itself is an homage to ultra-nationalist Charles Maurras; Benoît became an outspoken Nazi supporter). Here, the protagonist's masculinity is challenged and repeatedly reasserted, both in acts of violence and in the femme fatale falling in love with him. Reassertion of such classic cultural roles or stereotypes also operates in the collective sense: "we" might be faulty colonizers (in the use of alcohol), but "their" evil becomes a full justification. In the same years, more formulaic and light-hearted are the lost-world novels by Russian/Soviet author Vladimir Obruchev.

Interplanetary conflicts are strongly racialized in Jean De La Hire's 1908 *La Roue fulgurante* (*The Fiery Wheel*) and Gustave Le Rouge's 1908–9 *Le Prisonier de la planete Mars* / *La Guerres des vampires* (*The Vampires of Mars*). The hope of an interplanetary empire is central in the 1921 *La fine del mondo* (*The End of the World*) by Italian Fascist Futurist "Volt," in which an act of destruction is necessary for the departure of the "etherships" (*eteronavi*) which will establish an empire on Jupiter, the only way out of planetary ecodisaster. But the mission is opposed by pacifists; in a chilling ending, the protagonist blows up the house of European parliament. In Poland, Jerzy Żuławski's 1903–11 trilogy *Na Srebrnym Globe* (*On the Silver Globe*), *Zwycięzca* (*The Victor*), and *Stara Ziemia* (*Old Earth*), follows the vicissitudes of two men and a woman shipwrecked on the Moon; the sequels in the further future address the building of new communities and contacts with aliens, in what appears to be an attitude of mysticism leading to a renunciation of science and technology.

In the interwar years, the few examples of spatial SF are skeptical rather than overconfident or pessimistic. Prolific adventure writer José Moselli's 1925 *La Fin d'Illa* (*Illa's End*) is the cautionary tale of the emergence of an island where ancient documents tell of the conflict leading to the end of "Gondwana," a land that could boast cities fueled by solar energy, forcefields, and spaceships, but at the same time exploited genetically modified apes as servants, under a warmongering fascistic dictatorship. For what might be the first time, nuclear war is equated with total destruction of human civilization. A war is about to begin at the end of Maurice Renard's 1928 *Un Homme chez les microbes* (*A Man among the Microbes*). The tone is light and even comic in this sixty-year visit to a microscopic world, echoing classic satires and extraordinary voyages, until the protagonist is sent back home – but in the subatomic world two groups are about to wage war, and the choice of militarization on the "good's" side might not have the expected outcome. In a metafictional finale, the author steps in and cancels first the world and then the protagonist.

On the other hand, in Thea von Harbou's 1928 *Frau im Mond* (*The Woman in the Moon*), to which Fritz Lang's film adds technological emphasis, the clash between idealism and greed in the search for gold on the Moon is decided in the triumph of love. The final scene with the protagonist couple's embrace might be one of the most iconic in SF history.

Übermenschen and Übervillains

If many works above revolve around strong visionary figures, none of them reaches the absolute will to power incarnated by the protagonist of the leader of Italian Futurism (and later Fascist) Filippo Tommaso Marinetti's 1909 *Mafarka le futuriste* (*Mafarka the Futurist*), beginning with a disturbing chapter on a mass-rape scenario, a story in which a North African dictator, proud of his aeronautic feats, whose creation of an artificial "son" called Gazurmah seems to announce the destruction of the world in his attempt to "dethrone" the Sun, casting the world into darkness. Marinetti returned to SF in 1922 with *Gli indomabili* (*The Untameables*), which mixes racialism and revolutionary dreams in the description of a prison island populated by the formerly powerful Untameables. But SF's *Übermensch* figures are many, and only some cases are in the reactionary-colonialist vein. In 1906, Arnould Galopin's *Le Docteur Oméga* (*Doctor Omega*) uses some sort of "repulsion" technology to move his ship on land, under water, and in space; Galopin's Martians have more than an Orientalist touch. In the interwar years, Friedrich Freksa's vehemently racist 1931 work, *Druso oder die gestohlene Menschenwelt* (*Druso*), joins eugenics with the Atlantis myth and features a ruling caste whose influence and control is global, not national. One can also see strong racist themes in Finnish writer Sigurd Wettenhovi-Aspa's 1935 *The Diamondking of Sahara* (written originally in English, not Finnish), a technological feast with the Sahara turned into a forest.

Although the SF elements in these works are not dominant, Pierre Souvestre and Marcel Allain's immensely popular series of novels on virtually shape-shifting crime-lord Fantômas (thirty-two novels in 1911–13, with Gino Starace's illustrations crucial to the format) was seen as irrepressible, anti-bourgeois, and anarchist, seeming to many to reject any notion of sociality. The series was revived in 1925 by Allain, who penned another eleven novels – three of which appeared after the Second World War.

The "undergod" of Maurice Renard's 1908 *Docteur Lerne, sous-dieu* (*Doctor Lerne*) was a visionary gallery of transplants *à la* Moreau, involving humans, animals, plants, and machines, with an erotic element also stemming from brain exchange (at some point, the protagonist/narrator sees himself as "other"). Similar scientists were protagonists of many tales by Russian Alexander Belyaev: in his 1925 *Golova professora Douela* (*Professor Dowell's Head*), a dead ballerina's head is first explanted and kept alive then transplanted to the body of a dead singer; in the 1928 *Chelovek-amfibiya* (*The Amphibian*) a wounded child is cured with a transplant of shark gills; and in the 1930 "Хоŭmu-Тоŭmu" ("Hoity-Toity"), there seems to be friendship between the genius scientist and an elephant with a human brain.

Other cases seem to provide mirror reflections of the *Übermensch* figure. In Luigi Motta's 1903 *Il raggio naufragatore* (*The Shipwrecking Wray*) a villain is defeated with a mirror that returns the titular destructive ray to its creator. In 1899–1900, in the name of anti-American nationalism, Gustave Le Rouge and Gustave Guitton published *La Conspiration des milliardaires* (*The Dominion of the World*), an attempt at world domination through automata and psychic powers, countered by a group of heroes including, alongside idealists, a scientist who has devised an underwater transatlantic railway and a "psychic condenser." In the same vein, Le Rouge's own 1912–3 series *Le Mystérieux Docteur Cornelius* (*The Mysterious Doctor Cornelius*) is about two brothers leading a crime empire, one of them (the titular Cornelius) a cosmetic surgeon of uncanny abilities, defeated by an alliance involving a scientist, a millionaire, and a Lord.

Post-First World War bitterness drives Albert Robida's 1919 *L'Ingenieur von Satanas* (*The Engineer von Satanas*). Robida, whose writing turned very pessimistic in the latter stages of his career, creates a tale in which diabolical technology leads to global destruction. On the other hand, Maurice Renard's 1920 *Les Mains d'Orlac* (*The Hands of Orlac*) is a direct rejoinder to eugenicist mythology, in which a pianist has the hands of a criminal grafted onto his arms and is consequently driven to murder; here, the name of the scientist, Cerral, directly alludes to popular surgeon Alexis Carrel, the author of the widely circulated 1935 essay *Man, the Unknown*, which is both a lament for a dreaded modernity and a plea for eugenics as salvation for humanity. And in Russia, in Alexei Tolstoy's 1927 *Giperboloid inženera Garina* (*Engineer Garin and His Death Ray*), the titular "hyperboloid" is a death ray and an instrument for world dictatorship. There is much didacticism in this "red detective" tale, from lengthy scientific explanations to social snapshots starting, with the international jet set and including lower classes; the mad or at least fanatic scientist is eventually overturned by revolutionary forces, and, in an almost absurdist ending, ends up an outcast on an island. These superhero and mad-scientist strands of European SF would largely disappear in the 1930s.

Utopias

In this corpus, utopian texts appear from the beginning as a strong antinationalist and anti-separatist strand. In Germany, Theodor Herzl's 1902 *Altneuland* (*The Old-New Land*) features a visit to a social-democratic, nonnationalist Israel; and 1905 Nobel Peace Prize winner Bertha von Suttner's 1911 *Der Menschheit Hochgedanken: Roman aus der nächsten Zukunft* (*When Thoughts Will Soar: A Romance of the Immediate Future*, 1914) features an antinationalist utopia. In 1905, Anatole France's *Sur la Pierre blanche* (*The White Stone*), influenced by Edward Bulwer-Lytton and H. G. Wells, is a *roman philosophique* whose main frame is a conversation in Rome over classic epochs and readings, evoking a united European state, and closing on a far future in which life disappears.

Before the First World War, the signal utopia is Bogdanov's 1908 *Krasnaia Zvezda* (*Red Star*), in which a voyage on a barely described "eteronef" – perhaps an airship with radioactive propulsion – leads to the classic/static description of an advanced socialist Martian society, whose sexual equality has done away with gender roles. In a play on the double meaning of "red," the opposition is between the memories of ancient Mars (in which capitalism built the canals and was overturned by a revolution needing little violence) and a rapidly developing young Earth, which might become more pink.[4] In this double narrative, Bogdanov's utopia escapes the static model, tending instead towards what Tom Moylan calls "critical utopia." His 1913 prequel, *Inžener Mènni* (*Engineer Menni*) goes back to the construction of the canals to talk about culture and revolution, as well as the role of science. In the same years, a different approach to the critical utopia was Han Ryner's 1914 *Les Pacifiques* (*The Pacifists*), depicting an island where Westerners attempt violent colonization but are overcome by the islander's numbers; their eventual pardon is an acknowledgment of possible communication between the two worlds. And there is an ironic quest for beauty in the Hungarian Frigyes Karinthy's 1916 *Utazás Faremidóba* (*Voyage to Faremido*), which has Jonathan Swift's Gulliver meet benign intelligent machines who communicate through musical sounds.

Tolstoy's 1923 *Aelita* – which has shades of Wells, Benoît, and Edgar Rice Burroughs – portrays an advanced Martian civilization fighting scarcity of water, after the Martian irrigation system has been destroyed by civil wars and social unrest. Tolstoy's strategy is alliance, both in the love story between

---

[4] Bogdanov, like Andrej Platonov and Paul Scheerbart, was also a short-story author.

the Earth scientist Los and Aelita and in the cooperation between him and the "proletarian" fighter. Many ambiguities could be argued in the position of Earth people as source of vitalism for an ancient species: Tolstoy's utopia might be beckoning towards both a future and a past. Something similar could be said for a neglected work by one of German modernism/expressionism's leading authors, Alfred Döblin's 1924 *Berge Meere und Giganten* (Mountains seas and giants), a highly experimental novel of almost epic scope describing a future history through the twenty-seventh century, with a blend of sublime technophilia (Iceland's volcanoes are used to melt Greenland's ices), nature writing, and political conflicts. After a disaster, the ending of the work is rural, almost pastoral. A post-disaster reconciliation of technology and morality is also the hope in Ernest Pérochon's 1925 *Les Hommes frénétiques* (*The Frenetic People*), in a thirtieth-century technocratic future that can't control human passion, wars and radiations sterilize humanity, leaving only a single Adam/Eve couple; even without societal scope, the couple is a micro-utopia.

In Russia, Vladimir Mayakovsky's 1929 play *Banja* (*The Bathhouse*) voices both a scathing satire on Soviet bureaucracy and the hope for a return to socialist ideals. In Mayakovsky's play, a time machine reaches the future (despite the opposition of Soviet authorities) and distinguishes between the oppressed and bureaucrats (the future, incarnated in a woman figure, accepts the worthy and expels the unworthy). Written by another exponent of the Soviet dissenting left, Andrej Platonov, in 1928–9, *Čevengur* (*Chevengur*) is both a rural utopia, rejecting work and production, and a formally challenging work foregrounding the problem of contact with the outside, which implies the importance of desire. Above all, this is a novel, at no point a static description.

Written a few years before the Spanish civil war, Alfonso Martinez Rizo's 1932 *El amor dentro de 200 años* (*Love in Two Hundred Years*) is an anarchic utopia of highly technologized small communities, trying to overcome lingering conformism (with a rigid eugenic control over couples, and an all-controlling computer, which renders necessary a leader, if a kind one). Love (both straight and gay) is here the uncheckable force that might help defeat bureaucratic degeneration.

Later returns to utopia are German, by outstanding figures in fiction and theater, both despised by Nazis, and seem to be in the name of healing. In Hermann Hesse's 1943 *Das Glasperlenspiel* (*The Glass Bead Game*) a future Ruritania revolves around a male intellectual order devoting themselves to a "game" mixing philosophy and mathematics; and Austrian emigré Franz

Werfel's posthumous *Stern der Ungeborenen* (*Star of the Unborn*), written in 1945, presents a surreal, depopulated future California, with long-lived, almost incorporeal beings, a "winter garden" to rejuvenate war-shocked people, and wilderness all around – a story of exile with a Dantesque guide.

Bleak Times

The earliest dystopias are conservative. In 1901–2 Albert Robida wrote *L'Horloge des siècles* (*The Clock of the Centuries*), a story of inverted time (subjectively experienced as normal): teeth that have fallen out grow back; financial catastrophes disrupt corporations who have to return their capital to shareholders, and so forth. Robida's novel ends with the birth of steam power and Waterloo – which, curiously, might be the closest Robida comes to portraying a utopia, for at least the complicating factors of modernity (including possible revolutionary threats) have been displaced through this historical regression. On the other hand, Emilio Salgari's 1907 *Le meraviglie del Duemila* (*The Wonders of 2000*) is a story about the contemporary protagonist/visitor's inability to fit into a technological future, written by the most successful among Italian adventure authors. The harshest rejection of modernity, seen as destructive of spiritual values, was in Spain: Miguel de Unamuno's 1913 "Mecanópolis" ("Mechanopolis"), a short anti-science/technology/progress (and anti-culture) story, a pure statement of primitivism.

French pessimism looked like a closed loop of history and culture. Anatole France's 1908 *L'Île des pingouins* (*Penguin Island*) is a satire on an imaginary land in which a half-blind missionary baptizes penguins, a problem for God, who consults saints and theologians and transforms them into humans; the history of Penguinia will end up endlessly repeating the mistakes of human history. In 1910, in Jules Verne's *L'Éternel Adam* (*The Eternal Adam*), largely the work of his son Michel, far-future archeologists discover an ancient manuscript recounting the catastrophe that has wiped out an ancient civilization (our own), whose survivors start over and eventually build that future Empire.

In Russia symbolist poet and playwright Valerij Brjusov's 1907 "Respublika Južnogo Kresta" ("The Republic of the Southern Cross"), presents a future dystopian city in Antarctica, the capital of an industrial empire, enclosed in a dome, stricken by a disease that makes people do the contrary of what they say (*mania contradicens*). In this city, the bourgeoisie who try to maintain order are overcome by the populace. The trope of self-enclosure returns in Yevgeny Zamyatin's 1920–1 *My* (*We*), set centuries after a genocidal Two

Hundred Year War, in which a regimented city-state is surrounded by a Green Wall to keep at bay the post-apocalypse world, and people have been turned into numbers. The key is the love story between the protagonist scientist and the subversive woman, who plans to take control of the starship the scientist has helped to design. He does not report her, but the authorities discover his silent complicity in her diaries. Arrested and lobotomized, he nonchalantly witnesses her torture and execution. A reader of Wells, Zamyatin aims at a synthesis between literature and science (here summarized in a meditation on the square root of minus one). The protagonist is defeated by the One State, but never gives up his faith in knowledge, love, and art, hinting at a dynamic final situation in which his story might not be forgotten.

After Zamyatin, dystopias tend to be much less open-ended. In Karel Čapek's 1922 *Továrna na absolutno* (*The Absolute at Large*), the "absolute" is an uncanny byproduct of a matter/energy reactor, mysticism, wars, and booming nationalisms. The economy becomes the principal terrain of disorder; the absolute produces endless material goods generating a crisis of overproduction rather than a post-scarcity paradise. Science itself is no longer reliable in his melancholic 1922 play *Věc Makropulos* (*The Makropoulos Secret*), a story of immortality as apathy (turned into an opera with score by Leoš Janáček, performed in 1926), in which a 300-year-old woman destroys her father's longevity formula. This view of immortality is shared by André Maurois's 1931 *Le Peseur d'âmes* (*The Weigher of Souls*), while in Maurois's similarly disenchanted 1937 *La Machine à lire les pensées* (*The Thought Reading Machine*), the "Psi-Ki" ("psychograph") is first studied, then marketed as a tool to discover extramarital affairs, then quickly forgotten for lack of interest.

The most classic closed dystopia is Thea von Harbou's 1926 *Metropolis* (filmed the following year) starting with its multisensory opening, from a church and a procession to the voice of the city, and the downtrodden's request for food. Here the city's inhabitants are living food in a Tower of Babel-like allegorical multi-level deified machine, in which humans are to be discarded when unfit. The metropolis's subjects are called by number, but mothering is a haunting presence. The creation of an artificial woman might bring about new subjects, and new roles, as she wishes to be more than a toy (with echoes of both *Frankenstein* and *Moreau*) – but the final destruction, and the destruction of the woman, leaves no way out.

From different standpoints, many later dystopias are in fact anti-utopias, souring earlier hopes for progress. In Spain, this is the case for Luis

Araquistáin's 1923 collection *El archipiélago maravilloso* (The marvelous archipelago), a Swiftian visit to various mystical, primitivist, and eugenic places, and Salvio Valentí's 1933 *Dal éxodo al paraíso* (From exodus to paradise), an anarchist's view of bureaucratic socialism. Misogyny and antifeminism are to be found both in Karinthy's 1921 *Capillária*, a women-dominated society in which miniature males keep building phallic towers regularly destroyed by the women, and in Salvador de Madariaga's 1925 *La jirafa sagrada* (*The Sacred Giraffe*), about a seventieth-century African country called Ebania, where the victory of feminism has created a women-ruled nation and the birth of a male emancipation movement called *hominismo*.

The most frankly reactionary work is Léon Daudet's 1927 *Le Napus: Fléaus de l'an 2227* (*The Napus: The Great Plague of the Year 2227*), describing a farcical, unexplained incident, creating the ineffable all-destroying phenomenon of "napusification." No less surreal is André Maurois's 1928 *Voyage au pays des Articoles* (*A Voyage to the Island of the Articoles*), whose satiric targets are intellectuals (by a future antifascist), the story of a Pacific island in which 600 artists live. The artists have their every need provided for, but are so detached from real life that they require a zoo to study humans. In Russia, Mayakovsky's 1928 play *Klop* (*The Bedbug*) (originally with musical score by Shostakovich), betrayed little hope in the way his society is developing: a hibernating man wakes up in a Soviet world, along with an insect. In this world, bourgeois germs have survived, and both the man and the insect end up in a zoo.

In the 1930s the prevailing mood is despair. In Dutch Ferdinand Bordewijk's 1931 *Blokken* (*Blocks*) regimentation is literalized in a cubist architecture, a (communist?) geometrical state that has managed to suppress the curves and nuances of individuality. The Hungarian pacifist antifascist Mihály Babits's 1933, *Elza pilóta vagy a tökelétes társadalom* (The pilot Elza, or the perfect society) joins two plotlines: the story of a family caught in an endless war and the story of an artificial planet (from life to death). In France, Régis Messac builds two novels on the trope of unbreathable air. In his 1935 *Quinzinzinzili*, after a post-apocalyptic war, humanity might find a second start among the children of a small of group of survivors; but, innocent as they are, they rediscover not only love but also war (over the only surviving female), worshiping the titular god ... "qui es in coeli." His *La Cité des asphyxiés* (*The City of the Asphyxiated*) is an absurdist satire about an underground world in which the ruling caste, thanks to its monopoly on air, keeps the slave "Zéroes" in cruel bondage. In Karel Čapek's 1937 *Bílá nemoc* (*The White Disease*), a dictator is after Europe (starting with a small state analogous to Czechoslovakia), indifferent to a rising epidemic. A doctor (who only treats the poor as a kind of political strategy to persuade the rich to intervene against the war) blackmails the dictator, but is killed by the blind mob. In this work, no group, generation or class can be the agent of salvation.

If, in Italy, antifascist Corrado Alvaro's 1938 *L'uomo è forte* (*Man is Strong*) can save some faith in classic humanist intellectuals against his novel's Dostoyevskyan "Inquisitor," the French Jacques Spitz is savage in two novels from the same year. In *La Guerre des mouches* (The War of the Flies), mutant flies declare war on humans, and win out, keeping only a few specimens alive in the zoo. Targets for satire are attempts at evangelization, Mussolini's speeches, Soviet propaganda, and starving Germans eating fly-sausages. In the end Hitler himself might be among the zoo's inmates; maybe the flies are Nietzsche's *Übermensch*, and maybe specters of Nazism and appeasement. His *L'Homme élastique* (The Elastic Man) is also satiric, with an atomic miniaturization/expansion procedure used as cosmetic surgery, in sport, in medicine, in supporting nationalisms and new hierarchies (especially in Germany, where the Führer grows six meters tall) and to create "Lilliputian" minisoldiers, who become the new humanity.

The most ambivalent work is Ernst Jünger's *Auf den Marmorklippen* (*On the Marble Cliffs*), in which an idyllic pastoral people are threatened by unscrupulous people who create a dictatorship, while old values crumble down: is it anti-Nazi (for its description of camps and violence) or anticommunist? The author himself admitted the ambiguity. In Denmark, Karin Boye's 1940 *Kallocain* is a surveillance society, where truth drugs are used to detect rebellious thought; the main theme of the book, written in diary/memoir form, is the possibility of individual self, and of love, in dystopia.

By the middle of the twentieth century, at least in some countries, SF was ready for rebirth. In the USSR, Ivan Yefremov was publishing his earliest stories during the Second World War; in France, René Barjavel's 1943 *Ravage* (*Ashes, Ashes*) became an iconic tale of nationalist reconstruction, in which, after the collapse of electricity, survivors flock from Paris to Provence, creating a pastoral community under a ruthless patriarch. Here, as a fit work for the peak of Second World War tragedies, I would conclude with Spitz's 1945 surreal *L'Oeil du purgatoire* (*The Eye of Purgatory*), the story of a failed painter who volunteers for a test on the grafting of an artificial bacterion in the optic nerve. He discovers he can see the future, but that future recedes further and further, and the eyes come to see a world of death-in-life; eventually the painter begins glimpsing forms of desires incarnate, and the very extinction of the universe, before ending with a transcendently inverted vision of his own essential self, as it has been seen by others during his life. After the war, undoubtedly, SF in Europe was seeking new ways to see.

Rise of the Supermen: Science Fiction during the Second World War

ANDREW PILSCH

This chapter traces the history of SF during the Second World War, particularly in its US context.[1] During the war years, SF focused on narratives surrounding supermen, and not just the ones who wear tights and leap tall buildings.[2] As comic books invented the modern superhero, written SF became focused on narratives about genetically enhanced supermen. This "superman boom" occurred on two fronts: among SF fans who began to use tropes of the special and persecuted outsider as a rallying cry for creating a distinct SF fan culture, and among professional SF writers and editors who, when not writing stories about these genetic leaps, experimented on one another with systems of mental and physical enhancement such as Alfred Korzybski's General Semantics and L. Ron Hubbard's Dianetics. These supermen tropes were also used to bolster the US war effort in the form of comic books shipped in massive quantities to the troops at the front as both propaganda and entertainment. Tracing this history from the home front to the front lines reveals the complicated relationship SF had to fascist and eugenic politics during this period and also shows how rhetorical tropes of genetic supermen unified a surprisingly robust wartime SF scene.

The Home Front: "Fans are Slans"

Amateur fan historian Dal Coger recalls in a column for the fanzine *Mimosa* an important wartime visit to Al and Abby Lou Ashley in Battle Creek,

---

[1] I would like to dedicate this chapter to the memory of Candace Benefiel of the Texas A&M University Libraries. Candace, who passed away while this book was being edited, greatly helped in researching this chapter.

[2] My focus on Second World War SF and the superman reveals interconnections between written and graphic SF during this period. While not widely considered in criticism, for an in-depth analysis of the technological links between written SF and wartime science, specifically looking at Campbell's *Astounding*, see Edward M. Wysocki Jr, *An Astounding War* (CreateSpace Independent Publishing Platform, 2015).

Michigan, who had opened their home to any SF fans who happened to be passing through Battle Creek.[3] E. E. "Doc" Smith, author of the Lensman series and creator of the space opera genre, was a frequent guest. Coger writes that, at a gathering that included Neil de Jack and the fan artist Jack Wiedenbeck alongside Smith and the Ashleys:

> We all reveled in fan talk and someone came up with the idea, "Hey, wouldn't it be great if we could get fans together and have our own apartment house?" A. E. van Vogt's *Slan* had been published a year or so earlier as a serial in *Astounding* and someone had almost immediately asked, "Do you suppose fans are Slans?"[4]

A. E. van Vogt's *Slan* was one of the first truly important novels in SF history. During its initial serialization in *Astounding* and its subsequent hardcover publication by Arkham House in 1946 ("a time when nobody was touching science fiction in hard covers with a ten foot pole," as Robert Bloch observed), the novel – whose story follows the flight from a repressive future government of a slan (the book's term for genetically enhanced humans) named Jommy Cross – resonated with fans in a profound way.[5] "Fans are slans!" became a rallying cry during early fandom.

Owing in part to wartime paper shortages and the work done for the war effort by many involved in SF – E. E. Smith made explosives for the Army; Robert Heinlein, Isaac Asimov, and L. Sprague De Camp all did engineering work for the US Navy; James Blish served in the Army Dental Corps; Hal Clement flew B-24s in Europe; Fritz Leiber worked inspecting military aircraft, etc. – the professionally published magazines such as *Astounding* (whose July 1939 issue arguably inaugurated the Golden Age of American SF) were in recession and interest in fan culture was surging. The first science fiction convention had taken place in 1936 in New York and organizations such as FAPA (The Fantasy Amateur Press Association)[6] were allowing fans

---

[3] For a more detailed history of this period and the development of fan culture during the Second World War, please see my article on the topic: Andrew Pilsch, "Self-Help Supermen: The Politics of Fan Utopias in World War II-Era Science Fiction," *Science Fiction Studies* 41, 3 (2014), pp. 524–42.

[4] Dal Coger, "The Legendary Slan Shack," *Mimosa* 29 (December 2002), pp. 52–4.

[5] Quoted in John D. Haefele, *August Derleth Redux: The Weird Tale 1930–1971* (Lulu.com, 2010), p. 16.

[6] An amateur press association (APA) is a group of people who distribute written material (sometimes literary, sometimes journalistic) amongst themselves. FAPA was inspired by H. P. Lovecraft's participation in a variety of APAs during his lifetime. Specifically, FAPA consisted of a series of short fanzines sent to a single editor who mimeographed and collated the submissions before mailing them to all participants. See "APA," and "FAPA," *Fancyclopedia 3*, (1959), http://fancyclopedia.org/apa and http://fancyclopedia.org/fapa.

to interact with one another beyond the letter columns of "pros" (professionally produced magazines). As Jack Speer's *Fancyclopedia* explains, in the early 1930s, "a few clubs came into existence, fanzines took form and increased fannish interaction. About 1935, fandom broke away from its commercially motivated roots and became an independent organism."[7] Fandom began to see itself as a distinct culture from "pros" and even general SF readers, who might read SF novels and short stories but did not necessarily adopt the lifestyle associated with fan culture.

Against this background, then, the question asked at the Ashleys' house is important. Thanks in part to population movements brought about by the wartime economy, national contact was increasing amongst SF fans. The groups that formed during this period began to have arguments about the nature of fandom itself. Early fan Harry Warner recalled Jack Speer having suggested that "Practically all fans fell into the upper one-quarter of the population in intelligence, and the average is within the top 10 percent. Fen in the Army went up quickly," by which Warner suggests that promotion was quickly attained by many early fans.[8] In the same article, Warner quotes Al Ashley, who shared Speer's sentiments: "The average fan enjoys intellectual superiority over the average man. But that only means that as a select group we excel the human average. No effort would be needed to find other select groups which surpass the fen intellectually."[9] This attitude was fairly widely held amongst fans at the time.

As Warner stated in an interview published in *Mimosa*, all of this thinking was at least in part inspired by van Vogt's novel: "I think *Slan* may have inspired a lot of individuals at the time into thinking that maybe fans were a 'chosen race' because the Slans in the story were separate and different from the rest of humanity, and fans in those days did feel a sense of being 'different' somehow."[10] Given this view, fans began to see banding together as a key to their survival. At the same event in which Dal Coger recalled first hearing the suggestion that fans might be slans, the conversation about fans as evolutionary beings shifted to a discussion of fan cohabition:

But our idea of closer association was promptly named Slan Center.

---

[7] "Fandom," *Fancyclopedia 3* (1959), http://fancyclopedia.org/fandom.

[8] Quoted in Harry Warner Jr., "Al Ashley," in *All Our Yesterdays*, p. 1961. http://efanzines.com/AOY/AOY-21.htm. "Fen" was an early colloquial plural of "fan."

[9] Quoted in Warner Jr., "Al Ashley," n.p.

[10] Curt Phillips, "One Life, Furnished in Early Fandom," *Mimosa* 30 (August 2003), http://jophan.org/mimosa/m30/phillips.htm.

Our planning included a fanzine room where all occupants would share access to a mimeo, and apartments with northern light for the artists (Jack W.'s idea). What was behind this was the feeling of closeness, of being able to be open in our ideas, that we as fans could express most easily in each other's company. Everyone had experienced the raised eyebrows of mundanes when you tried to discuss science fictional ideas with them. Slan Center would make it possible to be openly fannish any time we were away from work.[11]

The Ashley's house became the first Slan Center, called Slan Shack – but when the group moved to Los Angeles toward the end of the war looking for more lucrative work *and* to be nearer Los Angeles's vibrant SF community, the idea of Slan Center as an actual, functioning autonomous development became a serious possibility. Publishing in their FAPA-distributed fanzine, the Ashleys further articulated the idea:

A suitable square block could probably be purchased for from three to five thousand dollars. Then an ultra modern group of homes, apartments, housing units, or whatever you wish to call them, would be built around the block. In the center, formed by the square, (in the collective backyard, if you will) a larger communal building would be constructed. This would serve as a meeting hall, library, publishing headquarters, central heating plant, and even an electric plant. If desirable, there could even be a small machine and woodworking shop for those who enjoy such hobbies.[12]

The period surrounding World War II can be thought of as the period of "fan utopias," in which readers of *Slan* took the idea of their own genetic superiority seriously and sought to manufacture a distinct fan culture.[13] Though Coger insists that no one took Slan Shack seriously, the Ashleys' article (and its detailed plan) suggests that Coger's is a revisionist history, specifically written to avoid the negative associations the idea later came to have.

This period came to an end with the arrival of Claude Degler into fandom. Degler was an itinerate fan who spent the war (where his 4-F status – the US Selective Service System's designation for those deemed unfit for military service – exempted him from the draft) hitchhiking between fan communes and attempting to organize something he called the Cosmic Circle. The stated goal of this organization played into another theme of fandom at the time: the discussion surrounding a national fan organization. Degler

[11] Coger, "The Legendary Slan Shack."
[12] Al Ashley and Abby Lu Ashley, "Slan Center," *En Garde* 6 (June 1943), pp. 3–4.
[13] Pilsch, "Self-Help Supermen."

anticipated that "fans returning from the war will want to find a well organized *United Fandom* they can be proud to rejoin."[14] The Cosmic Circle, Degler believed, would become the basis for this United Fandom. In addition to this modest goal, however, Degler also imagined United Fandom as a complete culture to a degree only hinted at in the Ashleys' account of Slan Center: "literature, music, history for *united fandom . . .* books for fan children."[15] Degler even, like the Ashleys, hinted at the creation of a fan utopia: a Cosmic Center on land he owned in rural Arkansas.

Degler's agitation for Cosmic Circle eventually came to create problems for fans. Warner's troubling suggestion that *Slan* let fans in the 1940s imagine themselves as a "chosen race" (an inflammatory position in a nation fighting an ideology of Aryan purity) was only intensified by Degler, who referred to the culture he sought to create with the Cosmic Circle as "fanationalism." Degler's call for a creation of fandom as a nation-state was not the first nor the last time that fandom flirted with extreme politics, but his call came at a time when fandom was specifically reeling from internal political strife. In 1937 Don Wollheim read a speech by John Michel entitled "Mutation or Die" at the Third Eastern Science Fiction Convention. In it, Michel argued that Hugo Gernsback's scientifiction "had made idealists and dreamers of fans, since it is the best form of escape literature ever invented."[16] The position Wollheim and Michel advocated became known as "Michelism" and advocated that fans become involved in the political creation of the future they wanted, primarily through membership in the Communist party.[17] In reaction, Sam Moskowitz created The New Fandom, which organized the first Worldcon in 1939, as a conservative reaction against Michelism.[18] The New Fandom was ultimately successful, but the split between Michelist and New Fandom members was particularly bitter, with Wollheim and Michel being ejected from fandom by having their membership in FAPA revoked.

Recalling painful memories from the Michelist period, Degler ultimately caused problems with the pro publishers that fandom, though increasingly seeing itself as autonomous from commercial publication, relied on for

[14] Claude Degler, "Cosmic Circle Commentator," *Cosmic Circle Commentator* 1 (September 1943), p. 3.

[15] Ibid., p. 2.

[16] "Michelism," *Fancyclopedia 3* (1959), http://fancyclopedia.org/michelism (last accessed June 12, 2018).

[17] Ibid., n.p.

[18] "New Fandom," *Fancyclopedia 3* (1959), http://fancyclopedia.org/new-fandom (last accessed June 12, 2018).

circulating information about amateur press associations (such as FAPA) and conventions. Specifically, as related in *Fancyclopedia*,

> [A] copy of the *Cosmic Circle Commentator* had come into the hands of *Amazing Stories*' editor [Raymond A.] Palmer. The declaration of existence of a super race smelled to him of Nazism, and the fanationalistic program seemed the horrid ultima of fans' movement away from the pros which he ... decried. Because of this ... he made it know [*sic*] ... that fans or fandom would not get into the letter departments in the future ... Some fans reacted by saying that Degler's ideas in some form had all been spoken in fandom before, and who the hell was Palmer to try to dictate to fandom ... Others, alarmed at the possibility that other pros mite [*sic*] follow Ziff-Davis's lead and cut fandom off from financial, recruiting, and publicity assistance made haste to inform Palmer that Degler didn't speak for fandom. Palmer modified his statement of the ban, but urged fen to return to the ways of their fathers.[19]

Faced with the loss of support from the prozines, Degler was similarly ejected from fandom and all talk of fanationalism and fan utopian settlements disappeared from fan discourse. As the War concluded, fandom began to settle into the pattern of national conventions now recognizable as SF fan culture. This story of superman-inspired nationalism and the view of fans as a master race of genetic superbeings was not the only strange occurrence on the home front during the Second World War, however. The activities of the pro writers producing the superman fiction that inspired fanationalism is equally odd and experimental.

"We 'Must' Study Psi"

The period from 1939 to 1945 not only represented the birth of modern fandom; it represented the transition from the scientifiction of Hugo Gernsback to the social SF of the Golden Age championed by John W. Campbell and his stable of star writers (including Isaac Asimov, A. E. van Vogt, and Robert Heinlein). Under Campbell's guidance, SF began to focus on the human response to futurity, rather than technological wonder. As James Gunn explains, in a Golden Age story,

> some significant element of the situation is different from the world with which we are familiar, and the characters cannot respond to the situation in customary ways, that is without recognizing that a changed situation requires

---

[19] "Claude Degler," *Fancyclopedia 3* (1959), http://fancyclopedia.org/claude-degler (last accessed June 12, 2018).

analysis and a different response. Or if the characters attempt to respond traditionally, without recognizing the need for a different response, they fail [20]

In Gunn's understanding of this period, the focus has shifted from gadgets and gizmos to the limit of human capability and perception.

Before the more nuanced tales Gunn describes, however, Campbell strongly encouraged authors to produce numerous stories of genetically superior superhumans, primarily during the first decade of his editorship at *Astounding*. Brian Attebery has an overview of the various memoirs recalling the form this pressure took.[21] This superman boom allowed professional writers a way of exploring human potential *as* a technological wonder, bridging Gernsback and the Golden Age. Like the fans described above, professional writers were also experimenting with making *themselves* supermen while documenting it in fiction. In addition to writing about supermen with fantastic physical and mental powers, the SF writers scene, especially the one organized around Robert A. Heinlein's Mañana Literary Society in Southern California in the early 1940s, experimented with various systematic approaches to human enhancement as a means of actualizing their own transformations into supermen. Where fandom read superman fiction as an allegory of their own alienation from mainstream society, the writers affiliated with Campbell's magazine during the superman boom sought to engage in human engineering through psionics, the occult, and, most famously, Count Alfred Korzybski's General Semantics, a system of non-Aristotelian thought marketed as a means beyond mankind's baser instincts.

While most of the writers associated with the superman boom moved on to other topics after the War (van Vogt, who wrote the most superman stories, was a notable exception), Campbell continued to believe in rational, real-world human enhancement for most of his career and would continue to put forward a credulous attitude toward the paranormal in his editorials in *Astounding*. Writing in 1959, the editorial titled "We 'Must' Study Psi" stands as a manifesto of sorts for Campbell's approach to paranormal research:

> You can't control a phenomenon by denying its existence. You can't control it by suppressing it either; suppression simply causes an energy-storage effect that leads to eventual explosive release . . .

[20] James Gunn, "Towards a Definition of Science Fiction," in Matthew Candelaria and James Gunn, eds., *Speculations on Speculation: Theories of Science Fiction* (Lanham, MD: Scarecrow, 2005), p. 7.

[21] Brian Attebery, "Super Men," *Science Fiction Studies* 25, 1 (1998), pp. 61–76.

A phenomenon can be controlled only by acknowledging it, studying it, understanding it, and directing it usefully.[22]

For Campbell, psionic and other paranormal human abilities represented the next frontier of exploration. However, unlike the way these phenomena would be treated by the New Age movement of the 1970s, Campbell rigorously rejected mysticism in favor of a kind of human, paranormal engineering: his focus was on expanding human potential in a rigorous fashion. Campbell's passion for such work was shared by his authors during the period of the superman boom. A. E. van Vogt was the most passionate proponent of Campbell's call for a human engineering. In his autobiography, he laments that "to describe human abilities, we use terms like creativity, intelligence, and so forth. These are not operational terms."[23] This language of "operational terms" appears throughout his fiction. For instance, in *The Weapon Shops of Isher*, van Vogt begins the novel by describing the plight of Cayle Clark, a "callidetic giant," who is manipulated by the libertarian Weapon Shops into a fight against the Empire of Isher on a far-future Earth. Clark leaves his home village to try his fate in the big city but is robbed on the plane by some card-sharps. His Weapon Shop handler, in seeking assistance from the Weapon Shop's Coordination Department has this conversation about Clark:

> "This is Lucy Rall, guardian of Imperial Potential Cayle Clark ... We measured him as a callidetic giant and are watching him in the hope that his rise will be so rapid that we can use him in our fight to prevent the empress from destroying the Weapon Shops with her new time weapon ... "
> "I see." The virile face was thoughtful. "What is his village index?"[24]

Typical of the breakneck and dreamlike logic of van Vogt's plots, this discussion of "callidetics" and "village index" is never returned to, but van Vogt does partly clarify what he means in his autobiography, much of which is taken up with documenting how he used his fiction and lived his life as a self-conscious attempt to escape this village logic and become fully a citizen of an urban modernity. For van Vogt, an engineering approach to human ability sought a way to shepherd humanity through technological change.

[22] John W. Campbell, "We 'Must' Study Psi," in Harry Harrison, ed., *Collected Editorials from Analog* (New York: Doubleday, 1966), p. 224.

[23] A. E. van Vogt, *Reflections of A. E. van Vogt: The Autobiography of a Science Fiction Giant with a Complete Bibliography* (Lakemont, GA: Fictioneer, 1975), p. 93.

[24] A. E. van Vogt, *The Empire of Isher: The Weapon Makers/The Weapon Shops of Isher* (New York: Orb, 2000), p. 57.

Van Vogt, who was, along with many in SF, heavily involved in the early days of Dianetics (before the group became the modern Church of Scientology), also sought the means to enact a properly modern mindset. After *Slan*, van Vogt's most famous and successful novel is *The World of Null-A* (1945). Though this work is still recognizably a superman narrative, the key difference is that the superhuman hero, Gilbert Gosseyn (meant, as van Vogt explained, to be pronounced "Go Sane"), acquires his powers through careful study of General Semantics. Treated as a futuristic regime of mental conditioning in the novel, General Semantics was an existing system of mental training first described by Alfred Korzybski in *Science and Sanity* (1933). Korzybski, who moved to the United States fleeing the increasing turbulence in prewar Europe, begins *Science and Sanity* mirroring van Vogt's concern about village mindset: "One of the gravest difficulties facing the world today is the passing from one historical era to another. Such passings, as history shows, have always been painful, and pregnant with consequences."[25] Korzybski argues that humanity has reached a state of advanced technology but is still mentally infantile, suggesting the chaos of 1930s Europe is "based on structural assumptions which are false to facts."[26] For Korzybski, these structural assumptions result from using the verb "is" to designate an existing relationship between a word and a thing. Korzybski calls this assumption of unity between label and object "Aristotelianism" and offers General Semantics as a "Non-Aristotelian" (or Null-A) system. By dissociating words from things, Korzybski argues that humans can escape animal thought patterns and arrive at a recursive mode of thinking about thinking about thinking (and so on). Korzybyski argues that Null-A practitioners can behave more rationally, free from the panic and fear that so often grip human thought.

In *The World of Null-A*, van Vogt uses his own training in General Semantics as a basis for imagining a superhero narrative. Gilbert Gossyn wakes in a major city with no memory. It is the evening before the trials for General Semantic practitioners hoping to become involved in the Null-A government. As Gossyn uncovers a conspiracy against this world, he dies and is reborn. Eventually, his Null-A training unlocks new mental abilities that allow him to control the shape of matter at a molecular level and experience profound oneness with the universe. With these newfound mental abilities, Gossyn is even able to teleport between planets.

---

[25] Alfred Korzybski, *Science and Sanity: An Introduction to Non-Aristotelian Systems and General Semantics*, 4th edn. (Forest Hills, NY: Institute of General Semantics, 1958), pp. xxxvi–xxxvii.

[26] Ibid., p. 42.

This revision of the superman narrative proved controversial. In "Cosmic Jerrybuilder," SF editor Damon Knight claims that *The World of Null-A* is "one of the worst allegedly-adult science fiction stories ever published."[27] In addition to a variety of other claims about the novel, Knight charges that "van Vogt has not bothered to integrate the gadgets into the technological background of his story, and he has no clear idea of their nature."[28] Of course, as we have seen, in the novel, Gosseyn's mental abilities *are* the gadgetry. This point is lost on Knight. While Gernsback fiction focuses on technology and Golden Age fiction focuses on human reactions to technology, in the period of the superman boom, as best exemplified by *The World of Null-A*, humans *are* the new technology.

In "Getting Out of the Gernsback Continuum," Andrew Ross suggests SF during the 1920s and 1930s created gadget-driven future stories as a means of articulating a "critical technocracy" in the present, as a counter-ideology to socialism during the Depression.[29] As I have been arguing here, the superman boom, similarly dismissed as naive wish-fulfillment in SF histories and scholarship, articulates a kind of human engineering that uses the superman narrative as a means of escaping from the ideology of total war that was driving the world to the brink of destruction in the years before Pearl Harbor. Through systematic approaches to creating supermen, such as Korzybski's General Semantics, SF writers both created fiction for their readers *and* sought to extend the real-world horizons of human knowledge and potential. Once again, we see the superman narrative, so prominently associated with the Nazis, doing work *for* American SF during the period of the War. In exploring how this narrative went to war, we can see how this trope contributed to the struggle against fascism and Nazi rhetoric of Aryan superiority. The mobilization of supermen narratives, however, was most prominent in the comic books sent to GIs on the front lines.

The Front Lines

Beyond providing inspiration to SF fans and writers on the home front as the United States emerged from the Great Depression, the superman narrative played an important role in another avenue of SF history: the comic book. Ian

---

[27] Damon Knight, *In Search of Wonder: Essays on Modern Science Fiction* (Chicago: Advent, 1967), p. 47.
[28] Ibid., p. 56.
[29] Andrew Ross, "Getting Out of the Gernsback Continuum," *Critical Inquiry* 17, 2 (January 1, 1991), p. 415.

Gordon's history marks the emergence of the modern comic book as a simultaneous emergence of the modern superhero. The comic book format was first invented as a means of publishing reprints of old comic strips in the early 1930s, but in 1934 Malcolm Wheeler Nicholson began publishing *New Fun Comics*, the first to print new material.[30] Wheeler's company – after Wheeler was "eased out" – began publishing *Detective Comics* in 1937 (which would launch Batman in issue #27) and *Action Comics* in 1938, which was launched to promote superhero stories in general and Superman in particular.[31] It is not widely noted, however, in histories of this period that the birth of the comic book and the rise to publishing prominence of the superhero comic book coincide with the superman boom in written SF.

Like the SF of the superman boom, superhero comics were potent means of wish-fulfillment and escapism for a nation traumatized by the Great Depression, an association widely documented in histories of early superhero comics. For instance, the opening pages of Larry Tye's *Superman: The High-Flying History of America's Most Enduring Hero* catalogs Superman-creator Jerry Siegel's personal isolation as a gawky, day-dreaming teen, the communal isolation of his predominantly Jewish, immigrant neighborhood in Cleveland, and the various emotional privations that impacted the American consciousness during the Depression (from military atrocities in Europe and Asia to the Lindbergh baby kidnapping).[32] "On the eve of his birth," writes Tye, "Superman's world was awash in heroes" as readers sought escape from a brutal world in simple, moral tales of absolute good triumphant over pervasive evil.[33] As a cheap form of entertainment in the era before television, comic book accounts of these heroic beings, like pulp magazines, exploded in popularity during the Depression.

When the United States entered the Second World War in 1941, these superheroes mobilized for war along with the rest of the populace. Characters such as the Sub-Mariner, The Shield, The Human Torch, and Wonder Woman all famously fought alongside America's soldiers. Most famously, the iconic cover of Captain America #1 features the hero punching Hitler. As Tye writes specifically of Superman but more generally of comics during this period:

---

[30] Ian Gordon, *Comic Strips and Consumer Culture, 1890–1945* (Washington, DC: Smithsonian, 2002), p. 131.

[31] Ibid., p. 131.

[32] Larry Tye, *Superman: The High-Flying History of America's Most Enduring Hero* (Random House Trade Paperbacks, 2013), pp. 1–11.

[33] Ibid., p. 11.

They got all the blood and guts they needed on the battlefield, and all the run-ins with the Nazis and Japanese. Watching Superman battle with Lex Luthor and other fantastic villains let them escape. It offered them a way to feel like kids again and reminded them of the lives back home that they were fighting to protect. No gift could matter more.[34]

Superhero comics primarily functioned, for the troops, as an escape from the realities of war. This escapism is strikingly emphasized in Quality Comic's *Military Comics*, which ran from August 1941 to October 1945. Like other anthology comics of the day (notably *Detective Comics*, which featured Batman), *Military* featured an anchor story from a popular hero, in this case Blackhawk, as well as a collection of other stories broadly organized around the central theme of the comic. Before the United States entered the war, *Military* published stories of Americans serving in the Chinese army against the Japanese, British tank units in North Africa, or stories of Army Air Corp pilots in training. While also featuring Miss America ("a typical American girl upon whom the spirit of the Statue of Liberty has bestowed magical powers"), the majority of the stories were realistic in character and serious in tone. Like *Detective*'s focus on stories of private eyes and cops, these stories were soldiers doing soldier stuff.[35]

By the 1945 issues, the tone had radically shifted. While the requisite Blackhawk story remained as serious as the 1941 issues, the majority of issues are full of humorous stories of GI life. Most tellingly, the Death Patrol, a recurring feature over the full run of *Military*, had evolved from a serious tale of the exploits of a crack team of misfits into a Three-Stooges-esque tale of bumbling attempts of the Patrol to escape from various prisons. These last issues even feature the stories of Choo Choo, a blonde bombshell attempting to make it as a star in the movie industry. These stories feature no connection to the military and prefigure the repackaging of *Military* as *Modern Comics* in November 1945. The stark contrast between the blood-and-guts of the 1941 issues and the light humor of the 1945 issues embodies Tye's point about the shifting need of comics during this period. Whereas the prewar issues of *Military* jingoistically make the case for America's entrance into the war, the wartime issues provide an escape from the everyday violence of wartime life for GIs at the front.

As Gordon notes, GIs consumed comic books at a voracious rate. He cites gender differences in comic readership in 1944, where for most age groups

---

[34] Ibid., p. 60.
[35] "Miss America," *Military Comics*, 2 (September 1941), 24.

differences between male and female readers hovered around 5 percent except for the draft eligible eighteen- to thirty-year-olds with a difference of 28 percent in favor of male readers.[36] Additionally, the Army's Library Service "distributed 100,000 copies [of *Superman*] every other month" accounting for "about 10 percent of the comic's sales."[37] "Comic books outsold the combined circulation of *Reader's Digest, Life,* and *The Saturday Evening Post* by a ratio of ten to one" at many post exchanges.[38] Tye further suggests that the inclusion of comics in the material distributed to soldiers had an ulterior motive: "The Navy strove to end illiteracy within its ranks in part by having the dialogue in a Superman comic shaved to single or double syllables, then rolling out to its sailors 15,000 copies a month of the easy-to-read books."[39]

One of the most striking features of these wartime comics is that the most popular hero, Superman, did not fight in the war. Recognizing that Superman's outsize abilities would prove a liability to the imaginations of wartime readers ("Couldn't he just fly over there and kill Hitler right now?"), Jack Liebowitz – co-owner of DC Comics – made the decision to keep Superman out of the war.[40] Given the escapism military readers sought in comic books, Liebowitz's decision paid off with the character being one of the few to survive the postwar collapse of the comic book industry. As Tye writes, "finding a role for real warriors in peacetime was hard enough, but it was impossible for fantasy characters meant to provide an escape."[41] As Gordon notes, this period featured Superman in patriotic settings on the covers but stories about fighting spies, saboteurs, and mad scientists inside. Reading the pattern of advertising and the content of the stories, Gordon concludes that while less successful characters tried to inspire soldiers by fighting alongside them, Superman reminded soldiers of why they fight: democracy, home life, and consumerism.[42]

As with fan nationalism and human engineering, the superman narrative in comics was ultimately mobilized during the war to market both the war effort (Superman was part of the War Department's push to sell war bonds) *and* the coming peace. While the superman narrative had its origins, in both written and graphic SF, in the Depression, the trope was repurposed during the war for a variety of purposes. However, the unifying thread between these stories is

---

[36] Gordon, *Comic Strips*, p. 139.
[37] Ibid., p. 140.
[38] Ibid., p. 140.
[39] Tye, *Superman*, p. 60.
[40] Ibid., pp. 58–9.
[41] Ibid., p. 64.
[42] Gordon, *Comic Strips*, pp. 137–45.

a focus on the aspirational quality of supermen narratives. Though they may appear escapist, focusing on the human as the central gadgetry of written SF and as the stupendous center of comic book narratives paved the way for the more nuanced exploration of later periods in SF history. However, these periods would largely abandon the superman as a narrative trope.

The Best Years of our Lives

After the horrors of the Second World War were absorbed, SF shifted away from superman narratives. In most SF, the immediate changes coincided with the emergence of what Isaac Asimov called "social science fiction," stories and novels that sought to show the human condition adapting to new technologies for the betterment of the social. Perhaps the most telling example of this shift, specifically regarding the superman as a wartime archetype, is Bernard Wolfe's *Limbo* (1952).[43] Virtually pre-determining much of the bioethical discourse of human enhancement, Wolfe creates a future Earth obsessed with the ideology of Immob, in which able-bodied humans willingly amputate their limbs as a means of preventing humanity's impulse toward war ("No Demobilization without Immobilization" is one Immob slogan). In addition to engaging the emergent discourse of cybernetics,[44] Wolfe refigures the superhero as a disabled body rather than a super-abled body and also draws parallels with the injured body of those returning from the war. Unlike the work of van Vogt and Campbell during the superman boom, these refigured, cyborg bodies strike an elegiac rather than a hopeful tone for the future.

In comics, Danny Fingeroth notes that it was not until 1949 that stories dealt with the emotional burden Superman faced:

> Previously, Superman's stories had never gone into the emotional ramifica-
> tions of the Man of Steel being the last survivor of a doomed planet. But in
> a world where the Nazi genocide of Eastern Europe's Jews was so recent,
> Jewish (and gentile) Superman writers were moved ... to explore territory
> that had previously been considered too deep for comics.[45]

The vast majority of superhero titles created during the Depression and drafted into the war effort folded because they were too closely associated

---

[43] Bernard Wolfe, *Limbo* (New York: Random House, 1952).

[44] N. Katherine Hayles has discussed the novel's critique of cybernetics in *How We Became Posthuman* (Chicago: Chicago University Press, 1999); see pp. 113–30.

[45] Danny Fingeroth, *Disguised as Clark Kent: Jews, Comics, and the Creation of the Superhero* (New York: Bloomsbury Academic, 2007), pp. 66–7.

with the traumas of war that soldiers returning home wished to forget. Of the vast array of Golden Age heroes, Superman, Batman, Wonder Woman, and Blackhawk were the only superheroes to survive in print into the 1960s. As with written SF, a laconic mood struck comics as they evolved beyond the superhero form. EC Comics, whose horror and war comics pushed the boundaries of the form in the 1950s, launched the wildly influential *Two-Fisted Tales* in 1952. Unlike the jaunty jingoism of Blackhawk or Captain America,

> "Two-Fisted Tales" ... explored the traumas and complexities of war. The principle artist of the book, Harvey Kurtzman, eschewed stereotypes, depicted gritty scenes of violence and deprivation, and gave the figures in his comics a manic dynamism that amplified some of the anxieties one might feel in the midst of combat. There was an adult complexity to these comic books, in other words, that was unusual for the medium.[46]

However, these stylistic innovations were snuffed out with the publication in 1954 of Fredric Wertham's *Seduction of the Innocent*. An early example of the moral panics that came to grip the United States in the postwar era, Wertham's book argued that comic books' violent escapism was behind the rising tide of juvenile delinquency seemingly gripping the nation. While associations with war significantly weakened the popularity of comic books in the United States, *Seduction of the Innocent* effectively stalled comic books as a form for more than a decade. Returning home with traumatizing memories of carnage to economic prosperity, the superman, birthed in the twin crucibles of global economic collapse and total war, no longer resonated as a cultural icon. Despite a key role in mobilizing the war effort at home and abroad, this figure was a casualty of demobilization and the rise of a peacetime economy. Additionally, the decline of the superhero mirrored the decline of the pulp industry whose boom during the Depression had first brought him to prominence. As Fingeroth notes, Americans "were living in the Golden Age of television drama, and in the era of the flowering of the modern film and novel," and the pulps, which had always had a seedy reputation, became significantly less culturally important.[47] Despite this decline in visibility, however, the fuller articulations of this postwar ennui would bear fruit with the flowering of literary SF after the war.

---

[46] Kerry Soper, "The Comics Go to War," *War, Literature & the Arts: An International Journal of the Humanities*, 25 (January 2013), pp. 1–20.

[47] Fingeroth, *Disguised as Clark Kent*, p. 66.

12

Utopia . . . : Science Fiction in the 1950s and 1960s

MALISA KURTZ

> As we begin to master the potentialities of modern science, we move toward an era in which science can fulfill its creative promise and help bring into existence the happiest society the world has ever known.
>
> US President John F. Kennedy[1]

The 1950s and 1960s represented a time of tremendous innovation for mankind in outer space. *Sputnik* launched in 1957; in 1961 Yuri Gagarin became the first man in space; and in 1969 the United States put the first man on the Moon, exciting the public's imagination of a coming new era of exploration and discovery. For the first time since SF had imagined it, space colonization appeared to be a real possibility. In SF of the period visions of intergalactic travel, space wars, and new frontiers proliferated, undoubtedly fueled by the historical context of the space race and the Cold War. The next chapter in this volume will take up the dark side of rocketry, grim anticipations of nuclear war – but much SF focused on the optimistic promises of space flight. The work of authors such as Isaac Asimov, Arthur C. Clarke, and Robert Heinlein (SF's mid-century "Big Three") became iconic texts of the Space Age, offering up grand prophecies of humanity's future across the galaxy.[2]

Donald A. Wollheim, long-time SF editor at Ace Books, argued that Asimov's *Foundation* trilogy was in particular "the point of departure for the full cosmogony of science-fiction future history," commending the series for its totalizing representation of future history.[3] According to Wollheim, because "there is only a limited number of general possibilities open to

---

[1] John F. Kennedy, "A Century of Scientific Conquest" in the National Academy of Science, *The Scientific Endeavor* (New York: Rockefeller Institute Press, 1965), pp. 311–19.

[2] Though Asimov's *Foundation* trilogy was initially published in serial form in *Astounding* (1942–50), in 1950 it was compiled as a single novel in what A. E. van Vogt called a "fix-up" with the addition of a new first chapter.

[3] Donald A. Wollheim, *The Universe Makers: Science Fiction Today* (New York: Harper & Row, 1971), p. 42.

human conjecture," all SF that followed Asimov ultimately reaffirmed "what all our mental computers state as the shape of the future" in the following historical steps:

1. Exploration of the Moon and planets in our solar system.
2. First flight to the stars.
3. The rise of a Galactic Empire.
4. The Galactic Empire blooms.
5. The Galactic Empire begins to decline.
6. An interregnum occurs when worlds revert to savagery and primitivism.
7. A Permanent Galactic Civilization is restored.
8. Man advances to explore the furthest ends of Creation in a "Challenge to God."[4]

Wollheim argued his outline, published in *The Universe Makers* in 1971, represented the ambition of contemporary SF, and indeed his consensus future captures the spirit of scientific exploration in the genre. However, this "shape of the future" and so-called cosmology also reveals, retrospectively, the hubris of 1950s and 1960s SF, which assumed space colonization was both inevitable and imminent and that escalating social, political, and ecological struggles on Earth would somehow soon be resolved through scientific advance. Wollheim's outline is therefore also indicative of how much space-oriented SF appealed to greater ideological assumptions about technological utopianism.

In this chapter, I examine how 1950s and 1960s SF and its tendency towards techno-utopianism, especially in the United States, reflects on specific developments in the genre as well as a more general sense of cultural supremacy in postwar America. Though SF was being published around the world at this time – primarily through novels in Britain, with new magazines emerging in countries such as France, Italy, and Mexico – as Edward James argues SF was still largely recognized as an American cultural product as a result of the country's postwar economic and cultural dominance.[5] Book publishing was more prolific than SF periodicals outside the United States, and this difference in publishing markets and literary histories inevitably affected SF themes across different countries; for instance, in Britain post-apocalyptic SF and disaster narratives boomed, largely influenced by the legacy of H. G. Wells, while in the Soviet Union authors used SF as social and political critique,

---

[4] Ibid., pp. 42–5.
[5] Edward James, *Science Fiction in the Twentieth Century* (Oxford: Oxford University Press, 1994), p. 54.

a movement ushered in by novels such as Ivan Yefremov's groundbreaking *Andromeda Nebula* (1957). The technological utopianism of American SF, however, is heavily influenced by the popularity of early pulps such as *Astounding*, which promoted stories that emphasized technological application and possibility.

"Technological utopianism" refers to the belief that scientific advance and technological development are capable of solving all of mankind's problems. In his 1985 study of the topic, Howard Segal argues that technological utopianism in American culture was not ignorant of the problems that could be caused through technological advance, but that "[t]hey simply were confident that those problems were temporary and that advancing technology would solve mankind's major chronic problems" including any material or psychological problems.[6] Importantly, techno-utopianism is not confined to the SF reader only; as Imre Szeman argues, techno-utopianism is "a discourse employed by government officials, environmentalists, and scientists from across the political spectrum."[7] While Szeman refers specifically to the techno-utopianism employed in the oil industry, his argument can be extended to consider how techno-utopianism overrides the sense of potential catastrophic change by assuming science will solve any energy, nuclear, or environmental disaster. Frederik Pohl and C. M. Kornbluth satirize this mentality in *The Space Merchants* (1952) through the novel's protagonist, Mitch, an advertising copywriter who firmly believes that "Science is *always* a step ahead of the failure of natural resources."[8] Technological utopianism thrived in the 1950s and 1960s when, alongside developments in space travel and atomic energy, vast progress was being made in domestic technologies and personal computing; 1962, for example, saw the emergence of the first video game, *Spacewar!*

Careful attention also needs to be given to how 1950s and 1960s SF (particularly the space/galactic narratives) developed in light of global historical change. For instance, postwar America was imbued with a sense of cultural superiority and a widely shared belief in the necessity of technological progress. Such ideological bias manifested globally in the form of policies such as The Marshall Plan, which provided "aid" under the guise of economic

---

[6] Howard P. Segal, *Technological Utopianism in American Culture* (Syracuse, NY: Syracuse University Press, 2005 [1985]), p. 21.

[7] Imre Szeman, "Oil, Futurity, and the Anticipation of Disaster," *South Atlantic Quarterly* 106, 4 (2007), p. 812.

[8] Frederik Pohl and C. M. Kornbluth, *The Space Merchants* (New York: Thomas Dunne Books, 2011 [1952]), p. 18.

imperialism; the Korean and Vietnam wars in which the United States was a primary force; the expansion of what Dwight D. Eisenhower called the military-industrial complex; and international competition for supremacy in the nuclear arms and space races. Outside North America, European colonialism was increasingly criticized by writers such as Aimé Césaire and Frantz Fanon, and decolonization and liberation movements grew throughout the global South. The techno-utopianism of 1950s and 1960s SF proliferated amidst this global context, and reflects a cultural milieu affected simultaneously by decolonization and new forms of imperialism. This chapter will explore how historical change across technoculture, nationalist ideology, and global politics shaped, and was simultaneously shaped by, SF narratives.

Genre and/as History

The works discussed in this chapter are part of what Leger Grindon calls a *cycle*, which is to say that these stories characterize a specific trend in SF and are not an exhaustive representation of the genre's diversity during the 1950s and 1960s. Scholarly criticism of SF from these decades reflects such diversity, as the 1950s has been heralded as both "the true classic era" and an era of stagnant generic growth.[9] Readers of SF will easily recognize other potential cycles such as the New Wave or cyberpunk; the next chapter, for example, will examine a different cycle in SF during the 1950s and 1960s, which emphasized the growing fear and pessimism towards scientific development after the atomic bombings of Hiroshima and Nagasaki. Though Grindon's notion of genre cycles comes from film genre theory, his distinction between modes, genres, cycles, and clusters is particularly useful for understanding SF. Grindon argues that cycles are a "distinctive and more focused category" than genres, and that cycles are held together by the production of specific works "produced during a limited period of time and linked by a dominant trend in their use of the genre's conventions."[10] The techno-utopianism of 1950s and 1960s SF might also be considered a cycle in that it "presents a variable ... treatment of a genre's fundamental conflicts under the influence of a particular time, place, and circumstance."[11] Held together by Wollheim's notion of the "cosmogony of science-fiction future history," SF's intergalactic tales reflect a specific cycle in the larger genre.

[9] James, *Science Fiction in the Twentieth Century*, p. 85.
[10] Leger Grindon, "Cycles and Clusters: The Shape of Film Genre History," in Barry Keith Grant, ed., *Film Genre Reader IV* (Austin, TX: University of Texas Press, 2012), p. 44.
[11] Ibid.

To begin, some of the techno-optimism in SF during these two decades inevitably stems from the residual effects of the genre's growth in pulp magazines from the 1930s through to the 1940s and the Golden Age of SF. Inheriting a tradition from the editorship of Hugo Gernsback and soon after from John W. Campbell, SF during the war emphasized stories firmly rooted in scientific plausibility and prediction. Robert Heinlein, who started his career in Campbell's *Astounding*, exemplified this commitment to rationalism in his own work and considered scientific accuracy a requirement of SF writing, arguing that one of the central premises of the genre was that "no established fact shall be violated . . . It may be far-fetched, it may seem fantastic, but it must *not* be at variance with observed facts."[12] The commitment to instrumental rationality carries into 1950s SF, particularly in works that came to be known as "hard science fiction." The term itself develops in the late 1950s, and Peter Schuyler Miller is credited for first using it in his 1957 review of Campbell's *Islands in Space*, which Miller called "very characteristic of the best 'hard' science fiction of its day."[13] Adherence to technoscientific rationality characterized "real" and hard SF for Miller and for many SF readers of the time, even though, paradoxically, narrative depictions of interstellar space travel overwhelmingly violate the accepted scientific theory that nothing can travel faster than light. The meaning of "hard SF" has shifted since the 1950s, but underlying its fuzzy definition is still the central assumption that the world can be understood through rational thought and scientific observation.

Works typically associated with hard SF most clearly exemplify the technological utopianism of 1950s and 1960s SF, as such narratives are generally premised upon introducing problems that can only be solved through a commitment to instrumental rationality. Part of the appeal of techno-utopian narratives in this postwar period arises from the decade's spirit of technological innovation and the sense that human ingenuity was capable of producing a new social renaissance. SF's sense of wonder became everyday reality as developments in domestic technologies flooded the marketplace – television, kitchen appliances, advancement in cars and flight proliferated as new products were introduced to consumers daily. SF captured the excitement of this period of rapid scientific advance, and soon the genre was no longer confined to the pulps but a part of suburban America's daily life. It is also during the 1950s and 1960s that developments in SF media brought the

---

[12] Robert A. Heinlein, "On the Writing of Speculative Fiction," in L. A. Eshbach, ed., *Of Worlds Beyond* (Reading, PA: Fantasy Press, 1947), p. 15.
[13] Peter Schuyler Miller, "The Reference Library," *Astounding Science Fiction* 60, 3 (November 1957), p. 143.

genre's themes directly to the living rooms of middle-class families – while certain television shows based on pulp figures such as *Buck Rogers* (1950–1) and *Flash Gordon* (1954–5) had short production spans, others such as *The Twilight Zone* (1959–64) and *Star Trek* (1966–9) continue to influence the genre. This postwar economic and cultural boom also symbolized the great promise of the American dream, or the potential for ordinary citizens to buy status, social standing, prestige, and a bright future. Wollheim's eight historical steps and outline of the "shape of the future" were therefore not only a quality of SF, but also an expression of the capitalist spirit: innovative, occasionally destructive, but also always capable of renewal and regeneration.

Stories such as Hal Clement's *Mission of Gravity* (1954 and serialized a year earlier in *Astounding*), Heinlein's *The Moon Is a Harsh Mistress* (1966), and Tom Godwin's "The Cold Equations" (1954) are examples of hard SF that extrapolated on science at the time to consider the difficulties man might encounter in space travel and colonization. In *Mission of Gravity*, for instance, Clement constructs an alien world, Mesklin, which carefully follows the principles of centrifugal force and gravitational pull. As the novel's two protagonists – the native Barlennan and human partner Charles Lackland – explore Mesklin they encounter several obstacles that are easily solved through application of the basic principles of physics. Like Clement's novel, hard SF during this time was consumed by space and imagining the discovery of new worlds, undoubtedly influenced by the space race. These explorations were often stories that reveled in testing the universal law of physics in new solar systems, and any conflict encountered is solved through pragmatic solutions.

Tom Godwin's "The Cold Equations" is considered exemplary of hard SF, though it also reveals how scientific rationalism disguises its own ideology under the name of "objectivity." Godwin's story takes place aboard an Emergency Dispatch Ship headed to supply an outer planet with much-needed medicine. When a stowaway (Marilyn) is discovered on board, the pilot (Barton) is forced to explain that she must be jettisoned, as the ship does not have enough fuel to complete its mission with excess weight aboard. Marilyn's weight compromises the mission to save the lives of six other men, and because she cannot pilot the vessel "there could be no alternative" for Barton except to "coldly, deliberately, take the life of a [wo]man."[14] Despite the story's refusal to succumb to sentimentality and its ability to follow through on the purely rational decision of ejecting Marilyn into space,

---

[14] Tom Godwin, "The Cold Equations," in R. Silverberg, ed., *The Science Fiction Hall of Fame: Volume 1, 1929–1964* (New York: Orb, 1998 [1954]), p. 449.

scholars such as Mark Bould and Sherryl Vint note celebration of such rationalism also "adamantly ignore[s] the story's systematic repression of all the human decisions that created the problem in the first place."[15] Similarly, Cory Doctorow questions the ethical implications of the story, asking why an author would construct a ship and mission with no margin for error in the first place; thus, for Doctorow, "The Cold Equations" is ultimately not about following the laws of physics so much as an excuse for "moral hazard" and "justifiable murder."[16]

The notion of "rationalism" in Godwin's story is not only intentionally designed; such knowledge is also privileged for a select few and women are clearly excluded from this category. Looking back on Godwin's story, it is hard to ignore how the story constructs the "laws" of the universe as the territory of men.[17] Barton spends pages dwelling on the difference between space-traveling men who know "the laws of nature" and girls who simply do not: "The men of the frontier knew – but how was a girl from Earth to fully understand?"[18] Just as Marilyn is jettisoned from Godwin's story, in many ways hard SF of the time occludes the concerns of women and people of color, and comes to assume the universal value of a particular brand of Western rationality and logic. Notably, hard SF's assumptions and its roots in patriarchal science were already being questioned in the 1950s by the feminist writings of authors such as Judith Merril. Merril's "Dead Center" (1954) and "The Lady Was a Tramp" (1956), for example, challenge the machismo of SF's space narratives. "Daughters of the Earth" (1952) in particular re-writes intergalactic narratives that have disregarded women's perspectives of space travel. The novella focuses on six generations of women (rather than a lone male protagonist, or a lone male protagonist and his sidekick alien), and, as Lisa Yaszek notes, "goes on to imagine an alternate history of humanity's fascination with space" in which women take a central role in space colonization and exploration.[19]

By excluding certain categories of people from its visions of the future, hard SF such as "The Cold Equations" implicitly defines the techno-utopian

---

[15] Mark Bould and Sherryl Vint, *The Routledge Concise History of Science Fiction* (New York: Routledge, 2011), p. 85.

[16] Cory Doctorow, "Cold Equations and Moral Hazard," *Locus Online*, www.locusmag .com/Perspectives/2014/03/cory-doctorow-cold-equations-and-moral-hazard (last accessed August 15, 2016).

[17] Godwin, "The Cold Equations," p. 463.

[18] Ibid.

[19] Lisa Yaszek, *Galactic Suburbia: Recovering Women's Science Fiction* (Columbus, OH: The Ohio State University Press, 2008), p. 36.

future as a space reserved for select "rational" and exceptional (and almost exclusively white) men. Heinlein's interplanetary wars (e.g., *Double Star, Starship Troopers, The Moon is a Harsh Mistress*), A. E. van Vogt's libertarian empires (e.g., *Slan, The Weapon Shops of Isher*), and Asimov's galactic histories all propagate visions of a future in which it is primarily men of European descent who survive, and with them their social prejudices and hierarchies. It is Asimov's Foundation series, however, which is arguably the quintessential example of how SF imagines empires founded upon the superior intelligence of a small minority of men. The trilogy follows the history of a crumbling empire whose demise risks destroying the scientific progress that has already been achieved. In an attempt to preserve this scientific knowledge and rebuild a new empire that will eliminate the "great human misery" of previous generations, Hari Seldon, a mathematician who has modeled the coming collapse, "establishe[s] two Foundations at 'opposite ends of the Galaxy' ... their location was so designed that in one short millennium events would knit and mesh so as to force out of them a stronger, more permanent, more benevolent Second Empire."[20] Both Foundations are meant to continue the project of scientific development after the decline of the Galactic Empire, but they are also intended to "guide" the emergence of a new empire; Seldon's calculations indicate that by following his "Plan" the coming dark can be reduced from 100,000 years to only 1,000. The terms of the Plan are openly anti-democratic; as the third book in the series describes it, the Seldon Plan intends to provide for the emergence of a Second Foundation to be led by a group of select scientists, as "[o]nly an insignificant minority ... are inherently able to lead Man through the greater involvements of Mental Science."[21] The Plan is meant to culminate in a second Empire, led in secret by the Second Foundation, whose knowledge and power is used to control the galaxy in what Wollheim would call a more "Permanent Galactic Civilization." Returning to the Foundation series in the 1970s and 1980s, Asimov complicated the original terms of the fantasy, casting significant doubt on the wisdom and desirability of the Seldon Plan; this thematic ambiguity was left unresolved when he died before completing the expanded series.

If the trilogy in its original form represents "the point of departure for the full cosmogony of science-fiction future history,"[22] it also represents the sense

---

[20] Isaac Asimov. *Foundation, Foundation and Empire, Second Foundation* (New York: Alfred A. Knopf, 2010 [1951–3]), p. 205.
[21] Ibid., p. 499.
[22] Wollheim, *The Universe Makers*, p. 42.

of exceptionalism cultivated through Golden Age SF and postwar cultural ideology. Asimov himself exemplified this sense of exceptionalism when in an interview with James Gunn he argued that "science fiction['s] ... very nature is intended to appeal (a) to people who value reason and (b) to people who form a small minority in a world which doesn't value reason."[23] Like the superior intelligence of members of the First and Second Foundation, Edward James notes that "SF fans naturally identified themselves with a minority who saw the world more clearly than their fellows."[24] Similarly, Roger Luckhurst argues that stories such as Asimov's Foundation series appealed to readers who were often marginalized because it enabled them to envision themselves as "elite engineers of imperial history, [transcending] the pettiness of everyday existence with uncanny scientific predictive power";[25] little wonder the series has inspired a diverse spectrum of fans ranging from Paul Krugman on the left to Newt Gingrich on the right. This sense of exceptionalism flourished particularly in the context of American SF, which dominated SF's mass market publishing and paperback industry.

Importantly, SF's orientation towards positivist science and "elite engineers" in the 1950s and 1960s is as much a symptom of the genre's techno-optimism as it is a reflection of US paternalism and imperialism. SF's techno-optimism reflects larger socio-cultural trends during this time, specifically in relation to the shared perception amongst governments, scientists, and the public that global advance was wedded to American cultural and technological advance. Edward Teller, the father of the Hydrogen bomb, for example, argued in 1962 that the United States needed to focus more on scientific innovation because "the whole dynamic civilization of the West, for which America is the spearhead, is based upon scientific and technological advancements."[26] Teller's statement reflects the push for exceptionalism that characterized US politics of the time, particularly in regards to the space race. Kennedy's expansion of space programs in the early 1960s was designed specifically to re-inspire confidence in American technological superiority, and in his speeches Kennedy made clear the idea that American success in space meant global success. In his address to Congress in May 1961 he argued, "Now it is time to take longer strides – time for a great new

---

[23] James Gunn, "An Interview with Isaac Asimov," in C. Freedman, ed., *Conversations with Isaac Asimov* (Jackson, MS: University of Mississippi Press, 2005), p. 54.

[24] James, *Science Fiction in the Twentieth Century*, p. 71.

[25] Roger Luckhurst, *Science Fiction* (Malden, MA: Polity Press, 2005), p. 724.

[26] Quoted in Milton Leitenberg, "The Present State of the World's Arms Race," *Bulletin of the Atomic Scientists* 28, 1 (January 1972), p. 17.

American enterprise – time for this nation to take a clearly leading role in space achievement, which in many ways may hold the key to our future on earth."[27] One wonders though who exactly the collective "we" is that Kennedy refers to in "our future on earth"; part of the problem of techno-utopianism is not just the assumption that technology will provide solutions to all of mankind's problems, but rather *whose* problems are selected as most important.

Manichean Allegories / Oppositions

The assumption that the scientific and social development of mankind will be possible through the genius of a small minority of rational experts is troubling on a number of fronts. First, it creates problematic hierarchal divisions which are clearly evident in 1950s and 1960s SF, divisions which ultimately support the construction of Manichean oppositions and a colonial gaze. Secondly, because techno-utopian SF fails to acknowledge the ideological biases behind these Manichean oppositions, it also fails to recognize its own complicity in reproducing imperialist ways of thinking. These imperialist frameworks are most evident through SF's deployment of the colonial gaze, and through the Manichean oppositions techno-utopian SF sets up between "white and black, good and evil, superiority and inferiority, civilization and savagery, intelligence and emotion, rationality and sensuality, self and Other."[28] Though Abdul JanMohamed refers to colonialist literary representations when he argues that such Manichean oppositions are "the dominant model of power" and therefore "the central feature of the colonialist cognitive framework,"[29] all the oppositions he identifies are equally applicable to the context of techno-utopian SF. From SF fandom's sense of exceptionalism to the very formation of the genre's primary images, techno-utopian SF creates divisions between characters who are "rational" (and therefore superior) and characters who are "irrational" (and inherently inferior), replicating colonial models of power. Aliens, robots, and disposable human others are central counterparts to SF's space heroes.

Consider, once again, Asimov's iconic robot novels, which are premised upon the idea that "robots would be allowed to free men of poverty and

---

[27] John F. Kennedy, "Special Message to the Congress on Urgent National Needs" (May 24, 2004), NASA (last accessed September 15, 2016).

[28] Abdul R. JanMohamed, "The Economy of Manichean Allegory: The Function of Racial Difference in Colonialist Literature," *Critical Inquiry* 12, 1 (1985), p. 63.

[29] Ibid.

toil."[30] Advancement in robotics, however, is only possible through the continued application of imperial power between humans and robots. Earthers despise robots and keep them hidden from view in fields, where they perform most of the agricultural and mining work to sustain Earth's over-populated cities, and though robots are more valued by Spacers they are also seen simply as tools to be used in colonizing new planets. However, this careful division between humans and robots is soon threatened by the development of advanced robotics and the creation of R. Daneel, a robot who looks, sounds, and to an extent thinks like humans. While both novels are murder mysteries, their central narrative tension is arguably not about solving the murder case but about detective Elijah Baley's struggle to come to terms with the fact that Daneel is "almost the same, but not quite."[31]

Though robots are treated merely as tools, the novels' need to consistently illustrate the difference between humans and robots makes clear that humans are threatened by the performative similarity of robots. Like Homi Bhabha's argument that mimicry exposes the ideological constructions and artificiality behind representations of power, Daneel threatens to expose the ambiguous framework behind what it means to be human.[32] To reassert power and ideological superiority, Asimov's novels establish a colonial framework under the codified "Three Laws of Robotics," which provides scientific justification for a robot's difference.[33] For example, the second law of robotics states that a robot must obey orders given to it by a human, a law intentionally designed to eliminate the idea of freewill while requiring submission to human power. Baley himself recognizes this in *The Caves of Steel* when he asks Daneel for the time despite having his own watch. Confused by why he would ask Daneel to perform such a trivial task, Baley recognizes the true psychological purpose of his command: "To give the robot a trivial order that he must fulfill emphasized his roboticity and, contrariwise, Baley's humanity."[34] Though asking for the time is a common question and Daneel responds to Baley's as any human would, the Three Laws of Robotics requires Daneel to respond where a human

---

[30] Isaac Asimov, *The Robot Novels: The Caves of Steel and the Naked Sun* (Garden City, NY: Doubleday, 1957), p. 348.
[31] See Homi Bhabha's discussion of mimicry in *The Location of Culture* (New York: Routledge, 1994), p. 122.
[32] Ibid.
[33] Tellingly, Asimov developed the Three Laws of Robotics upon John W. Campbell's suggestion. See James Gunn, *Isaac Asimov: The Foundations of Science Fiction* (Toronto: Scarecrow Press, 2005), p. 47.
[34] Asimov, *The Robot Novels*, p. 170.

might not – this artificially imposed rule represents the thin line between Daneel's "roboticity" and Baley's "humanity."

As the ultimate Other, robots perform the same function for both Earthers and Spacers: their difference as robots emphasizes the humanity and superior intelligence of the novels' human characters. SF's colonial gaze, then, makes possible the very premise of the Three Laws of Robotics. John Rieder argues the colonial gaze is one of SF's most recognizable conventions, where narrative voice and power are given to the (white, male) observer; as Rieder says, the cognitive framework of the colonial gaze in SF "distributes knowledge and power to the subject who looks, while denying or minimizing access to power for its object, the one looked at."[35] Though robots such as Daneel appear very similar to humans, the novel constructs a series of practices and beliefs to ensure that robots are ultimately never seen as human. In *The Naked Sun*, for example, Baley proclaims that Daneel is "logical but not reasonable"[36] in his detective work because Daneel cannot possibly understand Solaria's cultural differences. (Baley having been on Solaria for two days, however, obviously does.)

Though colonial narratives often represent the dispossessed as disposable and insignificant, robots are in fact critical to maintaining Solaria's economy and social structure in *The Naked Sun*. As Asimov's characters note, space colonization is possible only with "robots to help";[37] indeed, "one of the reasons the first pioneers left Earth to colonize the rest of the Galaxy was so that they might establish societies in which robots would be allowed to free men of poverty and toil."[38] Without acknowledging it, Asimov's novels point out a central fact about modern scientific advance: its roots are deeply intertwined in European settler-colonialism. In order to "free men of poverty and toil" Asimov's novels construct robots in an attempt to ignore the fact that social and scientific progress has historically been made at the expense of slave labor. As Sandra Harding points out, postcolonial histories of science and technology reveal how "modern sciences . . . emerged in Europe in part because of the resources provided to them by the Voyages of Discovery and subsequent stages of European expansion."[39] Thus when in 1963 Frederick Benham claimed "There is one powerful force working

---

[35] John Rieder, *Colonialism and the Emergence of Science Fiction* (Middletown, CT: Wesleyan University Press, 2008), p. 7.
[36] Asimov, *The Robot Novels*, p. 232.
[37] Ibid., p. 164.
[38] Ibid., p. 348.
[39] Sandra G. Harding, *Is Science Multi-Cultural: Postcolonialism, Feminism, and Epistemologies* (Bloomington, IN: Indiana University Press, 1998), p. 111.

constantly towards greater output per head and ever-rising standards of living. It is the march of science and invention; in technical progress lies the economic hope of mankind,"[40] his comment hides the fact that the global North's "ever-rising standards of living" have frequently been at the expense of people of color and the global South. Similarly, under the guise of objectivity, technoscientific SF such as Asimov's robot novels ignore how Western rationality and scientific progress have in fact been critical tools in the continuation of imperial violence.

Robots are necessary to Solaria's freedom and increased standards of living, and Solarians suggest they have also enabled social equality. Class has no function on Solaria and social competition has been eliminated. They have achieved this because "in place of the dispossessed are robots."[41] While Solaria may depict a post-racial future in which there is little social difference, comparison of robots with the dispossessed signifies that imperialist ideologies have not disappeared; they have merely been displaced onto non-human others. Colonial space narratives, such as *The Caves of Steel* and *The Naked Sun*, proliferate at a historical moment when on the world stage nations in the global South were challenging the very real dispossession enabled under colonial rule. Published between 1954 and 1957, Asimov's novels frame the 1955 Bandung conference and the first meeting of Asia's and Africa's newly independent countries. In the context of such postcolonial nationalism, Asimov's novels and their erasure of the historical struggles of the dispossessed seem both strikingly naïve and disturbingly imperialistic. This is perhaps a judgment even Asimov himself would agree with: when he later expanded the Foundation novels in the 1970s and 1980s he merged them with the robot metanarrative and revealed none other than a disguised R. Daneel Olivaw as both the secret power behind the throne of the Galactic Empire and the secret co-architect of the Seldon Plan, reversing the racialized logic of servant/master that had previously characterized the robot books.

Like many works published during the 1950s and 1960s Asimov's robot novels do not directly address colonialism or race, but their deployment of the colonial gaze reveals how such texts harbor the same imperialist tendencies they claim to eschew.[42] When texts such as Arthur C. Clarke's *Childhood's*

---

[40] Quoted in David Dickson, *The Politics of Alternative Technology* (New York: Universe Books, 1975), p. 35.

[41] Asimov, *The Robot Novels*, p. 313.

[42] *Black Man's Burden* (1961-2) by Mack (Dallas McDord) Reynolds is an exception to this and directly addresses issues regarding race and colonialism, though it also reproduces a colonial gaze by succumbing to stereotypes about "primitive" African societies.

End (1953) did confront questions of race in the future, they often imagined a post-racial future where "the convenient word 'nigger' was no longer taboo in polite society . . . [And it] had no more emotional content than such labels as republican or Methodist, conservative or liberal."[43] Just as Asimov's novels perpetuate a colonial gaze, Clarke's novel supports colonial ideologies which erase the very real struggles of African Americans. As Bould argues, "From the 1950s onwards, sf in the US magazine and paperback tradition postulated and presumed a color-blind future," but "the problem with such a gesture, of course, is that rather than putting aside trivial and earthly things, *it validates and normalizes very specific ideological and material perspectives*, enabling discussions of race and prejudice on a level of abstraction while stifling a more important discussion about real, material conditions" (my emphasis).[44] Such color-blind SF erases the historical struggles of people of color, trivializing and invalidating, for instance, the effects of Jim Crow laws, the struggles of civil rights movements, and the violence perpetuated under colonial and neo-colonial regimes.

Bould also points out the limitations of SF television during this time, particularly in the cosmopolitan fantasies of series such as *Star Trek* (1966–9), which depict a future free from racial prejudice even while "reveal[ing] the limitations of liberal discourse."[45] For instance, the series is often credited with airing the first interracial kiss in US television. In an episode from November 1968 titled, "Plato's Stepchildren," Captain Kirk and Lieutenant Uhura kiss, but the gesture is involuntary, as both Kirk and Uhura are manipulated by an alien species through telekinesis. Even while providing visions of a cosmopolitan future, then, the series positions aliens as the true reason behind the characters' desire. Furthermore, *Star Trek*'s depiction of an egalitarian future ultimately resubordinates all races to a white man and his Federation, both determined to assimilate all others into its ideological fold under the premise of equality and peaceful cooperation. By prioritizing technological progress or the exciting possibilities of space travel over thinking through the difficult challenges of social stratification, works such as Asimov's robot novels, Clarke's *Childhood's End*, and *Star Trek* ultimately normalize a colonial gaze.

---

43 Arthur C. Clarke, *Childhood's End* [1953] (New York: Del Rey, 1990), p. 83.
44 Mark Bould, "The Ships Landed Long Ago: Afrofuturism and Black SF," *Science Fiction Studies* 34, 2 (July 2007), pp. 177, 180.
45 Mark Bould, "Film and Television," in Edward James and Farah Mendlesohn, eds., *The Cambridge Companion to Science Fiction* (Cambridge: Cambridge University Press, 2003), p. 90.

Other space/alien stories during this time constructed similar Manichean oppositions between "us" and "them," including James Blish's *Cities in Flight* series (1950–62); Asimov's problematic exploration of race in *The Currents of Space* (1952) and the rest of his Galactic Empire series (1945–51); Heinlein's *Stranger in a Strange Land* (1961);[46] Frank Herbert's *Dune* (1965); Roger Zelazny's *This Immortal* (1965); and Robert Silverberg's *Thorns* (1967). Heinlein's *Starship Troopers* (1959) is one of the most controversial and obvious examples of such imperialist tendencies against the treatment of "alien" difference. The novel follows a soldier named Juan "Johnny" Rico as he enlists in the army and takes part in an interstellar war, also known as the "The Bug War," against an alien species. Heinlein's novel is an example of the SF Bould points to as embracing a form of multi-culturalism that erases the real histories of violence endured by people of color, thereby hiding its own colonialist attitude.

While the future of *Starship Troopers* claims to be a "democracy unlimited by race, color, creed, birth, wealth, sex, or conviction,"[47] it reserves its fear of difference and subsequent aggression for the alien "Bugs." Rico's instructor is the epitome of this mentality, and he claims that even if humans attempted to live through peace, "soon (about next Wednesday) the Bugs move in, kill off this breed which 'ain'ta gonna study war no more' and the universe forgets us."[48] For Rico, the only way to deal with the "invasion" of difference is, "Either we spread and wipe out the Bugs, or they spread and wipe us out."[49] As Brooks Landon points out, "one of the many galling assumptions in *Starship Troopers*," is "that contact with alien cultures would inevitably lead to war."[50] Heinlein's novel represents "one of the ways in which SF has managed to be at once a visionary and a blindered literature,"[51] particularly in regards to race and colonial histories of violence. Since its publication, *Starship Troopers* has been criticized for its militarism and violence, especially in light of growing resistance to the United States' involvement in the Vietnam War at the time; debate rages about whether the book and

[46] For discussion of how Heinlein's novel "portray[s] inward voyages in imperial terms" see David Higgins, "Psychic Decolonization in 1960s Science Fiction," *Science Fiction Studies* 40.2 (July 2013), pp. 228–45; p. 229.

[47] Robert Heinlein, *Starship Troopers* [1959] (New York: Penguin, 1987), p. 194.

[48] Ibid., p. 196.

[49] Ibid.

[50] Brooks Landon, *Science Fiction After 1900: From the Steam Man to the Stars* (New York: Routledge, 2002), p. 69.

[51] Ibid.

especially its 1997 film adaptation by Paul Verhoeven represent a fascist or an antifascist take on the future.[52]

Heinlein's division between humans and "Bugs" is only an extreme manifestation of the colonial gaze that underlies many SF texts. Whether as aliens or robots, non-human others abound in 1950s and 1960s SF, and they betray how SF reproduces, and in some cases openly supports, colonialist ways of thinking. If SF at this time frequently reproduced imperial frameworks, this was also due in part to the ideological atmosphere in US politics. The Cold War, the impact of McCarthyism, postwar American cultural supremacy, and escalating racial tensions after legal challenges to segregation such as Brown vs. Board of Education (1954), meant that politically and socially America was rife with social divisions between "us" and "them." Furthermore, policies such as the Immigrant Act, which restricted Asian immigration (until 1965) and the Bracero programs, which permitted cheap, exploitable labor from Mexico, ensured the values of white, middle-class America were protected from "hordes" of alien immigrants. Techno-utopian SF may have been consumed with the promises of atomic energy and space travel, but it was also ultimately symptomatic of greater socio-cultural forces that saw progress as the necessary advancement of Western science and civilization.

Whose Galaxy? The Times They Are a Changin'

Like Asimov's techno-utopian imaginings, Wollheim's consensus future sits easily on colonial frameworks perpetuated through SF's colonial gaze and its Manichean oppositions. However, SF's techno-utopian cycle begins to crumble in the late 1960s despite the achievement of America's first Moon landing in 1969 and the realization of Kennedy's dream. What happened? Historically, the world was changing once again. In 1966 delegates from around the world gathered in Havana for the first Tricontinental Conference of Solidarity of the Peoples of Africa, Asia, and Latin America. The gathered representatives shared a common purpose of coming together against contemporary forms of colonialism, neocolonialism, and imperialism, particularly as exhibited by the United States in Vietnam and Southeast Asia. Robert Young claims, "in many ways [the conference] represents the formal initiation of a space of international resistance of which the field of postcolonial theory would be

---

[52] See for example Joe Haldeman's *The Forever War* (1974), a well-known critique of Heinlein's militaristic agenda.

a product."[53] In the United States, Civil Rights Acts were signed in 1964 and 1968, and counter-cultural movements of the 1960s challenged middle-class American values.

Times were changing in SF as well. Alongside SF's techno-utopian cycle, SF also developed works that were biting critiques of the consumerism, Cold War paranoia, and conservatism that defined much of the 1950s and 1960s. With the New Wave and more diverse representation across the genre, SF would once again see the emergence of new cycles. As previously mentioned, feminist SF authors began to challenge SF's patriarchal frameworks; post-colonial science studies challenged modern science's claim to value-neutrality;[54] and authors such as Samuel Delany began to re-write SF's colonial gaze. Interestingly, Delany admired Heinlein's *Starship Troopers*, citing his revelation that Johnny Rico is black as an example of the genre's unique potential (though the text of the novel actually suggests Rico is of Filipino descent, not black). Like Asimov's and Heinlein's, Delany's stories are about space travel, colonization, and alien others, but his fiction in the 1960s takes a decidedly different tone. *The Einstein Intersection* (1967), for instance, reverses the colonial gaze by taking on the perspective of the alien, forcing the reader to adopt the position of the Other. Delany's *Nova* (1968), a typical space opera in many ways, also features an explicitly bi-racial protagonist, Lorq, who "knew that his mother's parents were on Earth, in a country called Senegal. His father's great-grandparents were also from Earth, from Norway."[55] Delany's works were in many ways still ground-breaking, and Delany recounts his experience of trying to publish *Nova* with John W. Campbell only to be told that readers could not relate to a black character.[56] Delany was one of several authors who would, as part of the New Wave, begin to challenge and expand the genre's boundaries through literary experimentation and radical social critique.

---

[53] Robert J. C. Young, *Postcolonialism: An Historical Introduction* (Oxford: Blackwell, 2001), p. 213.
[54] Harding, *Is Science Multicultural*, p. 61.
[55] Samuel R. Delany, *Nova* (New York: Vintage Books, 2002), p. 43.
[56] Samuel R. Delany, "Racism and Science Fiction," *The New York Review of Science Fiction* 120 (August 1998), www.nyrsf.com/racism-and-science-fiction-.html (last accessed September 15, 2016).

... or Bust: Science Fiction and the Bomb, 1945–1960

BRENT RYAN BELLAMY

In the atomic age ... survival cannot be safeguarded by self-defence: for self-defence with thermonuclear weapons means total destruction.

Mordecai Roshwald, *Level 7*[1]

The sublime is kindled by the threat of nothing further happening.

Jean-François Lyotard, "The Sublime and the Avant-Garde"[2]

If the 1950s witnessed a utopianism of the will, it also saw SF writers produce works that fit under the mantle of cynicism. Aftermath, contamination, fallout, radiation: many words describe the ways that the utopian hopes of SF from the long 1950s get dashed, and most can be traced back to the dual-technological innovation of nuclear fission. What the nuclear reactor promises, the atomic bomb threatens to take away. Promises of seemingly limitless energy deflate as the science-fictional imaginary turns from utopia to bust. The harnessing of the destructive power of the atom risks obliterating the nuclear-powered, techno-utopian worlds envisioned by the SF of the 1950s. But these busted chances did not necessarily spell the end of the pursuit of a harmonious social life for humanity. As Jean-François Lyotard might see it, the atomic bomb presents the ultimate fuel-source for the sublime imagination. However, tales of nuclear holocaust often feature survivors – so Lyotard's understanding of narrative's well-spring can also be put in positive terms. M. Keith Booker explains that some works "succumb to the temptation to see nuclear war as an almost positive event that interrupts the growth of alienation and routinization in American society."[3] A variety of post-

---

[1] Mordecai Roshwald, *Level 7*, ed. David Seed, *Library of American Fiction* (Madison: The University of Wisconsin Press, 2004 [1959]), p. 135.

[2] Jean-François Lyotard, "The Sublime and the Avant-Garde," in *The Inhuman: Reflections on Time* (Cambridge, MA: Polity Press, 1991), p. 99.

[3] M. Keith Booker, *Monsters, Mushroom Clouds, and the Cold War: American Science Fiction and the Roots of Postmodernism, 1946–1964. Contributions to the Study of Science Fiction and Fantasy*, Number 95 (Westport, CT: Greenwood Press, 2001), p. 65.

catastrophe fictions feature characters finding themselves in a new Eden – or they may find that they can acclimatize themselves to a radioactive world without modern convenience enough to enjoy this new life.[4]

From the infamous Trinity test in the Jornada de Muerto desert and its deployment in Japan, the bomb underwent many transformations in shape and kind. Super bombs, such as the MK IV or "Fat Boy" bomb, rely on nuclear fission – the splitting of an atom to release hundreds of millions of volts of electric energy. By the mid-1950s, the first fusion bombs were in development, such as the MK-17 or "Bravo." These weapons are also referred to as "thermonuclear" bombs because they fuse hydrogen isotopes into helium nuclei, which releases massive amounts of energy (just as with the reactions found in stars). Poul Anderson and F. N. Waldrop's "Tomorrow's Children" (first published in *Astounding Science Fiction*, March 1947) uses the conceit of a man flying a "stratojet" over the Mississippi to detail the bomb's nuclear devastation to the landscape. The story moves from the pilot's psychic anguish at seeing the destroyed landscape below to the people on the ground under that jet: "When one plane could carry the end of a city, all planes were under suspicion."[5] Yet, as early as the 1960s, the fear of bombers and air-raid sirens would be replaced by a dispersed sense of dread: the threat of nuclear missiles launched from one country to another. Germany first began the development of Intercontinental Ballistic Missiles (ICBMs) during the Second World War. After that, USSR scientists worked to develop ICBMs capable of delivering a thermonuclear warhead – the R7. The United States spent much of the 1950s working to develop similar technology, and it was not until 1954 that the Atlas missile program was given top priority. By September 1959, Atlas missiles were accepted into service. Both the USSR and US programs fed the doctrine of Mutually Assured Destruction during the early years of the Cold War.[6]

---

[4] Some SF stories imagine the removal of electric energy, without the impact of nuclear war. René Barjavel's novel *Ravage* (1943) pictures a newly pastoralized post-electricity France, and Fredric Brown's story "The Waveries" (originally published in *Astounding*, January 1945) features electromagnetic-radiation beings that block the use of electricity on Earth.

[5] Poul Anderson and F. N. Waldrop, "Tomorrow's Children," in Robert Silverberg, ed., *Mutants* (Rockville, MD: Wildside Press, 2009), pp. 15–16.

[6] Even as it shows the influence of Socialist Realism and fixates on the space race, Russian SF during the 1950s bears the traces of nuclear development. Ivan Yefremov's novel *Andromeda: A Space-Age Tale* (1957) imagines a vast galactic alliance and a peaceful communist utopia, which contrasts with much US nuclear fiction of the period, yet it contains the shadows of a familiar nuclear-holocaust reality: at one point in the novel a crew of cosmonauts investigates the radio silence of an alliance planet only to discover that most of the life on the planet has perished as the result of radioactive experiments.

Before SF authors became obsessed with imagining the world of horrors that the bomb would bring about, though, they had anticipated and even arguably inspired its invention. H. G. Wells predicted the invention of nuclear weapons long before their actual development, in a story Manhattan Project originator Leo Szilard says he read in the 1930s.[7] In his history of SF, Adam Roberts credits Cleve Cartmill's story "Deadline" (first published in *Astounding*, 1944) with describing the atomic bomb in detail nearly a year before it was deployed, which earned Cartmill an investigation by the US Army "Counter Intelligence Corps." The story had anticipated reality so well that they believed military security had been breached.[8] Later, the SF author Philip Wylie became involved in government nuclear policy – David Seed credits Wylie's *Tomorrow!* (1954) as one of the few nuclear-catastrophe novels to describe the atomic explosion.[9] Whether as inspired forecaster or techno-minded consultant, the SF writer and SF text enter and maintain a privileged relationship with knowledge production, specifically military knowledge, during the 1950s.

Though SF writers have been credited with envisioning atomic weapons, once those weapons became a reality, SF stories that picture post-nuclear devastation can be best described as extrapolative. The historian of science, David Nye, describes a shift in public opinion about science and technology during the post-Second World War period from the "illusion that science was intrinsically beneficent" to the reality of a world reshaped by the atomic bomb.[10] The outcome: terror returned to the technological object. No longer in the position of a writer such as Wells picturing an as-yet fictional future technology, SF writers in the wake of the atomic bomb could instead describe

---

Vladimir Ivanovich Savchenko makes a more direct connection in his first novel *Black Stars* (1960), which deals extensively with nuclear physics. In the novel "neutronium is mechanically and thermally indestructible," and is used to make antimatter, which results in an accidental fusion explosion. Though these two examples far from prove a trend, each text positions nuclear development as a distant yet real threat.

7 David Seed describes Hungarian physicist Szilard's surprise at Wells's "depiction of nuclear war" and how it suggested "the possibility of a chain reaction he was able to apply in the planning of the first atomic bomb." David Seed, *American Science Fiction and the Cold War: Literature and Film* (Edinburgh: Edinburgh University Press, 1999), p. 5.

8 Adam Roberts, *The History of Science Fiction* (New York: Palgrave Macmillan, 2005), p. 206.

9 Philip Wylie served in the Office of War Information, he was invited to report in the Hiroshima bombing, he served as special adviser to the Chairman of the Joint Committee for Atomic Energy, he was given a Q (i.e., maximum) security clearance to attend the Desert Rock A-bomb tests and brief publishers on the implications of the atomic age, and he served on the Federal Civil Defense Authority. Seed, *Science Fiction and the Cold War*, p. 15.

10 David E. Nye, "Atomic Bomb and Apollo XI: New Forms of the Dynamic Sublime," in *American Technological Sublime* (Cambridge, MA: The Massachusetts Institute for Technology Press, 1994), p. 225.

its effects on human bodies, communities, and ways of knowing. Theodore Sturgeon's "Thunder and Roses" (first published in *Astounding*, 1947) is set after a nuclear strike on the United States. The central character, Pete Mawser, wonders "how the slow increase of radioactivity in the air, as the nitrogen transmuted to Carbon Fourteen, would affect him if he kept healthy in every way. What happens first? Blindness? Headaches? Perhaps a loss of appetite or slow fatigue?"[11] Within ten years accessible knowledge about radiation had significantly advanced, and novelists, such as Pat Frank, used SF to explain nuclear radiation, as this character from *Alas, Babylon* (1959) does:

> Radiation's not a germ or a virus. You can eat or drink radioactive matter, like strontium 90 in milk. It can fall on you in rain. It can sift down on you in dust, or in particles you can't see on a day that seems perfectly clear. You can track it in the house on your shoes, or pick it up by handling any metal or inorganic matter that has been exposed. But you can't catch it by kissing a girl, unless, of course, she had gold teeth.[12]

Sturgeon and Frank, separated by a decade, display significantly differing levels of nuclear knowledge, yet both work to present facts about the effects of radiation. Diverging from such dramatic scenarios, Henri Queffélec's novel *Combat contre l'invisible* (1958), rather than illustrating the aftermath of nuclear war, elaborates the issues arising from living with nuclear-generated energy and radioactive substances in the wake of the Second World War.[13]

As radioisotopes leave imprints on human beings and offer a means to date geological events, so too the SF films of the 1950s are marked by nuclear fission's radioactive glow. Susan Sontag credits SF film with an advantage over written SF: "In the films it is by means of images and sounds, not words that have to be translated by the imagination, that one can participate in the fantasy of living through one's own death and more, the death of cities, the destruction of humanity itself."[14] This is particularly visible in films with explicit connections to nuclear weapons testing and other themes. Ishirō Honda's *Godzilla* (1954) famously features the ancient kaiju disturbed from its underwater lair by hydrogen bomb testing – and, debuting the same year in the United States as *Godzilla* did in Japan, Gordon Douglas's *Them!* (1954) is a giant-monster film about radioactively enlarged ants. Honda's *Rodan!*

---

[11] Theodore Sturgeon, "Thunder and Roses," in *Thunder and Roses: Stories of Science Fiction and Fantasy* (London: Michael Joseph, 1957), pp. 151–2.

[12] Pat Frank, *Alas, Babylon* (New York: J. B. Lippincot, 1959), p. 182.

[13] Queffélec's novel was published in English as *Frontier of the Unknown* (1960).

[14] Susan Sontag, "The Imagination of Disaster," in *Against Interpretation* (New York: Doubleday, 1986), p. 212.

The Flying Monster (1957), another giant-monster film, was released two years later in the United States than in Japan and featured the addition of nuclear bomb test footage before the start of the film. In another of Honda's films, *The Mysterians* (1957), an alien force seeks to invade Earth, having lost its own home planet to nuclear war and suffered mutations and population loss from radiation poisoning. While these 1950s films make explicit reference to monstrous nuclear origins, films in the 1960s, such as the late George A. Romero's *Night of the Living Dead* (1968), would sublimate nuclear anxiety into an encroaching zombic mass of unknowable otherness and mass suffering, giving birth to new genres and tropes in the process.

The bomb shelter becomes a key structure of 1950s post-catastrophe stories; indeed it would become a central setting for these stories as well. It represents a safe space, offers a site where culture might come to be preserved, and hints that a small group might survive into the near future. Philip K. Dick's short story "Foster, You're Dead!" (first published in *Star Science Fiction Stories 3*, 1955) imagines the desirability and marketability of commercialized bomb shelters. Mike Foster, the kid focalizing character, exists in the world of burgeoning 1950s consumer culture. He is the only person whose family does not have a shelter; he does not even have access to the public shelter. His schoolmates deride him and label his father "Anti-P," which stands for anti-preparedness. The world seems to be against him as he reads bunker advertising: "THE NEW 1972 BOMBPROOF RADIATION-SEALED SUBSURFACE SHELTER IS HERE!" It features an elevator, air conditioning, food and water decontamination, and an "e-z payment plan."[15] In the story Dick artfully captures the sense of a child who feels the sting of class difference. Foster suffers under the heavy weight of his peer's expectations. "Foster, You're Dead!" explores the impact of atomic knowledge on the confined space of the nuclear family unit.

But containment exists in the eye of the beholder. It either keeps the bad things *in* or keeps worse things *out*. Containment can mean protection and shelter, and it can also mean control. This two-sided logic organizes the structure of post-catastrophe 1950s SF. As containment appears to be about survival and preservation, its relationship with isolation means that it has correlate concepts in the enclave, the trusted inner-cloister, the thought police, and other ways of managing subversive ideas. The Order of Leibowitz in Walter Miller Jr.'s *A Canticle for Leibowitz* (1959) for instance,

---

[15] Philip K. Dick, "Foster, You're Dead!" in Jonathan Lethem, ed., *Selected Stories of Philip K. Dick* (Boston: Houghton Mifflin Harcourt, [1955] 2013), p. 160.

represents the containment of knowledge for its preservation, as the Order forms around a cloistered yet progressive attitude towards the use of technology. The impact of the atomic bomb on the imagination lands on the side of both the author and the critic. For instance, in John Wyndham's "The Wheel" (first published in *Startling Stories*, January 1952) when a boy literally reinvents the wheel he sends waves of fear through the community. The trajectory implied by the community's reaction is one that echoes the words of Theodor W. Adorno, "No universal history leads from savagery to humanitarianism, but there is one leading from the slingshot to the megaton bomb."[16] In Wyndham's tale, the boy's grandfather takes his grandson's place as a sacrificial scapegoat in the hopes that the boy has learned his lesson. Similarly about technological management, George Orwell's *Nineteen Eighty-Four* (1949) and Ray Bradbury's *Fahrenheit 451* (1953) fit alongside the cornerstone of 1950s bust stories, though they focus on top-down control and the limited capacity of individual freedoms rather than the day-to-day struggle for survival in a post-catastrophe setting.

Ray Bradbury's post-nuclear story "There Will Come Soft Rains" (first printed in *Collier's*, May 1950) operates on a containment logic. The automaton house itself provides a shell that preserves the cultural memory of a day in the life of the suburbanite Allendale, California family. The automated house performs the daily chores of subsistence – waking, clothing, cleaning, and feeding the family and so on – even in the face of the family's absence. Having long been obliterated, they are now nothing more than patches of remaining paint left behind. Their bodies sheltered the garage wall from the searing light of the atomic explosion, leaving "five spots of paint – the man, the woman, the children, the ball."[17] Bradbury intertwines the dialectic of memory and forgetting with that of containment and contamination. "There Will Come Soft Rains" works in the same way as these other nuclear-holocaust stories even though it has no characters in the traditional sense.

As with the robotic house overseeing the daily rhythms of family life, post-nuclear holocaust stories hinge on rhythms and durations. As with containment, temporality becomes a primary axis of organizing the story world. Judith Merril's *Shadow on the Hearth* (1950) features a woman who survives because she is in her basement doing laundry and then must bear the felt *longue durée* of radio broadcasts wondering if her husband will make it back

---

[16] Theodor W. Adorno, *Negative Dialectics* (London: Routledge, 2004), p. 319.
[17] Ray Bradbury, "August 2026: There Will Come Soft Rains," *The Martian Chronicles* (New York: Simon and Schuster [1950] 2012), p. 222.

from the city. Post-nuclear SF stories figure the new length of journeys without automobiles; the new length of days without electric light and without human company; the time of exposure to radiation; the new daily rhythm in a fallout shelter and without work or with new work; the number of generations before the outside or the Earth becomes safe once more; the number of generations before civilization returns; and the new distance from the past without tradition or technology. Containment and temporality work together, each restraining the other. New rhythms of life in these novels often play out within the bounded expectations of managed communities. Arthur C. Clarke's "If I Forget Thee, Oh Earth . . ." (first published in *Future*, September 1951), presents the ideological promise of safety the bunker presents.[18] It also reveals the expansive timescale associated with nuclear radiation. In the story, a father takes his son out for the first time, from what the reader assumes to be an underground bunker. Instead of being on the Earth's surface the man shows his son the view of Earth from space. The Moon colony has survived a massive nuclear war because of its remove from the Earth. The father leads his son to understand that he cannot go back to Earth during his lifetime and that it will be up to him to carry on this tradition of revealing their loss of the Earth to future generations.[19]

SF stories from the 1950s set after nuclear war balance on an atom's edge of containment and contamination; they revel in the loss or the preservation of knowledge; and they develop characters that face the hot winds of change blowing from the future. In the following pages, I elaborate the containment logic of several 1950s SF novels by Leigh Brackett, Mordecai Roshwald, Pat Frank, and Philip K. Dick. These novels move from a secret nuclear knowledge (Brackett) to the confined and enclosed space of a military bunker (Roshwald) and from a story that relies on the ways nuclear war structures the present (Frank) to one that shifts the nuclear apocalypse from the foreground and present to the background of the distant past (Dick).

Brackett's *The Long Tomorrow* (1951) charts the ways communities change in the aftermath of nuclear war. The New Mennonite pastoral community of Piper's Run is technology averse. Founded along a river around a small steam-engine manufactory and some warehouses, Refuge pushes against

---

[18] Another SF variant of the bunker trope appears in Fritz Leiber's "A Pail of Air" (*Galaxy Science Fiction*, December 1951), in which a boy survives living in a nest of blankets with his Pa, Ma, and Sis as it gets colder outside. The Earth has been dragged away from the Sun by a dark star and the family survives by melting frozen oxygen.

[19] For further reading on reproductive futurism see Rebekah Sheldon, *The Child to Come: Life after Human Catastrophe* (Minneapolis: University of Minnesota Press, 2016).

the limits of legal city size. According to the thirtieth amendment to the Constitution of the United States of America, "No city, no town, no community of more than one thousand people or two hundred buildings to the square mile shall be built or permitted to exist anywhere in the United States of America."[20] This amendment adapts a variant of bunker logic to the perceived problem of population. Much of the conversation in small communities focuses on the evil of cities and city living: "Megalopolis, drowned in its own sewage, choked with its own waste gases, smothered and crushed by its own population."[21] A third community, Bartorstown, offers the clearest exemplar of intertwining containment logic and temporality in *The Long Tomorrow*. The whispered legends of Bartorstown keep the idea of cities and civilization alive: Bartorstown shelters an underground prewar government installation. A research facility buried under a mountain houses a nuclear reactor power station and a working computer.

With the narrative's move into the cloistered environment of Bartorstown, the novel shifts its secondary characters' political aims from a decrying of cities and moral decay to a defense of nuclear power. While introducing the protagonist to the nuclear reactor that powers Bartorstown, one of the scientists assuages his fears, "Listen ... You're thinking of the bomb. This isn't a bomb. It isn't hurtful. We've lived with it here for nearly a hundred years. It can't explode, and it can't burn you. The concrete makes us safe. Look ... See? There's nothing to fear."[22] Despite this mouth-piece vocalization of the safety of nuclear technology, the position of the novel itself seems deeply ambivalent. During the tour of the high-tech facilities, the narrator offers a different viewpoint on the operation: "the power entrapped behind the concrete wall gave off its strength silently, untiringly, the deathless heart beating and throbbing in the rock."[23] This description makes nuclear energy anthropomorphic and cosmic simultaneously – both a living force and something unspeakably immense and old. Finally, the protagonist provides a third position, neither defensive nor uncertain, when he pragmatically muses: "The bomb is a fact. Atomic power is a fact. It is a living fact close down under my feet, the dreadful power that made these pictures. You can't deny it, you can't destroy it because it is evil and evil is like a serpent that dieth not but reneweth itself perpetually."[24] *The Long Tomorrow* offers a version of the

---

[20] Leigh Brackett, *Long Tomorrow* (New York: Ballatine, 1986 [1955]), p. 7.
[21] Ibid., p. 70.
[22] Ibid., p. 151.
[23] Ibid., p. 172.
[24] Ibid., p. 155.

hero–quest narrative with no return at the end, despite the knowledge gained by the protagonist. The novel builds a world caught in stasis, with some people yearning for a return to the way life was before, some people desperately fighting against any such thing, and others waiting for the time that history might begin again.

Providing the most in-depth exploration of bunker life, Roshwald's *Level 7* (1959) reads as though it were the journal of a military officer sequestered miles beneath the Earth's surface in a top secret, ultra-secure facility. Military command selects Officer X-127 along with X-107, X-117, and X-137 and assigns him to push-button duty on Level 7. Loudspeaker voices interrupt X-127 throughout the novel. In an early case of this kind of interruption, the voice explains the nature of the mission to X-127 and his colleagues. It says, "You are the defenders of truth and justice," and explains that the "infamous and treacherous" enemy has developed its attack capabilities to such an extreme that the offensive wing of the military needed to seek shelter underground to "protect our protectors."[25] X-127 conveys very clearly that he knows what atomic war implies: "Even if we were victorious, the damage up on top would be so disastrous and the atomic pollution so widespread that no living creature could exist there."[26] And so it does come to pass that X-127's predictions are correct. In *Level 7*, the nuclear war begins by accident. On the entry marked June 15 he writes, "The enemy and we, his satellites and our allies (or, as he prefers to put, his allies and our satellites), indeed the entire surface of the Earth, have been laid in ruins."[27] *Level 7* might very well be one of the most extreme cases both of containment and enclave mentality and of the total annihilation of life on Earth.

Calculated to the very inch, no space of Level 7 is wasted. Even excrement gets automatically vacuum-sealed and deposited alongside the remaining food in deep-freeze storage. In this and other ways, Roshwald depicts Level 7 as a finely tuned yet ultimately closed system. Early in the book X-127 makes a startling observation along these lines: "For one thing, we shall never run out of fuel. Everything here works by electricity from dynamos powered by an atomic reactor which can supply all the energy we want to a thousand years."[28] The bunker built to keep atomic war out is powered by a nuclear reactor: in the face of nuclear winter, Level 7 and all of its officers would be wholly reliant on nuclear power.

[25] Roshwald, *Level 7*, pp. 12–13.
[26] Ibid., pp. 14–15.
[27] Ibid., p. 134.
[28] Ibid., p. 29.

In the end, it is the atomic energy powering Level 7 that also spells its downfall. On October 8, X-127 writes, "Something went wrong with the reactor." He continues, "If it had been on the surface the reactor could have been stopped, isolated and repaired at leisure. If necessary, people could have been moved to a safe distance. But here on Level 7 there was no choice. The reactor had to be repaired where it was, and quickly, even with the danger of lethal radiation. Without light, the plants would have stopped supplying oxygen; and we would soon have died."[29] So the AE officers (Atomic Engineers) risked their lives and partly succeeded; the energy supply will continue. Unfortunately, so will the lethal radiation. The reactor will go on working simultaneously as a source of life and death.

Frank's *Alas, Babylon*, set in Fort Repose, Florida, follows a group of survivors who happen to be located far enough from military targets and lucky enough to have the wind blowing away from them on the night of the strikes that they not only avoid the initial devastation wreaked by the bombs, but the land that sustains them survives as well.[30] Despite at least one hundred pages of lead-up, the description of the attack is a mere two sentences long: "Very few actually saw an enemy aircraft or submarine, and missiles appeared only on the most sensitive radar screens. Most of those who died in North America saw nothing at all, since they died in bed, in a millisecond slipping from sleep into deeper darkness."[31] Though there are no bunkers present, the logic of containment found in Brackett's and Roshwald's novels still obtains here.

Just after the nuclear strike, the narrator explains the town's isolation. All that would be required to paste this elaboration into another post-apocalyptic story would be that the author changes the city name, so long as the settlement is of a similar size:

> Like most small towns, Fort Repose's food and drug supply was dependent upon daily or thrice weekly deliveries from warehouses in the larger cities. Each day trucks replenished its filling stations. For all other merchandise, it was dependent upon shipments by mail, express, and highway freight, from jobbers and manufacturers elsewhere. With the Red Alert, all these services halted and at once. Like thousands of towns and villages not directly seared by war, Fort Repose became an island.[32]

[29] Ibid., p. 178.
[30] While Fort Repose is a fictional town, Frank lived for quite some time in Tangerine, FL and reportedly based Fort Repose on the nearby town of Mount Dora.
[31] Pat Frank, *Alas, Babylon* (New York: J. B. Lippincot, 1959), p. 137.
[32] Frank, *Alas*, p. 117.

Most striking about this detailed look at how Fort Repose "became an island" is its relation to transportation. This passage reveals that what appears to be a stable and plentiful supply of food in the supermarket or petrol at the gas pump is in fact constantly in motion, shipped in daily – revealing that the circulation of commodities organized by a capitalist economy entails profound unpreparedness for the kind of isolating crises imagined in Frank's book.

As the narrator contemplates what isolation means for Fort Repose, the book exposes an infrastructural background. Later, the novel continues this line of thought through the central character: Randy realizes that "This disaster was perfectly predictable," and that "He had been a fool." Rather than stockpile preserved meat when his brother warned him of the impending war, he bought as much fresh meat as he could. If he could have anticipated one thing, it ought to have been the loss of electricity: "Even had Orlando escaped, the electricity would have died within a few weeks or months. Electricity was created by burning fuel oil in the Orlando plants. When the oil ran out, it could not be replenished during the chaos of war. There was no longer a rail system, or rail centers, nor were tankers plying the coasts on missions of civilian supply."[33] While the energy consumption of the previous elaboration of circulation was simply implied, trucks run on diesel or gasoline too. In Randy's assessment of his preparedness he explicitly names oil as the fuel source that would allow him to keep his meat fresh. In the novel, he and his group will now need to fish and gather to survive, which they do handily. In this manner, Alas, Babylon does a compelling job of mapping the circulation of goods and of energy.

In ten years, Philip K. Dick published five novels based on the conceit of nuclear catastrophe: The World Jones Made (1956), The Man Who Japed (1956), Vulcan's Hammer (1960), The Penultimate Truth (1964), and Dr. Bloodmoney, or How We Got Along after the Bomb (1965). The World Jones Made takes place in the wake of massive, global nuclear war that destroyed much of the United States, the USSR, and the People's Republic of China. An extra-national body, Fedgov, emerges to rule the world through the ideology of relativism. The Man Who Japed follows a media creator who works for the puritan government Morec (Moral Reclamation), which emerged as a response to an apocalyptic conflict; the jape is a joke that lands the protagonist in hot water. Vulcan's Hammer is similarly set after a nuclear war, only here the emergent state is known as Unity and it rules through artificial intelligence

---

[33] Ibid., p. 152.

units known as the Vulcan Series. In *The Penultimate Truth* warfare has left the surface of the Earth uninhabitable, and humanity lives underground in massive ant tanks. On the surface, the fighting continues between mechanized combatants known as "leadies." Finally, rather than distancing itself from nuclear conflict, *Dr. Bloodmoney* features tensions rising between the United States and the USSR and People's Republic in the 1980s even as the first manned mission to Mars launches. A decade earlier, Dr. Bruno Bluthgeld's nuclear experiments went wrong, unleashing radioactive fallout around the world. In his unpublished dissertation, "The Novels of Philip K. Dick," SF author Kim Stanley Robinson explains that these early SF novels by Dick critique forces he observed on the rise in the 1950s: "the power of large corporations, the power of the police, the power of centralized information, and the power of self-righteous moralism."[34] Robinson's assessment of these novels, as post-holocaust novels, situates them as using nuclear war "to disengage history and allow Dick to take it where he will," which paradoxically leads Dick to "construct dystopian societies much like ones that in other novels are linear extensions of our history, that require no cataclysm."[35] For Robinson, only *Dr. Bloodmoney* leads out of this dystopian cycle and succeeds in representing the effects of nuclear war.

However, in *The Man Who Japed* the background stands out as a crucial part of the history of apocalyptic storytelling. Outside the bounded territory of Morec, objects of the long-dead world molder and rot, forming ashy-grey substrata. Taking a closer look, the novel describes "remnants of the old. Tons of usable, partly usable, and ruined debris, objects of priceless worth, trinkets, indiscriminate trash."[36] These bits and pieces run the gamut from usable trash to useless treasure. The underfoot in this scene forms a kind of unremovable moral blight. Here the dustbin of history cannot be emptied out. Even nuclear inferno leaves some things intact.

Yet this unofficial space of memorialization is not the only one that exists in the novel. Later, the protagonist takes a child to a museum. At the core of the museum is an exhibit on the twentieth century in the form of "an entire white-stucco house" which

> had been painstakingly reconstructed, with sidewalk and lawn, garage and parked Ford. The house was complete with furniture, robot mannequins, hot food on the table, scented water in the bathtub. It walked, talked, sang

---

[34] Kim Stanley Robinson, "The Novels of Philip K. Dick," unpublished dissertation, University of San Diego (1982), p. 37.

[35] Robinson, "Philip K. Dick," p. 57.

[36] Dick, *The Man Who Japed*, p. 62.

and glowed. The exhibit revolved in such a way that every part of the interior was visible. Visitors lined up at the circular railing and watched as Life in the Age of Waste rotated by. Over the house was an illuminated sign: HOW THEY LIVED.[37]

The centrality of the domestic space of the house to the exhibit echoes of Bradbury's "There Will Come Soft Rains" – especially given what happens next:

> ... Over the exhibit the sign winked out. An ugly cloud of smoke rolled up, obscuring the house. Its lights dimmed, turned dull red, and dried up. The exhibit trembled, and, to the spectators, a rumble came, the lazy tremor of a subterranean wind.
>
> When the smoke departed the house was gone. All that remained of the exhibit was an expanse of broken bones. A few steel supports jutted, and bricks and section of stucco lay strewn everywhere.
>
> In the ruins of the cellar the surviving mannequins huddled over their pitiful possessions: a tank of decontaminated water, a dog they were stewing, a radio, medicines. Only three mannequins had survived and they were haggard and ill. Their clothing was in shreds and their skins were seared with radiation burns.
>
> Over this hemisphere of the exhibit the sign concluded: AND DIED.[38]

The Man Who Japed sets this calamity in the distant past, but makes it repeatable. Museum goers can watch again and again the smooth transition from the morally bankrupt Age of Waste to how life might have been after nuclear havoc was wreaked.

Though the way post-nuclear novels destroy their imagined worlds fluctuates, these visions articulate a shared vision of post-nuclear catastrophe. As David Nye puts it, "Nothing human beings had made was more powerful than the atom bomb exploded on July 16, 1945."[39] The event-like character of the bomb before and during the early days of the Cold War presents a shared object for the SF imaginary. With that in mind, one more version of containment should be placed in this archive. John Wyndham's *Day of the Triffids* (1951) and *The Kraken Wakes* (1953) take green spaces and the deep ocean, respectively, and render them nearly impassable. Both *Day of the Triffids* and *The Kraken Wakes* transpose nuclear anxiety onto the varied terrain of monstrosity and environmental change. They project an idea of the way that nature, whether through a science experiment gone wrong or the

---

[37] Ibid., p. 72.
[38] Ibid., p. 73.
[39] Nye, *Technological Sublime*, p. 227.

invasion of deep-sea dwelling extraterrestrial life, might seek to contain human life, activity, and mobility. Though mid-century bust narratives were certainly not aware of the full history of carbon emissions, pollutants, and plastics, in the age of climate disaster the atomic imaginary gains a renewed resonance as it depicts massive changes to the Earth that people alive today might very well witness.

14

Women in the Golden Age of Science Fiction

JANE DONAWERTH

Women writers flourished during the Golden Age of science fiction. In "What Can a Heroine Do? Or Why Women Can't Write" (1972), Joanna Russ, herself a writer of SF, argues that mainstream fiction before the 1970s limited female authors to stories about romance and marriage, or about tragic madwomen, while SF freed women writers because as a genre it is dedicated to "myths of human intelligence and human adaptability . . . exploring a new world conceptually . . . assessing the consequences of technological or other changes."[1] Indeed, women writers of the Golden Age explored utopian future worlds and technologies, imagined alternative modes of reproduction, and critiqued the value of weapons technology.

Each scholar defines the Golden Age differently. I use the term to refer to the decades when short stories were the primary venue for SF, from the 1920s advent of the genre of "scientifiction"[2] through a good part of the 1950s, when paperback novels began to outnumber short stories in the magazines. This time period is often termed the era of pulp fiction, since during the 1920s and 1930s most SF magazines were printed on paper made from wood pulp. I stretch the term "Golden Age" to include the "digest" magazines that became popular in the 1940s and 1950s and were half the size of the folio-size pulp magazines. I briefly discuss the conventions of SF and the portrayal of women in men's Golden Age SF, but I focus here on women in women's fiction, emphasizing the writers' use of SF conventions, their devising of narrative strategies to resist the conventional masculine point of view, and their construction (and deconstruction) of gender.

---

[1] Joanna Russ, "What Can a Heroine Do? Or Why Women Can't Write," in Susan Koppelman Cornillon, ed., *Images of Women in Fiction* (Bowling Green, OH: Bowling Green University Popular Press, 1972), pp. 17–18.
[2] "Scientifiction" was the term used by Hugo Gernsback for the scientific romances he published in the 1920s; see Chapter 8 of this volume.

None of the women of this period might be said to be canonical SF writers in the way that Isaac Asimov or Robert Heinlein were viewed. Some well-known women SF writers – Anne McCaffrey, Judith Merril, and Kate Wilhelm, for example – got their start in the magazines, but are best known for their later paperback novels and collections. While there were many women writers in the magazines, there was still widespread gender bias: a woman did not win the novella and short story Hugos (the Science Fiction Achievement Award voted on by fans and established in 1953) until Anne McCaffrey in 1968 and Ursula K. Le Guin in 1974, and no woman won the novella, novelette, or short story Nebula SF Awards (voted on by members of the Science Fiction Writers of America and established in 1965) until Anne McCaffrey in 1968, Vonda McIntyre in 1974, and Kate Wilhelm in 1969. Of the writers discussed later in this essay, who began their publishing in the SF magazines, the following have won major SF awards:

- Leigh Brackett won a Jules Verne Award, was a Guest of Honor at the World SF Convention, and was one of two credited writers for the film *The Empire Strikes Back*, which won a Hugo
- Marion Zimmer Bradley was given the World Fantasy Award for lifetime achievement
- Clare Winger Harris's first story was published because she won third place in a contest sponsored by Hugo Gernsback
- Lilith Lorraine, who pioneered the genre of SF poetry, won an Arizona State Poetry Prize and the Old South Award from the Poetry Society of Texas
- Katherine MacLean won a Nebula Award, was a Guest of Honor for WisCon, was named Author Emeritus by the Science Fiction Writers of America, and has received a Cordwainer Smith Rediscovery Award
- Anne McCaffrey, the first woman to win a Hugo and the first to win a Nebula, also won a Gandalf Award, an American Library Association Award for teen novels, a Robert A. Heinlein Award for her work in SF, was named a Grand Master by the Science Fiction Writers of America, and was inducted into the Science Fiction and Fantasy Hall of Fame
- Judith Merril was named Author Emeritus by the Science Fiction Writers of America, was inducted into the Science Fiction and Fantasy Hall of Fame, and her autobiography posthumously won a Hugo
- C. L. Moore was awarded a Forry Award, a Count Dracula Society Award for Literature, a World Fantasy Award for Lifetime Achievement, a Gandalf Lifetime Achievement Award, was inducted into the Science

Fiction and Fantasy Hall of Fame, and received a Cordwainer Smith
Rediscovery Award

- Kate Wilhelm has won three Nebula Awards, two Hugo Awards, and
  a Locus Award, has been a Worldcon Guest of Honor, and has been
  inducted into the Science Fiction and Fantasy Hall of Fame.[3]

Gender and Men's SF in the Magazines

SF by men in the Golden Age magazines evolved into an adventure genre
employing a point of view decidedly masculine and enthusiastically
scientific: stories were usually told by a young scientist or a bold male
explorer.[4] Men who wrote SF developed coded conventions that expressed
hopes for the benefits of science and American culture: the power and speed
of rocket ships, the defeat of aliens (often as a code for American or white
superiority), the exploring of a new planet (a re-telling of the pioneer
history of the United States), the advances of genetics, and the opportunities and dangers of smart technology (especially robots). Edmund
Hamilton's "The Sargasso of Space," published in *Astounding Stories*
in September 1931, is perhaps exemplary: a rocket ship is pulled off course
when its engine fails from leaking fuel tanks, and is drawn into the "dead
zone," a graveyard of rocket ships. The crew hunt through the abandoned
ships, finding one with enough fuel to get them to Neptune, but also finding
pirates who try to seize theirs. With the help of a brave girl held captive by
the pirates, they fend off the pirates and continue their journey. The story
epitomizes the adventure of space, the glamor of rocket travel, and the
problem-solving science that allows them to pump fuel through a quarter
mile of hoses back to their ship.

But brave girls are not always rewarded in men's SF: in Tom Godwin's
"The Cold Equations," published in *Astounding Stories* in August 1954, a girl
who bravely stows away in a cargo ship to visit her brother must be jettisoned
into space because her extra weight would mean the whole ship with a life-
saving cargo of medicines would miss its planetary rendezvous.

In the stories by men of the Golden Age, women are often portrayed in
one of three ways: domestic rewards for the hero, alien monsters, or heroes

---

[3] For awards to these writers, see the websites for the various awards, and the biographies
in Lisa Yaszek and Patrick B. Sharp, eds., *Sisters of Tomorrow: The First Women of Science
Fiction* (Middletown, CT: Wesleyan University Press, 2016).
[4] See Thomas D. Clareson, *Some Kind of Paradise: The Emergence of American Science Fiction*
(Westport, CT: Greenwood Press, 1985), pp. 81–102 and 157–224.

themselves who occupy roles very like those of Terran men.[5] For instance, in Nat Schachner's "Pirates of Gorm," published in May 1932 in *Astounding Stories*, spaceman Grant Pemberton is on a rocketship passenger liner captured by Ganymedan pirates, but foils their plans, despite their deployment of hordes of surgically induced zombie troops – and his reward is the lovely passenger he has rescued, Nona. In 1940s and 1950s illustrations and short stories in the pulps, Robin Roberts has pointed out, "The female alien's size and reproductive powers separate her from humanity and isolate her from the male hero, often symbolizing the powers of nature that men cannot control." As an example, Roberts cites Robert Gibson Jones's cover for *Fantastic Adventures* in May 1951 and the story it illustrates, Paul Fairman's "Invasion from the Deep": Llanni, an alien who lives deep in the ocean, in the illustration looms over men on a submarine deck; and in the story represents the powerful ocean that threatens but sustains the life of the protagonist Nick.[6] At times in men's pulp SF, women are heroic, in much the same manner as the men of the story, as in Philip Francis Nowlan's "Armageddon – 2419 AD," published in *Amazing Stories* in August 1928: in this tale, the scientist-narrator, Anthony "Buck" Rogers, succumbs to stasis from radioactive gases in an abandoned coal mine and wakes in a future where Chinese hordes have overrun the world – but Americans, who are fighting as guerillas, have established sexual equality, and his heroic partner is his brave wife Wilma.

These early stories, generally narrated by young male scientist-adventurers, celebrate the power of science and American culture through familiar SF codes (the rocket ship, the robot, etc.), and imagine a deeply patriarchal future. Nevertheless, there are exceptions. In "The Defenders," published in *Galaxy Science Fiction* in January 1953, Philip K. Dick satirizes the imperialist male point of view of SF through a naive scientist-soldier who learns too late that the robots designed to fight the next world war between the United States and Russia have instead made peace, and are beginning to solve the problem of feeding all humans. In Stanley G. Weinbaum's "A Martian Odyssey," instead of hostile aliens, spacemen discover many intelligent nonhumans on Mars – ostrich-like beings and crawling plant-

---

[5] In *Decoding Gender in Science Fiction* (New York: Routledge, 2002), esp. pp. 43–5, Brian Attebery examines the gender stereotypes in pulp SF mainly by men: male characters are usually athletic heroes (students or adventurers) or professors (older scientists), while female characters play the roles of assistants (daughters, housewives, victims to be rescued, or romantic rewards for the hero).

[6] Robin Roberts, "The Female Alien: Pulp Science Fiction's Legacy to Feminists," *Journal of Popular Culture* 21 (1987), pp. 36.

animals termed "biopods" – and a civilization equal to that of Earth. Subverting the convention of the daughter of the old scientist as reward for the young hero, Raymond Z. Gallun's "Old Faithful," published in *Astounding Science Fiction* in December 1934, pictures young scientist Jack Cantrill working with Yvonne, the daughter of his mentor, to communicate with a Martian who arrives on Earth, and, though fatally injured, leaves his spaceship as a model for human exploration. Here patriarchy is undermined by a sympathetic alien and by men and women represented as equal partners.

Decoding Genre Conventions in SF by Women: Rockets, Aliens, Genetics, Cyborgs

Women writers of the Golden Age often employ the codes of men's SF with irony or with a twist that critiques the ideology that generated such codes. These women are "resisting readers" of men's SF conventions.[7] For example, while the rocket signified masculinity in men's SF, it is used to ironic effect in Leslie F. Stone's "Out of the Void," published in 1929 in *Amazing Stories*. In this story, a young explorer, Dana Gleason, Jr., raised to hate women by a misogynous father, volunteers to pilot Professor Rollins' experimental rocket to Mars. Like Jules Verne's rocket in *From the Earth to the Moon* (1864), the ship is catapulted into space, and is propelled by a series of explosions. Ironically, however, the pilot who "mans" this first spaceflight (albeit with a last-minute partner, Richard Dorr), is a woman, raised by her father as his son. The power of the rocket, which ordinarily signals heroic masculinity, is presented with tongue-in-cheek hyperbole: "There was a deafening explosion, the force of which sent large pieces of machinery flying through the air, killing two mechanics ... and all but killing the Professor."[8] As they begin their trip together, Dorr tells Dana, "I know all your courageous deeds, your researches, your science, your war experiences ... but ... you *are* a woman ... You *are* at a disadvantage."[9] Surely this rocket, with its explosive launch that throws both astronauts off their feet, debunks the phallic symbol that is the tradition of men's SF. Moreover, the alien spaceship that returns to Earth with Dana's story, instead of the phallic spire of SF magazine covers, is a glass cylinder that seems suspended in space as it moves, rather than pulsing with engines.

---

[7] Judith Fetterley, *The Resisting Reader: A Feminist Approach to American Literature* (Bloomington: Indiana University Press, 1981), esp. p. xxii.
[8] Leslie F. Stone, "Out of the Void, Part I," *Amazing Stories* (August 1929), p. 450.
[9] Ibid., pp. 453–4.

The rocket Professor Rollins designs is the conventional penetrator of space, but the ship that returns is a container, holding aliens and humans together.[10]

And so it goes with many of the traditional SF codes in women's SF of the Golden Age. In Zenna Henderson's "The Substitute," published in August 1953 in *Imagination*, the alien who makes first contact with Earth is not the monster of many male writers, but an elementary school teacher's star pupil. In Rosel George Brown's "Car Pool," published in February 1959 in *If: Worlds of Science Fiction*, a Terran mom suffers not only the difficulties of temper tantrums and the flu season when it is her turn to drive children to school, but also the future tensions of interactions between xenophobic human children and vulnerable alien offspring. In these two stories, the significance of the code of alien is reversed, from danger to opportunity, and the stories explore co-existence.

Reversing the basic template of Golden Age SF often amounts to political critique. In Margaret St. Clair's "Quis Custodiet," published in July 1948 in *Startling Stories*, instead of pioneer spacemen conquering the problems of an alien world, Mirna, a future botanist, works to find extinct species on Earth or to hybridize them from mutated offspring, thus resisting those humans who continue to destroy Earth's vegetation in a post-nuclear-holocaust environment. The symbolic importance of human evolution in SF promoting the ideology of American progress is severely questioned in Alice Eleanor Jones's "Created He Them," published in the *Magazine of Fantasy and Science Fiction* in June 1955. In this near-future dystopia, because pollution of the Earth has reached such proportions that many humans are sterile, a woman stays in her oppressive marriage because she can have children, even though the state takes them away at the age of three to protect and educate them. Jones's story does not celebrate human progress, but instead laments society's errors and government's incompetence.

In men's SF, robots represent both the progress of (masculine) science in replacing work with leisure for humans, and also, as Amardeep Singh points out, "potential threats to the idea of humanness itself."[11] In "No Woman Born," first published in December 1944 in *Astounding*, C. L. Moore upends this SF code to call into question the reliability of the masculine point of view in SF and the male characters' definition of what it means to be human.

[10] On the story as container in women's fiction, see Ursula K. Le Guin, "The Carrier Bag Theory of Fiction" (1986), in *Dancing at the Edge of the World* (New York: Harper & Row, 1989), pp. 165–70.
[11] Amardeep Singh, "Robots," in Leigh Ronald Grossman, ed., *Sense of Wonder: A Century of Science Fiction* (Rockville, MD: Wildside Press, 2011), pp. 344.

Moore's story recounts the rehabilitation of Deirdre, a world-famous star in the future medium of television, after a theater fire has destroyed her body. Under the leadership of Dr. Maltzer, a team of scientists, sculptors, and engineers design and build a metal body for Deirdre that is worthy of her former grace, and after a year of therapy, she can again walk, talk, sing, and dance as a cyborg. Maltzer takes the view of traditional SF: to him, Deirdre is "a terrible mistake," "isn't female anymore," and he himself is a "Frankenstein" who brought "life into the world unlawfully."[12] But Deirdre has realized what Judith Butler in *Gender Trouble* later theorized, that "gender is a kind of persistent impersonation that passes as the real,"[13] in Moore's words, an "Illusion"[14] – indeed, that humanness is an impersonation. When Maltzer tries to commit suicide by jumping from his apartment window, Deirdre rescues him by her speed and strength. Both Maltzer and Deirdre's agent John Harris view Deirdre as stereotypically inferior, lacking the strength to withstand the dehumanization they fear her mechanical body will cause. Moore reverses the symbolism: the robotic body of Deirdre does not relieve her of work but enables it, and she is again a world-famous entertainer; her body is not a threat to her humanity but an elaboration of it. As Deirdre claims, "I'm not sub-human . . . I'm – superhuman."[15] The story thus critiques the ideology of the superiority of patriarchal science by reversing the gender of the traditional robot.

Narrative Strategies: Cross-Dressing as a Male Narrator

Women writers of Golden Age SF generally accept the convention of the male narrator as adventurer or scientist: they cross-dress as male narrators.[16] But they also deploy the convention in hyperbolic, parodic, ironic ways so

---

[12] C. L. Moore, "No Woman Born," *Astounding Science Fiction* 34, 4 (December 1944), pp. 152, 165–6.

[13] Judith Butler, *Gender Trouble: Feminism and the Subversion of Identity* (New York: Routledge, 1990), p. viii.

[14] Moore, "No Woman Born," p. 139.

[15] Ibid., p. 176.

[16] In *Vested Interests: Cross-Dressing and Cultural Anxiety* (New York: Routledge, 1992), pp. 6 and 141, Marjorie Garber argues that cross-dressing offers women the power of "blurred gender" and signals women's break with patriarchal social and erotic expectations. On the cross-dressing of women writers as male narrators in modern SF, see Jane Donawerth, *Daughters of Frankenstein* (Syracuse, NY: Syracuse University Press, 1997), pp. 109–76.

that the ideology that has generated the convention is resisted and questioned.

Frequently women writers parody the masculinity of the scientists of men's SF. Judith Butler has explained that such hyperbolic enactment of gender is one way to resist the idea of gender as a "natural" category.[17] In Miriam Allen deFord's "Featherbed on Chlyntha," published in 1957 in *Venture Science Fiction*, for example, the young male anthropologist, Duncan Keith, who narrates the story, is depicted as hyperbolically masculine, his comments suggesting extreme arousal as he views the female alien scientists who hold him captive. When alien Iri explains that she has been testing him for his "sexual equipment," as well as intelligence, he replies in Terran, which she does not understand, "Well, how about a practical demonstration, baby?"[18] While Iri explains the aliens' quest for a solution to their culture's growing sterility, he admires her breasts.[19] Duncan's exaggerated masculinity is amplified by his homophobia. When he learns that Chlynthans, like oysters on Earth, change from female to male during their lives, he explains, "I'd lost my appetite for Chlynthan girls now that I'd become aware of their future."[20] At first, Duncan's exaggerated heterosexual masculinity seems to provide a solution to Chlyntha's problems, and so to offer him release. He suggests that the Chlynthans solve their reproductive problems by changing from female-centered to male-centered sexuality. Chlynthan women traditionally have sex with as many mates as possible, to capitalize on their brief period of fertility (although the sexual equality and general happiness of Chlynthan women suggest other benefits to this social arrangement). Duncan tells his captors that he will aid them in cross-species fertilization if in a year his alternative plan hasn't worked: he misogynistically suggests that sterility is the fault of females, and so men should have sex with as many women as possible, rather than the current arrangement. In return, he asks to be released. His plan does work, and Chlynthan births double. However, deFord makes her narrator naive, undercutting his masculine confidence: the story ends not with Duncan returned to Terra, having placed males in the dominant position on Chlyntha, but with a museum tour that shows young Chlynthans viewing a stuffed alien – Duncan.

A second way in which women's Golden Age SF resists the male scientist point of view is the creation of a hypermasculine protagonist who is

---

[17] See Butler, *Gender Trouble*, p. 31.

[18] Miriam Allen deFord, "Featherbed on Chlyntha," *Venture Science Fiction* 1, 6 (November 1957), p. 54.

[19] Ibid., p. 56.

[20] Ibid., p. 63.

converted through the influence of a strong woman. In Leigh Bracket's "Retreat to the Stars," published in 1941 in *Astonishing Stories*, Arno, the coldly masculine alien through whose point of view the story is told, is planted as a spy inside the humans' renegade camp to prevent them from escaping genocide. Arno's dedication to serving the alien State, which exacts total obedience from him and even assigns him sexual partners, recalls American views of Nazis for this story written during the Second World War. Arno reports to his government when humans send out ships to garner food or metal for their secret plan, and finally tips off his government when humans complete the project. Rather than a secret weapon, though, the humans are building a giant escape vehicle that will take them to the stars, out of reach of oppression. However, while Arno has collected the information, he is increasingly impressed by their young leader, Ralph, and his partner, Marika. Arno at first finds Marika repulsive, with her "clear, authoritative eyes,"[21] but gradually comes to admire her loyalty and her "unwomanly strength"[22] – he falls in love, not only with Marika, but also with the grand sense of human community. Arno is converted, at the cost of his own death betraying the State's plan to attack, so that humans board their ship and leave the alien State far behind. Arno's is a certain kind of masculinity that misogynistically isolates itself, and Marika's strength mirrors that of American women who took over industrial production during The Second World War.

In an extremely grim short story, "Experiment," published in February 1953 in *The Magazine of Fantasy and Science Fiction*, Kay Rogers similarly sketches an alien male, Cobr, who buys a Terran female slave to ascertain what their culture means by "love," and is converted to an understanding of loyalty by the love songs the Terran woman plays. His conversion, however, does the Terran, who dies in captivity, no good, because his response to love is aesthetic appreciation of the arts of song and femininity rather than compassionate understanding of a fellow creature.

Women writers of the Golden Age also use multiple narrators to question the authority of the male scientist point of view. In Kathleen Ludwick's "Dr. Immortelle," published in Fall 1930 in *Amazing Stories Quarterly*, there are three points of view, one within the other (as in Mary Shelley's *Frankenstein*, the ur-SF novel published in 1818). The story begins and ends with an engineer who loved Linnie, the nurse who exposes the terrible actions of Dr. Immortelle, a mad scientist who steals blood from young children for transfusion so he can

---

[21] Leigh Brackett, "Retreat to the Stars," *Astonishing Stories* 3, 2 (November 1941), pp. 36.
[22] Ibid., p. 40.

remain young. The body of the story is told by Dr. Immortelle's former slave, who also loves Linnie, and has been the subject of Dr. Immortelle's experiments, in the process transformed from black slave to white assistant by transfusions from white children. And within his story, Linnie has a voice, although only an intermittent one. The multiple narrators, however, resist the pull of the single scientist narrator (Dr. Immortelle's point of view does not shape the story), and the nurse's voice also resists the picture of her we derive from the male narrators. The engineer, who in the traditional SF plot would have gained Linnie as his prize, sees Linnie as "the ideal nurse" full of "beauty and womanly grace."[23] Victor, the black man who idealizes her white beauty, says, "I reverenced Linnie . . . I intuitively sensed the incorruptible purity of her soul."[24] Linnie, however, is the voice of moral strength, castigating Dr. Immortelle for leaving the scene of a car accident, and accosting him when she recognizes him as the murderer of her little brother years before. Neither prize nor ideal, she dies in a Red Cross tent on a battlefield in World War I, a woman who has escaped the usual role of women in SF stories of the period.

Marion Zimmer Bradley's "The Wind People," published in February 1959 in *If: Worlds of Science Fiction*, similarly uses multiple narrators to undercut the authority of the scientific male narrator of traditional SF. The story is framed by Captain Merrihew's point of view, who sees the birth of Robin and the scandal of unmarried Dr. Helen Murray's pregnancy during shore leave as a problem because infants don't survive the rigors of space travel, and his ship is due to leave. The point of view is taken up by Helen, who stays, alone with her son Robin, since no shipmate claims partnership. Her point of view alternates with Robin's, who hears the voices in the wind of the secretive alien people of the world. As Robin reaches maturity, he reaches out sexually to his mother, who rejects him, and runs into the woods. There, Helen, too, hears the voices and sees the alien inhabitants, but fears miscegenation and views them as signs of her own madness. Robin is taken up by his alien father's people, and years later Captain Merrihew returns to discover only an absence. Thus the authority, compassion, and knowledge of the male explorer-scientist as framing narrator are undercut by the voices of Helen's resistance and Robin's desertion of humanity.

When women writers do shift to more frequent use of a female point of view in the late 1940s and 1950s, it is to underline the affordances of the

---

[23] Kathleen Ludwick, "Dr. Immortelle," *Amazing Stories Quarterly* 3, 4 (Fall 1930), pp. 562.
[24] Ibid., p. 567.

popular genre of the near-future dystopia. In Judith Merril's "That Only a Mother," published in *Astounding* in June 1948, a young woman, pregnant during a future world war, works in a factory and worries about the deformities suffered by many newborns because of military radiation.[25] Through the daily news, she also hears of infanticides carried out world-wide by fathers of such infants. But when her baby is born, she reports to everyone how delighted she is that her lovely Henrietta is not only healthy, but even superior, learning to speak before she can crawl and singing at eight months. The point of view shifts at the end to that of the father, on leave from the military, who realizes that his daughter has no limbs, and that his wife fails to recognize this. He deems his wife mad, and "his fingers tightened on his child,"[26] the implication being that he has killed the brilliant but disabled daughter named for him. Written just after the Second World War, this near-future dystopia asks, through its use of a female point of view on warfare, if it is not rather the fathers who release the toxins and kill their children, than the mothers who love their disabled children, who are mad.[27] Kate Wilhelm's "Android, Kill for Me," published in *Future Science Fiction* in May 1959, similarly switches viewpoints. On a future Earth where reproduction is regulated by eugenics, women are divided into intellectuals, who stay at home to create but are tied to male artists and expected to produce offspring continuously, and women who do not bear children but have affairs of their choice. The story is told from the point of view of Helen, a writer of romances for women, who despises her husband because he insults her and refuses intimacy except when it is time for another baby. Because of the couple's productivity, they are served by the advanced, Z-class android. "He" helps Helen with research for her novels and records her dictation. Eventually, Helen hints to him to kill her husband, devising a way that he can do so

[25] In "Hoping for the Best, Imagining the Worst: Dystopian Anxieties in Women's SF Pulp Stories in the 1930s," *Extrapolation* 50, 1 (Spring 2009), pp. 61–79, Alice Waters argues that dystopian stories by women in the 1930s reflect anxieties about women's lives in the United States, reading Leslie F. Stone's "The Great Ones" (1930) as focusing on anxiety about eugenics, an "intrusion of science into reproduction and family life," and C. L. Moore's "Greater Than Gods" (1939), as contrasting "a patriarchy characterized by military conquest" and "a matriarchy with resolute dedication to peace and community" (p. 64).

[26] Judith Merril, "That Only a Mother," *Astounding Science Fiction* 41, 4 (June 1948), p. 95.

[27] See Lisa Yaszek, *Galactic Suburbia: Recovering Women's Science Fiction* (Columbus: The Ohio State University Press, 2008), who argues that in their science fiction after the Second World War, in general narrated from the point of view of wives and mothers, women were mainly concerned with the impact of science on women and their families, rethinking women's agency, imagining new kinds of families and domesticity, and protesting technological warfare.

without actually disobeying robotic laws. She hopes to then be free to have an affair with a pilot she has been secretly meeting. At the end, the story changes to the "male" robot's viewpoint, who has heard too many of Helen's romances – he kills not only the husband, but also the pilot. As victor, he expects her "to melt into his arms."[28] In this story, Wilhelm cleverly reverses expectations for the characters whose points of view she employs: the woman is not tender-hearted, and the robot, assuming the masculine role, is not obedient.

Reversing Gender

In the 1970s and 1980s, women SF novelists frequently created reverse-gender alien worlds where women are in charge and hierarchical matriarchies are very like patriarchies.[29] The women writers of Golden Age short stories sometimes portray women in these traditionally masculine, reversed-gender ways, but often instead leverage the plot device of gender reversal to complicate how we think about women's roles, reimagining traditional female gender traits not as weak or inferior, but as heroic and world-saving. These women reverse gender and recast women's roles by writing into our futures heroic wives and mothers whose domestic skills are life-saving, scientific reproduction at cell level or in laboratories, sympathetic negotiators who save the world from aliens by their abilities to communicate, and female sexualities that transform the stereotype of the seductive woman into a practicing therapist.

Certainly there are simple gender reversals in many stories by women in the SF magazines. In Leslie Stone's "Men with Wings," published in *Air Wonder Stories* in July 1929, Lois is a flying warrior, and in Clare Winger Harris's "The Ape Cycle," published in *Science Wonder Quarterly* in Spring 1930, Sylvia is an airplane mechanic. Additionally, in Miriam Allen deFord's "Featherbed on Chlyntha," which we have already discussed, the standard plot of Earth woman captured by male aliens for reproductive use is reversed to Terran man captured by female aliens, but for the same reason. In a more sophisticated reversal, Judith Merril, writing under the pseudonym Rose Sharon in "The Lady was a Tramp," published in *Venture Science Fiction* in March 1957, reverses and so critiques the double standard. In Merril's story, Terry Carnahan, on his first assignment after training and in charge

---

[28] Kate Wilhelm, "Android, Kill for Me!," *Future Science Fiction* 10, 2 (May 1959), p. 48.
[29] See, for example, Marion Zimmer Bradley, *The Ruins of Isis* (1978); C. J. Cherry, *The Pride of Chanur* (1981); and Cynthia Felice, *Double Nocturne* (1986).

of the mathematical computations and complex machinery that allow jumps between stars, is assigned to a tramp merchant rocket. The story elaborates a parallel in its imagery between the *Lady Jane*, the once-lovely ship, and the medical officer, Anita Filmord, who saw to the five-man crew's physical, psychological, and, it turns out, sexual health: both are tramps, but together they transform the priggish lieutenant from territorial and scandalized, to understanding and willing to share. Through the gender reversal of mono-gamous men and polygamous woman, the story debunks the double stan-dard that served as the rule of SF at the time.

More frequently, however, SF stories by women in the magazines twist women's traditional roles into new visions of power: because of women's role as caretaker, they are better at science or governing than men.[30] In Clare Winger Harris's "The Fifth Dimension" (1928), for example, Ellen, the protagonist, recounts a déjà vu feeling that her husband dismisses, but the result is a neighbor's death. Later, when Ellen has a second such feeling, she forbids her husband to take a train that is then involved in an accident, killing many people. She theorizes that time is cyclical, and so subject to interven-tion: Ellen has a premonition because she has lived this time before, but time evolves, so she can prevent tragedy. Ellen explains why she is the one to envision this philosophically scientific answer: her husband John was "forced out ... in the business world," so no longer has the time for contemplation that she has.[31] In Harris's story, the role of middle-class wife allows Ellen to develop her intellectual powers.

Similarly, in "Into the 28th Century," Lilith Lorraine creates a future utopia where a youth revolution not only establishes a democratic, socialist state, but also is a catalyst for a women's movement that creates true equality between the sexes. As women grow into their new roles, new scientific discoveries allow near immortality and alternatives to the dangers of natural childbirth. Because of women's "finer sensibilities," they "have found ... compensation for [the loss of] motherhood" in becoming "mother of the World-State ... supreme in the realm of government." Lorraine has

---

[30] In "Science Fiction by Women in the Early Pulps, 1926–1930," I argued that women writers of the early pulp magazines drew on nineteenth-century women's technological utopias to infuse the new genre of SF with visions of technological transformations of domestic space, revisions of gender roles and societies based on sexual equality, and resistance to the SF tradition of the male-scientist narrative voice. See Jane L. Donawerth and Carol A. Kolmerten, *Utopian and Science Fiction by Women: Worlds of Difference* (Syracuse, NY: Syracuse University Press, 1994), pp. 137–52.
[31] Clare Winger Harris, "The Fifth Dimension," *Amazing Stories* 3, 9 (December 1928), p. 824.

reinvented the role of mother so that women oversee "the spiritual and intellectual guidance of our planet, the home of the human race."[32] Moreover, in Anne McCaffrey's "Freedom of the Race," published in *Science Fiction Plus* in October 1953, women defeat aliens who attempt to conquer humans to use Terran women as incubators. The women expose themselves to German measles early in their pregnancies, thus ensuring that alien offspring are born deformed or dead. They transform the traditional roles of women as nurses and child-bearers into heroic – but destructive – defenders of humanity.

In a stunning reimagination of women's role as reproducer of humanity, Katherine MacLean, in "And Be Merry . . ." published in *Astounding Science Fiction* in February 1950, imagines that Helen Berent, an endocrinologist who is also a conventional wife who has sacrificed her career as a scientist to follow her husband's travels as an archaeologist, decides this time to stay home to experiment on herself. Drawing on the early-twentieth-century discovery that some cells are "immortal" – that they can live on indefinitely outside the body, as long as proper environment and food are provided – MacLean has Helen turn her kitchen into a laboratory to use enzymes to break down and rebuild her own body at cellular level, with the unexpected consequence that she also is rejuvenated, thus opening the possibility of immortality for humans. The future of never dying so frightens her that she goes mad, to be rescued by her husband with the promise that, because cells mutate, she will eventually succumb to cancer. The story is a clever scientific extrapolation from cytological and endocrinological discoveries – but, more to our point, it is also a surprising reimagining of the role of woman, from biological mechanism for reproducing humans to female scientist who reproduces herself cell by cell.

Conclusion

Men who write about women in the Golden Age often resist the stereotypes to imagine a future that includes progress toward equality between the sexes. Nevertheless, the basic template depends on a male scientist as point of view, an adventure story centered on science that usually excludes women, and coded elements that signal future but stand in for patriarchal American values (the rocket ship for exploration and virility, the alien Other, the robot for

---

[32] Lillith Lorraine (pseudonym for Mary M. Dunn Wright), "Into the 28th Century," *Science Wonder Quarterly* 1, 2 (Winter 1930), p. 257.

technological progress). SF by women in the Golden Age also depends on this basic template, but more often than not resists or reverses its constituents. Women writers mock the phallic rocket through hyperbole, sympathize with the alien Other, and reverse the gender of the robot to make it stand for art rather than science. These female writers resist the masculine narrative voice by converting or multiplying the narrator, and eventually by giving women the point of view. Rather than outright reversing gender roles, women writers reimagine the meanings of feminine qualities, making wives and mothers and grandmothers the ones who save their loved ones or even the world. And women writers co-opt the science our culture attributes to men, making women scientists who invent new ways of reproduction and who nurture instead of destroy life.

15

Better Living through Chemistry: Science Fiction and Consumerism in the Cold War

LEE KONSTANTINOU

On July 24, 1959, US Vice President Richard Nixon and Soviet Premier Nikita Khrushchev held a series of informal discussions that came to be known as the Kitchen Debate. Nixon was in the Soviet Union to open the American National Exhibition, a six-week exhibit in Sokolniki Park, which was putatively designed to give Soviet citizens a "clearer picture of life in the United States."[1] In fact, the exhibit was "a tool of cultural diplomacy against the Soviet Communist regime."[2] It was a propaganda weapon in what one historian has called the "combat of commodities" between the first and the second worlds.[3] Against the enemy of international communism, the Exhibition mobilized the power of the American consumer economy: color televisions, automobiles, a full ranch home, and model kitchens. Over the course of the day, as they toured the exhibit, Nixon and Khrushchev publicly discussed the respective virtues of capitalism and socialism. Part of their exchange was filmed in a mock RCA television studio; another discussion happened away from television cameras, during a tour of one of the kitchens, but was reported by the *New York Times* and other outlets.[4] Nixon's argument for the superiority of capitalism invoked, among other examples, the sophistication of labor-saving devices available to American women. The Vice President averred that "what we want to do [in America] is make easier the

---

[1] Sarah T. Phillips and Shane Hamilton, *The Kitchen Debate and Cold War Consumer Politics: A Brief History with Documents*, 1st edn. (Boston: Bedford/St. Martin's, 2014), p. 1.
[2] Marilyn S. Kushner, "Exhibiting Art at the American National Exhibition in Moscow, 1959: Domestic Politics and Cultural Diplomacy," *Journal of Cold War Studies* 4, 1 (January 2002), p. 6.
[3] Stephen J. Whitfield, *The Culture of the Cold War*, 2nd edn. (Baltimore: Johns Hopkins University Press, 1996), p. 72.
[4] "The Two Worlds: A Day-Long Debate," *New York Times* (July 25, 1959).

life of our housewives."[5] Khrushchev decried Nixon's "capitalist attitude toward women," and dismissed many of the proffered devices as "merely gadgets."[6] "Don't you have a machine that puts food into the mouth and pushes it down?" he quipped.[7]

The Kitchen Debate is a classic emblem of how consumerism became politically significant during the Cold War. US propaganda extolling American consumerism meant in part to strike at a perceived weak point of Soviet industrial and social development. For many years, the Soviet Union had emphasized the production of the means of production (Group A, capital goods) and had concomitantly developed less fully its consumer economy (Group B goods). Nonetheless, during the Stalin and Khrushchev eras, the Soviet government "tied its legitimacy to consumption," especially emphasizing the material abundance of communism in the 1961 program of the Communist Party.[8] In the United States, meanwhile, the departure of women from wartime industries, the cultural effort to encourage women to return to domestic labor and so-called women's professions, a burgeoning consumer economy, and the industrialization of agriculture made the kitchen an important symbol of American power.[9] For American Cold Warriors, images of consumerist plenty (as well as labor-saving inventions for the household) therefore functioned as propaganda not only internationally but also domestically. Such propaganda suffused political rhetoric, magazine advertising, and other zones of cultural production in the early days of the Cold War.

This chapter will explore how such propaganda drew on the resources of SF, and how, in turn, SF responded to these appropriations of the genre's characteristic tropes. SF about consumerism largely, though not exclusively, operated in the mode of satire. This satire made use of both a ruthless Juvenalian mode (Frederik Pohl and C. M. Kornbluth's biting attack on advertising, *The Space Merchants*, being the most famous example), as well as a more tolerant Horatian mode (Hanna-Barbera's animated sitcom, *The Jetsons*, comes to mind). Much of the most important anti-consumerist SF was published in *Galaxy Science Fiction* under the editorship of H. L. Gold. Under Gold's guidance (1950–61), *Galaxy* became a hothouse for socially critical SF, serializing Robert Heinlein's *The Puppet Masters* (1951), Alfred Bester's *The*

---

[5] Phillips and Hamilton, *The Kitchen Debate and Cold War Consumer Politics*, p. 47.
[6] Ibid., pp. 47, 48.
[7] Ibid., p. 48.
[8] Natalya Chernyshova, *Soviet Consumer Culture in the Brezhnev Era* (London: Routledge, 2015), p. 2.
[9] Emilie Stoltzfus, *Citizen, Mother, Worker: Debating Public Responsibility for Child Care after the Second World War* (Chapel Hill, NC: The University of North Carolina Press, 2003).

Demolished Man (1952–3) and *The Stars My Destination* (1956–7), as well as the precursor novella to Ray Bradbury's *Fahrenheit 451*, "The Fireman" (1951). Kurt Vonnegut Jr. and many other prominent SF satirists also published in *Galaxy*. After 1961, Frederik Pohl continued supporting this critical mode when he took over the editorship of *Galaxy*, and he brought the same irreverent sensibility to the pages of *If*, which he edited at the same time. Though the prominence of this mode might be dismissed as a reflection of the idiosyncratic interests of a handful of editors, SF's participation in the Cold War debate about consumerism expressed larger concerns. At stake in the Cold War ideological struggle was control over how the future would be imagined, a subject about which SF writers thought they had a thing or two to say. Khrushchev's dismissal of the fruits of the American exhibit as "merely gadgets" already hints at how this debate drew on the resources of SF. SF is, after all, a literature of the gadget. The genre partly originated, as Grant Wythoff has suggested, from "a number of concrete practices all geared toward reckoning with technological revolutions in the fabric of everyday life."[10] In its devotion to "extremes of both technical detail and fantastic speculation," Hugo Gernsback's "scientifiction" was sometimes dismissed as merely a series of "gadget stories."[11] Fans and authors alike identified the gadget story, often ambivalently, as one of the major strains of SF.[12] Given this heritage, it shouldn't be a surprise that during the Cold War, anti-consumerist SF became an increasingly prominent means through which writers explored the implications of – and criticized – the mid-century Keynesian vision of prosperity guaranteed through the control of economic demand.

The prominence of anti-consumerist SF satire during the Cold War has already been widely noted among writers, editors, fans, and scholars.[13] In his classic study *New Maps of Hell* (1960), Kingsley Amis identified what he called the "comic inferno" as the most accomplished example of the subgenre, lavishly praising *The Space Merchants* as its premier achievement.[14] Despite the attention this subgenre has been given, I argue, existing scholarship has

---

[10] Grant Wythoff, "Introduction," in Hugo Gernsback, *The Perversity of Things: Hugo Gernsback on Media, Tinkering, and Scientifiction*, ed. Grant Wythoff (Minneapolis: University of Minnesota Press, 2016), p. 3.

[11] Ibid., p. 5.

[12] Robert A. Heinlein, "On the Writing of Speculative Fiction," in Rob Latham, ed., *Science Fiction Criticism: An Anthology of Essential Writings* (London: Bloomsbury Academic, 2017), p. 17.

[13] John Clute *et al.*, eds., "Satire," *SFE: Science Fiction Encyclopedia*, September 26, 2016, www.sf-encyclopedia.com/entry/satire (last accessed May 29, 2018).

[14] Kingsley Amis, *New Maps of Hell* (London: Penguin Classics, 2012).

not properly assessed the political significance of this Cold War tendency within SF. In my view, scholars have too easily arrived at either positive or negative assessments of the politics of this mode. (This chapter offers a more dialectical view.) John Clute has claimed that the early years of the Cold War saw the publication of SF that was, at least in the case of Pohl and Kornbluth, "on the cutting edge of social comment."[15] Against this view, William J. Burling writes that "socialist thought in United States Left-sf varies [in the 1950s] from considerably muted to non-existent" and that such fiction "rarely poses solid political questions or offers Left alternatives to capitalism."[16] SF's focus on consumerism might be viewed, from this perspective, as an evasion of larger questions of political economy. Mark Bould and Sherryl Vint, meanwhile, argue that Cold War SF was "as likely to be critical, as supportive, of hegemonic norms."[17] All of these claims contain a grain of truth, but they miss the degree to which SF was, in most cases, not solely supportive or critical of hegemonic norms. Rather, most of these mid-century writers and artists evinced profound ambivalence about consumerism. Clute is right to locate mid-century satirical SF – the sort of story one might read in the pages of *Galaxy* or *If* – as the avant-garde of a broader anti-consumerist discourse in American culture. *The Space Merchants* and similar works indeed anticipated a renaissance of social critique, including attacks on the advertising industry found in *Mad* (founded 1952), Vance Packard's *The Hidden Persuaders* (1957), J. B. Priestley's polemics against "Admass," and of course the Frankfurt School's critiques of the Culture Industry.[18] On the whole, early Cold War culture was far "more self-critical than we have previously imagined," and SF arguably led the way.[19] To be sure, such critiques were not only concerned with Cold War politics; they also offered forms of nascent media criticism and developed broader arguments about the dangers of conformity. But attacks on consumerism were often thinly coded – or not at all coded – manifestations of Cold War strife. The enemies of the state in *The Space Merchants* are, let us recall, derisively called "Consies." Beyond Cold War themes, these dissenters emphasized the failure of the consumer economy to

[15] Quoted in William J. Burling, "Marxism," in Mark Bould, Andrew M. Butler, Adam Roberts and Sherryl Vint, eds., *The Routledge Companion to Science Fiction* (London: Routledge, 2009), p. 242.

[16] Ibid.

[17] Mark Bould and Sherryl Vint, *The Routledge Concise History of Science Fiction* (New York: Routledge, 2011), p. 82.

[18] Vance Packard, *The Hidden Persuaders* (Brooklyn: Ig Publishing, 2007); Roger Fagge, *The Vision of J. B. Priestley* (London: Bloomsbury Academic, 2013).

[19] Morris Dickstein, *Leopards in the Temple: The Transformation of American Fiction, 1945–1970* (Cambridge, MA: Harvard University Press, 2002), p. xi.

meet spiritual needs, and its use of manipulative advertising to lull consumers into complicity, as well as the risks of overpopulation, resource depletion, and environmental degradation. Such critiques inevitably led critics to speculative modes of thought. After all, the danger consumerism posed was – for many of the middle-class writers and readers of these critiques – not perceived as imminent. Despite the seductions of the mid-century economy, these writers feared, the bill would someday soon come due.

In rendering their verdict on consumerism, mid-century SF writers could draw on a range of relevant precursors. Thinking in the most expansive terms, we might regard Jonathan Swift's *Gulliver's Travels* (1726) and Voltaire's novella "Micromégas" (1752) (as well as his short story "Plato's Dream" [1756]) as models of SF in the satirical-dystopian mode of comic inferno. The core strategy of such precursors is evident in the title of Voltaire's novella: small/big. SF satire rescales reality, reframing everyday life in disturbing ways, stretching out reality to grotesquely large (or compressing it into unsettlingly small) proportions. Such literary distortions of scale were, as Mark McGurl has suggested, banished from the mainline of Western realism and came to reside in the "ambiguously novelistic subgenre called scientific romance and then, later, science fiction."[20] Science fictional distortions of reality arguably always require some form of social criticism (the function that was eliminated from Western realism). As Pohl writes in his memoir, *The Way the Future Was*, when you "invent a society, you make a political statement about the one you live in. Every [SF] writer is in some sense a preacher."[21] On this view, the characteristic operations of satire (grotesque exaggeration, vicious irony, dissonant juxtapositions) sit well with the rigorous cognitive estrangement characteristic of SF more generally. One can therefore see why Kornbluth would call *Gulliver's Travels* the "earliest English science fiction novel which is still part of the living literature," in an essay that argues that "explicit social criticism" is central to SF.[22]

More squarely in the modern SF tradition, H. G. Wells's polemical novel, *When the Sleeper Wakes* (1899), is the most obvious precursor of early Cold War anti-consumerist satire. The novel depicts a future in which the ubiquity of advertising signals the corruption of the novel's future post-revolutionary

---

[20] Mark McGurl, "Gigantic Realism: The Rise of the Novel and the Comedy of Scale," *Critical Inquiry* 43, 2 (December 12, 2016), p. 408.

[21] Frederik Pohl, *The Way the Future Was: A Memoir* (New York: Ballantine Books, 1978), p. 17.

[22] C. M. Kornbluth, "The Failure of the Science Fiction Novel as Social Criticism," *Library of America: American Science Fiction: Classic Novels of the 1950s*, http://sciencefiction.loa .org/biographies/pohl_failure.php (last accessed May 1, 2017).

society. The titular sleeper, Graham, awakens from his cataleptic trance into a world where – "on every crest and hill, where once the hedges had interlaced, and cottages, churches, inns, and farmhouses had nestled among their trees" – he discovers power-generating windmills plastered with "vast advertisements."[23] There are "great fleets of advertisement balloons and kites."[24] Elsewhere, Graham encounters "violent advertisement[s]," a "tumult of light and colour," finding that "Babble machines of a peculiarly rancid tone were abundant and filled the air with strenuous squealing and an idiotic slang 'Skin your eyes and slide,' 'Gewhoop, Bonanza,' 'Gollipers come and hark!'"[25] Graham's encounters with violent, hectoring advertisements presage many anti-consumerist tropes in twentieth-century SF. Mid-century anti-consumerist SF also resembles non-science fictional satires of consumerism and mass society from the 1930s. The relevant precursors here are works by authors such as Nathanael West and Kenneth Fearing, or magazines such as *Ballyhoo* (1931–9).[26] Depression-era photographs, by Dorothea Lange, Margaret Bourke-White, and others, often "uncomfortably juxtapose[d] the fact of scarcity and the promise of abundance," making the failure of the consumer economy into a political scandal. "By the mid-1930s," Jackson Lears notes, "the trade press was running satirical lists of the mythical maladies copywriters had invented."[27] In all these precursors, critiques of technoscience, capitalism, and domestic technologies were already conjoined into a single rhetorical appeal. However, in all of these cases, the mode of critique is relatively straightforward. Wells suggests that advertising and consumerism are corrupting forces. Depression-era satirists emphasized the *failure* of capitalism to deliver the consumer goods promised by official pronouncements.

By contrast, mid-century SF evinced ambivalence about the meaning of consumerism. On the one hand, Cold War anti-consumerist SF used the tools of speculation to show how a consumer-led economy might harm human flourishing, rob life of deeper values, and promote complacency and conformity. On the other hand, these same stories understood that SF was implicated in the future-oriented ideologies that promoted growth and consumer plenty as the telos of economic policy. Given this paradox, SF that

[23] H. G. Wells, *When the Sleeper Wakes* (New York: Harper & Row, 1899), p. 161.
[24] Ibid., p. 163.
[25] Ibid., p. 265.
[26] Rita Barnard, *The Great Depression and the Culture of Abundance: Kenneth Fearing, Nathanael West, and Mass Culture in the 1930s* (Cambridge: Cambridge University Press, 1995).
[27] Jackson Lears, *Fables of Abundance: A Cultural History of Advertising in America* (New York: Basic Books, 1995), p. 194.

straightforwardly presented "Left alternatives to capitalism," as Burling puts it, would arguably evade interrogating its own conflicted ideological position. A closer look at *The Space Merchants* will illustrate the character of this conflict. Pohl and Kornbluth's 1952 novel – serialized from June to August 1952 in *Galaxy Science Fiction* under the title *Gravy Planet* – depicts a dystopian future in which corporations have colonized all governmental functions and public spaces. The House of Representatives and Senate now represent not American states but corporate firms, in proportion to those firms' financial might. The social world is divided between two great classes: precarious consumers (the overwhelming majority, many of whom rent individual stairs in skyscrapers to sleep on every night) and wealthy executives (a tiny but powerful minority who enjoy slightly more space in tiny studio apartments). Government-engineered overpopulation (meant to increase the consumer base) threatens to exhaust the Earth's resources, inspiring the rise of the Consies, radical conservationists who engage in sabotage and other acts of dissent against the consumer order. The novel's plot hinges on an effort by the Star Class copysmith, Mitch Courtney of Fowler Schocken Associates, to successfully sell consumers on the prospect of colonizing Venus, which is an uninhabitable hellhole – scalding hot, wracked by 500-mph winds, and chemically toxic to life. On the face of it, the novel seems to be an unambiguously critical attack on the politics of unlimited growth.

Yet the novel's ambivalence is evident in an early scene, in which Mitch tries to convince Jack O'Shea, the first man to land on Venus and return to Earth alive, that marketers can indeed shape consumer preferences using only language:

> "I'm going to ask you to spend the morning and afternoon with one of the world's great lyric poets: A girl named Tildy Mathis. She doesn't know that she's a poet; she thinks she's a boss copywriter. Don't enlighten her. It might make her unhappy.
>
> > 'Thou still unravish'd bride of quietness,
> > Thou Foster-child of Silence and slow Time – '
>
> That's the sort of thing she would have written before the rise of advertising. The correlation is perfectly clear. Advertising up, lyric poetry down. There are only so many people capable of putting together words that stir and move and sing. When it became possible to earn a very good living in advertising by exercising this capability, lyric poetry was left to untalented screwballs who had to shriek for attention and compete by eccentricity."
>
> "Why are you telling me all this?" he asked.

"I said you're on the inside, Jack. There's a responsibility that goes with power. Here in this profession we reach into the souls of men and women. We do it by taking talent and redirecting it. Nobody should play with lives the way we do unless he's motivated by the highest ideals."[28]

O'Shea reassures Mitch not to worry: his motives in promoting the colonization of Venus are pure. "I'm not in this thing for money or fame," he says. "I'm in it so the human race can have some elbow room and dignity again." Mitch is shocked at this answer and informs the reader that "the 'highest ideal' I had been about to cite was Sales."[29] The art of the copysmith, we learn, is to "convince people without letting them know that they are being convinced."[30] Much the same, the authors imply, could be said of the writer – not to mention the SF writer. Advertising cannot be treated merely as an object of science fictional critique, but should be rightly seen as a rival for ownership of the cultural authority to imagine the future. On this view, SF is itself a form of advertising, and advertising is not unlike SF. Each in its own way seeks to construct a vision of a good future.

The rivalry between SF and advertising was staged not only within individual stories but also within the paratexts surrounding these in SF magazines (which were themselves products of the postwar boom). Pohl's 1955 story, "The Tunnel Under the World," published in *Galaxy Science Fiction* under Gold's editorship, may at first seem less than subtle in its critique. The protagonist of that story, Guy Burckhardt, discovers that he and everyone in his town of Tylerton have died and been transformed into tiny robots. Living in a simulacrum of Tylerton, these robots relive a single day over and over and are subjected to experimental advertisements. The town has become a captive, undead focus group. The story's horror emerges, in part, from the aggressive nature of the ad campaigns. On the second version of the repeated day (June 15) that is represented in the story, Buckhardt is accosted with the following deafening pitch:

> Feckle, Feckle, Feckle, Feckle, Feckle, Feckle. Cheap freezers ruin your food. You'll get sick and throw up. You'll get sick and die. Buy a Feckle, Feckle, Feckle, Feckle! Ever take a piece of meat out of the freezer you've got and see how rotten and moldy it is? Buy a Feckle, Feckle, Feckle, Feckle, Feckle. Do

---

[28] Frederik Pohl and C. M. Kornbluth, *The Space Merchants* (New York: St. Martin's Press, 1987), pp. 37–8. The revised edition of the novel, published in 2011, only slightly modifies this scene. Frederik Pohl and C. M. Kornbluth, *The Space Merchants* (New York: St. Martin's Griffin, 2011), pp. 52–3.

[29] Pohl and Kornbluth, *The Space Merchants*, 1987, p. 38.

[30] Ibid., p. 51.

you want to eat rotten, stinking food? Or do you want to wise up and buy a Feckle, Feckle, Feckle – [31]

Pohl almost seems to be rewriting Wells's *When the Sleeper Wakes*. However, the editorial Gold writes for this issue of *Galaxy*, though it seems to reinforce the anti-consumerist themes of Pohl's story, complicates such a reading. In his editorial, Gold answers a long-standing reader question, explaining where SF writers get their ideas. He shows how aspiring writers can extrapolate future scenarios from everyday life, and he models the process of speculative thought by noticing a "premium" on a cereal box and then spinning out the economic, social, and political logic of giving away free gifts as a spur to consumption. "Where did they [premiums] start?" he asks. "How far have they come since then? By contrasting the present with the past, what influence might they have on the future?"[32] Gold concludes, "Imagine what would happen if that rate of growth continued! Who'd need money?"[33] The logic of endless, linear growth of the consumer economy here is also figured as the very motor of speculation. Overproduction is not only a potential subject for an interesting SF story, but is also what allows SF writers to manufacture an endless series of speculative stories, inspired by nothing more exotic than a cereal box. SF writers are, in short, themselves in the growth business. *They* are the ones who can convince you to move to Venus, even if Venus is an uninhabitable hellhole. This ideological function of SF has been widely noted, and in a 2011 essay by Neal Stephenson, celebrated.[34]

The consonance of these missions – the alignment of the future-oriented image-making of advertising and SF – is evident across mid-century culture. SF imagery supported the burgeoning space program and was used in advertising for military contractors. As Megan Prelinger documents, early aerospace industry advertising in specialist trade journals drew heavily on "pulp science fiction's visual vernacular of rockets and moonscapes."[35] Such advertising depicted technologies that tended "to run a few steps ahead of proven technological developments," using "science fiction vernaculars to tell true stories of emerging technology."[36] These advertisements played an especially important role between the launch of *Sputnik 1* and the start of the

[31] Frederik Pohl, "The Tunnel Under the World," *Galaxy Science Fiction* (January 1955), p. 15.
[32] H. L. Gold, "Yours For a Dime!," *Galaxy Science Fiction* (January 1955), p. 4.
[33] Ibid., p. 5.
[34] Neal Stephenson, "Innovation Starvation," *World Policy Journal* 28, 3 (September 21, 2011), pp. 11–16.
[35] Megan Prelinger, *Another Science Fiction: Advertising the Space Race 1957–1962* (New York: Blast Books, 2010), p. 14.
[36] Ibid., p. 15.

Apollo Program. Afterwards, "advertising became grounded in realistic representation" of existing technologies.[37] Robert Heinlein's "The Man Who Sold the Moon" also famously illustrates how a science fictional imagination could be yoked to an entrepreneurial agenda. Heinlein's 1951 novella offers a libertarian parable that takes a seemingly positive attitude toward advertising and consumer culture. Hoping to colonize the Moon, D. D. Harriman bribes, cajoles, and manipulates his way to success. He is described, alternately, as "the last of the Robber Barons," and "the first of the *new* Robber Barons."[38] At one point in the story, he cons the CEO of Moka-Cola into buying the rights to advertise on the Moon. The novella, whose focus is less on Moon colonization than on Harriman's monomaniacal will to succeed, has become a touchstone for writers who, like Stephenson, have hoped to revive the spirit of Golden Age SF in our supposedly more pessimistic time.[39] But what distinguishes "The Man Who Sold the Moon" isn't so much its techno-optimistic libertarian politics as Heinlein's means of emplotting Harriman's zany scheme. Harriman's greatest talent, it seems, isn't business acumen or technical knowledge but his endless capacity for wild speculation. Harriman repeatedly meets with resistance from unimaginative bureaucrats and businessmen; what he does better than his opponents is anticipate how economic, political, social, and technological trends will play out in response to his attempted seizure of the Moon. The technical details – the boring parts of the speculative process – are left for experts to work out. What Harriman most resembles, then, is an SF writer, modeled on Heinlein himself. Yet Harriman's drive comes to seem bittersweet, even tragic. Though he finally succeeds, he is forced to stay behind on Earth. "He looks as Moses must have looked, when he gazed out over the promised land," one character comments. So it goes with SF's entrepreneurial drive: the SF writer always only imagines a grand or terrible future; he can never live in it.

Even in mainstream corners of mid-century culture, SF satire similarly married complicity with critique. The television program *The Jetsons*, the Hanna-Barbera sitcom – which aired on ABC from 1962 to 1963 (before being revived in the 1980s) – offers a sophisticated, if also ambivalent, perspective

---

[37] Ibid., p. 222.

[38] Robert Heinlein, "The Man Who Sold the Moon," in *The Man Who Sold the Moon / Orphans of the Sky* (New York: Baen Books, 2013), p. 200.

[39] See the two Heinlein homage stories – Cory Doctorow's "The Man Who Sold the Moon" and Gregory Benford's "The Man Who Sold the Stars" – in Ed Finn and Kathryn Cramer, eds., *Hieroglyph: Stories and Visions for a Better Future* (New York: William Morrow, 2015).

on the politics of consumerism.[40] Members of the Jetson family constantly gripe about the difficulties new technologies bring into their lives, complaining about being overworked. And yet the show comically deflates their complaints. They are simultaneously the beneficiaries of consumer plenty and beleaguered by that plenty. The opening scene of the pilot episode, "Rosie the Robot," shows Jane doing morning push-button finger exercises, a preview of the episode's central conflict. Jane complains to George about the difficulty of domestic labor, and decides to buy a robot maid when the family Food-a-Rac-a-Cycle (which they purchased on credit) starts malfunctioning. "Housework gets me down," she tells her mother. Afraid to ask for a raise, George protests that when they were first married Jane "could punch out a breakfast like Mother used to make." For his part, George works as an "digital index operator" on the "referential unisonic digital indexer machine" at Spacely Space Sprockets. He whines about the "slave driving" conditions of his workplace; over one day, he presses a button five times. The opening episode also indirectly comments on the Cold War; when Elroy says that he is going to a Siberian salt mine with his class, Jane warns, "Don't pick fights with the little Russian boys," reminding viewers of the Cold War but also suggesting that the conflict might be over by 2062 (the year the show takes place). The plot of the pilot turns on George's effort to convince his boss, Cosmo Spacely, to give him a raise; Spacely has invited himself to dinner to eat the "home cooked" meal his own wife, Stella, won't make for him. When Rosie drops a pineapple upside down cake onto Spacely's head, Spacely fires George, but shortly thereafter rehires him (with a raise) because he likes the cake. The ambivalence toward consumerism I have already noted in various stories is self-evident in this episode (and in later episodes). What is *more* noteworthy is how the pilot, on the one hand, is openly suspicious of capital in the figure of Cosmo Spacely and, on the other hand, imagines an axis of worker–owner solidarity built around patriarchal domestic authority. In this and later episodes, George and Cosmo similarly struggle against nagging wives. Mid-century anti-consumerist critique often failed to recognize the home as an important site for the reproduction of capitalism. But these critiques also often tacitly posited the nuclear household as a zone of political conflict (coded as domestic conflict). Labor-saving gadgets – which promised

---

[40] Reboots of *The Jetsons* since its original run, including the 2017 DC Comics reboot, have tended to increase this sense of ambivalence – suggesting, for instance, that the reason the Jetsons live in such ultra-high skyscrapers is that the world beneath them has been devastated by nuclear war, pollution, or climate change.

if not domestic tranquility then domestic convenience – were in part designed to vouchsafe the submission of women.

Though offering a greater range of critical perspectives than has been commonly assumed, SF in this satirical mode often also expresses fatalism and quietism. Kornbluth, for one, was skeptical about the political power of the subgenre. In a 1957 lecture delivered at the University of Chicago, he suggested that "the science fiction novel is not an important medium of social criticism" when compared to "mundane" texts such as *Don Quixote, Uncle Tom's Cabin, The Jungle*, and the like.[41] The reason it isn't effective, he suggests, is that science fictional "symbolism lies too deep for action to result" and "that the science fiction story does not turn the reader outward to action but inward to contemplation."[42] As critiques of irony and satire have suggested, attacks on consumerism might themselves become just another consumer object, a niche product that allows one to enjoy one's consumption while continuing to feel superior to other, naïve consumers. There is also a well-studied question about the relation between satire and ideology. Media effects researchers have looked at audience interpretations of satirical figures such as Archie Bunker and Stephen Colbert, suggesting that ideology dramatically inflects reception. If you are inclined to agree with Archie Bunker, watching a satirical representation of your bigoted views might only reinforce those views.[43] Other researchers have suggested that conservative viewers interpret the Stephen Colbert of *The Colbert Report* as *reinforcing* rather than *undermining* their political opinions.[44] Beyond the question of whether satire is effective as political speech or action, the ambivalence of anti-consumerist science fictional satire can also be understood as an ambivalence about capitalism itself. As Sianne Ngai has suggested in her astute analysis of the concept of "the gimmick," modern labor-saving devices arouse ambivalent feelings precisely because "the device that 'saves' human labor contributes to both its intensification and elimination in the long run" in capitalist economies.[45] Such new technologies seem destined to fail to satisfy the human wants they have supposedly been developed to address.

---

[41] Kornbluth, "The Failure of the Science Fiction Novel as Social Criticism."
[42] Ibid.
[43] Neil Vidmar and Milton Rokeach, "Archie Bunker's Bigotry: A Study in Selective Perception and Exposure," *Journal of Communication* 24, 1 (March 1974), pp. 36–47.
[44] Heather L. LaMarre, Kristen D. Landreville, and Michael A. Beam, "The Irony of Satire: Political Ideology and the Motivation to See What You Want to See in the Colbert Report," *The International Journal of Press/Politics* 14, 2 (2009), pp. 212–31.
[45] Sianne Ngai, "Theory of the Gimmick," *Critical Inquiry* 43, 2 (Winter 2017), p. 471.

Behind the veneer of satire, therefore, one finds that anti-consumerist SF often takes a tragic turn. Fredric Brown's short story "Pi in the Sky" (*Thrilling Wonder Stories*, Winter 1945) envisions a version of the 1990s in which "advertising competition was so keen that there was scarcely a bare wall or an unbillboarded lot within miles of a population center" and in which "discriminating people could retain normal outlooks on life only by carefully-cultivated partial blindness and partial deafness which enabled them to ignore the bulk of that concerted assault upon their senses."[46] An eccentric businessman fights the world's advertising blindness by creating the illusion that the stars are moving, and he uses this illusion to advertise his brand of soap. Yet the story's comic premise takes a darker turn when the relocated stars accidentally misspell the businessman's name. He falls out of a window and, it is determined, dies of "apoplexy."[47] Nonetheless, the scheme works, and "sales of Sniveley Soap increased 915%!"[48] Robert Sheckley's "One Man's Poison" (*Galaxy Science Fiction*, 1953) similarly combines humor and primal suffering. The story describes the journey of two interplanetary astronauts, Casker and Hellman, who arrive at Helg, an abandoned planet circling a red dwarf, and who discover there that they have run out of food. They find an abandoned alien warehouse full of wondrous consumer products, each advertised with breathless copy: "VIGROOM! FILL ALL YOUR STOMACHS, AND FILL THEM RIGHT!" And: "BORMITISH – GOOD AS IT SOUNDS!"[49] When Hellman suggests the astronauts will need to deduce the nature of the Helgans from their consumer goods, Casker grouses, "All we do know is that they wrote a lot of lousy advertising copy."[50] Hellman, a former librarian, translates (and mistranslates) various alien consumer product labels in search of something edible, trying to figure out what is food, and what poison. Hellman's mistranslations of alien advertising copy drive comic set pieces involving giggling liquids, expanding goo, and other menaces. Yet the story's playfulness is circumscribed by human hunger. Casker's plaintive refrain, "There must be *something* here we can eat," suggests that consumer plenty may nonetheless ultimately leave one's stomach empty.[51]

[46] Fredric Brown, "Pi in the Sky," *Thrilling Wonder Stories* (Winter 1945), p. 51.
[47] Ibid., p. 59.
[48] Ibid., p. 66.
[49] Pohl, "The Tunnel Under the World," p. 38.
[50] Ibid., p. 39.
[51] Ibid., p. 38.

Philip K. Dick's fiction of the 1950s brings the same satiric ambivalence to its logical conclusion – planting the seeds of the more paranoid anti-consumerist art of the 1960s and 1970s. His short story, "Exhibit Piece," (*If*, 1954), is constructed around an opposition between the entrepreneurial freedom of Eisenhower-era America and the collectivist repression of the twenty-second century. George Miller, curator at the History Agency, is obsessed with the object of his study: the twentieth century. He dresses in the clothing of the era and wishes to escape his own society. When he discovers a gateway between his time and the American 1950s, his first encounter with the past happens in "a ranch-style California bungalow," where he discovers that he has an alternate family life – complete with wife and children.[52] After learning that the version of the 1950s he has stepped into is indeed real, Miller resolves to stay in the era of consumerist plenty and personal freedom. He finally settles "down in the easy chair and snapped on the television" in his "safe, comfortable living room," and reads a headline indicating that the version of the 1950s he now inhabits may shortly be destroyed by nuclear warfare.

RUSSIA REVEALS COBALT BOMB
TOTAL WORLD DESTRUCTION AHEAD[53]

It is almost as if the cosmos must punish Miller for his hubristic domestic comfort. Dick's "Sales Pitch" (*Future Science Fiction*, 1954) adopts a different attitude toward the Eisenhower era, transposing the social world of the 1950s onto a future in which white-collar workers commute through the solar system. An aggressive sales robot, called a fasrad, invades the home of Ed Morris, and refuses to leave until Morris agrees to purchase him. Dick came, in time, to regret the story's grim ending, in which Morris dies in a spaceship crash. In 1978, he suggested that "The logic of paranoia of this story should be deconstructed into its opposite; Y, the human-against-robot theme, should have been resolved into null-Y, human-and-robot-against-the-universe."[54]

Nonetheless, Dick's "logic of paranoia" anticipates his later fiction, especially *Ubik* (1969), as well as anti-consumerist New Wave SF such as J. G. Ballard's "The Subliminal Man" (*New Worlds*, 1963) and Pamela Zoline's "The Heat Death of the Universe" (*New Worlds*, 1967). Ballard's story takes the impasse at the heart of Dick's "Sales Pitch" to its ultimate end, imagining a near future in which the Keynesian imperative to increase consumption

---

[52] Philip K. Dick, "Exhibit Piece," *If* (August 1954), p. 65.
[53] Ibid., p. 75.
[54] Philip K. Dick, *Second Variety and Other Classic Stories* (New York: Citadel Press, 2002), p. 413.

transforms the "overcapitalized industrial system" into a complete control society.[55] One character in Ballard's story, Hathaway, worries that new electronic billboards will "transistorize our brains."[56] Mid-century Keynesian capitalism comes to be described as "a sort of communism."[57] Hathaway's lack of connection to the consumer economy is a sort of freedom; his interlocutor, the doctor Franklin, meanwhile discovers his own lack of freedom in the form of "three mortgages on his home, the mandatory rounds of cocktail parties, the private consultancy occupying most of Saturday which paid the instalments on the multitude of household gadgets, clothes and past holidays."[58] Fears of a recession lead economic planners to implement subliminal manipulation meant to increase consumer demand, a sort of economic stimulus via thought control. The story is thus about the hypothetical limits of the Keynesian consensus. Zoline's classic story, meanwhile, seems at first to go beyond the Keynesian consensus, placing mid-century consumerism into a cosmological context. "Heat Death" tells the story of Sarah Boyle, a housewife whose dissatisfaction with domestic life is cast against a cosmic and metaphysical backdrop, which frames a climactic emotional breakdown at the story's end. Yet, much like Thomas Pynchon in his short story "Entropy" (*The Kenyon Review*, 1957), Zoline transforms the second law of thermodynamics into an allegory for consumer capitalism's tendency toward wasteful overproduction. The heat death of the universe comes to stand for the empty abundance of the consumer economy. This economic order, Zoline suggest, relies on a picture of the nuclear family that relegates women like Sarah – "a vivacious and intelligent young wife and mother, educated at a fine Eastern college" – to wall themselves off from matters of ultimate concern.[59] Sarah is asked to ignore the way in which she is connected to "Time/Entropy/Chaos and Death."[60] "Heat Death" therefore also indirectly revisits the Kitchen Debate, reminding us why the kitchen had become a political combat zone. As if meaning to directly recall Gold's 1955 editorial, the story's narrator asks us to consider a cereal box as an "abstract object," seen from a non-American or even possibly nonhuman perspective.[61]

---

[55] J. G. Ballard, "The Subliminal Man," in *The Complete Stories of J. G. Ballard* (New York: W. W. Norton & Company, 2010), p. 422.

[56] Ibid., p. 413.

[57] Ibid.

[58] Ibid., p. 414.

[59] Pamela Zoline, "The Heat Death of the Universe," in *The Heat Death of the Universe and Other Stories* (Kingston, NY: McPherson & Co, 1988), p. 15.

[60] Ibid., p. 21.

[61] Ibid., p. 14.

The narrator observes that a "notice in orange flourishes states that a Surprise Gift is to be found somewhere in the packet," which leads Sarah's children to "request more cereal than they wish to eat."[62] By changing our cultural perspective on the box, Zoline invites us to understand that the domestic struggle of a mother, her fight against the rampant desires of her children, is connected to economic and political choices made at larger scales. And Sarah's quotidian consumer choices, likewise, have political consequences. Sarah's seemingly existential or cosmological crisis arguably arises (by allegorical substitution) from the American effort to control domestic – that is, socially reproductive – household management. The satirical themes we have so far discussed reach a grim non-satirical pinnacle with Ballard and Zoline. Their stories arguably perfect the anti-consumerist SF story, but in so doing dissolve its satirical veneer. The results are, arguably, emotionally suffocating.

As the 1960s came to a close, many writers and artists also took a more explicitly activist turn. Indeed, some authors began to imagine that they might appropriate advertising toward different ends. For his part, Ballard produced a series of five "conceptual advertisements" from 1967 to 1970 – first published in *New Worlds, Ambit*, and elsewhere – and republished in *Re/Search* in 1984.[63] "It occurred to me about a year ago," Ballard explained in an interview, "that advertising was an unknown continent as far as the writer was concerned, a kind of virgin America of images and ideas, and that the writer ought to move into any area which is lively and full of potential."[64] William S. Burroughs, who like Ballard briefly worked as a copywriter, also came to be interested in advertising. He imagined his fiction as a kind of anti-advertising. "Like the advertising people we talked about," he explains, "I'm concerned with the precise manipulation of word and image to create an action, not to go out and buy a Coca-Cola, but to create an alteration in the reader's consciousness."[65] As I have argued elsewhere, Burroughs took this project quite seriously, and his science fictional Nova trilogy as well as his novel *The Wild Boys* and its sequel *Port of Saints* can be fruitfully read as forms of SF that try to deploy

---

[62] Ibid.

[63] *Re/Search: J. G. Ballard* (San Francisco, CA: Re/Search Publishing, 1984).

[64] Quoted in Rick Poynor, "The Conceptual Advertising of J.G. Ballard," *Design Observer* (April 17, 2014), http://designobserver.com/feature/the-conceptual-advertising-of-jg-ballard/38432 (last accessed May 29, 2018).

[65] Conrad Knickerbocker, "William Burroughs," in Alfred Kazin, ed., *Writers at Work: The Paris Review Interviews* (New York: Viking, 1967), p. 174.

the techniques of advertising – and other "control systems" – in order to dismantle existing regimes of power.[66]

A few decades after the end of the Cold War, debates about consumerism have lost some of their heat. To be sure, anti-consumerist SF satires, especially in a dystopian mode, have become more common than ever, perhaps even commonplace. Nonetheless, the consumer economy has not seemed particularly threatened by such critiques. If anything, the market has warmly embraced anti-consumerist storytelling. Celebrated novels such as Neal Stephenson's *Snow Crash* (1992), David Foster Wallace's *Infinite Jest* (1996), Max Barry's *Jennifer Government* (2003), the Sonmi~451 novella in David Mitchell's *Cloud Atlas* (2005), Margaret Atwood's MaddAddam trilogy (2003–13), and Lauren Beukes's *Moxyland* (2008) have sustained the storytelling spirit inaugurated in the pages of *Galaxy* and *If*; animated television shows such as *Futurama* (1999–2013) and *Rick and Morty* (2013–) have followed the path first cleared by *The Jetsons*, and a systematic study of filmic adaptations of Philip K. Dick's fiction would require a monograph of its own. Yet anti-consumerist storytelling today may be less a way to criticize society than a way to join an established SF tradition. Anti-consumerist stories, just as much as the fascist *Jetsons*-like stories that haunt the protagonist of William Gibson's "The Gernsback Continuum" (1981), may now amount to little more than "semiotic ghosts."[67] And it may be the case, as Jill Lepore has argued, that "dystopia used to be a fiction of resistance; [today] it's become a fiction of submission, the fiction of an untrusting, lonely, and sullen twenty-first century, the fiction of fake news and infowars, the fiction of helplessness and hopelessness."[68] I will end, however, by suggesting that Cold War anti-consumerism was most politically significant at a time when the Keynesian model of state-led demand management seemed like a successful enterprise. A world of unrelenting growth was a world that seemed destined to choke to death on its own productivity. Today, the great dramas of consumption may have less to do with living in a world of plenty than in living in a world where the prospect of having access to consumption at all seems for many to be increasingly precarious, increasingly contingent, and increasingly out of reach to those who once took the availability of inexhaustible consumer

---

[66] See Chapter 2 of Lee Konstantinou, *Cool Characters: Irony and American Fiction* (Cambridge, MA: Harvard University Press, 2016).

[67] William Gibson, "The Gernsback Continuum," in *Burning Chrome* (New York: Harper, 2003), p. 35.

[68] Jill Lepore, "No, We Cannot," *The New Yorker* (June 5 and 12, 2017), p. 108.

goods for granted. For such people, the worries of George Jetson may seem like the worries of a happier time, though we would do well not to forget the sense of threat and dread – the risk of the mass annihilation through cobalt bomb – hanging over the heads of those who dreamed up those past visions of the future.

16

"The Golden Age of Science Fiction Is Twelve": Children's and Young Adult Science Fiction into the 1980s

MICHAEL LEVY

The title of this chapter is, of course, a play on the famous tendency of SF historians to refer to the "Golden Age of science fiction" that probably originates with a fan named Peter Scott Graham (though it has been claimed that he *actually* said that the Golden Age of science fiction is thirteen).[1] Graham points to the way many adult fans of the genre, regardless of when they grew up, remember the stories they read at twelve or thereabouts with a special glow of nostalgia – even an uncritical tendency to regard those works as the greatest SF stories ever written, with what's been published since as somehow just not quite up to snuff. Although such references to the good old days are endemic to all human culture, in a genre so obsessed with the "new" this has come to have greater significance; the more experienced an SF reader you are, the harder it can be to find the rush of the new that is one of the attractions of the genre. Thus the purpose of this chapter is to discuss the SF written for children and what were once called "juveniles," but are now called "young adults," during a time period that would be the Golden Age of science fiction in Graham's sense for a now-greying generation of older readers, which ran from the early twentieth century through the early to mid-1980s.

Literary fantasy specifically for children began to make a regular appearance in the mid- to late nineteenth century with such works as Charles Kingsley's *The Water Babies* (1863) and Lewis Carroll's *Alice in Wonderland* (1865), although examples of the genre can be found as early as 1749 in Sarah Fielding's *The Governess*.[2] But, oddly enough, comparable works of SF simply

---

[1] See Peter Nicholls and Mike Ashley, "Golden Age of SF," in John Clute, David Langford, Peter Nicholls, and Graham Sleight, eds., *The Encyclopedia of Science Fiction*, Gollanz, April 9, 2015, www.sf-encyclopedia.com/entry/golden_age_of_sf (last accessed May 15, 2018).

[2] See Michael Levy and Farah Mendlesohn, *Children's Fantasy Literature: An Introduction* (Cambridge: Cambridge University Press, 2016), p. 22.

didn't exist. This may well have been because the growing French and British tradition of the scientific romance, as practiced by Jules Verne (*Five Weeks in a Balloon*, 1851, *Journey to the Center of the Earth*, 1864), H. G. Wells (*The Time Machine*, 1895, *The Island of Doctor Moreau*, 1896), Sir Arthur Conan Doyle ("The Great Keinplatz Experiment," 1885, *The Lost World*, 1912) and others – not to mention earlier science fictional tales such as Mary Shelley's *Frankenstein* (1818) and various of Edgar Allan Poe's stories such as *The Narrative of Arthur Gordon Pym of Nantucket* (1838) and "Mellonta Tauta" (1849) – made such works unnecessary. These fictions, although intended for adults (and often reprinted in the pulp magazines as well), were widely viewed as child-friendly, or as "family reading." In Verne's case, this was particularly true of the early English-language editions, most of which had their considerable political content expunged, turning Verne's sometimes radical texts into appropriate reading material for young people.[3] Likewise, as discussed in more detail in Nathaniel Williams's chapter on the Edisonade earlier in this volume, early dime-novel narratives were often centered on child heroes and often possessed a dual intended audience, rather than being written specifically or only for children.

By the early twentieth century, some specialized stories emerged, more often in the United Kingdom than the United States and often seeing initial publication in various boys' magazines, where they could be linked with the more literarily accepted scientific romance tradition. Examples included John Mastin's religiously didactic *The Stolen Planet: A Scientific Romance* (1906), which concerns the adventures of two boys who build an anti-gravity-powered spaceship and fly it across the galaxy, watching planets collide and visiting various planetary civilizations, where they receive a variety of moral lessons; Fenton Ash's *A Trip to Mars* (1909), about two boys who save the life of the King of Mars, are abducted to his planet aboard a fabulous half-organic spaceship, and then help put down a revolt; and Garrett P. Serviss's *A Columbus of Space* (1911), which also uses an anti-gravity spaceship to convey its heroes to Venus, where they meet a variety of monsters as well as a telepathic humanoid civilization, a book that may have influenced Edgar Rice Burroughs's space fiction. Also worth mentioning are *The Mystery Men of Mars* (1933) by Carl Claudy, an *American Boy* magazine serial which combines Wells's Martians from *The War of the Worlds* (1898) and his Selenites from *The First Men in the Moon* (1901) in the oddest fashion, and *Planet Plane* (1936),

[3] See William Butcher. *Jules Verne Inédit: les Manuscrits Déchiffrés* (Nantes: ENS Editions Institute d'Histoire du Livre, 2015).

a rare "juvenile" novel by a major British SF writer John Wyndham (writing as John Beynon), which involves humanity's first flight to Mars and our discovery of a dying race of Martians who are on the verge of being succeeded by machine intelligences.

Children of the Golden Age

It wasn't until after the Second World War, however, that writing SF for children and older juveniles became regularized.[4] British children's writer John Kier Cross published a series of well-done SF stories, beginning with *The Angry Planet* (1945), that concerned children stowing away aboard a rocketship (a common motif) to Mars, where they meet decidedly non-humanoid vegetable life forms and become enmeshed in their deadly war. What clearly qualifies as the most distinquished children's SF novel of its day, American William Pène Du Bois's Newbery Award-winning *The Twenty-One Balloons* (1947), tells the story of a nineteenth-century utopian civilization located on the island of Krakatoa in the East Indies. This magical book somehow manages to combine great humor and serious utopian speculation on a child's level with the facts of the great volcanic eruption that wipes out not only the island but the utopian experiment. Other writers for younger children who produced excellent work were the Scot Ruthven Todd, whose *Space Cat* (1952) and sequels involve a number of delightful adventures; Eleanor Cameron, whose *The Wonderful Flight to the Mushroom Planet* (1954) and sequels received much praise in its day; Jay Williams's and Raymond Abrashkin's inventive *Danny Dunn* series, beginning with *Danny Dunn and the Anti-Gravity Paint* (1956); John M. Schealer's *Zip-Zip and his Flying Saucer* (1956), and its sequels; and Ellen MacGregor's much beloved *Miss Pickerell Goes to Mars* (1957).

In the late 1940s and early 1950s three significant figures emerged in SF for young people: Robert A. Heinlein, Isaac Asimov, and Andre Norton. Heinlein, of course, was already a major presence in the field when he began writing for children, the author at the center of John W. Campbell, Jr.'s *Astounding*-based "Golden Age." *Rocketship Galileo* (1947), the first of twelve volumes of "juvenile" SF published by Heinlein over a period of twelve years (a thirteenth volume intended for the series, *Starship Troopers* (1959) was rejected by Scribner, the publisher of his juveniles, and was instead

---

[4] A parallel might be drawn here to the way superhero comic books, originally consumed by adults during the wartime era, were deliberately reengineered as a children's genre in the early 1950s.

brought out by G. P. Putnam Sons for the adult market), feels rather creaky by modern standards. It concerns three teens (one of whom is Jewish) who, with the help of a scientist, build their own atomic-powered rocket and, upon arrival on the Moon, are attacked by Nazis who are plotting World War III from their secret lunar base. Defeating the Nazis, the boys also discover the remains of a dead lunar civilization. Despite its pulp feel, the book was better written than most SF previously published for children, and included a fair amount of accurate science. It also began an astonishingly rich period in Heinlein's career, establishing him as the premier author of SF for younger readers. High points in the series included *Starman Jones* (1953), one of the best portraits ever created of the crew of a working starship; *Time for the Stars* (1956), in which telepathically linked twin brothers age at different rates when one sets off on an interstellar voyage which triggers relativistic time dilation; *Citizen of the Galaxy* (1957), which concerns a young slave who, through many adventures and his own competence, eventually rises to become the head of a major corporation; and *Have Spacesuit – Will Travel* (1958), in which two human children, a benevolent space alien, and a spacesuit (which turns out to be sentient) are kidnapped by evil aliens. Each of these books combined an exciting story in which young people demonstrate their ability to mature and gain competence – frequently with the help of an adult mentor – with interesting science and engineering detail, fascinating sociological extrapolation, and a sense of optimism about humanity's future. Although Heinlein's juveniles invariably had male protagonists, it's also worth noting that most of them also featured strong secondary female characters, something which made the books popular with girl readers of SF from early on.

Isaac Asimov had also established himself as a major writer of adult SF when he began thinking about writing an SF series for children. Beginning with *David Starr: Space Ranger* (1952), the books were written under a pseudonym, Paul French, in part because they were originally intended to become a television series and Asimov didn't want his name connected to what he saw as the low quality of that medium.[5] Less ambitious than Heinlein's work and written for a somewhat younger and presumed male audience, the Lucky Starr books are space operas, featuring a young adult agent of Earth's Council of Science, who deals with a series of nefarious villains out to do damage to humanity. The first volume was followed by five more, finishing up with *Lucky Starr and the Rings of Saturn* (1958), in which Starr is instrumental in avoiding war with aliens from Sirius who have

---

[5] Isaac Asimov, *In Memory Yet Green* (New York: Doubleday, 1979), p. 620.

colonized the moon Titan. Although primarily intended to tell an exciting story, these books also display a variety of themes consistent with the liberal ideology common to the rest of Asimov's fiction, particularly the importance of diverse groups of people learning to live together in peace.

Andre Norton (Alice Norton) may not have been quite as innovative as Heinlein, but her children's books also told great stories in which young people succeeded in mastering their generally fascinating futuristic environments, and must be ranked well above Asimov's books for younger readers in quality. Although the majority of Norton's many novels were actually marketed to adults, she is to this day widely perceived as primarily a children's writer: witness the decision by the Science Fiction and Fantasy Writers of America, which had earlier named her a Grand Master, to create an award in her honor specifically for young adult SF and fantasy. High points among her juveniles include *Starman's Son: 2250 AD* (1952, also published as *Daybreak 2250 AD*), a believable post-holocaust tale in which a young mutant runs away from the clan that rejects him to prove himself as an explorer; *The Stars Are Ours!* (1954), in which a group of human scientists, determined to avoid the errors that have led their society to war, escape to the stars and found a new civilization dedicated to living in peace with the alien inhabitants of the planet they colonize; *Catseye* (1961), in which a young refugee gets a temporary job in an exotic pet store on an alien planet, discovers he can communicate with animals, and becomes involved in an attempted revolution; and *Quest Crosstime* (1965, also published as *Crosstime Agent*), which concerns travel between dimensions and an attempt to keep various predatory societies from preying on those that are less willing to use violence. Unlike Heinlein, who really devoted only a decade of his life to writing juvenile fiction, Norton continued to write such works until her death in 2005, often in the form of long-running series and continuations of her early work, frequently without the original juvenile label. As the years went by she increasingly made use of female protagonists and many girls who grew up to be SF readers learned to love the genre through her work.

Equally important as a group, however, were the authors of the Winston Juveniles series of SF novels, which were published in the 1950s. The Winston Juveniles, with their memorable end papers depicting spacemen, aliens, and other icons of SF, were developed in response to Scribner's success with Heinlein's juveniles and consisted of thirty-seven volumes published over a decade, though few were as memorable as the novels Heinlein produced. As a whole, the series was specifically aimed at boys. It included one short story anthology, edited by Lester del Rey, who was a mainstay for Winston, producing something like eight volumes under various pseudonyms, as well as a nonfiction work, *Rocket Through Space* (1957). The first volume in the series was Milton Lesser's merely competent *Earthbound* (1952), though Evan Hunter's *Find the Feathered Serpent* (1952), a time-travel story involving a quest to discover the origins of the Mayan god Quetzalcoatl, fared better. Other volumes included Arthur C. Clarke's *Islands in the Sky* (1952), an adventure story set on a space station, which paid close attention to the details of life in space; Poul Anderson's *Vault of the Ages* (1952), perhaps the high point of the series, a post-apocalyptic tale in which a young man discovers a vault containing humanity's lost technology, including the nuclear technology that had previously destroyed civilization; Jack Vance's *Vandals of the Void* (1953), an exciting story of space piracy; del Rey's *Step to the Stars* (1956), which centers on the actual building of a space station; and Ben Bova's *The Star Conquerors* (1959), an exciting military space opera featuring evil aliens, and battles in space. Other Winston volumes were written by Raymond F. Jones, Philip Latham, Robert W. Lowndes, Alan E. Nourse, Chad Oliver, and Donald A. Wollheim. In general, as this list should make clear, these novels were all written by professional SF writers, men (all the authors were male) who made their living writing SF for adults.

In the 1960s, even after the Winston Juveniles were no longer being published, this continued to be the trend; veteran and up-coming SF writers like Clarke (*Dolphin Island*, 1963), Robert Silverberg (*Time of the Great Freeze*, 1964), and Gordon R. Dickson (*Space Winners*, 1965) wrote the occasional novel for young readers. All were readable, but none were particularly memorable. Two new writers, however, soon broke the mold: Madeleine L'Engle and John Christopher.

L'Engle, who had no particular connection with genre SF, and who wrote as much for adults as for children, had been publishing since the mid-1940s, but first came to the attention of readers of the literature of the fantastic for a unique novel, *A Wrinkle in Time* (1962), the second SF novel to win the Newbery Award for outstanding children's literature (after *The Twenty-One Balloons*). In general it seems safe to say that L'Engle didn't care much about genres and simply wrote what she wanted to, visiting the realms of SF and fantasy when it suited her purposes. She was deeply interested in science, but the most important influence on the author's writing was undoubtedly her Christian faith, which imbued all of her books in various ways.

Over the years, the bibliographic universe of *A Wrinkle in Time* grew more and more complex, as L'Engle developed two overlapping plot lines, sometimes referred to as the Kairos and Chronos series, which together encompass some sixteen novels, some of them with overlapping characters, some of them science fictional and others entirely realistic. *A Wrinkle in Time* centers on Meg Murry, a bright but maladjusted thirteen-year-old daughter of scientists, and her youngest brother, Charles Wallace Murry, who is a genius and telepath. When their father disappears while working on something called a tesseract for the government, Meg sets out to find him and uncovers a wondrous universe filled with marvelous beings that are at once alien and supernatural, not to mention an evil force called the Black Thing that is out to conquer the universe. L'Engle's work, which sometimes calls to mind that of C. S. Lewis, centers directly on some of the most important issues facing young readers such as "death, social conformity and truth."[6] Meg Murry, as a female protagonist, also served as a conduit into SF for many girl readers. Other books in the immediate series include *A Wind in the Door* (1973), the National Book Award-winning *A Swiftly Tilting Planet* (1978), and *Many Waters* (1986).

British writer, John Christopher (the pen name for Sam Youd) began publishing in the late 1940s, writing dozens of novels under at least seven pseudonyms and moving back and forth between work for adults and for children over the course of his career. His most important work for younger readers is probably the Tripods trilogy, beginning with *The White Mountains* (1967), a loose variation on H. G. Wells's *The War of the Worlds* based in part on the question of what would have happened if the aliens hadn't succumbed to bacteria. Christopher postulates a post-apocalyptic world in which human beings, all of whom are controlled by "Caps" implanted on their heads, live a largely rural existence with the tripods overseeing everything. The novel's young protagonist, Will, is looking forward to receiving his cap at age fourteen, until he meets an odd, uncapped adult who persuades him to join the Resistance. As the series continues, Will gradually rises within the Resistance, and violent revolution breaks out. Unlike most American children's SF of the period, the trilogy ends after only partial human victory, with everything still in the balance and the tripods' defeat by no means clear. Christopher came back to the series some twenty years later with *When the Tripods Came* (1988), but this prequel tells us nothing of the eventual outcome of humanity's revolt. Among Christopher's other significant works of children's SF are The Sword of the Spirits trilogy, beginning with *The Prince in Waiting* (1970), which is set in a post-apocalyptic, medieval world, and the time-travel centered Fireball trilogy, beginning with *Fireball* (1981).

---

[6] Jean C. Fulton, "A Wrinkle in Time," in Fiona Kelleghan, ed., *Classics of Science Fiction and Fantasy Literature* (Pasadena, CA: Salem Press, 2002), pp. 597–8.

By the mid- to late 1960s, the authoring of SF novels for young readers became to a greater and greater extent the work of writers who, although they might occasionally publish an adult novel, more often wrote specifically for children and young adults – and this caused a significant change in the field. In 1963 British children's writer Joan B. Clarke published *The Happy Planet*, the first of several children's SF novels, which explored three post-apocalyptic societies, one highly technological, one pastoral, and the third cyborg. Another post-apocalyptic tale, Suzanne Martel's *Quatre Montréalais en l'an 3000* (1963), very probably the first French-Canadian SF novel, appeared in English as *The City Under Ground* (1964) and gained enduring popularity in both languages. Alexander Key's *Escape to Witch Mountain* (1968), which concerns the adventures of two orphans who discover that they are actually extraterrestrials with psi powers, remained popular for decades and was made into two motion pictures. Peter Dickinson's *The Weathermonger* (1968), the first volume of his Changes trilogy, mixed fantasy and SF, when a sleeping Merlin is awakened and, unhappy with modern technology, sends England back into the dark ages. A. M. Lightner's *The Day of the Drones* (1969) was a well-done post-apocalyptic tale set in Africa, one of the first children's SF novels to feature black protagonists and deal openly with racial prejudice.

SF for children and young adults was also being increasingly affected by the rise of contemporary realistic fiction for that audience in the form of such novels as *The Pigman* (1969) by Paul Zindel, *The Outsiders* (1970) by S. E. Hinton, and *The Chocolate War* (1974) by Robert Cormier, books dedicated to an often gloomy and frequently searing view of childhood and young adulthood, and in many cases a fear of what is to come. In her book *The Inter-Galactic Playground*, Farah Mendlesohn, comparing Heinlein's fiction and that of other early writers for young readers to that which followed, has suggested that, "Juveniles and YA science fiction are not quite the same things . . . Juvenile sf, like its adult progenitor, points outward . . . This is true even in the series juveniles such as the *Tom Swift* books."[7] Later SF, she suggests, written by children's and young adult (YA) writers, tends instead to "Accept the present because the future might be worse. It does not invite kids to engage."[8] Perry Nodelman's seminal essay "Out There in Children's Science Fiction: Forward into the Past" goes even further, arguing, as Mendlesohn summarizes it, that readers are often asked "to be dissatisfied with the promised future and regard

[7] Farah Mendlesohn, *The Inter-Galactic Playground: A Critical Study of Children's and Teens' Science Fiction* (Jefferson, NC: McFarland, 2009), 14.
[8] Mendlesohn, correspondence.

the present as the better option."[9] Nodelman was writing specifically about a very common motif in children's SF of the mid- to late twentieth century (one that has been reconstituted today in the current flood of YA dystopian novels): the escape from the futuristic but enclosed city into an outside world that seems more like our present day or even a bucolic past. He sums his point up thus: "Even the most terrifyingly negative adult sf tends to suggest, not that change is inherently bad, but that some kinds of change are less desirable than others . . . But when sf intended for young readers expresses the ambivalence typical of children's fiction, and makes claims for acceptance that balance its appeal to the desire for change, it inevitably dilutes the power of its own evocations of possibility."[10]

Thus, the work of Heinlein, Norton, the Winston Juveniles writers, and most other authors of this sort of fiction, can be seen as almost invariably optimistic about what the future holds, whereas much post-1960s YASF isn't particularly optimistic. Moreover, what's important in YASF, as is the case in non-fantastic YA fiction more generally, tends to be forming successful relationships with others rather than voyaging out into the unknown.

It should be noted, of course that these are tendencies, matters of emphasis, not absolutes, and there are always exceptions. Much recent YASF still allows for adventures, just as much earlier juvenile SF allowed for relationships. Something close to the traditional juveniles continued to be written (often by writers whose primary work is for adults), notable examples including Gregory Benford's *The Jupiter Project* (1975), Joan Vinge's *Psion* (1982), Pamela Sargent's *Earthseed* (1983), John Ford's *Growing Up Weightless* (1993), Charles Sheffield's *Higher Education* (1996), and Ann Halam's *Dr. Franklin's Island* (2001), all novels that have much more in common with, for example, Heinlein's *Farmer in the Sky* (1950) or Norton's *Catseye* (1961) than they do with most of the work by the writers to whom we are about to turn.[11]

YASF in the 1970s and 1980s

The sheer number of writers producing children's and YASF in the 1970s and 1980s is enormous and it is impossible to discuss all of them within the limits

---

[9] Summarized by Mendlesohn in *Inter-Galactic*, p. 15.

[10] Perry Nodelman, "Out There in Children's Science Fiction: Forward into the Past," *Science Fiction Studies* 12, 3 (November 1985), p. 294.

[11] These comments are not meant to disparage more recent young adult SF; the quality of the books we will now consider is every bit as high as that of the juveniles, and sometimes higher, but the authors are interested in somewhat different issues.

of this chapter. Among the major authors in this period, however, were Sylvia Louise Engdahl, Louise Lawrence, Robert C. O'Brien, Laurence Yep, William Sleator, H. M. Hoover, Monica Hughes, Jane Yolen, Robert Westall, and Peter Dickinson. Sylvia Louise Engdahl is best remembered for *Enchantress from the Stars* (1970), which stands out for its fusing of a science fictional plot with fairytale underpinnings, its anti-colonial theme, and its strong, competent heroine. This last is one of the hallmarks of the new YASF: suddenly female heroes were as common as male heroes and female concerns were given equal time.

Among Louise Lawrence's several excellent novels are *Andra* (1971), in which a girl in the far future, given the chance to directly experience the emotions of a boy from our era, incites a rebellion against her repressive government; her later *Children of the Dust* (1985), explores various attitudes towards rebuilding society after a nuclear war. Robert C. O'Brien's classic *Mrs. Frisby and the Rats of NIMH* (1971), which teeters engagingly between SF and animal fantasy, concerns sentient mice and rats, the latter the result of human experimentation, attempting to create their own utopian community; O'Brien's grim *Z for Zachariah* (1975) tells the carefully nuanced story of a teenager's survival in the wake of a nuclear war. Laurence Yep's *Sweetwater* (1973), is a tale of deep ecology and music involving the human colonists of an alien planet and their native hosts.

William Sleator, one of the most significant children's SF writers of the later twentieth century, wrote the genuinely horrific *House of Stairs* (1974) about five teens who, victims of a psychology experiment gone mad, are imprisoned in a sort of M. C. Escher painting made real and must constantly ascend and descend staircases and do various nonsensical tasks in order to receive food; Sleator's *Interstellar Pig* (1984) is the bizarre tale of a boy who discovers aliens, disguised as human adults on a seashore vacation, who are playing a virtual reality board game with world-shaking consequences. The prolific H. M. Hoover's best book is probably *The Rains of Eridan* (1977), which does a fine job of exploring parenting issues in a research station on an alien planet where the residents suddenly find themselves deeply terrified for no obvious reason. Monica Hughes's *The Keeper of the Isis Light* (1980) and sequels explore in touching detail the life of a human child who, abandoned in a harsh alien world and physically altered by her robot guardian so that she can survive, must eventually learn to coexist with new human colonists. Jane Yolen's *Dragon's Blood* (1982) and its sequels tell the story of a boy trained to raise dragon-like aliens in a harsh penal colony. Robert Westall's *Futuretrack 5* (1983) concerns a teen in a well-realized dystopian future who rebels against his assigned job, tending to a super computer. Peter Dickinson's magnificent *Eva* (1987) concerns a badly injured girl whose memory is transferred into the brain and body of a chimp. Also of note here is the lone foray into SF by one of children's and YA literature's giants: Virginia Hamilton's beautifully realized Justice trilogy, beginning with *Justice and Her Brothers* (1978), concerns a set of telepathic siblings who gradually realize that they are developing into a new sort of lifeform, one with the ability to replace humanity. Other talented and astonishingly diverse authors of YASF who can only be listed owing to space limitations include Nancy Bond, Isabelle Carmody, Nicholas Fisk, Douglas Hill, Diana Wynne Jones (one of the greatest YA writers but, again, primarily a fantasist), Jan Mark, the hilariously funny Daniel Pinkwater, Terry Pratchett (although he's better known for fantasy), Florence Randall, Philip Reeve, Gillian Rubenstein, Ann Schlee, Neal Shusterman, Zilpha Keatley Snyder, John Rowe Townsend, Simon Watson, and Cherry Wilder.

The major themes of children's and YASF, as should be clear from the above, have varied over the years, although every theme that is mentioned here does see at least occasional use in every time period. Early on, with the dime novels, various Edisonades, and Stratemeyer Syndicate books, even to some extent the pulps, the emphasis was on great inventions and awakening boys (regrettably, typically specifically boys) to the new world of technology that they would grow up to master. Also important was exploration, invariably through the use of technology, of other worlds, especially Mars, but also Venus, the Moon, and elsewhere. The opening of the American West and the memory of slavery were often implicit subtexts, with aliens standing in for Native Americans and robots, perhaps, for African Americans (and an assumed white child or teen reader). Heinlein, Asimov, Norton, and the various Winston Juvenile authors all used these themes to various degrees, but Heinlein in particular incorporated the importance not just of technical competence but also of social and political competence. His heroes became better engineers over the course of a book, but they also became people who could make their way through difficult social situations using their intellects, their growing knowledge bases, their physical competence, and especially their strong moral compasses. A Heinlein hero wasn't above trickery, but he always had the best interest of others (as well as himself) at heart; if the books had been filmed, their protagonists might well have been played by a young John Wayne.

As SF writers for adults who also wrote juveniles began to give way to true children's and YA writers, the traditional preoccupations continued to be of importance, but now had to share room with more personal and inward looking themes. As Mendlesohn argues, perhaps overgeneralizing: "The child and teen as *practical*, competent, inventive and assertive disappears in the mid-1980s. It is replaced by a child or teen for whom the emphasis is on *emotional* competence and practical *dependence*."[12] Paradoxically, however, another devastating new theme to gain importance in the new SF of the 1970s and 1980s is that adult leaders could not be trusted or, at the very least, were frequently wrong. Wise mentors, so common in earlier SF, are often absent from these books. We see this again and again in the realistic fiction of the period: witness Cormier's *The Chocolate War*, in which a new student at a Catholic school discovers that the Vice Principal, a Catholic Brother no less, is behind both a bogus candy sale and the various attacks on the protagonist after he refuses to take part in it. Mendlesohn cites Christopher and Dickinson as early exponents of this sort of plot. In the latter's *The Weathermonger*, the collapse of society is due in part to the actions of an evil pharmacist who has somehow revived Merlin (here described as a mutant), hooked him on morphine, and forced him to use his magic to destroy modern technology, thus driving England back into a pseudo-medieval state. Other, somewhat later examples include the monstrous psychologists of Sleator's above mentioned *House of Stairs*, and the negligent parents of his *Interstellar Pig*; the adult colonists overwhelmed by a combination of greed and terror in Hoover's *The Rains of Eridan*; the leader of the Isis colony in Hughes's *The Guardian of Isis* (1981), who has forced his people to give up technology; the titular character of Hughes's *The Isis Pedlar* (1982), who sets out to corrupt the colonists on Isis in order to steal their most valuable possessions; and the elders of Jeanne DuPrau's *City of Ember* (2003), who pursue policies that will probably lead to the death of everyone in their underground city. These tales do give their protagonists some room for heroic action – but, as often as not, it's no more than a matter of escaping from the crisis the adults have created. Even when the child protagonist wins, she or he is likely to be deeply scarred by the experience.

Another important theme in the postwar era, both for children's and adult SF, was the danger of nuclear war or other apocaplyptic incidents. These

---

[12] *Inter-Galactic*, p. 111. Beyond the scope of this chapter, however, she also points out that the competent children's and YA hero does make a significant return in the SF of the twenty-first century, presumably in such books as Phillip Reeve's *Mortal Engines* (2001), Nancy Farmer's *The House of the Scorpion* (2002), Suzanne Collins's *The Hunger Games* (2008), and James Dasher's *The Maze Runner* (2009), a period that is covered in Chapter 44 of this volume by Rebekah Sheldon.

stories sometimes describe the immediate impact of the catastrophic events, while others go on to depict how things work out long term. Among the many books that tell such stories are Poul Anderson's early *Vault of the Age* (1952), Suzanne Martel's *The City Under Ground* (1964), A. M. Lightner's *Day of the Drones* (1969), H. M. Hoover's *Children of Morrow* (1973), Robert C. O'Brien's *Z is for Zachariah* (1975), Elisabeth Mace's *Out There* (1978), Gudrun Pausewang's *The Lost Children of Schewenborn* (1983), Robert Swindell's *Brother in the Land* (1984), Gloria Miklowitz's *After the Bomb* (1985), Louise Lawrence's *Children of the Dust* (1985), and, somewhat later, Roderick Philbrick's grueling *The Last Book in the Universe* (2000) and Todd Strasser's *Fallout* (2013).

Also increasingly common are the many dystopian novels, some of which take an earlier nuclear or other apocalyptic event as their starting point, but primarily use it as the means to an end, the depiction of dystopia. We saw such plots in the work of Norton, Heinlein, and the Winston Juveniles, to some extent, but writers such as Lawrence, Sleator, and Hughes made even more use of dystopia. If a book centers on a child's emotions and inner life, and particularly on what the child or YA reader is angry about, after all, what better antagonist is there than society itself? Teens in particular often see themselves as living in a dystopia in any case. Just take what they hate about the restrictions placed on them by parents, schools, and acquaintances and translate it into SF. Hughes's *The Tomorrow City* (1973), Sleator's *House of Stairs*, Gregory Maguire's *I Feel Like the Morning Star* (1989), and du Prau's *City of Ember* (2003) are typical examples, and it probably isn't coincidence that most of these books involve children who are trapped within enclosed spaces, claustrophobic micro-cultures of a sort, where everything is gradually getting worse and breaking out is the only sane option. This dystopian theme will go on to dominate the SF of the late twentieth and early twenty-first centuries: witness the novels of Suzanne Collins, James Dasher, Veronica Roth, and their imitators.

The overthrow of dystopia, of course, implies the establishment of a new kind of society, one supposedly better than the generally very confining and often highly mechanized culture that has been overthrown. Noga Applebaum argues that much more recent YASF portrays technology negatively, essentially touting new societies that tend towards the pastoral and low-tech, and further suggests that this tendency more often reflects the technophobic attitudes of the adults involved in writing and publishing such books, particularly in the early 1980s, than those of the child and teen readers themselves.[13] Most of the genre's intended audience, after all, were becoming increasingly at home with computers and other high-tech gadgets. It might well be argued, however, that this change began a decade or more earlier, as SF for children became less the product of veteran SF writers for adults like Heinlein and Asimov, most of whom had a generally positive attitude towards technology – unlike the new children's writers who were revolutionizing the field. It seems probable that the truth of this argument comes down to which specific work of children's or YASF you are looking at.

YASF is a growing, thriving part of the great stream that is speculative fiction. It deals with some issues that are uniquely of interest to younger readers, but also tackles many of the themes that are prevalent in SF written for adults, merely presenting those themes in ways that younger readers will find applicable to their own lives. Most recently, Marek C. Oziewicz, in a highly theoretical volume, has argued that "YA speculative fiction ought to be recognized as one of the most important forges of justice consciousness for the globalized world of the 21st century,"[14] owing in part to its ability to "test-run scenarios that are theoretically possible but have not yet happened" and thus examine their moral implications in a concrete fashion. "Only speculative fiction," Oziewicz suggests, "offers the framework to engage in this sort of investigation, which often is a metadiscourse on justice writ large."[15] Such a claim speaks volumes about the importance of children's, juveniles, and YA fiction in helping to shape the ethical and political commitments of the adults its young readers someday become.

---

[13] Noga Applebaum, *Representations of Technology in Science Fiction for Young People* (New York: Routledge, 2010), p. 2.

[14] Marek C. Oziewicz, *Justice in Young Adult Speculative Fiction: A Cognitive Reading* (New York: Routledge, 2015), p. 4.

[15] Ibid., p. 12.

17

Spectacular Horizons: The Birth of Science Fiction Film, Television, and Radio, 1900–1959

SEAN REDMOND

Audio-visual SF is particularly hard to define; its codes, conventions, and repetitions are more fluid than (say) the expansive geography of the Western film, or the sharp stabs of Gothic horror sounding their way out of the radio. Vivian Sobchack suggests that there is a "plastic inconstancy"[1] in the types of iconography found in SF film and television, which Barry Keith Grant suggests "is a necessary result of the genre's extrapolative function, to project today's technology into tomorrow."[2] While audio-visual SF is undoubtedly difficult to pin down in terms of what it may look and sound like, there is, nonetheless, a consistency in the themes it addresses, the kinds of stories it tells, and in the way its future predictions and possibilities connect it to the hopes and fears of the present. It is not then simply a question of what film, television, and radio SF looks and sounds like, but the way it materializes – in its world-building imaginings – the future, and how it critically grapples with the technological transformations of its era.

That said, media specificity does have a central role to play in the way these stories are told and the future is enacted. The durational canvas of film is different from the serial and series format of television, which is itself different from the radio play. This omnibus chapter will explore each form of media in turn and address its central structures and themes, highlighting the key features of SF film, radio, and television. This chapter will also take note of those boundaries where different media converge and enter into cross-media dialogue in the first half of the twentieth century.

---

[1] Vivian Sobchack, *Screening Space: The American Science Fiction Film* (New Brunswick, NJ: Rutgers University Press: 1987), p. 75.

[2] Barry Keith Grant, "Sensuous Elaboration: Reason and the Visible in the Science Fiction Film," in Sean Redmond, ed., *Liquid Metal: The Science Fiction Film Reader* (London: Wallflower Press, 2004), p. 17.

Science Fiction Film

One can argue that SF was at the pulsating heart of the advent of cinema: not only is film a special effect but "trick films" and space operas took hold of its outputs from the end of the nineteenth century.[3] If cinema was at first felt to be a form of SF, set in a sea of spectacular attractions,[4] films soon emerged that dreamt the future and took its stories into outer space. One of the very first adventures into outer space was Georges Méliès's *Le Voyage dans la lune* (1902). As Phil Hardy notes:

> Méliès's film marks the real beginnings of the Science Fiction cinema. Where other film-makers had been content to poke fun at the new and emerging technologies of the 20th Century – X-rays, air flight, electricity, the motorcar – Méliès created a Science Fiction story and, in the process, identified the theme of space travel which became one of the abiding themes of the genre. Other directors isolated other themes and began to elaborate upon them, thus molding the genre, but it was Méliès who laid its foundation.[5]

Le Voyage dans la lune is fourteen minutes long, cost a record 10,000 francs to make, and was based upon Jules Verne's *From the Earth to the Moon* (1865) and H. G. Wells's *First Men in the Moon* (1901). With thirty scenes in total, the film tells the story of an expedition to the Moon where the scientists meet and defeat the Moon people. The film sets up a number of recurrent themes that are then carried into SF film more generally.

First, *Le Voyage dans la lune* brilliantly captures the relationship between modernity, subjectivity, and the difference "between the virtual and the real," a difference that Jonathan Bignell argues mirrors the machinery of cinema and the spatial transformations that occurred with industrialization. In the age of modernity one can move across identity positions as they are re-imagined in the exploration and time travel narratives that special effects cinema so powerfully produces or elicits. In the 1960 film version of *The Time Machine* (dir. George Pal), for example, Bignell argues that "time travellers and cinema spectators are displaced from the reality of their own present and their own real location in order to be transported to an imaginary elsewhere and an imaginary elsewhen."[6] One might term this a special type

---

[3] Dan North, *Performing Illusions* (London: Wallflower Press, 2008).
[4] Tom Gunning, "The Cinema of Attractions: Early Film, Its Spectator and the Avant-Garde," *Wide Angle* 8, 3–4 (Fall 1986), pp. 63–70.
[5] Phil Hardy, *The Overlook Film Encyclopedia: Science Fiction*, 3rd edn. (New York: Overlook, 1995), p. 18.
[6] Jonathan Bignell, "Another Time, Another Space: Subjectivity and the Time Machine," in Redmond, ed., *Liquid Metal*, p. 138.

of "heterotopia of time" or, better still, a heterotopia of special effects, outside or beyond the ordinary through which a synthesis of "special" irregular moments of time and space, conjoined with the wonder of special effects, transports one to new and spectacular horizons. This type of experience we might define as that which "entails a state of wonder, and one of the distinctions of this state is the temporary suspension of chronological time and bodily movement. To be enchanted, then, is to participate in a momentarily immobilizing encounter; it is to be transfixed, spellbound."[7]

Second, the film privileges white male scientists and inventors, and prophesizes about the power of science to shape the future purposefully. The ability to travel is engineered out of the ingenuity and exceptionalism of white scientists, supported by white visionaries and explorers who feel it is their right to visit new lands, to discover what is out there and to bring the civilizing effects of earth-bound whiteness with them. This trope is played out repeatedly from this point on in Western SF film (and radio and television), reaching its height in the Space Age Whiteness films of the 1950s and 1960s.[8] For example, in *Rocketship X-M* (dir. Kurt Nuemann, 1950), Dr. Karl Eckstrom (John Emery) is introduced as the "designer of the RXM, and as you all know one of the most brilliant physicists of the day." Eckstrom has engineered the first "man"-made spaceship to the Moon and is given the position of explaining its flight path, which he does through chalk diagrams and science-inflected vocabulary. Surrounded by politicians, journalists, and military personnel, he is given the power to speak and enact the future. This scene, often repeated in SF films of this period, centers the white scientist as the creator or progenitor of a productive science that affords humanity progress, advances civilization, and creates the conditions out of which new worlds are discovered. Through white scientists outer space is mapped from a white-centric point of view, and such "representations unconsciously reflect or embody the colonial imagination."[9] The message is that outer space isn't just to be visited and admired, but must be colonized by the white imagination.

Nonetheless, different representations of the scientist do emerge. According to Mark Bould, the dominant form taken in the 1930s was the

---

[7] Jane Bennett, *The Enchantment of Modern Life: Attachments, Crossings, and Ethics* (Princeton, NJ: Princeton University Press, 2001), p. 5.
[8] See Sean Redmond, "The Whiteness of Cinematic Outer Space," in Peter Dickens and James S Ormrod, eds., *The Palgrave Handbook of Society, Culture and Outer Space* (London: Palgrave, 2016), p. 337–54.
[9] E. Ann Kaplan, *Looking for the Other: Nation, Woman and Desire in Film* (London: Routledge, 1997), p. 42.

"mad scientist" and "mad science" movie intent on giving everything to his experiment even if that means unleashing terror on the world.[10] Often misunderstood, set on a plot of revenge, the mad scientist knows no reason and will do anything to get her or his invention into the world. Mexico's first fully realized SF film, *Los muertos hablan / The Dead Speak* (dir. Gabriel Soria, 1935), is centered on a scientist who steals corpses and uses them in experiments.

Third, *Le Voyage dans la lune* offers viewers visions of awe and wonder from the position of a wide-eyed child,[11] its visions and imaginings rendering one innocent before the fantasy, taking one's breath away as it does so. *Le Voyage dans la lune*'s space rocket scene that involves a spectacular crash landing on the Moon has become one of the iconic shots of film history, capturing the way space, time, and invention come together in new ways. SF film comes to tell its stories through these spectacular horizons: whether it be the futuristic constructionist sets of *Aelita: Queen of Mars* (dir. Yakov Protazanov, 1924), the expressionistic brutal futurism of *Metropolis* (dir. Fritz Lang, 1927), or the grand public optimism of public life in *Things to Come* (dir. William Cameron Menzies, 1936). SF spectacle often creates the conditions for the sublime in which the limits of the embodied self are breached, and the material conditions of one's existence liquefy.[12] We are asked to meet spectacle through the senses, leaving reason, logic, and language behind us. Drawing on Kant,[13] one can describe this type of awesomeness as the "dynamical sublime," measured by its unboundedness and formlessness – something, of course, visual effects help create since they work out of narratives of expanded geographies and seemingly exponential vistas of wonder.[14]

The importance of special effects can also be seen in industrial or commercial contexts: Lee Zavitz won the Academy Award for Visual Effects for *Destination Moon* (dir. Irving Pichel, 1950), and as Ben Walker suggests, SF film can be seen as a "technological showcase for current image creation technologies – technologies that perhaps only a few years before were science

[10] Mark Bould, *"Film and Television,"* in Edward James and Farah Mendlesohn, eds., *The Cambridge Companion to Science Fiction* (Cambridge: Cambridge University Press, 2003), p. 83.
[11] Grant, "Sensuous Elaboration," p. 18.
[12] See Giuliana Bruno, "Ramble City: Postmodernism and 'Blade Runner'," *October*, 41 (Summer 1987), pp. 61–74.
[13] See Immanuel Kant, *Observations on the Feeling of the Beautiful and Sublime* (Berkeley, CA: University of California Press, 1960).
[14] Michele Pierson, "No Longer State-of-the-Art: Crafting a Future for CGI," *Wide Angle* 21, 1 (January 1999), pp. 29–47.

fictions in themselves."[15] In defining SF, Darko Suvin suggests that it readily employs a "novum" or "cognitive innovation" that is scientifically instigated or realized. The novum is the narrative and visual catalyst for the way inventions can be realized and the physical rules and laws of that world transformed and transgressed. The novum is crafted out of current, real-world science but extended outward, so that predictions become possibilities enacted.[16] So, for example, 1950s SF film travelled to outer space before the technology had been developed to do so but while it was in development. These films drew on existing technologies and on scientific prediction to imagine what space travel would soon be like.

Fourth, *Le Voyage dans la lune* begins a cycle of "alien encounter" films that often involve conflict with (evil) aliens. For example, in *It! The Terror from Beyond Outer Space* (dir. Edward L. Cahn, 1958), a creature from Mars stows away on a spaceship escaping from its planet. The creature is intent on killing everyone on board, which it does through sucking all the moisture out of its victims. The creature – so antithetical to civilized life that it cannot be properly named – is driven by the logic of consumption, intent on harvesting human civilized life so that it thrives at the expense, or replacement, of everything human. This binary between good (humans) and evil (aliens), however, is often compromised in SF film as humanity is often shown to be less than the Other which it is pitched against. The Alien Other may be both technologically and intellectually superior, and our attempt to colonize outer space or to understand them may be shown to be destructive. In *A Message from Mars* (dir. Wallett Waller, 1913), the first full-length SF feature in the history of British cinema, Horace Parker (Charles Hawtrey), characterized as a selfish and arrogant man, is taught a series of valuable lessons by a visiting Martian. In *The Day the Earth Stood Still* (dir. Robert Wise, 1951) the alien Klaatu prophesizes that the security of Earth resides singularly in the hands of scientists. It is their rational approach to international affairs that will steer Earth away from the arms race and the slow creep to nuclear annihilation that Klaatu sees as happening through Cold War politics.

The 1950s must, of course, be read in the context of their particular historical juncture: in military terms this was also the age of atomic testing, with the first hydrogen bomb detonated at the Eniwetok atoll in the Marshall Islands on November 1, 1952. At the same time, the rhetoric of the Cold War

[15] Ben Walker, *The Digital Surreal* (2007), p. 3. Available at http://surfacedetail.com/wp-content/uploads/2008/09/the_digital_surreal.pdf.
[16] Darko Suvin, *Metamorphoses of Science Fiction: On the Poetics and History of a Literary Genre*, (New Haven: Yale University Press, 1979), p. 64.

created the impression that the Soviet Union was a persistent "invasion" threat to American national security. The Soviet Union's launch of the satellite Sputnik on October 4, 1957, followed by the 1959 launch of the spacecraft *Luna I*, which reached the vicinity of the Moon, intensified fears of Soviet technological power. A range of political and cultural tensions and contradictions took root in the 1950s, then, and SF film (television and radio) seemed best able to negotiate them.

First, the radioactive monster films of the period speak to the fear of nuclear proliferation and the human apocalypse it will create. The science–military nexus creates an alliance in the Cold War era that made tangible to the world the possibility of extinction through the arms race and the relentless testing of nuclear weaponry. The nuclear monsters, such as those found in *Attack of the Giant Leeches!* (dir. Bernard L. Kowalski, 1960) and *Attack of the Crab Monsters!* (dir. Roger Corman, 1957), are byproducts of the fallout from rocket tests or nuclear explosions. Similarly, nuclear testing awakes *Godzilla* (dir. Ishirō Honda, 1954), and the beginning of the film in which a fishing boat sinks in the water recalls directly the 1954 nuclear detonation at the Bikini atoll. The 1954 Bikini atoll bomb was then the biggest man-made explosion, until it was surpassed by the USSR's 50-megaton test in 1961. Three weeks after the Bikini bomb it emerged that a Japanese fishing boat, called *Lucky Dragon*, was within 80 miles (129 km) of the test zone at the time. Its twenty-three crew were severely affected by radiation sickness. As Tomoyuki Tanaka, the producer of the film, explains: "The theme of *Godzilla*, from the beginning, was the terror of the bomb. Mankind had created the bomb, and now nature was going to take revenge on mankind."[17]

Second, the Invasion Narrative films of the period can be seen as vehicles for playing out the politics of the Cold War between the USSR and American and other Western nation-states, including Britain. The alien invasion narrative is seen as merely a code for Soviet aggression and the imagined threat of nuclear, territorial, and geographical domination. In *Invasion of the Body Snatchers* (dir. Don Siegel, 1956), for example, the aliens silently arrive and secretly take over and copy humans. These simulacra are cold, pathological, and demonstrate a crowd/herd instinct as they seek and destroy all human life in their wake. These murderous clones, without individual personal freedoms to speak of, are here seen to embody the Soviet political system, and it is this embodiment that gets narratively transposed onto

---

[17] Steven Ryfle, "Godzilla's Footprint," essay appearing in *Gojira: The Original Japanese Masterpiece* DVD set, 2004.

a vulnerable/weak Western society precisely because ordinary people fail to recognize or resist the alien threat – until it is nearly too late, that is. The message that ordinary people must be ever vigilant and ever conscious of the communist Other is ever present in these Invasion Narrative texts.[18]

In Peter Hutchings's examination of British invasion narratives from the 1950s and 1960s, paranoia is connected to a set of distinctly British fears and concerns that emerged postwar.[19] Hutchings suggests that these films produce a rather despairing national mood, one which reflects the fragmented and unstable nature of British identity as it faced challenges to elements of tradition, and normative gender roles. As Hutchings argues:

> It seems from these films that Britain has lost its center and become fragmented, its population scattered in isolated groups and its institutions and hierarchies no longer as efficacious as they once were . . . It is as if Britain, displaced from an imperial history and the glories of the Second World War and caught up in a series of bewildering changes, is more open to self-doubts and an accompanying acknowledgement of its own limits.[20]

Third, the Invasion Narrative can be understood to be an exploration of racial tension. As Eric Avila contends, one of the fears of 1950s American life was the movement of black Americans into the inner city areas, producing a "white flight" into the newly established suburbs: "The rise of Hollywood science fiction paralleled the acceleration of white flight in postwar America and not only recorded popular anxieties about political and sexual deviants, but also captured white preoccupations with the increasing visibility of the alien Other."[21] In Earth-centered invasion films of the 1950s, the alien is coded as a racial Other, threatening the sanctity of these new white, civilized suburbs. But white flight is also played out in outer space, with the same power-saturated binary oppositions, and the same spatial geometries. Whiteness is known and knowable space: expansive, clean, it sits at the core of all the good and true physics in the cosmos. By contrast, the Alien Other is the dark cosmos magnified: chaotic, frenzied, intent on harvesting the light for its diabolical ends.

---

[18] Notably, the original by Jack Finney takes a much more ambiguous view of the invasion, imagining peaceful coexistence with the pod people once the invasion has been thwarted.

[19] Peter Hutchings, "We're the Martians Now: British Invasion Fantasies of the 1950s and 1960s," in Redmond, ed., *Liquid Metal*, pp. 337–46.

[20] Ibid., p. 339.

[21] Eric Avila, "Dark City: White Flight and the Urban Science Fiction Film in Postwar America," in Daniel Bernardi, ed., *Classic Hollywood: Classic Whiteness* (Minneapolis: University of Minnesota Press, 2000), p. 55.

Nonetheless, as noted above, space travel is positioned as a problematic activity, involving conquest and exploitation. These critical invasion narrative texts draw attention to the power struggles that occur in deep space, with the control and ownership of cargo, commodity, and people in open contestation. When these contests occur on alien planets, race and ethnicity are brought to the fore through the figure of the alien who very often comes to stand for the minoritarian Other, rendered grotesque next to the sublime power of whiteness. In these films there is often a necessary struggle over racial hegemony, but by the film's closure whiteness is often positioned as ultimately salvific. In *Rocketship X-M*, as the crew descends on Mars they see evidence of an advanced civilization in ruins. When they check the radiation levels they find high readings that suggest a nuclear war has taken place there. When the remnants of the civilization blindly stumble out from behind rocks, embodying an aggressive primitivism, Dr. Eckstrom prophetically comments, "From Atomic Age to Stone Age." What is being narratively constituted in these scenes is a commentary on the development and testing of nuclear weapons in the United States at the time: the film is a siren warning about what will happen if we continue down this road – the destruction of our cities and homes and a return to an age where the ostensibly civilizing frames of whiteness are not in place. However, it is also a critical commentary on the blindness of privileged whiteness that invests too heavily in the cold science of destruction at the expense of compassion and feeling. What is being transposed onto the people of Mars is the contention that the white techno-elite have brought about the means of their own annihilation. Nonetheless, the fact that it is white scientists who can bring this message back to Earth positions whiteness as ultimately redeemable, and able to free itself from its own dangerous extremes.

Finally, SF films of the 1950s can be said to address the growing postwar crisis in masculinity and femininity. Those monsters and aliens that are marked by rationality and linked to the purest of scientific forms are often encoded as hyper-masculine and it is this rationalized and hard masculinity that poses a threat to the natural order of things. Women, by contrast, often personify those values and actions which are under threat from such regulatory masculinity – they show emotion, demonstrate intuition, and are totally family centered. In short, in these 1950s invasion narratives an ideological battle takes place over what it means to be masculine and feminine in an increasingly rationalized and pluralized 1950s Western world. Biskind argues that *Them!* (dir. Gordon Douglas, 1954) "reflects the new prestige of science by placing male scientists at the center of world-shaking events," and that the ants in the film work as an "attack on women in a man's world" because "the ant society is, after all, a matriarchy presided over by a despotic queen."[22]

In all of these 1950s films there emerges what Susan Sontag defines as SF's "imagination of disaster."[23] Sontag argues that these films are about the "aesthetics of destruction, with the peculiar beauties to be found in wreaking havoc, making a mess. And it is in the imagery of destruction that the core of a good science fiction lies."[24] Sontag goes on to argue that these images and scenarios of destruction serve two complementary functions. First, they work to explore the "deepest anxieties about contemporary experience." Second, they are "strongly moralistic" fables that in their representations and resolutions provide a "utopian fantasy" space where all problems are easily resolved. As a consequence, Sontag concludes, "there is absolutely no social criticism, of even the most implicit kind, in science fiction films" of the 1950s.[25]

Michael Ryan and Doug Kellner, by contrast, suggest a more complex relationship between these films and their ideological content.[26] They argue that there are two types of dystopian/technophobic SF film texts: there are those texts oriented toward a conservative and essentialist paradigm which often involve a terrifying anti-humanist technology counterposed against an idealistic "natural" environment or social structure; and there are those texts that project liberal-critical viewpoints around technology and nature and which, consequently, challenge the conservative binary oppositions that structure such relationships. Ryan and Kellner argue that from a conservative perspective, "Technology represents artifice as opposed to nature, the mechanical as opposed to the spontaneous, the regulated as opposed to the free, an equalizer as opposed to a promoter of individual distinction, equality triumphant as opposed to liberty, democratic leveling as opposed to hierarchy derived from individual superiority."[27] In *Forbidden Planet* (dir. Fred M. Wilcox, 1956) the pathology of technoscience is

---

[22] Peter Biskind, "The Russians Are Coming, Aren't They? *Them!* and *The Thing*," in Redmond, ed., *Liquid Metal*, p. 321.

[23] Susan Sontag, "The Imagination of Disaster," in Redmond, ed., *Liquid Metal*, pp. 40–7.

[24] Ibid., p. 44.

[25] Ibid., pp. 43–5. Sontag's claims about the apoliticality of disaster films contrast with Fredric Jameson's 1971 essay "Metacommentary," which provides an embryonic view of the theory of utopia for which he would later become famous. See *PMLA* 86, 1 (January, 1971), pp. 9–18, especially pp. 16–17.

[26] Michael Ryan and Douglas Kellner, "Technophobia," in Annette Kuhn, ed., *Alien Zone: Cultural Theory and Contemporary Science Fiction Cinema* (New York: Verso, 1990), pp. 58–65.

[27] Ibid., p. 58.

personified more directly through the figure of Dr. Edward Morbius (Walter Pidgeon). Morbius is one of only two survivors of an expedition that landed on the planet Altair IV. He warns the rescue mission that has been sent out that they will be in danger if they land on the planet, at risk from an invisible monster that stalks it. They land, nonetheless, and Morbius eventually shows the landing party the advanced technology of the Krell people, who had once lived on the planet only to suffer a "mysterious" genocide just as they were about to make their biggest scientific breakthrough. Morbius demonstrates the power of one of these technologies, the "plastic educator," which increases human intelligence and allows him to build his robot, Robby, as well as the other advanced marvels at his home. However, the viewer subsequently learns that there is a price to pay for this increased brainpower; the machine is fueled by the subconscious mind, and the monster that has been let loose on Altair IV is actually Morbius's unleashed Id. At the end of the film Morbius attacks the monster and is fatally wounded in the process – as he dies so does the monster he gave birth to. As one of his last acts, Morbius presses a self-destruct button and just as the rescue team escapes into space Altair IV is blown to smithereens. The film thus suggests that if we come to live only in and through technology, we lose our humanity, and our connection with nature.

Radio Science Fiction

On the radio, musical and auditory soundscapes emerged for deep space, futuristic weaponry, advanced warfare, apocalypse, robots, sentient machines, alien creatures and messiahs, time travel, future cities, and more. So powerful was the language of radio SF that when Orson Welles narrated *War of the Worlds* on the Mercury Theater on Air Show, on Halloween, October 30, 1938, viewers phoned in believing that the Martians were really invading America. The power of the broadcast lay not only in the way it drew upon "live" news and documentary traditions to blur the boundary between fact and fiction, but also in the impressionable and alienating sounding of the alien spacecrafts, lasers, and alien creatures set within an orchestral and solo piano arrangement that constantly hinted at unexplainable danger.

One of the sonic instruments used to create this sense of otherworld strangeness was the theremin, invented by Léon Theremin, and whose manufacturing rights were bought by the Radio Corporation of America (RCA), naming the device the thereminvox. One of the first uses of the theremin was on *The Green Hornet Radio Show* (1936), which began its broadcast with a hornet-like hum from a theremin and the dialogue, "He hunts the biggest of all game." The theremin was used to amplify the super-human qualities of its titular hero. Other notable sound effect inventions included using an air-conditioning vent to produce the sound of the rockets in *Buck Rogers in the 25th Century*.

The centrality of the (super) hero to serial "adventure stories" at this time was clear. Aimed at children and young adults, radio shows such as *Buck Rogers in the 25th Century* and *Flash Gordon* had a huge audience and broadcast four to five times per week. *Buck Rogers*, which aired for the first time in 1932, told the story of Anthony (Buck) Rogers who, while working in a mine, was exposed to a gas that left him in suspended animation until the twenty-fifth century. Life in the twenty-fifth century is mostly utopian with a great deal of the worries, ills, and pains of past life eradicated, as new technologies and inventions have changed life, leisure, and work patterns for the better. However, the future is still marked by alien villains and it is the guile and bravery of the twentieth-century hero Buck that often saves the day. The message the serial offers viewers is that the heroism of today has an important hand in shaping a positive future.

Alex Raymond's *Flash Gordon* debuted in 1935 on the Mutual Broadcasting System and starred Gale Gordon as Flash. Set in a future in which Earth has been earmarked for destruction by the merciless Emperor Ming and the subjected people of Mongo, Flash – along with his "girlfriend" Dale Arden, Dr. Zarkov, and the rebellious Hawkmen – take on Ming in a Manichean battle between good and evil. Flash is American masculinity personified and the romantic coupling with Dale allows for the series to end with a perfect utopian marriage once Ming has been roundly defeated.

SF radio can be argued to have first developed its audience in the 1930s and lasted as a central conduit for future listening until the advent of television in the 1950s, when there was a migration away to the new magic box in the corner of the living room. However, there was a great deal of crossover between SF radio, film, television, and literature, so that shows developed, repeated, and adapted their formats depending on their media specificity. However, what began to emerge in the 1950s was a turn to serious, literate radio SF and a move away from these "juvenile" serial adventures. As M. Keith Booker argues,

> It was not until the 1950s that science fiction radio really hit its stride, even as science fiction was beginning to appear on television as well. Radio programs such as Mutual's *2000 Plus* and NBC's *Dimension X* were anthology series that offered a variety of exciting tales of future technology, with a special focus on

space exploration (including alien invasion), though both series also often reflected contemporary anxieties about the dangers of technology.[28]

One of the most significant literary serials was NBC's *Dimension X*, which ran between 1950 and 1951. *Dimension X* adapted short stories by acknowledged masters of SF literature, including Isaac Asimov, Robert Bloch, Ray Bradbury, Robert Heinlein, and Kurt Vonnegut. The first thirteen episodes of *Dimension X* were broadcast live and Norman Rose was heard as both announcer and narrator, with his famous opening line, "Adventures in time and space . . . told in future tense, " opening up the series to its own time-travel momentum.

This was in one sense darkly themed SF radio, full of the existential and melancholic fears of the age, and of future prediction built on a fear of what humankind had become and what outer space and future technologies might offer us. As with SF film of the 1950s, there was a foreboding sense of the future. For example, in the adaptation of Jack Williamson's 1947 novelette, "With Folded Hands," first published in an issue of *Astounding Science Fiction*, it is suggested that "some of the technological creations we had developed with the best intentions might have disastrous consequences in the long run."[29] "With Folded Hands" is set in a near future or perhaps parallel present, where Humanoids, small black robots, begin to take over the small town of Two Rivers. Their prime directive is to make humans happy, or "to serve and obey and guard men from harm." However, this becomes defined as total control, and results in the surveillance and maintenance of all human life, and when anyone fails to obey the prime directive, they are lobotomized and turned into passive humans happy to be slavishly led. The broadcast ends with Underhill, a seller of "Mechanicals" (unthinking robots that perform menial tasks), having failed in his mission to bring down the humanoids, being taken away to an uncertain if "happy" future. "With Folded Hands" prophesizes the dangers of letting too much technology into one's life, and warns of the power of dictatorial governments to control their populations by any means necessary.

Science Fiction Television

The Golden Age of Television occurred in the 1950s and SF became one of its mainstay and occasionally primetime genres. The technology of television

---

[28] M. Keith Booker, *Science Fiction Television* (Westport, CT: Praeger, 2004), p. 65.

[29] Larry McCaffrey, "An Interview with Jack Williamson," *Science Fiction Studies* 18, 2 (July 1991), www.depauw.edu/sfs/interviews/williamson54interview.htm (last accessed August 1, 2017).

rapidly entered the home in the United States, the United Kingdom, and Australia, to name but a small number of "early adopters," and its output centered on live drama, game shows, soap operas, westerns, SF, and news bulletins. Golden Age television was indebted to both radio and theatre, and drew upon the codes and conventions of film genres to furnish its scheduling patterns. In a very real sense, Golden Age television was "transmedia" at birth, a fusion of other forms and traditions, and this was particularly true of anthology shows rooted in SF like *Tales of Tomorrow* (1951–3), and *Science Fiction Theatre* (1955–7).[30]

One can divide the broad output of SF television into two related categories. First, there was SF documentary, either in animation form such as the Tomorrowland episodes within the Disneyland franchise (1955), or as science education programming such as the Bell Laboratory Science Series: *Our Mr. Sun* (1956). These offered both technophiliac and utopian promises of what science may bring the world, allowing invention and dreaming to imagine future worlds better than the present. For example, *Man in Space* (Tomorrowland, 1955) begins with Walt Disney opining, "many of the things that seem impossible today will become realities tomorrow," followed by an exploration of how man will eventually space travel. The exposition is supported by animation, history, and drawings, voice-over and special effects, so that the episode not only teaches but also spectacularly imagines the then-fiction of space travel.

Second, there was the subgenre of the (super) hero space opera such as *Flash Gordon*, *Captain Video and His Video Rangers*, *The Secret Files of Captain Video*, *Tom Corbett: Space Cadet*, *Space Patrol*, and *Rocky Jones: Space Ranger*. These often-future set series were aimed at both children and adults and set their narratives in binary good and evil terms. The heroes and their sidekicks stood for democracy, exceptionalism, and the American way of life, while their alien, ethnically coded enemies represented an insidious threat to these red, white, and blue threads of manifest destiny. Such shows

> tapped into America's fear of and wonder at the power of the atomic bomb, as well as the rapid technological developments ongoing in other fields, including television itself. Often produced on shoestring budgets, these series nevertheless excited the imagination of cold war viewers, who were increasingly uncertain about their future both at home and abroad. The message in

---

[30] See J. P. Telotte, "Introduction: The Trajectory of Science Fiction Television," in J. P. Telotte, ed., *The Essential Science Fiction Television Reader* (Kentucky: University of Kentucky Press, 2008), pp. 1–34.

all these series was often the same: the universe was in peril, and only the forces of the United States could put matters right.[31]

Set in the year 2254, *Captain Video and His Video Rangers* follows the adventures of a group of heroic soldiers, fighting for truth and justice against enemies racially and politically coded as evil incarnate. With their uniforms resembling United States Army combat gear, emblazoned with lightning bolts, they stood for American values in the age of Cold War uncertainty and fear of the racial Other.

As the "Master of Science," Captain Video was a scientific genius able to develop new technologies that would help win the relentless war against their diabolical enemies. Such inventions included a Cosmic Ray Vibrator, a static beam of electricity able to paralyze its target; the Electronic Strait Jacket; the Opticon Scillometer, a long-range, X-ray machine used to see through walls; the Discatron, a portable television screen which served as an intercom; and the Radio Scillograph, a palm-sized, two-way radio.

Captain Video and His Video Rangers was also important in terms of being one of the first SF series to involve its fans in the development of the show, and in extending its merchandising possibilities – both forerunners of the modern commodity-driven media landscape. The audience was encouraged to write in, to propose plot developments or to suggest new inventions and characters. For example, Tobor (the show's robot) and Dr. Pauli (an arch enemy) were killed when their diabolical schemes backfired, and yet they were brought back to life in later episodes because of outcries from the show's fanbase.

In terms of transmedia and merchandise extension, young fans of the show were invited to join the Video Rangers Club and to buy Captain Video merchandise, including helmets, toy rockets, games, and records. The series was adapted as six issues of Captain Video comics in 1955 and a fifteen-chapter movie serial, *Captain Video, Master of the Stratosphere* (released by Columbia Pictures in 1951, starring Judd Holdren and Larry Stewart). It was the first attempt by Hollywood to capitalize on a television program through deliberate merchandizing efforts and cross-pollination with other media to expand the audience and impact of the brand. DuMont, the show's producers, also attempted to build on the popularity of the show by developing *The Secret Files of Captain Video*, a thirty-minute, weekly adventure complete within itself

---

[31] Wheeler Winston Dixon, "Tomorrowland TV: The Space Opera and Early Science Fiction Television," in Telotte, ed., *The Essential Science Fiction Television Reader*, p. 93.

which ran concurrently with the serial from September 1953 until May 1954. One can see shows such as *Captain Video, Space Patrol*, and *Rocky Jones* as

> reassuring influences in a world that subconsciously teetered on the brink of destruction; threats were well defined, relatively easily contained, and seldom did anyone really get hurt. The real world was a far more unsettled place. If one sees that space opera series of the early 1950s served, for the most part, as instructional media, then one might also argue that they presented, in necessarily simplistic terms, a microcosm of events that were then being played out on the world political stage. Whether shot on film for verisimilitude or broadcast live using the barest of sets and minimal special effects, the space operas and other science fiction series of the era served primarily as socializing agents for a new generation, coming of age in a world that even their parents often could barely comprehend themselves.[32]

This dialogue between utopian dreaming and near dystopian despair seems to underwrite almost all of SF television in the Golden Age of television. On the one hand, heroes and invention and ingenuity were everywhere to be seen – we not only could see the stars but also believed we could shortly reach them. On the other hand, the fear of war, of nuclear weaponry, and of radical transformations in everyday life brought on by new technologies, meant the world felt unstable, in constant seismic movement.

Conclusion

While a great deal of early SF film, television, and radio is marked by its sense of wonder and utopian idealism, there is much SF that is haunted by dystopian sentiments and apocalyptic scenarios. Above any comparable genre, SF seems to be able to represent and reproduce the individual and collective fears, paranoia, and cultural and political transformations that exist in society. SF can do this because, by definition, it is delineated by the word fiction, and because its landscapes, narratives, and ideological centers are seemingly so far removed from the "realism" of the actual world by its time travel and future technology metaphors. SF exists in possible worlds and imaginable futures, but the myths that are (barely) buried in its fantastic belly are ones that speak to people in the signs and codes of their everyday lives. As Annette Kuhn summarizes: "There is the idea that science fiction films relate to the social order through the mediation of ideologies, society's representation of itself in and for itself – that films speak, enact, even produce

---

[32] Ibid., p. 95.

certain ideologies, which cannot always be read directly off films' surface contents."[33] What we see in the period from 1900 to 1960 is a blossoming of the themes and concerns of the genre, and a growing inter-relationship between the different media. Commercial intertextual and extra-textual relations sometime drive these relations by branding and merchandising, but they are also shaped by the politics of the age – by the yearning for new beginnings and by the fears of what may come.

[33] Kuhn, ed., *Alien Zone*, p. 10.

18

Fandom and Fan Culture in the Golden Age and Beyond

KAREN HELLEKSON

Fans, fandoms, and the study of fan culture are inextricably bound up with the history of SF.[1] Of course fans have always been engaging with texts, often in transformative ways: rewriting books or scenes, crafting new endings, literally scribbling in the margins of their paperbacks. But the current model of participatory fandom evident in Western culture, as it manifests across genres and across national boundaries, is based on a pattern created in SF fandom that began in the mid-1930s, mostly in the United States.[2]

Early SF fandom grew out of clubs dedicated to SF and weird fiction pulp magazines that began publishing in the late 1920s, such as *Startling Stories*, *Wonder Stories*, and *Weird Tales*. Clubs in Los Angeles, Philadelphia, and New York City were particularly active. New York groups included the Greater New York Science Fiction Club, the New York chapter of the national Science Fiction League (founded in 1934 by influential editor Hugo Gernsback), and the Brooklyn Science Fiction League.[3] These clubs formed, broke apart (often over political differences), and then reformed, nearly cyclically. In 1937 several New York organizations coalesced into the Futurians, SF's best-known fan club. Many of the club members were young – in their teens and twenties –

---

[1] *Fans* are people who actively engage with something – a text, objects such as coins, stamps, favored sports teams – and *fandom* is the community that fans self-constitute around that text or object. As such, fandoms vary greatly in their practices and expressions. What they all have in common is the desire to share an often passionate, affective response to the item in question with like-minded others. Fans today create and consume artworks, police community rules, and engage with each other in complicated, self-referential, multivocal discourses, the very expression of which constitutes the community. In order to best disseminate the artworks and texts associated with their fandom, fans tend to be early adopters of technology, be it hand letterpresses, VHS tapes, Photoshop software, or social media.

[2] On the importance of the US SF community to fan history generally, see also Karen Hellekson, "Fandom and Fan Culture," in Eric Carl Link and Gerry Canavan, eds., *The Cambridge Companion to American Science Fiction* (Cambridge: Cambridge University Press, 2015), pp. 153–63.

[3] Dave Kyle, "The Science Fiction League," *Mimosa* 14 (1993), pp. 17–24, www.jophan.org /mimosa/m14/kyle.htm (last accessed May 15, 2018).

and aspired to be writers or editors themselves. Members of this mostly male club included now-familiar names such as Isaac Asimov, Damon Knight, Sam Moskowitz, Frederik Pohl, Judith Merril, and Donald A. Wollheim, many of whom have written memoirs of their experiences in early fandom.[4]

As was common in early face-to-face fandom communities, personalities clashed, and differences of politics led to schisms. Some fan groups, for example, had sharply political focuses, with some early fans into communism (notably Pohl), and some fans into an application of rationality and science as a way for society to progress, with SF used as a tool to bring about a rational utopia. Those who did not hew to the party line would be cast out. Some strong personalities, including Wollheim, William S. Sykora, James V. Taurasi, and John Michel, clashed over the political direction they thought the fan clubs should take, with clubs rising and falling with tiring regularity as a result. According to the Fancyclopedia, "Sykora (along with Moskowitz, Wollheim, Michel, and several others) was at the center of the epic battles which shaped (and shook) fandom in the late 1930s. At the root was the SF (and science) focus of Sykora and Moskowitz versus the left-wing political focus of the Futurians such as Michel and Wollheim."[5]

As the published biographies of the major players reveal, the Futurians formed from a melding of at least four other New York-based fan clubs, including the Brooklyn Science Fiction League and the East New York Science Fiction League. The group, which had perhaps twenty members, some of whom shared lodgings and others of whom married, was founded by Wollheim and Michel. In 1945 it ended under the weight of lawsuits as seven members sued and countersued each other.[6] During their heyday, the Futurians were notable for their impact on SF as their fannish activity gave way to turning their passion into a business: many became writers, editors, and agents important in the field of SF. Knight and Merril went on to become editors of series of SF anthologies; Wollheim founded DAW books; Asimov,

---

[4] See, for instance, Isaac Asimov, *In Memory Yet Green: The Autobiography of Isaac Asimov, 1920–1954* (New York: Doubleday, 1980); Damon Knight, *The Futurians: The Story of the Science Fiction "Family" of the '30s that Produced Today's Top SF Writers and Editors* (New York: John Day, 1977); Sam Moskowitz, *The Immortal Storm: A History of Science Fiction Fandom* (Atlanta, GA: Atlanta Science Fiction Organization Press, 1954); Frederik Pohl, *The Way the Future Was: A Memoir* (New York: Ballantine Books/Del Rey, 1978); and others.

[5] J. B. Speer, "William S. Sykora (1913–[1994])," *Fancyclopedia* 31, 1 (1944) (fanzine). Speer's text, updated, is available online at *Fancyclopedia*, http://fancyclopedia.org (last accessed May 15, 2018). See also Chapter 11 of this volume, "Rise of the Supermen," for a detailed description of another vicious early fandom political dispute, this one centered around eugenics.

[6] Speer, "The Futurians" and "X Document," *Fancyclopedia 3*.

James Blish, Cyril Kornbluth, and Pohl became important writers; Virginia Kidd and Pohl were literary agents. All this activity grew out of the Futurians' synergistic activities.

These fans created two modes of expression that remain with SF fandom to this day: exchanging written texts (mostly nonfiction) and meeting up in person at a themed convention. These activities created a self-defined cohesive group organized around a common interest that we would now call a fandom. The texts that early fans exchanged comprised letter columns and fan magazines, first catalyzed by Hugo Gernsback in *Amazing Stories* and widely adopted across the field of SF production (in varying ways) over the subsequent decades. Gernsback provided an opening for fan engagement not only by creating the national Science Fiction League, with its area chapters, but also by including letter columns in the pulp magazines he published. He printed letters of comment sent in by readers and included the writers' street addresses. This permitted readers to get in touch with one another directly, to correspond, then meet up and network. In the first issue of *Amazing Stories* (1926), Gernsback writes, "How good this magazine will be in the future is up to you. Read *Amazing Stories* – get your friends to read it and then write us what you think of it. We will welcome constructive criticism – for only in this way will we know how to satisfy you."[7] Fans took this invitation seriously; they also considered it a mark of distinction when Gernsback published their letters or otherwise responded to them. Gernsback's willingness to engage in back-and-forth with the young fans of his "scientifiction" magazines was emulated by the fans themselves as they engaged with each other.

From this it was a short step to creating texts to share among one another. The first SF fan magazine, *The Comet*, edited by Raymond A. Palmer, appeared in May 1930, published out of Chicago.[8] A slew of others followed. Most had very small readerships, correspondingly small print runs – sometimes only as many copies as pages of carbon paper could be inserted in the typewriter – and erratic publication frequency. Fans could subscribe, or they could donate a fan magazine to receive one in exchange. Several libraries today hold extensive collections of these early SF and weird tales fan magazines in nonlending archives, including the University of California at

---

[7] Hugo Gernsback, "A New Sort of Magazine" (editorial), *Amazing Stories* 1, 1 (April 1926). Available at http://archive.org/stream/AmazingStoriesVolume01Number01/Amazing StoriesVolume01Number01_djvu.txt (last accessed May 15, 2018).

[8] N3F Editorial Cabal, "A Brief History of Science Fiction Fandom," *N3F* (April 1, 2003), http://n3f.org/2013/04/a-brief-history-of-science-fiction-fandom/; ZineWiki, *Comet*, http://zinewiki.com (last accessed May 15, 2018).

Riverside, the University of Iowa, Syracuse University, and Liverpool University, available for scholars to visit and study. The fact that fanzines were sent through the mail means that they are legally treated as personal correspondence. Copyright law thus forbids their being posted online, and quoting from them requires obtaining permission from the writer or his estate. This has curtailed scholarly work done on early-era fanzines, as viewing them and quoting from them are both difficult.

Physically, fan mags – the word *fanzine* was not coined until 1940[9] – were stapled-together pieces of ordinary-sized letter paper, sometimes folded in half. Often one side would remain empty so it might be addressed and the postage stamp affixed. Sometimes covers were made of colored heavy paper, and they often included artwork as well as the magazine's title. The writer would prepare the magazine on a typewriter, then reproduce it. Early modes of reproduction included simple carbon paper, Ditto machine (spirit duplication), hectograph, and mimeograph. Photocopying came later. Artwork, if included, would be hand-drawn, and might be colored by hand, so each copy would be unique. Sometimes the writer would paste in a photograph, often of a fan being profiled. Fan mags' content primarily provided extensions of the now-familiar letters of comment. Editorials and reviews of current issues of SF magazines would often be included. Fiction rarely appeared, and if it did, was often about the fans themselves. In fact, as J. B. Speer notes, the early meaning of the term *fan fiction* did not mean "fiction written by fans," but "fiction written about fans."[10]

As Neil Patrick Hayden describes, after fan magazines had been established, fans co-opted APAs (amateur press association, from groups formed in the late 1870s by the owners of hand letter presses to disseminate their work) for the SF world.[11] The Fantasy Amateur Press Association, or FAPA, was founded by SF fan and Futurian Donald A. Wollheim in 1937, who learned about APAs from weird tales writer H. P. Lovecraft. In this nifty mode of dissemination, which remains in use, fans would create a zine and then send a certain number of copies to a master editor, who would collate them and then mail the bundles to all the contributors.

[9] "Fanzine," *Science Fiction Citations* (2008), www.jessesword.com/sf/view/186 (last accessed May 15, 2018).
[10] J. B. Speer, "Fan Fiction," *Fancyclopedia 3*.
[11] Neil Patrick Hayden, "H. P. Lovecraft, Founding Father of SF Fandom," *Tor.com* (December 3, 2009), www.tor.com/blogs/2009/12/h-p-lovecraft-founding-father-of-sf-fandom (last accessed May 15, 2018).

Fans thus built their communities via the technologies then current: reproduction and postal mail. But they also met in person, as the vogue of fan clubs and SF leagues hints. The first World Science Fiction Convention, or Worldcon, was held in conjunction with the 1939 New York World's Fair over the Fourth of July weekend.[12] The World's Fair theme of "The World of Tomorrow" meshed nicely with science fictional interests. Worldcons have been held ever since, with a break during the Second World War. It is no coincidence that fandom became active during what is now known as the Golden Age of science fiction, which is usually dated from around 1939 (the date of the first Worldcon) to the 1940s or 1950s (depending on whom you ask). Indeed, the activities of the fans – who were the writers, editors, and consumers of SF literature – ended up not just constituting a fandom but the genre of SF itself.

Fandom in the 1940s, 1950s, and early 1960s saw the codification of many of the firsts noted above. Some fans organized their lives around fandom, with marriages and children resulting; FIAWOL (fandom is a way of life) became a catch phrase. Fans kept up extensive correspondences, published fanzines, and organized and attended conventions. Filk, or SF-related, fan-created and -sung songs, often with new lyrics to familiar tunes, became active in the early 1950s and remains popular today, with new genres such as Harry Potter-themed wizard rock (aka wrock). Cosplay, or costume play, debuted at the first Worldcon in 1939 when superfans Forrest J. Ackerman and Myrtle R. "Morojo" Douglas dressed in futuristic outfits from the 1936 film *Things to Come*.[13] It was later enshrined at many conventions as part of a big stage show, where fans would model the costumes they created.

SF magazines continued to publish new fiction, although the market contracted sharply in the 1950s as many magazines folded. Serializations of many novel-length SF texts by now-classic writers appeared, which would then go on to be published as stand-alone books. SF fandom was thus a fandom of literature, and it was being led by professional writers who were formerly among the first fans. This permitted, even encouraged, contact between writers and fans.

As David Hartwell outlines, fans continued to create a complex, often exclusionary vocabulary that cemented their role as insiders and

[12] J. B. Speer, "Worldcon," *Fancyclopedia 3*.
[13] An image of Ackerman and Morojo dressed up at the 1939 Worldcon is available online at www.racked.com/2016/5/9/11451408/cosplay-inventor-morojo-myrtle-r-douglas (last accessed May 15, 2018).

tastemakers.[14] Fanzines, APAs, and in-person conventions all continued, with local conventions and Worldcons important nexuses of connection. Histories of SF fandom in the 1940s and 1950s by Harry Warner Jr., an active fan and letter writer, describe fannish activities from an anecdotal point of view and highlight the personalities that populated this era and the culture they constructed.[15] Extensive letter writing by prominent fans bridged distances between fans and forged friendships and alliances. Zines provided a forum for fan essays, analysis, and, later, fan fiction. The retrospective works about this era by active fans such as Warner and histories of fandom such as those that appear in the fanzine *Mimosa* demonstrate a kind of fannish self-analysis that remains important as fans create and contextualize their experiences.

Science Fiction Media Fandom

The landscape of fannish activity changed in 1967. That year saw the publication of the first SF media zine, *Spockanalia*, which marked the rise of SF media fandom, as opposed to SF literature fandom. According to Joan Marie Verba, this *Star Trek* zine was created after fans saw the pilot of *Star Trek* at the 1966 Worldcon in Cleveland.[16] Naturally, a zine was the result. SF media fandom thus grew directly out of SF literature fandom, and its primary catalyst was *Star Trek*.[17] These early *Star Trek* media fans also initiated what has since become a staple in fandom: the save-the-show campaign, run by fans to try to resurrect a canceled show. Indeed, *Spockanalia* included an editorial that described a letter campaign to save the recently canceled program.

As the first-known fannish save-the-show campaign, Save *Star Trek* (1968–9) provides an example of fans banding together and influencing producers' decisions. When the show was threatened with cancellation after its first season, Harlan Ellison wrote a letter on December 1, 1966 to the membership of the Science Fiction Writers of America encouraging his

---

[14] David G. Hartwell, *Age of Wonders: Exploring the World of Science Fiction* [1985] (New York: Tor, 1996).

[15] Harry Warner Jr., *All Our Yesterdays: An Informal History of Science Fiction Fandom in the Forties* (Chicago: Advent, 1969) and *A Wealth of Fable: The History of Science Fiction Fandom in the 1950s*, 3 vols. (New York: Fanhistorica Press, 1976) (fanzine).

[16] Joan Marie Verba, *Boldly Writing: A Trekker Fan and Zine History, 1967–1987* (Minneapolis: FTL Publications, 1996), www.ftlpublications.com/bwebook.pdf (last accessed May 15, 2018).

[17] For more on this period in fan history, see Francesca Coppa, "A Brief History of Media Fandom," in Karen Hellekson and Kristina Busse, eds., *Fan Fiction and Fan Communities in the Age of the Internet* (Jefferson, NC: McFarland, 2006), pp. 41–59.

fellow authors to write letters to the broadcast network, NBC, to advocate for the show to be continued. Later, Gene Roddenberry spoke with a prominent fan, Bjo Trimble, and revealed to her that the show was also in danger of cancellation after its second season – a problem because a TV show needed at least three seasons to be placed into syndication, which would ensure its longevity. Bjo knew that letters from prominent writers would not be enough this time. She and her husband, John Trimble, concocted a save *Star Trek* campaign targeted instead to fans. Bjo did research to ensure that the letters would get read. She remembers, "I went around to secretaries of corporations and even secretaries on the Paramount lot, and asked what it is about a letter, the one and only letter per day you put on your boss's desk for attention, or even filing it instead of throwing it away, that gets it there. And they told me, so I used that as a basis on how to write a letter."[18] Another campaign for a fourth season failed, but fan activity later led to syndication and the expansion into original-cast films (and, eventually, new series). It is not hyperbole to suggest that fans ensured the longevity of the franchise.[19] Fan save-the-show campaigns continue today, with varying levels of success.[20]

As Francesca Coppa explains, women – and they were mostly women, in contrast to the boys and men who comprised fandom in the mid-1930s – engaged in media fandom in a primarily transformative mode. Not content to stick with letters of comment, essays, poems, and the occasional piece of fiction (which quickly morphed into entire zines dedicated to fan fiction), these *Star Trek* fans created vidding, a fannish art form pioneered by Kandy Fong, whose slide show, "What Do You Do With a Drunken Vulcan?," appeared in 1975. Fong used *Star Trek* film snippets literally picked up from the cutting room floor and played a slide show of still images to a popular filk song, which fans received enthusiastically.[21]

The genre evolved into video-recorded clips from the episode strung together, expertly edited on VHS tape and timed to a specific song.

---

[18] Michael Hinman, "History Is Written by the Victors: Bjo Trimble Talks about Saving *Star Trek*," *Airlock Alpha*, May 10, 2003, http://airlockalpha.com/1142/history-is-written-by-the-victors-html (last accessed May 15, 2018).

[19] "History of Star Trek Campaigns," *Fanlore* (wiki), https://fanlore.org (last accessed May 15, 2018).

[20] See Meredith Woerner, "Fan Campaigns that Actually Saved TV Shows," *io9*, January 12, 2012, https://io9.gizmodo.com/5875356/fan-campaigns-throughout-history-that-saved-scifi-and-fantasy-tv-shows (last accessed May 15, 2018).

[21] Francesca Coppa, "Women, *Star Trek*, and the Early Development of Fannish Vidding," *Transformative Works and Cultures*, 1 (2008), http://dx.doi.org/10.3983/twc.2008.0044 (last accessed May 15, 2018).

In continuing with the fannish penchant of turning technologies to their own ends, be they letter presses or videotape, fan vidders have lately turned to digital technologies, which permit them not only to clip images and sync them to music, but also to alter the images. In fan vids, also known as songtapes, images are chosen to fit the song lyrics, but the very best vids use this to create a new story – a romance, perhaps, between two characters not engaged thus canonically, transforming the original text into an art form that tells a new story by rereading and reconstructing images from a fannish point of view.

In addition to vidding, early media fandom was associated with zine culture, as Camille Bacon-Smith's ethnographic report describes.[22] Zines, which previously had been mostly news, reviews, and analysis, now turned to fan fiction. The homoerotic genre of "slash fiction" also gained prominence, so called because of the typographical slash used between character names to indicate a romantic relationship; Kirk/Spock slash remains the best-known example. Slash received quite a bit of critical attention, especially in the mid-1990s, not only because the communities that created it were interesting for scholars to study from an ethnographic point of view but also because of the recognition that slash dealt with rupture, rewriting, and the Other, thus placing slash, just like SF, in contrast to the mainstream.

The fannish zine culture has always relied on a gift economy, although this is now being called into question, as writers collected by Kristina Busse argue.[23] Fanzines have traditionally been sold for the cost of reproduction and postage, with any overage used to seed the next project or donated to a charity. Fans' fear of cease-and-desist orders from producers or adverse attention from writers or actors has resulted in a fannish convention of making no money from their projects, thus relegating fans to amateur status. Fans also attach disclaimers to their work to indicate that they understand they have no right to the characters or situations. So strong is this ethos that fan-created and -disseminated software for archiving fan fiction includes disclaimers on every page as a default setting. Fans perceive this fly-under-the-radar, make-no-money strategy as circumventing copyright law – although, as Rebecca Tushnet explains, many fan works would

---

[22] Camille Bacon-Smith, *Enterprising Women: Television Fandom and the Creation of Popular Myth* (Philadelphia: University of Pennsylvania Press, 1992).
[23] Kristina Busse, ed., "In Focus: Fandom and Feminism: Gender and the Politics of Fan Production," *Cinema Journal* 48, 4 (2009).

fall under fair use and parody anyway (with the latter term used in its legal sense).[24]

Early fan studies academic scholarship published in the 1990s describes how media fans, in Henry Jenkins's term, poached the work of producers in order to create something of value, and the creation and exchange of these new artworks in turn constituted the fannish group.[25] This reading of fan activity – which valorized the work fans did to analyze texts and construct new meanings, and placed fan works in opposition to that of the producers who created the canonical text – remains current, although in 2013 Jenkins and colleagues updated the ideas of fan–producer networking and dialogue to reflect changes in the fan environment, notably Internet trends.[26] Spreadable media, in which fan networks take on the role of distribution of content, complicates the fan–producer power divide as fan activities force a change in traditional modes of corporate control. Instead of top-down decrees from The Powers That Be, fans desired actual dialogue with the producers.

Just as media conventions spun off from SF fandom, so did other specialty fan conventions. For example, MediaWest*Con is an important annual convention devoted to SF media fandom, run entirely by fans and without guests. Another well-known convention, Vividcon, is dedicated to vidding. In addition, many local groups host fan conventions. In addition to fan-run conventions, for-profit organizations such as Creation Entertainment run them, and Comic-Con, formerly a haven for comic book fans, has expanded to become a giant media extravaganza, with producers and actors on hand to hawk the latest SF TV show or film. Filk, cosplay, zines, and fan-created artwork may all play important roles at these events. The convention model pioneered by early SF fans has thus been endlessly replicated and tweaked to reflect the specific interests of the fan group.

The advent of the Internet, with its attendant broadening of community, greatly affected fandom.[27] Suffice it to say here that fans continue to be early adopters of technology. For example, fans adopted blogging software, turning blogs into fan fiction archives. Letters of comment moved to blogging

---

[24] Rebecca Tushnet, "Legal Fictions: Copyright, Fan Fiction, and a New Common Law," *Loyola of Los Angeles Entertainment Law Journal* 17 (1997), pp. 641–86, http://digitalcommons.lmu.edu/cgi/viewcontent.cgi?article=1347&context=elr (last accessed May 15, 2018).

[25] See Henry Jenkins, *Textual Poachers: Television Fans and Participatory Culture* (New York: Routledge, 1992).

[26] Henry Jenkins, Sam Ford, and Joshua Green, *Spreadable Media: Creating Value and Meaning in a Networked Culture* (New York: New York University Press, 2013).

[27] This move online is addressed in detail later in this volume (see Chapter 45, "Convergence Culture: Science Fiction Fandom Today").

software's Comments section. Artwork was shared at dedicated sites like Deviantart, and new modes of fan art sprang up, including original artwork but also altered image sets, fandom-specific avatars, and GIFs. VCR-to-VCR creation of fan videos gave way to the use of specialized software to create the vids, and YouTube and other platforms were used to share them. Usenet, Yahoo groups, and blogging platforms such as LiveJournal have fallen to the might of Tumblr, whose "reblog" feature permits easy sharing.

Why SF?

Of course, not all fans center their activities around SF texts. Contemporaneous readers of Jane Austen's work would extend or rework her narratives. Sherlock Holmes had an early fandom; fans wrote and exchanged Holmes pastiches in what might be called the first fan fictions.[28] However, SF, supernatural, and so-called cult texts tend to draw especially active, vocal fans who work together to build a community around a source text. *Star Trek, Blake's 7, The X-Files, Xena: Warrior Princess, Buffy the Vampire Slayer, Battlestar Galactica, Twilight, Harry Potter, Doctor Who* – all these media sources have attracted particularly extensive fan activity as well as critical scrutiny from academics. And even texts like *The Man from U.N.C.L.E.* and *The Professionals* (1960s-era spy shows) and the Sherlock Holmes canon might be said to contain a kind of engagement with the technological that marks it as akin to SF, be it winning the day through cleverness and gadgetry or solving a crime by applying a rigorously scientific method.

Something about the fantastic in a text invites engagement, although notions vary of what that ineffable *something* is: the world-building? The characters? The situations? The blank spaces on the map, where the imagination of the fan can run wild with new stories? Whatever the reason, SF and other cult texts create a disrupted, nonrealistic world, where the Other – be it monster, alien, or angel – impinges on our construction of the real world, thus opening the everyday up to fabulous possibilities. This forces a questioning of the status quo and valorizes, even normalizes, those who struggle against it. However, as Sharon Marie Ross notes, the specific elements of a text that make it cult, and that thus invite affective engagement, may be less important than the sheer act of creating a social audience in the first place.[29]

---

[28] See Karen Hellekson and Kristina Busse, eds., *The Fan Fiction Studies Reader* (Iowa City: University of Iowa Press, 2014).

[29] Sharon Marie Ross, *Beyond the Box: Television and the Internet* (Oxford: Blackwell, 2008).

The Three Waves of Fandom

Fandom's three waves, as articulated by Jonathan Gray, Cornel Sandvoss, and C. Lee Harrington, have greatly broadened the definition of *fan*, and this is paralleled by changes in the culture industry.[30] The first wave celebrated fandom as cultural resistance. Epitomized by Jenkins's *Textual Poachers* (which in turn engaged theories by Fiske and De Certeau[31]), fans were seen as seizing the work of producers; fandom was a subculture of resistance to a dominant mass culture. The first wave of fandom pitted the producer against the consumer-fan; it also attempted to turn the "get a life!" pathologic mode of viewing fans to a more celebratory one while still retaining the fan as the Other.[32] The second wave engaged new media and saw a proliferation of self-identified fan communities, often bound together by the Internet. Following Bourdieu, second-wave fandom analyzed fan practices in terms of hierarchies of taste. Sociological analyses also abounded, with scholars focusing on fan identity construction. During this wave, producers sought to more overtly engage fans, so the relationship became less confrontational, although the fan remained the Other. Finally, third-wave fandom (the current cultural moment) has broadened the notion of what might be considered fannish to the everyday. Sports fans, comic book collectors, and Martha Stewart fans could be considered in much the same way that SF and media fans had been considered previously.

The third wave sees the fan as Us. During this phase, producers engage regularly with fans, even attempting to co-opt their passion and labor by attempting to turn it to create buzz and build viewership. The primary importance of third-wave fandom is its broadening of the stakes from relatively small subcommunities (fandoms) to a larger field: everyday life. As Gray *et al.* write of this wave, "Here fandom is no longer only an object of study in and for itself. Instead, through the investigation of fandom as a part of the fabric of our everyday lives, third wave work aims to capture fundamental insights into modern life."[33] The stakes are therefore greater: certainly first- and second-wave fandom studies still have much to offer, and useful, important work continues in these veins, but the project of the third wave is an inquiry of the contemporary moment of our culture even as we organize

---

[30] Jonathan Gray, Cornel Sandvoss, and C. Lee Harrington, *Fandom: Identities and Communities in a Mediated World*, 1st edn. (New York: New York University Press, 2007).

[31] John Fiske, *Reading the Popular* (New York: Routledge, 1989); Michel De Certeau, *The Practice of Everyday Life* (Berkeley: University of California Press, 1984).

[32] Joli Jenson, "Fandom as Pathology: The Consequence of Characterization," in Lisa A. Lewis, ed., *The Adoring Audience* (London: Routledge, 1992), pp. 9–29.

[33] Gray *et al.*, *Fandom*, 1st edn., p. 9.

and comprise it. Fan studies interrogates popular culture, but third-wave fandom takes the strategies of fan studies and applies it to an even broader field of play. Gray *et al.* later address the third wave of fandom by stressing the audience's position. The advent of the Internet meant that fans could find each other without the aid of in-the-know insiders; thus being "fannish" in the old sense of the term did not resonate with their experience. Although such people might call themselves fans (or be called fans by outsiders), they do not mean it in the restrictive sense that old-school "true" fans meant it.[34] Third-wave fandom accommodates this experience and makes meaning of it.

Gray *et al.* describe the projects of third-wave fandom as working on intrapersonal fan relationships in terms of consumption, resulting in, among other things, psychoanalytic and affective approaches. On a larger level, however, "third-wave research on fans extends the conceptual focus beyond questions of hegemony and class, to the overarching social, cultural, and economic transformations of our time, thereby offering new answers to the question of why we should study fans … Third-wave fan studies … tell us something about how we relate to ourselves, to each other, and to how we read the mediated texts around us."[35] Third-wave fan studies include analyses of the large concerns of race, gender, and heteronormativity, as well as the smaller worlds of women sports fans, comics, and gamers, which previously might not have been considered to fall within the realm of interest for fan studies because the fan groups did not self-describe as fans.[36]

Views of fandom have shifted in academic and popular discourse, first by valorizing fannish behavior, then by broadening fandoms' constituents, and finally by expanding fannish activity to the everyday, with lessons learned from the fannish experience used to explicate sociocultural practices more generally. Fandoms are creating new traditions that often do not fit the

---

[34] See Cornel Sandvoss, "The Inner Fan: Fandom and Psychoanalysis," in *Fans: The Mirror of Consumption* (New York: Polity, 2005).

[35] Gray *et al.*, *Fandom*, 2nd edn., p. 7.

[36] On race and heteronormativity, see the essays comprising the special issue on race and ethnicity in fandom, edited by Sarah N. Gatson and Robin Anne Reid, *Transformative Works and Cultures* 8 (2011), http://dx.doi.org/10.3983/twc.2011.0392 (last accessed May 15, 2018). On women sports fans, see Kim Toffoletti, *Women Sport Fans: Identification, Participation, Representation* (New York: Routledge, 2017). On comics, see J. Richard Stevens and Christopher Edward Bell, "Do Fans Own Digital Comic Books? Examining the Copyright and Intellectual Property Attitudes of Comic Book Fans," in Manuel Castells and Gustavo Cardoso, eds., *Piracy Cultures: How a Growing Portion of the Global Population Is Building Media Relationships through Alternate Channels of Obtaining Content* (Los Angeles: USC Annenberg Press, 2013). On gamers, see Megan Condis, *Gaming Masculinity: Trolls, Fake Geeks, and the Gendered Battle for Online Culture* (Iowa City: University of Iowa Press, 2017).

generalizations put forth about fan fiction and media fandom. Examples include *yaoi*/boys' love texts and artworks, soap opera scripts, anime fan fiction and costuming, and fantasies imagining fan relationships with musical artists. Moreover, the advent of the Internet means that community norms, formerly policed in person, are now policed within smaller, self-created communities that owe allegiance to no one but themselves, thus expanding the field of engagement. The seeds that SF fandom planted in the mid-1930s continue to bear fruit today. The fannish experience that early SF fans pioneered lives on in a multitude of new formats, and also the affective engagement and community that fandoms are built on, remain the bedrock of fan experience. SF fandom, in all its multitudes, as third-wave fandom has demonstrated, has pointed the way to assessments of ontological concerns in contemporary society.

19

Science Fiction and Its Critics

ROB LATHAM

SF is unique among popular genres in having a highly evolved critical discourse that has been generated and sustained *from within*, by prominent authors, editors, and fans. Decades before the first academic journal devoted to SF – *Extrapolation* – debuted in 1959, fanzines were offering penetrating and sophisticated analyses of major themes and trends in the field. The first SF fanzines emerged in the early 1930s, in the wake of Hugo Gernsback's *Amazing Stories*, offering platforms for critical discussion and exchange. Often their level of discourse barely rose above impressionistic banter, yet some fan editors – such as Arthur Wilson ("Bob") Tucker, editor of *Le Zombie*, and Robert A. W. ("Doc") Lowndes, editor of *Le Vombiteur* – consistently offered sharp, sarcastic critiques of pulp clichés, in what amounted to the first SF literary criticism. Tucker, in 1941, famously coined the term "space opera" in disparagement of the "outworn space-ship yarn" that filled the pages of pulps like *Thrilling Wonder Stories*, arguing that such hackwork merely aped the conventions of the Western "horse opera."[1]

Such harsh evaluations of the formulaic nature of much pulp SF were balanced by full-throated defenses of the genre as a wellspring of potent social commentary, an argument that foreshadowed later academic criticism by the likes of Darko Suvin and Carl Freedman. John B. Michel, for example, stoutly advocated for SF as a bulwark of progressive ideals, calling on authors to eschew mere escapism in favor of the depiction of utopian worlds governed by social justice. A member of the Futurian fan group that also included such future luminaries as Frederik Pohl and Donald A. Wollheim, Michel held a vision of SF strongly colored by his leftwing views – and, indeed, the Futurians were a significant part of the genre's own "cultural front" against

---

[1] See David Pringle, "What Is This Thing Called Space Opera?," in Gary Westfahl, ed., *Space and Beyond: The Frontier Theme in Science Fiction* (Westport, CT: Greenwood, 2000), pp. 35–47.

fascism in the 1930s.[2] Most significantly, this youthful cadre went on, during the subsequent decades, to positions of professional prominence within the field. After helming a series of minor pulps during the 1940s, Pohl became one of the genre's most important authors of social-satirical SF, including the classic 1953 novel *The Space Merchants* (co-authored with fellow Futurian C. M. Kornbluth), while Wollheim edited the first mass-market SF anthology, *The Pocket Book of Science Fiction*, in 1943, and – as SF editor at Avon and Ace Books – helped to initiate the paperback explosion of the 1950s. This career trajectory, from noted fan commentator to professional heavyweight, would come to characterize the field for the next several decades.

In terms of the development of SF criticism, it was three other Futurians – James Blish, Damon Knight, and Judith Merril – who led the way. By the early 1950s, all three were well-established authors, having penned such classic stories as "That Only a Mother" (Merril, 1948), "Not with a Bang" (Knight, 1950), and "Surface Tension" (Blish, 1952). While Knight and Blish had modest success as editors (piloting the short-lived digests *Worlds Beyond* and *Vanguard*, respectively), Merril was the most important anthologist in the field, releasing an annual "year's best" compilation from 1956 until 1968. All three worked to lift the artistic and intellectual standards by which SF was evaluated, promoting more rigorous forms of speculation, as well as more nuanced depictions of character and a more fluent prose style. Toward this end, they came together in 1956 to found the Milford Writers' Conference, hosted each year at Knight's home in Milford, Pennsylvania, where all three authors lived. These workshops brought together SF writers, both established and apprentice, to offer feedback on each other's work, swap advice about markets, and debate prevailing trends in the field. Prior to this time, as I have argued elsewhere,

> authors had dealt primarily with editors, whose particular creative values – and ideological crotchets – tended to permeate the work produced for them. What Blish, Knight, and Merril proposed to do was to foster a sense, especially among younger writers, of autonomous artistry, of pursuing a career in which an individual's imaginative vision could thrive simply because of the sheer diversity of available markets. Some older authors

[2] See Jerome Winter, "The Michelist Revolution: Technocracy, the Cultural Front, and the Futurian Movement," *The Eaton Journal of Archival Research in Science Fiction* 1,2 (November 2013), pp. 78–95 (online). Michel's notorious 1933 address to the Third Eastern Science Fiction Convention in Philadelphia, entitled "Mutation or Death," is available in Rob Latham, ed., *Science Fiction Criticism: An Anthology of Essential Writings* (London: Bloomsbury, 2017). For an insightful history of the fan group, see Damon Knight, *The Futurians* (New York: John Day, 1977).

looked askance at these developments, muttering darkly about an encroaching "Milford Mafia," but there can be little doubt that these conferences incubated some of the more ambitious work produced in the latter half of the decade and beyond.[3]

The Milford Conference dissolved in the early 1970s, with Blish moving to England to found a competing event while Knight helped run the newly established Clarion Writers Workshop at Michigan State University.

Yet, over and above their influence as authors, editors, and conference organizers, it was as literary critics that Blish, Knight, and Merril had their most significant impact on the development of the genre. For his part, Blish adopted a pseudonym for much of his nonfiction writing: William Atheling, Jr., adapted from an alias that modernist poet Ezra Pound had used for his music criticism. Blish's anonymity was preserved until Atheling's essays were gathered into the 1964 volume *The Issue at Hand*, whereupon the author doffed his mask, admitting that he had used the pen name so he could be brutally frank in his judgments without endangering his own professional status.[4] Published in fanzines such as Redd Boggs's *Sky Hook* (1948–57), Patricia and Richard Lupoff's *Xero* (1960–3), and Larry and Noreen Shaw's *Axe* (1961–3), Atheling's criticism helped to raise the standards for fan writing substantially during the 1950s and early 1960s. As his Pound-inspired alias suggested, Blish's aesthetic commitments extended well beyond the borders of the genre to encompass significant trends in modern world literature.[5] This was, in fact, the major contribution of Knight and Merril as well: to bring to the assessment of SF a robust, catholic sense of literary possibility.[6]

Blish threw down the gauntlet in his very first essay as Atheling, published in 1952, asserting that, if SF wanted to move out of the literary "ghetto" and "into

---

[3] Rob Latham, "A Genre Comes of Age: The Maturation of Science Fiction in the 1950s," in Steven W. Belletto, ed., *American Literature in Transition, 1950–1960* (Cambridge: Cambridge University Press, 2018), pp. 326–37. Critiques of the Milford crowd as a cultish "in-group" were still current in the late 1960s: see Paul Hazlett, "The Inside Story of the Milford Mafia," in *BeABohema* 6 (1969), pp. 28–31.

[4] James Blish, "Introduction," in *The Issue at Hand: Studies in Contemporary Magazine Fiction* by William Atheling, Jr. (Chicago: Advent, 1973), p. 1.

[5] Blish's abiding interest in modernist fiction and poetry is discussed in David Ketterer's biography of the author, *Imprisoned in a Tesseract: The Life and Work of James Blish* (Kent, OH: Kent State University Press, 1987), p. 281.

[6] In this regard, their criticism stands in counterpoint to the position articulated by James E. Gunn, for example, who has argued that SF should not be evaluated by the same criteria used to judge "mainstream" literature: see "The Protocols of Science Fiction," in James E. Gunn, ed., *Inside Science Fiction*, 2nd edn., (Lanham, MD: Scarecrow, 2006), pp. 141–5. Gunn's argument draws upon Samuel R. Delany's understanding of SF as a unique linguistic formation, radically distinct from "mundane fiction" – a viewpoint I discuss below.

the category of an art-form," SF criticism would "necessarily have to be more ambitious."[7] To this end, critics needed to hold SF writing at least to "minimum standards of competence" while at the same time urging writers to embrace "the huge body of available technique" and "the essential features of good narrative practice" (7–8). SF authors should not be content to repeat comfortable formulas, crafting cardboard worlds full of big ideas and stick-figure characters; instead, they needed to show the "acuity of observation" and "depth of emotional penetration" that gives flesh to fictional scenarios in any genre (7). In sum, "we are not interested in any form of fiction which cuts itself off from human life and human values" (9). In his essays, gathered in *The Issue at Hand* and his 1970 follow-up volume *More Issues at Hand*, Blish put this humanist criterion to the test, examining a range of themes and trends in contemporary SF, from religious speculation ("Cathedrals in Space," 1953) to the use of gadgets ("Things Still to Come," 1964) to the emergence of the New Wave ("Making Waves," 1970). Throughout, he remained committed to the belief that a good critic must be a "useful citizen, who is positively obliged to be harsh toward bad work" in order to insure that the genre truly grows and matures (3).

In one of his early essays, Blish singled out for praise the book reviews of Damon Knight, claiming they displayed "discipline and devotion," as well as "the sharpest kind of perception" (18). Certainly, Knight was not afraid to "be harsh toward bad work," having published a devastating critique of Golden Age stalwart A. E. van Vogt as a "Cosmic Jerrybuilder." This notorious essay, which mercilessly dismantled van Vogt's slapdash novel *The World of Null-A* (1945) and significantly damaged his literary reputation in the process, was originally published in Larry Shaw's fanzine *Destiny's Child* and subsequently gathered into Knight's 1956 collection *In Search of Wonder*, the first significant book-length work of criticism to focus on genre SF. The volume consists mostly of reprinted book reviews that originally appeared in professional magazines such as *Worlds Beyond*, *Science Fiction Adventures*, and *Future Science Fiction*, in a column Knight appropriately called "The Dissecting Table." Most other SF reviewers – such as P. Schuyler Miller, long-time columnist for *Astounding Science Fiction* – were content to offer cursory, impressionistic evaluations, but Knight delved deeper, providing rigorous and often tart assessments of current work in the field.

Knight's very first column, published in 1952, made his position crystal clear: "science fiction is a field of literature worth taking seriously, and . . .

---

[7] *The Issue at Hand*, p. 6. Subsequent references will be given as parenthetical page numbers in the text.

ordinary critical standards can be meaningfully applied to it."[8] What makes for successful SF, Knight asserts, "is not different from the thing that makes mainstream stories rewarding, but only expressed differently . . . not in small, everyday symbols, but in the big ones of space and time" (4). Like Blish, Knight embraces a credo that demands from SF a serious commitment to high literary ambition and humane values, and he lauds the writers who aspire, if only intermittently, to this elevated standard: Theodore Sturgeon, Henry Kuttner, C. L. Moore, and Blish himself. At the same time, he castigates the "chuckleheads" and the "half-bad writers" who either miserably fail at evoking credible worlds or else seem "on alternate pages [to be] a genius and an idiot" (63). Along the way, Knight coins critical terms he then uses to analyze specific works – such as "idiot plot" (a concept he attributes to Blish), which refers to a story "kept in motion solely by virtue of the fact that everybody involved is an idiot" (26). Such works constitute a collective embarrassment to the field, militating against its ever being taken seriously; like Blish, Knight is deeply concerned with the low-art stigma attached to the genre, though both clearly believe that SF writers, editors, and fans have no one to blame but themselves for this negative verdict, by settling too often for the formulaic and the second-rate.

In Search of Wonder was the first publication from Advent Press, a fan publishing house founded by Earl Kemp, a prominent member of the University of Chicago Science Fiction Club. Over the next two decades, Advent released a number of important works of SF criticism, reference, and bibliography, including the 1959 collection *The Science Fiction Novel: Imagination and Social Criticism*, edited by Basil Davenport. Featuring wide-ranging and insightful essays by Robert A. Heinlein, C. M. Kornbluth, Alfred Bester, and Robert Bloch, this volume was the fruit of a lecture series at the University of Chicago organized by the Science Fiction Club, one of the first academic symposia devoted to SF. The first-ever college-level class on SF was taught by Sam Moskowitz at New York City College in 1953, and within a decade regular courses on the subject were being offered at Colgate College and Stanford University.[9] In 1959, celebrated British novelist Kingsley Amis chose SF as the subject of a series of invited lectures at Princeton University, which were published the following year as *New Maps of Hell*, the first critical

---

[8] Damon Knight, *In Search of Wonder: Essays on Modern Science Fiction* (Chicago: Advent, 1967), p. 1. Subsequent references will be given as parenthetical page numbers in the text.
[9] See Richard Dale Mullen, "Introduction" to the special issue on "Science Fiction and Academe," *Science Fiction Studies* 23, 3 (November 1996). The history of SF studies in the classroom is also discussed in Chapter 30 of this volume.

study of the genre to be released by a major press (Harcourt, Brace & World). Science fiction criticism had begun to enter the academic and literary mainstream.

Probably the most significant vector for this incursion was the *Year's Best SF* series edited by Judith Merril, first for fan publisher Gnome Press and later for the mainstream houses Simon & Schuster and Delacorte (the paperback editions were released by Dell Books). Merril brought to this task a wide-ranging literary sensibility: volumes in the series mixed work by genre mainstays such as Isaac Asimov, Hal Clement, and Theodore Sturgeon with stories produced outside the perimeters of genre, by such luminaries as Eugène Ionesco, Isaac Bashevis Singer, and John Steinbeck. Merril was also one of the first stateside anthologists to take note of the glimmerings of a fresh sensibility in British SF, reprinting early stories by Brian W. Aldiss and J. G. Ballard. Indeed, during the 1960s, Merril would emerge as one of the most vocal advocates for so-called New Wave writing, as we shall see.

The *Year's Best* volumes featured, on top of the editor's eclectic selections, incisive and searching "summations" canvassing significant issues and trends within the field. In these summations, Merril gave voice to her conviction that SF is a form of fabulation that "add[s] emotional urgency and dramatic power to what are basically problems in philosophy and morality."[10] At the same time as it addresses perennial human problems through the lens of "fantasy," SF is also an important medium "for the expression of social criticism" (24). Indeed, for Merril, the abbreviation "SF" stood for a wide range of types of writing: science fiction, science fantasy, speculative fiction. Over the course of the eleven volumes in the series, Merril gradually settled on the final term as offering the most expansive remit possible for what the field can offer, seeing it as encompassing a broader range than the "specialized cult of science fiction" purveyed by the pulp and digest magazines. This narrow genre was, she asserted, "rapidly disappearing, as the essential quality is absorbed into the main body of literature" (44) – a convergence she heralded not only in these annual summations but also in her review column for *The Magazine of Fantasy and Science Fiction*, which ran from 1965 to 1969, where she reviewed the work of John Barth and William S. Burroughs alongside that of Clifford D. Simak and Samuel R. Delany.

---

[10] Merril's scattered critical writings, including her summations in the *Year's Best* volumes, were recently gathered into *The Merril Theory of Lit'ry Criticism*, edited by Ritch Calvin (Seattle: Aqueduct, 2016); the passage quoted above appears on page 17. Subsequent references to Merril's writings are to this volume and will be given as parenthetical page numbers in the text.

During the period Merril was reviewing for *F&SF*, the genre was being shaken by ferocious debates over the so-called "New Wave," a form of SF that favored inner over outer space, surrealistic techniques over linear exposition. Merril was, in fact, at the center of these squabbles, championing Ballard's "ontological explorations" of delirious mindscapes as the cutting-edge of speculative writing (121). Though this judgment was widely derided by proponents of Old Guard SF, it was merely the logical culmination of the Milford crowd's embrace of the modernist legacy – e.g., Blish's fondness for James Joyce's *Finnegans Wake* (1939), which deeply influenced his own SF writing.[11] Despite his rather waspish view of the New Wave as a series of "abortive experiments in the guise of finished work,"[12] Blish paved the way for these experiments with his wholehearted embrace of the modernist canon. For his part, Knight advanced a New Wave agenda as SF editor at Berkley Books, releasing the first stateside editions of Ballard's early novels and story collections; and, as editor of the *Orbit* series of anthologies, starting in 1966, he favored speculative fabulation over traditional hard SF. There is, in short, a clear line from the mid-1950s Milford Conferences to the late-1960s New Wave wars. As editor-critics, Knight and Merril helped to build and sustain a market for ambitious experimental work.

The authors most closely associated with the New Wave, in both Britain and the United States, were even more active critics than the Milford troika, producing a rich and fertile body of essayistic writing that deeply shaped the developing discourse of SF studies. Aldiss, Delany, Ursula K. Le Guin, Joanna Russ – all eventually received Pilgrim Awards from the Science Fiction Research Association for lifetime achievement in scholarship. While the 1950s generation of author-critics preferred to work within traditional genre formats (fanzine essays, review columns, book prefaces), this later cohort began to move into more overtly scholarly terrain. Aldiss, for example, wrote the first significant narrative history of modern SF: *Billion Year Spree* (1973), which was eventually updated and expanded as *Trillion Year Spree* (1986). This study offered a genealogy for the genre that has been immensely influential on subsequent critical surveys, tracing its roots to the Gothic novel, specifically Mary Shelley's *Frankenstein* (1818).

---

[11] See Grace Eckley, "*Finnegans Wake* in the Work of James Blish," *Extrapolation* 20,4 (1979), pp. 330–42.

[12] Blish (as William Atheling, Jr.), *More Issues at Hand* (Chicago: Advent, 1970), p. 129.

According to Aldiss, *Frankenstein* established the basic terms of what would become *the* classic SF scenario: "Hubris clobbered by Nemesis."[13] In other words, scientific overreaching, such as Victor Frankenstein's fabrication of his Creature, would inevitably run up against limits both natural and social; SF, for Aldiss, was thus an essentially *cautionary* genre. This assumption accords with the attitude of most New Wave writers, who chafed at what they saw as the out-of-control technophilia of John W. Campbell's Golden Age. In many ways, *Trillion Year Spree* was designed to re-balance the historical ledger, displacing the American pulp tradition from its presumed centrality in favor of a longer, darker, and more overtly "literary" lineage that included the foundational work of Shelley and H. G. Wells, alongside the corrosive dystopian satires of Yevgeny Zamiatin, Karel Čapek, and Stanislaw Lem. Aldiss's critical commitment to expanding the historical – and international – borders of the field was also evidenced by his central role, along with fellow authors such as Pohl and Harry Harrison, in the "World SF" association, which was founded in 1976 in order to promote a sense of the global reach of SF ideas and creative energies.[14] Over the course of his long career as an SF author, critic, and cultural ambassador, Aldiss did more to combat parochial viewpoints and advance a truly cosmopolitan agenda than perhaps any other single figure. His impact on the formation of scholarly institutions in the field – and the facilitation of links between academic critics and professional authors – can hardly be overstated, as witnessed by his presence on the editorial boards of *Science Fiction Studies, Extrapolation,* and *Journal of the Fantastic in the Arts.*

Indeed, *Science Fiction Studies,* which was founded in 1973 (the same year as the publication of Aldiss's history), was in its early years a welcoming environment for work by practicing author-critics, including Russ and Le Guin. Between 1973 and 1980, these two authors published five articles and reviews in the journal, including such path-breaking works as Le Guin's "American SF and the Other" (1975), which argues that the depiction of social otherness in the pulp tradition is largely regressive, and Russ's "*Amor Vincit Feminam*: The Battle of the Sexes in Science Fiction" (1980), which powerfully contrasts feminist utopias with misogynistic matriarchal dystopias written by male authors. Le Guin and Russ deserve to be seen as two of the main founders of feminist SF criticism during the 1970s, publishing scholarly work

---

[13] Brian W. Aldiss (with David Wingrove), *Trillion Year Spree: The True History of Science Fiction* (New York: Atheneum, 1986), p. 26.

[14] See Brian W. Aldiss, "World SF," *The New York Review of Science Fiction* 100 (1996), pp. 1, 4–5.

in numerous venues, including fanzines and semiprozines as well as academic journals. Their fearless criticism was an inspiration for later generations of feminist SF scholars, such as Marleen Barr, Sarah Le Fanu, and Jenny Wolmark.

Le Guin's criticism, which was gathered into the collections *The Language of the Night* (1979; revised and expanded in 1992) and *Dancing on the Edge of the World* (1989), is less ferociously barbed than Russ's, though no less shrewd in its critique of how SF tends to fumble its mission to challenge the status quo, especially when it comes to gender issues. Her 1976 essay "Is Gender Necessary?" – which articulates the agenda of her award-winning novel about androgynous aliens, *The Left Hand of Darkness* (1969) – makes clear that the best SF consists of "thought experiments" that can lead to "reversals of a habitual way of thinking," upsetting orthodoxies and opening up fresh speculative possibilities.[15] Always deeply self-critical, Le Guin revised this essay in 1988 to apologize for her own failures of imagination, acknowledging that her depiction of the nominally genderless Gethenians in the novel was deformed by heterosexism and a default masculinist bias. This sort of auto-critique, in which an author scrutinizes her fiction for unexamined ideological assumptions, was relatively new to the genre, showing the gradual convergence of cutting-edge SF with modes of critical thinking emerging in the academy during the 1970s.

For her part, Russ was actually an academic, teaching literature and creative writing at the University of Washington for many years. She was a prolific and versatile critic, whose work appeared in a wide range of venues: scholarly, fannish, and activist. Russ's critical writing, while invariably incisive, is often quite funny, evincing a biting wit that drips with sarcasm: her sinisterly titled *How to Suppress Women's Writing* (1983), for example, is structured like a guidebook, with instructions. Her collections, both published by major university presses, are *To Write Like a Woman: Essays in Feminism and Science Fiction* (1995), which gathers her academic articles alongside a handful of shorter pieces, and *The Country You Have Never Seen* (2005), which compiles her scattered essays and reviews. The latter includes the classic study "The Image of Women in Science Fiction," a scathing survey of the genre's depiction of female characters; according to Russ, most SF, despite chronicling strange societies set in the distant future or on far-flung planets, tends to portray the relationship between the sexes in quite

---

[15] Ursula K. Le Guin, "Is Gender Necessary (Redux)," in *The Language of the Night: Essays on Fantasy and Science Fiction*, rev. edn. (New York: HarperCollins, 1992), pp. 159.

traditional ways, reflecting the values of "the American middle class with a little window dressing."[16] Originally published in the literary journal *The Red Clay Reader* in 1970, the essay was reprinted four years later in the SF magazine *Vertex* before being gathered into *The Country You Have Never Seen*, released by Liverpool University Press. This trajectory is characteristic of the way in which, since the 1970s, the critical reflections of major SF authors, often incubated in small-press or journalistic markets, have gradually been absorbed into academic discourse.

Delany's critical career traces a similar arc: his early essays were published in fanzines, literary journals, and anthologies, such as *Lighthouse, The Little Magazine*, and *Quark*, were then eventually gathered into books released by trade and small imprints (e.g., Berkeley Books, Dragon Press), before finally being enshrined in revised editions by Wesleyan University Press. Indeed, few authors have more deeply influenced the scholarly conversation about the genre than has Delany – and none has more extensively incorporated the insights of critical theory directly into his fiction, as witnessed by his use of Michel Foucault's concept of "heterotopia" as a structuring principle for his 1976 novel *Triton* (aka *Trouble on Triton*). During the 1970s, Delany evolved an idiosyncratic approach to the analysis of SF that converged with the contemporaneous perspective of scholars like Darko Suvin: meticulously focusing on the way SF texts evoke worlds estranged from our own, his early essays analyze SF's capacity to reference concepts and events exceeding the bounds of mundane reality – which he calls SF's "level of subjunctivity."[17] Before Delany, few critics paid substantial attention to the language of SF, aside from bemoaning the genre's tendency towards purple prose. But in the wake of studies such as Delany's *The American Shore* (1978), which microscopically interprets a short story by Thomas M. Disch in a manner akin to Roland Barthes's parsing of Balzac in *S/Z* (1970), scholars have been compelled to acknowledge that SF's ability to summon alternative worlds is linked to the unique way in which it mobilizes its linguistic resources.

This group of New Wave author-critics – Aldiss, Le Guin, Russ, and Delany – may have been the most celebrated and influential, but they were just the tip of the iceberg. Virtually every major writer associated with this movement during the 1960s and 1970s produced a significant critical discourse that was eventually gathered in book form: Barry N. Malzberg's *The Engines of*

---

[16] Joanna Russ, "The Image of Women in Science Fiction," *The Country You Have Never Seen: Essays and Reviews* (Liverpool: Liverpool University Press, 2005), p. 206–7.

[17] Samuel R. Delany, "About 5,750 Words," *The Jewel-Hinged Jaw: Notes on the Language of Science Fiction* (New York: Berkley Windhover, 1977), p. 36.

the Night (1982), Norman Spinrad's *Science Fiction in the Real World* (1990), J. G. Ballard's *A User's Guide to the Millennium* (1996), Thomas M. Disch's *The Dreams Our Stuff Is Made Of* (1998), and the multifarious nonfiction musings of Harlan Ellison. This is unsurprising given that the New Wave was very much a self-reflexive movement, driven by a powerful critique of the genre status quo. As I have remarked elsewhere,

> The New Wave, as a political and an aesthetic formation ... represented an unprecedented moment in the history of popular genres when social-critical and literary-experimental impulses converged ... Rather than endorsing a tacit consensus regarding the outcome of technoscientific progress, SF began to explore visions of alterity rooted in contemporary anthropological, psychoanalytic, and gender theory, visions frequently elaborated through experimental narrative techniques. [18]

During the period, the most prominent single platform for the articulation of these alternatives, in both fiction and criticism, was the British magazine *New Worlds*, edited by Michael Moorcock from 1964 to 1971. In particular, the writings of in-house critics M. John Harrison and John Clute broke substantial new ground in the disciplined analysis of SF. Harrison, who for some time was Books Editor for the magazine, evolved an iconoclastic and uncompromising aesthetic that demanded the highest standards from SF, driven by the premise that the genre must "be radically changed from the inside by people who will not compromise."[19]

Like Merril in the 1950s, Harrison perceived the urgent need for the field to shed the remaining vestiges of its pulp past, embracing a speculative agenda that wedded SF with the literary avant garde, and few critics were more witheringly contemptuous of authors who were content to churn out escapist adventure stories. His 1971 essay "A Literature of Comfort" decried the purveyance of "a body of warm, familiar assumptions, reiterated from book to book and serving the same purpose as 'once upon a time'" – a tendency toward formulaic hackwork that reduced the genre to "a literature of shoddy, programmed pap."[20] On the other hand, Harrison celebrated the convergence of the best New Wave

---

[18] Rob Latham, "Assassination Weapons: The Visual Culture of New Wave Science Fiction," in Kembrew McLeod and Rudolf Kuenzli, eds., *Cutting Across Media: Appropriation Art, Interventionist Collage, and Copyright Law* (Durham, NC: Duke University Press, 2011), p. 278. The New Wave as a whole is discussed from a variety of critical perspectives in Part Two of this volume, following.

[19] Christopher Fowler, "The Last Rebel: An Interview with M. John Harrison," *Foundation: The Review of Science Fiction* 23 (October 1981), p. 7.

[20] M. John Harrison, "A Literature of Comfort," in Michael Moorcock, ed., *New Worlds Quarterly #1* (New York: Berkley, 1971), p. 183. *New Worlds* magazine was converted into a quarterly anthology series with this issue.

writing – by Ballard, Disch, Russ, and John Sladek – with the trenchant literary experiments of John Barth and William S. Burroughs. His ultimate posture amounts to a radicalization of the modernist aesthetic of Merril, Blish, and Knight, pushing their aspirations for a reformed SF into pugnacious demands for wholesale revolution, a transcendence of genre entirely.[21]

By contrast, Clute steered closer to the Milford troika's internalized critique, seeking to push SF towards a greater maturity of theme and style, while at the same time remaining sensitive to the sorts of pleasures the genre characteristically affords. One of the most protean critics the field has ever produced, Clute has generated a voluminous body of essays and reviews, as well as helming the most significant work of reference ever devoted to SF: *The Encyclopedia of Science Fiction*.[22] In the early 1970s, Clute began writing criticism for *New Worlds* that acknowledged the genuine accomplishments of even minor talents, such as Keith Laumer and Ben Bova, while warmly celebrating more sophisticated efforts by the likes of Moorcock and Ellison. In fact, virtually alone among *New Worlds'* stable of reviewers, Clute perceived the New Wave as less an epochal rupture with the genre's storytelling traditions than an offshoot that remained "deeply bound to the genre which gives it sustenance."[23] Over the past five decades, no one has more searchingly or systematically canvassed the genre's vast output to locate works that stand as milestones, not so much transcending the field as inspiring it towards fresh horizons. Indeed, Clute is, in all likelihood, the most ambitious and accomplished critic that SF, as a literary/cultural institution, has ever produced.[24]

From the 1980s onward, academic scholarship on SF has mushroomed exponentially: virtually every major university press releases relevant titles, with several – Liverpool, Wesleyan, Wales, Nebraska – offering dedicated lines on the subject. In any given year, one can find well over a hundred

---

[21] For a more extensive discussion of Harrison's role as author-critic during the New Wave era, see my "A Young Man's Journey to Ladbroke Grove: M. John Harrison and the Evolution of the New Wave in Britain," in Mark Bould and Michelle Reid, eds., *Parietal Games: Critical Writings by and on M. John Harrison* (Liverpool: Science Fiction Foundation, 2005), pp. 249–64.

[22] This *Encyclopedia* has gone through three editions: two in book form (1979 and 1993), co-edited with Peter Nicholls, and the most recent (2011–) as a growing online compendium, co-edited by David Langford (with Nicholls as Editor Emeritus and Graham Sleight as Managing Editor), which contains nearly 17,000 entries and over five million words – almost a third of which were produced by Clute himself.

[23] John Clute, *Strokes: Essays and Reviews 1966–1986* (Seattle: Serconia Press, 1988), p. 80.

[24] For a fuller discussion of Clute's critical work, see my "'The Job of Dissevering Joy from Glop': John Clute's *New Worlds* Criticism," *Polder: A Festschrift for John Clute and Judith Clute*, edited by Farah Mendlesohn (Baltimore, MD: Old Earth Books, 2005), pp. 28–39.

studies of major authors, themes, and cultural trends. We have come a long way from the day when SF criticism was confined to scattered fanzines, professional review columns, and anthology prefaces. Yet it is undeniable that this recent academic blossoming owes a tremendous debt to the long tradition of critical discourse produced by SF authors, editors, and fans.

PART II

★

THE NEW WAVE

20

Riding the New Wave

ANDREW M. BUTLER

In Gardner Dozois's history of SF after the Golden Age, there is a moment when he complains that "although it was easy enough even then to prove that the New Wave as such did not exist, the public insisted on reacting as if it did exist."[1] If this opinion were entirely true, the next few pages of this book would be blank – so I will assert that there is indeed such a thing as the New Wave, perhaps even several New Waves. The temptation is to assume a linear history to the genre, such as the parodic one offered by Barry Malzberg: "the primitive twenties, wondrous and colorful thirties, systematized and optimistic forties, quiet and despairing fifties, fragmented and chaotic sixties, expressionless seventies ... "[2] This straw history claims that Hugo Gernsback and John W. Campbell created an optimistic genre that celebrated engineering and technology, in which characterization and style played a distant fourth or fifth place to ideas, the sense of wonder, and action. John Clute refers to this as "Agenda" or as "First" SF, which is "born to advocate and enthuse and teach";[3] "the result was an SF universe written in the shape of Man. Women and other aliens had visiting rights only."[4]

In the straw history, Michael Moorcock and Harlan Ellison came along in the 1960s and between them introduced the genre to formal experimentation, literary value, swearing, and sex. While there is some truth to this straw history, it oversimplifies. Moorcock and Ellison did revolutionize the genre, but largely independently – and there had certainly been literary and

---

[1] Gardner Dozois, "Beyond the Golden Age – Part II: the New Wave Years," *Thrust Science Fiction in Review* 19 (1983), p. 12.

[2] Barry Malzberg, "The Wrong Rabbit," in James Gunn and Matthew Candelaria, eds., *Speculations on Speculation: Theories of Science Fiction* (Lanham, MD: Scarecrow Press, 2005), p. 245.

[3] John Clute, *Look at the Evidence: Essays and Reviews* (Liverpool: Liverpool University Press, 1995), p. 355.

[4] Ibid., p. 130.

pessimistic SF published in genre magazines before the 1960s, most notably by Alfred Bester, Robert Sheckley, and Theodore Sturgeon. The assertion of the New Wave as a break in time is as much a matter of its own publicity as anything else; it is a time-tested tactic of revolutionaries, after all, to rubbish the values of the previous age.

Towards the New Wave

The term "New Wave" was taken from Françoise Giroud's coinage of "nouvelle vague" in 1957, which described a group of young filmmakers (including Jean-Luc Godard, Claude Chabrol, and François Truffaut) who were revolutionizing the French film industry in the late 1950s and 1960s. Perhaps the earliest SF usage was in P. Schuyler Miller's review of American editions of novels by Kenneth Bulmer and John Brunner. Miller noted that the authors had been first published by John Carnell in *New Worlds*:

> I suspect it's a moot question whether Carnell discovered the "big names" of British science fiction – Wyndham, Clarke, Russell, Christopher – or whether they discovered him. Whatever is the answer, there is no question at all about the "new wave": Tubb, Aldiss, and to get to my point, Kenneth Bulmer and John Brunner.[5]

New Worlds had started as a British fanzine, *Novae Terrae* (1936–9), changing its name when Carnell became editor. He tried to make it a professional market, but the Second World War intervened and so this only happened from 1946. In accounts of British SF, Carnell has been presented as less adventurous than he actually was.[6] He published an editorial by J. G. Ballard, who argued that "science fiction must jettison its present narrative forms and plots ... it is *inner* space, not outer, that needs to be explored."[7] Ballard was to follow this impulse through in his fiction.

A year later, Moorcock argued that most SF lacks "passion, subtlety, irony, original characterisation, original and good style, a sense of involvement in human affairs, colour, density, depth and, on the whole, real feeling from the

---

[5] P. Schuyler Miller, "The Reference Library," *Analog Science Fact and Fiction* 68, 3 (1961), p. 166.

[6] See, however, Brian Aldiss, "John Carnell: Pioneer of Science Fiction," *SFWA Bulletin* 8, 2–3 (1972), pp. 7–8 and Michael Moorcock, "On Carnell," *SFWA Bulletin* 8, 2–3 (1972), p. 9. One account of this neglected period can be found in John Boston and Damien Broderick, *Building New Worlds, 1946–1959: The Carnell Era, Volume One* (San Bernardino, CA: Borgo Press, 2012) and *New Worlds: Before the New Wave, 1960–1964: The Carnell Era, Volume Two* (San Bernardino, CA: Borgo Press, 2013).

[7] J. G. Ballard, "Which Way to Inner Space?," *New Worlds* 118 (1962), p. 117.

writer,"[8] and went on to praise the work of Aldiss, Ballard, and Brunner. All three were published by Carnell, but *New Worlds*, like the rest of the SF magazine market, was struggling. The publisher, Roberts & Vintner, more associated with adult materials, bought *New Worlds* and its sister magazine, *Science Fantasy*, thinking them routes into more respectable markets. Moorcock was offered the chance of editing either and chose *New Worlds*; book and art dealer Kyril Bonfiglioni took the other, which he edited until 1966. Carnell, who had favored continuing *New Worlds* as a paperback original, started a series of anthologies, *New Writings in SF*. In the introduction to the first, he argued that this presented

> a radical departure in the field of the science fiction short story. As the name implies, not only *new* stories written for the series as well as s-f stories which would not normally be seen by the vast majority of readers, will appear in future editions, but *new* styles, ideas, and even *new* writers who have something worth contributing to the *genre*, will be presented.[9]

Carnell was to edit twenty-one volumes, with the reins passing to Kenneth Bulmer for nine after his death. As well as stories dealing with the hard sciences, Carnell looked for those that drew on "sociology, psychology, medicine, politics, genetics, and even religion" and began preferring the term "speculative fiction" to SF.[10]

The term "new wave" was to appear in a review of the fanzine *Beyond* in the "Amateur Magazines" column of *New Worlds*: "This one also carries fiction and like ZENITH [from Peter Weston] represents the 'new wave' of SF fans – the young ones demanding more serious SF criticism in fan magazines."[11] Presumably in response, a Chris Priest column in *Zenith-Speculation* 8 entitled "New Wave Prozines," reviewing *New Worlds* and *Science Fantasy* under their new editors, argues "the fact that they are experimenting – with favourable results – should ensure that these 'new-wave' Prozines are not only encouraged through loyalty alone."[12] Priest saw Moorcock as a competent writer, Ballard as having peaked and felt that "Keith Roberts, Thom Heyes [*sic*: Keyes] and Langdon Jones show unmistakable promise in not only style and idea, but quantity too."[13] The label "New Wave" was now attached to writers who had been emerging for about a decade already.

---

[8] Michael Moorcock, "Play With Feeling," *New Worlds* 129 (1963), p. 123.
[9] John Carnell, "Foreword," *New Writings in SF 1* (London: Dobson), p. 7.
[10] Ibid., pp. 8, 9.
[11] "Amateur Magazines," *New Worlds* 145 (1964), p. 126.
[12] Chris Priest, "New Wave Prozines," *Zenith-Speculation* 8 (1964), p. 11.
[13] Ibid., p. 10.

Pop Art and Surrealism

Moorcock seemed in his editorials and his selections to want to leave generic SF behind, in part by drawing on writers and visual artists who were parasitic upon SF. Eduardo Paolozzi, for example, had included the cover of *Amazing* (February 1952) for Don Wilcox's "The Iron Men of Venus" in a series of collages, *BUNK!*, presented using an epidiascope while he grunted at the Institute for Contemporary Arts. This 1952 lecture is also credited with inspiring the term "pop art." Paolozzi had an installation, "Patio and Pavilion," with photographer Nigel Henderson and architects Alison and Peter Smithson at the *This is Tomorrow* exhibition held at the Whitechapel Art Gallery (August 9 through September 9, 1956), consisting of three walls with a plastic roof surrounding a sandpit littered with found objects, creating the sense of a post-apocalyptic world where humanity would have to scrape together an existence from the relics that had survived the collapse of civilization.

This is Tomorrow was organized by artists and architects associated with the Independent Group and both Moorcock and Ballard had visited it. In another grouping, Richard Hamilton, John McHale, and John Voelcker juxtaposed images from *Forbidden Planet*, Vincent Van Gogh's sunflowers, Marlon Brando, Marilyn Monroe, and other popular cultural images. The catalogue used a black and white version of Hamilton's collage "Just What Is It That Makes Today's Homes So Different, So Appealing?" The appropriation of actors and actresses, pop stars, space imagery, consumer goods, and politicians and the collage aesthetic was to become central to a number of British-based New Wave writers, such as Ballard, Moorcock, Thomas Disch, and John Sladek. Many New Wave writers were to abandon narrative linearity in favor of other structural systems – alphabetical order, numerical order, lists, bureaucratic forms, questionnaires, flow charts – and juxtaposed paragraphs that might not immediately relate to each other. This reached its zenith in Ballard's condensed novels, collected in *The Atrocity Exhibition* (1970).

If Moorcock wished to distance his magazine from traditional SF, Paolozzi perhaps wanted to distance himself from traditional art culture, asserting at a lecture that "It is conceivable that in 1958 a higher order of imagination exists in an SF pulp produced in the outskirts of LA than in little magazines of today."[14] Paolozzi was to be profiled by *New Worlds*'s art editor Christopher

---

[14] Quoted in Lucy R. Lippard, *Pop Art* (New York: Praeger, 1966), p. 35.

Finch: "[For] Paolozzi the anonymous beauty of technology offers a model for art."[15] Finch introduced Paolozzi to Moorcock and then he became friends with Ballard, sharing the interest in car crashes which was to emerge in Ballard's own show at the Institute for Research in Art and Technology and the novel *Crash* (1973). Paolozzi was added to the masthead of *New Worlds* as "Aeronautics Advisor," but seems to have had little input into the magazine.[16]

Ballard was also to look back to earlier art, especially surrealism, arguing that "The art of Salvador Dalí is a metaphor that embraces the 20th century."[17] Ballard saw Dalí as a true naive, who is never certain whether something is real or imagined, and not caring. Ballard also categorized H. G. Wells, modern SF writers, Andy Warhol, and William S. Burroughs as naives. The latter was the focus of Moorcock's first *New Worlds* editorial: "Burroughs's own writing techniques are as exciting – and as relevant to our present situation – as the latest discovery in nuclear physics."[18] An article by Ballard in the same issue suggests that Burroughs created "the first authentic mythology of the age of Cape Canaveral, Hiroshima and Belsen."[19] Moorcock and Ballard were to embrace Dalí and Burroughs's exploration of sexualities to differing extents, and Burroughs's cut-up and fold-in techniques may have been an influence upon Moorcock's Jerry Cornelius stories.

New Worlds vs. the Genre Ghetto

But if Moorcock's debut paired these articles with fiction from soon-to-be New Wave stalwarts Aldiss, Ballard, Brunner, and Barrington J. Bayley, subsequent issues also included more traditional work by authors such as E. C. Tubb and Sydney J. Bounds, possibly using up inventory left over from Carnell. Moorcock was leading an attempt to break out of genre SF into what was seen as the mainstream – in the era of Marshall McLuhan's global village, the space race, *Doctor Who*, Dalekmania, and ongoing fears about the bomb. In his 1963 editorial, he had pointed to Anthony Burgess and Angus Wilson as writers competing with SF from the outside, but increasingly he wanted to take the battle to them. There was a potentially larger audience outside the genre ghetto, but it was hard to reach, and in the process he risked alienating

---

[15] Christopher Finch, "Language Lessons," *New Worlds* 174 (1967), p. 35.
[16] For more on Paolozzi and the New Wave see David Brittain, *Eduardo Paolozzi at New Worlds* (Manchester: Savoy Books, 2013).
[17] J. G. Ballard, "Salvador Dalí: The Innocent as Paranoid," *New Worlds* 187 (1969), p. 25.
[18] Michael Moorcock, "A New Literature for the Space Age," *New Worlds* 142 (1964), p. 2.
[19] J. G. Ballard, "Myth Maker of the 20th Century," *New Worlds* 142 (1964), p. 127.

his readers. Sales declined, and Moorcock was forced to publish the magazine himself – which Carnell had done with other British writers before selling to Roberts & Vintner. Aldiss called upon a variety of literary names such as J. B Priestley, Marghanita Laski, and Edmund Crispin, who were sympathetic to SF, to lobby the Arts Council, and was able to get £1,800 a year to support the publication. The downside of this from a commercial point of view was that this pushed the magazine further away from the genre. Two decades later, Peter Rønnov-Jessen suggests that Moorcock felt "that fandom has changed – that the readers, the fans no longer know what's good for them . . . New Wave sf had removed itself so far from traditional sf and the tastes of the average sf reader as to alienate that reader."[20] The positioning of the magazine had moved from SF to speculative fiction to just fiction.

Take the July 1967 issue as an example, published from Moorcock's Ladbroke Grove flat with Langdon Jones as associate editor and Charles Platt as designer. The cover is an M. C. Escher woodcut, *Relativity*, tying-in with an appreciation by Platt. A new serial began – Disch's *Camp Concentration*, a Faust-inspired narrative in which the protagonist Louis Sacchetti is sent to a military prison camp where he is injected with syphilis in the hope that this will raise his intelligence. Ballard contributed a story, "The Death Module," and Disch's friend and collaborator Sladek offered "1937 A.D.," a comic story in which a loser character in 1877 invents a time machine that takes him into an alternate version of 1937 and enables him to change the past. Sladek's fiction frequently blends SF with its own parody – especially in his engagement with the robot stories of Isaac Asimov in the *Roderick* novels (1980, 1983) and *Tik Tok* (1983). Pamela Zoline's "The Heat Death of the Universe" (1967) divides into fifty-three numbered paragraphs about an unhappy Californian housewife preparing for a children's party, intercut with reflections upon the nature of entropy. In some ways it is a realist story – but it only makes sense through the scientific parallels she makes. Entropy, decay, and chaos had become a central image of the New Wave, for example in the empty swimming pools, dried-up rivers, crystallizing forests, and collapsing communities of J. G. Ballard and in the early short stories of M. John Harrison. The latter's "Running Down" (1975) centers on Lyall, whose house is surrounded by car wrecks, damaged stone walls, and corpses of animals and whose wife prematurely ages and burns to death. Boundaries were being pushed – for example, James Sallis's editorial "Orthographies" cited Colin Wilson, James Joyce, Marcel Proust, André Gide,

---

[20] Peter Rønnov-Jessen, "Science Fiction in the Marketplace," in Ib Johansen and Peter Rønnov-Jessen, eds., *Inventing the Future: Science Fiction in the Context of Cultural History and Literary Theory* (Aarhus, Denmark: Seklos, 1985), p. 88.

Harry Mathews, Donald Barthelme, John Updike, Philip Roth, Susan Sontag, Robert Creeley, Charles Olson, Robert Lowell, James Wright, Jorge Luis Borges, the Tel Quel Group, with only Sladek and Disch to represent SF.[21] The same issue included Thomas Pynchon's story "Entropy" (1969), Ballard's essay on Dalí, and Moorcock on Mervyn Peake.

England Swings SF

While in London SF was being turned inside out, the effects were being felt in the United States. In 1965, the World Science Fiction Convention had made a then rare move out of North America to Britain, for Loncon 2. Among the visitors was writer and editor Judith Merril. Born in Boston in 1923, she had become part of the Futurians fan group in New York in the 1940s and went on to write fiction on her own as well as in collaboration with C. M. Kornbluth. In 1950 she had started editing anthologies, most notably *S-F: The Year's Greatest Science-Fiction and Fantasy* from 1956 to 1968. Having met many of the authors involved in *New Worlds* and *Science Fantasy*, she wrote features on the scene for *Fantasy and Science Fiction*. Merril "became an ardent convert and began preaching the new gospel vigorously as the ultimate form of science fiction."[22] Her anthology, *England Swings SF* (1968), included several pieces by Ballard, fiction by Moorcock, Aldiss, Platt, Disch, Keith Roberts, Bonfiglioni, Zoline, Daphne Castell, Josephine Saxton, and John Calder, and poetry by George Macbeth, Michael Hamburger, Bill Butler, and Peter Redgrove, among others.

Merril suggests her title alludes to Paolozzi's print series *Moonstrips Empire News* and Finch's celebration of them; in their eyes England in general and London in particular had become an image bank as part of and counterweight to media bombardment. English culture was taking over the west. "England Swings (Like a Pendulum Do)" was a Roger Miller hit record in 1965 – although Merril rejected the pendulum comparison[23] – and the phrase "London: The Swinging City" had been used as an article title in *Time* on April 15, 1966. That magazine's cover was a collage including mini-skirts, a Mini Cooper, a Jaguar, a Rolls Royce (with John Lennon and Paul McCartney of the Beatles), a Routemaster bus, and other icons that quickly became clichés and found their way in one form or another into New Wave fiction. British Pop Artists such as Peter Blake, David Hockney, and Richard

---

[21] James Sallis, "Orthographies," *New Worlds* 187 (1969), pp. 2–7.

[22] Lester Del Rey, "Rebellion: The New Wave and Art," *Starship* 16, 4 (1979), p. 26.

[23] Editorial matter in Judith Merril, ed., *England Swings SF: An Anthology of Speculative Fiction* (New York: Ace, 1970), p. 186.

Hamilton were already making a mark on the international scene and the Beatles had cracked America in 1964, followed by the Rolling Stones, The Kinks, The Animals, and other bands. As Rønnov-Jessen notes: "The sixties saw an eruption of popular art, music, literature; expressions of working-class culture which were soon co-opted by the establishment."[24] While a younger generation was challenging the older in terms of fashion, sexuality, and coolness, it often became tied up in capitalism and appropriated by advertising and mainstream culture.

England Swings SF was presented as being controversial, especially in its Ace paperback edition, where the publisher says that they are reprinting the book "not because we are in agreement or in disagreement with it, but because we think it is part of Ace's traditional service to science fiction."[25] In the main text, Merril rarely mentions the term New Wave, rather referring to the *New Worlds* group and similar terms. Aldiss, though, argues in his comments to his "Still Trajectory," "Really, I'm no part of the new wave (don't even like their stories madly)," but Merril goes on to note that "the 'new wave' still has a magazine to publish in"[26] because of Aldiss's campaign for the Arts Council grant. Aldiss's story became part of his novel *Barefoot in the Head: A European Fantasia* (1969), which imagined a European war with weaponized psychedelic drugs and was written in the style reminiscent of James Joyce. In 1962, Aldiss had completed but failed to sell *Report on Probability A* (1968), using experimental techniques from French novels in which events are described from a variety of points of view; Moorcock published a shorter version in *New Worlds* in 1967. A versatile writer, Aldiss would return to the New Wave style in his aptly named "Enigmas" series, which appeared mainly in the Bulmer-edited volumes of *New Writings in SF*.

Dangerous Visions

Meanwhile, Harlan Ellison pushed at the genre's boundaries of style and subject matter in an anthology, *Dangerous Visions* (1967). According to del Rey, Ellison's "mission appeared to be to make science fiction relevant to the events going on around him at the time."[27] This would have included the Black Civil Rights movement and marches and speeches by Martin Luther King, Malcolm X, and others, the growing feminist movement, the increasing use of recreational drugs, the emergence of the counterculture, the Vietnam

[24] Rønnov-Jessen, "Science Fiction in the Marketplace," p. 89.
[25] Editorial matter by Donald A. Wollheim in Merril, ed., *England Swings SF*, p. 2.
[26] Editorial matter in Merril, ed., *England Swings SF*, p. 279.
[27] Del Rey, "Rebellion," p. 26.

war and protests against it and so forth. SF has always been political – Merril had been a Trotskyist in the 1940s, for example – but Ellison's editorial introductions and afterwords were pushing things further. Working with the publisher Doubleday, he was able to incorporate more swearing and representations of more graphic sex than the American magazines had.

Samuel R. Delany argues that *Dangerous Visions* "is an island of an entirely different density and structure [to *New Worlds*], with an entirely different fall-out, [which] has been hopelessly confused with the New Wave because it was more or less contemporaneous with it."[28] The British New Wave appeared in a regular venue alongside polemics, reviews, art, and articles on culture and counterculture; Ellison offered a single venture, albeit with polemical introductions and authorial afterwords. It became a series of individual performances by authors given free rein, rather than a community that was sharing inspiration. Ellison edited a second volume, *Again, Dangerous Visions* (1970) with a new set of writers, and intended to include other active SF writers not in the first two volumes in a third, *Last Dangerous Visions*. (Evidently a Sisyphean task, this did not appear before Ellison's death in 2018.)

Dangerous Visions included thirty-three stories, with Aldiss, Ballard, Brunner, and Sladek from the *New Worlds* group, and a number of America-based authors including Poul Anderson, Lester del Rey, Philip José Farmer, and Fritz Leiber. Philip K. Dick's story, "Father of Our Fathers" could be taken as exemplary. He had started publishing in the 1950s, but was rarely published in the Gernsback–Campbell pulps such as *Astounding* and *Amazing*. A cut-down version of *Time Out of Joint* (1959) appeared in the Carnell *New Worlds* as a serial, and John Brunner had called Dick "The most consistently brilliant SF writer in the world"[29] – but he was not part of the New Wave. Most of Dick's fiction dealt with the question of the nature of reality and what it meant to be human, and frequently used mass media, hallucinogenic drugs, and evil corporations as part of his narrative tool box. Ellison wanted a story about drugs, ideally written while on drugs, and Dick produced a narrative in which the Chinese rule a world subdued by drugs. The protagonist, Tung Chien, has taken an illegal anti-hallucinogen that may have allowed him to see the real, alien, leader, or possibly to see God. While Dick had occasionally taken LSD and frequently used amphetamines, the story did more to cement his reputation as drug-crazed than anything else.

---

[28] Samuel R. Delany, "Reflections on Historical Models in Modern English Language Science Fiction," *Science Fiction Studies* 7, 2 (1980), p. 137.

[29] John Brunner, "The Work of Philip K. Dick," *New Worlds* 166 (1966), p. 142.

The two most important stories in *Again, Dangerous Visions*, a collection of forty-six stories by forty writers, were both by women. Ursula K. Le Guin's "The Word for World is Forest" was inspired by both her opposition to the war in Vietnam and her knowledge of aggression against indigenous people. She had already been publishing for a decade, becoming associated with what became called soft science fiction – more interested in sociology and psychology than in physics and chemistry. Joanna Russ had been selling stories for a similar amount of time, and her "When It Changed" depicted a member of an all-female society meeting her first man. It won the Hugo and Nebula awards, and was a prequel to the not-yet-published *The Female Man* (1975), a feminist showpiece that embraced New-Wave-style fragmentation, multiple points of view, and challenges to normative sexualities. In 1976, Moorcock was to give a rather mixed review to *Again*, arguing that the writers usually associated with the New Wave have been represented by uncharacteristically tame materials, whereas the old guard had experimented. *Again* "stands as a monument to the sf genre at a time when it is in a state of metamorphosis ... No other popular genre has such a monument, possibly because messianism is an integral part of the sf writer's temperament."[30]

The New Wave Dissipates

By then, *New Worlds* was again on the verge of collapse. The third part of a serialization of Norman Spinrad's *Bug Jack Barron* and Langdon Jones's "The Eye of the Lens," in which a woman argues with the crucified Christ, both appeared in the March 1968 issue, and led to complaints about the Arts Council sponsoring filth. John Menzies and W. H. Smith, the two major British magazine wholesalers and retailers, refused to stock *New Worlds*. Moorcock turned to writing more novels to subsidize the magazine, but the situation became hopeless when the Arts Council finally stopped its grant. Issue 200 was the last to be publicly distributed, with a further issue sent to subscribers. Moorcock, meanwhile, negotiated with Sphere to produce *New Worlds* as a quarterly paperback, although this schedule was not maintained. *New Worlds* 10 (1976) was the last to appear; only five issues appeared in magazine format between 1978 and 1979. This unhappy transition perhaps marks the end of the New Wave.

Experimental and groundbreaking fiction was appearing elsewhere. Original anthologies such as Robert Hoskins's *Infinity* (1970–3), Harry

---

[30] Michael Moorcock, "A Fiercer Hen," *New Society* 37, 721 (1976), p. 244.

Harrison's *Nova* (1970–4), Robert Silverberg's *New Dimensions* (1971–81), and Terry Carr's *Universe* (1971–87) all feature stories closer to *New Worlds* and *Dangerous Visions* in spirit than to *Astounding*. Damon Knight's *Orbit* (1966–80) soon acquired a reputation for its literary qualities and a number of the stories – Richard McKenna's "The Secret Place" (1966), Richard Wilson's "Mother to the World" (1968), Kate Wilhelm's "The Planners" (1968), and Robert Silverberg's "Passengers" (1968) – won Nebula Awards. Wilhelm appeared regularly, along with R. A. Lafferty and Gene Wolfe. Meanwhile, Delany edited four volumes of an anthology *QUARK/* (1970–1) with his wife, the poet Marilyn Hacker, featuring work by Bailey, Brunner, Disch, Harrison, Lafferty, Platt, Priest, Russ, Saxton, Sladek, and others, along with poetry. But *QUARK/* was met with some hostility and the publisher ended the series.

Not everyone welcomed the New Wave – some of the hostile writers ironically referred to themselves as Old Wave, while, as I have already said, several of the names associated with it rejected the label. In June 1968, *Galaxy* published two petitions, one against and the other in favor of the Vietnam War, with the old guard predominately supporting the war.[31] There was a risk of battle lines being drawn up. John J. Pierce started a fanzine, *Renaissance*, to attack the New Wave – and in his introduction to *Nebula Award Stories 4*, Poul Anderson insisted that "science fiction . . . remains more interested in the glamour and mystery of existence, the survival and tragedy of heroes and thinkers, than in the neuroses of some snivelling fagot,"[32] an apparent sideswipe at the New Wave.

The New Wave's Novelty

The New Wave editors trumpeted novelty, and Gardner Dozois argues that "the new writers were, literally and demographically, new people."[33] The tendency brought new people into writing SF; some of whom were never to appear again. David I. Masson abandoned fiction after his collection *The Caltraps of Time* (1968) – the first story of which, "Traveller's Rest" (1965), had been a huge influence on *New Worlds* writers, being set in an apocalyptic war with the characters experiencing time distortions. Anna Ostrowska's "Time Machine" (1976) can be seen as a rewrite of early *Doctor Who* stories in

---

[31] See Chapter 26, "New Wave Science Fiction and the Vietnam War."
[32] Poul Anderson, "Introduction," Poul Anderson, ed., *Nebula Award Stories 4* (London: Panther, 1971), p. 7.
[33] Dozois, "Beyond the Golden Age," p. 12.

a naive tone – she does not seem to have published since. Some contributors were wives, girlfriends, or acquaintances of the editorial team – "Period Piece" (1968) was written by J. M. Rose, Sallis's wife – and some contributors (especially Moorcock) used pseudonyms.

Del Rey argued that there had been "an influx of new writers who were generally totally disenchanted with science or the idea that there was a bright future of progress ahead,"[34] leading to a pessimistic tone in the narratives, an embrace of downbeat endings, and perhaps an anti-establishment politics. More importantly, "the writers were *primarily* interested in writing as a thing in itself."[35] The SF writers of the 1930s, 1940s, and arguably the 1950s had training in the sciences or engineering, but the new generation – who had of course grown up reading SF – more often had backgrounds in so-called soft sciences or the humanities. As early as 1964 Carnell argued that "One didn't have to have a degree in English Lit to understand for example what Edgar Rice Burroughs was writing about,"[36] implying you needed one to understand William S. Burroughs.

Del Rey records that in the period "a great many women began writing and achieving success in science fiction. To pick only a few of many names, there were Marion Zimmer Bradley, Ursula K. Le Guin, Anne McCaffrey, Vonda N. McIntyre, Joanna Russ, Pamela Sargent and Kate Wilhelm . . . Of all the changes going on in the field, this evolution was probably the healthiest and most promising for the future."[37] Many of these writers had broken through before the New Wave(s), although they found greater success in the 1970s. *New Worlds* rarely explored feminist ideas, with women appearing as goddesses or anima figures, objectified – Jacqueline Kennedy, Marilyn Monroe, or the Mona Lisa were just symbolic. Zoline was one exception to this blind spot, but she produced only a handful of stories. Saxton went on to write a couple of feminist SF novels and collections, but was largely silent in the genre after the mid-1980s.

Then, as now, SF was dominated by white writers. Moorcock's characters might change ethnicity between books or chapters – compare Jerry Cornelius in *The Final Programme* (1968) with *A Cure for Cancer* (1971) and Karl Glogauer in *Breakfast in the Ruins* (1972) – but there is a sense that this is as much for shock value as real insights into Black British identity. Delany was one of the few African-American genre writers of the period, but he rejected the New

[34] Del Rey, "Rebellion," p. 25.
[35] Ibid.
[36] Charles Platt, "Interview with John Carnell," *Beyond* 4 (1964), p. 4.
[37] Del Rey, "Rebellion," p. 28.

Wave label, arguing he was "sympathetic to [it] but not connected with it in any real way."[38] Delany had begun publishing at the start of the 1960s with Ace, with his intellectual interests and ethnic and sexual identities pushing him into more challenging work. His story "Aye, and Gomorrah" (1967) appeared in *Dangerous Visions*, and "Time Considered as a Helix of Semi-Precious Stones" (1968) appeared in *New Worlds*. His novel *Dhalgren* (1975) may not have been possible without New Wave iconoclasm – but he was looking outside the genre to Joyce's *Finnegans Wake* (1939) and other European experimental writers for his models.

Delany's fiction also included explicitly homosexual and bisexual characters, which had been rare but not unknown in magazine SF before 1960 and usually operated on the level of hints and connotations. A number of obscenity trials on both sides of the Atlantic – *Howl* in 1957, *Lady Chatterley's Lover* in 1960, *Naked Lunch* in 1966, *Last Exit to Brooklyn* in 1968 – found in favor of free speech and literary merit over censorship. Publishers could be braver in what they published. Del Rey noted "there was a rash of sex in science fiction, along with a 'daring' use of four-letter words."[39] Barry Malzberg, for example, in his deconstruction of the astronaut identity, included homosexuality in *Beyond Apollo* (1972) and *The Sodom and Gomorrah Business* (1974), while Ballard featured both straight and gay intercourse in *Crash*, his exploration of the erotics of technology in the form of the automobile.

The New Wave Legacy

One result of the New Wave was a growing academic acceptance of SF. *Foundation* (1972–) and *Science Fiction Studies* (1973–) were initially dominated by articles on proto-SF, New Wave works, and soft SF. Just as the Science Fiction Writers of America were honoring New Wave writers with Nebulas, they were also shortlisting mainstream authors such as Italo Calvino, Thomas Pynchon, and E. L. Doctorow on the ballots in the mid-1970s.

But the genre was moving on. Gernsback and Campbell, the architects of Agenda SF, had died in 1967 and 1971, and their influence had waned. In Britain there might have been more professional SF writers than ever before – but there was no regular magazine until the 1980s when a collective of editors set up *Interzone*. They enjoyed the relative freedom of book

[38] Delany, "Reflections on Historical Models," p. 137.
[39] Del Rey, "Rebellion," p. 28.

publication. Some of the *New Worlds* writers also appeared in *Interzone* – Aldiss, Ballard, Disch, Platt, among others – and some of the stories shared the New Wave's pop art aesthetic. Along the way it nurtured a new generation of writers – Stephen Baxter, Kim Newman, Keith Brooke – and helped pave the way for the British SF boom of the late 1990s and 2000s. The title *New Worlds* was resurrected by David S. Garnett for a series of original anthologies (1991–7).

Ballard achieved mainstream respectability with *Empire of the Sun* (1984), a novel which for some critics retrospectively explained his choice of images in his 1960s and 1970s SF. Moorcock maintained his countercultural edge, mixing Eternal Champion titles with the richly mythic Colonel Pyat quartet (1981–2006). Aldiss worked tirelessly as an anthologist, especially for Penguin, produced *Billion Year Spree: The True History of Science Fiction* (1972) – later expanded and reissued as *Trillion Year Spree* (1986) – and wrote novels that engaged with SF's history, *Frankenstein Unbound* (1973) and *Moreau's Other Island* (1980).

Meanwhile in America, Le Guin had emerged as a major talent – with *The Left Hand of Darkness* (1969) and *The Dispossessed: An Ambiguous Utopia* (1975), alongside other female writers such as Suzy McKee Charnas, C. J. Cherryh, James Tiptree Jr., and Joanna Russ. While their work was rarely experimental in form, the New Wave had freed up the possibility of political subject matter and sociological speculation, allowing fictional explorations of second wave feminism and paving the way for examinations of gender. The 1970s became an era of ideological exploration – with films such as *A Boy and His Dog* (1976), *Silent Running* (1972), *Slaughterhouse-Five* (1972), *Soylent Green* (1973), and *THX 1138* (1971) packing political and emotional punches rather than offering escapist fantasies. The director of the latter, George Lucas, would later direct *Star Wars* (1977), which returned to the values, iconography and plot of *Buck Rogers, Flash Gordon*, and the 1920s pulps, without the aesthetic values of pop art. *Star Wars* and the revived *Star Trek* would set the template for SF blockbusters which were consolatory rather than experimental.

The next attempt to shake up the genre from within was cyberpunk – with Bruce Sterling becoming the Moorcock to William Gibson's Ballard. Sterling's 1980s editorials were clear about their debt for ideas to Ballard and the New Wave, as well as to William S. Burroughs and Alfred Bester, for prose style to Raymond Chandler, and for narrative to Dashiell Hammett. On the other hand, very little of the fiction in the seminal anthology *Mirrorshades* (1986) is actually cyberpunk, and by then Sterling was already declaring the movement dead. Even so, as computers moved into our homes and onto our phones, the media landscape imagined in the 1960s became even more central to SF.

Arthur Byron Cover argues that "the term New Wave was and is only a verbal handle, enabling the critic to grab hold of a sieve through which he can pour the sandy water of his own observations."[40] There was certainly no single New Wave with an unambiguous meaning, although the attempt to fix a definition can cast an interpretative light on a given text. It probably was not even the dominant subgenre for SF readers in the 1960s. Delany recalls a memorable conversation in 1966 with Langdon Jones in which the latter outlined the traditional conventions of SF – a single man can change history, the universe is hospitable, and greater intelligence can solve greater problems – and "I had never before realized [that] they *were* genre conventions."[41] In questioning its basic assumptions in the New Wave period – whatever else the New Wave's larger legacy – SF was at the least refreshed and renewed.

[40] Arthur Byron Cover, "Cathedrals in Inner Space," *New York Review of Science Fiction* 3, 3 (1990), p. 8.
[41] Delany, "Reflections on Historical Models," p. 136.

21

New Wave Science Fiction and the Counterculture

SHANNON DAVIES MANCUS

In 1962, J. G. Ballard declared Golden Age SF defunct, presaging the rise of an avant-garde style that would come to be called New Wave. In an essay published in *New Worlds* – a serial SF magazine that would eventually become the flagship publication of the new mode – Ballard called for a paradigm shift, saying: "I think science fiction should turn its back on space, on interstellar travel, extraterrestrial life forms, galactic wars and the overlap of these ideas that spread across the margins of nine-tenths of magazine s-f . . . [the] biggest developments of the immediate future will take place, not on the Moon or Mars, but on Earth, and it is *inner space*, not outer, that needs to be explored. The only truly alien planet is Earth."[1]

Shortly after Ballard's declaration, a generation burnt out on wars, a militarized space race, and the stale narratives of the mainstream gained cultural, social, and political prominence, especially in the United States as well as in Allied Europe. In the United States, twenty million individuals turned eighteen between 1964 and 1970. A demand from industry for college-educated workers meant that a large part of this population became concentrated on campuses. The number of college degrees given out in the United States doubled between 1956 and 1967. Postwar economic abundance meant that many middle-class (mostly white) youth in that generation also had means with which to enjoy their leisure time while they were located in institutions of higher learning. A transnational counterculture emerged that fundamentally challenged the politics, culture, and ideology of the generation which came before it.

Countercultural figures and fellow travelers – including New Wave SF writers – were experiencing a master narrative fatigue. The stories that guided morality seemed not only stale, but dangerous. The bloody battles

---

[1] Reprinted in J. G Ballard, *A User's Guide to the Millennium: Essays and Reviews* (New York: Picador USA, 1996), p. 197.

of the civil rights movement and the Vietnam War gave lie to the idea that the United States and Allied powers were unmitigated forces for good in the world. The government and big business were not to be trusted. On the domestic front, old scripts about social roles seemed broken, as second- and third-wave feminism and the Stonewall uprising followed on the heels of the civil rights movement. Similarly, Golden Age SF plots seemed mired in stale – and potentially dangerous – ways of thinking. Tales of conquest echoed cultural narratives that justified imperialism. Science seemed either malignant – a tool of imperialist militaries – or otherwise naive, with fantasies of space exploration quickly reimagined as a new front in the Cold War, and space technology becoming yet another military tool. Authority of all types was under question, and not only new narratives, but new styles and forms were needed to capture the shifting intellectual zeitgeist. Colin Greenland, citing a film that claimed that "the moon belonged to the poets as long as it was out of reach," notes that "after 1969, not only was it within reach, but it had already been processed, converted into a golf-course, and littered with the remains of disposable gadgets."[2] Not only poets, but increasingly literary SF writers and youth movements at large needed a new domain through which to explore meaning, and it was largely to inner space that they turned.

The rejection of intergalactic adventure in favor of interstitial analysis constitutes a rebellion against stale generic conventions as well as the narratives that had guided the cultural zeitgeist up to the breaking point from which the counterculture emerged. New Wave writers, though they varied in age, were part of a cohort on an ontological precipice. A key part of this shared consciousness shift was the perception that enlightenment era thinking and "rational" politics had failed. A generation entering their teen-age years in the early 1960s looked around and saw their elders – the same bloc of people who expressed disgust and worry over the complicity of "good Germans" in the Second World War – turning a blind eye to the neglectful or egregious actions of the government toward the civil rights movement, endorsing the escalating American deployment to the front lines of the Vietnam War, and supporting leaders engaged in nuclear brinksmanship that threatened the very existence of life on the planet. Many saw the threat of "mutually assured destruction" and nuclear winter as more than just an existential threat; they saw it as evidence of the failure of the ethics of science, the effectiveness of traditionally democratic and liberal politics, and even

---

[2] Colin Greenland, *The Entropy Exhibition: Michael Moorcock and the British "New Wave" in Science Fiction* (London; Boston: Routledge & Kegan Paul, 1983), p. 46.

a failure of "rationality" itself. By the mid-1960s, many perceived the world to be on a precipice in which the boundaries of pre-existing notions of reality itself were up for grabs. Darko Suvin predicates the process of cognitive estrangement on the device of a "novum," which is a trope that is so radically outside our previous frame of reference that it compels us to break with what we know about reality and look at society anew. The imminent threat of nuclear holocaust may be considered a novum for the countercultural generation, who became cognitively estranged from the culture that they grew up in to such an extent that Ballard's statement that "the only true alien planet is Earth" rang true for many. That ontological shift necessitated the exploration of "inner space." New Wave SF proved an apt medium for this cognitively estranged population.

One of the first SF stories to deconstruct the failings of Western culture and to propose mind expansion and the collective unconscious as an antidote was Robert Heinlein's *Stranger in a Strange Land* (1961). Published around the same time as Ballard's essay declaring Earth alien and calling for a turn to inner space, *Stranger* won a Hugo Award and steadily grew in popularity over the course of the decade, necessitating a second printing in 1968 when it became fairly ubiquitous on college campuses. The novel follows the life and death of Michael Valentine Smith, the infant survivor of a failed human expedition to Mars. Retrieved from the red planet when he is twenty-five, Smith is rescued from the nefarious unified government that has coalesced after World War III. He learns about humanity from sensitive humans who eventually become his religious followers, and eventually imports Martian sensibilities to the wider world through a church he leads before he is stoned to death and ascends to heaven as an archangel. Throughout the book, the reader is coaxed to see the strangeness of humanity through the stranger Smith, and to identify with an alien morality that promoted alternative models for sexuality, altered consciousness, and new forms of spirituality. Much to the surprise and slight dismay of the author, many took the book as a script rather than as an intellectual excursion. The verb "to grok" entered the countercultural lexicon to describe the feeling of understanding something or someone so deeply as to almost become one with it. In Haight-Ashbury, groups took the community Smith forms as a model for their own pseudo-religious "nests," which were largely nudist communes that engaged in free sexuality. This includes "the Church of All Worlds," which gained official recognition as a religion in 1970 and persists to this day.

Though the topics that *Stranger* tackled were radical for its time, it was fairly traditional in structure. As SF continued to tackle topics of cultural relevance, many writers felt that traditional narrative storytelling was not up to the task – that the journey into inner space needed new forms of transport. Even before the New Wave emerged as a force, Ballard asserted that traditional forms of communication were not adequately suited unpacking a new reality and urged SF writers to abandon traditional narrative structure, lamenting, "I've often wondered why s-f shows so little of the experimental enthusiasm which has characterized painting, music and the cinema during the last four or five decades, particularly as these have become more whole-heartedly speculative, more and more concerned with the creation of new states of mind, constructing fresh symbols and languages where the old cease to be valid."[3]

The question of the creation of new states of mind was a vital one for the rejuvenation of the genre and – some felt – for the preservation of the species as atomic and environmental dangers loomed. Popular culture absorbed the weight of these fears and anxiety about the inability to change dominant ways of thinking. In 1965, the song "Eve of Destruction," written by P. F. Sloan and recorded by Barry McGuire, made the Billboard top 100. The anthemic song urges the listener to consider the dire consequences of continued complicity by couching stanzas that enumerate reasons for terror within the repetition of a chorus that accuses the listener of a break between cognition and reality. For example, some of the first lyrics invoke the obvious threat of nuclear war:

> Don't you understand, what I'm trying to say?
> And can't you feel the fear that I'm feeling today?
> If the button is pushed, there's no running away
> There'll be no one to save with the world in a grave

before admonishing the listener with what becomes the song's refrain:

> But you tell me over and over and over again my friend
> Ah, you don't believe we're on the eve of destruction.

The song goes beyond naming obvious frustration with the threat of atomic warfare to linking (albeit problematically) global racism and disillusionment with the promise of space exploration:

> Think of all the hate there is in Red China!
> Then take a look around to Selma, Alabama!
> Ah, you may leave here, for eight days in space
> But when you return, it's the same old place . . .

---

[3] Ballard, *A User's Guide*, p. 197.

And you tell me over and over and over and over again my friend
Ah, you don't believe we're on the eve of destruction.

The song, at mid-decade, gave voice to a nascent feeling in the counter-culture that a shift in global consciousness and the breaking of tired and dangerous thought patterns – "you tell me *over* and *over* and *over* and *over* again" – were needed to combat or avoid further mass atrocities. It makes sense, then, that in searching for forms appropriate to this task, counter-culture figures such as Abby Hoffman and the Diggers in San Francisco and New Wave writers such as Judith Merril and J. G. Ballard looked to other artistic movements that had rejected canonical methodologies in search of new realities which might prove less violent than the "real world." In particular, writers such as Thomas Pynchon and Ken Kesey drew inspira-tion from creative figures who had rejected master narratives after major wars, including the Dadaists and surrealists, who had sought to deconstruct dominant narratives after the mass casualties of WWI, and the Beats, who had critiqued post-WWII American culture. From the practices of post-WWI avant-garde artistic movements, New Wave writers like Merril, Pamela Zoline, and Giles Gordon sampled methodologies such as textual collaging: the surrealists believed that odd juxtapositions and rearrangements of sym-bols reveal more about the original subject of inquiry than the narratively unified whole, and that exploring the subconscious creates a kind of cognitive estrangement that allows for a break with old, violent forms of thinking and creates new realities. Drawing inspiration from the Beats, New Wave authors echoed themes of sexual experimentation, a substance-fueled methodology, and an antagonism to the idea of the American Dream that had been predicated on consumption and sold to the parents of the baby boomer generation.

Like the artistic counterculture movements that the nascent literary style drew from, there was strong institutional pushback against iconoclasm of form. This necessitated alternative outlets for publication and advocates who gave their time, money, and energy to champion new forms of SF. Chief among them, perhaps, was Michael Moorcock, who took over the publica-tion of *New Worlds* in London in 1964, and made it an outlet for controversial ideas and experiments in form, despite constant threats of bankruptcy and censorship. Under Moorcock's tenure, SF authors pushed the boundaries of form, playing with hybridizing genres from poetry, to screenwriting, to drawing. "The Four-Colour Problem" by Barrington Bailey, for example, not only switches between traditional narratives, illustrative schematics, and technical writing but also advocates for alternative reading practices of the text: a heading declaring the start of "Technical Section (II)" is marked with a star that directs the reader to an author's note that reads, "Readers who are uninterested in mathematics may omit this section without much loss."

J. G. Ballard himself, Moorcock's New Wave standard-bearer, was heavily influenced by the surrealists, claiming that Ernst and Dali had painted the vaunted inner space of his advocated artistic trajectory. Later, anthologist Judith Merril would employ surrealism in the structure of an anthology of stories by British New Wave authors (many of whom were originally published in *New Worlds*) by creating biographies of sorts for the authors by collaging together bits of texts culled from different sources.

In 1967, Harlan Ellison managed, after haggling with publishers and authors and investing quite a bit of his own money, to publish *Dangerous Visions*, an anthology of thirty-two original stories. The stories are meant to be "dangerous" in both form and content, and many harken back to earlier avant-garde techniques. In an introduction to his work, Harlan Ellison describes the work of David R. Bunch as "dada-like," and his story "Incident in Moderan" – which largely focuses on the conversation between a belligerent robot and weeping flesh blob on either side of a barricade planted in an immense plastic field – is a Tanguy-esque apocalyptic vision indeed. Elsewhere in the volume, the much-lauded "Riders of the Purple Wage" – the longest short story in the collection, which shared the Hugo Award for best novella that year – characterizes the subconscious, as the protagonist, Chib, does somnolent battle with "giants" called Un and Sub, as his sentient serpentine member ventures autonomously forth from the bed. The author, Philip José Farmer, elsewhere intrudes on the narrative with poetry that illuminates an event, and even with poetic lines that mimic the action being described:

> ... And then he and his crew and his
> ship
> Dip and hurtle headlong over
> The edge of the world
> And from what I hear, they are still
>
> f
> a
> l
> l
> i
> n
> g

It was not just SF authors, but other facets of the counterculture as well, that were repurposing the ideas of the post-First World War avant-garde. Groups like the Diggers, who were performative radicals who operated as a collective in Haight-Ashbury from 1968 to 1969, took direct inspiration from the Dadaists and surrealists: they constructed a huge square "Frame of Reference" that they encouraged people to walk through, burned money, and ran a "store" full of "liberated" products. Of the Diggers, Todd Gitlin notes that they "derived the precedent of artists injecting art like some wild drug into the veins of society; from the civil rights movement came the as-if, the idea of forcing the future by living in it, as if the obstacles, brought to a white heat, could be made to melt."[4]

This idea of counter-realities being drug-like in their ability to force people out of old patterns of thinking also functioned in the inverse. Figures such as Timothy Leary, Aldous Huxley, Ken Kesey, and the Merry Pranksters, who advocated for the literal ingestion of drugs in order to create powerful alternative consciousnesses, made arguments for experimentation that gained traction with the counterculture. The tradition of substance use and abuse in the writing process is certainly older than the Beats, but those particular iconoclastic proto-counterculture icons had direct influence on the artistic movements that would follow. William S. Burroughs, noted heroin addict and hero of many in the avant-garde in the 1960s, had previously dubbed himself "an explorer of psychic areas . . . a cosmonaut of inner space" and was an oft-cited inspiration to many New Wave writers as they began to develop psychedelic lines of inquiry.[5]

The attainment of altered states of consciousness through intoxicants or psychotropic substances was a thread from Beat culture that the nascent Hippie movement continued, receiving a boost as LSD became available. Initially used in university and government tests – most famously by Dr. Timothy Leary of Harvard – the psychotropic was readily available on the street by 1966. For a while the drug was legal, easy to transport, and cost effective: a dose that cost two or three dollars would trigger a trip that lasted eight to twelve hours.

In his book *The Electric Kool-Aid Acid Test* (1968), Tom Wolfe describes his adventures on the road with Ken Kesey and the Merry Pranksters, as they traveled around Mexico and the United States from 1963 through 1966. Kesey, author of *One Flew Over the Cuckoo's Nest* (1962) and mischievous advocate of

[4] Todd Gitlin, *The Sixties: Years of Hope, Days of Rage* (New York: Bantam Books, 1987), p. 224.
[5] Quoted in Greenland, *Entropy*, p. 57.

acid, preached about the power of the drug as a consciousness-changing agent as he and his band of counterculture provocateurs traveled in their school bus called *Further*. Wolfe's style, which combined reportage with literary flourishes and came to be known as "New Journalism," was especially apt for capturing the experience of the drug trips that were central to the Merry Prankster's exploits, as he experimented with intersubjective narration. Among Wolfe's observations of the psychedelic proto-hippies was the presence of the text *Stranger in a Strange Land*, and the ways in which the Merry band functioned like a "nest" as presented in Heinlein's vision, by living communally, engaging in alternative sexual arrangements, and seeking out a collective unconscious through the use of psychotropics.

Stranger in a Strange Land also continued to be popular on college campuses, where drug use flourished among students and activists. Todd Gitlin, the one-time president of Students for a Democratic Society and eventual author of *The Sixties: Years of Hope, Days of Rage*, describes how drugs – even the relatively tame psychotropic properties of marijuana – seemingly altered the perception of all aspects of reality, and caused radical shifts in thought patterns. He recalls that "Light took on properties of its own: take a look through this prism, this kaleidoscope, check out the color TV ... Stoned consciousness darted, flowed, went where it wanted to go, freed of rectilinear purpose and instruction. Routine talk seemed laughable; weird juxtaposition made perfect sense, sense made no sense at all ... just as anything you looked at, really looked at, might be transfigured in the seeing."[6] Gitlin claims that, initially, many of the people manufacturing drugs like LSD were not doing so purely for a profit motive, but instead distributed pure product at reasonable prices (and often gave free samples) because they "fancied themselves dispensers of miracles at the service of a new age" and saw themselves as distributing a vehicle for social change – and perhaps even world revolution.[7]

New Wave writers such as Philip K. Dick and Thomas M. Disch were interested in the juxtapositions caused by drug use in much the same way that they were drawn by surrealist ideals and methodologies. The idea of piercing the veil of the dominant reality in order to understand the cultural unconscious manifested itself in different ways. First, writers used psychotropics as a tool for story writing. For example, in his introduction to Philip K. Dick's short story "Faith of our Fathers," Ellison disclosed that he had

---

[6] Gitlin, *The Sixties*, p. 202.
[7] Gitlin, *The Sixties*, p. 214.

commissioned a piece by Dick to be written specifically under the influence of LSD, and that this short story is indeed a product of an acid trip. After holding court about how much art produced under the influence is dreck, he praises Dick as the exception to the rule, though he admits he doesn't know how usefully his example extends. "All I can venture is that the proper administration of mind-expanding drugs might open whole new areas to the creative intellect. Areas that have been, till now, the country of the blind."[8] The story is about a dystopic future in which a man, Tung Chien, is given what he believes to be harmless snuff that he was sold by a veteran peddler who is later revealed to be part of a resistance movement against the government. The "snuff" turns out to be an anti-hallucinogen that allows him to see that the Supreme Leader of the republic in which he lives is a hallucinatory byproduct of a drugged water supply. He reluctantly begins to cooperate with the resistance as they help him pass a rigged ideology test, which allows him to attain a higher government rank and be invited to the Supreme Leader's house. There, he encounters the being that pretends to be the Supreme Leader which he, under the influence of anti-hallucinogens once more, perceives to be God – an omnipotent, evil, draining force that denies him even the satisfaction of suicide. The grim tale plays with the boundaries of perception to a degree which prompts Ellison to note that if the story "doesn't nibble away at your sense of reality a little bit . . . check your pulse. You may be dead."[9] This was far from the only drug-themed exploration undertaken by Dick: many of his well-regarded works, including *A Scanner Darkly*, *Now Wait for Last Year*, and *Flow my Tears, The Policeman Said* feature drug use as a prominent plot device.

In addition to writing under the influence, many New Wave narrators also speculated about possible futures in which drugs play a significant role in the shaping of societies. Short stories such as "Multi-value Motorway" by Brian Aldiss and "No Direction Home" by Norman Spinrad took up the subject of a drug-centered culture after the potential popularity of this subject had been proven in 1965 by what would eventually come to be called the world's bestselling SF novel, *Dune*. In this popular and critically acclaimed novel, which was the first in a long series, the young protagonist Paul Atreides becomes embroiled in the battle to control the planet of Arrakis, home to *melange*, also known as "spice," a mind-enhancing drug that is the most valuable substance in the universe of the series. Various forms of ancient

---

[8] Harlan Ellison, ed., *Dangerous Visions: Thirty-three Original Stories* (Garden City, NY: Doubleday, 1967), p. 174.
[9] Ibid.

wisdom allow Atreides to become prescient, and he matures over the course of the novel into a messianic figure. A few years later, after LSD had been outlawed and the New Left had fallen apart, Brian W. Aldiss offered his own take on christological sensitivities in a universe where those who control drugs control reality with *Barefoot in the Head* (1969). The novel, which Adam Roberts has called an "exercise in exuberant drug-influenced surrealism," features a narrator who rises to the status of hallowed crusader but subsequently becomes increasingly muddled because of the hallucinogenic fallout from the weaponized psychotropics of the "Acid Head War."[10] This dark turn echoes the increasing prevalence of bad trips and the growing opposition to war. As the decade progressed, the youth population became more and more estranged from an increasingly troubling reality.

Whereas the beginning of the decade had provided an "alien" avatar for disaffected youth in the figure of Valentine Michael Smith from *Stranger in a Strange Land*, the end of the decade saw a new mass publication that featured a super-powered being from space that looked at the human race with a mixture of awe, dismay, and disgust. In 1968, Marvel released the first issue of *The Silver Surfer*, and the comic book soon became popular on college campuses.[11] The titular character – a silvery, bald, masculine, humanoid figure who traverses space on a cosmic surfboard – first debuted in an issue of the *Fantastic Four* in March 1966 as a herald for the villain Galactus, who sustained himself by eating inhabited planets. Stan Lee, the story's creator was initially confused when he noticed the addition of the offbeat form of transportation, prompting illustrator Jack Kirby to explain that he put the herald on a surfboard because he was "tired of drawing spaceships" (New Wave authors were apparently not the only population fatigued by certain tropes).

In the first issue, the Silver Surfer's backstory is revealed. Before he was granted cosmic powers, he lived as Norrin Radd on the planet Zenn-La. It is not an accident that the name of Radd's home world invokes the idea of mystical peace, as the beings there had ostensibly reached the peak of civilization, living in harmony. Nonetheless, Radd is restless, romanticizing the striving and exploration of earlier epochs in ways that are illegible to his

---

[10] Adam Roberts, *The History of Science Fiction* (Basingstoke and New York: Palgrave Macmillan, 2006), p. 247.

[11] As Ramzi Fawaz, has demonstrated, comics in the countercultural era provided ample opportunities to use cognitive estrangement to generate affinity for those considered outside the boundaries and definitions of personhood. See Ramzi Fawaz, *The New Mutants: Superheroes and the Radical Imagination of American Comics* (New York: New York University Press, 2016).

fellow citizens. When a malevolent force invades Zenn-La, he sees his opportunity and volunteers to act as emissary, only to encounter the God-like being Galactus, who is intent on consuming the planet. Radd bargains with him: he will serve as herald to Galactus, seeking out alternative planets to consume. He leaves behind his lover, Shalla-Bal, is infused with "Power Cosmic," and sets off, eventually encountering Earth and rebelling against Galactus's plans to destroy it. As punishment, Galactus creates a barrier around Earth which prevents the Silver Surfer from leaving the immediate vicinity of the planet, making him a captive witness to the disappointments of a species he sacrificed to save.

For the duration of the eighteen-issue series, Lee used the Surfer as a mouthpiece to meditate on the failings of human nature and the path civilization was taking. Readers are meant to identify with the Surfer's assessments as he is repeatedly cast out of human civilization for being different, and therefore potentially dangerous. Unlike the "otherness" of Smith in *Stranger*, the ostracizing of the Surfer often took on racial overtones. In issue five ("And Who Shall Mourn For Him?"), released in April of 1968, the Surfer falls from the sky after he steals a prototype device for penetrating dimensions from Mr. Fantastic of the Fantastic Four and unsuccessfully tries to use it to pierce the barrier that binds him to Earth. He is found by Al Harper, an African-American physicist, who shows the Surfer kindness. Upon waking, the Surfer asks him why he has helped when so many have refused friendship, and Harper implies an affinity between them based on difference, stating "Mebbe it's 'cause I know how it feels to be pushed around!" Harper believes he can help the surfer build a device to rend the cosmic impediment if he can acquire the money necessary for parts and the Silver Surfer dons a trench coat and sets off to try to earn an honest wage. In the process, the analogy between the Surfer and Harper is made more explicit, as he is turned away with comments such as "Did you get a look at his skin?" and "Not a chance! One look at you, and it's goodbye customers!"

Cognitive estrangement allowed New Wave authors opportunities not only for progressive critique, but also enough slack to question master narratives that not even the counterculture would have critiqued. For example, narratives that disrupted gender binaries or explored queer sex were considered groundbreaking for the time (see, in particular, Samuel R. Delany's Nebula award-winning "Aye, and Gomorrah"), but others went even further, using estrangement to assess the validity of disgust against even the most taboo sexual arrangements. Incest, particularly, crops up in a number of New Wave stories. Several of Michael Moorcock's novels, including *A Cure for Cancer* (1971), *The English Assassin* (1972), and *The Condition of Muzak* (1977), feature an ongoing epic in which the protagonist, though he switches names and sometimes genders, carries on a sexual relationship with his mother. The aforementioned "Riders of the Purple Wage" similarly naturalizes mother–son sexual relations, and Ellison's own "The Prowler in the City at the Edge of the World" features a grandfather who brings victims to his present for his granddaughter to murder so that she will agree to sexual congress with him. Theodore Sturgeon goes one step further in "If All Men Were Brothers, Would You Let One Marry Your Sister?" by introducing readers to a utopic race of beings who live in perfect harmony, and then having one of these ostensibly supreme beings, who is caught by the human protagonist having sex with his own daughter, systematically take apart the rational arguments for laws and taboos against incest. This list is not meant to imply that the authors themselves were advocating incest – some were even conservatively noting the perceived dangers of moral relativism; nevertheless, the preponderance of this motif in New Wave writing reveals a commitment to pushing the questioning of dominant ideology to the extreme.

This spirit of questioning everything also extended to the divine. Many prominent countercultural figures, such as the members of the Beatles, looked increasingly to figures like Maharishi Mahesh Yogi, who promoted forms of spirituality that included practices such as meditation and a focus on peace. Widespread interest in gurus such as Yogi represented a turn away from traditional Christian traditions toward Eastern mystic traditions and a communitarian spirituality that focused on the overcoming of the ego and the melting away of individualism. Hippies co-opted the wearing of beads and amulets as talismans, and practices that revolved around astrology, the I Ching, and yoga were common. This spiritual iconoclasm often manifested in New Wave writing as literary rebellions against the figure of God. In 1967, Moorcock released his novella "Behold the Man," which tracks a man by the name of Karl Glogauer as he travels backwards in time in the hopes of meeting Jesus. Instead, he discovers the historical Jesus is mentally impaired, and – as he has already performed a "miracle" by his mysterious appearance – steps into the mantle of fulfilling the biblical life of the purported son of God. The next year, in the introduction to *Dangerous Visions*, Ellison declared that "my own personal seminal influence for the fantasy that is the basis of all great speculative fiction is the Bible," and indeed, many of the stories contained in the anthology demonstrate that predilection. The visions of the divine are as grim as they are dangerous: "Evensong" narrates God's panicked flight as he flees from humankind, which has subsumed his dominant place in the universe; "Encounter with a Hick," presents God as a thoroughly demystified corporate presence; and in the post-apocalyptic "Shall the Dust Praise Thee?," God waits too long to return to Earth and raise his followers from the dead. The angels watch his impotent attempts in dismay before they discover the machine that was the agent of the planetary destruction, into which are carved the words "WE WERE HERE. WHERE WERE YOU?"[12]

A general sense of fatalism grew as the decade progressed. The nonviolent, love-based pranksterism of the counterculture took a darker turn as the US government more aggressively monitored and prosecuted activists, and the high profile assassinations of Martin Luther King and Bobby Kennedy seemed to point to a failure of rational politics. The New Left fractured and many abandoned the vows of nonviolence that had marked both early civil rights and early anti-war protests, taking up more militant stances instead. Rioting at the Democratic Convention in Chicago in 1968 involved many previously non-violent activists; in fact, in 1969 the Student Nonviolent Coordinating Committee (SNCC) decided to change the meaning of its acronym, dropping nonviolent and replacing it with "National." Students for a Democratic Society (SDS) also became more militant, and some members left to form the notorious Weather Underground, which had the stated goal of overthrowing the government of the United States and conducted multiple bombings, mostly against government properties, including the US Capitol building. In Britain "The Angry Brigade," a new left anti-war radical group began committing acts of terrorism on a small scale in 1967, but escalated to carry out twenty-six attacks between 1970 and 1971.

Even some of the cherished literature of the peace and love years was tainted by association or echoes of fatalism. In 1969, after the Manson family committed the murders of eight people, a rumor was started that Manson had based his cult and its behavior on *Stranger*, which gave many another excuse to condemn the counterculture. In 1970, even the Silver Surfer vowed to become savage in order to fight humanity on its own terms. The very last page of the original series is dominated by a close-up of the Surfer's face that emphasizes his blank white eyes and cavernous mouth opened in an enraged yell as he declares:

> Since a fiendish fate has trapped me here – with a hostile race in a nightmare world! I'll forget my heritage – blot out my space-born ethic – No longer will

---

[12] Ellison, *Dangerous Visions*, p. 328.

I resist their Earthly madness! No longer mine a lonely voice, pleading peace in a world of strife! From this time forth, the Silver Surfer will battle them on their own savage terms! Let mankind beware! From this time forth, the Surfer will be the deadliest one of all![13]

Out of the madness, not only did new attitudes emerge, but also a new literary style. Terry Eagleton, in his book *Literary Theory: An Introduction*, defines it thus: "Post-structuralism was a product of that blend of euphoria and disillusionment, liberation and dissipation, carnival and catastrophe, which was 1968. Unable to break the structures of state power, post-structuralism found it possible instead to subvert the structures of language."[14] Theorists like Foucault and Derrida, who were part of the failed student uprising to overthrow the French government, turned to deconstruction to strike at the heart of the narratives by dissembling their parts. During the rise of post-structuralism, Thomas Pynchon penned *Gravity's Rainbow* (1973). In contrast to the mechanics of *Stranger*, which alienated the readers by coaxing them to see through the eyes of an alien overwhelmed by the strangeness of human life and culture, Pynchon alienates the reader by weaving a text so dense that the most prominent companion book that seeks to unpack the references in the pages of the book is itself 383 pages long.[15] Featuring over 400 named characters and unfolding through leaps through time and space, flashbacks, and hallucinogenic breakdowns, Pynchon paints a picture of a species under constant threat from nefarious weapons and the ever-looming menace of insidious government surveillance. The controversial tale prompted strong reactions: *Gravity's Rainbow* shares the National Book Award and nearly won the Pulitzer, but was prevented from receiving the award by trustees who had unwavering objections to scatalogical content; for the first time in history, no Pulitzer was given that year. *Gravity's Rainbow*, intriguingly, was also nominated for the 1973 Nebula Award, a prize which ultimately went to Arthur C. Clarke for *Rendezvous with Rama* instead – a moment Jonathan Lethem famously called a "hidden tombstone marking the death of the hope that science fiction was about to merge with the mainstream."[16]

---

[13] Stan Lee, John Buscema, Jack Kirby, Joe Sinnott, Sam Rosen, and Art Simek, *The Essential Silver Surfer, Volume 1* (New York: Marvel Comics, 2001).

[14] Terry Eagleton, *Literary Theory: An Introduction* (Minneapolis: University of Minnesota Press, 2008), 123.

[15] Steven Weisenburger, *A Gravity's Rainbow Companion: Sources and Contexts for Pynchon's Novel*, 2nd edn., (Athens, OH: University of Georgia Press, 2006).

[16] Jonathan Lethem, "The Squandered Promise of Science Fiction," *Voice Literary Supplement* (June 1998), pp. 45–6

In any event, by the time *Gravity's Rainbow* was published, both counter-culture and the New Wave as a movement had largely dissolved. Though the counterculture and New Wave SF as movements were both fractious, contentious, and prevalent for relatively short periods of time, for many they left positive imprints on the subcultures that followed. Moorcock has said of Ellison's work collecting stories for *Dangerous Visions*: "He changed our world forever. And ironically, it is usually a mark of the world so fundamentally altered – be it by Stokeley Carmichael or Martin Luther King, Jr., or Lyndon Johnson, or Kate Millett – that nobody remembers what it was like before things got better."[17] The power of both movements is also proportional to the stakes of altering the dominant cultural narratives; as Gitlin observes, even from the beginning of the 1960s, "Governor George Wallace and Dr. Timothy Leary agreed that what was at stake was nothing less than Western Civilization, the only question being whether its demise was auspicious."[18]

[17] Moorcock in Harlan Ellison, ed., *Dangerous Visions: 35th Anniversary Edition* (New York: ibooks, 2002), p. xi.
[18] Gitlin, *The Sixties*, p. 206

Science Fiction Film, Television, and Music during the New Wave, 1960–1980

JEFFREY HICKS

Just as the New Wave changed SF literature on a fundamental level, it also influenced filmmakers and musicians to create works that broke with past traditions. In a 1965 editorial for *New Worlds* magazine, Michael Moorcock claimed that the field "need[s] more writers who reflect the pragmatic mood of today, who use the images apt for today, who employ symbols gathered from the world of today ... Like all good writing, SF must relate primarily to the time in which it is written; a writer must write primarily for his own generation."[1] New Wave authors did just that: they produced novels and stories that made free use of the social and political concerns of the sixties in an original and influential way.[2] The New Wave also shifted the genre's focus away from the "hard" SF of the Golden Age – much of it focused on fantasies about outer space – to what author J. G. Ballard called "inner space."[3] Ballard argued that, rather than spending so much effort creating futures controlled by the physical sciences, authors should instead look to new developments in the biological and social sciences and the possibilities they raise for more experimental forms of storytelling. Moorcock's emphasis on contemporaneity and Ballard's concept of inner space joined with a newfound interest in challenging colonial ideologies and exploring issues of race and gender in SF to create the ethos of New Wave SF.

It would, of course, be impossible to discuss *every* SF film, television program, or song from the 1960s to the 1980s in this brief chapter. My goal, instead, is to provide a general survey of important SF works in each medium, with an emphasis on those that more closely follow New Wave

---

[1] Michael Moorcock, "Symbols for the Sixties," *New Worlds* 148 (1965), p. 3.
[2] See Rob Latham, "The New Wave," in David Seed, ed., *A Companion to Science Fiction* (Malden, MA: Blackwell, 2005), pp. 202–16, and Rob Latham, "New Worlds and the New Wave in Fandom: Fan Culture and the Reshaping of Science Fiction in the Sixties," *Extrapolation: A Journal of Science Fiction and Fantasy* 47 (Summer 2006), pp. 296–315.
[3] J. G. Ballard, "Which Way to Inner Space?" *New Worlds* 118 (1962), pp. 2–3.

ideas as outlined above. Certainly work continued to be produced that was more aligned with Golden Age traditions, but that will not be my focus here. As a result, some important and popular texts – such as the TV series *Star Trek* (1966–9), which has deep roots in the Golden Age space-operatic imaginary – will receive somewhat less attention than they might have, at least when compared with other texts that more closely align with the ideologies associated with the New Wave.

SF Film

American SF films of the early to mid-1960s were primarily a hodge-podge of poorly costumed monsters, alien invasion stories, and Irwin Allen disaster adventures. There are a few exceptions, such as Ray Milland's *Panic in Year Zero!* (1962), Sidney Lumet's *Fail Safe* (1964), or John Frankenheimer's *Seconds* (1966), but the intensity and political subversiveness of *The Day the Earth Stood Still* (dir. Robert Wise, 1951) and *Invasion of the Body Snatchers* (dir. Don Siegel, 1956) would be discarded in the early 1960s in favor of more conventional SF tropes. Outside the United States, however, filmmakers adopted more experimental approaches, creating some of the most impressive films of the decade. Throughout the 1960s, several filmmakers associated with the French New Wave movement in cinema embraced SF, in the process challenging American conceptions of the genre and providing inspiration for both SF filmmakers and authors. Chris Marker's *La Jetée* (1962), Jean-Luc Goddard's *Alphaville* (1965), Roger Vadim's *Barbarella* (1968), and François Truffaut's adaptation of *Fahrenheit 451* (1966) blend avant-garde filmmaking techniques, small budgets, and a whole-hearted acceptance of the bizarre that would come to influence SF filmmakers for decades to come.

At the end of the 1960s, two mainstream films, one lowbrow and one highbrow, can register for us New Wave SF's decisive turn away from the Golden Age, inaugurating a line of films that are clearly marked by New Wave influences. Based on a 1963 Pierre Boulle novel, *La Planète des Sanges*, Franklin J. Schaffner's *Planet of the Apes* (1968) imagines a future where human beings have been supplanted by highly evolved apes as the dominant species on the planet. The film, which would eventually be followed by four sequels, a television adaptation, and two remakes, was quite successful, and it developed a strong cult following in part because of its ability to blend a novel concept with cringe-worthy costuming and special effects. *Planet of the Apes* may, at first glance, appear similar to the SF films of the early 1960s, or even perhaps to the *The Twilight Zone* television series with which it shares a writer – but, alongside such films as *The Omega Man* (dir. Boris Sagal, 1971) and *Soylent Green* (dir. Richard Fleischer, 1973), both also starring Charlton Heston, *Apes* worked to transform the familiar 1950s hero into a cynical, disillusioned mess, incapable of truly overcoming his circumstances. The idea that there really is no escape for Heston's Taylor, that the apes have won, must have come as a shock to viewers expecting human techno-superiority to save the day in the end. The famous final scene of the film, with its hero on his knees before a ruined, Ozymandian Statue of Liberty, instead blames humanity for a worldwide nuclear holocaust; in the first sequel, *Beneath the Planet of the Apes* (dir. Ted Post, 1970), a deeply embittered Taylor finishes the job himself, using a long-buried doomsday device to finally destroy the Earth.

Premiering in the same year, Stanley Kubrick's ambitious *2001: A Space Odyssey* transformed SF film forever. Kubrick's use of innovative techniques, new special effects technologies, and metaphysical themes ushered in a new approach to SF filmmaking that worked to engage a younger audience looking for visual representations of the 1960s counterculture. Rob Latham argues that in its moment "*2001: A Space Odyssey* was a cause célèbre within the sf genre, dividing old guard fans, who deplored the filmmaker's purported contempt for reason and scientific inquiry, from younger fans aligned with contemporary counterculture, who embraced its trippy imagery, its fusion of science and mysticism, and its tone of apocalyptic transcendence."[4] Adapting his 1951 short story, "The Sentinel," Arthur C. Clarke worked with Kubrick on both the screenplay for the film and the novel that accompanied it; together they created a film that, while still taking into account many of the practical realities behind artificial intelligence and space exploration, manages to challenge viewers' conceptions of space, time, and the origins of life. The "Starchild" sequence at the end of the film suggests the impossibility of truly understanding humanity's place in the universe, and Bowman's experiences capture the horror of the unknown and our inability to conceive of the truly alien.

The influence of *2001: A Space Odyssey* can easily be seen throughout the next decade, and the effects of the New Wave are readily apparent in the films of the 1970s as filmmakers embraced lower budgets and more experimental plots. Looking for resonant, contemporaneous storylines instead of blockbusters, directors and writers of SF film in the 1970s took risks that often

---

[4] Rob Latham, "'Lack of Respect, Wrong Attitude, Failure to Obey Authority': Dark Star, A Boy and His Dog, and New Wave Cult SF," in J. P. Telotte and Gerald Duchovnay, eds., *Science Fiction Double Feature: The Science Fiction Film as Cult Text* (Liverpool: Liverpool University Press, 2015), p. 205.

produced passionate cult followings even if they were not so profitable. Rob Latham suggests these films "began to absorb some of the attitudes and ambiences that New Wave fiction shared with youth counterculture: an abiding suspicion of technoscientific modes of knowledge, a casual contempt for social authority, and a downbeat assessment of the human prospect in the nuclear age."[5] Peter Watkins's film *Punishment Park* (1971) imagines a government-sponsored race through the desert for political prisoners bold enough to speak out against an authoritarian regime. In the same year, George Lucas released *THX-1138*, another film imagining the consequences of submitting to a totalitarian state. L. Q. Jones's adaptation of Harlan Ellison's *A Boy and His Dog* (1975) and Paul Bartel's *Death Race 2000* (1975) combine the low-budget special effects of the 1960s SF films with a pointed criticism not only of staid middle America, locked in complacency, but also the tendency to sacrifice the young to maintain the status quo. Together these films use their hyperbolic visions of the future to create a far bleaker response to Nixon's administration and the Vietnam War than their countercultural SF counterparts in the 1960s.

SF films of the 1970s also showcased the New Wave's interest in over-population and the environmental movement. Michael Campus's *Z.P.G.* (1972) is set on an Earth devastated by the environmental effects of pollution and reeling from the strain of an ever-growing populace. In an attempt to fight both pollution and a lack of resources, the world's government creates a moratorium on childbirth, displacing maternal desire with propaganda and life-like robotic children. Harry Harrison's 1966 novel *Make Room! Make Room!* was adapted into the 1973 Richard Fleischer film *Soylent Green*, and – while the film has since been remembered more for Charlton Heston's defiant denunciation of cannibalism – images of New Yorkers sleeping on staircases and being scooped into the beds of massive dump trucks created forceful visual warnings about a predicted population explosion.

In 1972, Douglas Trumbull brought his special effects magic to the eco-SF film *Silent Running*. The film stars Bruce Dern as Freeman Lowell, a rogue scientist attempting to preserve one of the last forests of Earth after the planet's ecosystem has been destroyed. After receiving orders from Earth to destroy the domes, Lowell, with the help of his robot friends, manages to save at least one of the remaining forests for the future. John Boorman presents an even more outlandish scenario in his 1974 film *Zardoz*, in which a select few of Earth's elite survive an unexplained apocalypse in a domed city protected by an energy field. After a wildly attired barbarian, played by a

---

[5] Ibid., p. 206.

mostly confused-looking Sean Connery, sneaks into the city, the surprisingly apathetic dome-dwellers find their perfectly planned immortal lives disrupted. In the nihilistic final act, Connery's Zed lowers the community's defenses, and the invading barbarians lay waste to the city and bring willing death to its inhabitants. While both of these films will be remembered more for their low-budget look and bizarre costuming, they also work to contest the belief in an easy technological fix for the then-current environmental problems affecting the planet, as would similarly dyspeptic eco-pessimistic films like the overpopulation thriller *Logan's Run* (dir. Michael Anderson, 1976), Jack Smight's post-nuclear film *Damnation Alley* (1977), and George Miller's apocalyptic *Mad Max* (1979) and its sequels.

Although the arrival of *Star Wars* (dir. George Lucas, 1977) and *Star Trek: The Motion Picture* (dir. Robert Wise, 1979) ushered in a return of Golden-Age-style space opera and the temporary foreclosure of more thoughtful SF film – as well as inaugurating the hegemony of trilogies, franchises, and eventually "cinematic universes" – many of the films mentioned above remain cult classics, and inspired the more innovative films of the 1980s and 1990s both inside and outside the SF genre. Even *Star Wars*, with its broken-down starships, its dirty, lived-in cityscapes, and its dyspeptic depiction of a brutal galactic dictatorship, can be seen as a deliberately revisionist space opera totally appropriate for the New Wave era – while the cycle of *Star Trek* movies inaugurated by *The Motion Picture* likewise emphasize the dangers and moral ambiguities of outer space, including a multi-movie arc depicting the agonizing death and troubled resurrection of beloved fan-favorite Spock (Leonard Nimoy).

SF Television

Star Trek (1966–9) – in its earlier, much more Golden-Age small-screen incarnation – remains itself perhaps the best-known American SF television show of the era. For three seasons, the crew of the starship *Enterprise* roamed the galaxy in search of the unknown. Despite the groundbreaking choices made in its casting and its numerous attempts to woo the counterculture, *Star Trek* was at its heart a space opera written in the more traditional mode of the Golden Age forged by John W. Campbell. The relegation of female characters – both crew and alien – to sexual conquests, the overtly colonial approach in the series of the "United Federation of Planets" towards alien civilizations and cultures, its extreme technological and scientific optimism, and the crew's unbelievable superiority over any alien species fit far more solidly with SF's Golden Age than with the New Wave, despite the series' increasing engagement with the counterculture and the fraught politics of the Vietnam War.[6]

As with *Star Trek*, the British SF mainstay *Doctor Who* (1963–present) seldom rose above traditional SF tropes in the 1960s and 1970s. *Doctor Who* depicts the adventures of a nearly immortal Time Lord from the Planet Gallifray, who traverses time and space in a cosmic machine called a TARDIS with his sidekick companions (usually though not always attractive young women from contemporary Britain). Despite the world of possibilities open to such a marvelous being, Mark Bould notes that "the series never really strays from the BBC's agenda of liberal neutrality nor shifts from an institutionalized, conservative reformism."[7] Bould further suggests that, despite its occasional focus on contemporary British sociopolitical issues such as pollution and overpopulation, the series consistently championed "traditional British democracy" while disavowing "Britain's ongoing history of colonial violence, oppression, and expropriation."[8] Nevertheless, *Doctor Who* continued to garner large audiences during these decades, bringing a weekly dose of SF into the homes of both British and American viewers – and, like *Star Trek*, it too developed a sort of nascent New Wave consciousness as the series aged, as in the environmentalist allegories undergirding many of the stories involving the mostly earthbound third Doctor (played by Jon Pertwee from 1970 to 1974).

In the United States, SF television was dominated by family-friendly action series that were popular if not exactly genre-challenging. From 1964 until 1970, producer Irwin Allen introduced *The Time Tunnel* (1966–7), *Lost in Space* (1965–8), *Voyage to the Bottom of the Sea* (1964–8), and *Land of the Giants* (1968–70). *Land of the Giants* eventually reached 110 episodes, making it one of the longest-running SF series. However, episode plots of these programs rarely rose above monster-of-the-week scenarios, and more time seemed to be spent on novelty than on character development. These series were joined by the children's shows *Fantastic Voyage* (1968–9), *Land of the Lost* (1974–6), and *The Tomorrow People* (1973–9) to create an archetypal model of SF television that features a handful of displaced scientists, children, and comic relief

[6] See, in particular, the chapter on *Star Trek* in H. Bruce Franklin's *Vietnam and Other American Fantasies* (Amherst: University of Massachusetts Press, 2000), discussed in Chapter 26, "New Wave Science Fiction and the Vietnam War."
[7] Mark Bould, "Science Fiction in the United Kingdom," in J. P. Telotte, ed., *The Essential Science Fiction Television Reader* (Lexington, KY: University Press of Kentucky, 2008), p. 215.
[8] Ibid., p. 218.

exploring the unknown while trying to survive a hostile environment populated by rubber monsters and the cheapest special effects cost-conscious producers could get away with.

Despite such mediocre fare, American SF television of this period will also be remembered for the haunting speculations offered by *The Twilight Zone* (1959–64) and *The Outer Limits* (1963–5). Some of the best TV work during the early years of the New Wave came in the form of the anthology series, and both *The Twilight Zone* and *The Outer Limits* presented episodes written by several established SF authors. In 1964, Harlan Ellison wrote two episodes of *The Outer Limits*, and stories from *The Twilight Zone* were taken from C. L. Moore, Harry Kuttner, Richard Matheson, Damon Knight, and Ray Bradbury. While not aligned specifically with the New Wave, both series presented stories that embraced Ballard's call to turn away from hard science and embrace the socio-psychological impact of exposure to the unknown.

In Britain, the short-lived anthology series *Out of this World* (1962) featured an adaptation of Philip K. Dick's story "The Impostor," along with episodes taken from stories by Isaac Asimov, John Wyndham, and Clifford D. Simak. The series was followed by the equally impressive *Out of the Unknown* (1965–71), which featured adaptations of work by both established SF authors and some of the more prominent members of the New Wave. Producer Irene Shubik worked with *New Worlds* founder and British SF agent John Carnell to find SF stories worthy of being televised, and together they presented work by Ballard, John Brunner, William Tenn, Kate Wilhelm, Frederik Pohl, and Ray Bradbury. Perhaps because of its insistence on using material from SF authors instead of studio writers, *Out of the Unknown* was known for bringing a more cerebral approach to SF at a time when American shows were focused more on lighter, family-oriented entertainment. This approach might also explain why the fourth series of the show, which relied on original material meant to imitate American SF television rather than adaptations, failed to generate a series renewal.

In 1973, New Wave icon Harlan Ellison created Canada's syndicated television series, *The Starlost* (1973–4), about a generational spaceship full of colonizers looking for a new home. In the series, something unexpected has happened to the ship, and isolated pods of passengers have created bizarrely individualized societies that have lost all touch with the ship's original mission or, often, with reality. The program focuses on a group of three intrepid escapees from a Quaker-like farming community, who work to unlock the mysteries of the ship so that they might change its current course before it leads them directly into a distant sun. Ursula K. Le Guin penned the third episode of the series, and its depiction of an all-male society kept alive by use of artificial insemination makes it one of the more thoughtful episodes. Despite its novelty, *The Starlost* was canceled after only sixteen episodes.

In 1970, Gerry Anderson, Sylvia Anderson, and Reg Hill created the series *UFO* (1970–1) for ITC Entertainment in the United Kingdom. The Andersons were better known for their marionette-driven children's programs such as *Thunderbirds* (1965–6), and *UFO* was their first foray into live-action television. The series, set in 1980, concerned an alien invasion and the group of shadowy government officials – named SHADO, for Supreme Headquarters Alien Defense Organization – tasked with stopping the extraterrestrial menace. SHADO operates out of a film studio in London, which helped to explain any odd occurrences on the premises and worked to minimize production costs for the Andersons. The series featured wild costumes, futuristic (and sometimes glaringly mundane) automobiles, a moon base, submarines, spacecraft, and a supersonic jet that, at first glance, might have connected the program more firmly to the Anderson's kid shows than to compelling SF. Yet the storylines were often surprisingly deep and far too dark to be considered suitable for youngsters. Throughout the series, the director of SHADO, Edward Straker, watches as his family is destroyed by his commitment to his post, and several episodes focus on the psychological strain forced on Straker by the seeming impossibility of his job. In the chilling episode "A Question of Priorities," Straker is sent away from his home by his ex-wife before he can say goodbye to his son, and as Straker drives away, he watches his son run after his car and into the path of a speeding motorist. Later, as his son lies in the hospital awaiting an urgently needed medication he had promised to deliver, Straker must make the decision to divert the sub-sonic SHADO plane containing his son's antibiotics to investigate a possible alien sighting. The episode ends with Straker's son's dying and his wife telling him she never wants to see him again.

Often confused as a children's show by BBC programmers and suffering from low ratings in American syndication, *UFO* failed to garner a second season. However, not wanting the initial work on a new season to be wasted, the Andersons followed *UFO* with *Space: 1999* (1975–7). *Space: 1999* capitalized on the popularity of *UFO*'s moon-base sequences by setting the entire series on a scientific outpost on Earth's moon. After an accident involving poorly handled nuclear waste, the moon base – and the Moon itself – are sent hurtling through space, headed for the unknown. Throughout the first season, the series regulars dealt with the dangers of nuclear power, the nature of post-humanity, and the causes and consequences of violence as the cast fought off an inevitable horde of menacing aliens, but unlike series such as *Star Trek*, *Space: 1999* often emphasized thought and consideration rather than brute force.

Perhaps the television program most thematically aligned with the New Wave, though, is the British series *The Prisoner* (1967–8). While Patrick McGoohan was filming the popular spy show *Danger Man* (1960–1, 1964–7), he imagined a series in which a government agent would be relocated to a luxury prison after retiring so that government secrets could never be shared. *The Prisoner* kept McGoohan's basic plot suggestions but added a complex hierarchical structure to the leadership of "The Village," and kept its purpose a mystery to both McGoohan's "Number Six" and to viewers. The episodes focused on themes of identity, agency, and structures of power, even as viewers were kept guessing about the series' ultimate aims. On the one hand, *The Prisoner* seems to stress the importance of individuality, but on the other, it constantly undercuts that message by suggesting leadership and power are ultimately hollow. The final episode stresses this idea by ending with McGoohan's character re-living the initial shots of the first episode and title credits. Like many New Wave texts, the series finale enraged many fans with its incomprehensibility and ambiguity, but while there have been re-make attempts and efforts to somehow update the spirit of the show, no one has been successful at recapturing the absurd magic of *The Prisoner*.

By the end of the 1970s, *Star Wars* had begun to usher in a new generation of action-adventure space operas in both the United States and Britain. In America, *Battlestar Galactica* (1978–9) and the reboot of *Buck Rogers in the 25th Century* (1979–81) attempted to cash in on a new-found interest in SF, and in Britain *Blake's 7* (1978–81) tried to compete (unsuccessfully) with those two American imports. It would take at least another decade before SF television returned to the thoughtful exploration of the impact of science and technology on humanity found in the best British SF series.

SF Music

Throughout the 1950s and the early 1960s, there were occasional nods to SF and science fictional concerns within popular music – but a handful of musical movements in the mid-1960s and 1970s began a more overt incorporation of SF themes in their lyrics and stage performances and an increased experimentation with technology and instrumentation that mirrors the moves of New Wave SF. Although it is difficult to measure just how much of an influence the New Wave had on music in these decades, it is clear that the psychedelic rock, progressive rock, and afro-futurist music scenes fully embody a connection to the counterculture, an emphasis on inner space, and a willingness to incorporate unorthodox, original approaches to their art and thus clearly resonate with the New Wave.

In the mid-1960s, counterculture movements promoted psychedelic "trips" induced through the use of drugs such as LSD as a way to explore inner space and achieve mind expansion. At the same time, rock musicians were experimenting with distorted guitars, electronic keyboards, studio recording effects, and the freer structural form of improvised jazz. This new style of music was dubbed psychedelic rock, and it quickly became the preferred soundtrack for those seeking to explore their own inner worlds. Psychedelic rock lyrics often used the imagery of fantasy literature, and towards the end of the decade, many artists began to add elements of SF into their compositions as well. In the United States, bands such as Jefferson Airplane and the Grateful Dead were early adherents, and established artists such as the Beach Boys began experimenting with a more psychedelic sound in the late 1960s. As with many music movements of the decade, however, the presence of psychedelic rock was more profoundly felt overseas. The base of a more SF-focused psychedelic rock in Britain was the aptly named UFO Club, home to bands such as the Soft Machine, who had taken their name from the first novel in William S. Burroughs's "Nova Trilogy," and Tomorrow, a band which featured future Yes guitarist Steve Howe.

UFO Club also frequently featured the earliest incarnation of Pink Floyd. In their early years, Pink Floyd experimented with loud psychedelic rock played against a backdrop of swirling lights with the intention of presenting music that was to be experienced rather than danced to. Two of the highlights of their set list were the space-themed songs "Astronomy Domine" and "Interstellar Overdrive," both of which were featured on the band's debut album, *The Piper at the Gates of Dawn* (1967). With these songs, Pink Floyd simulated the excitement, wonder, and potential terror of space exploration. "Astronomy Domine" begins with the sound of a dispassionate voice crackling through the distortion of a loudspeaker. The lyrics read like the itinerary of a cosmonaut's interplanetary journey as they reference the British SF comic *Dan Dare, Pilot of the Future*. Syd Barrett's guitar work alternates between long glissandos and staccato, mechanical pinging, creating the sound effect of a rocket traveling through space. Like "Astronomy Domine," "Interstellar Overdrive" seeks to recreate the experience of space travel, but this time strictly through the instruments of psychedelic rock. The sweeping guitar, bass, drums, and organ join together to create an aural landscape of outer worlds, a landscape through which the listener can journey without having to leave the confining bounds of Earth. SF themes would persist throughout Pink Floyd's psychedelic era. Their second album, *A Saucerful of Secrets* (1968), featured songs such as "Set the Controls for the Heart of the Sun" and "Let There Be More Light," whose lyrics reference a benevolent alien invasion similar to the one found in Arthur C. Clarke's novel *Childhood's End* (1953). Pink Floyd again paid tribute to Clarke with a song titled "Childhood's End," which was featured on the soundtrack of the Barbet Schroeder film *La Vallée* (1972).

Straddling the space between psychedelic and progressive rock, Hawkwind combined psychedelic rock's journeys to inner space with a more progressive sound that many have dubbed "space rock." Throughout the 1970s, Hawkwind was known for its sprawling, lengthy compositions and SF themes in songs such as "Silver Machine," and in the 1973 album *Space Ritual*. In the early 1970s, New Wave author Michael Moorcock began working with the band, contributing lyrics and the occasional vocal, and following them on tours. Moorcock's involvement peaked in 1975 with the release of *Warrior on the Edge of Time*, named for and heavily influenced by Moorcock's "Elric" saga. The songs on the album feature Moorcock's "eternal champion," who can see through all dimensions simultaneously. Instead of existing as a traditional Golden Age fantasy hero, however, Moorcock's champion is a darker and more compromised figure. Music historians Paul Hegarty and Martin Halliwell suggest that, "rather than conveying the omniscient perspective of an all-seeing figure, the brooding and spacey music suggests that the eternal champion has an uncertain role in a universe full of warriors and wizards whose motives are hard to gauge."[9] Here, the ideas of the New Wave begin to peek through, even if the form and structure of the story rely more on traditional fantasy tropes.

In the late 1960s and early 1970s, progressive rock arose largely from British countercultural movements. Maintaining the psychological and metaphysical aspects of psychedelic rock, progressive rock added an emphasis on complex compositions influenced by jazz, folk, and classical music and an even stronger dedication to new technology. Like psychedelic rock, progressive rock is also known for incorporating fantasy and SF themes into its lyrics and for its elaborate live productions and stage personas. Bands such as Jethro Tull, King Crimson, ELP, and Yes also often experimented with time

---

[9] Paul Hegarty and Martin Halliwell, *Beyond and Before: Progressive Rock since the 1960s* (New York: Bloomsbury Academic, 2011), p. 99.

signatures, Moog synthesizers, and decidedly non-rock instrumentation. Many such bands were quite deliberate about their deployment of SF, including at times epic songs and even entire concept albums built around SF themes and SF imagery.

Canadian super-group Rush began moving towards a more progressive sound on their album *2112* in 1976. Influenced directly by the work of Ayn Rand, the songs on *2112* depict a dystopian future where the universe is united under the totalitarian rule of the "Solar Federation," with the priests of the temple of Syrinx controlling every aspect of its citizens' lives. The group's next two albums, *A Farewell to Kings* (1977) and *Hemispheres* (1978), continued to blend elements of SF and fantasy into their lyrics in songs such as "Cygnus X-1 Book One: The Voyage Prologue," the eco-critical "Trees," and "Cygnus X-1 Book Two: Hemispheres." The lyrics from this period were combined with increased experimentation in non-traditional percussion, lengthier songs, and the use of synthesizers to create a cosmic sound that is synonymous with progressive rock. The songs on these albums, as with much of progressive rock, blend their challenges to authority with a yearning for a more traditional way of life and a championing of individualism that doesn't exactly match the feeling of the New Wave. Hegarty and Halliwell note:

> Potentially radical in projecting alternative futures, but also potentially conservative in recouping a lost past, the cultural politics of progressive bands are complex and sometimes undecidable. The interest in myths and mythology within an early to mid-1970s context reveal a more contested cultural politics – at times engaged politically, at others self-absorbed, escapist, or esoteric – than the participatory leftist politics of late 1960s counterculture.[10]

To find more of a New Wave spirit in music during the 1960s and 1970s, it might be better to consider the sounds of the burgeoning Afrofuturist movement. Inspired by a vision he had received in his late teens or early twenties, musician Sun Ra began melding jazz with SF themes in the 1950s. Often bringing SF-influenced props and costumes with him onstage, Sun Ra eventually became one of the founding artists of a growing Afrofuturist movement within jazz, pop, and rock music that peaked in the 1970s and still finds followers today. On albums such as *Monorails and Satellites, Vol. 1 and Vol. 2* (1968–9), *Space Probe* (1969), and *Space is the Place* (1973), Sun Ra and his Arkestra created music that took the listener on a trip through the universe,

---

[10] Ibid., p. 103.

blending newly created instruments with free improvisation to generate the cosmic sound the artist is known for.

George Clinton took Afrofuturism even further with his bands Parliament and Funkadelic. Clinton combined Parliament's more rhythm and blues sound with Funkadelic's rock roots to create the awesome power of P-funk. During the 1970s, Parliament released *Osmium* (1970) and *Up for the Down Stroke* (1974), but they failed to catch mainstream success until the band fully embraced the P-funk ethos in albums such as *Mothership Connection* (1975) and *The Clones of Dr. Funkenstein* (1976). These albums featured strong SF themes and the Afrofuturist agenda of placing African Americans directly in fields more commonly promoted as the domain of whites. At the same time, Funkadelic released the albums *Cosmic Slop* (1973) and *One Nation under a Groove* (1978), which, while not as specifically aligned with SF themes, furthered Clinton's political messaging and worked to inspire many of the funk and rap artists that would emerge in the 1980s. Throughout the late 1970s, Clinton created a Parliament–Funkadelic stage presence that featured both bands, an impressive SF-themed show complete with mothership, and an aura that became synonymous with Afrofuturism for the next several decades. These bands also contributed to spin-offs such as Bootsy Collins's Rubber Band and inspired other Afrofuturist artists and bands in the 1970s and 1980s such as Afrika Bambaataa and Warp 9.[11]

It seems only fitting to end this chapter with the late David Bowie's contributions to music and film in the 1970s, as no other artist did more to represent the ideas of the New Wave in popular culture during that decade. In 1976, Bowie appeared in the Nicolas Roeg film *The Man Who Fell to Earth*, playing Thomas Jerome Newton, an alien who comes to Earth in search of water for his dying planet. In the film, Newton builds a large company by patenting inventions from his planet in the hopes of using his wealth to construct a spaceship capable of transporting water back home. Very little time in the film is spent on elaborate special-effects sequences or on dazzling speculations of advanced technology. Instead, Roeg showcased Newton's alien-ness through Bowie's performance and appearance in the film. As Bowie's character slowly succumbs to alcoholism and the machinations of the United States government and a rival company, the viewer is drawn into Newton's despair, and shattered by images of his family back home slowly dying from thirst. The surreal sequences of Bowie watching multiple

---

[11] For more on Afrofuturism in music, especially the work of Sun Ra, see Chapter 25, "Afrofuturism in the New Wave Era."

televisions at once or his frantic bouts of sex and binge drinking give the film a distinctly Ballardian feel while almost completely eschewing the gosh-wow characteristics that would come to define post-New-Wave SF film a year later with the release of *Star Wars*.

Throughout the decade, Bowie incorporated SF themes into his music and performance, at one point committing his entire life to his alien alter ego, Ziggy Stardust. The song "Space Oddity," released as a single in 1969 and then as a track on his second album, chronicles the melancholy odyssey of "Major Tom" as he orbits the Earth in a cramped space shuttle. Part ode to the addictive properties of heroin and part reflection on the loneliness of space, "Space Oddity" would become one of Bowie's best-remembered songs. *Hunky Dory*, released in 1971, included the songs "Life on Mars?" and "Oh! You Pretty Things," which treated the coming of a new line of super-beings to replace the inferior human race. Bowie followed *Hunky Dory* with *The Rise and Fall of Ziggy Stardust and the Spiders from Mars* in 1972. Even before the release of the album, Bowie had been toying with a new, alien persona marked by outrageous costumes and a shock of brownish-red hair. In songs such as "Starman," "Ziggy Stardust," and "Suffragette City," and in his passionate stage performances, Bowie brought the title character to life. Ziggy Stardust, a bisexual, alien rock god celebrates the great excess of stardom even as he is eventually torn apart by it.[12] During this period, the Ziggy character became a central part of Bowie's public persona, and the album became a rallying cry for disaffected teens who saw themselves reflected in the Other of Bowie's performance.

By the end of the 1970s, *Star Wars* set the tone for SF film as well as television just as punk and New Wave left psychedelic and progressive rock in the past. While New Wave SF themes continued to be present in a handful of films in the 1980s, the technophilia of cyberpunk joined space opera as the dominant form of SF in popular culture. While the New Wave era soon receded, it nonetheless left its mark in the form of some of the most compelling and experimental works of film, television, and music of the postwar period, both inside and outside the niche SF marketplace.

---

[12] This theme is featured in a number of New Wave texts including Brian Aldiss's *Barefoot in the Head* and Norman Spinrad's story, "The Big Flash."

23

Science Fiction, Gender, and Sexuality in the New Wave

LAUREN J. LACEY

The years of SF's "New Wave" in the 1960s and 1970s coincided with an influx of women writers as well as increased emphasis on social and anthropological themes. Gender became an important area of inquiry in many works of the era, while sexuality was a focus for both traditional and New Wave authors at a time when "free love" and feminism were part of the larger cultural conversations. Writers who are typically cited as exemplars of these emphases on gender and sexuality in the New Wave include Ursula K. Le Guin, Joanna Russ, and James Tiptree, Jr. There are, however, many other writers whose works demonstrate the phenomenon, including but not limited to Eleanor Arnason, Octavia E. Butler, Angela Carter, C. J. Cherryh, Samuel Delany, Sonya Dorman Hess, Doris Lessing, Anne McCaffrey, Vonda N. McIntyre, Marge Piercy, Kit Reed, Lisa Tuttle, Kate Wilhelm, Chelsea Quinn Yarbro, and Pamela Zoline.

In order to offer a sense of the depth and diversity of these writers' explorations of gender and sexuality, this chapter works through examples of texts that engage in a variety of forms of intervention into dominant, often patriarchal and heteronormative, SF narratives. Given space constraints, most of the examples here are drawn from short fiction, with a few references to the many novel-length works that helped to reimagine gender and sexuality in SF. Below are discussions of stories that critique prevailing modes of masculinity, those that emphasize a shift of narrative focus to women and other "Others," some that explore gender roles that are reversed, revised, or otherwise remade, and, finally, narratives that focus on reimagining the very concepts of gender and sexuality.

Contextualizing Gender and Sexuality in SF

It is important to note that the women writers who became so significant during the New Wave were nowhere near the beginning of women writing

SF. There is Mary Shelley, of course, and other nineteenth-century antecedents, but even during the era that is frequently termed the "Golden Age" in SF, when the genre was supposedly all about masculine fantasy, there were plenty of women publishing in the field. Lisa Yaszek's *Galactic Suburbia* argues that Golden Age women writers, well before the 1960s, were engaged in strategically rewriting SF story types in ways that put wives and mothers at the center of the narratives.[1] Yaszek further emphasizes how feminist writers in the New Wave and later extend and develop ideas first explored by earlier writers, including tropes of female aliens, ultimately arguing that later writers offered radical solutions to some of the concerns around gender and sexuality that were first raised by their postwar counterparts.[2] Overt explorations of gender relations and sexuality did not begin in the New Age, but they did evolve during that time.

While it may not be accurate to say that women first entered SF in the New Wave, it is demonstrably true that they became a more important presence in the field during that time. Patricia Melzer argues, "Beginning with the New Wave in the 1960s, Western SF texts and criticism have developed from a mainly white, male, heterosexual genre into a more diverse body of texts with the potential to radically reconceptualize power relations. This development coincided with radical feminist interventions into male-defined liberation movements and theories."[3] An overt focus on power, in both its micro and macro level forms, can be seen in a wide range of texts from the New Wave. Furthermore, the feminist interventions Melzer describes were having a significant effect on literary fiction and literary criticism, so that conditions were ripe for SF writers to engage with feminism. Writers like Doris Lessing and Marge Piercy demonstrate how speculative narratives became important vehicles for authors who were already engaged with feminist ideas. Lessing's *The Golden Notebook* (1962) is a realistic narrative that explores issues related to both sexual and women's liberation in the era. In 1974, Lessing published *The Memoirs of a Survivor*, a dystopian narrative that works with science fictional devices to examine some of the same themes as her earlier work. Marge Piercy published several works in the 1960s and 1970s, nearly all of them fully engaged with feminist critique and creation. Her 1976 time-travel novel *Woman on the Edge of Time* combines a devastating analysis

---

[1] Lisa Yaszek, *Galactic Suburbia: Recovering Women's Science Fiction* (Columbus: The Ohio State University Press, 2008), p. 196.

[2] Ibid., pp. 200–1.

[3] Patricia Melzer, *Alien Constructions: Science Fiction and Feminist Thought* (Austin, TX: University of Texas Press, 2006), p. 5.

of economic, racial, and gender-based systemic violence in the 1970s with a feminist utopian vision of a future world in which gender distinctions do not even register and sexuality is both open and free. The prolific SF editors Ann and Jeff VanderMeer have noted "the great flowering of feminist speculative fiction in the late 1960s through the 1970s," and go on to say that "it is no surprise that this period of flowering coincided roughly with the flourishing of the New Wave literary movement because the New Wave created its own unique space by championing experimentation and literary values."[4] New Wave sensibilities increased the parameters of the genre of SF, creating space for many kinds of feminist interventions.

Critiques of Masculinity

But how did gender figure in the texts that did not challenge naturalizing discourses? Brian Attebery claims, "Until the 1960s, gender was one of the elements most often transcribed unthinkingly into SF's hypothetical worlds."[5] Any review of the work by some of the more prominent male writers through the 1960s and 1970s, however, suggests that the "unthinking" approach to gender and sexuality Attebery describes is alive and well there, along with overt objectification and sexualization of women, dismissive treatment of female characters, collapsing of women with animal and alien Others, frequent and unexamined portrayals or discussions of sexual violence, and general embracing of stereotypically dominating masculinity. Cordwainer Smith's "The Ballad of Lost C'Mell" (1962) features casual misogyny in a story about a golden-hearted, Orientalized, animalized prostitute's unvoiced love for a male hero. Harry Harrison's "A Criminal Act" (1967) embraces hyper-masculinity as well as weak and downright idiotic femininity. Larry Niven's New Wave story, "Cloak of Anarchy" (1972), claims women are always only a hair's breadth away from rape, and men are even closer to being rapists. Writers interested in interrogating the relationships among gender, sexuality, and power during the New Wave were reacting to and writing against a continued emphasis on patriarchal and misogynist tropes in much of the SF of the period.

Given the models of excessive masculinity in so many stories by male writers of the period, it is not surprising that many of the women who wrote

---

[4] Ann VanderMeer and Jeff VanderMeer, "Introduction," in Ann VanderMeer and Jeff VanderMeer, eds., *Sisters of the Revolution: A Feminist Speculative Fiction Anthology* (Oakland: PM Press, 2015), p. 1.

[5] Brian Attebery, *Decoding Gender in Science Fiction* (New York: Routledge, 2002), p. 5.

during the same era produced narratives that interrogated masculine identities. For example, "False Dawn" (1972), by Chelsea Quinn Yarbro, depicts a horribly violent dystopian future in which the female protagonist is, from the very first, always in danger of rape and murder by threatening males.[6] The story features a strong female heroine who is at risk in part because of her "mutant" status, but this strong woman spends the whole story avoiding dangerous men, and finally being raped by one. In the end, she is saved from murder by another man – also a mutant and someone with whom she has formed a kind of alliance. The story comes down to the good guy versus the bad guy, fighting over her body – though the story differs from some contemporaneous visions of rape culture in that it is focalized through a woman's perspective, and because the rapist's behavior is demonized not only as anti-social but as specifically a lesser form of masculinity.

More nuanced and complex critiques of masculinity can be found in many of the stories written by Alice Sheldon, writing both as James Tiptree, Jr., and as Raccoona Sheldon. The 1972 "And I Awoke and Found Me Here on the Cold Hill's Side," written under the name of James Tiptree, Jr., is made up of a conversation between a newly arrived reporter and a worker at a service port for spaceships – both male. The focus is on humans' drive to have sex with aliens, to the point of losing their attraction to one another: "Man is exogamous – all our history is one long drive to find and impregnate the stranger. Or get impregnated by him; it works for women too. Anything different-colored, different nose, ass anything, man *has* to fuck it or die trying. That's a drive, y'know, it's built in. Because it works fine as long as the stranger is human."[7] Sheldon takes aim at patterns of masculine desires based in exoticization and objectification. As Wendy Pearson points out, "rather than a tale of conquest, whether sexual or spatial, the red-headed man's narrative is one of failure, of the destruction of the soul. As a hard-bitten masculine hero, the storyteller simply doesn't cut it."[8] The male SF hero is dismantled in this story; his conquests lead to despair. Writing as Tiptree, Sheldon takes pains to ensure that women are affected too, but the entire story focuses on two men preparing to compete over alien sex opportunities, as the worker warns the reporter to stay away from *his* potential conquests.

---

[6] Chelsea Quinn Yarbro, "False Dawn," in Pamela Sargent, ed., *Women of Wonder: The Classic Years* (New York: Harcourt Brace and Company, 1995), pp. 234–48.

[7] James Tiptree, Jr. "And I Awoke and Found Me Here on the Cold Hill's Side," in Justine Larbalestier, ed., *Daughters of Earth: Feminist Science Fiction in the Twentieth Century* (Middletown, CT: Wesleyan University Press, 2006), p. 166.

[8] Wendy Pearson, "(Re)Reading James Tiptree Jr.'s 'And I Awoke and Found Me Here on the Cold Hill Side,'" in Larbalestier, ed., *Daughters of Earth*, p. 176.

In this story, the sex-crazed human is less a potential rapist than an unwitting victim of a dangerous biological drive, but in the end men driven by lust are doomed.

A later story written under the feminine pseudonym "Raccoona Sheldon" picks up some of the same themes but offers a more overt critique of masculine sexual identity: "The Screwfly Solution" (1977). This now-famous and deeply disturbing story features a scientist named Alan writing back and forth with his wife, Anne, who tells him about the increasing number of attacks on and murders of women in the United States. It turns out that aliens have infected human males with an exterminating agent in order to prepare their way; it works by turning the male sex drive into a frenzied violence machine. Alan, who has been working in Colombia, returns home only to succumb to the illness. The passage in which that transition happens is a disturbing commentary on the male gaze as it is trained not only on women, but on young girls: "And Amy would be there, too; he grinned at the memory of that prepubescent little body plastered against him. She was going to be a handful, all right. His manhood understood Amy a lot better than her mother did; no cerebral phase for Amy . . . But Anne, his exquisite shy one, with whom he'd found the way into the almost unendurable transports of the flesh."[9] His daughter, Amy, is sexualized, while his wife, Anne, is infantilized; Sheldon succinctly describes the way patriarchal values condemn females and destroy families. As his anticipatory daydream continues he realizes his sexual fantasy has become violent, and sees that he has been infected. The story concludes with Anne on her own, trying to survive and observing the aliens who have been preparing the planet for occupation. Writing under a female pen name, Sheldon takes a much more direct approach to a critique of masculinity here. Once again, men are dangerous to women – deeply so.

Of Kate Wilhelm, Pamela Sargent writes, "Her characters, in their subtle ways, reflect the changing roles of men and women."[10] Many of her stories do more than reflect, though, as they incorporate important analyses of the limits of old roles, and the potential of new ones. "No Light in the Window" (1963) is Wilhelm's story of a married couple, both of whom are vying for spots on an interstellar spaceship. The wife, Connie, worries incessantly that her husband, Hank, will be chosen while she will not. Extensive psychological testing is part of the selection process, and Connie broods over her

---

[9] Raccoona Sheldon, "The Screwfly Solution," in Tom Shippey, ed., *Oxford Book of Science Fiction Stories* (Oxford: Oxford University Press, 2003), p. 447.

[10] Pamela Sargent, "Introduction," in Pamela Sargent, ed., *Women of Wonder: The Classic Years* (New York: Harcourt Brace and Company, 1995), p. 17.

husband's ability to remain unruffled and calm in any situation, while she is anxious and nervous. In a significant critique of masculine ideals of emotional repression, Wilhelm's story reverses the usual values by having Dr. Zorin, the psychologist, choose Connie but not Hank, explaining to Connie, "'He's the very things you are not. He's brittle and inflexible and unyielding. He can't accept occasional failure and being human he must fail. He has never faced the possibility that one of you might not be selected."[11] Hank is dangerous because he has no way to cope. Traditional masculinity is deemed inferior to open and thoughtful femininity.

Shifting the Focus: Female and Feminized Perspectives

In addition to challenging masculinity as an ideal, feminist SF of the New Wave offers points of view, often female, that tend to change the terms of the entire conversation. Helen Merrick describes a transition from efforts to render women "visible" and/or to deny gender differences in earlier narratives, to "increasingly more complex characterizations ... with portrayals of women as fully 'human,' rather than 'female men'" in the 1960s.[12] Perhaps the most frequently cited example of such a story is Pamela Zoline's "The Heat Death of the Universe" (1967). It is a very New Wave story, in that it employs experimental form and only the barest science fictional trappings. The story is a list of items relevant to the life of a housewife: "(9) Sarah Boyle is a vivacious and intelligent young wife and mother, educated at a fine Eastern college, proud of her growing family which keeps her busy and happy around the house."[13] As it is here, the tone is at times distant and objectifying – scientific, even – as the items on the list come together to add up to the life of a housewife. "Heat Death" uses the defamiliarizing power of science fictional writing to interrogate Sarah Boyle's daily existence.

The reader encounters lots of list items about housekeeping, personal appearance, as well as time, love, and entropy: "(35) Sarah Boyle has at times felt a unity with her body, at other times a complete separation. The mind/body duality considered. The time/space duality considered.

---

[11] Kate Wilhelm, "No Light in the Window," in Larbalestier, ed., *Daughters of Earth*, p. 105.
[12] Helen Merrick, "Gender in Science Fiction," in Edward James and Farah Mendlesohn, eds., *The Cambridge Companion to Science Fiction* (Cambridge: Cambridge University Press, 2003), p. 246.
[13] Pamela Zoline, "The Heat Death of the Universe," in Larbalestier, ed., *Daughters of Earth*, p. 131.

The male/female duality considered. The matter/energy duality considered. Sometimes, at extremes, her Body seems to her an animal on a leash, taken for walks in the park by her Mind."[14] Binary logic and the dichotomies that prop up everyday existence are not so very far from the surface of a typical housewife's life, it turns out. Mary E. Papke writes, "Like some of the work that Kate Wilhelm, Judith Merril, Marion Zimmer Bradley, and Anne McCaffrey produced around the same time, Zoline's story explores relational spaces, those shared by mothers and children, husbands and wives, domestic economy and the public sphere."[15] The shift is not just one of point of view, from men to women, but also from quest and conquer narratives to stories that delve into interpersonal relationships, and into the social structures that house those relationships.

Another story that works to shift perspective as well as narrative focus is Lisa Tuttle's "Wives," (1979). In this thoroughly defamiliarizing story, the reader follows Susie, first introduced as "Jack's wife," who "woke, her eyes open and her little nose flaring, smelling something beneath the sulphur smell. One of those smells she was used to not noticing, when the men were around. But it was all right, now. Wives could do as they pleased, so long as they cleaned up and were back on their proper places when the men returned."[16] It turns out Susie is a wife to a human man, but is herself a member of a nonhuman native species on a planet that has been colonized by human men. The story engages in strong critiques of gender roles and norms, imperialism (which the text links to dangerous forms of masculinity), and heteronormativity. Through violence and brutality, the men have created a suburban haven for themselves on an alien planet, complete with compliant and well-behaved housewives.

Susie follows her usually suppressed instincts and finds another of her kind who is in heat: "Over her skintight (which was bound more tightly than Susie's had been) Doris wore a low-cut dress, her three breasts carefully bound and positioned to achieve the proper, double-breasted effect. Gaily patterned and textured stockings covered her silicone-injected legs, and she tottered on heels three centimetres high."[17] Obviously, an underlying theme here is that femininity of the kind desired by the men is utterly false and fully a matter of subjugated beings conforming to ideals imposed upon them.

[14] Ibid., p. 137.
[15] Mary E. Papke, "A Space of Her Own: Pamela Zoline's 'The Heat Death of the Universe,'" in Larbalestier, ed., *Daughters of Earth*, p. 145.
[16] Lisa Tuttle, "Wives," in Larbalestier, ed., *Daughters of Earth*, p. 190.
[17] Ibid., p. 191.

Susie convinces Doris to escape the camp with her for a touching lovers' interlude, after which Susie attempts to recruit other "wives" to rebel with her. She does not want to go back to being the human Jack's wife, but the others resist her arguments because they don't think rebellion is possible given the strength and sheer cruelty of the colonizing men. Susie is killed by her own people, a death she understands and accepts because otherwise she might be a liability to all of them as they attempt to convince the men that they are harmless. The narrative ends when Jack returns and either doesn't notice that Susie has been replaced by another alien/wife, or doesn't care: "'Three tits and the best coffee in the universe,' he said with satisfaction, squeezing one of the bound lumps of flesh on her chest. 'With this to come home to, it kind of makes the whole war-thing worthwhile.'"[18] "Wives" offers the perspective of a colonized species that is forced to enact human femininity, thereby illustrating just how unnatural and constructed the role of a "wife" really is.

Revised and Remade Roles

Feminist narratives of the time also devote significant energy to revising genre and gender expectations with characters and plots that subvert norms. Anne McCaffrey is one of the most popular writers associated with the period. Her work is sometimes considered to be too conventional to be associated with either the New Wave or feminist SF; Josephine Saxton calls her "a writer of romance – fantasy without polemic – which endorses the very situation which feminist writers abhor."[19] There is certainly romance to be found in McCaffrey's works (and not all of it heterosexual), but patriarchal norms are problematized rather than simply reproduced. For example, the Harper Hall Trilogy focuses on the Harpers of Pern, who are teachers, ambassadors, and politicians as well as singers and musicians. The first book, *Dragonsong* (1976) follows Menolly, a young girl with an exceptional gift for music who comes from a small fishing village where gender roles operate in strict accordance with tradition, and where her talents are, at best, unappreciated. Menolly runs away from home, challenges gender conventions about harpers, and ultimately succeeds at Harper Hall in order to become a powerful figure on Pern. Marleen S. Barr argues that Menolly's story "critiques master narratives about

---

[18] Ibid., p. 198.
[19] Josephine Saxton, "Goodbye to all that . . ." in Lucie Armitt, ed., *Where No Man Has Gone Before: Women and Science Fiction* (New York: Routledge, 1991), p. 214.

female artists' inferiority,"[20] and it seems clear that the trilogy intervenes in genre expectations about who will succeed on quests and who will claim power, at the same time as it directly addresses the problems with traditional gender roles.

McCaffrey also published stories about a sentient spaceship that work to revise genre expectations. Andrew Butler argues, "Existing narrative structures needed to be remodelled to allow more female characters, or dropped altogether in favour of feminine or feminist ones,"[21] which is precisely what happens in these stories. In "The Ship Who Sang" (1961), McCaffrey tells the story of a spaceship who sings, thinks, and feels – who loves. It is, like the stories described above, about relationships; in this case, the relationship between the ship, Helva, and her pilot, a man called Jennan: "Helva didn't know that she fell in love with Jennan that evening . . . As a shell-person, she considered herself remote from emotions largely connected with physical desires."[22] Helva was born with such debilitating birth defects that her parents had to choose between her death and her existence as a "shell person," linked to and only able to experience the world through technological interfaces. Helva does not see herself as disadvantaged or disabled, though; she has the ability to travel between stars, after all. The story relates her experiences finding, and then losing, Jennan. They both sacrifice – he, his life, and she, him – in order to save strangers. This is not a colonizing vision of interstellar travel, but rather a narrative that delivers a posthuman adventure based in caring and symbiotic relationships.

Vonda N. McIntyre's works also trouble assumptions about gender and sexuality. "Of Mist, and Grass, and Sand" (1973) introduces Snake, a strong healer heroine who has had deep training and is able to perform powerful feats of healing with her snakes. The story itself is heartbreaking because, as she tries to help desert people who don't understand her medicine, those people kill her smallest snake, Grass, whose talents lie in helping people dream and easing deathbed suffering. Again, rather than a colonial narrative of conquest, this is a complex tale of village politics, outsider status, and, indeed, the potential for love. In addition to Snake's gender-reversing powerful abilities, McIntyre introduces a culture in which triad marriages are the norm. The 1978 novel set in the same world, *Dreamsnake*, won the Hugo,

---

[20] Marleen S. Barr, *Lost in Space: Probing Feminist Science Fiction and Beyond* (Chapel Hill: University of North Carolina Press, 1993), pp. 11–12.

[21] Andrew M. Butler, *Solar Flares: Science Fiction in the 1970s* (Liverpool: Liverpool University Press, 2012), p. 142.

[22] Anne McCaffrey, "The Ship Who Sang," in Sargent, ed., *Women of Wonder*, pp. 174–5.

Nebula, and Locus awards for best novel. As Butler explains in relation to that novel, "The quest has traditionally been a masculine narrative structure, with the hero discovering his strengths as he journeys across a landscape, but McIntyre appropriates it for a story that puts the questioning of sex and gender at its heart."[23] Thus, like McCaffrey, McIntyre tells of a female quester on a world with alternative family structures – both revisionist moves that defamiliarize gender and sexuality and remake them into sites of potential and becoming.

One other example can help to round out the discussion of how women writers during the New Wave addressed genre and gender conventions. Eleanor Arnason's "The Warlord of Saturn's Moons" (1974) is a metafictional narrative set in a dystopian near future where air pollution is rampant, in which we read about a writer and the story she is creating. It begins, "Here I am, a silver-haired maiden lady of thirty-five, a feeder of stray cats, a window-ledge gardener, well on my way to the African violet and antimacassar stage."[24] Instead of a story of a questing woman forging her own path, Arnason gives us the quintessential spinster figure of patriarchal dictates – no gender reversal there. However, like Menolly and Snake, this woman is a creator, an artist, who is during the story engaged in the process of writing a somewhat trite science fictional space fantasy. She lives in a clearly inhospitable world: "Maybe I should call the Air Control number (dial AIR-CARE) and complain. But it takes a peculiar kind of person to keep on being public-spirited after it becomes obvious it's futile."[25] Her outlet is clearly her writing; as she makes tea, she explains, "All the while my mind is with my heroine, smiling grimly as she pilots the power-sledge between bare cliffs."[26]

Arnason's story is partly an exploration of escapism, and its dangers, but it is also a reworking of the SF story that undermines the stability of the conventions of the genre. As Barr argues, "Many feminist authors adhere to an established postmodern literary trait: they rewrite master narratives. More specifically, they rewrite patriarchal master narratives and reveal them to be patriarchal fictions which form the foundation of constructed reality."[27] In Arnason's narrative, the romantic adventure of SF, which upholds master

---

[23] Butler, *Solar Flares*, p. 141.
[24] Eleanor Arnason, "The Warlord of Saturn's Moons," in Sargent, ed., *Women of Wonder*, p. 335.
[25] Ibid., p. 340.
[26] Ibid., p. 336.
[27] Marleen S. Barr, *Feminist Fabulation: Space/Postmodern Fiction* (Iowa City: University of Iowa Press, 1992), p. 12.

narratives of heteronormative romance as well as imperialism, is revised through the lens of the ignored and isolated woman who creates the tale. The end of the story is: "Enough for today, I think and put down my pencil. Tomorrow, I'll figure out a way to get 409 off Sophamine. Where there's life there's hope and so forth, I tell myself."[28] The narrator/writer has agency in the process of creation, and therefore there is hope.

Reimagining Gender and Sexuality

Perhaps the most significant intervention into representations of gender and sexuality that writers embraced during the New Wave was to focus the capacity of SF to defamiliarize and estrange onto the underlying assumptions of the gender binary and heteronormativity. In an era when feminism and free love movements coincided with new poststructuralist theories from the likes of Michel Foucault and Jacques Derrida, SF offered a literary venue for exploring the possibilities of futures and alternative societies in which gender and sexuality were radically deconstructed and reconfigured along profoundly denaturalizing lines.

In Sonya Dorman Hess's "When I Was Miss Dow" (1966), the reader shares the perspective of an alien whose planet is being explored by humans, and who takes on the form of a human female in order to infiltrate their society. Of the humans, the alien explains, "They come first as explorers, and perhaps realize we are a race of one sex only, rather amorphous beings of proteide; and we, even baby I are Protean also, being able to take various shapes at will."[29] The gender binary simply does not exist on this world or for this character until humans arrive. This alien absorbs the "female Terran pattern" and is assigned by the alien power structure to "the colony's head biologist," Dr. Arnold Procter: "He is a nice, pink man with silver hair, soft-spoken, intelligent."[30] As a temporary human, the alien who is Miss Martha Dow is struck by the imbalances in human gender roles: "Though absorbed in his work, Dr. Proctor isn't rude to interrupters. A man of unusual balance, coming as he does from a culture which sends out scientific parties that are 90 percent of one sex, when their species provides them with two."[31] In the end, the alien is close to the biologist until his death, at which point Miss Dow mourns him – and then returns to the alien body. Like Tuttle's "Wives,"

[28] Arnason, "The Warlord," p. 343.
[29] Sonya Dorman Hess, "When I Was Miss Dow," in Sargent, ed., *Women of Wonder*, p. 185.
[30] Ibid., p. 186.
[31] Ibid., p. 187.

Hess's story is about gender performance, but it is also an exploration of the thought processes of a being who has no gender.

In 1972 Joanna Russ first published "Nobody's Home," a far-future narrative where teleportation is a simple, everyday occurrence, genetic augmentation has led to super-intelligence, and families are structured to embrace a wide range of sexualities and arrangements. The story follows Jannine, the "temporary family representative" of a group of "eighteen adults (two triplet marriages, a quad, and a group of eight)."[32] Russ's novel *The Female Man* (1975) is perhaps one of the best-known works to address gender and sexuality in a New Wave fashion. In it, she explores several different worlds and their relationships to the gender and sex identities of characters. There is alternate history, utopian "Whileaway," and a dystopia where men and women are literally at war. It is a novel about the restrictions of the time of the novel's production, and about the potential to reimagine gender and sexuality in entirely new ways.

Samuel R. Delany's *The Einstein Intersection* (1967) is a challenging text (typical for Delany) that focuses on the beings who now inhabit a post-nuclear Earth. These beings, like those in Hess's story, can take on human genetic structures, but for them it seems to be a more permanent state. Within the pseudo-human society the beings create, there are males, females, and androgens. The first story Delany sold, "Aye, and Gomorrah . . ." (1967), examines the "Spacers," androgynous humans who lack birth-sex identities owing to a neutering procedure that allows them to live in space. Later, in 1976, Delany would go on to publish *Triton: An Ambiguous Heterotopia*, partially in response to Ursula K. Le Guin's *The Dispossessed* (1974), in which there are dozens of different sexes that occupy nine categories. As Butler writes of the highly complex novel, "Delany's comedy of manners, arguably obscured by his metafictional apparatus, is of a society where race and sex are not fixed, and where sexuality can be rewired on a more or less permanent level."[33] Delany's works make full use of the formal experimentation made permissible by the New Wave in order to thoroughly reconfigure the parameters of possibility for gender and sexuality.

I conclude with one of the most important feminist works of the New Wave: Ursula K. Le Guin's *The Left Hand of Darkness*. Novel-length works have much more capacity to explore the range of issues and interventions described above, and *Left Hand*, first published in 1969 and winner of both the

---

[32] Joanna Russ, "Nobody's Home," in Sargent, ed., *Women of Wonder*, p. 253.
[33] Butler, *Solar Flares*, p. 156.

Hugo and Nebula awards, delves into each of those areas. It is set on Gethen, a planet peopled by individuals who are neither male nor female, but who have the potential to be either during periods of sexual activity. The novel defamiliarizes sexual identity, recoding it as a function of desire.[34] Centering on the relationship between a lone human male, Genly Ai, and a person indigenous to the planet, Estraven, the narrative problematizes human masculinity and its assumptions, interrogates the way sexuality is tied to gender imbalances in our world, and insists that the only way forward for Genly Ai is to remake his understanding of subjectivity, so that it can be seen as something in flux rather than as fixed and stable. Like many of the texts discussed above, Le Guin's novel situates a critique of gender roles within a larger exploration of power as it functions both to restrict and to monitor subjectivities. Offering depictions of how social institutions, political landscapes, and individual lives play out on Gethen, *Left Hand* calls careful attention to the ways in which gender and sexuality are constructed on Earth.

Left Hand and the many other feminist works of the New Wave recode the meaning of gender in SF, changing forever the ways in which we imagine humanity's present and future. Robert Heinlein's *Stranger in a Strange Land* (1961) and Joe Haldeman's *The Forever War* (1974), along with a number of other novels of the period, denaturalize heteronormative monogamy and reorient readers to the possibilities of alternative social and personal arrangements. Octavia E. Butler's long-term commitment to examinations of the functioning of power in relation to subjectivity begins in the late 1970s with *Patternmaster* (1976) and continues into her classic *Kindred* (1979) and beyond. Angela Carter's revised fairy tales in *The Bloody Chamber* (1979), dystopian gender-bending in *The Passion of New Eve* (1977), and surrealist reimaginings in *The Infernal Desire Machines of Doctor Hoffman* (1972), all integrate New Wave experimentation with science fictional elements and deeply feminist inquiries into gender and sexuality. The list of relevant works is long and rich, reflecting the diverse approaches writers employed to integrate formal experimentation with deep social critique and inquiry during the New Wave.

---

[34] See Lauren J. Lacey, *The Past That Might Have Been, the Future That May Come: Women Writing Fantastic Fiction, 1960s to the Present* (Jefferson, NC: MacFarland & Company, Inc., 2014), especially pp. 154–7.

24

Shestidesyatniki: The Conjunction of Inner and Outer Space in Eastern European Science Fiction

LARISA MIKHAYLOVA

The processes influencing SF in Eastern European countries differed significantly from the ones leading to the formation and development of New Wave SF in the United Kingdom and the United States. First, the transformation started a few years earlier – at the end of the 1950s, boosted by the death of Stalin in 1953, the leadership of Nikita Khrushchev, and the negating of Stalin's methods at the XXth Communist Party of the Soviet Union Congress in 1956. This period of Soviet history, which features the abolition of the Gulag system, the easing of some cultural and artistic restrictions, and a general trend toward a policy of peaceful coexistence with other nations, came to be known as the "Khrushchev Thaw." The first Sputnik flight on October 4, 1957, and launching the first man in space on April 12, 1961, were for most people within the Soviet Union a source of hope that a new, wiser, better era had really started. Second, much of the novelty of the New Wave in Western Europe and the United States stemmed from the rejection of the stereotypes that had accumulated during the Golden Age on the pages of the American pulp magazines (such as the cult of an Earthman as a conqueror, mad scientists, bug-eyed monsters, and lack of depth in characterization). These stereotypes did not resonate as deeply in pre-1950s USSR SF; thus, the New Wave in the Soviet Union was informed by a different set of conventions and expectations, more rooted in the particular cultural and political trends during the time of the thaw.

If we think of SF as a movement, not a genre, the most productive approach to its study is similar to the study of any other evolving movement – be it social or artistic. It necessarily has three main components:

- *authors*, feeling the demand of society, and writing the
- *works*, which immediately become a source of discussions and interpretation, the most popular of them spawning sequels, not necessarily written by the original author, and
- *readers*, the fans, who ultimately organize themselves into a fandom.

In the case of this chapter, that *reader* is a researcher, who grew up in the 1960s in Moscow as a fangirl, and who in the 1970s defended a PhD thesis on the evolution of modern SF, creating one of the first university courses in the Soviet Union on the History of English Language SF in 1980, which later was transformed into a course in History and Translation of SF, serving as a basis for publication of a Russian SF magazine *Supernova* (www.snovasf.com). This chapter reflects the corpus of SF books available to an avid reader in the Soviet Union of the era, like myself.

Soviet SF before the Shestidesyatniki Generation

Alexei Tolstoy's famous *Aelita* (1923) and *Engineer Garin and his Death Ray* (1927) and Alexander Belyaev's versatile novels (*Amphibious Man* [1926], *Air Seller* [1929], *A Man Who Lost His Face* [1929], *Star KETS* [1936], etc.) were all written before the war, and naturally they reflect the conventions and themes of the era in which they were written. But Alexander Kazantsev's novel *Arctic Bridge* (1941 excerpts, 1946 in full) marked the beginning of a new era. In this novel a bridge – a tube channel with vacuum-propelled carriages for transport – is constructed in the Arctic Sea, joining the USSR and the United States. The first real American Exhibition of 1959 in Moscow was still almost twenty years in the future for the author when he wrote it upon returning from the New York World's Fair in 1939, where he was the main engineer of the Soviet pavilion (the very same fair on whose premises the first Worldcon was held). This book served for Soviet readers of the 1940s and 1950s as a depiction of wonderful possibilities lying within reach for people who manage to transgress ideological boundaries and work together – as a broad gesture of global symbolism, in Kazantsev's novel the bridge is built from both ends to meet in the middle.

In the USSR, restoration of the country after the Second World War helped fuel the fast-paced industrial development of the era, with many SF creators as active participants. Their enthusiasm originated in the early years after the Great October Revolution of 1917, fed by the newly freed creativity of former peasants who managed to become engineers and industrial builders, and who transformed the country through a combination of applied science and a desire to make it a better place for the coming generations. Unfortunately, the party bosses decided that the addition of a lash was needed as an impetus, which led to the creation of the infamous Gulag labor camps. Still, the core belief that socialism held the potential for the creation of a better future survived even among those enthusiasts who were thrown into these labor camps. Indeed, several SF writers continued writing after their release from the labor camps – Yan Larry (1900–77), Oles Berdnyk (1926–2003), Mikhail Belov (1910–2000).[1] Though counterintuitive, the strong social convictions of these authors outweighed their Gulag experiences. The Soviet vision – which included great plans to bring electricity to Siberian construction sites and to build new cities in the Arctic – still held promise for these authors, and even the harsher aspects of Soviet social control (as exemplified by the Gulag system) were considered necessary for the country to stand on its feet and provide opportunities for the younger generation. Within the circle of SF writers and readers such enchantment with the future was not contrary to the logic of scientific progress.

This dream of progress was also fueling the dedicated efforts of geologists who explored uncharted regions of Siberia and the Arctic to provide vital resources needed to support the growth and industrialization of the country – nickel, tin, aluminum, tungsten, copper, titanium, uranium, etc. In the 1950s, geology became one of the most popular professions. And some of those geologists grew into SF writers.

Ivan Yefremov (1908–1972)

The most influential of such geologists-turned-writers was Ivan Yefremov, who headed more than twenty survey expeditions in the Urals, Altai, and Yakutia. His first collection, "Five Compass Points," praised by Alexei Tolstoy for its "elegant and concise style,"[2] was published in 1944 and contained five stories "about the extraordinary." His stories evoke that famous science fictional "sense of wonder." Possessing an eidetic memory, Yefremov created clear and expressive visual representations in his stories, and at the same time drew widely on a variety of philosophical and aesthetic traditions when creating his characters and plots. Yefremov applied a wide

---

[1] A Far Eastern (the Russian far east is a region of Russia beyond Siberia by the Okhotsk Sea, from Vladivostok to Kamchatka) author from Khabarovsk, Mikhail Belov liked to repeat in the 1990s that he did not regret the 1930s because of the great deeds and dreams that emerged in that era – V. Karatsupa, V. Burya 2013 http://archivsf.narod.ru/1911/michael_belov/index.htm (last accessed November 20, 2017).

[2] Чудинов П. К. Иван Антонович Ефремов (P. K. Chudinov, Ivan Antonovich Yefremov) (Moscow: Nauka, 1987), Chapter 5.

geologic frame to paleontological developments, thus creating in 1940 a new science – taphonomy – which makes it possible to predict the areas where fossils are buried. This new scientific technique was a bold step forward in geological sciences before the computer era. Without the defense of a thesis, on the basis of his published articles Yefremov was awarded a PhD degree while still nominally an undergraduate student at the Leningrad Mining Academy. Yefremov's intense research into geology and the study of the emergence of life on Earth shaped his philosophical and scientific convictions and influenced his creative principles. His later career was connected to the USSR Academy of Sciences' Paleontological Institute: Moscow's Paleontological museum's most spectacular exhibits of dinosaurs were excavated during Ivan Yefremov's expeditions to Mongolian Gobi in 1946–8 and were found in full accordance with his taphonomy. In his story *Diamond Tube* (1944), on the basis of geologic comparison, Yefremov predicted a discovery of diamond fields in Yakutia, which actually happened in 1954. In another documented connection between Yefremov's scientific vision and his creative endeavor, Soviet physicist Yuri Densuyk's invention of holography was inspired by reading Yefremov's novella *Shadow of the Past* (1945).

The book that made Yefremov arguably the most famous Russian SF writer of the era, both in the Soviet Union and abroad, was his novel *Andromeda Nebula* (1957). *Andromeda Nebula* is set in the world of the fortieth century AD. The novel is often categorized by literary critics as portrayal of a kind of communist utopia, but it should be noted that although the novel is certainly about a communist society, Yefremov never considered his vision to represent an unattainable ideal. In this novel, Yefremov extrapolates a far-future human history in which human explorations of the universe lead to the establishment of the Great Ring of the Worlds. In thinking of this future state of humanity, Yefremov, with his systematic mind, came to the conclusion that such exploration would be possible only through combining the resources of Earth and significantly changing people themselves. Thus, the study of Eastern systems of self-control and meditation combined with the Hellenic traditions of harmonious physical training and the perception of beauty bring forth a picture of a society within the novel where individual development enriches everyone. This society is multicultural in the sense that characters cherish the cultural traditions of their distant progenitors – be they Ukrainian, Russian, African, Indian – but only in ways which make life more colorful (how they dress for special occasions, dance, cook, or sing). Otherwise, they share common values enabling them not just to coexist but to be good stewards of the planet, with easy access to educational and recreational areas for everyone. The highest organ is called Academy of Joy and Sorrow, because the balance of these emotions in a person epitomizes striving for happiness, and the development of society depends upon it. The Great Ring of the Worlds is established as mainly an information system connecting civilizations of the Universe. Interstellar travel demands considerable resources, and thus expeditions are not very numerous. But these resource demands do not stop exploration. In fact, the captain of the starship *Tantra*, whose crew's adventures start the novel, is born in space when his parents are flying to another star.

For Yefremov, the development of ethics was a pressing matter. Humankind simply does not have the luxury to remain "an archaeopteryx of the spirit," as Stapledon's Odd John defined it.[3] The novel *Razor's Edge* (1963) similarly explores how we might overcome the faults and vices of so-called "human nature." As a true evolutionist, Yefremov did not consider human nature unchangeable – but saw the inability to control impulses as a serious obstacle to consistent improvements. Ethics in his hands thus becomes a project of evolutionary engineering. Yefremov weaved principles of Tantric yoga into his book, the title of which is an expression of the dialectic possibility to tread right. Readers follow one of the protagonists – an artist and a sculptor, Dayaram – to a Himalayan monastery, where he treads a difficult path to master himself. He is also searching for a way to catch and express beauty. The Russian protagonist, a physician and psychophysiologist, Ivan Girin, and a girl he meets and falls in love with – a gymnast, Seraphima – participate in a discussion about beauty and nudity, against the parochial attitudes of hostile critics to Konenkov's wooden sculpture.[4] An adventure plotline about treasure hunters looking near the Indian shores for a Black Crown of Alexander the Great adorned with powerful jewels intertwines with the stories of Girin and Dayaram, adding to the novel's entertainment and bringing together aspects of physical and spiritual journeys in this novel, which Yefremov himself considered his "favorite child."

In Yefremov's next novel, *The Bull's Hour* (1969), set almost a thousand years after the Era of the Great Ring started, a spaceship named *Temnoye Plamya* (Dark Flame) goes to visit distant Earth relatives who fled to another

---

[3] "Man, I suppose, is about as clever along his own line as the earliest birds were at flight. He's a sort of an archaeopteryx of the spirit." Olaf Stapledon, *Odd John and Sirius* (New York: Dover, 1972), p. 27.

[4] Sergey Konenkov (1874–1971), a sculptor often called 'the Russian Rodin'. The work causing the discussion can be seen here https://s-media-cache-ako.pinimg.com/564x/07/bc/47/07bc477be0e708a5d9c2c1744f8c2a90.jpg (last accessed November 12, 2017).

galaxy in the Lynx constellation during a period of conflict and unrest. This novel, like others by Yefremov, takes up the theme of vanquishing the destructive urges in human thought and behavior. A fitting metaphor for the novel, "the bull's hour" is the darkest time before dawn. In a series of letters penned in 1968 to a specialist in ancient Chinese mythology, we find Yefremov reflecting on how he arrived at the metaphor of the "bull's hour" as a central image for the novel. Though Yefremov's depiction of the planet Tormans (or Yan-Yakh) is characterized by hints of a Maoist-style socialism, readers connected to government saw the depiction of the planet as a commentary on the stagnations of late-stage USSR political and economic conditions. This led to a search of Yefremov's house a month after the writer's death, followed by an order to cease the publication of a series of his collected works, as well as a command to remove all references to *The Bull's Hour* from entries on Yefremov in biographical essays and encyclopedias.

In *The Bull's Hour* Yefremov shows how the Earthling crew members immerse themselves in the life of Tormansians, and even the centuries-long tradition of self-discipline doesn't preclude the strong compassion they feel and a desire to help these distorted people overcome their degrading circumstances. Some of the Earth people perish, including the captain of the *Temnoye Plamya*, Fay Rodis – but before stopping her heart she orders the ship not to retaliate, but to fly away. Their open-mindedness shows the people of Yan-Yakh that it is possible to live without fear, negating the lies they were fed about a totally corrupt Earth and breaking the vicious circle of distrust.

A fit comparison would be with the Prime Directive in the world of *Star Trek* (1966–), established by Gene Roddenberry and the initial writers of the series as the leading principle of interaction between civilizations. The Prime Directive states that that pre-warp societies are only to be observed, not directly contacted by the Federation, and that relations with post-warp nations are to be established on the principles of reciprocity.[5] And, while "The Cage" with a woman as Number One was rejected as a *Star Trek* pilot by the National Broadcasting Company (NBC) in 1965, Yefremov made a woman the captain of his spaceship for the first time in the Soviet SF, and Fay Rodis instantly became one of his most popular characters.

Feminist principles are further explored and expressed in Yefremov's highly emotional philosophical-adventure novel, *Thais of Athens* (1971,

---

[5] In fact, it cannot be considered a violation in this case, as Tormansians were already in possession of interstellar flight, and they were not alien as such, but former people of Earth poisoned by deliberate lies.

English translation by Maria K. in 2010[6]). Yefremov's reader is returned to Hellenic Greece, but in the time of Alexander the Great. As in *The Razor's Edge*, we delve into the philosophy, but not of beauty *per se*, but rather beauty's role in the rise and fall of civilizations. Haetera Thais follows Alexander, but her personal development goes contrary to the conqueror's plans. She gradually understands that there is hardly anything more worthy on this Earth than to promote knowledge and to be the artist's inspiration. And she departs with her true friend – black priestess Eris – to Uranopolis, a city promoting the equality of people and the development of their talents.

In historical novels Yefremov condenses the ways which might help to reach the world of future peace and exploration. *Thais of Athens* is also about the worlds of love, and was more appreciated by the female readers of the era, but Yefremov's feminism – in the variant akin to *Women Who Run With the Wolves* (1992) by Clarissa Pinkola Estés – gained some ground in the hearts of male readership as well.

Yefremov's books are all a result of metasynthesis on the basis of his experience as a scientist accustomed to wide comparisons and his extensive reading of literature gathered with the help of his numerous correspondents in Europe and the United States. Foreign books were very difficult to obtain in Soviet times other than in translation, and Yefremov sent request lists to the scholars and writers with whom he corresponded: Poul Anderson, Arthur C. Clarke, Everett Olson, Friedrich von Huene, and many others.[7] His whole foreign language library at home – over 2000 volumes, containing, for example *The Lord of the Rings* and *Dangerous Visions* – resulted from such orders, which he usually compensated for by sending his books and art albums in return. The library was used during his lifetime as a source of materials by several translators, among them Zinaida Bobyr, the first translator of Ray Bradbury and J. R. R. Tolkien into Russian, by writers – including the Strugatsky brothers in the 1960s – and later researchers of SF. Showing a unique talent, Yefemov's works exist in dialogue with trends in global SF. His interest in Eastern culture and philosophy combined with his development of dialectics within SF brings to mind the works of another deep dialectician in SF, also very interested in Eastern philosophy: Ursula K. Le Guin.

Though Ivan Yefremov was indeed a leading figure of Soviet SF in the 1950s and 1960s, after his death his legacy was attacked by certain forces in the

---

6 I. Efremov, *Thais of Athens* (London: TA Productions Ltd, 2010).

7 Переписка Ивана Антоновича Ефремова (I. A. Yefremov's Correspondence) (Moscow: Veche, 2016).

KGB, and his name was excluded even from scientific publications – but his story is illuminating, as it reveals the true force of the Yefremov fandom that fought for a full restoration of his esteem against official attempts to subdue the memory of him.[8] In the following pages of this chapter we will observe his influence more than once.

Arkady Strugatsky (1925–1991) and Boris Strugatsky (1933–2012)

The Strugatsky brothers appeared in Ivan Yefremov's house in 1958 with a manuscript of their novella about Venus exploration, *The Land of Crimson Clouds*, which (on Yefremov's and Kirill Andreyev's recommendations) was accepted for publication in Detgiz – one of the central Moscow publishing houses. Although Arkady, the elder brother, a Japanese translator, had written a novel at the end of the 1940s, and even published a novella on the aftermath of the Bikini atomic bomb tests in 1956, *The Land of Crimson Clouds* served to introduce a new pair of voices in Soviet SF. Arkady's brother and co-author, Boris Strugatsky, was able to leave his career as an astronomer and dedicate himself entirely to literary pursuits from 1963 onwards. The Strugatskys were also writing about the extraordinary, but mostly looking for less traditional ways to express it. The style of their prose – dynamic, yet layered with subtle overtones – was decidedly oriented towards the personalization of their characters, making them closer to the tastes of modern-day readers and in sync with New Wave trends in SF in England and the United States. One can get a sense of these literary sensibilities in a letter from Arkady to Boris written on September 29, 1957: "We shouldn't shy from connecting slight sentimentality with adventure, with a pinch of philosophy and a grain of lewdness."[9] This proposed blending of genres and styles to make the material accessible and interesting to a wide population, including senior high school students, is characteristic of their thinking early in their career. The debut book discussed in this letter was never translated into English, and the authors preferred not to include it in their later collected

---

[8] See the article by Lev Borkin on the protest letters, "In Defense of Ivan Yefremov, a Paleontologist and Science Fiction Writer (1974)," *Studies in the History of Biology* 8, 1 (2016), pp. 94–120, www.noogen.su/iefremov/about/borkin.pdf (Russian, abstract in English; last accessed November 12, 2017).

[9] Геннадий Прашкевич, Дмитрий Володихин. Братья Стругацкие. Москва: Молодая гвардия, серия ЖЗЛ, 2012. Гл. 1, разд. 12 (G. Prashkevich and D. Volodikhin, Strugatsky Brothers. Moscow: Molodaya Gvardia, Biographies series, 2012, Chapter 1, paragraph 12).

works because of the "overt romanticism"[10] of the plot, but the characters introduced there – navigator Krutikov, geologists and biologists Dauge and Yurkovsky, engineer Bykov – acted in a number of further stories and novellas (as the Strugatskys defined most of their works, rather than novels).

The evolution of the authors' style and the scope of their stories progressed rapidly. Gradually the contours of the Earth in the twenty-second century started to become more palpable in the shorter and longer works that centered around the Noon world. The Noon cycle includes, besides the title novella *Noon: The 22nd Century* (1961), eight longer works written between 1960 and 1986: *Destination Amalthea* (1960), *Probationers* (1961), *Escape Attempt* (1962), *Far Rainbow* (1963), *Hard to be a God* (1964), *The Final Circle of Paradise* (1965), *Prisoners of Power* (1969), *Space Mowgli* (1971), *The Kid from Hell* (1974), *Beetle in an Anthill* (1980), and *The Time Wanderers* (1986). As in Yefremov's novels on the future, the society of the Noon world is governed by a global meritocratic council of scientists and philosophers, and the most discussed side of its depiction is a theory of education; teachers are the most respected profession. As many attentive fans of the Strugatskys have noted, this cycle reflects both a dream of the Shestidesyatniki generation – that is, those socially active people who worked and created in the 1960s Soviet Union – and the skepticism felt by this generation about the actual achievability of this dream. Or, rather, the disillusionment felt by those in this generation who despaired that social improvement could be realized during their lifetime. Lasting social transformation cannot proceed so quickly and easily; moreover, it is not irreversible, as reality in modern Russia shows.

In retrospect, the book that reflected the creative spirit of the 1960s best was the Strugatskys' 1965 novel *Monday Begins on Saturday* (translated into English by Leonid Renen). Andrew Bromfield's 2005 translation for Seagull Publishing has the title *Monday Starts on Saturday*. In my opinion, a more fitting translation would have been *Monday Starts on Saturday Night*, which would help convey the central idea involved: science is so fascinating in itself that researchers work practically nonstop, skipping weekends.[11] To stay away for even a day from such an adventure as scientific research – be it outer space or magic, as in the Institute of Wizardry and Witchcraft in this case – is an absolute loss of time. That was the Soviet spirit of the 1960s, not ordered from

---

[10] Б. Стругацкий. Комментарии к пройденному / А. и Б. Стругацкие. Собр. Соч в 11 тт, т. 1. – М., АСТ, 2011. С. 638 (B. Strugatsky, Comments to the Ways Trodden. In A. and B. Strugatsky, Collected works in 11 vols. Moscow: AST, 2001, Vol. 1, p. 638.)

[11] In the USSR of the 1960s only Sunday was a break in a working week, not Saturday and Sunday.

above but developing from the heart and from the inquisitiveness of the mind. The Strugatskys reflected this mighty movement and wrote "a fairy tale for junior researchers," spreading this inquisitiveness into a rich sphere of magic reflected in Slavic and World folklore, combining fairy figures with the realities of Soviet scientific research. Mixing genres in this book produced an exhilarating cocktail, blending modern science with millennia-old Baba Yaga, Yanus Bifrons, invisibility capes, and magic wands, resulting in a vibrant variant of science fantasy, or urban fantasy. The book also includes shades of irony and social criticism, noting wryly the modern tendency to implement bureaucratic routines within the field of scientific research. This irony can be seen in the title of one of the novel's parts – "Vanitas Vanitatum." To many SF fans in Russia this book remained the symbol of the time, when big strides in the country's economy and science seemed to promise even brighter perspectives in the future.

But the times were changing. Irony in the Strugatskys' later books turned into sarcastic satire in *Tale of the Troika* (1968) and *Snail on the Slope* (1972), and later into a gloomy rejection of any possibility of an optimistic outcome for their characters, or for the human race in general. Their *Roadside Picnic* (1971, publ. 1972) – and the subsequent adaptation of the novella by Andrey Tarkovsky as a film in 1979 – reveals this divide in a more pronounced form. The novella – dealing with the mess left after a visit by some irresponsible extraterrestrial visitors, the supposed picnickers – borders on a post-apocalyptic narrative; the zone where these incomprehensible and often destructive artifacts are found brings the characters to the limit of their endurance, and mostly defeats them. Andrey Tarkovsky in his film *Stalker* (1979) juxtaposes the rational and irrational positions of a physics professor and a writer, both of whom are left behind by a down-to-earth "stalker," a treasure hunter, who does not possess any illusions about the hardness of the world but still hopes for something better. In the film he returns home even more disillusioned, whereas the book contains the opposite message: reaching the coveted Golden Ball that is believed to fulfill any wish, Redrik Shukhart (the stalker has a name in the novella) finds in his heart the urge to wish for "happiness to all, for free." In making adjustments to the script, though, the authors agreed to the gloomier conclusion for the film.

The Strugatskys' books of the second half of the 1960s to an extent served the same role as Harlan Ellison's *Dangerous Visions* by criticizing encroaching bureaucracy and by making fun of doublethink. But as their career progressed, the authors gradually drew less and less palatable pictures of life in general, driven by doubts of a possibility for our human race to overcome trials and tribulations stemming from human nature itself (as in *Doomed City*, 1972, publ. 1989). Hence, we witness their almost paranoid vision of limits to scientific development and the failure to penetrate the barriers of our ignorance in *Definitely Maybe* (1974), or the introduction of space explorers who change so completely upon their return to Earth that they became a threat that needs to be exterminated (*Beetle in an Anthill*, 1979). By the 1980s, this spirit of despondency overcomes all the productive urges of the Strugatskys' characters.

Despite, or because of, this pessimism, the Strugatskys' books obtained a huge following, with their fans calling themselves "Ludeny" after the next stage of human evolution in their novel *The Time Wanderers*.

Stanislaw Lem (1921–2006)

For collectors of Soviet-era SF publications the most esteemed find is a hardcover series called the Library of Contemporary Science Fiction, published by Molodaya Gvardia in 1965–76 – twenty-eight volumes with an embossed silver and red crescent on the cover and a print run of 250,000 copies each. This collection was initiated by Yefremov, who also recommended some of the novels and stories for inclusion and translation from his home library, and the project was run by a group of writers and editors – Kirill Andreyev, Ariadna Gromova, Bella Klyueva, Eremey Parnov, Arkady Strugatsky, Sergey Zhemaitis. The main objectives of the collection were to showcase SF and to serve as a testament to the emergence of SF as a major contemporary branch of literature. The collection included both Soviet and foreign authors.

A number of regular SF divisions in widely distributed magazines like *Tekhnika-Molodezhi, Nauka ee Zhizn, Khimia ee Zhizn, Znanie-Sila* were founded in the 1960s and attracted growing attention to SF. Fan clubs likewise started to form all around the Soviet Union. Like all fans elsewhere, they discussed the books and films they liked, and also engaged in the process of translating and publishing SF from various languages. The main series – *Zarubezhnaya Fantastyka*, or ZF in short – was published by Mir publishing house, where a strong group of editors managed to create an elite list of SF classics from the United States and the United Kingdom, supported by anthologies of SF by authors from many European countries (135 books in the series: forty-one in the 1960s, plus a dozen anthologies and books without the series logo of such important works as Ray Bradbury's *Fahrenheit 451*). Mir also published some Soviet SF writers in translation into foreign languages.

At least one such edition was directly organized by Ivan Yefremov – he introduced the Strugatsky brothers to his acquaintance, the British SF scholar and translator Alan Myers, whose translation of the novella *Far Rainbow* was published as a paperback in 1967 by Mir.[12]

In the Mir series, and also in the Znanie almanacs (thirty-six issues, anthologists K. Andreyev, Ye. Brandis, V. Dmitrevsky, Ye. Parnov, R. Rybkin, and V. Babenko, among others), a prominent place was allotted to SF from Eastern European countries: East Germany, Bulgaria, Romania, Czechoslovakia, Yugoslavia, Hungary, Poland. Among this group, the most influential author was Poland's Stanislaw Lem – who, like the Strugatskys, would become famous among Anglophone SF fans as well.

Lem is often called a genius of paradoxes. Born in 1921 to a family of a doctor in Lvov, he described his childhood years in an autobiographical novel *High Castle* (1966). During the Second World War he joined the Resistance, and fought to liberate Poland from the fascists. In 1946 he moved to Krakow and finished his medical education at Jagiellonian University, where he conceived a passion for the methodology of science and started writing SF stories. In his work he manages to convey the seductive joys of scientific research, never forgetting the dangers of the new knowledge and skills but never agreeing to the sanctity of the existing structures, either. The works of the Strugatsky brothers and Stanislaw Lem attracted wide critical attention, and shared certain similarities in both form and content, though Marc Amusin argues that the Strugatskys were evolving in the tradition of Dostoyevsky and appealing to the emotions, whereas Lem was moving toward more abstract, logical constructions, as if insulating his characters *from* emotions.[13] The existentialist mode of his works somewhat reminds one of Kafka's style, but Lem mobilizes satire to fend off bureaucratic totalitarianism. There is laughter (though bitter laughter) in Lem, where Kafka succumbs to despair.

The Star Diaries (1954, expanded until 1971), describes the space voyages of Ijon Tichy in the grotesque satirical tradition of François Rabelais and Jonathan Swift.[14] Another cycle is built around an astronaut Pirx, and written

---

[12] The edition of *Far Rainbow* by the Strugatsky brothers in A. Myers's translation is presented at https://fantlab.ru/edition53501 (last accessed November 13, 2017).

[13] Амусин, Марк, Драмы идей, трагедия людей. Знамя (M. Amusin, "Dramas of Ideas, Tragedies of People," *Znamya* 7 (2009).

[14] English translations of selected stories were published in two volumes: *The Star Diaries*, by Michael Kandel (New York: The Seabury Press, 1976) and the second, *Memoirs of a Space Traveler: Further Reminiscences of Ijon Tichy*, by Joel Stern and Maria Swiecicka-Ziemianek (New York: Harcourt Brace Jovanovich, 1982).

in a more realistic manner, without absurdist inclusions. The tone varies from brighter glimpses of the spacefaring future in the early *Tales of Pirx the Pilot* (translated into English by Louis Iribarne in 1979) to gloomier visions deriving from Lem's changed opinion on the miniscule probability of ever meeting another civilization of sentient beings during a lifetime or even several lifetimes, as seen in the novel *Fiasco* (1986 translation by Michael Kandel). Humorous baroque-style stories about the exploits of Trurl and Klapaucius, "constructors" among robots, are collected in *The Cyberiad: Fables for the Cybernetic Age* (1964, translated by Michael Kandel in 1974).

Philosophical essays of the Enlightenment are another source of inspiration and favorite genre of Lem's – another time, like our own, when ideas spread faster than social structures and the morality expected to accommodate them. Lem's oeuvre is almost equally divided into fiction and philosophic-methodological essays, containing the author's thoughts on the problems resulting from the developments of cybernetics in the modern world. The most important of these essays are collected in a book, *Summa Technologiae* (1963; translated by Joanna Zylinska for the University of Minnesota Press in 2013). Essays from his two-volume critiques on SF, *Fantastyka i futurologia* (1970), were partially translated in the single-volume *Microworlds: Writings on Science Fiction and Fantasy* (edited by Franz Rottensteiner, 1984); his essay on SF declaring Philip K. Dick "A Visionary Among the Charlatans" was especially notorious among both SF creators and SF fans.

At times Lem's prose turned towards the highly metafictional, even experimental. In the collection *A Perfect Vacuum* (1971, transl. by Kandel in 1979) Lem uses a trope implemented by Jorge Luis Borges to express his thoughts on space, society, and culture as if reviewing fictional books, while in *Imaginary Magnitude* (1973; translated by Marc E. Heine in 1984) he collected introductions to nonexistent books to the same end.

However, despite the inventiveness of such work, *Solaris* remains by far the most well-known and influential novel by Lem. Written in 1961, it tells about almost a century of unsuccessful attempts to establish contact with the Ocean – the planet-enveloping sentient being on the planet Solaris. There start to appear "visitors" on the station, materialized from the researchers' memories, reversing the polarity of examiner and examinee. This telepathic duplication of personality structure by the "blind" Ocean – which has managed to read the men as an open book while ignoring all their attempts at meaningful contact – initially appears to be an ominous sign of communication impossibility between humans and the Ocean. But the complex evolution of one such phantasm, Harey, who decides to terminate her existence when she sees she is causing torment to the one she loves – is not an absence of a contact. It is rather a reaction and volition, harboring hope for communion. And this hope makes the primary protagonist, Kelvin, stay on the station above Solaris and continue the study. In his preface to a Russian edition Lem pressed his intention to accept the thought that the "Unknown will be meeting us among the stars."[15] Despite the author's scorn of Steven Soderbergh's screen adaptation of the novel in 2002 – "I didn't call it 'Love in Outer Space'"[16] – Andrey Tarkovsky's 1971 film managed to convey exactly Lem's concept of a mighty Unknown which will be forever a magnet for the human mind, and which won't be perceived unless felt and accepted as a part of ourselves.

During the 1960s the elder SF writers kept publishing (such as Georgy Gurevitch, Alexander Kazantsev, Georgy Martynov) and dozens of new writers entered the field, with an important trend towards developing deeper characterization and delving into psychological problems of inner space, each of them deserving a special chapter: Valentina Zhuravleva, Genrikh Altov, Dmitry Bilenkin, Olga Larionova, Kir Bulychev, Sever Gansovsky, and others. One novel of particular note appeared at this time which may serve as a representative of the whole: *Self-Discovery* by Vladimir Savchenko, a specialist in cybernetics and a philosopher from Kiev.[17] Savchenko's protagonist in this novel discovers a method for duplicating human beings, which becomes a meditation on the nature of human identity and selfhood.

Soviet SF Film, Television, and Fandom

In the United States, television in the 1960s gave *Star Trek* to the SF lovers in the English-speaking world, casting a well-conceived vision of future space exploration for a popular audience. Nothing of the kind had developed in Soviet television by then. Despite the existence of good acting schools and a great theatrical tradition, television series were not supported as an art form

[15] Лем С. Предисловие к русскому изданию / В мире фантастики и приключений. Сост. Е. Брандис и Вл. Дмитревский. – Л., 1963,c. 137 (S. Lem, Preface to a Russian edition. In Ye Brandis and V. Dmitrevsky, eds., *V mire fantastiki I priklyuchenij* (Leningrad: Lenizdat, 1963), p. 137.

[16] Stanislaw Lem, "The Solaris Station" (December 8, 2002). *Stanislaw Lem – The Official Site*. http://english.lem.pl/arround-lem/adaptations/soderbergh/147-the-solaris-station?showall=&start=1 (last accessed September 13, 2016).

[17] Vladimir Savchenko, *Self-Discovery* (Открытие себя, 1967), trans. Antonina Bouis (New York: Macmillan, 1979).

by the state. A descendant of a rich radio theatre tradition, SF teledrama was in the 1960s only starting to develop from recorded theatre performances to television series with specially produced props, high production values, and complex, ongoing storylines.[18]

There were two major ways that visually fantastic imagery was developing in the Soviet cinema: fairy tale films (which in the 1960s were widely known and very popular with both children and adults; over ten such films appeared during the decade), and popular science films, which combined feature elements with a narrative explaining scientific principles and laws. The master in this sphere was Pavel Klushantsev. Lack of regular cultural contacts led to a peculiar situation when his *Planeta Bur* (*Stormy Planet*, 1963) was revamped in the United States and turned into *Voyage to the Planet of Prehistoric Women* (1968). Klushantsev devised many special effects to render weightlessness on the screen, show hovercrafts, and depict otherworldly landscapes, which subsequently influenced such well-known SF masters as Stanley Kubrick and George Lucas. These developments allow us to say that, despite a very limited number of SF films (just under a dozen of them in the 1960s), fantastic cinema also was going through a period in which filmmakers were actively searching for how to represent the moral aspects of technical progress and to make imagined landscapes more convincing. The most popular of these films, *Amphibious Man* (*Человек-амфибия*, 1961), was a screen adaptation of A. Belyaev's novel about a bioengineered boy saved from incurable lung disease by having shark's gills implanted into him. A Soviet version of a sympathetic "biochemical" android attracted the viewers' attention by his genuine interest in understanding people in *His Name Was Robert* (*Его звали Роберт*, 1967). In 1967 a first part of the *Andromeda Nebula* film was issued, which was less nuanced than the book but gave a significantly more expressive picture of a future society than the mere episodic glimpses in earlier films. Music and songs from the films on space exploration created the background for public events.[19] SF art likewise received a mighty push in the 1960s and was actively represented at exhibitions promoted by the magazine *Tekhnika-Molodezhi*, published in books and highlighted on the book covers. Most of these hardcover books were

---

[18] One should mention in this respect a two-part 1968 *Solaris* filmed by Boris Nirenburg (screenplay Nikolai Kemarsky, cast Vasily Lanovoy, Vladimir Etoosh, Anatoly Katsinsky, and Antonina Pilyus).

[19] E.g., songs written by Vano Muradeli and Evgeny Dolmatovsky for the film *Toward Your Dreams* (Мечте навстречу, 1963, screenplay by Oles Berdnyk, among others) "There will be blooming appletrees on Mars" and "I am the Earth sending forth my sons and daughters with love."

illustrated with black and white pictures inside. And although no SF magazines appeared, there were still periodical publications such as an almanac *Мир приключений* (1955–90, 90,000–115,000 copies, edited by Yefremov and Arkady Strugatsky among others)[20] from Detgiz publishing house aimed predominantly at children and young adults, and thus widening the reading base for SF literature.

By the 1980s over one hundred SF fan clubs existed all over the country; books were in high demand. Clubs published several fanzines, the earliest fan magazine being *Gusli kota Vasiliya* (Sverdlovsk, 1966), and the longest running being *Oversun* and *Semechki* (Lipetsk). But librarians didn't have any systematic reference guides for the younger generation, which slowed both the popular spread of SF culture and inhibited early efforts to study the genre broadly. The first general guide in SF literature published for all the libraries in the USSR – *Mir glazami fantastov* (Мир глазами фантастов. М., Книга, 1985) – had a difficult birth. As a science editor of this book, which was compiled by a group of enthusiastic bibliographers of Lenin State Library, Zinaida Shalashova, Arnold Gorbunov, Irina Semibratova, and others, I regretted to observe how the manuscript volume diminished twice after going to the Central Committee of the Communist Party (CPSU) three times, as three general secretaries changed during the process of its publication – a victim of the inevitable prepublishing censorship in those days. Still, it was an important step, legitimizing the inclusion of SF into the system of modern literature in libraries' collections, organizing readers' conferences, and stimulating further study of the genre.

By the end of the 1980s the map of SF in the Soviet Union included, beyond the best-known prominent authors, a varied and thriving fandom, whose members during the next decades were to become anthologists and authors themselves, creating the next wave of SF, albeit in a very different country from the one in which Yefremov and the Strugatskys rose to fame.

---

[20] The series is well represented at the SF Russian portal Fantlab at www.fantlab.ru/series352 (accessed on November 12, 2017).

25

Afrofuturism in the New Wave Era

MARK BOULD

African Americans have written SF since the late nineteenth century, but it is generally accepted that they did not contribute to SF's specialty magazine-and-paperback tradition until Samuel R. Delany's *The Jewels of Aptor* (1962). Such an absence is hardly accidental, as SF was shaped by, often embraced and sometimes championed racial and colonial ideologies.[1] However, genre SF emerged between 1910 and 1930 – during the height of Jim Crow, when many states enshrined "one drop" hypodescent in law, and "blood fraction" states became effectively one-drop states – so some genre SF writers were undoubtedly, by these definitions, "black," whether they knew it or not.

In February 1926 – mere weeks before Gernsback launched the first specialty SF magazine – the National Association for the Advancement of Colored People's (NAACP's) *The Crisis*, edited by W. E. B. Du Bois, published a questionnaire on the representation of African Americans, the responsibility of black writers to their community, and their treatment by publishers. In the resulting symposium, published between March and November, Countee Cullen outlined the need to produce truly representative characters, Langston Hughes insisted on the author's right to creative freedom, and Jesse Fauset decried the power of white publisher bias, which would always favor certain kinds of writers, fictions, and representations. These issues continue to shape African-American culture, including the degree and kinds of its engagement with SF. Furthermore, as Kodwo Eshun notes, Black Atlantic culture has historically been dominated by "the practice of counter-memory" and its "ethical commitment to history, the dead, and the forgotten," against which "the manufacture of conceptual tools that could analyze and assemble counterfutures was understood as [a] dereliction of duty."[2]

---

[1] See John Rieder, *Colonialism and the Emergence of Science Fiction* (Middletown, CT: Wesleyan University Press, 2008).

[2] Kodwo Eshun, "Further Considerations of Afrofuturism," *CR: The New Centennial Review* 3, 2 (2003), p. 288.

Genre SF in the 1930s did contain progressive elements, emerging in part from popular front politics shaped by the US Communist Party's involvement in African-American causes; probably of greatest significance here were the Futurians, a group of left-wing fans, including C. M. Kornbluth, Frederik Pohl, Richard Wilson, and Donald A. Wollheim, who went on to become writers, editors, and agents. Allen DeGraeff's *Human and Other Beings* (1963) reprints sixteen stories by leftists such as Kornbluth, Pohl, Wilson, Theodore R. Cogswell, and Mack Reynolds, and others from SF's more liberal wing. However, rather than adopting African-American perspectives, they typically draw upon the metaphorical potential of aliens and other SF conceits to comment indirectly and often ambiguously on America's racist and racializing structures.

Pohl's contribution to Harlan Ellison's *Dangerous Visions* (1967) anthology is more direct. In "The Day After the Day the Martians Came," journalists cram Mr. Mandala's Cape Kennedy motel, awaiting the returning of a probe with Martians aboard and recycling old racist jokes, substituting "Martian" for whichever race or nationality appeared in the originals. As dawn breaks, Mandala opines that, "Outside of the jokes, I don't think that six months from now anybody's going to remember there were ever such things as Martians. I don't believe their coming here is going to make a nickel's worth of difference to anybody."[3] African-American bellboy Ernest disagrees: "Going to make a difference to some people. Going to make a *damn* big difference to me."[4]

While Pohl played an important editorial role in the development of the American New Wave, Reynolds was a mainstay of the politically, culturally, and aesthetically conservative *Analog* magazine throughout the period. Nonetheless, from 1961 to 1973, he wrote a story sequence, fixed-up as the North Africa trilogy (1972–8), in which African Americans lead a successful pan-African socialist revolution.

For the most part, though, the New Wave – on both sides of the Atlantic – avoided thinking about race. While J. G. Ballard savages the hollowness of the white bourgeoisie, their whiteness is unremarked; his bourgeois bundles of alienation and compulsion are white because that is the default appearance of the bourgeoisie, not because their color is significant to his satire. This is related to the color-blind future that genre SF, from the 1950s onward, often presumed, showing humankind "as one race, which has emerged from an

---

[3] Frederik Pohl, "The Day After the Day the Martians Came," in Harlan Ellison, ed., *Dangerous Visions* (New York: Edgeworks Abbey, 2009), p. 32.
[4] Ibid., p. 33.

unhappy past of racial misunderstandings and conflicts."[5] Paradoxically, this assumption reinforced the whiteness of SF futures; if race was no longer an issue, white-authored works struggled to imagine people of color in their color-blind futures. For example, Robert Silverberg's *Tower of Glass* (1970) depicts a twenty-fourth century in which most Asians and Africans died in wars, and automation has eradicated the proletariat. When android workers, who massively outnumber humans, contemplate revolution, their several factions are clearly derived from African-American struggles: some continue quietly to serve, awaiting a messiah who will recognize their worth and liberate them; some organize and agitate for legislation that acknowledges them as humans; and some turn to self-defense and revolution. Philip K. Dick's alternate history *The Man in the High Castle* (1962) at least has the courtesy to turn the ethnic cleansing typical of much SF world-building into a plot point: the Nazis, who won the war, are pursuing a Final Solution in Africa.

Thomas Disch and John Sladek's *Black Alice* (1969) is probably the most significant attempt by white New Wave writers to engage with American racial politics. An eleven-year-old heiress is abducted, medicated so as to turn her skin black – the efficacy of the drug is the novel's only SF element – and entrusted to the care of an elderly black woman, who used to run a brothel. A satire on the long hypocritical history of the color-line, it is not as precise as William Melvin Kelley's *A Different Drummer* (1962), as inventive as Ishmael Reed's *Mumbo Jumbo* (1972), as scathing as George Schuyler's *Black No More* (1931), or as despairing as Chester Himes's *Plan B* (1983; written 1969–72), but it does indict the instrumentalist and hysterical violence of both "normalized" and extremist white supremacism.

As such comparisons suggest, African-American authors did produce prose SF outside genre venues. Several such novels teeter on the brink of radically rupturing the worlds they depict, without ever quite becoming overtly science-fictional. John A. Williams wrote four such novels.[6] *The Man Who Cried I Am* (1967), set in a very slightly alternate near past (May 1964, closely resembling February 1965), culminates with the protagonist uncovering two

---

[5] Edward James, "Yellow, Black, Metal and Tentacled: The Race Question in American Science Fiction," in Philip John Davies, ed., *Science Fiction, Social Conflict and War* (Manchester: Manchester University Press, 1990), p. 47. See also De Witt Douglas Kilgore, *Astrofuturism: Science, Race, and Visions of Utopia in Space* (Philadelphia: University of Pennsylvania Press, 2003).
[6] On this cycle of novels, see Mark Bould, "Come Alive By Saying No: An Introduction to Black Power Sf," *Science Fiction Studies* 102 (2007), pp. 220–40, and Kalil Tal, "'That Just Kills Me': Black Militant Near-Future Fiction," *Social Text* 71 (2002), pp. 65–91.

conspiracies: a group of Western nations have formed an alliance to ensure newly independent African nations do not merge into a pan-African federation; and the United States plans to genocide its 22 million black citizens should struggles for equality become too disruptive. In *Sons of Darkness, Sons of Light* (1969), the US occupation of Vietnam has escalated to a nuclear standoff with China. A respected civil rights activist hires a Mafia hitman to assassinate racist cops who get away with murdering black people. Credit, however, is claimed by a militant organization, which plans to hold Manhattan hostage in exchange for reparations and reforms. The novel ends with this revolution hanging in the balance. *Captain Blackman* (1972) recapitulates the history of African-American military service as the injured eponymous protagonist, serving in Vietnam, timeslips between periods and conflicts. In the last chapter, set thirty years in the future, the military has been resegregated so it is more effective at suppressing black domestic insurgency. However, light-skinned soldiers, trained in Africa by Blackman, have infiltrated the positions necessary to seize control of global communications systems and America's nuclear arsenal. In *Jacob's Ladder* (1987), a newly independent West African country, attempting to maintain Cold War neutrality by developing its own nuclear capability, is brought to heel by the United States.

A similar inability to get to the yearned-for future is found in: Sam Greenlee's *The Spook Who Sat By the Door* (1969), in which the first black CIA agent uses his training to fashion street gangs into a revolutionary army; Blyden Jackson's *Operation Burning Candle* (1973), the protagonist of which assassinates well-known white supremacists at the Democratic convention, a reality-rupturing symbolic act intended to kickstart the revolution; Nivi-kofi A. Easley's *The Militants* (1974), in which the protagonist drifts away from the revolution to enjoy a phallocentric interracial pornotopia of hedonistic consumerism; and Randall Robinson's *The Emancipation of Wakefield Clay* (1978), which charts the protagonist's political awakening when his Division is deployed as a "peacekeeping force" to help the white South African government suppress a black revolution.[7] In contrast, Julian Moreau's wish-fulfillment fantasy *The Black Commandos* (1967) is utterly science-fictionalized. Through sheer determination, Denis Jackson develops superhuman speed, strength and

---

[7] In Chicano Hank Lopez's *Afro-6* (1969), Afro-Latino John Ríos's black revolutionary forces also take Manhattan hostage. Similar white-authored novels include Warren Miller's sympathetic *The Siege of Harlem* (1964), Alan Seymour's anguished *The Coming Self-Destruction of the USA* (1969), Edwin Corley's opportunistic *Siege* (1969), and Wilson Tucker's elegiac *The Year of the Quiet Sun* (1970).

intellect, trains an army to similar peaks of ability, and equips them with his superscientific inventions, so as to overthrow America's racist power structure in just ninety days.

A number of African writers also made use of science-fictional devices. For example, Algerian Mohammed Dib's *Who Remembers the Sea* (1962) offers a phantasmagoric vision of life under French occupation during the anti-colonial liberation struggle, while Congolese Sony Labou Tansi's irreal, grotesque *Life and a Half* (1979) is a nightmarish tale of life in the postcolony under a brutal dictator.

Music

Afrofuturist music can be traced back at least as far as Duke Ellington's "Ballet of the Flying Saucers" (*A Drum is a Woman*); in the same year, his essay "The Race for Space" (1957) identified love, respect, dignity, and freedom as the keys to space. In 1958, his nine-piece Spacemen issued *Cosmic Scene*, and the sleeve of Betty Carter's avant-bop *Out There with Betty Carter* depicted, against a luminous blue sky full of stars, an American rocket cruising beneath a Sputnik-like satellite, from out of which she peers. The major figure to emerge in the 1950s, though, was Sun Ra, one of the leading jazz composers and orchestra leaders of the second half of the twentieth century. Late in the decade, he formed the Arkestra, with whom he performed, recorded, and endlessly rehearsed until his death in 1993. The Arkestra's line up – like its name – was subject to constant change, but his key long-term collaborators included vocalist June Tyson and saxophonists Marshall Allen and John Gilmore. An exponent of free jazz, jazz fusion, avant-garde jazz, and world music, Sun Ra also pioneered electronic keyboards, using a Solovox as early as "Deep Purple" (1953), a prototype Minimoog in live performances in 1968, and a modular Moog on *My Brother the Wind* (1969).

From 1952, the year in which he legally changed his name from Herman Poole Blount to Le Sony'r Ra, he would describe a visionary experience from 1936 or 1937 (or the late 1940s) in which aliens teleported him to Saturn and told him to speak to the world through his music; later, he claimed to come from Saturn. He developed an Astro Black Mythology, drawing on Ancient Egyptian mysticism, Gnosticism, Kabbalah, black nationalism, numerology, Rosicrucianism, and freemasonry, which he expressed elliptically, in fragments, contradictions, non sequiturs, cut-ups, and other "equations" that developed a range of science-fictional conceits: his music came from a celestial plane, so it should not be called avant-garde since that term merely identified the current limits of terrestrial music; it was imperative to do impossible things with instruments, to play notes that do not exist in the earthly realm, so as to access the music of outer space, and thus prepare listeners for living there; he would end wars by unleashing "nerve-music," unearthly sounds beyond explanation that would stop combatants in their tracks as they turned to encounter this new thing.

Groundbreaking and prolific, Sun Ra experimented continuously, releasing around 120 albums between 1956 and 1993. The best material he recorded in Chicago in the 1950s is on *The Heliocentric Worlds of Sun Ra*, Volumes 1 and 2 (1965, 1966), *Interstellar Low Ways* (1966), and *We Travel the Spaceways* (1967), in New York in the 1960s on *The Magic City* (1965), *Cosmic Tones for Mental Therapy* (1967), and *Atlantis* (1969), and subsequently from Philadelphia on *Space is the Place* (1973), *Pathways to Unknown Worlds* (1975), the funk-influenced *Lanquidity* (1978), *Sunrise in Different Dimensions* (1981), *Cosmo Omnibus Imagiable Illusion* (1988), and *Somewhere Else* (1993).

If Sun Ra came from space, Jimi Hendrix came from the future. In his much shorter career, his science-fictionalized psychedelic rock strained against the technological limits of guitars, amplifiers, and recording equipment, while his sexualized dandy persona broke new ground in what it was possible for a black performer to get away with in front of white America. He showed that it was possible to burst through constraints, to sidestep the apocalypse, sonically depicted in the agonies of the twelve-and-a-half minute "Machine Gun" (*Band of Gypsys*, 1970), and to find a better world, such as the thirteen-and-a-half minute ambient aquatopia of "1983 . . . (A Merman I Should Turn to Be)" (*Electric Ladyland*, 1968).

George Clinton's Parliament-Funkadelic, some of whose overlapping personnel also performed as Bootsy's Rubber Band, Brides of Funkenstein, and Parlet, were central to 1970s Afrofuturist music and imagery. Dozens of musicians and singers came and went, but at the core were Clinton, bass guitarist Bootsy Collins, keyboardist Bernie Worrell, and lead guitarist Eddie Hazel (Pedro Bell and Overton Loyd contributed distinctive, surreally science-fictional sleeve art). Together, they distilled psychedelic, countercultural, and urban energies into a raunchy, phallocentric mix. They revolutionized recording and production with experiments in sound collage, echoplexing, computer-altered vocals, guitar pedals, improvised lyrics, puns and other wordplay, and revitalized live performance with effects-heavy stage shows, including absurd costumes and characters, and a flying saucer.

Funkadelic was formed in 1964 as an unnamed musical group to back Clinton's doo-wop act, The Parliaments, who had been performing since the late 1950s. When Clinton lost control over The Parliaments' name, he developed Funkadelic as a Hendrix/Sly Stone-influenced psychedelic funk rock band, with uncredited vocals by the Parliaments. Their key albums are *Maggot Brain* (1971), *Cosmic Slop* (1973), *Standing on the Verge of Getting It On* (1973), *One Nation Under a Groove* (1978), and *Uncle Jam Wants You* (1979). Psychedelic elements faded through the decade in favor of tighter guitars, increasing electronica, a more R&B sound, and greater conceptual coherence.

Clinton briefly reformed Parliament in 1970 as a psychedelic soul act, releasing *Osmium* (1970), which could as easily have been by Funkadelic. Parliament relaunched again in 1974 as R&B-orientated funksters, and they were most responsible for developing P-Funk's SF imagery and ideas. The title track on *Chocolate City* (1975) offers playful utopian social commentary on the relative powerlessness of people of color, even in chocolate cities where white flight to the vanilla suburbs produces majority black populations. It imagines African Americans running not just such cities but the nation, proposing Muhammad Ali and Aretha Franklin for President and First Lady, and cabinet posts for Richard Pryor and Stevie Wonder. *The Mothership Connection* (1975) extends this utopian vision, imagining black people in space, albeit not as Starfleet officers but as pimps in interplanetary Cadillacs – like the sleeve photo's finger-clicking, thigh-flashing Clinton, dressed in a home-made spacesuit, bursting out of a UFO hatch, silver knee-high platform boots spread wide. It also introduced the first of P-Funk's cartoonish pantheon, Star Child, who has come from the stars to bring the funk to our benighted planet. *The Clones of Dr. Funkenstein* (1976) introduces the eponymous emperor of intergalactic funk, the wild-haired scientist-inventor of the Bop Gun: if you are shot with it, you cannot resist the funk. *Funkentelechy vs. the Placebo Syndrome* (1977) pursued funk self-realization by declaring war on consumerism and disco, and added the all-style-no-substance pimp Sir Nose D'Voidoffunk – inspired by the Pinocchio Theory, outlined on Bootsy Collins's *Ah ... The Name is Bootsy, Baby!* (1977), which states that if you fake the funk your nose will grow. *Motor Booty Affair* (1978), whose gatefold included a pop-up Atlantis, depicts an aquatopia populated by fish, mermaids, African tribes, and Mr. Wiggles, the funk's underwater envoy; on "Aqua Boogie," Sir Nose refuses to get in the water because swimming is just dancing and thus, in his opinion, as uncool as the funk. *Gloryhallastoopid (Or Pin the Tale on the Funky)* (1979) argues that funk created the universe.

On the sleeve of *Trombipulation* (1980), elephant-trunked Sir Nose reclines among the pyramids as storm clouds gather in the distance.

Other American Afrofuturist musicians of this period include Anthony Braxton, Labelle, and Earth, Wind & Fire. Jamaica's Lee "Scratch" Perry, recording and producing since the mid-1960s, effectively invented reggae with "People Funny Boy" (1968) and dub with *Upsetters 14 Dub Blackboard Jungle* (1973), but would not move into an obviously Afrofuturist phase until the 1980s. Nigerian Fela Kuti, who started recording in the mid-1960s, fused Ghanaian highlife and Yoruba drumming with jazz and funk into an Afrobeat sound. His political radicalization, inspired by his encounter in 1970 with the Black Power movement, culminated in *Zombie* (1976), which used the metaphor of the undead feeding on the living to criticize the Nigerian army; in response, soldiers destroyed the commune where he lived, killing his mother.

Film

By the 1970s, after several decades of white flight, people of color made up 25–40 percent of Hollywood's domestic audience, prompting studios and independents to turn to blaxploitation – low- and medium-budget films with black protagonists and a degree of African-American creative input (although not necessarily writers and directors). In addition to crime and action movies, blaxploitation took other generic forms, including westerns, horror, and fantasy.[8]

---

[8] On blaxploitation horror, see Harry M. Benshoff, "Blaxploitation Horror Films: Generic Reappropriation or Reinscription?," *Cinema Journal* 39, 2 (2000), pp. 31–50, and Steven Jay Schneider, "Possessed by Soul: Generic (Dis)Continuity in the Blaxploitation Horror Film," in Xavier Mendik, ed., *Necronomicon Presents Shocking Cinema of the Seventies* (London: Noir, 2002), pp. 106–20. Blaxploitation horror and fantasy films include *Blacula* (dir. Crain 1972), *Bone* (dir. Cohen 1972), *Ganja & Hess* (dir. Gunn 1973), *Scream Blacula Scream* (dir. Kelljan 1973), *Abby* (dir. Girdler 1974), *The House on Skull Mountain* (dir. Honthaner 1974), *Sugar Hill* (dir. Maslansky 1974), *Coonskin* (dir. Bakshi 1975), *JD's Revenge* (dir. Marks 1976), *Death Dimension* (dir. Adamson 1978), and *Nurse Sherri* (dir. Adamson 1978). Other films of interest include *The Plague of the Zombies* (dir. Gilling 1966), *Night of the Living Dead* (dir. Romero 1968), the Planet of the Apes franchise (1968–73), *Le Frisson de vampires* (dir. Rollin 1970), *The Omega Man* (dir. Sagal 1971), *The Beast Must Die* (dir. Annett 1974), *Vampira* (dir. Donner 1975), *Dawn of the Dead* (dir. Romero 1978), *Born in Flames* (dir. Borden 1983), and *The Brother from Another Planet* (dir. Sayles 1984). The LA Rebellion group of African-American filmmakers typically opposed neo-realism to blaxploitation excess, a tension evident in *Welcome Home Brother Charles* (dir. Fanaka 1975), but later turned to more fantastic forms with *To Sleep with Anger* (dir. Burnett 1990), *Daughters of the Dust* (dir. Dash 1991), and *Sankofa* (dir. Gerima 1993).

Blaxploitation's SF content might be slight.[9] For example, *Black Samurai* (dir. Adamson 1977), a James Bond knock-off starring Jim Kelly, merely features high-tech gadgetry, including a long sequence of an actual prototype jetpack, while *The Spook Who Sat by the Door* (dir. Dixon 1973), co-written and co-produced by Sam Greenlee, bears the same relationship to the genre as his novel. It is, however, particularly effective in capturing a sense of protagonist Freeman's "double consciousness." Lawrence Cook is unobtrusive as the mild-mannered integrationist and slick as the concerned bourgeois liberal he ostensibly becomes after leaving the CIA but, when he drops these masks, he is physically, sexually, and intellectually potent. At the end of the film, as he dies from a gunshot wound, the radio reports a wave of uprisings sweeping American cities.

Blaxploitation is typically more conservative about black liberation. In *Abar, the First Black Superman* (dir. Packard 1977), the eponymous leader of the Black Front of Unity, who gains superpowers, is given "positive" connotations by overtly comparing him to the early, civil-rights-era (rather than the later, more radical) Martin Luther King, whose "I Have a Dream" speech plays over the closing shots. While *Abar* ultimately rejects revolutionary struggle, *The Black Gestapo* (dir. Frost 1975) condemns black militancy, equating it with criminality, fascism, and "anti-white racism," and confusedly comparing protagonist General Ahmed to King, Malcolm X and the Black Panthers. Matters spiral out of his control when his right-hand man sets up an armed self-defense force and, without Ahmed's knowledge, uses it to take over the Mafia's drug business. In a more obviously science-fictional vein, *Space Is the Place* (dir. Coney 1974) depicts the cosmic struggle between Sun Ra and the Overseer, which takes the terrestrial form of black pride community versus black capitalist individualism. It opens with Ra wandering in an alien garden in which he intends to establish a black colony, free from white interference, and pondering whether he should transport colonists there by "isotope transportation transmolecularisation" or teleport them through music; it concludes with his return there, reversing the Middle Passage, and destroying the Earth behind him.

The majority of blaxploitation SF is concerned with surgical or chemical transformation. In *Change of Mind* (dir. Stevens 1969), the brain of white District Attorney David Rowe, diagnosed with terminal cancer, is transplanted into the body of Ralph Dickson, a brain-dead African American.

---

[9] See Mark Bould, "Paying Freedom Dues: Marxism, Black Radicalism, and Blaxploitation Sf," in Ewa Mazierska and Alfredo Suppia, eds., *Red Alert: Marxist Approaches to Science Fiction Cinema* (Detroit: Wayne State University Press, 2016), pp. 72–97.

Rowe must learn to deal with white people seeing him as a black man, the film repeatedly emphasizing the greater physical stature he now enjoys (or endures – at one point, he imagines he has been given a robot body). He loses white political allies by prosecuting a racist white sheriff for murdering a black prostitute, but the black community rallies to his support – only to abandon him when, having discovered the sheriff's innocence, he drops the case. In contrast, the loud comedy *The Watermelon Man* (dir. Van Peebles 1970) ends with an embrace of blackness and community. Thanks to a homemade tanning lotion, white racist insurance salesman Jeffrey Gerber overnight turns black. When he goes jogging, the police assume he is a fleeing criminal. His neighbors, fearing property values will drop, try to buy his house. His hitherto liberal wife cannot cope with sharing her home with a black man. Ultimately, rather than waking up from this "nightmare," as the studio intended, Gerber develops black pride, moves to an African-American neighborhood, and with other working-class black men secretly trains for combat.

While both films strongly associate black working-class masculinity with excessive physicality, *The Thing with Two Heads* (dir. Frost 1972) and *Blackenstein* (dir. Levey 1973) go further, linking it to animality. In the former, Maxwell Kirshner, a racist white surgeon who has perfected a brain transplant technique, keeps a now-two-headed gorilla caged in his laboratory, creating an uncomfortable association with the African-American death row convict onto whose body his own head will be transplanted. In the latter, a quadriplegic Vietnam veteran undergoes experimental DNA therapy to restore his limbs, developing a simian brow and hairy paws before going on the rampage. *Dr. Black, Mr. Hyde* (dir. Crain 1976) gives such transformations a rather different set of connotations. When award-winning African-American medical researcher Dr. Henry Pride tests a new serum on a black rat, it loses pigmentation, kills the other occupants of its cage, and dies. He tries it on a terminal black patient, who also turns white and violent, before expiring. Finally, he tests it on himself and begins intermittently to transform into a prostitute-murdering brute. He becomes stronger, his features become heavier and – most significantly – he turns white. His descent into murderous animalistic violence is not, as in earlier adaptations of Stevenson's novel, into simian negritude but into ashen pallor, into whiteness.

Comics

African-American creative input into mainstream comics was far more tenuous than in blaxploitation film, but the emergence of black superheroes –

including Marvel's Black Panther (1966), Falcon (1969), Luke Cage (1972), Blade (1973), Brother Voodoo (1973), Misty Knight (1975), Storm (1975), and Black Goliath (1975), and DC's John Stewart/Green Lantern (1971), Bumblebee (1976), Tyroc (1976), and Black Lightning (1977) – was a visible development in Afrofuturist representation. Black superheroes also began to appear in African comics, including South Africa's Jet Jungle (1965) and Mighty Man (1975) – the former also appeared in a radio serial, the latter in a 1978 isiZulu movie – and Nigeria's Powerman, aka Powerbolt (1975).

Stan Lee and Jack Kirby's Black Panther was introduced in *Fantastic Four* #52 and #53 (1966). When an unknown African chieftain presents the team with an amazing flying vehicle, the Thing asks "How does some refugee from a Tarzan movie lay his hands on this kind of gizmo?"[10] Sue and Johnny are similarly incapable of believing it could have been created by Africans. But Wakanda, a nation hitherto hidden away in equatorial Africa, combines tradition with high technology, thanks to a large supply of vibranium, an otherwise rare extraterrestrial mineral. Its ruler, T'Challa, also wears the skin-tight, short-caped costume and cowl of the Black Panther, in which guise he nearly defeats his superpowered visitors, before they become allies against Klaw, who killed T'Challa's father.

In 1968, after other thankless appearances with the Fantastic Four and Captain America, T'Challa relocated to New York, joined the Avengers, and also appeared with Daredevil and Doctor Doom; in 1972, he was briefly renamed the Black Leopard so as to distance him from the Black Panther Party. With *Jungle Action* #5 (1973), Black Panther was finally given his own feature; from #6 writer Don McGregor and a number of artists, primarily the African American Billy Graham, began the detailed development of T'Challa and Wakanda. Marvel's first multi-issue story arc, "Panther's Rage," ran for thirteen issues (1973–5), in which T'Challa returns from the United States, with his African-American lover, singer-turned-social-worker Monica Lynne, to a Wakanda dislocated by his absence. He must triumph over suspicions of his new outsider ways, win back the loyalty of the people he left behind to govern on his behalf, and fight a series of costumed villains, giant white gorillas, and an army of dinosaurs before facing would-be conqueror Erik Killmonger. The "Panther vs. the Klan" arc – T'Challa and Monica investigate her sister's murder by the Ku Klux Klan – stuttered and stalled through 1975, and was unresolved when *Jungle Action* was cancelled.

[10] Reprinted in Reginald Hudlin and John Romita, Jr., *Black Panther: Who Is Black Panther?* (New York: Marvel, 2009), p. 2.

Prior to Black Panther, *Jungle Action* merely reprinted old Atlas comics stories about white colonial adventurers. Their faded relevance faded further as McGregor name-dropped Arethra Franklin, Isaac Hayes, Roberta Flack, Ella Fitzgerald, James Baldwin, Eldridge Cleaver, and John Shaft. Graham's explosive splash-panels and splash-pages disrupted conventional lay-outs, emphasizing the protagonist's muscular agility; his most striking images are those of Black Panther tied to a burning cross by the Klan, a black Christ who breaks free and strikes down his enemies. However, the comic, while often bold, nonetheless reiterates racialized binaries (civilized/primitive, technology/tradition), and hedges its political bets: major black characters issue pronouncements against revolutionary struggle, describe Baldwin and Cleaver as merely bitter individuals, and reiterate southern myths about Reconstruction.

Black Panther soon returned in his own title, which lasted for fifteen issues (January 1977 to May 1979), with Jack Kirby writing and drawing the first dozen. Initially, T'Challa joins wealthy rogue archeologists pursuing ancient artifacts with cosmic connections, depoliticizing the character by excluding African and American racial contexts. However, Adilifu Nama argues, because white culture overwhelmingly ties black figures to jungles, urban or otherwise, it was "racially and politically progressive."[11] Regardless, by #8 T'Challa was en route to Wakanda to resume his role of ruler and protector.

DC's first black superhero also negotiated between urban and cosmic realities. His creators, Dennie O'Neil and Neal Adams, who were later responsible for the *Superman vs. Muhammad Ali* special (1978), had already shaken up Green Lantern by embedding him and Green Arrow in socially conscious narratives. In his 1971 debut, John Stewart's substitute Green Lantern is tasked with protecting a racist politician. Hal Jordan, the actual Green Lantern, questions the Guardians of the Universe's wisdom, seeing Stewart as just an angry black man with a poor attitude towards authority – and is apparently validated when Stewart does not stop a gunman from shooting at the politician. But Stewart, busy saving a policeman's life at the time, knew the politician staged the "assassination attempt." A recurring character throughout the decade, Stewart became the main Green Lantern from 1984 to 1988, before returning to a more intermittent role.

Luke Cage, created by Archie Goodwin, John Romita Sr., and George Tuska, was the first black superhero to have his own title, which ran from

---

[11] Adilifu Nama, *Super Black: American Pop Culture and Black Superheroes* (Austin: University of Texas Press, 2011), p. 48.

1972 to 86 as *Hero for Hire* (#1–16), *Luke Cage Power Man* (#17–49), and *Power Man and Iron Fist* (#50–125). His origin story reworks that of Captain America while recalling various unethical experiments on black subjects, such as the Tuskegee Syphilis Study. Carl Lucas, wrongfully imprisoned and keen to avenge himself on the former friend who framed him, hopes to speed his parole by participating in Dr. Noah Burstein's electrobiochemical experiments in cell regeneration. When the process goes wrong, Lucas transforms into a hypermuscular figure with bullet-proof skin, able to punch his way through the prison walls to freedom. Believed dead, he returns to New York and disguises himself as a costumed superhero. He sets up office as a private eye above the Gem, a crumbling 42nd Street cinema that only shows old westerns, neatly triangulating Cage's brand of "hero for hire" with the implicitly outdated white models provided by Humphrey Bogart's Sam Spade/Philip Marlowe and by Alan Ladd's Shane.

Unlike other superheroes, Luke Cage has no secret identity. Always-already perceived as an angry black buck, he plays it to the hilt, even as thought-bubbles, in which he thinks about himself in the third person, reveal that he is consciously playing a role for a white-dominated culture. This is nicely captured in #17 (1974), when Cage decides that to attract media coverage, and thus generate business, he needs a fancier name. He rejects "The Ace of Spades" as "too ethnic" and "Super–" because it has been used before, although whether by DC's Superman or blaxploitation's Super Fly remains unclear. He breaks off midway through "The Avenging __," leaving the reader to contemplate what noun might follow (background characters often stop in the same way, midway through hurling a racial epithet).[12]

The comic had a rapid turnover of writers and artists. Early issues told more-or-less standalone stories, with the occasional multi-parter and some longer narrative threads eked out. Cage was pitted against low-rent villains[13] – although in #9 he pursues Doctor Doom to Latveria over an unpaid bill, where the Faceless One, drawing parallels with American slavery, tries to enlist his aid in a robot uprising.[14] Billy Graham drew the most dynamic early issues: while other artists showed explosive action within the frame, Graham exploded the frame. His *Black Panther* collaborator, Don McGregor, wrote

---

[12] Reprinted in *Essential Luke Cage, Power Man*, Vol. 1 (New York: Marvel, 2005), unpaginated.

[13] Such as Colonel Mace, who in #3 tricks Vietnam veterans into taking Manhattan hostage to protest their treatment, so he can rob Wall Street.

[14] Cage later briefly joins the Fantastic Four, becomes a part-time member of The Defenders, and, decades later, the leader of The Avengers and a member of Black Panther's Crew, but mostly he remains a street-level superhero.

six issues (#28, 30–4 (1975–6)) of conventional-seeming stories that subtly reconceptualized Cage, situating him more effectively within a community and contemporary politics. "The Fire This Time!" (#32) responds to James Baldwin's plea in *The Fire Next Time* (1963) for young black men to move beyond rage over everyday systemic racism to compassion. A black family, who have scrimped and saved to afford a home in a nice, if vanilla, suburb, hire Cage to protect them from Wildfire, who is trying to burn them out. One neighbor eggs the flamethrower-wielding villain on, while others merely watch, not lifting a finger to help (unsurprisingly, Wildfire turns out to be just another disgruntled white suburbanite). In the following issues, Cage remains in touch with the family, attending the funeral of the son who died from smoke inhalation, and trying to help the traumatized daughter. McGregor also fleshed out Cage's relationships with recurring regular characters – girlfriend Claire Temple, who works with the reformed Burstein in a free clinic; DW, the film student who manages the Gem; Quentin Chase, a white police detective with whom a rapport develops – and made them more central to the narrative, transforming Cage in the process.

Marv Wolfman broke these ties, and abandoned these innovations, by relocating Cage to Chicago, but his new isolation was undone when he teamed up with wealthy white martial artist Iron Fist, an enduring homo-social bond established in Chris Claremont's rather soap-opera-ish seven-issue run, and Mary Jo Duffy's subsequent twenty-seven issues. Tony Isabella introduced Misty Knight, a black ex-cop turned bionic detective, and transformed Bill Foster, a recurring black scientist character, into Black Goliath. At DC, Isabella reworked Luke Cage as a more obviously positive character: Olympic champion Jefferson Pierce becomes a teacher at his old high school and, as Black Lightning, fights local crime. His superhero mask includes an afro wig, ensuring that he looks too ghetto to ever be connected to the respectably middle-class Pierce.

Genre SF

At least five African-American writers debuted in genre venues in this period. The major writer to do so in the 1970s was Octavia E. Butler. Her Patternist novels (1976–84) chart the evolution of two posthuman species, the psionic Patternists and the superhuman but bestial Clayarks. Focused on the hard truths of survival, these SF neo-slave narratives explore the terrible dilemmas faced by individuals and groups forced to negotiate between their own sense of themselves and indifferent, sometimes hostile, systems of power. Similar conflicts underpin Butler's later novels – the Xenogenesis or Lilith's Brood trilogy (1987–9), the Parables series (1993–8), and *Fledgling* (2005) – and *Kindred* (1979), her most straightforward reworking of the slave narrative.[15]

John M. Faucette's *Crown of Infinity* (1968) struggles with the disjuncture between Stapledonian magnitudes of cosmic space and time – civilizations fall and rise, humanity dies out, a posthuman remnant ascends to galactic supremacy – and credible characters, bathetically undermining its sense of scale. *The Age of Ruin* (1968), a post-apocalyptic adventure, was intended as social commentary on urban gangs, but it urges mutual tolerance only after many violent scenes. Both were published as halves of Ace Doubles, but Faucette fell out with editor Wollheim, who refused to publish a novel about a black protagonist caught up in race wars on another planet. *The Warriors of Terra* (1970), published by the more marginal Belmont, is a fast-moving space opera with an air of improvisation. Captured by the alien Morgia, Ran Hudson leads a slave revolt. In a reversal of the Middle Passage, and against immense odds, he brings a spaceship across the Barrens, an immense interstellar void, back home to Earth. A prequel, *Siege of Earth* (1971), commissioned by the even more marginal Modern Promotions, is an ostensibly anti-Vietnam War novel that consists almost entirely of scenes of mass destruction. Faucette published the non-SF *Disco Hustle* (1978) with Holloway House, and then disappeared until the self-published *Black Science Fiction* (2002) collected thirty-nine stories, only one of them published during the intervening decades.[16]

In the early 1970s, Charles R. Saunders published African-set sword-and-sorcery adventure fiction in amateur magazines. "The City of Madness" (1974), his first story featuring Imaro, was reprinted in Lin Carter's *The Year's Best Fantasy* (1975) for DAW, founded in 1971 by Wollheim after leaving Ace. DAW soon invited Saunders to fix up a number of related stories as the novel *Imaro* (1981), which he followed with *The Quest for Cush* (1984), *The Trail of Bohu* (1985), and *The Naama War* (2009).

Steven Barnes's first story, "Moonglow," appeared in 1974; his second, "The Locusts" (1979), a collaboration with Larry Niven, was nominated for a Hugo. He later co-authored novels with Niven, Jerry Pournelle, and his

---

[15] Butler's transformative impact on the SF field can be registered by the discussion of her work in so many subsequent chapters of this book, but see especially Isiah Lavender's Chapter 35 on "Contemporary Science Fiction and Afrofuturism," covering the period in which she rose to international prominence.

[16] Mark Bould, "Space/Race: Recovering John M. Faucette," in Isiah Lavender III and Lisa Yaszek, eds., *Afrofuturism through Time and Space* (Columbus, OH: Ohio State University Press, forthcoming).

wife Tananarive Due; his solo novels include the cyberpunk-ish *Aubrey Knight* (1983–94) and the *Bilalistan* (2002–3) alternate history series.

Samuel Delany, one of the key SF writers to emerge in the 1960s, eschewed the New Wave label. Never prolific at short lengths, his stories nonetheless appeared in such quintessential New Wave venues as *Dangerous Visions*, Michael Moorcock's *New Worlds* and Pohl's *If* and *Worlds of Tomorrow* magazines, and in the *Quark* anthologies Delany co-edited with Marilyn Hacker.[17] Pohl was also the editor responsible for Delany's major 1970s novels, *Dhalgren* (1975) and *Triton* (1976), while most of his early novels appeared among Wollheim's Ace Doubles. *The Jewels of Aptor, The Fall of the Towers* trilogy – *Captives of the Flame* (1963), *The Towers of Toron* (1964), *City of a Thousand Suns* (1965) – and the Nebula-winning *The Einstein Intersection* (1967) are set long after global nuclear wars, in archaic yet superscientific posthuman futures. In Delany's baroque space operas – *The Ballad of Beta–2* (1965), *Empire Star* (1966), the Nebula-winning *Babel–17* (1966), *Nova* (1968) – feudal power, identified with the charismatic heirs of corporate fortunes, resurfaces in an era of interstellar capitalism, while assorted outsiders try to make a buck, defeat a nemesis or save the Earth from aliens. In both types of novels, writers, poets, musicians, and other artists play significant roles, and Delany quietly incorporates an uncommon array of races and ethnicities.

As US involvement in Vietnam escalated, *The Jewels of Aptor* and *Captives of the Flame* identified the economic determinants of foreign wars, as well as their role as distractions from domestic issues – by creating irreal enemies, the state can persuade its unfree population that they are in fact free and fighting to free others. *The Ballad of Beta–2*, recalling grubby McCarthyist oppression, argues that social norms are relative and often manipulated by power, and that conformism is unethical because it presumes to fix the uncertainty and flux of life. Delany combines such ideas with post-structuralist thinking in *Dhalgren* and *Stars in My Pocket Like Grains of Sand* (1984), and more challengingly in his consciously pornographic novels, *The Tides of Lust* (1973),[18] *The Mad Man* (1994), *Hogg* (1995; written 1969–73) and the science-fictional *Through the Valley of the Nest of Spiders* (2012). Although Delany's queerness only becomes evident with *Empire Star*'s decadent literary allusions to Oscar Wilde and Bosie, Paul Verlaine and Arthur

---

[17] He won a Nebula for "Aye and Gomorrah . . . " (1967), and both Nebula and Hugo for "Time Considered as a Helix of Semi-Precious Stones" (1968).

[18] It was reissued as *Equinox* (1994), Delany's preferred title, with a hundred years arbitrarily added onto the ages of all the sexually active children in it, rendering it rather less transgressive.

Rimbuad, Jean Cocteau and Raymond Radiguet, and Colette and Henry Gauthier-Villars, it is easier in retrospect to read his anti-conformism as more rooted in sexuality than race. Nonetheless, from *Empire Star* onwards, Delany's fiction addresses the dynamics and legacies of slavery, most fully in the neo-slave narratives of *Stars in My Pockets* and the *Nevèrÿon* sword-and-sorcery series (1979–87), Delany's most substantial account of economics' role in shaping societies, subjectivities and sexualities.

Delany's post-structuralism also starts to emerge in *Empire Star*,[19] through the conceit of multiplex consciousness – the ability to see things from multiple viewpoints simultaneously, and to balance determinism, relativism, and dynamicism without collapsing them into each other. Such a mode of consciousness effectively places everything under erasure, endlessly deferring meaning. The novel's temporal loops embody this perspective, as does a final chapter that relates events in no particular sequence: can the reader hold them all simultaneously in mind, or does s/he succumb to the desire to order them into conventional linearity? *Babel–17* features an alien language without a first-person pronoun. The absence of signifiers through which to (mis)-recognize oneself as a (unified) subject generates a consciousness radically different from that experienced by monadic humans, whose languages deny their fluid intersubjectivity and thus amputate their sense of being. Both *The Einstein Intersection* and *Nova* turn to myth – Orpheus and the Tarot, respectively – as a linguistic and cultural code through which meaning is generated yet, in combination with other determinants, is kept in flux, never resolved. Introducing his graphic novel *Empire* (1978), illustrated by Howard V. Chaykin, Delany wrote of trying to capture, or create, the "experience of constant de-centered de-centeredness, each decentering on a vaster and vaster scale"[20] – efforts that come to fruition in *Stars in My Pocket*, which brings Derridean *différance* into the heart of space opera, once considered the most debased of SF forms.

In 1975, Delany returned to SF with a major late-modernist novel, *Dhalgren*, set in lawless, decaying Bellona, a diverse American city populated by violent gangs, countercultural remnants, and the few middle-class families who have not yet fled. It follows the misadventures of a newcomer, the Kidd, an

---

[19] Structuralist and post-structuralist theory underpins much of Delany's criticism in *The Jewel-Hinged Jaw: Notes on the Language of Science Fiction* (1977), *The American Shore: Meditations on a Tale of Science Fiction* (1978), *Starboard Wine: More Notes on the Language of Science Fiction* (1984) and later volumes.

[20] Samuel R. Delany and Howard V. Chaykin, *Empire: A Visual Novel* (New York: Berkley Windhover, 1978), n.p.

aspiring poet, amnesiac and adrift. In part a study of the relationship between discourse and subjectivity, representation and sexuality, it reiterates through detailed descriptions of Kidd's straight, gay, and group sexual encounters the fluidity of identity and desire. The final sixth of the novel reproduces his journal, including his edits, amendments and commentary, which also opens up the gulf between experience and its representation: language can never reproduce phenomena as they unfold because the very act of representation counters immediacy, subjecting experience to predetermined linguistic frameworks. *Triton* (1976), a travelogue through, as the subtitle puts it, *An Ambiguous Heterotopia*, explores similar ideas.[21] Bron Helstrom, a former sex-worker from Mars, now lives on Triton, where body shape and psychology can be altered and any sexual desire gratified. However, his sexual orientation requires female subservience to male dominance. He is profoundly patriarchal in an era in which patriarchy has been displaced and all the old romantic clichés about possession now seem like the dominance displays they always were. When he surgically transforms himself into the kind of woman he would like, she has no more success in finding a mate to dominate her.

Conclusion

It is unclear, even within a specific medium, how well acquainted African-American SF creators of the New Wave era were with each other's work: blaxploitation filmmakers preferred to adapt familiar, white-authored SF characters, such as Superman, Frankenstein's monster, and Jekyll and Hyde; Clinton claims not to have known about Sun Ra; the rarely mentioned Faucette admits to not knowing Delany was black; and although the protagonist of Delany's *The Einstein Intersection* is a black guitarist, the novel seems enamored of Ringo Starr, not Hendrix. It is also not clear how much of a cross-over audience there was between media: Butler's Patternist novels may have been influenced by her personal love of comics,[22] but did her own readers keep up with the adventures of Black Panther or Luke Cage?

However this remarkable range of work from the 1960s and 1970s was experienced at the time, it did not exist as "Afrofuturism." The retrospective

---

[21] "Heterotopia" is Michel Foucault's term for "a place of difference"; the subtitle indicates that the novel is a riposte to Ursula Le Guin's *The Dispossessed: An Ambiguous Utopia* (1974).

[22] See Gerry Canavan, *Octavia E. Butler* (University of Illinois Press, 2016), especially chapter 2.

formulation of an Afrofuturist tradition inevitably does violence to history even as it preserves that which might otherwise be lost. The misdescription of this array of creative endeavors as a relatively coherent phenomonenon changes them even as it restores them, obscures them while also making them visible. But it provides a strategic identity and a heritage for subsequent generations of SF creators and audiences of color. And like so many Afrofuturist works of the New Wave era, from Black Panther to *Kindred*, it reconciles the contradiction Eshun identified, showing that analyzing and assembling counterfutures requires the practice of countermemory.

26

New Wave Science Fiction and the Vietnam War

DAVID M. HIGGINS

The Vietnam War (known in Vietnam as Kháng chiến chống Mỹ, or the Resistance War against America) was central to the cultural moment in the 1960s to 1970s when Americans lost faith in their nation and its leaders to a historically unprecedented degree, and this loss of confidence was reflected within the SF of the era and its aftermath. The Vietnam War signaled the death knell, for many, of the United States' imperialistic self-confidence: after the Tet Offensive in 1968, Americans could no longer believe General Westmoreland's optimistic assurances that the Vietnam conflict was progressing toward a timely resolution, and trusted journalists such as Walter Cronkite began expressing influential public doubt regarding Washington's official narrative of the war. Televised images of protestors being beaten by the police in Chicago during the 1968 Democratic National Convention and scenes of students being shot by the National Guard at Kent State University in 1970 reinforced the widespread sense that the United States had become an unjust and repressive police state, and worldwide outrage exploded in 1969 when the atrocities of the My Lai massacre (and the government's attempts to cover it up) became public. After Daniel Ellsberg leaked the Pentagon Papers in 1971 and *The New York Times* published Nick Ut's iconic photo of nine-year-old Vietnamese napalm victim Phan Thi Kim Phuc in 1972, there could no longer be any question, for many, that the United States was a nation bereft of moral currency and corrupt at the highest levels (a perspective ultimately reinforced by the Watergate scandal and President Nixon's resignation – and subsequent pardon – in 1974).

SF registered the impact of these extraordinary events: As H. Bruce Franklin notes in *Vietnam and Other American Fantasies* (2000), American SF during the 1960s and 1970s "shaped and was shaped by the nation's encounter with Vietnam."[1] Gene Roddenbury's *Star Trek* (1966–9), for example, offers

---

[1] H. Bruce Franklin, *Vietnam and Other American Fantasies* (Amherst: University of Massachusetts Press, 2000), p. 151.

an imaginative exploration of the ethics of military and cultural intervention in foreign affairs. Rick Worland observes that *Star Trek* operates as a Cold War parable, with the Federation playing the role of NATO striving to contain the Soviet-style aggression of the warlike Klingons (and simultaneously struggling against the mysterious Romulans, who vaguely mirror the threat of the communist Chinese). After the show's first season, the Enterprise increasingly strives to protect and extend the Federation's domain of influence as a counterbalance to Klingon expansion and hegemony: Worland notes that by the second season of the series "the Klingons and the Federation were firmly established as two ideologically opposed superpower blocs that compete for the hearts and minds of Third World planets."[2]

Several *Star Trek* episodes comment directly on the United States' involvement in Vietnam. As Franklin demonstrates, the progression of these episodes reveals increasing disillusionment concerning the war during the late 1960s. Early episodes, such as "City on the Edge of Forever" (April 6, 1967) and "A Private Little War" (February 2, 1968), advocate a grudging support for the conflict, but later episodes such as "The Omega Glory" (March 1, 1968) and "Let That Be Your Last Battlefield" (January 10, 1969) reveal exhaustion, cynicism, and a loss of national confidence concerning both the war and the US military and political leaders. In "City on the Edge of Forever," Kirk falls in love with a social worker named Edith Keeler during a time travel visit to the 1930s, but he discovers that he must not interfere with the historical circumstances of her death, because if she survives she will create a peace movement that will prevent the United States from entering the Second World War. Franklin suggests that Keeler thus functions as "an embodiment of a dangerously misguided peace movement," and the episode as a whole invites viewers to see Cold War conflicts like the war in Vietnam as regrettable but necessary.[3] Similarly, in "A Private Little War," the Enterprise discovers a conflict-in-progress between the "villagers" and the "hill people" on a planet called Neural; the villagers have been armed with advanced weapons by the Klingons, and Kirk ultimately decides that the Federation must similarly arm the hill people in order to maintain a balance of power. Kirk justifies his decision to McCoy with a specific reference to the Vietnam conflict, arguing that preserving the Cold War "balance of power" was "the only solution"[4] in

---

[2] Rick Worland, "Captain Kirk: Cold Warrior," *Journal of Popular Film and Television* 16, 3 (1988), p. 110.

[3] Franklin, *Vietnam*, p. 139.

[4] Quoted in Franklin, *Vietnam*, pp. 142–3.

Vietnam, even if the brutal methods by which this was carried out are difficult to accept.

"A Private Little War" also reflects the deeply held American myth that there was a pre-existing internal division between the pro-Communist North Vietnamese and the anti-Communist South Vietnamese. It was not until after the release of the Pentagon Papers in 1971 that Americans confronted the degree to which the entire conflict in Vietnam had been engineered by the United States to contain Chinese communism against the popular wishes of nearly the entire population of Vietnam, and many Americans today still have little awareness of how the people of Vietnam understood and experienced the war. Even in the absence of this historical awareness, however, popular sentiment concerning the war's perceived necessity eroded in the late 1960s, particularly after the Tet Offensive. This shift in popular support for the war can be seen reflected in "The Omega Glory," a *Star Trek* episode in which the *Enterprise* discovers a world that has experienced a parallel evolution with our own Earth. On this planet, Omega IV, an unceasing war between the Kohms (Communists) and the Yangs (Yankees) has reduced both sides to mindless barbarism, and Kirk must eventually re-awaken human sentiment in the Yangs by reminding them of the true meaning of the ideals enshrined in the United States' Constitution and the "Star-Spangled Banner."[5] Similarly, in "Let That Be Your Last Battlefield," the crew of the *Enterprise* discovers yet another pointless and devastating conflict: a war between two races on an alien world (one colored white on the left and black on the right, and the other colored black on the left and white on the right) who are locked in battle against one another because of a long history of systemic racial oppression. This conflict, which simultaneously allegorizes both the Vietnam War and the tensions of the civil rights movement, ultimately devastates their entire world, and the episode (like "The Omega Glory") rejects the show's earlier advocacy for the necessity of war and instead demands a radical transformation of American politics and foreign policy.[6]

Many other cultural productions during the 1960s and 1970s, such as comic books and SF films, also register an ever-increasing sense of cynicism, disillusionment, and despair emerging from US involvement in the Vietnam conflict. Lincoln Geraghty notes that *Planet of the Apes* (1968), for example, offers a bleak Vietnam-era failure of the traditional American

[5] Franklin, *Vietnam*, p. 146.
[6] Ibid., p. 148.

frontier narrative: "Whereas traditionally the space of the mythical West in previous incarnations of Western and SF films implied positive rebirth," Geraghty observes, "here it has become a countercultural wasteland of death and destruction. The frontier myth is no longer relevant or positive for an American society undergoing tremendous social and cultural change while the nation struggles to fight a needless war in South East Asia."[7] Matthew J. Costello further notes that superhero comics during this period "revealed not unity and moral certainty but division and moral ambiguity."[8] Captain America and Iron Man, for example, both visit Vietnam in the pages of Marvel comics during the 1970s; according to Costello, however, they both have difficulty "defining the enemy and asserting the morality of US action."[9] During one story arc in the 1970s Captain America even renounces his allegiance to the United States altogether, becoming "Nomad: The Man without a Country" after discovering his loathed enemy HYDRA had infiltrated the US government as high as the presidency itself.

SF prose authors, in particular, were deeply divided in their attitudes toward Vietnam, and this division was especially observable in the June 1968 issue of *Galaxy* magazine, which showcased two dramatic opposing full-page advertisements listing the names of SF writers, artists, and editors advocating for and against the war. The pro-war list included recognizable figures such as Poul Anderson, Marion Zimmer Bradley, John W. Campbell, Robert A. Heinlein, Larry Niven, Jerry Pournelle, and Jack Vance, while the anti-war list includes what Franklin refers to as "almost the entire vanguard of an emerging kind of science fiction" often thought of as the New Wave.[10] This anti-war list included Samuel R. Delany, Philip K. Dick, Thomas Disch, Harlan Ellison, Damon Knight, Ursula K. Le Guin, Judith Merril, Gene Roddenberry, Joanna Russ, Norman Spinrad, Kate Wilhelm, and many others.[11]

Franklin suggests that the pro-war SF authors articulate the (often unconscious) imperial fantasies that supported the war; the New Wave authors, in contrast, offer what he describes as "conscious anti-imperialist fantasies that

---

[7] Lincoln Geraghty, *American Science Fiction Film and Television* (New York: Berg, 2009), p. 41.
[8] Matthew J. Costello, "U.S. Superpower and Superpowered Americans in Science Fiction and Comic Books," in Eric Carl Link and Gerry Canavan, eds., *The Cambridge Companion to American Science Fiction* (New York: Cambridge University Press, 2015), p. 132.
[9] Ibid., p. 132.
[10] Franklin, *Vietnam*, p. 152.
[11] Franklin observes that both ads had also appeared previously in the March issue of the *Magazine of Fantasy and Science Fiction*, separated then between eighty-four pages of fiction and reviews. Franklin, *Vietnam*, p. 152.

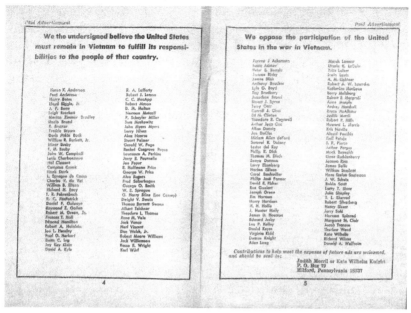

26.1 Pro- and anti-Vietnam War ads in the June 1968 issue of *Galaxy Science Fiction*.

developed in opposition to it."[12] From Franklin's perspective – which echoes the view articulated by James William Gibson's book *The Perfect War: Technowar in Vietnam* (1986) – the war *itself* must be understood as a science fictional event that embodies fantasies of American technological omnipotence and dreams of inevitable progressive imperial expansion.[13] Pro-Vietnam-War SF registers these imperial fantasies in works such as Heinlein's *Starship Troopers* (1959) and *Glory Road* (1963), in Joe Poyer's story "Null Zone" (1968), in Jerry Pournelle and Stefan Possony's *The Strategy of Technology* (1970), and in Roy L. Prosterman's story "Peace Probe" (1973).

New Wave authors, who were in various ways sympathetic to the anti-war movements and postwar countercultures, responded with several anti-war stories: Norman Spinrad's "The Big Flash" (1969) satirizes the idea of winning the war through the use of nuclear weapons; Harry Harrison's "Commando Raid" (1970) criticizes the economic imperialism inherent to Western humanitarian interventions; Gene Wolfe's "The HORARS of War" (1970) offers

---

[12] Franklin, *Vietnam*, p. 166.
[13] In addition to Franklin, see also James William Gibson, *The Perfect War: Technowar in Vietnam* (New York: The Atlantic Monthly Press, 1986).

what Andrew Butler calls "a metaphor for the dehumanizing impact of war and the necessary programming of military training"[14]; Kate Wilhelm's "The Village" (1973) re-imagines the My Lai massacre taking place within the United States; Harlan Ellison's "Basilisk" portrays returning Vietnam veterans as tragic scapegoats pursued by angry townsfolk; and Ronald Anthony Cross's "The Heavenly Blue Answer" (1987) offers a story in which a veteran returns home to find America "Orientalized" by Asian influences that shatter cozy distinctions between self and enemy.

Two Allegories of Vietnam: *The Forever War* and *The Word for World Is Forest*

Nearly all existing scholarship agrees that two novels in particular best represent the New Wave's critique of the Vietnam War: Joe Haldeman's serialized novel *The Forever War* (1972–4) and Ursula K. Le Guin's *The Word for World Is Forest* (1972). *The Forever War* is frequently understood as a critical response to the celebratory militarism of *Starship Troopers*, and it uses the science-fictional trope of an inscrutable interstellar conflict to condemn the brutal absurdity of the growing military industrial complex and imperial war economy of the Vietnam era. *The Forever War* tells the story of William Mandella, a physics student drafted to fight in an interstellar battle against an alien race called the Taurans. Mandella and his fellow soldiers, under the influence of homicidal military posthypnotic suggestions, brutally wipe out a base of the Tauran "teddy bears," who lack the technological resources to defend themselves. Not long afterwards (at least from his perspective), Mandella's ship is damaged by advanced Tauran weaponry that has been developed in the years since he left Earth; such inconsistencies in military technology occur because interstellar travel at extreme speeds causes relativistic effects. (Mandella experiences days or weeks of travel, for example, while years, decades, or even centuries pass on Earth and on Tauran worlds.) When Mandella and his fellow soldier Marygay Potter return to Earth, they discover a dramatically transformed human society (one which is disorienting to them because of changes in sexual norms), and they have difficulty adapting to civilian life. They are separated after re-enlisting, yet they both survive (against all odds) until the end of the war, only to discover at the end of their relativistic travels that the far-future human society they eventually

---

[14] Andrew M. Butler, *Solar Flares: Science Fiction in the 1970s* (Liverpool: Liverpool University Press, 2012), p. 97.

rejoin has ultimately developed a friendly alliance with the Taurans and now regards the entire embarrassing war as "a monument to human stupidity."[15]

The Forever War is similar to many other Vietnam War narratives because it centers on the experience of a soldier who finds himself trapped within a conflict that seems inexplicable and absurd. It is different from many Vietnam War narratives, however, because Haldeman exposes the hard-edged economic and political causes of the war rather than portraying the conflict as somehow existentially meaningless. Peter C. Rollins suggests that realist Vietnam narratives such as Ron Kovic's film *Born on the Fourth of July* (1976), Philip Caputo's *A Rumor of War* (1977), Robert Mason's *Chickenhawk* (1983), and W. D. Ehrhart's *Vietnam-Perkasie* (1978) often fail to apprehend the war's causes,[16] and Owen W. Gilman similarly argues that Vietnam has been "resistant" to "reductive efforts" to give it a coherent sense of meaning.[17] Gilman notes that Barry Levinson's film *Good Morning, Vietnam* (1987) opposes the sharp fury of Robin Williams's improvisational comedy against the primal horror of the war's essential senselessness.[18] Gilman also argues that Michael Herr's *Dispatches* (1977) – a work of New Journalism widely considered one of the most powerful literary works to emerge from the Vietnam conflict – draws upon "official pronouncements" from the war in order to highlight its absurdity.[19] Peter McInerney echoes this suggestion, arguing that *Dispatches* captures the sense that all the facts about the war somehow fail to communicate the war's deeper truth,[20] and he concludes that most literary works foreground "the impossibility of creating any 'absolute truth' about Vietnam" whatsoever.[21] Steffen H. Hantke also observes that Vietnam narratives with fantastical elements – such as Larry Heinemann's *Paco's Story* (1987), Tim O'Brien's *In the Lake of the Woods* (1994), Jack Dann's anthology *In the Fields of Fire* (1987), and Bruce McAllister's *Dream Baby* (1987) – often fail to achieve meaningful closure; he concludes that "Vietnam literature has appropriated the impossibility of its

---

[15] Joe Haldeman, *The Forever War* (New York: Thomas Dunne Books, 1974), p. 259.
[16] Peter C. Rollins, "The Vietnam War: Perceptions Through Literature, Film, and Television," *American Quarterly*, 36, 3 (1984), p. 422.
[17] Owen W. Gilman, "Vietnam, Chaos, and the Dark Art of Improvisation," in Michael Anderegg, ed., *Inventing Vietnam* (Philadelphia: Temple University Press, 1991), p. 232.
[18] Ibid., p. 235.
[19] Ibid., p. 245.
[20] Peter McInerney, "'Straight' and 'Secret' History in Vietnam War Literature," *Contemporary Literature* 22,2 (Spring 1981), p. 191.
[21] Ibid., p. 203.

endeavor," consistently portraying the war as inscrutable, unreal, bewildering, and senseless.[22]

In contrast to narratives that foreground a disorienting postmodern sense of fragmentation and by refusing to assign ultimate meaning to the Vietnam War, Haldeman's *The Forever War* concludes with a critical interrogation of the war's economic and imperialistic underpinnings. The representative of humanity who debriefs Mandella upon his return home reveals that "Earth's economy needed a war" back when the conflict began and the "old soldiers" in command at the beginning of the twenty-first century (veterans of the Vietnam era) provoked the war under "false pretenses" for economic purposes; they manufactured an interstellar Gulf of Tonkin incident in order to orchestrate a conflict that offered "a nice hole to throw buckets of money into."[23] Rather than portraying the war as a senseless horror, Haldeman exposes the war's true origins: the struggle against the Taurans, just like the Vietnam conflict, was manufactured to support an imperial war economy. The Taurans are a communist clone race with "no concept of the individual,"[24] yet rather than annihilating them, far-future humanity has ultimately moved to emulate the Taurans, abolishing "wealth," "back salary," "compound interest," "money," and "credit," while at the same time developing alternative social norms (and abandoning the heterosexual nuclear family structure) to mirror the Taurans' clone culture.[25]

Haldeman's refusal to adhere to what John Carlos Rowe calls the disorienting "personalist epistemology" that characterizes many Vietnam narratives enables *The Forever War* to overcome the pervasive aura of mystification that has often been produced around the conflict.[26] Evan Carton observes that the widespread portrayal of the Vietnam experience as disorienting and traumatic serves to mystify the war's historical context; the insistence on the war's senselessness, in other words, often obscures the war's actual causes.[27] Phil Beidler, drawing on Hannah Arendt, describes this mystification as a form of "banality" that forecloses "critical openings" and leaves little space for deeper and more thoughtful contemplation about

[22] Steffen H. Hantke, "The Uses of the Fantastic and the Deferment of Closure in American Literature on the Vietnam War," *Rocky Mountain Review of Language and Literature* 55, 1 (2001), p. 79.

[23] Haldeman, *The Forever War*, p. 263.

[24] Ibid., p. 261.

[25] Ibid., p. 259.

[26] John Carlos Rowe, "Eye-Witness: Documentary Styles in the American Representations of Vietnam," *Cultural Critique*, 3 (1986), pp. 126–7.

[27] Evan Carton, "Vietnam and the Limits of Masculinity," *American Literary History* 3, 2 (Summer 1991), p. 296.

the war.[28] In his view, science-fictional works like Kurt Vonnegut's *Hocus Pocus* (1990) overcome this banality to a much greater degree than mass-market Vietnam novels such as William Franklin Leib's *The Fire Dream* (2003) or Danielle Steel's *Message from Nam* (1990). At the same time, even Vonnegut's novels critical of Vietnam and the Cold War – such as *Slaughterhouse-Five* (1969) and *Breakfast of Champions* (1973) alongside *Hocus Pocus* – engage in such multi-layered postmodern satire that it becomes difficult to hold anyone in particular responsible for the war; Americans are all implicated in the war's bleak absurdity. Although this is certainly true to some degree, *The Forever War* offers what Fredric Jameson might characterize as a more intricate "cognitive mapping" of the war's causes; in contrast to the radical postmodern loss of stable reference observable in Vonnegut's parodies, Haldeman shows that it is possible to explore the personal experience of trauma and disorientation experienced by soldiers while at the same time situating such individual traumas within a larger context of historical awareness regarding unjust imperial economics.

Although there is almost universal agreement that *The Forever War* functions as a challenge to the celebratory militarism of Heinlein's *Starship Troopers*, little critical attention has been paid to Delany's trilogy *The Fall of the Towers* (first published as a collected omnibus in 1970) despite the fact that Delany reveals in his autobiography *The Motion of Light in Water* (1988) that he wrote the series in response to *Starship Troopers* during a moment when he was strongly influenced by the ongoing background of the Vietnam conflict.[29] *The Fall of the Towers* is, in many ways, Delany's own version of *The Forever War*, especially insofar as Delany (like Haldeman) prioritizes the simultaneity of objective knowledge and subjective experience in relation to a seemingly incomprehensible and unimaginably brutal military conflict. In the trilogy, a far-future human empire struggles against a mysterious enemy that seems to threaten it from remote (and radioactive) areas of the world; ultimately, however, the people of the empire discover that the war they have been fighting is a social hallucination provoked by the empire's economic and social inequities, and the war is being waged within a deadly cyberspace simulation that randomizes soldiers' deaths in order to diminish the Empire's underprivileged surplus population. During this war, two outside cosmic superpowers – the benevolent Triple Mind and the malevolent

---

[28] Phil Beidler, "Bad Business: Vietnam and Recent Mass-Market Fiction," *College English* 54, 1 (January 1992), p. 74.

[29] Samuel R. Delany, *The Motion of Light in Water: Sex and Science Fiction Writing in the East Village* (Minneapolis: University of Minnesota Press, 2004), p. 193.

Lord of the Flames – struggle to influence the empire's culture. Throughout the trilogy, Delany pays close attention to the alienating complexity of imperial economics, and one of the narrative's central arguments is that individuals must develop what Jameson would call deeper and more accurate "cognitive maps" in order to demystify the economic, social, and political causes of a seemingly incomprehensible war. At the same time, however, Delany (like Haldeman) rejects the notion that human subjectivity can be optimized through military brainwashing, and *The Fall of the Towers* (perhaps more than almost any other New Wave response to the Vietnam War) draws attention to the irreducible validity of individual subjectivity and its complex relationship with objective knowledge.

Ursula K. Le Guin's novel *The Word for World Is Forest*, like Haldeman's *The Forever War*, is frequently cited as one of the New Wave's most powerful responses to the Vietnam conflict. The novel, which is part of Le Guin's Hainish cycle and was originally published in Ellison's *Again, Dangerous Visions* (1972), offers shocking portrayals of rampaging commandos using "firejelly" (a fantastical version of napalm) to immolate innocent forest-dwelling natives who impede imperial profiteering. Le Guin wrote the story in 1968, and the novella uncannily anticipates the outrage that would accompany the public exposure of the My Lai massacre in 1969 and the publication of the Phan Thi Kim Phuc napalm photo in 1972.

The Word for World Is Forest takes place on a densely forested world called Athshe; this planet is called "New Tahiti" by the settlers from Terra (Earth) who colonize it and establish a logging industry there. The Terrans enslave the native population of the planet, a smaller fur-covered forest-dwelling humanoid race they call "creechies," and force them to perform industrial labor against their will. The Athsheans, led by a former slave named Selver, eventually rise up against the Terrans and liberate their world using guerilla resistance tactics, but not before Terran Captain Don Davidson unleashes psychotic commando fury upon them, unable to accept that Terrans (with their superior technology) might be defeated by what he regards as super-stitious teddy bears. Despite his victory over Davidson, Selver laments that the Athsheans have now learned to use violence in a way that had never previously been part of their culture; the master's house, as Audre Lorde might suggest, has been dismantled by the master's tools, and the Athsheans can never fully heal from the brutal cultural influence of Terran colonization.

As Hantke notes, *The Word for World Is Forest* frames the United States' involvement in Vietnam as an expression of "the myth of the American frontier, westward expansion, the Indian Captivity Narrative, [and] the cautionary tale of going native and succumbing to sin and corruption."[30] Le Guin portrays Davidson as a traditional frontier hero, yet as she draws the reader into his first person perspective, we're invited to experience revulsion at his racist, sexist, and imperialist worldviews: he believes that New Tahiti was "literally made for men" and that once "the primeval murk and savagery and ignorance" are eliminated, the world will offer a new paradise, "a real Eden."[31] He denies the personhood of the Athsheans (despite his willingness to sexually exploit them): "This isn't slavery," he notes, "slaves are humans. When you raise cows, you call that slavery? No. And it works."[32] Ultimately, Le Guin reveals how the attitudes embodied by countless American western heroes like Davidson contain dangerously homicidal elements: "The fact is," Davidson reflects to himself toward the end of the story, "the only time a man is really and entirely a man is when he's just had a woman or killed another man."[33] Le Guin's portrayal of Athshe as a new American West (from the perspective of Terran colonizers) thus exposes the injustices of both the Vietnam War and a deeper history of US colonization of indigenous peoples throughout the United States.

The Word for World Is Forest – much like Michael Cimino's Vietnam film The Deer Hunter (1978) and Norman Mailer's novel Why Are We in Vietnam? (1967) – ultimately suggests that the United States' psychotic determination to treat Vietnam as a new Western frontier exposes irrational fantasies of unfettered mastery that remain psychologically unresolved within American culture. John Hellmann notes that The Deer Hunter functions as a deconstruction of the traditional American western insofar as it "presents Vietnam as a frontier landscape so hostile that America, having come as hunter with dreams of omnipotence, is held captive in it and forced to confront the full implications of its own impulses."[34] Rubin Rabinovitz offers a similar argument about Why Are We in Vietnam?, a story of two young boys hunting in the Alaskan wilderness who ultimately fail to come to terms with their conflicted inner feelings and enjoy catharsis through killing and technological superiority over nature. According to Rabinovitz, Mailer's novel suggests that the United States "is being ravaged by the effects of repressed

---

[30] Steffen H. Hantke, "Disorienting Encounters: Magical Realism and American Literature on the Vietnam War," Journal of the Fantastic in the Arts 12, 3 (2001), p. 270.

[31] Ursula K. Le Guin, The Word for World Is Forest (New York: Tor, 1972), p. 12.

[32] Ibid., p. 18.

[33] Ibid., p. 96.

[34] John Hellmann, "Vietnam and the Hollywood Genre Film: Inversions of American Mythology in The Deer Hunter and Apocalypse Now," in Michael Anderegg, ed., Inventing Vietnam (Philadelphia: Temple University Press, 1991), p. 65.

irrationality" and he proposes that "it is time Americans made an attempt to confront and understand their irrationality."[35]

The Word for World Is Forest forwards precisely this argument about the effects of repressed irrationality in regard to the Terran colonizers on Athshe and (by extension) in regard to the United States' imperialist drive toward conquest in Vietnam. Le Guin's Athsheans possess an advanced ability to explore and resolve their unconscious impulses (which they refer to as Gods) by means of deep dreaming, and Selver is astonished by the Terran inability or refusal to dream. Because Terrans like Davidson cannot dream, "they take poison to let loose the dreams in them, but it only makes them drunk or sick."[36] Worse, Terrans "go about in torment killing and destroying, driven by the gods within, whom they will not set free but try to uproot and deny. If they are men, they are evil men, having denied their own dark gods, afraid to see their own faces in the dark."[37] From Le Guin's perspective, which is echoed by Cimino and Mailer, the United States' imperial conquest of Vietnam is driven by an unconscious and unexamined fantasy of political, economic, and technological mastery that reflects the worst of the nation's most violent urges.

The Forever War and *The Word for World Is Forest* each reflect New Wave SF's critical attitudes toward the Vietnam War and loss of confidence in the United States toward its national leaders in a larger sense. Additionally, these representative novels register epochal shifts occurring within British and American imperial fantasy during the Cold War era. John Rieder proposes in *Colonialism and the Emergence of Science Fiction* (2008) that early SF as a recognizable genre emerges from colonial contexts, and it has always been historically implicated within the production of imperial imaginings.[38] Early science fictional works, such as Edgar Rice Burroughs's *A Princess of Mars* (1917), often celebrated imperial expansion and conquest. After Western European decolonization in the wake of the Second World War, however, imperialism gained a negative reputation in the Western popular imaginary (even as imperial practices continued under newly hegemonic regimes of neoliberal globalization), and SF narratives often turned toward heroic tales of counter-imperial struggle and anti-authoritarian uprising, especially during and after the Vietnam War.

---

[35] Rubin Rabinovitz, "Myth and Animism in *Why Are We in Vietnam?*" *Twentieth Century Literature* 20, 4 (October 1974), p. 304.

[36] Le Guin, *The Word for World Is Forest*, p. 56.

[37] Ibid., p. 57.

[38] See John Rieder, *Colonialism and the Emergence of Science Fiction* (Middletown, CT: Wesleyan University Press, 2008).

Certain strands of SF, such as *Starship Troopers*, continued to glorify militaristic imperial expansion during and after the Vietnam years. As Tim Blackmore notes, an entire industry of militarist authors (including Jerry Pournelle, David Drake, David Feintuch, S. M. Sterling, Harry Turtledove, and David Weber) "valorize war culture without questioning it" despite the United States' failures in Vietnam.[39] What's striking, however, is that *both* militaristic SF *and* the more liberal-leaning New Wave imaginings invite Western readers to identify with (or as) colonized heroes struggling toward liberation; on both the Right and the Left, SF protagonists are framed as freedom fighters staging a decolonizing struggle against an oppressive establishment. Cold War SF often, therefore, thrives on the pleasures of imperial masochism, or the enjoyment that comes from imaginatively occupying the position of a subaltern victim. Heinlein gestures in this direction with *Stranger in a Strange Land* (1961), a book that suggests we must all liberate our subjectivities from the interior colonization of conventional norms in order to become psychic supermen, and even an apparently proto-fascist work like his *Starship Troopers* can be read as anti-colonial satire (the approach taken by Paul Verhoeven in his 1997 film adaptation). Frank Herbert's *Dune* (1965) frames an agent of extreme privilege, Paul Atreides, as a Lawrence of Arabia figure who leads a quasi-Arabian subaltern population in an anti-colonial uprising. The central pleasure of Philip K. Dick's *The Man in the High Castle* (1962) arguably comes from imagining the United States as a defeated and colonized nation, and 1960s television shows like *The Prisoner* (1967–8) imagine authoritative male action heroes trapped within Kafkaesque bureaucratic and administrative systems struggling to recover a lost sense of agency and power.

SF texts that in some way *explicitly* engage with the Vietnam conflict force writers and readers to explore the contradictions of imperial masochism in the Cold War era. After 1968 in particular, Vietnam forces American SF writers (and editors) who are in any way associated with the Left to identify simultaneously with and against American imperial power as such. Take, for example, New Wave writer and editor Judith Merril. In her autobiography, *Better to Have Loved* (2002), Merril describes the conflicting identifications she experiences as an American living in London during a time of escalating opposition to the Vietnam War. Her British friends express their relief at having passed the torch of the white man's burden to the United States:

[39] Tim Blackmore, "Hot For War: Jerry Pournelle and David Drake's Regendered Battlefield," *War, Literature, and the Arts* 14 (2002), p. 195.

"Now that you Americans have taken over the world and we don't have to worry about it anymore," she recalls them saying to her, "what are you going to do with it?"[40] British New Wave writers such as Michael Moorcock, J. G. Ballard, and Brian Aldiss are able to take cover within what Paul Gilroy describes as a kind of postcolonial melancholia that disavows imperial injustices and rejects the burden of guilt for postwar imperial atrocities: "There was something telling," Merril says, "in the fact that the particular group of people I knew in Britain were all terribly relieved they were no longer running the world."[41]

As an American, Merril could not share in such relief; her US citizenship forced her to simultaneously identify with (guiltily) and against (passionately) US imperial activities in Southeast Asia. "At some point," she recalls, "I realized I had to go home and see if there was a revolution I could join. If there wasn't one, I felt strongly that I couldn't go on being an American citizen."[42] Le Guin echoes a similar sentiment: in one introduction to *The Word for World Is Forest* (reprinted in *The Language of the Night*), she notes that she wrote the story in 1968 while living in London:

> 1968 was a bitter year for those who opposed the war. The lies and hypocrisies redoubled; so did the killing. Moreover, it was becoming clear that the ethic which approved the defoliation of forests and grainlands and the murder of noncombatants in the name of "peace" was only a corollary of the ethic which permits the despoliation of natural resources for private profit or the GNP, and the murder of the creatures of the earth in the name of "man." The victory of the ethic of exploitation, in all societies, seemed as inevitable as it was disastrous.[43]

Le Guin, like Merril, was driven to participate in revolutionary opposition to the imperial aggression of her own nation, and her anti-war sentiment drove her writing to such an extent that she feels compelled to contextualize and explain the anti-war polemic she voices in *The Word for World Is Forest* in her later introduction to the re-published novella.[44]

Le Guin and Haldeman each explore complex experiences of identification and disidentification with both perpetrators and victims of imperial militarization. In some ways, both of their Vietnam novels participate in an imperial

---

[40] Judith Merril and Emily Pohl-Weary, *Better to Have Loved: The Life of Judith Merril* (Toronto: Between the Lines, 2002), p. 167.

[41] Ibid., p. 167.

[42] Ibid.

[43] Ursula K. Le Guin, *The Language of the Night: Essays on Fantasy and Science Fiction*, ed. Susan Wood (New York: Berkley Books, 1979), p. 141.

[44] Ibid., pp. 141–2.

masochism that enables Western readers to identify with and see themselves as victims of empire. This dynamic of identification, however, is never easy or unproblematic; it is always troubled and self-contradictory. In *The Forever War*, for example, Haldeman offers a critique of the senseless and violent bureaucracy that drives the Western military industrial complex; yet, at the same time, the educated white male soldier is offered as the victim of the faceless system with whom we are invited to identify: he is drafted against his will, dismembered in battle, and ultimately becomes a diasporic refugee from a home he can never return to. In *The Word for World Is Forest*, Le Guin invites readers to shift between different perspectives and identifications. Seeing the world from Captain Davidson's point of view invites us to experience revulsion at the psychotic masculinist power fantasies that drive the expansion of empire; experiencing the world from Selver's perspective is a Fanonian exploration of the inescapable psychic and corporeal violence inherent to anticolonial resistance. The chapters told from the perspective of Lyubov, the colony's Terran anthropologist, place the reader in the position of contributing to imperial violence and simultaneously seeking to oppose it – exactly the contradictory position both Merril and Le Guin feel themselves occupying.

In both novels, readers are invited to identify as both victims and perpetrators of imperial violence. Yet the texts are also caught in a kind of historical narcissism. The absence at the core of both texts is, of course, Vietnam itself: neither narrative attempts to understand or relate to actual Vietnamese people, who are structurally and ideologically absent from the texts. Nonetheless, these two narratives problematize imperial masochism – readers can't simply enjoy frictionless imaginative identification with colonized subjects, and they must consider their own role within the imperial system.

Reappropriating Vietnam

A multitude of other science fictional imaginings, however, offer more frictionless opportunities for American audiences to identify as subaltern victims in unsettling ways. Indeed, as Franklin notes, a disturbing national trend emerged after Vietnam to "reverse the roles of victim and victimizer" by appropriating iconic images from the war and replacing Vietnamese victims with American soldiers.[45] Franklin demonstrates how iconic moments from *The Deer Hunter* and *P.O.W.: The Escape* (a 1986 film starring

---

[45] Franklin, *Vietnam*, p. 17.

DAVID M. HIGGINS

David Carradine) each transform the widely popularized 1968 photo of a Saigon police chief shooting a Viet Cong prisoner into reverse-images in which American soldiers are instead executed by Viet Cong captors.[46] Such images constitute one part of a much larger POW/MIA narrative, a cultural paranoia that countless American soldiers were being held captive and tortured by the Vietnamese after the war. (This myth would even become the psychic backdrop for Captain Kirk's illegal mission to recover Mr. Spock from the jungle-like Genesis Planet in *Star Trek III: The Search for Spock* [dir. Leonard Nimoy, 1984].) According to Franklin, this myth was intentionally fabricated by the Nixon administration in order to deadlock the Paris negotiations and deflate the antiwar movement, the last in a shifting series of arguments for why the Vietnam War could never be ended.[47] Another variation of the reimagining of the 1968 execution photo occurs in a November 1988 issue of *The 'Nam* from Marvel Comics in which photojournalists are re-framed as the enemies doing the harmful "shooting" that ultimately costs the United States the war.[48] Each of these images performs the fantasy work of transfiguring the country into the victim of the war rather than the aggressor.

James William Gibson and Susan Jeffords both observe that such victimization fantasies give rise to the post-Vietnam paramilitary hero, a figure who struggles alone in a guerilla conflict against overwhelming forces in order to recover and reclaim a sense of dominant masculinity that is supposedly threatened by the United States' loss in Vietnam. As Gibson says, "American men – lacking confidence in the government and the economy, troubled by changing relations between the sexes, uncertain of their identity or their future – began to *dream*, to fantasize about the powers and features of another kind of man who could retake and reorder the world. And the hero of all these dreams was the paramilitary warrior. In the New War he fights this battle of Vietnam a thousand times, each time winning decisively."[49]

The dominant 1980s paramilitary hero is, of course, Sylvester Stallone's Rambo, a former POW who fights countless guerilla-style retributive battles. Rambo characters, however, also populate numerous speculative fictional imaginings during the 1970s and 1980s. Blackmore argues that Pournelle's and

---

[46] Ibid., pp. 15–17.
[47] Ibid., p. 178.
[48] Ibid., pp. 19–21.
[49] James William Gibson, *Warrior Dreams: Paramilitary Culture in Post-Vietnam America* (New York: Hill and Wang, 1994), p. 11. See also Susan Jeffords, *The Remasculinization of America: Gender and the Vietnam War* (Bloomington: Indiana University Press, 1989).

430

Drake's SF heroes are often paramilitary mercenaries who "rise above their hired-soldier status" in order to redeem a threatened sense of heroic masculinity.[50] Similarly, John McTiernan's *Predator* (1987) elevates Arnold Schwarzenegger into a Rambo-style role: his character, Major Alan "Dutch" Schaefer, becomes a paramilitary guerilla warrior in a jungle conflict where he is threatened by both CIA corruption and by the alien Predator itself, a relentless and invisible enemy that hunts its American prey with deadly traps and ambushes. The paramilitary victim-hero, like Dutch, often fights two battles: one against a savage and relentless enemy (like the Predator) who functions as a twisted allegory for the victorious Viet Cong; and one against the US government itself, which is portrayed as corrupt beyond redemption.

Much tech-oriented SF continues to elevate such "victim heroes" into sacred icons during and after Vietnam, and such narratives often celebrate the power of militarized technoscience to redeem the United States from impotency and moral decline. Tricia Jenkins, for example, suggests that *The Six Million Dollar Man* (1974–8) and *The Bionic Woman* (1976–8) center upon wounded military heroes whose bodies are healed and augmented by cybertechnology; such narratives, in her view, "create reassuring, nationalist messages about American superiority."[51] Gibson similarly observes that techno-thriller novels and films – such as Tom Clancy's *The Hunt for Red October* (1984), which was adapted into a blockbuster film in 1990 – function to restore faith in patriarchal family values and American techno-military superiority at a time when both seemed undermined by defeat in Vietnam. Gibson suggests that "the 1970s were a time of deep crisis for war and the warrior, as well as an institutional crisis for what I call 'technowar,' the military's paradigm of capital-intensive, high-technology warfare and the claims to vast economic resources this mode of warfare requires."[52] Technowar may have failed in Vietnam, but this very failure was ideologically transformed within various cultural narratives into a defeat and victimization that paradoxically legitimizes even greater investments in military technoscience and masculine domination. This is the essence of imperial masochism: imaginatively appropriating the position of the victim, as Dianne Enns observes, enables the victim-subject to adopt a "status beyond critique" that seemingly

---

[50] Blackmore, "Hot For War," p. 194.

[51] Tricia Jenkins, "Nationalism and Gender: The 1970s, *The Six Million Dollar Man*, and *The Bionic Woman*," *The Journal of Popular Culture* 44, 1 (2011), p. 97.

[52] James William Gibson, "Redeeming Vietnam: Techno-Thriller Novels of the 1980s," *Cultural Critique* 19 (Autumn 1991), p. 183.

legitimizes the exercise of violent power.[53] The United States lost the war in Vietnam, the story often goes, because it did not allow itself to win; corrupt bureaucrats, the liberal media, and a misguided peace movement held its true power in check, and the only way to recover from this emasculating defeat was to cut loose with unchecked masculine power and technological superiority. This loss is re-framed as an imperial rape–revenge narrative, and the tragic failure to exercise imperial hegemony becomes the legitimizing basis for the expression of new forms of imperial might, such as the militarization of domestic police forces in the "war on drugs" in the 1980s and beyond.

One of the most popular and enduring examples of SF's post-Vietnam shift toward imperial masochism can be seen in *Star Wars* (1977), a film which arguably gave birth to the most popular SF franchise of the postwar period. *Star Wars* invites audiences to identify with heroic guerilla resistance fighters struggling against a corrupt and evil empire (without the friction of ever being forced to identify themselves as agents of such an empire). The tensions between pro-war militarism and New Wave fear and loathing within the SF of the Vietnam era often provoked a cultural yearning for a more innocent time, and scholars such as Butler and Geraghty suggest that the first *Star Wars* film was a significant cultural landmark because it "reversed the feeling of loss after Vietnam and literally replaced it with *A New Hope.*"[54] Le Guin's river camp of Endtor from *The Word for World Is Forest* becomes transformed by this logic into the forest moon of Endor, and the complex subaltern teddy bears of Athshe become the comical Ewoks of *Return of the Jedi* (1983), who join "us" in defeating a remorseless invading hyperpower. Although *A New Hope*'s portrayal of outlaw heroes fighting a guerilla resistance against a technologically superior empire clearly invokes Vietnam-era concerns, Robert G. Pielke observes that audiences are "supposed to have a good time with the film without being troubled, upset, or otherwise provoked to deep thought,"[55] and many regard the moral absolutism of the *Star Wars* films as a hollow remedy to the dark tensions of the early 1970s and a harbinger of the succeeding the Reagan era. Perhaps the most striking imaginative aspect of *Star Wars*, however, is the franchise's consistent determination that the ultimate heroes, whether they be the Rebels of the *New Hope* era or the Resistance from *The Force Awakens* (2015), *must* be desperately outnumbered

[53] Diane Enns, *The Violence of Victimhood* (University Park: Pennsylvania State University Press, 2012), p. 6.

[54] Geraghty, *American Science Fiction Film and Television*, p. 60.

[55] Robert G. Pielke, "*Star Wars* vs 2001: A Question of Identity," *Extrapolation* 24, 2 (Summer 1983), p. 145.

and outgunned freedom fighters struggling against imperial power. This is one of the strangest legacies that the Vietnam War has created for American SF: American audiences, who are the privileged beneficiaries of imperial globalization, are constantly invited to identify with anticolonial guerilla freedom fighters (like the Viet Cong), despite the almost total absence of any attempt whatsoever to understand actual Vietnamese perspectives concerning one of the most brutal and devastating wars in either Vietnamese or American history.

27

New Wave Science Fiction and the Dawn of the Environmental Movement

REBECCA EVANS

In his afterword to "Riders of the Purple Wage," Philip José Farmer's contribution to Harlan Ellison's groundbreaking New Wave anthology *Dangerous Visions* (1967), Farmer writes: "Ten years ago, I would have been close to ecstasy if I could have worked on a space project. Rockets, Moon landings, airlocks, and all that. But in the past eight years I've been increasingly interested in, and worried over, terrestrial problems. These are population explosion; birth control; the rape of Mother Nature; human, and animal, 'rights'; international conflicts; and especially mental health. I'd like to see us explore space, but I don't think we have to."[1] Farmer's comment points toward the overlap – historical, thematic, and attitudinal – between two burgeoning fields: modern environmentalism on the one hand and the emergence of New Wave SF on the other. This chapter will trace the interactions between the environmental movement and the New Wave, exploring their historical coincidence (both came into their own in the 1960s and 1970s), common themes (with speculative strategies influencing environmental discourse and environmental themes filtering through SF), and their shared orientation toward dystopia (with both environmentalism and New Wave SF tending toward dire imaginations of future decline).

Speculative Strategies and the Environmental Movement

The stirrings of what would become modern environmentalism began before the 1960s and 1970s. The conservation movement, for instance, can be traced at least as far back as the middle of the nineteenth century, to British debates about deforestation in India and growing American concern about

---

[1] Philip José Farmer, "Afterword" to "Riders of the Purple Wage," in Harlan Ellison, ed., *Dangerous Visions* (London: The Orion Publishing Group, 2012), p. 110.

the erosion of wilderness spaces in the rapid development of the West. (This concern would develop into a schism between conservationists, who believed that natural spaces and resources should be judiciously managed for maximum human usage, and preservationists, who supported the preservation of wilderness on the basis of its intrinsic value.) Meanwhile, questions about overexploitation, pollution, and public health were voiced by figures such as Karl Marx and Friedrich Engels throughout the Industrial Revolution and continued in the late nineteenth and early twentieth centuries through work by Alice Hamilton and Jane Jacobs in the burgeoning fields of occupational and public health. Nonetheless, environmentalism as we know it today began in earnest in the 1960s and 1970s, with rising anxiety about overpopulation and pollution in the 1960s and linked waves of environmental "consciousness," research, advocacy, and legislation in the 1970s.

Each of the individual issues that would coalesce into the environmental movement – pollution, pesticides, air and water quality, overpopulation, nuclear power, energy resources – has its own history that can be told separately, but the movement is best understood as a network of activist issues that reached a tipping point in the 1960s. We can thus trace the development of modern environmentalism through a chain of significant events, some in the realm of print and some in the realm of politics: the publication of Rachel Carson's *Silent Spring*, which brought the lasting effects of exposure to toxic pesticides such as dichlorodiphenyltrichloroethane (DDT) into the public view, in 1962, and of Stewart Udall's *The Quiet Crisis*, which warned about the pollution and overconsumption of natural resources, in 1963; the passage of the Clean Air Act, the Wilderness Act, and the Water Quality Act in 1963, 1964, and 1965, respectively, in the United States; and the publication of *The Population Bomb*, Paul Ehrlich's apocalyptic warning of the dangers posed by global population overgrowth, in 1968. In the 1970s, all these threads of warning began to be woven into a recognizable international movement. The year 1970 saw the celebration of the first Earth Day, the notorious publication of the first "Dirty Dozen" list identifying the twelve US members of Congress with the worst environmental records, and the establishment of a range of American environmental agencies, most notably the Environmental Protection Agency and the National Resources Defense Council. In 1971, Canadian activists founded Greenpeace. In 1972, the Club of Rome published *The Limits to Growth*, which projected possible futures based on the variables of "population, industrialization, pollution, food production, and resource depletion"; meanwhile, the United Nations held the Conference on the Human Environment and established its Environment

Programme.[2] In 1973, the United States passed the Endangered Species Act. In 1975, Edward Abbey's novel *The Monkey Wrench Gang* described a form of radical environmental activism that would inspire the founding of the advocacy organization Earth First! in 1979; in 1978, the discovery of toxic industrial waste polluting the water supply in the Love Canal neighborhood of New York led to the establishment of Superfund in 1980. Concerns about natural resources, oil spills, and renewable energy surfaced throughout the decade; meanwhile, the partial meltdown at the Three Mile Island nuclear power plant in 1979 rekindled longstanding anxieties about nuclear energy. It is no surprise, then, that the 1970s are often called "the environmental decade."

As environmentalism emerged in the 1960s and 1970s, it took shape as a necessarily *predictive* as well as descriptive field. Many of the environmental disasters that activists, writers, and policymakers sought to address were at least partially located in the future, objects of prevention as much as cure. Another way to put this is that, as environmentalism developed, it borrowed from SF speculative strategies in general and the genres of apocalypse and dystopia in particular. Enjoining the public to see in the present the early stages of ecological disaster, environmental advocates produced a variety of speculative writing that, like so much dystopian fiction, warned of what was to come.

Perhaps the most literary use of SF in environmental advocacy writing comes in the opening chapter of Carson's *Silent Spring*, "A Fable for Tomorrow." Flirting with fairy tale, the first chapter opens: "There was once a town in the heart of America where all life seemed to live in harmony with its surroundings."[3] Carson tells readers of lush vegetation, abundant wildlife, pristine landscapes, before pivoting into fantasy: "Then a strange blight crept over the area and everything began to change. Some evil spell had settled on the community ... Everywhere was a shadow of death." Livestock die off; humans sicken and die; birds weaken and vanish; insects fail to appear; plants wither and die. The science fictional culprit is revealed dramatically: "In the gutters under the eaves and between the shingles of the roofs, a white granular powder still showed a few patches; some weeks before it had fallen like snow upon the roofs and the lawns, the fields and streams." This white powder is not "witchcraft" or "enemy action": "the people had done it themselves." As the

[2] Donella H. Meadows, Dennis L. Meadows, Jorgen Randers, and William W. Behrens III, *The Limits to Growth: A Report for the Club of Rome's Project on the Predicament of Mankind* (Washington, DC: Potomac Associates, 1974), p. 29.
[3] Rachel Carson, *Silent Spring* (New York: Mariner Books, 2002), p. 1.

chapter draws to a close, Carson marks these pages as somewhere between documentary and fiction: "This town does not actually exist," she writes, but "every one of these disasters has already happened somewhere."[4] As *Silent Spring* progresses through its excoriation of the incautious use of pesticides, it shifts between meticulous documentation of environmental and medical phenomena and speculation about the afterlives of those phenomena. Carson's book thus calibrates nonfictional observation with fictional speculation: the dangers she discusses are present enough to be confirmed, but still oriented enough toward the future that the warning capacity of the dystopian mode proves useful.

Such speculative strategies recur throughout the major texts of the modern environmental movement's early decades, even as those texts explicitly renounce the techno-utopianism of pre-New Wave SF. *The Population Bomb*, for instance, rejects science fictional modes. Ventriloquizing the reader's possible skepticism regarding his dire predictions, Ehrlich writes, "But ... surely Science (with a capital 'S') will find a way for us to occupy the other planets of our solar system and eventually of other stars before we get all that crowded," then rebukes the fantasy: "Interstellar transport for surplus people presents an amusing prospect," but "enough of fantasy"; the time has come for hard facts.[5] Nonetheless, Ehrlich's book is predicated on speculative dystopian prediction – on the extrapolation of certain destructive trends in the present (namely, population growth in relation to global food production) into catastrophic futures. The same can be said of *The Limits To Growth*, which sets out to describe possible outcomes should the human population continue to grow; though the book consists of a series of simulated possibilities rather than a single predicted scenario, it nonetheless engages in a futuristic practice of speculation that juxtaposes the dystopian future – which, it suggests, seems from the vantage point of 1972 likely to occur – with the utopian alternative that could be achieved were humankind to make significant and global adjustments to its patterns of growth and consumption. Meanwhile, on the more utopian side, R. Buckminster Fuller's *Operating Manual for Spaceship Earth* (1968) and James Lovelock's *Gaia* (1979) both borrow from SF as they seek to describe ecology on the planetary scale – Fuller with his comparison of the Earth to a spaceship, and Lovelock with his description of the planet and its various systems as responsive and coherent, if

---

[4] Ibid., pp. 1–3.
[5] Paul Ehrlich, *The Population Bomb* (New York: Ballantine Books, 1968), pp. 20–1.

not sentient. As the modern environmental movement grew, then, it came to rely on strategies of speculation that show the influence of SF.

Environmental Pessimism: Eco-Dystopia in the New Wave

The New Wave has tended to be defined by two qualities: a new attention to literary style and formal experimentation, and a turn away from utopian visions of engineering and technological development to, as Darren Harris-Fain puts it, a "growing pessimism about humanity's present and future" that was as likely to discuss social as it was scientific extrapolation.[6] As we shall see, the New Wave's pessimism – as well as certain strands of its qualified optimism – often encompassed possible ecological futures.

One could argue that the New Wave's turn toward the so-called "soft" sciences simply made the genre more open to environmental questions. However, it seems at least as likely that the widespread cultural engagement with environmental issues in the 1960s helped to shape the New Wave's often dystopian interest in the "soft" sciences. As indicated by the comment by Farmer with which this chapter opened, the New Wave's shifts in subject matter were a response to the cultural anxieties that fueled such movements as environmentalism. It is not surprising, then, that the issues to which the environmental movement had turned its attention make frequent appearances in New Wave SF. Indeed, if part of the New Wave's increased prestige is thanks to the perception that, unlike earlier SF, it was willing to reject escapism and interrogate pressing social issues, the treatment of environmental themes can be seen as contributing to the New Wave's sense of cultural significance.

In keeping with the general New Wave trend toward pessimism, dystopia tended to serve as the movement's dominant ecological mode, with contemporaneous environmental concerns extrapolated into disastrous futures. In the introduction to the anthology *The Ruins of Earth* (1971), Thomas Disch lays out the parameters of this dystopian extrapolation: whereas earlier anxieties about nuclear apocalypse were so totalizing that ignoring them was the only option, he writes,

> Now, in 1971, it isn't possible to look the other way. It is the daytime, suburban side of existence that has become our nightmare. In effect the

---

[6] Darren Harris-Fain, "Dangerous Visions: New Wave and Post-New Wave Science Fiction," in Eric Carl Link and Gerry Canavan, eds., *The Cambridge Companion to American Science Fiction* (Cambridge: Cambridge University Press, 2015), p. 32.

bombs are already dropping – as more carbon monoxide pollutes the air of Roseville, as mercury poisons our waters, our fish, and ourselves, and as one by one our technology extinguishes the forms of life upon which our own life on this planet depends. These are not catastrophes of the imagination – they are what's happening.[7]

New Wave writers plumbed these ecological catastrophes in their dystopian visions, though not always with as explicit a purpose as in Disch's case.

One of the most frequent topics of New Wave environmental dystopias was overpopulation. Though, as Brian Stableford notes, pre-New Wave SF writers had turned their attention to overpopulation in the 1950s, the subject became a matter of major concern for writers associated with the New Wave.[8] Perhaps the most famous SF treatment of overpopulation is offered in John Brunner's novel *Stand on Zanzibar* (1968). *Stand on Zanzibar* adopts experimental formal strategies to toggle between individual characters' plotlines and world-building interludes as it depicts a world so crowded that, were each living person to be given only a one-by-two-foot space, they would fill the surface area of the titular island. Brunner won the Hugo, the British Science Fiction Association (BSFA) Award, and the Prix-Tour Apollo Award for his novel, which has received critical admiration for its highly stylized prose and innovative form.[9] However, even before *Stand on Zanzibar* and *The Population Bomb* turned overpopulation into a buzzword in 1968, New Wave writers frequently explored the concept. Early short stories by J. G. Ballard ("The Concentration City" [1957] and "Billennium" [1962]) describe claustro-phobic cityscapes stuffed with residents, while Anthony Burgess's *The Wanting Seed* (1962) discusses the increasingly violent population control measures taken to address an overcrowded world. Brian Aldiss's *Earthworks* (1965) depicts the aftermath of a cascading series of disasters caused by overpopulation, particu-larly in terms of industrial farming and food scarcity; Harry Harrison's *Make Room! Make Room!* (1966) also charts the relationship between overpopulation and food, following a network of characters through a catastrophically crowded late twentieth-century version of New York. Philip K. Dick takes an even more fantastical approach in *The Crack in Space* (1966), which depicts

[7] Thomas M. Disch, "On Saving the World," in Thomas M. Disch, ed., *The Ruins of Earth: An Anthology of Stories of the Immediate Future* (New York: G. P. Putnam's Sons, 1971), pp. 2–3. *The Ruins of Earth* is divided into four sections: "The Way It Is," "Why It Is the Way It Is," "How It Could Get Worse," and "Unfortunate Solutions."

[8] Brian Stableford, "Science Fiction and Ecology," in David Seed, ed., *A Companion to Science Fiction* (Malden, MA: Blackwell Publishing, 2008), p. 137.

[9] For more on Brunner's formal innovations, see Ursula Heise, *Sense of Place and Sense of Planet: The Environmental Imagination of the Global* (New York: Oxford University Press, 2008), pp. 68, 76–9.

political machinations against a backdrop of desperate efforts to address over-population, including the seclusion of millions of people in cryopreservation and the colonization of other planets. Meanwhile, Roger Zelazny's *The Dream Master* (1966) focuses primarily on the psychological effects of living on an overcrowded planet.

In the late 1960s and 1970s, overpopulation remained a common topic, migrating into dystopian SF film and television as well as fiction. In some works, such as Robert Heinlein's *I Will Fear No Evil* (1970) and T. J. Bass's Nebula-nominated *The Godwhale* (1974), overpopulation serves as back-ground to societies plagued by many other ills. Others – most notably the thriller/SF film *Soylent Green* (1973), a (less than strict) adaptation of Harrison's *Make Room! Make Room!* – focus on horrific systematic responses to overpopulation, such as the transformation of human remains into the film's titular substance in order to feed the planet's ever-increasing masses. Similarly, *Logan's Run* (1976) imagines a future Earth in which everybody who reaches the age of thirty is killed in order to control the population and thus avoid restricting the lifestyles of the living. Akin to *Soylent Green* and *Logan's Run* in their suspicion of government responses to overpopulation are the *Star Trek* episode "The Mark of Gideon" (1969), in which a corrupt ruler manufactures an epidemic to reduce a problematically large population, and the *Population Bomb*-inspired film *Z.P.G.* (1972), in which a couple risks the death penalty by rebelling against draconian anti-reproduction policies. (By contrast, in Robert Silverberg's *The World Inside* [1970–1], the dystopian aspect is government's *encouragement* of overpopulation via flawed policies promoting constant reproduction in its cramped cities.) In New Wave SF, then, dystopian treatments of overpopulation took many forms, ranging from the straightforward depiction of unpleasant living conditions to the paranoia-infused narration of nightmarish systemic responses to an over-populated world.

Alongside overpopulation, pollution emerged in the 1960s and 1970s as a dystopian subject for the New Wave. Environmental advocacy from Carson's *Silent Spring* to Keep America Beautiful's infamous "Crying Indian" commercial showed how pollution operated on a frightening spec-trum of spatial and temporal scales, ranging from the accumulation of mountains of trash to the dispersal through air, soil, and water of chemicals invisible to the naked eye, which persisted almost indefinitely in bodies and ecosystems. As concerns about pollution grew, New Wave writers probed the dystopian boundaries of the polluted future. James Blish's "We All Die Naked," for instance, which appeared alongside other novellas by Silverberg and Zelazny in the disaster collection *Three for Tomorrow* (1969), is a satiric account of trash management in a hyperbolically polluted future Earth, with garbage taking over massive bodies of water and floating through the streets of flooded cities. Likewise, another Brunner novel, the Nebula-nominated *The Sheep Look Up* (1972), depicts an America in which food, water, and air have all been rendered hopelessly toxic by an unchecked swell of pollution. Meanwhile, in Kate Wilhelm's *Where Late the Sweet Birds Sang* (1976), pollution has caused such pervasive health problems that human society has not merely shifted toward dystopia, but collapsed entirely into apocalypse, with the threat of human extinction lurking. (In fact, in Wilhelm's telling, near or total extinction may be the only way to reverse the pollution; loving accounts of the post-collapse landscape seem almost to celebrate the end of human-inflicted filth.) Indeed, even when pollution is not the central topic, it permeates the New Wave: many of the works discussed above, especially *Make Room! Make Room!*, included pollution in their accounts of overpopulation's unsavory effects.

The New Wave also incorporated less focused and issue-based environmental critiques into its dystopian futures. Accounts of ecological catastrophe, for instance, persisted throughout the 1960s and 1970s, both in explicitly environmentalist anthologies such as *The Ruins of Earth* and in the less straightforwardly political disaster novels of J. G. Ballard. Anointed by Judith Merril and Michael Moorcock alike as the rising star of the British New Wave, Ballard published a series of natural disaster novels in the 1960s, including *The Wind from Nowhere* (1961), *The Drowned World* (1962), *The Burning World* (1964), and *The Crystal World* (1966).[10] Each novel depicts a different mysterious ecological catastrophe on a global scale – an overwhelming wind, a tropical flood submerging everything except far northern territories, a drought, and a strange plague of crystallization turning everything it touches into a lifeless gem. While *The Burning World* explains the drought as the byproduct of pollution, the climatic transformations of *The Drowned World* are described as the result not of human intervention but rather of a solar fluke, and the origins of the disasters of *The Wind from Nowhere* and *The Crystal World* are more enigmatic. Though the imagery of environmental catastrophe saturates the prose, ecological disaster is deployed less to critique particular environmentally destructive practices than as an opportunity for meditation on the end of civilization. These novels

---

[10] See Robert Latham, "The New Wave," in David Seed, ed., *A Companion to Science Fiction* (Malden, MA: Blackwell Publishing, 2008), pp. 207, 209.

operate as allegories for contemporary socioecological issues, not as specific extrapolations of those issues into the future.

Alongside these more dramatic environmental outcomes, another strand of eco-dystopia emerged in what we might call the post-natural New Wave. Philip K. Dick's *Do Androids Dream of Electric Sheep?* (1968), for instance, incorporates nascent anxieties about endangered species and a general distancing of modern society from the natural world into a post-nuclear landscape. In Dick's barren world, nonhuman animals have been rendered so rare by fallout that they serve as extraordinary status symbols, and even electric replicas are cherished; meanwhile, human-presenting androids take on more and more work while being denied human rights. As bounty hunter Rick Deckard tracks down android rebels, Dick leads readers along the ever more slippery boundary between the "real" and the "unreal." The end result is a novel that probes the widening gap between human society and the "natural" world, even as it questions the fetishizing of that distinction. This theme of the dystopian separation of man from nature emerges frequently in New Wave work. Farmer's "Riders of the Purple Wage," for instance, depicts a society divided between radicals who retreat into the wilderness and the artificially controlled lives lived by the rest of the population. Likewise, Pamela Zoline's "The Heat Death of the Universe," originally published in *New Worlds* and reprinted in Judith Merril's groundbreaking anthology *England Swings SF* (1968), describes a California housewife's claustrophobic frustration with her suburban life: as she "imagines a whole world which has become like California, all topographical imperfections sanded away with the sweet smelling burr of the plastic surgeon's cosmetic polisher," we are told that her eyes are "bluer far and of a different quality than the Nature metaphors which were both engine and fuel to precedent literature. A fine, modern, acid, synthetic blue," like "the promising, fat, unnatural blue of the heavy tranquilizer capsule" or "the deepest, most unbelievable azure of the tiled and mossless interiors of California swimming pools."[11] These anxieties about the social separation from nature are amplified in the film *Silent Running* (1972), which describes an ecologist's determined attempt to preserve the last specimens of botanical life after plants go extinct. In such works – influenced less by specific environmental policy issues than by the general nostalgia for nature associated with environmental consciousness – we see a dystopian extension of mainstream environmental writer Edward

---

[11] P. A. Zoline, "The Heat Death of the Universe," in Judith Merril, ed., *England Swings SF* (Garden City, NY: Doubleday & Company, 1968), pp. 315, 319.

Abbey's more intangible warning: "If industrial man continues to multiply his numbers and expand his operations he will succeed in his apparent intention, to seal himself off from the natural and isolate himself within a synthetic prison of his own making" – will, indeed, "make himself an exile from the earth."[12]

Environmental Optimism: Critical Ecotopias

In keeping with the environmental movement's general trend toward pessimism and the prediction of disaster, dystopia remained the major mode of New Wave environmental SF. However, utopian strands of environmentalism emerged cautiously in the 1960s and 1970s as well. Indeed, arguably the most famous work of environmental utopia – Ernest Callenbach's novel *Ecotopia* (1975) – was published during this period. *Ecotopia* is set in the late 1990s and follows fictional journalist Will Weston as he explores the titular state, which seceded from the United States in 1980; the novel alternates between Weston's journalistic dispatches and his personal diary entries. (In this way, Callenbach's entry into the utopian canon echoes the genre's most common structural conceit, honed from Sir Thomas More to Edward Bellamy to Charlotte Perkins Gilman: the recorded or recollected experience of a traveler moving through unfamiliar terrain.) As Weston's research brings him further and further into Ecotopian society, he discovers the significant differences between Ecotopia and his home state: not only do the Ecotopians, as their name would suggest, prioritize sustainability and resource management; they also enjoy more permissive sexual and gender norms, generally reject mass culture, and purposefully incorporate recreational mock warfare into the social fabric to safely dissipate aggression. (Racial difference is treated rather less satisfyingly: as Weston explains, black residents of Ecotopia live in self-enforced segregation, which "is surely one of the most disheartening developments of all of Ecotopia, and . . . clouds the future of our nation as well."[13]) By the novel's end, Weston has fallen in love with an Ecotopian woman and decides to stay. His decision is clearly intended to prompt Callenbach's readers to make the same choice – to begin, in other words, to make an Ecotopia in their own lives and societies.

However, the utopianism of *Ecotopia* is rare in the context of the New Wave. Even outside the strictly dystopian decline and disaster narratives

[12] Edward Abbey, *Desert Solitaire: A Season in the Wilderness* (New York: Touchstone, 1990), p. 169.
[13] Ernest Callenbach, *Ecotopia* (New York: Bantam Books, 1990), p. 110.

discussed above, New Wave writers were reluctant to leave pessimism behind. Almost universally, then, even the more optimistic New Wave treatments of environmental themes contain a lurking element of dystopia or at least of the possibility of it. In other words, if environmentalism translated easily into dystopian warnings in the 1960s and 1970s, New Wave writers took a more cautious approach to environmental utopia: it may be possible, they tended to suggest, but it is by no means the most likely outcome.[14]

Ambivalent environmental utopias divide into two categories in the New Wave. The first concerns the post-scarcity utopia, in which depleted and harsh environments force their inhabitants to band together in the pursuit of building a sustainable (or, put less delicately, survivable) society. Into this category fall some of the most famous works of 1960s and 1970s SF, including Frank Herbert's Hugo- and Nebula-winning novel *Dune* (1965) and a number of Ursula K. Le Guin's novels, including the Hugo- and Nebula-winning *The Left Hand of Darkness* (1969) and the Hugo-, Nebula-, and Locus-winning *The Dispossessed* (1974). In *Dune*, a "space opera" steeped in 1960s counter-cultural mysticism, protagonist Paul Atreides leads the enigmatic Fremen against the scheming Emperor and his minions, who wish to use the harsh desert planet of Arrakis to mine melange, a hallucinogenic substance with great technical value for space travel. The planet's environment is so unforgiving that those who travel on it must use "stillsuits," which preserve and recycle every drop of water from the wearers' bodies; however, as "planetary ecologist" Liet-Kynes reveals, Arrakis is the subject of a *longue durée* terra-forming permaculture project meant to restore water and life to the planet's surface. *Dune*'s influence on environmentalism cannot be overstated: in its attention to the interaction between bodies and environments, its articulation of crucial principles of ecological ethics ("The highest function of ecology," Liet-Kynes tells us, "is understanding consequences") and its willingness to imagine ecology on a *global* scale, *Dune* opened up new horizons for environmental literacy in the realm of SF.[15] Nonetheless, its utopianism is

---

[14] Following Tom Moylan's influential categorization in *Demand the Impossible*, we might define all of these texts as "critical utopias"; indeed, Moylan identifies *Ecotopia*, Ursula K. Le Guin's *The Dispossessed*, and Marge Piercy's *Woman on the Edge of Time* as such. However, though Moylan in *Scraps of the Untainted Sky* reserves the term "critical dystopia" for works written after the late 1980s, these works arguably operate in that mode as well, offering both a dystopian probable future and the faint possibility of utopian outcomes. See Tom Moylan, *Demand the Impossible: Science Fiction and the Utopian Imagination* (London: Methuen Publishing, 1986), pp. 9–11 and *Scraps of the Untainted Sky: Science Fiction, Utopia, Dystopia* (Boulder, CO: Westview Press, 2000), p. 186.

[15] Frank Herbert, *Dune* (New York: Ace Books, 1990), p. 272.

tempered: Arrakis's environment is not lush, beautiful, or even particularly comfortable; indeed, its inhabitants are arguably committed to sustainability only because of the dire consequences they face.

The same can be said of Le Guin's quasi-utopian novels *The Left Hand of Darkness* and *The Dispossessed*. In *The Left Hand of Darkness*, which is set on the planet of Gethen, environmental utopianism is a less explicit concern than gender and utopia: on Gethen, people are ambisexual, fluctuating between gender expressions depending on the dynamics of their romantic and sexual partnerships; as a result, both gendered hierarchy and violent conflict are entirely absent. Nonetheless, as Le Guin hints, the harshness of the environment also contributes to Gethen's social stability: as one expert explains, "in the end, the dominant factor in Gethenian life is not sex or any other human thing: it is their environment, their cold world. Here man has a crueler enemy even than himself."[16] In *The Dispossessed*, which traces the distinctions between two planets – Urras, which is torn between capitalism and socialism, and Anarres, a barren moon that is home to an anarchist society – this relationship between ecological scarcity and utopian outcomes is made even more explicit. Anarres's equitable, non-hierarchical social organization clearly would not exist if not for the harshness of its landscape and the very real need for total cooperation and cohesion. *The Dispossessed* is often subtitled "an ambiguous utopia": if some of that ambiguity comes in the protagonist's recognition that the social structures on Anarres are not always as purely utopian as they set out to be, it is also partially defined by the brutality of Anarres's environmental conditions. In Le Guin, as in Herbert, then, environmental utopias (societies characterized by permacultural practice) are imaginable only in the context of stark and dangerous environmental limitations.

The second category within the New Wave's environmental utopianism concerns what we might call the *cautionary* utopia, in which a utopian future is presented, but formally placed in the narrative context of a dystopian alternative. In these works, environmental utopia is not promised or even extrapolated, but instead held up against its dystopian counterpart – which, it is generally hinted, is the likelier outcome of present trends. In the New Wave of the 1970s, this was expressed primarily in

---

[16] Ursula K. Le Guin, *The Left Hand of Darkness* (New York: Ace Books, 1987), p. 96. See also Fredric Jameson's account of this dynamic in "World Reduction in Le Guin: The Emergence of Utopian Narrative," *Science Fiction Studies* 2, 3 (1975), pp. 221–30, where Jameson traces "the inseparability of utopia and scarcity of Le Guin's work."

ecofeminist SF, most notably in the work of Joanna Russ and Marge Piercy.[17] Russ's Nebula-nominated novel *And Chaos Died* (1970), for instance, could be categorized as one of the overpopulation dystopias described above; the future Earth from which its protagonist hails is over-populated and prone to acts of violence. However, the planet on which he crash-lands is an eco-political utopia whose telepathic inhabitants live in harmony with their environment and with each other. *And Chaos Died* thus incorporates environmental dystopia (overpopulation) and environmental utopia (sustainability): the former is clearly marked as more probable from Russ's 1970 perspective, but she holds out the latter as a still-possible alternative. (Russ would return to this multi-world structure in *The Female Man* [1975].) Marge Piercy's *Woman on the Edge of Time* (1976) takes a similar path, following protagonist Connie's traumatic time in a mental hospital as she communicates with two future societies: a feminist and environmental utopia in which pollution, dissociation from nature, and social strife have been almost entirely eliminated; and a patriarchal dystopia. As the novel makes explicit, these futures are both possible in Connie's (and Piercy's) present; it is up in part to Connie to help determine which path Earth will take. In short, Russ and Piercy write ecofeminist utopias only in the context of explicit patriarchal eco-*dystopias*: utopianism is held out as a possibility, but always with the call that, unless action is taken, dystopia is the more likely outcome. All in all, then, New Wave environmental utopias are generically mixed: picking up on the New Wave's trend toward pessimism, dystopia always lurks in the period's environmental SF, even when it is not the central mode.

As environmentalism and the New Wave grew alongside one another, then, both themes and genres flowed between the two fields. Environmentalism borrowed dystopian and speculative strategies to under-score the potency of its warnings; meanwhile, the New Wave turned its attention to environmental themes as it sought to distance itself from what many writers saw as the escapist techno-utopianism of earlier SF. With dystopia as their common language and the human influence on ecology as their common subject, New Wave SF and the environmental movement partnered in constructing the environmental zeitgeist of the 1960s and 1970s.

---

[17] This coincidence of feminist and utopian fiction is not particular to texts dealing with environmental themes; indeed, in the twentieth century, feminist writers have produced the bulk of utopian texts.

28

Stagflation, New Wave, and the Death of the Future

GREG CONLEY

Late twentieth-century economics were tumultuous and often disastrous. From the slowdown of the postwar boom economy to the extended recessions of the 1970s, the period was marked by deep economic fluctuation – and New Wave SF noticed. Many writers focused on the increasing deregulation of capitalist interests and the diminishing influence the governments of the world had on their own economies. They depicted near- and far-future dystopias with unregulated corporate economies that destroy the lives of their citizens, futures in which corporations – or governments that behaved like corporations – ran everything. Depending on the author's inclination, these corporations could engage in environmental destruction, economic exploitation, war-mongering, brutal suppression of dissent, and even, in the case of works such as Philip K. Dick's "Faith of Our Fathers" (1967) and Stanislaw Lem's *The Futurological Congress* (1971), covert drugging of the population as a means of social control. Some of the authors discussed in this chapter may not have identified as New Wave, but regardless of their aesthetic allegiance they all took part in SF's growing interest in the breakdown of the postwar boom and the emergence of neoliberal capitalism in the 1970s.

Economic Turmoil

SF authors certainly had plenty of problems in the economic sphere to inspire them.[1] During the New Deal years in the United States, a group of economists, opposed to the theories of John Maynard Keynes, had argued that the economy must be *less* regulated; only then, they said, would inflation, unemployment, and other social ills disappear. Through most of the New Deal era, no one listened – their most vocal supporter, Milton

[1] Naomi Klein, *The Shock Doctrine* (New York: Picador, 2007), p. 23.

Friedman, was described as "a pixie or pest" by *Time* as late as 1969.[2] But as the New Deal ran out of energy, governments began to shift their views, and neoliberal austerity and deregulation began to be tested – perhaps most famously in Chile. Augusto Pinochet hired many of Friedman's students after he took control of Chile's government. He even brought Friedman himself in as a consultant.[3] The world watched as Pinochet transformed the country, cutting government spending by 25 percent in six months and completely opening the country to foreign trade; this was accompanied by a turn to autocracy, ultimately leading to the murders of thousands in football stadiums.[4] Thus began the "fifty-year campaign for total corporate liberation" that was still ongoing in the 2010s.[5]

In *The Shock Doctrine* Naomi Klein dates the wholesale adoption of such *laissez-faire* doctrines in the United States and other first-world countries to the 1980s, with the rise of Reaganomics and Thatcherite policies[6] – but in fact the shift started earlier, in the 1970s. The official story is that "the triumph of deregulated capitalism has been born of freedom, that unfettered free markets go hand in hand with democracy" – but "this fundamentalist form of capitalism has consistently been midwifed by the most brutal forms of coercion."[7] That is one of the social changes SF authors were most drawn to in the 1970s – the coercive elements of the union of corporate capitalism and the neoliberal state as they sought to monetize all aspects of contemporary life, including basic functions of social order that had once been the role of government to provide.

The change of the 1970s was certainly a shock for those who lived through it. Many had never lived in anything but an economy of consistent growth.[8] The stereotypical placidity of the 1950s and the cultural revolution of the 1960s gave way to a widespread sense of instability, uncertainty, and pessimism in the 1970s. While it would be a simplification to say that the New Wave was wholly pessimistic while the concurrent older styles were wholly

---

[2] Ibid., p. 21.
[3] Ibid., pp. 94, 99.
[4] Ibid., p. 99.
[5] Ibid., p. 23.
[6] Ibid., pp. 21–2.
[7] Ibid., pp. 22–3.
[8] The period between 1947 and 1973 "marked the most sustained period of rapid economic growth in world history." GDP nearly tripled; US median income grew by nearly 50 percent; energy costs declined "by an annual average of 5 percent ... " Thomas Borstelmann, *The 1970s: A New Global History from Civil Rights to Economic Inequality* (Princeton, NJ: Princeton University Press, 2011), ebook edn., loc. 985.

optimistic,[9] the trend of pessimistic criticism grew at a rate that nearly mirrors the freefall of the economy. A new kind of dystopia appeared, characterized by the New Wave's emphasis on technique and psychology as well as the deregulation of capitalist economies and the rise of the corporate state.

Death of the Present: Economic Collapse

The widescale economic changes of the period – both at the level of policy and at the level of political ideology – came about in part as a result of a floundering economy. In many countries, not only the United States and Britain, unemployment rose even as inflation lowered the value of currency.[10] Economists called this perverse situation "stagflation"; they had once believed it impossible. Inflation so badly devalued American currency that the Nixon administration severed the dollar's fixed exchange rates.[11] The Organization of the Petroleum Exporting Countries (OPEC) embargo in 1973 only made matters worse – famously, the gasoline shortage was so bad that lines stretched for blocks. Stations locked their pumps at night and drivers sealed their vehicles' gas caps.[12] The Carter administration (1977–80) tried to stem inflation. In 1978 it announced a program to limit both wages and prices; it didn't work.[13] The administration also assumed the oil crisis earlier in the decade was one of a kind and couldn't be repeated. Unfortunately, oil prices surged again, in 1979 and 1980,[14] as did food and housing prices.[15]

Even at the start of the crisis the answer to the growing malaise of the 1970s was seen to be deregulation and unfettered capitalism. Stewart Udall, former Secretary of the Interior, argued in a 1972 *Atlantic* article that the country was rushing toward disaster. Writing about oil and transportation, he asked, "Given the fact that we are already at the edge of an energy crisis of this

---

[9] See Damien Broderick, "New Wave and Backwash: 1960–1980," in Edward James and Farah Mendlesohn, eds., *The Cambridge Companion to Science Fiction* (Cambridge: Cambridge University Press, 2003), p. 55.

[10] Borstelmann, *The 1970s*, loc. 1010.

[11] Ibid., p. 3307.

[12] Brian Resnick, "What America Looked Like: The 1970s Gas Crisis," *The Atlantic* (2012), www.theatlantic.com/national/archive/2012/05/what-america-looked-like-the-1970s-gas-crisis/257837 (last accessed 21 May, 2018).

[13] W. Carl Biven, *Jimmy Carter's Economy: Policy in an Age of Limits* (Chapel Hill, NC: University of North Carolina Press, 2002), p. 185.

[14] Ibid., p. 191.

[15] Ibid., pp. 191–3.

magnitude, why are our government and industry leaders not discussing appropriate growth-limits policies?" He went on to complain that "For its part, the private sector has been dominated by oil and auto industries whose executives have been unable even to contemplate production plateaus and low horsepower engines."[16]

The once-common New-Deal-era assumption that a regulated economy worked best was displaced by a turn to the autonomy of financial institutions and corporations. The new economic regime maintained that "the market alone" was best able to "allocate resources and stimulate growth."[17] When absolutely required, government interference should be as limited as possible. "Since that time all nation states have been at the mercy of financial disciplining" from either the effects of the market or the direct intervention of financial institutions.[18]

Greil Marcus, writing about Ronald Reagan and Margaret Thatcher, argues that poverty was not a symptom of the new societal order, but rather the "linchpin" of it.[19] Many New Wave writers of the 1970s recognized the same problem: the rhetoric of deregulation implies a willingness to let millions, even billions suffer for the benefit of capital. This altered view of the relationship between government and corporate interests affected SF in the 1970s and early 1980s. Dystopias could be rooted in many concepts, from authoritarian snooping to ecological disaster, but the 1970s saw the rise of the specifically economic dystopia, in which capitalist practices (rather than war or natural disaster) destroy the world, and the people in it. Novels such as John Brunner's *The Sheep Look Up* (1972), Frederik Pohl's *Gateway* (1977), Ursula K. Le Guin's *The Dispossessed* (1974), and James E. Gunn's *Kampus* (1977) all feature worlds ruined by rampant capitalism, with mass suffering caused by the effects of unfettered actions of the market upon human beings, necessary social and cultural institutions, and the larger natural world.

Unfit for Human Consumption

William Gibson once claimed that when he started writing in the early 1980s, SF "tended not to depict income inequality. It tended to pretend that

[16] Udall, Stewart, "The Last Traffic Jam," *The Atlantic* (Oct. 1972), www.theatlantic.com/magazine/archive/1972/10/the-last-traffic-jam/303367 (last accessed 21 May, 2018).

[17] Borstelmann, *The 1970s*, loc. 1010.

[18] David Harvey, *The Condition of Postmodernity* (Oxford: Blackwell Publishing, 1990), pp. 164–5.

[19] Greil Marcus, *Lipstick Traces: A Secret History of the Twentieth Century* (Cambridge, MA: Harvard University Press, 1990), EPub edition, n.p.

capitalism didn't exist . . . [Characters] don't seem to have salaries or any-thing. There doesn't seem to be any money. There don't seem to be any products."[20] Despite the general tendency Gibson identifies, however, in fact many New Wave and post New Wave authors *did* write about money and products – and, often, sale of products that should be free or easily attainable but are instead subjected to market forces.[21]

John Brunner shocked the reader early in his novel *The Sheep Look Up* with just such an example. Air is a resource that might seem difficult to monetize – but early in the novel we see a section titled "Signs of the Times." It reads:

THIS BEACH NOT SAFE FOR SWIMMING
NOT Drinking Water
UNFIT FOR HUMAN CONSUMPTION
Now Wash Your Hands
(Penalty for noncompliance $50)
FILTERMASK DISPENSER
Use Product once only – maximum 1 hour
OXYGEN 25¢[22]

These ads serve not only to illustrate the ecological dangers ubiquitous in Brunner's dystopia, but also the effects of unregulated capitalism on the environment and the emergence of a world in which all needs are controlled by capital. Will corporations be willing to clean up after themselves if they can make *even more* money selling gas masks and canned oxygen to the populations devastated by pollution? Later in the novel, Brunner says no. Businesses make millions selling home water filters while foreign aid supplies are drugged to cause mass killings in developing countries. The result is not a return to the happy conditions of postwar economic growth but rather widespread misery and social chaos. Still, the answer is less regulation; in a snippet from a newspaper, we see a senator accusing "chlorophyll addicts" of "hamstringing American business, already staggering under the load of high unemployment and recession, by insisting that our manufacturers comply with regulations ignored by foreign competition."[23] The report goes on to mention riots in fishing villages and violent dust storms.

---

[20] Erika M. Anderson, "William Gibson Talks to Ema about Getting the Future Right," *PaperMag.com* (2015), www.papermag.com/william-gibson-talks-to-ema-about-getting-the-future-right-1427658486.html (last accessed 21 May, 2018).

[21] Such narratives naturally have much in common with the sort of ecodystopias discussed in the previous chapter, which similarly depict a world ravaged by unfettered consumption.

[22] John Brunner, *The Sheep Look Up* (Dallas, TX: Benbella Books, 2003), p. 3.

[23] Ibid., p. 74.

Deep in denial, characters in the novel ignore obvious signs like poison-resistant rats and mass drugging until, in nearly every case, they are dead or disfigured. In the end, a statistical analyst suggests that for the "long, happy, healthy future for mankind" we would need to "exterminate the two hundred million most extravagant and wasteful of our species."[24] He means, of course, the Americans – who the novel implies will eventually do the job themselves. Brunner's sharp and brutal satire suggests corporate capitalism, supported by a government no longer offering any resistance or providing any protections to its citizens, will end the world.

Just a year before *The Sheep Look Up* was released, Stanislaw Lem published *The Futurological Congress* (1971). It is primarily a study of layered hallucination and the nature of perceived reality. However, Lem begins the narrative with a futurologists' conference at a Hilton hotel in Costa Rica, meant to figure out how to save the world from itself; among the problems are a debilitating population explosion.[25] Governments are so violent that no one bats an eye when the American ambassador's guards shoot an attendee as "the result of a simple misunderstanding, which [ended] with an exchange of diplomatic notes and official apologies."[26] The satirical tone helps to underline the point: the United States is so hated in this world that armed diplomatic guards must keep the listening crowd under cover of their guns and ultimately kill a man for sneezing. When the narrator, Ijon Tichy, sees the scale of the surveillance state, which includes a widespread network of informers, the reader can only think of the existing spy networks of both the United States and the USSR. The network is so large, he says, "it must have cost the government plenty to maintain them – funds which might have been better spent improving the economic situation in Costa Rica."[27] Lem criticizes the government for spying on its own citizens; he goes further and points out the expenditure should go to fixing things, and in particular the economy.

The novel goes on to explore hallucinations, the entire city having been drugged by the government in an attempt to put down a protest. The narrator seems to wake up in the future and marvels at how wonderful everything appears to be – actually the result of hallucinatory drugs given to everyone at all times. Even in the false future, though, businesses continue to dodge responsibility. In an odd note within the vast catalog of strangenesses

[24] Ibid., p. 363.
[25] Stanislaw Lem, *The Futurological Congress* (Orlando, FL: Harcourt, 1985), p. 1.
[26] Ibid., p. 5. On the previous page we learn that someone in the crowd tried to throw rotten tomatoes at the US contingent of the conference.
[27] Ibid., p. 33.

Tichy describes, we find that the company who runs futuristic television prefers to settle lawsuits for accidents caused by their sets instead of fixing the problem. Even here there is no sense of political accountability or even ethical responsibility on the part of corporations – only monetary transactions intended to minimize cost and maximize profit.

A New Frontier to Exploit

The breakdown of economic growth fueled a return of a sort to frontier fantasy; if resources are running out locally, go explore, and then exploit, new realms! But in the hands of dyspeptic, economically minded New Wave authors many of these supposed new frontiers proved sterile or toxic rather than reinvigorating. Instead the image of corporations and government-corporation conglomerates spreading out through the cosmos, pillaging as they went, filtered into SF work of the period. Samuel R. Delany's *Nova* (1968) centers on the crew of a ship trying to hit it big in a world where two conglomerates ruthlessly mine the Outer Colonies of the super-element Illyrion, necessary for space travel. In Isaac Asimov's *The Gods Themselves* (1972), two separate universes exploit the differences in the laws of physics to create never-ending energy, with the result that both universes teeter on the edge of destruction. And in Ridley Scott's classic SF–horror hybrid *Alien* (1979), the Weyland-Yutani corporation sends crews out to acquire ruthless killing machines at great risk to their workers, none of whom have consented to these dangers, all in the name of corporate profit.

Even in the 1970s works by pre-New Wave authors (such as Asimov) show the growing influence of New Wave concerns. A work like Frederik Pohl's *Gateway*, with one foot in both Golden Age and New Wave sensibilities, shows just how widespread these concerns had become – ultimately winning the novel the Hugo, Nebula, and Campbell Awards. The novel follows Robinette – or Bob – Broadhead through his meetings with a computer psychiatrist. In flashback we get his life story, from his time in the shale mines to his big, lucky break that made him rich. In between, we see a world destroyed by economic and ecological disasters. Bob worked in a shale mine because they had to use oil as fertilizer to grow yeast and bacteria for food. He wins the lottery, which he spends on the travel expenses to get to Gateway. That's the space station from which prospectors take blind runs in alien spaceships, trying to discover scientific and archeological artifacts left behind by the "Heechee," an advanced alien race that seems to have disappeared millennia before humans built their first rocket. The humans can operate the ships' autopiloting systems, but cannot pilot them themselves, or even anticipate where a given ship will go or how long the journey will take; thus a huge proportion of the trips end with the death of the prospector.

Much of the novel deals with Bob's fear of prospecting – most prospectors live in penury until they are forced by their poverty to take a dangerous gamble on a trip in a Heechee vessel – and his relationships with a handful of other prospectors, including Klara, the woman he comes to love. His team appears near a black hole and the only way to escape is to jettison one of two linked ships. Bob ends up in the ship to be jettisoned, but as the result of an accident the other ship goes into the black hole instead. His entire team, including Klara, dies – but the mission report earns Bob enough money to make him rich for life.

In *Gateway*, as in *Sheep Look Up*, corporate interests have helped ruin the economy and the environment, but this time there is no hope for anybody; this time the entire planet is devastated. The alien artifacts offer the only hope for humankind's salvation – and the search for them has been turned over entirely to a corporation. *Gateway* thus stands as an accusation, a working out of the logical conclusion to corporatism – and, most importantly, what it means to live in a culture that assumes corporatism is not a choice but a fact of life. Indeed, Pohl's entire corpus across his career can be read – and has been read, by David N. Samuelson – as overtly critical of "incompetents, power-grabbing manipulators, and such communal vices as war, waste, overbreeding" as well as gullibility.[28] Samuelson claims Pohl's work had been concerned with "issues of production and consumption, and matters of social and economic regulation" even as far back as the 1950s.[29] In *Gateway*, we find evidence of corporate manipulation of macro-scale economic and political powers as well as micro-scale human lives and desires. Like a lottery, the corporation can afford to offer huge sums to desperate would-be prospectors because almost no one will cash in.

The world is already nearly destroyed, and the only hope to fix it (the unfettered market) destroys individual lives. Both these problems have been and are perpetrated by corporate interests. But the novel centers instead on the psyche of Bob Broadhead. Half the novel is set in his psychiatrist's office! Bob's "gullibility" is in thinking he just needs more money, more nameless women, and he'll be fine. He buys into the corporate, capitalist system that gave him his psychological injuries. He gets to Gateway by wasting money

[28] David N. Samuelson, "Critical Mass: The Science Fiction of Frederik Pohl," *Science Fiction Studies* 7, 2 (1980), p. 80. See also the reading of Pohl's earlier work in Chapter 15.
[29] Ibid., p. 81.

on a lottery. He gets off Gateway by winning an unwinnable situation – while nearly every other character in the novel disappears into oblivion.

The kind of gullibility here is of acceptance, accepting that the world just *is* the way it is, without any idea of changing it. Notably, Pohl eventually wrote lesser-known sequels to *Gateway* featuring more traditional iconoclasts who want to change the system; Bob himself becomes one of them. But in this widely read and award-winning novel we see instead a man beaten down so far by his own cultural assumptions that he suffers continually – but nonetheless he cannot see outside them. He sacrifices the love of his life to corporate interests because that is the only way for him to escape the poverty imposed by the same sorts of corporate interests he serves – but he doesn't escape at all, and is instead permanently traumatized by the loss. In the way Klara is forever stuck in the black hole, Bob is stuck in a kind of never-ending loop between economic polarities. He does not escape one world (poverty) for another (riches); he ignorantly moves around inside the same economic system. Bob is as much a victim of the corporate world when he's rich as when he's poor, because he can't envision any way out of the system itself, which runs everything from food production to space travel.

Schools and Moons

If everything is ruined and the corporations manipulate everyone, it would seem as though there's no hope. However, it was only natural that some authors would try to write a way out of the capitalist wasteland. Roger Zelazny's *Damnation Alley* (1969) features a nihilist biker crossing the nuclear holocaust in the middle of North America to deliver medical supplies to a distant group of survivors. Philip K. Dick's *Flow My Tears, the Policeman Said* (1974) includes college campuses ringed with militarized police forces, keeping the subterranean students locked away from society at large. In Michael Anderson's *Logan's Run* (1976), the top-down solution to the end of the world is to isolate a small population and to euthanize them at the age of thirty, to conserve materials; the titular Logan runs from this scheme and discovers natural resources have redeveloped. And William Gibson's *Neuromancer* (1984) displays a dystopia so commercially fraught that one of the main characters jacks into a computer and turns off her own mind so she can have sex for money without physical or emotional discomfort.

Two novels that grapple in especially interesting ways with the philosophical, as well as the adventurous, solutions to the capitalist nightmare are James E. Gunn's *Kampus* (1977) and Ursula K. Le Guin's *The Dispossessed*

(1974). They are presented out of chronological order because *Kampus* portrays a problem while only hinting at solutions, while *The Dispossessed* explores a solution and finds it satisfactory.

Kampus portrays a dystopian future in which students at college campuses are all revolutionaries with no causes to support. *Kampus*, like other works of New Wave SF, is a satire of youth culture, and another cutting one, showing not just youth's foolishness but the sinister hands of the system manipulating discontent and maintaining the status quo. College campuses are militarized, with every student a gun-toting revolutionary in some clique or other. The professors teach behind bullet-proof glass and anything is fair game within the confines of the campus walls. Outside is an eerie, old-fashioned America that sends its children to work out their anger issues and come back for typical office jobs. But this world is not like the others discussed so far. Everyone gets money from the government, from a surplus caused by "cybernated abundance."[30] But when the main character, Gavin, goes home after being expelled from college, his father delivers a speech straight out of the 1950s:

> You can be satisfied with the guaranteed annual income when you're young and single, when you have no responsibilities and can live on bread and peanut butter ... When you've got a wife and a family ... you want something better for them than the minimum. You want walls around you that you own, a home that's yours, and you want a job to go to, something important to do.[31]

Gavin calls his father out on these claims, which his father disavowed in his own youth. Gavin's father goes on to say they had to do without to get Gavin through school – a lie, since the government pays for college for everyone from the "abundance." Since Gavin's father has a job and both his parents get their government-mandated minimum allowance, Gavin wonders what his parents could possibly have done without. "Plenty of things," according to his father. "Trips to Europe, new cars, a better house, clothes, a vacation home, a boat, lots of things we thought about and knew we couldn't afford."[32] Even in the midst of utopian plenty the same consumer ideas Pohl targeted rise up in the minds of the most ardent anti-establishment revolutionary.

Kampus offers a solution, at least for Gavin – he meets a co-op group who grow their own food, living as far away from others as possible. The members

---

[30] James E. Gunn, *Kampus* (New York: Bantam Books, 1977), p. 124.
[31] Ibid., p. 124.
[32] Ibid., p. 125.

have spirited debate every night and work every day, in a particularly American utopian ideal. The novel argues that the world's present course is untenable, *even if* technology were to solve all economic problems. The same cultural ideas would shape the new world into a worse one, with children assuming they have to fight authority when there isn't any to speak of and with the staunch middle classes working for what they don't have even when they have everything they need. The satire is grimly effective, showing the assumptions of capitalism could survive even the death of capitalism itself.

The Dispossessed seems to offer more overt solutions to world problems. While Le Guin dislikes most critical readings of her work, she also admits it was one of her most obviously didactic works, given that it is a "utopia."[33] In *The Dispossessed*, Shevek, a physicist in an anarchic society, solves the latest problems in unifying physics, creating a temporal theory that could lead to such advances as faster interstellar travel and instantaneous communication across vast interstellar distances. With some caveats – the novel is an "ambiguous utopia" after all – the novel suggests that socialist anarchism might be the only foil for capitalism. At the least, it vilifies capitalism in such a way that the novel stands as one of the greatest post-New Wave indictments of the philosophy of corporatism and its unconscious assumptions. The novel hinges on the ways in which those unconscious assumptions affect other ideas, behaviors, and cultural and scientific advancements.

Shevek is a native of Anarres, the moon of a planet called Urras. The settlers of Anarres were members of a radical group of anarchists who objected to all forms of commerce and governance. Their influence was so great the governments of Urras failed to squelch the movement, and cut a deal with it: the anarchists got the moon all to themselves to set up their perfect Odonian society – named after their martyred leader, Odo – and Urras got rid of them. Shevek is an Odonian physicist who communicates with scientists on Urras after a long period of isolation, and eventually – despite vehement protest – goes to Urras to meet with scientific leaders to develop his Unified Theory of Temporal Physics. Over the course of his trip, he is horrified with how fundamental the transactional nature of capitalism is in every relationship – not only between ruler and worker, but man and wife, father and child, and, perhaps most chillingly for Shevek, between scientist and state.

---

[33] Ursula K. Le Guin, "A Response, by Ansible, from Tau Ceti," in Laurence Davis and Peter Stillman, eds., *The New Utopian Politics of Ursula K. Le Guin's The Dispossessed* (Oxford: Lexington Books, 2005), p. 306.

Shevek compares the "operations of capitalism" to barbaric rites.[34] These operations are not even primarily monetary, according to the novel's portrayal of capitalism. They are rather power plays, dominance games. Shevek "had thought to bargain with them, a very naïve anarchist's notion. The individual cannot bargain with the state. The state recognizes no coinage but power: and it issues the coins itself."[35] His fellow scientists on Urras turn out to be chauvinists, racists, classists, and spies, both foreign and domestic. They are *unable* to be anything else in their capitalist system. The novel equates the most objective, intelligent class (naturally, in an SF novel, the scientists) as transactional villains. That implies *anyone* engaging in the capitalist enterprise turns into such villains.

The novel alternates settings. One chapter is set in Shevek's past on Anarres, the next in the present on Urras. This shape allows us to contrast the capitalist world with the anarchist. While Shevek and the reader recognize problems in the anarchist system and its need for certain kinds of reforms – the most obvious being the impossibility of orchestrating work usefully without something that will tend toward governance – the realities of life on Urras are worse.

In the end the novel even brings we humble Earthlings into the fracas as a third, maximally dystopian term outside the Urras–Anarres binary. Shevek, in fleeing the Urrasti police after a protest, finds sanctuary in the Earth embassy. The ambassador tells Shevek about Earth.

> My world, my Earth, is a ruin. A planet spoiled by the human species. We multiplied and gobbled and fought until there was nothing left, and then we died. We controlled neither appetite nor violence; we did not adapt. We destroyed ourselves. But we destroyed the world first. There are no forests left on my Earth. The air is grey, the sky is grey, it is always hot.[36]

She goes on to describe ruined cities, a populace of half a billion that was once nine billion, and how she can only envy Urras. She says that she cannot understand why the workers were protesting. "The rich are very rich indeed, but the poor are not so very poor. They are neither enslaved nor starving. Why aren't they satisfied with bread and speeches? Why are they supersensitive ... "[37] She sees a police state in which protestors are abused and killed – all for asking for more money, for rights – and sees it as a vast improvement over her own ruined home. She calls Urras a paradise.

---

[34] Ursula K. Le Guin, *The Dispossessed* (New York: HarperCollins, 2015), p. 130.
[35] Ibid., p. 271.
[36] Ibid., p. 347.
[37] Ibid., p. 341.

But Shevek says of Urras that "There is nothing you can do that profit does not enter into, and fear of loss, and the wish for power. You cannot say good morning without knowing which of you is 'superior' to the other, or trying to prove it."[38] Annares is not perfect, but it has raised children to whom this behavior is utterly alien. His inability to comprehend capitalist, power-hungry behavior is his greatest strength. He finally gets past his mental walls and comes up with his Unified Theory as he begins to realize that insisting on total certainty in science is equivalent to looking for power or ownership. "He had been demanding a security, a guarantee, which is not granted, and which, if granted, would become a prison."[39] Because of his culture, his upbringing, he is able to do something no scientist has ever done, not even a scientist from the super-developed Hainish worlds. And the novel implies that Shevek's discoveries will lead to the development of the ansible, the faster-than-light communication technology used in many of Le Guin's other Hainish novels.[40]

The Dispossessed not only criticizes capitalist, commercial culture – it implies the way to create the perfect human and scientific unification is to be an anarchist from a world with no ownership, without even a word for ownership. The novel does not so much criticize capitalism as attack the idea that capitalism is a fundamental tenet of human behavior. The novel thus speaks back against the growing assumption in the 1970s, which gained international prominence in the 1980s and ultimately became a foundational assumption of even ostensibly left political parties by the 2000s, that capitalism is a natural and unalterable feature not only of the human species but of all possible social relations, on any world, and that anything that interfered with the unfettered operation of the market is thus an "inefficiency" that needed to be eliminated. The disjuncture between these worldviews, already becoming unavoidable in the 1970s, would only intensify in the next major period in SF history, the cyberpunk era, which would foresee a humanity that would be either liberated or destroyed by the emergence of a wholly autonomous economic-industrial sphere, also known as the rise of the machines.

---

[38] Ibid., p. 345.

[39] Ibid., p. 279.

[40] The ansible is itself an important utopian revision of earlier SF works, allowing for instantaneous sharing of ideas without the possibility of colonial exploitation, resource extraction, or galactic genocide (as are made possible by such fantastic inventions as hyperspace and warp drive).

29

Science Fiction in the Academy
in the 1970s

RITCH CALVIN

The academia [*sic*] is invading science fiction, they tell us, and it will never
be the same again.

Cy Chauvin[1]

Let's take science fiction out of the classroom and put it back in the gutter
where it belongs.

Dena Benatan Brown[2]

The university is where it's always belonged.

William Tenn[3]

On Tuesday, September 22, 1953, Sam Moskowitz convened the first college-
level SF class for the City College of New York. Part of the impetus was the
increased popularity of SF, and part of the impetus was the opportunity to
assemble an anthology to sell. The class had eleven students. At the time,
Moskowitz was the editor of *Science Fiction+*, and he pulled in a number of
guest lecturers, including Isaac Asimov, Lester del Rey, Murray Leinster,
Robert Sheckley, Theodore Sturgeon, and Fletcher Pratt.[4] Moskowitz states
that many of the authors agreed because of the prestige of lecturing at college
and saw it as a form of validation.[5]

In 1962, Mark R. Hillegas "taught the first academic course in the nation,
and possibly the world, in science fiction." The course was capped at fifty
students and filled. It garnered attention outside the university, including an
article by the *New York Times*. "By 1965," Hillegas notes, "Southern Illinois
University knew about the Colgate course and hired me partly because of it.

[1] Cy Chauvin, "Review of *SF: The Other Side of Realism* by Thomas D. Clareson," *Amazing Science Fiction* (January 1973), p. 108.
[2] "Dena Brown," *Fancyclopedia 3* (April 18, 2017), n.p.
[3] Willam Tenn, "Jazz Then, Musicology Now," *The Magazine of Fantasy and Science Fiction* (May 1972), p. 113.
[4] Sam Moskowitz, "The First College-Level Course in Science Fiction," *Science Fiction Studies* 23, 3 (November 1996), p. 415.
[5] Ibid., p. 414.

The shift was underway."[6] During the spring semester of 1973, James Gunn offered his second general SF course at the University of Kansas. The course had 165 students, 60 more than the previous offering.[7] For the two courses, Gunn had 270 students. At the end of the term, they distributed a questionnaire – inside the class and out – to determine students' attitudes about and familiarity with SF. They concluded, if somewhat unscientifically, that primary, secondary, and post-secondary students "are more interested in science fiction than any other audience."[8]

The movement of SF into the academy – and the ways in which it happened – has a complicated and particular history. For example, Larry McCaffrey suggests that SF has been a "respectable" genre in Europe far longer than in the United States. He notes that H. G. Wells, Karel Čapek, Olaf Stapledon, Aldous Huxley, George Orwell, Italo Calvino, and Stanislaw Lem were all accepted as "legitimate" within the European literary tradition.[9] The acceptance of SF as "literature" in Europe might suggest that SF was adopted and considered within both critical circles and the academy. Even so, Andy Sawyer and Peter Wright note that the association of SF with mass-market genre has kept it from literary and critical acceptance.[10] SF, from both inside and outside the field, has long been viewed as a marginal genre, as "trash," or as something better suited to the "gutter." Those sentiments are simultaneously warranted and unwarranted. Literary critics as well as literary academics have, indeed, long held genre fiction in contempt. Genre fiction operates as the marked term that negates its own worth. The origins, content, and readership of genre fiction all negated it as legitimate literature, or as literature "proper." Nevertheless, of all the genre forms, including detective fiction, noir, the western, and romance, SF has made the earliest and most consistent inroads

[6] Mark Hillegas, "Colgate and the First Course in Science Fiction," *The Mage* 4 (Winter 1985), p. 14.

[7] Barry Baddock and James Gunn, "Science Fiction Readership on Campus," *Extrapolation* 15, (May 1974), p. 148.

[8] Ibid., p. 151.

[9] Larry McCaffrey, "Introduction," in Larry McCaffrey, ed., *Across the Wounded Galaxies: Interviews with Contemporary American Science Fiction Writers* (Urbana: University of Illinois Press, 1990), p. 3.

[10] Andy Sawyer and Peter Wright, "Introduction," in Andy Sawyer and Peter Wright, eds., *Teaching Science Fiction* (Basingstoke: Palgrave Macmillan, 2011), p. 1. Tellingly, when Sawyer and Wright discuss the integration of SF into the classroom, they turn to its history in the United States. Nevertheless, the British critical journal *Foundation* appeared in 1972, after *Extrapolation* and a year before *Science Fiction Studies* appeared in the United States. It would seem that very little work has been done on SF in the academy (at least in English). A full study of the integration of SF into the academy in Europe, Latin America, Africa, and Asia, though beyond the scope of this chapter, is in order.

towards academic respectability.[11] By 2016, most colleges and universities in the United States offered a class devoted to SF (science fiction, speculative fiction, science fantasy, etc.), and, even more significantly, SF texts (stories, novels, shows, films) were dispersed and taught in all kinds of courses. SF's assimilation in the academy is well under way. Nevertheless, over forty years after the rapid colonization of the academic hallways that occurred in the 1970s, many of us still get those sideways glances when we tell people what we study and teach, and we feel the need to justify SF as a legitimate field of inquiry.

Science Fiction and the Scholar

As noted above, too many critics, scholars, and academics have viewed SF (and, indeed, all genre literature) as sub-literary.[12] That judgment, arguably, resides in the age-old high–low distinction so prevalent in the academy and, to a lesser extent, in society at large – a distinction that critics and the academy have helped foster and maintain.

For better or worse, one of the most prominent arbiters of the academy, at least in terms of English literature and instruction, has been the Modern Language Association (MLA). The MLA, at least for some, serves as the arbiter of "proper" language use and style, and arguably by extension, as an arbiter of "proper" fields of study; while the former is achieved via the *MLA Handbook for the Writers of Research Papers*, the latter is achieved via the annual MLA Conference. The first MLA Conference was held in New York in 1883 (with forty people in attendance), and a conference has been held every year since (except the war years), growing to as many as 10,000 attendees. For many of those years, the MLA determined a set number of topics, panels, and seminars. In 1957, the MLA held its first "Literature and Science" panel (General Topic #7) – signaling, in part, a sign of the times, and, in part, an interest in the confluence of arts and the sciences. As James Gunn, Jack Williamson, Lisa Yaszek, and many others have noted, the events of the Second World War brought about an increased interest in science and

---

[11] For example, James Gunn writes that as late as 2005 it was difficult to get SF courses approved, though he claims there are more courses taught at colleges and universities on SF than on the detective, western, or romance. See *Inside Science Fiction*, 2nd edn. (Lanham, MD: Scarecrow, 2006), p. 80.

[12] See, for example, Gunn, "Introduction," p. xxi; Mark Hillegas, *The Future As Nightmare: H. G. Wells and the Anti-Utopians* (New York: Oxford University Press, 1967), p. 7; Alvin Toffler, "Review of *Future Perfect* by H. Bruce Franklin," *Technology and Culture* 8, 1 (January 1967), p. 152.

technology, but also an increased sense that SF might have something to say about the dangers of technology. The "Literature and Science" panel was held again in 1958 (indeed, every year until at least 1978). Still, "literature and science" is not really the same thing as "science fiction."

In 1958, the MLA held its first panel explicitly devoted to SF, "The Significance of Science Fiction," with Thomas D. Clareson of Wooster College as discussion leader. Clareson attributes the development to an "impulsive outburst" at the 1957 MLA meeting in Washington, DC, in which someone in the audience shouted, "'I'd rather have talked about science fiction.'"[13] Writer and teacher Jack Williamson has called Clareson the "foremost pioneer" of the "serious academic study of science fiction."[14] In that same year, and in support of the "MLA Conference on Science Fiction," Clareson established *The Newsletter of the Conference on Science-Fiction of the MLA*, which eventually became *Extrapolation*. Peter Nicholls asserts that "*Extrapolation*'s existence as the earliest public platform for sf studies significantly advanced them."[15] Eleven years later, Clareson was also one of the founding figures of the Science Fiction Research Association (SFRA), which is an international organization dedicated to the proposition of teaching SF at all levels.[16]

In 1961, Mark Hillegas submitted "A Draft of the Science-Fiction Canon" to the MLA Conference. The list consisted of a compilation of suggestions given to Hillegas by members of the "MLA Conference on Science Fiction" and offers 108 titles, in reverse chronological order, from *The Sound of His Horn* in 1960 back to *Mundus alter et idem* from 1607. In 1970, the Conference held a panel on "Science Fiction and Myth." While SF certainly has legitimate ties to mythology, the linking of SF and myth was part and parcel of a strategy of legitimation. The 1972 conference saw its first panel dedicated to a science fiction writer, in this case Kurt Vonnegut, followed by Doris Lessing in 1973.

---

[13] Thomas D. Clareson, "Now That We Are Twenty-Five," *Extrapolation* 25, 4 (Winter 1984), p. 291.

[14] Jack Williamson, "On Science Fiction in College," *Science Fiction Studies* 23, 3 (November 1996), pp. 375–6.

[15] Peter Nicholls, "Extrapolation [magazine]," *SFE: The Encyclopedia of Science Fiction* (December 24, 2015), n.p.

[16] Patricia S. Warrick, one-time president of the SFRA, wrote an origin story of the SFRA in "Now We Are Fifteen: Observations on the Science Fiction Research Association by Its President," *Extrapolation* 254 (Winter 1984), pp. 360–8. According to Warrick, Fred Lerner made a suggestion at the St. Louis Worldcon to create an organization that would preserve the history of science fiction and "promote its study as serious literature" (p. 364). A group, including Lerner, Clareson, Virginia Carew, Darko Suvin and Ivor Rogers met in Buffalo, and they developed the concept of the SFRA. Carew hosted the first annual SFRA conference at Queensborough Community College in 1970.

The next two years saw panels on "Utopian/Dystopian Literature," arguably also interconnected with SF (especially after the Second World War) and also another strategy of legitimation for SF-interested scholars.

Volume 10, issue 2 of *Extrapolation* (1970) offers a transcript of a roundtable held at an MLA Conference (New York, 1968). The roundtable, organized by Scott Osborn and entitled "MLA Forum: Science Fiction: The New Mythology," featured H. Bruce Franklin, Isaac Asimov, Darko Suvin, and Frederik Pohl (Judith Merril was unable to attend). Clareson reports that "well over 500"[17] people attended the two-and-a-half hour forum, including Robert Silverberg, Joanna Russ, Lester del Rey, Harrison Mill, Samuel Grafton, Philip Klass, Jerry Freeman, John Grimaldi, and Sophia Morgan. In fact, the panel ran one-hour-and-forty-five minutes over the allotted time. The panel consisted of two scholars and two novelists, demonstrating a working relationship between writers and scholars (that will be called into question later in this chapter); it also demonstrated some of the resistance to subjecting SF to academic criticism at all. In their concluding remarks, Franklin recommends attendees to subscribe to *Extrapolation* ("the journal of criticism of sf" and attend the annual conference, while Silverberg points out "the irrelevance of much that has been said up here today."[18]

In an essay in a special issue of *The Magazine of Fantasy and Science Fiction* (1972), William Tenn (Philip Klass) also addresses the question of SF and the academy. Tenn notes that interest in SF may just be another "fad" or "boom," but he suggests that this fad may be different because it takes place in the university. Tenn notes, "And the university is where it's always belonged. Science fiction, after all, is nothing but dramatized concept, ideation made into flesh of character and line of narrative. It's come home at last to its origins, to the one place where the hard sciences become abstract, where the social sciences build reality, where the new frontiers of esthetics and metaphysics are measured off."[19] Similarly, Mark Hillegas notes that something happened between 1967 and 1973 to cause the boom in courses and the interest in the study of SF.[20] Both writers suggest multiple sources, including technological change, social instability, and shifts in the academy. However,

---

[17] Thomas D. Clareson, "Launching Pad," *Extrapolation* 10, 2 (May 1969), p. 50.
[18] "MLA Forum: Science Fiction: The New Mythology," *Extrapolation* 10, 2 (May 1969), p. 113.
[19] William Tenn, "Jazz Then, Musicology Now," *The Magazine of Fantasy and Science Fiction* (May 1972), p. 113.
[20] Mark Hillegas, "Second Thoughts on the Course in Science Fiction," in Willis E. McNelly, ed., *Science Fiction: The Academic Awakening* (Shreveport, LA: College English Association, 1974), p. 16.

they both acknowledge that students now arrived at campus already reading SF, and that a newer generation of professors grew up reading SF.

Gary K. Wolfe addresses the explosion of publications in the 1970s. "It has often been suggested that this boom in SF scholarship was essentially opportunistic"[21] – that is, beleaguered English departments have used the allure of pop culture and SF to draw in students. Wolfe suggests that that tells only part of the story. "Some of the growth in SF studies, then, must be attributed to the growth in stature and the maturation of the genre itself."[22] Wolfe concludes that "the influence of structuralism, feminism, deconstructionism, and a seemingly endless fascination with postmodernism have helped topple the traditional 19th-century based realistic novel from its privileged status in the canon and opened up critical discourse to a far wider range of texts than might have been discussed a decade or two earlier."[23]

Hand-in-hand with the papers presented at academic conferences, especially the MLA, both book and journal publications contributed to the legitimation of SF within the academy. In the very first issue of *Extrapolation*, Clareson suggests that the SF scholar faces four specific tasks, including the creation of "accurate, cumulative bibliographies" (of both primary and secondary works), the creation of "accepted critical criteria in order to judge a work," the development of a comprehensive history of the genre (including histories of various geographic and national traditions), and the establishment of the relationship between SF and the known science of its period of creation.[24] Indeed, Clareson frequently renews his calls for works of these four kinds in his editorials of the next twenty-seven years.

Clareson himself began compiling and publishing such bibliographic resources in the second issue, with "A Checklist of Articles Dealing with Science Fiction" (with Edward S. Lauterbach), which includes works in newspapers, magazines, and journals (such as *The Bulletin of the Atomic Scientists*, *The English Journal*, *Michigan Alumnus Quarterly Review*, *Modern Fiction Studies*, *The Georgia Review*, *Science*, and *The Bulletin of Bibliography*).[25] In 1972, Clareson published *Science Fiction Criticism: An Annotated Bibliography* (Kent State Press), which contains 821 entries divided into General Studies;

---

[21] Gary K. Wolfe, "History and Criticism," in Neil Barron, ed., *Anatomy of Wonder 4: A Critical Guide to Science Fiction* (New Providence, NJ: R. R. Bowker, 1995), p. 486.
[22] Ibid., p. 487.
[23] Ibid., p. 487.
[24] Thomas D. Clareson, *Extrapolation: A Science-Fiction Newsletter: Volumes 1–10, December 1959–May 1969* (New York: Johnson, 1970 [reprint]), p. 1.
[25] Ibid., pp. 29–34.

Literary Studies; Book Reviews; The Visual Arts; Futurology, Utopia, and Dystopia; Classroom and Library; Publishing; Specialist Bibliographies, Checklists, and Indices; and The Contemporary Scene. In 1975, Marshall B. Tymn picked up where Clareson left off and compiled and published an annotated checklist of academic and critical works on SF from 1972 to 1973. Tymn (sometimes with Roger Schlobin) published a (more or less) annual checklist of critical works in *Extrapolation* until 1986. *Extrapolation* also published occasional bibliographies of individual authors, including Jules Verne (issues 2.1 and 3.2), H. P. Lovecraft (3.1), Aldous Huxley (6.1), and J. R. R. Tolkien (10.1).

A fifth issue for the SF scholar is that of the thematic development of SF. Patrick Parrinder suggests that "SF courses in English departments are normally run on either thematic or historical lines."[26] Neil Barron's "Library and Reference Resources," in Jack Williamson's *Teaching Science Fiction* (1980), offers an annotated checklist which identifies resources that would assist in thematic approaches to SF,[27] and Marshall Tymn's annual checklists do so, as well. In a 1974 essay, Orval Lund describes how he teaches his SF class thematically, focusing on "the necessity of moral responsibility for the scientist, the human need for religious beliefs, and the question of a purpose for human life in the universe."[28] In a special issue of *Science Fiction Studies* on SF and academe (1996), James Gunn published "Teaching Science Fiction," in which he offers twenty-three thematic groupings of stories, including changing attitudes, aliens and alienation, the nature of reality, and the future of humanity.[29]

Finally, for a sixth issue, Darko Suvin suggests that SF scholars must develop a theory of SF. In an essay that appeared in a special issue of *The Magazine of Fantasy and Science Fiction* on "SF and the Academy" (1972), Suvin makes his case for the need for both criticism and theory. He argues – perhaps somewhat self-servingly – that no literary genre exists without "criticism – oral or written, gossipy or scholarly." However, for Suvin not just any kind of criticism will do: for one, criticism itself must set out its own premises so that it can be evaluated (improved or rejected), and, for another, criticism that deals with the theory of SF "is particularly imperative for this

---

[26] Patrick Parrinder, *Science Fiction: Its Criticism and Teaching* (London: Methuen, 1980), p. 137.
[27] Jack Williamson, *Teaching Science Fiction: Education for Tomorrow* (Philadelphia: Owlswick, 1980), pp. 242–58.
[28] Orval Lund, Jr., "SF in the Classroom: II. SF as an Undergraduate Course," *Extrapolation* 15, 2 (May 1974), p. 144.
[29] James Gunn, "Teaching Science Fiction," *Science Fiction Studies* 23, 3 (November 1996), p. 384.

genre, in order to identify it and so make rational inquiry into it possible in the first place." [30] For Suvin, a definition is mandatory. Books that do not do this are "prejudiced blather" – of which he says Sam Moskowitz is guilty. He "accuses" Moskowitz of the "we-just-know-what-it-is," "gossipy" variety of criticism. [31] Instead, he argues that SF needs "'meaty' critics" to establish the formal and historical parameters of SF. Suvin concludes, "Once these are at least approximately established, writing monographs about writers and forms, historical surveys, and cross-references between SF and anything else you wish (science, sociology, futurology) is a matter of application and field prestige." [32]

In "History and Criticism," Wolfe suggests that SF criticism as we now understand it derived via three primary trajectories, including fans writing letters in pulps and fanzines (the tradition from which Sam Moskowitz emerged), from writers commenting on the field (he includes James Blish [as William Atheling, Jr.] and Damon Knight, and I would add Judith Merril), and from "mainstream" critics and academically trained scholars. [33] For example, Blish published *The Issue at Hand* (1964) and *More Issues at Hand* (1972), and Knight published *In Search of Wonder* (1956) and *Turning Points: Essays on the Art of Science Fiction* (1977). Merril edited her anthology series from 1956 until 1968, and her Books columns in *The Magazine of Fantasy and Science Fiction* from 1965 through 1969, in which she worked through a critical assessment of an ever-changing field. Furthermore, her two-part essay, "What Do You Mean? Science? Fiction?" appeared in early volumes of *Extrapolation* (1966).

Wolfe also notes that academic criticism and analysis have a much-longer-than-one-might-expect history. He notes, for example, the contributions of J. O. Bailey and E. F. Bleiler. Bailey's *Pilgrims through Space and Time* (1947) was based on his 1934 dissertation. [34] Bleiler's *The Checklist of Fantastic Literature* appeared the following year. In 1952, James Gunn published parts of his Master's thesis in an SF magazine, *Dynamic Science Fiction*, [35] a move that Wolfe sees as "emblematic of the whole history of SF scholarship. [36]

Academic presses were engaged in SF criticism from an early date, as far back as the early 1940s. However, despite Raymond Williams's short piece,

---

[30] Darko Suvin, "Books: Against Common Sense: Levels of SF Criticism," *The Magazine of Fantasy and Science Fiction* (May 1972), p. 124.

[31] Ibid., p. 125.

[32] Ibid., p. 125.

[33] Gary K. Wolfe, "History and Criticism," pp. 483–4.

[34] Ibid., p. 485.

[35] Gunn, *Inside Science Fiction*, p. 15.

[36] Wolfe, "History and Criticism," p. 485.

"Science Fiction," which first appeared in *The Highway*, the journal of the Workers' Educational Association in 1956,[37] most historians of SF agree that the real turning point for the legitimacy of academic SF criticism was Kingsley Amis. For example, Gunn writes that "critical acceptance of the genre was given significant impetus" by Amis's interest in SF.[38] According to Frederik Pohl, "The Seminar Committee of Princeton University invited Kingsley Amis ... to deliver a series of lectures in Princeton's Christian Gauss Seminars in Criticism. Amis accepted, and for his subject he elected to discuss science fiction in its modern form."[39] Pohl wryly notes that we have no record of whether or not the Committee was pleased by Amis's choice of lecture topic. Pohl reports that the lectures were well attended by faculty and even better attended by New York editors and publishers. The lectures were collected and published as *New Maps of Hell* (1960). Leslie Flood comments that Amis "performs a useful service in attempting to analyse, for his own amusement and possibly the edification of the uninitiated, the background, current trends, and the prospects of science-fiction,"[40] and Alfred Bester, noting that the book caused "quite a stir" upon publication, agrees with Amis's "sensible and gently expressed opinions."[41] Pohl writes, "Examinations of science fiction have appeared often in the past decade, but this is not merely the newest of them. It is the best,"[42] adding that "his conclusion is that science fiction is indeed worthwhile, containing in it something of special value which is not to be found, except in trace quantities, anywhere else at all."[43] The cover of the book boldly announces, "This is the book that made science fiction grow up." Overall, Amis offers a defense of (some parts of) the genre, and develops a critical set of evaluative criteria.

In 1966, H. Bruce Franklin released *Future Perfect: American Science Fiction of the Nineteenth Century.*[44] His study of early SF places the roots of SF within the

---

[37] Williams offers his own typology of SF, suggesting three "modes or norms," which he defines as "Putropia, Doomsday, and Space Anthropology." He notes that he dislikes the first two modes "intensely": "The modes are interesting because they belong, directly, to a contemporary structure of feeling, whereas the rest of SF, for the most part, is merely a profitable exercise of a formula." *The Highway*, 48 (December 1956), pp. 41–5.

[38] Gunn, *Inside Science Fiction*, p. 8.

[39] Frederik Pohl, "Review of *New Maps of Hell* by Kingsley Amis," *If* (July 1960), p. 100.

[40] Leslie Flood, "Review of *New Maps of Hell* by Kingsley Amis," *New Worlds Science Fiction* 105 (April 1961), p. 126.

[41] Alfred Bester, "Review of *New Maps of Hell* by Kingsley Amis," *The Magazine of Fantasy and Science Fiction* (July 1961), p. 81.

[42] Pohl, "Review of *New Maps of Hell* by Kingsley Amis," p. 100.

[43] Ibid., p. 101.

[44] In an email to the author of this chapter, Franklin notes that *Future Perfect* was rejected by seventeen publishers before it was accepted by Oxford University Press.

nineteenth century and traces examples to many well-known writers. In between the selections of fiction, Franklin weaves an origin story that seeks to historicize the emergence of SF and to lend the genre credibility, either by example or by affiliation. At the time of its publication, Merril called the collection "witty, informative, literate, imaginative, well-selected, and – fresh."[45] P. Schuyler Miller argues that while Bailey and Moskowitz listed titles and analyzed plots, "Franklin's book stands in a class by itself."[46] He further suggests that "You may find this form of literary analysis unconvincing and even painful, but you can't complain that it is superficial, as is most of the discussion of current science fiction by members of the literary 'Establishment.'"[47] In a 1995 review (at the time of a reissue), Wolfe notes that Franklin's anthology made SF seem as though "SF was far from an occasional aberration during the 19th century, but rather a lively tradition, an acceptable mode of writing that was visited more than once by Poe, Hawthorne, O'Brien, Bierce, and Bellamy, and at least on occasion by Melville, Twain, Thomas Wentworth Higginson and a number of other lesser-known writers."[48] Wolfe concludes, "This is a collection which ought to be in every SF student's library, but for different reasons than those in 1966. Then, it seemed almost an admonishment of how far SF had fallen from the main-stream; now, it seems a reminder of how far back we've come."[49]

In 1967, Robert Scholes articulated a formal model of speculative fiction in *The Fabulators*, published by Oxford University Press. In her review of the book, Virginia Carew suggests that Scholes's model allows for too much to be read as SF (e.g., Iris Murdoch) and fails to consider important genre texts (e.g., *The Einstein Intersection*).[50] In the same year, Mark Hillegas published *The Future as Nightmare* (also Oxford University Press). While Hillegas con-centrates primarily on H. G. Wells, his precursors, and his influences, Carew focuses her review on the tone of the book, noting that Hillegas does not "have that half-a-worm-in-my-apple reaction that most professors of English have, sometimes hypocritically."[51] Indeed, many of the early books were

---

[45] Judith Merril, "Books, September 1966," in Ritch Calvin, ed., *"The Merril Theory of Lit'ry Criticism": The Nonfiction of Judith Merril* (Seattle: Aqueduct, 2016), n.p.

[46] P. Schuyler Miller, "Review of *Future Perfect* by H. Bruce Franklin," *Analog* (October 1966), p. 159.

[47] Ibid.

[48] Gary K. Wolfe, "Review of *Future Perfect* by H. Bruce Franklin," *Locus* 411 (April 1995), p. 50.

[49] Ibid., p. 50.

[50] Virginia Carew, "Review of *The Fabulators* by Robert Scholes," *The Magazine of Fantasy and Science Fiction* (July, 1968), p. 60.

[51] Ibid., p. 61.

quite defensive in their justifications of topic. Three years later, Robert M. Philmus published *Into the Unknown: Science Fiction from Francis Godwin to H. G. Wells* (University of California Press), another early example of an examination of SF history and genre development. In chapter 1, Philmus offers a definition of SF, and then traces an early history of the genre, culminating with Wells – not so much an "evolution" as "a more-or-less chronological perspective."[52] As was common enough in the early days of SF criticism, Philmus reads SF as a new kind of myth (cf. the early MLA seminars). Reviews of the book were mixed; however, Joanna Russ concedes that "there is good – and new – material here for a theory of science fiction."[53]

The following year, Clareson published *SF: The Other Side of Realism* (Bowling Green University Popular Press), a "heterogeneous"[54] collection of twenty-six essays on SF, with an introduction by Clareson. Several of the essays here are reprinted from *Extrapolation* (Delaney, Hillegas, Merril) and two are reprinted from elsewhere (Franklin, Lem), but the bulk of them are original to the collection. Again, the reviews were mixed, though Peter Nicholls concludes that Clareson's book "clearly emerges as the most considerable work on the subject in a long time – if not ever . . . It seems to me a necessary book for anybody who takes science fiction seriously."[55] In *New Worlds for Old: The Apocalyptic Imagination, Science Fiction, and American Literature* (Indiana University Press, 1974) David Ketterer takes a different approach. Although he argues that his book will offer a "relatively sophisticated appreciation and theoretical understanding of science fiction" in a book-length study,[56] Clareson argues that the book suffers from

---

[52] Charles Clay Doyle, "Review of *Into the Unknown* by Robert M. Philmus," *Eighteenth-Century Studies* 4, 3 (Spring 1971), p. 352.

[53] Joanna Russ, "Review of *The Shape of Utopias* by Robert C. Elliott and *Into the Unknown* by Robert M. Philmus," *College English* 33, 3 (December 1971), p. 372.

[54] Darko Suvin, "Review of *SF: The Other Side of Realism* by Thomas D. Clareson," *College English* 34, 8 (May 1973), p. 1148

[55] Peter Nicholls, "The Sun Shines in Bowling Green: Review of *SF: The Other Side of Realism* by Thomas D. Clareson," *Foundation* 4 (July 1973), p. 94. In 1973, R. D. Mullen established *Science Fiction Studies* at his home campus at Indiana State University. The journal moved to Canada for a brief time and was edited there by Darko Suvin, Marc Angenot, and Robert Philmus. It returned to the United States in 1992 to Depauw University, and it remains there under the guidance of Arthur B. Evans, with an editorial board of Istvan Csicsery-Ronay, Jr., Veronica Hollinger, Joan Gordon, Rob Latham, Sherryl Vint, and Carol McGuirk. While the *Encyclopedia of Science Fiction* casts the journal as overly academic, filled with jargon, a 1994 essay in *The Chronicle of Higher Education* describes it as the "most theoretical scholarly publication" on SF and the "most daring": Jim Zook, "Daring Journal of SF Theory," *The Chronicle of Higher Education* (June 1, 1994), A: 8.

[56] David Ketterer, *New Worlds for Old: The Apocalyptic Imagination, Science Fiction, and American Literature* (Bloomington: Indiana University Press, 1974), p. ix.

a narrowness of definition, which serves Ketterer's thesis regarding apocalyptic fiction, but which ignores the rich history in SF that celebrates technological innovation and the perfectibility of man and society.[57]

In 1976, Neil Barron published the first iteration of *Anatomy of Wonder:
Science Fiction* (Bowker, revised 1981, 1987, 1995, and 2004).[58] Part I contains
selections from four historical essays (Philmus, Clareson, Ivor Rogers, and
Joe de Bolt and John R. Preiffer) and an essay on juvenile SF (Francis Molson),
each with a bibliography for further reading. Part II consists of seven
bibliographies or checklists of critical texts, awards, and collections – six of
these by Barron and one by H(al) W. Hall. Barron intends the book for four
audiences, including school libraries, interested readers, faculty, and students.
In his review, Lester del Rey calls *Anatomy* "probably the most significant and
valuable bibliographic tool in the history of the field to date."[59] While
Anatomy does not offer a theory or critical interpretive framework, it offers
a substantive and (generally) accurate survey of the available sources and
resources. Further, it fulfills Clareson's call for accurate bibliographies, and its
publication by a major imprint signals a legitimacy and acceptance.[60]

In 1979, at the close of a decade of fervor and ferment, Darko Suvin
published *Metamorphoses of Science Fiction: On the Poetics and History of
a Literary Genre* (Yale University Press). Originally published as *Pour une
poétique de la science-fiction* in 1977, the much shorter work was reworked
and reorganized for an English-speaking audience.[61] A few SF magazines took
notice. Joe Sanders, echoing the sentiments raised above regarding the
academic usurpation of hallowed territory, notes that it was "inevitable"
that a university press would publish something on SF, but that he can only
recommend the book with "serious reservations."[62] In the same issue, Patrick
S. Diehl offers a "Second Opinion," which is much less favorable. He calls the

---

[57] Thomas D. Clareson, "Review of *New Worlds for Old* by David Ketterer," *American
Literature* 47, 2 (May 1975), p. 301. A sort of roundtable on *New Worlds for Old* appears in
Science Fiction Studies 6 (July 1975), with comments by Robert Canary, C. S. Fredericks,
and Ursula K. Le Guin, with a response from Ketterer.

[58] The second edition of the book (1981) added essays on various national SF traditions
(German, French, Russian, Italian, Japanese, Chinese), and "Classroom Aids" by
Marshall Tymn. The fourth edition (1995) was substantively revised, with four new
essays in Part I, and eight new essays (not by Barron) in Part II, including "History and
Criticism" by Wolfe, and "Teaching Science Fiction" by Dennis Kratz.

[59] Lester del Rey, "Review of *Anatomy of Science Fiction* by Neil Barron," *Analog Science
Fiction/Science Fact* (December 1976), p. 168.

[60] J. B. Post, "Review of *Anatomy of Wonder* by Neil Barron," *RQ* 16, 4 (Summer 1977), p. 336.

[61] Patrick S. Diehl, "A Second Opinion: Review of *Metamorphoses of Science Fiction* by Darko
Suvin," *Science Fiction and Fantasy Book Review* 1, 7 (August 1979), p. 86.

[62] Joe Sanders, "Review of *Metamorphoses of Science Fiction* by Darko Suvin," *Science Fiction
and Fantasy Book Review* 1, 7 (August 1979), pp. 85–6.

book "less than successful" and notes that Suvin "fails to relate his abstractions convincingly to the concrete particulars of individual texts."[63]

Unsurprisingly, given the general movement of SF and SF studies into the academy, and the book's grounding in Marxism and literary and cultural theories, academic journals were more likely to take notice. A number of journals, including *Nineteenth-Century Fiction*, *World Literature Today*, *MLN*, and *Revue française d'études américaines*, published reviews of *Metamorphoses*. John Dean asserts that *Metamorphoses* is "the most authoritative and well-thought-out analysis of the SF genre to date" even if sometimes "downright abstruse and circumlocutory."[64] Dagmar Barnouw, a sometime contributor to *Science Fiction Studies*, concludes that Suvin's text "fill[s] a great need for informed, critical and sympathetic examination of a most interesting contemporary literary phenomenon," even if Suvin's concepts of "science" and "estrangement" are too broadly defined and too conveniently pliable.[65] Tom Lewis contends that the "increasing esteem that science fiction has enjoyed during the past decade" is largely due to Suvin's *Metamorphoses*.[66] Lewis concludes that Suvin's "efforts have produced more than a study in the poetics and history of a literary genre: he has also provided a suggestive model for future genre studies."[67] George Slusser, longtime contributor to SF scholarship, takes a more critical view of the text, and argues that Suvin develops his Marxist, materialist framework, which itself prevents him from grappling with the question of why SF has failed to live up to its dialectical potential. "It is almost, then, as if Suvin, instead of defining his genre, avoids defining it out of fear that the 'subversive' form might turn out simply another handmaiden of bourgeois ideology."[68]

In this condensed and targeted history of the development of SF scholarship, from the 1950s through the 1970s, we can see the ways in which the scholarship addresses the "needs" as set out by Clareson and Suvin. These books, essays, and journals work toward developing a set of critical research tools for the scholar and the student. Even so, the scholars and the works they

---

[63] Diehl, "A Second Opinion," p. 86.

[64] John Dean, "Review of *Metamorphoses of Science Fiction* by Darko Suvin," *Revue française d'étude américaines* 9 (April 1980), pp. 176–7.

[65] Dagmar Barnouw, "Review of *Metamorphoses of Science Fiction* by Darko Suvin," *MLN* 95, 5 (December 1980), p. 1466.

[66] Tom Lewis, "Review of *Metamorphoses of Science Fiction* by Darko Suvin," *World Literature Today* 54, 4 (Autumn 1980), p. 703.

[67] Ibid., p. 704.

[68] George Slusser, "Review of *Metamorphoses of Science Fiction* by Darko Suvin," *Nineteenth-Century Fiction* 35, 1 (June 1980), p. 75. For further consideration of the long-term influence of the Suvinian paradigm on the study of SF, see Chapter 46 of this volume.

have produced have not succeeded fully. In his essay "Academic Criticism and Science Fiction" (1992), Gary Westfahl argues that critics and scholars have failed in their larger goal, "to transform science fiction into a respected field of literary study. That is, today there are no jobs for science fiction scholars, there is no wiser concern for science fiction research, there is no discernible interest in science fiction criticism at all ... they have been completely unable to convince other critics that science fiction is a worthwhile field for literary criticism."[69] Westfahl (and others) imagined that the category of SF would stand alongside the traditional, recognized, areas of study, such as medieval studies or Shakespeare, of contemporary US literature, and that departments would also hire someone in SF studies. While some universities do have research units that focus on SF (e.g., University of California, Riverside), they remain the exception to the rule.

Science Fiction and the Classroom

The relationship between the study of SF and the teaching of SF is inter-connected. While one might assume that professors and teachers need to study SF, to develop rubrics and analytic models, to develop syllabi before teaching the material, that was not exactly what transpired, according to Gunn, Williamson, Clareson, and others. Indeed, as SF shifted into the public consciousness, as people simultaneously grew alarmed at the scientific and technological horrors around them and saw that it addressed many of these issues, and as the younger generation clamored for new courses that included SF because it addressed those existential fears, universities, colleges, and high schools scrambled to find people to teach a topic that most were unfamiliar with and unprepared to teach.

Gunn notes that a number of writers, including "Lester del Rey and Ben Bova and Harlan Ellison saw, in the academic interest, disaster for science fiction."[70] They all feared that teachers were teaching/using SF for the wrong reasons, that they had the wrong backgrounds and allegiances, and that they would turn off students and readers.[71] For example, in 1974, writers at a conference at Kean College of New Jersey complained bitterly of their experiences – teachers were butchering SF.[72] In an editorial for *Analog*

---

[69] Gary Westfahl, "Academic Criticism of Science Fiction: What It Is, What It Should Be," *Monad: Essays on Science Fiction* 2 (March 1992), p. 80.
[70] Gunn, *Inside Science Fiction*, p. 21.
[71] Ibid., p. 22.
[72] Ibid.

(June 1974), Bova contends that "if these classes result in disillusionment, then these hard-won gains will evaporate."[73] As Bova reckons it, in the rush to fill a perceived need to teach SF in the classroom, insufficient professional standards are being applied. His evidence consists of an experience with a "lovely, leggy blond engineer" who has merely read a bit of SF but has been deemed "qualified" enough by school admin to let her teach.[74]

While Bova's example may be simultaneously titillating and extremely sexist, he was correct that that was often the process. Donald Hassler, for example, notes that Kent State was seeking to boost enrollments, and asked him to teach a class on SF, even though he "knew little about modern SF."[75] The class filled and administration asked him to continue, at which point he began to solidify his SF background. In the November 1974 *Analog*, Gunn responds directly to Bova's concerns, arguing that some teachers may well be unqualified, but that that would hold true for any new discipline or field. According to Gunn, "Science fiction teaching will develop its own criteria, its own canon, its own tools, and we can agree on this – it behooves those of us who have vested interests in its welfare to contribute our ideas and see that they are heard."[76]

Definitively determining the numbers of courses offered in any given year proves difficult, though several individuals have made attempts. In 1971, Gordon Dickson (then president of the Science Fiction Writers of America) claimed that 150 courses in SF were being taught in the United States.[77] In that same year, Williamson published descriptions of the seventy college-level courses that were submitted in response to his questionnaire.[78] A year later Clareson writes in *F&SF* that the number had doubled.[79] In 1974, Williamson published an essay in Bretnor's *Science Fiction, Today and Tomorrow* in which he claims to have catalogued "250 science fiction and fantasy courses offered in American colleges during that past two or three years."[80] In "The Education of a Science Teacher" (1974), James Gunn suggests that

---

[73] Ben Bova, "Teaching Science Fiction," *Analog Science Fiction Science Fact* (June 1974), p. 6.

[74] Ibid., p. 176.

[75] Donald Hassler, *"Re: SF and the Academy – Request for Input,"* email to the author, 28 June 2016, n.p.

[76] Gunn, *Inside Science Fiction*, p. 92.

[77] Jack Williamson, "Science Fiction Comes to College," *Extrapolation* 12, 2 (May 1971), p. 67.

[78] Ibid., pp. 67–78.

[79] Thomas D. Clareson, "SF: The Academic Dimensions," *The Magazine of Fantasy and Science Fiction* (May 1972), pp. 116–23.

[80] Jack Williamson, "Science Fiction, Teaching and Criticism," in Reginald Bretnor, ed., *Science Fiction: Today and Tomorrow* (Baltimore: Penguin, 1974), p. 309.

hundreds, if not thousands, of courses are offered.[81] In his "Introduction" to the first edition of *Anatomy of Wonder* (1976), Neil Barron suggests that, in 1975, "many hundreds" of courses were taught at colleges and universities.[82] In 1996, *Science Fiction Studies* published an issue dedicated to the question of Science Fiction in Academe. For the issue, Robert Mullen and Arthur B. Evans sent out a questionnaire. They published the 404 course descriptions they received.[83] Clearly, then, the estimates vary widely, and the methods of gathering accurate numbers are suspect. As Williamson notes, people do not always respond to questionnaires. Furthermore, access to course catalogs was difficult in a pre-Internet era.

A secondary question to that of whether or not SF was "fit" for the classroom is that of how to offer it. For many professors, the desire was to offer stand-alone courses, or courses solely focused on SF as literature, or to teach SF as social commentary. Indeed, the numbers cited above address those courses. Others, however, argued that SF should not be a topic in and of itself, but should be integrated into other courses and not just English department courses. For example, at the MLA regional meeting in Detroit (1971), Clareson notes that many participants said that they would not "relegate" SF to a specially designated course since they preferred to integrate SF into their regular classes.[84] Similarly, Patrick Hogan wonders whether we should have separate SF courses.[85] "The time may have come for an evaluation of activities on college and university campuses masquerading, if the term may be used gently, as science fiction."[86] Instead, many argue that SF is best taught and learned embedded within other sorts of courses.

In the special issue of *F&SF* (1972), Clareson notes that SF and SF-related courses are already taught in "History, Anthropology, Sociology, Political Science, and the History of Science."[87] In his rebuttal to Bova in *Analog* (1974), Gunn notes that "teachers of science fiction are not just in English but in history, sociology, engineering, political science, anthropology, religion, philosophy, chemistry, physics, and many more disciplines, no doubt."[88]

---

[81] Gunn, *Inside Science Fiction*, p. 8.

[82] Neil Barron, "Introduction," in Neil Barron, ed., *Anatomy of Wonder* (New York: Bowker, 1976), p. xxi.

[83] R. D. Mullen, "Science Fiction in Academe," *Science Fiction Studies* 23, 3 (November 1996), p. 374.

[84] Clareson, "SF: The Academic Dimensions," p. 117.

[85] Patrick G. Hogan, Jr., "SF in the Classroom: 1. Opportunities and Limitations," *Extrapolation* 13, 2 (May 1972), p. 110.

[86] Ibid., p. 110.

[87] Clareson, "SF: The Academic Dimensions," p. 116.

[88] Gunn, "Teaching Science Fiction," p. 92.

Similarly, Hillegas in 1985 offers a list of course titles offered by non-English Department faculty that include SF, including Science and Contemporary Culture, Religious Dimensions of Science Fiction, and Man and His Environment.[89] Certainly, SF, as a mode of literature, draws upon the literary tradition; furthermore, the critical modes of both reading and evaluating SF draw upon literary criteria and models. However, SF also draws upon physics, biology, psychology, sociology, history, philosophy, and economics, among others. Perhaps even more importantly, SF helps us understand and respond to scientific, technological, social, political, personal, and aesthetic change. In order to fully understand these changes, SF texts should be integrated into the entire curriculum. Arguably, in the 1970s, both of these developments occurred simultaneously. As Barry Baddock suggests, "The Western world of the twentieth century, full of advertising slogans and television sets, distraction and trivialization, renders the 'pursuit of discrimination' more difficult than ever. 'In an environment such as this,' [Frank] Whitehead says, 'the future adult, in his own interests both as citizen and as individual, desperately needs to be equipped with some degree of critical awareness.'"[90]

Extrapolation, which began as a resource for researchers and teachers, began a series of essays entitled "SF in the Classroom." These ranged in focus and topic, but included Patrick Hogan on the pitfalls of SF-only courses (1972), Andrew J. Burgess on teaching religion through SF (1972), John R. Pfeiffer on teaching SF at the Air Force Academy (1972), Orval A. Lund on developing an elective English course (1974), Baddock and Gunn on SF readership among college students (1974), Stanley Schmidt on teaching science through SF (1976), Richard D. Erlich on teaching SF in a writing class, and John Morressy on teaching SF to both English and non-English majors (1979).

In 1979, *Science Fiction Studies* published a transcript of a discussion on "Teaching Science Fiction: Unique Challenges," which was a Special Session at the 1978 MLA (New York). The panel included Gregory Benford, Samuel R. Delany, Robert Scholes, and Alan Friedman as moderator. Like Schmidt above, Benford describes several strategies for teaching SF in a physics department. He offers several strategies, including the "softer" strategy of comparing two writers' notions of the scientists' career, to examining writers'

[89] Hillegas, "Colgate and the First Course in Science Fiction," *The Mage* 4 (Winter 1985), p. 14.
[90] Barry Baddock, "SF in the Classroom: A Look at Student Projects," *Extrapolation* 17, 1 (December 1975), p. 31.

"scientific habits of mind," to the "really tough part" of teaching physics.[91] Delany, on the other hand, offers a way to help readers who cannot read SF, by focusing on the word-by-word construction of science fictional worlds.[92] Scholes, drawing on Delany's remarks, suggests that we, as teachers, should begin with texts that draw upon a more familiar social and political background. We should avoid, at least initially, texts that overly defamiliarize the world.[93] Finally, respondent Friedman draws on C. P. Snow's "two cultures" argument, and suggests that basic facts about science are often beyond non-scientists and basic facts about the humanities (particularly literature) are often beyond science students. All four participants, in one way or another, suggest that teaching SF throughout the disciplines would be useful.

In sum, the development of academic SF criticism began in the 1950s, picked up steam in the 1960s, and reached full speed in the 1970s. Critical resources, critical criteria, and pedagogic integration all flourished in the 1970s. SF became a staple in classrooms, journals, and conferences. Further, SF criticism infiltrated a wide range of disciplines. As Williamson summarizes: "I look back on the 1970s as a golden age of sf in the classroom."[94]

---

[91] John Woodcock, *et al.*, "Teaching Science Fiction: Unique Challenges (Proceedings of the MLA Special Session, New York, December 1978)," *Science Fiction Studies* 6, 3 (November 1979), pp. 249–62.

[92] Ibid., pp. 251–4.

[93] Ibid., p. 255.

[94] Jack Williamson, "On Science Fiction in College," *Science Fiction Studies* 23, 3 (November 1996), p. 376.

PART III

★

AFTER THE NEW WAVE

30

The Birth of the Science Fiction Franchise

STEFAN RABITSCH AND MICHAEL FUCHS

Stardate, September 8, 1966 – an iconic day in the history of popular SF. On that day, the first episode of *Star Trek* (NBC, 1966–9) was broadcast on US television. At the time, it was anything but clear that *Star Trek* would become one of the largest and most lucrative franchises in SF history. Encompassing six live-action series, an animated series, and thirteen movies, more than a hundred novels, some fifty video games, dozens of comics, and a number of analog games, *Star Trek* has become a popular culture juggernaut, nurturing a multi-million dollar merchandizing and licensing ecology.

Fast-forward to August 6, 2016: The official fiftieth anniversary *Star Trek* convention is underway in Las Vegas, Nevada. Among the many *Star Trek* alumni (actors, writers, producers, makeup artists, etc.) in the audience, William Shatner takes command of the stage in his bombastic Shatner/Kirk persona and delivers an assertion that hits fans in the room and around the globe like a chroniton torpedo (i.e., shields were useless): "First of all, *Star Wars* created *Star Trek*." Apart from the unsettling implications of Captain James T. Kirk mentioning the "other" SF franchise at a *Star Trek* convention, Shatner's statement – not unlike that chroniton torpedo – was clearly out of temporal phase; after all, *Star Wars* (dir. George Lucas, 1977) was released a decade after *Star Trek*. However, Shatner had a point. When Paramount began to understand the scope of *Star Wars*' success, the studio started scouring their archives for an intellectual property it could develop into something that could rival *Star Wars*. The result was *Star Trek: The Motion Picture* (dir. Robert Wise, 1979). Shatner thus not only scored an accurate hit whose impact shattered a foundational belief of Trekkies around the globe, but, more importantly, highlights the cross-fertilization between "the big two," which has so often been neglected.

As *Star Trek* and *Star Wars* diversified and expanded following aggressive licensing and merchandizing strategies, various companies launched major intellectual properties, nurtured them, and re-envisioned them. However, "the big two" remained a testing ground for business models and strategies, which other franchises then imitated and developed further. However, it would be shortsighted to claim that SF franchises were "born" at the intersections between these two popular culture behemoths; that would be only part of the story of the "birth" of SF franchises, as the *Star Wars* and *Star Trek* franchises did not come out of a cultural vacuum. Not only did they emerge at a critical juncture between the SF blockbusters of the 1970s and SF's televisual turn in the 1980s, but they also developed out of socio-economic processes that can be traced back to the late nineteenth and early twentieth centuries.[1]

Indeed, we would be remiss to discuss the birth of SF franchises without looking at other genres and the development of the entertainment industry after the Second World War (or even at a franchise like the long-running British series *Doctor Who* [BBC, 1963–89, 2005–], which predates *both* franchises, or comics anchors like Superman and Batman, who precede all three by decades). Accordingly, in this chapter, we will map the evolution of SF franchises in four intersecting (and increasingly overlapping) stages:

Stage 1: Postwar economic growth and the rapid rise in consumerism fueled the US media industry in the 1950s. Responding to this increasing commercialization of American life, SF magazines, radio drama, and film serials laid the groundwork for a period of grand aspirations, attempts, and false starts (including the first golden age of SF television).

Stage 2: This first period led to the emergence of the SF blockbuster in the 1970s. In the wake of the cross-fertilization between *Star Wars* and *Star Trek*, a growing number of SF films were serialized in the 1980s and early 1990s.

Stage 3: Heralded by TV shows like *Battlestar Galactica* (ABC, 1978–9) and *Buck Rogers in the Twenty-Fifth Century* (NBC, 1979–81), the televisual turn at the end of the 1980s translated into a second Golden Age of SF television. *The X-Files* (Fox, 1993–2002, 2016–18), *Babylon 5* (PTEN, 1994–7, TNT, 1998), *Stargate SG-1* (Showtime / Sci Fi, 1997–2007), and *Farscape* (Sci Fi, 1999–2003) emerged during that time, while *Star Trek* and *Star Wars* continued to grow: *Star Trek Generations* (dir. David Carson, 1994) launched a sequence of The Next Generation (TNG) movies complementing a total of four spin-off series, while

---

[1] See Jan Johnson-Smith, *American Science Fiction TV: "Star Trek," "Stargate" and Beyond* (New York: I. B. Tauris, 2005), pp. 48–64.

the *Star Wars* prequel trilogy (dir. George Lucas, 1999–2005) added to its expanded universe.

Stage 4: Toward the end of the twentieth century, the *Matrix* franchise harbingered the emergence of prefabricated transmedia ventures. Since then, we have entered the era of media convergence, which has witnessed the rapid growth of SF video game franchises (e.g., *Wing Commander*, *Halo*, *Mass Effect*, and *BioShock*), the proliferation of prequels and sequels (e.g., *Prometheus* [dir. Ridley Scott, 2012], *Alien: Covenant* [dir. Ridley Scott, 2017], and *Blade Runner 2049* [dir. Denis Villeneuve, 2017]), and the perpetual reboot. These insta-franchises, whether ultimately successful (e.g., *The Hunger Games* and *The Walking Dead*) or not (e.g., *Jupiter Ascending* and *Defiance*), have become the norm for launching SF titles and/or adding to already existing ones.

As media franchising has become the default business model, the use of the term has proportionally inflated, as practically everything is – or may become – a franchise today.

Approaching the Tentacular Beast: Characterizing SF Franchises

Before diving into these socio-economic developments, however, there is a proverbial elephant in the room: What, in fact, is a franchise? Franchises usually display five defining features (to varying degrees, of course): (1) their capitalist impetus, (2) their global reach, and (3) a core storyworld, which is continually expanded through (4) serialization across media and (5) exploited through licensing. Accordingly, SF franchises are primarily a Western, albeit globally dispersed, phenomenon. They manifest as transmedia universes that form the nucleus of sprawling commercial ecologies governed by multi-national corporations.

The *Oxford English Dictionary* defines a franchise as a "general title, format, or unifying concept used for creating or marketing a *series* of products (esp. films, television shows, etc.)."[2] It also lists a *New York Times* movie review of the 1936 gangster flick *Public Enemy's Wife* (dir. Nick Grinde) as the first instance the term was used to describe a body of intellectual property – Warner Bros.' "G-men Franchise" (*Little Caesar* [dir. Mervyn LeRoy, 1931],

---

[2] "Franchise." *Oxford English Dictionary* (2017), https://en.oxforddictionaries.com/definition/franchise (last accessed May 15, 2017); our emphasis.

The Public Enemy [dir. William A. Wellman, 1931], and *G Men* [dir. William Keighley, 1935]). This early reference to a series of thematically connected films as a "franchise" demonstrates that the term has a long-standing history in the entertainment industry, an industry whose business cycles and models have always followed recognizable patterns of repetition, serialization, and adaptation.

In addition, the term also denoted a "geographic area of varied nature and extent in which an individual or corporation could ... exercise public jurisdiction" in the fifteenth century.[3] In view of these etymological roots, understanding SF franchises as media ecologies is just as relevant as acknowledging questions of ownership and property rights. Indeed, SF franchises belie strict vertical hierarchies; instead they are reminiscent of imperial power structures, with an imperial center (the primary/core text[s] and trademark/copyright holder) and the colonies (the "ancillary" texts/paratexts and licensees) surrounding it.[4]

Even though participatory fan cultures may perform rebellious gestures questioning this hierarchy, as they poach elements from the source text for their own creative purposes,[5] they are still accessories to corporate interests.[6] After all, fans who wear T-shirts of their favorite franchises provide not only free promotion, but, in fact, pay for the merchandise they advertise to other potential buyers. Indeed, regardless of how invested we may be in fictional worlds like *Doctor Who*, *Star Trek*, or *Star Wars*, the discourses of Western techno-science and free market capitalism ultimately define and govern them as property ecologies.

In order for any SF story to become a franchise, it must have the potential for sustained and sustainable growth, narratively and financially. The vastness of SF and fantasy worlds lends itself to franchise-building precisely because of their fictional worlds' vastness. Spatial and/or temporal expansiveness allow an imagined world to accommodate serialized stories

---

[3] Ibid.

[4] See Dan Hassler-Forest, *Science Fiction, Fantasy, and Politics: Transmedia World-Building Beyond Capitalism* (Lanham, MD: Rowman & Littlefield, 2016).

[5] See Henry Jenkins, *Textual Poachers: Television Fans and Participatory Culture* (New York: Routledge, 1992), Henry Henkins, *Fans, Bloggers, and Gamers: Exploring Participatory Culture* (New York: New York University Press, 2006), and the hundreds of essays influenced by Jenkins's thinking.

[6] See Jonathan Gray, Cornel Sandvoss, and C. Lee Harrington, "Introduction: Why Study Fans?," in Jonathan Gray, Cornel Sandvoss, and C. Lee Harrington, eds., *Fandom: Identities and Communities in a Mediated World* (New York: New York University Press, 2007), pp. 1–16; and Derek Johnson, "Fan-tagonism: Factions, Institutions, and Constitutive Hegemonies of Fandom," in Gray, Sandvoss and Harrington, eds., *Fandom*, pp. 285–300.

which sustain diverse environments and develop a wide range of characters across media.[7] As Patti McCarthy, for example, explains in relation to *Star Wars*: "If you see a moon in the background of a particular video game, you can be sure it has a name, a culture, a history, and a people that might appear later in another game, or has/will be featured in a new book."[8] Alternatively, temporal discontinuity and multi-verses offer an equal degree of expansiveness. Major comic book worlds implemented the latter model to build their franchises decades before the recent surge in reboots.

This recent proliferation of reboots and remakes has foregrounded the fact that many SF franchises did not start out as franchises despite the grand aspirations of their respective "creators"; rather, they became and/or were grown into franchises. As fictional worlds expand, the question of what is marketed and policed as the "official story" becomes an increasingly thorny issue, as *continuity* and *consistency* present manifold challenges. Lucasfilm, for example, introduced the Holocron continuity database in 2000 to hierarchize the *Star Wars* canon, which featured six levels of canonicity. These ranged from G-canon for "George Lucas Canon," which included not only the always latest versions of the movies, but also production notes and other statements made by Lucas, down to N-canon, "Non-Canon," which included what-if stories such as *Star Wars: Infinities* (2001–4). As Disney's reboot in November 2014 – which "de-canonized" all material other than the six films and the *Clone Wars* TV show (Cartoon Network, 2008–13, Netflix, 2014) – has shown, however, *any* canon is mutable.

This mutability suggests that these transmedia storyworlds are perhaps best understood in Deleuzo-Guattarian terms: a transmedia storyworld grows "organically," similar to a rhizome.[9] In an ideal form, a transmedia narrative may be inaugurated in one core medium which is supported by ancillary media nodes. As time passes, the narrative core could migrate to another medium, ultimately resulting in a multidirectional ecology, which may question easy binaries between "core" and "ancillary" texts. Indeed, as Karin Littau has argued, the *Alien* franchise helps us "think about media history as not constituted by relations of discrete, 'pure' media, but by an ecology of intermedial borrowings, joinings, and convergences," similar to

---

[7] See Mark J. P. Wolf, *Building Imaginary Worlds: The Theory and History of Subcreation* (New York: Routledge, 2012).

[8] Patti J. McCarthy, *The Lucas Effect: George Lucas and the New Hollywood* (Amherst, NY: Teneo Press, 2014), Kindle edition, loc. 3127.

[9] Gilles Deleuze and Félix Guattari, *A Thousand Plateaus: Capitalism and Schizophrenia*, trans. Brian Massumi (Minneapolis: University of Minnesota Press, 1987), pp. 3–25.

Darwinian adaptation.[10] These transmedia narratives sustain rich, diverse, and immersive worlds, but they also limit economic risks in that they capitalize on the strengths of different media in order to counterbalance their respective limitations and thus maximize profitability.[11]

Post-Second World War Consumerism, Adaptations, and Selling Stuff

In the wake of the Second World War, consumerism began to increasingly influence US values, attitudes, and behaviors, as everyday life in the United States became overtly commercialized. Advertising across media and the commercialization of entertainment products fed into an explosion of mass culture in the 1950s. Tellingly, in the same decade, US business management scholars began to study franchising, a business model which emerged in the late nineteenth to early twentieth century (depending on one's definition of "franchising").[12] Business management scholar David Schwartz linked the mushrooming of franchises in the 1950s to "corporate desires to build sales volume across a range of retail and service industries."[13] Similarly, the culture industry had already produced proto-franchises before the Second World War. Some of these proto-franchises, like Edgar Rice Burroughs's *Barsoom* stories, *Buck Rogers*, and *Flash Gordon*, originated in comic strips and/or pulp magazines, which were quickly adapted to other media, first radio and then usually movie serials. However, few of these worlds developed into larger property ecologies, since television, as one of the main engines driving mass culture in the 1950s, was still in its infancy.

While their initial lifespan was perhaps rather short, superhero comics of the 1930s and 1940s foreshadowed the commercial appeal of fantastic stories. The Golden Age of Comics was initiated with the publication of the first Superman story in *Action Comics* #1 (1938). Coinciding with shifts in mass marketing, superheroes were arguably commodities first, and vehicles for stories only second. Tellingly, DC Comics laid claim to their caped son of Krypton by way of trademark rather than copyright laws. Thus, Superman, Inc. was founded solely for the purpose of licensing in 1939. As a result,

---

[10] Karin Littau, "Media, Mythology and Morphogenesis: *Aliens*," *Convergence* 17, 1 (2011), p. 22.

[11] Henry Jenkins, *Convergence Culture: Where Old and New Media Collide* (New York: New York University Press, 2006), pp. 93–130.

[12] Derek Johnson, *Media Franchising: Creative License and Collaboration in the Culture Industries* (New York: New York University Press, 2013), p. 35.

[13] Ibid.

Superman not only protected the citizens of Earth, but soon sold everything from cornflakes and bubble gum to gasoline and sportswear. As Ian Gordon has argued, "Superman was not so much a character who helped sell comic books as a product that comic books sold."[14] Batman, Captain America, and Wonder Woman were developed along similar lines, with *Batman Incorporated* (2010–13) even going as far as reflecting on the industrialized production of stories centering on the caped crusader, as Bruce Wayne has made his crime-fighting endeavors more effective by licensing his gear and trademarking his "secret" identity, which wannabe-superheroes across the globe may license.

This commercial approach is tied to the boom in mass culture and consumerism that suffused US culture at that time, which, in turn, is interconnected with the rise of television. Television was potent and pervasive, since it quickly succeeded in penetrating the homes of millions of Americans. Television was initially perceived as a threat to a movie industry struggling with the dissolution of the vertically integrated studio system since the Supreme Court's 1948 Paramount Decision. Over the next decade and a half, "New Hollywood" began to grow into an array of media corporations for whom television broadcasting became a vehicle to learn about and advertise to audiences. Normalizing the white middle-class family to the detriment of other cultural formations, television programs, and the property ecologies they were a part of and/or grew into, first nurtured, then catered to, and ultimately fulfilled, at least in part, their consumerist sensibilities.

In particular, westerns quickly mushroomed on the small screen, often by way of adapting existing titles (e.g., *The Lone Ranger* [ABC, 1949–57] and *Hopalong Cassidy* [NBC, 1949–54]).[15] Westerns such as *The Gene Autry Show* (CBS, 1950–6) were ideologically valuable, since they instructed the younger generations in what it meant to be a good American (e.g., Autry's "Cowboy Commandments" or the Lone Ranger's "moral code"). At the same time, they were highly lucrative avenues for merchandising and licensing and reached deep into baby boomers' pockets.

With President Kennedy's "New Frontier" – and thus *Star Trek*'s "final frontier" – not too distant, horse operas and space operas, which had already cross-fertilized in pulps as well as radio and movie serials, continued

---

[14] Ian Gordon, *Comic Strips and Consumer Culture, 1890–1945* (Washington, DC: Smithsonian, 1998), p. 134.
[15] On *Hopalong Cassidy*'s franchising, see Michael Kackman, "Nothing On But Hoppy Badges: *Hopalong Cassidy*, William Boyd Enterprises, and Emergent Media Globalization," *Cinema Journal* 47, 4 (2008), pp. 76–101.

influencing each other. As a result, SF television was inaugurated by a flurry of juvenile space opera titles (e.g., *Captain Video and His Video Rangers* [DuMont, 1949–55] and *Flash Gordon* [DuMont, 1954–5]), most of which led to short-lived spin-offs, companion programs, and/or tie-in titles that were broadcast on the radio and published in magazines concurrently. Most importantly, however, networks and advertisers made excessive use of the commercial opportunities presented by their respective franchises. For example, while DuMont was only short-lived as a network, *Captain Video and His Video Rangers* still set benchmarks: the show was sponsored by Post Consumer Brands, PowerHouse candy, and Skippy peanut butter, and it was also used to sell DuMont's own brand of television sets. Special collectables, such as photos of the cast, a "secret seal" ring, plastic spacemen figures, and "membership cards" for fans, were offered as premiums together with these products. Although aimed at young adults, these serial space operas soon gathered significant numbers of adult viewers, which led to more diversification in the form of SF anthology shows (e.g., *Science Fiction Theater*, syndicated, 1955–7), which then paved the way for more sophisticated SF drama in the next decade.

Outside the United States, franchising attempts in the 1950s led to the development of successful, albeit short-lived, transatlantic property ecologies (e.g., *Quatermass*) and laid the groundwork for an icon of nuclear fear and trauma that could be resurrected ad infinitum (Godzilla). Created by Nigel Kneale for the BBC, Bernard Quatermass was a professor and leading scientist in the British space program. He first appeared in 1953 in the successful TV serial *The Quatermass Experiment*, which was soon followed by a second (*Quatermass II*, BBC 1955) and a third serial (*Quatermass and the Pit*, BBC 1958–9). When the second installment aired, Hammer Films released their film adaptation of the first serial, titled *The Quatermass Xperiment* (dir. Val Guest, 1955). Apart from upping the horror factor, they made significant changes to the story, especially its protagonist, in order to cater to the American market. Quatermass was no longer a pensive, troubled scientist, but rather a rough-and-tumble action-hero academic. The transatlantic adaptation worked, and the film, released as *The Creeping Unknown* in the United States, became Hammer's highest-grossing film up to that point. Hammer's adaptations of the second and third serials followed in 1957 and 1967, respectively. The cross-culture market adaptation of *Quatermass* stands as a perhaps neglected precursor for the *Doctor Who* franchise, which, prior to its breakthrough on the American market in 2005 (the event which, arguably, turned it into a franchise in the first place) was a largely British phenomenon.

In an entirely different part of the world, the American foreign policy measures which eventually ended the Second World War and the commercial successes of creature features released in the early 1950s gave birth to a monster that stands at the center of the longest continuously running movie franchise according to the Guinness World Records – Godzilla. The original movie (dir. Ishirō Honda, 1954) required nearly twice the budget the production company Toho invested in its second big film of the year, Akira Kurosawa's now-iconic *Seven Samurai*. In order to whet the audience's appetites for *Godzilla*'s release, Toho produced a radio play based on the script, which was serially broadcast between July and September. The concerted marketing efforts were successful, as would-be patrons stood in line for hours waiting for tickets.[16] Like all monsters, Godzilla is a vehicle onto which different interpretations may be projected. However, the general understanding is that the monster symbolizes the unbelievable force of the atomic bomb and the invincibility of the US military.

When Hollywood became interested in the Japanese movie, this critical stance toward America raised concerns (to say the least). Still, Joseph E. Levine, who had distributed international films in the United States in the previous decade, secured the American rights to the movie for $25,000 (*Godzilla* had made about $420,000 at the Japanese box office). Whereas Levine's earlier foreign releases were subtitled and screened in arthouse cinemas, *Godzilla* underwent a more complex adaptation for the American market and turned into *Godzilla, King of the Monsters!* (dir. Ishirō Honda and Terry O. Morse, 1956). Unlike later films in the series, *Godzilla* was not dubbed in its entirety. In addition, the American version changed the chronology and removed some subplots. These adaptations arguably aimed not only at selling *King of the Monsters*, but, more importantly, at developing Godzilla into an iconic monster equal to Universal's monsters of the 1930s and 1940s, which had been resurrected in numerous sequels and had even received the shared universe/crossover treatment in *House of Frankenstein* (dir. Erle C. Kenton, 1944) and *House of Dracula* (dir. Erle C. Kenton, 1948).

Since the original movie, Toho has produced more than thirty *Godzilla* movies and co-produced one with the American studio UPA (*Invasion of the Astro-Monster* aka *Monster Zero* [dir. Ishirō Honda, 1965]). In addition to *King of the Monsters*, the American versions of *King Kong vs. Godzilla* (dirs. Ishirō Honda and Thomas Montgomery, 1963) and *Godzilla* (dirs. Koji Hashimoto and R. J. Kizer, 1985) feature additional content, as does the Italian colored

[16] Ed Godziszewski, "The Making of *Godzilla*," *G-Fan* 12 (1994), p. 39.

489

and expanded re-cut of the first movie in the series (*Godzilla* [dirs. Ishirō Honda, Luigi Cozzi, and Terry O. Morse, 1977]). Toho first re-booted the series with *The Return of Godzilla* (dir. Koji Hashomoto, 1984), a second time with *Godzilla 2000* (dir. Takao Okawara, 1999), and a third time with *Shin Godzilla* (dirs. Hideaki Anno and Shinji Higuchi, 2016). In addition, there have been two "American" reboots, both of which were titled *Godzilla* (dir. Roland Emmerich, 1998, dir. Gareth Edwards, 2014). The 1998 reboot is particularly interesting from a transnational point of view, as TriStar Pictures and Centropolis co-produced the film. The Japanese media giant Sony had owned TriStar since 1989, while Roland Emmerich's Centropolis is officially headquartered in Germany. Sony, in particular, made sure that its investments in the Godzilla trademark paid off, as Geoff King explains in his book *New Hollywood Cinema* (2002):

> The *Godzilla* video is distributed by Sony Music Operations, part of the Sony Corporation's music division, Sony Music Entertainment . . . The soundtrack album . . . achieved sales of more than one million: it was released on Epic Records, a label owned by Sony Music Entertainment. Sony Pictures also has extensive interests in television production through the Columbia TriStar Television Group. To a roster including hit shows such as *Wheel of Fortune* and *Jeopardy* was added the animated *Godzilla: The Series* . . . There is an online computer game produced by Columbia TriStar Interactive and two games have been developed for the GameBoy platform.[17]

Preceding the origins of the "big two" SF franchises in the United States, the original *Godzilla* movie is at the heart of a sprawling property ecology whose corporate evolution and transnational reach show how convoluted the franchising process is. Indeed, as early as 1963, the American toy manufacturer Ideal Toy Corp. created a *Godzilla* board game. In the same year, a *Godzilla* model kit was released. The year after, the Japanese company Marusan began to sell *Godzilla* figures. In terms of success, these toys were rather negligible; however, these merchandizing strategies laid the groundwork for schemes George Lucas and company would perfect in later decades.

Botched Attempts, False Starts, and the "Big Two"

The commercial success of space opera and rocket men shows of the 1950s, which reached beyond their juvenile target audience, slowly convinced networks and studios of the economic viability and practicality of producing SF

---

[17] Geoff King, *New Hollywood Cinema: An Introduction* (London: I. B. Tauris, 2002), p. 69.

television geared towards an adult audience.[18] Drawing on radio anthologies and serial drama, and building on the success of anthology shows such as *Tales of Tomorrow* (ABC, 1951–3), Rod Serling's *The Twilight Zone* (CBS, 1959–64) inaugurated the first golden age of SF on television. Together with *The Outer Limits* (ABC, 1963–5), Serling's program embodied the commercial potential among adult viewers.[19] Although successful, these series did not immediately grow into larger property ecologies quite simply because their lack of a unified world complicated world-building efforts and their commercial reach paled in comparison with other formats. Yet, similar to some SF movies of the 1950s, these shows provided fertile ground for remakes and adaptations in the 1980s and 1990s, respectively (*The Twilight Zone* [CBS, 1985–9], *The Twilight Zone* [UPN, 2002–3], *The Outer Limits* [Showtime, 1995–2000, Sci Fi, 2001–2]). Around the same time in the United Kingdom, the BBC launched *Doctor Who* (1963–89), which would "becom[e] the longest continuously running science fiction series in television history."[20] As already intimated, however, *Doctor Who* remained predominantly a British phenomenon until it was resurrected in the early 2000s. Even so, the show's transtemporal premise, and especially a protagonist who could repeatedly "regenerate" into new versions of the character played by new actors, laid the groundwork for a storyworld that became a global franchise largely as a result of its 2005 breakthrough on the American market.

American SF television diversified in the 1960s, as networks expanded their competitive programming. Every time a network released a new title, the others tried to match it with a similar format. Amidst this wave of new programs, two intellectual properties loom large. While Irving Allen's *Lost in Space* (CBS, 1966–8) was arguably more successful during its initial run, the fictional world of Gene Roddenberry's *Star Trek*, which seemingly failed in the 1960s, proved to be the bedrock of what has since become one of the biggest SF franchises.

Star Trek eventually became a success despite its repeated failures. Gene Roddenberry committed the pitch for the series to paper on March 11, 1964 in a document simply titled "STAR TREK is ... " First, he approached CBS,

---

[18] See Mark Jancovich and Derek Johnston, "Film and Television, the 1950s," in Mark Bould, Andrew M. Butler, Adam Roberts and Sherryl Vint, eds., *The Routledge Companion to Science Fiction* (London and New York: Routledge, 2009), pp. 74–5.

[19] See Peter Wright, "Film and Television, 1960–1980," in Bould *et al.*, eds., *The Routledge Companion to Science Fiction*, pp. 93–4.

[20] Jay P. Telotte, "The Trajectory of Science Fiction Television," in Jay P. Telotte, ed., *The Essential Science Fiction Television Reader* (Lexington: University Press of Kentucky, 2008), p. 16.

who ultimately rejected his proposal despite showing strong interest in his ideas, as they were concerned about the potential competition for Irving Allen's show. Roddenberry also had little luck at MGM. His next stop, NBC, proved more successful. TV executives were, however, still on the fence about the practicality, feasibility, and profitability of producing an SF show with what was then considered a large recurring main cast visiting new alien places on a weekly basis. The expansive potential of *Star Trek*'s humanist vision of the future, combined with an ideologically uplifting and allegorically potent premise, could initially not compensate for the show's poor economic performance.[21]

The unlikeliness of *Star Trek* becoming a multi-million dollar franchise may be sketched out by way of a few anecdotal examples. On the one hand, they point to the commercial challenges and limits of mass market SF prior to the successful SF blockbusters of the 1970s; on the other, they also reveal ambiguities of people like Roddenberry who tried to navigate the vagaries of the industry on the grounds of idealism while also wanting to make a pretty penny. Despite reservations, NBC committed funds and asked Roddenberry to develop a pilot episode. The test screenings of the original pilot, "The Cage," were not successful; executives and the test audience concluded that the story was "too cerebral," among other things. Consequently, Roddenberry had to make compromises and concessions to keep the show alive. Interestingly, he did not budge on another issue studio executives were even more concerned with – product placement and sponsors, especially the tobacco industry. Roddenberry stood his ground and argued that people on a starship in a supposedly more advanced future would not smoke cigarettes and poison their bodies; he kept the *Enterprise* smoke-free. This decision, however, left a dent in the show's profitability.

At the same time, Roddenberry did not shy away from commercializing some of the key principles that inform the *Star Trek* future. For example, the Vulcan IDIC, short for Infinite Diversity in Infinite Combinations, was introduced as the central principle of Vulcan philosophy. According to Vulcan logic, the entire cosmos is but infinite permutations of infinite manifestations of the same whole. As a concept and as a symbol, the IDIC was first introduced in the third-season episode "Is There in Truth

---

[21] See Chris Gregory, *Star Trek: Parallel Narratives* (London, Macmillan, 2000); and Matthew W. Kapell, ed., *Star Trek as Myth: Essays on Symbol and Archetype at the Final Frontier* (Jefferson: McFarland, 2010); and Jon G. Wagner and Jan Lundeen, *Deep Space and Sacred Time: Star Trek in the American Mythos* (Westport: Praeger, 1998); and Ina Rae Hark, *Star Trek* (London: BFI, 2008); and Stefan Rabitsch, *Star Trek and the British Age of Sail: The Maritime Influence throughout the Series and Films* (Jefferson: McFarland, 2018).

No Beauty?" (October 18, 1968). Spock (Leonard Nimoy) wore an IDIC pendant designed by Roddenberry. Initially, the pendant would have taken an even more prominent role solely for the purpose of selling replicas through Lincoln Enterprises, Inc., a mail order catalog company whose origins are shrouded in ambiguity. Ultimately, Majel Barrett Roddenberry and Betty Trimble ran the business, which allowed Gene to sell items from the show that the studio would otherwise throw away. Nimoy and other cast members were dismayed and the script was subsequently changed to tone down the "sales pitch" for the IDIC pendant. Even so, it went on sale at $ 7.50 in 1969.

Despite two fan letter campaigns – the first of their kind – credited with earning *Star Trek* a second and third season, the show still failed and was cancelled in 1969.[22] It was actually not until the early 1970s when *Star Trek* began to generate more revenue and its popularity rose to unanticipated levels. Unbeknownst to the network at first, the economic potential of *Star Trek* was revealed in ever-more expanding fan activities and a measureable growth of new viewers of a show that, ironically, had been cancelled. The show's rights were sold into syndication, which meant that it would be available on smaller, local stations where it was shown in continuous reruns. Syndication introduced *Star Trek* to a much larger market and new audiences, in particular young adults and twentysomethings. Although viewers longed for more, there was nothing to satisfy their desires. Around that time, fans organized the first conventions where like-minded aficionados could exchange their ideas and engage in fan activities (costume contests, merchandise trading, filking,[23] etc.). There, they could also meet the show's creator(s) and cast. The growing demand for more *Star Trek* was met with the short-lived *Star Trek: The Animated Series* (NBC, 1973–4), which, despite winning an Emmy, became too expensive to produce. *Star Trek*'s initial failure, combined with the relatively short run of *Lost in Space* and *The Twilight Zone*, showed studios that mass-market SF was not economically viable; there were simply not enough people watching it.

In hindsight, while the New Wave kept sweeping through SF literature, Stanley Kubrick's visually dazzling and technically sophisticated *2001: A Space Odyssey* (1968) stands as a lone sentinel anticipating the blockbusting success

---

[22] See also Chapter 18 of this volume.
[23] A particular form of fan culture and fan labor, filk music is a genre that draws on American folk music (especially social justice songs), appropriating it to accommodate science fiction and fantasy themes. Filk artists have been active since the 1950s, but their output has proliferated since the rise of big fan conventions in the 1970s.

of SF extravaganzas on the silver screen in the late 1970s. Apart from re-runs, the decade witnessed a few cautious attempts at growing franchises by way of developing television spin-offs of SF movies. The short-lived *Planet of the Apes* (CBS, 1974), the animated series *Return to the Planet of the Apes* (NBC, 1975–6), and *Logan's Run* (CBS, 1977–8) are cases in point. Even though the films they were based on offered potentially expansive storyworlds, economically they were not yet viable. Despite a failed remake in 2001, *The Planet of the Apes* franchise began a successful series of reboot films in 2011. Other SF television titles of the 1970s, such as *The Six Million Dollar Man* (ABC, 1973–8), and *The Bionic Woman* (ABC, 1976–7, NBC, 1977–8), were largely "ephemeral."[24] Adaptations from film to TV to grow SF franchises proved unsuccessful not least because television simply could not yet challenge big movie productions. However, someone who considers himself "a product of the television age" made a little movie set a long time ago in a galaxy far, far away which had a tremendous impact on the shape of SF franchises to come.[25]

The story of *Star Wars* begins with the rise of its creator, George Lucas. His award-winning student film *Electronic Labyrinth: THX 1138 4EB* (1967) turned Lucas into a filmmaking prodigy. However, the feature film based on his project, *THX 1138* (1971), flopped at the box office. While Lucas was dissatisfied with the lack of commercial success the movie enjoyed, more importantly, he became incredibly frustrated with the way the entertainment industry operated, as Warner Bros. tampered with the film in ways Lucas disagreed with. Unfortunately for Lucas, that experience repeated itself only a short time later, when Universal hired editors to cut *American Graffiti* (1973). Surprisingly, Lucas's second cinematic release became a gigantic hit, grossing more than $100 million and earning Academy Award nominations in five categories, including Best Picture and Best Director. Suddenly, Lucas transformed from a young filmmaker to a commercially successful writer and director.

Lucas, however, did not know of his sudden rise to superstardom when he started planning life after *American Graffiti*. Originally, Lucas meant to direct *Apocalypse Now* next but eventually gave up on the idea and turned to developing *Star Wars*. Lucas approached United Artists and Universal, but both studios passed up on the project. Alan Ladd, Jr. of Twentieth-Century Fox, however, was quick to pick it up. Lucas signed a deal memo in mid-July of 1973, which stipulated that Fox would not intervene in the production.

[24] Telotte, "The Trajectory of Science Fiction Television," p. 16.
[25] George Lucas quoted in Dale Pollock, *Skywalking: The Life and Films of George Lucas* (Cambridge, MA: Da Capo, 1999), p. 12.

After the release of *American Graffiti* on August 1, Fox feared that Lucas would demand more money, since he had not signed an official contract. Lucas, however, did not want more money – he wanted control. Accordingly, he asked for merchandizing as well as sequel rights and requested that Lucasfilm produce the movie. While Fox's negotiators could not quite imagine why Lucas insisted on obtaining the merchandizing rights, *Star Wars* "was designed around toys," as Lucas has put it.[26]

After Hasbro had launched the action figure industry in 1963 with the release of G. I. Joe, Mego had become the dominant player in the American market by the mid-1970s, selling action figures based on DC and Marvel Comics superheroes and villains, television shows (such as the original *Star Trek* series, but also *The Waltons*), and movies (including *Planet of the Apes*). Since Mego failed to see the potential of *Star Wars* tie-in products, Kenner stepped in. Famously, Kenner underestimated the demand for *Star Wars* toys and sold "Early Bird Certificates" during the holiday season 1977, which entitled kids to receive one of the first four *Star Wars* action figures once they were available. Kenner went on to sell more than 40 million *Star Wars* toys in 1978 and more than 50 million the year after.[27]

While some scholars have gone as far as claiming that "more than anything else, *Star Wars* was the *toys*," *Star Wars* is so much more than *just* the toys.[28] In fact, similar to contemporary blockbusters, the *Star Wars* universe began to take shape before the first movie had even been released. In what turned out to be excellent marketing ploys, the *Star Wars* novelization was published in November 1976, theatrical trailers were first shown during the holiday season 1976, and *Star Wars* was also heavily advertised on television. Releasing a novelization ahead of the film might not have been a groundbreaking idea (indeed, it was a staple during the early days of cinema), but the aggressive promotion in cinemas six months ahead of *Star Wars*' release certainly was. However, one should be aware that both the novelization and the movie trailers were primarily meant to appease Fox, as the movie was originally scheduled for release in late 1976. Still, Lucasfilm,

---

[26] George Lucas quoted in John Baxter, *Mythmaker: The Life and Work of George Lucas* (New York: HarperCollins, 1999), p. 174.

[27] David Diamond, "Arsenal of Killer Toys is Growing," *Ellensburg Daily Record*, June 19, 1980, p. 8; Louise Cook, "Toymakers are Ready Months Ahead of Santa," *The Free Lance-Star*, February 18, 1980, p. 18.

[28] Robert Buerkle, "Playset Nostalgia: LEGO *Star Wars: The Video Game* and the Transgenerational Appeal of the LEGO Video Game Franchise," in Mark J. P. Wolf, ed., *LEGO Studies: Examining the Building Blocks of a Transmedial Phenomenon* (New York: Routledge, 2014), p. 132.

under the tutelage of marketing director Charles Lippincott, concertedly marketed the movie at SF conventions, including the 1976 San Diego Comic Con (back then not the commercialized beast the convention is today) and the 1976 Worldcon where members of the production team exhibited props and showed multimedia presentations, in order to create some hype.

As the intended release date drew closer, a new problem emerged – barely any cinema wanted to book *Star Wars*, which is why Fox decided to offer it in a package with *The Other Side of Midnight*, which was based on a bestselling novel and expected to become an enormously successful movie. It didn't, but *Star Wars* became an instant hit. Despite the initial success *Star Wars* had in the few cinemas in which it originally screened, industry insiders believed interest in the movie (and the emerging franchise) would quickly fade. However, Lippincott continued finding new licensees, which "renewed interest" and "brought in new audiences."[29] After a first-day opening in thirty-two cinemas and a first-weekend opening in forty-three cinemas, *Star Wars* played in close to 1,100 cinemas across the United States two months later and ended up grossing more than $220 million during its initial run in the United States. The worldwide release between fall 1977 and spring 1978 and American reissues between 1978 and 1982 only increased revenues, and the first film had earned about $530 million (on a budget of $11 million) at the box office by the time the Original Trilogy concluded.

Of course, despite periods of hibernation (particularly in the 1980s), the *Star Wars* franchise has only grown since then – from an R2-D2 aquarium and *Star Wars* fishing gear to Wookie Crocs and Death Star waffle makers, there is barely a product in our capitalist world that one cannot purchase with the *Star Wars* logo slapped onto it. As a result, despite the original film's enormous return on investment, its box office success pales in comparison with the billions of dollars the entire franchise has made since 1977 (not to mention the unclear amounts of money licensees have made from *Star Wars* products).[30] In December 2015, *Fortune* presented estimates for *Star Wars* revenues since 1977 (in billion dollars), as shown in the table on p. 497.

In other words, the movies have generated only about 30 percent of the total revenue, while toys and other merchandize account for about 40 percent. Tellingly, Thomas Elsaesser has argued that movies have become little

---

[29] Ibid.

[30] See Sean Guynes and Dan Hassler-Forest, eds., *Star Wars and the History of Transmedia Storytelling* (Amsterdam: Amsterdam University Press, 2017) for a recent book-length treatment of the industry surrounding the *Star Wars* films.

Box office (adjusted for inflation)	7.3
Home entertainment	5.7
Toys and other merchandize	17.0
Video games	4.3
Intellectual property	4.0
Misc. (books, licensing, income generated through *Clone Wars*)	3.7
Total	42.0

Source: Jonathan Chew, "Star Wars Franchise Worth More Than Harry Potter and James Bond, Combined," *Fortune*, December 24, 2015, http://fortune.com/2015/12/24/star-wars-value-worth (last accessed May 15, 2017).

more than "bill-board[s] stretched out in time."[31] By way of "copyright[ing] everything [one] could think of" (as Lippencott has put it), *Star Wars* anticipated this development and established many of the promotional efforts which have become the standard by now.[32]

The Tentacles Just Keep Growing: From Media Convergence to the Perpetual Reboot

If the birth pangs of SF franchises are located in the consumerism and the commercialization of the media industry between the 1950s and the 1970s, then what has followed since amounts to repetition, permutation, and expansion. While the underlying characteristics of franchises and franchising have barely changed, the corporate transmedia mass market has quite simply become more convoluted. The SF blockbusters in the wake of *Star Wars* (e.g., *E.T.: The Extra-Terrestrial* [dir. Steven Spielberg, 1982] and *The Terminator* [dir. James Cameron, 1984]) led to sequels and TV spin-offs. In our age of media convergence, franchising has since become a multidirectional explosion of strategies and media forms. The SF franchise beast has spawned a host of new tentacles (e.g., video games, increased seriality and complexity, reboots, and web-based content), which allow for only cursory observations.

The financial successes of – and the technological advancements brought forth by – SF blockbusters like *Star Wars* fed into the increasingly reciprocal

[31] Thomas Elsaesser, "The Blockbuster: Everything Connects, but Not Everything Goes," in Jon Lewis, ed., *The End of Cinema as We Know It: American Film in the Nineties* (London: Pluto Press, 2002), p. 11.

[32] Charles Lippincott quoted in Stephen Lepitak, "Star Wars Marketing Man Charles Lippincott on the Real Force Behind the Franchise's Success," *The Drum*, December 1, 2015, www.thedrum.com/news/2015/12/01/star-wars-marketing-man-charles-lippincott-real-force-behind-franchises-success (last accessed May 15, 2017).

cross-fertilization of media. Exemplified by series such as *Battlestar Galactica* (ABC, 1978–9), *V* (NBC, 1983–5), and *Alien Nation* (Fox, 1989–90), the televisual turn of the mid-1980s marks a milestone in media convergence. Television became more visual owing to increased budgets and the erosion of traditional network structures. For example, the straight-into-syndication sales strategy of *Star Trek: The Next Generation* (1987–94) maximized the show's marketability, recouping its relatively high budget of more than $1 million per episode. The proliferation of cable, satellite, and pay-TV channels made narrowcasting economically attractive and viable.[33] Productions like *Babylon 5* heralded the age of what television scholar Jason Mittell has called "complex television."[34] Tightly constructed and rigorously policed by J. Michael Straczynski, the *B5* universe did not, however, spawn a sprawling property ecology, as direct-to-DVD telefilms and the short-lived spin-off series *Crusade* (TNT, 1999) failed to make a bang. Shows such as *The X-Files* and the remake of *Battlestar Galactica* (Sci Fi, 2003–09), on the other hand, quickly became "must-see-television." The hype surrounding these shows anticipated a ubiquitous tool of SF franchising in the twenty-first century: The launch of an SF universe is usually marketed as an "event"; built up (or even launched) by pre-release announcements and trailers.

Blockbusters such as *Jurassic Park* (dir. Steven Spielberg, 1993), *Stargate* (dir. Roland Emmerich, 1994), *Independence Day* (dir. Roland Emmerich, 1996), and *X-Men* (dir. Bryan Singer, 2000) were released while the second golden age of SF television was in full swing. These films provided the material for franchise structures in varying degrees. While the *Jurassic Park* sequels (dir. Steven Spielberg, 1997, dir. Joe Johnston, 2001) failed to match the original's success at the box office and the animated spin-off *Escape from Jurassic Park* was cancelled before it was released, the reboot/sequel *Jurassic World* (dir. Colin Trevorrow, 2015), and *Jurassic World: The Fallen Kingdom* (dir. Juan Antonio Bayona, 2018), together with IDW acquiring the comic book rights from Topps Comics and the video game *Jurassic Park Evolution* (Frontier Development, 2018), set the dinosaur-filled world on track for future franchising endeavors. On the other hand, the TV adaptation of *Stargate* and its excessive growth (three live-action TV shows, a short-lived animated series, and two direct-to-DVD films) bespeak the limits of franchising strategies: *Stargate* was essentially "milked dry" by too much formulaic repetition and unsustainable growth, which ultimately led to its economic exhaustion. A similar fate befell *Star Trek*

---

[33] See Johnson-Smith, *American Science Fiction TV*, pp. 64–73.
[34] Jason Mittell, *Complex TV: The Poetics of Contemporary Television Storytelling* (New York: New York University Press, 2015).

when *Star Trek: Enterprise* (UPN, 2001–5) was cancelled. However, as Ina Rae Hark has suggested, franchise fatigue had arguably already set in with *Star Trek: The Next Generation*.[35] The *Star Wars* prequel trilogy, arriving with a deeply mixed critical reception despite obvious profitability, coincided with the economic bonanza of fantasy franchises – *Lord of the Rings* (2001–3), *Harry Potter* (2001–11), *Twilight* (2008–12) – which effectively provided newer, more expansive franchising models at the dawn of the twenty-first century, and new global fan communities to sustain them.

In terms of SF franchises, the new millennium was hailed in by *The Matrix*, which marked another milestone in media convergence because of its aggressive transmedia storytelling approach. The *Matrix* franchise was arguably the first transmedia venture conceived for the global mass market. The core nodes of the three films (1999–2003) were intricately expanded upon and interwoven with an anthology of nine animated short films (*The Animatrix* [2003]) and three video games (*Enter the Matrix* [2003], *The Matrix Online* [2005–9], *The Matrix: Path of Neo* [2005]).

In some ways, the commitment to transmedia heralded by the *Matrix* franchise was fully embraced only some years later when Marvel launched its colossal Marvel Cinematic Universe (MCU) with *Iron Man* (dir. Jon Favreau, 2008). In the film's post-credit scene, Nick Fury (Samuel L. Jackson) tells Tony Stark (Robert Downey, Jr.), "Mr. Stark, you've become part of a bigger universe – you just don't know it yet." When Stark then appeared in the post-credit scene of *The Incredible Hulk* (dir. Louis Leterrier, 2008), released just six weeks after *Iron Man*, the implications of Fury's self-reflexive statement became clear: *Iron Man* was not a stand-alone movie, but rather part of a network of films. Of course, Marvel laid the groundwork for its cinematic universe over decades, as stories originally introduced in comics feed into the movies and ancillary materials. However, in the summer of 2015, Marvel Comics' editor-in-chief Axel Alonso made explicit the radical shift the Marvel Universe has experienced in the past decade, as he wondered: "What was your first encounter with the Marvel Universe? Did you pull a comic book off a spinner rack . . . or did you float out of a movie theater, your mind blown by what you saw on the Silver Screen[?]"[36] The rhetorical question signals that

---

[35] See Ina Rae Hark, "Franchise Fatigue? The Marginalization of the Television Series after *The Next Generation*," in Lincoln Geraghty, ed., *The Influence of "Star Trek" on Television, Film and Culture* (Jefferson, NC: McFarland, 2008), pp. 44–69.

[36] Axel Alonso quoted in Esteban Cepero, "Marvel Releases an Official Look at the All-New, All-Different Marvel Titles," *MoviePilot* (July 3, 2015), https://moviepilot.com/posts/3352116.

the primacy of the comic books is passé – the Marvel Universe now centers on the movies, with the comics (and other media) functioning as extensions to the cinematic universe. With combined global box office earnings of more than 12 billion dollars over the first sixteen movies and movies scheduled for release until 2028,[37] the MCU is most definitely here to stay and has provided a template for the DC Extended Universe, the Universal Monsters "Dark Universe," and arguably, Disney's approach to its post-2012 ownership of the *Star Wars* universe.[38]

Aside from the shared universe tactic to franchising, video games have become a super-tentacle of the SF franchise beast. Their growth, complexity, and potentials are still incalculable. With too many SF game titles on the market to map comprehensively, BioWare's *Mass Effect* franchise serves as a paradigmatic example, not least because it was also an ambitious attempt at transmedia storytelling. Launched in 2007, the first installment of *Mass Effect*, an action role-playing game, introduced players to a space opera that created an immersive universe by drawing on the most successful elements of the biggest SF franchises in film, on TV, and the expansive imagination of hard SF literature. Subsequently grown in two sequel games (2010, 2012), with each being expanded by way of downloadable content, the narrative world of *Mass Effect* was also dispersed via novels, a series of graphic novels as well as mini-comics, digital games on mobile platforms, and a largely unsuccessful animated film, *Mass Effect: Paragon Lost* (dir. Atsushi Takeuchi, 2012). The latest addition to the *Mass Effect* rhizome, *Mass Effect: Andromeda* (2017), has met with mostly lukewarm criticism, likely indicating another case of franchise fatigue. Still, big SF video game franchises such as *Mass Effect, BioShock*, and *Halo* are undoubtedly harbingers of the shape of things to come.

The recent surge in prequel/sequel production, and the reboot craze in particular, added significantly to the output of SF franchises. Indeed, we have effectively entered the age of the perpetual reboot. Perhaps best understood as the remediation, reconfiguration, and repackaging of already existing intellectual properties, SF reboots are a franchising strategy for catering to an insatiable mass market hungry for repetition (with difference). In that sense, reboots contribute to the dispersal of narratives, as they can be inserted at any stage to continue intellectual properties. While the lines of the different kinds of reboots are, of course, not clear-cut, two types of reboots

---

[37] See Martin Flanagan, Mike McKenny, and Andy Livingstone, *The Marvel Studios Phenomenon: Inside a Transmedia Universe* (New York: Bloomsbury, 2016), p. 36.

[38] On the MCU, see also Matt Yockey, ed., *Make Ours Marvel: Media Convergence and a Comics Universe* (Austin: University of Texas Press, 2017).

have recently proliferated. On the one hand, moderate reboots are character-ized by prequel/sequel/interquel structures, spruced-up aesthetics and pro-duction values, perhaps some retconning, and the full transmedia franchise treatment (i.e., excessive advertising, merchandising, and the eventification that coincides with the rollout of a reboot, such as in *Alien: Covenant, Jurassic World* and *Star Trek: Discovery* [CBS, 2017–]). More radical reboots are, on the other hand, perhaps best defined as parodies, following Linda Hutcheon's comprehensive understanding of the term. Such reboots go ahead and engage in extensive reimagining to the point that they change essential premises and world-building rules of the source texts, effectively becoming "repetition[s] with critical distance," thus marking "difference rather than similarity."[39] J. J. Abrams's reboot of *Star Trek* (2009), and Ronald D. Moore's re-imagined *Battlestar Galactica* serve as cases in point.

By the middle of the second decade of the twenty-first century, franchises became the default label to conceptualize, launch, market, consume, and talk about SF phenomena in general. By now at least in part transmedial in nature, every mass market SF title, whether original, reimagined, and/or rebooted, is launched as a prefabricated merchandising and licensing behe-moth. Rising like a Cthulhian monster, the SF franchise beast, insatiable as ever, seems to be fully awake now, spreading its tentacles far and wide.

[39] Linda Hutcheon, *A Theory of Parody: The Teachings of Twentieth-Century Art Forms* (London: Methuen, 1985), p. xii.

31

Science Fiction and Postmodernism in the 1980s and 1990s

PHILLIP E. WEGNER

Early in his essay "The Aesthetics of Singularity" (2015) Fredric Jameson points out that sometime in the early 1980s there emerged an increasingly nagging sense, a veritable structure of feeling, that something had changed in our world: "At that time, it was clear that there was a turn in all the arts away from the modernist tradition, which had become orthodoxy in the art world and the university, thereby forfeiting its innovative and indeed subversive power."[1] This something soon would be named *postmodernism*, a notion whose currency Jameson would play no small part in helping to establish. The dramatic ascendancy of the concept-term postmodernism stands as one of the most important intellectual developments of the decade.

The notion of postmodernism rapidly expanded beyond its original academic context. This fact is underscored in the April 1988 "Nice Issue" of *SPY* magazine – which also features a cover image of a tuxedo-clad, thumbs-up Donald Trump seated on a box that proclaims he is "A Heck of a Guy" – with its "Guide to Postmodern Everything: The Rise and Fall of a Great American Buzzword." The feature's author, Bruce Handy, notes that while, "The word *postmodern* used to mean something, in much that same way that *prehistory*, say, means things that happened in the epoch before history was invented, or that *canine* means 'of dogs'"; the term has become

> hard to pin down . . . It can mean anything that's sort of old but sort of new, a little bit ironic, or kind of self-conscious – like movies that steal bits from old movies, or photographs of the photographer. It's used in reference to creative endeavors that never had a modernist movement to begin with – art forms such as music videos, rap songs and panty hose design. It's culture-speak, shorthand for *Stuff That's Cool in 1988*. It's the postmodern (you know

---

[1] Fredric Jameson, "The Aesthetics of Singularity," *New Left Review* 92 (2015), p. 103.

what we mean) version of *groovy*, except that using it makes you sound smart.[2]

SF would very much come to be among the "cool stuff" to which the term postmodernism would be indiscriminately applied. However, such reductive uses obscure the fact that the relationship that developed in the 1980s and 1990s between SF and postmodernism was in fact far more complex and multiform, each helping transform the other in sometimes surprising ways. There have already been excellent surveys of the formal and thematic relationships between SF and postmodernism, and thus my claims in what follows will be historical in nature.[3] If the 1980s and 1990s were the time when SF emerged as a significant means of understanding the nature of the contemporary – a situation that increasingly seemed science fictional – it was also when SF itself became postmodern.

A number of the most influential theorists of postmodernism were conversant with SF and drew upon it regularly to exemplify the transformations they took as characteristic of an emerging situation. For example, in his landmark book, *Postmodernism, or, the Cultural Logic of Late Capitalism* (1991), Jameson himself illustrates some of his most important insights through discussions of fiction by Philip K. Dick and J. G. Ballard. Moreover, in the book's first endnote, Jameson refers to cyberpunk as "the supreme *literary* expression if not of postmodernism, then of late capitalism itself."[4] In another comment added to the book's opening chapter, Jameson points toward the recent appearance of "a new type of science fiction, called *cyberpunk*, which is fully as much an expression of transnational corporate realities as it is of global paranoia itself: William Gibson's representational innovations, indeed, mark his work as an exceptional literary realization within a predominantly visual or aural postmodern production."[5]

One of the figures to whom Jameson acknowledges "a great debt" for his formulation of postmodernism is the French social theorist Jean

---

[2] Bruce Handy, "Guide to Postmodern Everything: The Rise and Fall of a Great American Buzzword," *Spy* (April 1988), pp. 101–2. A year earlier, Dick Hebdige similarly notes, "when it becomes possible to describe all these things as 'postmodern' (or more simply, using a current abbreviation, as 'post' or 'very post') then it's clear that we are in the presence of a buzzword." See Dick Hebdige, "A Report on the Western Front: Postmodernism and the 'Politics' of Style," *Block* 12 (1986–7), pp. 4–26.

[3] See Veronica Hollinger, "Science Fiction and Postmodernism," in David Seed, ed., *A Companion to Science Fiction* (Oxford: Blackwell, 2005), pp. 232–47.

[4] Fredric Jameson, *Postmodernism, or, the Cultural Logic of Late Capitalism* (Durham, NC: Duke University Press, 1991), p. 419.

[5] Ibid., p. 38. Jameson did not develop a full reading of these innovations until more than two decades later, in an essay to which I will return below.

Baudrillard.[6] In his own deeply influential book, *Simulacra and Simulation* (1981) – a copy of which appears early in *The Matrix* (dir. Wachowski siblings, 1999), and from which Morpheus takes the phrase, "the desert of the real" – Baudrillard claims that Ballard's *Crash* (1973) – the first novel in his urban disaster trilogy, which also includes *Concrete Island* (1974) and *High Rise* (1975) – "is the first great novel of the universe of simulation, the one with which we will all now be concerned – a symbolic universe, but one which, through a sort of reversal of the mass-mediated substance (neon, concrete, car, erotic machinery), appears as if traversed by an intense force of initiation."[7]

Another major theorist of postmodernism who draws inspiration from SF is the American feminist scholar Donna Haraway.[8] In her landmark work, "A Cyborg Manifesto" – originally published in 1985 under the title, "Manifesto for Cyborgs: Science, Technology, and Socialist Feminism in the 1980s" – Haraway observes, "The cyborgs populating feminist science fiction make very problematic the statuses of man or woman, human, artefact, member of a race, individual entity, or body."[9] Haraway's examples include works by Octavia E. Butler, Samuel R. Delany, Anne McCaffrey, Vonda McIntyre, Joanna Russ, James Tiptree, Jr., and John Varley. Four years later, in her essay "The Biopolitics of Postmodern Bodies," Haraway expands upon her earlier observations in an extended discussion of Butler's fiction, in which she also argues that the alien Oankali of Butler's "Xenogenesis" trilogy (later retitled "Lilith's Brood"), "live in the postmodern geometries of vast webs and networks, in which the nodal points of individuals are still intensely important."[10]

In his 1992 volume *Constructing Postmodernism*, the literary scholar Brian McHale asserts that SF, "far from being marginal to contemporary 'advanced' or 'state-of-the-art' writing, may actually be *paradigmatic* of it." McHale further maintains:

> This is so in at least two respects. First, SF is openly and avowedly ontological in its orientation, i.e., like "mainstream" postmodernist writing it is self-

---

[6] Ibid., p. 399.

[7] Jean Baudrillard, *Simulacra and Simulation*, trans. Shelia Faria Glaser (Ann Arbor: The University of Michigan Press, 1994), p. 119.

[8] Baudrillard and Haraway are, along with Darko Suvin, the only scholars to be included in the collection, *Fifty Key Figures in Science Fiction*. See Mark Bould, Andrew M. Butler, Adam Roberts, and Sherryl Vint, *Fifty Key Figures in Science Fiction* (London: Routledge, 2010).

[9] Donna Haraway, "A Cyborg Manifesto," reprinted in *Simians, Cyborgs, and Women: The Reinvention of Nature* (London: Routledge, 1991), p. 178.

[10] Donna Haraway, "The Biopolitics of Postmodern Bodies," in *Simians, Cyborgs, and Women*, p. 228.

consciously "world-building" fiction, laying bare the process of fictional world-making itself. Secondly, SF constitutes a particularly clear and demonstrable example of an intertextual field, one in which models, materials, images, "ideas," etc. circulate openly from text to text, and are conspicuously cited, analyzed, combined, revised, and reconfigured. In this it differs from "mainstream" postmodernism only in the openness and visibility of the process. It is precisely this relative openness of intertextual circulation in SF that makes it so valuable as a heuristic model of literature in general, and postmodernist literature in particular.[11]

McHale's observations point toward another fundamental change then already well underway. To grasp the nature of such a change, however, we first need to reformulate postmodernism in Jameson's expanded sense: "not as a style but rather as a cultural dominant."[12] For McHale, as for many of the critics who focus on SF's postmodern turn, the term refers to such formal and stylistic features as heightened self-reflexivity, lowered affect, an ontological or spatial emphasis, and a willful poaching, quotation, or pastiche of earlier texts and genres. Such a formal approach then enables critics to find postmodern traits in texts from earlier historical situations, the work of Philip K. Dick, with its blurring of the boundaries between nature and culture and the artificial and the real, then becoming paradigmatic of the postmodern. While, as we shall see, such stylistic features are fundamental aspects of the postmodernism of 1980s and 1990s SF, Jameson helps bring into focus a more general mutation occurring in this moment in a cultural logic to which *all* cultural productions must be understood, in terms of both their contents and their forms, as responses, or as particular modes of symbolic action. In this sense, there can be no cultural texts produced in the postmodern context of the 1980s and 1990s – an "economic situation and the cultural 'structure of feeling'," which, Jameson maintains, "somehow crystallized in the great shock of the crises of 1973"[13] – that are not postmodern. Indeed, as we shall see below, even the decision, always still possible (residual and emergent practices surrounding and defining the dominant and effective center), to adhere to older formal protocols, such as those of modernism, becomes an instructive "symptom" of the situation to which it responds.

One significant symptom of these new realities lies in the dramatic transformation that takes place in the status of SF, within both an academic

---

[11] Brian McHale, *Constructing Postmodernism* (London: Routledge, 1992), p. 12.
[12] Jameson, *Postmodernism*, p. 4
[13] Jameson, *Postmodernism*, p. xx.

context and the culture as a whole. Jameson points out that a "fundamental feature" of postmodernism, in a variety of media and practices, is

> the effacement in them of the older (essentially high-modernist) frontier between high culture and so-called mass or commercial culture, and the emergence of new kinds of texts infused with the forms, categories, and contents of that very culture industry so passionately denounced by all the ideologues of the modern, from Leavis and the American New Criticism all the way to Adorno and the Frankfurt School. The postmodernisms have, in fact, been fascinated precisely by this whole "degraded" landscape of schlock and kitsch, of TV series and *Reader's Digest* culture, of advertising and motels, of the late show and the grade-B Hollywood film, of so-called paraliterature, with its airport paperback categories of the gothic and the romance, the popular biography, the murder mystery, and the science fiction or fantasy novel: materials they no longer simply "quote," as a Joyce or a Mahler might have done, but incorporate into their very substance.[14]

An early indication of the changing status of SF can be found in Larry McCaffery's 1988 essay, "The Fictions of the Present." McCaffery, an influential champion of cyberpunk, offers the following assessment of postmodern literary production more generally:

> Crucially, however, that "daily world" was frequently portrayed as an ambiguous construct in constant flux, a mass of information, words, and images whose "meaning" was deferred, whose very "reality" was suspect, unknowable. In short, this daily world was a shifting, fabulous entity greatly resembling the poststructuralist text, a world whose depiction required a definition of "realism" flexible to accommodate the claims to "realistic aims" made by writers as different as Robert Coover, Raymond Carver, Larry McMurtry, Joyce Carol Oates, Walter Abish, Toni Morrison, William Gibson, Max Apple, and Leslie Silko.[15]

Like all such lists, McCaffery's is an exercise in canon formation, a performative rather than a constative utterance aimed at convincing his readers on what they should spend their time. Moreover, while McHale is correct in his own engagement with McCaffery's essay to point out that "the myth of the collapse of hierarchical distinctions in postmodern culture is just that, a myth, and the institutions for the production, distribution, and consumption of high culture continue to be distinct from those for popular culture,"[16] what he misrecognizes, or what he is perhaps not yet in

---

[14] Jameson, *Postmodernism*, pp. 2–3.
[15] Larry McCaffery, "The Fictions of the Present," in Emory Elliot, ed., *Columbia Literary History of the United States* (New York: Columbia University Press, 1988), p. 1164.
[16] McHale, *Constructing Postmodernism*, p. 226

a position in the early 1990s to recognize, is that McCaffery's inclusion of Gibson among some of the most celebrated writers of the latter part of the twentieth century helps reorganize those very institutions. Already underway by the late 1980s is the crack up of what Mark McGurl more recently identifies as the "Program Era" in American literature, the moment of the hegemony of a university creative writing program style, which privileges Jamesian psychological realism and precludes "the shoddy inauthenticity of genre fiction of all kinds,"[17] including SF, as hallmarks of "good" or "serious" (high) literature. This opens up in the first decades of the twenty-first century, the possibility on the part of some of the most interesting and influential writers – Margaret Atwood, Junot Díaz, Louise Erdrich, Kazuo Ishiguro, Jonathan Lethem, Cormac McCarthy, David Mitchell, Mikael Niemi, Colson Whitehead, and Charles Yu, among others – to produce works identified as SF. Not surprisingly too, the moment in which McCaffery is writing also witnesses a new seriousness within the academic context of both the study of SF, and of SF studies as an institutional and disciplinary locus.

If in the 1980s and 1990s, SF becomes foundational for the theorization of postmodernism, such theorization also shapes how we understand changes then underway in the generic practice itself. David Pringle bookends his still valuable, *Science Fiction: The 100 Best Novels* (1985), with George Orwell's *Nineteen Eighty-Four* (1949) and William Gibson's *Neuromancer* (1984).[18] While Pringle's selection of *Neuromancer* as his last novel is most immediately a consequence of the date of his book's release, it has the additional benefit of framing a significant historical period within the genre's history – a period I identify in *Shockwaves of Possibility* as SF's second "modernist" moment, emerging after the Second World War in the work of Leigh Brackett, Ray Bradbury, Alfred Bester, Dick, and others, and coming to full fruition in the 1960s New Wave generation of writers, including Ballard, John Brunner, Samuel R. Delany, Thomas Disch, Harlan Ellison, Ursula K. Le Guin, Michael Moorcock, Joanna Russ, Norman Spinrad, and James Tiptree Jr. (Alice Bradley Sheldon).[19] Whatever its achievements, as well as its very real limits, the energies of this second modernist moment were largely spent by the end of the 1970s, and the conservative turn of the 1980s resulted in an

---

[17] Mark McGurl, *The Program Era: Postwar Fiction and the Rise of Creative Writing* (Cambridge, MA: Harvard University Press, 1990), p. 103.

[18] David Pringle, *Science Fiction: The 100 Best Novels: An English-Language Selection, 1949–1984* (London: Xanadu, 1985).

[19] Phillip E. Wegner, *Shockwaves of Possibility: Essays on Science Fiction, Globalization, and Utopia* (Oxford: Peter Lang, 2014), p. 26.

environment less hospitable to the formal experimentation and dangerous visions of science fictional modernism.

The early 1980s also witnessed the rise of cyberpunk.[20] Cyberpunk needs to be understood as postmodern in at least three different senses: first, broadly, as a specific response to the historical situation (late capitalism) from which it emerges, but also, second, within the history of the genre, in terms of its rejection of the technocratic optimism of pre-Second World War US SF and its ambivalence concerning the modernist radicalisms of the New Wave. In these aspects, the low-affect, apolitical "mirrorshades" cool of cyberpunk proved to be an ideal fit for the new climate of the Thatcher–Reagan era. Third, in its celebration and scintillating original figurations of information technologies and a nascent phase of globalization and its poaching from a variety of genres and styles, cyberpunk quickly came to be understood, as I have suggested above, as exemplary of postmodern fiction more generally.[21] Or, as McHale quipped, "if cyberpunk did not exist, postmodernist critics like myself would have had to invent it."[22]

No single text better exemplifies the complex intertwining of postmodernism and SF than the novel understood to found cyberpunk: Gibson's 1984 debut, *Neuromancer*, first published in the New Ace Science Fiction Specials series edited by Terry Carr. Indeed, Veronica Hollinger claims that "Science fiction 'officially' became postmodern in 1984, with the publication of William Gibson's now-classic Cyberpunk novel."[23] The year 1984 proved to be an extraordinary one more generally for cultural production, representing to postmodernism what 1922 is to an earlier modernism. First appearing that year were such key postmodern fictions as Kathy Acker's *Blood and Guts in High School*, Martin Amis's *Money*, Julian Barnes's *Flaubert's Parrot*, Don DeLillo's *White Noise*, and Milan Kundera's *The Unbearable Lightness of Being*; debut novels by Iain Banks (*The Wasp Factory*), Tom Clancy (*The Hunt for Red October*), Louise Erdrich (*Love Medicine*), and Jay McInerney (*Bright Lights, Big City*); film and video productions such as James Cameron's *The Terminator*, the Coen brothers' directorial debut, *Blood Simple*, Brian De Palma's *Body Double*, Jim Jarmusch's *Stranger Than Paradise*, Nam June Paik's *Good Morning, Mr. Orwell*, Michael Radford's *Nineteen Eighty-Four*, John Sayles' *The Brother from Another Planet*, Ridley Scott's "1984" Apple Macintosh commercial, and Wim Wender's *Paris,*

---

[20] On cyberpunk generally, see also Chapter 32 in this volume.
[21] Wegner, *Shockwaves*, p. 36.
[22] McHale, *Constructing Postmodernism*, p. 13.
[23] Hollinger, "Science Fiction and Postmodernism," p. 236.

Texas; and landmark theoretical statements including Jameson's first major essays on postmodernism, the second and third volumes of Michel Foucault's *Histoire de la sexualité*, and the English translation of Jean-François Lyotard's *The Postmodern Condition*. Also published that year was another monumental work of SF, *Stars in My Pocket Like Grains of Sand*, by Samuel R. Delany, one of the most important writers to come to prominence in the 1960s. If *Neuromancer* marks the full emergence of postmodernism in SF, *Stars in My Pocket* stands as a last monument to the modernist New Wave. The coincidence of the publication in 1984 of these two works thus offers an extraordinary opportunity not only to measure the distance between modernist and postmodern SF, but further to assess the cultural situation to which they both invariably respond.

One of the curious aspects of McCaffrey's placement of *Neuromancer* among other postmodern literary landmarks lies in his characterization of Gibson's cyberpunk SF as "realism." A few years later, Jameson similarly claims, "Under those circumstances, where a formerly futurological SF (such as so-called cyberpunk today) turns into mere 'realism' and an outright representation of the present, the possibility Dick offered us – an experience of our present as past and as history – is slowly excluded."[24] What this means is spelled out in Jameson's 2015 essay, "A Global Neuromancer." Jameson claims that the formal innovations of Gibson's novel are two-fold. On the one hand, the novel's most well-known figuration, that of cyberspace, is not a representation of an emerging digital information space, but rather "an abstraction to the second degree," a narrative presentation of an "unrepresentable totality, which until now only SF has uniquely possessed the representational means to designate ... that of finance capital itself, as it constitutes one of the most original dimensions of late capitalism (or of globalization or of postmodernity, depending on the focus you wish to bring to it)."[25] Jameson further argues:

> that in the face of the impasses of modernism, which proved unable to handle the new incommensurabilities of that greatly enlarged and as it were post-anthropomorphic totality which is late or third-stage capitalism, science fiction, and in particular this historically inventive novel of Gibson, offered a new and post-realistic but also post-modernistic way of giving us a picture and a sense of our individual relationships to realities that transcend our

[24] Jameson, *Postmodernism*, p. 286.
[25] Fredric Jameson, "A Global Neuromancer," in *The Ancients and the Postmoderns: On the Historicity of Forms* (New York: Verso, 2015), pp. 229–30.

phenomenological mapping systems and our cognitive abilities to think them.[26]

The novel's other and less appreciated innovation is located in its figure of "simstim," the technologically mediated capacity to project one's consciousness into another body. Simstim serves as a symptom of bodily experience in postmodernity, "another testimony to our unreal life in Guy Debord's society of the spectacle, our life among what Jean Baudrillard calls simulations (a term significantly preserved in the very term simstim). Here, then, we have a second and different type of abstraction from the real; and indeed what is essential is to see that in Gibson these two abstractions are dialectically related."[27] Jameson then concludes,

> Global versus local? This is indeed the form expressed by the twin presence and opposition between the exploration of cyberspace and the utilization of simstim; but it projects this rather glib contemporary formulation as what it is, namely a contradiction rather than a simple alternation or even a choice of perspectives . . . The two poles are two dialectically linked dimensions which structure our daily lives in this society, and confirm the paradoxical proposition that we are both too abstract and too concrete all at once.[28]

Whatever its achievements, *Neuromancer* reaches its limits in an inability to mediate between the global and local. In the concluding section of his 1984 essay, Jameson posits the notion of "cognitive mapping" as a placeholder for an aesthetic practice to come that will produce just such mediations, "a pedagogical political culture which seeks to endow the individual subject with some new heightened sense of its place in the global system."[29] Any such aesthetic will surely be, Jameson maintains, collective in nature.

It is in its treatment of the collective dimensions of contemporary life that Gibson's vision collapses back into postmodern ideological fantasy (an imaginary resolution to a real contradiction). For example, Jameson suggests that the novel's "heist plot" – a plan to break into the orbiting palazzo of the corrupt Tessier-Ashpool clan, and free the Artificial Intelligence they control – offers "a distorted expression of the utopian impulse insofar as it realizes a fantasy of non-alienated collective work."[30] *Neuromancer* posits such a fantasy in opposition to the forms of work life it could still imagine in 1984 to be dominant: "The crowd, he saw, was mostly Japanese. Not really

---

[26] Jameson, "Global," p. 234.
[27] Ibid., p. 235.
[28] Ibid., p. 237.
[29] Jameson, *Postmodernism*, p. 54.
[30] Jameson, "Global," p. 225.

a Night City crowd. Techs down from the arcologies. He supposed that meant the arena had the approval of some corporate recreational committee. He wondered briefly what it would be like, working all your life for one zaibatsu. Company housing, company hymn, company funeral."[31] Case's work is decidedly without the deadening day-to-day monotony experienced by those employed in bureaucratic corporations; however, it is also without the securities such employment makes available – life-time job guarantees, housing, high wages, recreation time, and health care. Case's labor is fully contingent and flexible – freelance and temporary. The price for Case of failure in such an economy is also made clear early on: "Night City was like a deranged experiment in Social Darwinism ... Biz here was a constant subliminal hum, and death the accepted punishment for laziness, careless-ness, lack of grace, the failure to heed the demands of an intricate protocol."[32] The postmodern utopia of *Neuromancer* thus ultimately resolves into a figure for what the economist Michel Aglietta names post-Fordism, and William Davies has more recently characterized as "combative neoliberalism."[33]

The novel's related fantasies of the collective "meat" spaces of the con-temporary city are evident in this description of Case's one-time home of "BAMA, the Sprawl, the Boston-Atlanta Metropolitan Axis"[34]:

> The landscape of the northern Sprawl woke confused memories of child-hood for Case, dead grass tufting the cracks in a canted slab of freeway concrete.
>
> The train began to decelerate ten kilometers from the airport. Case watched the sun rise on the landscape of childhood, on broken slag and the rusting shells of refineries.[35]

Andrew Ross notes that a nascent punk culture offered cyberpunk,

> an image-repertoire of urban culture in postindustrial decay for white sub-urban youths whose lives and environs were quite removed from daily contact with the Darwinist street sensibility of "de-evolved" city life. It is perhaps no coincidence that none of the major cyberpunk writers were city-bred, although their work feeds off the phantasmatic street diet of Hobbesian lawlessness and the aesthetic of detritus that is assumed to pervade the

---

[31] William Gibson, *Neuromancer* (New York: Ace, 1984), p. 37.

[32] Ibid., p. 7

[33] William Davis, "The New Neoliberalism," *New Left Review* 101 (2016), p. 124. For a valuable linking of postmodernism and post-Fordism, see David Harvey, *The Condition of Postmodernity: An Enquiry into the Origins of Cultural Change* (Oxford: Basil Blackwell, 1989).

[34] Gibson, *Neuromancer*, p. 43.

[35] Gibson, *Neuromancer*, p. 85.

hollowed-out core of the great metropolitan centers. This urban fantasy, however countercultural its claims and potential effects, shared the dominant, white middle-class conception of inner-city life. In this respect, the suburban romance of punk, and, subsequently, cyberpunk, fashioned a culture of alienation out of their parents' worst fears about life on the mean streets.[36]

Moreover, in what could very well serve as a description of the setting of *Neuromancer*'s realist contemporary, McInerney's *Bright Lights, Big City*, Ross points out that "All through the 1980s, this romance ran parallel with the rapid growth of gentrified Yuppie culture in the 'abandoned' zones of the inner cities, where the transient thrills of street culture served up an added exotic flavor for the palates of these pioneers in their newly colonized spaces."[37]

Delany, on the other hand, is very much "city-bred," and, as we might anticipate, the urban and collective imaginaries at work in *Stars in My Pocket* are radically different from those found in *Neuromancer*. This is especially the case in the novel's great utopian vision of southern Velm, the home of the protagonist, Marq Dyeth. Velm is a world co-inhabited by two radically different species, the humans to which Marq belongs biologically, and the three-sexed Evelmi. The intermingling of these communities allows the development of a wild proliferation of identities far beyond the binaries of male and female and straight and gay, as well as extraordinary queer kinships. Of his home and family, Marq observes:

> Perhaps the greatest generosity of my universe is that in so much it's congruent with the worlds of others, which I suppose is finally just one with the generosity of my evelm parents, who thought my unique position among humans quite charming and were proud of it, and my human parents, who from time to time worried if, as distinct from more usually sexually oriented males, gay or straight, I might not encounter some social difficulty, say, of the same sort as I might have had in some societies had I been a nail-biter myself. But both spoke, both agreed on who I was, that I was a ripple that shored their stream, so that their universe, with all its idiosyncratic wonder, unique to my eyes, has still, always, seemed a part of mine.[38]

This combination of difference and congruity makes the novel's utopia one of unexpected encounters – encounters enabled by the very texture of the urban space itself:

---

[36] Andrew Ross, *Strange Weather: Culture, Science and Technology in the Age of Limits* (New York: Verso, 1991), p. 146.

[37] Ibid.

[38] Samuel R. Delany, *Stars in My Pocket Like Grains of Sand* (Middletown, CT: Wesleyan University Press, 2004), pp. 342–3.

Tingling heels drying, we walked down the resilient woven flooring of the shadowy tunnel. Here and there along the arched ceiling or the curved wall, a meter-wide vent, or sometimes a three-meter-wide vent, let in light.

...

The hollow-eyed face looked down. "This is where you come for sex?"

"And sculpture." I nodded for him to follow me between two high vegetal shapes of plastic with a ring of taste plates at licking level. "At least, for the day-to-day variety when you want to spend less than twenty minutes at it on your way somewhere else."[39]

This passage and what follows makes evident that the novel's urban spaces stand as a transfigured image of the urban, and especially queer, communities Delany inhabited in the New York City of the 1960s and 1970s. Delany later reflects that such spaces encouraged "interclass contact and communication conducted in a mode of good will."[40]

However, the project inaugurated in *Stars in My Pocket* remains incomplete: originally intended as the first book of a two-volume narrative, it turned out to be Delany's last major work of SF. Over the years, a range of possible answers have been suggested as to why Delany did not complete the work: the explosive onset of the AIDS crisis, the end of his eight-year-long relationship with Frank Romeo, and the general neoliberal remapping of the Manhattan cityscape – the last documented in Delany's extraordinary nonfiction book, *Times Square Red, Times Square Blue* (1999). However, there may be something in the very nature of what Delany undertakes here that makes its completion in the new situation of postmodernism impossible.

Throughout the novel, Delany stresses the precariousness of Velm's community. First, it is threatened on the intergalactic plane by the rising tide of the fundamentalist political alliance known as the Family. Former allies of the Dyeths violently denounce, soon after allying themselves with the Family, the collective's queer kinships: "A disease is not innocent, and this equation of unnatural crime with innocence is, in itself, a disease, which can only be cured by the most primitive means: quarantine, fire, prayer."[41] In this way, the Family figures the deeply homophobic Moral Majority founded by Jerry Falwell only five years before the novel's publication and coming to increasing prominence during the Reagan presidency. At the same time, Delany raises the possibility that Velm itself may be on the verge of "Cultural

---

[39] Ibid., p. 225.

[40] Samuel R. Delany; *Times Square Red, Times Square Blue* (New York: New York University Press, 1999), p. 111.

[41] Ibid., p. 303.

Fugue," a situation where "socioeconomic pressures ... reach a point of technological recomplication and perturbation where the population completely destroys all life across the planetary surface."[42] Finally, there is growing concern on Velm itself over the "tragedy of the north," in which the relationships between humans and Evelmi increasingly degenerate into violence.[43]

In order to complete his second volume, Delany would have had to resolve these various crises. Such challenges, considered in spatial terms, are fundamentally ones of scaling: how to translate the successes of the local urban community figured in Velm onto the wider levels of the nation, the planet, and the intergalactic federation. Jameson points out in the concluding section of *Postmodernism* that similar issues in the 1960s confront a variety of radical political movements: "Since the crisis of socialist internationalism, and the enormous strategic and tactical difficulties of coordinating local and grassroots of neighborhood political actions with national or international ones, such urgent political dilemmas are all immediately functions of the enormously complex new international space in question."[44] Unable to effect a movement across scales, these projects lose their momentum and ultimately collapse. Similarly, and not unlike *Neuromancer*, finding it impossible to mediate between its "local" collective space and its more "global" contexts, Delany's novel arrives at an impasse. As a result, the dominant tone in *Stars in My Pocket* comes to be a bittersweet, nostalgic one – a paean to the unrealized possibilities of the 1960s.

The common situation shared by *Stars in My Pocket* and *Neuromancer* is thus in part that of the closure in the mid-1980s of the dynamic political and cultural sequence known as the "sixties" – a fact that another event in 1984, Reagan's re-election, would forcefully bring home. The response in each case is, of course, radically different – an imagining in Gibson's text of strategies for surviving, negotiating, and even flourishing in an emergent present, and a re-affirmation in Delany's unfinished narrative of his fidelity to missed opportunities. However, neither strategy – acquiescence or intransigency – proves in the longer run to be satisfactory.

The relationship I have been tracing out between Gibson's and Delany's novels, and the way they become emblematic of the situation in which SF finds itself in the 1980s, can be represented as shown in Figure 31.1.

---

[42] Ibid., p. 66.
[43] Ibid., p. 209.
[44] Jameson, *Postmodernism*, p. 413.

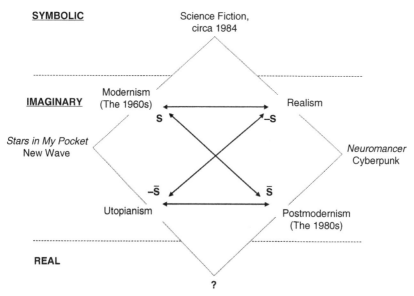

31.1 A Greimas square mapping science fiction's relationship to modernism, realism, utopianism, and postmodernism.

Such a presentation has the value of not only highlighting the deadlock characteristic of postmodernism, but also the imperative, not unlike Jameson's call for an aesthetics of cognitive mapping, to develop narrative strategies beyond both the New Wave and cyberpunk, or beyond modernism and postmodernism.[45] The formulation of post-cyberpunk or post-postmodern narrative practices was undertaken in many of the most significant works of SF to appear in subsequent decades.[46] These included what Marlene Barr names the late 1980s and early 1990s "feminist fabulations" of such writers as Octavia E. Butler (especially *Parable of the Sower* [1993]), Doris Lessing, Pamela Sargent, and Joan Slonczewski; and the novels Tom Moylan identifies as inaugurating the "critical dystopia" tradition: Kim Stanley Robinson's *The Gold Coast* (1988) and Marge Piercy's *He, She and It* (1991).[47]

However, a prefiguration of such a new direction is offered in another debut novel to appear in 1984, one that was also published, albeit to

[45] For a discussion of how this re-imagined semiotic square operates, see Phillip E. Wegner, *Periodizing Jameson: Dialectics, the University, and the Desire for Narrative* (Chicago: Northwestern University Press, 2014).

[46] Wegner, *Shockwaves*, pp. 37–42.

[47] See Marlene S. Barr, *Feminist Fabulation: Space/Postmodern Science Fiction* (Iowa City: University of Iowa Press, 1992); Tom Moylan, *Scraps of the Untainted Sky: Science Fiction, Utopia, Dystopia* (Boulder, CO: Westview, 2001).

much less fanfare, in Carr's New Ace Science Fiction Specials series: Robinson's *The Wild Shore*. *The Wild Shore* – the first of Robinson's "Californias trilogy," which also includes *The Gold Coast* and *Pacific Edge* (1990) – is set in southern California, sixty years after a surprise nuclear attack on the United States has reduced the nation to a scattering of isolated agricultural communities. The novel touches on only two such communities, those occupying the remains of the Onofre Valley and San Diego, as well as their inhabitants' fraught contacts with the Japanese military who patrol the coast.

Throughout the trilogy, Robinson retraces the historical development of SF. He begins with a version of one of the dominant postwar sub-genres, the nuclear post-apocalypse – a subgenre also regularly mined by another California-based writer and one of the great precursors to the New Wave, Philip K. Dick. (Dick's work is the topic of Robinson's doctoral dissertation, also first published in a revised form in 1984.) Robinson then moves backward with *The Gold Coast* to the late nineteenth-century precursor to SF – formed through the fusion of the literary utopia and naturalism – the dystopia.[48] Finally, Robinson brings his trilogy to its conclusion with a contemporary version of the now five-century-old practice of the narrative utopia. Recapitulating the history of SF enables Robinson to clear a space for its reinvention in forms adequate to emerging global realities – exactly the work he undertakes in his masterpiece of the 1990s, the trilogy of *Red Mars* (1993), *Green Mars* (1994), and *Blue Mars* (1996).

And yet, to tell the story in this way ignores the ways *The Wild Shore* is aware of the narrative challenges that must be surmounted. Most significantly, the novel highlights the limits imposed by the older cognitive mappings of the nation-state, especially as these are championed by an ascendant neo-conservatism (in 1984 as much as today):

> "You tell them they can make this country what it used to be. They can help. But we all have to work together. The day will come. Another Pax Americana, cars and airplanes, rockets to the moon, telephones. A unified country." Suddenly, without anger or whispery passion, he said, "You go back up there and tell your valley that they join the resistance or they oppose it."[49]

---

[48] For an exploration of the genetic connection between naturalism and dystopia, see Phillip E. Wegner, *Life Between Two Deaths, 1989–2001: US Culture in the Long Nineties* (Durham, NC: Duke University Press, 2009), pp. 117–24.
[49] Kim Stanley Robinson, *The Wild Shore* (New York: Ace, 1984), p. 106.

These limits are made even more evident through the device of the book-within-the-book, a travel narrative entitled, *An American Around the World: Being an Account of a Circumnavigation of the Globe in the Years 2030 to 2039:*[50]

> I asked him if he could tell me why the weather had become so much colder on the California coast since the war.
>
> . . .
>
> "It's a complicated question. It's generally agreed that the war did alter the world's weather, but how it effected the change is still debated. It's estimated that three thousand neutron bombs exploded on the continental United States that day in 1984, not too much long term radiation was released, luckily for you, but a lot of turbulence was generated in the stratosphere – the highest levels of air – and apparently the jet stream altered its course for good.
>
> . . .
>
> "California has been strongly affected, no doubt about it – like moving fifteen degrees of latitude north – but a few other parts of the world have been just as strongly affected, or even more so. Lots of rain in northern Chile – and my, is that washing all the sand off the Andes into the sea. Tropical heat in Europe during the summer, drought during the monsoon – oh, I could go on and on. It has caused more human misery than you can imagine."[51]

In this passage, Robinson offers a full-blown announcement of what subsequently will emerge as a major figure for shared global realities and the imperative to think beyond the nation on new planetary scales: an "anthropocence" produced by a human-made, terraforming climate change.

In *The Wild Shore*, we are presented less with the solutions than the articulation of the fundamental problems that will be tackled not only in Robinson's later work, but in other post-cyberpunk SF: the narrative mapping of the relationships between the individual body, the local, and the global; and the forging of the tools to "think globally" so we might "begin to grasp our positioning as individual and collective subjects and regain a capacity to act and struggle which is at present neutralized by our spatial as well as our social confusion."[52] That *The Wild Shore* is intended as no more than the beginning of such a project is indicated by its closing lines: "This damp last page is nearly full. And my hand is getting cold – its getting so stiff I can't make the letters, these words are all big and scrawling, taking up the last of the space, thank God. Oh be done with

[50] Ibid., pp. 118–19.
[51] Ibid., pp. 202–4.
[52] Jameson, *Postmodernism*, p. 92.

it. There's an owl, flitting over the river. I'll stay right here and fill another book."[53]

The fact that Robinson, along with many others, decided to do likewise, to stay here and fill another book, accounts for the continued relevance of post-cyberpunk SF in the post-postmodern or global situation we all now inhabit. A brief sampling of writers who contributed in the late 1980s and 1990s to a burgeoning environmental and global turn in SF and a revitalization of the utopian energies of the earlier New Wave would include, in addition to those mentioned above, the US writers Sheri Tepper and Terry Bisson; the great Scottish authors, Iain M. Banks, whose monumental Culture series launched with *Consider Phlebas* (1987), and Ken MacLeod, whose debut novel, *The Star Fraction* (1995), and the opening of his "Fall Revolution" quartet (1995–9), is described by Robinson as "revolutionary science fiction";[54] and members of booms in Canada – Margaret Atwood, Cory Doctorow, Nalo Hopkinson, Robert J. Sawyer, Karl Schroeder, Peter Watts, and Robert Charles Wilson – and Great Britain – Neil Gaiman, Peter Hamilton, Gwyneth Jones, Ian McDonald, China Miéville, Allan Moore, Philip Pullman, Alastair Reynolds, Geoff Ryman, and Charles Stross. All of this work helps clear the space for the emergence in the new millennium for what Eric D. Smith theorizes as "postcolonial science fiction," perhaps the most effective "literary and cultural expression of globalization."[55]

---

[53] Robinson, *The Wild Shore*, p. 371.
[54] Ken MacLeod, *The Star Fraction* (New York: Tor, 2001), endorsement.
[55] Eric D. Smith, *Globalization, Utopia, and Postcolonial Science Fiction* (New York: Palgrave Macmillan, 2012), p. 6.

32

Cyberpunk and Post-Cyberpunk

GRAHAM J. MURPHY

Cyberpunk emerged in the early to mid-1980s initially to describe a cadre of authors whose thematic interests and narrative motifs were strikingly similar. The term originated with Bruce Bethke's short story "Cyberpunk" (1983) and was bestowed by editor Gardner Dozois onto the early fictions of William Gibson, Bruce Sterling, Rudy Rucker, John Shirley, and Lewis Shiner, although later entrants into the cyberpunk pantheon soon appeared. Cyberpunk marries the *cyber-* of cybernetics with the countercultural *punk* attitude of the 1970s, and this attitude is evident in the at-times tempestuous attitude cyberpunks had towards earlier SF. For example, Bruce Sterling edited the *Cheap Truth* fanzine in the earliest days of the Movement, as cyberpunk was initially known, and in his nom de plume "Vincent Omniaveritas" he sketched out cyberpunk's countercultural attitude: "Extrapolations, that once held some intellectual validity, have now become distorted folk tales, passed down through generations. SF's vision of the future has become a *Punch and Judy* show, ritualized, predictable, and only fit for children."[1] Or, "Sue Denim," aka Lewis Shiner, pitted the young upstarts against the establishment in his speculations on the 1985 Nebula Awards: "The voices of repression range from the senile babblings of Robert Heinlein to the California vapidity of Larry Niven to the moist-eyed urgency of Kim Stanley Robinson; arrayed against them are William Gibson, Lewis Shiner, and Jack Dann . . . For every Heinlein that smites a Gibson, thousands more will rise in his place. The SF revolution is crying out for literacy, imagination, and humanity; it needs only a victory in the Nebulas to shatter the giant's terracotta feet. Up against the wall, Heinlein!"[2]

---

[1] Bruce Sterling (as Vincent Omniaveritas), "Cheap Truth Magazine, Issue #9," *Totse.com*, totseans.com/totse/en/ego/on_line_zines/cheap09.html.

[2] Lewis Shiner (as Sue Denim). "*Cheap Truth* Magazine, Issue #10." *Totse.com*, totseans.com/totse/en/ego/on_line_zines/cheap10.html (last accessed May 25, 2018).

It was this punk attitude that energized cyberpunk; after all, cyberpunk's literary motifs certainly didn't originate in the eighties. Cyberpunk's genetic imprint can be found in such diverse offerings as Samuel Delany's *Nova* (1968), Philip K. Dick's *Do Androids Dream of Electric Sheep?* (1968), Joanna Russ's "When It Changed" (1972) and *The Female Man* (1975), Thomas Pynchon's *Gravity's Rainbow* (1973), James Tiptree, Jr.'s "The Girl Who Was Plugged In" (1973), John Brunner's *The Shockwave Rider* (1975), John Varley's "Overdrawn at the Memory Bank" (1976), among others. Nevertheless, stories such as Gibson's "The Gernsback Continuum" (1981) embody the revolutionary punk swagger. The story follows an American photojournalist hired to photograph the architectural remnants of a never-realized future, a "1980s that never happened. An architecture of broken dreams."[3] When the photographer begins seeing visions of an alternate America, he goes to Merv Kihn, who explains he is witnessing "semiotic phantoms, bits of deep cultural imagery that have split off and taken on a life of their own."[4] One such vision is of a white, blond, and likely blue-eyed American family standing in front of a futuristic city common to SF of earlier decades, prompting the narrator to recall, "It had all the sinister fruitiness of Hitler Youth propaganda."[5] In one deft sentence, Gibson's story efficiently dismisses Golden Age visions of the future as akin to Hitler Youth propaganda, and it is these extrapolations that were vociferously rejected by cyberpunk.

Gibson gave the fledgling movement its gravitational locus and Sterling sets the scene in the documentary *No Maps for These Territories* (dir. Mark Neale, 2000): "When Lewis Shiner and I . . . were first reading Gibson's work in manuscript, we looked at it and said 'Look, this is breakthrough material. This guy is really doing something different. Like we gotta put down our preconceptions and pick up on this guy from Vancouver. It's the way forward.' A hole had opened up in consensus reality and we just saw daylight." Gibson's first novel, *Neuromancer* (1984), begins a trilogy that continues with *Count Zero* (1986), and *Mona Lisa Overdrive* (1988). The story follows Henry Dorsett Case, a crippled computer hacker who is recruited by the cyborg assassin Molly Millions, whom we've earlier encountered in "Johnny Mnemonic" (1981). The duo teams with the psychologically damaged Armitage and sociopathic Peter Riviera to pull off a series of heists for a mysterious employer. *Neuromancer* is in part modeled upon the hard-

---

[3] William Gibson, "The Gernsback Continuum," *Burning Chrome* (New York: Ace, 1987), p. 25.
[4] Ibid., pp. 29–30.
[5] Ibid., p. 33.

boiled detective fictions of Dashiell Hammett and Raymond Chandler, so Gibson's near-future is not only awash with diverse, often illicit, technologies but also told from the street-level of hustlers, criminals, and opportunists, a familiar narrative *topos* that Gibson expertly crafted in such stories as "Johnny Mnemonic," "Burning Chrome" (1982),[6] "New Rose Hotel" (1984), and "The Winter Market" (1985). In the end, "Sue Denim" witnessed the Nebula victory he longed for in his *Cheap Truth* editorial: *Neuromancer* won the 1985 Nebula Award for Best Novel, as it did the 1985 Hugo Award and the 1984 Philip K. Dick Award, the first (and only) time one book has won all three awards.

A significant problem for early cyberpunk, however, was Gibson's success: the popularity of his narrative vision eclipsed the diversity of cyberpunk's earliest practitioners. For example, John Shirley's *City Come A-Walkin'* (1980), published four years earlier, is tonally similar to *Neuromancer*, but his *Song Called Youth* series – *Eclipse* (1985), *Eclipse Penumbra* (1988), and *Eclipse Corona* (1990) – is more socio-politically engaged in its exploration of neo-fascism in the techno-digital age. Lewis Shiner's *Frontera* (1984) involves colonizing Mars while *Deserted Cities of the Heart* (1988) features mushroom-induced psychedelic visions that involve time travel to an ancient Mayan age. Rudy Rucker's *Ware* tetralogy – *Software* (1982), *Wetware* (1988), *Freeware* (1997), and *Realware* (2000) – follows the evolutionary paths of different kinds of robots ('boppers'), robot–human hybrids ('meatbops'), intelligent symbiotes ('moldies'), and so forth. Bruce Sterling's *The Artificial Kid* (1980) is set on the distant planet of Reverie where Arti, the novel's protagonist, sells videos of himself engaged in bloodsport combat with his fellow fighters, all for the amusement of the socio-economically privileged classes. On the other hand, his *Schismatrix* series – "Swarm" (1982), "Spider Rose" (1982), "Cicada Queen" (1983), "Sunken Gardens" (1984), "Twenty Evocations" (1984), and *Schismatrix* (1985) – takes place over the span of nearly 200 years and is set in the sprawling Shaper/Mechanist universe, a far-future posthuman era defined by ongoing conflict between the Shapers, who modify their bodies chiefly through genetic modifications, and the Mechanists, adherents to cybernetic augmentations. Finally, his *Islands in the Net* (1988) addresses the difficulties of living off the grid and is set in locales largely ignored in cyberpunk, including Grenada, Singapore, and the African continent.[7]

---

[6] "Burning Chrome" coined the term "cyberspace," which would quickly enter the English lexicon, although *Neuromancer* certainly popularized it.

[7] For further detail, see Mark Bould, "Afrocyberpunk Cinema: The Postcolony Finds its own Use for Things," in Graham J. Murphy and Lars Schmeink, eds., *Cyberpunk and Visual Culture* (New York: Routledge, 2018), pp. 213–34.

In spite of the initial popularity, there was also an increasing sense that for all its revolutionary bluster,[8] cyberpunk amounted to nothing more than a clever marketing campaign. After all, as famed SF editor David Hartwell once remarked in conversation, Sterling brought an idea for a cyberpunk anthology to Hartwell, who promptly told Sterling he didn't have enough authors to assemble a collection. Sterling then went on a recruitment campaign to complete the project, and the release of *Mirrorshades: The Cyberpunk Anthology* (1986) effectively completed the rebranding of the Movement into the easily marketable *cyberpunk*. It was therefore always a retail category and cyberpunk impersonators and knock-offs quickly cashed in, although such novels as K. W. Jeter's *The Glass Hammer* (1985), Walter Jon Williams's *Hardwired* (1986), Robert Charles Wilson's *Memory Wire* (1987), and *Mirrorshades* alumnus Tom Maddox's *Halo* (1991) were better than most. In any event, Shiner categorically dismissed later cyberpunk as "sci-fiberpunk" in his *New York Times* editorial "Confessions of an Ex-Cyberpunk" (1991): "Other writers had turned the form into formula: implant wetware (biological computer chips), government by multinational corporations, street-wise, leather-jacketed, amphetamine-loving protagonists and decayed orbital colonies."[9] It also probably didn't help that Sterling's introductory remarks to *Mirrorshades* readily packaged cyberpunk: "Certain central themes spring up repeatedly in cyberpunk. The theme of body invasion: prosthetic limbs, implanted circuitry, cosmetic surgery, genetic alteration. The even more powerful theme of mind invasion: brain–computer interfaces, artificial intelligence, neurochemistry – techniques radically redefining the nature of humanity, the nature of the self."[10] Shiner would not be the first movement-era writer to declare cyberpunk dead. Sterling returned to conduct his own autopsy for *Interzone* in "Cyberpunk in the Nineties" (1998): "But today, it must be admitted that the cyberpunks ... are no longer a Bohemian underground. This too is an old story in Bohemia; it is the standard punishment for success. An underground in the light of day is a contradiction in terms. Respectability does not merely beckon; it actively envelops. And in this sense, 'cyberpunk' is even deader than Shiner admits."[11]

---

[8] The revolutionary energy would eventually be substituted with a more "retrofit" outlook. Sterling eventually writes "cyberpunk is in some sense a return to roots," chiefly acknowledging the importance of 1960s-era authors, including Philip José Farmer, Alfred Bester, and others. "Preface," *Mirrorshades* (New York: Ace Books, 1988), pp. x–xi.

[9] Lewis Shiner, "Confessions of an Ex-Cyberpunk." *New York Times* (7 January 1991), lysator.liu.se/lsff/mb-nr10/Saxat.txt (last accessed May 25, 2018).

[10] Bruce Sterling, Preface to *Mirrorshades*, p. xiii.

[11] Bruce Sterling, "Cyberpunk in the Nineties," *Interzone* 48 (1991), http://lib.ru/STERLINGB/interzone.txt (last accessed May 25, 2018).

While literary cyberpunk's influence may be open to debate, it has arguably "been the most relevant and influential as a visual aesthetic."[12] After all, *Neuromancer*'s opening line is the visually rich "the sky above the port was the color of television, tuned to a dead channel";[13] or, Pat Cadigan's "Pretty Boy Crossover" (1986) features one of its characters, Bobby, trading his corporeal self for a "pretty boy" digital simulation where he can perpetually dance on the video screens of the hottest nightclubs. Given this visual preponderance, it is understandable why cinematic cyberpunk underwent its own evolution. Its benchmark consists of a trifecta of titles: *TRON* (dir. Steven Lisberger, 1982), *Blade Runner* (dir. Ridley Scott, 1982), and *Videodrome* (dir. David Cronenberg, 1983). With its neon-saturated and polluted urban sprawl, overcrowded streets, futuristic and anachronistic technologies, and incessant advertising, coupled with the fact that it is an adaptation of Dick's *Do Androids Dream of Electric Sheep?*, *Blade Runner* is arguably the most influential cinematic vision of cyberpunk: Scott Bukatman writes that "cyberpunk provided *the* image of the future in the 1980s" and the "aesthetic of cyberpunk was almost defined by *Blade Runner*."[14] *Videodrome*, however, is certainly no pushover: with its graphic and hallucinatory interrogation of media, mind-control conspiracies, and techno-organicism, Cronenberg's bizarre cinematic journey is "the most significant sf film of the 1980s, and is certainly – and very early on – the most cyberpunk."[15] Finally, *TRON* is important in its own right as the film's depiction of the internal digital space of video games "set the standards for representing game space and still resonates in the popular cultural sensibility. With its 90°-angled grid-structure, the overlay of physical and virtual space, and the dark background lit with neon circuitry, *TRON* provided the space beyond the screen with its original blueprint".[16]

[12] Pawel Frelik, "'Silhouettes of Strange Illuminated Mannequins': Cyberpunk's Incarnations of Light," in Murphy and Schmeink, eds., *Cyberpunk and Visual Culture*, p. 81.
[13] William Gibson, *Neuromancer* (New York: Ace, 1984), p. 3. Famously, what once suggested a grey, overcast day now suggests a clear, bright blue sky, as the default color of a "dead channel" has shifted with the times.
[14] Scott Bukatman, *Blade Runner*, 2nd edn. (New York: Palgrave Macmillan, 2012), pp. 50, 58.
[15] Peter Nicholls, "*Videodrome*," in John Clute, David Langford, Peter Nicholls, and Graham Sleight, eds., *The Encyclopedia of Science Fiction* (February 6, 2017), www.sf-encyclopedia.com/entry/videodrome (last accessed May 25, 2018).
[16] Murphy and Schemink, eds., *Cyberpunk and Visual Culture*, p. 102. A case can be made to include *WarGames* (dir. John Badham, 1983), which includes teenaged hacker David (Matthew Broderick) whose playful hacking of a super-computer almost triggers a nuclear war with Russia.

It is tempting to argue the revolutionary energy infusing cyberpunk effectively died by the start of the 1990s, epitomized by Shiner's eulogy, the rote sci-fiberpunk crowding the bookshelves, the critically panned but marginally successful *The Lawnmower Man* (dir. Brett Leonard, 1992), the financial and critical failure of *Johnny Mnemonic* (dir. Robert Longo, 1995), and the commercial and critical bomb that was Billy Idol's *Cyberpunk* (1993), an album for which Idol admits his "creative instincts and possibly even my taste seemed to abandon me this time around."[17] At the same time, cyberpunk was undergoing necessary transformations from its 1980s splendor. For example, a consistent critique was cyberpunk's celebration of white, masculinist, heteronormativity that largely ignored the progressive influence of 1970s-era feminist SF. A 1990s-era feminist influx into cyberpunk produced Misha's *Red Spider White Web* (1990), Marge Piercy's *He, She and It/Body of Glass* (1991), Pat Cadigan's *Synners* (1991), Maureen F. McHugh's *China Mountain Zhang* (1992), Laura J. Mixon's *Glass Houses* (1992), Mary Rosenblum's *Chimera* (1993), and Melissa Scott's *Trouble and Her Friends* (1994). Cadigan deserves special attention because as the only woman included in the *Mirrorshades* anthology, she cemented herself as the Queen of Cyberpunk with such short stories as "Rock On" (1984), "Pretty Boy Crossover," "Roadside Rescue" (1985), and the novel *Mindplayers* (1987), itself a fix-up novel comprising "The Pathosfinder" (1981), "Nearly Departed" (1983), "Variation on a Man" (1984), and "Lunatic Bridge" (1987). *Synners* defies a quick summary, but the novel features genetic implants, computer hackers, the commodification of dreams, corporate exploitation of burgeoning markets, digital uploads of consciousness, and the evolution of an artificial intelligence. Karen Cadora argues *Synners* subverts "cyberpunk's masculinist conventions in important ways,"[18] chiefly by virtue of implantable sockets that destabilize traditional masculinity: "these cyberpunks plug wires deep into their own brains. They are the penetrated, not the penetrating. Cadigan's male cyberpunks are automatically feminized by virtue of their entry into the matrix."[19]

Interestingly, penetration is also central to Scott's *Trouble and Her Friends*. The story follows retired hackers and former lovers Trouble and Cerise as their tracking of someone impersonating Trouble pulls them back into one another's orbit and the hacking domain of Seahaven. What emerges is

---

[17] Billy Idol, *Dancing with Myself* (New York: Touchstone, 2014), pp. 290–1.
[18] Karen Cadora, "Feminist Cyberpunk," in Graham J. Murphy and Sherryl Vint, eds., *Beyond Cyberpunk: New Critical Perspectives* (New York: Routledge, 2010), pp. 158.
[19] Ibid., p. 162.

a conflict between the old-school hackers – white, straight, male, who rely solely on their manual hacking skills – and the more-recent hackers, who use implanted brainworm technology to hack digital databases. This new generation of hackers is clearly coded as women, queer, and/or persons of color and they are dismissed by the old-school hackers for relying on the implanted "worm" and therefore not being true hackers. In a roundtable discussion at the International Conference on the Fantastic in the Arts, Scott once acknowledged she was annoyed by cyberpunk's conservatism and wrote *Trouble and Her Friends* as an explicit rebuttal to cyberpunk's white, straight, masculinism. It clearly resonated with readers: *Trouble and Her Friends* won the 1995 Lambda Literary Award for Gay and Lesbian Science Fiction and Fantasy.

While feminist or feminist-oriented cyberpunk may have been altering literary cyberpunk's narrative landscapes, Neal Stephenson's *Snow Crash* (1992) inherited the cyberpunk crown, joining Gibson's *Neuromancer* on *Time* magazine's list of 100 all-time best English-language novels post-1923. *Snow Crash* is a sprawling novel that follows pizza deliverer, hacker, and sword-wielder Hiro Protagonist and courier Y.T. (Yours Truly) as they navigate both a virtual world called the Metaverse and a balkanized America whose enclaves are ruled by private organizations, organized religion, and/or the mafia. Hiro's and Y.T.'s skills are put to the test when facing an info-apocalypse based on a Sumerian *ur-language* which infiltrates the brain, reduces the user to a babble-spewing shell, and facilitates neurological reprogramming. The antagonists L. Bob Rife, a Christian fundamentalist, and Raven, a nuclear-bomb wielding Aleut, distribute the Snow Crash virus through an addictive drug, tainted blood, and/or a computer program that attacks hackers and leaves them vulnerable, if not brain dead. In addition to its ongoing popularity – *Variety* reported on September 28, 2017 that Amazon and Paramount Television were developing a *Snow Crash* adaptation – *Snow Crash* continues cyberpunk's trend of "equating unchecked capitalist relations with dystopian futures."[20]

At the same time literary cyberpunk was undergoing metamorphosis, its two most prominent figures – William Gibson and Bruce Sterling – were again testing their collaborative mettle (following their co-written story "Red Star, Winter Orbit" [1983]) by travelling into an alternate version of the past with *The Difference Engine* (1990). In their co-authored novel, Gibson and Sterling depict an alternate history in which Charles Babbage has succeeded

---

[20] Lisa Yaszek, "Cultural History," in Mark Bould, Andrew M. Butler, Adam Roberts, and Sherryl Vint, eds., *The Routledge Companion to Science Fiction* (London and New York: Routledge, 2009), p. 196.

in constructing the Difference Engine and the Analytical Engine, steam-powered computers that radically reshape the direction of the Industrial Revolution, the British Empire, and the world at large. *The Difference Engine* depicts a British Empire that, as a direct result of Babbage's technological achievements and Ada Lovelace's programming skills, is more powerful than its real-world nineteenth-century counterpart, a vast British North America (i.e., Canada) that has maintained imperial stability, a then-fledgling United States that is both fragmented and geo-politically stunted, an Ireland that never suffered through the Great Famine (1845–9), and plenty of other alterations to the historical record. As John Clute writes for *The Encyclopedia of Science Fiction, The Difference Engine* depicts "a cruel and polluted Dystopia, a land dominated by calculation, measurement and severely 'practical' reason. Vast arterial roads ransack a choking London; huge masonical edifices house the new totalitarian bureaucracy which operates the Engines; and a conscious AI is a-borning."[21] Nevertheless, *The Difference Engine* resonated with readers as it translated cyberpunk's obsession with Alvin Toffler's future shock by projecting the force of technological change into a different epoch. It was nominated for several awards, including the British Science Fiction Award (1990) and the Nebula Award (1991), and helped popularize *steampunk* as a marketable niche within science fiction.

Of course, while *The Difference Engine* may have popularized this niche label, steampunk existed prior to Gibson and Sterling's influential novel. In fact, these cyberpunk forefathers arrived well after K. W. Jeter coined the term *steampunk* in a letter of April 1987 to *Locus* to encapsulate alternate history fictions set amidst the backdrop of an industrial steam-powered era. This alternate history aesthetic can be carbon-dated to such novels as Jeter's *Morlock Night* (1979) and *Infernal Devices* (1987), Tim Powers's *The Anubis Gates* (1983), and James P. Blaylock's *Homunculus* (1986), although Peter Nicholls and David Langford's entry on steampunk for *The Encyclopedia of Science Fiction* draws attention to such proto-steampunk novels as Christopher Priest's *The Space Machine* (1976), Michael Moorcock's *The Warlord of the Air* (1971), William Kotzwinkle's *Fata Morgana* (1977), John Mella's *Transformations* (1975), and Steven Utley and Howard Waldrop's "Black as the Pit, from Pole to Pole" (1977). Following the success of *The Difference Engine*, however, steampunk has evolved, even at times eclipsed, cyberpunk's

---

[21] John Clute, "William Gibson," in John Clute, David Langford, Peter Nicholls, and Graham Sleight, eds., *The Encyclopedia of Science Fiction* (August 18, 2017), www.sf-encyclopedia.com/entry/gibson_william (last accessed May 25, 2018).

contemporaneous development, including *Mirrorshades* alumnus Paul Di Filippo's three novellas – "Victoria" (1991), "Walt and Emily" (1993), and "Hottentots" (1995) – collected as *The Steampunk Trilogy* (1995), Ann and Jeff VanderMeer's anthologies *Steampunk* (2008), *Steampunk II: Steampunk Reloaded* (2010), and Ann VanderMeer's *Steampunk III: Steampunk Revolution* (2012), and Sean Wallace's anthology *The Mammoth Book of Steampunk* (2012), to name only a sliver of titles from an otherwise voluminous corpus of work. Nicholls and Langford also draw attention to "China Miéville's *King Rat* (1998), *Perdido Street Station* (2000) and several later works [that show] a debt to urban fantasy generally, and Steampunk in its darker aspects" and YA author Phillip Reeve, "arguably one of the prime movers in what followed, with at least seven very popular steampunk novels, from *Mortal Engines* (2001) to *Scrivener's Moon* (2011)."[22] And, of course, steampunk wasn't restricted to prose: Alan Moore and Kevin O'Neill's *The League of Extraordinary Gentlemen* (1999–2007; 2009–), Joe Kelly and Chris Bachalos's *Steampunk: Manimatron* (2000–2), and Bill Willingham, Sergio Davilla, and Joe Benitez's *Legenderry: A Steampunk Adventure* (2013–14) are only three steampunk comic book titles while video games, notably *The Chaos Engine* (Amiga 1993), which was inspired by *The Difference Engine*, also trade heavily in steampunk motifs. As a result, steampunk has increasingly gained steam and "has gone far beyond [such] markers [as] gaslit alleys, intrepid urchins, steam-powered machines, and technologies that never were" to also include such locales as "Canada, New Zealand, Wales, ancient Rome, Australia, alternate California, and even the postapocalypse."[23] In fact, steampunk has arguably achieved the pinnacle of cultural endurance and saturation thanks to fashion and cosplay: clothing styles include "retro elements, most commonly from the Victorian era with such retro-tech accessories as motorists' or pilots' goggles (preferably brass-framed) and clockwork components. This design aesthetic fed back into art objects, paintings, and more books – often young-adult – which attracted more young writers. Steampunk in this expanded sense became a widespread phenomenon that is still current."[24]

While steampunk may have a stronger claim to the do-it-yourself *punk* aesthetic that had initially defined cyberpunk, cinematic cyberpunk recovered

---

[22] Peter Nicholls and David Langford, "Steampunk," in Clute, Langford, Nicholls, and Selight, eds., *The Encyclopedia of Science Fiction*, www.sf-encyclopedia.com/entry/steampunk (last accessed May 25, 2018).

[23] Kelly Link, ed., *Steampunk! An Anthology of Fantastically Rich and Strange Stories* (Somerville, MA: Candlewick Press, 2011), p. ix.

[24] Nicholls and Langford, "Steampunk."

from the disappointing returns of *Johnny Mnemonic* and *The Lawnmower Man* to maintain its foothold in the nineties thanks to a handful of films: *Strange Days* (dir. Kathryn Bigelow, 1995), *eXistenZ* (dir. David Cronenberg, 1999), *The Thirteenth Floor* (dir. Josef Rusnak, 1999), and *The Matrix* (dir. Wachowski siblings, 1999). *Strange Days* is very Cadigan-esque with its pulsing, end-of-millennium celebrations and recordable and implantable memories and experiences known as SQUID recordings (Superconducting Quantum Interference Device). The film follows Lenny Nero (Ralph Fiennes) and Lornette "Mace" Mason (Angela Bassett) who get caught up in the murders of Jeriko One (Glenn Plummer) and Iris (Brigitte Bako) when they come into possession of a SQUID that unravels a wider conspiracy. *The Thirteenth Floor*, loosely based on Daniel F. Galouye's *Simulacron-3* (1964), follows Douglas Hall (Craig Bierko), who is accused of murdering multibillionaire Hannon Fuller (Armin Mueller-Stahl), whose company has created a virtual reality simulation of Los Angeles, *c.* 1937. The avatars within this simulated 1930s-era Los Angeles are unaware they are computer programs, but Hall eventually learns he too is living in a vast simulation, *c.* 1999. Hall eventually ventures offline to the real world of 2024 and discovers he was a puppet in a much larger and more complicated drama. Cronenberg's *eXistenZ* fuses cyberpunk motifs with the body horror and bodily transgressions typically associated with Cronenberg's oeuvre, much like his earlier *Videodrome*. In *eXistenZ*, futuristic video gamers are biotechnologically linked to their games via game pods that attach to ports surgically implanted into players' spines. The film follows Allegra Geller (Jennifer Jason Leigh), the creator of the *eXistenZ* organic reality system, as she goes on the run with Ted Pikul (Jude Law) following an assassination attempt. As Geller tries to save *eXistenZ*, reality slowly begins to dissolve into surrealism in typical Cronenbergian fashion. Although these movies were box-office failures and garnered disparate reviews[25] – *eXistenZ* earned respectable reviews; *Strange Days* was divisive for critics; *The Thirteenth Floor* was largely trashed – they remain important contributions to cinematic cyberpunk, particularly in their use of visual iconography that dissolves the boundaries between "real" and "virtual" domains, a thematic motif that achieved box-office success with *The Matrix*.

Keanu Reeves regained a wealth of cyberpunk credibility[26] with his turn as Neo in the Wachowskis' *The Matrix, The Matrix Reloaded* (2003), and

---

[25] As per box office revenues reported on The Internet Movie Database and movie reviews available on Rotten Tomatoes.

[26] As the star of the titular *Johnny Mnemonic*, Reeves is partly to blame for his wooden performance in an otherwise atrocious film (visuals notwithstanding).

The Matrix Revolutions (2003). *The Matrix* follows hacker Neo who is recruited by Trinity (Carrie-Anne Moss) and Morpheus (Laurence Fishburne) into a larger conflict with Agent Smith (Hugo Weaving) and the Artificial Intelligences controlling the world. Neo learns he is living in a simulation and that he is nothing more than a battery servicing the needs of sentient machines that are waging an ongoing war with the remnants of humanity in the underground city of Zion. Morpheus follows the prophecy of the Oracle (Gloria Foster) and believes he has found 'the One' who will bring an end to the war. Neo doubts himself until he eventually embraces the prophecy and learns to manipulate the digital code of the matrix, temporarily besting Agent Smith and flying off like Superman to the refrain of Rage Against the Machine's "Wake Up." The sequels continue Neo's development as he settles into his role as the One, wages his ongoing battles against Agent Smith, and helps to broker a truce. *The Matrix Revolutions* ends with a beautiful sunrise beaming over the city and the Oracle (Mary Alice, replacing the now-deceased Foster) professing her belief that Neo now heralds a bright future. *The Matrix* and *The Matrix Reloaded* received generally positive reviews – *The Matrix Revolutions* was savaged by critics – and the series was a financial boon for Warner Bros. In addition, the trilogy's success resides "not only through its wealth of references for the scholar and the film fan, but also through the complexity of the narrative, which is contained within the Hollywood film structure. The potency of the films thus lies in their ability to appeal to both the popular audience and the cultural theorists."[27] *The Matrix* franchise,[28] coupled with scores of book-length critical studies and academic articles, ensured cyberpunk remained "fresh" heading into the new millennium.

Part of cyberpunk's endurance in the 1990s and into the first decade of the twenty-first century was also a result of its (albeit mixed) adaptation into television. Originally broadcast as *Max Headroom: 20 Minutes into the Future* on British Channel 4 (1985) followed by a video, music, and talk show (1985–7), the Americanized *Max Headroom* debuted on ABC and ran for two seasons from 1987 to 1988. It sparked a cultural phenomenon: Max Headroom appeared in the Art of Noise's *Paranoimia* music video (1986), as the spokesperson for New

---

[27] Stacy Gillis, "Introduction," *The Matrix Trilogy: Cyberpunk Reloaded* (New York: Wallflower Press, 2005), p. 3.
[28] The trilogy is supplemented by other materials that comprise the franchise, such as animated short films bundled as *The Animatrix* (2003), a series of video games that started with *Enter the Matrix* (Shiny Entertainment 2003), and *The Matrix Comics* web-based comic series.

Coke, and on countless merchandise items. Although Scott Bukatman considers this *Max Headroom* a diluted version of its British counterpart, it did address cyberpunk "aspects of spectacular culture (including violent spectator sports . . . information control and the invasion of privacy, television evangelism, and terrorism and the media)."[29] *VR.5* ran on the Fox network in 1995 and featured Sydney Bloom (Lori Singer), a young woman who, upon learning she can enter virtual reality, agrees to run missions for the secretive Committee. Chris Carter's *The X-Files* made two explicitly cyberpunk-ish episodes – "Kill Switch" (1998) and "First Person Shooter" (2000) – written by William Gibson and Tom Maddox. In roughly the same period, Carter also launched *Harsh Realm* (1999–2000) on Fox which follows Lt. Thomas Hobbes (Scott Bairstow), who finds himself fighting for his life when he is trapped inside a military simulation, although the fight didn't last long: it was cancelled shortly after it premiered. *Dark Angel* survived longer on Fox, completing two seasons from 2000 to 2002, and it followed Max Guevara (Jessica Alba), a genetically enhanced runaway from the Manticore project who is hiding from secret government agents all the while searching for other Manticore escapees. She is assisted chiefly by Logan Cale (Michael Weatherly), an underground, paraplegic cyber-journalist, and a group of friends she maintains in her public life as a bicycle courier. Joss Whedon returned to television after *Buffy the Vampire Slayer* (1997–2003), *Angel* (1999–2004), and *Firefly* (2002) with *Dollhouse* (2009–10) starring *Buffy* and *Angel* alumnus Eliza Dushku as Echo, an Active or Doll, who has her entire personality wiped and alternate personalities uploaded before she is pimped out by a clandestine organization to wealthy clients for any number of so-called missions. Finally, *Mr. Robot* (2015–) follows cybersecurity engineer and hacker Elliot Alderson (Rami Malek), who joins the hacktivist team *fsociety*, headed by Mr. Robot (Christian Slater).

Cyberpunk has also a notable history in comic books; in fact, one of cyberpunk's chief precursors was the visual narratives collected in French magazine *Métal Hurlant*, particularly Jean "Moebius" Giraud's illustrations of Dan O'Bannon's "The Long Tomorrow" (1975–6). Bukatman addresses how "Moebius's compacted urbanism, Phillip Druillet's saturated darkness and Angus McKie's scalar exaggerations" visually influenced *Blade Runner*; similarly, Gibson has acknowledged *Neuromancer*'s indebtedness to Moebius and *Métal Hurlant*.[30] The visual aesthetics in cyberpunk comic books are

---

[29] Scott Bukatman, *Terminal Identity: The Virtual Subject in Post-Modern Science Fiction* (Durham, NC: Duke University Press, 1993), p. 67.

[30] Bukatman, *Blade Runner*, p. 26; Jeff Verona, "Heroes and Villains: Ventures and Adventures in the Comic Book Industry," in Gary Westfahl, George Slusser, and Eric

also evident in Frank Miller and Geof Darrow's *Hard Boiled* (1990–2), Paul Pope's *Heavy Liquid* (1999–2000), Robert Venditti and Brett Weldele's *The Surrogates* (2005–6), Warren Ellis and Steve Pugh's *Hotwire: Requiem for the Dead* (2009) and *Hotwire: Deep Cut* (2010), Philip K. Dick and Tony Parker's *Do Androids Dream of Electric Sheep?* (2009–11), and Rick Remender, Sean Murphy, and Matt Hollingsworth's *Tokyo Ghost* (2015–16), a series that also features steampunk-ish visual aesthetics. The standout English-language series, however, is undoubtedly Warren Ellis and Darick Robertson's *Transmetropolitan* (1997–2002). The story features the trials and tribulations of gonzo-journalist Spider Jerusalem, who seeks the truth in a world awash with corruption and saturated with media and technological wonders. Jerusalem routinely finds himself at odds with the powers of authority, including two presidents ("The Smiler" and "The Beast"), all the while struggling against gradual urban decay, the slippery slope towards dystopia, and the responsibilities of his own fame. Spider even breaks the fourth wall on occasion and speaks directly to the reader, imploring them to learn the lessons of his own cyberpunk exploits.

The notion of "post-cyberpunk" gained some early traction in the new millennium, assisted in no small part by James Patrick Kelly and John Kessel's *Rewired: The Post-Cyberpunk Anthology* (2007), a collection of short stories that includes more-recent offerings by *Mirrorshades* alumni Sterling, Gibson, Cadigan, and Di Filippo coupled with Greg Egan's "Yeyuka" (1997), Gwyneth Jones's "Red Sonja and Lessingham in Dreamland" (1996), Charles Stross's "Lobsters" (2001), Paolo Bacigalupi's "The Calorie Man" (2005), Mary Rosenblum's "Search Engine" (2005), and Cory Doctorow's "When Sysadmins Ruled the Earth" (2006), to name a few titles. In their introduction, Kelly and Kessel explain post-cyberpunk in this fashion:

> The punk in post-cyberpunk [PCP] continues to make sense if it is pointing toward an attitude: an adversarial relationship to consensus reality. This attitude is just south of cynicism but well north of mere skepticism. It has to do with a reaction to a world in which humanity must constantly be renegotiated ... The characters in a PCP story need this healthy dose of attitude because their relationship to reality is different from ours ... reality itself is everywhere mediated, and what comes between the characters and reality must constantly be interrogated.[31]

S. Rabkin, eds., *Science Fiction and Market Realities* (Athens, OH: University of Georgia Press, 1996), pp. 184–93; p. 191.

[31] James Patrick Kelly and John Kessel, "Hacking Cyberpunk," in James Patrick Kelly and John Kessel, eds., *Rewired: The Post-Cyberpunk Anthology* (San Francisco: Tachyon Books, 2007), p. xii.

Nevertheless, differentiating between "cyberpunk" and "post-cyberpunk" seems akin to splitting hairs, especially considering the cyberpunk label is unwilling to give up the ghost, as shown by Pat Cadigan's *The Ultimate Cyberpunk* (2002) or *Cyberpunk: Stories of Hardware, Software, Wetware, Evolution, and Revolution* (2013), edited by Victoria Blake and featuring the usual suspects – Gibson, Sterling, Cadigan, Shiner, Rucker, Di Filippo, and Shirley – and such unlikely entrants as Kim Stanley Robinson ("Down and Out in the Year 2000" [1986]), David Marusek ("Getting to Know You" [1998]), or Daniel H. Wilson ("The Nostalgist" [2009]). At the same time, cyberpunk, post-cyberpunk, or cyberpunk-ish novels of the new millennium include Justina Robson's *Silver Screen* (1999) and *Mappa Mundi* (2001), Richard K. Morgan's Takeshi Kovacs series (*Altered Carbon* [2002], *Broken Angels* [2003], and *Woken Furies* [2005]) and *Market Forces* (2004), Marianne de Pierres's Parrish Plessis series (*Nylon Angel* [2004], *Code Noir* [2004], and *Crash Deluxe* [2005]), Daniel Suarez's *Daemon* (2006) and *Freedom* (2010), Adam Sternbergh's *Near Enemy* (2015), K. C. Alexander's *Necrotech* (2016), Matthew de Abaitua's *The Destructives* (2016), or Annalee Newitz's *Autonomous* (2017). Cyberpunk aesthetics have even filtered into such young adult titles as M. T. Anderson's *Feed* (2002), Cory Doctorow's *Little Brother* (2008) and *Homeland* (2013), James Dashner's *The Morality Doctrine* series (*The Eye of Minds* [2013], *The Rule of Thoughts* [2014], *The Game of Lives* [2015]), Patrick Ness's *More Than This* (2013), and Ernest Cline's *Ready Player One* (2011), to again name a few titles. At the same time, Lars Schmeink, channeling Brian McHale, points to the phenomenon of *biopunk* as a cyberpunk sub-variety "which has since grown into a larger and more varied cultural formation" and, by the end of the twentieth century, "the genetically engineered posthuman has brought forth a cultural formation of *biopunk* that spans many different forms of culture."[32] Biopunk examples in Schmeink's study include Margaret Atwood's *MaddAddam* trilogy (*Oryx and Crake* [2003], *The Year of the Flood* [2009], and *MaddAddam* [2013]), Bacigalupi's award-winning *The Windup Girl* (2009), the film *Splice* (dir. Vincenzo Natali, 2009), or the video game *BioShock* (Irrational Games and Looking Glass Studios [2007]). Nevertheless, the ongoing work from yesterday's cyberpunks, including such forefathers as William Gibson (*The Peripheral* [2014]) and Bruce Sterling (*Pirate Utopia* [2016]), coupled

---

[32] Lars Schmeink, *Biopunk Dystopias: Genetic Engineering, Society, and Science Fiction* (Liverpool: Liverpool University Press, 2016), pp. 7–8.

with an endurance despite competition from steampunk and biopunk, show a thriving market for cyberpunk in the twenty-first century.

It bears noting that cyberpunk is not a strictly North American phenomenon. For example, Japanese cyberpunk was a popular cinematic subgenre in Japan, organized chiefly around such directors as Shigeru Izumiya (*Death Powder* [1986]), Shin'ya Tsukamoto (*Tetsuo: The Iron Man* [1989]), and Shozin Fukui (*√964 Pinocchio* [1991], *Rubber's Lover* [1996]). Although largely unknown outside Japan, *Death Powder* is "arguably the first film of Japan's extreme cyberpunk movement, exemplifying the invasive, corporeal surrealism that would follow over the next ten years."[33] Japanese cyberpunk rejected much of what had been popularized in North American cyberpunk to instead focus on visions of "industrial scrap – *Tetsuo* – and makeshift laboratories built from crude and dated equipment – *Rubber's Lover* – lending a DIY aesthetic to their overall ethos."[34] Finally, Japanese cyberpunk was often set in "the present-day, real-life cyberpunk city of Tokyo, suggesting that anxieties over rapid modernity are not some far-off venture but something that should be worried about now,"[35] anxieties that also formed the core of much Japanese anime and manga, particularly Katsuhiro Ōtomo's *Akira* (1982–90 [manga]; 1988 [anime]) and Masmune Shirow's *Ghost in the Shell* franchise.

Ōtomo's voluminous *Akira* is set in post-World War III Neo-Tokyo and follows the adventures of Tetsuo Shima and Shōtarō Kaneda as they navigate a complex and bloody world featuring post-apocalyptic biker gangs, biological mutations, and secret military agencies. It is on this sprawling canvas of "nuclear blasts, high-speed bike chases, and profuse gunplay [that] Ōtomo used the protagonists' predicament to explore the value of friendship, the isolation and disillusionment of youth subcultures, and the state of the subject faced with corrupt, irresponsible authorities."[36] *Akira* achieved remarkable success, in part a result of Ōtomo's anime adaptation as well as its import by Marvel Comics' Epic Comics imprint that translated and digitally colorized *Akira* for a North American audience. Masmune Shirow's *Ghost in the Shell* franchise has also proved immensely popular in domestic and international markets with its ongoing tales of Major Motoko

[33] Mark Player, "Post-Human Nightmares – The World of Japanese Cyberpunk Cinema," *Midnight Eye* (May 13, 2011), www.midnighteye.com/features/post-human-nightmares-the-world-of-japanese-cyberpunk-cinema (last accessed May 25, 2018).

[34] Ibid.

[35] Ibid.

[36] Abraham Kawa, "Comics Since the Silver Age," in Bould, *et al.*, eds., *The Routledge Companion to Science Fiction*, p. 165.

Kusanagi, a cyborg officer and squad leader of Public Security Section 9, who struggles with her identity as a "'ghost' of human essence [that] inhabits a state-of-the-art 'machine,' at times rendering the soul, as well as the flesh and blood understanding of human life, as mere data – a freely transferable artificial intelligence desperately seeking to maintain its own singularity and identity."[37] *Ghost in the Shell* has therefore proved to be both successful and immensely important as a transmedia product, including *Ghost in the Shell* (1989–1990 [manga]; 1995 [anime]); *Ghost in the Shell 2: Man–Machine Interface* (1991–7 [manga]); *Ghost in the Shell 2: Innocence* (2004 [anime]); *Ghost in the Shell: Stand Alone Complex* (2002 [TV animation]); *Ghost in the Shell: S.A.C. 2nd GIG* (2004 [TV animation]); *Ghost in the Shell: Stand Alone Complex The Laughing Man* (2005 [original video animation]); *Ghost in the Shell: Stand Alone Complex Individual Eleven* (2006 [original video animation]; *Ghost in the Shell: Stand Alone Complex – Solid State Society* (2006 [anime]); *Ghost in the Shell: The New Movie* (2015 [anime]), and Hollywood's *Ghost in the Shell* (dir. Rupert Sanders, 2017), although this Hollywood version was a critical and financial failure, in part because of the whitewashing controversy surrounding casting Scarlett Johansson in the lead role.

Cyberpunk has also gone increasingly global. For example, *Sleep Dealer* (dir. Alex Rivera, 2008) is set largely in Mexico and focuses on three intersecting characters: Memo Cruz, a young hacker who is forced to leave his home and find work in Tijuana as a node worker ("sleep dealer"); Luz Martínez, an idealistic journalist who uploads her daily memories and experiences to an online vlog on a pay-per-play basis; and, Rudy Ramirez, a drone pilot whose missions to secure corporate water rights are the subject of a *Cops*-style television show called *Drones*. As Sherryl Vint writes regarding Memo's experiences, "in contrast to what we expect of heroes in cyberpunk fiction, whose mastery within cyberspace transforms their marginal position in the material world into one of mastery within cyberspace, Memo remains marginalized in both material and virtual realms,"[38] although both Luz and Rudy undergo their own marginalization in this digital global economy. Of course, marginalization and global economics are familiar for residents of Cuba, and in his study of the relationship between SF and Cuba's social reality, Juan C. Toledano Redondo notes that "despite the late publication

---

[37] Paul Wells, "Animation," in Rob Latham, ed., *The Oxford Handbook of Science Fiction* (Oxford: Oxford University Press, 2014), p. 192.
[38] Sherryl Vint, "Cyberwar: The Convergence of Virtual and Material Battlefields in Cyberpunk Cinema," in Murphy and Schmeink, eds., *Cyberpunk and Visual Culture* (New York: Routledge, 2018), p. 265.

and limited publication of cyberpunk texts, they were absorbed quickly in Cuba during the late 1990s, condensing the evolution of the subgenre into just a few years."[39] Toledano Redondo points to such Cuban authors as Yoss (José Miguel Sánchez), Vladimir Hernández Pacín, and Michel Encinosa Fú in such collections as *Timshel* and *Reino eterno: Cuentos de fantasía y ciencia ficción* (Eternal Kingdom: Stories of fantasy and science fiction, Yoss, 1989; 1999*), Interfase: Selección de cuentos cyberpunk* and *Nova de cuarzo* (Hernández Pacín, 1997; 1999), and *Niños de neón* (Fu, 2001) to show how "Cuban cyberpunk style rebels against both socialist realism and imperialistic late-capitalism."[40]

Perhaps cyberpunk's most widespread influence resides with the multi-billion dollar gaming industry. Scholars have pointed out the pervasive "cyberpunk-ness" of role-playing games (e.g., *Cyberpunk 2020*, R. Talsorian Games, 2010) and video games that maintain the visual aesthetic established by even the earliest cyberpunk, including *Final Fantasy* (Square Enix, 1987–present), *Neuromancer* (Interplay, 1988), *System Shock* (Looking Glass, 1994) and *System Shock 2* (Irrational Games, 1999), *Shadowrun* (BlueSky, 1994), *Sid Meier's Alpha Centauri* (Firaxis, 1999), *Rez* (Sega, 2001), *Darwinia* (Introversion, 2005), *Dystopia* (Puny Human Games, 2007), the *Mass Effect* franchise (Bioware, 2007–present), *Deus Ex: Human Revolution* (Square Enix, 2011), *Remember Me* (Dontnod Entertainment, 2013), and *Watch Dogs* (Ubisoft, 2014).[41] Since the gaming industry remains healthy, there is every reason to believe cyberpunk will continue to influence it.

In the end, cyberpunk has diversified and infiltrated popular culture to such an extent that it is difficult to think of it as a definable genre or subgenre; instead, Thomas Foster, drawing upon the work of Lawrence Grossberg, explains it isn't so much a "genre, which is organized around 'the existence of necessary formal elements,' [as] a cultural formation [which is] a historical articulation of textual practices with 'a variety of other cultural, social,

---

[39] Juan C. Toledano Redondo, "From Socialist Realism to Capitalism: Cuban Cyberpunk," *Science Fiction Studies* 32, 3 (November 2005), p. 450.

[40] Ibid.

[41] See Stina Attebery and Josh Pearson, "'Today's Cyborg is Stylish': The Humanity Cost of Posthuman Fashion in *Cyberpunk 2020*," in Murphy and Schmeink, eds., *Cyberpunk and Visual Culture*, pp. 55–79; Mark R. Johnson, "The History of Cyberspace Aesthetics in Video Games," in Murphy and Schmeink, eds., *Cyberpunk and Visual Culture*, pp. 139–54; Stephen Joyce, "Playing for Virtually Real: Cyberpunk Aesthetics and Ethics in *Deus Ex: Human Revolution*," in Murphy and Schmeink, eds., *Cyberpunk and Visual Culture*, pp. 155–73; and Jenna Ng and Jamie Macdonald, "'We Are Data': The Cyberpunk Imaginary of Data Worlds in *Watch Dogs*," in Murphy and Schmeink, eds., *Cyberpunk and Visual Culture*, pp. 174–89.

economic, historical and political practices.'"[42] As a cultural formation, cyberpunk has always already been extrapolating upon techno-mediated realities while it continues to integrate "worlds that were formerly separate: the realm of high tech, and the modern pop underground."[43] Cyberpunk has experienced "a sea change into a more generalized cultural formation"[44] since it first burst forth in the 1980s and it continues to evolve and expand in response to changing global conditions. We are arguably living in cyberpunk's futures, so our cyberpunk fictions – past, present, and future – are more important today than they have ever been.

[42] Thomas Foster, *The Souls of Cyberfolk: Posthumanism as Vernacular Theory* (Minneapolis: University of Minnesota Press, 2005), p. xvi. See Murphy and Schmeink's *Cyberpunk and Visual Culture* for an exploration of cyberpunk as a "cultural formation."

[43] Sterling, *Mirrorshades*, p. xi.

[44] Foster, *The Souls of Cyberfolk*, p. xiv.

33

Science Fiction Film and Television in the 1980s and 1990s

NICOLE DE FEE

SF film and television productions of the 1980s and 1990s follow, in many ways, rather predictable patterns. We still see the tried and true space opera; we see alien invasions and takeovers; we see creature features of various forms. Predictability and even cliché aside, though, SF films and television series of the 1980s and 1990s also register the new political concerns and cultural anxieties of their day: in the 1980s, the acceleration of the military industrial complex, the intensifying fear of nuclear war, and the ever-mounting tensions with the Soviet Union, and in the 1990s the opportunities and pitfalls associated with the end of the Cold War and the emergence of the United States as the world's only "hyperpower."[1]

Although other chapters offer a more detailed discussion of the cultural form of the SF franchise,[2] I would be remiss not to address three major SF franchises of the late 1970s, beginning with George Lucas's 1977 *Star Wars* (later rechristened *Episode IV: A New Hope*). Its sequel, *The Empire Strikes Back* (dir. Irvin Kershner, 1980), is often heralded as *the* SF movie of the 1980s (a quick Google search will put *Empire* at the top of just about every major SF list of the 1980s), and the franchise now spans four decades and multiple media contexts. The original *Star Wars* trilogy radically shifted the ways in which audiences viewed and consumed SF, inaugurating aesthetic sensibilities, merchandising opportunities, and blockbuster box-office expectations that continue to define SF film today. In addition to *Star Wars*, there are two other major franchises of the late 1970s that have found continued success over the course of four decades: *Star Trek* and *Alien*. After returning to the big screen with *The Motion Picture* (dir. Robert Wise, 1979), *Star Trek* saw five sequels with its original cast before returning to television with the era-defining *Star Trek: The Next Generation* in 1987;

---

[1] The British journalist Peregrine Worsthorne coined the term in 1991.
[2] See Chapter 30 of this volume.

Star Trek: Generations (dir. David Carson, 1994) would eventually bridge the gap between the two franchises. *Alien* (dir. Ridley Scott, 1979), too, would yield three sequels over the next two decades as well as two crossovers with the Predator franchise and two more prequels (and counting) in the twenty-first century, as well as producing multiple transmedia spinoffs of its own; the film was novel and influential in its merging of horror, SF, and action, as well as its early deployment of a female action hero.

Rather than proceeding chronologically, this chapter takes a thematic approach, grouping SF film and television of the period into a number of broadly conceived categories: "future war," apocalypse, and disaster fantasies; science run amuck; aliens; superhero and comic book-inspired narratives; and time travel.

Future War

The title of Chris Hables Gray's essay "'There Will Be War!': Future War Fantasies and Militaristic Science Fiction in the 1980s" sums up one of the decade's SF subgenres.[3] Gray argues that SF of the 1980s is fundamentally "pro-war" and "focuses around the same metaphors and concepts that preoccupy the command and planning leadership of the US military itself and that shape the way it conceives of postmodern war." Furthermore, a significant part of "postmodern war" is "the necessity for cybernetically connected man–machine weapon systems – cyborg soldiers."[4] Opening the weekend before Halloween, on October 26, 1984, ten days before the presidential election between Ronald Reagan and Walter Mondale – at a time when Reagan's campaign slogan was "It's Morning in America," which proclaimed that a new, and presumably brighter day is coming – *The Terminator* presents the antithesis of this optimism. Here the future is not a consumer paradise but rather a ruined civilization and a dead world, utterly beholden to military machines and industrial capital. Indeed, the *Terminator* franchise will prove paradigmatic of my analysis of SF films in the 1980s and 1990s, fitting to one extent or another in every category that follows.

The Terminator and *RoboCop* (dir. Paul Verhoeven, 1987) are the most significant "cyborg soldiers" of the 1980s, a list to which we should also add the "universal soldiers" of the 1990s: *Universal Soldier* (dir. Roland Emmerich, 1992) and *Universal Soldier: The Return* (dir. Mic Rogers, 1999). Each version of

---

[3] Chris Hables Gray, "'There Will Be War!': Future War Fantasies and Militaristic Science Fiction in the 1980s," *Science Fiction Studies*, 21, 3 (November 1994), pp. 315–36.
[4] Ibid., p. 316.

the "man-machine weapon system" offers a different visual of the cyborg soldier as uncanny doppelgänger: the Terminator is an artificially intelligent robot masquerading as a human, while Robocop is a murdered police officer and the Universal Soldiers are former Vietnam soldiers who died in combat and are reverse engineered into precision fighting machines.[5] Focused on war and violence in general, rather than cyborgs or genetically enhanced soldiers in particular – but still including plot threads involving man–machine synergy (hypertechnologized soldiers) and augmented human capacity (psychic soldiers) – are David Lynch's 1984 film adaptation of *Dune* and Paul Verhoeven's darkly prescient satire of resurgent fascism, *Starship Troopers* (1997).

The war machine, as a kind of political abstraction or even filmic shorthand, evolved in significant ways during this era, particularly with respect to the ongoing growth of the military-industrial complex and the emergence of nonconventional warfare. In 1994 the United States launched the first Predator Drone, and GPS guided munitions were in full effect by 1995; these developments were not lost on SF filmmakers. There were a number of militaristic sci-fi/alien/fantasy films of the 1980s and 1990s, several of them blockbusters, many of them featuring Arnold Schwarzenegger. In addition to the aforementioned *Terminator* franchise – perhaps his most famous role – Schwarzenegger found his niche in SF action films throughout the 1980s and 1990s in such films as *Predator* (dir. John McTiernan, 1987) and *Total Recall* (dir. Paul Verhoeven, 1990). Schwarzenegger provided an almost ideal body with which and on which to enact violence, as well as to illustrate the conflict between human and machine; as Carl Freedman argues, "Arnoldian antihumanism is constructed through an intricate, plausible glorification of the machine as such, and the visual-libidinal satisfactions thus enabled – satisfactions sufficiently powerful and desirable … are derived primarily from the concrete, cinematically demonstrable superiority of machine steel to human flesh."[6] Furthermore, "what the Terminator *enacts*, what he allows the viewer to relish vicariously, is an all-too-human rage against the human body."[7] This "rage against the body" applies not just to the Terminator, but is an

---

[5] Gray also extends his argument beyond true SF into other fictions and includes Tom Clancy in his discussion of future-war fantasies. Perhaps the closest to this may be the ABC miniseries *Netforce* in 1994; this was Clancy's foray into an early version of what would now be understood as cyberterrorism.

[6] Carl Freedman, "Polemical Afterword: Some Brief Reflections on Arnold Schwarzenegger and on Science Fiction in Contemporary American Culture," *PMLA*, 119, 3 (May 2004), p. 543.

[7] Ibid., original emphasis.

important factor in many SF films involving technology and the body and, by extension, all living things.

Apocalypse and the Aftermath

Many of the future war scenarios bleed into visions of the apocalypse (again, perhaps most famously *The Terminator* and its sequels). In the 1980s, many apocalypse narratives and Cold War fears worked in conjunction. In the early part of the decade, both American and British television addressed this fear: *The Day After* (ABC, 1983), *Testament* (PBS, 1983), and *Threads* (BBC, 1984) imagine worlds where relations between the United States and the USSR lead to World War III. NBC's 1983–4 *V: The Miniseries* and *V: The Final Battle* portray a version of World War III that echoes the Holocaust of the Second World War in the human fight against alien colonization and annihilation. Even the Japanese felt panic of a seemingly imminent United States/USSR World War III. *Fumoon* (dir. Hisashi Sakaguchi, 1980) examines mounting tensions between the United States and the USSR and atomic testing leading to the creation of mutants. *Akira* (dir. Katsuhiro Ōtomo, 1988), considered to be the greatest animated SF film of all time, imagines a dystopic post-World War III Tokyo (though it does not indicate that the war was a byproduct of US–USSR relations). Australia and New Zealand also produced post-apocalyptic narratives during the late 1980s, which were not related to World War III or nuclear annihilation. *The Quiet Earth* (dir. Geoffrey Murphy, 1985) adapted from the novel of the same name finds a man waking alone on Earth under the belief that his work on DNA and radiation has created the empty planet. Much of the story revolves around Hobson's attempt to accept the death of his son, which has left him questioning his culpability in humanity's destruction. Perhaps the most significant of the Australian post-apocalyptic films is the *Max* series, which has had enduring pop culture influence all the way into a twenty-first-century fourth installment, *Mad Max: Fury Road*, all directed by George Miller. The first in the series is *Mad Max* (1979), taking place just before the apocalyptic social breakdown that will characterize the situation of the later films. Both *The Quiet Earth* and the *Mad Max* series provide a completely different perspective on the post-apocalyptic narrative from the more Western- or urban-themed versions of the aftermath of nuclear war. Paul Williams argues that one of the reasons the Australian and South Pacific regions are suited to a wealth of post-apocalyptic SF narratives (in film, comics, and print) has to do with the history of atomic bomb testing in the region, as well as the vastness of the Outback that allows for, Williams argues, imperialist fantasies to be played out in a time when there is seemingly nothing left to colonize. Australia provides "a post-apocalyptic landscape [that] is an expression of two converse impulses: the terrifying contemplation of the empty space of the world after nuclear war, and the exhilaration that this blank canvas is the stage for feats of adventure and heroism."[8] Even though Aunty Entity belts out that "we don't need another hero" in *Beyond Thunderdome* (1985), in most post-apocalyptic narratives of the period we end up with unlikely heroes and a vision of possible human resurgence, rather than final annihilation.

The rising crisis of the AIDS epidemic throughout the 1980s and into the 1990s corresponded with a wave of SF that examines humanity's destruction at the hands of incurable and untraceable viruses rather than nuclear or ecological collapse. The first of what would be grouped under AIDS cases appeared in 1981.[9] Kinji Fukusaku's 1980 film *Day of Resurrection* (also known as *Virus*) opens the decade with a virus that has nearly destroyed the human race. It narrowly predates what would become the AIDS epidemic and ushers in a wave of viral outbreak and viral apocalypse films, including to varying degrees *Alien 3* (dir. David Fincher, 1992), *Daybreak* (dir. Alan Brown, 1993), and even David Cronenberg's *The Fly* (1986), as well as many episodes of televised SF series (including multiple entries in the TNG-era *Star Trek* canon alone). Even a campy film like *C.H.U.D. II: Bud the CHUD* (dir. David Irving, 1989) exemplifies the sort of viral/apocalypse narratives that we see throughout the 1980s – biomedical manipulation, military-industrial-complex takeover, secret military experiments, attacks on suburbia, and, of course, renewed interest in zombies.

Even more films involving viral outbreaks were made in the 1990s. If the 1980s gave us an incurable disease, the 1990s gave us advances in biological engineering that seemed by turns utopian and apocalyptic. The first successful intracytoplasmic sperm injection in vitro fertilization occurred in 1992; the Human Genome Project which sought to map and sequence all genes in

---

[8] Paul Williams, "Beyond *Mad Max III*: Race, Empire, and Heroism on Post-Apocalyptic Terrain," *Science Fiction Studies* 32, 2 (July, 2005), p. 301.

[9] Originally called Gay-Related Immune Deficiency (GRID), by the middle of 1981 the disease became known as AIDS and was originally thought to be limited to intravenous drug users in the gay community. In 1983, the first female cases of AIDS were being reported, indicating that the disease could be contracted through heterosexual sex. Throughout the decade reports of infection grew from close to 300 a year to nearly 40,000 by the end of the 1980s, with over eighty countries reporting cases. For more on the specific connections between the AIDS crisis and 1980s and 1990s SF, see K. Thor Jensen, "How the AIDS Crisis Influenced Science Fiction," geek.com, www.geek.com/culture/how-the-aids-crisis-influenced-science-fiction-1702080 (last accessed June 5, 2017).

DNA began in 1990; use of DNA in criminal law also gained traction during this decade. In film and television, biomedical tampering and biomedical warfare became primary features of the viral outbreak narrative: for example, ABC's 1994 miniseries *The Stand* based on the Stephen King novel of the same name, and Michael Crichton's 1995 *Outbreak*. Alien DNA splicing is central to *Species* (dir. Roger Donaldson, 1995) and *Species II* (dir. Peter Medak, 1997) as well as to *The X-Files'* series mythology. Movies like *Jurassic Park* (dir. Steven Spielberg, 1993) and *The Lost World: Jurassic Park II* (dir. Steven Spielberg, 1997), both of which were major box office hits, eschewed the viral apocalypse but intensified the notion of unchecked science as a potential menace to human beings.

The mid- to late 1990s produced a string of natural disaster films, frequently thinly veiled allegories for the growing awareness of ecological crises: *Twister* (dir. Jan de Bont, 1996), *Dante's Peak* (dir. Roger Donaldson, 1997), *Volcano* (dir. Mick Jackson, 1997), *Deep Impact* (dir. Mimi Leder, 1998), and the biggest blockbuster of them all, Michael Bay's 1998 *Armageddon*. Most of these films are more action and suspense than anything else, and may only marginally have SF elements to them (*Armageddon* being the strongest exception). However, most of these films involve advances in technology ahead of their time, aimed at not only trying to predict but ultimately trying to stop natural disasters and save humanity through scientific ingenuity.

Mad Science

As *Jurassic Park* and its many imitators attest, science can be a double-edged sword. A significant amount of films throughout the 1980s and 1990s are concerned with the dangers / fears of technology, such as *The Terminator*, *Altered States* (dir. Ken Russell, 1980), *Looker* (dir. Michael Crichton, 1981), *Blade Runner* (dir. Ridley Scott, 1982), *Tron* (dir. Steven Lisberger, 1982), *Videodrome* (dir. David Cronenberg, 1983), *Brainstorm* (dir. Douglas Trumbull, 1983), *Weird Science* (dir. John Hughes, 1985), *Back to the Future* (dir. Robert Zemeckis, 1985), *Short Circuit* (dir. John Badham, 1986), *RoboCop, Innerspace* (dir. Joe Dante, 1987), *Jurassic Park*, and *Mimic* (dir. Guillermo del Toro, 1997). These films vary widely in their tone and style, from the light and lighthearted to the dark and brooding, but each film in some fashion explores the concept of technology's potentially threatening relationship to humanity – often without any compensatory utopian potential or positive application. For instance, David Cronenberg explores the tension between the deadly and the erotic in the human–

technology interface in such notable and influential films as *Videodrome*, *The Fly*, and *eXistenZ* (1999). Cronenberg's imagery in these films is often grotesque, with biomechanical representations that chart territory similar in some ways to the dark paintings of H. R. Giger, whose own work blends the mechanistic and the human in ways simultaneously disturbing and erotic, largely within a science-fictional context.[10]

Even though the threat of nuclear war is the background of John Badham's 1982 film *WarGames*, the film also highlights the fears surrounding technology, especially around personal computing;[11] the computer in the 1980s leads to mischief at best, nuclear war at worst. *Tron* eradicates the line between human and machine. *Weird Science* light-heartedly plays upon this fear as well: Gary and Wyatt create the woman of their dreams simply by using a doll and a computer. However, even the threat of war lingers in that film, as the boys accidently create a nuclear missile with their home computer as well.

A subset of technology gone awry is the subject of mind control, a category that crosses the two decades and overlaps with other areas. In film, again we again see *Altered States*, *Videodrome*, and *RoboCop* in the 1980s, as well as Cronenberg's *Scanners* (1981), *Star Trek II: The Wrath of Khan* (dir. Nicholas Meyer, 1982), *Dreamscape* (dir. Joseph Ruben, 1984), and *They Live* (dir. John Carpenter, 1988). Various television shows similarly addressed mind control at various points during their series' run: *Doctor Who* (1963–89), *Alf* (1986–90), *Teenage Mutant Ninja Turtles* (the animated series 1987–96), *Star Trek: The Next Generation* (1987–94). This interest in manipulation and mind control – and the attendant Gnostic, Philip.-K.-Dickian suggestion that reality itself may be a lie – extends into the next decade with *Total Recall*, *Jacob's Ladder* (dir. Adrian Lyne, 1990), *The X-Files* (1993–2002, and films), *Men in Black* (dir. Barry Sonnenfeld, 1997) and its sequels, and, most influentially, *The Matrix* (dir. Wachowski siblings, 1999) and its sequels.

The preoccupation of these types of films with 1980s technology, the human body, and mind control is a natural segue into the boom of virtual reality films of the 1990s. The first crop of virtual reality headsets in the late

[10] H. R. Giger was also the artist who created much of the sinister imagery found in the *Alien* franchise, including the famous Xenomorph.

[11] The first personal computer was introduced in the mid-1970s, but computers were not a household item until about 1983. *Time Magazine* declared 1982 "the year of the computer"; in 1984 Apple introduced the Apple Macintosh, and in 1985, Microsoft introduced the first Windows operating system.

1980s was too high a price point for the average person,[12] but by 1991 there were VR group arcade games. *The Lawnmower Man* (dir. Brett Leonard, 1992) brought VR to a larger audience by depicting VR as being capable of increasing human intelligence. In 1993 and 1995, Sega and Nintendo, respectively, introduced VR gaming consoles. Following *The Lawnmower Man* were a handful of VR movies of the early 1990s: *Arcade* (dir. Alex Pyun, 1993), *Brainscan* (dir. John Flynn, 1994), *Virtuosity* (dir. Brett Leonard, 1995), *Strange Days* (dir. Kathryn Bigelow, 1995), and *Johnny Mnemonic* (dir. Robert Longo, 1995) in the first half of the decade, most of them quite forgettable.[13] The second half of the decade though gave us some standouts in terms of both VR and SF; the three most noteworthy are *Dark City* (dir. Alex Proyas, 1998), *The Thirteenth Floor* (dir. Josef Rusnak, 1999), and, of course, *The Matrix*.

All things being equal, most would argue that *The Matrix* is the standout film of the 1990s, and much has been written on the film's style, influence, philosophy, even its impact on teacher education; see, for instance, the discussion of the film in the context of the cyberpunk and post-cyberpunk moment in Chapter 32 of this volume. Remixing the basic coordinates of *The Terminator*'s robot future for the hyperconnected Internet era, *The Matrix* not only charted new territory for the SF film but also helped transform the action film more broadly. The movie pioneered a specific form of stylized action sequences called "bullet time" that had yet to be either seen or used successfully in a blockbuster film up to that point. Now, the visual style that originated with *The Matrix* has been used so much that it has almost become cliché and trite, registering the film's immense influence and popularity.

The Alien Body and the Other

The body as a subject of difference marks both major and minor films of the decade.[14] *Alien* and its sequel *Aliens* (dir. James Cameron, 1986) provide a paradigmatic example. The threat that appears for the first half of *Alien* is the alien that impregnates humans in order to reproduce and destroy, thus repurposing our bodies for its own designs. But we soon discover a second

---

[12] The EyePhone VR platforms ranged in price from approximately $9000 to almost $50,000.

[13] Michael Crichton's *Disclosure* differs somewhat from the other VR films in that it more or less uses VR to further the plot of the movie, whereas VR *is* the point of the other films.

[14] For what is perhaps the most definitive source on the subject of the body/other/cyber-organisms, see Donna Haraway, "A Cyborg Manifesto: Science, Technology, and Socialist-Feminism in the Late Twentieth Century," in *Simians, Cyborgs, and Women: The Reinvention of Nature* (London: Routledge, 1991), pp. 149–81.

threat that the emergency of the Xenomorph has blinded us to: Ash, secretly a robot, who has been programmed to *protect* the alien so that the corporation they work for can monetize it. In Ash's calculus, humans are expendable; only the profit of the company counts. The 1986 sequel, *Aliens*, presents us with an "artificial human" so lifelike that he is nearly indistinguishable from the humans, but who has been programmed with safeguards to prevent him from becoming a threat; in a sense, Bishop's character conforms with – or plays off – a version of Isaac Asimov's famous Laws of Robotics. Since the newer versions of the artificial humans cannot hurt humans or allow harm to come to humans, the threat now is not in the "robot" but rather in the actual human, Carter Burkes (Paul Reiser), whose inhuman allegiance is once again to the corporation above all. In the seven years between the two films we thus see the development of human greed and mid-decade fears of corporate takeover allegorized as something that might colonize everything so completely that they will even take over our bodies.

The artificial human or cyborg also stands in for a missing piece of the self, or of the traditional family (now believed lost). The replicant Rachel in *Blade Runner* is the "daughter" to Dr. Eldon Tyrell, a.k.a., "the father" of all the replicants; Lois, an all-purpose robotic maid in Michael Crichton's 1984 *Runaway*, replaces the deceased mother and wife in the Ramsay home, as Schwarzenegger's reprogrammed, now-heroic T-800 replaces John Connor's lost father in *Terminator 2: Judgment Day* (dir. James Cameron, 1991). Driven by hormones and a basic teenage male desire for sex, Gary and Wyatt's need for female human connection in *Weird Science* drives them to create their version of a perfect woman who, though created by machine, teaches them to be more human and how to respect women.

Other films involving aliens overlap with space travel, colonization, mind control, and space war. There are malicious invasions and there are kind invasions. Spielberg's major blockbuster of the early 1980s, *E.T.* (1982), sets the tone for aliens who are not around to harm humans but are in fact vulnerable to our paranoia, an outlook common to its many imitators, particularly in material directed at children like *The Flight of the Navigator* (dir. Randal Kleiser, 1986), *Batteries Not Included* (dir. Matthew Robbins, 1987), and *Alf* (NBC, 1986–90). Even in movies for adults, alien otherness frequently provided a source of transcendent inspiration or hope, as in *Starman* (dir. John Carpenter, 1984), *Coccoon* (dir. Ron Howard, 1985), and *Contact* (dir. Robert Zemeckis, 1997). But just as commonly we see aliens as an external threat requiring tremendous violence to repel, as in *V: The Series* (1983–4), *Predator*, *They Live*, *Mars Attacks* (dir. Tim Burton, 1996), and *Independence Day* (dir.

Roland Emmerich, 1996), to name only a few entrants in an incredibly popular subgenre.

The subject of aliens would be incomplete without a discussion of Fox's *The X-Files*, which ran from 1993 to 2002 before moving to films (and ultimately returning to television with the original cast in 2016). Drawing on 1990s interest in conspiracy, paranoia, and the occult, the show was highly popular both critically and culturally during its height, and remains influential on SF television today. *The X-Files* seemed to reawaken a popular fascination with aliens, linking it to distrust of both governmental and corporate authority. The show's blending of stand-alone cases-of-the-week with a series-long mythos involving an imminent alien invasion has since become paradigmatic in the industry.

Superheroes

The 1980s and 1990s also saw a proliferation of superhero- and comic book-inspired films. The two biggest franchises of the 1980s and 1990s were both DC Comics heroes: Superman and Batman. Richard Donner's 1978 *Superman* sets the stage for superhero movies to follow. There were three *Superman* sequels in the 1980s, with *Superman III* (dir. Richard Lester, 1983) and *Superman IV: The Quest for Peace* (dir. Sidney J. Furie, 1987) each attempting to capitalize on the 1980s zeitgeist: computers and the threat of nuclear war (with diminishing returns). Tim Burton's 1989 *Batman* established a darker and grittier template for the superhero film than the brightly colored and grinning Christopher Reeves Superman – though its sequels would abandon grit and develop a campiness that would echo the *Batman* TV series of the 1960s. The period inaugurated a superhero craze that, with ebbs and flows, has continued to the present, including filmic treatments of Swamp Thing, Supergirl, Howard the Duck, the Teenage Mutant Ninja Turtles, the Rocketeer, failed attempts at Captain America and the Fantastic Four, the Mighty Morphin Power Rangers, Spawn, and many more. Needless to say, both the Terminator and Matrix franchises overlap with this subgenre as well: the "good" Terminator of *T2* uses the outsized strength, single-mindedness, and indefatigability of the original Terminator to save lives rather than kill them, while the full emergence of Neo's powers in the virtual world allows him to fly away like Superman at the end of *The Matrix* (albeit with a black trench coat rather than a bright red cape).

On television, *The Incredible Hulk* (CBS, 1978–2) was probably the most notable comics-inspired series, and there were three made-for-TV movies that followed the series in the late 1980s: *The Incredible Hulk Returns* (NBC, 1988), *The Trial of the Incredible Hulk* (NBC, 1989), and *The Death of the Incredible Hulk* (NBC, 1990). During its run of *The Incredible Hulk*, CBS also ran *Captain America* and *Captain America II: Death Too Soon* (1979). There were a handful of other made-for-TV films, such as *The Justice League of America* (CBS, 1997) and *Black Scorpion* and *Black Scorpion II: Aftershock* (Showtime, 1995, 1997). While there were several films and television shows inspired by comics and superheroes that attempted to capitalize on the success of *Superman* and *Batman*, most failed or flew under the radar; not until Brian Singer's 2000 *X-Men* movie would there be a major revitalization of the comic book superhero genre in film.

Then there is Joss Whedon's *Buffy the Vampire Slayer* – not a superhero in traditional comic terms, nor properly SF by some traditional definitions, but still worthy of mention here. The 1997 series, though a spinoff of the 1992 film of the same name, featured a much darker version of Buffy than the campy early 1990s film. (Though primarily devoted to vampire slaying, Buffy also often fought science-fiction-inspired foes on occasion, most notably the Frankenstein pastiche Adam built by the military in season four and the technophilic "Evil Nerd Trio" in season six.) The series was a cult hit, inspired multiple transmedia spinoffs, and still has a legion of fans, even producing one of the first academic groups devoted to dedicated pop culture analysis of a single television series, Buffy Studies (later expanded to Whedon Studies).

Time Travel

Time travel in SF in the 1980s and 1990s runs the gamut during these two decades from the light-hearted and frivolous to the serious and horrific. A handful address space/time paradox overtly: *Millennium* (dir. Michael Anderson, 1989), the *Back to the Future* trilogy, *Star Trek: The Voyage Home* (dir. Leonard Nimoy, 1986), *First Contact* (dir. Jonathan Frakes, 1996), *Twelve Monkeys* (dir. Terry Gilliam, 1995), *Bill and Ted's Excellent Adventure* (dir. Stephen Herek, 1989) and *Bill and Ted's Bogus Journey* (dir. Peter Hewitt as Pete Hewitt, 1991), and *Peggy Sue Got Married* (dir. Francis Ford Coppola, 1986). (Again, *The Terminator* and *Terminator 2: Judgment Day* make important appearances in yet another category.) As with the other categories, the idea of time travel seems to dialectically produce both optimistic and bitterly pessimistic possibilities, with even the most comedic entries in time-travel fiction simultaneously producing dark speculations about free will, human nature, and the fight for control of the future; even the characters from the ultra-light-hearted *Back to the Future* find themselves briefly trapped in a night-marish alternate timeline as a result of their travels in *Back to the Future, Part II* (dir. Robert Zemeckis, 1988).

Time travel was popular on television as well, as in the long-running British television series *Doctor Who* (which had its first run from the early 1960s through 1989) and *Quantum Leap* (1989–93), as well as a frequently deployed trope on *Star Trek: The Next Generation* and its sequel series. Here, too, time travel produces both possibility (Sam Beckett uses the Quantum Leap Accelerator to set right what once went wrong; the Doctor uses his time machine to save the Earth time and time again) and catastrophe (on all three series, essentially any major deviation from the "official" timeline results in disaster). The shorthand developed in popular time travel narratives of the period has produced a consensus theory of time travel that is startlingly conservative in its orientation; nearly any attempt to change the past is horrendously ill-fated or actively malicious, and the true "point" of nearly every time travel story becomes not to change the present or to control the future but rather to become reconciled with the past (however bad you once thought it is, or actually was). With few exceptions, like the minor, highly local improvements allowed in *Quantum Leap* and the ending of the original *Back to the Future*, nearly any conceivable change will either prove impossible (like the vicious time loops in *Twelve Monkeys* and the *Terminator* series) or else inevitably be for the worse (*First Contact*, "Yesterday's Enterprise," *Back to the Future, Part II*, and so on).

Toward the End of the Century

I agree with Vivian Sobchack's claim to some degree: "If we are to make evaluative statements, few SF films are great; most are not even good."[15] This chapter concerned itself mostly with films and television that remain highly recognizable, highly influential, or both. Of course, there are some questionable moments; while *C.H.U.D. II: Bud the C.H.U.D.* captures campily major concerns of the late 1980s, it is hard to argue that the film is good or even worthy of inclusion in this chapter, entertaining as I find it. No such list could be exhaustive; while I feel I have encompassed a broad scope here, had space permitted, it might have been a worthwhile pursuit to look at a B-film like Roger Corman's 1980 *Battle Beyond the Stars* as a response to the *Star Wars*

---

[15] Vivian Sobchack, *Screening Space: The American Science Fiction Film* (New Brunswick, NJ: Rutgers University Press, 2004), p. 20.

blockbusters, or the ways in which Chris Carter's other TV show of the mid-1990s, *Millennium*, explored in its own terms enduring fears of government conspiracy and bio-warfare (through supernatural and religious backdrops). I might also have turned to the new, intense nostalgia for the 1980s in texts ranging from *Stranger Things* (2016–) and *Ready Player One* (book 2011, film 2018) to recent reboots and revivals of the *Ghostbusters*, *Star Wars*, *Star Trek*, *Mad Max*, *Blade Runner*, *Tron*, *Terminator*, and *Alien* franchises (among others).

Sobchack likewise notes that "the SF film is ever aware – thematically and visually – that we have to live in our own future, and that future, unknowable as it may finally be, is very real."[16] What we see from SF films from the late 1970s on, through the end of the century/millennium, is how dramatically that vision of the future changes, and how persuasively and enduringly it comes over the period to be seen not as a space of hope or potential renewal so much as a space of permanent menace, disaster, and threat.

[16] Ibid., p. 103.

34

"Strangers to Ourselves": Gender and Sexuality in Recent Science Fiction

VERONICA HOLLINGER

> How might we encounter the difference that calls our grids of intelligibility into question without trying to foreclose the challenge that the difference delivers? What might it mean . . . to be willing, in the name of the human, to allow the human to become something other than what it is tradition-ally assumed to be?
>
> Judith Butler[1]

Stories for "Posthumans"

In a recent review of a 2013 anthology of stories titled *21st Century Science Fiction*, critic John Clute raises, in his own inimitable style, an alarm about what he sees as the anthology's overall failure "to awaken from the unflagged quantum-entanglement dream of classic sf into regions less congenial." "The allure of *Homo sapiens*-compliant sf is great," he observes. "As a species, we do not do well with strangeness." Clute's rather devastating final claim is that, in our own particularly fraught early twenty-first century, "the stories that make us feel most human are no longer the stories that tell us the truth."[2] Taking my cue from Clute, I want to focus in this chapter on a selection of Anglo-American SF novels and stories that are not "*Homo sapiens*-compliant" but which instead make use of SF's powers of estrangement to challenge some of our comfort-able ideological investments in ourselves as sexed and gendered human beings. In this new millennium of economic globalization and climate crisis, under the influence of increasingly transformative developments in technoscience, and in the context of an ethical responsibility to the ideals of social justice, we can no longer (if we ever could) afford to be nostalgic for less complex and more "human" ways of being in the world.

---

[1] Judith Butler, *Undoing Gender* (New York: Routledge, 2004), p. 33.
[2] John Clute, "*21st Century Science Fiction*, edited by David G. Hartwell and Patrick Nielsen Hayden," *The New York Review of Science Fiction* 328 (December 2015), pp. 4–5.

Questions about gender and sexuality are inextricably tangled up in questions about who is or is not to be recognized as fully human. The equations for what Adrienne Rich named "compulsory heterosexuality"[3] are simple and fearsomely coercive: "sexual desire [for the opposite sex] follows from [hetero]sexual orientation that in turn follows from feminine/masculine behaviours thought to follow from biological [female/male] sex."[4] Those subjects who fail to perform gender appropriately, or whose sexual expression does not adhere to the norms of "the heterosexual matrix," risk being relegated to what queer/feminist theorist Judith Butler refers to as "abject zones within sociality."[5] Such abjected individuals are "unintelligible" insofar as they disrupt the conventional alignments among genders, bodies, and sexualities. Counterintuitively, Butler argues that gender takes priority, retroactively constituting "sex" according to always-already historically determined assumptions about appropriate roles for women and men.[6] Historian Thomas Laqueur draws much the same conclusion, pointing out that, based on the historical evidence, "sex ... is situational; it is explicable only within the context of battles over gender and power."[7]

As a future-oriented narrative genre, SF has the potential to imagine differently. Most noticeably since the feminist movements of the 1970s, and under the influence of later lesbian and gay, queer, and trans theories and practices – as well as responding to the dizzying pace of technoscientific change since the second half of the twentieth century – a growing number of SF stories have worried away at the fabric of unreflective and conventional ideas about "women" and "men" and "sex." Through its estranged worlds and its multiplicity of futures, through the sense of wonder invited by its novums, and perhaps most importantly through its critical potential as "the literature of change," that is, its commitment to the idea of historical change

[3] Adrienne Rich, "Compulsory Heterosexuality and Lesbian Existence," *Signs* 5, 4 (Summer 1980), pp. 631–60.
[4] Mari Mikkola, "Feminist Perspectives on Sex and Gender," in *The Stanford Encyclopedia of Philosophy* (Stanford: Stanford University Press, 2011), p. 10.
[5] Judith Butler, *Bodies That Matter: On the Discursive Limits of "Sex"* (New York: Routledge, 1993), p. 243 n. 2. The heterosexual matrix is "that grid of cultural intelligibility through which bodies, genders, and desires are naturalized" (Butler, *Gender Trouble: Feminism and the Subversion of Identity* [New York: Routledge, 1990], p. 151 n. 6). Power works on both the body and the psyche. As Karen Barad explains, "The relationship between the material and the discursive is one of mutual entailment. Neither is articulated/articulable in the absence of the other; matter and meaning are mutually articulated" ("Posthumanist Performativity: Toward an Understanding of How Matter Comes to Matter," *Signs* 28, 3 [2003], p. 822).
[6] Butler, *Bodies That Matter*, pp. 5–6
[7] Thomas Laqueur, *Making Sex: Body and Gender from the Greeks to Freud* (Cambridge, MA: Harvard University Press, 1990), p. 11.

through time, SF is particularly well suited to exploring alternative ways of being/doing human.

Second-wave feminism amply demonstrated the social constitution of gender roles (feminine/masculine), although often assuming bodies (female/male) to be biologically determined. But bodies too, as Butler and others have argued, are to a significant extent socially constituted and historically determined, even as they make their own demands on both the individual and the social. Under the onslaught of contemporary technoscientific advances, we might consider that not even "nature" is natural these days.

I begin, therefore, in the brilliantly imagined and radically unnatural far-future universe of Greg Egan's *Schild's Ladder* (2001), in which human beings have been extinct for 19,000 years. The novel's incredibly powerful posthuman characters exist virtually and/or corporeally and/or in as many copies of themselves as they desire. Egan provides no physical descriptions: his characters are unmarked by sex, race, ethnicity, age, or any of the other differential attributes by which we categorize human beings. Into this universe limps the hugely outmoded spaceship of the Anachronauts, a sorry remnant of humanity who have survived through cryogenic suspension and been literally resurrected into the future. The Anachronauts travel from planet to planet ostensibly to witness the future unfolding – "to witness what humanity would become." Specifically, they are looking for signs of "the eternal struggle between women and men,"[8] signs, that is, that heterosexual gender binarism still prevails and that, therefore, "human nature" is still human nature. For the Anachronauts, the absolute distinction between nature and culture is a given. Although Egan's posthumans have long since abandoned any investment in the idea of a "natural" humanity,

> Nobody could bring themselves to break the news that the sole surviving remnant of human sexual dimorphism was the retention, in some languages, of different inflections of various parts of speech associated with different proper names – and that expecting these grammatical fossils to be correlated with any aspect of a person's anatomy would be like assuming from similar rules for inanimate objects that a cloud possessed a penis and a table contained a womb.[9]

For the Anachronauts as for Egan's readers, gender as the division of human beings into women and men is a fact of life, if not *the* fact of life. To consider that it might be historically contingent upon a particular version of the

---

[8] Greg Egan, *Schild's Ladder* (London: Gollancz, 2003 [2001]), p. 129.
[9] Ibid.

human, one that may well be technologically superseded by our posthuman progeny, is both profoundly unsettling and, at the same time, deeply resonant with the sense of wonder that permeates this fascinating novel. Egan imagines a post-gender world in which there are no more conventionally coherent links between and among gender, sex, and sexuality. For some readers, as for the Anachronauts, this will mark the absolute annihilation of our essential humanity; for others this will fulfill the promise of a great liberation. After all, we can already see how the lines between nature and culture are blurring as we embark on our own technological self-fashioning.

Schild's Ladder locates its posthumans on the other side of some unimaginable technological singularity, all too quickly bypassing questions about how this utopian future, which can look back on a "nineteen-thousand year era in which no sentient being had died at the hands of another,"[10] has come into existence. There are no sexual–political conflicts in the novel because there are no more women and men. *Schild's Ladder* is about the sublime affective power of the physical universe, not about the struggles of materially sexed bodies upon which these politics are constructed and upon which they act.

In contrast, Kim Stanley Robinson's *2312* (2012), another novel of the posthuman future, raises ethical, philosophical, and political questions about the work required to create and to maintain a more just society. Its singularity is less an abrupt break than a gradual and benign techno-evolution that takes place over the course of several centuries. Robinson's characters, unlike Egan's, are always materially embodied: his two protagonists are biologically both female and male; although one identifies as a woman and the other as a man, each has borne children during the course of their long lifetimes. One of the most striking textual features of *2312* is the many interruptions to the narrative by long sequences of fictional historical, scientific, and philosophical fragments variously referred to as "lists" or "extracts." One fragment in "Extract (7)" notes that "prenatally selected bisexuality has the strongest positive correlation with longevity," and another fragment notes that "principal categories of self-image for gender include feminine, masculine, androgynous, gynandromorphous, hermaphroditic, ambisexual, bisexual, intersex, neuter, eunuch, nonsexual, undifferentiated, gay, lesbian, queer, invert, homosexual, polymorphous, poly, labile, berdache, hijra, two-spirit ..."[11] Comparatively speaking, our own present-day efforts at

---

[10] Ibid., p. 205.

[11] Kim Stanley Robinson, *2312* (New York: Orbit, 2012). Like Robinson, Egan also imagines a multiplicity of sexualities: in one scene in *Schild's Ladder*, an "ex-acorporeal" is reduced to helpless laughter by his first experience of embodied sexuality; his disgruntled partner

inclusiveness, such as in the acronym "LGBTQ2S" – lesbian, gay, bisexual, transgender, queer, two-spirited – appear very narrowly conceived.

Robinson imagines that, given the choice, many individuals would value some kind of multi-sexual and imaginatively enhanced embodiment. Taking up some of the arguments of contemporary posthumanist philosophy, *2312* supports the idea that "human" has never been a stable category and that it will inevitably mean something different in the future.[12] *2312* does not support the categorical distinction between the human and the posthuman that partially structures *Schild's Ladder*. Instead, it imagines a gradual expansion of the ways in which we can be human; as one of the characters argues, "it isn't being *post* human, it's being *fully* human. It would be stupid not to do the good things when you can, it would be *anti* human."[13]

Stories for "Women"

In different ways, *Schild's Ladder* and *2312* both speculate about technocultural futures in which the constraints and injustices of real-world gender politics no longer hold sway over posthuman subjects who inhabit worlds of multiplex sexualities. There are no more "women" and "men" in any meaningful sense in these novels, since the lives of their characters have little to do with the social roles assigned to individuals on the supposed basis of "naturally" sexed female and male bodies. Not coincidentally, one of the most significant threads in feminist theory since the 1980s, much influenced by postmodern thought, has been a careful critique of the identity politics, the "gender realism,"[14] that was so foundational to 1970s second-wave feminist theory and practice, and which tended to treat "woman" as a universal and ahistorical category.

Lesbian sadomasochism (S/M) activist Pat Califia's short story, "The Hustler" (1988), is a pointed critique of this kind of "gender realism." In the story's near future, women have overcome their centuries of personal and political repression and are now the ruling "sex." Dramatizing a historical opposition between politically acceptable feminism and its abjected outlaw sister, lesbian S/M, the first-person narrator, a butch "top," muses to herself:

suggests that "Next time you want an authentic embodied experience, just simulate it" (p. 123).
[12] See Rosi Braidotti's eco-feminist study of philosophical posthumanism, *The Posthuman* (Oxford: Wiley, 2013).
[13] Robinson, *2312*, p. 100.
[14] Mikkola, "Feminist Perspectives on Sex and Gender," p. 7.

It's just fine with me that men don't run the world any more, that the war has stopped, and that we're trying to stop contaminating the planet. But I can't help but wonder why so many of us have not profited greatly from the women's revolution, despite the fact that we are women. Perhaps it's because I'm just not the right kind of woman.[15]

Lesbian S/M is "unintelligible" in the context of heterosexual femininity and, since all human beings purportedly must "have" gender, lesbian S/M becomes a "perversion" that marginalizes its practitioners and renders them less than fully human, even to many feminists.

At the same time, the 1980s – the last decade of the Cold War – were a period of conservative backlash against women's demands for gender equality and social justice, a moment encapsulated in the title of Susan Faludi's bestseller, *Backlash: The Undeclared War against American Women* (1991). One of the most accomplished speculative fictions of this period, Margaret Atwood's *The Handmaid's Tale* (1985), is a bleak dystopian extrapolation of this "undeclared war." In the novel's near future, the fundamentalist state of Gilead obsessively exerts absolute control over women and their sexuality, efficiently color-coding them according to their perceived functions. Handmaids, whose sole function is to bear children, must always wear red; unmarried daughters wear white; widows wear black; and so on. Sterile women, lesbians ("gender traitors"), nuns, and "incorrigibles" – "Discards, all of us"[16] – are utterly abjected as disposable "Unwomen" and condemned by the state to work at toxic waste disposal sites, a sure sentence of death.[17] In a kind of grim irony, the patriarchs of Gilead share the same commitment to "gender realism" as those feminists who reify the idea that there is a "right kind of woman." An ironic "Historical Notes" coda to the discovered manuscript that is the novel, set at a "Gilead Studies" academic conference decades after the regime has fallen, dyspeptically suggests that rigid gender normativity and assumed male supremacy persist even in its much more optimistic future.

In the context of postmodern technoculture, Donna Haraway's "A Manifesto for Cyborgs" was one of the period's most influential disruptions

---

[15] Pat Califia, "The Hustler," in *Macho Sluts: Erotic Fiction* (Boston: Alyson, 1988), p. 179. See also Califia's substantial "Introduction" to *Macho Sluts*, pp. 9–27.

[16] Margaret Atwood, *The Handmaid's Tale* (Toronto: McClelland and Stuart, 1986 [1985]), p. 233.

[17] Among other things, *The Handmaid's Tale* is a warning about taking for granted the gains for women of the second-wave feminist movement. Atwood's protagonist, Offred, is conscious of her own complicity in the gradual establishment of Gilead's dystopian regime; in this sense, the novel is also a critique of the problematic concept of postfeminism: "We lived, as usual, by ignoring. Ignoring isn't the same as ignorance, you have to work at it" (ibid., p. 3).

in the ongoing intellectual history of "woman." Originally published in 1985, like *The Handmaid's Tale*, Haraway's "Manifesto" suggested a new way to think about the subject in technoculture – as a cyborg, "a hybrid of machine and organism, a creature of social reality as well as a creature of fiction."[18] Haraway argued that the most appropriate and effective collective action for this kind of fragmented subject would be based on a politics of affinity rather than identity: "With the hard-won recognition of their social and historical constitution, gender, race, and class cannot provide the basis for belief in 'essential' unity. There is nothing about being 'female' that naturally binds women."[19] Especially since the 1980s, there has been a growing realization that human subjects are constituted at the intersections not only of gender and sexuality, but also of the many other identity markers through which we differentiate ourselves and each other.

Haraway honors the radical challenges to gender essentialism in the SF of "theorists for cyborgs"[20] such as Joanna Russ, James Tiptree, Jr. (Alice Sheldon), Vonda M. McIntyre, and John Varley, and in the pioneering SF of African-American writers such as Samuel R. Delany and Octavia E. Butler. Hybrid subject/ivities are at the core of Butler's classic Xenogenesis trilogy, for example. The first book, *Dawn* (1987), introduces readers to black protagonist Lilith Iyapo; she has become a captive of the alien Oankali, for whom sexual pleasure between females and males is mediated by a "third sex," the ooloi. Throughout the ensuing books, hybrid families of human and Oankali, enabled by the aliens' advanced biotechnological skills, produce "construct" children, literal biological hybrids. In Butler's work, as in the SF of newer writers such as Jamaican-Canadian Nalo Hopkinson, African-American Nisi Shawl, and of non-Anglo-American writers such as East Indian Vandana Singh and South African Lauren Beukes, sex, gender, and race are inextricably bound together in the constitution of characters and events.

Whether gender is "real"/natural or "artificial"/cultural, it remains a salient marker of the human. Not everyone dreams of a post-gender world. A passionate desire to be recognized as fully human is at the heart

---

[18] Donna Haraway, "A Manifesto for Cyborgs: Science, Technology, and Socialist Feminism in the 1980s," reprinted in Elizabeth Weed, ed., *Coming to Terms: Feminism, Theory, Politics* (New York: Routledge 1989 [1985]), p. 174.

[19] Haraway continues: "There is not even such a state as being 'female,' itself a highly complex category . . . Gender, race, or class consciousness is an achievement forced on us by the terrible historical experience of the contradictory social realities of patriarchy, colonialism, and capitalism . . . Painful fragmentation among feminists (not to mention among women) along every possible fault line has made the concept of *woman* elusive, an excuse for the matrix of women's domination of each other" (ibid., p. 179).

[20] Ibid.

of Shariann Lewitt's "A Real Girl" (1998), a post-cyberpunk story marked by the theoretical fragmentation of "woman" as the subject of feminism and by the growing influence of queer theory and its critiques of essences and identities. Lewitt's narrator/protagonist is an artificial intelligence who, in an anti-Cartesian commitment to embodiment and sexual difference, is about to be downloaded into a cloned female body: "To my normal perception of myself and the world, I am four pounds of neural computing circuitry in a box ... I am two hundred years old."[21] The "I" of Lewitt's story identifies "herself" as both a woman and a lesbian. In order to join her lover, with whom she has enjoyed a technologically enabled virtual relationship, in the physical world, she is determined to take on "authentic" human corporeality and become "a real girl" – achieving, as it were, an "intelligible" alignment between her self-identity and her sexed embodiment.

This suggests how it is possible to read "A Real Girl" as, among other things, an allegory of transsexual subjectivity.[22] Lewitt's AI prepares to be downloaded into a body that, she is convinced, will guarantee her status as an authentic woman. Like many trans persons, she is invested in gendered identity in a way that directly counteracts assumptions such as Judith Butler's about gender as a culturally constituted performance. Certainly for Lewitt's AI, gender is ontologically real and crucial to her sense of herself. At the very least, the particular kind of "gender realism" to which "she" is committed suggests the contingency of these concepts and their dependence, at least in part, on the claims made on subjectivity by embodied identity.

At the same time, the subject constructed in Lewitt's story – a two-hundred-year-old lesbian artificial intelligence about to be downloaded into an eighteen-year-old cloned body – has so little to do with common-sense categories such as "real" and "girl" that the rules of heteronormativity are rendered meaningless. Virtually anyone can lay claim to attributes such as "real" and "girl": we are all constantly striving to pass the Turing tests of gender. In this sense, "A Real Girl" takes on a fine ironic resonance

---

[21] Shariann Lewitt, "A Real Girl," in Nicola Griffith and Stephen Pagel, ed., *Bending the Landscape: Original Gay and Lesbian Writing: Science Fiction* (Woodstock, NY: Overlook, 1998), pp. 266–7.

[22] Technologically enabled sex changes in SF are often imagined to be easy and accessible, for example in stories such as Delany's *Triton* (1976), Varley's "Options" (1979), and Egan's "Closer" (1992). This kind of fantasy hardly reflects the very real difficulties experienced by many trans persons, both inside and outside the context of formal transition.

as a literalization of Simone de Beauvoir's famous dictum that "One is not born, but rather becomes, woman."[23]

Stories for "Men" and "Women"

Since the 1990s there has been increasingly productive attention paid to the theoretical opposition between representationalism and performativity, initially explored by Judith Butler and developed more recently by theorists such as new materialist feminist Karen Barad. In this view, material-discursive regimes such as the heterosexual matrix are never innocent: they are not merely "sayings" but also "doings" that seek to bind subjects within normative systems.[24] In Barad's words, "representationalism is the belief in the ontological distinction between representations and that which they purport to represent; in particular, that which is represented is held to be independent of all practices of representing."[25] In fact, of course, gendered subjects do not exist prior to their constitution through the performative regimes of compulsory heterosexuality. At the same time, however, we are not completely at the mercy of these forces; otherwise, nothing would ever change, not even in SF stories.

As might be expected, many stories about gender and sexuality are structured around the struggle to resist often conflicting representations of "real" women and "real" men and, as such, we can read them as themselves performative utterances rather than as "mere" representations – that is, they seek to affect readers, to engage with them critically, and to invite them to consider how things might be otherwise. Perhaps this is even more pronounced in SF stories that cannot claim, as can realist narratives, merely to be representational of some pre-existing reality.

An appreciation for the powerful potential of SF as a literature of change led to the inauguration, in 1991, of the James Tiptree, Jr. Literary Award, which aims to encourage the expansion and exploration of gender in SF. A legendary figure in the field as a writer of darkly gripping feminist-oriented

---

[23] Simone de Beauvoir, *The Second Sex* [1949], trans. Constance Borde and Sheila Malovany-Chevallier (New York: Vintage, 2009), p. 330. As Mikkola notes, when gender and sex are theorized as in a more fluid relationship, "one can be a woman without being a female" (p. 19).

[24] For example, when the doctor announces that "it's a girl," this appears to be a simple description, the representation of an already existent entity; in Butler's argument, it is the first in an ongoing series of discursive and material practices that performatively constitute the child *as* a "girl" (*Bodies That Matter*, p. 232).

[25] Barad, "Posthumanist Performativity," p. 804.

short stories, Tiptree was eventually "outed" in 1977 as a woman: Alice Hastings Bradley Sheldon. Performing as a male writer enabled her writing, and her output declined noticeably after her "real" identity was discovered. Tiptree remains a paradigmatic figure of trans-textual performance and gender fluidity within the SF field.

John Kessel's complex and thought-provoking novella, "Stories for Men," won the Tiptree Award in 2002. Set in an apparently utopian matriarchal lunar colony, it uses the familiar SF strategy of gender-role reversal to tell a contemporary version of "the battle of the sexes," a trope that can be traced back at least as far as Leslie F. Stone's pulp extravaganza, "The Conquest of Gola" (1931). At the center of Kessel's novella is Erno, a discontented seventeen-year-old who falls under the spell of Tyler, an older man working to incite a men's revolution. In this women-ruled colony, men are second-class citizens who cannot vote or own property, recalling the disaffections of first-wave feminists of the late nineteenth and early twentieth centuries.

Kessel embeds a real-world book inside his story, intertextually connecting his imagined future with the historical past of a specific ideology of masculinity: Tyler gives Erno a copy of *Stories for Men*, a collection edited by Charles Grayson and originally published in 1936 (republished in a new edition in 2011). The conflict in the novella is between the matriarchy's efforts to reshape masculinity – in spite of its apparently innocent motto: "We do not seek to change men, but to offer them the opportunity to be other than they have been" – and a revolutionary conspiracy of men to take back power, inspired by a model of "authentic" masculinity.[26] The collection of grim stories in *Stories for Men* (by writers such as James T. Farrell, James M. Cain, and Dashiell Hammett) is supposed to provide this model: as Tyler says, positioning himself on the side of "gender realism," these are stories about "elemental manhood," but "Erno still had trouble grasping exactly the metaphor Tyler intended when he used the term 'man'."[27] Ultimately Erno refuses to participate in the violence the conspirators are planning: "So that this is the story of how Erno discovered that he was not a man."[28]

Motherhood rather than manhood is at the center of Eugene Fischer's short story, "The New Mother" (2015) – another Tiptree Award winner – which imagines a world in which some women no longer require men for reproduction; the result is a firestorm of moral and political panic. A new

---

[26] John Kessel, "Stories for Men" (2002), in Gardner Dozois, ed., *The Year's Best Science Fiction: Twentieth Annual Collection* (New York: St. Martin's Griffin, 2003), p. 258.

[27] Ibid., p. 267.

[28] Ibid., p. 301.

sexually transmitted disease called "Gamete Diploidy Syndrome" (GDS) is the story's novum; this "disease" induces pregnancies in women and renders men sterile: "Their genetically identical children will themselves be carriers, and will similarly begin auto-impregnating when they reach puberty."[29] Public panic results in calls for everything from cutting off federal funding for prenatal care for GDS mothers to forced sterilization; recalling Judith Butler's arguments about "intelligible" gender and "intelligible" sexuality, questions are raised as to whether these women and their children are in fact still human, since "natural" women reproduce through heterosexual congress. As one politician argues, "If we don't handle this correctly, it could literally be the end of mankind."[30] Tess Mendoza, Fischer's point-of-view character, who is covering the issue for a magazine article, concludes that "The battle lines are shaking out as a woman's right to choose versus a man's right to exist."[31]

Tess is in a lesbian partnership and has become pregnant through sperm donation. The story thus draws attention to already existing "unnatural" reproductive technologies. Are GDS pregnancies only another example of the many "unnatural" ways in which humans can reproduce these days? Or are GDS mothers and their clone-children "unintelligible," no longer the same species as "naturally" born human beings? "The New Mother" does not answer these questions. Instead, what Fischer gives readers is a sequence of scenes opening out to an utterly unpredictable future of difference in the relationships between women and men, a future which begs the question about the meaning of human being in the face of such difference.

Stories for "Queers"

Since we do not live in the far future of Egan's *Schild's Ladder*, the performative force of representationalist discourse in the constitution of gendered subjects remains rigidly coercive, even at the level of the pronouns that are applied to both people and things. While "she" and "he" and "it" are representational indices for specific individuals and objects,[32] they also signal

---

[29] Eugene Fischer, "The New Mother" (*Asimov's Science Fiction* [April/May 2015]), https://medium.com/@glorioushubris/the-new-mother-9df848da415b (last accessed May 23, 2018).

[30] Ibid.

[31] Ibid.

[32] *He, She and It* is the title of Marge Piercy's 1992 SF novel, which acknowledges the influence of both William Gibson's cyberpunk fiction and Haraway's cyborg theory. As the title suggests, the novel is centrally concerned with gender issues, especially in

that the recognition of an individual's humanity depends upon her or his prior recognition as "having" gender; gendered pronouns therefore also function as performatives that confer a crucial status on subjects in the social. SF has provided some striking examples of reimagining how pronouns work in order to transform gender representation at the level of the text. The result, in some cases, has been the construction of queer and queer-feminist worlds in which traditional differential identity categories no longer bind subjects and subjectivities.

The pioneering work in this context is Ursula K. Le Guin's *The Left Hand of Darkness* (1969). Le Guin's use of the masculine pronoun to reference the non-gendered aliens of the planet Gethen is highly effective in demonstrating the irrelevance of sexual binarism among the Gethenians. At the same time, however, the novel attracted a fair amount of criticism for performing the erasure of female subjects implied in the use of the conventionally universal "he." As many readers argued, the result was simply that all Gethenians appeared to be men.[33] In contrast, in her novel *Woman on the Edge of Time* (1976), Marge Piercy imagines a feminist utopia in which the end of women's oppression is suggested by the abandonment of gendered pronouns. In Piercy's future Mattapoisett, "per" is the universal pronoun which disrupts the performativity of gender constitution; it is impossible to identify a character's sex when "per" appears in the narrative. And in an efficacious reversal of *The Left Hand of Darkness*, on some of the many worlds of Samuel R. Delany's space epic *Stars in My Pocket Like Grains of Sand* (1984), "woman" is the default universal designation: "'she' is the pronoun for all sentient individuals of whatever species who have achieved the legal status of 'woman.' The ancient dimorphic form 'he,' once used exclusively for the gendered indication of males ... has been reserved for the general sexual object of 'she' ... regardless of the gender of the woman speaking or the gender of the woman referred to."[34]

terms of its construction of the android Yod. Yod is initially programmed by "its" male creator to function as a weapon, but is then reprogrammed to incorporate "feminine" attributes such as empathy and affection as well. Piercy's text is a significant exploration of the connections – affective, ethical, and political – between artificial and human subjects.

[33] Le Guin herself explored her problematic use of the male pronoun in some detail in her essay, "Is Gender Necessary?," originally published in 1976 and revised as "Is Gender Necessary? Redux" in 1987. In the latter she noted that "Men were inclined to be satisfied with the book, which allowed them a safe trip into androgyny and back, from a conventionally male viewpoint" (*Dancing at the Edge of the World: Thoughts on Words, Women, Places* [New York: Grove, 1989]), p. 16.

[34] Samuel R. Delany, *Stars in My Pocket Like Grains of Sand* (1984) (New York: Bantam, 1985), p. 78.

On the other side of their technological singularity, the posthumans of *Schild's Ladder* consider gendered words to be "grammatical fossils," completely lacking in performative force.[35] In Anne Leckie's very popular Tiptree-Award-winning space opera, *Ancillary Justice* (2013), which is set, like *Schild's Ladder*, in a vast posthuman universe, terms for gender remain crucially important. Echoing Delany's strategy in *Stars in My Pocket*, humans in the Radchaii Empire are no longer differentiated by gender: "she" is the universal pronoun. This relatively minor tweak to conventional English has results that are quite different from Le Guin's use of the universal "he," because "she" is exactly *never* the universal in the world of Leckie's readers. It functions to bring all sexed identities into question: heterosexuality as the horizon of expectations disappears. For the most part, it is impossible to know which of the characters are female and which are male, so that all sex in the novel is queer sex. Like *Stars in My Pocket*, Leckie's novel, the first of the *Imperial Radch* trilogy, imagines a post-gender world, and constructs it discursively through the performative force of its revisionary pronouns.

Leckie's protagonist, Breq, is "a corpse soldier,"[36] the sole remaining body of the many bodies that were enslaved to the artificial intelligence that controlled – that *was* – the Justice of Toren, a vast troop carrier in the Radchaii fleet: "I had once had twenty bodies, twenty pairs of eyes, and hundreds of others that I could access if I needed or desired it."[37] Breq is not human, although "she" wears a (technologically enhanced) human body. By the end of the third book in Leckie's trilogy, *Ancillary Mercy* (2015), the question of who is human has become superseded by the posthuman question of who counts as a "significant being" in a universe inhabited not only by humans and AIs, but also by the very powerful and wonderfully alien Presgar, who have no compunction about destroying any species who do not appear to them to be "significant." By this point in the trilogy, the cast of characters has grown to include AIs who are ships and space stations, as well as various species of humans and aliens. Breq's final revolutionary move is to make the case to the Presgar that "we AIs are not only a separate species from human, but also Significant."[38] In the face of intense human opposition to the fact of their "property" claiming such rights, the Presgar envoy concludes that

---

[35] Egan, *Schild's Ladder*, p. 129.
[36] Anne Leckie, *Ancillary Justice* (New York: Orbit e-book, 2013), n.p.
[37] Ibid., n.p.
[38] Anne Leckie, *Ancillary Mercy* (New York: Orbit e-book, 2015), n.p.

"The question of their Significance will, I suspect, be contentious, but the question has been raised and I judge it to be a valid one."[39]

Leckie's *Imperial Radch* trilogy is an exciting and witty series that has been compared in scope and tone to the Culture novels of the great Iain M. Banks. It takes advantage of the space opera subgenre not only to erase gender difference in language, but also to literalize an ethics of expansive inclusiveness. In the radically heterogeneous universe of Leckie's trilogy, the privileged term is "significant" – certainly not "human," although perhaps posthuman.

In a 2009 special issue of *Science Fiction Studies* on sexuality, writer Candas Jane Dorsey, dissatisfied with what Clute would later term *"Homo-sapiens-compliant sf,"*[40] called for "a breakthrough of paradigm . . . a real imagined future where our ideas of gender are so far gone that a modern reader is lost in the subjunctivity."[41] All the diverse ways in which recent SF has imagined genders and sexualities differently may not amount to Dorsey's "singularity of queer,"[42] but they do suggest the expansiveness with which SF stories have imagined the possibilities for post/human being. In its opposition to identity categories of all kinds, including most emphatically the gender binarism of normative heterosexuality, queer is a concept that opens out to unknowable futures and provides rich ground for speculative exploration. José Esteban Muñoz's *Cruising Utopia* movingly emphasizes the commitment of queerness to the future: "Queerness is not yet here . . . We have never been queer, yet queerness exists for us as an ideality that can be distilled from the past and used to imagine a future. The future is queerness's domain."[43] This is the future toward which stories such as Robinson's *2312*, Lewitt's "A Real Girl," and Fischer's "The New Mother" gesture; not surprisingly, these stories all end inconclusively, suggesting not only their inability to imagine what might come next, but also their reluctance to prescribe in advance how such futures of difference might unfold.

As if she were thinking through speculative fiction, Judith Butler has argued that "there is a certain departure from the human that takes place in order to start the process of remaking the human."[44] In *Undoing Gender*

---

[39] Ibid., n.p.

[40] Clute, "*21st Century Science Fiction*," p. 4.

[41] Candas Jane Dorsey, "Some Notes on the Failure of Sex and Gender Inquiry in SF," *Science Fiction Studies* 36, 3 (November 2009), p. 390.

[42] Ibid.

[43] José Esteban Muñoz, *Cruising Utopia: The Then and There of Queer Futurity* (New York: New York University Press, 2009), p. 1.

[44] Butler, *Undoing Gender*, pp. 3–4.

(2004), she references "the 'New Gender Politics' . . . a combination of movements concerned with transgender, transsexuality, intersex, and their complex relations to feminist and queer theory."[45] Most of the stories I have discussed here can be framed within this new politics, demonstrating the power of science-fictional estrangement to suggest new directions for considering the nature of human nature. These stories literally make us "strangers to ourselves," in Julia Kristeva's lovely phrase;[46] in the process, they suggest that "human being" is not a fixed entity but a process of constant transformation into something other. This is as it should be: "the stories that make us feel most human are no longer the stories that tell us the truth."[47]

---

[45] Ibid., 4.

[46] Julia Kristeva, *Strangers to Ourselves*, trans. Leon Roudiez (New York: Columbia University Press, 1991).

[47] John Clute, *"21st Century Science Fiction,"* p. 4.

35

Contemporary Science Fiction and Afrofuturism

ISIAH LAVENDER III

As a historical phenomenon, Afrofuturism emerges in parallel with its sister genre, science fiction, at the dawn of modernity, in response to the singular risks and possibilities afforded by industrial capitalism. Today Afrofuturism appears ubiquitous – in music, in dance, in art, in film. While some people might think of Sun Ra, Flying Lotus, or even Outcast in terms of musical Afrofuturism, Janelle Monáe immediately comes to mind with her albums *The ArchAndroid* (2010) and *The Electric Lady* (2013) and *Dirty Computer* (2018), as well as the elaborate backstory of her black cyborg alter ego Cindi Mayweather who pops up in various songs across both studio albums. At Chicago's Tuley Park, Afrofuturism dance therapy exists as a class, led by Discopoet Khari B and author Ytasha Womack, to help people release stress. Graphic artists John Jennings and Stacey Robinson collaborated on an art exhibition, later made into a visual book, *Black Kirby: In Search of the MotherBoxx Connection* (2013) inspired by Afrofuturism and Hip Hop sensibilities to represent black history in comics form. Film shorts coming from the African continent, such as Kenyan director Wanuri Kahiu's *Pumzi* (2009) and Ghanaian director Frances Bodomo's *Afronauts* (2014), track the growth and reach of Afrofuturism, which also includes African-American singer Beyoncé's visual album *Lemonade* (2016). Likewise, the growing importance of Afrofuturist imagery in such feature films and Internet television series as Stephen Norrington's *Blade* (1998), the Wachowski sisters' *The Matrix* (1999), and *Luke Cage* (2016), signal the ongoing importance, and undeniable *coolness*, of this aesthetic.

While the significance of these new avenues for Afrofuturism cannot be underestimated, the printed word remains an important lens through which to understand the full dimensions of Afrofuturism. To that end, this chapter focuses on the works of Octavia E. Butler, some of her contemporaries (Jewelle Gomez, Steven Barnes, and Walter Mosley), and the next generation of African-American writers inspired by Butler as well as Samuel R. Delany

(Nalo Hopkinson, Tananarive Due, Nisi Shawl, Colson Whitehead, Nnedi Okorafor, and N. K. Jemisin). Although Butler emerges as an SF writer after the New Wave experimentation of the 1960s and 1970s, she clearly combines soft and hard sciences, like sociology and genetics, along with her interests in race, gender, and religion in her writing to such an extent that so many different scholarly niches claim her as one of their own – historians, social scientists, multiculturalists, literary theorists, feminists and queer studies, and undoubtedly others. Butler's talent and creativity led to her being the first SF writer to receive a MacArthur "genius" grant, in 1995.

To better understand Butler's Afrofuturist legacy, this chapter first discusses the early 1990s articulation of Afrofuturism as a theoretical innovation by thinkers like Mark Dery, Alondra Nelson, and Kodwo Eshun, before turning to her key post-New Wave works.

Theory and Historicism

When Mark Dery coined the term "Afrofuturism" in 1993 to describe art that explores issues of science, technology, and race from technocultural and science fictional perspectives, he did so primarily in reference to contemporary art, music, and literature. Dery states, "Speculative fiction that treats African-American themes and addresses African-American concerns in the context of twentieth-century technoculture – and, more generally, African-American signification that appropriates images of technology and a prosthetically enhanced future – might, for want of a better term, be called 'Afro-futurism.'"[1] Despite the clear critical importance of Dery's founding term, Samuel R. Delany, Greg Tate, and Tricia Rose deserve enormous credit for participating in the set of interviews conducted by Dery. They underpin his intervention with their keen insights of and about black cultures and how these cultures relate to SF, while Dery merely poses the questions, and frames these thinkers with his brief introductory essay. If anything, the theoretical dynamism inspiring Afrofuturism clearly belongs to these black scholars with whom Dery was mainly just the interlocutor.

Nonetheless, Dery's influential definition led the first generation of Afrofuturist scholars to treat Afrofuturism as an emergent art form appearing in the wake of the Second World War, one that is uniquely suited to thinking about issues of social justice in a global and technology-intensive world. Afro-

---

[1] Mark Dery, "Black to the Future: Interviews with Samuel R. Delany, Greg Tate, and Tricia Rose," *South Atlantic Quarterly* 92, 4 (1993), p. 736.

British scholar Kodwo Eshun improves Dery's original definition, extending it to black music, which he describes as a sonic fiction, whereby blacks accept "a perpetual fight for human status, a yearning for human rights, a struggle for inclusion within the human species . . . any intimation of an AfroDiasporic futurism, of a 'webbed network' . . . which routes, reroutes and criss-crosses the Black Atlantic."[2] This unending fight by black people for human inclusion across time and space produces precisely such a networked consciousness connecting the past, present, and future via creative production. Eshun makes room for the future inclusion of a necessarily different African SF, which had yet to truly materialize at this point in the late twentieth century, through his webbed network. Oddly, there appears to be a flattening narrative effect where Africa seems an extended Dark Continent trope in Black American mainstream literature. Yet, as we will see, Afrofuturists across the African diaspora have worked around this inertial dampening through native scientific applications that appear supernatural or magical.

A second early Afrofuturist scholar, sociologist Alondra Nelson, clarifies this webbed network as a chronotopal awareness, a time–space mindfulness.[3] Nelson writes: "Who we've [black people] been and where we've traveled is always an integral component of who we can become."[4] In other words, "our imaginings of the future are always complicated extensions of the past."[5] Nelson also challenged the white monochrome futures of SF when she edited the Afrofuturism issue of the journal Social Text in 2002, in which she and her contributors explore how Afrofuturism provides "unique analytical frameworks for interpreting black cultural production, as imagery of the near-future" by black artists.[6] Afrofuturism, therefore, offers a future-oriented worldview that appreciates history. Feminist SF critic Lisa Yaszek agrees with Nelson when she states: "Afrofuturism is not just about reclaiming the history of the past, but about reclaiming the history of the future as well."[7] Afrofuturism goes well beyond black technological use as Dery asserts.

Inspired by Dery's vision of a future-oriented black aesthetic practice as well as the proliferation of award-winning anthologies featuring speculative fiction

---

[2] Kodwo Eshun, *More Brilliant than the Sun: Adventures in Sonic Fiction* (London: Quartet, 1998), p. 00[–006].

[3] For more information on the chronotope notion, see Mikhail M. Bakhtin, *The Dialogic Imagination: Four Essays*, trans. Caryl Emerson and Michael Holquist (Austin: University of Texas Press, 1981).

[4] Alondra Nelson, "AfroFuturism: Past-Future Visions," *Color Lines* (2000), p. 34.

[5] Ibid., p. 35.

[6] Alondra Nelson, "Introduction: Future Texts," *Social Text* 20, 2 (2002), p. 9.

[7] Lisa Yaszek, "An Afrofuturist Reading of Ralph Ellison's *Invisible Man*," *Rethinking History* 9, 2/3 (2005), p. 300.

by black artists, groundbreaking studies including Elisabeth Leonard's *Into Darkness Peering: Race and Color in the Fantastic*,[8] DeWitt Douglas Kilgore's *Astrofuturism: Science, Race, and Visions of Utopia in Space*,[9] Sandra M. Grayson's *Visions of the Third Millennium: Black Science Fiction Novelists Write the Future*,[10] Sharon DeGraw's *The Subject of Race in American Science Fiction*,[11] Marleen S. Barr's *Afro-Future Females: Black Writers Chart Science Fiction's Newest New-Wave Trajectory*,[12] and my own *Race in American Science Fiction*[13] demonstrated the affordances and limitations of genre fiction – especially in its printed forms – as a vehicle for imagining brave new futures in full color. In doing so, these anthologies emphasized the centrality of storytelling/narrative/print fiction to the Afrofuturist project. This ongoing critical explosion continues with recent collections and books like my own *Black and Brown Planets: The Politics of Race in Science Fiction*, André M. Carrington's *Speculative Blackness: The Future of Race in Science Fiction*, and Paul Youngquist's *A Pure Solar World: Sun Ra and the Birth of Afrofuturism*. [14]

Not surprisingly, the rise of Web 2.0 and the increasing availability of affordable digital communication tools in recent years have encouraged scholars to turn their attention to Afrofuturism as it is expressed across media. In particular, works such as Adilifu Nama's *Black Space: Imagining Race in Science Fiction Film*, Sandra Jackson and Julie E. Moody-Freeman's *The Black Imagination: Science Fiction, Futurism, and the Speculative*, and Reynaldo Anderson and Charles E. Jones's *Afrofuturism 2.0: The Rise of Astro-Blackness* have been crucial for understanding the significance of Afrofuturism in media including film, comic books, and digital art.[15]

---

[8] Elisabeth A. Leonard, ed., *Into Darkness Peering: Race and Color in the Fantastic* (Westport, CT: Greenwood Press, 1997).

[9] DeWitt D. Kilgore, *Astrofuturism: Science, Race, and Visions of Utopia in Space* (Philadelphia: University of Pennsylvania Press, 2003).

[10] Sandra M. Grayson, *Visions of the Third Millennium: Black Science Fiction Novelists Write the Future* (Trenton, NJ: African World Press, 2003).

[11] Sharon DeGraw, *The Subject of Race in American Science Fiction* (New York: Routledge, 2007).

[12] Marleen S. Barr, ed., *Afro-Future Females: Black Writers Chart Science Fiction's Newest New-Wave Trajectory* (Columbus: Ohio State University Press, 2008).

[13] Isiah Lavender III, *Race in American Science Fiction* (Bloomington: Indiana University Press, 2011).

[14] Isiah Lavender III, ed., *Black and Brown Planets: The Politics of Race in Science Fiction* (Jackson: University Press of Mississippi, 2014); André M. Carrington, *Speculative Blackness: The Future of Race in Science Fiction* (Minneapolis: University of Minnesota Press, 2016); Paul Youngquist, *A Pure Solar World: Sun Ra and the Birth of Afrofuturism* (Austin, TX: University of Texas Press, 2016).

[15] Adilifu Nama, *Black Space: Imagining Race in Science Fiction Film* (Austin, TX: University of Texas Press, 2008); Sandra Jackson and Julie E. Moody-Freeman, eds., *The Black Imagination; Science Fiction, Futurism, and the Speculative* (New York: Peter Lang Press,

Over the past decade Afrofuturist criticism has grown well beyond its initial mandate. While scholars continue to explore contemporary black artists in light of Dery's initial conception, they often do so from the new vantage points afforded by digitally enabled research and publishing practices. For instance, increased access to the archives of prominent African-American artists has led scholars to rethink the role of scientific research in Octavia E. Butler's socially oriented SF, while the recent discovery of W. E. B. Du Bois's early twentieth-century science fantasy "The Princess Steel" (*c.* 1908–10) gestures toward the rich history of African-American authors who have long used genre fiction to convey challenging political ideas to readers.[16] Meanwhile, events such as the 2012 "Five Continent" SF reading in Second Life, with Ghanaian writer Jonathan Dotse representing all of Africa, and the publication of pan-African SF anthologies including Ivor W. Hartmann's *AfroSF* series[17] and Nerine Dorman's *Terra Incognita*[18] ask readers to rethink Afrofuturism as a globe-spanning tapestry of creative voices and aesthetic practices linking historic African-American, contemporary black Atlantic, and pan-African authors together in provocative new ways. Indeed, digitization of archival research has enabled the recovery of a centuries-old diasporic speculative tradition and the turn to e-publishing has enabled the seemingly meteoric rise of a new, pan-African SF with complex ties to its Western counterparts.

In this respect, Afrofuturism purposefully subverts the prevailing power narratives of white SF. Groups such as Larry Correia and Brad Torgersen's Sad Puppies and Vox Day's Rabid Puppies tried so hard to preserve white prestige through slate voting for the Hugo Awards in the mid-2010s. Puppygate represents the conservative backlash by white fan groups attempting to undermine the triumphs of Nnedi Okorafor and N. K. Jemisin, among others, in winning Hugo Awards for daring to portray Afrocentric futures in their work. Black writer and activist Ytasha L. Womack similarly expands Afrofuturism by freshly describing it as "both an artistic aesthetic and a framework for critical theory [that] combines elements of science fiction,

---

2011); Reynaldo Anderson and Charles E. Jones, eds., *Afrofuturism 2.0: The Rise of Astro-Blackness* (Lanham, MD: Lexington Books, 2016).

[16] W. E. B. Du Bois, "The Princess Steel," introduced by Adrienne Brown and Britt Rusert, *PMLA* 130, 3 (2015), pp. 819–29. Rusert and Brown's extraordinary find signals Afrofuturism's continual expansion into the past as well as its ongoing urgency.

[17] Ivor W. Hartmann, ed., *AfroSF: Science Fiction by African Writers* (Storytime, 2012) and *AfroSFv2* (Storytime, 2015).

[18] Nerine Dorman, ed., *Terra Incognita: New Short Speculative Stories from Africa* (Short Story Day Africa, 2015).

historical fiction, speculative fiction, fantasy, Afrocentricity, and magic realism with non-Western beliefs."[19] Womack's expansive delineation acknowledges the Afrofuturist contribution of black writers such as Tananarive Due, Okorafor, and Jemisin, who do not essentially use science and technology in ways normally understood as such. Stretching Afrofuturism's definition incorporates SF by black writers on all sides of the Atlantic Ocean if not the entire globe. Clearly, Womack subconsciously recognizes something without articulating it. Afrofuturism is diminished when it is only thought of in terms of technoculture. This weird flattening effect reoccurs by excluding what might be deemed the fantastic to solely concentrate on Western, largely American, notions of science and technology. That is to say, much SF concerns the interactions between politics and technoscience and the influence they exert on culture. Afrofuturism certainly engages with technoculture on some levels. But no place exists for an African SF which does not necessarily look like Black American SF.

Expanding Afrofuturism essentially involves native scientific practices that reflect a sense of the supernatural. Native science means the accumulated knowledge(s) of traditional practices like story, dance, song, art, and other societal rituals that have been discredited by the Western notion of "rational 'self' versus mystical 'other,'" basically a form of pattern recognition.[20] Some of these societal rituals relate to conjuring and the knowledge that goes into the exact mixing and measuring of components that go into medicines. Conjurers perform the mythical, but construct their own knowledge of the natural world through observable phenomena, practice, and training just like scientists. Gloria Naylor's novel *Mama Day* (1998) serves as a strong example of native science here, as the character of Miranda (Mama) Day practices conjuring in Willow Springs to benefit her family and community. The novel is not considered Afrofuturist – but it should be thought of in this way. Dery recently concedes that Afrofuturism contests "the positivist, rationalist, materialist biases of the Enlightenment project by reasserting the value of intuition and the unconscious; of the pre-industrial, mythic modes of modeling the world."[21] But this candid acknowledgment does not overturn the critical neglect of Afrofuturism's supernatural element in the intervening years since his neologism became synonymous with a black SF.

[19] Ytasha L. Womack, *Afrofuturism: The World of Black Sci-Fi and Fantasy Culture* (Chicago: Lawrence Hill, 2013), p. 9.
[20] Colin Scott, "Science for the West, Myth for the Rest?: The Case of James Bay Cree Knowledge Construction," in Sandra Harding, ed., *The Postcolonial Science and Technology Studies Reader* (Durham: Duke University Press, 2011), p. 176.
[21] Mark Dery, "Afrofuturism Reloaded: 15 Theses in 15 Minutes" (2016), www.fabrikzeitung .ch/afrofuturism-reloaded-15-theses-in-15-minutes (last accessed June 9, 2017).

Butler and Afrofuturism

Butler's *Wild Seed* (1980) provides a perfect illustration of this Afrofuturist strand. Butler weaves her own longstanding interest in genetics with a native scientific practice enhanced by a sense of the supernatural in her fourth Patternist novel, though first in the series' internal chronology.[22] *Wild Seed* recounts the beginning of the long relationship between Anyanwu and Doro, both immortal, from the interior of Africa to the antebellum South over the course of 150 years as well as their joint and separate attempts to build a race of long-lived people through selective breeding. At the time of their meeting in 1690, Anyanwu is nearly 300 years old, while Doro has seen nearly four millennia pass. A gifted healer with absolute mastery of her physiology, Anyanwu can transform her body in myriad ways. By local accounts of the surrounding African villages, many of them filled with her descendants, Anyanwu practices witchcraft. Meanwhile, Doro's greatest gift lies in his ability to wear other people's bodies, consume them, and then transfer to another one nearby. Simply put, he steals bodies, he trades bodies, and he breeds bodies. Doro can also track people with special abilities as well as those with psionic potential. Although he convinces Anyanwu to leave her African surroundings, she goes with him to America for two reasons: first, she wants immortal children, and, second, she wants to protect her children from Doro's veiled menace.

Specifically, the shape-shifting protagonist Anyanwu exemplifies the indigenous scientific bent of Afrofuturism. She utilizes her supreme knowledge of biology to survive beyond time. In some situations, she improves her senses and physical strength and in others she alters her gender and skin color. She even transforms into other creatures like a leopard, eagle, or dolphin in the direst of circumstances. The species boundary does not trouble her. In fact, Anyanwu has given birth to children as well as fathered them. She can heal and repair all of her own physical injuries as well as manufacture medicines for others within her body: science and magic in perfect combination. Famed theorist Donna Haraway likens Anyanwu to "an African sorceress [with] powers of transformation."[23]

---

[22] For the omnibus version of the book series and its disowned fifth book, see Octavia E. Butler, *Seed to Harvest* (New York: Grand Central, 2007) and *Survivor* (New York: Doubleday, 1978). My analysis here is indebted to Amandine Faucheux and our co-authored essay "Tricknology: Theorizing the Trickster in Afrofuturism," *MOSF Journal of Science Fiction* 2, 2 (2018).

[23] Donna J. Haraway, "A Cyborg Manifesto: Science, technology and socialist-feminism in the late twentieth century," in *Simians, Cyborgs, and Women: The Reinvention of Nature* (New York: Routledge, 1991), p. 179.

Nonetheless, Anyanwu, like a mad scientist, experiments on her own body to produce life-saving remedies. For example, when she first agrees to go off with Doro, his current body sickens from a small cut on his hand while walking through an African jungle. Anyanwu nips his infected hand, caresses it with her tongue, analyzes the illness, and dispenses a precise medication within her saliva. Although she has no name for microorganisms, Anyanwu explains to a convalescing Doro that "there were things in your hand that should not have been there . . . living things too small to see" and that she "can feel . . . and know" by taking "them into [her] body" to "kill them."[24] She then manufactures the medicine in her saliva and shares it. Her actions reflect a native scientific practice based on her own understanding of microbiology that appears to be magic.

Butler's novel blends science and the supernatural to produce an expanded Afrofuturism. Nowhere is this idea more apparent than when Anyanwu transforms herself into an old, genteel and affluent white slaveholder, Edward Warrick of Avoyelles Parish, Louisiana. Anyanwu flawlessly camouflages herself in the Deep South of the antebellum era to protect her gifted family from white people and from an estranged Doro. But Doro finds her after a ninety-nine-year separation, though Anyanwu refuses to subordinate herself, be his slave. To her surprise, Doro slightly amends his breeding program to have a companion through the ages after she begins shutting down her biological functions as a final escape. Butler demonstrates what Delany, Tate, Eshun, and others know about Afrofuturism and how it provides a science fictional return to the New World's traumatic beginnings for black people as well as a way forward.

Butler's second series, the Xenogenesis trilogy, comprising *Dawn* (1987), *Adulthood Rites* (1988), and *Imago* (1989) – later rebranded as *Lilith's Brood* – continues her exploration of genetics and slavery with an alien twist. The trilogy's basic storyline entails a nuclear holocaust on Earth that surely would have extinguished humanity if an alien species known as the Oankali had not been passing through the solar system and decided to rescue what remained of the dying human population. As it so happens, the entirely alien and downright repulsive Oankali are gene traders and they find humanity's genetic material irresistible – specifically, our cancers. The Oankali's uncontrollable acquisitive nature derives from their own biology and it demands a trade with humanity to further evolve themselves by combining the explosive growth of cancerous cells with their existing mastery of the

---

[24] Octavia E. Butler, *Wild Seed* (New York: Popular Library, 1980), p. 29.

genome. This undesired trade, ostensibly for mutual benefit, establishes a newfangled slave narrative. The Oankali modify the human genome via biological engineering involving a cross-species reproduction without conscious permission. In simple terms, they mix themselves with the captive human species to create something new much like Doro's breeding program in the Patternist series. The Oankali generation starship functions as a slave ship for the coming interstellar middle passage resulting from the ongoing genetic experimentation. In this respect, Afrofuturism provides a perhaps sharper focus on race and racism throughout the trilogy and how these social conventions play out with the alien species at first contact. Through it all the Oankali also evince Butler's characteristic pessimism, even misanthropism; the Oankali identify two conflicting human genes – hierarchical tendencies and intelligence – that always result in extinction when paired together (hence the nuclear apocalypse), a crisis on the level of species-being that only merging with the Oankali can solve.

Using Afrofuturism as an interpretive framework, readers intuit how Butler intelligently links the alien colonization theme with slavery's history to demonstrate a complex view of a capitalist American society and the inherent dangers of the differences it produces in terms of racial ideologies, neocolonial relations of exploitation and domination, political agendas, queer futurities, post-human theorizing, and more.

Butler's third series, the Parable books, including *Parable of the Sower* (1993) and *Parable of the Talents* (1998), renews her obsession with slavery's vestiges, namely racism, oppression, and violence, and also delivers an extreme answer to these color line issues in the dystopian near future. Environmental, political, and economic emergencies converge and trigger societal turmoil in the books, resulting in a swift revival of slavery to cope with a changing America; businesses, politicians, and religious leaders all fight to provide answers for a fallen nation while only exacerbating the chaos. As an Afrofuturist text, *Parable of the Sower* presents in alarming fashion decaying public education systems, escalating energy, food, and water expenses, unimpeded violence and crime, drug addiction, homelessness, deregulation of minimum wages, global warming, drought, failing religions, and a dismantled space program, among many other disasters. As literary scholar Madhu Dubey believes, the "dystopia presented" by Butler "is so closely extrapolated from current trends ... that it produces a shock of familiarity rather than estrangement."[25] *Parable of the Talents*

---

[25] Madhu Dubey, "Folk and Urban Communities in African-American Women's Fiction: Octavia Butler's *Parable of the Sower*," *Studies in American Fiction* 27, 1 (1999), p. 106.

continues this downward trend as Butler depicts a United States dominated by anarchy, religious zealotry, slavery, and violence that falls under the sway of the Church of Christian America, who send wayward souls to brutal reeducation camps. The Parable books feel recognizable now in this moment; it did not escape notice in 2016 that *Parable of the Talents* depicts the rise of a white ethno-nationalist politician on the slogan "Make America Great Again," nearly twenty years in advance of the election of Donald Trump. The feeling of estrangement iconic to the science fictional experience does not represent Afrofuturism here; rather, the Afrofuturist jolt hinges on surviving this grim imitation of reality.

Although Butler's Parable books feel portentous and dire – especially as the series was ultimately left unfinished by Butler's death[26] – she demonstrates hope through community building. Surviving together despite the many challenges of this world's backdrop depends on diversity as Lauren shapes a multiracial group capable of coping with the intensifying problems after the sacking of her neighborhood, Robledo. Butler stresses the importance of community and education through Lauren, and how these specific things help with adaptation and safeguarding human existence. "Embrace diversity / Or be destroyed" as Lauren writes in her Earthseed book.[27] Achieving "unity in diversity," as Dubey states, "is necessarily risky and difficult, requiring the ability to interpret unfamiliar cultural codes and the alert balancing of suspicion and trust typical of urban social interactions."[28] From an Afrofuturistic standpoint, Butler's positive message, concerning diversity as a cultural change mechanism, lances through her dystopian setting because Lauren and her group only manage to survive through teamwork and adaptive learning on a continual basis.

Butler's two standalone novels, *Kindred* (1979) and *Fledgling* (2005), and the stories contained in her short story collection, *Bloodchild* (1995, expanded 2005), similarly explore the possibility of a different tomorrow in the best Afrofuturist way, where the future, combined with science, technology, and black themes, demonstrates a maturing humanity overcoming manmade social obstacles like race, ethnicity, and gender – at least potentially. Butler's best-known novel, *Kindred*, a neo-slave narrative,[29] features the time-

---

[26] For details on the drafts of the unfinished *Parable of the Trickster*, its possible sequels, and its interpretive ramifications on the two existing Parables books, see Gerry Canavan's *Octavia E. Butler* (Champaign, IL: University of Illinois Press, 2016).

[27] Butler, *Parable of the Sower*, p. 197.

[28] Dubey, "Folk and Urban Communities in African-American Women's Fiction: Octavia Butler's *Parable of the Sower*," p. 113.

[29] For a comprehensive explanation of the term, see Ashraf H. A. Rushdy, *Neo-Slave Narratives: Studies in the Social Logic of a Literary Form* (New York: Oxford University Press, 1999).

travelling Dana Franklin, a twentieth-century black woman, who seeks to preserve her own life by repeatedly saving her white slave-holding ancestor Rufus Weylin. Butler uses what Toni Morrison identifies as "rememory" in her own neo-slave narrative *Beloved* to bring the past into the present.[30] Rememory compels us to confront slavery's harsh reality and the agonizing problems this practice generated globally hundreds of years into the future, namely racism, oppression, and racial violence. Claiming this terrible past is an Afrofuturist function in that we can change our historical perception of it, drain the power of its memory haunting us, and alleviate fears of the peculiar institution ever returning – even as *Kindred* itself leaves Dana herself brutally traumatized and ultimately permanently mutilated by her experiences.

Butler's final book, *Fledgling*, also concerns blood relationships and genetics. In this SF-inflected vampire novel, Butler depicts another species, known as the Ina, quietly living among humans. As a genetically engineered half-Ina, half-human, Shori Matthews wakes in a cave without memory and must discover who she is and what happened to her family. Shori represents a successful genetic experiment, splicing African DNA with Ina DNA, granting her access to daylight when the uniformly blond and pale Ina are confined to the night. Butler displaces our racial paradigm with a different species, where Shori is the focus of bigotry, intolerance, and hatred amongst the Ina, particularly the Silk family, without the need to discuss human racism's bitter history although the white supremacy analogy becomes impossible to miss. Scientific experimentation resulting in a "black" vampire heroine reads like Afrofuturism in that Butler purposefully breaks the white vampire tradition reflected by Bram Stoker's *Dracula*.[31]

Butler's Contemporaries

In keeping with the importance of Octavia E. Butler to SF and Afrofuturism, briefly discussing a few of her contemporaries (barring Samuel R. Delany, the worthy subject of an earlier chapter) such as Jewelle Gomez, Steven Barnes, and Walter Mosley becomes imperative. For instance, Gomez writes about a 200-year stretch of time from 1850 antebellum Louisiana to 2050 in a black lesbian vampire's life in *The Gilda Stories* (1991) – from the moment the runaway slave is turned to the moment vampires are outed globally. While Steven Barnes has been consciously writing quality SF for more than thirty-

[30] Toni Morrison, *Beloved* (New York: Knopf, 1987), p. 43.
[31] For sketches of the potential *Fledgling* sequels, see again Canavan, *Octavia E. Butler*.

five years, roughly thirty solo or co-authored novels, the overwhelming presence of Butler and Samuel Delany simply dwarf him, causing critical neglect. His Aubry Knight trilogy – *Streetlethal* (1983), *Gorgon Child* (1989), and *Firedance* (1993) – features Knight as a black fugitive anti-hero, a former mob enforcer and null-boxer (think zero-gravity mixed-martial arts) in a techno-dystopian future. Knight brings down a mob cartel in a gritty Los Angeles, defeats a megalomaniacal television evangelist plotting to re-enslave America, and overthrows a totalitarian regime in Pan-Africa in the respective books. Barnes's multiracial future, accented by cyberpunk and Afrocentricity, qualifies as Afrofuturism with a black man kicking butt much like Marvel Comics heroes Luke Cage and the Black Panther. Interestingly, Aubry Knight discovers that he is directly descended from the Ibandi people, a tribe of African warriors which happens to be the subject of the later "Ibandi" series – *Great Sky Woman* (2006) and *Shadow Valley* (2009) – set in a mythical Africa thirty thousand years in the past at the foot of Mount Kilimanjaro. Although this connection is ephemeral at best, it demonstrates Barnes's historical attentiveness to portraying blacks positively in the speculative genres. Africa's prominent role in his fiction desegregates troublesome depictions of Africa as the Dark Continent by white SF writers with Barnes offering an alternative vision of ancient African mythology.

Arguably, the Insh'Allah series – consisting of *Lion's Blood* (2002) and *Zulu Heart* (2003) – represent Barnes's best work in the genre. Barnes presents an alternate history of the United States where Africa and Islam hold sway in the Deep South in this plantation saga, replete with an Islamic calendar, paradox events, and enslaved Europeans. Barnes utilizes the power of race to tell his counterfactual account of antebellum America, where an Irish boy, Aidan O'Dere, captured and sold into slavery in the New World, and Kai ibn Jallaleddin ibn Rashid, the privileged second son of a powerful black noble, forge an unlikely master–slave friendship on the Dar Kush plantation. History changes when Socrates chooses not to drink the poison hemlock around 400 BC, Europe remains plague-ridden, locked in the dark ages, steam power and air technologies develop on the African continent allowing its peoples to conquer the world, and Arabic becomes "the great trading tongue."[32] Possibly the greatest symbolic paradox of the text, a giant black colossus, standing on an island in the harbor of what would be New Orleans, mirrors the Statue of Liberty on Ellis Island except this black statue mirrors the spirit and dreams of an African empire in the New World.

---

[32] Steven Barnes, *Lion's Blood* (New York: Warner, 2002), p. 141.

From an Afrofuturist perspective, Barnes suggests that humanity's violent nature is universal and that blacks would have enslaved whites and treated them just as harshly given the opportunity. Race and racism become permeable; thus we can see ourselves with fresh, perhaps, alien eyes through the distortion of our national memory.

Better known for his hardboiled detective fiction series featuring the characters Easy Rawlins in his Los Angeles-set fiction and Leonid McGill in his New York City-set fiction, Walter Mosley does not limit himself to one genre amongst the forty-eight books written to this point in his career. His forays into SF touch upon Afrofuturist themes featuring black heroes, technoculture, and future visions of race: *Blue Light* (1998), *Futureland: Nine Stories of an Imminent World* (2001), *The Wave* (2005), *47* (2005), *The Tempest Tales* (2008), *The Last Days of Ptolemy Grey* (2010), and *Inside a Silver Box* (2015). Mosley believes in the promises of SF, "future[s] full of possibility, alternative lives ... a black president, a black world, or simply hav[ing] a say in the way things are. This power is the first step in changing the world."[33] Mosley clearly experiments with such possibilities in his writing.

For instance, in *The Last Days of Ptolemy Grey*, using urban violence and Los Angeles as a starting point, Mosley relates how Ptolemy Grey, a ninety-one-year-old black man suffering from dementia, must cope with the drive-by murder of his caretaker and favorite grand-nephew, Reggie. This storyline seems normal – but then Mosley gives it an Afrofuturist injection, wherein Grey, at the behest of his seventeen-year-old friend and new caretaker Robyn, volunteers for an experimental drug program that fully restores his mind and vigor while quickly burning out his body, costing him his life in a few short weeks. Lucidity restored, Grey goes about avenging his nephew and ensuring his family's material future. Mosley certainly makes a wry comment on black people unsuspectingly imperiled by medical experiments like the Tuskegee Experiment by having Grey gladly sacrifice his life for a few weeks of clarity.[34] Seen from a black cultural viewpoint, though, Mosley offers a grim hope for justice in the black community through this unlikely hero.

---

[33] Walter Mosley, "Black to the Future," in Sheree R. Thomas, ed., *Dark Matter: A Century of Speculative Fiction from the African Diaspora* (New York: Warner, 2000), pp. 405–6.

[34] This infamous forty year-long experiment overseen by the US Public Health Service concerned studying syphilis and its progression in rural Black men in Alabama under the pretense of free health care provide by the government.

Afrofuturism's Next Generation

Many of Butler's contemporaries still write and write well, but Afrofuturism's next generation has already emerged with the likes of Nalo Hopkinson, Tananarive Due, Nisi Shawl, Colson Whitehead, Nnedi Okorafor, N. K. Jemisin, and many others. These talented black SF writers testify to Butler's continuing legacy and her enormous influence on them should be obvious.

Nalo Hopkinson's work, by far, has garnered the most scholarly acclaim of the new generation, with many academics classing her stories on par with both Butler and Delany while also insisting on her inclusion as a member of the big three black SF writers at the beginning of the twenty-first century. Debatably, her best-known works remain *Brown Girl in the Ring* (1998) and *Midnight Robber* (2000). The first of these excitingly mixes Afro-Caribbean folklore, organ theft, gangs, and a single, black teenaged-mother protagonist within a dystopian Toronto and the second features an entire black Caribbean planet named Toussaint, interdimensional travel, and a cyberpunk feel interwoven with Caribbean myth as a young black girl comes of age. In both novels, if not all of her work, Hopkinson strongly critiques the dilemmas of modern black life and empowers black people to create their own futures.

Primarily recognized as a horror writer, Tananarive Due's African Immortals series – *My Soul to Keep* (1997), *The Living Blood* (2001), *Blood Colony* (2008), and *My Soul to Take* (2011) – introduces a mysterious group of undying Ethiopian men, with advanced science, technology, music, and knowledge, all blood-linked until one of the Life-Brothers shares his gift with his most recent wife and child, setting up an epic battle between good and evil that plays itself out through the four novels. While Due advances her own black vampire mythology, she provides us with positive images of blacks using science and technology to impact the world.

Nisi Shawl's steampunk novel *Everfair* (2016) offers an alternate history of the Congo region's brutal exploitation by Belgium's King Leopold II in the name of wealth and power, where the indigenous African population learns about steam power much earlier resulting in the birth of a new country amidst the horror of colonization. Shawl's important novel directly engages racial politics through steampunk by asking the essential "what if" question that drives much of SF itself. Her answer delivers on Afrofuturism's promise of imagining a different tomorrow for black people while addressing the historical whitewashing of this human tragedy. Colson Whitehead (like Butler, a MacArthur genius grant awardee) similarly explores an alternate history for black people in his *The Underground Railroad* (also 2016), which literalizes the metaphor by positing an actual subway transporting escaped slaves to freedom, while his *Zone One* (2011) imagines a zombie future for the United States, centered on a black protagonist whose racial identity he reveals only very late in the novel, as a pointed reversal of his readers' assumptions.

Inspired by her own Nigerian heritage, Nnedi Okorafor's novels blend elements of fantasy, the supernatural, and SF. Her first adult novel, *Who Fears Death* (2010), takes place in a far-future Sahara Desert after the apocalypse, where vestigial technologies exist alongside magic, while its prequel, *The Book of Phoenix* (2015), explains how the apocalypse came about because of genetic experimentation conducted on corporately owned and designed black people in the United States. Both novels feature young black women as protagonists struggling against greater powers. Okorafor's novella *Binti* (2015) and its sequels tell the story of a young Himba woman, talented in advanced mathematics, who accepts admittance to the premier galactic university, and how this journey changes her life when her starship is attacked by aliens. Clearly, Okorafor directs her creative energies toward the intersections of identity politics and futurity as she carefully navigates the different histories of Africa and black America.

N. K. Jemisin's *The Fifth Season* (2015) and its sequels introduce us to the world of The Stillness, a geologically unstable supercontinent that experiences catastrophic seismic activity on a frequent basis, where magic and science coexist. The main characters perilously traverse the unstable land seeking refuge from a xenophobic society and mastery of the earth science–magic orogeny. Admittedly, Jemisin's novel veers more toward fantasy, but the way she constructs, critiques, and rethinks oppressive systems demonstrates a keen Afrofuturist sensibility. The 2016 Hugo Award wins for Jemisin's *The Fifth Season* as best novel[35] and for Okorafor's *Binti* as best novella bode well for Afrofuturism. To end this academic treatment of Afrofuturism with a bit of black vernacular, race be a science fiction itself, and Afrofuturism learns it to us real good, real good.

---

[35] Jemisin also won the Hugo for *The Fifth Season*'s sequel, *The Obelisk Gate* (2016), making her the first author to win back-to-back Hugos in over twenty years, and then again for *The Stone Sky* (2017), the first time a trilogy has won three consecutive Hugos.

36

Science Fiction and the Revenge of Nature: Environmentalism from the 1990s to the 2010s

ERIC C. OTTO

This Last Story

Curiosity about the fate of a dying Earth leads protagonist Clio Finn of Kay Kenyon's debut novel *The Seeds of Time* to pilot her team of time divers into the near future, where they record the final transmission of a New York radio broadcast. The message of "this last story" is clear to the team and to readers of the 1997 SF book: the ecological disaster engulfing the people of the future resulted from a "failure of imagination."[1] The broadcaster remarks, "We could not sustain ourselves, our populations, our rampant development, our consumerism, our combustion engines, our sprawling cities. And we could not imagine life without them."[2] The material world that enables human activity is finite, and becomes exhausted, because modern industrial civilization demanded more of ecosystems than ecosystems could deliver. Population growth, sprawl, consumer capitalism, and the combustion engine constituted the physical and ideological fabric of this civilization; twentieth- and early twenty-first-century humanity could neither reconsider nor abandon them. The people of *The Seeds of Time*'s late twenty-first century learn the bitter lesson of this failure.

With this last story, Kenyon stresses two roles for imagination in guiding humanity's engagements with the nonhuman world. First, the continued viability of these engagements depends on our ability to conceive alternatives to practices that carry on as if ecosystems are boundless and unalterable. There are options other than an economic system that motivates the mass consumption of material goods. There are options other than an energy system that thickens Earth's CO_2 blanket. These options just need to be

[1] Kay Kenyon, *The Seeds of Time* (New York: Bantam, 1997), p. 79.
[2] Ibid., p. 80.

imagined, at the same time as we find the will to want them and to bring them into existence. In her other appeal for imagination, Kenyon highlights a stimulus for thinking and acting beyond unsustainable human activities. Concluding his message, the broadcaster implores, "Nurture your world, your habitat well. They are finite gifts. Imagine them lost and you will cherish them the more."[3] A creative foresight informed by extrapolating current observations of an endangered Earth into a plausible future of heightened ecological and social loss can prompt new ways of being in the world. In Alexa Weik von Mossner's words, awareness of how we are threatening ecosystems – awareness of risks – "takes its starting point in the observation of past and present occurrences, combined with a projection of their potential future developments."[4]

Apocalyptic Ecological Critique

The environmental SF written between 1990 and today includes more examples of Kenyon's second role for imagination. Its creators are more focused on engaging our awareness of risks than on detailing alternatives. To be sure, preeminent works like Kim Stanley Robinson's Mars trilogy (1993, 1994, 1996) and N. K. Jemisin's *The Fifth Season* (2015) and its sequels are centrally attentive to new ways of thinking and being, the former imagining a more ecologically responsive politics and economics, and the latter imagining a more ecologically responsive cultural lore. But a survey of work ranging from David Brin's *Earth* (1990) through Amy Thomson's *The Color of Distance* (1995), T. C. Boyle's *A Friend of the Earth* (2000), Kelpie Wilson's *Primal Tears* (2005), M. M. Buckner's *Watermind* (2008), Bong Joon-ho's *Snowpiercer* (2013), Paolo Bacigalupi's *The Water Knife* (2015), and more reveals that the environmental SF of the last quarter century has largely employed what Gerry Canavan calls "apocalyptic ecological critique," approaching environmental issues "in almost exclusively negative terms."[5] As such, these works sustain the prevailing critical strategy of the canonical environmentalism that precedes them. In her 1962 book, *Silent Spring*, Rachel Carson condemned the use of toxic insecticides by documenting their immediate consequences and imagining their long-term, damaging effects. She dedicated one chapter, "The Other Road," to envisioning alternatives. Three decades later,

---

[3] Ibid.
[4] Alexa Weik von Mossner, "Science Fiction and the Risks of the Anthropocene: Anticipated Transformations in Dale Pendell's *The Great Bay*," *Environmental Humanities* 5 (2014), p. 206.
[5] Gerry Canavan, "Ecology 101," *SFRA Review* 314 (2015), p. 20.

apocalyptic ecological critique was still ascendant. Bill McKibben concluded *The End of Nature* (1989) by calling readers to a "more humble way of life," but his book's chief argument was that "We have killed off nature" and replaced it with something of our own making.[6]

There is a clear sense when reading *Silent Spring*, *The End of Nature*, and other texts of environmentalism's first few decades that late twentieth-century society was starting to see its ways of living as incompatible with local and global ecological fitness, and its primary mode of expressing this observation was through narratives of ecological loss. With its attention to "the Coming Climate Catastrophe," "The Revenge of Gaia," and more, post-1990s environmentalism sustains this apocalypticism.[7] This is not to say it has stagnated in a decades-long pessimistic mode. Rather, the persistence of imagining the world lost reflects a holding pattern for environmentalist thinking in the last quarter century, when entrenched ideas of nature's material inexhaustibility have proved difficult to shake. In an atmosphere of increasing denial, rather than moving on to optimistic celebrations of human ingenuity, environmentalists have instead embraced the educative potential of a sustained focus on the hazards of human behavior.

The twentieth anniversary of Earth Day in 1990 drew renewed attention to an environmental movement that had been expanding its numbers of lobby-ists, national organization members, and grassroots activists in response to the anti-environmental political temperament of the 1980s. Two years later, the "Rio 'Earth Summit' signaled the emergence of global environmentalism as a powerful force calling for environmental protection."[8] But even before that, in the 1960s, various forms of strategic negation had started to influence public opinion about environmental issues. Back then, the chemical industry campaigned against Rachel Carson with brochures and personal attacks. In the 1970s, the aerosol industry denied the role of chlorofluorocarbons in the depletion of ultraviolet-absorbing stratospheric ozone, with one of its hired scientists insisting "human activities were too small to have any impact on the atmosphere."[9] Industry interest groups sowed doubts about research

---

[6] Bill McKibben, *The End of Nature* (New York: Anchor, 1989), pp. 186, 96.

[7] See James Hansen, *Storms of My Grandchildren: The Truth About the Coming Climate Catastrophe and Our Last Chance to Save Humanity* (New York: Bloomsbury, 2009); and James Lovelock, *The Revenge of Gaia: Earth's Climate Crisis and the Fate of Humanity* (New York: Basic Books, 2006).

[8] Riley E. Dunlap and Aaron M. McCright, "The Climate Change Denial Campaign," *Scholars Strategy Network* (2013), p. 1.

[9] Naomi Oreskes and Erik M. Conway, *Merchants of Doubt: How a Handful of Scientists Obscured the Truth on Issues from Tobacco Smoke to Global Warming* (New York: Bloomsbury, 2010), p. 114.

on acid rain in the 1980s and 1990s. Climate change science is the most recent target of these efforts by polluting industries to deflect criticism and muddy the conversation. As Peter J. Jacques notes, anti-environmentalist strategists have also adopted "environmental skepticism," "positioning the discourse *not* as a rejection of environmental public interest values, but instead positioning themselves as a prudent minority up against the environmental radicals that control Goliath."[10] Environmental issues are real, these skeptics note, but human activity is not responsible for them.

Anti-environmentalist counter-politics has compelled environmentalism to do more educating and convincing than it does imagining alternatives. While the influence of those Naomi Oreskes and Erik M. Conway call "merchants of doubt," and Jacques calls "skeptics," cannot be assessed, we can at least observe that modern industrial society acts as if their strategies are working – as if we are convinced the science is wrong and humanity is indeed too small to matter. However, we are in fact leaving enough of "a pervasive and persistent signature on Earth" to name our epoch "the Anthropocene."[11] The rate of species extinction today "is estimated to be 100 to 1,000 times more than what could be considered natural," and this is largely due to habitat loss associated with land development.[12] Large-scale agricultural fertilizer use has added excessive amounts of nitrogen into oceans around the world, resulting in vast areas deprived of oxygen and therefore of plant and animal life. Greenhouse gas emissions through the burning of fossil fuels have warmed the planet during what should be a global cooling period, with consequences including more frequent droughts, higher sea levels, and species extinctions.[13]

Given the way modern society continues to behave in the face of mounting scientific evidence that many of its activities endanger global ecological health, it is no wonder that environmentalism links environmental advocacy "strategically to apocalyptic thought," though to some dismay.[14] Doug

---

[10] Peter J. Jacques, *Environmental Skepticism: Ecology, Power and Public Life* (New York: Ashgate, 2009), p. 44.

[11] Colin N. Waters, *et al.*, "The Anthropocene Is Functionally and Stratigraphically Distinct from the Holocene," *Science* 351 (2016), p. 1.

[12] Johan Rockström, *et al.*, "A Safe Operating Space for Humanity," *Nature* 461 (2009), p. 474.

[13] Waters, *et al.*, "The Anthropocene," p. 6.

[14] Graham Huggan, "From Arctic Dreams to Nightmares (and Back Again), Apocalyptic Thought and Planetary Consciousness in Three Contemporary American Environmentalist Texts," *ISLE: Interdisciplinary Studies in Literature and Environment* 23 (2016), p. 73.

Henwood, for example, claims "Dystopia is for losers."[15] In his estimation, it would be better "to spin narratives of how humans are marvelously resourceful creatures who could do a lot better with the intellectual, social, and material resources we have."[16] Jenny Price sees hopelessness in "apocalypse-style environmental thinking: OMG, we've destroyed the entire earth!"[17] But if Kay Kenyon's near-future broadcaster wants us to imagine the world lost, it is not because we should give in to the inevitability of an eco-apocalyptic historical trajectory. Instead, like many environmentalists, he thinks that if we imagine the worst for Earth, we will act in ways to prevent such a future from happening. There is not a lack of mobilizing optimism in environmentalism as much as there is not yet an audience large enough for such optimism. The will to imagine alternatives – the utopian impulse – must first be energized by an understanding that modern society faces a moment when alternatives need to be imagined.

Humanity's the Culprit

Today's environmental SF facilitates this understanding. Its body of work is quite vast and comprehensive of most of the major environmental issues that have garnered attention not only in the last quarter century, but also in the years since Carson's *Silent Spring*. As the issue that has prompted most attention to anthropogenic environmental impacts, climate change dominates as a theme across recent environmental SF, enough so that "cli-fi," although not always SF, has emerged as its own subgenre. Stories of overpopulation appear less as we move away from the overpopulation anxiety of the 1960s and 1970s, an anxiety captured academically in Paul and Anne Ehrlich's 1968 book *The Population Bomb*, and captured creatively in Harry Harrison's 1966 book *Make Room! Make Room!* and its 1973 film adaptation *Soylent Green*. Some works duplicate the neo-Malthusian concerns of environmentalism's early years by highlighting the pressures of general human population growth on natural resources and other species. Other works update these concerns not by thinking simply about the impact of more bodies, but instead about the impact of additional bodies as people adopt

---

[15] Doug Henwood, "Dystopia Is for Losers," in Sasha Lilley, David McNally, and Eddie Yuen, eds., *Catastrophism: The Apocalyptic Politics of Collapse and Rebirth* (Oakland, CA: PM Press, 2012), p. xv.

[16] Ibid.

[17] Jenny Price, "Resilience!," *Resilience: A Journal of the Environmental Humanities* I (2013), n.p.

modern ways of living. Also voicing anxieties about ozone depletion, biodiversity loss, drought, and more, environmental SF brings anthropogenic ecological issues to the forefront of our attention using genre tools ideally suited to imagine loss.

Published in June of 1990, very soon after Earth Day 20, Brin's *Earth* is an appropriate starting point for analyzing environmental SF of the 1990s–2010s. *Earth* leaves few environmental issues out of its pages, setting the tone for later works whose broad attention to the many faces of ecological degradation attests to their understanding of the collective impact of seemingly detached environmental problems. The year is 2038, and although industry has "stopped spewing chlorine compounds into the air," ozone depletion-related UV exposure blinds domestic and wild animals.[18] People must cover up when outside or else guarantee skin cancer. There are ten billion humans on the planet, creating a drain on resources that some say can be solved with "a grim Malthusian solution" – allowing five billion to die – and others say should be met by placing billions in a temporary freeze, to be resuscitated when things are better in three hundred years.[19] Around the world, one hundred arks house species that no longer have viable habitats; full restoration of these habitats is expected "in only a few centuries."[20] After years of population flux, blue and bowhead whales are extinct, and while other whale species fare better, hope for them wanes as computer models forecast a collapse of the ecosystems supporting the cetacean diet.

By 2038, oil has run out, with sedimentary basins having been "probed, palpated, steamed, and sucked dry."[21] Television shows of the decade depict twentieth-century oilmen as "shortsighted fools, even rapists," and an environmental engineer who travels the world in search of new sources of fresh water to exploit wonders if future generations will look back on him the same way.[22] On top of ozone depletion, population-related social and environmental stress, species extinction, energy crisis, and water crisis, global warming is causing the Greenland ice sheet to retreat and coastal areas to flood. Summing up this widespread, anthropogenic environmental decline, the engineer thinks:

---

[18] David Brin, *Earth* (New York: Bantam, 1990), p. 13.
[19] Ibid., pp. 68–9.
[20] Ibid., p. 14.
[21] Ibid., p. 72.
[22] Ibid.

All over the planet there were problems crying out for solutions, not tomorrow, but right now. Nations and cities wanted water shifted, pumped and diked. As the seas rose and rains migrated unpredictably, so did his labors, as governments strove desperately to adapt. Great changes were at work, in the air and land and oceans. They were the sort of global transformations one read of in the very rocks themselves . . . such as when one long epoch of geological stability would come suddenly and violently to an end, leaving everything forever recast.[23]

The concluding sentence in this passage distinguishes a new epoch, one that recognizes the geological impact of modern industrial humanity: the Anthropocene.

Employing science fictional extrapolation, *Earth* calls attention to human activities that culminate in 2038's ecosystemic and social turmoil. The book's advertised plot, however, reads with more apocalyptic immediacy than do *Earth*'s environmentalist appeals. While investigating the escape of a mini black hole he created, which has fallen into Earth's core, a physicist discovers an even larger, more threatening black hole consuming the planet. In about two years, Earth will start suffering major earthquakes and volcanoes, and soon after will be swallowed in its entirety. The combination of this apocalypticism with the book's detailed attention to real concerns about global warming, biodiversity loss, and other anthropogenic environmental crises can be read as representing these concerns as additional examples of hyperbolic, catastrophic thinking. But Brin is being more thoughtful than that. In one darkly humorous scene, the physicist concludes that the more dangerous black hole – the Beta – is too complex to have been created by humans, meaning "'*We're not guilty*. We haven't destroyed ourselves and our world!'"[24] The Beta is either natural or, the physicist suspects, a weapon sent to Earth by a more advanced civilization. Thus, what at first seems to read as the novel's conflation of environmental jeremiad with the grandiose apocalypticism of the thriller genre becomes instead a powerful indictment of modern humanity. No, we didn't create the superweapon that might destroy Earth, but as one character reflects, *"We know humanity's the culprit."*[25] We have found plenty of ways to help the aliens with their alleged mission. With or without the Beta – even with or without the physicist's black hole – the planet is doomed, because of us.

---

[23] Ibid.
[24] Ibid., p. 395.
[25] Ibid., p. 367.

Things We Do to Ourselves

In their 1991 treatise, *Our Angry Earth*, SF deans Isaac Asimov and Frederik Pohl argue that "almost all these current threats to human life have in common is that they are what are called 'anthropogenic' processes: they are things we do to ourselves."[26] Environmental SF since 1990 attends to this central assertion of both Brin's and Asimov and Pohl's texts. While this might not make recent environmental SF much different from earlier works such as John Brunner's *The Sheep Look Up* (1972), Ursula K. Le Guin's *The Word for World is Forest* (1976), and Neal Stephenson's *Zodiac* (1988), for example, the number of creators now underlining humanity's suicidal devotion to self-toxification and self-destruction is at an all-time high. Also at an all-time high is the number of environmental concerns expressed in SF as the genre echoes and reflects on the anxieties voiced more and more in the larger culture.

Productive action on one of these anxieties – ozone depletion – mostly predates the 1990s, but the ozone issue demonstrates that scientific and popular distress about environmental crises can successfully motivate change. In 1985, scientists from the Natural Environment Research Council (NERC) published a foundational paper on stratospheric ozone depletion.[27] After accounting for thirty years of data on mean values for the natural fluctuation in levels of ozone over Antarctica, the scientists found historical decreases in the radiation-shielding gas. The NERC team noted that the only prominent difference between the atmosphere observed in earlier decades and the one observed as ozone levels above Antarctica trended downward was the higher concentration of human-produced compounds. Previous research had already established a theoretical link between these compounds and the degradation of ozone, but many people, especially in industry, doubted the connection, much less the media's reporting on the cataclysmic risks of ozone-depleting gases.[28] However, within the next two years, scientists verified the connection between the chemicals and the hole in the ozone layer, and by the end of the 1980s, the Montreal Protocol had codified an international phasing out of ozone-depleting gases. As Oreskes and Conway note, "American people had already started to change their habits" years before, trading out certain household products for less harmful ones.[29]

---

[26] Isaac Asimov and Frederik Pohl, *Our Angry Earth* (New York: Tor, 1991), p. 21.

[27] J. C. Farman, B. G. Gardiner, and J. D. Shanklin, "Large Losses of Total Ozone in Antarctica Reveal Seasonal ClOx/NOx Interaction," *Nature* 315 (1985), pp. 207–10.

[28] See, for example, Walter Sullivan, "Issue and Debate," *The New York Times* (31 March 1975), p. 36.

[29] Oreskes and Conway, *Merchants of Doubt*, pp. 117–18.

Environmental SF after 1990 was written with full knowledge that governments, industries, and individuals were taking action on ozone depletion. Nevertheless, several works from this period integrate the destruction of the ozone layer into their plots, sustaining the productive apocalyptic critique employed in science and the press while also advancing caution about celebrating the positive outcome of the ozone debate too soon. A character in *Earth*, for example, questions whether the phasing out of chlorine compounds will have enough of an immediate, rehabilitative effect to matter for the species suffering from years of UV overexposure. Brin imagines action on ozone depletion to come later than it actually did, but his book takes up the issue of ozone loss in a manner similar to others that followed it – that is, by drawing attention to long-term ecological impacts. Set in 2048, Starhawk's *The Fifth Sacred Thing* (1993) accurately attributes the ban on chlorofluorocarbons to the 1990s, but then like *Earth* reflects on the extended period of time between the cessation of their use and the date when the ozone layer will be fully restored. (Coincidentally, the book's prediction of the latter date – around 2068 – aligns with recent scientific projections.[30]) A character in Bruce Sterling's *Heavy Weather* (1994) includes "CFCs in the ozone" on his list of reasons why "'the weather's never gonna calm down and be normal.'"[31] The ozone hole killed off the albatross in Thomson's *The Color of Distance* and, in Mark Budz's *Clade* (2003), the world outside the habitable, bioremediated areas is lifeless, owing in part to "unfiltered UV."[32] The invading, extraterrestrial organism in Joan Slonczewski's *The Highest Frontier* (2011) proliferated under Earth's heightened UV levels; at the same time humans see increasing rates of melanoma and vision loss.

Ozone depletion is not as fundamental to the plots of any of these works as, say, water pollution is to Buckner's *Watermind* or drought is to Wanuri Kahiu's short film *Pumzi* (2009). In the former, water pollution is *the* antagonist; in the latter, drought is *the* motivating environmental and social context for the protagonist's actions. But in much the same way as writers have foregrounded other environmental crises by situating their stories within worlds afflicted by these crises, the treatment of ozone loss in these books demonstrates the continued effort of environmental SF to underpin the reality of broad anthropogenic ecological change. Species loss is not central to *Earth*'s plot either, but the story takes place in a future when steep declines

[30] See Paul A. Newman, *et al.*, "When Will the Antarctic Ozone Hole Recover?" *Geophysical Research Letters* 33 (2006), p. 3.
[31] Bruce Sterling, *Heavy Weather* (New York: Bantam, 1994), p. 210.
[32] Mark Budz, *Clade* (New York: Bantam, 2003), p. 115.

in biodiversity join ozone depletion, pollution, drought, overpopulation, and global warming as evidence of modern humanity's heavy ecological footprint. *Earth's* comprehensiveness has not been matched in other works of environmental SF, but the subgenre as a whole collectively emphasizes a wide range of human activities and their consequences.

From the near future, characters in *The Fifth Sacred Thing* look back on the animal "'die-offs'" of the late twentieth century, and they mourn "the long-gone whales."[33] The book is about a small, San Francisco community that heeds the lessons of the past and strives to live more sustainably. Threatening their ecotopia is an outside group motivated toward violence and possession by an adherence to patriarchal hierarchy and concepts of ownership and private property. While the San Franciscans lament and learn from biodiversity loss, their invaders maintain the value system that, in the book's critique, enabled the extinction of species. Also giving us a future perspective on biodiversity loss, T. C. Boyle's *A Friend of the Earth* imagines most mammals and sea animals to be extinct by 2025. Its protagonist traces "the sixth great extinction" to "us ... man ... progress"; "everything was poached and encroached out of existence."[34] There are no more seahorses on Earth in Karen Traviss's *City of Pearl* (2004), and as we learn what species a secret mission from Earth seeks to obtain from an off-planet gene bank, we understand why: "It was simply a long list of commercial crops ... a shopping list worth billions."[35] Centered on the story of a part-bonobo, part-human woman whose mother was a surrogate in a bonobo restoration program, Wilson's *Primal Tears* is concerned not only with the fate of endangered apes but also with "'spotted owls and Del Norte salamanders and coho salmon and wolverines and grizzly bears.'"[36] The book attributes the loss of these species to habitat destruction and human overpopulation.

Anxiety about the future of species links these novels, as anxieties about other anthropogenic environmental crises link other works. But environmental SF does not have a monopoly on foregrounding such anxieties. Instead, the subgenre employs a number of speculative conventions that uniquely support an effective, perspectival examination of species loss, ozone depletion, global warming, and so forth as human-created problems. One of these conventions gives us the outlook from the future, its rhetorical intent aligning with philosopher Jean-Pierre Dupuy's proposal for us to imagine

[33] Starhawk, *The Fifth Sacred Thing* (New York: Bantam, 1993), pp. 239, 372.
[34] T. C. Boyle, *A Friend of the Earth* (New York: Penguin, 2000), pp. 281, 9.
[35] Karen Traviss, *City of Pearl* (New York: EOS, 2004), p. 255.
[36] Kelpie Wilson, *Primal Tears* (Berkeley, CA: Frog, 2005), p. 28.

ourselves in a disastrous future and then to act now in the way we should have acted to prevent that future.[37] This imploration vis-à-vis biodiversity loss – among other ecological issues – is implied in *A Friend of the Earth*'s 2025, *Snowpiercer*'s 2031, *Earth*'s 2038, *The Fifth Sacred Thing*'s 2048, and captured well in this exchange from Budz's *Clade*:

> "Species have always vanished. That's what evolution, survival of the fittest, is all about."
>
> "Yes. But we sped up the process exponentially. Human beings out-evolved evolution. Except for cockroaches and a few other highly adaptive organisms, the biosphere couldn't keep pace with us. *We* almost couldn't keep pace with us."[38]

Asked if the mass extinction of the book's "ecocaust" was different from any previous mass extinction, the latter character observes, "'We could have prevented it from happening.'"[39]

In more galactic tales, it is often not from future humans that we learn about the consequences of our actions, but instead from alien species who recount their own experiences with environmental change brought on by human activity. In *City of Pearl*, the protector of planet Bezer'ej infers a connection between humans and an invasive population of "isenj": "'Millions of bezeri died from [isenj] pollution. The marine ecosystem is very fragile. I thought that would be something [humans] understood from experience.'"[40] With its isenj reproducing and spreading "'across their own world and its moon,'" *City of Pearl* joins *Primal Tears* in implicating population growth, as such, in environmental devastation.[41] (Though not presenting the outsider view of an alien, a character in the latter book doesn't want to reproduce, because he insists that overpopulation causes "global warming, pollution, the energy crisis, hunger, war, disease."[42]) In Yoss's *A Planet for Rent* (2001), aliens surveilled humans for thousands of years, waiting "until they were mature enough to be adopted by the great galactic family" of advanced species across the universe.[43] The aliens intervened, however, when they saw that humans "were incapable of intelligent self-government or of using their natural resources rationally."[44] Objecting to fossil and nuclear fuel, industry

---

[37] See Slavoj Žižek, *First as Tragedy, Then as Farce* (London: Verso, 2009), p. 151.
[38] Budz, *Clade*, p. 103.
[39] Ibid., p. 104.
[40] Traviss, *City of Pearl*, p. 176.
[41] Ibid.
[42] Wilson, *Primal Tears*, p. 11.
[43] Yoss, *A Planet for Rent*, trans. David Frye (New York: Restless, 2015), p. 11.
[44] Ibid.

and science, human population growth, polluting businesses, and the decimation of the Siberian tiger, the aliens seize control of Earth and turn it into a tourist destination, where they themselves fail as custodians of the planet and its population.

More recent works to take advantage of the rhetorically effective, alien perspective on anthropogenic environmental degradation are John Scalzi's *Fuzzy Nation* (2011) and Nnedi Okorafor's *Lagoon* (2014). In the former book, when a native of planet Zarathustra learns how to speak the language of the humans who are prospecting there, he says about them, "They have machines and tear the ground and trees and make the air stink. The trees are where we live and where our food is. When they come we do not stay. They do not see us because we see how they kill animals who come close. We go and we hide."[45] Here, environmental destruction and species loss are not represented as the consequences of more human bodies, but instead as the results of the actions of those bodies, however many there are. As petrofiction, Okorafor's book takes a close look at another one of these actions and its consequences: offshore oil drilling. The novel opens with a swordfish who is angry at the "burrowing and building creatures from the land," the humans who "brought the stench of dryness . . . the noise and made the world bleed black ooze that left poison rainbows on the water's surface."[46] The swordfish sabotages an oil hose with its sharp upper bill, and moments later a loud noise signals the effort of an alien species to fulfill the wishes of the swordfish and other sea animals by cleansing Nigeria's coastal waters of oil pollution. Endowing the sea animals with new abilities, the aliens commit to destroying offshore drilling facilities and expediting Nigeria's shift away from the oil economy and into an era of environmental sustainability.

Whether it communicates to us using the outlooks of future humans, the perspectives of aliens, or simply the observations of present-day protagonists (as in Buckner's *Watermind* and Liz Jensen's *The Rapture* [2009]), today's environmental SF affirms the anthropogenic origins of ecological loss. Ozone depletion and species decline are consequences of human activity, as science says they are, and as the fiction cited above reinforces. Water pollution cannot *not* be anthropogenic, considering documented cases of industrial leaks, spills, gushers, runoffs, and residues. Deforestation and the risks of fossil-fuel dependence – again, humanity's the culprit. SF has its stories for every one of these issues. Nicola Griffith's *Slow River* (1995) and

---

[45] John Scalzi, *Fuzzy Nation* (New York: Tor, 2011), p. 305.
[46] Nnedi Okorafor, *Lagoon* (New York: Saga, 2014), p 3.

Buckner's *Watermind* don't even need to imagine loss, but instead take the loss that already exists and novelize it. Indeed, as *Slow River* reminds us, "One mistake with a wastewater plant and . . . you could have PCBs and lead and DDT running free in our water system."[47] This is a fact upon which Griffith builds a tale about what is less a "mistake" and more a result of an indifferent economic model that rewards the developers of a patented bioremediation technology at the same time as it rewards another company for cost-cutting its way around using this technology. In the end, the victims of *Slow River*'s tragedy put a human face on the ecological costs of modern society.

Watermind imagines water pollutants and e-waste developing into a sentient colloid, and so it is more of the literary fantastic than Griffith's book. We can't expect to see a clump of nano-trash self-organize within a toxic stew of leached estrogen, strontium-90, and discarded appliances. However, we can verify that the fictional colloid's base of operation – Devil's Swamp in Louisiana – "was proposed for the Superfund National Priority List" in 2004.[48] The swamp is the location of a hazardous waste site and a key point of origin for the environmental justice movement. In August 2015, authorities found "high levels of PCB and mercury in the water that could be dangerous to human health."[49] As for deforestation, *A Friend of the Earth* is clear on its social origins, with the book's chapter-by-chapter oscillation between the late 1980s and mid-2020s connecting the ongoing decimation of "the great hardwood forests" during the former time period to a "100 percent" deforested Sri Lanka and its extinct elephants in the latter, imagined time period.[50] Sterling's *Heavy Weather* considers "Clear-cutting the jungles in Indonesia and Brazil" among "the planet's truly monumental ecoblunders," and a character in Jeanette Winterson's *Stone Gods* (2007) repeats the sentiment, counting the loss of virgin forests among the evidence of the "gutting" of his Earth-like planet, Orbus.[51]

Our Place in the World

Given the breadth of attention to environmental issues within and across recent environmental SF, these issues might seem to serve as atmospherics.

---

[47] Nicola Griffith, *Slow River* (New York: Ballantine, 1995), p. 33.
[48] M. M. Buckner, *Watermind* (New York: Tor, 2008), p. 28.
[49] Kevin Frey, "Warning: State Agencies Report Contamination in Devil's Swamp, Bayou Baton Rouge," *WAFB News Baton Rouge, LA* (2015), n.p.
[50] Boyle, *A Friend of the Earth*, pp. 72, 101.
[51] Sterling, *Heavy Weather*, pp. 139–40; Jeanette Winterson, *The Stone Gods* (Orlando, FL: Harcourt, 2007), p. 56.

One might argue that the literary function of Earth's ozone depletion, global warming, species extinction, drought, and pollution in Slonczewski's *The Highest Frontier* is to justify the off-planet setting of the book and its protagonist's presence there. Something similar could be claimed about Ben Bova's *The Precipice* (2001) or Tobias S. Buckell's *Arctic Rising* (2012) – that global warming and oil conflict in both are current-event substitutes for nuclear war or any number of apocalyptic circumstances frequently employed in SF to provide a stage for primary conflict. Likewise, we might see drought and the privatization of water in Alex Rivera's *Sleep Dealer* (2008) as backdrop to the film's primary focus on immigrant labor along the US–Mexico border. However, environmental SF must be defined not only by its attention to the ways anthropogenic crises color its plots, but also by the ways these crises structure the lives of its characters within the distressing material conditions that accompany certain human behaviors. It is the dire nature of this structuring that demonstrates, as Gerry Canavan says of Margaret Atwood's *Oryx and Crake* (2003) and *The Year of the Flood* (2009), "the urgent necessity of radically changing our social relations and anti-ecological lifestyles – of choosing to make a better *social* world before it is too late for the natural one."[52]

Nowhere is this urgency more palpable than in Octavia E. Butler's *Parable of the Sower* and Bacigalupi's *The Water Knife*. With the former published in 1993 and the latter in 2015, these novels epitomize the ways in which environmental SF of the 1990s–2010s has sustained the request of Kay Kenyon's radio broadcaster, imagining loss in hopes that readers will see the need to shift course. While not as explicitly focused on global warming as Kim Stanley Robinson's Science in the Capital trilogy (2004, 2005, 2007), Bacigalupi's *The Windup Girl* (2011), Gordon Van Gelder's edited collection *Welcome to the Greenhouse* (2011), and others, *Parable of the Sower* and *The Water Knife* are fictions "concerned with anthropogenic climate change or global warming as we now understand it" and thus may be considered among the growing body of cli-fi.[53] Butler's book expresses anxieties about global warming when, for example, its protagonist observes, "People have changed the climate of the world" and "Sea levels keep rising with the warming

---

[52] Gerry Canavan, "Hope, But Not for Us: Ecological Science Fiction and the End of the World in Margaret Atwood's *Oryx and Crake* and *The Year of the Flood*," *Literature Interpretation Theory* 23 (2012), p. 155.
[53] Adeline Johns-Putra, "Climate Change in Literature and Literary Studies: From Cli-Fi, Climate Change Theater and Ecopoetry to Ecocriticism and Climate Change Criticism," *WIREs Climate Change* 7 (2016), p. 267.

climate."[54] In *The Water Knife*, cities everywhere have "taken hits ... from climate change."[55]

As near bookends to the body of environmental SF considered in this chapter, these two novels reflect the characteristics of this body by resisting narrow categorization as climate fiction. Rebecca Tuhus-Dubrow writes, "Climate change is unprecedented and extraordinary, forcing us to rethink our place in the world," and certainly cli-fi is at the forefront of using narrative to provoke this rethinking.[56] As Patrick D. Murphy notes, "Recent large-scale studies of climate change, the politics around it, and the need to move to a different economic model for the world here at the end of growth all address an increasingly inescapable conclusion: the problem is not one of means but one of recognition, acceptance, and will to act."[57] But environmental SF of the last twenty-five years has demonstrated that anthropogenic ecological degradation, *in general* – not only climate change – is unprecedented and extraordinary and demands recognition, acceptance, and will to act. Environmental SF has been working for years to connect a breadth of environmental issues to human activity, taking as its starting point the lesson that humans can and do induce ecological loss.

Given their close attention to the consequences of drought, *Parable of the Sower* and *The Water Knife* might, along with *Sleep Dealer* and *Pumzi*, be called "dry-fi." Both books imagine the privatization of dwindling water supplies to foster deep class divide, social and personal corruption, and lasting ecological decline. Rather than identifying either climate change or drought as discrete origins of the degraded conditions that set social turmoil and ecological ruin into motion, these books join those they bookend in demonstrating the inseparability of environmental crises. In both, the United States is hot, parched, and laden with toxins. However, climate change, drought, and pollution constitute devastating totalities that structure all personal and social activity. Neither crisis is more or less significant than the others but instead part of a whole that would be more accurately spoken of using the language of relatedness customary in ecological thinking. Seeking better terminology for what we face, Kim Stanley Robinson notes, "the phrase 'climate change' is an attempt to narrate the ecological situation. We use the term now as a synecdoche to stand for the totality of our damage to the biosphere,

[54] Octavia E. Butler, *Parable of the Sower* (New York: Aspect, 1993), pp. 50, 105.
[55] Paolo Bacigalupi, *The Water Knife* (New York: Alfred A. Knopf, 2015), p. 140.
[56] Rebecca Tuhus-Dubrow, "Cli-Fi: Birth of a Genre," *Dissent* (2013), p. 61.
[57] Patrick D. Murphy, "Pessimism, Optimism, Human Inertia, and Anthropogenic Climate Change," *Interdisciplinary Studies in Literature and Environment* 21 (2014), p. 149.

which is much bigger than mere climate change, more like a potential mass extinction event."[58] Recent environmental SF has avoided such synecdoche, even when its individual works seem to warrant some sort of literary taxonomy (e.g., cli-fi, dry-fi) as the result of a particular issue's presence in their narratives.

Robinson proposes to replace the prevailing "words and phrases" approach to understanding ecological disaster with a narrative approach.[59] Instead of talking about "global warming, climate change, sustainable development, decarbonization," and more, he offers this: "This coming century looks like the moment in human history when we will either invent a civilization that nurtures the biosphere while it supports us, or else we will damage it quite badly, perhaps even to the point of causing a mass extinction event and endangering ourselves."[60] A prolific writer of environmental SF during the time period addressed in this chapter, Robinson has embraced this more comprehensive, narrative approach to imagining loss and urging changes in human behavior. In the last quarter century, environmental SF as a whole has embraced this approach, its texts highlighting a collection of anthropogenic environmental issues, all of which encourage us to rethink our relationship with Earth.

---

[58] Kim Stanley Robinson, "Still, I'm Reluctant to Call This Pessimism," in Gerry Canavan and Kim Stanley Robinson, eds., *Green Planets: Ecology and Science Fiction* (Middletown, CT: Wesleyan University Press, 2014), p. 243.

[59] Ibid.

[60] Ibid., p. 244.

37

Science Fiction and the Return of Empire: Global Capitalism, Tom Cruise, and the War on Terror from the 2000s to the 2010s

DAN HASSLER-FOREST

"Live. Die. Repeat." When the critically lauded but commercially disappointing SF film *Edge of Tomorrow* (dir. Doug Liman, 2014) was released on home video, the original poster's tagline entirely overshadowed the bland official film title.[1] This far more provocative alternative title not only has some active bearing on the film's plot, in which a foot soldier in a losing war against invading aliens relives the same day over and over again until he learns how to defeat them – it also has great symbolic resonance for a futuristic war film produced and released after the United States military has been involved with its own "Live. Die. Repeat" scenario for the past fifteen years of the War on Terror.

While this pulpy and cleverly structured fantasy lacks any noticeable ambition to provide an elaborate allegorical representation of post-9/11 geopolitics, its central conceit does offer an uncanny reflection of key tensions underlying the historical period in which it was made. Like so many popular fantasies of the 2000s and 2010s, it translates the political and ideological debates surrounding the ongoing War on Terror into the pleasurable fantasy of the alien invasion genre. *Edge of Tomorrow* adapts familiar genre fiction into a form that legitimizes American policies while also articulating deeply felt frustrations and anxieties about this kind of military escalation. Its endless war is made meaningful in the context of twenty-first-century global capitalism, where the absence of political and economic alternatives has mired us in an ongoing feedback loop of self-perpetuating crises. Like so many other twenty-first-century SF texts that appeared in this period, *Edge of*

---

[1] The film's original title *All You Need Is Kill*, after the English translation of the Japanese "light novel" on which it was based, had been rejected by the studio because of concerns over the centrally placed word "kill."

596

Tomorrow makes commonly shared fantasies, fears, and tensions about the War on Terror pleasurable by embedding them within the narrative and aesthetic conventions of SF as situated within historically specific conditions of media production, distribution, and reception.

This creates a contradiction that in many ways typifies SF as a popular genre. As John Rieder has pointed out, the history of SF is marked both by the recurrence of recognizable themes, styles, and motifs and as a cultural practice embedded within what he calls the "mass cultural genre system."[2] Moving away from a Suvinian approach, which perceives SF as a clearly defined and politically subversive genre, I instead follow more recent work that approaches it as a "selective tradition"[3] in which political and ideological contradictions do not merely coexist but proliferate. By the same token, I locate SF as a genre that currently leaves its greatest cultural footprint in those narrative media that are central to the mass cultural system in the twenty-first century: film and television.[4] While SF literature obviously remains a dynamic and lively cultural form, it has arguably become less central to the genre than it was throughout most of the previous century. For this reason, my main focus throughout this chapter will be on SF film and television, with occasional references to other media.

The fact that *Edge of Tomorrow*'s ending is so much less compelling than the cleverly constructed series of temporal reboots that precedes it is not because of any specific failing on the four credited screenwriters' part: I would rather argue that it reveals how difficult it has become for us to even imagine this kind of closure. What has sustained the imperial might of American neoliberal capitalism in the twenty-first century is the fundamentally limitless nature of the political, ideological, and military conflicts that make up the War on Terror. Michael Hardt and Antonio Negri, whose theoretical work on the imperial nature of global capitalism has profoundly shaped this debate, have framed America's twenty-first-century hegemony in precisely such terms: the post-9/11 War on Terror is no geopolitical conflict in the traditional sense, but instead represents "a general omni-crisis, when the state of

---

[2] See John Rieder, *Science Fiction and the Mass Cultural Genre System* (Middletown, CT: Wesleyan University Press, 2017), pp. 33–5.

[3] Andrew Milner, *Locating Science Fiction* (Liverpool: Liverpool University Press, 2012), p. 178.

[4] While video games also make up a substantial component of this century's mass cultural system, the medium's relationship to narrative is more ambiguous (and, indeed, contested) than film and television, while it also remains a more "enclosed" subculture that resides further from the cultural mainstream.

war and thus the state of exception become indefinite or even permanent, as they do today."[5]

The many cultural, economic, and ideological contradictions of global capitalism have found various forms of expression in twenty-first-century SF. Indeed, one would expect a genre so thoroughly invested in imagining alternative futures to reflect the multiple faces of a historical period in which the very idea of any alternative to the current political system is flatly denied. Indeed, the conspicuous absence of utopian thinking in twenty-first-century SF film and television clearly expresses this stifling lack of meaningful political and ideological options. In this socio-cultural context, we have even become so desperate to identify moments of promise and potential in futuristic narratives that we cling to the most minimal, thoroughly ambiguous twists in overwhelmingly dystopian SF texts: *Children of Men* (dir. Alfonso Cuarón, 2006), *Snowpiercer* (dir. Bonn Joon-ho, 2013), and *Elysium* (dir. Neill Blomkamp, 2013) are just a few influential films that have grappled with the frustrating impasse of our allegedly "post-historical," "post-ideological" sensibility, in which even the most heroic attempt to transform the existing order leads – at best – to ambivalent results.[6] Similarly, the rapid ascent of dystopian storyworlds in young adult book series like *The Hunger Games* (2008–10) and *The Maze Runner* (2009–16), and their many transmedia offshoots, further illustrates the sense of impotence that defines global capitalism's "futurelessness."[7]

While there obviously remains a wide variety of cultural production in twenty-first-century SF, the general tendency has moved away from the kind of faith in human progress that long defined the genre. The most vivid illustration of this failure of utopian imagination in popular SF is the early 2000s reboot of the *Star Trek* franchise (1966–). A series that used to be the very embodiment of liberal-democratic utopianism first floundered in a half-hearted attempt to allegorize the War on Terror as an endless "Temporal Cold War" in the awkward and poorly received *Enterprise* (2001–5). Shortly thereafter, the storyworld was rebooted in a newly incarnated film series, the first of which

---

[5] Antonio Hardt and Michael Negri, *Multitude: War and Democracy in the Age of Empire* (Harmondsworth: Penguin Books, 2005), p. 8.

[6] Gerry Canavan, "'If the Engine Ever Stops, We'd All Die': *Snowpiercer* and Necrofuturism," *Paradoxa* 26 (2014), pp. 1–26.

[7] Franco "Bifo" Berardi, *Futurability: The Age of Impotence and the Horizon of Possibility* (London and New York: Verso Books, 2017). Even the work of Kim Stanley Robinson, whose Mars Trilogy (1994–7) has often been cited as a key work of late twentieth-century utopian SF, has in recent years taken on a more negative turn, foregrounding instead the seemingly inevitable crises of resource shortage and disastrous climate change.

(dir. J. J. Abrams, 2009) redefined the starship's ongoing mission as a thoroughly militarized quest for revenge against the perpetrators of the ostentatiously 9/11-like destruction of the planet Vulcan. Embracing the genre's suddenly-fashionable "gritty and dystopian" visual *and* political register even more fully, the aptly titled *Star Trek Into Darkness* (dir. J. J. Abrams, 2013) piled on the War on Terror references even higher, offering up one set piece after another in which buildings, starships, and entire city blocks are wiped out by spectacular terrorist attacks.

So even though positive visions of a better future have been in short supply in the post-9/11 years, there has been no shortage of SF productions that reproduce some of the War on Terror's most basic characteristics. Without claiming to offer an exhaustive or complete list, I would propose that there are three recurring key concerns that have informed public debates on the War on Terror and which resonate strongly in twenty-first-century SF film and television:

1. *Surveillance*: As a technological means of social control, surveillance has long been a prominent feature of dystopian SF, with variations of Orwell's infamous two-way "Telescreens" featuring prominently in influential genre classics like *Metropolis* (dir. Fritz Lang, 1927), *Modern Times* (dir. Charlie Chaplin, 1936), and, of course, George Orwell's novel, *1984* (1949). But with the ubiquity of panoptic security cameras in metropolitan areas, the digitization of government data and intelligence networks, and the adoption of sweeping new legislation after 9/11, surveillance quickly became central to any understanding of the War on Terror. As a regular thematic motif, surveillance as a form of political control can be recognized in twenty-first-century TV series like *Fringe* (2008–13) and *Person of Interest* (2011–16), and in films such as *The Island* (dir. Michael Bay, 2005), *A Scanner Darkly* (dir. Richard Linklater, 2006), *The Dark Knight* (dir. Christopher Nolan, 2008), *Moon* (dir. Duncan Jones, 2009), *Inception* (dir. Christopher Nolan, 2010), *Source Code* (dir. Duncan Jones, 2011), *Looper* (dir. Duncan Jones, 2012), and *Captain America: The Winter Soldier* (dir. Russo brothers, 2014).

2. *Victimhood*: The narrative motif of the United States (or, more broadly, "the West") as the victim of an unprovoked and unforeseeable attack took hold with remarkable ease after the tragic terrorist attacks on the World Trade Center and Pentagon. Popular culture was quick to provide abundant narratives that confirmed this ahistorical and irresponsible political position, with war movies and disaster epics providing symbolic

expressions of victimized Americans heroically surviving a 9/11-like assault. The television reboot of *Battlestar Galactica* (2004–9), which I discuss in more detail later in this chapter, is a wonderfully ambiguous example, while SF films that have recently adopted this trope include *The Mist* (dir. Frank Darabont, 2007), *Cloverfield* (dir. Matt Reeves, 2008), *The Road* (dir. John Hillcoat, 2009), *Monsters* (dir. Gareth Edwards, 2011), *Battle: Los Angeles* (dir. Jonathan Liebesman, 2011), the aforementioned *Star Trek* movies, and *10 Cloverfield Lane* (dir. Dan Trachtenberg, 2016).

3. *Posthuman warfare*: Following the US actions in Afghanistan and the "shock-and-awe" invasion of Iraq that followed soon after the 9/11 attacks, the dominant discourse regarding American military action became increasingly focused on posthuman forms – most notably drone strikes, which increased dramatically during the Obama administration. The growing resistance to deployment of foot soldiers in remote high-risk zones, together with the economic incentive to invest in military-industrial technology, transformed both public and political perceptions of the War on Terror, especially from 2009 onwards. The SF genre's longstanding fascination for robots, cyborgs, and technological extensions of the human body made for a seemingly natural connection with emerging discourses on the War on Terror. Surely the key SF text that expresses and negotiates the basic fantasies and fears of posthuman warfare is *Iron Man* (dir. Jon Favreau, 2008) and its sequels. But there are many other examples of twenty-first-century SF films that offer representations of this phenomenon, including *A.I.: Artificial Intelligence* (dir. Steven Spielberg, 2001), *WALL•E* (dir. Andrew Stanton, 2008), *Never Let Me Go* (dir. Mark Romanek, 2010), *Man of Steel* (dir. Zack Snyder, 2014), *Ex Machina* (dir. Alex Garland, 2015), and Scarlett Johansson's remarkable "posthuman trilogy" *Her* (dir. Spike Jonze, 2013), *Under the Skin* (dir. Jonathan Glazer, 2013), and *Lucy* (dir. Luc Besson, 2014).

In order to chart some of the key ways in which SF films have responded to the larger context of global capitalism, post-9/11 intensified neoliberalism, and the War on Terror, this chapter will engage with popular SF representations of these three themes in this chapter through a singular case study: an analysis of the SF oeuvre of Tom Cruise.

In a catalogue of the Hollywood SF films of the 2000s and 2010s, Cruise's iconic presence is striking: he appeared in four high-profile features that also elegantly span the fifteen-year period in question. Besides forming a fairly manageable body of work in terms of quantity, these four films also neatly (though quite accidentally) foreground themes that have become iconic signifiers of the post-9/11 era: in *Minority Report* (dir. Steven Spielberg, 2002), the concept of ubiquitous surveillance and pre-emptive policing; in *War of the Worlds* (dir. Steven Spielberg, 2005), the ambivalent anxieties about monstrous and unpredictable threats to American hegemonic power that have been used to justify its own War on Terror; in *Oblivion* (dir. Joseph Kosinski, 2013), drone technology and the anxieties surrounding posthuman warfare; and in the aforementioned *Edge of Tomorrow*, a productive intersection of all three motifs, which together come to embody the neoliberal era's creeping sense that traditional notions of causality and linear progression increasingly break down in what Paul Virilio has described as capitalism's "war on Time."[8]

This quartet of SF blockbusters thereby perfectly encapsulates what I would describe as the contradictory logic of global capitalism's "structure of feeling" – Raymond Williams's helpful term for articulating the dialectical tension between residual and emergent energies that together make up the complex sensibility of any given cultural moment.[9] Moreover, this concept allows us to see cultural texts – even those with Tom Cruise in them – not as expressions of a single hegemonic ideological position, but as complex and internally contradictory expressions of "meanings and values as they are actively lived and felt."[10]

But besides the coincidental fact that this handful of SF blockbusters conveniently illustrates some of the main themes, motifs, and forms of imagery that have come to represent popular imaginations of the War on Terror, the figure of Tom Cruise himself provides a useful icon for coming to terms with the cultural logic of the 2000s and 2010s. It has been fashionable for film critics, journalists, and authors of online think-pieces in recent years to describe Cruise as "the last movie star," a relic of industrial capitalism's relative stability that has somehow survived amidst the more precarious and unpredictable age of "flexible accumulation."[11] One particularly influential article even argues that Cruise's residual stardom has increasingly been threatened by "YouTube and internet journalism."[12]

---

[8] Paul Virilio, *Speed and Politics* (Cambridge, MA: MIT Press, 2006), p. 69.
[9] Raymond Williams, *Marxism and Literature* (Oxford: Oxford University Press, 1977), p. 132.
[10] Ibid.
[11] David Harvey, *The Condition of Posmodernity* (London: Wiley Blackwell, 1989), p. 147.
[12] Amy Nicholson, "How YouTube and Internet Journalism Destroyed Tom Cruise, Our Last Great Movie Star," *LA Weekly* (May 20, 2014).

Nevertheless, while it may be tempting to imagine him as the nostalgic embodiment of the studio era and Hollywood stardom, Tom Cruise is also a celebrity who has proved to be almost preternaturally adept at navigating an environment that demands subjects to become an "entrepreneur of the self."[13] In the early 1990s, just as the end of the Cold War ushered in the age of truly global capitalism and increased deregulation, he founded his own production company, Cruise/Wagner Productions. This entrepreneurial move enabled him to gain a much higher degree of control over the movies he starred in, and especially over his own financial stake in these productions.[14] While he is therefore indeed one of the last remaining movie stars whose name has enough drawing power to "open" a big Hollywood movie, he is also among the first to benefit in so many ways from the neoliberal climate of flexibility and media diversification. Both onscreen and off, Tom Cruise has become one of the true icons of global capitalism in the post-9/11 age.

Minority Report: Post-9/11 Premediation and Ubiquitous Surveillance

Appearing in cinemas a little more than a year after the attacks of September 11, 2001, *Minority Report* was one of the first SF blockbusters to map out the key fantasies, tensions, and anxieties that would become pivotal in cultural representation of the emerging War on Terror. Based on a short story by Philip K. Dick, that most prophetic and insightful of twentieth-century SF authors, the film depicts a future in which the use of genetically engineered human mutants dubbed "Precogs" has allowed for the creation of a police department of "PreCrime." Tom Cruise plays a PreCrime detective tasked with investigating crimes that have not yet occurred, who must go on the run from his own department when he is himself found guilty of committing a future crime.

In the film's structural conceit, the three mutant Precogs pick up future violent crimes and record them as memories. The input they receive is recorded by the PreCrime police department's elaborate technological apparatus, yielding the name of the killer, the name of the victim, and a bunch of video footage that resembles a pretentious film student's attempt to deliver a dramatic dream sequence, complete with fisheye lenses, a bombardment of

---

[13] Maurizio Lazzarato, *Signs and Machines: Capitalism and the Production of Subjectivity* (Cambridge, MA: MIT Press, 2014), p. 52.
[14] Edward J. Epstein, "Tom Cruise Inc," *Slate* (June 27, 2005).

Dutch angles, and disorienting extreme close-ups. One of the film's clever ironies is that the PreCrime detectives must become creative filmmakers in order to solve / prevent the crime: in what has become *Minority Report*'s most iconic image, Cruise works his way through the chaotic and disjointed audiovisual material in search of a coherent narrative, quickly putting together a film scene that establishes character, setting, and motivation. The resulting film sequence gives him the "evidence" he needs before he can dash off and prevent the crime he has just reconstructed on film before it actually occurs.

While the film had been in development for well over a decade, when it was finally released in June 2002 its themes of ubiquitous surveillance, trauma, and the uncanny fantasy of turning back time for highly mediated events tapped directly into the emergent post-9/11 structure of feeling. The way in which the film organizes its seemingly flawless department of PreCrime perfectly articulates the fantasy of a high-tech, thoroughly professional, and fully militarized police force that clearly operates entirely for the common good: the PreCrime task force expresses the logic Hardt and Negri also identify in America's imperial geopolitics, operating "not on the basis of force itself but on the basis of the capacity to present force as being in the service of right and peace."[15] Cast in his familiar role as a mid-level Everyman professional, Tom Cruise[16] is initially a true believer in the system: as someone who has suffered tremendous personal loss, his dedication to his job in PreCrime's militarized police force derives from his desire to save others from a similar fate, while at the same time acting out his desire for vengeance on the (future) perpetrators he consigns to a lifetime in a suspended-animation prison.

The film's provocative play[17] with conflicting modes and registers of time and temporality resonates on at least two levels in the context of the post-9/11 cultural logic of neoliberal capitalism: firstly, it grapples productively with the desire to turn back time on tragedy, specifically by associating the detailed analysis of audiovisual material with the ability to stop or even reverse the

[15] Michael Hardt and Antonio Negri, *Empire* (London and Cambridge, MA: Harvard University Press, 2000), p. 15.

[16] While Cruise obviously plays various different characters in the movies I discuss in this chapter, I refer to him each time simply as Tom Cruise: partly for the sake of simplicity, and partly to underline how we experience him in all these roles firstly *as a movie star* rather than as a particular character.

[17] Thomas Elsaesser has grouped the film within a larger corpus of recent "mind-game films," a subgenre that he sees as "indicative of a 'crisis' in the spectator-film relation" (16). See his "The Mind-Game Film," in Warren Buckland, ed., *Puzzle Films: Complex Storytelling in Contemporary Cinema* (Chichester: Blackwell Publishing, 2009).

actions being depicted – as if studying the endlessly repeated footage of the airliners striking the World Trade Center towers would ultimately allow us to avoid those very events. The hypermediated digital era in which those attacks occurred is further underlined and exaggerated on the one hand in Cruise's compulsive and drug-fuelled addiction to his home entertainment system, as he spends his evenings compulsively interacting with video recordings of his dead son. On the otherhand, we see in the film a cultural and commercial context organized with remarkable prescience, where the equivalent of Big Data is used to track individuals wherever they go, as the urban landscape constantly bombards everyone in it with personalized advertising.

Richard Grusin has used *Minority Report*'s ambivalent treatment of time to illustrate his concept of "premediation," a form of logic that "insists that the future itself is also already mediated, and that with the right technologies . . . the future can be remediated before it happens."[18] While Grusin previously focused on the dialectical tension that informs all forms of media representation in his book *Remediation* (co-authored with Jay David Bolter),[19] he has more recently argued that the post-9/11 media landscape is dominated by a kind of affective subjectivity that short-circuits the public's relationship to mediated temporality, and, therefore, our basic understanding of historicity. For the double logic of premediation intensifies this dialectical movement into a contradictory theory of the political nature of commercial media, "imagining the future in terms of new media practices and technologies and on extending the media networks of the present so that they seem to reach indefinitely into a securely (if indeterminately) colonized future."[20]

To unpack this idea a little further: Grusin's logic of premediation, while not entirely new to the post-9/11 age, represents an intensification not just of the media-saturated world that postmodernists like Jean Baudrillard described as a "bombardment of signs,"[21] but also as an extension of the War on Terror's doctrine of systemic pre-emption. American military conflicts of the twenty-first century have primarily been wars that correspond eerily with *Minority Report*'s PreCrime program. The 2003 invasion of Iraq is the most obvious example of this kind of pre-emptive strike, with the United States invading another nation based on speculation about possible future

[18] Richard Grusin, "Premediation," *Criticism* 46, 1 (2004), p. 19.
[19] Richard Grusin and David Jay Bolter, *Remediation: Understanding New Media* (Cambridge, MA: MIT Press, 2000).
[20] Grusin, "Premediation," p. 37.
[21] Jean Baudrillard, *Simulacra and Simulation* (Stanford: Stanford University Press, 1988).

crimes. But just as the film's convoluted plot revolves around Cruise's discovery that those in power can manipulate the available data to use the Precogs' prophetic abilities simply to further their own interests, it has similarly become a matter of public record that the formal reasons for military action in Iraq had similarly been fabricated.

Minority Report thus serves as a potent example of the double logic of post-9/11 premediation and the kind of thinking that underlies the flimsy political justifications for the War on Terror. Its double logic of premediation strengthens the hold this historical event has had on twenty-first-century politics, ideology, and culture, as a singularity that one of the editors of this collection once described as something "to which we imagined ourselves to be permanently bound and to which we, even now, somehow feel at risk of return."[22] The film's adaptation of Philip K. Dick's famously circular and frequently unknowable narrative logic therefore perfectly sums up one central aspect of the post-9/11 era and its deeply contradictory sense of historicity.

In characteristic pop-cultural form, the film doesn't resolve this contra-dictory logic, but rather intensifies it. Not only does the finale try to have it both ways with an ambiguous "happy ending" that could also quite plausibly be read as an extended dream sequence. It is also as intoxicated by its depiction of a media-saturated and fully panoptic society as it is critical of it. As what has since become a paradigmatic twenty-first-century SF film, *Minority Report* thus dramatizes some of the key themes that would continue to dominate the War on Terror. It tapped into an emerging narrative trope that quickly proliferated across popular culture, most noticeably in popular TV narratives, which all foregrounded neoliberalism's more flexible modes of mediated temporality – sometimes in ways that seemed to embrace global capitalism's system of flexible accumulation, in procedurals like *24* and *CSI*, and – somewhat more rarely – in ways that questioned or even challenged this new cultural logic, like *The Wire*, *Fringe*, and *Person of Interest*.

Minority Report thus articulated with uncanny precision the War on Terror's basic logic of preemptive action, ubiquitous surveillance, and inten-sified pre-, re-, and hypermediation. But if this first collaboration between blockbuster director Steven Spielberg and "last great movie star" Tom Cruise gave us an appropriately ambivalent summation of the contradictions that

---

[22] Gerry Canavan, "Terror and Mismemory: Resignifying September 11 in *World Trade Center* and *United 93*," in Véronique Bragard, Christophe Dony and Warren Rosenberg, eds., *Portraying 9/11: Essays on Representations in Comics, Literature, Film and Theatre* (Jefferson, NC: McFarland, 2011), p. 119.

inform post-9/11 American politics and culture, their second collaborative venture into SF, which appeared three years later, can be read as a sequel in more ways than one.

War of the Worlds: Refugees from the War on Terror

The second Hollywood adaptation of H. G. Wells's genre-defining novel (1897) was explicitly promoted, discussed, and received as an attempt to infuse a genre classic with imagery and themes that connected directly to the remediation of 9/11 and its aftermath. Reviews invariably brought up how the film's depiction of a large-scale alien invasion resembled mediations of the terrorist attacks, how certain lines from the script (like Tom Cruise's daughter asking "Is it the terrorists?" as a first response to the alien's appearance) clearly acknowledged this connection, and creative personnel involved in the production gave numerous interviews that foregrounded this element. Spielberg, for instance, proclaimed in one promotional interview that he felt this particular narrative had special significance "in the shadow of 9/11," and that "this story's time had come again" ("Revisiting the Invasion"). Why, then, would it make sense to position this futuristic action-disaster film as a particularly timely piece? What made it resonate so strongly within the context of post-9/11 American culture? And what sets it apart from its predecessor and mirror image, the previous Cruise/Spielberg collaboration *Minority Report*?

Central to understanding the structure of feeling that defines this twenty-first-century adaptation of Wells's classic novel is the structuring fantasy its narrative has articulated across its cumulative history. At its core, the novel expresses the imperialist's ambivalence about the violence and destruction colonialism in its many forms has perpetuated throughout capitalism's long and barbaric history.[23] The thrill of the story's sensational depictions of Western civilization being savagely torn apart by alien invaders with highly advanced military technology resides in its quite obvious turning of the tables on geopolitical dynamics – whether the alien onslaught is being compared explicitly to Britain's occupation of India, as in Wells's novel, or related to Cold War anxieties, as in the fondly remembered 1953 film.

Similarly, the 2005 film expresses what Slavoj Žižek has described as the seemingly irrational desire to see global capitalism's world of unearned

---

[23] John Rieder, *Colonialism and the Emergence of Science Fiction* (Middletown, CT: Wesleyan University Press, 2008), p. 5.

wealth and privilege destroyed. In his widely read response to the 9/11 attacks, he confronts the central question why the imaginary landscapes of American popular culture have been so preoccupied with this kind of imagery:

> The fact that the September 11 attacks were the stuff of popular fantasies long before they actually took place provides yet another case of the twisted logic of dreams: it is easy to account for the fact that poor people around the world dream about becoming Americans – so what do the well-to-do Americans, immobilized in their well-being, dream about? About a global catastrophe that would shatter their lives – why? This is what psychoanalysis is about: to explain why, in the midst of well-being, we are haunted by nightmarish visions of catastrophes.[24]

In the case of *War of the Worlds*, this type of reading clearly makes sense. The absolutely merciless campaign of terror and destruction waged by the Martian tripods, here depicted as towering, mobile skyscrapers, both questions and reinforces the War on Terror's most basic logic. On the one hand, we are treated to an overwhelming deluge of spectacular footage showing the American landscape (starting in the nondescript suburbs of New Jersey before moving into America's rural heartland) being obliterated in ways both pleasurable and terrifying; while on the other, these atrocities are committed by non-human bodies that easily represent an evil "Other" undeserving of empathy or, indeed, the extension of even the most basic *human* rights.

Like so many post-9/11 fantastic films that used a similar narrative logic, the terrorist attacks on New York are reimagined as the spectacular assault of a completely alien, often faceless invader. From the Godzilla-like creature in *Cloverfield* to the disposable alien bodies of the Chitauri in *Marvel's The Avengers* (dir. Joss Whedon, 2012), popular SF depictions of the attacks take enormous pleasure in the depiction of urban terror, while also strengthening the most common-sense cultural and political shorthand that emerged in the wake of the attacks: the notion that they were not just exceptional, but had also been unprovoked, unforeseeable, and unimaginable. Thus, by reframing the dominant media representation of the 9/11 attacks from within the context of Hollywood spectacle, the War on Terror's political narrative received further ideological justification by emphatically portraying America/"the West" *as victims*.

But clearly, *War of the Worlds* doesn't function entirely in the register of rah-rah pro-military films like *Independence Day* (dir. Roland Emmerich, 1996),

---

[24] Slavoj Žižek, *Welcome to the Desert of the Real* (London and New York: Verso, 2002), p. 17.

Black Hawk Down (dir. Ridley Scott, 2002), or *Battle: Los Angeles*, with their genocidal fantasies of superhero-soldiers killing "anything that's not human."[25] While the most obvious ideological reading is that of a grossly exaggerated dramatization of the 9/11 terrorist attacks, the film's visual and narrative trajectory at the same time closely resembles an *inversion* of the War on Terror, with Tom Cruise's character representing another blue-collar worker (in this case, a stevedore) who is made into a refugee by the sudden invasion of impossibly superior technological forces. Its presentation of the invasion, while representing its own undeniably impressive form of audio-visual spectacle, deliberately avoids scenes in which iconic urban landmarks are destroyed. Instead, the narrative, following the form of its source novel, depicts Tom Cruise's first-person experience of the alien invasion as he struggles to get his two estranged children to safety.

In this sense at least, *War of the Worlds* offers a provocative portrait of a family displaced by a military force whose tactics closely resemble Dick Cheney and Donald Rumsfeld's "shock-and-awe" approach to fast-paced military action. Such a reading is strengthened by the way in which the American landscape is suddenly transformed within the film from the familiar imagery of suburbs, ferries, and pastoral spaces of refuge to an unpredictable and deeply unstable environment full of potentially lethal obstacles. The scene in which the theft of Cruise's car (itself stolen from a neighborhood friend) culminates in the alien attack on an overloaded ferry resonates even more strongly a decade after the film's release, as images of Syrian refugees displaced by the War on Terror's spiraling effects have become a devastating part of the daily international news cycle.

Tom Cruise's second SF epic thus adopts the same double logic that many have also recognized in the post-9/11 reboot of TV series *Battlestar Galactica* (2004–9). The new show's "re-imagining" of the 1970s space opera placed far more emphasis on the traumatic impact of the sneak attack that reduces human civilization to the "ragtag fleet" of survivors led by the eponymous starship, obviously reframing the narrative as one with renewed relevance for the twenty-first century's unstable geopolitical context. But at the same time, the show's depiction of military occupation during the third season's "New Caprica" story arc resonated strongly with the contemporaneous American occupation of Iraq. Inverting the series' opening situation, in which the human survivors unsubtly stood in for Americans traumatized and confused

---

[25] Gerry Canavan, "'I'd Rather Be in Afghanistan': Antinomies of *Battle: Los Angeles*," *Democratic Communiqué* 26, 2 (Fall 2014), p. 41.

after a devastating and disorienting terrorist attack, the narrative just as easily reverses this scenario by having the humans represent the oppressed victims of invasion and occupation by a vastly superior military force.

By adopting this kind of fluid, ambivalent, and even contradictory structure in terms of their symbolic representation of the War on Terror, both *Battlestar Galactica* and *War of the Worlds* reflect an emerging post-9/11 structure of feeling. By heightening this central contradiction rather than attempting to resolve it, viewers are invited to "adopt a critical, self-reflective frame toward our post-9/11 world."[26] And while this invitation to adopt a critical perspective is more explicit in *Battlestar Galactica* – in the same way that more highbrow SF films like *Children of Men* and *Snowpiercer* use the genre to critique political and ideological positions – *War of the Worlds* is all the more potent for its own internal contradictions.

This becomes most obvious in the screenplay's notoriously whiplash-inducing pivot towards the very end. In its oft-derided final act, the film moves abruptly from an increasingly dire post-apocalyptic drama of blue-collar American families becoming third-world refugees to a bizarrely contrived happy ending that is as disingenuous as it is grossly artificial. And while Wells's novel is itself somewhat notorious for the anticlimactic *deus ex machina* that puts a sudden end to the seemingly unstoppable alien invasion, the way in which screenwriter David Koepp adapted it for the post-9/11 age illustrates the deeper connection between the traumatic attacks and catharsis associated with military violence.

For while both the book and the 1953 film end with humanity's repentance and resignation, the Tom Cruise film finds occasion for visually spectacular (though narratively nonsensical) military action in the film's ending. As everyone even vaguely familiar with the century-old popular narrative is well aware, the Martians turn out to have no resistance to common Earth bacteria, and are halted in their global genocide as they succumb abruptly to the common cold. While this ending has always seemed like a desperate ploy by an author who has written himself into a corner, it also plays into a resilient Western narrative tradition of finding redemption by learning humility. The now-common postcolonialist interpretive perspective on Wells's novel strongly supports such a reading, as the imperialist power of Great Britain is ultimately redeemed by undergoing an experience that is

---

[26] Brian L. Ott, "(Re)Framing Fear: Equipment for Living in a Post-9/11 World," in Tiffany Potter and C. W. Marshall, eds., *Cylons in America: Critical Studies in Battlestar Galactica* (New York: Continuum, 2008), p. 14.

a short-term approximation of what it has inflicted on the colonial realms it has conquered.

Considering how swiftly and how thoroughly narratives surrounding the attacks of 9/11 were tied up with imperial militarism and the emerging War on Terror, it is no surprise that the 2005 film ends with such a weird display of American military prowess. In the scene in question, Tom Cruise comes across a platoon of soldiers, alerting them to the fact that one of the alien tripods' impenetrable shields is clearly no longer operational. Having spent the duration of the film on the run from the invincible invaders – with the exception of one scene where he straps a bomb to his chest and allows himself to be caged in order to rescue his daughter – Cruise finally becomes the man of action we know from countless other films, guiding the soldiers towards a pointless but noisily cathartic destruction of two tripods.

In part, this ending is clearly predicated by what are often interpreted as "demands of the marketplace," or what can at least be understood as a standard film-industrial convention. Such common-sense conventions prescribe, for instance, that Hollywood action spectacles released as summer tentpole movies end not only on a note of reassurance, but also with a spectacular set piece in which the central conflict is unambiguously resolved, and the audience is treated to a spectacular and literally explosive climax.[27] But these industrial conventions also reflect and strengthen ideological positions and discursive formations: in this case, the cultural association between victimization and military retaliation cements the political justification of the War on Terror. The both seemingly pointless and thoroughly redundant military attack on the dying aliens therefore serves the vital purpose of once more associating narrative closure and emotional catharsis with conventional depictions of heroic military action.

Thus, *War of the Worlds* demonstrates the structural ambivalence of science-fictional responses to the post-9/11 era and the War on Terror. While it reproduces on the one hand the increasingly common discursive notions of American victimhood and exceptionalism, it also unavoidably opens itself up to a more counter-intuitive reading, as Tom Cruise's all-American hero is forced into the role of a refugee displaced by an impossibly superior invading force that uses Rumsfeldian shock-and-awe tactics.

---

[27] Prototypical Hollywood blockbusters *Jaws* (dir. Steven Spielberg, 1975) and *Star Wars* (dir. George Lucas, 1977) are obvious examples of this all but ubiquitous narrative and aesthetic template, while the post-9/11 monster movie *Cloverfield* (dir. Matt Reeves, 2008) offers a rare example of the horror genre's more ideologically subversive refusal to provide a reassuring restoration of the status quo.

The startling dissonance between the film's depiction of post-9/11 America as an apocalyptic environment and the bizarrely gung-ho militarism and gross sentimentality of its off-putting finale perfectly encapsulates this post-historical structure of feeling.

Oblivion: Imperial Administration and Posthuman Warfare

The first Tom Cruise SF film that wasn't also a collaboration with Spielberg, *Oblivion* is easily the most poorly received of the four films discussed in this chapter. Moving beyond the celebrated footage of an abandoned and over-grown Manhattan in the similarly themed post-9/11 SF horror film *I Am Legend* (dir. Francis Lawrence, 2007), *Oblivion* imagines a full-fledged return to nature: modern urban landscapes survive only in the form of ruined vestiges protruding from recently formed mountain ranges. While the film was praised for its elaborate visual depiction of a radically depopulated post-human Earth, its screenplay was justifiably criticized for its patchwork of elements from classic SF plots.

The film's plot, which manages to be impossibly convoluted while also seeming completely derivative, revolves around a new beginning for human-ity after a disastrous war with an alien species. Tom Cruise once again plays an Everyman technician, tasked this time around with servicing large machines siphoning water off the Earth's surface, supposedly intended for the human survivors who are in the process of relocating to another planet. But to the surprise of no one who has ever seen an SF movie, it is soon revealed that Cruise and his partner are actually being controlled by the very same evil alien species that has forced the last groups of human survivors into a life of underground resistance to the invaders and their unwitting human troops while stealing the planet's natural resources.

The film's representation of posthuman warfare resonates fully with the emergent logic of the War on Terror and its ongoing state of exception. Like *Minority Report* and *War of the Worlds*, the text itself is profoundly contra-dictory, offering a patchwork of clichés resulting in a sense of Jamesonian pastiche without much ideological or narrative coherence. What therefore makes it so compelling in the context of post-9/11 American SF is precisely its double logic, as it invites us to identify first with an imperial force that depends on drone warfare and militarized security forces to maintain its own privilege, and second with the rebels fighting an asymmetrical battle against a technologically superior occupying force.

As an actor whose movie stardom is unavoidably associated with the famously reactionary militaristic *Top Gun* (dir. Tony Scott, 1986), Tom Cruise as a military technician plays into expectations that associate his persona by default with hegemonic American power. The fact that his team partner is a white woman with whom he also forms a romantic couple further strengthens his implicit embodiment of heteronormative masculinity and American imperial rule. In many ways, the first section of the film veers dangerously close to self-parody, as Cruise spends his days policing the sublime landscapes of post-apocalyptic New York before retiring to his spot-less penthouse apartment to have sex in his private swimming pool. As a grossly unsubtle satirical portrait of imperial power and white privilege, the contrast between the spectacular posthuman landscapes and the sterile luxury apartment they inhabit is the first obvious indication of what becomes the film's first big reversal.

This narrative U-turn occurs when Cruise learns that he has been fighting a rather different war than he thought he was. This revelation resembles his trajectory in *Minority Report*, as the plot slowly reveals that the seemingly flawless system of PreCrime in fact represents a corrupt and easily abused exercise of biopower in its most literal sense. But while that older film's impressive use of drone technology in the form of its spider robots cleverly prefigures the Obama-era War on Terror, the film nevertheless remained primarily invested in human bodies as fundamental to the militarized police force that was so central to global capitalism's imperial power. In that older film, the characters' various uses of technology, from Cruise's virtuoso use of disembodied multi-touch interfaces to the police force's goofy jetpacks, function as *extensions* of their bodies, which remain the primary site of agency.

The most provocative aspect of *Oblivion* is its representation of drone technology that operates independent from human decision-making. It is therefore all the more telling that Cruise, while depicted on many of the movie's posters as a soldier in quasi-military uniform holding a rifle, in fact plays the role of a low-ranking technician whose only function is to service the machinery of imperial warfare. His instructions are received via computer screens, and while he has a few close calls with the dangerous-seeming rebel scavengers, or "Scavs," in the film's early scenes, his task is neither to fight the war nor even to direct its robotic soldiers, but rather to perform the maintenance required to keep the technology from malfunctioning. One of *Oblivion*'s cleverest ironies is therefore how it reduces *Top Gun*'s archetypal

Cold Warrior from "best of the best" fighter pilot to a glorified janitor fixing expensive military equipment in a war being fought entirely by drones.

The way the film represents the technocratic nature of the War on Terror in the Obama era is as chilling as it is eerily familiar: Cruise plays a literal cog in the military machinery engaged in a never-ending war waged against a faceless, nameless enemy that is forced to hide out in caves and underground shelters. These Scavs are so thoroughly dehumanized that they most closely resemble a science-fictional incarnation of *homo sacer*, the extra-legal figure of pure abjection "who *may be killed and yet not sacrificed*,"[28] and whose troubling existence as an ongoing state of exception both constitutes and disrupts the basic coordinates of biopolitical power in the modern age.

While the blankly derivative *Oblivion* remains too stubbornly invested in traditional "Hero's Journey" narrative tropes to be considered a radical political film, it nevertheless offers a compelling negotiation of the tensions that connect the posthuman turn to the War on Terror in what has become the "drone age." I use the term "posthuman" here to indicate the long overdue shift away from liberal humanism, and a way of seeing the human body and mind not as a privileged unit that exists separately from the world it inhabits, but as a fluid, contested, and irreducibly multiple site of agency and identity.[29] Posthumanism offers a theoretical perspective that demands not only the acknowledgment of humanity's dependence on and membership of a larger environment of organic and non-organic agents, but also its fundamental reliance on technology.

Both aspects figure prominently in *Oblivion*, but the posthuman hybridization of the organic and the technological is especially crucial to the film's reflection of the post-9/11 era of drone warfare. This is not only a question of the obvious and rather unsubtle prominence of military drones, represented in the film not as the harmlessly anthropomorphic robot sidekicks of *Silent Running* (dir. Douglas Trumbull, 1972) or *Star Wars*, but as the inscrutable and seemingly unstable extensions of a thoroughly alien intelligence. This preoccupation with posthuman consciousness is made even more explicit when it is revealed that Tom Cruise himself is not, in fact, "real," but exists only as a clone: merely one of an army of identical bodies, grown on board the aliens' spaceship and programmed to carry out his assigned tasks as the more powerful actual drones' organic servant.

---

[28] Giorgio Agamben, *Homo Sacer: Sovereign Power and Bare Life* (Stanford: Stanford University Press, 1998), p. 12.

[29] Robert Pepperell, *The Posthuman Condition* (London: Intellect Books, 2003), p. 20.

Of course, *Oblivion* ultimately fails to follow through on the radical implications of this plot point, retreating instead into a conservative fantasy of purity and authenticity in pastoral life and sexual reproduction. But it nevertheless foregrounds profound anxieties that are specific to cultural representations of the post-9/11 War on Terror. Its depiction of military conflict illustrates on the one hand the uncanny nature of posthuman warfare, as Cruise slowly grasps not only the fact that the drones he services are something other than a neutral and technocratic peacekeeping force, but even that he is himself a technological construct whose existence blurs the boundary between the "artificial" and the "authentic." On the other hand, there is also a great deal of self-reflexive weight in an SF scenario that depicts the "last great movie star" as a mass-produced body servicing an oppressive and exploitative imperial occupying force.

"Live. Die. Repeat."

Ending once more, then, back where we began, the most recent of these four Tom Cruise SF movies brings together aspects of all three previous films. In *Edge of Tomorrow*, the double logic of premediation that was so prominently on display in *Minority Report* resurfaces in the film's seemingly endless repetition of warfare and global catastrophe. Just as media depictions of future crimes allow a militarized police force to avoid them, the accumulation of information about the future battle ultimately makes Tom Cruise able to alter the timeline and establish a viable future. At the same time, the film's struggle against a technologically superior invading force represents an inversion of America's War on Terror that resembles *War of the Worlds'* remarkably similar approach. But as in the post-9/11 film adaptation I focused on in this chapter, the conflict is once again resolved through military action that relies crucially on the combination of weaponized intelligence and a thoroughly flexible, high-tech army force.

Finally, the technocratic drone warfare against a fully "othered" alien invasion that was depicted so ambivalently in *Oblivion* recurs here in different form, with Tom Cruise once again being taught to develop a deeply intimate relationship with the military technology on which the fate of mankind comes to depend. And while *Edge of Tomorrow* is clearly more comfortable with the posthuman hybridization of the organic and the artificial, it demonstrates a similar anxiety about posthumanism's more radical implications, ultimately retreating into the safe haven of celebrity fetishization and heterosexual romance. But *Edge of Tomorrow* provides especially uncanny insight into the War on Terror in its compulsive repetitiveness: it is at its best when it fully embraces the notion that imperial warfare exists – like Tom Cruise's stardom – in a self-perpetuating process of endless repetition: a geopolitical tragedy repackaged as spectacular farce.

In many ways, these four films and their reflection of larger post-9/11 cultural discourses of surveillance, victimhood, and posthuman warfare also typify mainstream media production. As hugely expensive media products, these films obviously hedge their bets by incorporating provocative and topical themes, but do so in ways that are oblique enough to remain politically ambivalent and thoroughly pleasurable. In other fields of cultural production, including SF literature, these themes have often penetrated in ways that are more radical, more critical, and more obviously political. Influential post-9/11 SF novels like William Gibson's *The Peripheral* (2014), Neal Stephenson's *Seveneves* (2015), and Nnedi Okorafor's *Binti* trilogy (2015–7) all engage with these very same themes in profoundly different ways, while SF-inspired art installations like the anti-drone "Not a Bug Splat" project also brings all three categories together without engaging with narrative media production at all.[30] But while these other forms clearly illustrate the wide range of registers and varied genres of SF production in the twenty-first century, they also confirm how negotiations of surveillance, victimhood, and posthuman warfare continue to haunt the SF genre as the War on Terror continues, with no end yet in sight: Live. Die. Repeat.

---

[30] See https://notabugsplat.com (last accessed May 23, 2018).

38

Comic Books from the 1980s to the 2010s

AARON KASHTAN

Science fiction has been a major genre in comic books since the inception of the medium, and has only grown in importance since the 1980s, the decade when graphic novels such as *Watchmen* helped make comics an artistically and culturally viable medium. While often closely associated with the super-hero genre, the SF genre is also an entity in its own right, and contemporary SF comic books are highly diverse in terms of subject matter, artistic style, and publication format. This chapter offers a broad overview of SF comic books published since the 1980s, focusing primarily on American comics and on foreign comics that have been published in America, and seeking to present a broad big-picture overview of the field rather than an analysis of individual works.

The period covered in this chapter corresponds with the period during which American comics production was dominated by superheroes as a genre and by the direct market (i.e., specialty comic book stores) as a channel of distribution. In the Golden and Silver Ages, comic books were a major genre, and the modern genre of superhero comics was heavily influenced by writers and editors immersed in SF culture, such as Gardner Fox, Julius Schwartz, and Mort Weisinger. Having lost most of their massive postwar popularity thanks to factors such as the 1950s anti-comics campaign and the rise of television, comics suffered a major period of contraction in the 1970s. Newsstand sales of comic books declined, and comic book stores, which appealed primarily to hardcore fans and collectors, became the primary distribution mechanism for comic books. One result of this was the virtual disappearance of formerly major genres, such as SF, as super-heroes became the primary comic book genre. Titles such as *Unknown Worlds of Science Fiction* and *Mystery in Space* barely survived the turn of the 1980s. Thus, in the so-called "mainstream" section of the comics market (i.e., Marvel and DC), the most influential SF comics were in fact superhero comics with SF elements. However, SF continued to be an important genre of so-called "independent" comics, that is, comics published by companies other than Marvel and DC, and distributed through comic book stores. In the 2000s and 2010s, non-superhero SF comics began to emerge as a distinct genre of the commercial comics marketplace. SF has been a less important genre of "art" or "alternative" comics, which tend to be more realistic in approach.[1]

This essay is organized economically rather than thematically or chronologically, examining each of the various segments of the American comics marketplace in turn, although this distinction is somewhat artificial because all these segments of the industry influence each other. I begin with the superhero genre, which was the commercial center of the industry for most of the period from the 1980s to the 2010s, and then discuss other SF comics that are published by mainstream corporate publishers but don't belong to the superhero genre. Third, I examine SF comics published by independent publishers and small presses. Fourth, I discuss foreign SF comics available in English. I conclude by discussing SF comics that are intended for children or that adapt stories from other media. These areas have historically had a marginal economic role in the industry, but have rapidly grown in importance in the second decade of the twenty-first century. Despite its brevity, this overview indicates the breadth and diversity of contemporary SF comics.

Superhero and Non-Superhero SF at Marvel and DC

Since the start of the 1980s, the superhero genre has dominated the American comic book industry, in terms of both economics and public perception, and has been the most prominent venue for SF in American comics. Of course, superheroes and SF are overlapping but distinct genres. According to Pete Coogan, one of the three defining elements of a superhero, along with "mission" and "identity," is "superpowers – extraordinary abilities, advanced technology, or highly developed physical, mental, or mystical skills."[2] Superhero narratives most often become science-fictional when the superhero's powers have a counterfactual but scientifically plausible origin, however loosely defined (e.g., Superman, Green Lantern, or Iron Man) or when the comic takes place in a futuristic or outer-space setting. Superhero comics

---

[1] For a broad historical overview of American comics, see Jean-Paul Gabilliet, *Of Comics and Men* (Jackson, MS: University Press of Mississippi, 2013) and Roger Sabin, *Comics, Comix and Graphic Novels: A History of Comic Art* (London: Phaidon Press, 2001).

[2] Peter Coogan, *Superhero: The Secret Origin of a Genre* (Austin, TX: MonkeyBrain Books, 2006).

whose heroes have no powers (e.g., Batman) or powers derived from magic (e.g., Dr. Strange) may not be SF at all, or may become SF only through the introduction of fantastic inventions. Even when a hero's powers do have a scientific origin, his or her adventures might be generically distinct from SF; for example, Captain America derives his powers from a super-soldier serum, but most of his adventures have nothing to do with SF. Moreover, superhero comics typically take place in large shared universes which have elements of other genres as well as SF; for instance, the Marvel Universe has been used as the setting for SF, fantasy, horror, western, and detective stories, among other generic modes.

Despite all that, SF is a central element of many superhero comics. Many of the Silver Age superhero comics of the 1950s and 1960s were influenced by then-current scientific issues, including the Cold War space race and arms race, and this influence continues to be visible in superhero comics of later decades. In the Marvel Universe, the X-Men, the Hulk, and Spider-Man all get their powers as a result of radioactivity. In the case of the X-Men, the premise that the characters' parents were all exposed to radiation was gradually dropped, but genetic mutation has always been the central topic of the franchise. In *The Incredible Hulk* # 377 (1991), Peter David (borrowing from an earlier story by Bill Mantlo) established that the Hulk was a split personality of Bruce Banner, which turned into a separate entity thanks to exposure to gamma radiation. Many Marvel superheroes have historically been scientists, including Reed Richards, whose initial space flight was an attempt to beat the Soviets into space. *Iron Man* has been centrally concerned with the ethics of technology and engineering; one notable *Iron Man* story arc, "Armor Wars" (#225–232, 1968), was about Tony Stark's attempt to deal with the theft of his technology by villains. The Marvel Universe also includes a heavy dose of space opera. The X-Men fight on behalf of the exiled queen of the Shi'ar aliens to save the universe from the M'Krann Crystal (#108, 1977); later, the same aliens put Phoenix (Jean Grey) on trial for her potentially universe-destroying abilities, leading to her death. Jim Starlin's Warlock and Captain Marvel comics of the 1970s were influenced by or at least closely resembled New Wave SF, and spawned a whole subgenre of "cosmic" Marvel comics, including Starlin's own *Infinity Gauntlet* crossover (1991) and Dan Abnett and Andy Lanning's revival of the *Guardians of the Galaxy* franchise (2008–10). The latter spawned two feature films and a spinoff comic starring Rocket Raccoon and his verbally challenged tree-monster friend Groot. Many Marvel stories have included time travel and alternate futures, such as

"Days of Future Past" (*Uncanny X-Men* #141–42, 1963), in which Kitty Pryde's future self seeks to prevent the creation of a dystopian future.

The DC Universe has been just as heavily influenced by science. The modern DC Universe was effectively created by writers and editors steeped in Golden Age SF, such as Gardner Fox, John Broome, Mort Weisinger, and Julie Schwartz. While all but the latter were long since retired by the 1980s, their influence was still visible. For example, Gardner Fox was responsible for the notion that the DC Universe consists of multiple alternate universes separated by different vibrational frequencies – e.g., Earth-1, where the modern DC heroes live, and Earth-2, where the Golden Age heroes live. Numerous DC crossover events, including "Crisis on Infinite Earths" (1985), "Zero Hour" (1994), "Infinite Crisis" (2005), "Final Crisis" (2008), and "Flashpoint" (2011), have since been devoted to untangling (and retangling) the continuity problems resulting from DC's scheme of multiple Earths.

Many of DC's heroes, including the Silver Age Atom (Ray Palmer) and Flash (Barry Allen), are scientists, but after the Silver Age, science usually had a less prominent role in DC than in Marvel comics. However, many DC comics are set in outer space or feature alien protagonists. For example, one of the most memorable *Green Lantern* runs, by Steve Englehart and Joe Staton (1985–8), was about Hal Jordan's creation of an Earth-based Green Lantern Corps whose other members included members of various alien species. Starfire, one of the protagonists of *New Teen Titans* (1980–c.1984), is the princess of an alien planet, and in *New Teen Titans* #23–6 (1982), she and her teammates liberate her home planet from her evil sister Blackfire. DC's most obviously science-fictional series is *The Legion of Super-Heroes*, set in the thirtieth or thirty-first century and starring teenage heroes from various alien worlds. While the Legion has mostly focused on adventure stories and soap-opera drama, it also has a political subtext. Longtime Legion writer Paul Levitz has explicitly stated that the Legion reflects his vision of how humanity will have to change in order to survive to the thirtieth century, and in the 1990s Mark Waid and his co-writers established diversity as one of the Legion's core values.

Some of the most important SF superhero comics have been set outside the primary Marvel and DC universes. The most important author of SF superhero comics is Alan Moore. His early work includes non-superheroic SF comics like *The Ballad of Halo Jones* (1984–6) and *D.R. and Quinch* (1983–5), but his 1982 revival of the 1950s British Captain Marvel knockoff Marvelman (renamed Miracleman when published in America) inaugurated a series of comics that radically question the premises of the superhero narrative.

Moore (with various artistic collaborators) establishes that Miracleman's powers are the result of government experiments based on alien body-switching technology. Miracleman fails to prevent his deranged ex-sidekick Johnny Bates from destroying the entire city of London, but proceeds to establish a benevolent global dictatorship which he rules from a tower built on London's ruins. The theme of superheroes taking over the world also appeared in *Squadron Supreme* (1985–6) by Mark Gruenwald and various artists. Moore and David Lloyd's *V for Vendetta* (1982–9) takes place in a Britain that has succumbed to fascism after a nuclear war; the hero, a sort of Batman parody, sacrifices his life to defeat the fascist government and replace it with anarchy. Moore's most famous and successful work is *Watchmen* (1986–7), illustrated by Dave Gibbons and loosely based on the Charlton Comics heroes of the 1960s. In an alternate version of the 1980s where Nixon is still president and the Soviet intervention in Afghanistan threatens to lead to nuclear war, a group of forcibly retired superheroes resume their secret identities in order to solve a murder. However, it turns out the murderer is one of their own, who seeks to defuse the Cold War by convincing the world that an alien invasion is coming. Most of Moore's later major works, such as *From Hell* (1991–8), are not SF, but he has continued to publish comics such as *The League of Extraordinary Gentlemen* (1999–2007), *Promethea* (1999–2005), and *Tom Strong* (1999–2006) that are in various ways homages to classic SF.

At the same time as *Watchmen*, DC also published the other major example of so-called "deconstructionist" superhero comics: Frank Miller's *Batman: The Dark Knight Returns* (1986), set in a dark dystopian future in which Batman returns from retirement in order to save his city from corruption and crime. Moore and Miller's grim, realistic, serious take on the superhero genre had a massive and not always positive influence on the subsequent development of the genre. Miller and Dave Gibbons's *Martha Washington* series (1990) is also relevant to SF; its hero is a black female soldier who seeks to restore the United States after a second Civil War.

Watchmen and *DKR* created a trend toward comics that were grim, gritty and violent, often for no good reason. However, they also inspired some important superhero comics with SF content, such as Warren Ellis's *Stormwatch* (1996–8), and *The Authority* (1999–2002), about a heavily interventionist superhero team. Another Ellis title set in the same universe is *Planetary* (1998–2009), drawn by John Cassaday, which consists of a series of self-referential pastiches on classic genre characters like Tarzan and Doc Savage. Kurt Busiek and Brent Anderson's *Astro City* (1995–) goes in the opposite direction, taking the premises of the superhero genre for granted but exploring the private lives and emotions of both super- and non-super inhabitants of a superhero universe. A contemporary of Moore is Grant Morrison, who has produced a large body of SF-influenced superhero work. Morrison and Chas Truog's *Animal Man* (1988–90) drew upon (pseudo)scientific concepts such as Rupert Sheldrake's morphogenetic field and David Bohm's implicate order, and Morrison and Howard Porter's first *JLA* storyline (1997) introduced a new team of superheroes who turned out to be Martians in disguise. Morrison's *All-Star Superman* (2005–8), probably the best modern Superman comic, has significant SF content. Morrison's primary non-superhero SF work is *WE3* (drawn by Frank Quitely), from 2004, an Incredible-Journey-esque story about three pets who seek their freedom after being turned into cyborg soldiers. Robert Kirkman, Cory Walker, and Ryan Ottley's *Invincible* (2003–) inverts the superhero narrative by revealing that the hero's Superman-esque father is actually an agent of an imperialist alien race; subsequent Invincible stories involve other alien races, alternate dimensions, and time travel.

Besides their influence on the superhero genre, *Watchmen* and *DKR* helped to spawn a number of other adult-oriented and auteurist comic books which had no superhero content, including many SF comics. To understand how this happened, we need to take a detour into the independent comics market that developed in the 1980s.

Independent Presses and the Rise of the Imprint

An early precursor to the independent comics market was the underground comix movement that started in the late 1960s and early 1970s. Underground comix appealed to a counterculture audience and often contained extreme depictions of sex and violence. They were able to evade the restrictive Comics Code because they were sold in venues such as head shops, while the Code only applied to comics sold on newsstands. The core underground comix, like R. Crumb's *Zap*, had little if any SF content. The major SF creator who worked for the underground market was Richard Corben, whose works, such as *Den* and *Mutant World*, use a distinctive airbrushed style of coloring. The undergrounds inspired other "ground-level" comics that were stylistically closer to mainstream comics and had a mix of underground and mainstream creators, including Mike Friedrich's *Star*Reach* (1974–9). A related phenomenon was the comics magazines published in the 1960s and 1970s by companies such as Warren and Skywald, which similarly evaded the Comics Code because of their larger format. Warren, in particular, published a wide range of SF material, particularly in the magazine *1984* (1979–83, later renamed *1994*).

In the 1970s, phenomena such as declining newsstand sales and the rise of organized comics fandom helped lead to the creation of the direct market, in which comics were sold by publishers to specialized comic book stores, often via a distributor as middleman. Several new companies, including Pacific, First, and Eclipse, were founded with the intent of publishing comics specifically for direct market distribution. Creators at these companies owned their work, unlike Marvel and DC, which operated strictly on a work-for-hire basis, and like the undergrounds, the independents published a wide range of material instead of just superheroes. Most of the 1980s independent companies published at least some SF comics; for example, Eclipse published Tim Truman's *Scout* (1985–7) about a Navajo hero in a post-apocalyptic United States, and Pacific and Eclipse both published Bruce Jones's SF anthology series *Alien Worlds* (1982–5). Eclipse also published Larry Marder's *Tales of the Beanworld* (1985–93), which is completely unclassifiable, but resembles SF in its creation of a fictional world that operates by bizarre but internally consistent rules.

But the independent publisher most notable for SF was First, whose masterpiece was Howard Chaykin's *American Flagg!* (1983–9), a sex-heavy political satire about a porn star turned cop. First also published Mike Baron and Steve Rude's *Nexus*, which looks like a superhero comic because the protagonist has powers and a costumed identity, but is closer to SF. Nexus is not a superhero, but an executioner who uses his fusion-kasting powers to kill mass murderers, on behalf of a godlike alien called the Merk. Rude's artwork draws upon both Russ Manning (of *Magnus, Robot Fighter* fame) and Dr. Seuss, and *Nexus* is full of bizarre aliens and outer space environments. John Ostrander and Tim Truman's *Grimjack* (1983–), also published by First, resembles a hard-boiled detective story in tone, but is set in the "pan-dimensional city" of Cynosure, a nexus of multiple realities which is explicitly compared to Michael Moorcock's Tanelorn. Other notable SF comics from other publishers include Jan Strnad and Dennis Fujitake's *Dalgoda*, starring a dog-headed alien explorer (Fantagraphics, 1984–6), and Mark Schultz's *Xenozoic Tales* (Kitchen Sink, 1987–96), an adventure story taking place in a post-apocalyptic world dominated by dinosaurs.

The only major 1980s indie publisher that still primarily publishes comic books is Dark Horse, whose most famous SF publication was its long series of *Star Wars* adaptations (see p. 630 below). However, Dark Horse's most important early SF title was Paul Chadwick's *Concrete* (1986–). Like the

Thing of the Fantastic Four, Concrete is a human trapped in a body made of rock, but the similarity ends there: *Concrete* is not a superhero comic but a series of philosophical meditations, often involving Concrete's relationship to his bizarre body.

Besides Dark Horse, few of the independent publishers survived the 1990s, but they had a massive impact on the development of SF comics. The independent publishers showed that creator-owned comics with a more highbrow orientation were viable, and both DC and Marvel responded by creating their own creator-owned imprints. Marvel's creator-owned imprint, Epic, lasted from 1982 to 1994, and was named after the preexisting anthology magazine *Epic Illustrated* (1980–6). The most notable SF feature from this magazine, Jim Starlin's *Metamorphosis Odyssey*, was spun off into a comic book, *Dreadstar* (1982–95), published under the Epic imprint. Epic published such other SF comics as Elaine Lee and Michael Wm. Kaluta's *Starstruck* (1982–91) and Bill Sienkiewicz's *Stray Toasters* (1988). After Epic folded, Marvel showed little interest in publishing SF comics set outside the Marvel Universe. DC's creator-owned and adult-oriented imprint, Vertigo, lasted much longer, and helped turn SF into a comics genre that rivals superheroes in commercial and artistic importance.

DC's Vertigo imprint was founded by Karen Berger in 1993 as a new branding for several existing titles, most of which were fantasy and horror titles with vestigial superhero elements, e.g., *Sandman*, *Hellblazer*, and *Doom Patrol*. In 1996, DC founded a parallel imprint called Helix, which was intended to publish SF titles, and whose creators included SF writers like Michael Moorcock and Lucius Shepard. Helix itself only lasted until 1998, but its most successful title, Warren Ellis and Darick Robertson's *Transmetropolitan* (1997–2002) – about a Hunter S. Thompson-esque muckraking journalist in a cyberpunk future America – was absorbed into the Vertigo imprint. Subsequently, Vertigo showed a willingness to branch out beyond the horror and fantasy genres. Other early Vertigo titles with SF elements were Paul Pope's *Heavy Liquid* (1999–2000) and *100%* (2002–3). Besides *Transmetropolitan*, Vertigo's most notable SF title was Brian K. Vaughan and Pia Guerra's *Y: The Last Man* (2002–8), in which a plague kills all the male creatures on Earth except the protagonist and his pet monkey. This title was a notable exploration of gender issues, and helped make Vaughan a superstar. Paul Cornell and Ryan Kelly's Vertigo title (2012–13), about the UFO phenomenon, was nominated for a Hugo, but lasted only fourteen issues.

A development that paralleled the creation of Vertigo was the rise of Image Comics. Founded in 1992 by seven fan-favorite artists who were unhappy with the working conditions at Marvel, Image began by publishing superhero comics, which were just like Marvel comics but with more violence. However, over the course of the 1990s and 2000s, Image diversified its output and became a venue for more innovative work. Around the turn of the 2010s, thanks largely to Vertigo's unfavorable licensing deals, high-profile creators like Brian K. Vaughan started taking projects to Image that would previously have been natural fits at Vertigo. The most notable such project, and the most important SF comic of the 2010s, is Vaughan and Pia Guerra's *Saga* (2012–) about two lovers and new parents who come from warring alien worlds. At heart, *Saga* is a story about family, parenthood, and aging, but it derives much of its charm from bizarre unexplained details such as a lie-detecting cat and a forest of rocket ships. Besides many comics-specific awards, *Saga* won the 2013 Hugo for Best Graphic Story. Image titles such as *Saga* and *The Walking Dead* have helped to significantly expand the audience for comic books beyond the traditional demographic of white teenage- to middle-aged men.

Other image comics with SF content include: Matt Fraction and Christian Ward's *ODY-C* (2014–), an all-female SF version of Homer's Odyssey; Jeff Lemire and Dustin Nguyen's *Descender* (2015–), a space opera that takes place in the aftermath of a robot uprising; Vaughan and Cliff Chiang's time travel story *Paper Girls* (2015–); Kelly Sue DeConnick and Valentine De Landro's *Bitch Planet* (2014–), a deeply feminist story about a dystopian world where "non-compliant" women are held in an offworld prison; and Babs Tarr, Cameron Stewart and Brenden Fletcher's *Motor Crush* (2017–), about futuristic motorcyle racing. Image also publishes Matt Fraction, Fábio Moon and Gabriel Bá's *Casanova* (2006–), about a dimension-jumping gender-ambiguous thief who resembles Michael Moorcock's Jerry Cornelius. Jonathan Hickman, whose most successful work is his SF-influenced take on the Fantastic Four, has published a number of other SF projects through Image, including *Pax Romana* (2007–8), *The Manhattan Projects* (2012–, with Nick Pitarra) and *East of West* (2013–, with Nick Dragotta).

Another important group of SF comics published by Image is the oeuvre of Brandon Graham and his circle. Graham's major solo works, *King City* (2007–) and *Multiple Warheads* (2009–), are absurdist, pun- and sex-fests that concentrate more on world-building than on narrative and are drawn in a graffiti-esque style. In 2012, Graham and artist Simon Roy revived an old Image superhero title, *Prophet*, and turned it into a bold and challenging work of SF, full of bizarre, deliberately under-explained alien worlds and creatures. *Prophet*'s sister title, Joe Keatinge and Sophie Campbell's *Glory* (2011–), was an equally unconventional SF version of Wonder Woman. Keatinge and Leila del Duca subsequently created *Shutter*, a title that blends SF and fantasy in a similar fashion to *Saga*. Graham's current anthology title, *Island*, contains a significant amount of SF work, including Roy's generation-starship story "Habitat."

Other commercial publishers have contributed to the rise in SF comics. Dark Horse publishes Carla Speed McNeil's originally self-published *Finder* (1996–), a work of "aboriginal science fiction" whose most notable story, "Talisman," is a poignant meditation on reading. Dark Horse also publishes the highly metafictional works of Matt Kindt, including *MIND MGMT* (2012–15), about a mind-manipulating spy organization, and *Dept. H.* (2016–), an undersea murder mystery. Brian Clevinger and Scott Wegener's *Atomic Robo* (2007–), currently published by IDW, is a humor series about a goofy robot adventurer who was built by Nikola Tesla.

The other legacy of the underground comics of the 1960s was the rise of the "alternative" or "art" comics market. Alternative comics differ from "mainstream" or independent comics by having more of an artistic than a commercial orientation and by typically having a single writer/artist. Alternative comics were originally distributed via the direct market, but are now typically published as graphic novels, which are becoming a respected literary genre.

SF has not been a major genre of either the alternative comic book or the graphic novel, which have been dominated by realistic genres such as autobiography, history, and journalism. One exception is Jaime Hernández's *Love and Rockets* (1982–), coauthored with his brothers Gilbert and Mario, the title of which reflects its partial focus on SF. Jaime's heroine, Maggie Chascarillo, is a "prosolar mechanic" whose early adventures involve robots and spaceships. However, Jaime mostly dropped the SF elements from Maggie's stories as his focus shifted toward realistic stories informed by his Chicano heritage. Charles Burns's *Black Hole* (1995–2005), in which Seattle teenagers become mutants as a result of a sexually transmitted disease, is perhaps the most notable alternative comic with SF elements. Another current alternative comic of SF interest is Michel Fiffe's *Copra* (2012–), which is a tribute to John Ostrander's 1980s DC comic *Suicide Squad*, but has stronger SF elements because of its use of collage and mixed-media techniques to depict otherworldly phenomena.

The comic strip, which played a pivotal role in the history of SF thanks to works like *Flash Gordon* and *Buck Rogers*, was already a moribund medium by the 1980s, and dedicated SF comic strips are almost nonexistent. However, the greatest recent American comic strip, Bill Watterson's *Calvin & Hobbes*, has many SF elements. Several storylines revolve around six-year-old protagonist Calvin's cardboard box, which can be a duplicator, a transmogrifier, or a time machine, and one of Calvin's alter egos is the interplanetary adventurer Spaceman Spiff. The decline of SF in comic strips was paralleled by the rise of webcomics, which include a wide variety of SF works. The field of webcomics is so broad and diverse that a comprehensive survey is impossible, so I mention only a few examples. Perhaps the first webcomic that achieved broad popularity among SF readers was Pete Abrams's *Sluggy Freelance* (1997–). Randall Munroe's Hugo-winning webcomic *xkcd* (2005–) describes itself as "a webcomic of romance, sarcasm, math, and language," and shows deep familiarity with both science and SF. Tom Siddell's *Gunnerkrigg Court*, published in print form by IDW, is a boarding-school story taking place in a space-opera milieu. Phil and Kaja Foglio's "gaslamp fantasy" webcomic *Girl Genius* has won four Hugo awards, while Howard Tayler's *Schlock Mercenary*, about a mercenary company in a space-opera milieu, has been nominated for five, and Andrew Hussie's sprawling multimodal *Homestuck* (2009–16) achieved widespread popularity and fandom among Internet denizens.

Foreign-Language SF Comics

The previous account mostly focused on American comics, but SF comics from non-Anglophone countries have had a major impact on Anglo-American comics. This section concentrates on works originally published in English or available in English translation; unfortunately, a large number of foreign SF comics have yet to be translated.

The British and American comics industries are tightly linked, especially since the "British invasion" of writers like Alan Moore and Grant Morrison in the 1980s. However, there is also an independent tradition of British SF comics. Most British comics creators who work for the American market have previous experience with the weekly comic magazine *2000 AD* (1977–). This magazine is most famous as the home of John Wagner and Carlos Ezquerra's creation Judge Dredd, a fascistic lawman in "Mega City-One," a dystopian future city that covers the North American continent. Out of the massive body of Judge Dredd material, a good place to start is Wagner and

Colin MacNeil's "America" (1990–1), which explores Mega-City One's democracy movement. Other important *2000 A.D.* strips include Pat Mills and Kevin O'Neill's *Nemesis the Warlock*, Gerry Finley-Day and (originally) Dave Gibbons's *Rogue Trooper; ABC Warriors*, by Pat Mills and various artists; and *Strontium Dog*, written by John Wagner and Alan Grant. For the American market, Wagner, Grant and longtime *Judge Dredd* artist Mike McMahon created *The Last American* (Epic, 1990–1), about an American soldier awakened from cryogenic sleep after a nuclear war. *2000 AD* also relaunched the classic British comic *Dan Dare*, which subsequently became the flagship strip of the relaunched *Eagle* magazine (1982–94). Grant Morrison and Rian Hughes's *Dare* (1990–1), a politically charged parody of Dan Dare, appeared in the *2000 AD* spinoff *Revolver*.

Britain's first SF comic for a primarily adult audience was Galaxy Media's *Near Myths* (1978–80). While short-lived, this magazine launched the careers of Grant Morrison and Bryan Talbot. Morrison's first major work, *Zenith* (drawn by Steve Yeowell), appeared in *2000 AD* from 1987 to 1992. Talbot's *The Adventures of Luther Arkwright*, begun in *Near Myths* and concluded in 1989, is probably the outstanding British SF comic since the 1970s. Drawn in an experimental black-and-white style, it stars a Jerry Cornelius-esque hero with the power to travel between alternate realities, who fights on the Royalist side in an alternate Britain where the English Civil War never ended. The color sequel, *Heart of Empire* (Dark Horse, 1999), resumes the story many years later when the Royalists have won and have transformed Britain into an imperialist superpower.

SF is a major genre in French and Belgian comics (known as *bandes dessinées*, or BD), which have historically enjoyed a far higher cultural status than American comics and have been recognized as the "ninth art." SF was a key element of classic Franco-Belgian adventure, including Hergé's *Tintin* (1929–86) and Edgar P. Jacobs's *Blake et Mortimer* (1946–77, later continued by others). In the 1960s and 1970s, French-language comics, previously consumed mostly by children, sought to reach a more adult audience. A key contributor to this effort was *Métal hurlant*, founded by Jean Giraud (aka Moébius), Philippe Druillet, and Jean-Pierre Dionnet in 1974 and published by Les Humanoïdes Associés. Moébius is the leading creator of French SF comics. His solo works include *The Airtight Garage* (originally "The Airtight Garage of Jerry Cornelius") and the surrealistic, wordless *Arzach*. With Chilean film director Alejandro Jodorowsky, he created *The Incal*, an unclassifiable series that blends cyberpunk dystopia and mysticism. A minor character from *The Incal*, the warrior known as the Metabaron, became the protagonist of a spinoff series by Jodorowsky and Juan Giménez. Druillet's major work, *Lone Sloane*, is light on narrative but is drawn in an ornate, psychedelic style. Other notable SF artists published in *Métal hurlant* included Enki Bilal, Caza, and Hermann. Les Humanoïdes Associés also published SF graphic novels like Bilal's *Nikopol Trilogy*, a postapocalyptic story involving Egyptian gods; and Jean-Claude Mézières and Pierre Christin's *Valerian*, about the titular buffoonish "spatiotemporal agent" and his more sensible partner and girlfriend Laureline. Through its American incarnation *Heavy Metal* (1977–), *Métal hurlant* helped popularize adult-oriented French comics among American audiences. *Heavy Metal* and *Métal hurlant* have both had a significant impact on American comics and SF cinema; for example, *Heavy Metal* inspired the 1981 cult animated film of the same name, and Moébius and Mézières both did production designs for the film *The Fifth Element* (dir. Luc Besson, 1997).

French SF comics are not limited to the *Métal hurlant* group. Jacques Lob and Jean-Marc Rochette's *Le Transperceneige* (1982), published by Casterman, was the basis of Bong Joon-Ho's 2013 film *Snowpiercer*. François Schuiten and Benoît Peeters's *Les Cités obscures* (1983–, variously translated as *Stories* or *Cities of the Fantastic*), inspired by Calvino's *Invisible Cities*, is a series of interrelated SF/fantasy narratives with an architectural focus. One early volume, *Fever in Urbicand*, is about a mysterious alien cube whose steady growth threatens to overwhelm a city. More recent Francophone SF comics translated into English include Denis Bajram's *Universal War One* (2008–9) and Frederik Peeters's *Aâma* (2011–14). The British publisher Cinebook has translated a wide range of both current and classic French SF comics, including Roger Leloup's *Yoko Tsuno* (1970–) and Léo's *Aldebaran* (1994) and its sequels. SF comics in European languages other than French are rare in English translation.[3]

Probably the largest category of SF comics available in English is manga (Japanese comics). The modern Japanese comics industry is essentially the creation of Osamu Tezuka (1928–89), known as the "God of Comics," although he drew inspiration from Disney and from older Japanese visual traditions. Tezuka's vast body of work includes many SF comics which have been translated into English, such as *Astro Boy* (1952–68), *Phoenix* (1956–89), *Black Jack* (1972–83) and *Ode to Kirihito* (1970–1). In Japan, manga are an important mass medium; in 2006, manga represented over 25 percent of all

---

[3] One major exception is Héctor Germán Oesterheld and Francisco Solano López's *El Eternauta* (1957–59), perhaps the most highly acclaimed Argentine comic.

books sold.[4] One reason for manga's massive success is its appeal to a broader range of demographics than American comics. Indeed, manga may be categorized by the demographic groups they appeal to, such as *shonen* (young boys), *shojo* (young girls), *seinen* (adult men) and *josei* (adult women). However, in America, manga did not achieve widespread popularity until after Epic's 1988 publication of Katsuhiro Ôtomo's *Akira*, a cyberpunk saga of a teenager with psychic powers. *Akira* helped introduce American audiences to the narrative and visual style of manga, which differs significantly from that of American comics, as well as pioneering new computer coloring techniques. Manga remained a niche category of the American comics market until the early 2000s, when companies like Viz and TokyoPop succeeded in getting manga distributed via chain bookstores like Borders. The resulting "manga boom" peaked around 2007 and is now in decline, but manga remains a massive industry, and thousands of manga volumes have been published in America, many of them with SF content.

A good starting point for readers unfamiliar with manga is Makoto Yukimura's *Planetes* (1999–2004), a lyrical slice-of-life story about garbage-collecting astronauts. Other works in a similar vein include Kou Yaginuma's *Twin Spica* (2001–9) and Hisae Iwaoka's *Saturn Apartments* (2006–11). One of Japan's most acclaimed manga creators is Naoki Urasawa, whose works include the medical thriller *Monster* (1994–2001), the conspiracy theory story *20th Century Boys* (1999–2007), and *Pluto* (2003–9), an adaptation of a chapter of *Astro Boy*. Masamune Shirow's *Ghost in the Shell* (1989–1990) was highly popular in America in both its manga and anime forms. All these works are aimed at the *seinen* demographic. SF is a major genre of *shonen* manga, which often focuses on action and combat. Akira Toriyama's wildly popular *Dragon Ball* (1984–95), whose anime adaptation helped popularize anime in America, has SF content in that the protagonist and several of the villains are aliens. Later *shonen* manga with SF content include Hiromu Arakawa's steampunk epic *Fullmetal Alchemist* (2001–2010) and Hajime Isayama's *Attack on Titan* (2009–), whose protagonists seek to defend the remnants of the human race from man-eating giants. *Shojo* manga was pioneered by the "Year 24 Group" (consisting of artists born around 1949, the twenty-fourth year of the Showa era), many of whose works were science fictional, including Moto Hagio's "They Were Eleven" (1975) and *A, A Prime* (1984); and Keiko Takemiya's *To Terra* (1977–80). Later *shojo* manga with SF premises include Saki

[4] JETRO (Japanese External Trade Organization). "Manga Industry in Japan," 2006, http://facweb.cs.depaul.edu/noriko/JapanTrip08/JETRO-market_info_manga.pdf (last accessed June 18, 2018).

Hiwatari's *Please Save My Earth* (1986–94) and the various works of the CLAMP collective, such as *Chobits* (2000–2) and *Clover* (1997–9). A work that stands outside the mainstream of manga is Hayao Miyazaki's *Nausicäa of the Valley of Wind* (1982–94), about a princess who seeks to save her post-apocalyptic world from ecological catastrophe. Drawn in a style resembling European comics, it inspired the film of the same name and helped launch Miyazaki's career as Japan's most acclaimed animation director.

Neglected Categories: Comics for Young Readers and Transmedia Comics

An often ignored but economically important category of SF comics is adaptations of SF works in other media. Licensed-property comics were the industry's most popular comic book genre prior to the rise of superheroes in the 1960s, and have again grown in popularity in the past decade.

Licensed-property comics are often dismissed for being uncreative (as Image publisher Eric Stephenson controversially argued in a 2014 speech) and for being mere potboilers produced by second-tier talent. In the late 2000s and the 2010s, IDW helped to dispel this stereotype by producing high-quality comics adaptations of media franchises like *Doctor Who*, *Ghostbusters*, *Star Trek*, *Transformers*, and *G.I. Joe*. Perhaps IDW's most critically acclaimed adaptation is James Roberts and Alex Milne's *Transformers: More Than Meets the Eye* (2012–), notable for its witty dialogue. One franchise which is almost a subgenre on its own is *Star Wars*. Marvel Comics's *Star Wars* adaptation lasted 107 issues, and its massive success helped save the company from bankruptcy in the late 1970s. When Dark Horse acquired the *Star Wars* license in 1991, it cemented their reputation as the industry's then-leading publisher of licensed-property comics. Dark Horse also published adaptations of franchises like *Aliens*, *Predator*, *Terminator*, *RoboCop*, and the Whedonverse. In 2015, Marvel reacquired the Star Wars license. The first issue of its new Star Wars series sold an unheard-of total of nearly a million copies, making it easily the bestselling comic book of 2015.

Despite the longstanding ideological association between comics and children, actual children largely stopped reading comics after the 1980s; indeed, Michael Chabon's 2002 Eisner Awards keynote speech castigated the industry for having abandoned younger readers. In the 2010s, this situation started to reverse itself thanks to the efforts of mainstream publishers like Scholastic to market comics to children. Thanks largely to the phenomenal success of the non-SF author Raina Telgemeier, children's and young adult comics and graphic novels are currently the most commercially successful segment of the American comics industry. Scholastic's publications include *Harry Potter* cover artist Kazu Kibuishi's *Amulet* (2008–), a fantasy work with SF elements, and Mike Maihack's *Cleopatra in Space*, a space opera starring the time-traveling young queen of Egypt (2014–). Notable children's SF comics from other publishers include Ben Hatke's *Zita the Spacegirl* (2011–14) and Hope Larson's adaptation of Madeleine L'Engle's *A Wrinkle in Time* (2015).

Conclusion

Contrary to the common stereotype that comics are exclusively dominated by superheroes and/or by realistic graphic novels, SF comics are a major genre and are likely to grow in importance in the future. Contemporary SF comics offer a broad range of subject matter, a diverse array of characters, and a wide variety of artistic styles, and are published in multiple formats and for many different audiences. As comics grow in commercial and cultural importance, and as the economic and transmedial links between comics and other media grow stronger, accounts of the contemporary SF genre will increasingly need to take comics into account.

39

Video Games and Virtual Lives: Science Fiction Gaming from the 1980s to the 2010s

PAWEL FRELIK

There is more than one history of science fiction gaming, as there is more than one history of any other medium of the genre – but this chapter asserts that the odds against successfully writing the former are bigger than in the case of SF literature or film or television, and for a number of reasons, too. Writing histories of cultural forms is as much a task of historical investigation as it is of constructing what Raymond Williams called "selective tradition";[1] in the case of SF video games this chapter will demonstrate there are as many as four reasons why the task is particularly fraught with arbitrariness. Two of them apply to practically all medial forms of the genre, including literature, and the other two remain specific for digital games.[2] Given that reference volumes do need, after all, to propose at least *some* historical trajectory, the chapter will then offer two possible ways of thinking about a history of SF video games and virtual environments.

The most obvious among the reasons why a history of SF video games cannot be written is that *all* cultural histories are constructs, but this caveat concerns literature and film as much as other media – so for the purposes of this discussion I will disregard this particular line of argument. The same concerns the fluidity of the very definition of SF. In other SF media, the arbitrariness of this definition underwrites the discourses of exclusion and

Acknowledgment: The research involved in the preparation of this chapter was supported by a grant from the Polish National Science Center 2014/13/B/HS2/01159.

[1] Raymond Williams, *Marxism and Literature* (Oxford: Oxford University Press, 1977), pp. 115–17.

[2] Given the transnational nature of the game industry, which for Nick Dyer-Witheford and Greig de Peuter exemplifies the global flows of cognitive capitalism, it must be noted it is difficult to work with national origins in game production. See Dyer-Witheford and de Peuter, *Games of Empire: Global Capitalism and Video Games* (Minneapolis: University of Minnesota Press, 2009). The location of the development studio is usually a criterion, but the international mobility of designers and artists and corporate mergers may blur clear-cut identifications.

inclusion as well as the distinction between genre and non-genre SF – but this distinction does not obtain in video games, since the medium has not evolved internal hierarchies of high/low so characteristic of other cultural forms. Though avid SF readers and viewers, many game designers approach the question of genre with far less rigor than their counterparts in other media. As a result, the game world has not witnessed the sorts of intra- or extra-genre legitimation wars that SF has fought in literature, film, and television.[3]

Systemic problems inherent in writing histories of video games in general are the third obstacle in the way of writing a comprehensive history of SF games. Video game histories – because of the medium's shorter tenure and the decentralization of the industry – are particularly susceptible to shifts in the presentation of digital heritage. In his meta-overview of games scholarship, Jaakko Suominen identifies four distinct, albeit partly overlapping, approaches: enthusiast, emancipatory, genealogical, and pathological.[4] The enthusiasts highlight what is commonly perceived as paradigmatic milestones: "the best-of," "the most," and "the classic" publications, most notably heavily illustrated coffee-table books with mostly generic textual commentary. Enthusiastic histories are very much informed by a latter-day version of Thomas Carlyle's theory of Great Men and Max Weber's vision of charismatic authority (as well a ludic version of auteurism, which possesses some traction in independent games but is practically useless with larger projects), in which the identity of key game producers is sometimes retained but most focus is bestowed on supposedly groundbreaking titles. Emancipatory approaches provide "contra-dictory, alternative, and enriching perspectives on history, or rather histories, of games."[5] They are often grounded in the enthusiastic approach but enhance it with a New Historicist energy that complicates easy chronological narratives and relativizes their construction. The genealogical school of gaming histories focuses on archiving and the "triad of a game, player, and gaming device," rather than the context outside this limited network, including social condi-tions and industry considerations.[6] Finally, pathological approaches – the term need not be immediately construed as pejorative – focus on deep media archeology and "deep excavations" of "the pre- and protohistories of games, which can also lead to a tendency to underline ruptures, anomalies, material,

[3] Roger Luckhurst, "The Many Deaths of Science Fiction: A Polemic," *Science Fiction Studies* 21, 1 (1994), pp. 35–50.
[4] See Jaakko Suominen, "How to Present the History of Digital Games: Enthusiast, Emancipatory, Genealogical, and Pathological Approaches," *Games and Culture* 12, 6 (2017), pp. 544–62.
[5] Ibid., p. 553.
[6] Ibid., p. 555.

embodied, and experiential as well as experimental aspects of contemporary game cultures."[7] Combinations of these approaches are possible, but most game histories can be located within only one of these four categories.

Beyond writing general game histories, the last reason for the medium's resistance to coherent historical narratives concerns even more specific problems related to the genre system of the medium. As most game critics note, ludic genres are primarily defined by type of haptic and cognitive engagement as well as the mode of presentation of the world.[8] This leads to a disjuncture between layers, each of which may exhibit their own "genre": the thematic layer, which is predominantly expressed in narrative as well as in graphics and sound, and the ludic layer, related to the mode of activity. To this duo, Maria Garda adds the functional dimension, whose modalities include such classifications as casual, hardcore, and retro.[9] Individual games may thus share any of these three classificatory layers with other titles, but also differ from others in only one aspect. Games belonging to the same franchise and thus sharing a thematic genre (which invites treating them as unified albeit dispersed transmedia texts) may thus differ functionally owing to their ludic genre. The *Halo* franchise is a good example of this. Like many transmedia narratives, it spans multiple media, but central to its nexus are video games. The core titles of the saga are all first-person shooters, but *Halo Wars* (2009) and *Halo Wars 2* (2017) are real-time strategy games while *Halo: Spartan Assault* (2013) and *Halo: Spartan Strike* (2015) are twin-stick shooters.

This genre system in video games makes it more difficult to compare titles and their use of SF tropes. For all their aesthetic and thematic differences, it is entirely possible to discuss together *2001: A Space Odyssey* (dir. Stanley Kubrick, 1968), *Alien* (dir. Ridley Scott, 1979), *Blade Runner* (dir. Ridley Scott, 1982), and *Arrival* (dir. Denis Villeneuve, 2016) since they all share formal qualities as well as institutional contexts of production and distribution. In the gaming medium, such comparisons would be much more problematic. Although all three titles can be nominally described as space opera, juxtaposing *Homeworld* (1999), *EVE Online* (2003), and *Mass Effect* (2007) makes little

[7] Ibid., p. 556.
[8] Mark J. P. Wolf, "Genre and the Video Game," in *The Medium of the Video Game* (Austin, TX: University of Texas Press, 2001), pp. 113–34; Dominic Arsenault, "Video Game Genre, Evolution and Innovation," *Eludamos. Journal for Computer Game Culture* 3, 2 (2009), pp. 149–76. Like texts in other media, games are not pure generically: terms like role-playing, third-person shooter, survival horror, etc. may refer to different aspects of the same title.
[9] Maria Garda, *Interaktywne fantasy. Gatunek w grach cyfrowych* [*Interactive Fantasy: Genre in Digital Games*] (Łódź: University of Łódź Press, 2016).

practical sense, since, belonging to diverse gaming genres, they construct their meaning differently and offer their players dramatically different rewards and pleasures.

Consequently, any attempt to write a continuous history of SF games needs to address these issues – answers to which, I insist, prove even more difficult than in other SF media. The historiographical difficulties are further aggravated by two qualities of the medium: its decenteredness and its relatively short cultural tenure. With the former, unlike in literature, film, and television, SF video games are not tied to the fixed cultural networks of dedicated publications, events, channels, and venues. There are, naturally, some developers who have manifested a penchant for SF,[10] such as the Canadian company Bioware, whose games are all either SF or fantasy, but most producers – both AAA and independent – move fluidly between thematic genres and seem to be more attached to specific ludic categories. With the latter, games evade periodization: time scales involved are smaller and sub-genre monikers within the tentative category of SF games are driven less by inspirational and aesthetic trends and more by technological innovation in hardware and software. Writing about early film, Brooks Landon suggested that all productions belonging to what Tom Gunning labeled "cinema of attractions" can be considered SF due to the centrality of technological spectacle.[11] Since technological affordances and limitations play an even more crucial role in video games and because the goal of most texts identified as games[12] is to unravel rules governing gamespaces, there is a similar temptation to consider *all* video games "science fiction." Naturally, the overly broad claim that *Mafia* (2002) and *Grand Theft Auto V* (2013) are somehow SF has little practical use or analytical value. At the same time, the intersection of games and SF is characterized by several unique qualities that cannot be found in other, analog or digital, media of the genre.

The most important of these is the participatory nature of the medium. Much can be said about the imaginative and ergodic efforts involved in

---

[10] Frequent mergers, takeovers, and shared development in the industry, particularly in the AAA sector, make the unified genre identity even more problematic.

[11] Brooks Landon, "Diegetic or Digital? The Convergence of Science-Fiction Literature and Science-Fiction Film in Hypermedia," in Anette Kuhn, ed., *Alien Zone II: The Spaces of Science-Fiction Cinema* (London: Verso, 1999), p. 32. Tom Gunning, "The Cinema of Attraction: Early Film, Its Spectator and the Avant-Garde," *Wide Angle* 8, 3–4 (1986), pp. 63–70.

[12] The term is not as clear as one might immediately assume. Definitional battles, both within academia and fandom, around the so-called walking simulators, apps, and digital environments reveal significant disparities as to what various communities of players consider a "game."

interacting with other media,[13] but video games are the only major medium that requires actual action from the player for a text to become available. The complexity of such participation may vary depending on the ludic genre, but, in most cases, the player's decisions depend on the understanding of the principles and rules of the gameworld. Probing them is, arguably, inherently science-fictional – SF games are thus spaces for speculation and extrapolation, modes of thinking that constitute the very essence of SF.

Equally importantly, much SF has always been centrally informed by the apprehension of worlds as systems that are internally consistent, complex, and consequential – three adjectives that also describe the most fundamental properties of all functioning video games. Games are inherently informed by algorithmic-ness and procedurality,[14] within which interdependence and causality are the primary principles of gameworld construction. Because of this, video games bring to SF a more direct mode of engagement with the ideas and structures identified with the genre and provide frameworks which allow for experiential and simulated testing of these ideas and concepts. Thus, if SF is a cultural discourse that has showcased the systemic nature of constructs from individual machines to planetary ecologies, then video games can be perceived as a privileged medial form for both diegetic and formal transmission of this perspective: both diegetically but also – even more importantly – formally.

This close affinity notwithstanding, mapping the development and con-tinuity of how games have engaged such science fictional preoccupations constitutes a challenge. All genre researchers agree that the beginnings of the video game medium are inextricably intertwined with SF through *Spacewar!* (1962), one of the first video games, which brought the nascent gaming culture into cultural visibility and spawned the entire genre of space combat games. The cultural hype of early arcade games also influenced some of the late 1970s and early 1980s SF filmmaking, including *Star Wars* (1977), *Tron* (1982), and *The Last Starfighter* (1984). Beyond these beginnings, however, as the medium exploded, first in the 1970s and then on the subsequent genera-tions of home consoles starting in the early 1980s,[15] the games have

---

[13] See Espen Aarseth, *Cybertext: Perspectives on Ergodic Literature* (Baltimore, MD: Johns Hopkins University Press, 1997), p. 1.

[14] See Ian Bogost, *Unit Operations: An Approach to Videogame Criticism* (Cambridge, MA: MIT Press, 2008) and Ian Bogost, *Persuasive Games: The Expressive Power of Videogames* (Cambridge, MA: MIT Press, 2010).

[15] Technically, the first generation of consoles is usually dated to the release of Magnavox Odyssey in 1972, and the second to the market debut of the Fairchild Video Entertainment System in 1976.

proliferated across multiple platforms and genres, whose sheer numbers in the last two decades of the twentieth and the first two of the twenty-first century make it almost impossible to construct coherent historical narratives of the medium.

In the face of all these difficulties, and regardless of the obstacles mentioned earlier, I would, nevertheless, like now to propose two alternative ways of thinking about the history of SF video games. The first of these histories, which can be tentatively called the canonical, focuses on individual titles and, in some ways, reflects similar efforts in other media. The second history of SF games privileges instead ludic genres whose characteristics resonate particularly closely with an SF conceptual core and attaches much less importance to specific games. Neither aspires to being completist and authoritative, but their respective genealogies represent two very different methods of thinking about SF at large.

The canonical history of SF games relies on chronology and spans Suominen's enthusiast and emancipatory approaches. It also aligns closely with the popular perception of what the "best science fiction games" are. In some ways, this historical narrative is equivalent to the more general history of landmark video games from which all non-SF titles have been removed. Although the titles in this canon vary considerably, they are largely narratively complex games. This bias remains consistent with the nature of much of SF criticism: its narrative obsession and its reluctance to consider the visual and aural layers of cultural texts separately from their narrative layer.[16] While there are several strategy games among the classics here, the core canon relies on three gaming genres which have sustained, in the field of SF studies, almost undivided critical attention: first- and third-person shooters and role-playing games. These three types of games function as most effective containers for narratives in the form readily imported from other visual media. The cinematic qualities of many contemporary games, as well as their partly overlapping systems of production, align SF games with SF cinema, while the episodic structure of missions and quests within titles resonates with many qualities of television drama series. These similarities are crucial since the canonical history of SF games features a number of titles whose narrative and aesthetic assets can be easily appreciated by audiences educated

---

[16] Tanya Krzywinska and Esther MacCallum-Stewart's "Digital Games" (2009), the first systematic discussion of SF games, follows this approach and features the list of landmark titles, whose majority fit my characterization. See "Digital Games," in Mark Bould, Andrew M. Butler, Adam Roberts, and Sherryl Vint, eds., *The Routledge Companion to Science Fiction* (New York: Routledge, 2009), pp. 350–61.

in other SF media. In fact, most titles in this canon can be – in narrative or visual terms – conceived as gaming analogs of pre-existing cinematic and televisual SFs, both specific titles and broader intra-SF conventions.

This equivalency is most readily exemplified by games tied to narrative franchises. The *Star Wars* universe has produced a number of successful titles across a range of genres and for various demographic groups, including *X-Wing* (1993) and *TIE Fighter* (1994), *Star Wars: Knights of the Old Republic* (2003), and the *Star Wars Battlefront* games (2004, 2005) as well as their recent reboots (2015, 2017). The same concerns the *Aliens* franchise, in which several games, most prominently *Aliens vs. Predator* (1999) and *Aliens vs. Predator 2* (2001), continue to enjoy significant popularity. Frank Herbert's landmark novel has inspired a number of games. Their reputation can be perceived as problematic, but at least one title has been highly regarded: *Dune II: The Building of a Dynasty* (1992), a real-time strategy game, was a considerable critical and commercial success and has centrally influenced many later titles, including the sprawling *Command & Conquer* franchise (1995–2013), in itself an umbrella for three distinct game lines, and the *StarCraft* games and expansions (1998–2016).[17]

Outside multi- and transmedia franchises, many canonical games correspond in narrative terms with the principal thematic conventions of literary and cinematic SF. The cult classic *Doom* (1993) is more revered for the visceral dynamic of its gameplay as well as its influence on the entire first-person shooter genre and other aspects of the gaming culture than for any particular narrative or aesthetic value, but it is undoubtedly an SF game to the core. Along with the entire *Doom*/*Quake* clade of first-person shooters it has spawned, *Doom* represents action SF at its most kinetic and functions as a gaming analog of *Transformers* movies. Later classics, which also expanded their narrative layer, can be juxtaposed with certain thematic conventions even more easily. The *Fallout* series (1997–2015) remains the hallmark among post-apocalyptic titles. The *Deus Ex* quadrilogy (2000–16) constitutes the most accomplished version of the nexus of themes grouped as cyberpunk: near-future temporality, dystopian urban locations, conspiracy theories, posthuman augmentation, and social critique. *BioShock* (2007) has gathered accolades for its retrofuturistic and steampunk aesthetic as well as its critical engagement of Ayn Rand's ultra-capitalist conception of objectivism, which aligns itself with SF's critical powers. Praised for the complexity of world-building, the *Mass Effect* trilogy (2007–12), possibly the most coherent

---

[17] Interestingly, none of over fifty *Star Trek* games released since 1971 for various platforms has gone down in the medium history as particularly memorable outside the series fandom.

narrative arc ever developed in a game series, draws heavily on space opera and centrally relies on the trope of galactic war. Finally, *Portal* (2007) and *Portal 2* (2011), first-person puzzle games, can be viewed as dialoging with the scientific bent of hard SF.

As in literary, cinematic, and televisual SF, the degree of reliance on complex narrative varies, as do visual registers. The *Borderlands* series (2009–15) can be seen as a response to the original *Mad Max* movies, while the subsequent *Gears of War* games (2006–16) are perhaps best understood as offering an interactive version of the alien-invasion blockbuster experience. The *F.E.A.R.* series (2005–14) clashes SF themes with the supernatural and, finally, at the narratively diluted end of the spectrum, there are a number of zombie games, ranging from the kinetic *Left 4 Dead* (2008) to the more decision-oriented *The Last of Us* (2013).

Aesthetically, the great-titles canon largely reflects the increasing aural and visual spectacularity and parallels the upward trajectory of high-resolution hyper-realistic graphics, the tendency that has also informed cinematic and televisual production in the genre over the last two decades. There are, naturally, exceptions: *Borderlands* utilizes comics-like graphics, the *Halo* franchise has never fully transcended a certain simplification of its visual layer, and some of the early titles, including *Fallout* (1997) and *Half-Life* (1998), have not aged gracefully when it comes to graphics. In general, however, big-budget games have favored life-like graphics, emphasizing the convergence of all digital media, but also registering the bifurcation between ambitious narratives and spectacular graphics, the opposition that needs not to be entirely mutually exclusive.

All the above titles can be arranged and expanded into a chronological history of SF video games, but one should not expect the sort of cohesive narrative offered by comprehensive histories of literary or cinematic SF. The overarching narratives of both histories proper (e.g., Adam Roberts's *History of Science Fiction* [2006]) and anthologies (e.g., Arthur B. Evans *et al.*'s *Wesleyan Anthology of Science Fiction* [2010]) envision the genre as an accreting chain of recurring and constantly dialoging figures, tropes, and scenarios that collectively make up the genre's mega-text.[18] Similar interdependencies can be found in SF games, but they concern more formal aspects of game mechanics, gameplay, and world construction within individual ludic genres, rather than diegetic echoes and resonances. Consequently, the canonical

---

[18] Damien Broderick, *Reading by Starlight: Postmodern Science Fiction* (London: Routledge, 1994), pp. 57–60.

history of SF games resembles more a string of critically acclaimed and commercially successful titles, whose narrative and technological continuities operate predominantly within specific franchises and ludic genres, and less an integrated tapestry of used and revised themes and tropes.

The second approach to constructing a history of SF video games eschews identifying milestones whose narratives replicate the genre's preoccupations in other media. Instead, it assumes the science-fictionality of games themselves and proposes that the nature and mechanics of certain gaming genres resonate with SF's intrinsic qualities. While first-person shooters, racing games, and role-playing games are flexibly themable[19] and their fictional worlds can be changed at will, several types of games correlate more intimately with SF's conceptual and philosophical underpinnings. In the same way in which the first canon of SF video games is dominated by the three gaming genres which often host complex narratives, the second canon privileges genres that stage and activate the types of experience that SF has long sought to represent and incite. The first- and third-person shooters and role-playing game conventions of the first canon often intertwine in individual titles. Similarly, even more fundamental affinities can be discerned between the three genres that, to my mind, constitute the core of the second version of SF game history: simulations, massively multiplayer online games, and first-person walkers. All three are often open-world games, although the exact degree of this openness may vary. Central to them, though, is the thematization of gamespace, whose descriptions derive from the games' database and which transforms directional storyline into multivalent.[20] Naturally, almost all games involve some form of traversing space, but the three genres of the second canon position spatiality in the very center of gaming experience and as their narrative pivot. Notably, this spatial turn runs against SF's privileging of time as the new dimension of modernity that has replaced space but reflects the unique character of video games as digital texts.

In each of the three categories, the excellence of individual titles is less important to their sense of science-fictionality than their qualities consonant with the genre's preoccupations. This also means that the titles mentioned below should not be treated as hallmarks of this historical narrative but as exemplars of more general qualities that are inherently science-fictional and can be found in numerous gaming texts.

---

[19] Jesper Juul, *Half-Real: Video Games between Real Rules and Fictional Worlds* (Cambridge, MA: MIT Press, 2005), p. 189.

[20] McKenzie Wark, *Gamer Theory* (Cambridge, MA: Harvard University Press, 2007), p. 69.

Simulation video games are the broadest category among the three and an umbrella term for a wide array of smaller groupings driven by copying or performing various tasks, often imitating real-life activities. Many titles in these categories focus on mundane or highly specialized activities, but several simulation subgenres dramatically expand their scope. As David Higgins notes, SF and globalization have a special relationship, which makes the genre a useful site for analyses of "globalization's conditions and conse-quences" – but Higgins also cautions that broad perceptions of the process "fail to isolate a sense of the origins and consequences of globalization with useful specificity."[21] Globalization does not need to be understood here only in the socio-economic terms of late capitalism, but also as a more general awareness of ecological interconnectivity and planetarity. If the latter term is to be understood not only in social and political terms originally suggested by Gayatri Chakravorty Spivak, but as an admission of the integrated (albeit hardly harmonious) wholeness, then simulation games seem to be perfectly equipped for its expression.[22]

Will Wright's *SimEarth* (1990) is one of the earliest examples of such global aspirations. Although ostensibly realistic, the game enforces upon the player a position that is nothing short of fantastic, one of a god-like entity that sidesteps the passage of time and can affect the development of the entire globe.[23] Equally extrapolative is a flat hierarchy of all multicellular organisms, which allows the players to evolve non-hominid sapient species, a motive long present in the genre. Because of its difficulty, *SimEarth* was a commercial failure, but Wright returned to the same idea in *Spore* (2008) and there has been a line of similar games, many favoring the scenario of space colonies on alien planets. Not all have equally ambitious scope and focus on the manage-ment of smaller-scale habitats, but, regardless whether they utilize in-game characters or feature a god-like perspective, most compel the players to consider and calculate a wide range of environmental entanglements and living conditions. Some titles, such as *Space Colony* (2003) and *RimWorld* (2013), are set on fictional planets, but Mars has also proved to be a strong inspiration in the twenty-first century. Some of these are more economically minded, like *Offworld Trading Company* (2016) or *Mars Industries* (2016), while others,

[21] David M. Higgins, "Introduction: Science Fiction and Globalization," *Science Fiction Studies* 39, 3 (2012), p. 370.

[22] See Gayatri Chakravorty Spivak, *Death of a Discipline* (New York: Columbia University Press, 2005), pp. 71–102.

[23] Sabine Höhler, *Spaceship Earth in the Environmental Age, 1960–1990* (New York: Routledge, 2015), p. 137.

including *Sol 0: Mars Colonization* (2016), *Take on Mars* (2017), and *Mars 2030* (2017), pay more attention to the ecological contexts of colonization efforts.

Of special interest among SF-themed simulators are space flight simulators, again a super-label that encompasses military, trading, and exploratory varieties, often combined in individual titles. *Elite* (1984) is often credited as a particularly influential title because of its open-ended, non-sequential gameplay, and graphics.[24] While the general goals of the game have remained generally comparable in the two sequels *Frontier: Elite II* (1993) and *Frontier: First Encounters* (1995) as well as the rebooted *Elite: Dangerous* (2012), space flight simulators have grown increasingly complex. Many titles in this group possess clear win/lose conditions and scoring systems, but some of the most interesting examples include space simulators that lack such structures and offer vast fictional (although many are based on actual astronomical charts and atlases) universes with no narrative and no gameplay goals. Whether the name "game" – as opposed to "an astronomical simulation" or "a digital environment" – is appropriate for such texts is debatable, but they certainly resonate with a number of SF's preoccupations. They foreground the vastness of the universe and are prime examples of science fictional world-building at its grandest. In some ways, they can be thought of as imaginary frameworks within which space operas stage the adventure of their protagonists and cultures. However, by removing individual purpose and agency, story-less space simulators compel the players to confront the relativity and, ultimately, insignificance of humanity within the universe, a position that has informed a number of SF novels, most recently Liu Cixin's *Remembrance of Earth's Past* trilogy (2008–10, English trans. 2014–16).

Alessandro Ghignola's *Noctis IV* (2000) is one of the earliest examples of simulators almost devoid of narrative. Set in the 90,000-light-year-wide galaxy named Fylterion, *Noctis IV* allows the player to land on and explore billions of procedurally generated worlds – and nothing more. The game's native resolution of 320 x 200 pixels has aged considerably, but the aesthetic awe at the size of its universe seems to hold. Phillip Scuderi noted that *Noctis IV* is terrifying as it foregrounds humanity's "deep-set fears of our own mortality, transience and ultimate inconsequentiality and sharp exposure to *Noctis'* determinism does nothing to assuage them."[25] Among later texts in

---

[24] See Alison Gazzard, "The Platform and the Player: exploring the (hi)stories of *Elite*," *Game Studies*, 13, 2, (2013), http://gamestudies.org/1302/articles/agazzard (last accessed September 15, 2017).

[25] Phillip Scuderi, "Footprints in Moondust." *The Escapist* (19 July 2006), www.escapistmagazine.com/articles/view/video-games/issues/issue_54/325-Footprints-in-Moondust (last accessed September 15, 2017).

this category is *Space Engine* (2016), more properly a 3D astronomy program using star catalogs and procedural generation to create a cubical universe with Earth at the center. Ostensibly a scientific tool with a community of users responsible for add-ons, spacecraft models, and fictional planetary systems, *Space Engine* is quintessentially science-fictional in its integration of unlimited space travel and capacity for in-game photography whose qualities locate the program in the same visual tradition as Hubble space footage and digital graphics of imaginary worlds. *No Man's Sky* (2016) is one of the most recent examples of games that showcase large-scale spatial exploration. Although it does possess narrative, action sequences, and survival mechanics, the game's main asset is a procedurally generated fictional universe of 18 quintillion planets, many with their own ecosystems. While the players can choose to follow the task-oriented gameplay, the game's uniqueness clearly resides in its exploratory dimension within which *No Man's Sky* does not seem to have a point[26] and privileges the freewheeling flights of imagination which are, nevertheless, firmly grounded in scientifically rigorous principles of universe construction.

The second gaming genre that foregrounds SF's conceptual preoccupations are massively multiplayer online games (MMO), capable of supporting thousands of players simultaneously and featuring persistent open worlds. As frameworks, MMOs mobilize different gaming genres from first-person shooters to real-time strategies, but in most a pre-conceived narrative remains secondary in relation to the social interactions of live players who, beyond the general rules provided by software, often develop closely knit communities with their own jargons, social structures, customs, and lores open to full-blown ethnographic research.[27] While the majority of MMO games are fantasy-themed, there are several that are SF-oriented fiction, and it is precisely the complexity of rules and principles governing the social and economic systems of these universes that makes them important for SF.

Most notable among them is *EVE Online* (2003). Like practically all MMOs, it possesses narrative structures, but the game owes much of its cult status to the construction of the gameworld and the furious intensity of player interactions. Unlike in other games of its class, in *EVE Online* all players interact on the same server (there is a separate one for China only, though), which results in

---

[26] Peter Suderman, "*No Man's Sky* is an existential crisis simulator disguised as a space exploration game." Vox.com (August 27, 2016), www.vox.com/2016/8/27/12646008/no-mans-sky-game-review-existential-crisis (last accessed September 15, 2017).

[27] Bonnie A. Nardi, Celia Pearce, and Tom Boellstorff, *Communities of Play: Emergent Cultures in Multiplayer Games and Virtual Worlds* (Cambridge, MA: MIT Press, 2011).

a decisively more intricate network of allies and enemies. *EVE* is also, arguably, one of the most difficult video games ever produced with an infamously steep learning curve and high new user attrition rates. The biggest challenge is the complexity of gameplay involving constant calculations and strategic planning, while the structure of the game renders systematic study difficult.[28] For Darren Jorgensen, this makes *EVE* a quintessential SF game: not because of the thematic skinning but because of the "numerical verisimilitude," which he sees at work in much hard SF since the pulp era.[29] At the same time, *EVE Online* centrally utilizes the extrapolated logic of late capitalism with shifting commercial and military alliances and ruthless competition for resources by means both legal, including corporate takeovers and alliances, and illegal: piracy, "player scams, subterfuge, and betrayals."[30]

The relevance of SF-themed massively multiplayer online games for the genre consists in their representation of complex systems. Where many gaming genres, most notably first-person shooters, offer severely simplified versions of their fictional worlds, MMOs like *EVE* force the players to confront the gritty detail of imaginary futures. The principal calculations and strategies required may not be very different from what free agents in the real world have to contend with when going up against steep competition occasionally much bigger than themselves. However, if SF reflects, among other things, the interconnectedness of world systems and the rigor of their operations, MMO games excel among all ludic genres in delegating to the players the task of working out and negotiating these connections.

The third and the last gaming genre that occupies a prominent position in this conception of the SF game history is walking simulators, also known as first-person walkers – originally a derogative denomination – or games of exploration. The games in this group have been praised for innovativeness and uniqueness of experience, while at the same time, they have attracted a considerable amount of criticism and even disdain in various gaming communities – perhaps in both cases because they challenge many definitions of digital games. Despite their name, they rarely simulate any specific activity, but many do share with simulations the absence of goals and tasks that most other ludic genres position in front of the players. Although SF accounts for only a portion of the titles usually grouped in the category,

---

[28] Nicholas Taylor, Kelly Bergstrom, Jennifer Jenson, Suzanne de Castell, "Alienated Playbour: Relations of Production in *EVE Online*," *Games and Culture* 10, 4 (2015), p. 4.
[29] See Darren Jorgensen, "The Numerical Verisimilitude of Science Fiction and *EVE-Online*," *Extrapolation* 50, 1, pp. 134–47.
[30] Taylor *et al.*, "Alienated Playbour," p. 5.

walking simulators seem to offer a unique experience when cast in the speculative mode of SF or fantasy. While realistic "walkers" – a colloquial name styled after "shooters" – predominantly rely for their effect on either accurate, hyper-realistic environs or arresting stories, the status of speculative titles as secondary world creations makes it impossible for players to fall back on familiar geographies and thus encourages a species of engagement absent from mimetic games.

The relatively cultural ephemerality of walking simulators results from their existence outside commercial flows and the fleeting nature of their experience. Some titles also push the envelope of SF games by turning away from ideological entanglements and offering intricate constructs whose primary engagement is largely aesthetic, the status that has been treated with suspicion in many SF communities. *Verde Station* (2014) and *Tacoma* (2017) are both set aboard empty space stations, environments whose contained character allows for greater cohesion. The players are tasked with discovering the back story behind abandonment, but the relatively uncomplicated narratives that emerge are arguably less important than the experience of moving through evocative spaces. In *Master Reboot* (2013), the player's point of view shifts to a virtual space inside a computer, but the essence of the experience remains the same. SF walkers thus activate exploratory pleasures by downplaying the centrality of storytelling tension and originality. Some of them are certainly open to narrative and ideological interpretations. *Tacoma*'s anti-corporate sensibility rings clear at the end of the game, but it is the player's affective faculty that the game seems to target. The moodiness of exploration of recently inhabited spaces combined with the mapping of the station and the structure of tasks requiring repeated visits to some locations clearly privilege exploratory wonder so characteristic of numerous fantastic traditions that fed into the twentieth-century conception of SF.

The two approaches to formulating a history of SF games are in some ways conflicting and draw two very different landscapes of the medium, but neither is in any way more authoritative than the other. They certainly reflect disparate ways of thinking about the genre of SF as well as the medium of games, not to mention the more general issues of canon formation and historiography. Within SF, they also emphasize two distinct – although, it needs to be emphasized, not mutually exclusive, and frequently overlapping in various proportions – types of ludic experience. The canonical history preserves continuity with earlier media of the genre and privileges the cerebral dimension, which also lends itself more readily to the conveyance of overt ideological critique that, as a genre, SF has been resolutely committed to in the last few decades. The conceptual history, on the other hand, attaches more importance to the philosophical dimension of the genre as well as its commitment to world-building as a value in itself. It also reinvigorates the genre's investment in the construction of spaces, which informed earlier fantastic narratives but has been since eclipsed in literature, film, and television by adventure-driven narrative focus. With both things being equal, however, I would argue that while the canonical history does not differ methodologically from similar ludic narratives of other genres, the second, conceptual perspective is better equipped to address the specific intersections of SF and digital games.

40

Twenty-First Century Chinese Science Fiction on the Rise: Anti-Authoritarianism and Dreams of Freedom

HUA LI

Chinese science fiction has garnered increasing visibility among both academic specialists and general readers in the West as an increasing number of English translations of Chinese SF works have become available. In the wake of Chinese writer Liu Cixin's *The Three-Body Problem* (2008, translated to English 2014) receiving the 2015 Hugo Award for Best SF Novel and Hao Jingfang's "Folding Beijing" receiving Best Novelette the next year in 2016, alongside the ever-growing global importance of the Chinese economy, this worldwide interest in Chinese SF is likely to increase. The rise of Chinese SF in the twenty-first century has become part of the new literary wave of global SF. This chapter examines two major Chinese novels, Chan Koonchung's *The Fat Years* (2009, translated to English 2011) and *The Three-Body Problem*, which represent two branches of contemporary Chinese SF: socially engaged SF and hard SF. My discussion will focus on the anti-utopian nature of the two novels and reveal various interactions between imagined utopias, narrative paradigms, and ideology.

Over the past three decades, many literary studies of utopia have rejected the notion of utopia as a static ideal, and have sought to broaden the scope of utopian inquiry in both narrative form and theme. The utopian critics have begun to investigate various narrative devices in more recent utopian fiction, which typically engage readers "in a complex dialogue, rather than merely aiming to secure their unquestioning assent to the writer's sociopolitical agenda."[1] Chris Ferns observes that utopian fiction written before the twentieth century "may be identified as primarily centralist and authoritarian in orientation – a dream of order conceived of in a world of disorder."[2] These utopian works, such as

---

[1] Chris Ferns, *Narrating Utopia: Ideology, Gender, Form in Utopian Literature* (Liverpool: Liverpool University Press, 1999), p. x.
[2] Ferns, *Narrating Utopia*, p. 14.

Thomas More's *Utopia* and Tommaso Campanella's *The City of the Sun*, empha-sized order and social control under the premise that such control would be imposed on humanity in its own best interest. The reality of modern dictatorship has given rise to rethinking the premises of order and social control – and sometimes downgrading their importance as a result. Therefore, the thematic concerns of many utopian works in the twentieth century have instead adopted a variety of forms of dystopias, anti-utopias, and dreams of freedom.

When we look at the subgenre of SF in modern and contemporary China, we can also see this change in utopian vision from a powerful China free from poverty, civil war, and foreign invasion towards a communist China achiev-ing its Four Modernizations of industry, agriculture, national defense, and science and technology, and finally to anti-utopia and dystopia with the themes of anti-authoritarianism and the pursuit of liberty. Chinese SF narra-tives from various periods have varying characteristics in both style and theme, and play varying social and political roles. However, a utopian vision, an emphasis of science and technology, and an emphasis on political implica-tions have remained salient characteristics throughout the subgenre's development.

Chinese SF before the Twenty-First Century

As a literary genre, Chinese SF enjoyed four periods of flourishing during the twentieth century. The first period was during the late Qing and early Republican eras, which witnessed the emergence of Chinese SF as a new literary genre. *Tales of the Moon Colony* has generally been identified as the first piece of Chinese SF; it was written in 1904 by an anonymous author with the pen name Huangjiang Diaosou. *Tales of the Moon Colony* was an incomplete work of thirty-five chapters, each of which was serialized in the magazine *Illustrated Fiction* from the twenty-first to the sixty-second issue off and on in 1904. The novel is a shoddy imitation of *Five Weeks in a Balloon* by the famous French popular novelist Jules Verne, though it prefigures such tropes as the sick man of Asia, the iron house, and cannibalism that appeared later in Lu Xun's stories.[3] Because of the incomplete and unfinished nature of *Tales of the Moon Colony*, "Tales of Mr. New Braggadocio," a short story written by Xu Nianci with the pen name Donghai Juewo in 1905, can be considered the earliest complete work of Chinese SF. The introduction and reception of

---

[3] For an insightful analysis of this novel, see Nathaniel Isaacson, "Science Fiction for the Nation: Tales of the Moon Colony and the Birth of Modern Chinese Fiction," *Science Fiction Studies* 40, 1 (March 2013), pp. 33–54.

Western SF in China at the turn of the twentieth century catalyzed the formation of SF as a transplanted Chinese literary genre. Meanwhile, early Chinese SF was also a product of the "revolution in fiction" advocated by Liang Qichao in the late Qing period. In the 1930s and 1940s, some SF works continued to be written and published till the 1940s, such as Lao She's *Cat City* (1933), Gu Junzheng's collection of *Under the North Pole* (1939), and Xu Dishan's "Gills of Iron Fish" (1940). Though not considered as a bona fide literary genre during this early period of time, SF was a conscious choice of various Chinese intellectuals and writers of the time as one of the means to promote a scientific outlook and thus modernize Chinese culture and society. The utopian motif of the rise of China has identified its pedigree in such early works as Liang Qichao's *The Future of New China* (1902), *Tales of the Moon Colony*, and "Tales of Mr. New Braggadocio." In these works, a better Chinese society is achieved through technological advances and a newly constitutional government.

In Mao Zedong's highly regimented state-socialist China, SF witnessed a boom of sorts during the 1950s and 1960s. Under heavy influence from Soviet Russian SF, Chinese SF narratives brimmed with optimism about the coming communist utopia, and trumpeted visions of technology reigning supreme over a compliant nature. Science and technology would not generate negative unintended consequences, but would instead help usher China into a new earthly paradise just around the corner. Utopian visions of a communist heaven on Earth were presented in such novels as Zheng Wenguang's *Caprices of Communism*.[4] In addition to utopian communist SF, science-popularization SF was a major form in the 1950s.

However, Chinese SF faded into dormancy during the Cultural Revolution (1966–76), when political chaos and regimentation halted almost all literary and artistic creation. Following the death of Mao in 1976 and the subsequent post-Mao cultural thaw of the late 1970s and early 1980s, the Deng Xiaoping-led party-state's reaffirmation of science and technology as driving forces of modernization rekindled further writing of Chinese SF. Both forms of 1950s SF were revived in the late 1970s and early 1980s with some changes. During

---

[4] *Caprices of Communism* was written during the period of the Great Leap Forward (1958–9) by Zheng Wenguang. It was partially serialized in the twenty-third and twenty-fourth issues of *Chinese Youth* in 1958. Though Zheng was not satisfied with this work, he still included it in the collection of his selected works entitled *Zheng Wenguang qishi shouchen ji congshi wenxue chuangzuo wushijiu zhounian jinian wenji* [A Collection of Works to Commemorate Zheng Wenguang's Seventieth Birthday and Fifty-ninth Anniversary of Creative Writing] (1999). The collection was printed and published by Chinese SF critic Wu Yan with personal funds, and presented to Zheng at Zheng's seventieth birthday.

the 1980s, more Golden Age Western SF works were introduced to China and translated into Chinese, such as the works of Arthur C. Clarke and Isaac Asimov; meanwhile, the classical Western SF works of Jules Verne were reprinted. Some SF magazines and magazines specifically designed to popularize science and technology emerged, including *Science, Art and Literature, Ocean of Science Fiction, Wisdom Tree, Illustrated Science,* and *Scientific Epoch.* Responding to Deng Xiaoping's political call to look ahead to the future with hope instead of dwelling on the recent past of the Cultural Revolution with trepidation, Chinese scientists and SF writers mostly presented a rosy vision of China's future, though there were a small number of SF works that engaged in heartfelt reflection on problems of the Cultural Revolution, such as Ye Yonglie's "The Black Shadow" (1981) and Zheng Wenguang's "The Mirror Image of the Earth" (1980). Writers generally adopted the simplistic belief that science and technology would inevitably bring a bright future to China, much as 1950s SF had done. Most narratives made do with a simple plot and characterization, except for a select few written by such veteran writers as Ye Yonglie, Zheng Wenguang, and Tong Enzheng. Partly reminiscent of 1950s SF, politicized visions of a future utopian communist society remerged in novels such as Ye Yonglie's *Xiao Lingtong Travels to the Future* (1978). During this period, science-popularization SF reached its apogee with such works as Wan Huankui's "The Woman who Puffs Smoke Rings" (1982), Lu Zhaowen's "The Sweet Water Lily" (1981), and Zhao Yuqiu's "Fishery" (1980). These works played an instrumental role in popularizing science and technology, along with introducing juvenile readers to creative visions of future technological advances.

It was also during the late 1970s and 1980s that Chinese SF writers started to debate some issues related to the genre itself. For example, what is the nature of SF, literature or science? Should SF focus more on the scientific angle or the literary angle? Some writers consciously improved the artistic and aesthetic quality of their science fictional works. Chinese SF would have developed more smoothly in the 1980s if there had been no government-orchestrated campaign to "eliminate spiritual pollution" during the early part of that decade.[5] The tightened political controls stemming from the party-state's campaign against "spiritual pollution" and its 1989 martial-law decree and military crackdown on unarmed protestors combined to leave Chinese SF in the doldrums from the mid-1980s to the mid-1990s. Though many writers

---

[5] For a detailed overview of the history of Chinese SF, see Dingbo Wu, "Looking Backward: An Introduction to Chinese Science Fiction," in Dingbo Wu and Patrick D. Murphy, eds., *Science Fiction from China* (New York: Praeger, 1989), pp. xi–xli.

continued to write "for the drawer" during these years, their works seldom got published until a partial easing up of political controls during the late 1990s.

Some Chinese SF critics regard the development of Chinese SF during the different periods in the twentieth century as lacking in continuity. I would concede that Chinese SF narratives contrasted significantly in style, theme, and function from one period to the next. However, the continuities are in many ways even more striking. Though Chinese SF in the early twentieth century was far from amounting to a full-fledged literary genre – these narratives typically read more like science fantasy than SF – various salient characteristics of these early works re-appear in later Chinese SF narratives throughout the twentieth century. For example, the utopian visions about future society presented in *Tales of the Moon Colony* and "Tales of Mr. New Braggadocio" reemerged as a communist utopia in such SF works as *A Communist Capriccio* in the 1950s and *Xiao Lingtong Travels to the Future* in 1978. Though Xu Nianci, Lu Xun, and Gu Junzheng advocated that SF should help popularize science and technology among readers of Chinese fiction, this function did not really take place until the 1950s and 1980s, when scientific-popularization SF became an important subgenre in China. This emphasis on technology and science laid a foundation for the prosperity of "hard" or "serious" SF from the 1990s on. In addition, the tradition of incorporating political implications in early Chinese SF continued into the 1990s and has reappeared in many works of contemporary Chinese SF penned by authors such as Liu Cixin, Han Song, and Wang Jinkang.

During the late 1990s and afterwards, Chinese SF reached a new phase of diversification, with an expansion of narrative techniques and themes occurring. More recent Western SF works and writers of the New Wave movement and cyberpunk were introduced to China, and have exerted great influence on Chinese SF readers and writers. The field has been expanding quickly, though SF still has a rather small readership compared with mainstream literature. However, the overly optimistic view about scientific and technological progress has changed since the 1990s, for the old utopian elements in SF have been reconfigured in a far more critical way. The new millennium ushered in dystopian or anti-utopian Chinese SF such as Wang Jinkang's *The Ant Life* (2007), along with Han Song's *Subway* (2010) and *My Homeland Does Not Dream* (2011). In these works, Chinese writers cast a critical eye on the sociopolitical system in a seemingly utopian society brought about by advanced science, technology, and economic development. The emergence of Chinese anti-utopian SF has been a response to the changing sociopolitical circumstances of contemporary China.

The following sections focus on the anti-utopian and dystopian qualities of *The Fat Years* and *The Three-Body Problem*. I argue that this quality is manifested through the characters' continuous and risk-taking efforts to oppose a static and ostensibly perfect society, and to strive instead to expand its sociopolitical, spatial, and technological horizons. The anti-utopian quality is also reflected in the following narrative strategies: transformation of traditional utopian narrative elements such as the traveler's tale and classical dialogue, and the application of new narrative techniques borrowed from realist literature, such as double-voiced discourse, open-ended finales, and novelistic treatment of characters and plot development. These variations in form are the consequence of the interaction between the narrative paradigm and the sociopolitical ideals embodied in the utopian societies depicted in the two novels. At the ideological level, the two authors have undertaken a sober yet creative response to the party-state's high-flown rhetoric about building a harmonious Chinese society, focusing almost single-mindedly on fast economic growth, and enabling China's self-styled "peaceful rise" in the world. They have cautioned readers that technological and economic progress might become the instruments for the imposition of an even more regimented tyranny, and help achieve a revival of totalitarianism.

The Content and Form of *The Fat Years*

Chan Koonchung was born in Shanghai in 1952, and worked in Hong Kong as a writer and journalist before moving to Beijing early in the twenty-first century. The experience of the narrator Lao Chen in *The Fat Years* overlaps much with Chan himself. He observed China's contemporary sociopolitical development and was inspired to write the novel by the Chinese government's response to the global financial crisis of 2008–9 and by its policy of imposing an authoritarian harmony on society.[6] Chan has a deep concern about contemporary China as well as its past and future. This obsession with China is manifested in his "China Trilogy," of which *The Fat Years* is the first volume.[7]

---

[6] Julia Lovell, "Preface," in Chan Koonchung, *The Fat Years*, trans. Michael Duke (New York: Nan A. Talese, 2011), p. x.

[7] Following *The Fat Years: A Novel* (New York: Random House, translated in 2011) and *The Unbearable Dreamworld of Champa the Driver* (London: Doubleday, translated in 2014), Chan Koonchung published his third fiction about Mainland China titled *The Second Year of Jianfeng: An Alternative History of New China*, completing what some critics have called Chan's "China Trilogy."

The Fat Years was published in Chinese in 2009, and translated into English in 2011. It is a near-future novel with a realistic exposé of the sociopolitical system in contemporary China. In the novel, China's Golden Age of Ascendancy officially begins in 2011, when the global economy spins out of control and descends into a protracted crisis. From that time on and throughout all of China, practically everybody is living comfortably and feeling both spiritually and materially satisfied. Inside the country, there has been no social upheaval; the society is more harmonious than ever. However, a small minority of Chinese people feel that something has gone wrong, and are searching for the missing month between the onset of the global economic crisis and the beginning of China's new Golden Age. They yearn to find out why nearly all Chinese people have undergone a transformation to such an elated spiritual state.

On the one hand, the narrative presents a utopia, which is dubbed China's Golden Age and derives from the machinations of the Chinese Communist Party's (CCP) and the Chinese people's collective amnesia. On the other hand, the narrative simultaneously portrays the negation and demystification of this Golden Age by the awakened few who refuse to forget the past, preferring to live in a "good hell" where people remain aware of the many severe shortcomings in their sociopolitical system. The first-person narrator Lao Chen serves as both a public and a private narrator, and is torn between these two narrative forces. The novel presents a satirical double-voiced discourse of the ruling CCP rhetoric that celebrates its harmonious society and its Chinese dream focusing mainly on burgeoning state power instead of rising opportunities for the individual.

In Mikhail Bakhtin's investigation of the dialogic nature of language, he argues that an imaginative writer may exploit someone else's discourse for the writer's own purposes "by inserting a new semantic intention into a discourse which already has, and which retains, an intention of its own."[8] *The Fat Years* lends itself well to such a Bakhtinian reading. Chan's use of double-voiced discourse is achieved and complicated by the participation of a multitude of narrative voices throughout the novel – the high-ranking CCP official He Dongsheng, the narrator Lao Chen, and various focalizers such as Fang Caodi, Zhang Dou, and Little Xi. This critical approach to Chan's satire of China's Golden Age teases out the novel's complex use of irony and its cautionary implications.

---

[8] Mikhail Bakhtin, *Problems of Dostoevsky's Poetics*, trans. Caryl Emerson (Minneapolis: University of Minnesota Press, 1984), p. 189.

The majority of the novel is narrated by Lao Chen, and is based upon his observations of Chinese society and his interactions with other characters. Lao Chen thus serves as a public narrator, who conjures forth a fictional world while having a narrow or parochial understanding of it. Lao Chen brings in the voices of the majority in Chinese society including intellectuals, former political dissidents, foreign reporters, scholars, religious leaders, and even janitorial support staff. He unreflectively shares most people's impression that "there is no possible way for China to be any better than it is today."[9] Similarly, intellectuals have stopped criticizing the government, and have all become extremely satisfied with the current state of affairs, and no foreigners dare to offend the CCP and thus risk denial of a visa. The sociologist Hu Yan advises the central government to defuse the controversy over official restrictions on religion by treating it more as a normal part of life. Chinese Christians thereby exhibit a mild form of dogmatic self-satisfaction. Even the cleaning lady tells Lao Chen that life is much better today than previously. As a public narrator, Lao Chen presents an unreflective official articulation of Party-based discourse about a Chinese-style utopia.

While presenting this vision of a practically perfect society as a public narrator, Lao Chen occasionally switches his role to that of a private narrator with an authoritative voice and a more reflective recognition of reality. As a private narrator, he is sympathetic with voices of an awakened minority who regard the Golden Age as a fake paradise. Lao Chen thus articulates a second group of voices who demystify the supposed utopia. This minority group of voices consists of various focalizers whose "consciousness is responsible for the perceptions, thoughts, feelings, or orientations to the scene that the narrator relays."[10] These people have all been taking one or another type of drug for an extended period, including antidepressants, painkillers, corticosteroids (to treat asthma), and various analgesics. This might be the reason why they have not forgotten the past, and remain fully aware that something has gone wrong with society. They are also relatively marginalized people within society: Xiao Xi is a former lawyer who has become an Internet-based political activist; Fang Caodi is a drifter who works as a jack-of-all-trades; Zhang Dou is a former child-slave-laborer who has become an aspiring guitarist; and Dong Niang is a high-class prostitute. They refuse to indulge

---

[9] Chan, *The Fat Years*, p. 270.
[10] Susan Sniader Lanser, *The Narrative Act: Point of View in Prose Fiction* (Princeton: Princeton University Press, 1981), p. 142.

themselves in the bread-and-circuses carnivalesque society and to give in to amnesia about the nation's checkered past.

If we place this double-voiced discourse and the narrator Lao Chen in a traditional utopian narrative paradigm, we can see that this novel is an outgrowth or transformation of the traditional traveler's tale. In traditional utopian fiction, the traveler is always an outsider, and accidentally happens upon a utopia. The traveler moves from place to place in a random and arbitrary order so as to witness the various excellent features of this utopian society; the role of the individual in the utopian society is focalized through a single typical citizen.[11] In *The Fat Years*, Lao Chen plays the role of traveler, but he is not a passive observer from an outside world. He is on the one hand an insider of this utopian society and actively engaged in its social life. On the other hand, Lao Chen casts a critical light on the sociopolitical system, and eventually becomes a traitor to this utopia.

Traditional utopian fiction always contains a classical dialogue that helps explain the sociopolitical system of the given utopian society. *The Fat Years* also contains lengthy dialogues of this sort in its finale. These dialogues disclose how the Golden Age was implemented by means of the Chinese government strategy in its "Action Plan for Achieving Prosperity amid Crisis." These dialogues are between He Dongsheng and the awakened minority following the latter's kidnapping of He. These dialogues adopt the mode of interrogation as a rhetorical tool. The questions asked by Lao Chen and his friends are designed to ferret out the hidden official agenda of the one-party state's ruling elite. He Dongsheng discloses that the Party has taken advantage of the unprecedented global economic crisis to "implement a genuine dictatorship, guarantee action at the bottom on every order from the top, and build a firm foundation for China's Golden Age of Ascendancy that was just waiting to blossom out of the nation's growing power."[12]

In order to facilitate the Action Plan, the government starts to secretly add MDMA (the recreational narcotic ecstasy) to all of China's drinking water reservoirs and bottled beverages on the same day that the government announces the beginning of China's Golden Age. However, the national leaders remain sober and under control by maintaining their own separate and uncontaminated sources of drinking water. The chemical keeps the populace intoxicated so as to forestall complaints about the government and just let its officials do whatever they please. Consequently, China soon

---

[11] Ferns, *Narrating Utopia*, pp. 13–21.
[12] Chan, *The Fat Years*, p. 232.

achieves the world's highest ratings on the happiness index. People gradually lose all their memories of important historical events, including the twenty-eight days between the beginning of the global economic crisis and the day that the Action Plan gets implemented. Taking advantage of this collective amnesia, the government revises or deletes whatever it wants to alter regarding the country's historical past. In his role as translator of *The Fat Years*, Michael Duke indicates that the style of He's monologue is no less significant than its content. The way He patronizingly lectures Lao Chen and his friends is exactly the way the CCP addresses the Chinese populace from on high. The content of his lecture has far more to say about the realities of contemporary China than about its possible future. Many of the novel's "Strategic Plans" have already been implemented in reality.[13]

The double-voiced discourse of the Golden Age is also presented through the contrasting imagery of a good hell versus a fake paradise. These images of a good hell and a small group of awakened people have been borrowed from the early twentieth-century writer and social critic Lu Xun. In Lu's "Preface" to his first collection of short stories, *Call to Arms*, he compares China in the 1920s to an iron house without any doors or windows. Most people remain asleep within this house, for merely a few of them have awakened. Lu hopes that these few awakened people could wake up their sleeping confreres and together escape death by breaking apart the iron house.[14] In Chan's novel, China in the contemporary Golden Age closely resembles Lu's iron house. Most people are effectively sleepwalking through the supposedly harmonious and affluent Golden Age, and remain unaware of the fact that they are facing immanent suffocation from their unaccountable government's autocratic suppression of truth and its unwillingness to learn from its calamitous errors of the past. Nobody except for a small minority remember the often harrowing past, attempt to wake up the sleepwalking majority, and insist on truth-telling in the public sphere.

Chinese literature's *locus classicus* of a "good hell" is from Lu Xun's essay "The Good Hell That Was Lost." Lu wrote this essay in 1925 to describe the hellish conditions of Chinese society under the rule of various war-mongering regional warlords. The essay takes the reader to a legendary realm of the past in which the devil defeats God and subsequently rules over all three realms of heaven, Earth, and hell. Yet the devil is unprepared to

---

[13] Michael Duke, "Translator's Notes," in Chan, *The Fat Years*, p. 297.

[14] Xun Lu, "Preface to the First Collection of Short Stories *Call to Arms*," in Yang Xiany, trans., *Selected Works of Lu Xun*, 4 vols. (Beijing: Foreign Languages Press, 1956), vol. 1, pp. 1–7.

govern such an expansive empire, and no longer gives sufficient attention to his original realm of hell. Some of hell's demons therefore travelled to the human realm to ask for help with returning hell to normalcy. Having agreed with this request, Man fought victoriously against the devil, forcing the devil to withdraw from hell in retreat. "Man then wielded absolute power over hell, his authority exceeding that of the devil."[15] However, when the demons again raised an outcry about what they saw as improper rule of hell, they became rebels against Man, who punished them there as a result. Only at this juncture did the demons realize that they had lost their good hell. Lu's essay suggests that during China's warlord period (1916–27), the difference between living under the rule of one regional warlord or another amounts to nothing more than living in a relatively good hell or a relatively bad hell.

In *The Fat Years*, instead of making a contrast between a good hell and a bad hell, the author contrasts a good hell with a fake paradise. Chan summarizes China's good hell as follows: "During the Cultural Revolution and the beginning of [the era of Economic] Reform and Opening, everyone knew that the true facts were being suppressed."[16] However, during the seemingly paradisiacal Golden Age, China's populace has become mostly oblivious to the true facts. People have fallen under the illusion that they are following their own reading preferences and freely choosing what they read, but they have lost the capacity to discern that most books have been politically bowdlerized, with much of history having been censored. The private narrator Lao Chen draws a clear distinction between a good hell and a fake paradise: "In a good hell, people are aware they are living in hell, and so they want to transform it, but after living for a long time in a fake paradise, people become accustomed to it and they actually believe that they are already in paradise."[17]

By borrowing the literary motifs of a good hell and the awakened minority, the author engages in an ongoing discussion of the ideas Lu Xun expressed several decades ago, and inspires the reader to delve beneath the glittering surfaces of China's so-called Golden Age. The nation's growing wealth and power have brought about a higher standard of living to most of its populace, but Chinese society and culture still resemble an iron house. Most of the people inside this iron house seem unaware of the fact that they have no basic rights or freedoms – nor the ability to think critically or outside the box that the Party line sets out for them. Contemporary Chinese society

[15] Lu, "The Good Hell That Was Lost," in *Selected Works of Lu Xun*, p. 344.
[16] Chan, *The Fat Years*, p.143.
[17] Ibid., p. 144.

and culture remain much the same in essence as what Lu Xun lamented back in the 1920s. Readers in the People's Republic, where the novel is officially banned yet often available through various unofficial channels, may well ask themselves: Would I rather live in a good hell or a fake paradise?

The Content and Form of *The Three-Body Problem*

In contrast with Chan Koonchung and his hard-hitting political satire and allegory, Liu Cixin is best known for his hard SF works such as *The Wandering Earth* (2000), *Ball Lightning* (2005), and the trilogy *Remembrance of Earth's Past* (2006, 2007, and 2010, better known in the United States by the name of its first entry, *The Three-Body Problem*). Besides hard SF, Liu has also written a group of works that are set in the future and yet haunted by the swirl of recent events in Chinese politics and its global context. These works include the critical utopian novel *China 2185* (1989), the novella "Mirror" (2004), and his alternate histories – the short stories "The Western Ocean" (1998) and "Butterfly Effect" (2001). Although these works were written at various stages of Liu's career, they bear a key unifying characteristic: a focus on the impact of science and technology on human behavior and social systems.

Although *The Three-Body Problem* has been commonly regarded as a typical hard SF novel, of a type with many similar works in the West, its political and ideological implications are significant. Liu's depiction of the Trisolaran civilization reflects certain aspects of contemporary China: existence and development are the premises for everything; the government-mandated construction of a harmonious society comes at the price of suppressing individual freedom, personal emotions, and literature and art. It is at this point that *The Three-Body Problem* shares a common thematic concern with *The Fat Years*: anti-utopia – specifically, in their expression of anti-authoritarianism and support for more freedom of thought and expression.

The Three-Body Problem is the first volume of Liu's trilogy *Remembrance of Earth's Past*. The novel was first serialized in *Science Fiction World* in 2006, and published in book form in 2008; it was translated into English in 2014. Similar to *The Fat Years*, the novel presents a contrast between a good hell on Earth and a fake paradise on Trisolaris. The double-voiced discourse of the fake paradise of Trisolaris and the good hell of Earth comes across to the reader through different focalizers – Ye Wenjie on Earth and Listener 1379 on Trisolaris. Both of them are so disappointed with their society that they rebel against it, and subsequently embark on a quest for a better life on another planet.

Ye Wenjie is an astrophysicist. During the Cultural Revolution, her father has been persecuted to death by a group of female Red Guards. Meanwhile, both her mother and her younger sister have betrayed her father in order to protect themselves. Later, Ye joins the Inner Mongolia Production and Construction Corps and is dispatched to the Greater Khingan Mountains with other educated youth to work as lumberjacks. While living and working in the Greater Khingan Mountains, she is deeply influenced by Rachel Carson's *Silent Spring* (1962). It is because of her fondness for this ideologically incorrect book that an erstwhile friend is able to frame her and get her locked up in jail for a time. Having witnessed the madness and violence of the Cultural Revolution along with the reckless clear-cutting of forests in the Greater Khingan Mountains, she becomes disillusioned with human nature and humankind in general. She becomes a researcher at the Red Coast Base – a secret research institute that is probing extraterrestrial intelligent life and civilizations.

Ye accidentally discovers that the Sun could be used to amplify radio waves sent out from Earth. She thereupon secretly sends out radio signals from Earth to various parts of the universe. These signals are picked up by the Trisolaran civilization, which is four light-years away from Earth, and located on a planet of the nearest stellar system from Earth, Alpha Centauri. The civilization on Trisolaris has been extinguished and then reborn for many cycles as a result of the irregular motions of the three suns in this system. The Trisolaran civilization has striven to migrate to other stars where the climate was eternally mild. Ye is soon warned by a pacifist in Trisolaris named Listener 1379 not to answer any radio call from Trisolaris. If she were to answer, the Trisolaran civilization would be able to ascertain the location of Earth, and Earth would soon be invaded and conquered by the Trisolaran civilization. However, Ye ignores this warning and sends out more radio signals in the hope that an advanced civilization will arrive to save humanity and the Earth from evil. After receiving Ye's response, the Trisolaran civilization formulates their plan for a massive migration to Earth. They first send two super intelligent "sophons" to Earth to prevent mankind from making further progress in science. Meanwhile, the Trisolaran Fleet has set sail toward the solar system and will arrive at Earth after some four hundred and fifty years. On Earth, more and more people join Ye and her fellow activist Evan's Earth–Trisolaris Organization, which is making preparations for a visit from the Trisolaran civilization.

This novel is an inversion of the traditional extraterrestrial colonization story, in which human civilization longs to leave Earth behind and conquer or colonize Mars or some other planet or moon. In this novel, Earth becomes the paradise that the extraterrestrial civilization longs to conquer and colonize. Through the eyes of Ye and Listener 1379, the novel presents a sharp contrast between how humankind and the Trisolarans perceive Earth and Trisolaris.

For Ye, Evans, and their fellow enthusiasts, human society on Earth resembles hell. They are extremely disappointed with human nature and the devastating effects of industrial civilization on Earth's natural environment and ecology. They pessimistically believe that human civilization is no longer capable of improving itself on its own. They pin all their hopes on Trisolaran civilization to "reform human civilization, to curb human madness and evil, so that the Earth can once again become a harmonious, prosperous, sinless world."[18] Ye and her friends believe in a sort of salvationist fantasy about the Trisolaran civilization on account of their admiration for advanced science and technology. They assume that an extraterrestrial civilization at a higher stage of scientific and technological prowess would have necessarily developed a superior form of society and civilization – and that this would necessarily redound to Earth's benefit upon the extraterrestrials' arrival here.

However, the technologically utopian realm of Trisolaris is a world of endless isolation in the eyes of Listen 1379. Listener 1379 is one of the very small number of individuals who are not satisfied with this seemingly perfect society on Trisolaris. Again, this is reminiscent of Lu Xun's scenario of the minority of people inside his ominous iron house who have awakened. Similar to the private persona of Lao Chen in *The Fat Years*, Listener 1379 is an intellectually privileged observer of his would-be utopia, and also finds this utopia to be deeply flawed.

The narrative device of classical dialogue between the traveler and the ruler of the utopian society also appears in this novel. There is a lengthy dialogue between Listener 1379 and the Trisolaran "Princeps," the title of the highest-ranking political leader of the Trisolaran civilization. It is through these dialogues and Listener 1379's confession that the reader learns about the nature of the Trisolaran rule – absolute authoritarianism. The Trisolaran Princeps tells Listener 1379 that Trisolaran civilization also experienced free and democratic societies in the past, and left behind rich cultural legacies. However, they now generally believe that this type of civilization was too weak to survive for very long, and thus undesirable. The ultimate goal to

---

[18] Cixin Liu, *The Three-Body Problem*, trans. Ken Liu (New York: Tor Books, 2014), p. 314.

survive the alternate Chaotic and Stable Eras stimulates the Trisolaran civilization to develop advanced science and technology, and a highly efficient, centrally organized, and extremely authoritarian social structure, out of which estrangement or alienation have arisen. They can manipulate nine out of the eleven dimensions of the nano-scale world; they thus regard humans on Earth as little more than primitive insects, because mankind is still confined within a three-dimensional world. In this advanced civilization, individuality, spirituality, and emotions have all been eliminated. Individuals do not have names, and are identified merely by their post numbers and job titles. If any adult Trisolarans lose the ability to work, the government simply disposes of them by mandatory dehydration and burning – by force if necessary. All emotions such as fear, sorrow, anger, resentment, pleasure, and fondness for beauty have been thoroughly suppressed. Calmness and numbness are the only two mental states that they have promoted and cultivated for survival value. In Listener 1379's eyes, Earth is a paradise in spite of its civilization's much lower level of technology and various other imperfections.

In Listener 1379's dialogue with the Princeps, we encounter the same sort of cold-blooded autocratic rhetoric that peppers the entrenched leaders' discourse in *The Fat Years*, such as existence being the premise for everything, extreme authoritarianism, fight for survival, and spiritual monotony. Through Listener 1379's rebellion against the heartless dictates of his civilization, the author offers a cautionary note that future advances in science and technology will not necessarily lead to a more humane society or more satisfying way of life for the populace. Instead, it may lead to extreme authoritarianism, aggressive territorial expansionism, and the withering or even disappearance of freedom, individuality, and compassion.

In *The Dark Forest* and *Death's End*, the two sequels to *The Three-Body Problem*, Liu Cixin continues to explore the relations between existence, technology and totalitarianism, and expands their interactions to outer space – this time on a much more cosmic scale. He presents a vision of the alienation of posthumanity and describes the nature of the universe as a "dark forest" (a place where anything that makes a sound gets eaten). The plot of *The Dark Forest* develops around the Wallfacer Project – a strategic plan that humanity launches to find some way to cope with the ubiquitous Trisolaran sophons on Earth and resist the upcoming arrival of the Trisolaran Fleet within four hundred years. An astronomer and sociologist named Luo Ji is one of the four Wallfacers, and discovers the nature of the universe to be a dark forest. Consequently, he successfully sets up a mechanism of deterrence by threatening to reveal the locations of both Earth and Trisolaris to the universe at large, forcing the Trisolaran droplet probes and fleet to stay away from the Solar System. Luo becomes the "Swordholder" of the deterrence system, and humanity enters the Deterrence Era. In *Death's End*, the Trisolaran civilization takes the risky move of attacking the Earth upon Luo's retirement as the "Swordholder," with an eye to colonizing it. Earthlings subsequently trigger the mechanism of deterrence that uncovers the cosmic coordinates of Trisolaris by sending gravitational waves out across the universe. Consequently, both the Trisolaran civilization and the Solar System are destroyed by an unknown advanced civilization in space – though the story goes on with a small number of human survivors who escape the destruction by fleeing to another star, and ultimately another universe.

The two sequels present three dystopian worlds: the universe, posthuman spaceships, and the doomed Earth. The Darwinian theory of "survival of the fittest" on Earth is extended to the "dark forest theory" of the Universe. Because of the limited resources in the universe, the cosmos becomes an immense battlefield. "Every civilization is an armed hunter stalking through the trees like a ghost" in a dark forest.[19] In order to survive, universal laws of physics such as the speed of light can be manipulated and weaponized. When humans truly enter space, and are freed from the Earth, they have to follow the dark forest theory and cease to be human. This is what happens to both of the Earth's two major spaceships, *The Bronze Age* and *The Blue Planet*; when Earth's space fleet is attacked by the Trisolaran probes, only seven spaceships survive to escape from the doomed solar system. When spiritual bonds with Earth subsequently snap, the spaceship passengers suffer total spiritual alienation. "Space was like a distorting mirror that magnified the dark side of humanity to the maximum."[20] In order to obtain enough fuel, parts and food to support the space journey, the two ships *The Bronze Age* and *The Blue Planet* attack five other spaceships. In this posthuman world on the spaceships, an absolute autocracy and its new ethical code are established within five minutes. "The boundlessness of space nurtured a dark new humanity in its dark embrace."[21]

Human civilization on Earth also changes when facing this doomsday battle. By means of this ultimate crisis on Earth, Liu Cixin explores the complex relation between technology and totalitarianism. "Science and technology contributed to the elimination of totalitarianism; yet when crises

---

[19] Cixin Liu, *The Dark Forest*, trans. Joel Martinsen (New York: Tor Books, 2015), pp. 484–5.
[20] Cixin Liu, *Death's End*, trans. Ken Liu (New York: Tor Book, 2016), p. 409.
[21] Liu, *The Dark Forest*, p. 458.

threatened the existence of civilization, science and technology could also give birth to a new totalitarianism."[22] During the Deterrence Era, human society "reaches unprecedented heights of civilization: human rights and democracy reigned supreme in most places. On the other hand, the entire system exists within the shadow of a dictator," namely the Swordholder.[23] During the Post-Deterrence Era, a ruling system even more ancient than totalitarianism, namely theocracy, reappears and achieves ascendancy. In the era of the ultimate crisis, such human merits as having a conscience and a sense of duty are no longer esteemed, but are instead viewed as expressions of mental illness. Cheng Xin, the last Swordholder, finally pushes the human world into the abyss because of her love of humankind in its earlier civilized condition.

By presenting these dystopian visions in the two sequels, Liu cautions humankind that "the combination of supertechnology and an ultimate crisis could throw humankind back into a dark age."[24] This cautionary note echoes what Liu and Chan explored in *The Three-Body Problem* and *The Fat Years* respectively. As a response to contemporary China's sociopolitical circumstances, the anti-utopian and dystopian quality has become one of the salient characteristics in Chinese SF in the twenty-first century.

[22] Liu, *Death's End*, p. 132.
[23] Ibid.
[24] Ibid., p. 133.

41

Ciencia Ficción / Ficção Científica from Latin America

RACHEL HAYWOOD FERREIRA

Latin American SF has come into its own as a field of study in the last twenty years, but SF has been written in Latin America since the early days of the genre in the nineteenth century. This chapter discusses the full history of the *ciencia ficción/ficção científica* of Spanish America and Brazil.[1] The most extensive and consistent SF traditions in the region are those of Argentina, Brazil, Mexico, Cuba, and, increasingly, Chile, but SF has been produced in all Latin American countries. US–Mexican borderlands SF and the SF of Puerto Rico are also often discussed in conjunction with Latin American SF owing to significant intersections and commonalities of language, geography, and sociopolitical realities.

Latin America is an extremely heterogeneous region, with great linguistic, geographic, racial, historical, economic, and cultural diversity. At the same time, Latin American nations have a great deal in common: they form part of the Global South, sharing Iberian colonial pasts; they have heterogeneous populations; they suffer from uneven modernity and widespread income inequality; and a central issue for all of them has historically been the definition and consolidation of national identity. Therefore any history of Latin American SF will necessarily be rife with exceptions, but looking at the genre in the region as a whole provides a broader array of cultural products and makes visible patterns of theme and variation that might otherwise escape our notice.

What is Meant by Latin American Science Fiction: SF, the Canon, and Neighboring Genres

Andrew Milner has described SF as "a selective tradition, continuously reinvented in the present, through which the boundaries of the genre are

---

[1] While this region is most accurately referred to as "Ibero-America," I will generally prefer "Latin America," the more frequently used term in the field.

continuously policed, challenged and disrupted, and the cultural identity of the SF community continuously established, preserved and transformed. It is thus essentially and necessarily a site of contestation."[2] The identity of Latin American SF is particularly in flux in comparison with its Northern counterparts because the regional Latin American SF community and national SF communities are less established and smaller in size, because Latin American SF has only recently been the subject of sustained critical attention, because of the reputation of SF as a "borrowed" genre in Latin America, and because other genres with reputations more literary and more local appear to occupy some of the same territory as SF. Definitions of what is and is not SF in Latin America are necessarily affected by many factors: by the role of the definer or the hat(s) s/he is wearing at the time (bibliographer, publisher, reader, scholar, writer); by whether one's individual background or field of study centers more around genre fiction or the literary canon; and by what one's society and/or one's field of study values. In short, what is meant by Latin American SF depends upon whom you ask, when you ask, and for what purpose. There are a great deal more works of SF and works that can be usefully read through a science-fictional lens to be found in Latin America outside the books, magazines, and websites that carry the genre label.

Latin American SF is often described as more connected with canonical literature or disconnected from mass culture than SF written in the North.[3] Many Latin American writers have used science-fictional elements in their work without identifying as genre writers. This can happen, as it can in the North, because science-fictional tropes permeate modern culture, and mainstream writers may use them to explore and extrapolate from contemporary reality. For example, Juan José Arreola, Carlos Fuentes, and Marcela del Río have been described as Mexican writers who have not thought of themselves as participants in a particular genre,[4] and Argentine writers such as Jorge Luis Borges, Adolfo Bioy Casares, and Julio Cortázar are also frequently cited as canonical authors of science-fictional or SF-adjacent texts. While mainstream

---

[2] Andrew Milner, *Locating Science Fiction* (Liverpool: Liverpool University Press, 2012), pp. 39–40.

[3] See for example: Luis C. Cano, *Intermitente recurrencia: La ciencia ficción y el canon literario hispanoamericano* (Intermittent Recurrence: Science Fiction and the Spanish American Canon) (Buenos Aires: Corregidor, 2006), pp. 18, 262; Silvia Kurlat Ares, "Argentinean Science Fiction" in Lars Schmeink, ed., *A Virtual Introduction to Science Fiction: Online Toolkit for Teaching SF* (2013), pp. 1–11. http://virtual-sf.com/?page_id=806 (last accessed June 18, 2018).

[4] Gabriel Trujillo Muñoz, *Biografías del futuro: La ciencia ficción mexicana y sus autores* (Biographies of the Future: Mexican Science Fiction and Its Authors) (Mexicali, Mexico: Universidad Autónoma de Baja California, 2000), p. 17.

writers such as these do not self-identify as SF writers, this is not to say they are divorced from the genre. Still, Pablo Capanna's characterization of Argentine SF as "a science fiction that resists recognizing itself as such" remains widely applicable in Latin America.[5]

The publication of works as mainstream fiction that could be published as SF can occur in Latin America, as in the North, out of an author's, publisher's or bookseller's desire to avoid genre stigma and ghettoization, but this genre-avoidance is more prevalent in Latin America. Likewise, the describing of works as mainstream fiction that could be described as SF is more prevalent, as critics and others strive to define their fields of interest in more canonical, socially acceptable terms. Much of the (un)conscious reasoning behind this phenomenon comes from the Latin American canon itself. Historically, the Latin American literary canon has always privileged realistic fiction. Latin American fiction is expected to be engaged: to represent local themes and issues, educate the people and address their problems, and work toward social justice by denouncing evils and abuses in society and by instigating change.[6]

SF has neighboring genres that border, overlap, and intermingle. Latin American genre fiction also has these generic neighbors and the tendency to form hybrids with them, but some of these neighboring genre labels, such as the fantastic and magic realism, have been preferred by writers and critics over SF to an exaggerated degree when describing Latin American fiction. Unlike SF, these genres are not seen as foreign, and they enjoy literary cachet at home and abroad, with their respectability solidified by, for example, the edition of the *Antología de la literatura fantástica* [*Anthology of Fantastic Literature*] by Borges, Bioy Casares, and Silvina Ocampo in 1940 and the Nobel Prizes of magic realist writers such as Miguel Ángel Asturias (1967) and Gabriel García Márquez (1982). This is not to take issue with the correct application of these other labels or with the application of multiple genre labels to a work. The problem is when science-fictional works are mislabeled or unlabeled,[7] when magic realism, for example, is viewed as the Latin

---

[5] Pablo Capanna, *El mundo de la ciencia ficción* (The World of Science Fiction). (Buenos Aires: Ediciones Letra Buena, 1992), p. 177. All translations in this chapter are mine.

[6] In this context magic realism has had its cake and eaten it too, being considered realistically engaged as well as appreciated for its fantastic elements. In recent decades Northern countries have often privileged the translation of works of Latin American magic realism, the poster children of the canonical Boom literature of the 1960s–1970s, over that of other Latin American fictions, often leading to a somewhat skewed vision of Latin American literature abroad.

[7] For more on the mislabeling, unlabeling and dual labeling of Latin American SF, see Rachel Haywood Ferreira, *The Emergence of Latin American Science Fiction* (Middletown, CT: Wesleyan University Press, 2011), pp. 8–11.

American version of SF,[8] or when it is assumed that magic realism describes all of Latin America all of the time. As Daniel Croci wrote as early as 1985, "Spanish America today is no longer completely reflected in Macondo. Despite our dependency, fragmentation, marginal and peripheral condition, we have technified and industrialized. Our new world is no longer that magical mixture of aboriginal mythic universe and ambitious Spanish chimera, neither is it – only – the decadence and frustration of that world that García Márquez depicts magnificently."[9]

SF, then, has been condemned in Latin America both for what it is and what it is not perceived to be. Like Northern SF, it has been seen as a lesser literature, as escapist, children's stories, pulp fiction. It has also been judged as not fulfilling Latin American literary expectations: being unrealistic, not dealing with concrete social and political problems as directly as realist fiction does, even as distorting reality.[10] In addition, SF in Latin America is often seen as an imported or borrowed or foreign genre and suffers from negative associations with political and cultural colonialism and neocolonialism. Roberto de Sousa Causo, for example, has characterized a common Brazilian attitude toward SF as "not [being] a good match for Brazilian reality,"[11] and Miguel Ángel Fernández Delgado has described a perception of Mexican SF writers as cultural sell-outs, "guided by the *malinchismo* that could be assumed in the cultivators of a literary movement that came from outside."[12] Such ideas are beginning to change, but these preconceptions remain challenges for writers of SF in Latin America.

[8] This happened most notably in James Gunn's introduction to the Latin American section of *The Road to Science Fiction* (*Volume 6: Around the World* [Clarkston, GA: White Wolf, 1998] pp. 480–3), but it has also been a fairly common assumption.

[9] Daniel Croci, "Tesis para una nueva literatura fantástica nacional" (Thesis for a New National Fantastic Literature), in Augusto Uribe, ed., *Latinoamérica fantástica* (Fantastic Latin America) (Barcelona: Ultramar Editores, 1985), p. 132.

[10] Elton Honores, *Narrativas del caos: un ensayo sobre la narrativa de lo imposible en el Perú contemporáneo* (Chaos Narratives: An Essay on the Narrative of the Impossible in Contemporary Peru) (Lima: Cuerpo de la metáfora, 2012), p. 9.

[11] Roberto de Sousa Causo, *Ficção científica, fantasia e horror no Brasil, 1875 a 1950* (Science Fiction, Fantasy and Horror in Brazil, 1879–1950) (Belo Horizonte: Editor UFMG, 2003), p. 247.

[12] Miguel Ángel Fernández Delgado, "Introducción," in Miguel Ángel Fernández Delgado (ed.), *Visiones periféricas: Antología de la ciencia ficción mexicana* (Peripheral Visions: Anthology of Mexican Science Fiction) (Mexico D.F.: Lumen, 2001), p. 14. The exception to these rules is Cuba, particularly after 1979, when SF, under the aegis of the Soviet seal of approval, is well regarded by the Cuban government and by literary critics and is considered engaged, even militant and an instrument for revolutionary change. See Daína Chaviano, "Veinte años de ciencia ficción en Cuba" (Twenty Years of Science Fiction in Cuba), *Revista Unión* 1 (1986), pp. 122–3; Daína Chaviano, "Science Fiction and Fantastic Literature as Realms of Freedom," *Journal of the Fantastic in the Arts*

What is Meant by *Latin American* SF: Characteristics

Because it is still a relatively new field of study, the defining characteristics of Latin American SF have been evolving particularly rapidly, as new knowledge is added and the full scope of genre production in Latin America emerges. "What's Latin American about it?" is indeed one of the central questions underlying the study of Latin American SF; in order to understand the answers, it is essential to understand the history and context behind them. Case in point: perhaps the most frequently cited characterization of Latin American SF is that it is "soft," based on the social rather than the hard sciences. In part this is to be expected: Latin America is much more a consumer than a producer of science and technology, and notable contributions have been made by Latin American SF writers and critics with backgrounds in the social sciences.

But the description of Latin American SF as soft requires qualification: Latin American SF is *predominantly* soft or perhaps *tends toward* the soft. Latin American SF often emphasizes humanistic values either over knowledge of the hard sciences or in concert with that knowledge. The "softness" of Latin American SF has been explained by many critics from a variety of useful angles. Andrea Bell and Moisés Hassón provide literary context for this quality: "An ever-present concern with meeting essential human needs has, to varying degrees over time, informed the thematic and stylistic elements of virtually all literary genres in Latin America, and so it is also with science fiction."[13] Pablo Capanna sheds light on the "soft" designation from a comparative standpoint: "Perhaps the most common feature is that our authors do not write sf based on science, as happens in industrial countries where science is a socially prestigious activity and technology permeates daily life ... Here authors write science fiction based on science fiction."[14] Finally, Mexican writer and critic Pepe Rojo addresses the soft–hard line and the impact of science in the periphery: "When speaking to the rest of the world, the distinction between hard and soft science fiction becomes blurry. Mauricio-José Schwarz, a Mexican SF author, used to say that some people find it funny that there could be such a thing as science fiction in Mexico, to which he always replied that even if his country didn't produce much science

---

15, 1 (2004), p. 5; Juan Carlos Toledano Redondo, "Sputniks cubanos: De como la URSS ocupó la imaginación de una generación" (Cuban Sputniks: How the USSR Occupied the Imagination of a Generation), *Kamchatka* (July 2015), pp. 187–98.

[13] Andrea Bell and Moisés Hassón, "Prelude to the Golden Age: Chilean Science Fiction, 1900–1959," *Science Fiction Studies* 25, 2 (1998), p. 297.

[14] Pablo Capanna, "La ciencia ficción y los argentinos," *Minotauro* 10 (1985), p. 56

or technology, it sure did suffer from them. Maybe the way to characterize 'World SF' is not as hard or soft, but sharp, when it works well."[15]

There are Latin American SF writers who come from the hard sciences and who write hard (or at least hard*er*) SF; this is especially true of nineteenth-century SF authors, and among those writing around the 1950s and the time of the Cold War,[16] and among some of the more recent writers working in cyberpunk. Just as the harder moments in Latin American SF parallel some of the harder moments in Northern SF, the upswing in softer SF in the 1960s at the height of the Golden Age of SF in Latin America parallels the upswing in soft SF during the New Wave in the North.[17] Northern SF trends do affect trends in Latin American SF, but events in regional and global arenas are equally strong impulses behind changes in the genre there. If Latin American SF is somewhat softer than Northern SF, then, this softness is more than a reflection of the state of Latin American development: it reflects cultural concerns, strengths, and values, and it reflects global events and movements, and discoveries in politics, culture, and science. Hard SF in Latin America is not an aberration, soft SF is not a rule, and there is a lot of gray area in between the two.

In describing SF written outside the United States, Istvan Csicsery-Ronay neatly summarizes some of the characteristics of Latin American SF; he writes: "[S]f outside the US ... is more prone to social concreteness, to present-centeredness, to stylistic affectation reflecting psychological or literary complexity, and to a fatalism in the face of history."[18] The tendency toward present-centered narratives goes hand-in-hand with a less optimistic historical outlook. Luis Cano has discussed these tendencies in Latin American SF in detail, contrasting the more linear, future-centric SF of the North with Latin American SF's greater focus on an uncertain present and the history that led to it, and tracing "the progressive extinction of the optimistic vision of a future filled with promises and possibilities for change."[19] This pessimism stems both from diminishing hopes that change could be brought about in Latin America through the development and control of technology

---

[15] Pepe Rojo, "Desperately Looking for Others," *Los Angeles Review of Books* 24 (May 2016), lareviewofbooks.org/article/desperately-looking-others (last accessed May 29, 2018).

[16] See Rachel Haywood Ferreira, *Emergence* and "How Latin America Saved the World and Other Forgotten Futures," *Science Fiction Studies* 43, 2 (2016), pp. 207–25.

[17] See Yolanda Molina-Gavilán, *Ciencia ficción en español: Una mitología moderna ante el cambio* (Lewiston, NY: Edwin Mellen, 2002), p. 44.

[18] Istvan Csicsery-Ronay, "The Global Province (Review)," *Science Fiction Studies* 26, 3 (1999), p. 484.

[19] Cano, *Intermitente recurrencia*, p. 72.

and, in the political arena, from continuing local and global oppressions and inequalities. This is not to say that there is no optimism in Latin American SF, indeed there are periods that lean towards optimism, and these periods tend to parallel periods of greater optimism in Northern SF in response to global events (see the next section for further discussion). However, in a region that has a history of hard-won fights for independence, ongoing national power struggles, and economic dependence, attitudes toward the future are less sanguine. Since these populations have historically been witnesses rather than actors when it comes to reaping any economic benefits of technology or participating in political negotiations that have shaped the world, it is not surprising that the historical outlook and the SF might trend less optimistic than those of Latin America's Northern neighbors.

The tendency toward social concreteness in Latin American SF is in large part a result of the aforementioned "ever-present concern with meeting essential human needs" in a region where these needs are immediate and pressing. One corollary of this tendency is that Latin American SF is often more overtly political than SF in the North. National politics are a frequent theme, including explorations and denunciations of abuses of power and corruption, and a frequent subtext is the struggle to establish national identity, and to maintain that identity in the face of Northern political, economic, and cultural influence. SF has proved an excellent vehicle for negotiating these issues: looking backward to consider the legacies of discovery, conquest, and colonization,[20] and looking at the present day or extrapolations therefrom to attack neoimperialism and neocolonialism in all of their forums, from politics to big business and consumer culture.[21]

The stylistic emphasis that has been noted in Latin American SF can be explained from two somewhat overlapping perspectives. From one approach Latin American SF is seen as more literary, as more closely linked to mainstream literature than its Northern counterpart, particularly in times when canonical literature put a premium on literary experimentation and complexity, for example during modernism and the Boom. An alternate focus views even Latin American SF that is consciously written as genre fiction as more

---

[20] See Rachel Haywood Ferreira, "Second Contact: The First Contact Story in Latin American Science Fiction," in Brian Attebery and Veronica Hollinger, eds., *Parabolas of Science Fiction* (Middletown, CT: Wesleyan University Press, 2013), pp. 70–88 and Andrea L. Bell and Yolanda Molina-Gavilán, eds., "Introduction," in *Cosmos Latinos: An Anthology of Science Fiction from Latin America and Spain* (Middletown, CT: Wesleyan University Press, 2003), p. 17.
[21] Andrea Bell, "Science Fiction in Latin America: Reawakenings," *Science Fiction Studies*, 26, 3 (1999), p. 443.

literary than Northern SF because of the relative absence of a pulp tradition in Latin America and of US pulp influence in the region.

Some of the other characteristics that have been used to describe Latin American SF include the incorporation of Latin American myths, both myths originally associated with Latin America by European colonizers (El Dorado, Atlantis) and myths born in the new world (the "City of the Caesars" in Chile; Brazilian cultural myths such as Brazil as tropical paradise and racial democracy; foundational myths such as La Malinche in Mexico).[22] Latin American SF is also inclined toward urban settings, stemming from settlement patterns in colonial times as well as internal migrations and the ensuing associations of cities as focal points of national life and culture; this stands in marked contrast, for example, to the trope of the frontier and the value placed on individualism in US SF.[23] The challenges of print publication and the relatively smaller market share for SF in Latin America have also impacted the genre, leading to a prevalence of short stories over longer fiction or multi-volume works. This has also meant that the Internet and electronic media have been an especially important development for Latin American writers and fans, easing the process of getting one's work published, fostering writer and fan communities, and facilitating the continued publication of fanzines and prozines that otherwise might be forced by standard costs or hyperinflation to join the throng of SF magazines in Latin America that have folded after only a handful of issues.

If there is one characteristic of Latin American SF that is universally recognized, it is the significant influence of Northern SF on the genre in the region, but that influence, as well as the global nature of the genre itself, has been understood in various ways. Latin American SF has often been described as a synthesis of North–South inputs, a synthesis expressed by Sergio Gaut vel Hartman as "mestización a la fuerza" [forced hybridization],[24] or by Ivan Carlos Regina and others in terms of a Southern "antropofagia" [cannibalism] of Northern tropes.[25] Some consider Northern SF to be the major influence on

---

[22] See Bell and Hassón, "Prelude to the Golden Age," p. 292; M. Elizabeth Ginway, *Brazilian Science Fiction: Cultural Myth and Nationhood in the Land of the Future* (Lewisburg, PA: Bucknell University Press, 2004), p. 16; M. Elizabeth Ginway, "A Working Model for Analyzing Third World Science Fiction: The Case of Brazil," *Science Fiction Studies*, 32, 3 (2005), p. 489.

[23] See Ginway, *Brazilian Science Fiction*, p. 23.

[24] Sergio Gaut vel Hartman, "Prólogo" (Prologue) in Uribe, ed., *Latinoamérica fantástica*, p. 11.

[25] See Ivan Carlos Regina, "Manifesto Antropofágico da Ficção Científica Brasileira – Movimento Supernova" (Cannibal Manifesto of Brazilian Science Fiction) [1988] *D. O. Leitura* 12, 138 (1993), p. 8; Ginway, *Brazilian Science Fiction*, pp. 139–43.

Latin American SF writers; others view the influence from the Latin American literary canon and mainstream as predominant. The type and degree of influence vary across countries, time periods, and individual authors and continue to be an issue of cultural politics and debate.

SF as a genre clearly has its historical roots and traditional stronghold in the North; however, it is increasingly being recognized that SF has been and is being written all over the world, and it bears mentioning how Latin American SF functions within this global genre paradigm. Latin American writers and texts certainly participate in and belong to the genre, and Latin American SF has important contributions in perspective, theme, and content to make to the genre as a whole. The missing piece is the actual sharing of these contributions, integrating them into the SF megatext, since influence has historically been primarily a one-way street. A central challenge is the dearth of translations of Latin American SF into other languages.[26] It is notable that (eventual) translation of SF is assumed or considered likely from North-to-South, but that Latin American SF is written for a national audience,[27] with South-to-North translation *not* assumed to be in the picture and multilingual readers from outside the Spanish-speaking world far from the norm. In 2000 Gabriel Trujillo Muñoz asserted Mexican SF's achievement of a conscious and distinct identity within the global SF movement, and he followed that assertion with a call for his fellow writers to contribute to a greater degree of much-needed transculturation within the genre as a whole:

> Not to accept, passively, the fashionable trends of the dominant culture without contributing new ideas and concepts that impact it in the opposite direction: from the periphery to the center. This attitude is a point of departure for national science fiction on the verge of the twenty-first century. Not remaining on the local stage repeating imported designs, but using that which is local to build a creative platform that resounds at the Latin American level, at the international level.[28]

The awareness of the need for a genre that better reflects global diversity exists, but in order to achieve this the North needs to have access to and to understand what the South has to say.

---

[26] The landmark *Cosmos Latinos* anthology edited by Bell and Molina-Gavilán has all too little company in the Anglophone arena, for example.

[27] See J. Andrew Brown and M. Elizabeth Ginway, "Introduction," in J. Andrew Brown and M. Elizabeth Ginway, eds., *Latin American Science Fiction: Theory and Practice* (New York: Palgrave Macmillan, 2012), p. 10 and Ginway, *Brazilian Science Fiction*, pp. 247–8, n. 194.

[28] Trujillo Muñoz, *Biografías del futuro*, pp. 355–6.

Making Waves

As with Northern SF, the history of Latin American SF can be described in waves. While Northern SF trends have played a role in the formation of these waves, there are many other elements that affect the evolution of the genre in Latin America. The catalysts that spark trends and turning points in the genre in Latin America are international and regional, broad and narrow: political events and scientific developments; literary trends, individual or groups of writers, even single works; changes in the market from the rise of genre magazines to the emergence of genre publishers or imprints; literary prizes, symposia, and fan clubs that foster genre identity and cohesion. Each country in Latin America traces its local history with the genre differently, but some general trends and commonalities have emerged that may provide both useful indicators of larger regional orientations and a contextual backdrop against which individual cases may be viewed.

The long nineteenth century

Latin American SF written during this time period was scattered between countries and within the oeuvres of writers. There were no local schools or communities of SF, and connections to the genre were through Northern works rather than intra-Latin American influence. Among the impulses that turned writers toward the emerging genre and influenced their choice and use of science-fictional tropes were, in the political arena, national independences and processes of consolidation, and the ongoing construction of national identities. The sciences were also extremely influential, as in the nineteenth century, "The obsolete legal discourse of Spanish colonization was replaced by scientific discourse as the authoritative language of knowledge, self-knowledge, and legitimation."[29] The long nineteenth century encompasses the heights of positivistic technophilia, during which it seemed possible that the giant strides forward in transportation, communication, medicine, and more might leapfrog Latin America toward the forefront of the world stage, as well as the ensuing technophobic lows, when science failed to fulfill its earlier promise in sufficient measure. In literary circles, translations of the works of Edgar Allan Poe, Jules Verne, H. G. Wells, and other writers of early SF arrived with little delay in Latin America, where they mingled with the national foundational fictions being written across the region. Science fictional works were published in newspapers, in mainstream

---

[29] Roberto González Echevarría, *Myth and Archive: A Theory of Latin American Narrative* (Durham, NC: Duke University Press, 1998), p. 103.

magazines, or by mainstream publishers as one-offs or as part of the body of an established writer's works. Popular themes and tropes included fantastic journeys in space and time, usually utopian or dystopian in nature; tales influenced by theories of evolution and also devolution and eugenics; the creation of artificial life; and the importance of alternative as well as orthodox sciences, particularly during Spanish American modernism. Among the principal authors of this period are Juana Manuela Gorriti, Eduardo L. Holmberg, and Leopoldo Lugones in Argentina; Joaquim Manuel de Macedo and Aluísio Azevedo in Brazil; Francisco Miralles in Chile; Pedro Castera, Amado Nervo, and Martín Luis Guzmán in Mexico; Clemente Palma in Peru; Horacio Quiroga in Uruguay and Argentina.[30]

Between the wars (c.1920 to early 1950s)

In a wave schema of Latin American SF this time period forms something of a trough, although it includes a number of writers and texts that are landmarks in the genre. SF ebbs during these decades in part owing to the continued popularity of realism in the wake of the impact of phenomena like the Mexican Revolution and the Great Depression. There was not a significant pulp era in Latin American SF, nor were there genre magazines or editors like Hugo Gernsback or John W. Campbell around whom the genre could coalesce.[31] This period is one of relative hibernation for SF in Latin America,[32] with genre elements dissolving into the mainstream, particularly into works of fantastic or "adventure" fiction. Major writers include: Borges and Bioy Casares in Argentina; Gastão Cruls, Monteiro Lobato, and Menotti del Picchia in Brazil; Francisco Urquizo and Diego Cañedo in Mexico. We also see the emergence of a few forebears of genre SF such as Jerônimo Monteiro in Brazil and Ernesto Silva Román in Chile.

---

[30] For fuller details of authors and works for all time periods see Yolanda Molina-Gavilán, Andrea Bell, Miguel Ángel Fernández Delgado, M. Elizabeth Ginway, Luis Pestarini, and Juan Carlos Toledano Redondo, "Chronology of Latin American Science Fiction, 1775–2005," *Science Fiction Studies* 34, 3 (2007), pp. 369–431, and the Latin American entries in the John Clute, David Langford, Peter Nicholls, and Graham Sleight, eds., *Encyclopedia of Science Fiction*, www.sf-encyclopedia.com; for more on the long nineteenth century, see the contents and bibliography of Haywood Ferreira, *Emergence*. A very useful source for this section has also been Roberto de Sousa Causo, "Uma sistematização histórica dos períodos e tendências da ficção científica brasileira, do século XIX ao presente" (A Historical Systematization of the Periods and Tendencies of Brazilian Science Fiction, from the Nineteenth Century to the Present), unpublished manuscript.
[31] See Bell, "Science Fiction in Latin America," p. 441 and Sousa Causo, *Ficção científica*, pp. 233–93.
[32] Cano, *Intermitente recurrencia*, pp. 149–50.

The Golden Age (mid-1950s to c.1970)

The SF of this time period in Latin America is commonly referred to as Golden Age SF, genre SF, or modern SF. It is now that writers are first identifying themselves as genre authors writing as part of an identifiable movement in Latin America and/or in individual countries. The beginning of this wave is usually dated by the publication of the novel *Los Altísimos* (The Superior Ones) by Chilean writer Hugo Correa in 1959, the Argentine magazine *Más Allá* (Beyond) (1953–7), or the original *El Eternauta* (The Eternaut) comic by H. G. Oesterheld and Francisco Solano-López (1957–9), and by political phenomena such as the Cuban Revolution and the Cold War. The ending of the Golden Age is usually associated with the Moon landing, with the growing tide of social and political movements, both local and global, and with increasingly repressive dictatorial governments in Latin America. This era combines the optimism of the space race and the possibilities of atomic energy with the flip-side pessimism of ICBMs and the atomic bomb. The 1950s is largely a decade of unabashed technophilia and a rise in hard SF in Latin America, but the next decades criticize the 1950s SF for its "optimistic attitude toward the use of science, for its vision of a better future when the evidence against this is accumulating before our very eyes."[33] The 1960s and 1970s see increasing pessimism with regard to technology and growing interest in the social sciences, social problems, and softer SF along with stylistic experimentation, as discussed above. The SF marketplace experiences a mini-boom during this time period. We see the rise of genre magazines that include stories by local writers for the first time, for example: *Más Allá* and *Minotauro* (Minotaur) in Argentina, *Crononauta* (Crononaut) in Mexico, the *Magazine de Ficção Científica* (Magazine of Science Fiction) in Brazil, and *Espacio-tiempo* (Space-Time) in Chile. Influential genre publishers and imprints emerge, such as Francisco (Paco) Porrúa at Ediciones Minotauro in Argentina and Gumercindo Rocha Dorea and his Edições GRD in Brazil, and anthologies of national and international Latin American SF appear in ever greater profusion. All of this activity gives rise to the first SF fan clubs; to several national and international symposia and conventions (in Argentina Bairescon [1967] and Mardelcon [1968] and in Brazil the Simpósio de FC/SF Symposium [1969]); and to the first works of SF criticism written in Latin America, most famously Pablo Capanna's *El sentido de la ciencia ficción* (The Meaning of Science Fiction) (1966) and André Carneiro's *Introdução ao Estudo da "Science*

---

[33] Trujillo Muñoz, *Biografías*, p. 345.

Fiction" (Introduction to the Study of "Science Fiction") (1967), both of which, however, focus largely on Anglophone SF. Latin American SF writers that emerge in these years include: H. G. Oesterheld and Angélica Gorodischer in Argentina; continued production by Jerônimo Monteiro plus new authors André Carneiro, Fausto Cunha, Dinah Silveira de Queiroz, and Rubens Teixeira Scavone in Brazil; Hugo Correa in Chile; Ángel Arango, Óscar Hurtado, and Miguel Collazo in Cuba; Álvaro Menén Desleal in El Salvador; Arreola, Diego Cañedo, Colombian-born René Rebetez, Chilean-born Alejandro Jodorowsky, and Carlos Olvera in Mexico; José Adolph in Peru; Luis Britto García in Venezuela, and numerous others.

The Slump (1970s to mid-1980s)

Almost across the board Latin American SF experiences a slowdown during some or all of this time period, primarily as a result of the rise of repressive political regimes and widespread economic instability and social unrest. Beleaguered publishers tend to stick to safer bestseller-type works. Paradoxically, however, SF is able to survive because its reputation as a popular, marginal genre makes government censors believe it to be less of a threat; SF is also employed by genre and mainstream writers to disguise politically sensitive ideas.[34] Some of the principal authors in the genre continue to write SF, and important new authors emerge, among them Gorodischer and Carlos Gardini in Argentina; Carneiro, Cunha, Herberto Sales, and Ignácio de Loyola Brandão in Brazil; Correa and Elena Aldunate in Chile; Arango in Cuba; Cañedo and Costa Rica-born Alfredo Cardona Peña in Mexico; Adolph in Peru; Tarik Carson in Uruguay. This was a period of continued stylistic experimentation, with popular themes including dystopia, apocalypse, and allegorized political critiques.[35]

Revivals (mid-1980s to the present)

At least two waves of SF have emerged in Latin America in recent years, one beginning in the mid-1980s and another around 2000, with many writers from both generations continuing to publish today. The first surge in SF occurred as many Latin American nations transitioned from dictatorship to democracy. Latin American SF from this period shows an increase in local settings, characters, and perspectives, with the priority for a Latin American and/or

---

[34] For more see Bell and Molina-Gavilán, "Introduction," pp. 9–10 and Capanna, *El mundo*, pp. 184–5.
[35] Sousa Causo, "Uma sistematização," n.p.

national SF crystalizing in places such as Regina's "Cannibal Manifesto of Brazilian Science Fiction," Brazilian cyberpunk or *tupinipunk*,[36] and nationally and regionally themed anthologies. Fan organizations proliferate, as do magazines and fanzines of increasing longevity, particularly after the advent of the Internet; among the publications in Argentina alone are: *El Péndulo* (Pendulum) (second period), *Minotauro* (second period), *Sinergia* (Synergy), *Cuásar* (Quasar), and *Axxón* (est. 1989, 276 issues and 42 million views and counting). New literary prizes such as the Premio David in Cuba, the Premio Más Allá in Argentina, and the Premio Puebla in Mexico are also a major stimulus for the resurgence in SF. There is something of a sea change in Latin American SF around the turn of the millennium, with the emergence of a new generation of writers who draw inspiration from currents like cyberpunk and post-cyberpunk, steampunk, the New Weird, and genre fusions, especially with horror. The genre has also received increasing scholarly attention in the first two decades of the twenty-first century both in Latin America and in the North, though institutional support and acceptance has been slower to come in Latin America. Important initial groundwork has been laid in the publication of bibliographies, genre histories, and theoretical studies of Latin American SF: guidebooks and compasses for a field that is rapidly coming into its own. If SF has yet not broken out of the genre ghetto and gained broader acceptance in Latin America, and if Northern SF influences remain important, still, SF in Latin America is self-sustaining and it has achieved a sense of national and regional identity in the twenty-first century. A necessarily truncated list of writers from this period includes: Gardini, Marcelo Cohen, and Alejandro Alonso in Argentina; Jorge Luiz Calife, Braulio Tavares, Roberto de Sousa Causo, Gerson Lodi-Ribeiro, and Ana Cristina Rodrigues in Brazil; Jorge Baradit and US–Argentine Mike Wilson in Chile; Daína Chaviano and Yoss (José Miguel Sánchez Gómez) in Cuba; Gabriel Trujillo Muñoz, José Luis Zárate, Pepe Rojo, and Bef (Bernardo Fernández) in Mexico.

What SF Brings to Latin America and What Latin America Brings to SF

SF is often touted for its ability to help Latin American writers think outside boxes. This ability is often expressed in terms of freedoms, albeit

---

[36] A term coined by Roberto de Sousa Causo; see Ginway, *Brazilian Science Fiction*, pp. 151–65.

largely the mixed-blessing freedoms of the outsider: freedom from the norms of regional sociopolitical dialogues, freedom from the limitations of national literary and cultural expectations, freedom from SF genre expectations, and even the greater freedom to innovate of the writer who does not make a living from his/her craft.[37] SF is also seen as an instrument for bringing about national and regional change and as a tool for understanding Latin America's uneven modernity, both by evaluating the social impact of modernization projects[38] and in its role as "a catalyst for all of these contradictory realities, as a fermenter of the chaos that obsesses us."[39] In addition to the initial divergence between mainstream and genre writers, a diversity of perspectives exists within the genre itself. M. Elizabeth Ginway identifies three main ideological groups, for example, in the Brazilian SF community, "those who believe in the universalist principles of science fiction, those who believe that science fiction should adopt the principles of high art and literary experimentalism, and those who believe in a distinct nationalist contribution of Brazilian science fiction."[40] In the end, what SF brings to Latin America can be different for different people.

The Global South and the economic periphery have contributed to the SF megatext for over a century and have an important role to play. As a genre associated with the Global North, SF can suffer from what Capanna has aptly described as "the incapacity, characteristic of all imperial centers in history, to understand what occurs far from the center of power, or how those who live in the periphery think."[41] The economic periphery is one place to turn in searching for renewal, revision, and extension of the SF megatext. Latin America brings an infusion of new regional and local myths, of cultures and cultural fusions, of literary traditions and hybrid formations, of linguistic variety. It provides alternate experiences of encounter, colonization, and independence from which to write, as well as explorations into measures of

[37] See Kurlat Ares, "Argentinean Science Fiction," p. 8; Molina-Gavilán et al., "Chronology," p. 369; A. E. van Vogt, "Prólogo" (Prologue), in Bernard Goorden and A. E. van Vogt, eds., *Lo mejor de la ciencia ficción latinoamericana* (The Best of Latin American Science Fiction) (Barcelona: Ediciones Martínez Roca, 1982), p. 11.

[38] Cano, *Intermitente*, p. 23.

[39] Gabriel Trujillo Muñoz, "*El futuro en llamas*: Breve crónica de la ciencia ficción mexicana" (The Burning Future: A Brief Chronicle of Mexican Science Fiction), in Gabriel Trujillo Muñoz, ed., *El futuro en llamas* (The Burning Future) (Mexico City: Vid, 1997), p. 26.

[40] Ginway, *Brazilian Science Fiction*, p. 141.

[41] "Entrevista con Pablo Capanna (Interview by Eduardo Carletti)," *Axxón*, 106 (2000), axxon.com.ar (last accessed Sepetember 16, 2016).

superiority or success that lie outside the hard sciences. Latin American SF brings the genre new stories and just plain more stories. With all that Latin American SF has to say, it is earnestly to be hoped that publication, translation, and distribution continue to increase, enabling it to be heard better at home and abroad.

42

Science Fiction and the Global South

HUGH CHARLES O'CONNELL

There's a specter haunting Western SF, and that specter is the Global South. Today, SF from the Global South is a fast-growing field in both production and critical studies of SF – but European and American SF has *always* been haunted by the Global South. For example, Mark Bould traces the history of Africa's representation in the roots of Western SF to Jules Verne in 1863, while also making the case for African SF's own sporadic but increasing development across the twentieth century.[1] Similarly, Debajani Sengupta frames the history of Bengali SF from 1882 to 1974 as "a myth formation of the new industrial age."[2] Indeed, SF has such a long and abiding presence in the Global South that its tropes have seeped into the literary mainstream with, among many others, Salman Rushdie's *Grimus* (1975), Nadine Gordimer's *July's People* (1981), Ben Okri's *The Famished Road* (1991), and Amitav Ghosh's Clarke Award winner, *The Calcutta Chromosome* (1995). SF as a putatively Western genre – "as Western as Coca Cola," as Uppinder Mehan once quipped – has thus always been haunted by the alter-trajectories and histories provided by Global South SF, just as the Global South has often functioned (as critics like John Rieder and Patricia Kerslake have argued) as the spectral Other against which the techno-rational SF imagination pits itself.[3] Rather than repeat this critical work, this chapter focuses instead on the advent of a fully realized Global South SF in the twenty-first century as part of the global turn in SF production and consumption, marking the advent of a true "World SF," in Lavie Tidhar's terms.[4]

---

[1] Mark Bould, "Introduction: Africa SF," *Paradoxa* 25 (2013), p. 25.

[2] Debajani Sengupta, "Sadhanbabu's Friends: Science Fiction in Bengal from 1882 to 1974," in Ericka Hoagland and Reema Sarwal, eds., *Science Fiction, Imperialism and the Third World: Essays on Postcolonial Literature and Film* (Jefferson, NC: McFarland, 2010), p. 115.

[3] Uppinder Mehan, "The Domestication of Technology in Indian Science Fiction Short Stories," *Foundation* 74 (1998), p. 54.

[4] Tidhar dates the advent of a true world SF to the 2005 publication of *Internova*, produced by international writers themselves, rather than by Anglo-American editors and authors,

The reasons for the recent growth of Global South SF in the twenty-first century include a number of overlapping and co-determining factors at the cultural, formal-aesthetic, and political levels. The globalization and popularization of SF has led to a change in genre producers' and consumers' demographics. Rieder remarks that the "steady displacement of the white male SF community's centrality to the SF subculture by more and more writers and readers marked by gender and racial difference" follows its rise from a niche to a mass cultural dominant.[5] Moreover, this culturally ascendant SF and its imbrication with globalization and neoimperialism are related to changes in the formal-aesthetics of postcolonial literature. For example, Eric D. Smith argues that magical realism gives way to SF as the dominant non-mimetic form in contemporary postcolonial literatures, marking the transition from colonialism to full globalization,[6] a shift that similarly marks the advent of the Global South as a socio-political concept.

In terms of genre, however, Global South SF doesn't often hew closely to strict definitions. It eschews the rigidity of Western niche market-driven distinctions by drawing on different "ontological motivations,"[7] and often utilizes a more do-it-yourself approach to publishing by taking advantage of digital platforms and smaller presses. As Chinelo Onwualu, author and co-editor of *Omenana*, a prominent venue for African genre fiction, attests: "*Omenana* doesn't really conform to some of the rigid conceptions of genre that are evident in Western markets. Because here magic and the supernatural are not discrete entities, the line between fantasy and reality is often nonexistent. However, while genre is often a largely marketing concept, there is a clear line between what we know as realistic fiction . . . and the speculative."[8]

In order to delimit this expansive and growing body of SF, then, this chapter primarily considers twenty-first-century Global South SF from Africa, the Middle East, and the Indian subcontinent. Rather than offering a comprehensive overview of each one of these locations, it highlights key thematic and historical points of reference for the development of Global South SF, as well as significant authors and anthologies, with particular

---

be they well-meaning or looking to "drink in exotic locales." Lavie Tidhar, "The Aliens Won: SF Around the World and Back Again," *World Literature Today* 84, 3 (2010), p. 39.

[5] Although his reference points are to North American SF and especially indigenous SF and Afrofuturism, these ideas can be generalized to the global expansion of SF. John Rieder, *Science Fiction and the Mass Cultural Genre System* (Middletown, CT: Wesleyan University Press, 2017), p. 139.

[6] Eric D. Smith, *Globalization, Utopia, and Postcolonial SF* (London: Palgrave, 2012), pp. 9–12.

[7] Istvan Csicsery-Ronay, "What Do We Mean When We Say 'Global Science Fiction'? Reflections on a New Nexus," *Science Fiction Studies* 39, 3 (2013), p. 481.

[8] Personal email correspondence, March 14, 2017.

attention paid to Africa as the largest growth area. This approach is in no way meant to efface the very real social, historical, cultural, and political differences that proliferate within each region, let alone across them. Instead, it is meant to highlight the strategies that this wider body of Global South SF employs in its often-fraught relationship to the advent of global modernity.

What unites the SF of the Global South perhaps more than other traits is its decentering of the West as the singular site and progenitor of futurity. Global South SF places its own original and striking futures – utopian, dystopian, ambiguous, and/or ambivalent – at the center of its SF worldbuilding. As Ivor Hartmann, the editor of *AfroSF*, the first anthology dedicated solely to SF written by Africans, writes:

> SciFi is the only genre that enables African writers to envision a future from our African perspective. Moreover, it does this in a way that is not purely academic and so provides a vision that is readily understandable through a fictional context. The value of this envisioning for any third-world country, or in our case continent, cannot be overstated nor negated. If you can't see and relay an understandable vision of the future, your future will be co-opted by someone else's vision, one that will not necessarily have your best interests at heart.[9]

This decentering often takes place alongside a postcolonial critique that interrogates SF's relationship to technoscience, for example, critiquing technoscience's relationship to capitalist neoimperialism and forms of modernization and development predicated on environmental degradation, racism, sexism, imperialism, and instrumentalization. As such, Global South SF often engages with the legacies of imperialism (classical and neo-) that have made the Global South the purview of what Kodwo Eshun calls the Western "futures industry," that is, a site of perpetual dystopia that needs the investment of the West to secure and direct its future.[10]

Gulf Futurism, the Iraq Wars, and the Arab Spring

One of the key movements in Middle Eastern and Arabic SF is the Gulf Futurism aesthetic, coined by Sophia Al Maria in "The Gaze of Sci-fi Wahabi," and spread by tech and culture magazines like *Dazed*,[11] *Bidoun*,

[9] Ivor Hartmann, "Introduction," in Ivor Hartmann, ed., *Afro SF: Science Fiction by African Writers* (Story Time Press, 2012), p. 7.
[10] Kodwo Eshun, "Further Considerations on Afrofuturism," *CR: The New Centennial Review* 3,2 (2003), p. 290.
[11] See especially: Karen Orton, "The Desert of the Unreal," *Dazed*, 2012, www.dazeddigital .com/artsandculture/article/15040/1/the-desert-of-the-unreal (last accessed May 15, 2017).

and Bruce Sterling's columns for *Wired*. It's a thoroughly postmodern aesthetic that draws on influences from Jean Baudrillard to Philip K. Dick and juxtaposes the oil-fueled high-tech, consumerist modernization of Middle Eastern cities with desertscapes, rural villages, traditional elements of Islamic culture, and the futurological destruction wrought by the video game logic of the Gulf wars. Like many late capitalist aesthetics, it contrasts images of uneven development, rampant wealth and social inequality, political exclusion and repression, and the cross-cutting of traditionalism with libertarian hypermodernism. Its influence can be found in the music and videos of Fatima Al Qadiri, urban planning and development in Dubai, the planned utopia of Masdar City,[12] and the recent, largely dystopian and surreal speculative and SF literary output of authors like Ahmed Khaled Towfik, Nael Eltoukhy, Mohammad Rabie, Basma Abdel Aziz, and Ahmed Naji from Egypt, Ahmed Saadawi and Hassan Blasim from Iraq, and the Bangladeshi author Saad Z. Hossain.

The Invasion of Iraq provides the backdrop for Saad Z. Hossain's *Escape from Baghdad!* (2012), a brisk, surreal farce that follows the travails of two Iraqi black marketers in league with a former Ba'athist torturer and a member of the US military as they seek to escape arrest in Baghdad and recover a forgotten treasure in Mosul. However, the novel slowly morphs into an investigation of one of the oldest SF tropes: transcending the human–god barrier and creating eternal life. As contemporary gulf futurist SF, the novel draws on a rich array of Druze theology, the history of Arabic alchemy and science, and contemporary transhumanism intermixed with direct references to *Frankenstein* and *The Island of Dr. Moreau*, all set against the backdrop of contemporary post-invasion Iraq. A different take on the Frankensteinian motif is offered by Ahmed Saadawi's *Frankenstein in Baghdad* (2014/2018), winner of the 2014 International Prize for Arabic Fiction. In this novel, a body assembled from fragments of bomb victims comes to life and takes revenge upon the perpetrators of the bombings.

The works collected in *Iraq + 100*, conceived and edited by the Iraqi author and filmmaker Hassan Blasim, forgo the present in order to imagine a future Iraq 100 years after the start of the 2003 invasion. Blasim first came to attention with his deeply surreal and absurdist speculative story collections that have been republished as *The Corpse Exhibition* (2014). *Iraq + 100* draws on the extrapolative aspects of SF to not only reflect on the conditions of the

---

[12] See M. Irene Morrison's review of Towfik's *Utopia* and its relationship to the Masdar City project and issues related to gulf futurism more broadly in *Paradoxa* 27, 2nd edn. (2016), pp. 271–6.

present but also, as Fredric Jameson would put it, to create the present as the closed, mock past of some future possibility in order to restore a dimension of historicity.[13] As Blasim notes, the desire was that "writing about the future would give [the collection's authors] space to breathe outside the narrow confines of today's reality"[14] and "to imagine a Modern Iraq that has some-how recovered from the West's brutal invasion."[15] Despite its deep roots in Arabic culture, including some of the first depictions of other planets and space travel in Sumerian, Assyrian, and Egyptian classical texts, Blasim argues that SF is a largely absent genre in contemporary Iraqi and more generally Arabic literature due to cultural and political constraints.[16] This view is shared by the Egyptian writer Ahmed Khaled Towfik, author of *Utopia* and often heralded as "the Arab world's first author to pen horror and science fiction thrillers."[17] Thus *Iraq + 100* represents the first collection of its kind from the Middle East and has prompted Comma Press to begin work on a similar Palestinian volume, *Nakba + 100*.

The stories collected in *Iraq + 100* are nearly all stylistically strong examples of original contemporary SF. However, notwithstanding the utopian note struck by the introduction, many of the stories are ambivalent or even pessimistic about the future. Anoud's "Kahramana" finds a woman refugee trapped in an Iraq that is divided between the "Islamic Empire of Wadi Hashish" and the "American Annex of Sulaymania," neither offering freedom or respite. Blasim's "The Gardens of Babylon" presents an Iraq that has escaped "the violence [of] the age of oil and religious extremism"[18] to create a new Babylon. This digitech "playground," developed on an ideology of "creative freedom," ushers in a new era of "peace and prosperity through imagination."[19] Yet, climate change has created a water crisis, and water slowly replaces oil as the engine of a violence the narrator had hoped his country had escaped.

---

[13] Fredric Jameson, *Archaeologies of the Future: The Desire called Utopia and other Science Fictions* (London: Verso, 2005), p. 288.

[14] Hassan Blasim, "Foreword," *Iraq + 100* (Manchester: Comma Press, 2016), p. v.

[15] Ibid., p. vii.

[16] For a longer history, see Ada Barbaro, *La fantascienza nella letteratura araba* (Science Fiction in Arabic Literature), (Roma: Carocci Editore, 2013).

[17] Hala Khalaf, "Emirates Lit Fest 2017: Egyptian author Ahmed Khaled Towfik on the Dissemination of Arabic Science Fiction," *The National*, 8 March 2017, www.thenational .ae/arts-life/emirates-airline-festival-of-literature/emirates-lit-fest-2017-egyptian-author-ah med-khaled-towfik-on-the-dissemination-of-arabic-science-fiction (last accessed May 17, 2017).

[18] "The Gardens of Baylon," in *Iraq + 100*, p. 13.

[19] Ibid. pp. 11, 12.

In a more utopian register, Ali Bader's "The Corporal" revisits the conventions of classical utopias like Edward Bellamy's *Looking Backward* (1888) by having a soldier who was killed in "the American War" in 2003 sent back to his home of Kut 100 years later to discover it a renewed, secular, technological, and ecological paradise rather than "choked with dust and flies" as he remembered it.[20] In a nod to a number of Global South SF texts' ironic reversals in which the ill conditions of the Global South are cast onto the West – perhaps most identified with Abdourahman Waberi's utopian satire *In the United States of Africa* (2006/2009) – it is now the United States that is torn apart by fundamentalist religious violence, and owing to the narrator's religious inclinations, he is arrested as an illegal refugee. A similar reversal animates Ibrahim al-Marashi's pilgrimage narrative "Najufa," in which advanced AI and robotic technology allow for a grandfather and his son to return to the holy sites of a now peaceful Iraq, while the United States splinters under Christian sectarian violence. Still other stories like Zhraa Alhaboby's "Baghdad Syndrome," Diaa Jubaili's "The Worker," and Khalid Kaki's "Operation Daniel" represent a desire to recover what has been lost by the successive wars and corrupt governments before it is sold to foreign governments and antique collectors, destroyed in a cultural revolution, or more metaphorically lost as people go blind from the "Baghdad Syndrome" as a result of chemical exposure from the US–UK invasion.

Although Blasim laments the relative lack of an SF tradition in contemporary Arabic literature, there is a trend of Egyptian dystopia related to the Arab Spring: Ahmed Khaled Towfik's *Utopia* (2008/2011), Nael Eltoukhy's *Women of Karantina* (2013/2014), Basma Abdel Aziz's *The Queue* (2013/2016), Mohammad Rabie's *Otared* (2014/2016), and Ahmed Naji's *Using Life* (2014/2017). These novels imagine a near future wherein privation and immiseration are met with indifference from the ruling elites. Moreover, the novels are often imbued with a laconic boredom and ennui. In Towfik's *Utopia*, slated to be filmed because of its immense popularity in Egypt, we find bored, hedonistic rich youths in a corporate-libertarian fortress who idle their days away in a haze of drugs, sex, rape, and violence. The story involves a proposed trip to kill one of the "Others" from the dystopian outside and collect their arm as a trophy. Although not as violent as Towfik's novel, Naji's *Using Life*, with a plot revolving around the Society of Urbanists and their manipulation of architecture as a form of social control, is similarly steeped in boredom, drugs, and sex. Aziz's *The Queue* forgoes the hedonism of these

---

[20] "The Corporal," in *Iraq + 100*, p. 52.

novels. However, its *Waiting-for-Godot*-meets-*We* dystopian narrative presents life at a standstill, with an ever-growing, permanent queue of citizens waiting for the "Gate" to open in order to apply for routine procedures. Personal electronic devices become modes of surveillance, and the micromanaging of all behavior works to dull agency and even mask complicity. What ties these works together most, though, as Mark Bould attests of Towfik's *Utopia*, is often their inability to "admit" or "countenance" a successful third worldist anti-imperial revolution.[21] Instead they focus attention on techno-utopia's inhuman inverse and the growing chasms that separate the haves from the have-nots in post-Arab Spring dystopias that are predicated on surveillance and other technoscientific aspects of control.

Indian SF

In a manner similar to Blasim, Indian SF author and editor Anil Menon has bemoaned the lack of originality in Indian SF, its imagination still enthralled by a colonial-era attachment to Western motifs.[22] At the same time, however, he points towards a "new era" of Indian SF authors producing original Indian SF that is aesthetically, culturally, and politically linked to contemporary conditions in the subcontinent, including Pradip Ghosh, Ashok Banker, Samit Basu, Priya Chabria, Abha Iyengar, Manjula Padmanabhan, Anushka Ravishankar, Anshumani Rudra, Pervin Saket, Vandana Singh, and Kaushik Vishwanathan. For Sami A. Khan, this new era includes a notable dystopian turn, seen most prominently in Rimi Chatterjee's *Signal Red* (2005) and Mainak Dhar's *Zombiestan* (2012), which "create dystopias indicting the distortions of religion," and Ruchir Joshi's *The Last Jet-Engine Laugh* (2001) and Shovon Chowdury's *The Competent Authority* (2013), which "portray dystopias that critique multiple aspects of a developing India."[23] Manish Jha's filmic dystopia *Matrubhoomi: A Nation Without Women* (2003) should also be added to this list.

Of these authors, the most well known within SF studies is Vandana Singh, author of the short story collection *The Woman Who Thought She Was a Planet*

[21] Mark Bould, "From Anti-Colonial Struggle to Neoliberal Immiseration: Mohammed Dib's *Who Remembers the Sea*, Sony Labou Tansi's *Life and a Half* and Ahmed Khaled Towfik's *Utopia*," *Paradoxa* 25 (2013), pp. 41–2.
[22] Anil Menon, "World-Building in a Hot Climate," *World SF Blog*, 12 May 2010. https://worldSF.wordpress.com/2010/05/12/original-content-world-building-in-a-hot-climate-by-anil-menon (last accessed May 17, 2017).
[23] Sami A. Khan, "The Others in India's Other Futures," *Science Fiction Studies* 43, 3 (2016), p. 479.

(2008), the novellas *Of Love and Other Monsters* (2007), and *Distances* (2008), and other uncollected short fiction. As Eric D. Smith essays in reference to *Love and Other Monsters*, part of the originality of Singh's fiction is that it "insists on themes of infinity, interdimensionality, and indeed, universality, frequently underpinned by a referential framework of mathematics."[24] These same issues permeate her short story "Life-pod"[25] (2007) and the novella *Distances* (2008) with their discoveries of a meta-universe underwriting our own. Both turn on the relationship between mathematics and art and on related issues of instrumentality versus a kind of neo-Kantian aesthetics of the free play of the imagination. Within these narratives, the imbrication of art and mathematics points towards the need for a "meta-language" beyond the "verbal or mathematical"[26] to represent the relationship between the recently discovered "meta-universe" and what we had traditionally experienced as the universe; or, to put it slightly differently, to map what amounts to the totality of reality. The advanced mathematics this requires is referred to as poetry. Yet in each story, the successful mapping carries the threat of destroying the artistry of the process through a creeping instrumentality and suggestions of capitalist competition to take advantage of the discovery.

In *Distances*, the beauty of mathematics as poetry is in its incompleteness, which renders a certain utopian possibility of difference as the very substance of the universal. The artistic mapping of hyperspace is thus simultaneously presented with a deeply disturbing complement in which the instrumentalization of nature contains the risk of turning "pathic" as a sick and totalizing rationality in Theodor Adorno's terms. To be sure, both narratives end on a reflective moment of undecidable possibility that echoes the very ambiguity and ambivalence of Global South SF itself, in which SF mediates the interminably intertwined narratives of modernization and rationality as well as radical utopian possibility under the real subsumption of global capitalism.

The African Genre Fiction Boom

Perhaps the greatest event undergirding the Global South SF boom is the recent explosion of African SF. One of the most striking features of Mark

---

[24] Eric D. Smith, "Universal Love and Planetary Ontology in Vandana Singh's *Of Love and Other Monsters*," *Science Fiction Studies* 43, 3 (2016), p. 515.

[25] Vandana Singh, "Life-pod," in Bill Campbell and Edward Austin Hall, eds., *Mothership: Tales from Afrofuturism and Beyond* (College Park, MD: Rosarium Publishing, 2013), pp. 111–19.

[26] "Life-pod," in *Mothership*, p. 115

Bould's list of indigenous African SF from the twentieth century is the amount stemming from mainstream or literary writers, including Mohammad Dib, Sony Labou Tansi, Ngũgĩ wa Thiong'o, Ben Okri, Buchi Emecheta, and Ousmane Sembene, among others.[27] This highlights the significance of SF within African literature, while also drawing attention to the lack of a distinguishable genre tradition prior to the twenty-first century.

As is perhaps fitting for laying the foundations of an SF genre movement, much of the production has taken place in the form of short stories in anthologies like *AfroSF: Science Fiction by African Writers Vol. 1* (2013), *Lagos 2060: Exciting Sci-Fi Stories from Nigeria* (2013), *AfroSF: 5 Novellas Vol. 2* (2015), *Terra Incognita: New Short Speculative Stories from Africa* (2015), and *Imagine Africa 500* (2016); the founding of new African genre-specific magazines like *Omenana* and *Jungle Jim*; African literary blogs like *Brittle Paper* and genre-specific special issues of African literary journals such as *Jalada's* "Afrofuture(s)" (2015); and the increasing publication of stories in SF venues (both print and web) like *Expanded Horizons, Lightspeed, Tor.com, Strange Horizons, Clarkesworld, Interzone, Apex Magazine,* and *The Manchester Review* 18, among others. Across these various venues, a number of authors have or are beginning to rise to prominence, including Lesley Arimah, Lauren Beukes, Mame Bougouma Diene, Dilman Dila, Stephen Embleton, Ivor Hartmann, Tendai Huchu, Sarah Lotz, Biram Mboob, Dayo Ntwari, Chiagozie Fred Nwonwu, Efe Okogu, Nnedi Okorafor, Chinelo Onwualu, Sofia Samatar, Wole Talabi, Tade Thompson, and Nick Wood.[28] While it would be impossible to do justice to every volume, story, or author of this boom, drawing attention to a few key tropes – the Anthropocene, the neuropolitical, and revisionist narratives concerning first contact and space exploration – can emphasize the original contribution of African SF to the larger field of contemporary world SF.

The Anthropocene marks the impact of humanity on the geologic scale. However, as Christophe Bonneuil and Jean-Baptiste Fressoz argue, it develops unequally, with the Global South suffering from the outsized contributions by the Global North.[29] Owing to this unequal contribution, they argue, it is better to think of the Anthropocene as a series of overlapping

---

[27] Bould, "Introduction: Africa SF."

[28] For resources on African SF authors and works, see Geoff Ryman, "100 African Writers of SFF," *Strange Horizons*, http://strangehorizons.com/100-african-writers-of-sff (last accessed June 13, 2018) and *The African Speculative Fiction Society*, www.africansfs.com/home (last accessed June 13, 2018).

[29] Christophe Bonneuil and Jean-Baptiste Fressoz, *The Shock of the Anthropocene* (London: Verso, 2016).

practices in order to distinguish the "human" from the particular social processes that are most responsible. Especially pertinent for Global South SF are the Thanatocene (war and the technology and fuels necessary to carry it out), the Phagocene (commodity proliferation and consumption), and the Capitalocene (the development of the "technostructure" necessary for the development of the global capitalist world-system).

In his study of recent African "postcrisis" SF, Matthew Omelsky argues that African SF authors "are pioneers of an aesthetic turn to articulate the ontological paradox that we may soon face: that life may one day exist on an Earth that no longer sustains life."[30] Wanuri Kahiu's short film *Pumzi* (2010) and Okogu's "Proposition 23," Omelsky argues, gesture toward a renewal of the Fanonian new human and revolutionary strategies adapted for a postcrisis Africa. Similar themes underwrite the work of "Naijamerican" author Nnedi Okorafor,[31] especially *Who Fears Death* (2010) and its prequel *The Book of Phoenix* (2015). These novels, seamless hybrids of SF, future-dystopian world-building, and fantasy – dubbed "magical futurism"[32] – depict a world ravaged by environmental apocalypse let loose by war, consumption, and development. In the cosmology of the novels, the goddess Ani pulls the Sun down from the sky to scorch the Earth in order to punish humans, particularly the Okeke black population. Following the conventions of fantasy, but adding an Afro-feminist twist, it is Onyesonwu's destiny to rewrite the Great Book of Ani and bring forth the green space that she dreams of that resides "*outside* the Great Book,"[33] ending both the enslavement of her people and leading to a new postcrisis utopia. The prequel, *The Book of Phoenix*, explores the time just prior to Ani's punishment. Rather than the postcrisis Sudan of *Who Fears Death*, much of the novel is set in a future, hyper-modern, technologically advanced United States under the effects of climate change. Most significantly, the novel explores the uneven development of the factors leading to the Anthropocene and Ani's punishment, as well as how and why the Okeke and specifically women came to be the scapegoats for the United States' techno-capitalist accelerationism that ostensibly brings about the end of the modern world. As such, it underscores the false equivalence of the

---

[30] Matthew Omelsky, "'After the End Times': Postcrisis African Science Fiction," *Cambridge Journal of Postcolonial Literary Inquiry* 1, 1 (2014), p. 36.

[31] The term is Okorafor's own preference over Nigerian-American for the way that it creates continuity rather than separation.

[32] "Nnedi Okorafor: Magical Futurism," *Locus Online* (May 17, 2015), www.locusmag.com /Perspectives/2015/05/nnedi-okorafor-magical-futurism (last accessed May 17, 2018).

[33] *Who Fears Death*, p. 287.

human in the Anthropocene, and focuses on the uneven development of contributing factors.

Similar scenes of Anthropocentric environmental desolation recur frequently throughout African SF, including Mame Bougouma Diene's strikingly original *Hell Freezes Over* (*AfroSF Vol. 2*) which narrates humanity's postcrisis attempts to build a final outpost before the world is covered by rising ocean waters. In contrast to the desertification of Okorafor's novels, it presents "the future as an endless field of ice."[34] However, it depicts the similar development of a cosmology critical of capitalist modernization bolstered by instrumental rationality, tracing this all the way back to Plato's Cave. Both Okorafor and Diene render stark, ravished landscapes in which the techno-capitalist development of the preceding centuries is responsible for creating the conditions of its own destruction. Each also presents a woman protagonist who must struggle to make her postcrisis civilization more equitable, as it is marked by slavery and systemic rape. In this, they provide a particularly feminist critique of the phallocentric hubris of capitalist modernity and its fallout.

Other African writers present a different take on the environmental postcrisis narrative and its relation to technology. Contrasting with the technologically barren landscapes of Okorafor and Diene, authors like Lauren Beukes, Efe Okogu, and Sofia Samatar explore how technology is used to subdue populations in postcrisis societies. Rather than capitalist accelerationism and the Anthropocene bringing about the end of modernity and capitalism, capitalist technoscience thrives in advanced authoritarian settings in the form of what Omelsky refers to as "neuropolitical" power. Building on the work of Michel Foucault and Achille Mbembe, Omelsky acknowledges that while power continues to "encompas[s] the bio- and necropolitical" in the futurological societies of African SF, it is accompanied by "futural technologies" that "enable the control of the body itself, its cognitive and neurological networks, in what might be called the 'neuropolitical.'"[35] In Beukes's *Moxyland*, we see this in the way that humans are policed through shocks delivered by the cellphones that connect them to society, the use of organ liquidating bio-agents to control protestors, and perhaps most strongly through corporate nano-advertising that increases a person's cognitive ability at the same time that it makes them dependent on a soft drink and produces a neon logo on their skin. *Zoo City* places a fantasy twist on this where those

---

[34] Mame Bougouma Diene, "Hell Freezes Over," in Ivor W. Hartmann, ed., *AfroSFv2: 5 Novellas* (A StoryTime Publication, 2015), p. 113.

[35] Omelsky, "End Times," p. 42

who have committed murder are psychically and physically linked with an animal. Humans suffer debilitating consequences if their animal is too far from them and even die if the animal is killed.

While Beukes's fiction focuses on near-future South African settings where the consequences of climate change are still in the early phases of being registered through worsening resource conflict, immiseration, and refugee migration, Efe Okogu's "Proposition 23" (*AfroSF Vol. 1*) and *An Indigo Song for Paradise* (*AfroSF Vol. 2*) present distant futures ravaged by the catastrophic effects of the Anthropocene as particularly filtered through the Thanatocene with nuclear war. Nonetheless these worlds maintain their technoscientific capabilities. In "Proposition 23," neuropolitical control is most evident through the novum of the "neuro": an enhanced, somatic nanotech-enabled version of the Internet that keeps everyone tied to society and under government control. Those found guilty of violating government decrees have their neuro disabled and join the "undead" in a feral existence outside society. *An Indigo Song*, an example of the parallel worlds subgenre, follows a character who has been transplanted from a fairly idyllic, utopian space of lush nature (resembling the green space vision of Okorafor's novel and Kaihu's *Pumzi*) to the last refuge of post-nuclear fallout humanity, Paradise City. Rather than the direct neuropolitical control of "Proposition 23," the novella presents Paradise through one of the revolutionary characters as "an illusion, a simulation on a hyper-dimensional computer ... Unfortunately, the game being played on the PC's mainframe is Empire. The Graphic User Interface displays Paradise but deep beneath the City, a ravenous beast of a machine seeks the corruption of your mind and the destruction of your soul."[36] The work of Kaihu, Okorafor, and Okogu operates within the critical dystopian register, requiring collective action to stake a utopian space for life after the apocalypse. Shifting the reference from colonialism to neoimperialism, they echo a common refrain in Afrofuturism and African SF – that the apocalypse has already happened – and are narratives about the violence and possibilities of life after death. And in a motif that recurs throughout Okorafor's work, they insist on a fidelity to revolution, even when its outcomes cannot be known in advance.

The short fiction of Sofia Samatar, recently collected in *Tender* (2017), similarly engages with many of these environmental and neuropolitical concerns, but it is often more intimate and slow-burning, told through elliptical and meditative narratives. For example, "How to Get Back to the Forest" includes teenagers whose minds and moods are controlled by

---

[36] Efe Okogu, "An Indigo Song for Paradise," in Hartmann, ed., *AfroSFv2*, p. 466

implanted bugs, and the bio-engineered narrator of "Tender" has a heightened sensitivity to radioactive toxicity. Isolation, dystopia, environmental devastation, and resource crises similarly haunt "The Closest Thing to Animals" and "The Red Thread."

Another current trend in contemporary African SF is the first contact narrative, or what Rachel Haywood Ferreira theorizes as "second contact due to the degree to which the original historical circumstances and the colonial legacy inform content and perspective." Such second contact narratives "rewrite, shanghai, and subvert both historical and science fictional accounts of contact."[37] Perhaps the best known in this register is Neill Blomkamp's alien-apartheid film *District 9* (2009). Despite its surface anti-imperialist politics, which suggest an allegory "of collective class identity across racial, cultural, and national divisions – among those in the now-universal state of exception whom corporate sovereignty has reduced to bare life" in neoliberal late capitalism,[38] the film was widely critiqued by post-colonial SF critics as a problematic "diversionary and compensatory ... spectacle of racial violence,"[39] as well as for its racist portrayal of Nigerians. As such, it served as an impetus for Okorafor's own second contact narrative, *Lagoon* (2014). By setting her narrative in Lagos, Nigeria, Okorafor sought to offer a more balanced and positive portrayal of Black Africans. Purposefully replaying the arrival of the waves of European colonizers by the sea, *Lagoon*'s aliens first crash-land in the ocean just off the coast of Nigeria before emerging on Bar Beach. The novel complicates the colonial overtones of the second contact narrative by acknowledging both the disruptive violence and the benefits of "change and technology" that accompany the aliens' arrival.

Alien contact also runs across Tade Thompson's "Notes from Gethsemane" (*AfroSF Vol. 1*), his novel *Rosewater* (2016), and novella *The Last Pantheon* (*AfroSF Vol. 2*), co-authored with the equally notable Nick Wood. In "Notes from Gethsemane," a biological entity crash-lands in Nigeria, forming a crater of sentient alien biomass that is perceived as a threat by governmental agencies, but also promises access to total knowledge of the world through communion and integration. *Rosewater* expands

---

[37] Rachel Haywood Ferreira, "The First Contact Story in Latin American Science Fiction," in Brian Attebery and Veronica Hollinger, eds., *Parabolas of Science Fiction* (Middletown, CT: Wesleyan University Press, 2013), p. 70.

[38] Smith, *Globalization*, p. 158

[39] John Rieder, "Race and Revenge Fantasies in *Avatar*, *District 9*, and *Inglourious Basterds*," *Science Fiction Film and Television* 4, 1 (2011), pp. 44, 45.

upon and transforms the ideas from the earlier story, pushing them in a more complex direction. Similar biological alien entities have crash-landed at multiple sites in the world, including Nigeria. As a result of the introduction of these entities, some humans have been rendered "sensitives" due to the bonding of an alien fungus with their skins. These sensitives are able to connect with a shared information realm known as the xenosphere. It's a complex narrative that moves back and forth in time, slowly unfolding the complex logic of this alien entity and the truth behind the xenosphere. *Rosewater* reverses the quasi-utopian ending of the earlier story and substitutes a slow motion alien environmental invasion as slow apocalypse.

Thompson and Wood's *The Last Pantheon* (*AfroSF Vol. 2*) shifts gears and takes up the theme of aliens as the origin of the human species. The novella combines aspects of superhero comic book lore, first contact, and alternate history[40] and uses a series of short entries that jump back and forth through time, largely in South Africa and Nigeria, to tell the story of Black Power and the Pan African, superhero and super villain, respectively. A deceptively complex novella, the superhero aspects mirror other recent treatments that look to the suspect and authoritarian underpinnings of the superhero. This is then filtered through a (neo)colonial political lens as the narrative moves across significant moments of political crisis in African history, calling into question the complicity of "keeping the peace" with enforcing the corrupt and/or neoimperial status quo. It also works within the first contact genre in a way that resonates across a lot of contemporary African SF, including Okorafor's *Binti: Home* (2017), Nwonwu's "Masquerade Stories" (*AfroSF Vol. 1*), Dila's *The Flying Man of Stone* (*AfroSF Vol. 2*), and Andrew Dakalira's *VIII* (*AfroSF Vol. 2*), whereby early African rites and rituals (and in this case humanity itself) have their roots in alien cultures.

If second contact narratives often reflect colonization, space exploration narratives take up the racialized question of who gets to imagine space, emphasizing the Global South's fraught relationship with a capitalist modernity that has often denied its contemporaneity, let alone futurity. This is the subtext of Deji Bryce Olukotun's *Nigerians in Space* (2014) and its follow-up, *After the Flare* (2017). Sofia Samatar's "Request for an Extension on the *Clarity*"

---

[40] While alternate history is not a dominant SF form for Global South SF, both Tade Thompson and Nick Wood have written intriguing and important contributions to the genre. Thompson's "Bootblack" (2017) published in *Expanded Horizons* uses time travel to retell the 1919 Welsh race riots, http://expandedhorizons.net/magazine/?page_id=3968 (last accessed May 15, 2018). More of a "true alternative history" in Karen Hellekson's terminology, Nick Wood's richly poetic novel *Azania Bridges* (2016) imagines a contemporary South Africa in which Apartheid still exists.

provides a similar consideration on this claim to space exploration. In "Request," the unnamed African-American female protagonist tends to a near Earth orbital, maintaining it so that it can "receive transmissions from our distant ships."[41] The story hinges on the nature of this simple word "our," as it slowly reveals that the narrator is not seen as a real participant in space exploration. Instead, she is a "bridge" or "janitor"; "I'm an astronaut, but not astronaut enough ... I'll never be famous. I don't explore. I'm too close to home."[42] Coupled with questions about the relationship and power of African pseudo-scientific knowledge about aliens and advanced technology versus Western knowledge about Africa, the story is a powerful meditation not only on who gets to imagine space, but what the epistemological and cultural value of such imagination is, an especially powerful question for the role of Global South SF.

These questions surrounding second contact and space exploration introduce a final thematic concern worth noting for its role in Global South SF: cultural recovery. We can see this issue at work in Chiagozie Fred Nwonwu's "Masquerade Stories" (*AfroSF Vol. 1*), a potent narrative about the antinomies between authenticity and technology, nativism and diaspora, and the use and abuse of tradition that recalls Frantz Fanon's essays on national consciousness and national culture in *The Wretched of the Earth*. The issues surrounding cultural recovery, cultural revolution, and the opposition of indigenous to Western knowledge systems are perhaps most central to the stories that comprise Dila's *A Killing in the Sun* (2014), probably the first single-authored volume of SF short stories published by an indigenous African author in English. The opening story, "The Leafy Man," pits "native medical science," which the protagonist, Japia, explicitly differentiates, "to the dismay of the community ... from spirit worship," against the "Pest and Germ Control Corporation."[43] The story sets the tone for many of Dila's by offering a dialectical mediation that subverts the uncritical acceptance of either tradition or science, Africa or the West.

This dialectic plays out most strongly in Dila's loosely connected future dystopian narratives, "Lights on the Water," "A Wife and a Slave," and *The Flying Man of Stone*, in which a postcolonial pseudo-utopia formed on a reifying notion of pre-European African cultural purity is revealed as dystopian in effect. In these stories, the possibility of a Fanonian futurity is stamped out by an anti-imperialism that turns against the future in favor of an

---

[41] Sofia Samatar, "Request," in *Tender* (Easthampton, MA: Small Beer Press, 2017), p. 179.

[42] Ibid., pp. 184, 185

[43] Dilman Dila, *A Killing in the Sun* (Johannesburg: Black Letter Media, 2014), p. 4.

ossified traditionalism in which the violence of imperialism becomes recursive rather than surpassed. Whether magic versus technology, tradition versus modernization, alien versus human, art versus propaganda, or even on a more formal level, fantasy versus SF, Dila's works privilege complex ruminations that reveal the imbrication of these elements in a way that points towards the larger combined and uneven development of global modernity.

Conclusion: Global South SF and Ambivalence

Building on Ferreira's concept of the "second contact narrative," it is hard not to read Global South SF as a formal meta-SF, that is, as an intervention into the form of SF itself. Rather than repeating the development of SF's Western history and development in a stagist manner – an African pulp age or the new Indian Golden Age – Global South SF reboots and remixes tropes and forms to create a space for thinking and imagining utopian interventions in our precarious global present and postcrisis futures. In this light, it is a dual de-centering of the form and content of SF and a desire for newness not repetition, while also a mode of commenting on the very complicity of aspects of the SF ideological imagination that hamstring such possibility. The specter of Global South SF thus haunts the traditional(ist) discipline of SF studies. It is not simply assimilable to its traditional categories, yet nor is it entirely separate from them. Instead, it calls on scholars to reconsider the apparitional absent-presence of the Global South in SF's development and past critical studies, as well as the way it transforms our understanding of current SF scholarship and literary production, circulation, and reception under globalization.

43

Science Fiction Film and Television of the Twenty-First Century

SHERRYL VINT

The twenty-first century has been simultaneously exciting and disappointing for SF film and television. There is proportionally more SF on screens large and small, and while much of this is formulaic and derivative, there are also fresh visions as more artists embrace how SF provides a vernacular for interrogating the present. SF has become a significant force in the industry, reflected in the fact that the San Diego ComicCon is now one of the most prominent venues for announcing new films and series of any genre. Along with this growing popularity of SF texts, the twenty-first century has seen the transformation of media industries through new digital technologies of distribution, especially streaming applications and their providers, such as Amazon, Hulu, and Netflix.[1] This shift makes this period radically distinct from earlier eras.

It is increasingly difficult to talk about film and television as separate media, because actors, directors, and producers move fluidly between them, and consumers increasingly experience all filmed texts through the same distribution platform. This chapter will discuss recent film and television thematically rather than segregated by media, although it is important to note that they remain distinct in many ways, chief among them budget for visual spectacle, where film retains an edge (although this, too, is fading), and narrative structure, with television remaining more open-ended. The final relevant issue is the emergence of transmedia storytelling, a marketing strategy for integrating stories set in the same fictional world across a number of texts in different media, which grew out of fan practices for extending a text's narrative world.[2] Speculative titles have a central place in transmedia production.

---

[1] See Amanda Lotz, *The Television Will Be Revolutionized*, 2nd edn. (New York: New York University Press, 2014).
[2] See Henry Jenkins, *Convergence Culture: Where Old and New Media Collide* (New York: New York University Press, 2008).

The End of the World as We Know It

Unsurprisingly, given how the 9/11 attacks shifted culture toward the military and the xenophobic, one of the most prevalent themes is alien invasion. This recent wave of alien invasion texts is often about hidden enemies, at times ones who pass as human, emblematizing fears of sleeper cells. Television in particular might be understood as a site where audiences sought to restage the trauma of the attack in a narrative context that transformed the over-whelming-because-incomprehensible into conspiracy, enabling a kind of control over events even while reveling in spectacles of destruction. Many shows drawing on this iconography lasted only a single season, but their frequency suggests an ongoing impulse to use SF to come to terms with a new awareness of vulnerability. *Threshold* (CBS, 2005) drew these connections most overtly, linking a secret contingency plan to stop alien invasion with a plot about infection that transforms some humans into hybrids working to terraform the Earth for alien occupation. Team members experience violent, hallucinatory dreams connected to the show's mythology, further symbolizing the post-traumatic stress disorder that fuelled contemporary American culture.

The show was quickly cancelled, the trauma perhaps not sufficiently displaced into an SF world. *Surface* (NBC, 2005) and *Invasion* (ABC, 2005) had similar plots – the former invaders from beneath the sea, connected to biotech malfeasance; the latter reinventing *Invasion of the Body Snatchers* (dir. Don Siegel, 1956) – and also lasted only one season. More successful were the cult hit *Lost* (ABC, 2004–10), the grim reboot of *Battlestar Galactica* (Sci-Fi, 2003–9),[3] and the military-centered *Falling Skies* (TNT, 2011–15). *Lost* defies summary, although this tale about survivors of a plane crash clearly works through 9/11 trauma, including questions about hidden agendas and allegiances. It is notable chiefly for the complex and shifting mythology through which it captured its fans' attention during the week between episodes, the most successful effort at that time to use social media tools to dominate the market. It is one of the key examples of the emerging layered and interactive style of storytelling that critic Jason Mittell calls "complex tv."[4]

Like the original 1978–9 series, *Battlestar Galactica* is about the last survivors of the human race, struggling to find a new home. The rebooted *Battlestar* features a more beleaguered humanity, beset as much by internal struggles

---

[3] The network rebranding as SyFy happened in 2009.

[4] Jason Mittell, *Complex TV: The Poetics of Contemporary Television Storytelling* (New York: New York University Press, 2015).

between civilian and military authority as by their android antagonists (this time their own sentient Cylon servants, who rebelled). Its main twist was a new "model" of Cylon that could pass for human, and the show thus explored complex storylines about divided loyalties, sleeper agents, and interspecies relations, including a sequence about a human colony living under Cylon occupation and turning to terrorism. Beloved by fans and critics, it ultimately endorsed a future in which human and Cylon species merged, creating a new culture that was revealed to be the origin of our own, a hybrid child becoming the first human ancestor on our Earth, the new home they ultimately find. On March 27, 2009, series creator Ron Moore and several cast members were invited by the United Nations to participate in a panel discussion about human rights, terrorism, child soldiers, and religious reconciliation, all themes explored by the series.

Falling Skies was far more simplistic and jingoistic, and quickly lost critical support, but it retained one of the largest cable audiences throughout its run. It depicts a heroic group of humans, led by a Revolutionary War history professor, fighting against an occupying alien force that devastated the planet six months before the events of the series. It flirts with themes about hybridity but ultimately endorses a purely human victory via a bioweapon. A plethora of other series explore similar terrain, including *Defiance* (SyFy, 2013–15), notable because it was released simultaneously with a massively multiplayer online role-playing game which outlasted the series; *The 4400* (CBS, 2004–7); *Colony* (USA, 2015–18), which shows much of Los Angeles occupied as if it were Baghdad; *The Event* (NBC, 2010); *Extant* (CBS, 2014–15); and *Braindead* (CBS, 2016), the last more satire than SF, speaking to how the imagery of SF is ready-to-hand for political allegory.

Invasion films range from the banal to the brilliant, with the nadir point marked by *Battlefield Earth* (dir. Roger Christian, 2000), an adaptation of L. Ron Hubbard's 1982 novel, and the apex by *Under the Skin* (dir. Jonathan Glazer, 2013), a stunning and compelling vision of humanity through the eyes of an alien for whom we are a food source, loosely based on Michel Faber's 2000 novel. Notable especially for its aesthetic innovations, including incorporation of unscripted interactions of lead Scarlet Johansson with men in Glasgow, the film conveys meaning through image rather than dialogue or narrative. Other influential invasion films include Matt Reeves's *Cloverfield* (2008), which eschews the usual spectacle set pieces to show an alien invasion of New York filmed on hand-held camera from the periphery, by people without a larger context to understand what is going on. More recently, *10 Cloverfield Lane* (dir. Dan Trachtenberg, 2016) similarly reoriented the viewer's position in a familiar plot by telling the story of a woman "rescued" from a car accident by a man who holds her captive in an underground bunker, insisting it is to protect her from aliens. In the last act, what seems to be a horror narrative about a crazed abductor reveals that he has indeed been telling the truth, although his methods remain suspect. The Korean *Save the Green Planet!* (dir. Jan Joon-hwan, 2003) uses the idea of believing in an alien invasion to explore the sociopathy of contemporary class politics.

Attack the Block (dir. Joe Cornish, 2011) depicts class and race relations in a London council housing estate using alien invasion, demonstrating the heroism of its black teenaged hero Moses (John Boyega – before his fame in the new *Star Wars* cycle) as it offers a glimpse of the larger context of systemic racism and economic deprivation that inform his petty crime. *District 9* (dir. Neill Blomkamp, 2009) received a lot of critical attention for its depiction of race relations in South Africa via the metaphor of alien refugees, but it falls into its own racial stereotypes about African people, blunting its theme of hybridity. More compellingly, *Monsters* (dir. Gareth Edwards, 2010), whose director went on to direct an influential *Godzilla* remake (2014), puts his alien invasion in Mexico and explores the damage done to that country by the histrionic US militarization of the border. This film portrays the aliens in a sympathetic light: they do damage, but only as a side-effect of defending themselves against the US military. One of the most-discussed films, James Cameron's *Avatar* (2009), reverses the invasion plot to excoriate the US military and corporate profit motive, aligning its sympathetic humans with the alien Na'vi, whose world is being destroyed by human colonialism. Embraced as a film with environmental themes by some, *Avatar* is also uncomfortably close to colonial adventure fiction in which a white savior is the only one able to protect valuable indigenous heritage, a familiar plot since at least Edgar Rice Burroughs's *A Princess of Mars* (1912), which was adapted as the dreadful *John Carter* (dir. Andrew Stanton, 2012). *Avatar*'s spectacular achievement in special effects, pioneering a new and more immersive kind of 3D alongside new computer-generated imagery techniques that digitally map actor's bodies, created a beautiful vision of Pandora that enthralled its fans.[5] This technology is also featured in the stunning visuals of Guillermo del Toro's *Pacific Rim* (2013), an anime-influence tale of mecha fighting kaiju.

The post-apocalyptic dominates the SF imaginary into the twenty-first century, visible in films such as *The Day After Tomorrow* (2004) and *2012* (2009),

[5] See James Chapman and Nicholas J. Cull, *Projecting Tomorrow: Science Fiction and Popular Cinema* (London: I. B. Taurus, 2013).

both directed by Roland Emmerich, known for his *Independence Day* (1996), recently given a sequel in *Independence Day: Resurgence* (2016). Films such as *Safety Not Guaranteed* (dir. Colin Trevorrow, 2012) and *Seeking a Friend for the End of the World* (dir. Lorene Scafaria, 2012) are dramas with an SF frame, pointing to the degree to which the genre's apocalyptic imagination shapes quotidian sensibilities. Spanish and Latin American films such as *2033* (dir. Francisco Laresgoiti, 2009), *Los últimos días* (The Last Days; dir. Pastor brothers, 2013), and *Fase 7* (Phase 7; dir. Nicolás Goldbart, 2010) show that these preoccupations are not solely American, although *Fase 7*, the most interesting in this list, uses the motif of a possible zombie plague to explore US control over Latin American politics.

Popular young adult (YA) series such as *The Hunger Games* (films 2012, 2013, 2014, 2015), *The Maze Runner* (films 2014, 2015, 2018), and *Divergent* (films 2014, 2015, 2016, 2017) show a future of economic and often environmental devastation, in which the teenaged generation is required to restore prosperity from the ruins, a pattern repeated in television's *The 100* (CW, 2014–), also adapted from YA fiction. J. Michael Straczynski's *Jeremiah* (Showtime, 2002–4), the first attempt to create an SF series on one of the premium channels, also falls into this pattern, although it was only moderately successful, perhaps because it was much earlier.

Some of these tales of rebuilding America from ruins use SF to allegorize elements of US occupations abroad by imagining them experienced by American citizens. *Jericho* (CBS, 2006–8) focuses on the aftermath of a nuclear attack, while *Revolution* (NBC, 2012–14) addresses rebuilding following an electromagnetic pulse attack that destroys even electricity. Both pit a "real" America of democratic values against a "fake" America embodied in military and/or political figures who use the rebuilding as an opportunity to augment their own wealth, suggesting that increasingly the trauma of the 2008 economic crisis was more pressing than the memory of 9/11. Cancelled mid-narrative, both series were completed in comic book form. The Michael Bay-produced series *The Last Ship* (TNT, 2014–18), which began as a story about fighting a viral pandemic but moved into one of rebuilding, like TNT's *Falling Skies*, remains jingoistic and pro-military: in its "split America" the civilian forces are the suspect ones. *The Walking Dead* (AMC, 2010–) and its spin-off *Fear the Walking Dead* (AMC, 2015–) use a similar premise of plague, but quickly reveal themselves to be straightforward allegories about the struggle over who deserves to live in a world of ever-dwindling resources.

Another common narrative is resetting time or history to avoid disaster, expressing nostalgia for a pre-9/11 world. This pattern is evident in Duncan

Jones's *Source Code* (2011), in which a critically injured veteran is able not only to thwart a second terrorist attack but also to transform his simulated reality of the first attack into a new world in which neither happened. This longing appears in time-travel television series such as *Odyssey Five* (Showtime, 2002); *Flashforward* (ABC, 2009–10); *Journeyman* (NBC, 2007); *Timeless* (NBC, 2016); *Terra Nova* (Fox, 2011), about a project to reboot human civilization by going back to the Late Cretaceous and thus avoiding an oil crisis; and *Wayward Pines* (Fox, 2015–16), a similar idea but projected thousands of years into the future.

The only *Star Trek* series on television in this period, *Enterprise* (UPN, 2001–5), is dominated by dour narratives about a major terrorist attack on Earth and an apparently unending "temporal cold war." The return of *Star Trek* to the small screen with *Discovery* (CBS All Access, 2017–) is shaped by new contexts of television production and distribution: produced by CBS, it is available only to subscribers of the network's streaming service, not part of its broadcast offerings. Set about a decade before the original series, *Discovery* promises a more complex examination of the difficulty of creating a diverse community than was offered by the hopeful liberal optimism of Gene Roddenberry's original, and includes the first openly homosexual character in the franchise, as well as an ethnically diverse cast. It seems designed to reimagine the *Star Trek* universe along darker lines, following in the path of the rebooted *Battlestar Galactica*, which many judged to exemplify SF's capacity for addressing political themes. *Discovery* tries to offer us critical perspectives on our contemporary political struggles, not the utopian vision of a future in which we have transcended them, previously the series' hallmark. Focused on a protagonist (Spock's never-before-mentioned adopted sister, who is Starfleet's first mutineer) who is doubly alienated from both human and Starfleet cultures, and set in a period in which the Federation is newly at war with the Klingon Empire, *Discovery* provides another point of view on Roddenberry's future, the original series optimism filtered through *Enterprise*'s reactionary values.

Sociotechnical Imaginaries

As we entered the twenty-first century, many icons previously found only in SF became part of daily life. Films such as *Inception* (2010) and *Interstellar* (2014), both directed by Christopher Nolan, imagine futuristic technologies – programmable dreams, the renewal of space travel – but these innovations serve mainly as backgrounds for stories about human relationships and the renewal of hope for a future. *Interstellar* echoes ecological themes explored in Danny Boyle's more understated *Sunshine* (2007), about an international group of astronauts on a mission to reignite the dying sun. *Europa Report* (dir. Sebastián Cordero, 2013) and *The Last Days on Mars* (dir. Ruairi Robinson, 2013) both imagine sinister outcomes to the discovery of life on other planets, and *Apollo 18* (dir. Gonzalo López-Gallego, 2011) fuses this idea with contemporary found-footage horror, representing itself as the secret that explains why NASA moon missions came to an end.

Franklyn (dir. Gerald McMorrow, 2008), which shifts between a contemporary political thriller and a steampunk adventure, uses the mapping between quotidian and speculative realities to show how damaged people cope with psychic injury through such constructions. *Womb* (aka *Clone*; dir. Benedek Fliegauf, 2010) portrays a woman whose grief over her husband's death leads her to gestate his clone, whom she raises. Alex Rivera fuses cyberpunk imagery and military drones in *Sleep Dealer* to interrogate the US fantasy of extracting resources from Mexico, including the labor-power of its citizens, while militarizing the border to prevent Mexican people from sharing in this wealth. US television has been less successful in quotidian SF, with both *Defying Gravity* (ABC, 2009), a workplace drama about astronauts on a long-term mission, and *Intelligence* (CBS, 2014), about a CIA operative enhanced with a microchip in his head, lasting only a season.

British television, in contrast, has garnered success and critical acclaim with *Black Mirror* (Channel 4, 2011–14; Netflix, 2016–), an anthology series set in the near future about the possible implications of social media technology. For example, the dark "Fifteen Million Merits" shows a dystopian future of economic austerity where even heartfelt outrage against this system is commodified into another media program, via a reality competition similar to *America's Got Talent* (NBC, 2006–). *Black Mirror* skillfully reveals how fully immersed we are in mediated, perhaps fictionalized realities, extrapolating technologies such as Siri or Twitter just slightly into the future, ultimately exploring how alienating such fusions of self and technology can be. Spike Jonze's *Her* (2013), about a man, Theodore, who falls in love with his operating system, explores similar territory, but pushes things slightly more toward SF with its interest both in Theodore and the AI, Samantha, who goes on to a posthuman existence. One of the most acclaimed recent series is *Mr. Robot* (USA, 2015–), about a hacker, Elliot Alderson (whose surname is surely meant to evoke *The Matrix*'s Neo, aka Thomas Anderson), who seeks to bring down global capital personified in the figure of Evil Corp. In the first season the antisocial and depressed Elliot seems to be recruited by the hacktivist group fsociety led by Mr. Robot, but by the season's end we discover Elliot has multiple personality disorder and *is* Mr. Robot. Their hack succeeds, and the second and third seasons explore what it means to live in the aftermath of such transformative protest, moving beyond Neo's exhilarating but perhaps ultimately empty speech about how a new future is going to begin that concludes the original *Matrix*.

Many texts explore related questions about surveillance and hacking, increasingly automated and mediated relations, and the possibility of AI. Created beings are almost always imagined as female, reflecting the gender bias of a sociotechnical imaginary that insistently characterizes personal assistant software as feminine. Andrew Niccol's *Simone* (2002) imagines replacing temperamental actresses, but its protagonist ultimately finds that the software too has a mind of its own, while *The Congress* (dir. Ari Folman, 2013), based on a Stanisław Lem story, takes this a step further and shows an aging actress replaced by her eternally youthful simulacra. *Eva* (dir. Kike Maillo, 2011), *The Machine* (dir. Carodog W. James, 2013), *Automata* (dir. Gabe Ibáñez, 2014), *Ex Machina* (dir. Alex Garland, 2014), and *Chappie* (dir. Neill Bloomkamp, 2015) all explore artificial beings that achieve consciousness and generally are sympathetic to AIs enslaved to human protocols. *Ex Machina* offers a dilemma for its viewers, since Ava's creator is so clearly a masculinist bully, and yet Ava too seems sinister in the film's final scenes when she embraces her freedom rather than bind herself to the sympathetic male character, Caleb. *Eva* embodies its AI as a child, her true identity not revealed until near the end of the film, and asks difficult questions about what it means to love a potentially dangerous created being.

Transcendence (dir. Wally Pfister, 2014) imagines a human uploaded into a machine consciousness. The film wavers between embracing this transhumanist dream and echoing an earlier generation of films about AI entities, such as *Colossus: The Forbin Project* (dir. Joseph Sargent, 1970) and *Demon Seed* (dir. Donald Cammell, 1977) – in that era, mostly male, influenced by *2001: A Space Odyssey* (dir. Stanley Kubrick, 1968) – in which an AI promising it knew what was best was a genocidal threat. *Transcendence*'s Will uses his superior networked intellect to make tremendous scientific advances in regenerative medicine and environmental melioration, and his projects transform the economy of a dying town, but nonetheless his inhumanity labels him a threat. The film's confusing conclusion sees audience sympathies suddenly shifted back to Will, even as the military attack on him succeeds, destroying not only his consciousness but the entire networked communications system upon which much of our social world rests. The film speaks powerfully to our ambivalence about how much we have already fused with our technology.

Eternal Sunshine of the Spotless Mind (dir. Michel Gondry, 2004) metaphorically conflates the human mind with a computer, imagining a technology for editing memory, and asking what remains of the self if formative experiences of interaction with others are treated as disposable. *Self/Less* (dir. Tarsem Singh, 2015) explores the idea of uploading consciousness directly to another host body, and is mainly an allegory about how the rich extend their lives by consuming those of the poor: the body donor is forced into this contract by necessity. The most significant film using this metaphor is *Get Out* (dir. Jordan Peele, 2017), which fuses a horror-film scenario of taking over another's body technologically to comment on the history of racist destruction of black lives by white supremacy in America.

On television, *Almost Human* (Fox 2013–14) fuses a police drama exploring contemporary biotech with the SF twist of partnering an android, who has emotional programming, and a human, who has had one leg replaced by cybernetic prosthetic. The critically praised *Person of Interest* (CBS, 2011–16) began as an episodic drama about a group helping people in danger, identified via cases deemed irrelevant by an AI programmed to anticipate terrorism (these dangers were mundane, not terrorist). By the finale, it transformed into a futuristic thriller about rival ideologies regarding surveillance and civic freedom, with groups in possession of two differently programmed AIs competing for hegemony. *Humans* (Channel 4 and AMC, 2015–), based on the Swedish program *Real Humans* (SVT1, 2012–13), explores a class of robots designed for labor who achieve consciousness and pays particular attention to the way that we integrate domestic technologies into our social and familial routines. HBO's *Westworld* (2016–), based on Michael Crichton's 1973 film, transposes this tale of terror about out-of-control technology that risks human lives into an interrogation of the dark side of human desire, premised on the idea that the robots (now called "hosts") in the theme park actually remember the sadistic and sexual abuse repeatedly enacted upon them. The first season highlights the growing agency of the female hosts in particular, while the second season draws attention to the colonial and racist dynamics of the park's fantasies.

Biotech industries and genomics have a central place in twenty-first-century film and television, much of it formulaic thrillers: *Repo Men* (dir. Miguel Sapochnik, 2010), about the visceral repossession of artificial organs in default, redeems itself with a final sequence showing that its typical action victory is a dream from within an artificial consciousness, and yet someone else has become controlled by debt to pay for it. Danny Boyle's *28 Days Later*

(2002) reinvented zombies as viral pandemic, and has spawned endless imitations and sequels. The British *Survivors* (BBC, 2008–10), about rebuilding in the aftermath of a viral pandemic, based on a 1970s series, omits the zombies and focuses on the struggle over what kind of society will be rebuilt after the crisis, which, it eventually suggests, may have been engineered.

Several films explore the ethics of genetic engineering and of medical professionals who cross ethical lines. *Teknolust* (dir. Lynn Hershman Leeson, 2002) is a story about a female scientist who creates three self-replicating cyborgs using her own DNA and sends them into the world to reproduce, a biting commentary on mediated relationships. *Code 46* (dir. Michael Winterbottom, 2003) merges an empathy virus, human cloning, and the stark segregation of the privileged and the impoverished to tell a story about love not being able to overcome all. *Splice* (dir. Vincenzo Natali, 2009) explores the relationship between a couple who create a new hybrid life form, that includes human DNA, which they try to raise as a child. The creature turns against them in an incestuous, gothic-tinged tale of family dysfunction. The more sinister element of the conclusion, however, is the female scientist's willingness to enter into a patent relationship regarding the hybrid foetus she carries, the product of rape.

Television series imagined superpowers as a genetic mutation in *Heroes* (NBC, 2006–10) and the attempted reboot *Heroes Reborn* (NBC, 2015), and in *No Ordinary Family* (ABC, 2010–11). *Heroes* stands out because it adopted a global rather than an American-centric perspective and for its diversity of casting, something that has improved overall, although much remains to be done. The widely embraced Netflix series *Sense8* (2015–18), which combines genetic mutation and social media themes, is noted for its diversity across gender and ethnic difference. *Cleverman* (Sundance, 2016) draws on stories from Australian and New Zealand aboriginal culture, translated into a superhero paradigm, and emphasizes issues such as racism, the politics of border patrol, and questions of immigration and identity. *Paradox* (BBC, 2009) and *ReGenesis* (The Movie Network, 2004–,8) are both about investigations of disaster, the latter imagining a fictional CDC (Centers for Disease Control)-like agency that works across Canada, Mexico, and the United States. Such series blur the lines between SF and contemporary drama.

Ronald Moore's *Helix* (SyFy, 2014–15), about a pandemic, began with similar attention to realistic detail about outbreaks, but quickly descended into a convoluted plot about sinister posthumans and corporate plans for world takeover, ignoring more promising plotlines about the commodification of biology. *Orphan Black* (Space, 2013–17), a widely acclaimed series, makes such questions central to its exploration of a group of women who discover they are clones, part of an experiment in regenerative medicine. The series is praised for its careful attention to scientific detail, including responding to ongoing court decisions, but it is rightfully celebrated most for the phenomenal performance of series lead Tatiana Maslany, who makes each clone distinct. The series takes on issues including the patenting of DNA, the rise of personalized medicine through DNA sequencing, and a DIY culture of body modification that has increasingly turned toward biotech methods of self-enhancement.

A Genre in Transition

A very diverse body of media texts can be called SF in the twenty-first century, from the crassly commercial to the overtly avant-garde. The massive number of franchise cycles and interrelated transmedia texts dominate common perceptions of the genre, and the frequency of this kind of SF has increased in the past decade. The early years of the twenty-first century were a transitional period, ending some 1990s series such as *Men in Black* (dir. Barry Sonnenfeld, 1997, with sequels in 2002 and 2012), *The Matrix* (1999, two sequels in 2003), *Alien vs. Predator* (films 2004, 2007), and the 1990s-era cast in *Star Trek: Nemesis* (dir. Stuart Baird, 2002). The 2010s saw a number of superhero films and sequels, such as *Spider-Man* (2002, 2004, 2007), *The Amazing Spider-Man* (2012, 2014),[6] *Hulk/The Incredible Hulk* (2003–8), *Fantastic Four* (2005, 2007), *X-Men: The Last Stand* (2006), and *Superman Returns* (2006) and *Man of Steel* (2013), in some cases rebooting a property with new actors and a new creative vision multiple times in less than a decade.

The real commercial success, however, came after the first *Iron Man* (dir. Jon Favreau, 2008), which launched a massive and integrated set of Marvel texts – over a dozen films to date, with Iron Man, Captain America, Thor, and the Avengers headlining several films, and minor players such as *Guardians of the Galaxy* (dir. James Gunn, 2014; 2017) and *Ant-Man* (dir. Peyton Reed, 2015) also getting their own films. The integrated Marvel universe encompasses spin-off series *Agents of S.H.I.E.L.D.* (ABC, 2013–) and *Agent Carter* (ABC, 2015–16) on network television, and *Daredevil* (2013–), *Jessica Jones* (2014–), *Luke Cage* (2016–), and *Iron First* (2017–) on Netflix. Marvel has mapped out further films and television series for this franchise into 2020. Although late to this strategy, DC is attempting to duplicate it with *Man of Steel* (dir. Zack

---

[6] The property then moved to the Marvel franchise, which created a new *Spider Man* series beginning with *Homecoming* (2017) and continuing with *Into the Spider-Verse* (2018).

Snyder, 2013) introducing a new kind of Superman, and numerous character cameos in *Batman v. Superman: Dawn of Justice* (dir. Zack Snyder, 2016), leading up to *Justice League* (dir. Zack Snyder, 2017) and ideally more films. DC has a number of television series, including *Arrow* (CW, 2012–), *Gotham* (Fox, 2014–), *The Flash* (CW, 2014–), *Legends of Tomorrow* (CW, 2016–), and *Supergirl* (originally CBS, now CW, 2015–); those airing on the CW are integrated with one another, but DC lacks Marvel's ambitious transmedia strategy.

Michael Bay saw financial success with his *Transformers* series (2007, 2011, 2014). Attempts were made to continue the *Terminator* series in film (2003, 2009, 2015) and on television *The Sarah Connor Chronicles* (Fox 2008–9), but none met with the success of the original trilogy. Similarly, *The X-Files* moved to cinema with *I Want to Believe* (dir. Chris Carter, 2008) and attempted a television reboot (Fox, 2016–18) but never found a sufficient audience. Many franchises, however, were successfully revived, generally by casting younger actors in the parts and ignoring established films, including *X-Men* (2011, 2014, 2016) and *Star Trek* (2009, 2013, 2016). *Star Wars* long had a franchise plan in place, and Lucas wrapped up his three prequel films, opening the way for J. J. Abrams to begin the sequel films with *The Force Awakens* (2015): the scale of the planned spin-off films will rival Marvel's cinematic franchise. Finally, *The Planet of the Apes* series was remade twice in this period, an unsuccessful version by Tim Burton in 2001, and a reinvention of the franchise with a focus on animal rights rather than human error (films 2011, 2014, 2017).

This waning imagination is also evident in the number of videogame adaptations, including multiple *Resident Evil* films (2002, 2004, 2007, 2010, 2012, 2017) and an astonishing number of remakes or reboots of earlier films and series, including *Rollerball* (dir. John McTiernan, 2002), *Solaris* (dir. Steven Soderbergh, 2002), *The Stepford Wives* (dir. Frank Oz, 2004), *The Day the Earth Stood Still* (dir. Scott Derrickson, 2008), *Death Race* (dir. Paul W. S. Anderson, 2008), *The Crazies* (dir. Breck Eisner, 2010), *Tron: Legacy* (dir. Joseph Kosiniski, 2010), *The Thing* (dir. Matthijs van Heijningen, 2011), *Prometheus* (dir. Ridley Scott, 2012), *Total Recall* (dir. Len Wiseman, 2012), *Robocop* (dir. José Padilha, 2014), *Jurassic World* (dir. Colin Trevorrow, 2015), *Mad Max: Fury Road* (dir. George Miller, 2015), *Blade Runner 2049* (dir. Denis Villeneuve, 2017), and *Ghost in the Shell* (dir. Rupert Sanders, 2016). Television saw the attempted reboot of the *Bionic Woman* (NBC, 2007) and *V* (ABC, 2009–11), and a successful relaunch of *Doctor Who* (BBC, 2005–), which also prompted the spin-off series *Torchwood* (BBC, 2006–11).

Many adaptations of print SF were released on film and some on television, including multiple Philip K. Dick adaptations: films in 2002, 2003, 2006, 2007, 2011; on television, *The Man in the High Castle* (Netflix, 2015–) and *Minority Report* (Fox, 2015). Beloved SF texts came to the big screen, such as *The Time Machine* (dir. Simon Wells, 2002); *I, Robot* (dir. Alex Proyas, 2004); *War of the Worlds* (dir. Steven Spielberg, 2005); *I Am Legend* (dir. Francis Lawrence, 2007); *The Invasion* (dir. Oliver Hirschbiegel, 2007), another update of *Invasion of the Body Snatchers*; *Watchmen* (dir. Zack Snyder, 2009); *Ender's Game* (dir. Gavin Hood, 2013); *Predestination* (dir. Spierig brothers, 2014), based on Heinlein's "All You Zombies"; *High-Rise* (dir. Ben Wheatley, 2015); and *Arrival* (dir. Denis Villeneuve, 2016), based on Ted Chiang's "Story of Your Life." Hulu adapted Margaret Atwood's *The Handmaid's Tale* (2017), and, at the time of writing this chapter, an adaption is in development for Cixin Liu's highly regarded *The Three-Body Problem* (dir. Fanfan Zhang, 2018) and its sequels.

At the same time, however, SF is also being embraced by independent filmmakers to create some of the most interesting works in contemporary cinematic culture. These include Robert LePage's *Possible Worlds* (2000), which interrogates the philosophical conjecture that reality might be the fantasy of a disembodied brain in a vat; Werner Herzog's *Wild Blue Yonder* (2005), an environmentalist film that fuses footage taken from a NASA mission with that of life under Antarctic ice, stitched together by a lose narrative about an alien who came to this world after his own was devastated; Wong Kar-wai's *2046* (2004), a beautiful meditation on the nature of love and loss, projected into this future year; and Gregg Araki's *Kaboom* (2010), a humorous look at struggles with sexual identity among a group of college students, which includes an alien encounter. Alfonso Cuarón's *Gravity* (2013), an Oscar winner, the story of an astronaut struggling to return to Earth after an accident in space, demonstrates that the equation of SF with overwhelming visual effects does not necessarily mean that the plot must be a banal story of military adventure.[7]

A number of films use SF premises to push their characters into startling confrontations with themselves and humanity in general: William Eubank's *Love* (2011) tells the tale of a lonely astronaut stranded in orbit after he witnesses the destruction of life on Earth by nuclear war; Lars von Trier's exquisitely painful *Melancholia* (2011) uses the coming destruction of the world by collision with another planet to force his

---

[7] See Mark Bould's *Science Fiction* (New York: Routledge, 2012) for a fuller discussion and refutation of the long-standing idea that SF cinema is necessarily inferior to print SF due to its emphasis on spectacle.

characters out of habituated convention; Mike Cahill's *Another Earth* (2011) gives his characters a glimpse at a second chance to make crucial life choices when a duplicate Earth suddenly appears in the sky; and Jeff Nichols's *Midnight Special* (2016) offers a more intimate look at what it might be like to parent a child who develops superhuman abilities. Richard Kelly uses SF motifs in both *Donnie Darko* (2001) and *Southland Tales* (2006) to critique the erosion of democratic values in contemporary culture, the latter film especially pointing toward the way that media-driven political spectacle is always-already a kind of SF fantasy. Shane Carruth demonstrates the range of SF cinema in two impressive but very different films: the minimalist *Primer* (2004), about a group of entrepreneurial friends who accidently invent time travel and use it to try to give themselves an edge in the stock market, a story that ends in paranoia and uncertainty, and the lush *Upstream Color* (2013), a complicated tale about interspecies entanglement, non-verbal communication, and ecosystem lifecycles.

Both *Primer* and *Donnie Darko* are also part of a group of films that explore the paradoxes of time travel. While on television time-travel series tend toward making particular historical (and personal) trajectories turn out the "right" way – *12 Monkeys* (SyFy, 2015–18), *Timeless* (2016, 2018), and the Spanish *El Ministerio del Tiempo* (La1, 2015; Netflix 2016–) – the film tradition focuses more on exploring the implications of duplicating oneself in time. The thriller *Looper* (dir. Rian Johnson, 2012) images a world of mobsters in 2074, who send people to be murdered, ensuring no bodies are ever found, and is propelled by a young character refusing to kill an older version of himself. *Los cronocrímenes* (dir. Nacho Vigalondo, 2007) features a series of humorous yet poignant misunderstandings as a man who accidentally travels to the past confronts another version of himself. The television series *Life on Mars* (BBC One, 2006–7; remade by ABC, 2008–9) sends a present-day police officer into the 1970s, its mystery plot making it similar to the paradox films. The announced series *Confederate* (HBO) and *Black America* (Amazon) will take on the difficult legacy of slavery by imagining alternative histories of the US Civil War, but the controversy that has greeted their announcement suggests that this historical trauma perhaps remains too fresh to be processed via mass-market speculative fiction. Kevin Wilmott's film *Confederate States of America* (2004) explored similar terrain but he doubly distanced viewers: it is made as if it were a documentary broadcast by the BBC in a world in which the South won the Civil War, providing an outsider view on this alternative reality.

Giving the pressing economic crises of the twenty-first century, however, perhaps the most important contribution of SF film and television of this period is its ability to offer compelling visions of the true costs of this situation. Even trite franchise films such as *The Purge* series (films 2013, 2014, 2016; television 2018) speak to the deep-seated anger about systemic inequity that lacks a clear political mode of expression. Terry Gilliam's *The Zero Theorem* (2013) satirizes a superficial world of material accumulation that crushes the human spirit through its enslavement to "productive" activity that lacks a larger purpose. Many films use SF to envision the problems with capitalist social relations and the inequity they create, but they too often tend to tack on happy endings that "solve" the problem by including those previously excluded rather than by addressing the structural systems that will continue to exclude some. *Elysium* (dir. Neill Blomkamp, 2013) exemplifies this problem; for all its failings, however, the fact that the horizon of utopian thinking in the film is access to healthcare means that it says a lot about our contemporary moment. Similarly, *In Time* (dir. Andrew Niccol, 2011), which uses time as currency, visualizes how the rich live longer by consuming the life energies of the laboring poor; *Upside Down* (dir. Juan Diego Solanas, 2012), which images a world of dual gravity with an upper level of privilege and a lower level of deprivation; and *Branded* (dir. Jamie Bradshaw and Alexander Doulerain, 2012), in which personified corporate brands literally consume the bodies of their adherents, all use SF's power to make metaphors literal to illuminate something about contemporary economic systems that is otherwise obscured.[8]

Joon-ho Bong's *Snowpiercer* (2013) presents a provocative vision of the violence of capitalist social relations, and Gerry Canavan offers a cogent reading of the film as emblematic of the centrality of greed and accumulation to neoliberal paradigms of social worth, which translates into allowing market systems to produce death worlds for the sake of profit.[9] *Moon* (dir. Duncan Jones, 2009) provides a more intimate reflection on these same forces in its story of a lonely miner working on the Moon to extract a new power source. He discovers that he is not due to rotate home in a few weeks, as he thought, but is in fact a clone of the original miner, nearing the end of his

[8] See Sherryl Vint, "Imagining Beyond Capital: Representation and Reality in Science Fiction Film," in Kennan Ferguson and Patrice Petro, eds., *After Capitalism: Horizons of Finance, Culture, and Citizenship* (New Brunswick: Rutgers University Press, 2016), pp. 106–21.

[9] Gerry Canavan, "'If the Engine Ever Stops, We'd All Die': *Snowpiercer* and Necrofuturism," in Mark Bould and A. Rhys Williams, eds., *Paradoxa 26: SF Now* (Fall 2014), pp. 41–66.

lifespan, destined to be incinerated and replaced by one of the many entities stored in the station like so many labor-power spare parts. Jones gestures toward a happy ending in his conclusion, in which this clone manages to escape to Earth, hoping to expose to consumers the real cost of their clean energy, but the film's final line – a snide comment from a radio call-in show – suggests that public apathy rather than lack of knowledge is what prevents change.

Television series since the 2008 economic crisis, particularly those from Canada, also foreground economics in their world-building. Series such as *Continuum* (Showcase, 2012–15), *Killjoys* (Space 2015–), *Dark Matter* (Space, 2015–), *The Expanse* (SyFy, 2015–) – based on novels by James S. A. Corey – all project a future of open class struggle in which governments protect the interests of corporations rather than people. Following trends in contemporary Hollywood, these series feature more diverse casts than has been true of SF in the past, and *contra* the survivalist ethics of many post-apocalyptic series, in these the true enemy is corporate structures of profit, not just other people, although some people do become tools of these systems. *Continuum* is the most interesting among them, showing the transformation of future police officer Kiera Cameron, who is sent back to our present by a malfunction in a terrorist bomb. These future terrorists fight the "corporate congress" and at first Kiera retains her law-and-order conservative ethic as she joins the contemporary police force and tries to return to the future. Yet incidents she sees in her job, which sacrifice civil liberties in the service of protecting property, transform her over the seasons, so by the series end she recognizes the injustice of her future, which privileges profit over people, and fights against the seeds of this coming order in our present.

As the twenty-first century continues, and the boundaries between SF and other culture continue to dissolve in media SF and beyond, SF will continue to be a robust tool for illuminating our present moment and, ideally, will urge us to challenge and change its injustices. Media SF has never been so central to the media landscape overall as it is in the twenty-first century, and if much of this output remains conventional and repetitive, another sizeable portion is genuinely innovation and pushes the genre toward new possibilities. It has become axiomatic to say that the contemporary world increasingly resembles SF, and this truism has some relevance here, as series such as *Mr. Robot* or films such as *Her* remind us: we live in a world filled with the kinds of technologies that were once found only in SF and this fact inevitably skews contemporary storytelling toward science. Moreover, speculative techniques are being embraced by an increasingly diverse population of artists, from the Black Speculative Arts influences visible in *Black Panther* (dir. Ryan Coogler, 2018) and *Pumzi* (dir. Wanuri Kahiu, 2009), a short film about water shortage and renewal set in a future Kenya, to the Brazilian series *3%* (Netflix, 2016–), which uses SF motifs to show the intensifying struggle between the privileged and the marginalized that shapes so much of contemporary reality. Overall, SF has moved to the center of twenty-first-century popular media and thus can have a powerful future – but only if it resists continual industry pressure to make more of what has proved to be lucrative.

44

Dystopian Futures and Utopian Presents in Contemporary Young Adult Science Fiction

REBEKAH SHELDON

The human prospect in the twenty-first century is not an altogether happy one.

Jason Moore, *Capitalism in the Web of Life*

The last two decades have been a golden age for young adult literature, which has become a mainstay of publishing houses and big-budget Hollywood film production. While this might be said of several SF subgenres, SF for young adults has proved especially fertile. These fictions, however, are not fully analogous to the New Wave and post-New Wave habits of extrapolation and speculation that have come to define SF written for adults. This is because young adult SF is not simply scaled to fit a younger reader; it is first and foremost *young adult fiction*. Its primary generic conventions come from the tradition of children's and young adult literature, which are themselves part and parcel of the century-long effort to regulate and control what knowledge children receive and when they receive it. That this purpose is out of sync with the typical concerns of SF (despite their parallel historical origins in the Victorian period) makes their recent alliance in the late twentieth and early twenty-first centuries both intriguing and in need of interpretation.[1]

It is important to note that contemporary young adult science fiction (hereafter YASF) does not take part in the full range of scenarios that SF might provide it. Few are the alien first contact stories, space operas, near future noirs, or cyberpunk westerns common in the adult genre. With some exceptions, YASF takes only two forms: post-apocalypses and dystopias. Both subgenres pit their characters against inimical systems in quests for survival

---

[1] From this perspective, the mid-century history of science fiction written for juveniles and explored by Farah Mendelsohn in multiple works of criticism become legible as versions of nonfiction guides and instruction manuals.

and revolution; both take their science fictional aspects from their extrapola-tions of bleak futures. While SF has been understood since Darko Suvin as a literature of ideas that uses extrapolation as a means to defamiliarize the present, the story of the future is quite different for YASF in its contemporary mode; for young adult dystopias and apocalypses, the bleak future is an argument for *preserving* the present, often at any cost.

Like everything else written in the twenty-first century, contemporary SF written for young adults is an index of the anxiety of the Anthropocene. Children's and young adult literatures have always been concerned with the proper production of future adults; as Jason Moore writes, however, the "human prospect in the twenty-first century is not an altogether happy one."[2] We might take this proposition one step further. The human prospect in the twenty-first century is one of the immanence of finitude. The shockwaves of extinction can't help but impact as *future*-full and as anthropocentric a construction as the teenager.

Crisis and Young Adult Fiction

Adolescence first took shape through the designation of youth as a distinct developmental period marked by heightened potential for crisis. G. Stanley Hall's 1906 *Youth* (a condensed version of his two-volume *Adolescence* intended for teachers and parents) described adolescence as "the spring season of emigration" because it is "the normal time of emancipation from the parental roof."[3] Adolescence inaugurates a "moratorium"[4] period in which childhood restrictions have not yet turned to adult responsibilities. Restrictions and responsibilities are both partially suspended so that the adolescent may "make wide comparison" and so "choose wisely."[5] The very necessity of that freedom to produce properly self-mastering adult-hood, however, opens the possibility that youth may *not* choose wisely, that they might (to use the language of the period) court error, wayward devel-opment, and, finally, degeneracy.

From its inception, then, the teen has been figured as a state of crisis in need of management before the final fixity of adult form. The difficulties of

---

[2] Jason Moore, *Capitalism in the Web of Life* (London: Verso Books), p. 1.
[3] G. Stanley Hall, *Youth: Its Education, Regime, and Hygiene* (New York: D. Appleton & Co., 1906), p. 127.
[4] Nancy Lesko, *Act Your Age!: A Cultural Construction of Adolescence* (New York: Routledge, 2012), p. 105.
[5] Hall, *Youth*, p. 127.

providing teens with the right kind of freedom backed by the right sort of subtle instruction, as advocated by progressive educators like Hall, only deepened in the post-Second World War period to which most scholarship tracks the full efflorescence of teen culture and the beginning of the young adult novel. Publications like *Seventeen Magazine*, manifestos like "The Teen's Bill of Rights," and social forms like the dancehalls, canteens, and drive-ins of the late 1940s and early 1950s may have positioned themselves as spaces where teens could be teens, but all were carefully overseen by adult editors, film censors, writers, educators, and advocates.[6] Such instances of *in loco parentis*, however, operated on what would come to be the characteristic compromise of young adult culture. Ideal consumers, teens were encouraged to develop a distinct culture apart from the expectations of normative adulthood but only insofar as they could be lead back to the domestic interior.[7] In this sense, the trajectory of the teen figure as it developed in postwar American culture reflected the *Bildungsroman* tradition from which it emerged. Like the heroes of the coming of age story, the protagonists of the new story of teenagehood broke with the customs of their provincial homes in order to adventure in new lands, endure trials, and eventually establish a new home place.

Crisis is not only the stock in trade of the teen figure but also the structuring principle of literature for young adults. Young adult novels have the dual task of shaping young readers toward the proper reproduction of normative adulthoods by appearing to offer alternative choices *while also* reassuring adult readers that no other choice was ever really possible. As one of many technologies that maintain the construction of the adolescent as a figure, young adult novels stage adolescence as a necessary crisis between the twin stabilities of childhood and child-rearing. In works of YASF, this staging takes on civilization-scale scope, posing crises in political reproduction in order to endorse a particular vision of political maturity.

Postmodern Young Adult Fiction

Considering postmodern young adult fiction, Roberta Seelinger Trites observes that the protagonists "must learn about the social forces that have

---

[6] For a wonderful source of archival images and discussion of publishing practices in the 1940s and 1950s, see Michael Barson and Steven Heller, *Teenage Confidential: An Illustrated History of the American Teen* (New York: Barnes and Noble, 1998).

[7] For more on the history of teen culture, see Grace Palladino, *Teenagers: An American History* (New York: Basic Books, 1997).

made them what they are" in order to negotiate their place in the social system.[8] This she contrasts with earlier juveniles and *Bildungsromane* whose vocation was education toward the goal of eventual mastery. For example, in works like Robert Cormier's *The Chocolate War* (1974), the adult world merely extends the ugliness of the playground, and adults in power (principals, police) bear as little love for the questioning, rebellious child as do the schoolyard bullies who curry favor with adult power. In these novels, no one develops; they merely grow up to greater reach and legitimation. The ironic final passages of William Golding's *Lord of the Flies* (1954) make this point by comparing the children's fatal war games on the island with the adult wars that brought the naval gun boat close enough to save them. In another Cormier novel, *I Am the Cheese* (1977), US government officials from the Witness Relocation Program keep fifteen-year-old Adam Farmer in a private sanatorium after his parents' death. This pastoral concern, however, is revealed by the novel's end as an interrogation technique aimed at assessing how much Adam's father might have revealed before his death, a death almost certainly caused by the people charged with protecting him. Fragmented into two distinct narrative threads, the scenes of Adam's "therapy" occur in between the main first-person present-tense narrative of Adam's bike journey to visit his father in the hospital. The second narrative line, eventually revealed as a delusion that Adam has been using to evade the interrogator's questions, recapitulates the *Bildungsroman* storyline but as fantasy. The final paragraph is identical to the opening paragraph, literalizing Adam's restricted development as a closed loop.

In contemporary YASF the social forces Trites notes have become even more hyperbolically overweening. Either they are *all-worlds* in which the private is totally dominated by the political order (as in the dystopian tradition) or else they are *no-worlds* whose apocalypses have decimated the divide between the public and the private. In either case, contemporary YASF traps teens in worlds in which they can neither achieve adult mastery nor retain the moral conviction attributed to childhood. In these books, the only possibility for growth is in escape or revolution. The escape or revolution extolled by contemporary YASF led back to the world of the reader's present, now recognizably enshrined as the better of two poor options. In these scenarios, it is not enough that the teen retain something of the moral conviction attributed to childhood. These Manichean worlds include no

[8] Roberta Seelinger Trites, *Disturbing the Universe: Power and Repression in Adolescent Literature* (Iowa City: University of Iowa Press, 2004), p. 3.

space for the subterfuges Adam employs; they are lethal arenas, both lawless and tightly controlled. Contemporary young adult dystopias hyperbolize the overweening institutional power and ambivalent menace of postmodern fiction, but differ from those older fictions by casting the teen as the restoration of rational adult authority.

While late-twentieth-century fictions for adolescents thus expressed doubt about the possibility of reproduction, their contemporary analogues script teens into wresting back a lost normalcy. The new concern might be said to begin with the publication of Lois Lowry's *The Giver* in 1993. In this text, we see a break between the entrapped teen of postmodern young adult literature, and the emergence of a YASF literature of the twenty-first century that would couple the primary task of marshaling the teen to adulthood with a newfound certainty that the teen is the only source of salvation for the whole community.

Dystopias have a funny duality, and young adult dystopias doubly so. Broadly, the dystopian vocation might be said to differ from the utopian only in its choice of narrative vehicles. Where utopias identify a social ill and then sketch out solutions to that ill, dystopias identify a social ill and then exaggerate it. This definition of dystopia would bring it in line with the more general mission and method of SF as a form of cognitive estrangement. Far more commonly, however, the dystopia appears more narrowly construed as "a rhetorical *reductio ad absurdum* of a utopian philosophy."[9] The first construction gives dystopia the radically anti-essentialist and historicist leanings of much SF criticism; the second relies on often unstated ideas about human nature in order to indict forms of social organization that pull against the grain of that nature. Dystopias in this second sense show young adult readers the vacuity of everything they might want in favor of the realist utopia of what they already have, specifically life under late capitalism. Like the mid-century dystopias they mimic, these young adult dystopias privilege consumer choice, unregulated markets, freedom from government control, and passionate individualism. In line with Margaret Thatcher's famous assertion that "there is no alternative" to capitalism, contemporary young adult dystopias set the promise of social protections against the expression of individual choice as if human nature were responsible for their mutual exclusion.

For the teen protagonist, this takes the form of an inverted utopia. Beginning in her utopian setting, the protagonist moves from assimilation

[9] Balaka Basu, Katherine Broad, and Carrie Hintz, "Introduction" in Balaka Basu, Katherine Broad, and Carrie Hintz, eds., *Contemporary Dystopian Fiction for Young Adults: Brave New Teenagers* (New York: Routledge, 2013), p. 2.

and acceptance to an encounter with difference that reveals the true dystopia of her world – a pattern evident in such well-known works as Suzanne Collins's *The Hunger Games* (books 2008–10; films 2012–15) and Veronica Roth's *Divergent* series (books 2011–13; films 2014–16), among others. In this way, the contemporary dystopian teen hero comes to recognize the faults of her home and the aspects of the human experience her society has chosen to forgo. For the teen reader, these novels encourage the abandonment of the utopian promise of radical difference as a childish fantasy that can only lead to dystopian conformity. The adult world, the mature choice, is already here in the everyday life worlds of late capitalism and any adult who suggests otherwise should be treated as a potentially menacing authoritarian.

These two vectors of adult–child figuration frame the narrative momentum in *The Giver*. The story concerns twelve-year-old Jonas, a contented and successful young man in "the community," an unnamed utopian compound that practices the Sameness as the first principle of social harmony. In the community, no one wants for anything. Children are born through genetic manipulation and raised for the first year by professional nurturers, which allows the community to set limits on population growth. Those same children are bestowed on a family perfectly constituted to raise them well. The Elders make sure that couples are well suited and that every child grows naturally and gracefully into the right kind of work. When those children are ready to marry and raise children, they too will apply for a partner and children and thus they will live until they move to the house for childless adults, and thence to the House of the Old. Developmental staging in the community is perfectly calibrated for every stage of the lifecycle. Such perfect calibration, however, is purchased through total control over nature: animal life is non-existent, the sky is sunless and cloudless, no one can see color or hear music, and all adults are required to take a pill to quell sexual urges.

Like the Eloi of H. G. Wells's *The Time Machine*, people in the community live lives of safety and pleasure but in ignorance of strong emotion – pain and death equally as much as joy and love. Jonas can see the lack only because he has been chosen for a special position as the Receiver of Memory. The novel relates his first year of training for this position, a year in which the former Receiver of Memory must give Jonas all the memories of human history that had been passed along to him. The novel frames this experience as a movement into adulthood and as a loss of childhood innocence ("he wanted his childhood again"[10]) that he alone must bear. As a result of his sacrifice,

---

[10] Lois Lowry, *The Giver* (New York: Houghton Mifflin Harcourt, 2014), p. 152.

everyone else in the community can remain cushioned and protected, in a state of extended infancy as if literalizing the derogation of state protections as "nanny state-ism." In this sense, the former Receiver (now Giver) acts as the father to Jonas's adulthood, exposing him to the memories both painful and pleasurable that shepherd Jonas's dawning awareness. Indeed, one of the most important moments of this sentimental education is not a memory at all but a recording of Jonas's father in his role as Nurturer lethally injecting an inadequate child. Jonas's new knowledge of his father's job and his realization of the lies his father has told about it complete Jonas's alienation. It is in the wake of this exposure that Jonas finally begins to express stereotypical features of teenhood: sarcasm, irony, and helpless rage.[11]

What happens next for Jonas, however, both cites and also breaks the pattern with postmodern YAF. Hearing Jonas's newfound disaffection, the Giver tells him that he might have a plan. "A plan for what?" Jonas asks. "There's nothing. There's nothing we can do. It's always been this way."[12] Like Adam before him, Jonas acknowledges his own incapacitation in the grip of the powerful social forces of the adult world. The Giver, however, turns Jonas's paralysis around by reasserting the importance of history. "It's true that it has been this way for what seems forever. But the memories tell us that it has not *always* been."[13] The new narrative pattern now comes fully into view. From good utopian citizen, figured as a state of perpetual childhood, emerges an émigré to a strange new world: ours. Jonas chooses love and pain, color and war, desire and family, individuality and consumption: a conjunction summarized by a memory of a Christmas evening spent with three generations opening presents around a brightly lit tree. But he doesn't just choose it for himself. He accepts the Giver's plan to release the memories to the entire community. "If you get away, if you get beyond, if you get to Elsewhere, it will mean that the community has to bear the burden themselves, of the memories you had been holding for them." The Giver's plan is to expand his pedagogical role to encompass the whole community, to force *their* maturation. "I think that they can, and that they will acquire some wisdom. But it will be desperately hard for them."[14] Jonas's sacrifice will save his community by restoring it to its long delayed adulthood.

The Giver ends in ambiguity, without closure and with no sense of Jonas's own personal wellbeing. Unlike the circularity inherent in *I Am the Cheese*,

[11] Ibid., p. 192.
[12] Ibid., p. 193.
[13] Ibid.
[14] Ibid., pp. 194–5.

however, Jonas's adventures do lead to a real egress for him and to change of some kind for his community. Building on this new pattern, twenty-first-century young adult dystopias are far less coy about the redemptive sacrifice of their teen heroes. Scott Westerfeld's Uglies series (2005–7) even goes so far as to include a final novel in the series that takes up the narrative after the end of total social control, as do some of the books in Lowry's The Giver Quartet (1993–2012). Westerfeld's quintology also employs the inverted utopia pattern. Like Jonas, the young adult protagonist, Tally Youngblood, is first forced to confront the desirability of her world, particularly of the required cosmetic surgery and the pleasure-rich life of the New Pretties in New Pretty Town, and then by becoming a part of a rebel community with a radically different mode of life. In *Uglies*, that mode of life comes in the form of the Smokies, a rustic do-it-yourself commune in the forests beyond New Pretty Town. While not as clearly a version of the reader's consensus world, the Smokies valorize individuality, innovation, and hard work over social conformity, vapid prettiness, and leisure. As in *The Giver*, social control and social protections come paired to the loss of individuality and interiority.

Mary J. Couzelis remarks that some contemporary dystopian novels "risk making the future look so bad that young readers are grateful for their contemporary societies as they are."[15] In the contemporary dystopias I have described so far, this gratitude appears less as a risk than as a desirable outcome. The salvation made possible by the young adult hero for his dystopian community brings that community back into familiar social forms. Another major recent type of young adult dystopia, related to the inverted utopia discussed above, are dystopias that target a specific social institution figured as recent and that long for the restoration of a remembered past. This is true of *The Giver* in its configuring of our world as the nostalgic past of the novel's present, but this is a homogenous and universalized past.

For both *Divergent* and James Dashner's 2009 *The Maze Runner* the specific social institution is educational testing, particularly the high-stakes testing instituted by the 2001 No Child Left Behind Act. In the closed society of *Divergent*, all sixteen-year-olds must undergo an immersive psychological test to determine their aptitude for life in any one of five factions, each defined by a virtue, and then to apprentice to the faction through a series of specialized tests. As in *The Giver*, these virtues (courage, kindness, wisdom, honesty, and

---

[15] Mary J. Couzelis, "The Future is Pale: Race in Contemporary Young Adult Dystopias," in Basu et al., eds., *Contemporary Dystopian Fiction for Young Adults*, p. 133.

self-sacrifice) were selected over the full range of human characteristic (understood as innate) in order to institute social harmony and avert warfare and greed. The test determines a young adult's primary virtue, but only insofar as one virtue stands out. Tris, the protagonist, expresses a range of virtues and so is labeled a divergent.

Balaka Basu, in her reading of the novel, points out that many of the characters admire the faction system, but as it had once been.[16] This retrospective nostalgia for a time before the factions weakened preserves the value of education in general while questioning the inflexibility of testing categories. *The Maze Runner* is even more explicit in its condemnation of testing. Over the course of the novel, the teen boys who find themselves trapped in the eponymous maze learn that they have been put there as part of an elaborate experiment overseen by ominously cold adults who claim that the teens' entrapment is urgently necessary for the wellbeing of humanity. It is also far more self-conscious about the genre environment in which it is operating. As with Lowry's Jonas, *The Maze Runner's* protagonist Thomas finds that he cannot adapt to the rules of his social world. However, in an ironic twist, and as an echo of the earlier postmodern fiction we have reviewed, Thomas's rebellion allows him to find the way through the maze and thus to pass the tests that the adults have set for them. Rather than the inverted adult–child relations of *The Giver*, in *Maze Runner* the test itself leverages the expectation of teen rebellion and seeks to employ it for sinister adult purposes. By the end, Thomas and the surviving boys have become even more deeply ensnared. Suzanne Collins's *Hunger Games* is in some sense the central example of these No Child Left Behind allegories; while *Hunger Games* allegorizes testing as a life-or-death game of competitive survival, its real contribution to this subgenre is its canny recognition of the social benefits provided by the spectacle of the games.

School likewise forms one of the targets for satire in M. T. Anderson's YA dystopia, *Feed* (2002). A novel about connectivity, in which the world's wealthiest get biotechnological implants that enhance their cognition with smart-phone like features, the irony of the book is that the feed in fact enforces disconnection. The effortlessness of consumption (which the novel calls a new form of dream literacy) means that the teen protagonists need never know the conditions under which their products were made and distributed. The pervasive entertainment media even finds a way to turn as

---

[16] Balaka Basu, "What Faction Are You In? The Pleasure of Being Sorted in Veronica Roth's *Divergent*," in Basu *et al.*, eds., *Contemporary Dystopian Fiction for Young Adults*, p. 28.

visceral and disquieting an experience as the skin lesions that afflict many Americans into a desirable condition, a kind of fashion statement – and once they have become popular, it is a small leap to artificially producing them as cosmetic enhancements for those unlucky enough to not have acquired them naturally. What gets lost in the translation from the lesions as medical condition to desirable enhancement is the suggestion that something has gone deeply awry in the environment, something that might pose a threat to human health.

The novel encourages the reader to see education as one of the institutions that enforce social unknowingness through ignorance of history. Titus, the privileged protagonist, explains why school is now trademarked as School™:

> School™ is not so bad now, not like back when my grandparents were kids, when the schools were run by the government, which sounds completely like, Nazi, to have the government running the schools? Back then, it was big boring, and all the kids were meg null, because they didn't learn anything useful, it was all like, da da da da, this happened in fourteen ninety-two, da da da da, when you mix like, chalk and water, it makes nitroglycerin, and that kind of shit? And nothing was useful?[17]

Education is clearly important to Anderson, and state-funded liberal arts education even more so. That Titus makes this speech himself, a speech that he clearly repeats from adults, reflects the pervasive effects of adult logics. At the same time, it slyly ironizes YA dystopias like *The Giver* for their depiction of government-supported programs as "completely, like, Nazi." Like *The Giver*, *Feed* proffers the present as the space of redemption, yet it does so by tying possible dystopian futures to contemporary incipiencies. It is both the dismantling of the public school system (and the broader notion that any government support leans to authoritarianism) and also the ills of the school system (and the rote repetition of isolated facts) that come under Anderson's scrutiny.

At the conclusion of the novel, Titus relates a capsule summary version of the events of the novel as if he were writing the ad copy for a major motion picture. "It's about this meg normal guy, who doesn't think about anything until one wacky day, when he meets a dissident with a heart of gold."[18] As in young adult fiction in postmodernity, the social reproduction promised by the teen love story never culminates in adulthood. They never learn to "resist the feed" as Titus puts it,[19] and nor does their love bring them into wise adulthood. Violet dies. Titus's only act of rebellion comes when he drains his bank account

---

[17] M. T. Anderson, *Feed* (Cambridge, MA: Candlewick Press, 2002), p. 109.
[18] Ibid., p. 297.
[19] Ibid., p. 298.

by ordering hundreds of pairs of the same pants. Unlike the YA novel in postmodernity, however, here the source of institutional power is identical to the self. Violet dies because the feedware has been damaged and it is tied into all of her body's regulatory and nervous systems. Over the course of the novel, she slowly loses control over her body. Titus's reckless shopping responds nihilistically to the recognition Violet's imminent death gives him that there is no outside to the feed – at least as far as one's will is concerned. The lesions imply, however, that death need not come from inside. Biotechnological control over natures of various forms may fail too. In so many ways, Titus's generation is "set against the backdrop of America in its final days."[20]

It is in the light of *Feed's* extrapolative near future and its poorly maintained illusion of control that the meanings of the several settings in Collins's *Hunger Games* come most fully into focus. In the Capitol, for example, Collins builds a hyperbolic extrapolation of contemporary uneven wealth distribution practices in the United States, while conditions in the Arena prefigure the imminent economic and environmental collapse engendered by overconsumption. The districts furthest away from the Capitol suffer under the dual burden of poverty via the expropriation of their natural resources and police surveillance and enforcement of punitive state policies. Far from the most clearly dystopian Gilead, however, Katniss's home district of District 12 stands at the threshold of the novel's own internal utopia in the form of the forbidden woods in which Katniss and Gale hunt for game. One of the novel's very first images of happiness happens between Katniss and Gale as they share a meal of berries and bread in the forest while mocking the ersatz wealth of the Capitol. Katniss's description of flinging a wild berry, catching it in her mouth, and breaking the skin with her teeth so that the berry's "tartness explodes across my tongue"[21] conjoins environmental and erotic innocence, both unsullied and unselfconscious. The series closes with Katniss returning to District 12, this time as a young mother. In the full narrative arc, we can see the way in which an idealized present or romanticized past completes the hero's quest by reproducing proper social reproduction as political stasis.

Apocalypse: A Brief Conclusion

As I have endeavored to demonstrate, the genre of YA dystopia tends to nostalgically affirm the past, including the present as the past of a collectively

---

[20] Ibid., p. 297.
[21] Suzanne Collins, *The Hunger Games* (New York: Scholastic Press, 2009), p. 8.

worse future. Fredric Jameson's argument that utopianism subsists under late capitalism as a longing for difference finds deeply equivocal expression in these novels, which leverage that longing instead toward the conservation of the present.[22]

Contemporary dystopias circulate alongside a range of pre- and post-apocalyptic extrapolations. While apocalypse and dystopia both hinge on some large-scale crisis, apocalyptic YA fictions are if anything *less hopeful* than their dystopian equivalents. Dystopian fictions hold out the longing for the restoration of the present or the near past as their ethical and pedagogic spur to the reader. For apocalyptic YA fiction, reproduction of all kinds is formally unimaginable.[23] The crisis is not only of political organization, therefore, but rather of the conditions of reproducibility for the planetary forces that sustain human institutions. Paolo Bacigalupi's protagonist Nailer, in his post-apocalyptic YA novel *Ship Breaker* (2010), for example, can only save himself; Sherri Smith's Fen, in her post-apocalyptic YA novel *Orleans* (2014), struggles to save herself and one other, an adopted child. Susan Beth Pfeffer's *Life as We Knew It* (2008) and Karen Thompson Walker's *Age of Miracles* (2012) offer even less: their planetary apocalypses don't mean that the young adult's quest for social reproduction ends, but rather that there is no more end for them to reach and so neither protagonist leaves her family of origin. However, with the exception of Walker's stand-alone novel, these are also series books. The future continues beyond any hope of salvaging a nostalgic past. In this sense, while dystopias are the more abundant genre, my hope is that the future is in apocalypse.

---

[22] Fredric Jameson, "Progress v. Utopia; or, Can We Imagine the Future," *Science Fiction Studies* 9, 2 (July 1982), pp. 147–58.

[23] It's worth noting that another strain of teen dystopias focuses on the teen as a literal source of reproduction via cloning and organ harvesting. See, for example, Neal Schusterman, *Unwind* (New York: Simon & Schuster, 2009) and Nancy Farmer, *The House of the Scorpion* (New York: Atheneum Books, 2002). YA zombie apocalypses might also fit under this heading.

45

Convergence Culture: Science Fiction Fandom Today

PAUL BOOTH

Fandom in the twenty-first century takes many forms and has many consequences. It is both mainstream and unconventional, both dependent on digital technology and eschewing of technological innovation, both aware of its history and certain that it is groundbreaking. Fandom today is a mix of contradictions and continuities, remarkable in its everydayness and yet certain to continue to be influential in the future. It is the very definition of a "convergence culture," as it remains tethered to older traditions while still innovating in new ways.[1]

Perhaps nothing illustrates the paradoxes of SF fandom today better than the fandom surrounding the *Star Trek* franchise (TV: 1966–69, 1973–74, 1987–94, 1993–99, 1995–2001, 2001–5, 2017–; films: 1979, 1982, 1984, 1986, 1989, 1991, 1994, 1996, 1998, 2002, 2009, 2013, 2016). As this chapter was being written, in the fiftieth year since the premiere of the original series, *Star Trek* had long been lauded as a groundbreaking work of SF by fans and non-fans alike. But the sheer enormity of the franchise has meant that fandom around the text – the type of convergence fandom today – cannot be completely typified as only one thing. When Henry Jenkins wrote his highly influential *Textual Poachers* in 1992 on *Star Trek* fandom, fan communities were certainly diverse and rich.[2] But today the sheer variety of fandom is manifested in the way different fan groups embrace different aspects of the franchise. Some Trekkers are die-hard Original Series fans and denigrate those who admire the "Kelvin Timeline" of the post-2009 films; others see those films as breathing new life into a dying franchise. Some see *Star Trek* as a symbol of "old" SF fandom – the one from which zines and K/S slash fiction

---

[1] Henry Jenkins, *Convergence Culture: Where Old and New Media Collide* (New York: New York University Press, 2006).
[2] Henry Jenkins, *Textual Poachers: Television Fans and Participatory Culture* (New York: Routledge, 1992).

emerged[3] – while others see *Star Trek* as presenting brave new worlds of fan invention. Some "Questarians" may be more fannish around *Galaxy Quest* (1999), a parody of *Star Trek*.[4] Others may never have seen *Star Trek* but know it only through the way allusions to it – or even direct references to it – are integrated into mainstream popular culture artifacts like the sitcom *Big Bang Theory* (2007–). The 2017 CBS All Access series *Discovery* may have led to new fans and even to new mainstream popularity, but *Star Trek* fans are still the butt of jokes, even from people associated with the production themselves (as with William Shatner's infamous 1986 "Get a Life" sketch on *Saturday Night Live* [1975–]).[5] Even as other SF and SF-adjacent properties like *Harry Potter* and the Marvel Cinematic Universe have garnered wide popularity, *Star Trek* has never really shaken the perception that fandom is "a scandalous category in contemporary culture, one alternately the target of ridicule and anxiety, of dread and desire" – even as the Trek model of fandom has proven incredibly enduring and influential, templating the sorts of fan publications and conventions that now dominate mainstream entertainment.[6]

It is impossible to fully describe the state of fandom today except to say that it is as varied as popular culture is. And, as digital technology has both extended the reach of fan communities and expedited communication between them, fandom has become a more *de facto* identity for young people than ever before. The ubiquity of social media and the interactions engendered within them make many interactions appear fannish even if they are not deliberately so. Today, fans are using different forms of media to practice their fandom, multiple fan groups make use of fandom in different ways, and fandom has become a focus of fan and academic thought. In addition, one of the biggest developments in fandom is the way fans from the 1980s and 1990s are today in charge of production on a number of key, important media franchises.

This chapter explores the ways that fandom is becoming a more mainstream identity for many audience members and reflects on the importance

---

[3] Slash fiction is the fan practice of reading the closeness of male characters in media texts as homosexual desire; the term "slash" comes from the punctuation mark between K/S – Kirk *slash* Spock, the original *Star Trek* slashed pair.

[4] Matt Hills, "Recognition in the Eyes of the Relevant Beholder: Representing 'Subcultural Celebrity' and Cult TV Fan Cultures," *Mediactive* 2, 2 (2003), pp. 59–73; Lincoln Geraghty, *Living with "Star Trek": American Culture and the "Star Trek" Universe* (London: I. B. Tauris, 2007).

[5] Paul Booth, "Reifying the Fan: *Inspector Spacetime* as Fan Practice," *Popular Communication* 11, 2 (2013), pp. 2–13; Paul Booth, *Playing Fans: Negotiating Fandom and Media in the Digital Age* (Iowa City, IA: University of Iowa Press, 2015).

[6] Jenkins, *Textual Poachers*, p. 15

of convergence for fan audiences. Convergence culture becomes a useful metaphor for understanding the often contradictory ways that fandom interacts with mainstream media culture today.[7] Contextually, fandom in the twenty-first century has no descriptive center, but is an amalgam of overlapping and sometimes competing social and cultural interests that reveal themselves in a wide variety of forms and media.

Fandom and Media Technology

Fans are often instrumental users of new technology.[8] Fans "have the ability, the desire, and the technology to interact, change, and play with the media."[9] New types of mediation – including the development of interactive tools, social media, and digital technologies – have altered *how* fans can interact with favored texts; more traditional fannish output such as fanzines have been changed by this type of technology. Digital technology has opened up conversations about fandom and affect online, especially as new technologies like Tumblr trade in affective communication.[10] Digital technology has made fandom seem more mainstream – sharing work on Tumblr or Twitter, or creating content on DeviantArt, or any of the hundreds of other social channels people use to communicate about their interests, makes it seem as though *everyone* is a fan. At the same time, as "fans can use digital technology like Tumblr to reach others, create new works, and develop new ways of interacting with their media texts and communities, their work becomes more visible and more approachable."[11] Fandom becomes more obvious just as viewer activities become more fannish. Online, everyone can appear to be a fan, even if they are not actually participating in fan communities.

While the technology may be different, the underlying impetus for fandom, the community of like-minded fans, has not changed much.[12] Despite the fact that many young people log on to social media sites like Tumblr and feel like they have "discovered" or "invented" fandom, the long history of fannish activities and behaviors predates even the motion picture camera,

---

[7] Jenkins, *Convergence Culture*, p. 2.
[8] danah boyd and Nicole Ellison, "Social Network Sites: Definition, History, and Scholarship," *Journal of Computer-Mediated Communication* 13, 1 (2007), pp. 210–30.
[9] Booth, *Playing Fans*, p. 5.
[10] Alexander Cho, "Queer Reverb: Tumblr, Affect, Time," in Ken Hillis, Susanna Pasonen, and Michael Petit, eds., *Networked Affect* (Cambridge, MA: MIT Press, 2015), pp. 43–58.
[11] Paul Booth, *Digital Fandom 2.0* (New York: Peter Lang, 2016), p. 222.
[12] Ibid.

some emerging in the nineteenth century with texts like Sherlock Holmes and authors like Jane Austin.[13] And, just because fans may post about their favorite novel or TV show doesn't mean that they are necessarily part of a *fandom*. Communicating about a favorite text means moving from relatively quiet fannishness to more public fandom.

Mark Deuze notes that this convergence of traditional practice and newer technology has an industrial side – namely that we must see convergence as "recombinantly driven by an industry desperate for strong customer relationships, technologies that are increasingly cheap and easy to use, and a media culture that privileges an *active audience*."[14] As much as fans help drive technology use, so too do the media industries want to engender more controllable fan work, blurring the lines between amateur audience creation and professional media production. "That is, both media fans and the media industries must continually negotiate, navigate, and adjust to the presence of each other in tandem with changing paradigms of technological discourse in our digital society."[15] For example, Karen Hellekson notes that Lucasfilm runs an annual *Star Wars* fan film competition where fans can make and upload their own films using their own digital technology content.[16] Although the fans' work is made and given away for free, it can be used by Lucasfilm both as free advertising and as a tool for funneling fandom into acceptable genres. Digital tools and technologies may make it easier for fans to communicate with each other, and even with media producers, but it also makes it easier for corporations to harness that communication into marketable demographics, free advertising, and fan labor.[17]

At the same time, as much as digital technology opens up the scope of fandom to allow (almost) anybody and any practice to be seen as "fannish," so too have some fans spurned the visibility and normalization that digitization has wrought. Attempting to stay "under the radar," as many SF slash fans did in the pre-digital era, some fans eschew digital technology and more

---

[13] See, among others, Roberta Pearson, "Bachies, Bardies, Trekkies, and Sherlockians," in Jonathan Gray, Cornel Sandvoss, and C. Lee Harrington, eds., *Fandom: Identities and Communities in the Digital World* (New York: New York University Press, 2007), pp. 98–109; Francesca Coppa, "A Brief History of Media Fandom," in Karen Hellekson and Kristina Busse, eds., *Fan Fiction and Fan Communities in the Age of the Internet* (Jefferson, NC: McFarland, 2006), pp. 41–60.

[14] Mark Deuze, "Convergence Culture in the Creative Industries," *International Journal of Cultural Studies* 10, 2 (2007), p. 244, emphasis mine.

[15] Booth, *Playing Fans*, p. 1.

[16] Karen Hellekson, "The Fan Experience," in Paul Booth, ed., *Companion to Media Fandom and Fan Studies* (Malden, MA: Wiley Blackwell, 2018), pp. 65–76.

[17] Abigail De Kosnik, "Fandom as Free Labor," in Trebor Scholz, ed., *Digital Labor: The Internet as Playground and Factory* (New York: Routledge, 2013), pp. 98–111.

openly practice their fandom in person or in face-to-face situations like conventions or small clubs.[18] Intimate fan clubs still exist; zines are still printed; conversations still dominate. For instance, a local *Doctor Who* fan club near me meets on a monthly basis; the only digital interaction that occurs is the occasional email if there has been a time change in the meeting. Meetings are virtually luddite – they consist of individuals sharing information they have learned about the series, discussion over particular episodes, and watching the show.

In fact, for many people in today's convergence culture, exposure to fandom and fan cultures occurs *not* through Tumblr or other digital technologies, but through fan conventions, which have become big business in the twenty-first century. Since the 1930s SF fans have been meeting in person to hear from keynote speakers, speak on fan-run panels, converse in hallways, cosplay (dress in costume[19]), purchase items in the dealer's room,[20] or just generally exist in physical proximity with other fans. One area of growth within fandom in convergence culture, especially as it goes along with the convention circuit, is the collecting of merchandise as a particularly innovative fan practice. Many fans collect toys, games, books, art, models, or other elements related to their favorite SF entity.[21] Thanks to cheaper goods and 3D printing technologies, fans can also create their own merchandise or customize their own action figures.[22]

The aura around conventions seems to have shifted from what were once seen as geeky and small affairs for socially awkward adults to now multi-million dollar events with over 130,000 attendees.[23] Fan conventions encompass entire swaths of fandom, from artists, to creators, to individuals who just want to spend time with other fans. Families attend, and whole weekends can be spent on the experience. They are also not inexpensive. Entrance fees can run into the hundreds of dollars (often quite a bit more, especially when

[18] Camille Bacon-Smith, *Enterprising Women: Television, Fandom and the Creation of Popular Myth* (Philadelphia, PA: University of Pennsylvania Press, 1992); Constance Penley, *Nasa/Trek: Popular Science and Sex in America* (London: Verso, 1995).

[19] See Nicolle Lamerichs, "Stranger than Fiction: Fan Identity in Cosplay," *Transformative Works and Cultures* 7 (2010), doi:10.3983/twc.2011.0246.

[20] Lincoln Geraghty, *Cult Collectors: Nostalgia, Fandom and Collecting Popular Culture* (London: Routledge, 2014).

[21] Ibid.

[22] See Matt Hills, "From Dalek Half Balls to Daft Punk Helmets: Mimetic Fandom and the Crafting of Replicas," *Transformative Works and Cultures* 16 (2014), http://dx.doi.org/10.3983/twc.2014.0531; Victoria Godwin, "GI Joe vs. Barbie: Anti-Fandom, Fashion, Dolls, and One-Sixth Scale Action Figures," *The Journal of Fandom Studies* 3, 2 (2015), pp. 119–33.

[23] Melanie Kohnen, "'The Power of Geek': Fandom as Gendered Commodity at Comic-Con," *Creative Industries Journal* 7, 1 (2015), pp. 75–8.

considering VIP packages that include autographs and photographs with stars).[24] Individual autographs and photographs can run into the hundreds as well – some stars can clear hundreds of thousands of dollars in a single weekend.[25] Not all conventions today are huge; some are more intimate affairs with just a few hundred attendees. Fan conventions run the gamut from corporate affairs (Creation Entertainment runs a large empire of *Supernatural* and *Star Trek* conventions, among others), to fan-run events.[26] Fan-run conventions also thrive, including some of the oldest conventions like WisCon (a feminist SF convention which started in 1977 and is held every year in Madison, Wisconsin) and newer conventions like fan vidding[27] convention Vividcon (which has run since 2002).

Indeed, although digital technology may be changing some aspects of fan culture, many traditional analog practices still remain.[28] A sort of "hybrid fandom" exists today, where fans use digital technology to enact traditional practices. Hybrid fandom explores not the ways that technology determines fan usage, but rather how fans use technology in particular ways. Too often, as Matt Hills notes, "online/Web 2.0/social media-enabled fandoms have been studied in isolation from offline fan experiences and identities, treated as separate objects of study, partly because they are often easier to study online as naturally occurring data."[29] Fans use digital technology like Twitter and Tumblr to augment their feelings of fandom, rather than to replace them. Fans use Twitter to post photos of filming in locations in order for other fans to converge on the physical location (e.g., using the hashtag #SetLock for *Sherlock* fandom, or #DWSR for *Doctor Who* Set Report). Fans use technology to enact in-person practices. Fandom in the convergence era isn't about simply replacing one form of technology (e.g., print) with another (e.g., digital), but rather finding the best tools and

[24] Paul Booth, *Crossing Fandoms: SuperWhoLock and the Contemporary Fan Audience* (London: Palgrave Macmillan, 2016); Lynn Zubernis and Katherine Larsen, *Fandom at the Crossroads: Celebration, Shame and Fan/Producer Relationships* (Newcastle: Cambridge Scholars Press, 2012).

[25] Lesley Goldberg, "Stars Getting Rich Off Fan Conventions: How to Take Home 'Garbage Bags Full of $20s,'" *Hollywood Reporter* (September 29, 2016), www.hollywoodreporter .com/live-feed/stars-getting-rich-fan-conventions-933062 (last accessed June 4, 2018).

[26] Booth, *Crossing Fandoms*.

[27] Vidding is the fan practice of editing clips of a media text together, set to music, often to create a new reading of the original text.

[28] Paul Booth and Peter Kelly, "The Changing Faces of *Doctor Who* Fandom: New Fans, New Technologies, Old Practices?" *Participations*, 10, 1 (2013), pp. 56–72; www .participations.org/Volume%2010/Issue%201/5%20Booth%20&%20Kelly%2010.1.pdf (last accessed June 4, 2018).

[29] Matt Hills, "The 'Imaginary Opponents' of Digital Fandom (and Fan Studies)," foreword to Booth, *Digital Fandom 2.0: New Media Studies*, p. xiii.

technologies with which to practice – indeed, to explore – how emotional connection and affect can function in twenty-first century fan cultures.

Convergent Uses of Fandom

The way that science fiction fans *use* their fandom – their fannish emotional energy and affect – in a convergence culture has become a major focus of contemporary fans studies. "Use" here refers not just to the way that fans join communities, discuss their favorite shows, make fan vids, write fan fiction, design costumes, knit creatures, create art, or any of the hundreds of other ways that fandom is actually *practiced* by fans. Rather, in a convergence culture, fandom has also been used as a means to an end – what do people do with the fandom that they experience? The power of the fan affects the media environment. Although no chapter can cover the entirety of ways people use fandom, this discussion will be a useful step for others to explore these topics in more depth.

Much work on fandom in the twenty-first century explores the critical way that fans engage in discussion about social issues, both from a progressive and from a regressive vantage point. Fans are often socially active. For Jenkins, convergence culture discusses how "citizens [are] starting to apply what they have learned as consumers of popular culture towards more overt forms of political activism."[30] If the tools of fandom include foregrounding discussion, mobilizing groups of people, and being critical of the media while also enjoying it, then these skills and principles of "access, participation, reciprocity, and peer-to-peer ... communication," he argues, can be applied to the political forum as well as cultural arenas.[31] Here, fandom is seen less as a way of showing the appeal of a particular SF program or book, and more about "the democratic potentials found in some contemporary cultural trends."[32] Fan engagement is a type of "mobilization through media engagement" – where "fans organized themselves and took collective action."[33] Viewing a particular fandom through this lens allows the fan researcher to discover ways that fandom leads to, or promotes, a more socially aware viewer, and one motivated to make change.

---

[30] Jenkins, *Convergence Culture*, p. 208.
[31] Ibid.
[32] Ibid., p. 247.
[33] Ashley Hinck, "Theorizing a Public Engagement Keystone: Seeing Fandom's Integral Connection to Civic Engagement through the Case of the Harry Potter Alliance," *Transformative Works and Cultures* 10 (2011), doi:10.3983/twc.2012.0311, 2.2.

In a later article with Sangita Shresthova, Jenkins discusses how, by promoting social change, fan groups can tap into "the affective and imaginative properties of popular culture to inspire a more intense connection with their supporters."[34] In this respect, socially aware fans use their favorite media texts as a lens through which positive social change can be enacted. One of the most common groups touted as an example of this politically motivated move from fandom is the Harry Potter Alliance.[35] This group, founded by Andrew Slack in 2005, originally collected donations at "Wizard Rock" shows by the band Harry and the Potters. The organization grew into a fully-fledged nonprofit organization that focused on raising money and awareness for campaigns such as literacy, United States immigration reform, economic justice, gay rights, sexism, labor rights, mental health, body image, and climate change.[36] The group uses the works of J. K. Rowling as an exemplar for "real-world" change. For instance, in the Harry Potter series, a group of magical creatures known as House Elves are held in indentured servitude – verging on slavery. The Harry Potter Alliance uses this fictional representation as a way of talking about the millions of people around the world who are forced to work for little-to-no compensation in terrible conditions, and to help raise money to end this world problem. As Ashley Hinck put it in 2011, this sort of fandom uses "media as cultural resources" where fans have "opportunities to redefine themselves and their social roles."[37]

The Harry Potter Alliance is not the only fan-focused organization enabling social change – others include Nerdfighters, Imagine Better, and Racebending. Racebending is particularly instructive for how fandom can be used to augment socially aware and critical interventions with the media. First discussed in reference to M. Night Shyamalan's *The Last Airbender* (2010), which infamously cast white actors to play the main protagonists instead of using the original anime's East Asian and Inuit-influenced characters,

---

[34] Henry Jenkins and Sangita Shresthova, "Up, Up, and Away! The Power and Potential of Fan Activism," in Henry Jenkins and Sangita Shresthova, eds., "Transformative Works and Fan Activism," *Transformative Works and Cultures* 10 (2012), doi: 10.3983/twc.2012.0435.2012, 1.5, quoting Liesbet van Zoonen, *Entertaining the Citizen: When Politics and Popular Culture Converge* (Lanham, MA: Rowman & Littlefield, 2005), pp. 206–29.

[35] Henry Jenkins, "Cultural Acupuncture": Fan Activism and the Harry Potter Alliance," in Lincoln Geraghty, ed., *Popular Media Cultures* (London: Palgrave Macmillan, 2015), pp. 65–74; Hinck, "Theorizing a Public Engagement Keystone"; Karin E. Westman, "The Weapon We Have Is Love," *Children's Literature Association Quarterly* 33, 2 (2008); Henry Jenkins, "Fan Activism as Participatory Politics: The Case of the Harry Potter Alliance," in Matt Ratto and Megan Boler, eds., *DIY Citizenship: Critical Making and Social Media* (Cambridge, MA: MIT Press, 2014).

[36] See Harry Potter Alliance, Wikipedia, 2016.

[37] Hinck, "Theorizing a Public Engagement Keystone," 2.2.

racebenders sought to correct this overt "whitewashing" of the series through social media campaigns and protests.[38] More recent racebending activity has included the imagining of Hermione in the *Harry Potter* series as a black character (rather than a white one as cast in the films), an overture that started on Tumblr and, as some see, has reached maturation with the casting of a black actress as Hermione in the stage show *Harry Potter and the Cursed Child* (London, 2016).[39]

It's important to realize that many of these groups continue to operate even after the conclusion of the series they are fans of; indeed, an important movement that emerged in 2012 and is still going strong is the Hawkeye Initiative, a collective work that satirizes the depiction of women in comic books.[40] This large and dispersed group collects comic-book-style images of male superheroes posed in the same types of poses that women superheroes are normally depicted in. This fan art makes clear the overt sexism in much comic art. Throughout these different organizations and groups, fandom has been used for particular political and social means – whether it is cultural representations (e.g., gender and race) or political change (e.g., charity work), fandom can be harnessed and used for particular goals.

Protective Fandom

The flip side of socially aware fannish work is the way that fandom can also be used for a more regressive or reactionary agenda. We might term this type of fandom a *protective* fandom, as it seeks not to open up fandom and fan groups to more inclusive and diverse groups, but to draw borders around who *is* and who *is not* considered a fan. In this way, the fans who police these boundaries appear to be trying to protect what they see as their type of fandom from what they interpret as interlopers, or new fans who want to change the fannish stage. These "new" fans are often Othered in important ways – gender being a major one, but youth, political leaning, and ethnicity

---

[38] See Lori Kido Lopez, "Fan Activists and the Politics of Race in *The Last Airbender*," *International Journal of Cultural Studies* 15, 5 (2011), pp. 431–45.

[39] Alanna Bennett, "What a 'Racebent' Hermione Granger Really Represents," *Buzzfeed* (February 1, 2015), www.buzzfeed.com/alannabennett/what-a-racebent-hermione-granger-really-represen-d2yp (last accessed June 4, 2018).

[40] Suzanne Scott, "The Hawkeye Initiative: Pinning Down Transformative Feminisms in Comic-Book Culture through Superhero Crossplay Fan Art," *Cinema Journal* 55, 1 (2015), pp. 150–60; Jennifer McGee, "Putting Men in the Male Gaze: The Hawkeye Initiative and Visual Argument" (2015), http://aska-r.aasa.ac.jp/dspace/bitstream/10638/5679/1/0033-007-201503-033-039.pdf (last accessed June 4, 2018).

being others.[41] Protective fandom is a specific type of anti-fandom, a term that refers to "the realm ... of those who strongly dislike a given text or genre, considering it inane, stupid, morally bankrupt and/or aesthetic drivel."[42] However, rather than anti-fandom of a particular text, these protective fans are more anti-fans of particular types of fans.[43] This protective fandom aura can be seen in varied arenas of fandom, including video game fandom and SF fandom.

Perhaps the most well-known aspect of protective fandom (or at least one of the most controversial aspects) is an amorphous group known as GamerGate.[44] Ostensibly a group formed over allegations that video game designer Zoe Quinn had a relationship with the games journalist who wrote about her game *Depression Quest* (2013), GamerGate soon grew into a more protective role, attempting to police the boundaries of video games (and video game fandom) from the "belief that videogames were being overrun by feminists and social justice warriors, and that (white, male) gamers were maligned victims."[45] The impetus of this protective fandom stemmed from an intense hatred and resentment of how video games – long held as the bastion of an assumed white male player – had become more inclusive. The method of this fandom involved sending death and rape threats to numerous female players and critics, doxxing many women on Twitter.[46] Although members of GamerGate denied that it was, the larger community of video game fans saw it as Simon Parkin notes: "GamerGate is an expression of a narrative that certain video-game fans have chosen to believe: that the types of games they enjoy may change or disappear in the face of progressive criticism and commentary, and that the writers and journalists

---

[41] Kristina Busse, "Geek Hierarchies, Boundary Policing, and the Gendering of the Good Fan," *Participations* 10, 1 (2013), pp. 73–91; www.participations.org/Volume%2010/Issue%201/6%20Busse%2010.1.pdf (last accessed June 4, 2018).

[42] Jonathan Gray, "New Audiences, New Textualities: Anti-Fans and Non-Fans," *International Journal of Cultural Studies* 6, 1 (2003), p. 70.

[43] See Rebecca Williams, "'Anyone Who Calls Muse a *Twilight* Band Will Be Shot on Sight': Music, Distinction, and the 'Interloping Fan' in the *Twilight* Franchise," *Popular Music and Society* 36, 3 (2013), pp. 327–42; Matt Hills, "'Twilight' Fans Represented in Commercial Paratexts and Inter-fandoms: Resisting and Repurposing Negative Fan Stereotypes," in Anne Morey, ed., *Genre, Reception, and Adaptation in the "Twilight" Series* (Farnham, UK: Ashgate, 2012), pp. 113–30.

[44] See Shira Chess and Adrienne Shaw, "A Conspiracy of Fishes, or, How We Learned to Stop Worrying About #GamerGate and Embrace Hegemonic Masculinity," *Journal of Broadcasting and Electronic Media* 59, 1 (2015), 208–20.

[45] Bethan Jones, "#AskELJames, Ghostbusters, and #GamerGate: Digital Dislike and Damage Control," in Booth, ed., *Companion to Media Fandom and Fan Studies*, pp. 415–30.

[46] Doxxing is the act of revealing personal information, like home addresses and phone numbers, of people online.

who cover the industry coordinate their message and skew it to push an agenda."[47] Decried for both their methods and their agenda, GamerGaters are, nevertheless, aspects of a fan culture that perform their fandom in a convergence culture.

Another aspect of protective fandom can be found in SF fandom, most notably with the appearance of the Sad and Rapid Puppies slate-voting groups at the 2013 Hugo Awards. This award is one of the most prominent in SF fandom, and the only one given out as based on votes from the fans themselves. In an attempt to thwart what they saw as an increase in socially aware and specifically feminist/anti-racist SF literature, a group of white male authors led by Larry Correia started promoting specifically action and non-"message" works of SF. This group, the Sad Puppies, wasn't particularly malicious, but did attempt to exorcise the Hugos of more liberal and progressive SF. Later, a group of fans known as the Rapid Puppies, led by alt-right supporter Vox Day, spearheaded a more overtly racist and sexist agenda, attempting to disrupt the Hugos even further. As Katie Wilson describes, Day "has been outspoken about his hatred of social justice warriors, his belief that rape is sometimes permissible, and his conservative political leanings. Using similar language and outlets as the men's rights activists, Day and his followers have firmly aligned themselves with the men's rights movement."[48]

The Sad and Rapid Puppies both attempted to protect what they saw as key elements of *their* fandom from "outsiders" – or, perhaps, as they might put it, "fake fans." Their attempts to disrupt the Hugos by stacking the ballots against progressive and feminist literature, SF by LGBT authors, and more racially aware works stems from a belief that their fandom is under attack. Indeed, Worldcon itself – the convention where the Hugos are held annually – is a more traditional fan convention than the comic cons and media cons that have sprung up more recently. First held in 1939, Worldcon is the premiere SF convention in the world. It is held in various cities, all of which must "bid" to host, and each proposed hosting city must, by Worldcon's constitution, be at least 500 miles away from the site of the previous convention. Many of Worldcon's attendees are older, white, and male (although certainly not all of them). But the fact that the Sad and Rapid

[47] Simon Parkin, "Gamergate: A Scandal Erupts in the Video-Game Community," *The New Yorker* (October 17, 2014), www.newyorker.com/tech/elements/gamergate-scandal-erupts-video-game-community (last accessed June 4, 2018).

[48] Katie Wilson, "Red Pillers, Sad Puppies, and Gamergaters: The State of Male Privilege in Internet Fan Communities," in Booth, ed., *Companion to Media Fandom and Fan Studies*, pp. 431–45.

Puppies have been shut down on multiple occasions – the Hugos allow "No Award" to trump any particular nominee, and the Puppies have mostly lost to "No Award" – means that the demographics of fandom are not necessarily related to its progressive politics and cultural importance. The Puppies (of various influences) may seek to protect their fannish boundaries, but more progressive fans seem to be more influential.

Convergence of Fandom, Aca-Fandom, and Meta-Fandom

An additional aspect of fandom in the twenty-first century that highlights a convergence of different aspects of the fan experience is the way fandom itself has become a significant subject of discussion in both fannish and academic circles. As fandom has become more mainstream and more visible, more people have become interested in fannish history and explorations of what it means to be a fan today (and what it meant in the past). From a fannish perspective, such writings about fandom might be termed "meta-" (although the term can also mean other things), as in meta-essays where fans discuss fandom itself.[49]

One consequence of an increased awareness of fandom and fan practices is an overt fandom *of fandom itself*. This has manifested itself in some fan practices that have created entire canons and texts out of miniscule amounts of information, like *Inspector Spacetime* (2011) fandom.[50] A few brief mentions of *Inspector Spacetime* – an obvious parody of *Doctor Who* (1963–) – on NBC's comedy series *Community* (2009–15) led to an entire online community of work constructing both the text and the fandom of this fake show. Much of the fan work surrounding *Inspector Spacetime* was, in fact, based on a love of fan practices in general. This work included writing outlines and scripts for early seasons of the show, casting the show throughout its fake fifty-year history, and even holding panels at fan conventions about the show, pretending that it had actually been produced.

The same type of "fandom of fandom" is apparent with the fan-created amalgam *SuperWhoLock* (2012) as well.[51] A mash-up of *Supernatural* (2004–), *Doctor Who*, and *Sherlock* (2010–), *SuperWhoLock* creates an entire world where

---

[49] Jenna Kathryn Ballinger, "Fandom and the Fourth Wall," *Transformative Works and Cultures* 17 (2014), http://dx.doi.org/10.3983/twc.2014.0569 (last accessed June 4, 2018).
[50] Booth, "Reifying the Fan"; Booth, *Playing Fans*.
[51] Nistasha Perez, "GIF Fics and the Rebloggable Canon of *SuperWhoLock*," in Paul Booth, ed., *Fan Phenomena: "Doctor Who"* (Bristol, UK: Intellect, 2013), pp. 148–57; Booth, *Playing Fans*; Booth, *Crossing Fandoms*.

these three shows exist in the same universe. The fans, making Gif Fics, fan art, and videos, among other things, have created the entire canon of the series without there actually being crossovers in the texts themselves. Although certainly fandoms of fake shows existed before *Inspector Spacetime* and *SuperWhoLock*, the effect of convergence means that more fans can contribute and generate additional aspects of the fan experience to the creation of these fannish moments.[52]

Since at least the 1990s, fandom has been a subject of academic analysis as well (although the history could be traced back further if scholars open up fan studies to examine non-mediated fandom like sports or non-Eurocentric fandom[53]). Researchers Jonathan Gray, Cornel Sandvoss, and C. Lee Harrington have outlined three "waves" of fan studies research: the first details opening up fandom as a worthwhile area of study; the second sees fandom as an exemplar of other cultural and social institutions; and the third examines how fandom is shown in other aspects of civic and cultural life.[54] As a topic of academic analysis, fandom has proven fruitful for examining changing modes of spectatorship,[55] active audience studies,[56] popular culture studies,[57] participatory cultures,[58] and many other avenues of both qualitative and quantitative research.

Fandom is also taught in college, with more and more university level classes leveraging the critical literacy and creative potentiality of fandom for their students.[59] Indeed, fandom itself teaches many lessons outside the classroom as well.[60] This has not been without controversy, as some university classes have been seen to violate some norms of fan communities.

---

[52] See Questarian fandom; Hills, "Recognition in the Eyes"; Lincoln Geraghty, *Living with "Star Trek": American Culture and the "Star Trek" Universe* (London: I. B. Tauris, 2007).

[53] See Rebecca Wanzo, "African American Acafandom and Other Strangers: New Genealogies of Fan Studies," *Transformative Works and Cultures* 20 (2015), http://dx.doi .org/10.3983/twc.2015.0699 (last accessed June 4, 2018).

[54] Jonathan Gray, Cornel Sandvoss and C. Lee Harrington, Introduction to *Fandom: Identities and Communities in the Digital World* (New York: New York University Press, 2007), pp. 1–17.

[55] Nicholas Abercrombie and Brian J. Longhurst, *Audiences: A Sociological Theory of Performance and Imagination* (London: Sage, 1998).

[56] Victor Costello and Barbara Moore, "Cultural Outlaws: An Examination of Audience Activity and Online Television Fandom," *Television & New Media* 8, 2 (2007), pp. 124–43.

[57] John Fiske, "The Cultural Economy of Fandom," in Lisa A. Lewis, ed., *The Adoring Audience: Fan Culture and Popular Media* (New York: Routledge, 1992), pp. 30–49.

[58] Jenkins, *Convergence Culture*; Leora Hadas, "The Web Planet: How the Changing Internet Divided *Doctor Who* Fan Fiction Writers," *Transformative Works and Cultures* 3 (2009), http://dx.doi.org/10.3983/twc.2009.0129 (last accessed June 4, 2018).

[59] Booth, *Digital Fandom 2.0*.

[60] Paul Booth, "Fandom: The Classroom of the Future," in Anne Kustritz, ed., "European Fans and European Fan Objects: Localization and Translation," *Transformative Works and Cultures* 19 (2015), http://dx.doi.org/10.3983/twc.2015.0650 (last accessed June 4, 2018).

A prominent example is a 2015 course at the University of California, Berkeley, which asked students to respond to fans online without their knowledge or permission. Many of the fans did not wish to be subject to academic scrutiny. So, along with academic investigation, many fan scholars also are concerned with the ethics of fandom in the twenty-first century.

If fandom is becoming an important academic subject, those of us who teach and study fandom are becoming more aware of our own place within fannish circles. Along with a convergence of technologies, a convergence of uses, and a convergence of cultural sensibilities, there has also been a convergence of academics who are fans and fans who are academics. The term "aca-fan," popularized by Jenkins, notes this hybridized identity, where academics reveal their own fannishness in order to represent their identity more authentically. Examining the subject position of the academic as a fan means repositioning the supposed objectivity of academia and revealing the subjectivities that undergird all academic analysis.[61]

Finally, another consideration in the mainstreaming of fandom is recognizing the power of fans in terms of media corporations. As digital technology has developed more intimate(-seeming) connections between the media industries and audiences, fans have become more aware of, and can participate in, interactions with those industries. In the 1960s, as other chapters have discussed, fan letter-writing campaigns (like Bjo Trimble's work with *Star Trek*) helped to popularize fannish interests to CBS, the network that aired *Star Trek*. Today, the multitude of ways that fans can use their fannish interest for corporate ends means that fandom can have an even more significant effect than in the past. Beyond written letters, fans today can Tweet,[62] crowdfund to support a franchise,[63] contact media producers via social

[61] Matt Hills, "Media Academics *as* Media Audiences: Aesthetic Judgments in Media and Cultural Studies," in Jonathan Gray, Cornel Sandvoss, and C. Lee Harrington, eds., *Fandom: Identities and Communities in the Digital World* (New York: New York University Press, 2007), pp. 33–47.

[62] Megan M. Wood and Linda Baughman, "*Glee* Fandom and Twitter: Something New, or More of the Same Old Thing?" *Communication Studies* 63, 3 (2012), pp. 328–44; Tim Highfield, Stephen Harrington and Axel Bruns, "Twitter as a Technology for Audiencing and Fandom: The #Eurovision Phenomenon," *Information, Communication & Society* 16,3 (2013), pp. 315–39; Inger-Lise Kalviknes Bore and Jonathan Hickman, "Continuing *The West Wing* in 140 Characters or Less: Improvised Simulation on Twitter," *The Journal of Fandom Studies* 1, 2 (2013), pp. 219–38.

[63] Paul Booth, "Crowdfunding: A Spimatic Application of Digital Fandom," *New Media & Society* 17, 2 (2015), pp. 149–66; Matt Hills, "*Veronica Mars*, Fandom, and the 'Affective Economics' of Crowdfunding Poachers," *New Media & Society* 17, 2 (2015), pp. 183–97;

media,[64] and can become knowledgeable about the way the media industries work in order to enact change.[65] For example, understanding sponsorship and product placement, fans of the television series *Chuck* (2007–12) took to fast-food restaurant Subway – a sponsor of the show – to order thousands of dollars worth of subs in order to demonstrate their commitment to the show.[66] This type of corporate fandom highlights the numerous ways that fans can use their own fannishness for industrial ends – and how they can be used by those same industries as free labor.[67]

Conclusion: Fandom as Model of Consumption

There is no way that a chapter of this size could encompass all the variety of fandom today, and it is my hope that interested readers will explore much of the literature on fandom that has been published recently. Nevertheless, it is apparent that while some fannish trends are unique to today's convergence culture, others are simply continuations of practices that have a long and varied history. Digital technology has certainly aided fandom in reaching greater numbers of people, in creating more varied communities, and has increased communication across space and time. But it has not changed everything, nor has it made fandom itself different. People still practice fandom in their own unique ways, and use fandom for many things – often contradictorily and often with abandon.

One way that we can see the power and influence of fandom today is with the rise of what Matt Hills has called "textual gamekeepers" – "'official producers are fans who combine communal knowledge with professional industry-insider status."[68] Showrunners in the convergence era, people like Russell T. Davies and Steven Moffat (*Doctor Who*), Joss Whedon (*Buffy the Vampire Slayer, Dollhouse, Firefly*), Ronald D. Moore (*Battlestar Galactica*), J. J. Abrams (*Lost, Star Trek, Star Wars*), Eric Kripke (*Supernatural*), and Tim

---

Suzanne Scott, "The Moral Economy of Crowdfunding and the Transformative Capacity of Fan-ancing," *New Media & Society* 17, 2 (2015), pp. 167–82.

[64] Bertha Chin, "Social Media, Promotional Culture, and Participatory Fandom," in Natalie T. J. Tindall and Amber Hutchins, eds., *Public Relations and Participatory Culture: Fandom, Social Media and Community Engagement* (London: Routledge, 2016), pp. 8–12.

[65] Booth, *Playing Fans*.

[66] Christina Savage, "Chuck Versus the Ratings: Savvy Fans and 'Save Our Show' Campaigns," *Transformative Works and Cultures* 15 (2013); http://dx.doi.org/10.3983/twc .2014.0497 (last accessed June, 2018).

[67] Booth, *Playing Fans*.

[68] Matt Hills, *Triumph of a Time Lord: Regenerating Doctor Who in the Twenty-First Century* (London: I. B. Tauris, 2010), p. 57.

Kring (*Heroes*), grew up as fans themselves.[69] A generation of media producers has been influenced by a half-century of fan work.

Fans have influenced both media production and media consumption for
decades. And yet fandom in the convergence era seems as fresh and as new as
if it were just a few years old. It's a constantly evolving and changing
subculture; what is fannish today is old tomorrow. Fandom is at the center
of today's media and SF cultures, and fans today have more resources at their
fingertips than any other group of fans in the past. Fandom is as varied as the
popular culture than spawns it, and in that respect, fandom has become
ubiquitous. Fandom is us.

---

[69] See Suzanne Scott, "Who's Steering the Mothership? The Role of the Fanboy Auteur in
Transmedia Storytelling," in Aaron Delwiche and Jennifer Jacobs Henderson, eds.,
The Participatory Cultures Handbook (New York: Routledge, 2013), pp. 43–52.

46

Theorizing SF: Science Fiction Studies since 2000

JOHN RIEDER

The first thing to be said about the field of SF studies since 2000 is that it is growing. The bibliography of SF criticism and scholarship on the *Science Fiction Studies* website lists fifty-six monographs published from 2000 through 2002; ten years later, from 2010 through 2012, that number doubles to 112.[1] It is safe to say that this increase in the volume of SF-related scholarship points to an increasing (if still far from universal) acceptance of SF as a legitimate object of study within academic circles. While some might lament the incipient normalization of a field of studies that has often prided itself upon its oppositional status with respect to the literary and academic status quo, I would argue that, first of all, the vigorous presence of Marxist, feminist, and LGBTQ work in the field shows no sign of abating, and, second, that the evidence points toward a healthy maturation of SF studies based not only upon the critical and theoretical framework established by Darko Suvin, Fredric Jameson, and others, but also and perhaps even more on the foundational scholarship of bibliographers such as E. F. Bleiler and Thomas Clareson, historians such as I. F. Clarke, and the encyclopedists John Clute and Peter Nicholls. A good portion of what is produced in the field has been and continues to be straightforward and traditional criticism and scholarship, albeit on nontraditional subject matter. An excellent recent example is Robert Crossley's *Imagining Mars* (2011), which updates a scholarly conversation within literary history that reaches back through Robert M. Philmus's *Into the Unknown* (1970) to Marjorie Hope Nicolson's *Voyages to the Moon* (1948).[2] Yet there are also new directions emerging in twenty-first century SF studies,

---

[1] "Bibliographies and Chronologies of Science Fiction," *Science Fiction Studies*. www.depa uw.edu/sfs.

[2] See Robert Crossley, *Imagining Mars: A Literary History* (Middletown, CT: Wesleyan University Press, 2011); Robert M. Philmus, *Into the Unknown: The Evolution of Science Fiction from Frances Godwin to H. G. Wells* (Berkeley: University of California Press, 1970); and Marjorie Hope Nicolson, *Voyages to the Moon* (New York: Macmillan, 1948).

two of which seem to me paramount: first, the articulation and spreading influence of a historically oriented genre theory that has been steadily displacing an older formalist approach; and second, the participation of SF studies in an ongoing, generations-old deconstruction and decentering of the categories of "Man," "Reason," and "the West" that now connects SF studies with posthumanism, the critique of globalization, human–animal studies, critical race studies, postcolonialism, indigenous studies, and the ecological humanities, among other fields.

The final decades of the twentieth century witnessed a paradigm shift in genre theory, but that shift had a muted and delayed effect on SF studies. Although throughout most of the twentieth century the genre theory guiding Anglo-American literary studies was dominated by an ahistorical, formalist set of assumptions – Northrop Frye's *Anatomy of Criticism* exemplifies this approach at its best – the last decades of the century saw a significant movement toward a theory of genres that treated them as mutable, historical phenomena (e.g., Alistair Fowler's *Kinds of Literature*).[3] One of the key elements of this shift to the historical involves attending to common usage rather than expert identification in the definition of genres. Within SF studies, however, Darko Suvin's thesis concerning SF as the "literature of cognitive estrangement" as advanced in his essay "On the Poetics of the Science Fiction Genre" (1972) and fully elaborated in *Metamorphoses of Science Fiction* (1979) argued for an unusually rigorous exclusion of common usage in order to defend the worthy examples of SF from being confused with the paraliterary masses in their neighborhood.[4] Suvin shaped the conversation well into the first decade of the twenty-first century, not so much commanding assent (many indeed found much to disagree with in his work) as dictating the questions and issues that shaped critical debate, as in China Miéville's influential anti-Suvinian essay "Cognition as Ideology."[5] Indeed, the Suvinian paradigm continues to act as the framework for a good deal of work, whether in substantial agreement with it (e.g., Philip E. Wegner's

[3] Northrop Frye, *Anatomy of Criticism* (Princeton: Princeton University Press, 1967); Alistair Fowler, *Kinds of Literature: An Introduction to the Theory of Genres and Modes* (Cambridge, MA: Harvard University Press, 1982).
[4] Darko Suvin, "On the Poetics of the Science Fiction Genre," *College English* 34, 3 (December 1972), pp. 372–82; and *Metamorphoses of Science Fiction: On the Poetics and History of a Literary Genre* (New Haven: Yale University Press, 1979); and see Chapter 29 of this volume.
[5] China Miéville, "Cognition as Ideology," in China Miéville and Mark Bould, eds., *Red Planets: Marxism and Science Fiction* (Middletown, CT: Wesleyan University Press, 2009), pp. 231–48.

Shockwaves of Possibility) or in revisionist adaptation of it (Seo-Young Chu's *Do Metaphors Dream of Literal Sleep?*).[6]

Nonetheless a radical break from the formalist assumptions underlying Suvin's definition of SF has gained momentum in recent years. Mark Bould and Sherryl Vint's essay "There Is No Such Thing as Science Fiction" explains its provocative title by announcing that "genres are never, as frequently perceived, objects which already exist in the world and which are subsequently studied by genre critics, but fluid and tenuous constructions made by the interaction of various claims and practices by writers, producers, distributors, marketers, readers, fans, critics, and other discursive agents."[7] In their jointly authored *Routledge Concise History of Science Fiction* Bould and Vint adapt Bruno Latour's Actor-Network Theory to describe the ways various agents "recruit" texts into the genre for a panoply of different reasons.[8] My essay "On Defining SF, or Not: Genre Theory, SF, and History," which received the institutional benediction of the Science Fiction Research Association's Pioneer Award in 2012, argues similarly that "the multiplicity of definitions of SF does not reflect widespread confusion about what SF is, but rather it results from the variety of motives the definitions express and the many ways of intervening in the genre's production, distribution, and reception that they pursue."[9]

All of this breaks from genre formalism by asserting, as John Frow puts it, that "genres have no essence: they have historically changing use values."[10] Texts do not belong to genres but rather use them or, more precisely, enable the use of them.[11] Genre identification is not just a question of ascertaining the properties of textual objects, then, but also and crucially involves the agency of the subjects positing genre categories, and therefore study of a genre entails examining the motives, the context, and the effects of those subjects' more or less consciously and successfully executed projects. Hence the emphasis on common usage. What begins to come into view at this point, instead of a set of

---

[6] Phillip E. Wegner, *Shockwaves of Possibility: Essays on Science Fiction, Globalization, and Utopia*. Ralahine Utopian Studies, Vol. 15 (Oxford: Peter Lang, 2014); Seo-Young Chu, *Do Metaphors Dream of Literal Sleep? A Science-Fictional Theory of Representation* (Cambridge, MA: Harvard University Press, 2011).

[7] Mark Bould and Sherryl Vint, "There Is No Such Thing as Science Fiction," in James Gunn, Marleen Barr, and Matthew Candelaria, eds., *Reading Science Fiction* (New York: Palgrave Macmillan, 2009), p. 48.

[8] Mark Bould and Sherryl Vint, *Routledge Concise History of Science Fiction* (New York: Routledge, 2011).

[9] John Rieder, "On Defining Science Fiction, or Not: Genre Theory, SF, and History," *Science Fiction Studies* 37, 2 (July 2010), p. 204.

[10] John Frow, *Genre* (London and New York: Routledge, 2006), p. 134.

[11] Frow, *Genre*, p. 2.

formal possibilities to be sorted out in the interest of understanding some sort of universal grammar of narrative possibilities à la Frye, is the vista of historically shifting systems of genre practice lodged within the overarching framework of ever-evolving and mutating regimes of publicity – ways of producing and distributing, attending and responding to, collecting and classifying, preserving and adapting and retelling and reclassifying stories.

Therefore the shift to the historical paradigm of genre theory has profound methodological implications regarding the object of study and the evidence relevant to critical investigation of the genre: "We need to look beyond the text as the locus for genre, locating genres within the complex interrelations between texts, industries, audiences, and historical contexts."[12] Within twenty-first century SF studies the best examples of scholarship looking beyond the conventional texts to examine the complex interrelations between texts and audiences are afforded by studies of SF fandom. The letters to the editor pages of early SF magazines form a crucial evidentiary archive for John Cheng's study of the interdependence of the popularization of scientific discourses, the emergence of SF within pulp genre practices, and the growth of SF fandom.[13] Justine Labalestier's history of *The Battle of the Sexes in Science Fiction* similarly draws heavily upon the letters to the editor pages of the early SF magazines.[14] In both of these cases, a literary history is being written that identifies the genre, not as a set of formally or thematically similar texts, but rather as a set of protocols and values negotiated by and within a community of practice, and these negotiations take place fluidly and heterogeneously both at the locus of production and various sites of reception.

If we shift our attention from the early SF magazine milieu to later twentieth and early twenty-first century fandom, the phenomenon of SF fan fiction likewise directs us toward the agency of communities of practice. Thus Karen Hellekson, in her introduction to the collection of essays *Fan Fiction and Fan Communities in the Age of the Internet*, identifies the object of study as the "fantext," which means "the entirety of stories and critical commentary written in a fandom."[15] Hellekson maintains that "the

---

[12] Jason Mittell, *Genre and Television: From Cop Shows to Cartoons in American Culture* (London and New York: Routledge, 2004), p. 10.

[13] John Cheng, *Astounding Wonder: Imagining Science and Science Fiction in Interwar America* (Philadelphia: University of Pennsylvania Press, 2012).

[14] Justine Larbalestier, *The Battle of the Sexes in Science Fiction* (Middletown, CT: Wesleyan University Press, 2002).

[15] Karen Hellekson and Kristina Busse, eds., *Fan Fiction and Fan Communities in the Age of the Internet: New Essays* (Jefferson, NC: McFarland, 2006), p. 7.

intertextuality of fannish discourse" results in "the ultimate erasure of a single author as it combines to create a shared space, fandom, that we might also refer to as a *community* . . . The community of fans creates a communal (albeit contentious and contradictory) interpretation [of the fantext] in which a large number of potential meanings, directions, and outcomes co-reside."[16] This "communal interpretation" appears at the horizon of critical practice once genre theory has shifted its focus away from the formal dimensions of single-authored texts to the collective work in progress of a community of practice.

A corollary to this emphasis on the communal and collective is a re-positioning of the place of the single-authored text itself. Once the interpreta-tion and evaluation of any given text or relatively small set of texts is set into dialogue with the collective, conventional practice of the genre, a dialectical analysis of typicality and individuality comes into play. It is obvious enough that every text is an intertext and that seriality and repetition are privileged topics of investigation when one is dealing with examples of franchise fiction or fan fiction. But such topics may be just as pertinently and usefully applied to the work of Philip K. Dick or Ursula K. Le Guin, in particular to the question of what gives such texts their canonical status in the academy.

It is worth noting that an inspection of the online *Science Fiction Studies* bibliography shows that focusing on a single author's work remains one of the most typical strategies – arguably *the* most typical strategy – of mono-graphs in the field since 2000. Not all the authors who receive such attention are canonical, but there is definitely a preponderance of attention to a small group of canonical authors comprised of Philip K. Dick, Jules Verne, Ursula K. Le Guin, and H. G. Wells (eight studies each of Dick and Verne, six of Le Guin, four of Wells; other authors to whom more than one monograph has been devoted since 2000 are J. G. Ballard, Octavia E. Butler, Samuel R. Delany, William Gibson, and Gene Wolfe, with two each). But canonical texts like those of Dick or Le Guin cannot be taken as indications of what is essential to a genre that has no essence, nor can the canonical text be taken as representative of the genre simply because of its canonicity. A text's canoni-city may indeed depend upon its high literary value, but this observation of the text's individual distinction simultaneously raises the collectively oriented question of why and how a particular canon – in this example the canon of higher literary education – is being constructed, a question which shortly leads to the inevitable observation that there are multiple SF canons

---

[16] Hellekson and Bose, eds., *Fan Fiction*, pp. 6–7, emphasis in text.

constructed by different communities of practice for different purposes. It may turn out that extended, durable canonicity has as much to do with a text's being able to serve the disparate purposes of multiple communities as it has to do with satisfying any one set of criteria for excellence.

Another consequence of the shift from thinking of the genre as a set of texts to thinking of it as a way of using texts has been a robust expansion of SF studies from mostly literary subjects to a more broadly defined set of semiotic practices. This shift is easy to see in the reference materials being produced for the field. The table of contents of the 1995 *Anatomy of Wonder 4: A Critical Guide to Science Fiction* is divided into two sections: "Primary Literature" and "Secondary Literature and Research Aids." Print narrative texts are clearly the dominant focus of the chronologically arranged chapters in the "Primary Literature" section, with some attention along the way to film and television, and separate sections on young adult fiction and poetry. The 2009 Routledge Companion to Science Fiction, in contrast, includes not only separate chapters on film, television, and comics (including one on anime and manga) but also a chapter on "SF tourism" and one on digital games. The 2014 *Oxford Handbook of Science Fiction*, edited by Rob Latham, pushes further into cultural practices other than narrative fiction by including chapters on animation, music, performance art, architecture, theme parks, advertising and design, and "UFOs, Scientology, and Other SF Religions."[17]

As such examples suggest, the distance that work based on historical genre theory establishes between itself and the Suvinian paradigm's focus on "the literature of cognitive estrangement" shows up very clearly in the status enjoyed – or, rather, no longer enjoyed – by the category of "literature." The now-classic expositions of the historical development and class function of this category are Raymond Williams's 1977 chapter on the topic in *Marxism and Literature* and Pierre Macherey and Etienne Balibar's essay, originally published in French in 1974, on "Literature as Ideological Form."[18] As Williams shows, the word literature changed from merely designating printed matter, in the seventeenth century, to designating writing of a sophisticated quality, in the eighteenth. During the course of the nineteenth

---

[17] Neil Barron, ed., *Anatomy of Wonder 4: A Critical Guide to Science Fiction* (New Providence, NJ: R. R. Bowker, 1995); Mark Bould, Andrew M. Butler, Adam Roberts, and Sherryl Vint, eds., *The Routledge Companion to Science Fiction*. (London and New York: Routledge, 2009); Rob Latham, ed., *The Oxford Handbook of Science Fiction* (Oxford: Oxford University Press, 2014).

[18] Raymond Williams, *Marxism and Literature* (Oxford: Oxford University Press, 1977); Pierre Macherey and Etienne Balibar, "Literature as an Ideological Form: Some Marxist Propositions," trans. James Kavanagh, *Praxis* 5 (1981), pp. 43–58.

and early twentieth centuries it then came to serve a crucial purpose in the curriculum of higher education. As the study of vernacular national traditions replaced the study of classical languages, the distinction afforded to canonical texts, formerly a linguistic one, turned into a generic one, institutionalizing what Macherey and Balibar call "two practices of the same language."[19] The prestige thereby afforded to "literature" establishes the inferior status conferred upon "genre fiction" that would later underwrite Suvin's dismissal of 95 percent of what is published as SF as unworthy of study.[20] With the advent of a historical genre theory, however, the hierarchical differentiation of literature and genre fiction ceases to be a given of higher educational practice and instead turns into a topic calling for historical research, and the tension between academic genre categorization and the practices pursued in the general culture serves not to exclude mere genre fiction from serious attention but rather to present itself as a crucial object of study.

The continuing relevance of Suvin's analysis of the strategies of cognitive estrangement in SF thus takes place within an increasingly decisive rejection of Suvin's special pleading for the political and thematic distinction of the genre's *form*. This is not only a matter of questioning the ideological commitment to a certain version of cognition built into the theory, as Miéville does; or the specificity of the strategy of cognitive estrangement to SF, as Chu's analysis must lead one to do; or of casting doubt upon its historical acumen, as Roger Luckhurst does in his work on the impurity and hybridity that characterize SF's late-nineteenth-century emergence.[21] It has even more to do with detaching the notion of form itself from structuralist notions of a universal grammar, seeing it instead as an accretion of repeated strategies of responding to widespread ideological and commercial pressures and opportunities. According to this logic, whatever ideological power a genre derives from its form and genealogy depends decisively upon the unequal access afforded to cultural resources by the class-based and institutionally circumscribed positions of its various practitioners.

What then accompanies the opening up of SF studies to the wide range of cultural practices covered in the *Oxford Handbook* is an entire release from any burden of demonstrating thematic or formal coherence across those widely divergent practices of SF – as it perhaps must do in order to negotiate the gaps separating such disparate media and venues. Video games, for instance, which constitute one of the most heavily capitalized and pervasive

---

[19] Macherey and Balibar, "Literature as an Ideological Form," p. 47.
[20] Suvin, "On the Poetics of the Science Fiction Genre," p. 381.
[21] Roger Luckhurst, *Science Fiction* (London: Polity Press, 2005), pp. 15–29.

of contemporary science fictional practices, "are not representations, or images, or narratives, or codes, or sets of rules ... [but rather] the video game is an enactive event that takes place across the biomechanical assemblage formed by the user's body, the hardware system, and the software program."[22] Thus Pawel Frelik writes in the *Oxford Handbook* chapter on video games "that the exclusive narrative approach imported from SF literary and film studies is biased, unproductive, and – most importantly – insufficient to address some of the most relevant aspects of the medium."[23] But even within literary and film studies of SF where notions of the text remain consonant with the concept of "literature," discarding Suvinian special pleading for SF's peculiar exercise of "cognitive estrangement" opens the way to the project of investigating its cognate relation to neighboring popular genres such as detective fiction or the western, and therefore to a more broadly based approach to topics such as colonialism and race in SF as well.

At this point the effects of the paradigm shift in genre theory dovetail with the second major trend in twenty-first-century SF studies I wish to discuss here: the ongoing deconstruction of Man, Reason, and the West. Just as the category of "literature" needs to be rethought once historical inquiry exposes its complicity with the exercise of class power, or as, in the last quarter of the twentieth century, the American Western entered a heavily revisionist phase once the historiography of the American West ceased to idealize the concept of the frontier and began to view US westward expansion as a typical example of imperialist and capitalist territorial appropriation,[24] SF studies in the twenty-first century are being reshaped by critical challenges to the cultural status and privilege of science. These challenges are not a twenty-first-century phenomenon. They have their roots deep in the twentieth-century Western Marxist tradition, where Theodor Adorno and Max Horkheimer's *Dialectic of Enlightenment* establishes a critique of the social and ecological impact of Western technoscience that reverberates to the present, and in the epistemological and sociological critique of the practices and self-understanding of science launched by Thomas Kuhn's groundbreaking analysis of *The*

---

[22] Colin Milburn, *Mondo Nano: Fun and Games in the World of Digital Matter* (Durham, NC: Duke University Press, 2015), p. 57.

[23] Latham, ed., *Oxford Handbook*, p. 228. See also Pawel Frelik's contribution (Chapter 39) to this volume.

[24] John Rieder, "American Frontiers," in Eric Carl Link and Gerry Canavan, eds., *The Cambridge Companion to American Science Fiction* (Cambridge: Cambridge University Press, 2015), pp. 167–9.

Structure of Scientific Revolutions.[25] More recently a historiography of science has come to prominence that radically revises claims that the scientific method emerges from dedication to the pursuit of pure knowledge or an objective disassociation of scientific research from political and institutional constraints (e.g., Steven Shapin and Simon Schaffer's 1985 study of Thomas Boyle and Thomas Hobbes).[26] It is on the basis of all of these intellectual developments that Bruno Latour argues, "technoscience is part of a war machine and should be studied as such," and Donna Haraway in her "Cyborg Manifesto" (1985) identifies the figure of the cyborg as "the illegitimate offspring of militarism and patriarchal capitalism."[27] Perhaps the scope of this ongoing critique of Western scientific practices is best captured in the widespread adoption in the twenty-first century of the notion of the Anthropocene to designate the epochal, geological impact of human activity – and especially of Western industrial capitalism – on the planet, in the form of climate change and species extinction.[28]

The decentering of anthropomorphism evident in the concept of the Anthropocene – a decentering that transforms human shaping of the environment from the godlike exercise of reason to something more like the impact of the giant comet that ended the age of the dinosaurs – comes to bear on SF studies in a number of closely related ways, starting with the discourse of posthumanism. Posthumanism is the theoretical exploration of the impact of cybernetics and the development of artificial intelligence on the status of the human subject, and therefore, of course, on the exercise of reason and the meaning of technology. In his 1991 essay "The SF of Theory," on the work of Jean Baudrillard and Donna Haraway, Istvan Csicery-Ronay sets the stakes of the problem very high: "The development of communications-technologies and the culture surrounding them has transformed every conceivable aspect of human and terrestrial life into an

---

[25] Theodor W. Adorno and Max Horkheimer, *The Dialectic of Enlightenment*, ed. Gunzelin Schmid Noerr, trans. Edmund Jephcott (Stanford: Stanford University Press, 2002); Thomas Kuhn, *The Structure of Scientific Revolutions* (Chicago: University of Chicago Press, 1962).

[26] Steven Shapin and Simon Schaffer, *Leviathan and the Air-Pump: Hobbes, Boyle, and the Experimental Life* (Princeton: Princeton University Press, 1985).

[27] Bruno Latour, *Science in Action* (Cambridge, MA: Harvard University Press, 1987), p. 172, quoted in Roger Luckhurst, "Bruno Latour's Scientifiction: Networks, Assemblages, and Tangled Objects," *Science Fiction Studies* 33,1 (March 2006), p. 7; Donna Haraway, *Simians, Cyborgs, and Women: The Reinvention of Nature* (New York: Routledge, 1991), p. 151.

[28] See e.g., Donna Haraway, *Staying with the Trouble: Making Kin in the Chthulucene* (Durham, NC: Duke University Press, 2016), pp. 44–7.

aspect of a cybernetic control model."[29] The transformation of life into information in this description of a thesis shared by Baudrillard and Haraway echoes the analysis of contemporary thought articulated in the deconstructionist philosophy of Jacques Derrida, who pronounced in his manifesto-like essay "Structure, Sign, and Play in the Discourse of the Human Sciences" in 1968 that the history of Western philosophy had until recently been the history of continually displacing and reinscribing its "center" – that is, that which acts as an originary reference and thereby makes the concept of structure possible and coherent, whether that function had been performed in the name of truth, god, the good, or the law. According to Derrida, a rupture had taken place in Western discourse precisely because the concept of the center had lost its aura of necessity, so that it had become instead "necessary to begin thinking that there was no center, that the center had no natural site, that it was not a fixed locus but a function ... This was the moment when language invaded the universal problematic; the moment when, in the absence of a center or origin, everything became discourse."[30]

From the perspective of posthumanism, the moment Derrida speaks of is consonant with and inseparable from the moment when thought itself is forced to confront the possibility that human consciousness is reducible to a mechanism. The crucial thing about the transformation of human life into "an aspect of a cybernetic control model" is that the human subject's sovereignty over itself has disappeared into a linguistic chain of signifiers, because the speaking human subject is no longer being identified with a body that originates a voice but with a position and a function within language. As one of the major analysts of posthumanism, N. Katherine Hayles, has put it, language no longer is understood to be operating according to a binary opposition between presence and absence (referring back to the originating presence of a center), but instead one between pattern and randomness.[31] Thus the linguistic subject no longer produces truth according to some regime of referential signification, but rather as an effect of patterning, a quasi-grammatical, structural effect that may be inevitable and inescapable but is not therefore foundational. Discourse

[29] Istvan Csicsery-Ronay, Jr., "The SF of Theory: Baudrillard and Haraway," *Science Fiction Studies* 18, 3 (November 1991), p. 389.
[30] Jacques Derrida, *Writing and Difference*, trans. Alan Bass (Chicago: University of Chicago Press, 1978), p. 280.
[31] N. Katherine Hayles, *How We Became Posthuman: Virtual Bodies in Cybernetics, Literature, and Informatics* (Chicago: University of Chicago Press, 1999), p. 44.

becomes a truth-machine, truth itself an epiphenomenon of this mechanical, cybernetic process.

There is a camp within posthumanism that embraces this dematerialization of the subject as a mode of liberating the consciousness from its bodily limitations, maintaining the unqualified sovereignty of reason over technical manipulation in looking forward to a neo-religious "rapture of the nerds" in which human consciousness can be uploaded into computers and freed from the body and death. The prevailing tendency within SF studies, however, follows both Hayles's compelling criticism of the conceptual and methodological errors that lead to the reduction of human subjectivity to mere information and her cogent arguments for the importance of attending to embodiment in order to understand not only the human subject but also information itself and informational processing machines. Yet Hayles's critique of the notion that human consciousness is reducible to a computer program is also, precisely, an emphatic continuation of the Derridean decentering of Man and Reason because it is an attack on a delusion of sovereignty that generates a fantasy of human "enlightenment" being able to separate itself from the body, the planet, and the past.

The topic of posthumanism entered SF studies in the 1990s as a more or less inevitable response to the cyberpunk movement. It continues to thrive in the twenty-first century partly because of its relevance to digital media, since the cyberpunk movement itself seems in retrospect to have been a harbinger of the contemporary gaming industry. However, the robustness of posthumanism has at least as much to do with the way the analysis of cybernetic networking intersects with the study of contemporary political and economic conditions as well as with posthumanism's anti-anthropocentric alliance with human–animal studies.

The weaving together of the political, economic, and literary implications of posthumanism is exemplified by Steven Shaviro's *Connected, or What It Means to Live in a Network Society*, in which Shaviro combines an analysis of the networks of publicity and consumption constructed by contemporary transnational corporations with his own network of readings connecting philosophical and political economic texts with the SF of Ken Jeter, Philip K. Dick, and many others. Shaviro, like Hayles, opposes the illusion of separation engendered by what Hayles calls the informatization of discourse: "The physical and virtual worlds should not be opposed; rather, they are two coordinated realms, mutually dependent products of a vast web of social, political, economic, and technological changes."[32] Thus, he argues, the virtualization of the subject explored in cyberpunk and posthumanist theory depends upon a concomitant virtualization of money most evident in the speculative instruments of finance capital developed in the last quarter of the twentieth century: "The phenomena of virtual reality – from cyberpunk disembodiment to prosthetic hyperembodiment, and from distributed, artificial intelligence to concentrated corporeal enhancement – all depend on the frantic exchange and circulation of money, or on what Marx [in the second volume of *Capital*] called the accelerated turnover of capital."[33] The target of Shaviro's critique is the neoliberal regime of accumulation analyzed by David Harvey, Manuel Castells, and Antonio Negri and Michael Hardt, and although the precision, imagination, and erudition of Shaviro's work is extraordinary, his marshalling the robust Marxist legacy of SF studies against neoliberal globalization is typical.[34]

Shaviro's emphasis on networks of exchange, identifying the objects of analysis as positions within such networks rather than as discreet, pre-given things, depends upon a fundamental commitment to semiotics but at the same time coheres with the shift away from structuralist formalism to a historical genre theory in its dedication to examining the collective construction of objects and practices in carefully historicized, socially embedded contexts. Anne Balsamo similarly writes of technologies that they "are not merely objects: they are best understood as assemblages of people, materialities, practices, and possibilities."[35] The body itself is also, increasingly, a semiotic construction negotiated along the medical and juridical lines offered by contemporary political and economic arrangements. According to Susan Squier in an essay on SF and transplant medicine, for instance, "the value and significance of a human organ ... is *produced* through a complex set of institutional negotiations."[36] Squier articulates a position with wide relevance to current SF studies when she maintains that SF, which once offered "imaginative emancipation" by creating "magical new worlds," instead "now shocks us by its resemblance

---

[32] Steven Shaviro, *Connected, or What It Means To Live in a Network Society* (Minnesota: University of Minnesota Press, 2003), p. 130.

[33] Shaviro, *Connected*, p. 128.

[34] Shaviro *Connected*, pp. 128–9, and cf. Wegner, *Shockwaves of Possibility*, and Eric D. Smith, *Globalization, Utopia, and Postcolonial Science Fiction: New Maps of Hope* (New York: Palgrave Macmillan, 2012).

[35] Anne Balsamo, *Designing Culture: The Technological Imagination at Work* (Durham, NC: Duke University Press, 2011), p. 31.

[36] Susan Squier, *Liminal Lives: Imagining the Human at the Frontiers of Biomedicine* (Duke University Press, 2004), p. 178.

to fact."[37] SF is now itself one of those sites of cultural negotiation "integral to the normalization and institutionalization of . . . the relation between body, body part, and identity; and the notion that even the death of the self is subject to social and scientific construction."[38]

Squier's invocation of the cultural construction of death itself points toward the contemporary governance model Michel Foucault calls biopolitics. As Sherryl Vint parses the term, under biopolitical governance "the old right to 'take life or let live' is now complemented and at the same time transformed by the new power 'to make live and to let die.'" Biopolitics thus entails "a shift from governing humans as legal or civil subjects toward governing the biological life of the species."[39] Here another convergence of political, juridical, and scientific discourses opens up to the ongoing deconstruction of Man and Reason in SF studies. The itinerary of Donna Haraway's work from her cyborg manifesto of 1985 to her *Companion Species Manifesto* of 2003 pioneered an alliance between posthumanism and human–animal studies most fully explored in Sherryl Vint's 2010 book *Animal Alterity*. Vint takes her point of departure both from Haraway and from Derrida's 1997 series of lectures *The Animal That Therefore I Am*:

> Combining the poetic with the philosophical or juridical [concepts of the animal distinguished in Derrida's work], then, will enable us to recognize the extent to which our entire philosophical tradition of subjectivity has been premised upon the separation of human from animal. SF, more than any other literature, can defy this separation because its generic premises enable us to imagine the animal quite literally looking at and addressing us from a non-anthropocentric perspective.[40]

The "our" in "our entire philosophical tradition of subjectivity" brings up the third element in the triad of Man, Reason, and the West. A historical examination of Western juridical and scientific constructions of the category of the human in relation to race, colonialism, and indigeneity, and of the way SF has participated in or challenged those constructions, has meant that critical race studies and postcolonial theory have had a stronger impact on SF studies in the first decade and a half of the twenty-first century than throughout the twentieth. Engagement with race in SF studies gets

---

[37] Squier, *Liminal Lives*, p. 213.

[38] Squier, *Liminal Lives*, p. 183.

[39] Sherryl Vint, *Animal Alterity: Science Fiction and the Question of the Animal* (Liverpool: Liverpool University Press, 2010), pp. 16–17, quoting Michel Foucault, *Society Must Be Defended: Lectures at the College de France 1975–1976* (New York: Palgrave Macmillan, 2003), p. 241.

[40] Vint, *Animal Alterity*, pp. 5–6.

seriously under way with the construction of Afrofuturism in Mark Dery's "Black to the Future" in 1993, and is solidified with the inclusion of major artists like Sun Ra, Samuel R. Delany, and Octavia E. Butler in a tradition of African-American SF writing dating back to the Harlem Renaissance in Sheree R. Thomas's groundbreaking anthology *Dark Matter* in 2000.[41] Both depictions of race and examination of the work of non-white writers have subsequently established themselves as major topics in SF studies. Alongside that development has come a spate of anthologies and critical studies on the topics of colonialism and postcolonialism in SF. My *Colonialism and the Emergence of Science Fiction* argues for the ubiquity and inescapability of references to colonial history, deployment of colonial discourses, and engagement with colonial ideologies in the development of SF up to the Second World War.[42] Although much of the burden of this account is devoted to the widespread and commonplace construction of apologetic fantasies that naturalize colonial and imperial oppression of colonized peoples and expropriation of their land and resources, the decentering effect of encounters with non-Western cultures on conceptions of the human and the possible is in a sense the book's hero.

The most recent episode in the deconstruction of the West in SF studies ties it together firmly with the deconstruction of Man and Reason. This is the elaboration of an indigenous strain of SF whose main exponent has been the Anishinaabe scholar Grace W. Dillon. In the introduction to her 2012 anthology of indigenous SF, *Walking the Clouds*, Dillon challenges the traditional Western notion of what constitutes the "science" in "science fiction" by juxtaposing Western science with "Indigenous scientific literacies," also known as "traditional ecological knowledge" or TEK.[43] Arguing that "Native/Indigenous/Aboriginal sustainable practices constitute a science despite their lack of resemblance to taxonomic Western systems of thought," Dillon crafts a wholly positive engagement with what is of lasting value in Suvin's analysis of cognitive estrangement in SF, radically destabilizing – or better, refreshing – what counts as cognitive as well as

---

[41] Mark Dery, "Black to the Future: Interviews with Samuel R. Delany, Greg Tate, and Tricia Rose," *South Atlantic Quarterly* 92, 4 (1993), pp. 735–78; Sheree R. Thomas, ed., *Dark Matter: A Century of Speculative Fiction from the African Diaspora* (New York: Time Warner, 2000).

[42] John Rieder, *Colonialism and the Emergence of Science Fiction* (Middletown, CT: Wesleyan University Press, 2008).

[43] Grace L. Dillon, "Imagining Indigenous Futurisms," in Grace L. Dillon, ed., *Walking the Clouds: An Anthology of Indigenous Science Fiction* (Tucson: University of Arizona Press, 2012), pp. 1–12.

what counts as strange.[44] The way Dillon's emphasis on sustainability speaks to the work of the other scholars mentioned here in posthumanism, human–animal studies, and postcolonialism makes much of twentieth-century SF's enthrallment to the ideological celebration of technological progress seem increasingly untenable, if not merely quaint. It also reorients the utopian potential of SF away from fantasies of technological transcendence of planetary limits or the discovery of inexhaustible energy sources and towards the project, as Donna Haraway puts it, of trying to make that slice of the geological record called the Anthropocene as thin as possible. The ambitions motivating the deconstruction of Man, Reason, and the West are now being aimed at combining SF's negotiation of common usage with the struggle for economic and political justice, indigenous resurgence, and ecological survival.

[44] Dillon, "Imagining Indigenous Futurisms," p. 7.

Select Bibliography

Aarseth, Espen. *Cybertext: Perspectives on Ergodic Literature*. Baltimore, MD: Johns Hopkins University Press, 1997.

Adorno, Theodor W. and Max Horkheimer. *The Dialectic of Enlightenment*, ed. Gunzelin Schmid Noerr, trans. Edmund Jephcott. Stanford: Stanford University Press, 2002.

Aldiss, Brian W. *Billion Year Spree* with co-author David Wingrove. London: Weidenfeld & Nicholson, 1973. (Later republished as *Trillion Year Spree*. New York: Atheneum, 1986.)

Alkon, Paul K. *Origins of Futuristic Fiction*. Athens: University of Georgia Press, 1987.

Science Fiction Before 1900: Imagination Discovers Technology. New York: Routledge, 2002.

Allen, Kathryn. *Disability in Science Fiction: Representations of Technology as Cure*. New York: Palgrave Macmillan, 2013.

Amis, Kingsley. *New Maps of Hell*. London: Penguin Classics, 2012.

Anderson, Jeffrey E. *Conjure in African American Society*. Baton Rouge: Louisiana State Press, 2005.

Anderson, Reynaldo and Charles E. Jones, eds. *Afrofuturism 2.0: The Rise of Astro-Blackness*. Lanham, MD: Lexington Books, 2015.

Applebaum, Noga. *Representations of Technology in Science Fiction for Young People*. New York: Routledge, 2010.

Ashley, Mike and Robert A. W. Lowndes. *The Gernsback Days: A Study of the Evolution of Modern Science Fiction from 1911 to 1936*. Holicong, PA: Wildside Press, 2004.

Asimov, Isaac. *In Memory Yet Green*. New York: Doubleday, 1979.

Asimov, Isaac and Frederik Pohl. *Our Angry Earth*. New York: Tor, 1991.

Asma, Stephen T. *On Monsters: An Unnatural History of Our Worst Fears*. Oxford: Oxford University Press, 2009.

Attebery, Brian. *Decoding Gender in Science Fiction*. New York: Routledge, 2002.

"Super Men." *Science Fiction Studies* 25, 1 (1998), pp. 61–76. www.jstor.org.lib-ezproxy .tamu.edu:2048/stable/4240674.

Attebery, Brian, and Veronica Hollinger, eds. *Parabolas of Science Fiction*. Middletown, CT: Wesleyan University Press, 2013.

Bacon-Smith, Camille. *Enterprising Women: Television, Fandom and the Creation of Popular Myth*. Philadelphia, PA: University of Pennsylvania Press, 1992.

Bakhtin, M. M. *The Dialogic Imagination: Four Essays*, trans. Caryl Emerson and Michael Holquist. Austin: University of Texas Press, 1981.

Ballard, J. G. *A User's Guide to the Millennium: Essays and Reviews*. New York: Picador USA, 1996.

"Which Way to Inner Space?" *New Worlds* 118 (1962).

Ballinger, Jenna Kathryn. "Fandom and the Fourth Wall." *Transformative Works and Cultures*, 17 (2014). http://dx.doi.org/10.3983/twc.2014.0569.

Banerjee, Anindita. *We Modern People: Science Fiction and the Making of Russian Modernity.* Middletown, CT: Wesleyan University Press, 2013.

Barr, Marleen S. *Feminist Fabulation: Space/Postmodern Fiction.* Iowa City: University of Iowa Press, 1992.

    Lost in Space: Probing Feminist Science Fiction and Beyond. Chapel Hill: University of North Carolina Press, 1993.

Barr, Marleen S., ed. *Afro-Future Females: Black Writers Chart Science Fiction's Newest New-Wave Trajectory.* Columbus: Ohio State University Press, 2008.

Barron, Neil, ed. *Anatomy of Wonder 4: A Critical Guide to Science Fiction.* New Providence, NJ: R. R. Bowker, 1995.

Barthes, Roland. *The Eiffel Tower and Other Mythologies*, trans. Richard Howard. Berkeley: University of California Press, 1997.

Bartkowski, Frances. *Feminist Utopias.* Lincoln, NE: University of Nebraska Press, 1989.

Basu, Balaka, Katherine Broad, and Carrie Hintz, eds. *Contemporary Dystopian Fiction for Young Adults: Brave New Teenagers.* New York: Routledge, 2013.

Baudrillard, Jean. *Simulacra and Simulation.* Stanford: Stanford University Press, 1988.

Beaumont, Matthew. *The Spectre of Utopia: Utopian and Science Fictions at the Fin de Siècle.* Bern: Peter Lang, 2012.

Bell, Andrea and Yolanda Molina-Gavilán, eds. *Cosmos Latinos: An Anthology of Science Fiction from Latin America and Spain.* Middletown, CT: Wesleyan University Press, 2003.

Berardi, Franco "Bifo." *Futurability: The Age of Impotence and the Horizon of Possibility.* London and New York: Verso Books, 2017.

Berger, Albert I. *The Magic That Works: John W. Campbell and the American Response to Technology.* San Bernadino: Borgo, 1993.

Berman, Marshall. *All That Is Solid Melts Into Air: The Experience of Modernity.* London: Verso, 2010.

"Bibliographies and Chronologies of Science Fiction." *Science Fiction Studies.* www.depauw.edu/sfs.

Blacklock, Mark. *The Emergence of the Fourth Dimension: Higher Spatial Thinking in the Fin de Siècle.* Oxford: Oxford University Press, 2016.

Bleiler, Everett F. *Science-Fiction: The Early Years.* Kent, OH: Kent State University Press, 1990.

Bleiler, Everett F., and Richard J. Bleiler. *Science-Fiction: The Gernsback Years: A Complete Coverage of the Genre Magazines Amazing, Astounding, Wonder, and Others from 1926 through 1936.* Kent, OH: Kent University Press, 1998.

Blish, James (as William Atheling, Jr.). *More Issues at Hand.* Chicago: Advent, 1970.

Bogost, Ian. *Persuasive Games: The Expressive Power of Videogames.* Cambridge, MA: MIT Press, 2010.

    Unit Operations: An Approach to Videogame Criticism. Cambridge, MA: MIT Press, 2008.

Bonneuil, Christophe, and Jean-Baptiste Fressoz. *The Shock of the Anthropocene.* London: Verso, 2016.

Booker, M. Keith. *Monsters, Mushroom Clouds, and the Cold War: American Science Fiction and the Roots of Postmodernism, 1946–1964. Contributions to the Study of Science Fiction and Fantasy*, Number 95. Westport, CT: Greenwood Press, 2001.

    Science Fiction Television. Westport, CT: Praeger, 2004.

Booker, M. Keith, and Anne-Marie Thomas, eds. *The Science Fiction Handbook*. Chichester, UK: Wiley-Blackwell, 2009.

Booth, Paul. *Digital Fandom 2.0*. New York: Peter Lang, 2016.

    Playing Fans: Negotiating Fandom and Media in the Digital Age. Iowa City, IA: University of Iowa Press, 2015.

Boston, John and Damien Broderick. *Building New Worlds, 1946–1959: The Carnell Era, Volume One*. San Bernardino, CA: Borgo Press, 2012.

    New Worlds: Before the New Wave, 1960–1964: The Carnell Era, Volume Two. San Bernardino, CA: Borgo Press, 2013.

Bould, Mark. "Come Alive By Saying No: An Introduction to Black Power Sf." *Science Fiction Studies* 102 (2007), pp. 220–40.

    "Introduction: Africa SF," *Paradoxa* 25 (2013).

    Science Fiction. New York: Routledge, 2012.

    "The Ships Landed Long Ago: Afrofuturism and Black SF." *Science Fiction Studies* 34, 2 (July 2007).

Bould, Mark, and Sherryl Vint. *The Routledge Concise History of Science Fiction*. New York: Routledge, 2011.

    "There Is No Such Thing as Science Fiction." In James Gunn, Marleen Barr, and Matthew Candelaria, eds., *Reading Science Fiction*. New York: Palgrave Macmillan, 2009, pp. 43–51.

Bould, Mark, Andrew M. Butler, Adam Roberts, and Sherryl Vint, eds. *Fifty Key Figures in Science Fiction*. London: Routledge, 2010.

    The Routledge Companion to Science Fiction. London and New York: Routledge, 2009.

Bova, Ben. "Teaching Science Fiction." *Analog Science Fiction Science Fact* (June 1974).

Braidotti, Rosi. *The Posthuman*. Oxford: Wiley, 2013.

Bretnor, Reginald, ed. *Science Fiction: Today and Tomorrow: A Discursive Symposium*. New York: Harper and Row, 1974.

Broderick, Damien. *Reading by Starlight: Postmodern Science Fiction*. London: Routledge, 1994.

Brooke-Rose, Christine. *A Rhetoric of the Unreal*. Cambridge: Cambridge University Press, 1981.

Brown, Bill. *Reading the West: An Anthology of Dime Novel Westerns*. Boston: Bedford/St. Martin's, 1997.

    "Science Fiction, the World's Fair, and the Prosthetics of Empire, 1910–1915." In Amy Kaplan and Donald E. Peas, eds., *Cultures of United States Imperialism*. Durham, NC: Duke University Press, 1993.

Brown, J. Andrew and M. Elizabeth Ginway, eds. *Latin American Science Fiction: Theory and Practice*. New York: Palgrave Macmillan, 2012.

Bukatman, Scott. *Blade Runner*. 2nd edn. Palgrave Macmillan, 2012.

    Terminal Identity: The Virtual Subject in Post-Modern Science Fiction. Durham, NC: Duke University Press, 1993.

Busse, Kristina. "Geek Hierarchies, Boundary Policing, and the Gendering of the Good Fan." *Participations* 10, 1 (2013).

    "In Focus: Fandom and Feminism: Gender and the Politics of Fan Production," *Cinema Journal* 48, 4 (2009).

Butler, Andrew M. *Solar Flares: Science Fiction in the 1970s*. Liverpool: Liverpool University Press, 2012.

Campbell, John W., ed. *Astounding* (1937–71).

The Best of John W. Campbell. New York: Ballantine, 1976.

Canary, Robert H. "New Worlds for Old?" *Science Fiction Studies*, 2, 2 (1975).

Canavan, Gerry. "The Suvin Event." In Darko Suvin, *Metamorphoses of Science Fiction*, ed. Gerry Canavan. New York: Ralahine Utopian Studies, 2016.

Canavan, Gerry, and Kim Stanley Robinson. *Green Planets: Ecology and Science Fiction*. Middletown, CT: Wesleyan University Press, 2014.

Candelaria, Matthew. "Before We Begin: Some Notes on Early SF Criticism." In James Gunn and Matthew Candelaria, eds., *Speculations on Speculation*. Lanham, MD: Scarecrow, 2005.

Capanna, Pablo. *El mundo de la ciencia ficción*. Buenos Aires: Ediciones Letra Buena, 1992.

Carrington, André M. *Speculative Blackness: The Future of Race in Science Fiction*. Minneapolis: University of Minnesota Press, 2016.

Carson, Rachel. *Silent Spring*. New York: Mariner Books, 2002.

Carter, Paul. *The Creation of Tomorrow: Fifty Years of Magazine Science Fiction*. New York: Columbia University Press, 1977.

Cheng, John. *Astounding Wonder: Imagining Science and Science Fiction in Interwar America*. Philadelphia: University of Pennsylvania Press, 2012.

Chu, Seo-Young. *Do Metaphors Dream of Literal Sleep? A Science-Fictional Theory of Representation*. Cambridge, MA: Harvard University Press, 2011.

Clareson, Thomas D., ed. *Extrapolation: A Science-Fiction Newsletter: Volumes 1–10, December 1959–May 1969*. Reprint. New York: Johnson, 1970.

Some Kind of Paradise: The Emergence of American Science Fiction. Westport, CT: Greenwood Press, 1985.

Clarke, I. F. *Voices Prophesying War: Future Wars, 1763–3749*. Oxford: Oxford University Press, 1993.

Clute, John. *The Darkening Garden: A Short Lexicon of Horror*. Cauheegan: Payseur and Schmidt, 2006.

Look at the Evidence: Essays and Reviews. Liverpool: Liverpool University Press, 1995.

Pardon This Intrusion: Fantastika in the World Storm. Essex, UK: Beccon Publications, 2011.

Clute, John, and Peter Nicholls, eds. *The Encyclopedia of Science Fiction*. 3rd edn. New York: St. Martin's Press, 1993.

Coogan, Peter, *Superhero: The Secret Origin of a Genre*. Austin, TX: MonkeyBrain Books, 2006.

Coppa, Francesca. "A Brief History of Media Fandom." In Karen Hellekson and Kristina Busse, eds., *Fan Fiction and Fan Communities in the Age of the Internet*. Jefferson, NC: McFarland, 1996, pp. 41–59.

Costello, Matthew. *Comic Books and the Unmasking of Cold War America*. New York: Bloomsbury Academic, 2009.

Cox, J. Randolph. *The Dime Novel Companion*. Westport, CT: Greenwood Press, 2000.

Crossley, Robert. *Imagining Mars: A Literary History*. Middletown, CT: Wesleyan University Press, 2011.

Crowe, Michael J. *The Extraterrestrial Life Debate, 1750–1900*. New York: Dover Publications, 1999.

Csicsery-Ronay, Istvan, Jr. "Science Fiction and Empire." *Science Fiction Studies* 30, 2 (2003), pp. 231–45.

 The Seven Beauties of Science Fiction. Middletown, CT: Wesleyan University Press, 2008.

Daston, Lorraine and Katherine Park. *Wonders and the Order of Nature*. New York: Zone Books, 1998.

DeGraw, Sharon. *The Subject of Race in American Science Fiction*. New York: Routledge, 2007.

De Kosnik, Abigail. "Fandom as Free Labor." In Trebor Scholz, ed., *Digital Labor: The Internet as Playground and Factory*. New York: Routledge, 2013.

Delany, Samuel R. *Jewel-Hinged Jaw: Notes on the Language of Science Fiction*. New York: Berkley Windhover, 1977.

 The Motion of Light in Water: Sex and Science Fiction Writing in the East Village. Minneapolis: University of Minnesota Press, 2004.

 "Racism and Science Fiction." *The New York Review of Science Fiction* 120 (August 1998), www.nyrsf.com/racism-and-science-fiction-.html. Reprinted in Sheree R. Thomas, ed., *Dark Matter: A Century of Speculative Fiction from the African Diaspora*. New York: Warner Books, 2000.

 Starboard Wine: More Notes on the Language of Science Fiction. Pleasantville, NY: Dragon Press, 1984.

Del Rey, Lester. *The World of Science Fiction: The History of a Subculture*. New York: Del Rey, 1977.

Denning, Michael. *Mechanic Accents: Dime Novels and Working-Class Culture in America*. London: Verso, 1987.

Derrida, Jacques. *The Animal That Therefore I Am*, ed. Marie-Louise Mallet, trans. David Wills. New York: Fordham University Press, 2008.

Dery, Mark. "Afrofuturism Reloaded: 15 Theses in 15 Minutes" (February 1, 2016), www.fabrikzeitung.ch/afrofuturism-reloaded-15-theses-in-15-minutes/.

 "Black to the Future: Interviews with Samuel Delany, Greg Tate, and Tricia Rose." In Mark Dery, ed., *Flame Wars: The Discourse of Cyberculture*. Durham, NC: Duke University Press, 1997.

Deuze, Mark. "Convergence Culture in the Creative Industries." *International Journal of Cultural Studies* 10, 2 (2007).

Dickson, David. *The Politics of Alternative Technology*. New York: Universe Books, 1975.

Dillon, Grace L., ed. *Walking the Clouds: An Anthology of Indigenous Science Fiction*. Tucson: University of Arizona Press, 2012.

Disch, Thomas M. *The Dreams Our Stuff Is Made Of: How Science Fiction Conquered the World*. New York: Simon & Schuster, 1998.

Doctorow, Cory. "Cold Equations and Moral Hazard." *Locus Online* (March 2014), www.locusmag.com/Perspectives/2014/03/cory-doctorow-cold-equations-and-moral-hazard/.

Donawerth, Jane L. *Frankenstein's Daughters: Women Writing Science Fiction*. Syracuse, NY: Syracuse University Press, 1997.

Donawerth, Jane L. and Carol A. Kolmerten, eds. *Utopian and Science Fiction by Women: Worlds of Difference*. Syracuse, NY: Syracuse University Press, 1994.

Dorman, Nerine, ed. *Terra Incognita: New Short Speculative Stories from Africa*. South Africa: Short Story Day Africa, 2015.

Dorsey, Candas Jane. "Some Notes on the Failure of Sex and Gender Inquiry in SF." *Science Fiction Studies* 36, 3 (November 2009), pp. 389–90.

Dyer-Witheford, Nick, and Greig de Peuter *Games of Empire: Global Capitalism and Video Games*. Minneapolis: University of Minnesota Press, 2009.

Eaton Journal of Archival Research in Science Fiction (journal). 2013–.

Ehrlich, Paul. *The Population Bomb*. New York: Ballantine Books, 1968.

Ellison, Harlan, ed. *Dangerous Visions*. Reprint edition. London: The Orion Publishing Group, 2012.

Eshun, Kodwo. "Further Considerations of Afrofuturism." *CR: The New Centennial Review* 3, 2 (2003), pp. 287–302.

   More Brilliant than the Sun: Adventures in Sonic Fiction. London: Quartet, 1998.

Evans, Arthur B., ed. *Vintage Visions: Essays on Early Science Fiction*. Middletown, CT: Wesleyan University Press, 2014.

Extrapolation (journal). 1959–.

Fancyclopedia 3. http://fancyclopedia.org.

Fanlore. https://fanlore.org.

Fanon, Frantz. *The Wretched of the Earth*, trans. Constance Farrington. New York: Grove Press, 1963.

Fawaz, Ramzi. *The New Mutants: Superheroes and the Radical Imagination of American Comics*. New York: NYU Press, 2016.

Fempec (journal). 1999–.

Ferns, Chris. *Narrating Utopia: Ideology, Gender, Form in Utopian Literature*. Liverpool: Liverpool University Press, 1999.

Fiske, John. "The Cultural Economy of Fandom." In Lisa Lewis, ed., *The Adoring Audience: Fan Culture and Popular Media*. New York: Routledge, 1992.

   Reading the Popular. New York: Routledge, 1989.

Fitting, Peter, ed. *Subterranean Worlds: A Critical Anthology*. Middletown, CT: Wesleyan University Press, 2004.

Flanagan, Martin, Mike McKenny, and Andy Livingstone.*The Marvel Studios Phenomenon: Inside a Transmedia Universe*. New York: Bloomsbury, 2016.

Foster, Thomas. *The Souls of Cyberfolk: Posthumanism as Vernacular Theory*. Minneapolis: University of Minnesota Press, 2005.

Foucault, Michel. *Society Must Be Defended: Lectures at the College de France 1975–1976*. New York: Palgrave Macmillan, 2003.

Foundation (journal), 1972–.

Fowler, Alistair. *Kinds of Literature: An Introduction to the Theory of Genres and Modes*. Cambridge, MA: Harvard University Press, 1982.

Franklin, H. Bruce. "America as Science Fiction: 1939." In George Slusser, Eric S. Rabkin, and Robert Scholes, eds., *Coordinates: Placing Science Fiction and Fantasy*. Carbondale: Southern Illinois Press, 1992, pp. 107–23.

   Future Perfect: American Science Fiction of the Nineteenth Century – An Anthology. New Brunswick, NJ: Rutgers University Press, 1966.

   Vietnam and Other American Fantasies. Amherst: University of Massachusetts Press, 2000.

Frayling, Christopher. *Mad, Bad and Dangerous? The Scientist and the Cinema*. London: Reaktion Press, 2006.

Freedman, Carl. *Critical Theory and Science Fiction*. Middletown, CT: Wesleyan University Press, 2000.

Frelik, Pawel. "Of Slipstream and Others: SF and Genre Boundary Discourses." *Science Fiction Studies* 113 (2011), pp. 20–45.

Frow, John. *Genre*. London and New York: Routledge, 2006.

Fuller, R. Buckminster. *Operating Manual for Spaceship Earth*. Carbondale: Southern Illinois University Press, 1968.

Geraghty, Lincoln. *American Science Fiction Film and Television*. New York: Berg, 2009.

 Cult Collectors: Nostalgia, Fandom and Collecting Popular Culture. London: Routledge, 2014.

Gernsback, Hugo. "A New Sort of Magazine." *Amazing Stories* 1.1 (April 1926), http://archive .org/stream/AmazingStoriesVolume01Number01/AmazingStoriesVolume01Numbe r01_djvu.txt.

Gibson, James William. *The Perfect War: Technowar in Vietnam*. New York: The Atlantic Monthly Press, 1986.

 Warrior Dreams: Paramilitary Culture in Post-Vietnam America. New York: Hill and Wang, 1994.

Ginway, M. Elizabeth. *Brazilian Science Fiction: Cultural Myth and Nationhood in the Land of the Future*. Lewisburg, PA: Bucknell University Press, 2004.

Gordon, Ian. *Comic Strips and Consumer Culture, 1890–1945*. Washington DC: Smithsonian, 2002.

Gray, Chris Hables. "'There Will Be War!': Future War Fantasies and Militaristic Science Fiction in the 1980s." *Science Fiction Studies* 21, 3 (November, 1994), pp. 315–36.

Gray, Jonathan, Cornel Sandvoss, and C. Lee Harrington. *Fandom: Identities and Communities in a Mediated World*, 2nd edn. New York: New York University Press, 2017.

Grayson, Sandra M. *Visions of the Third Millennium: Black Science Fiction Novelists Write the Future*. Trenton, NJ: African World Press, 2003.

Greenland, Colin. *The Entropy Exhibition: Michael Moorcock and the British "New Wave" in Science Fiction*. London and Boston: Routledge & Kegan Paul, 1983.

Grossman, Leigh Ronald, ed. *Sense of Wonder: A Century of Science Fiction*. Rockville, MD: Wildside Press, 2011.

Grusin, Richard. "Premediation." *Criticism* 46:1 (2004).

Grusin, Richard and David Jay Bolter. *Remediation: Understanding New Media*. Cambridge, MA: MIT Press, 2000.

Gunn, James. *Isaac Asimov: The Foundations of Science Fiction*. Toronto: Scarecrow Press, 2005.

 Inside Science Fiction. 2nd edn. Lanham, MD: Scarecrow, 2006.

 "Teaching Science Fiction." *Science Fiction Studies* 23, 3 (November 1996), pp. 377–84.

Gunn, James, and Matthew Candelaria, eds. *Speculations on Speculation: Theories of Science Fiction*. Lanham, MD: Scarecrow Press, 2005.

Gunning, Tom. "The Cinema of Attractions: Early Film, Its Spectator and the Avant-Garde." *Wide Angle* 8, 3 and 4 (Fall 1986).

Guynes, Sean, and Dan Hassler-Forest, eds. *Star Wars and the History of Transmedia Storytelling*. Amsterdam: Amsterdam University Press, 2017.

Haraway, Donna. *Simians, Cyborgs, and Women: The Reinvention of Nature*. London: Routledge, 1991.

 Staying with the Trouble: Making Kin in the Chthulucene. Durham, NC: Duke University Press, 2016.

Hardt, Michael, and Antonio Negri. *Empire*. London and Cambridge, MA: Harvard University Press, 2000.
  Multitude: War and Democracy in the Age of Empire. Harmondsworth: Penguin Books, 2005.
Hardy, Phil. *The Overlook Film Encyclopedia: Science Fiction*. 3rd edn. New York: Overlook, 1995.
Hartmann, Ivor W., ed. *AfroSF: Science Fiction by African Writers*. Storytime, 2012.
Hartwell, David G. *Age of Wonders: Exploring the World of Science Fiction*. [1985]. New York: Tor, 1996.
Harvey, David. *The Condition of Postmodernity*. Oxford: Blackwell Publishing, 1989.
Hassler-Forest, Dan. *Science Fiction, Fantasy, and Politics: Transmedia World-Building Beyond Capitalism*. Lanham, MD: Rowman & Littlefield, 2016.
Hayles, N. Katherine. *How We Became Posthuman: Virtual Bodies in Cybernetics, Literature, and Informatics*. Chicago: University of Chicago Press, 1999.
Haywood Ferreira, Rachel. *The Emergence of Latin American Science Fiction*. Middletown, CT: Wesleyan University Press, 2011.
  "How Latin America Saved the World and Other Forgotten Futures." *Science Fiction Studies* 43, 2 (2016), pp. 207–25.
  "Second Contact: The First Contact Story in Latin American Science Fiction." In Brian Attebery and Veronica Hollinger, eds. *Parabolas of Science Fiction*. Middletown, CT: Wesleyan University Press, 2013, pp. 70–88.
Heinlein, Robert. "On the Writing of Speculative Fiction." In L. A. Eshbach, ed. *Of Worlds Beyond*. Reading, PA: Fantasy Press, 1947.
Heise, Ursula. *Sense of Place and Sense of Planet: The Environmental Imagination of the Global*. New York: Oxford University Press, 2008.
Hellekson, Karen and Kristina Bose, eds. *Fan Fiction and Fan Communities in the Age of the Internet: New Essays*. Jefferson, NC: McFarland, 2006.
  The Fan Fiction Studies Reader. Iowa City: University of Iowa Press, 2014.
Higgins, David M. "Introduction: Science Fiction and Globalization." *Science Fiction Studies* 39, 3 (2012), pp. 369–73.
  "Psychic Decolonization in 1960s Science Fiction." *Science Fiction Studies* 40, 2 (July 2013), pp. 228–45.
Hillegas, Mark. *The Future As Nightmare: H. G. Wells and the Anti-Utopians*. New York: Oxford University Press, 1967.
Hills, Matt. *Triumph of a Time Lord: Regenerating Doctor Who in the Twenty-First Century*. London: I. B. Tauris, 2010.
Hoagland, Ericka, and Reema Sarwal. *Science Fiction, Imperialism and the Third World: Essays on Postcolonial Literature and Film*. Jefferson, NC: MacFarland, 2010.
Höhler, S. *Spaceship Earth in the Environmental Age, 1960–1990*. New York: Routledge, 2015.
Hollinger, Veronica, and Joan Gordon, eds. *Edging into the Future: Science Fiction and Contemporary Cultural Transformation*. Philadelphia: University of Pennsylvania Press, 2002.
Jackson, Sandra, and Julie E. Moody-Freeman, eds. *The Black Imagination: Science Fiction, Futurism, and the Speculative*. New York: Peter Lang, 2011.
James, Edward. *Science Fiction in the Twentieth Century*. Oxford: Oxford University Press, 1994.

James, Edward, and Farah Mendlesohn, eds. *The Cambridge Companion to Science Fiction.* Cambridge: Cambridge University Press, 2003.

James, Simon J. *Maps of Utopia: H. G. Wells, Modernity and the End of Culture.* Oxford: Oxford University Press, 2012.

Jameson, Fredric. *Archaeologies of the Future: The Desire called Utopia and other Science Fictions.* London: Verso, 2005.

"Metacommentary." *PMLA* 86, 1 (January, 1971), pp. 9–18.

Postmodernism, or the Cultural Logic of Late Capitalism. Durham, NC: Duke University Press, 1991.

"Progress v. Utopia; or, Can We Imagine the Future." *Science Fiction Studies* 9, 2 (July 1982), pp. 147–58.

Jenkins, Henry. *Convergence Culture: Where Old and New Media Collide.* New York: New York University Press, 2008.

Textual Poachers: Television Fans and Participatory Culture. New York: Routledge, 1992.

Jenkins, Henry, Sam Ford, and Joshua Green, *Spreadable Media: Creating Value and Meaning in a Networked Culture.* New York: New York University Press, 2013.

Johnson, Derek. *Media Franchising: Creative License and Collaboration in the Culture Industries.* New York: New York University Press, 2013.

Johnson-Smith, Jan. *American Science Fiction TV: Star Trek, Stargate and Beyond.* New York: I. B. Tauris, 2005.

Jones, Gywneth. *Deconstructing the Starships.* Liverpool: Liverpool University Press, 1999.

Journal of the Fantastic in the Arts (journal). 1990–.

Juul, Jesper. *Half-Real: Video Games Between Real Rules and Fictional Worlds.* Cambridge, MA: MIT Press, 2005.

Kerslake, Patricia. *Science Fiction and Empire.* Liverpool: Liverpool University Press, 2010.

Ketterer, David. *New Worlds for Old: The Apocalyptic Imagination, Science Fiction, and American Literature.* Bloomington: Indiana University Press, 1974.

Kilgore, De Witt Douglas. *Astrofuturism: Science, Race, and Visions of Utopia in Space.* Philadelphia: University of Pennsylvania Press, 2003.

Knight, Damon. *The Futurians.* New York: John Day, 1977.

In Search of Wonder: Essays on Modern Science Fiction. Chicago: Advent, 1967.

Konstantinou, Lee. *Cool Characters: Irony and American Fiction.* Cambridge, MA: Harvard University Press, 2016.

Kornbluth, C. M. "The Failure of the Science Fiction Novel as Social Criticism." Library of America: American Science Fiction: Classic Novels of the 1950s. http://sciencefiction.loa.org/biographies/pohl_failure.php.

Kristeva, Julia. *Strangers to Ourselves.* Trans. Leon Roudiez. New York: Columbia University Press, 1991.

Kuhn, Annette, ed. *Alien Zone.* London: Verso, 1990.

Kyle, Dave. "The Science Fiction League." *Mimosa* 14 (1993), www.jophan.org/mimosa/m14/kyle.htm.

Lacey, Lauren J. *The Past That Might Have Been, the Future That May Come: Women Writing Fantastic Fiction, 1960s to the Present.* Jefferson, NC: MacFarland, 2014.

Landon, Brooks. *Science Fiction After 1900: From the Steam Man to the Stars.* New York: Routledge, 2002.

Langer, Jessica. *Postcolonialism and Science Fiction.* New York: Palgrave Macmillan, 2012.

Larbalestier, Justine. *The Battle of the Sexes in Science Fiction*. Middletown, CT: Wesleyan University Press, 2002.

Larbalestier, Justine, ed. *Daughters of Earth: Feminist Science Fiction in the Twentieth Century*. Middletown, CT: Wesleyan University Press, 2006.

Latham, Rob, ed. *The Oxford Handbook of Science Fiction*. Oxford: Oxford University Press, 2014.

   Science Fiction Criticism: An Anthology of Essential Writings. London: Bloomsbury, 2017.

Lavender III, Isiah. *Race in American Science Fiction*. Bloomington: Indiana University Press, 2011.

Lavender III, Isiah, ed. *Black and Brown Planets: The Politics of Race in Science Fiction*. Jackson: University Press of Mississippi, 2014.

   Dis-Orienting Planets: Racial Representations of Asia in Science Fiction. Jackson: University Press of Mississippi, 2017.

Le Guin, Ursula K. *Dancing at the Edge of the World: Thoughts on Words, Women, Places*. New York: Grove, 1989.

   The Language of the Night: Essays on Fantasy and Science Fiction, ed. Susan Wood. New York: Berkley Books, 1979.

Lem, Stanislaw. *Microworlds: Writings on Science Fiction and Fantasy*. New York: Harcourt, 1985.

Leonard, Elisabeth A., ed. *Into Darkness Peering: Race and Color in the Fantastic*. Westport, CT: Greenwood Press, 1997.

Lethem, Jonathan. "The Squandered Promise of Science Fiction." *Village Voice* (1998). www.verysilly.org/lethem/lethems_vision.html.

Levy, Michael, and Farah Mendlesohn. *Children's Fantasy Literature: An Introduction*. Cambridge: Cambridge University Press, 2016.

Link, Eric Carl, and Gerry Canavan, eds. *The Cambridge Companion to American Science Fiction*. Cambridge: Cambridge University Press, 2015.

Liu, Cixin. "Beyond Narcissism: What Science Fiction Can Offer Literature." *Science Fiction Studies* 40, 1 (March 2013), pp. 22–32.

Locus (journal). 1968–.

Lofficier, Jean-Marc, and Randy Lofficier. *French Science Fiction, Fantasy, Horror and Pulp Fiction*. Jefferson, NC: McFarland and Company, 2000.

Lovelock, James. *Gaia: A New Look at Life on Earth*. New York: Oxford University Press, 1979.

   The Revenge of Gaia: Earth's Climate Crisis and The Fate of Humanity. New York: Basic Books, 2006.

Luckhurst, Roger. "The Many Deaths of Science Fiction: A Polemic." *Science Fiction Studies* 21, 1 (1994), pp. 35–50.

   Science Fiction. Malden, MA: Polity Press, 2005.

   Science Fiction: A Literary History. London: British Library, 2017.

Mackay, Robin, and Armen Avanessian, eds. *#Accelerate: The Accelerationist Reader*. Falmouth: Urbanomic, 2014.

Malmgren, Carl. *Worlds Apart: Narratology of Science Fiction*. Bloomington: Indiana University Press, 1991.

Manuel, Frank E., and Fritzie P. Manuel. *Utopian Thought in the Western World*. Cambridge, MA: Harvard University Press, 1979.

March-Russell, Paul. *Modernism and Science Fiction*. Basingstoke: Palgrave Macmillan, 2015.

Marinetti, Filippo Tommasso. "The Founding and Manifesto of Futurism" [1909]. In Lawrence Rainey *et al.*, eds. *Futurism*. New Haven: Yale University Press, 2009.

Marx, Karl, and Engels, Friedrich. *Communist Manifesto*. www.marxists.org/archive/marx/works/1848/communist-manifesto/ch01.htm.

Marx, Leo. *The Machine in the Garden: Technology and the Pastoral Ideal in America*, 2nd edn. New York: Oxford University Press, 2000.

Mattelart, Armand. *Networking the World, 1794–2000*, trans. Liz Carey-Libbrecht and James A. Cohen. Minneapolis, MN: University of Minnesota Press, 2000.

Mazierska, Ewa, and Alfredo Suppia, eds. *Red Alert: Marxist Approaches to Science Fiction Cinema*. Detroit: Wayne State University Press, 2016.

McCaffery, Larry, ed. *Across the Wounded Galaxies: Interviews with Contemporary American Science Fiction Writers*. Urbana: University of Illinois Press, 1990.

McCarthy, Patti J. *The Lucas Effect: George Lucas and the New Hollywood*. Amherst, NY: Teneo Press, 2014.

McGurl, Mark. *The Program Era: Postwar Fiction and the Rise of Creative Writing*. Cambridge, MA: Harvard University Press, 1990.

McHale, Brian. *Constructing Postmodernism*. London: Routledge, 1992.

McKibben, Bill. *The End of Nature*. New York: Anchor, 1989.

Meadows, Donella H., Dennis L. Meadows, Jorgen Randers, and William W. Behrens III. *The Limits to Growth: A Report for the Club of Rome's Project on the Predicament of Mankind*. Reprint edition. Washington DC: Potomac Associates, 1974.

Melzer, Patricia. *Alien Constructions: Science Fiction and Feminist Thought*. Austin, TX: University of Texas Press, 2006.

Mendlesohn, Farah. *The Inter-Galactic Playground: A Critical Study of Children's and Teens' Science Fiction*. Jefferson, NC: McFarland, 2009.

Merril, Judith, ed. *England Swings SF: Stories of Speculative Fiction*. Garden City, NY: Doubleday, 1968.

The Merril Theory of Lit'ry Criticism, ed. Ritch Calvin. Seattle: Aqueduct, 2016.

Merril, Judith, and Emily Pohl-Weary. *Better to Have Loved: The Life of Judith Merril*. Toronto: Between the Lines, 2002.

Miéville, China, and Mark Bould, eds. *Red Planets: Marxism and Science Fiction*. Middletown, CT: Wesleyan University Press, 2009.

Milburn, Colin. *Mondo Nano: Fun and Games in the World of Digital Matter*. Durham, NC: Duke University Press, 2015.

Milner, Andrew. *Locating Science Fiction*. Liverpool: Liverpool University Press, 2012.

Modern Masters of Science Fiction (series). University of Illinois Press, 2013–.

Moorcock, Michael. "A New Literature for the Space Age." *New Worlds* 142 (1964).

"Symbols for the Sixties," *New Worlds* 148 (1965).

Moore, Jason. *Capitalism in the Web of Life*. London: Verso Books.

More, Thomas. *Utopia*. With commentary by China Miéville and Ursula K. Le Guin. London: Verso, 2016.

Moretti, Franco, "The Slaughterhouse of Literature." *Modern Language Quarterly* 61 (2000), pp. 207–27.

Moskowitz, Sam. *Explorers of the Infinite*. Cleveland: World Publishing Company, 1963.

Strange Horizons: The Spectrum of Science Fiction. New York: Scribner, 1976.

Mosley, Walter. "Black to the Future." In Sheree R. Thomas, ed. *Dark Matter: A Century of Speculative Fiction from the African Diaspora.* New York: Warner, 2000, pp. 405–6.

Moylan, Tom. *Demand the Impossible: Science Fiction and the Utopian Imagination.* London: Methuen Publishing, 1986.

  Scraps of the Untainted Sky: Science Fiction, Utopia, Dystopia. Boulder, CO: Westview Press, 2000.

Moylan, Tom, and Raffaella Baccolini, eds. *Dark Horizons: Science Fiction and the Utopian Imagination.* London: Routledge, 2003.

Mullen, Richard Dale. "Science Fiction in Academe." *Science Fiction Studies* 23, 3 (November 1996), pp. 371–4.

Muñoz, José Esteban. *Cruising Utopia: The Then and There of Queer Futurity.* New York: New York University Press, 2009.

Murphy, Graham J., and Lars Schemink, eds. *Cyberpunk and Visual Culture.* New York: Routledge, 2018.

Murphy, Graham J., and Sherryl Vint. *Beyond Cyberpunk: New Critical Perspectives.* New York: Routledge, 2010.

Murphy, Patrick D. "Pessimism, Optimism, Human Inertia, and Anthropogenic Climate Change." *Interdisciplinary Studies in Literature and Environment* 21 (2014), pp. 149–63.

Nama, Adilifu. *Black Space: Imagining Race in Science Fiction Film.* Austin: University of Texas Press, 2008.

  Super Black: American Pop Culture and Black Superheroes. Austin: University of Texas Press, 2011.

Nardi, Bonnie A., Celia Pearce, and Tom Boellstorff. *Communities of Play: Emergent Cultures in Multiplayer Games and Virtual Worlds.* Cambridge, MA: MIT Press, 2011.

Nelson, Alondra. "Introduction: Future Texts." *Social Text* 20, 2 (2002).

New York Review of Science Fiction (journal), 1988–.

Nicolson, Marjorie Hope. *Voyages to the Moon.* New York: Macmillan, 1948.

Omelsky, Matthew "'After the End Times': Postcrisis African Science Fiction," *Cambridge Journal of Postcolonial Literary Inquiry* 1, 1 (2014).

Otto, Eric C. *Green Speculations: Science Fiction and Transformative Environmentalism.* Columbus: Ohio State University Press, 2012.

Oziewicz, Marek C. *Justice in Young Adult Speculative Fiction: A Cognitive Reading.* New York: Routledge, 2015.

Page, Michael. *The Literary Imagination from Erasmus Darwin to H. G. Wells: Science, Evolution, and Ecology.* Aldershot: Ashgate, 2012.

Panshin, Alexei, and Cory Panshin. *The World Beyond the Hill: Science Fiction and the Quest for Transcendence.* Los Angeles: J. P. Tarcher, 1989.

Paradoxa (journal). 1995–.

Parrinder, Patrick. *Learning from Other Worlds: Estrangement, Cognition, and the Politics of Science Fiction.* Durham, NC: Duke University Press, 2001.

  Science Fiction: Its Criticism and Teaching. London: Methuen, 1980.

Pearce, C. *Communities of Play: Emergent Cultures in Multiplayer Games and Virtual Worlds.* Cambridge, MA: MIT Press, 2011.

Pepperell, Robert. *The Posthuman Condition.* London: Intellect Books, 2003.

Penley, Constance. *NASA/Trek: Popular Science and Sex in America.* London: Verso, 1995.

Philmus, Robert M. *Into the Unknown: The Evolution of Science Fiction from Francis Godwin to H. G. Wells*. Berkeley: University of California Press, 1970.

Pick, Daniel. *Svengali's Web: The Alien Enchanter in Modern Culture*. New Haven: Yale University Press, 2000.

Pilsch, Andrew. "Self-Help Supermen: The Politics of Fan Utopias in World War II-Era Science Fiction." *Science Fiction Studies* 41, 3 (2014), pp. 524–42.

Pohl, Frederik. *The Way the Future Was: A Memoir*. New York: Ballantine Books, 1978.

Prelinger, Megan. *Another Science Fiction: Advertising the Space Race 1957–1962*. New York: Blast Books, 2010.

Pringle, David. *Science Fiction: The 100 Best Novels: An English-Language Selection, 1949–1984*. London: Xanadu, 1985.

Redmond, Sean, ed. *Liquid Metal: The Science Fiction Film Reader*. London: Wallflower Press, 2004.

Rickman, Gregg, ed. *The Science Fiction Film Reader*. New York: Limelight Editions, 2004.

Rieder, John. *Colonialism and the Emergence of Science Fiction*. Middletown, CT: Wesleyan University Press, 2008.

  "On Defining Science Fiction, or Not: Genre Theory, SF, and History." *Science Fiction Studies* 37, 2 (July 2010), pp. 191–210.

  Science Fiction and the Mass Cultural Genre System. Middletown, CT: Wesleyan University Press, 2017.

Roberts, Adam. *The History of Science Fiction*. Basingstoke: Palgrave Macmillan, 2006.

  Science Fiction. 2nd edition. London: Routledge, 2006.

Robinson, Kim Stanley. "Still, I'm Reluctant to Call This Pessimism." In Gerry Canavan and Kim Stanley Robinson, eds., *Green Planets: Ecology and Science Fiction*. Middletown, CT: Wesleyan University Press, 2014.

Rockström, Johan, *et al.* "A Safe Operating Space for Humanity." *Nature* 461 (2009), pp. 472–4.

Rogers, Brett and Benjamin Stevens. *Classical Traditions in Science Fiction*. Oxford: Oxford University Press, 2015.

Ross, Andrew. *Strange Weather: Culture, Science and Technology in the Age of Limits*. London: Verso, 1991, pp. 101–36.

Russ, Joanna. *How to Suppress Women's Writing*. Austin, TX: University of Texas Press, 1983.

  "The Image of Women in Science Fiction." *The Country You Have Never Seen: Essays and Reviews*. Liverpool: Liverpool University Press, 2005.

  To Write Like a Woman: Essays in Feminism and Science Fiction. Bloomington: Indiana University Press, 1995.

Sabin, Roger. *Comics, Comix and Graphic Novels: A History of Comic Art*. London: Phaidon Press, 2001.

Sargent, Lyman Tower. *Utopianism: A Very Short Introduction*. Oxford: Oxford University Press, 2010.

Sargent, Pamela, ed. *Women of Wonder: The Classic Years*. New York: Harcourt Brace and Company, 1995.

Sawyer, Andy, and Peter Wright, ed. *Teaching Science Fiction*. Basingstoke: Palgrave Macmillan, 2011.

Scholes, Robert, and Eric Rabkin. *Science Fiction: History, Science, Vision.* New York: Oxford University Press, 1977.

Science Fiction Film and Television (journal). 2008–.

Science Fiction Studies (journal). 1973–.

Seed, David. *American Science Fiction and the Cold War: Literature and Film.* Edinburgh: Edinburgh University Press, 1999.

 A Companion to Science Fiction. Oxford: Blackwell, 2005.

 Science Fiction: A Very Short Introduction. Oxford: Oxford University Press, 2011.

Segal, Howard. *Technological Utopianism in American Culture.* [1985]. Syracuse, NY: Syracuse University Press, 2005.

Shaviro, Steven. *Connected, or What It Means To Live in a Network Society.* Minneapolis: University of Minnesota Press, 2003.

Sheldon, Rebekah. *The Child to Come: Life After the Human Catastrophe.* Minneapolis: University of Minnesota Press, 2016.

Shippey, Tom, ed., *Fictional Space.* Oxford: Basil Blackwell, 1991.

Smith, Eric D. *Globalization, Utopia, and Postcolonial Science Fiction: New Maps of Hope.* New York: Palgrave Macmillan, 2012.

Sobchack, Vivian. *Screening Space: The American Science Fiction Film.* New Brunswick, NJ: Rutgers University Press, 1987.

Sontag, Susan. "The Imagination of Disaster." In Sean Redmond, ed., *Liquid Metal: The Science Fiction Film Reader.* London: Wallflower Press, 2004.

Stableford, Brian. *New Atlantis: A Narrative History of Scientific Romance.* Rockville, MD: Wildside Press, 2016.

 Science Fact and Science Fiction. New York: Routledge, 2006.

 "Science Fiction and Ecology." In David Seed, ed., *A Companion to Science Fiction.* Malden, MA: Blackwell Publishing, 2008.

Stephenson, Neal. "Innovation Starvation." *World Policy Journal* 28, 3 (September 21, 2011).

Sterling, Bruce. "Cyberpunk in the Nineties." *Interzone* no 48, 1991, pp. 39–41.

 "Preface." *Mirrorshades: The Cyberpunk Anthology.* New York: Ace, 1988, pp. ix–xvi.

Sullivan, Walter. "Issue and Debate." *The New York Times* (March 31, 1975), p. 36.

Suvin, Darko. *Metamorphoses of Science Fiction: On the Poetics and History of a Literary Genre.* New Haven: Yale University Press, 1979. 2nd edn. ed. Gerry Canavan. New York: Ralahine Utopian Studies, 2016.

 Positions and Presuppositions in Science Fiction. Basingstoke: Macmillan, 1988.

Szeman, Imre. "Oil, Futurity, and the Anticipation of Disaster." *South Atlantic Quarterly* 106, 4 (2007).

Tal, Kalil. "'That Just Kills Me': Black Militant Near-Future Fiction." *Social Text* 71 (2002), pp. 65–91.

Telotte, J. P., ed. *The Essential Science Fiction Television Reader.* Kentucky: University of Kentucky Press, 2008.

Thomas, Sheree R., ed., *Dark Matter: A Century of Speculative Fiction from the African Diaspora.* New York: Warner, 2000.

Toledano Redondo, Juan C. "From Socialist Realism to Capitalism: Cuban Cyberpunk." *Science Fiction Studies* 32, 3 (November 2005), pp. 442–6.

Tringham, N. R. *Science Fiction Video Games*, Boca Raton, FL: CRC Press, 2014.

Trites, Roberta Seelinger. *Disturbing the Universe: Power and Repression in Adolescent Literature*. Iowa City: University of Iowa Press, 2004.

Tuhus-Dubrow, Rebecca. "Cli-Fi: Birth of a Genre." *Dissent* (2013).

Tye, Larry. *Superman: The High-Flying History of America's Most Enduring Hero*. New York: Random House, 2013.

Tymn, Marshall B., ed. *Science Fiction: A Teacher's Guide and Resource Book*. Mercer Island, WA: Starmont, 1988.

VanderMeer, Ann, and Jeff VanderMeer. "Introduction." In Ann VanderMeer and Jeff VanderMeer, eds., *Sisters of the Revolution: A Feminist Speculative Fiction Anthology*. Oakland: PM Press, 2015.

Vint, Sherryl. *Animal Alterity: Science Fiction and the Question of the Animal*. Liverpool: Liverpool University Press, 2010.

Science Fiction: A Guide for the Perplexed. London: Bloomsbury, 2014.

Wark, Mackenzie. *Gamer Theory*. Cambridge, MA: Harvard University Press, 2007.

Molecular Red: Theory for the Anthropocene. London: Verso, 2015.

Warner, Harry, Jr. *All Our Yesterdays: An Informal History of Science Fiction Fandom in the Forties*. Chicago: Advent, 1969.

A Wealth of Fable: The History of Science Fiction Fandom in the 1950s. New York: Fanhistorica, 1976.

Wegner, Phillip E. *Life Between Two Deaths, 1989–2001: US Culture in the Long Nineties*. Durham, NC: Duke University Press, 2009.

Periodizing Jameson: Dialectics, the University, and the Desire for Narrative. Chicago: Northwestern University Press, 2014.

Shockwaves of Possibility: Essays on Science Fiction, Globalization, and Utopia. Ralahine Utopian Studies, Vol. 15. Oxford: Peter Lang, 2014.

Westfahl, Gary. "Academic Criticism of Science Fiction: What It Is, What It Should Be." *Monad: Essays on Science Fiction* 2 (March 1992), pp. 75–96.

Hugo Gernsback and the Century of Science Fiction. Jefferson, NC: McFarland, 2007.

The Mechanics of Wonder: The Creation of the Idea of Science Fiction. Liverpool: Liverpool University Press, 1998.

Space and Beyond: The Frontier Theme in Science Fiction. Westport, CT: Greenwood, 2000.

Williams, Keith. *H. G. Wells, Modernity and the Movies*. Liverpool: Liverpool University Press, 2007.

Williams, Raymond. *Marxism and Literature*. Oxford: Oxford University Press, 1977.

"Science Fiction." *Science Fiction Studies* 15, 3 (November 1988).

Tenses of Imagination. London: Peter Lang, 2010.

Williamson, Jack, ed. *Teaching Science Fiction: Education for Tomorrow*. Philadelphia: Owlswick, 1980.

Wittenberg, David. *Time Travel: The Popular Philosophy of Narrative*. New York: Fordham University Press, 2013.

Wolf, Mark J. P. *Building Imaginary Worlds: The Theory and History of Subcreation*. New York: Routledge, 2012.

Wollheim, Donald. *The Universe Makers: Science Fiction Today*. New York: Harper & Row, 1971.

Wolmark, Jenny. *Aliens and Others: Science Fiction, Feminism and Postmodernism*. Iowa City: University of Iowa Press, 1994.

Womack, Ytasha L. *Afrofuturism: The World of Black Sci-Fi and Fantasy Culture*. Chicago: Lawrence Hill, 2013.

Wythoff, Grant. "Introduction." In Hugo Gernsback, *The Perversity of Things: Hugo Gernsback on Media, Tinkering, and Scientifiction*, ed. Grant Wythoff. Minneapolis: University of Minnesota Press, 2016.

Yaszek, Lisa. *Galactic Suburbia: Recovering Women's Science Fiction*. Columbus: The Ohio State University Press, 2008.

Yaszek, Lisa, and Patrick B. Sharp, eds. *Sisters of Tomorrow: The First Women of Science Fiction*. Middletown, CT: Wesleyan University Press, 2016.

Yockey, Matt, ed. *Make Our Marvel: Media Convergence and a Comics Universe*. Austin: University of Texas Press, 2017.

Young, Elizabeth. *Black Frankenstein: The Making of an American Metaphor*. New York: New York University Press, 2008.

Žižek, Slavoj. *First as Tragedy, Then as Farce*. London: Verso, 2009.

Zubernis, Lynn, and Katherine Larsen. *Fandom at the Crossroads: Celebration, Shame and Fan/Producer Relationships*. Newcastle: Cambridge Scholars Press, 2012.

Index

Index

Index